W9-BVN-438

DISCOVER

Northern California

MOON

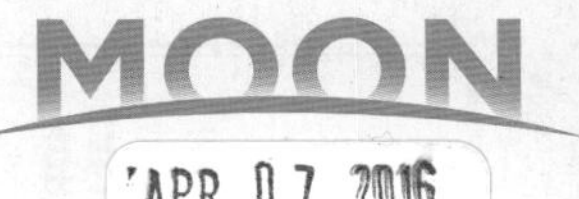

NORTHERN CALIFORNIA

ELIZABETH LINHART VENEMAN & CHRISTOPHER ARNS

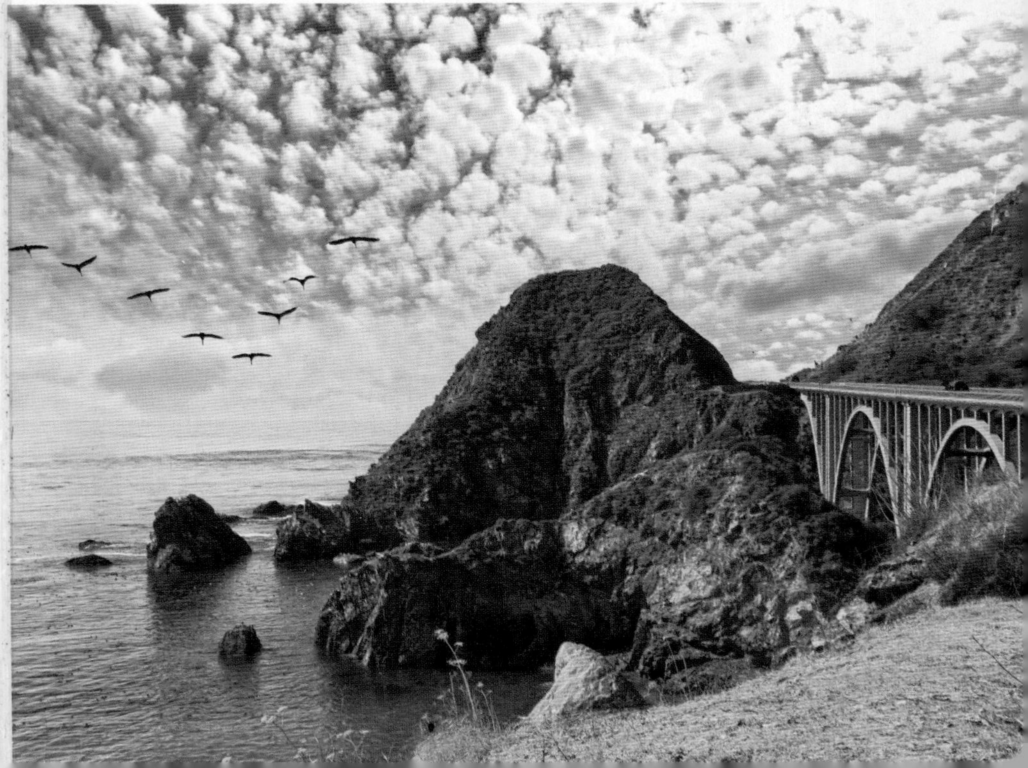

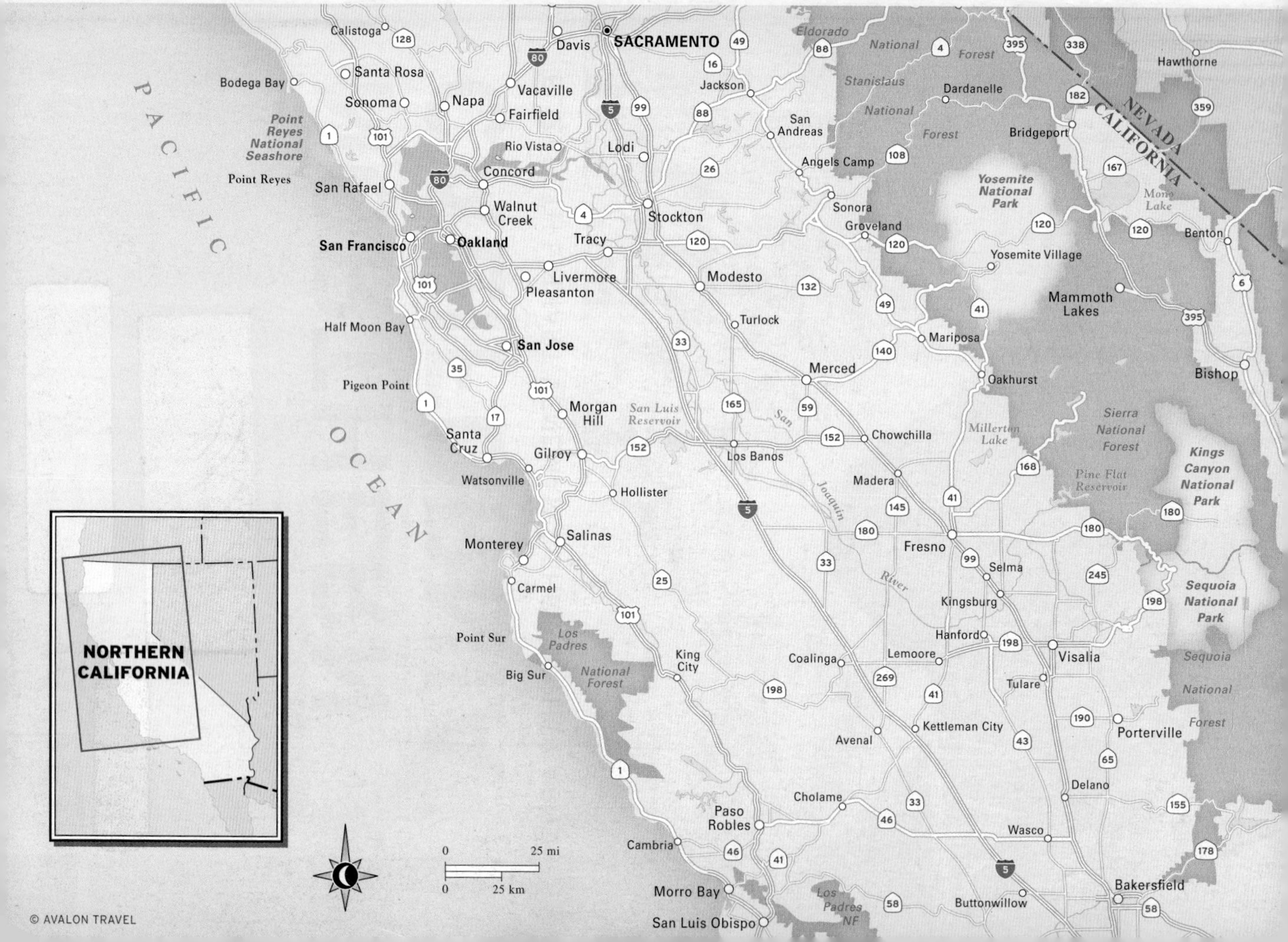

NORTHERN CALIFORNIA
PACIFIC OCEAN
SACRAMENTO
San Francisco
Oakland
San Jose
Calistoga
Santa Rosa
Bodega Bay
Sonoma
Napa
Davis
Vacaville
Fairfield
Point Reyes National Seashore
Point Reyes
San Rafael
Rio Vista
Lodi
Concord
Walnut Creek
Stockton
Tracy
Livermore
Pleasanton
Modesto
Half Moon Bay
Turlock
Pigeon Point
Morgan Hill
San Luis Reservoir
Merced
Santa Cruz
Gilroy
Watsonville
Hollister
Los Banos
Chowchilla
Madera
San Joaquin River
Monterey
Salinas
Carmel
Fresno
Selma
Kingsburg
Hanford
Lemoore
Visalia
Coalinga
Point Sur
Los Padres National Forest
King City
Big Sur
Tulare
Kettleman City
Avenal
Porterville
Delano
Cholame
Paso Robles
Wasco
Cambria
Morro Bay
San Luis Obispo
Los Padres NF
Buttonwillow
Bakersfield
Jackson
San Andreas
Angels Camp
Sonora
Groveland
Eldorado National Forest
Stanislaus National Forest
Dardanelle
Bridgeport
Yosemite National Park
Yosemite Village
Mariposa
Oakhurst
Millerton Lake
Mammoth Lakes
Sierra National Forest
Pine Flat Reservoir
Kings Canyon National Park
Sequoia National Park
Sequoia National Forest
Mono Lake
Benton
Bishop
Hawthorne
NEVADA
CALIFORNIA
0 25 mi
0 25 km
© AVALON TRAVEL

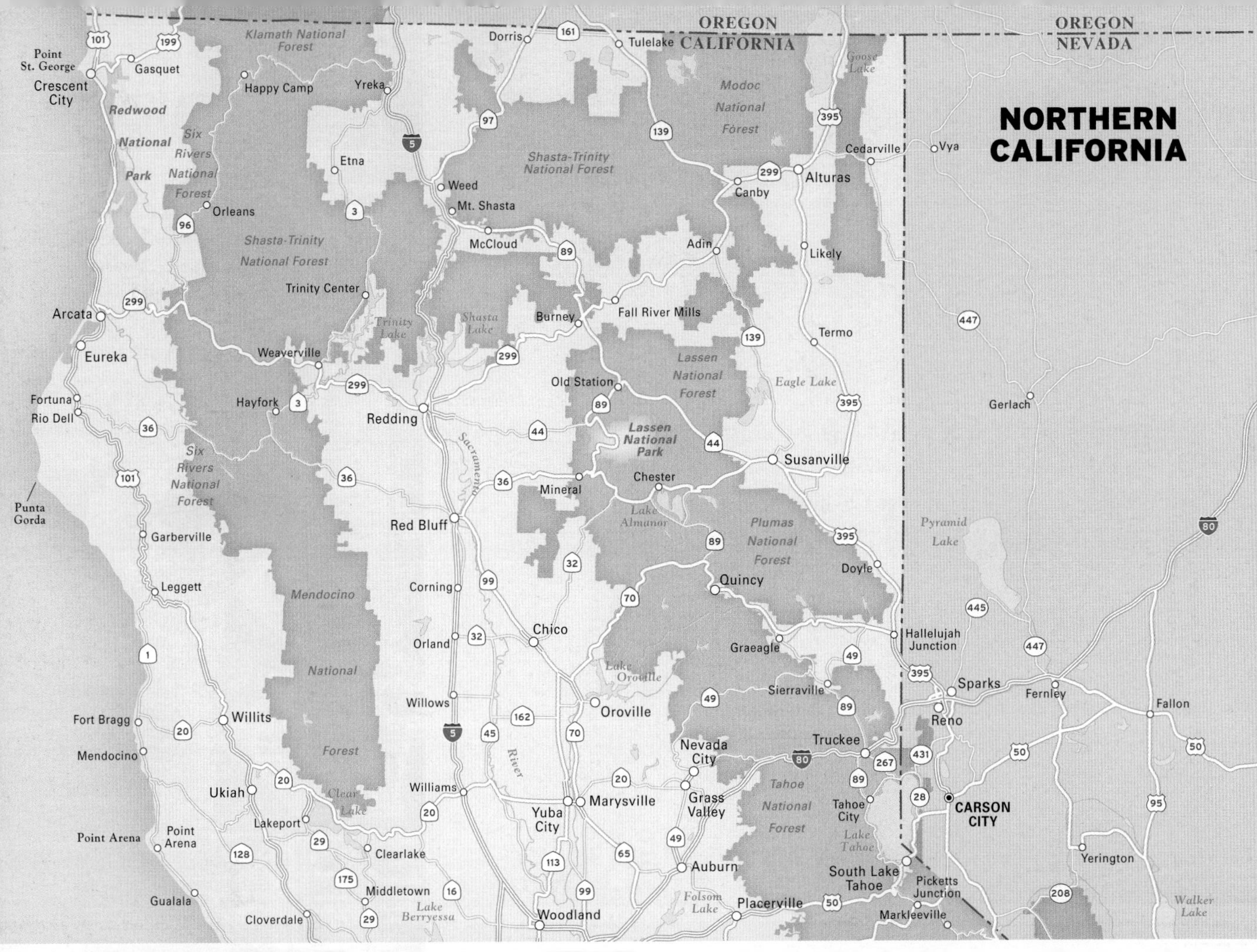
NORTHERN CALIFORNIA
OREGON
CALIFORNIA
OREGON
NEVADA
Point St. George
Crescent City
Gasquet
Redwood National Park
Six Rivers National Forest
Klamath National Forest
Happy Camp
Yreka
Dorris
Tulelake
Modoc National Forest
Goose Lake
Cedarville
Vya
Etna
Weed
Mt. Shasta
Shasta-Trinity National Forest
Alturas
Canby
Orleans
McCloud
Adin
Likely
Trinity Center
Trinity Lake
Shasta Lake
Burney
Fall River Mills
Termo
Arcata
Eureka
Weaverville
Lassen National Forest
Eagle Lake
Old Station
Gerlach
Fortuna
Rio Dell
Hayfork
Redding
Sacramento
Lassen National Park
Susanville
Chester
Mineral
Lake Almanor
Punta Gorda
Red Bluff
Plumas National Forest
Pyramid Lake
Garberville
Doyle
Corning
Quincy
Leggett
Mendocino National Forest
Chico
Orland
Hallelujah Junction
Graeagle
Lake Oroville
Sierraville
Sparks
Fernley
Fallon
Willows
Oroville
Reno
Fort Bragg
Willits
River
Nevada City
Truckee
Mendocino
Tahoe National Forest
Williams
Ukiah
Clear Lake
Grass Valley
Tahoe City
Marysville
Yuba City
CARSON CITY
Point Arena
Lakeport
Lake Tahoe
Clearlake
Auburn
Yerington
South Lake Tahoe
Middletown
Pickets Junction
Gualala
Lake Berryessa
Folsom Lake
Placerville
Walker Lake
Cloverdale
Woodland
Markleeville
101
199
97
5
139
395
3
299
96
89
447
44
36
1
32
99
70
445
49
80
162
45
20
267
431
28
50
95
128
29
175
16
113
65
208

Contents

If you can't decide between the beach or the mountains, city nightlife or quaint historical towns, and sleeping in luxury or roughing it, then Northern California is your ultimate destination. Dense in urban culture, awash in vineyards, and with some of the most scenic landscapes in the world, Northern California is a multi-faceted gem. Yosemite National Park, Lake Tahoe, Big Sur, and San Francisco are among the top 10 on most travelers' bucket lists. But beyond these headliners are lesser-known acts: towering coastal redwood trees, Gold Rush-era ghost towns, and a smoldering volcano, just to name a few.

San Francisco is the cultural heart of Northern California. Fine art, radical ideas, and world-class cuisine mix easily in this cosmopolitan city that loves its politics as much as its nightlife. In Wine Country, locals beckon you to enjoy life one sip at a time. Natural wonders and wide-open spaces dare outdoorsy types to climb Yosemite's granite peaks, hike among redwoods in Sequoia and Kings Canyon, ski Tahoe's powdery slopes, and dip their toes into the enchanting sea at Big Sur.

Whether you're a visitor discovering its wonders for the first time or a seasoned native looking to explore its hidden treasures, Northern California awaits.

Clockwise from top left: California poppies; vineyard on the Russian River; a wave breaking near the shore in Santa Cruz; Roosevelt elk near Humboldt County; giant sequoia tree in Mariposa Grove at Yosemite National Park; the Golden Gate Bridge.

Planning Your Trip

Where to Go

San Francisco

The politics, the culture, the food—these are what make San Francisco world famous. Dine on **cutting-edge cuisine** at high-end restaurants and offbeat food trucks, tour classical and avant-garde **museums,** bike through **Golden Gate Park** and explore its hidden treasures, and stroll along **Fisherman's Wharf,** where barking sea lions and frenetic street performers compete for attention.

San Francisco Bay Area

Surrounding San Francisco is a region as **diverse** as the city itself. To the north, **Marin** offers **wilderness** seekers a quick reprieve from the city, while ethnic diversity and intellectual curiosity give the **East Bay** a **hip, urban edge.** On the southern **Peninsula, beaches** and **farmland** are within quick driving distance of the entrepreneurial culture of Silicon Valley and **San Jose.**

Wine Country

Northern California's Wine Country is famous for a reason. This is the place to **pamper yourself** with excellent wines, fantastic food, and **luxurious spas. Napa** offers all of the above in spades, while **Sonoma** is the place to catch a bit of history and to enjoy a **mellow atmosphere.** The **Russian River** adds **redwoods** and a bit of river rafting to the mix.

North Coast

For deserted beaches, towering redwoods, and scenic coastal towns, cruise north along **The Redwood Coast.** Explore Russian history at Fort Ross on the **grassy bluffs** of the **Sonoma Coast,** be romanced by **Mendocino's** small-town charm and nearby wineries, and discover the quirky, **hippie charm** of towns like **Arcata** and **Trinidad.**

Shasta and Lassen

At the southern end of the volcanic Cascade Range are **geologic wonders** alongside plentiful outdoor recreation. Rent a houseboat on **Shasta Lake** or spend a few days climbing or skiing dramatic **Mount Shasta.** You can traverse nearby **lava tunnels** or travel south to hike through **boiling mud pots** and fumaroles at **Lassen Volcanic National Park.**

Previous page clockwise from top: a California harbor seal in Big Sur; an ornate Victorian in Eureka; the Transamerica Pyramid in San Francisco. **This page:** San Francisco's Chinatown Gate.

Lake Tahoe

Bright blue skies, **granite mountains,** and **evergreen forests** surround jewel-like **Lake Tahoe.** Glossy hotels and casinos line the **South Shore,** while the low-key **North and West Shores** beckon with **quiet beaches** and miles of hiking, biking, and ski trails. Nevada's **East Shore** specializes in **uninhibited** good times, while the **Truckee-Donner** area adds a bit of **Old West flavor** to the outdoor scene.

Sacramento and Gold Country

The political epicenter of California is the Gold Rush-era town of **Sacramento.** More history awaits on the **winding scenic highways** that crisscross **Northern Gold Country.** Tour abandoned mines, raft some **high-octane white water,** go wine-tasting in the **Shenandoah Valley,** or explore the caves, caverns, and big trees of **Southern Gold Country.**

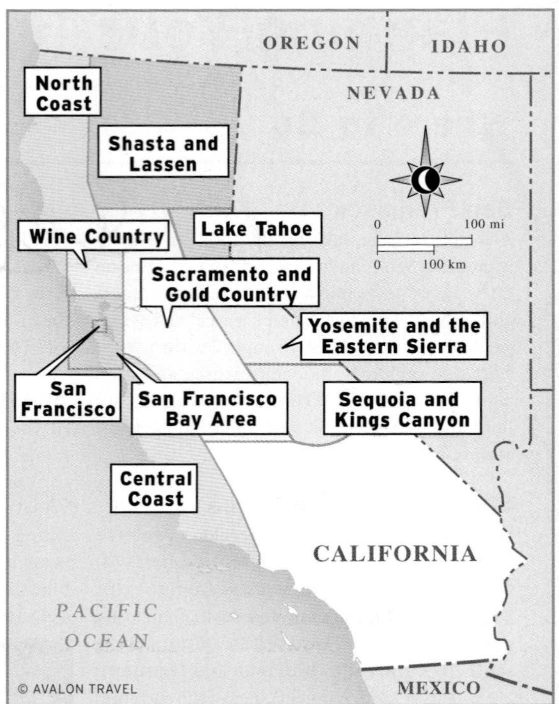

Lake Tahoe

Yosemite National Park

Yosemite and the Eastern Sierra

The work of Ansel Adams and John Muir has made Yosemite a **worldwide icon.** Thousands crowd into **Yosemite Valley** to view the much-photographed **Half Dome, Bridalveil Fall,** and **El Capitan.** On the eastern side of the Sierras, **Mono Lake** and **Mammoth Lakes** provide more **scenic wilderness** to explore.

Sequoia and Kings Canyon

Aside from the dramatic **rugged terrain,** the real draws to this central Sierra region are the **giant sequoias** in the **General Grant Grove** and the **General Sherman Tree.** Visit the **Giant Forest Museum,** take an invigorating hike up to **Moro Rock,** and duck into glittering **Crystal Cave,** which is as beautiful as its name suggests.

Central Coast

Some of the most beautiful and most **adventurous coastline** in the world is along Highway 1—the **Pacific Coast Highway.** Go surfing and wine-tasting in **Santa Cruz.** Witness **gray whales** and sea lions off the rugged **Monterey Bay,** and then explore their environment at the **Monterey Bay Aquarium.** Camp and hike the **unspoiled wilderness** of **Big Sur,** and then tour **grandiose Hearst Castle** in San Simeon.

When to Go

Northern California's best feature is its all-season appeal. **Yosemite's waterfalls** are at their peak in **spring,** when the crowds are fewer. This is also a great time to visit **Big Sur**—lodging rates drop, as do the number of visitors, while blooming wildflowers make for colorful road trips.

Mark Twain may never have said the famous, "The coldest winter I ever spent was a summer in San Francisco," but it doesn't make the statement any less true. Unsuspecting visitors are frequently surprised by the **wind and fog** that blow through the city **June-August.** Regardless,

autumn in Napa Valley

summer remains Northern California's travel season; expect crowds at popular attractions, wineries, national parks, and campgrounds.

Fall is a wonderful time to visit, as the summer crowds have left, but winter rain and snow have not yet closed Yosemite, Shasta, or Tahoe. **September** in particular is San Francisco's "summer," with **warm sunny days** and little summer fog.

In **winter,** Tahoe draws crowds for **skiing and snowboarding.** Unfortunately, it also draws **heavy traffic** along **I-80,** which can close because of snow and related accidents. **Yosemite's roads are closed** in winter, including **Highway 120** and the **Tioga Pass,** which links the Eastern Sierra to the west entrance of the park. **Heavy rains** can also flood Wine Country roads, leaving travelers stranded.

Before You Go

The most central place to **fly** into is **San Francisco International Airport** (SFO), but you can avoid some of the hassle of this large facility by flying into smaller airports in Oakland, San Jose, or even Sacramento.

Unless your trip is focused on San Francisco, plan to **rent a car** to explore the rest of the region. Winter drivers should carry **tire chains** for unexpected snows in the high Sierra.

Book hotels early and buy **tickets** for big-name attractions (like Alcatraz in San Francisco) in advance, especially in summer. If you plan to visit any well-known restaurants, make those reservations early as well. Lodging and **campground reservations** are particularly essential in **Yosemite and Big Sur.**

Summer fog is likely along the coast and is pretty much guaranteed in San Francisco, making the air damp and chilly. Bring **layered clothing,** especially a wind-resistant coat and a warm sweater, as well as sunscreen.

To visit the United States from abroad, you'll need your **passport** and possibly a **visa.**

Best Day Trips

Many of California's most famous destinations are within a short drive of **San Francisco.** Less than two hours away, **Wine Country** is one of the best day trips out of San Francisco. You can indulge and pamper yourself all day and still have time to fall asleep in the city that night. Though doable in a day, the **Central Coast** and the **Eastern Sierra** are better suited to an overnight stay or a weekend getaway.

San Francisco

Three days are perfect for a whirlwind romance with the city of San Francisco.

Day 1

Start your day with breakfast at the **Ferry Building.** Grab a latte at **Blue Bottle Café** or graze from one of the many on-site vendors before taking a two-mile stroll along the Embarcadero to **Fisherman's Wharf.** Then circle back to Pier 33 and hop on a (booked in advance) ferry to **Alcatraz** to tour the former island prison. Back on land, walk west on Bay Street for about six blocks, then board the Powell-Mason **cable car** at the intersection of Bay and Taylor Streets. Hop off for some window shopping and lunch at **Union Square.**

In the afternoon, head to the Sunset District to explore verdant **Golden Gate Park.** The fabulous **de Young Museum** is directly across from the **California Academy of Sciences.** Art lovers and science geeks can part ways here or squeeze in a trip to enjoy both! Near Golden Gate Park, visit the **Haight,** the hippie enclave made famous in the 1960s. Enjoy the finely crafted

view of downtown San Francisco

cocktails and nibbles at **Alembic** or head back downtown to splurge on dinner at **Farallon.** End the day with martinis at the swank **Top of the Mark.**

Day 2

North Beach is home to **Mama's on Washington Square,** whose specialty "m'omelettes" have made this joint a local favorite for decades. After brunch, stop in at **City Lights,** the legendary Beat Generation bookstore, then enjoy an old-school cappuccino at **Caffé Trieste.** Climb to the top of **Coit Tower** to catch a great view of the city skyline—look west to find crooked **Lombard Street.**

Spend the afternoon in the hip Mission District. Order an authentic Mission burrito at **La Taqueria** or sweets from **Tartine Bakery.** History buffs should visit 18th-century **Mission Dolores.** End your stay in the Mission with thin-crust pizzas and classic cocktails at **Beretta.**

Day 3

Get an early start for breakfast at popular **Dottie's True Blue Café.** Afterward, spend a few hours discovering the world of science at the **Exploratorium,** or, if the weather cooperates, explore **The Presidio** and take a hike along **Crissy Field.** Stop for coffee and a snack at **Warming Hut Bookstore & Café,** then it's off to the ultimate San Francisco photo op, the **Golden Gate Bridge.**

Marin Excursion

Extend the love affair with a side trip to wander the redwoods in Marin. **Muir Woods National Monument** is home to acres of staggeringly beautiful redwood forest just north of San Francisco. The **Muir Woods Visitors Center** is a great place to begin your exploration. Hike the **Main Trail,** a paved boardwalk through the beautiful redwoods. Pick up a self-guided trail leaflet at the visitors center and follow the interpretive numbers along the way to learn about the flora and fauna of this unique ecosystem.

Fill up on a hearty lunch of British comfort food at **The Pelican Inn.** Dark wood and a long trestle table give a proper Old English feel to the dimly lit dining room. It's just a short walk from the restaurant to lovely **Muir Beach,** perfect for wildlife-watching and beachcombing. End the day with oysters and drinks at the Farley Bar at **Cavallo Point Lodge.** Snag a blanket and a seat on the porch to watch the fog roll in over the Golden Gate Bridge.

a spotted owl in Muir Woods National Monument

Wine Country

Napa Valley is about 50 miles north of San Francisco, making it an ever-popular day trip. If you plan to tour Wine Country, choose one region to explore. **Napa** and **Sonoma** are closest to San Francisco, about one hour's drive. Traffic on the winding two-lane roads in these regions can easily become clogged with day-trippers, especially on weekends. To avoid the crowds, try to get an early start or visit on a weekday. Most wineries close by 4pm, and some are open only by appointment.

One Day in Napa

50 MILES, 1-1.5 HOURS FROM SAN FRANCISCO

In downtown Napa, get your bearings at the **Oxbow Public Market.** Shop, nibble pastries, and sip a cup of coffee, or just pick up some picnic supplies before hopping over to the Silverado Trail. Drive north to **Rutherford** and enjoy some bubbly at **Mumm,** followed by some cabernet at **Frog's Leap,** a famously fun and relaxed Napa winery. Get back on Highway 29 and lunch in St. Helena at **Long Meadow Ranch,** where the excellent farm-to-table cuisine and rustic chic atmosphere, plus wine- and olive oil tasting is the perfect all-in-one stop.

Give your taste buds a rest and stroll through the **Culinary Institute of America,** where the country's top chefs are trained, or soak in some steamy mud at **Dr. Wilkinson's Hot Springs Resort** in easygoing **Calistoga.** Afterward, you'll undoubtedly be hungry, so take a table next to the floating fireplace at the Michelin-starred **Solbar.** From Calistoga, the drive back to San Francisco will take two hours.

Overnight: Stay the night at **Indian Springs** before spending a second day exploring Sonoma.

One Day in Sonoma

40-50 MILES, 1-1.5 HOURS FROM SAN FRANCISCO

From Napa, Highway 121 winds west through the **Carneros wine region.** Stop off for a bit of bubbly at gorgeous **Domaine Carneros,** where the views and gardens are almost as impressive as the sparkling wines. From Highway 121, Highway 12 twists north into **Sonoma.** Stretch your legs in Sonoma Plaza and explore the charming downtown area.

Sonoma Mission

Local Favorites

the ghost town of Bodie

- **San Francisco's Ferry Building:** Home to a famous farmers market and the city's foodie mecca (page 31)
- **Angel Island State Park:** More recreation options—and fewer crowds—than Alcatraz (page 101)
- **Año Nuevo State Park:** The winter home of massive elephant seals (page 137)
- **Lassen Peak:** A 10,000-foot mountain that also happens to be an active volcano (page 303)
- **Donner Memorial State Park:** A peaceful spot for a picnic lunch far from Tahoe's crowds (page 374)
- **Bridalveil Fall:** The most accessible waterfall in Yosemite (page 451)
- **Bodie State Historic Park:** California's spookiest ghost town (page 500)
- **Devils Postpile National Monument:** A mind-boggling natural rock formation in the Eastern Sierra (page 506)
- **Crystal Cave:** An underground oasis among the redwoods (page 535)
- **Monterey Bay Aquarium:** An educational and fun destination that's worth a return trip (page 573)
- **Bixby Bridge:** The state's second-most famous bridge (page 606)

male elephant seal at Año Nuevo State Park

Stop in at the **Sonoma Mission** for a bit of history, and then grab a lunch at **the girl and the fig,** housed in the historic Sonoma Hotel. If the sunshine is calling, you may want to get picnic supplies at the **Basque Boulangerie Cafe** and head over to **Gundlach Bundschu Winery,** which boasts some of the best picnic grounds in the valley.

Then it may be time for a massage at the **Garden Spa at MacArthur Place** or a short hike at **Jack London State Historic Park** in quaint Glen Ellen, north on Highway 12. Practically next door, **Benziger Family Winery** offers more tasting opportunities, plus tractor tours of their beautiful hilltop vineyards.

If you have time for one more winery, be sure to visit **Chateau St. Jean** in Kenwood, where the manicured gardens, white chateau turrets, and expansive patio impress as much as the wine itself.

From here, it's only 11 miles to downtown **Santa Rosa,** where you can catch U.S. 101 south to San Francisco, 52 miles and a little over an hour away. To grab a bite before you head back, double back to Glen Ellen and dine on farm-to-table comfort food at the **Glen Ellen Star.**

Overnight: Spend the night at the **Gaige House** in Glen Ellen or the **Sonoma Hotel** on the plaza in Sonoma.

Monterey and Big Sur

One Day in Monterey Bay

112 MILES, 2 HOURS FROM SAN FRANCISCO

Attractions in Santa Cruz and Monterey, plus charming Carmel, can easily fill your itinerary. From San Francisco, take U.S. 101 south to Highway 17 through the redwoods to the laid-back town of Santa Cruz. Ride the rides on the **Santa Cruz Beach Boardwalk,** then rest on the beach.

Once you've had your fill of sun, continue an hour south to Monterey and the **Monterey Bay Aquarium.** Jump over to charming **Carmel-by-the-Sea** and dig your toes into the white sand at **Carmel Beach** as the sun goes down. Splurge on dinner at **Casanova.**

Overnight: The delightful **La Playa Hotel** in Carmel provides a quick launch to the coastal wonders of Big Sur the next day.

Julia Pfeiffer Burns State Park

Two Days in Big Sur
140 MILES, 3 HOURS FROM SAN FRANCISCO

Big Sur captures the best qualities of the Northern California coast: windswept beaches and pounding surf, verdant state parks with majestic redwoods, and the literary solitude of the Beat writers. Although possible as a day trip, this region is best done with two days.

Part of Big Sur's appeal is the drive along the Pacific Coast Highway, lined with historic bridges, pastures of grazing sheep, and breathtaking cliffs. The **Bixby Bridge** marks the official entrance to Big Sur. Stop at **Pfeiffer Big Sur State Park** to hike through the redwoods to Pfeiffer Falls.

The next day, don't miss breakfast at **Deetjens.** Thumb through the books at **Henry Miller Memorial Library,** then make your way south and walk the short trail to **McWay Falls** in **Julia Pfeiffer Burns State Park.** Toward Big Sur's southern end, **Limekiln State Park** offers another waterfall hike.

Overnight: Experience high-end camping at **Treebones Resort,** or book a budget-friendly ocean-view room at **Ragged Point Inn.** Make reservations in advance for both on summer weekends. If you have a third day, it's easy to make your way to Hearst Castle from here.

Return Option via Highway 1
70 MILES, 1.5 HOURS FROM PESCADERO TO SAN FRANCISCO

Add some variety to your return route by following coastal Highway 1 north of Santa Cruz. Turn east in Pescadero onto Pescadero Creek Road and follow it to the town's sole stop sign. Enjoy lunch at **Duarte's** paired with one of their famous bloody Marys. Continue east on Pescadero Creek Road until it meets Highway 84 in La Honda. Follow gorgeous Highway 84 east as it twists and turns through coastal redwoods, eventually coming to a crossroads in **Woodside.** Stop at **Alice's Restaurant** for biker-themed burgers and a beer, then roll north along Skyline Boulevard (Hwy. 35) through more scenic redwoods and past numerous county parks before returning to the urban landscape of I-280 north to San Francisco.

Yosemite and Tahoe

From San Francisco, it's just a four-hour drive to either **Lake Tahoe** or **Yosemite National Park.** Combine a trip to both in summer by crossing through Yosemite via Tioga Pass Road (Hwy. 120). On the eastern side of the Sierra, scenic U.S. 395 leads north almost to the Nevada border, and road-trippers can take forested Highway 89 west to its junction with U.S. 50 to continue to South Lake Tahoe.

One Day in Yosemite
200 MILES, 4 HOURS FROM SAN FRANCISCO

From the north, **Yosemite National Park** is most easily accessed from Highway 120 through the Big Oak Flat entrance; in winter, use Highway 140 through the main Arch Rock entrance.

In **Yosemite Valley,** hop aboard the Valley Shuttle for a scenic exploration of the valley's sights, especially **Bridalveil Fall, El Capitan,** and **Half Dome.** The best way to experience Yosemite's beauty is on one of its many trails. Enjoy a leisurely stroll around **Mirror Lake,** scale a waterfall on the **Mist Trail,** or test your powers of endurance on the way to **Upper Yosemite Fall.** Afterward, reward your efforts with a pit stop at the **Ahwahnee** bar to soak in the valley views.

Overnight: It takes advance planning to score a campground reservation in Yosemite Valley, especially in summer. Try your luck with one of the first-come, first-served campgrounds such as **Tamarack Flat** or **Tuolumne Meadows** (summer only)—but be sure to get there before noon.

Yosemite National Park

Two Days in Yosemite

Highway 120 becomes Tioga Road as it continues east through Yosemite's high country. This seasonal road is only open late spring-late fall, so plan your trip in the spring and fall to avoid the crowds. Along the way, gape at jaw-dropping vistas from **Olmsted Point,** gaze at crystal-clear alpine lakes and grassy **Tuolumne Meadows,** and explore some of Yosemite's rugged high-elevation backcountry on a hike to **Cathedral Lakes.** Tioga Road peaks at Tioga Pass as it leaves the park, descending to the arid desert along U.S. 395. Here, abandoned ghost towns like **Bodie State Historic Park** and saline **Mono Lake** characterize the drier eastern Sierra.

One Day in Tahoe

190 MILES, 3.5-4 HOURS FROM SAN FRANCISCO OR YOSEMITE VALLEY

U.S. 50 enters the Tahoe region on the popular **South Shore** of Lake Tahoe. Stop in at one of the casinos across the **Nevada** state line, or take in the lay of the land on the **Heavenly** gondola. Highway 89 heads west to glittering **Emerald Bay,** where you can hike the **Rubicon Trail** to **Vikingsholm Castle.** Continue north on Highway 89 to reach the **North and West Shores,** which hold Tahoe's legendary appeal. The lively center of **Tahoe City** has plenty of restaurants, hotels, and campgrounds to keep you close to the lake for the night.

Overnight: Spend the night at the **Pepper Tree Inn** in Tahoe City, or camp at General Creek Campground in **Sugar Pine Point State Park** (reservations recommended in summer).

Two Days in Tahoe

In the morning, take Highway 89 east to **Truckee.** Along the way, you'll pass Squaw Valley, which may merit a detour through **The Village at Squaw Valley.** While in Truckee, enjoy the Old West vibe and stop for lunch at the **Bar of America,** a town institution since 1974. On your way home, stop by **Donner Memorial State Park.** Although the park history tells a grim tale, the hiking trails around the lake are

Best Outdoor Adventures

the Pacific Crest Trail in Yosemite National Park

Northern California is rich with opportunities for getting outdoors. From surfing the Pacific coast to climbing the tallest mountain, you can do it all. Choose your own adventure to begin.

- **Backpacking:** Lost Coast (page 251), Pacific Crest Trail (pages 307, 359, 379, 508), Yosemite National Park (page 482)
- **Bicycling:** Point Reyes National Seashore (page 97)
- **Camping:** Yosemite's Tuolumne Meadows (page 477), Humboldt Redwoods State Park (page 255)
- **Canoeing:** Russian River (page 203)
- **Caving:** Mercer Cavern (page 436), Crystal Cave (page 535)
- **Fishing:** Lake Berryessa (page 170), Mendocino Coast (page 232)
- **Hiking:** Yosemite Valley (page 454), Sequoia National Park (page 536), Big Sur (page 609)
- **Horseback riding:** Mount Shasta (page 319), Yosemite Valley (page 456), Grant Grove (page 525)
- **Mountain climbing:** Mount Shasta (page 316), Mount Whitney (page 531)
- **Rock climbing:** Yosemite Valley (page 457)
- **Skiing:** Tahoe's North Shore (page 356), Badger Pass in Yosemite (page 462)
- **Snowboarding:** Mount Shasta (page 318), Tahoe (page 338)
- **Surfing:** Santa Cruz (page 564)
- **Swimming:** Eel River (page 255), Lake Tahoe (page 366), South Yuba River State Park (page 410)
- **Tidepooling:** Fitzgerald Marine Reserve (page 130)
- **Whale-Watching:** Bodega Bay (page 219)
- **White-Water rafting:** South Fork American River (page 414)

quite beautiful. After your last taste of the Sierra, it is 184 miles back to San Francisco (3.5 hours).

Tahoe in Winter

Nothing says winter like sliding down the slopes at Tahoe. Numerous ski resorts line the lake and mountains. **Heavenly** rules the roost on the South Shore, while **Squaw Valley** draws snowboarders and skiers on the North and West Shores. Cross-country skiers should head to **Royal Gorge** in the Truckee-Donner area.

Highway 89 and U.S. 50 are the main arteries to the Tahoe area, and they can become congested and blocked by snow into spring. Bring tire chains and plenty of patience—in inclement weather, it can take up to eight hours to drive here from San Francisco.

Classic Road Trips

The classic tour of Northern California is behind the wheel. Don't miss a chance to drive up the **Pacific Coast Highway,** with its quaint towns, giant redwoods, and untamed beaches. Cruising down **Highway 49** in the Gold Country is another favorite, where mining towns, some seemingly preserved in amber, detail California's boom-time beginnings. But less visited destinations like Mount Lassen and Mount Shasta, with their glaciers, steaming fumaroles, and beautiful desolation, celebrate the state's wild side. To add to the experience, a multitude of **scenic two-lane highways** makes driving from one destination to the next a treat in and of itself.

North Coast

HIGHWAY 1 TO U.S. 101 IN CRESCENT CITY

400 Miles, 9 Hours from San Francisco

Crashing surf, towering redwoods, and rocky beaches typify the rugged Northern California coast. Highway 1 and U.S. 101 twist apart and converge again for almost 400 miles from San

the rugged Sonoma coast

Francisco to Crescent City, culminating in one of the state's best and most scenic road trips.

From San Francisco, travel north over the Golden Gate Bridge to the Bay Area's playground, Marin County. Following Highway 1, stop for a short hike amid coastal redwoods at **Muir Woods National Monument** before continuing north past Stinson Beach to **Point Reyes National Seashore,** where a wealth of hiking and biking opportunities await. Slurp oysters at **Hog Island Oyster Co.** or stock up on gourmet cheese at **Cowgirl Creamery** for a picnic later. Just an hour north is **Bodega Bay,** where Alfred Hitchcock's *The Birds* was filmed. From January to May, you may even spot whales off the coast.

Guerneville makes a fun detour inland from Highway 1. Spend the night at **Creekside Inn and Lodge** and dip your toes—or a canoe—in the **Russian River.** Back on Highway 1, stop for a dose of history at **Fort Ross State Historic Park,** a reconstructed Russian fort. As Highway 1 winds north, the artsy enclave of **Mendocino** beckons. Wander through the **Mendocino Coast Botanical Gardens** and consider spending the night at one of the many quaint B&Bs.

Highway 1 rejoins U.S. 101 in Leggett and enters the famed Redwood Coast. From **Humboldt Redwoods State Park** near Garberville to **Del Norte Coast Redwoods State Park,** this 150-mile stretch is rich with hiking and camping opportunities. Cruise the **Avenue of the Giants** and pitch a tent in **Humboldt Redwoods State Park** or snag a campsite at **Prairie Creek Redwoods.** Del Norte Coast Redwoods is the last of the redwoods before **Crescent City.**

Shasta and Lassen

These northern peaks and parklands are some of the state's most spectacular and least visited. Mount Shasta is a paradise for outdoor enthusiasts year-round. You can hike or climb to the summit in the summer and ski down its slopes in winter. Shasta Lake, by contrast, is best in summer, when boating, fishing, and waterskiing can fully be enjoyed. Because of its high elevation and rocky terrain, Mount Lassen's roads are closed late fall-spring, making it a mid- to late summer destination.

Most services are found in Redding and Red Bluff, which are also the best access points from **I-5.** Each destination can be a road trip in itself, but you can also make a loop via **Highway 89.** It is a thrilling way to see both peaks and to make the most of a trek this far north.

SACRAMENTO TO MOUNT SHASTA

220 Miles, 3.5-4 Hours

From Sacramento, it takes about 2.5 hours of driving north on I-5 to get to the small city of **Redding,** the gateway for both **Shasta Lake** and **Mount Shasta.** From Redding, continue north on I-5 for just eight miles until you come to Shasta Lake. Turn west on Highway 151 to explore looming **Shasta Dam.** After marveling at its size, head over to the other side of I-5 to experience a natural wonder by touring the **Lake Shasta Caverns.**

Next, take advantage of what Shasta Lake does best: watery summer fun. Head over to the **Bridge Bay Resort** where you can rent all you need to go boating, waterskiing, or fishing out on the lake's many fingers and inlets. You can even book a room for the night. Or make the most of your time on the lake by renting a houseboat or camping at the **Hirz Mountain Lookout Tower,** with views of both Mount Shasta and Mount Lassen.

From Shasta Lake, head north on I-5 for 40 miles to **Castle Crags State Park,** where you can try your hand at rock climbing and scale granite faces, domes, and spires. Or you can hike the **Crags Trail to Castle Dome,** a 5.5-mile round-trip with spectacular views.

Next stop is Mount Shasta, only 15 miles up I-5, where more climbing and hiking opportunities await. The **Gray Butte Trail** is a moderate 3.4-mile hike to a small peak. If the big peak is too irresistible, you can opt for a multiday trek summiting **Mount Shasta.** Winter offers equally fun outdoor adventures, when you

Mount Shasta

a houseboat on Shasta Lake

can spend all day skiing and snowboarding at **Mount Shasta Ski Park.**

After a full day on the hiking, climbing, or skiing trails, snag a campsite at **Lake Siskiyou Camp & Resort** or opt for a greater indulgence and reward at the **Shasta MountInn Retreat & Spa.**

MOUNT SHASTA TO LASSEN

100 Miles, 2 Hours

Once you have had your fill of Mount Shasta, head east on Highway 89. The scenic two-lane road winds through mountainous terrain and across wild rivers. One of the best sights along the way is **McArthur-Burney Falls,** claimed to be the most beautiful waterfall in California. This can either be a quick stop, as the falls are near the parking lot, or you can take the time to do a short hike nearby.

You'll enter **Lassen Volcanic National Park** shortly after leaving McArthur-Burney Falls. Because you are entering from the north, you can make a quick stop at the **Loomis Museum** before pressing south to **Lassen Peak.** The beauty and the views on the trail make the effort worthwhile. Nearby is another treat, **Bumpass Hell,** where you can hike surrounded by smoking fumaroles and boiling mud pots.

Camp at either **Manzanita Lake** or **Summit Lake Campground.** From the park, it is less than 200 miles (3-3.5 hours) back to Sacramento.

Gold Country

SACRAMENTO TO NORTHERN AND SOUTHERN GOLD COUNTRY

180 Miles, 4-4.5 Hours

A tour through Gold Country is a road trip rich in history, beautiful scenery, outdoor adventure, and even wine-tasting. Highway 49 runs for 127 miles through the heart of Gold Country from Nevada City to Jamestown. Sacramento is near the Northern Gold Country and is a great place to start a historical tour. You can easily extend this trip to Yosemite via Highway 120 (2 hours), or continue east on U.S. 50 in Placerville to reach Lake Tahoe in a mere 1.5 hours.

In **Sacramento,** start your day early with a tour of the **Capitol Building** and see where all the big decisions are made. Walk over to **Old Sacramento,** where you'll find the Gold

the Capitol Building at dusk

Rush-era part of this town lovingly preserved. To really drink in the atmosphere, step into **Fat City Bar and Café** to enjoy comfort food served in a 19th-century dining room.

Take I-80 east for 32 miles until you reach Auburn in Northern Gold Country, then detour north on Highway 49 for 23 miles to **Grass Valley.** Stop at the **Empire Mine State Historic Park** and get a feel for the toil, hardship, and occasional wild luck that shaped the Gold Country. Charming Grass Valley offers food and shopping, or go straight to **Nevada City,** only three miles away, and spend the afternoon strolling its narrow streets. The **Outside Inn** offers unique rooms that border the creek.

Head back south on Highway 49 for one hour to reach **Placerville.** Take a thrilling white-water rafting trip on the American River near Coloma, or tour **Marshall Gold Discovery State Historic Park,** the site where James Marshall discovered gold in 1848. Next hit the wineries and orchards around **Apple Hill** and taste the Gold Country's best vintages. Consider staying nearby at the **Historic Cary House Hotel.** If you plan to stick by the river, the **American River Resort** has campsites as well as cabins.

It is 60 winding miles from Placerville down Highway 49 to Angels Camp, the heart of **Southern Gold Country.** Visit the **Angels Camp Museum and Carriage House,** which beautifully showcases 30 carriages and wagons from the Gold Rush era. Grab a bite at the **Sidewinder Café,** then venture east for eight miles on Highway 4 to **Murphys** and descend 162 feet below the ground into **Mercer Caverns.**

Head down to **Columbia,** where most of downtown is part of the **Columbia State Historic Park.** Stroll the preserved streets of this Gold Rush boomtown to get a feel for what life was like when the mines operated. Stick around for dinner at the **Columbia City Hotel Restaurant,** where fine dining meets Old West elegance.

Accommodations await a short jog west on Highway 108 in **Jamestown,** where the **National Hotel** has been in operation since 1859. In the morning, stop by the **Mother Lode Coffee Shop** for a hearty breakfast before returning to Sacramento (2 hours, 114 miles).

San Francisco

Look for ★ to find recommended sights, activities, dining, and lodging.

Highlights

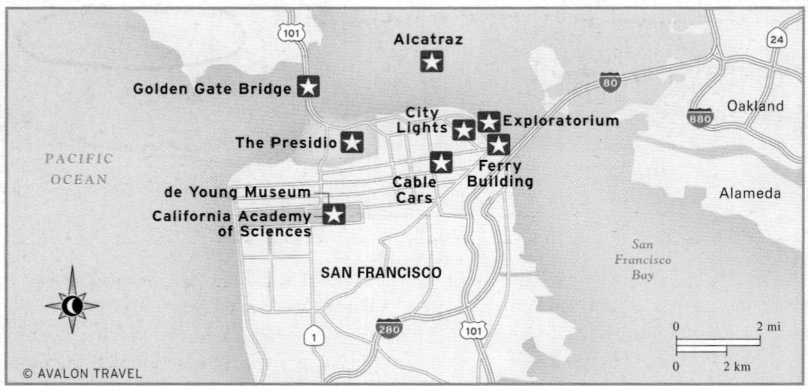

★ **Cable Cars:** Nothing is more iconic than climbing San Francisco's steep hills on a historic cable car (page 30).

★ **Ferry Building:** The 1898 Ferry Building has been renovated and reimagined as the foodie mecca of San Francisco. The thrice-weekly farmers market is not to be missed (page 31).

★ **Exploratorium:** Kids and adults love to explore San Francisco's innovative and interactive science museum. The exhibits are meant to be touched, heard, and felt (page 34).

★ **City Lights:** The Beat generation lives on at this landmark bookstore, widely considered the best in the city (page 36).

★ **Alcatraz:** Spend the day in prison . . . at the historically famous former maximum security penitentiary in the middle of the bay. Audio tours bring to life the cells that Al Capone, George "Machine Gun" Kelly, and Robert "Birdman of Alcatraz" Stroud called home (page 37).

★ **The Presidio:** The original 1776 El Presidio de San Francisco is now a national park. Tour the historical buildings that formerly housed a military hospital, barracks, and fort—all amid a peaceful and verdant setting (page 43).

★ **Golden Gate Bridge:** Nothing beats the view from one of the most famous and fascinating bridges in the country. Pick a fogless day for a stroll or bike ride across the span (page 43).

★ **de Young Museum:** The de Young is the showpiece of Golden Gate Park, with a mixed collection of media. Don't miss the 360-degree view from the museum's tower (page 46).

★ **California Academy of Sciences:** With a four-story rainforest, a state-of-the-art planetarium, and an underwater aquarium home to 38,000 animals, the Academy of Sciences thrills visitors of all ages (page 47).

The regular grid pattern found on maps of San Francisco leaves visitors unprepared for the precipitous inclines and stunning water views in this town built on 43 hills.

Geographically and culturally, San Francisco is anything but flat, and what level ground exists might at any moment give way. While earthquakes remake the land, social upheavals play a similar role, reminding locals that the only constant here is change. In the 1950s, the Beats challenged postwar conformity and left a legacy of incantatory poems and independent bookstores. The late 1960s saw a years-long Summer of Love, which shifted consciousness as surely as quakes shift tectonic plates. Gay and lesbian liberation movements sprung forth in the 1970s, as did a renewed push for women's rights. Since then, a vibrant culture of technological innovation has taken root and continues to rapidly evolve as groundbreaking companies and tech visionaries choose to make the city their home.

Although San Francisco is one of the most visited cities in the United States, it often seems like a provincial village, or a series of villages that share a downtown and a roster of world-class icons. Drive over the Golden Gate or the Bay Bridge as the fog is lifting and your heart will catch at the ever-changing beauty of the scene. Stand at the base of the Transamerica Pyramid, hang off the side of a cable car, or just walk through the neighborhoods that make the city more than the sum of its parts. Despite the hills, San Francisco is a city that cries out to be explored on foot.

PLANNING YOUR TIME

Try to spend at least one weekend in San Francisco, and focus your time downtown. Union Square makes a great home base, thanks to its plethora of hotels, shops, and easy access to public transportation, but it can be fairly dead at night. With a full week, you can explore Golden Gate Park's excellent museums—the de Young and the California Academy of Sciences. You can easily spend another full day exploring the Presidio and taking a scenic, foggy stroll across the Golden Gate Bridge.

San Francisco's weather tends toward blanket fog and chilly wind, with bright spots of sun being the exception. Come prepared with a warm coat and a sweater and leave the shorts at home.

Previous: the Golden Gate Bridge; lanterns in Chinatown. **Above:** Transamerica Pyramid.

San Francisco

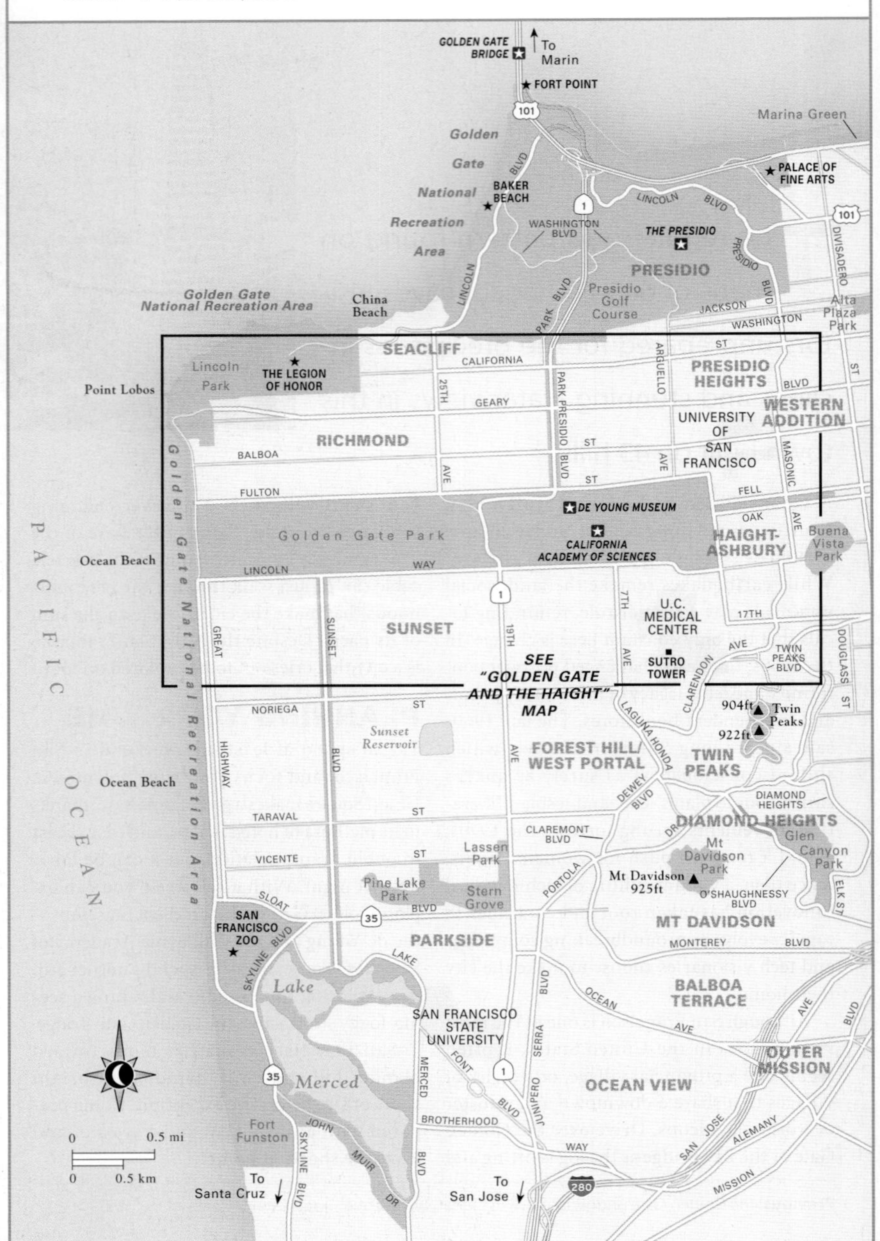

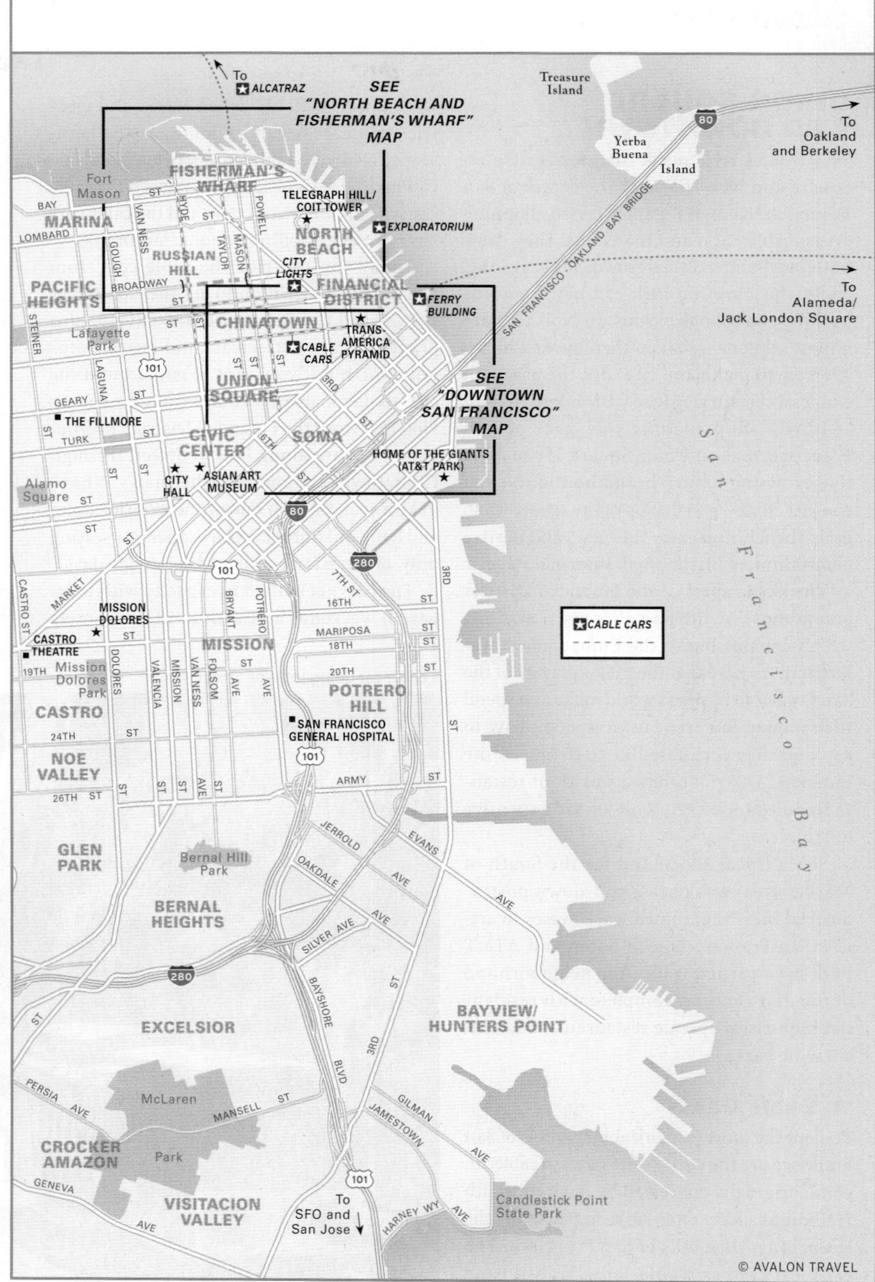
To ALCATRAZ
SEE "NORTH BEACH AND FISHERMAN'S WHARF" MAP
Treasure Island
Yerba Buena Island
To Oakland and Berkeley
To Alameda/ Jack London Square
SAN FRANCISCO - OAKLAND BAY BRIDGE
Fort Mason
FISHERMAN'S WHARF
MARINA
TELEGRAPH HILL/ COIT TOWER
EXPLORATORIUM
NORTH BEACH
RUSSIAN HILL
CITY LIGHTS
PACIFIC HEIGHTS
FINANCIAL DISTRICT
FERRY BUILDING
CHINATOWN
Lafayette Park
TRANS-AMERICA PYRAMID
CABLE CARS
UNION SQUARE
SEE "DOWNTOWN SAN FRANCISCO" MAP
THE FILLMORE
CIVIC CENTER
SOMA
HOME OF THE GIANTS (AT&T PARK)
CITY HALL
ASIAN ART MUSEUM
Alamo Square
San Francisco Bay
MISSION DOLORES
CASTRO THEATRE
Mission Dolores Park
MISSION
POTRERO HILL
CASTRO
SAN FRANCISCO GENERAL HOSPITAL
NOE VALLEY
GLEN PARK
Bernal Hill Park
BERNAL HEIGHTS
EXCELSIOR
BAYVIEW/ HUNTERS POINT
McLaren Park
CROCKER AMAZON
VISITACION VALLEY
To SFO and San Jose
Candlestick Point State Park
CABLE CARS
© AVALON TRAVEL

Sights

UNION SQUARE AND DOWNTOWN

Wealth and style mark the areas of Union Square and Nob Hill near the center of San Francisco. Known for their lavish shopping areas, cable cars, and mansions, they draw both local and visiting crowds all year long. Sadly, the stunning 19th-century mansions built by the robber barons on Nob Hill are almost all gone—shaken then burned in the 1906 earthquake and fire. But the area still exudes a certain elegance with a dash of noir.

If you shop in only one part of San Francisco, make it Union Square. If you don't like browsing luxury brand boutiques, you can just climb up to the top of the square itself, grab a bench, and enjoy the views and the live entertainment on the small informal stage.

The skyscrapers of the Financial District create most of the San Francisco skyline, which extends out to the Embarcadero waterfront. It's here that the major players of the San Francisco business world make and spend their money. But even businesspeople have to eat, and they certainly like to drink, so the Financial District offers a wealth of restaurants and bars. Hotels tend toward expensive tall towers.

SoMa (local shorthand for the South of Market area) was once a run-down postindustrial mess that rented warehouses to artists. San Francisco's tech boom and AT&T Park have turned it into *the* neighborhood of the 21st century, complete with residential high-rises, upscale restaurants, and chichi wine bars.

★ Cable Cars

Perhaps the most recognizable symbols of San Francisco are the **cable cars** (www.sfcablecar.com), originally conceived by Andrew Smith Hallidie as a safer alternative for traveling the steep, often slick hills of San Francisco. The cable cars ran as regular mass transit from 1873 into the 1940s, when buses and electric streetcars began to dominate the landscape. Dedicated citizens, especially "Cable Car Lady" Friedel Klussmann, saved the cable car system from extinction, and the cable cars have become a rolling national landmark.

Today you can ride the cable cars from one tourist destination to another for $6 per ride. A full day "passport" ticket ($15, also grants access to streetcars and buses) is totally worth it if you want to run around the city all day. Cable car routes can take you up Nob Hill from the Financial District, or from Union Square along Powell Street, through Chinatown, and out to Fisherman's Wharf. Take a seat, or grab one of the exterior poles and hang on! Cable cars have open-air seating only, making for a chilly ride on foggy days.

The cars get stuffed to capacity with tourists on weekends and with local commuters

a cable car going to Hyde Street Pier

at rush hours. Expect to wait an hour or more for a ride from any of the turnaround points on a weekend or holiday. But a ride on a cable car from Union Square down to the Wharf is more than worth the wait. The views from the hills down to the bay inspire wonder even in lifetime residents. To learn a bit more, make a stop at **The Barn** (1201 Mason St., 415/474-1887, www.cablecarmuseum.org, 10am-6pm daily Apr.-Sept., 10am-5pm daily Oct.-Mar., free), the home and nerve center of the entire fleet. Here a sweet little museum depicts the life and times of the cable cars while an elevated platform overlooks the engines, winding wheels, and thick steel cable that keeps the cars humming. You can even glimpse into the 1873 tunnels that snake beneath the city.

Grace Cathedral

A local icon, **Grace Cathedral** (1100 California St., 415/749-6300, www.gracecathedral.org, 7am-6pm Mon.-Fri., 8am-6pm Sat., 8am-7pm Sun.) is many things to many people. The French Gothic-style edifice, completed in 1964, attracts architecture and Beaux-Arts lovers by the thousands with its facade, stained glass, and furnishings. The labyrinths—replicas of the Chartres Cathedral labyrinth in France—appeal to meditative walkers seeking spiritual solace. Concerts featuring world music, sacred music, and modern classical ensembles draw audiences from around the bay and farther afield.

Grace Cathedral opens its doors to the community as a vibrant, active Episcopal church. The doctrine of exploration and tolerance matches well with the San Francisco community, of which the church remains an important part.

★ Ferry Building

In 1898, the City of San Francisco created a wonderful new Ferry Building to facilitate commuting from the East Bay. The rise of the automobile after World War II rendered the gorgeous construction obsolete, and its aesthetic ornamentation was covered over and filled in. But then the roads jammed up and

the Ferry Building

Downtown San Francisco

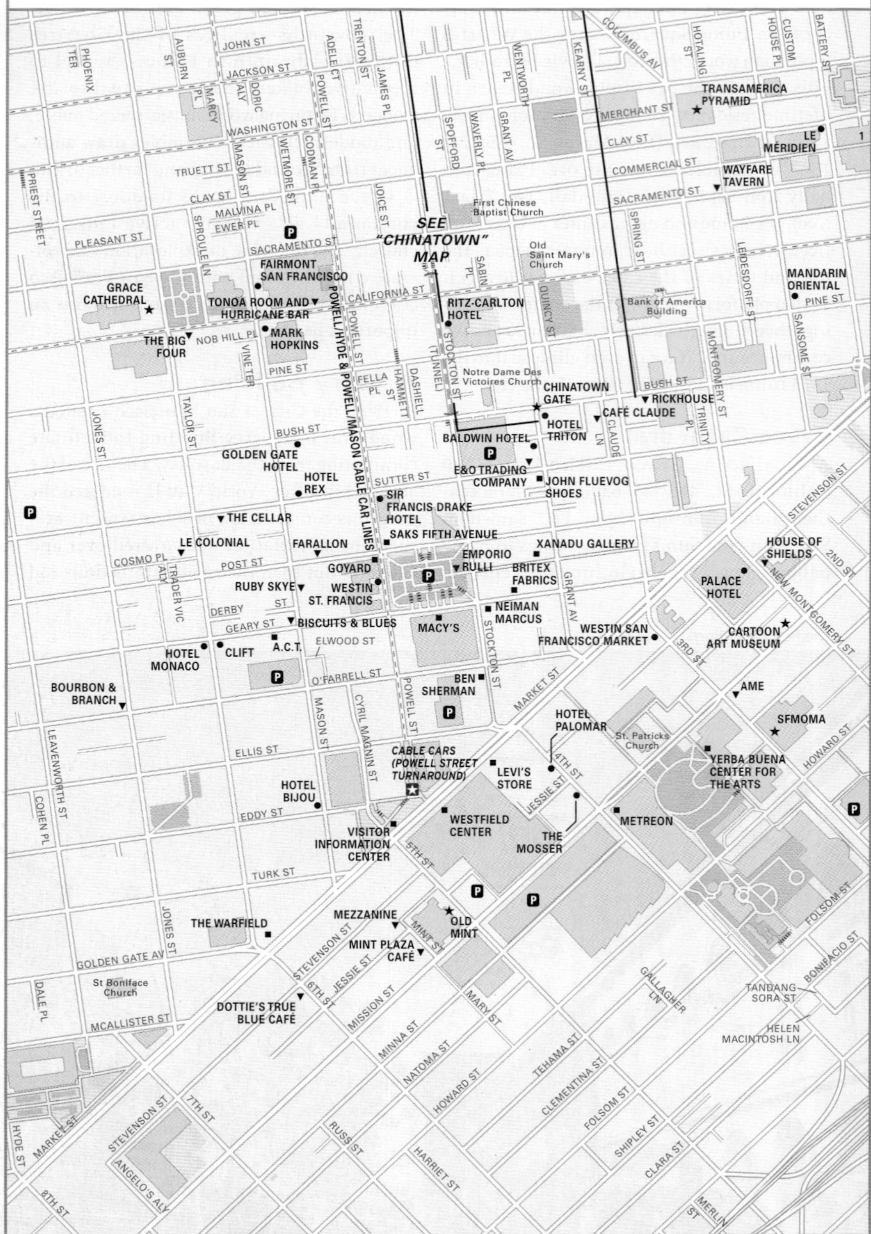

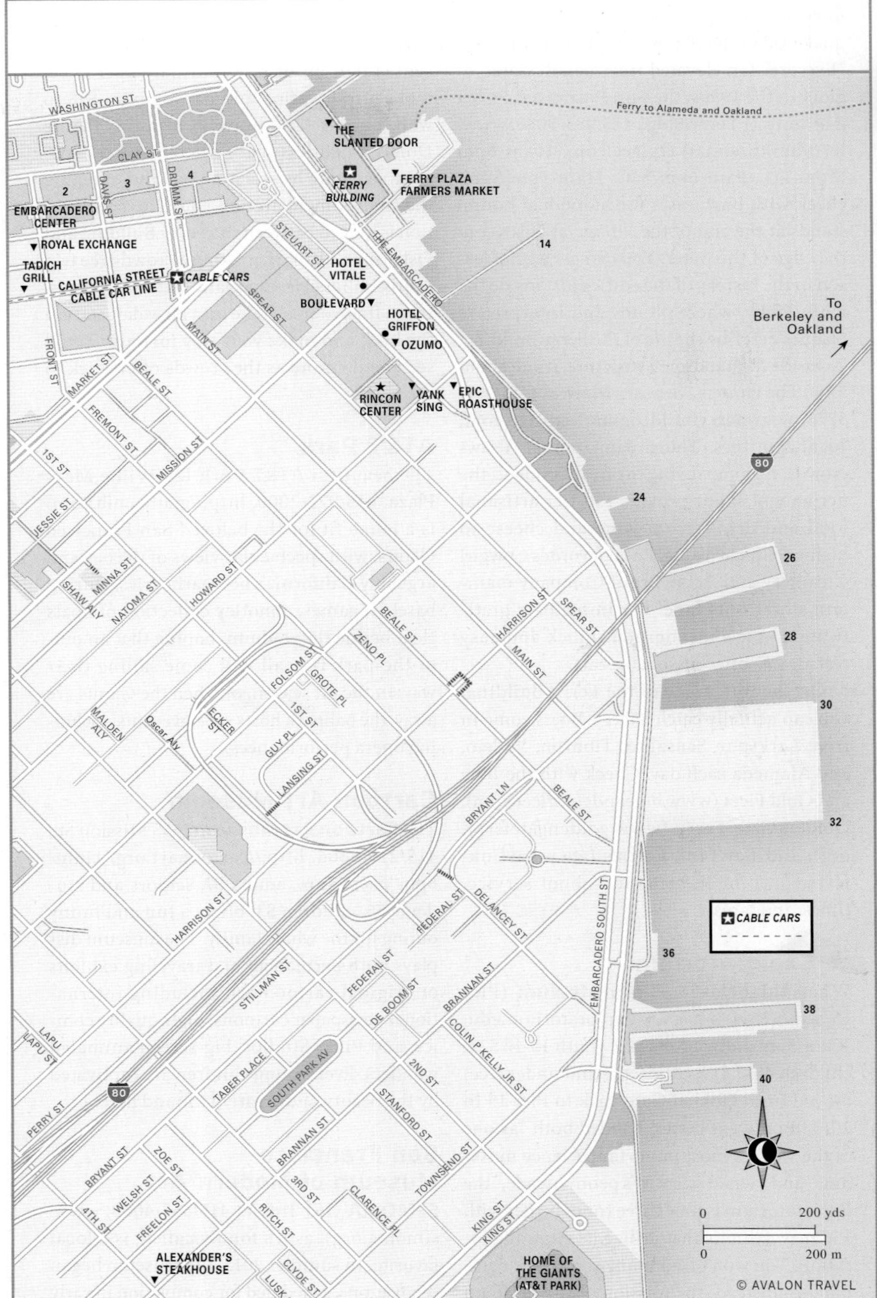
Ferry to Alameda and Oakland
THE SLANTED DOOR
FERRY BUILDING
FERRY PLAZA FARMERS MARKET
EMBARCADERO CENTER
ROYAL EXCHANGE
TADICH GRILL
CALIFORNIA STREET CABLE CAR LINE
CABLE CARS
HOTEL VITALE
BOULEVARD
HOTEL GRIFFON
OZUMO
RINCON CENTER
YANK SING
EPIC ROASTHOUSE
To Berkeley and Oakland
ALEXANDER'S STEAKHOUSE
HOME OF THE GIANTS (AT&T PARK)
WASHINGTON ST
CLAY ST
DAVIS ST
DRUMM ST
STEUART ST
THE EMBARCADERO
SPEAR ST
MAIN ST
FRONT ST
MARKET ST
BEALE ST
FREMONT ST
MISSION ST
1ST ST
JESSIE ST
MINNA ST
SHAW ALY
NATOMA ST
HOWARD ST
ZENO PL
FOLSOM ST
GROTE PL
MALDEN ALY
Oscar Aly
ECKER ST
GUY PL
LANSING ST
HARRISON ST
BRYANT LN
DELANCEY ST
FEDERAL ST
STILLMAN ST
DE BOOM ST
BRANNAN ST
COLIN P KELLY JR ST
EMBARCADERO SOUTH ST
LAPU
LAPU ST
PERRY ST
TABER PLACE
SOUTH PARK AV
2ND ST
STANFORD ST
TOWNSEND ST
BRYANT ST
ZOE ST
WELSH ST
4TH ST
FREELON ST
3RD ST
RITCH ST
CLARENCE PL
KING ST
CLYDE ST
LUSK ST
80
14
24
26
28
30
32
36
38
40
2
3
4
CABLE CARS
0
200 yds
200 m
© AVALON TRAVEL

ferry service began again, and the 1989 earthquake led to the removal of the Embarcadero "Eyesore" (an elevated freeway). Restored to glory in the 1990s, the **San Francisco Ferry Building** (1 Ferry Bldg., 415/983-8030, www.ferrybuildingmarketplace.com, 10am-6pm Mon.-Fri., 9am-6pm Sat., 11am-5pm Sun., check with businesses for individual hours) stands at the end of the Financial District at the edge of the water. You can get a brief lesson in the history of the edifice just inside the main lobby, where photos and interpretive plaques describe the life of the Ferry Building.

Inside the handsome structure, it's all about food. The famous **Farmers Market** (415/291-3276, www.ferrybuildingmarketplace.com, 10am-2pm Tues., Thurs., 8am-2pm Sat.) draws crowds. Accompanying the fresh produce, the permanent shops provide top-tier artisanal food and drink, from wine and cheese to high-end kitchenware. Local favorites Cowgirl Creamery and Acme Bread Company maintain storefronts here. For immediate gratification, a few incongruous quick-and-easy restaurants offer reasonable eats.

On the water side of the Ferry Building, you can actually catch a ferry. Boats come in from Larkspur, Sausalito, Tiburon, Vallejo, and Alameda each day. Check with the Blue and Gold Fleet (www.blueandgoldfleet.com), Golden Gate Ferry (www.goldengateferry.org), and Bay Link Ferries (www.baylinkferry.com) for information about service, times, and fares.

★ Exploratorium

When the beloved **Exploratorium** (Pier 15, 415/528-4444, www.exploratorium.edu, 10am-5pm daily, adults $29, youth 13-17 $24, children 4-12 $19, children 3 and under free) moved from Golden Gate Park to Pier 15 in 2013, it only got better. Lauded both "as one of the world's most important science museums" and "a mad scientist's penny arcade," the Exploratorium is now three times bigger with 150 new exhibits that utilize its stunning location. You won't find many screens or computers—instead, the mission of the museum is to educate (and entertain) with playful displays on physics, motion, perception, and the senses. For an utterly unusual experience, make a reservation and pay an extra $15 to walk blindly (and bravely) into the Tactile Dome, a lightless space where you can "see" your way only by reaching out and touching the environment around you. The new location is lodged between the Ferry Building and Fisherman's Wharf, making a crowd-free trip nearly impossible, especially on the weekends. If you find yourself here on a busy day, start in the back and make your way forward: You'll see and do more as the crowds often stick to the front.

AT&T Park

The beautiful **AT&T Park** (24 Willie Mays Plaza, 415/972-2000, http://giants.mlb.com) is a home fit for the beloved San Francisco Giants, with spectacular views of the bay and arguably California's best garlic fries. During baseball games, a motley collection of boats float beside the stadium, hoping that an out-of-the-park fly ball will come sailing their way. In the off season, or when the Giants are away, the ballpark hosts special events, including opera performances.

Cartoon Art Museum

The **Cartoon Art Museum** (655 Mission St., 415/227-8666, http://cartoonart.org, 11am-5pm Tues.-Sun., adults $7, seniors and students $5, children $3) offers a fun and funny outing for the whole family. The museum displays both permanent and traveling exhibits of original cartoon art, including international newspaper cartoons, high-quality comics, and Pixar Studios' big-screen animated wonders. Even young children are captivated by the beauty and creativity found here.

San Francisco Museum of Modern Art

SFMOMA (151 3rd St., 415/357-4000, www.sfmoma.org), as it's fondly called, is a local favorite. In summer 2013, the museum began renovations, scheduled for completion in early

2016. The makeover will more than double its gallery space for its permanent collections, including those of Ansel Adams, Henri Matisse, and Shiro Kuramata. There will also be plenty of room for the special exhibitions installed each year. In the meantime, visitors can scratch their modern art itch in various locations around the Bay Area where SFMOMA has loaned out some of its permanent collection. Visit the website for exhibit locations and updated visitor information once the renovation is complete.

NORTH BEACH AND CHINATOWN

The massive Chinese migration to California began almost as soon as the news of easy gold in the mountain streams made it to East Asia. And despite rampant prejudice and increasingly desperate attempts on the part of "good" Americans to rid their pristine country of these immigrants, the Chinese not only stayed but persevered and eventually prospered. Many never made it to the gold fields, preferring instead to remain in bustling San Francisco to open shops and begin the business of commerce in their new home. They carved out a thriving community at the border of **Portsmouth Square,** then center of the young city, which became known as Chinatown. Along with much of San Francisco, the neighborhood was destroyed in the 1906 earthquake and fire. Despite xenophobic attempts to relocate Chinatown as far away from downtown San Francisco as possible, the Chinese prevailed and the neighborhood was rebuilt where it originally stood. Today visitors see the post-1906 visitor-friendly Chinatown that was built after the quake, particularly if they enter through the **Chinatown Gate** (Grant Ave. and Bush St.), at the edge of Union Square. In this historic neighborhood, beautiful Asian architecture mixes with more mundane blocky city buildings to create a unique skyline. Small alleyways wend between the touristy commercial corridors, creating an intimate atmosphere.

Farther up Grant, North Beach is an odd

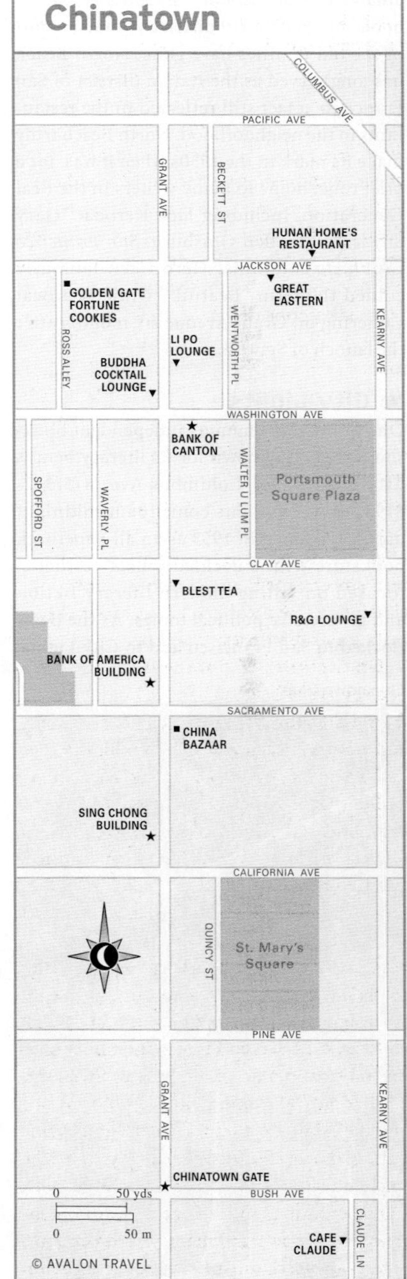

amalgam of old-school residential neighborhood and total tourist district. Although most of the old families have gone, North Beach has long served as the Italian district of San Francisco, a fact still reflected in the restaurants in the neighborhood. North Beach truly made its mark in the 1950s when it was, for a brief time, home to many writers in the Beat Generation, including Jack Kerouac, Gary Snyder, and Allen Ginsburg. *San Francisco Chronicle* columnist Herb Caen famously coined the term "Beatnik" while at a Beat gathering on Grant Avenue six months after the launch of Sputnik.

★ City Lights

One of the most famous independent bookshops in a city known for its literary bent is **City Lights** (261 Columbus Ave., 415/362-8193, www.citylights.com, 10am-midnight daily). It opened in 1953 as an all-paperback bookstore with a decidedly Beat aesthetic, focused on selling modern literary fiction and progressive political tomes. As the Beats flocked to San Francisco and to City Lights, the shop put on another hat—that of publisher. Allen Ginsberg's *Howl* was published by the erstwhile independent, which never looked back. Today they continue to sell and publish the best of cutting-edge fiction and nonfiction. The store is still in its original location on the point of Columbus Avenue, though it's expanded somewhat since the '50s. Expect to find your favorite genre paperbacks along with the latest intriguing new works. The nonfiction selections can really make you take a step back and think about your world in a new way, which is just what founder Lawrence Ferlinghetti wanted.

Chinatown Gate

Coit Tower

Built in 1933 as a monument to her beloved firefighters, **Coit Tower** (1 Telegraph Hill Blvd., 415/249-0995, http://sfrecpark.org, 10am-6pm daily May-Oct., 10am-5pm daily Nov.-Apr., adults $7, ages 12-17 $5, under age 12 $2, call for tour times) has beautified the city just as benefactor Lillie Hitchcock Coit intended. Inside the art deco tower, the walls are covered in the recently restored frescos painted in 1934 depicting city and California life during the Great Depression. For a fee (adults $7, youths $5, children $2, children 4 and under free), you can ride the elevator to the top, where on a clear day, you can see the whole city and bay. Part of what makes Coit Tower special is the walk up to it. Rather than contributing to the acute congestion in the area, consider taking public transit to the area and walking up Telegraph Hill Boulevard through Pioneer Park to the tower and descend down either the Filbert or Greenwich steps toward the Embarcadero. It's long and steep, but there's no other way to see the lovely little cottages and gardens of the beautiful and quaint Telegraph Hill.

Lombard Street

You've no doubt seen it in movies, on TV, and on postcards: **Lombard Street,** otherwise known as "the crookedest street in the world." Much of Lombard Street is a drab commercial artery connecting the Golden Gate Bridge with Van Ness Avenue, but the section that visitors flock to spans only one block, from Hyde Street at the top to Leavenworth Street at the bottom. However, the line of cars waiting their turn to drive bumper-to-bumper can be just as legendary as its 27 percent grade. Bypass the car and take the hill by foot. The unobstructed vistas of San Francisco Bay, Alcatraz Island, Fisherman's Wharf, Coit Tower, and the city are reason enough to add this hike to your itinerary, as are the brick steps, manicured hydrangeas, and tony residences that line the roadway.

Fisherman's Wharf

Welcome to the tourist mecca of San Francisco! While warehouses, stacks of crab pots, and a fleet of fishing vessels let you know this is still a working wharf, it is also *the* spot where visitors to San Francisco come and snap photos. **Fisherman's Wharf** (Beach St. from Powell St. to Van Ness Ave., backs onto Bay St., www.fishermanswharf.org), reachable by Muni F line and the Hyde-Powell cable car, sprawls along the waterfront and inland several blocks, creating a large tourist neighborhood.

The Wharf, as it's called by locals, who avoid the area at all costs, features all crowds, all the time. Be prepared to push through a sea of humanity to see sights, buy souvenirs, and eat seafood. Still, many of the sights of Fisherman's Wharf are important (and fun) pieces of San Francisco's heritage, like the **Fisherman's and Seaman's Memorial Chapel** (Pier 45, 415/674-7503, http://fishermanswharfchapel.org), and the **Musée Mécanique** (Pier 45, 415/346-2000, www.museemechanique.org, 10am-7pm Mon.-Fri., 10am-8pm Sat.-Sun., free), an arcade dating back over a century.

★ Alcatraz

Going to **Alcatraz** (www.nps.gov/alcatraz), one of the most famous landmarks in the city, feels a bit like going to purgatory; this military fortress turned maximum-security prison, nicknamed "The Rock," has little warmth or welcome on its craggy, forbidding shores. While it still belonged to the military, the fortress became a prison in the 19th century to house Civil War prisoners. The isolation of the island in the bay, the frigid waters, and the nasty currents surrounding Alcatraz made it a perfect spot to keep prisoners contained, with little hope of escape and near-certain death if the attempt were ever made. In 1934, after the

City Lights

North Beach and Fisherman's Wharf

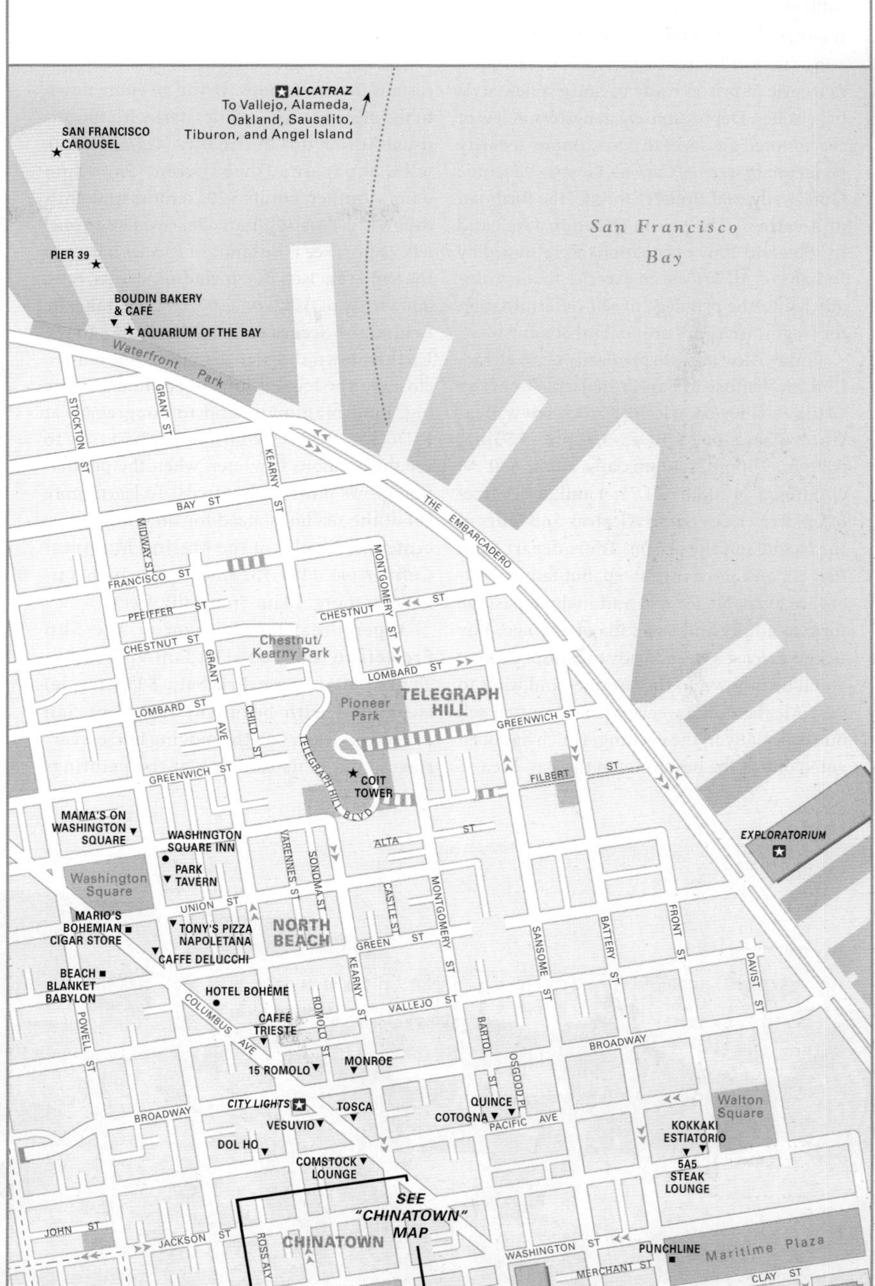
ALCATRAZ
To Vallejo, Alameda, Oakland, Sausalito, Tiburon, and Angel Island
SAN FRANCISCO CAROUSEL
San Francisco Bay
PIER 39
BOUDIN BAKERY & CAFÉ
AQUARIUM OF THE BAY
Waterfront Park
STOCKTON ST
GRANT ST
KEARNY ST
BAY ST
THE EMBARCADERO
MIDWAY ST
FRANCISCO ST
MONTGOMERY ST
PFEIFFER ST
CHESTNUT ST
Chestnut/ Kearny Park
GRANT AVE
LOMBARD ST
CHILD ST
Pioneer Park
TELEGRAPH HILL
GREENWICH ST
TELEGRAPH HILL BLVD
COIT TOWER
FILBERT ST
MAMA'S ON WASHINGTON SQUARE
WASHINGTON SQUARE INN
ALTA ST
EXPLORATORIUM
PARK TAVERN
Washington Square
VARENNES ST
SONOMA ST
CASTLE ST
UNION ST
MARIO'S BOHEMIAN CIGAR STORE
TONY'S PIZZA NAPOLETANA
NORTH BEACH
GREEN ST
SANSOME ST
BATTERY ST
FRONT ST
DAVIS ST
CAFFE DELUCCHI
BEACH BLANKET BABYLON
HOTEL BOHÈME
COLUMBUS AVE
ROMOLO ST
VALLEJO ST
CAFFÉ TRIESTE
POWELL ST
BARTOL ST
OSGOOD PL
BROADWAY
MONROE
15 ROMOLO
CITY LIGHTS
TOSCA
QUINCE
COTOGNA
PACIFIC AVE
Walton Square
VESUVIO
KOKKARI ESTIATORIO
DOL HO
COMSTOCK LOUNGE
5A5 STEAK LOUNGE
SEE "CHINATOWN" MAP
JOHN ST
JACKSON ST
ROSS ALY
CHINATOWN
WASHINGTON ST
PUNCHLINE
Maritime Plaza
MERCHANT ST
CLAY ST

military closed down its prison and handed the island over to the Department of Justice, construction began to turn Alcatraz into a new style of prison ready to house a new style of prisoner: Depression-era gangsters. A few of the honored guests of this maximum-security penitentiary were Al Capone, George "Machine Gun" Kelly, and Robert Stroud, "the Birdman of Alcatraz." The prison closed in 1963, and in 1964 and 1969 occupations were staged by Indians of All Tribes, an exercise that eventually led to the privilege of self-determination for North America's original inhabitants.

Today Alcatraz acts primarily as an attraction for visitors to San Francisco. **Alcatraz Cruises** (Pier 33, 415/981-7625, www.alcatrazcruises.com, 9:10am-3:50pm, 5:55pm, 6:30pm, 9:30pm, 9:40pm daily, adults $30-37, children 5-11 $18.25-21.75, 4 and under free) offers ferry rides out to Alcatraz and tours of the island and the prison. Tours depart from Pier 33, and prices are steep, but family tickets are available for $90 and include passage for two adults and two kids of any age. Buy tickets at least a week in advance, especially if you'll be in town in the summer and want to visit Alcatraz on a weekend. Tours often sell out, especially in the evening, which has been voted one of the best tours in the Bay Area.

Pier 39

One of the most visited spots in San Francisco, **Pier 39** (www.pier39.com) hosts a wealth of restaurants and shops. If you've come down to the pier to see the sealife, start with the unusual **Aquarium of the Bay** (415/623-5300, www.aquariumofthebay.com, 9am-8pm daily summer, adults $20, seniors and children $12). This 300-foot, clear-walled tunnel lets visitors see thousands of species native to the San Francisco Bay, including sharks, rays, and plenty of fish. For a special treat, take the Behind the Scenes or Feed the Sharks tours. Farther down the pier, get close (but not *too* close) to the local colony of sea lions. These big, loud mammals tend to congregate at K-Dock in the West Marina. The best time to see the sea lions is winter, when the population grows into the hundreds. To learn more about the sea lions, head for the interpretive center on Level 2 of the **Marine Mammal Center** (415/289-7325, www.marinemammalcenter.org, 10am-5pm daily, free).

A perennial family favorite, the **San Francisco Carousel** (10am-7pm Sun.-Thurs., 10am-8pm Fri.-Sat., $3 per ride) is painted with beautiful scenes of San Francisco. Riders on the moving horses, carriages, and seats can look at the paintings

Alcatraz

Ghirardelli Square

or out onto the pier. Kids also love the daily shows by local street performers. Depending on when you're on the pier, you might see jugglers, magicians, or stand-up comedians on the **Alpine Spring Water Center Stage** (show times vary, free).

San Francisco Maritime National Historical Park

The real gem of the Wharf is the **San Francisco Maritime National Historical Park,** which spreads from the base of Van Ness to Pier 45. At the **visitors center** (499 Jefferson St., 415/447-5000, 9:30am-5pm daily), not only will rangers help you make the most of your visit, but you can also get lost in the labyrinthine museum that houses an immense Fresnel lighthouse lens and engaging displays that recount San Francisco's history. For $5 you can climb aboard the historical ships at permanent dock across the street at the **Hyde Street Pier.** The shiniest jewel of the collection is the 1886 square-rigged *Balclutha,* a three-masted schooner that recalls times gone by, complete with excellent historical exhibits below deck. There are also several steamboats, including the workhorse ferry paddle-wheel *Eureka* and a cool old steam tugboat called the *Eppleton Hall.* Farther down at Pier 45, World War II buffs can feel the claustrophobia of the submarine **USS *Pampanito*** (415/775-1943, www.maritime.org, 9am-close daily, adults $12, children 6-12 $6, under 6 free) or the expansiveness of the Liberty Ship **SS *Jeremiah O'Brien*** (415/544-0100, www.ssjeremiahobrien.org, adults $12, children 5-12 $6, children under 5 free).

The 1939 Art Deco **Aquatic Bathhouse Building** (900 Beach St., 415/561-7100, www.nps.gov/safr, 10am-4pm daily, adults $5, children free), built in 1939, houses the Maritime Museum, where you can see a number of rotating exhibits alongside its brilliant WPA murals.

Ghirardelli Square

Jammed in with Fisherman's Wharf and Pier 39, **Ghirardelli Square** (900 North Point St., www.ghirardellisq.com), pronounced "GEAR-ah-DEL-ee," began its life as a chocolate factory in 1852, but has since reinvented itself as an upscale shopping, dining, and living compound. While no longer a factory, despite the large river of chocolate snaking through the room, the **Ghirardelli Chocolate Manufactory** (900 North Point St., 415/474-3938, www.ghirardelli.com, 9am-11pm Sun.-Thurs., 9am-midnight Fri.-Sat.) anchors the corner of the square. Here you can browse the rambling shop and pick up truffles, wafers, candies, and sauces for all your friends back home. Finally, get in line at the ice cream counter to order a hot-fudge sundae. These don't travel well, so you'll have to enjoy it here. Once you've finished gorging on chocolate, you can wander out into the square to enjoy more shopping (there's even a cupcake shop if your teeth haven't dissolved yet) and an unbelievably swank condo complex overlooking the bay.

MARINA AND PACIFIC HEIGHTS

The Marina and Pacific Heights shelter some of the amazing amount of money that flows in the City by the Bay. The Marina is one of the San Francisco neighborhoods constructed on landfill (sand dredged up from the bottom of the ocean and piled into what was once a marsh). It was badly damaged in the 1989 Loma Prieta earthquake, but you won't see any of that damage today. Instead, you'll find a wealthy neighborhood, a couple of yacht harbors, plenty of open space, great dining, and shopping that only gets better as you go up the hill.

Palace of Fine Arts

The **Palace of Fine Arts** (3301 Lyon St.) was originally meant to be nothing but a temporary structure—part of the Panama Pacific Exposition in 1915. But the lovely building designed by Bernard Maybeck won the hearts of San Franciscans, and a fund was started to preserve the Palace beyond the Exposition. Through the first half of the 20th century, efforts could not keep it from crumbling, but in the 1960s and 1970s, serious rebuilding work took place, and today the Palace of Fine Arts stands proud, strong, and beautiful. It houses the **Palace of Fine Arts Theater** (415/567-6642, www.palaceoffinearts.org), which hosts events nearly every day, from beauty pageants to conferences on the children's musical theater.

Fort Mason

Once the Port of Embarkation from which the United States waged World War II in the Pacific, **Fort Mason Center** (Buchanan St. and Marina Blvd., 415/345-7500, www.fortmason.org, parking up to $12) now acts as home to numerous nonprofit, multicultural, and artistic organizations. Where soldiers and guns departed to fight the Japanese, visitors now find dance performances, independent theatrical productions, art galleries, and the annual "epic foodie festival" **Eat Drink SF** (http://eatdrink-sf.com). At any time of year, a number of great shows go on in the renovated historical white and red buildings of the complex; check the online calendar.

Other fun features include installations of the **Outdoor Exploratorium** (www.exploratorium.edu/outdoor, dawn-dusk daily). Found all over Fort Mason, the Exploratorium exhibits appeal to all five senses (yes, even taste) and teach visitors about the world around them. You'll taste salt in local water supplies, hear a foghorn, and see what causes

the Palace of Fine Arts

the parking lot to crack and sink. It's free, and it's fascinating—download a map from the website, or grab a guide from installation 5, Portable Observatories.

★ The Presidio

It seems strange to think of progressive, peace-loving San Francisco as a town with tremendous military history, yet a visit to **The Presidio** (Bldg. 105, Montgomery St. and Lincoln Blvd., 415/561-4323, www.nps.gov/prsf, visitors center 10am-4pm Thurs.-Sun., free) will remind visitors that this used to be an army town. Capping the northwestern part of the city, the Presidio has been a military installation since 1776, when the Spanish created their El Presidio del San Francisco fort on the site. In 1846 the United States army took over the site (peacefully), and in 1848 the American Presidio military installation formally opened. When defense budgets shrank at the end of the Cold War, the military turned it over to the National Park Service, making it a historical park in 1994.

While there is plenty of history and architecture here to thrill any military buff, the Presidio's nearly three square miles are filled with miles of hiking trails, restored wetlands, forests, and foreboding cliffs that offer spectacular views of the Golden Gate and the Marin Headlands.

To orient yourself among the more than 800 buildings that make up the Presidio, start at the visitors center in the beautiful Main Post. You'll also find the **Walt Disney Family Museum** (104 Montgomery St., 415/345-6800, www.waltdisney.org, 10am-6pm Wed.-Mon., adults $20, children 6-17 $15) and George Lucas's **Letterman Digital Arts Center** (Chestnut St. and Lyon St., www.lucasfilm.com), where you can snap a photo with a life-size Yoda statue. More history can be found at **Crissy Field,** which runs along the bay and includes the World War II grass airfield, and Civil War-era fortifications at the breathtaking **Fort Point** (end of Marine Dr., 415/556-1693, www.nps.gov/fopo, 10am-5pm Fri.-Mon.).

★ Golden Gate Bridge

People come from the world over to see and walk the **Golden Gate Bridge** (U.S. 101/Hwy. 1 at Lincoln Blvd., 415/921-5858, http://goldengatebridge.org, southbound cars $7, pedestrians free). A marvel of human engineering constructed in 1936 and 1937, the suspension bridge spans the narrow "gate" from which the Pacific Ocean enters the San Francisco Bay. Pedestrians are allowed on the **east sidewalk**

the historic Presidio

the Golden Gate Bridge

(5am-6:30pm daily Nov.-Apr., 5am-9pm daily Apr.-Oct.). On a clear day, the whole bay, Marin Headlands, and the city skyline are visible. Cyclists are allowed on both sidewalks (check the website for times), but as the scenery is stunning, be aware of pedestrians and cyclists not keeping their eyes on where they are going.

The bridge itself is not golden, but a rich orange color called "international orange" that shines like gold when the sun sets behind it on a clear evening. But newcomers to the city beware—not all days and precious few evenings at the bridge are clear. One of the most beautiful sights in San Francisco is the fog blowing in over the Golden Gate late in the afternoon. Unfortunately, once the fog stops blowing and settles in, the bridge is cold, damp, and viewless, so plan to come early in the morning, or pick spring or autumn for your best chance of a clear sight of this most famous and beautiful of artificial structures.

CIVIC CENTER AND HAYES VALLEY

Some of the most interesting neighborhoods in the city cluster toward its center. The Civic Center functions as the heart of San Francisco. Not only is the seat of government here, so are venerable high culture institutions: the War Memorial Opera House and Davies Symphony Hall, home of the world-famous San Francisco Symphony. Visitors who last visited San Francisco a decade or more ago will notice that the Civic Center has been cleaned up quite a lot in the last few years. It's now safe to walk here—at least in the daytime.

As the Civic Center melts into Hayes Valley, you'll find fabulous hotels and restaurants serving both the city's politicos and the well-heeled. At this area's far western edge sits Alamo Square, possibly the most photographed neighborhood in San Francisco. Among its stately Victorians are the famous "painted ladies," a row of brilliantly painted and immaculately maintained homes. From the lovely Alamo Square Park (Hayes St. and Steiner St.), the ladies provide a picturesque foreground to the perfect view of the Civic Center and the rest of downtown.

City Hall

Look at San Francisco's **City Hall** (1 Dr. Carlton B. Goodlett Pl., 415/554-6079, www.sfgov.org,

San Francisco City Hall

8am-8pm Mon.-Fri., free) and you'll think you've somehow been transported to Europe. The stately Beaux-Arts building with the gilded dome is the pride of the city and houses the mayor's office and much of the city's government. Enjoy walking through the parklike square in front of City Hall (though this area can get a bit sketchy after dark). The inside has been extensively renovated after being damaged in the Loma Prieta earthquake in 1989. You'll find a combination of historical grandeur and modern accessibility and convenience as you tour the Arthur Brown Jr.-designed edifice.

Asian Art Museum

Across from City Hall is the **Asian Art Museum** (200 Larkin St., 415/581-3500, www.asianart.org, 10am-5pm Tues.-Wed. and Fri.-Sun., 10am-9pm Thurs., adults $15, seniors $10, ages 13-17 $10, children under age 13 free), with enormous Ionic columns. Inside you'll have an amazing window into the Asian cultures that have shaped and defined San Francisco and the Bay Area. The second and third floors of this intense museum are packed with great art from all across Asia, including a Chinese gilded Buddha dating from AD 338. Sit down on a padded bench to admire paintings, sculpture, lacquered jade, textiles, jewels, and every type of art object imaginable. The breadth and diversity of Asian culture may stagger you; the museum's displays come from Japan and Vietnam, Buddhist Tibet, and ancient China. Special exhibitions cost extra—check the website to see what will be displayed on the ground floor galleries when you're in town. Even if you've been to the museum in the past, come back for a browse. The curators regularly rotate items from the permanent collection, so you'll probably encounter new beauty every time you visit.

MISSION AND CASTRO

Perhaps the most famous, or infamous, neighborhoods in the city are the Mission district and the Castro district. The Castro is the heart of gay San Francisco, complete with naughty shops, leather bars, and all sorts of, uh . . . adult festivals. It has become pretty touristy, but you can still find the occasional jewel here. Just don't expect the Halloween party you've heard about—the city has cracked down, and Halloween has become sedate in this party-happy neighborhood.

With its mix of Latino immigrants, working artists, and high paid tech workers, the Mission is a neighborhood bursting at the seams with idiosyncratic energy. Changing from block to block, the zone manages to be blue-collar, edgy, and extremely gentrified all at once. While the heart of the neighborhood is still Latin American, with delicious burritos and *pupusas* around every corner, it has also become the "it" neighborhood for the new tech economy. Many older businesses have given way to million-dollar condos and pricey boutiques, but the neighborhood has also emerged as *the* dining district in a city famous for its food.

Mission Dolores

Mission Dolores (3321 16th St., 415/621-8203, www.missiondolores.org, 9am-4:30pm daily May-Oct., 9am-4pm daily Nov.-Apr., donation adults $5, children $3), formally named Mission San Francisco de Asís, was founded in 1776. Today the mission is the oldest intact building in the city, having survived the 1906 earthquake and fire, the 1989 Loma Prieta quake, and more than 200 years of use. You can attend Roman Catholic services here each Saturday, or you can visit the Old Mission Museum and the Basilica, which house artifacts from the Native Americans and Spanish of the 18th century. The beauty and grandeur of the mission recall the heyday of the Spanish empire in California, so important to the history of the state as it is today.

GOLDEN GATE PARK AND THE HAIGHT

Dominating the western half of San Francisco, **Golden Gate Park** (main entrance at Stanyan St. at Fell St., McLaren Lodge Visitors Center at John F. Kennedy Dr., 415/831-2700, www.golden-gate-park.com) is one of the city's most enduring treasures. Its over 1,000 acres include lakes, forests, formal gardens, windmills, museums, a buffalo pasture, and plenty of activities. Enjoy free concerts in the summer, hike in near solitude in the winter, or spend a day wandering and exploring scores of sights.

At the eastern end of the park, the neighborhood surrounding the intersection of Haight and Ashbury Streets (known locally as "the Haight") is best known for the wave of countercultural energy that broke out in the 1960s. The area initially was a magnet for drifters, dropouts, and visionaries who preached and practiced a heady blend of peace, love, and psychedelic drugs.

The door to the promised new consciousness never swung fully open, and then it swung shut with a resounding bang. Today thousands of visitors stand at the iconic intersection, and what they see is Ben & Jerry's. The district is still home to plenty of independent businesses, including vintage stores, lots of places to get pierced and tattooed, and of course, head shops.

★ de Young Museum

Whether you are an art aficionado or not, the **de Young Museum** (50 Hagiwara Tea Garden Dr., 415/750-3600, http://deyoung.famsf.org, 9:30am-5:15pm Tues.-Thurs. and Sat.-Sun., 9:30am-8:45pm Fri. Apr.-Nov., 9:30am-5:15pm Tues.-Sun. Dec.-Mar., adults $10, seniors $7, children 13-17 $6, children 12 and under free) in Golden Gate Park is a must-see. The collection is staggering in its size and breadth: You'll view everything from pre-Colombian art to

Mission Dolores, the oldest surviving structure in San Francisco

17th-century ladies' gowns. Painting, sculpture, textiles, ceramics, "contemporary crafts" from all over the world, and rotating exhibits range from King Tut to the exquisite Jean-Paul Gautier collection. Competing with all of that is the building itself.

The museum's modern exterior is wrapped in perforated copper, while the interior incorporates pockets of manicured gardens. Poking out of the park's canopy is a twisted tower that offers a spectacular 360-degree view of the city and the bay. Entrance to the tower, lily pond, and art garden are free. Surrounded by sphinxes and draping wisteria, you can enjoy an art-filled picnic lunch.

★ California Academy of Sciences

A triumph of the sustainable scientific principles it exhibits, the **California Academy of Sciences** (55 Music Concourse Dr., 415/379-8000, www.calacademy.org, 9:30am-5pm Mon.-Sat., 11am-5pm Sun., adults $35, students, seniors, and children 12-17 $30, children 4-11 $25, children 3 and under free) drips with ecological perfection. From its grass-covered roof to its underground aquarium, visitors can explore every part of the universe. Wander through a steamy endangered rainforest contained inside a giant glass bubble, or travel through an all-digital outer space in the high-tech planetarium. More studious nature lovers can spend days examining every inch of the Natural History Museum, including favorite exhibits like the 87-foot-long blue whale skeleton. The Academy of Sciences takes pains to make itself kid-friendly, with interactive exhibits, thousands of live animals, and endless opportunities for learning. How could kids not love a museum where the guards by the elevators have butterfly nets to catch the occasional escaping insect? On Thursday nights (6pm-10pm, $12), the academy is an adults-only zone, where DJs play music and the café serves cocktails by some of the city's most renowned mixologists.

Japanese Tea Garden

The **Japanese Tea Garden** (75 Hagiwara Tea Garden Dr., 415/752-4227, http://japaneseteagardensf.com, 9am-6pm daily Mar.-Oct., 9am-4:45pm daily Nov.-Feb., adults $7, seniors $5, children 5-11 $2, children 4 and under free) is a haven of peace and tranquility that's a local favorite within the park, particularly in the spring. The planting and design of the garden began in 1894 for the California Exposition. Today the flourishing garden

the de Young Museum

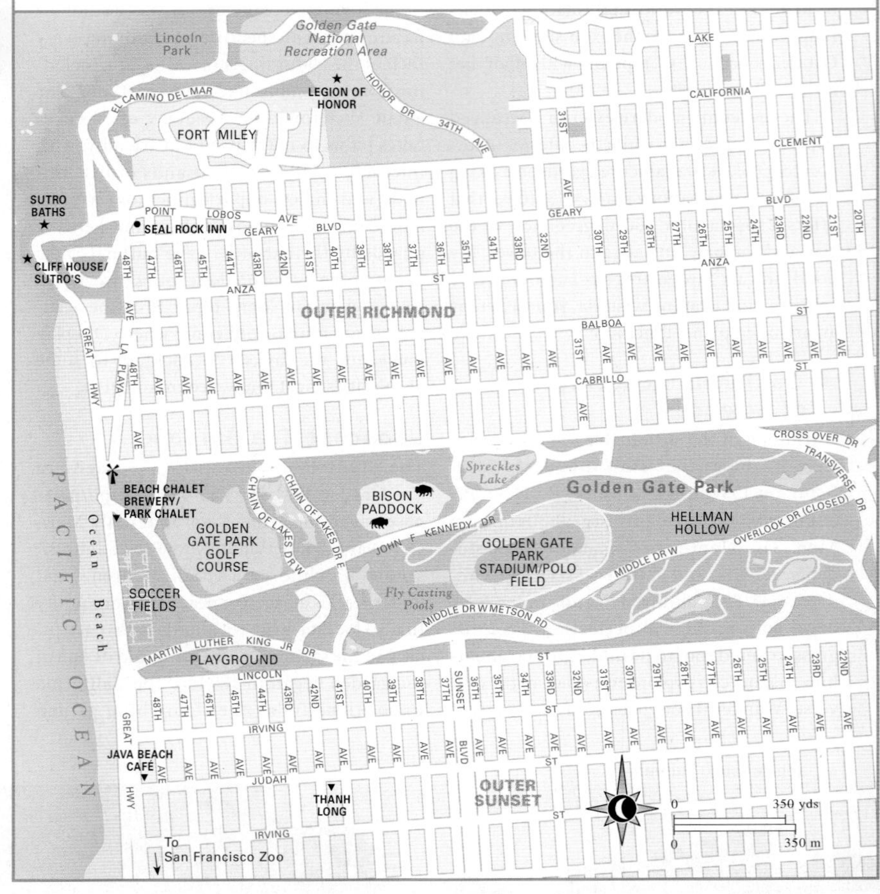

displays a wealth of beautiful flora, including stunning examples of rare Chinese and Japanese plants, some quite old. As you stroll along the paths, you'll come upon sculptures, bridges, ponds, and even traditional *tsukubai* (a tea ceremony sink). Take one of the docent-led tours and conclude your visit with tea and a fortune cookie at the tea house.

San Francisco Botanical Gardens

Take a bucolic walk in the middle of Golden Gate Park by visiting the **San Francisco Botanical Gardens** (1199 9th Ave. at Lincoln Way, 415/661-1316, www.sfbotanicalgarden.org, 7:30am-6pm daily early Mar.-Sept., 10am-5pm daily Oct.-early Mar., adults $7, students and seniors $5, ages 5-11 $2, families $15, under age 5 and city residents with ID free). The 55-acre gardens play home to more than 8,000 species of plants from around the world, including a California Natives garden and a shady redwood forest. Fountains, ponds, meadows, and lawns are interwoven with the

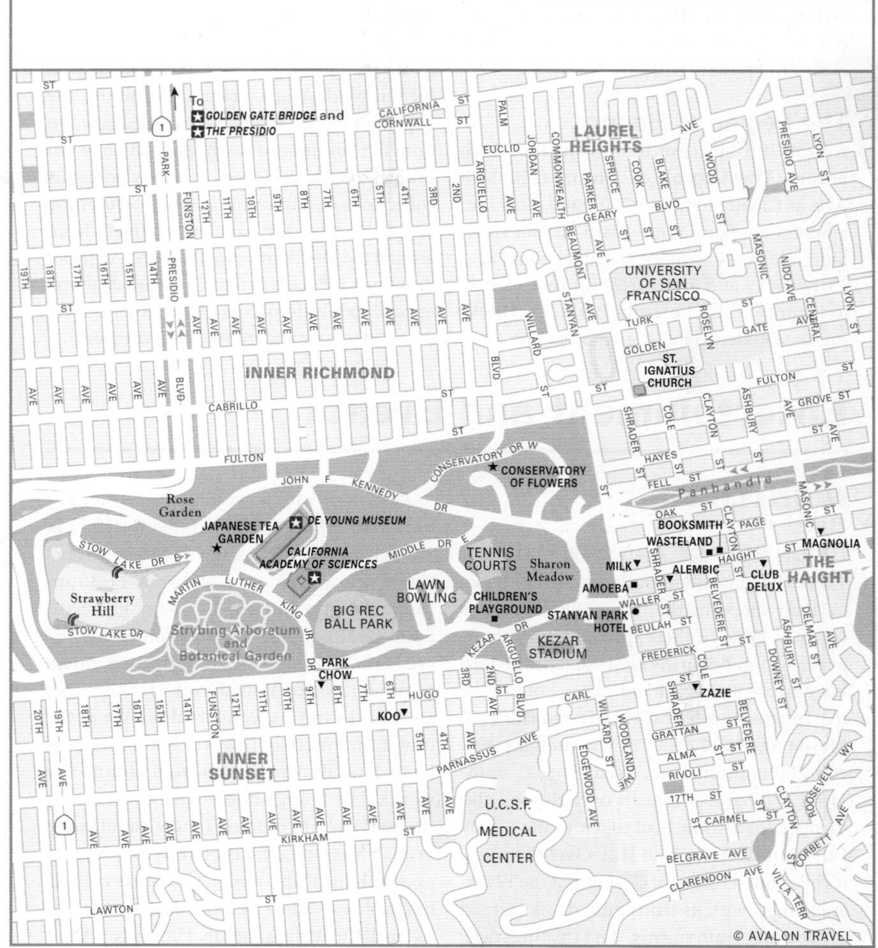

flowers and trees to create a peaceful, serene setting in the middle of the crowded city. The Botanical Gardens are a great place to kick back with a book and a snack; the plants will keep you in quiet company as you rev up to tackle another round of touring.

Conservatory of Flowers

For a trip to San Francisco's Victorian past, step inside the steamy **Conservatory of Flowers** (100 John F. Kennedy Dr., 415/831-2090, www.conservatoryofflowers.org, 10am-4:30pm Tues.-Sun., adults $8, students and seniors $5, ages 5-11 $2, children under 5 free). Built in 1878, the striking wood and glass greenhouse is home to over 1,700 plant species that spill out of containers, twine around rainforest trees, climb trellises reaching the roof, and rim deep ponds where eight-foot lily pads float serenely on still waters. Surrounded by the exotic flora illuminated only by natural light, it is easy to transport yourself to the heyday of colonialism when the study of botany was in its first bloom. Plus, it is one of the best places to explore on a rainy day. Strollers are not permitted inside; wheelchairs and power chairs are allowed.

The Legion of Honor

A beautiful museum in a town filled with beauty, **The Legion of Honor** (100 34th Ave. at Clement St., 415/750-3600, http://legionofhonor.famsf.org, 9:30am-5:15pm Tues.-Sun., adults $10, seniors $7, students and ages 13-17 $6, 12 and under free) sits on its lonely promontory in Lincoln Park, overlooking the Golden Gate. A gift to the city from philanthropist Alma Spreckels in 1924, this French Beaux-Arts style building was built to honor the memory of California soldiers who died in World War I. From its beginning, the Legion of Honor was a museum dedicated to bringing European art to the population of San Francisco. Today visitors can view gorgeous collections of European paintings, sculpture, and decorative arts, ancient artifacts from around the Mediterranean, thousands of paper drawings by great artists, and much more. Special exhibitions come from the Legion's own collections and museums of the world.

Entertainment and Events

NIGHTLIFE

Bars

UNION SQUARE AND DOWNTOWN

These ritzy neighborhoods are better known for their shopping than their nightlife, but a few bars hang in there, plying weary shoppers with good drinks. Most tend toward the upscale. Some inhabit major hotels, like the **Tonga Room and Hurricane Bar** (950 Mason St., 415/772-5278, www.tongaroom.com, 6pm-10pm Sun., Wed.-Thurs., 6pm-11pm Fri.-Sat.), where an over-the-top tiki theme adds a whimsical touch to the stately Fairmont Hotel on Nob Hill. Over the years, it's been on the brink of closing, but the 1940s-era lounge, with its fruity rum drinks served in coconuts, "rain storms," and floating stage, is so beloved that San Franciscans demanded it be designated a historical landmark.

Another hopping tiki lounge can be found at **Le Colonial** (20 Cosmo Pl., 415/931-3600, www.lecolonialsf.com, 5pm-close daily). Follow the dimly light staircase above the French Vietnamese restaurant and pick from the large and tropical cocktail menu. The thumping sounds of the DJs seem to clash with the 1950s colonial decor, but once the dance floor fills up and you're halfway through their signature "Scorpion Bowl," it feels like the most happening spot in sweltering Indochina.

Part live-music venue, part elegant bar, **Top of the Mark** (999 California St., 415/392-3434, www.intercontinentalmarkhopkins.com, 4:30pm-11:30pm Mon.-Thurs., 4:30pm-12:30am Fri.-Sat., 5pm-11:30pm Sun.) has something for every discerning taste in nighttime entertainment. Since World War II, the views and drinks in this wonderful lounge at the top of the InterContinental Mark Hopkins Hotel have drawn visitors from around the world. The lounge doubles as a restaurant that serves light dinners (and a champagne brunch on Sunday). Live bands play almost every night of the week. The dress code is business casual or better and is enforced, so leave the jeans at home. Have a top-shelf martini, and let your toes tap along.

The cocktail craze is alive and well at the **Rickhouse** (246 Kearny St., 415/398-2827, www.rickhousesf.com, 5pm-2am Mon., 3pm-2am Tues.-Fri., 6pm-2am Sat.). While it was listed as one of the top 10 whiskey bars in the country by *GQ* in 2013, Rickhouse truly specializes in cocktails made from long-forgotten spirits and fresh ingredients, or in the parlance of our times, the "retro-fresh cocktail." Grab a seat upstairs or down in the all-wood bar, and sample a Rye Maple Fizz or go in on a massive rum punch, served in a hollow clam shell. Get here before the after-work crowd, or you may not get in at all.

FINANCIAL DISTRICT AND SOMA

All those high-powered business suit-clad executive types working in the Financial District need places to drink too. One of these is the **Royal Exchange** (301 Sacramento St., 415/956-1710, http://royalexchange.com, 11am-11pm Mon.-Fri.). This classic pub-style bar has a green-painted exterior, big windows overlooking the street, and a long, narrow barroom. The Royal Exchange serves a full lunch and dinner menu, a small wine list, and a full complement of top-shelf spirits. But most of all, the Exchange serves beer. With 73 taps pouring out 32 different types of beer, the hardest problem will be choosing one. This businesspeople's watering hole is open to the public only on weekdays; on weekends they host private parties.

The **House of Shields** (39 New Montgomery St., 415/284-9958, www.thehouseofshields.com, 2pm-2am Mon.-Fri., 3pm-2am Sat.-Sun.) has been in the city since 1908. The original incarnation was an illegal speakeasy during the prohibition era (it even has an under-street tunnel to the neighboring Sheraton Hotel). After an extensive remodeling in 2010 by celebrity chef Dennis Leary, the House of Shields has reopened serving upscale cocktails (with upscale prices) in the gorgeous interior. Expect a huge crowd during happy hour, which thins out after 8pm or so.

Secret passwords, a hidden library, and an art deco vibe make **Bourbon and Branch** (505 Jones St., 415/346-1735, www.bourbonandbranch.com, 6pm-2am Mon.-Sat., reservations suggested) a must for lovers of the brown stuff. Tucked behind a nameless brown door, this resurrected 1920s-era speakeasy evokes its Prohibition-era past with passwords and secret passages. A business-class elite sips rare bourbon and scotch in secluded booths while those without reservations step into the hidden library.

CHINATOWN

Nightlife in Chinatown runs to dark, quiet dive bars filled with locals. Perhaps the perfect Chinatown dive, **Li Po Lounge** (916 Grant Ave., 415/982-0072, www.lipolounge.com, 2pm-2am daily, cash only) has an appropriately dark and slightly spooky atmosphere that recalls the opium den it once was. Cheap drinks and Chinese dice games attract locals, and it's definitely helpful to speak Cantonese. But even an English-speaking out-of-town visitor can get a good cheap (and strong!) mai tai or beer. The hanging lantern and Buddha statue behind the bar complete the picture. Another local favorite is the **Buddha Cocktail Lounge** (901 Grant Ave., 415/362-1792, noon-2am daily, cash only), or "Buddha Bar" just across the street.

NORTH BEACH AND FISHERMAN'S WHARF

North Beach is famous for its watering holes, but perhaps its most iconic is **Vesuvio** (255 Columbus Ave., 415/362-3370, www.vesuvio.com, 6am-2am daily) for the simple reason that Jack Kerouac loved it. Not much has changed since then, except its jukebox, which has only gotten better. This cozy bi-level hideout is an easy place to spend the afternoon with a pint of Anchor Steam.

Up one of North Beach's grimiest alleys is one its best kept secrets. **15 Romolo** (15 Romolo Place, 415/398-1359, www.15romolo.com, 5pm-2am Mon.-Fri., 11am-2am Sat.-Sun.), on the first floor of the Basque Hotel, feels like a hidden speakeasy. It serves fresh, inventive cocktails and a menu that will encourage you to stay and dine here instead of brave the North Beach restaurant crowds (the kitchen serves food until 1:30am). The bar is smallish and can get crowded on the weekend, so come on a weeknight if you prefer a quiet drink.

Drinking is such a long-standing tradition in North Beach that most of its bars have been around for nearly a half century. **Comstock Saloon** (155 Columbus Ave., 415/617-0071, www.comstocksaloon.com, noon-2am Mon.-Fri., 4pm-2am Sat., 4pm-midnight Sun.), opened in 2009, has edged its way in, bringing with it the city's retro-fresh craze. Although the cocktail menu may be tailored to today's taste, the vibe works to recall the city's early days. The heavy ornate bar and a meat-and-potato menu (think chicken livers and steak) conjure the 1860s, somehow making it feel modern and relevant.

MARINA AND PACIFIC HEIGHTS

Perched on top of Russian Hill alongside the humming cable car line is **Bacchus** (1954 Hyde St., 415/928-2633, www.bacchussf.com, 5:30pm-midnight daily), a tiny watering hole catering to locals who love vino. It offers an array of wines, sake cocktails, and even delivered-to-your-table sushi from nearby Sushi Groove. DJs sometimes spin on Thursday and Friday nights.

Weekend nights in the Marina can feel like a college party with all of the twentysomethings traipsing from bar to bar. One of the oldest bars in the neighborhood is the **Bus Stop** (1901 Union St., 415/567-6905, 10am-2am Mon.-Fri., 9am-2am Sat.-Sun.), a sports bar with plenty of cheap drinks, TV screens, and even a Ms. Pacman arcade game. It gets pretty packed on the weekends, so if you're looking for a less raucous time, head over to the Presidio. Equally old school, the **Final Final** (2990 Baker St., 415/931-7800, www.finalfinalsfsportsbar.com, noon-2am daily) also bills itself a sports bar, complete with a couple pool tables, but for the older, more polished Marina set.

All that's really left of the original Matrix club is the ground it stands on, but the **MatrixFillmore** (3138 Fillmore St., 415/563-4180, www.matrixfillmore.com, 9pm-2am Sun.-Mon. and Wed.-Thurs., 8pm-2am Fri.-Sat.) claims huge mid-20th-century musical fame. The Matrix, then a live music venue, was opened by Marty Balin, so that his freshly named band, Jefferson Airplane, would have a place to play. Subsequent acts included the Grateful Dead, Janis Joplin, and the Doors. Today the MatrixFillmore's Lincoln-log fireplace and top-shelf cocktails appeal to the quiet drinking crowd on weeknights and the bridge-and-tunnel singles scene on the weekend. DJs spin techno most nights, though you can catch an occasional live act here too. There's valet parking at Balboa Cafe down the street.

CIVIC CENTER AND HAYES VALLEY

Hayes Valley bleeds into Lower Haight (Haight St. between Divisadero St. and Octavia Blvd.) and supplies most of the neighborhood bars. For proof that the independent spirit of the Haight lives on in spite of encroaching commercialism, stop in and have a drink at the **Toronado** (547 Haight St., 415/863-2276, www.toronado.com, 11:30am-2am daily). This dimly lit haven maintains one of the finest beer selections in the nation, with a changing roster of several dozen microbrews on tap, including many hard-to-find Belgian ales.

Channeling a shipwreck in the middle of the Caribbean, the hipster **Smuggler's Cove** (650 Gough St., 415/869-1900, http://smugglerscovesf.com, 5pm-1:15am daily) has been named one of America's best bars by *Esquire, Times of London, Food & Wine* magazine, and *Playboy.* You can select from over 400 different types of rum. The cocktail menu reads like an index of rum drinks from the heyday of tiki bars, many using fire as a key ingredient.

If what you really want is a dive bar, **Place Pigalle** (520 Hayes St., 415/552-2671, http://placepigallesf.com, 5pm-2am Mon.-Tues., 2pm-2am Wed.-Sun.) is the place for you. This hidden gem in Hayes Valley offers beer and wine only, a pool table, lots of sofas for lounging, and an uncrowded, genuinely laid-back vibe even on weekends.

MISSION AND CASTRO

These neighborhoods seem to hold a whole city's worth of bars. The Mission, despite a recent upswing in its economy, still has plenty of no-frills bars, many with a Latino theme. And, of course, men seeking men flock to the Castro's endless array of gay bars. For lesbians, the Mission might be a better bet.

Dalva (3121 16th St., 415/252-7740, http://dalvasf.com, 4pm-2am daily) is a small but

served nightly and features a surprisingly varied and upscale menu combining California cuisine with the mystical flavors of New Orleans. Yum!

Bringing jazz to the high culture of Hayes Valley is **SFJazz Center** (201 Franklin St., 866/920-5299, http://sfjazz.org, hours vary Tues.-Sun.). The stunning 35,000-square-foot space boasts state-of-the-art acoustics. It's designed to feel like a small club, thanks to steep seating that brings the large audience close to the performers. Since opening in 2013, it has already drawn major acts such as Herbie Hancock and the Afro Cuban Allstars.

Comedy

San Francisco's oldest comedy club, the **Punch Line** (444 Battery St., 415/397-7573, www.punchlinecomedyclub.com, shows 8pm, 10pm Tues.-Sun., cover varies) is an elegant and intimate venue that earned its top-notch reputation with stellar headliners such as Robin Williams, Ellen DeGeneres, and Dave Chappelle. An on-site bar keeps the audience primed.

Cobb's Comedy Club (915 Columbus Ave., 415/928-4320, www.cobbscomedy.com, shows 8pm, 10:15pm Thurs.-Sun., cover varies, two-drink minimum) has played host to star comedians such as Louis CK, Sarah Silverman, and Margaret Cho since 1982. The 425-seat venue offers a full dinner menu and a bar to slake your thirst. Be sure to check your show's start time—some comics don't follow the usual Cobb's schedule.

THE ARTS

Theater

San Francisco may not be a known as a big theater town, but it does boast a number of small and large theaters. One perk is that many big New York shows come here to work out the kinks before their stints on Broadway. A great way to grab last-minute theater tickets (or for music or dance shows) is to walk right up to **Union Square TIX** (Union Square, 415/433-7827, www.tixbayarea.com, 10am-6pm daily). TIX sells same-day, half-price, no-refund tickets to all kinds of shows across the city. If you've got your heart set on a specific musical or play in a big theater, get to the booth early in the day and steel yourself for possible disappointment—especially on weekends, when many top-shelf shows sell out. TIX also sells half-price tickets to same-day shows online—check the website at 11am daily for up-to-date deals.

If you really, really need to see a major musical while you're in San Francisco, check out **SHN** (www.shnsf.com). SHN operates the Orpheum, the Curran, and the Golden Gate Theater—the three venues where big Broadway productions land when they come to town.

UNION SQUARE AND DOWNTOWN

Just up from Union Square, on Geary Street, the traditional San Francisco theater district continues to entertain crowds almost every day of the week. The old Geary Theater is now the permanent home of **A.C.T.** (415 Geary St., 415/749-2228, www.act-sf.org, shows Tues.-Sun., $22-82). A.C.T. puts on a season filled with big-name, big-budget productions. Each season sees an array of high-production-value musicals such as *Old Hats,* American classics by the likes of Sam Shepard and Somerset Maugham, and intriguing new works; you might even get to see a world premiere. Don't expect to find street parking on Geary. Discount parking is available with a ticket stub from A.C.T. at the Mason-O'Farrell garage around the corner. Tickets can be reasonably priced, especially on weeknights, but do be aware that the second balcony seats are truly high altitude—expect to look nearly straight down to the stage, and take care if you're prone to vertigo.

The **Curran Theater** (445 Geary St., 888/746-1799, www.shnsf.com, $105-250), next door to A.C.T., has a state-of-the-art stage for classic, high-budget musicals. Audiences have watched *Les Misérables, Phantom of the Opera,* and *Chicago* from the plush red velvet seats. Expect to pay a premium for tickets to these musicals, which can sometimes run at the Curran for months or even years. Check the schedule for current shows, and leave children under age five at home—they won't be permitted in the Curran.

NORTH BEACH AND CHINATOWN

There's one live show that's always different, yet it's been running continuously since 1974. This musical revue is crazy, wacky, and offbeat, and it pretty much defines live theater in San Francisco. It's **Beach Blanket Babylon** (678 Green St., 415/421-4222, www.beachblanketbabylon.com, shows Wed.-Sun., $25-100). Even if you saw Beach Blanket Babylon 10 years ago, you should come to see it again; because it mocks current pop culture, the show evolves almost continuously to take advantage of tabloid treasures. Although minors are welcome at the Sunday matinees, evening shows can get pretty racy and liquor is involved, so these are restricted to attendees 21 and over. You'll never forget the hats.

CIVIC CENTER AND HAYES VALLEY

Located in seedy Mid-Market area, both the **Orpheum Theater** (1192 Market St., 888/746-1799, www.shnsf.com, $50-200) and the **Golden Gate Theater** (1 Taylor St., 888/746-1799, www.shnsf.com, $50-200) run touring productions of popular Broadway musicals. Neither theater allows children under five. At the very San Franciscan **EXIT Theatre** (156 Eddy St., 415/931-1094, www.theexit.org, up to $15), down in the Tenderloin, you'll see plenty of unusual experimental plays, many by local playwrights and some even written by the audience. The theater also shows some burlesque and singer-songwriter acts. The EXIT also participates in the annual San Francisco Fringe Festival (www.sffringe.org).

Classical Music and Opera

Right around the Civic Center, culture takes a turn for the upscale. This is the neighborhood where the ultrarich and not-so-rich classics lovers come to enjoy a night out. Acoustically renovated in 1992, **Davies Symphony Hall** (201 Van Ness Ave., 415/864-6000, www.sfsymphony.org) is home to Michael Tilson Thomas's world-renowned San Francisco Symphony. Loyal patrons flock to performances that range from the classic to the avant-garde. Whether you want to hear Mozart and Mahler or classic rock blended with major symphony orchestra, the San Francisco Symphony does it.

The **War Memorial Opera House** (301 Van Ness Ave., 415/621-6600, www.sfwmpac.org), a Beaux-Arts style building designed by Coit Tower and City Hall architect Arthur Brown Jr., houses the **San Francisco Opera** (415/864-3330, http://sfopera.com) and **San Francisco Ballet** (415/861-5600, www.sfballet.org). Tours are available (415/552-8338, 10am-2pm Mon., $5-7).

Cinema

San Franciscans love their movies. There are a lot of great neighborhood theaters, many of which are just one or two screens. Your best option is the **Castro Theatre**

the ornate Castro Theatre

(429 Castro St., 415/621-6120, www.castrotheatre.com, $8.50-11), a grand movie palace from the 1920s that has enchanted San Francisco audiences for almost a century. The Castro Theater hosts everything from revival double features (from black-and-white through 1980s classics) to musical movie sing-alongs, live shows, and even the occasional book signing. The Castro also screens current releases and documentaries about queer life in San Francisco and beyond. Once inside, be sure to admire the lavish interior decor. If you get to your seat early, you're likely to be rewarded with a performance of the Mighty Wurlitzer pipe organ before the show.

For a more modern and upscale moviegoing experience, go to the **Sundance Kabuki Theater** (1881 Post St., www.sundancecinemas.com/kabuki.html, $9.75-15.50). The "amenity fee" pays for reserved seating, film shorts rather than commercials, and bamboo decor. The Kabuki has eight screens, all of which show mostly big blockbuster Hollywood films, plus a smattering of independents and the occasional filmed opera performance. The Over 21 shows are in the two theaters connected to full bars.

Shopping

UNION SQUARE

For the biggest variety of department stores and high-end international designers, plus a few select boutiques, locals and visitors alike flock to Union Square (bounded by Geary St., Stockton St., Post St., and Powell St.). The shopping area includes more than just the square proper: More designer and brand-name stores cluster for several blocks in all directions.

The big guys anchor Union Square. **Macy's** (170 O'Farrell St., 415/397-3333, www.macys.com, 10am-9pm Mon.-Sat., 11am-8pm Sun.) has two immense locations, one for women's clothing and another for the men's store and housewares. **Neiman Marcus** (150 Stockton St., 415/362-3900, www.neimanmarcus.com, 10am-7pm Mon.-Wed., Fri.-Sat., 10am-8pm Thurs., noon-6pm Sun.) is a favorite among high-budget shoppers, and **Saks Fifth Avenue** (384 Post St., 415/986-4300, www.saksfifthavenue.com, 10am-7pm Mon.-Sat., 11am-7pm Sun.) adds a touch of New York style to funky-but-wealthy San Francisco.

Levi's (815 Market St., 415/501-0100, www.levi.com, 9am-9pm Mon.-Sat., 10am-8pm Sun.) may be a household name, but this three-floor fashion emporium offers incredible customization services while featuring new music and emerging art. Levi's got its start outfitting gold miners in 1849, so it's literally a San Francisco tradition. Guys should head to the outpost of **Ben Sherman** (55 Stockton St., 415/593-0671, www.bensherman.com, 10am-8pm Mon.-Sat., 11am-7pm Sun.) for stylish threads from the British-based outfitter that has been dressing cool mods for almost five decades.

Fluevogers unite! There's an outpost of the popular **John Fluevog Shoes** (253 Grant Ave., 415/296-7900, www.fluevog.com, 10am-7pm Mon.-Sat., 11am-6pm Sun.) here. The Canadian designer's artistic creations have appeared on the pages of *Vogue* and on the feet of notable celebrities like Scarlett Johansson and the White Stripes.

The bones of fashion can be found at **Britex Fabrics** (146 Geary St., 415/392-2910, www.britexfabrics.com, 10am-6pm Mon.-Sat.), which draws designers, quilters, DIYers, and costume geeks from all over the Bay Area to its legendary monument to fabric. If you're into any sort of textile crafting, a visit to Britex has the qualities of a religious experience. All four floors are crammed floor-to-ceiling with bolts of fabric, swaths of lace, and rolls of ribbon. From $1-per-yard grosgrain ribbons to $95-per-yard French silk jacquard and $125-per-yard Italian wool coating, Britex has it all.

Even if you're not in the market for some fine Asian antiques, make a trip down Maiden Lane to **Xanadu Gallery** (140 Maiden Ln. 415/392-9999, www.xanadugallery.us, 10am-6pm Tues.-Sat.). The collection is impressive and spans from Asian to Africa to Latin America with such rarities as an amber snuff bottle from China to Papua New Guinea clam shell currency. However, the real draw is the address. Built in 1948 and designed by Frank Lloyd Wright, the building, though unassuming from the outside, is awash in light and sensuous curves. It is one of San Francisco's treasures, and only made more beautiful by the selection and arrangement of the art inside.

If shopping in Union Square makes you crave the good life, then there is no better place to browse than **Goyard** (345 Powell St., 415/398-1110, www.goyard.com, 10am-6pm Mon.-Sat., noon-5pm Sun.), the French maker of steamer trunks. There is nothing like the collection of handmade luggage (which does include wallets, totes, and overnight bags), to remind you of days when travel (at least for the rich) involved steamships sailing across the Atlantic.

MARINA AND PACIFIC HEIGHTS

The shopping is good in the tony Marina and its elegant neighbor Pacific Heights. **Chestnut and Union Streets** cater to the Marina's young and affluent residents with plenty of clothing boutiques and makeup outlets. Make a stop at **Books Inc.** (2251 Chestnut St., 415/931-3633, www.booksinc.net, 9am-10pm Mon.-Sat., 9am-9pm Sun.), one of the best bookstores in the city. You'll find everything from fiction to travel, as well as a great selection of magazines.

Fillmore Street is the other major shopping corridor. It is funkier than its younger neighbors in the Marina, probably because of its proximity to Japantown and the Fillmore. You'll still find fancy threads and accessories at places like **Marc by Marc Jacobs** (2141 Fillmore St., 415/447-9322, www.marcjacobs.com, 11am-7pm daily) and plenty to brighten up your home at the pricey **Jonathan Alder** (2133 Fillmore St., 415/563-9500, www.jonathanadler.com, 10am-7pm Mon.-Sat., 11am-5pm Sun.).

You'll also find some great secondhand stores; after all, the well-heeled need somewhere to take last season's fashions. **Seconds to Go** (2252 Fillmore St., 415/563-7806, 10am-5:30pm Mon.-Sat., noon-5pm Sun.) has great deals, but **GoodByes Consignment Shop** (3483 Sacramento St., 415/674-0151, www.goodbyessf.com, 10am-6pm Mon.-Wed., Fri.-Sat., 10am-8pm Thurs., 11am-5pm Sun.) is perhaps the best high-end consignment store in the city. A bit out of the way, but well worth the walk, GoodByes also has a men's store (3464 Sacramento St.) and a women's sale store (3464 Sacramento St.) for even better bargains just across the street.

HAYES VALLEY

In Hayes Valley, adjacent to the Civic Center, shopping goes uptown, but the unique scent of counterculture creativity still permeates. This is a fun neighborhood to get your stroll on, checking out the art galleries and peeking into the boutiques for clothing and upscale housewares, and then stopping at one of the lovely cafés for a restorative bite to eat.

Ver Unica (437B Hayes St. and 526 Hayes St., 415/431-0688, www.verunicasf.com, 11am-7pm Mon.-Sat., noon-6pm Sun.) is a vintage boutique that attracts locals and celebrities with high-quality men's and women's clothing and accessories dating from the 1920s to the 1980s, along with a small selection of new apparel by up-and-coming designers.

The corset takes center stage at unique **Dark Garden** (321 Linden St., 415/431-7684, www.darkgarden.net, 11am-5pm Sun.-Tues., 11am-7pm Thurs., 11am-8pm Fri.-Sat.). Custom fitting and design doesn't come cheap, but you'll get quality. An assortment of lingerie is also sold here.

Paolo Iantorno's boutique **Paolo Shoes**

(524 Hayes St., 415/552-4580, http://paoloshoes.com, 11am-7pm Mon.-Sat., 11am-6pm Sun.) showcases his collection of handcrafted shoes, for which all leather and textiles are conscientiously selected and then inspected to ensure top quality.

For those who worry that San Francisco is losing its quirkiness, **Zonal Home Interiors** (568 Hayes St., 415/255-9307, www.zonalhome.com, 11am-6pm Tues.-Sat., noon-5pm Sun.) works to keep the city's rent-controlled apartments decked out in shabby chic. Inside this one man show is an odd but cool collection of antique iron beds, refurbished tables and cabinets, and original work from local artists.

You can hardly walk 10 feet without passing a sweet shop selling macarons. The original is **Miette** (449 Octavia St., 415/626-6221, www.miette.com, 11am-7pm daily), a cheery European-inspired candy shop, sister store to the Ferry Plaza bakery (415/837-0300). From double-salted licorice to handmade English toffee, the quality confections include imports from England, Italy, and France.

MISSION

In a city known for its quirky style, the Mission was the last neighborhood with a funky, easy-on-the-wallet shopping district. Sadly, the days are gone when you could buy cool vintage clothes by the pound, but **Valencia Street** is still the most vibrant and diverse neighborhood for shoppers in the city.

The last vintage and secondhand holdout is the local favorite, **Schauplatz** (791 Valencia St., 415/864-5665, 1pm-7pm Mon., Wed.-Sat., 1pm-6pm Sun). It might be a bit more expensive than your average Goodwill, but you'll be wowed by the fabulous and unusual apparel. Surf the racks for everything from 1940s dresses to vintage sunglasses. **Harrington Galleries** (599 Valencia St., 415/861-7300, www.harringtongalleries.com, 11am-6pm Mon.-Tues. and Thurs.-Sat., noon-5pm Sun.) has anchored this corner of 17th and Valencia Streets since 1968 and sprawls over 15,000 feet, selling stylish vintage and contemporary home furnishings, accents, and even some clothes. The tagline, "a lifestyle emporium" is more than accurate and the beautifully maintained store, with cozy and fun displays, is worth a visit.

For something more contemporary, the **Bell Jar** (3187 16th St., 415/626-1749, https://belljarsf.com, noon-7pm Mon.-Sat., noon-6pm Sun.) has everything, from dresses and jewelry to art books and soaps, you need to make you and your home a stylish trendsetter of the 21st century. A bit more extreme is **Five and Diamond** (510 Valencia St., 415/255-9747, www.fiveanddiamond.com, noon-8pm Mon.-Thurs., 11am-9pm Fri.-Sat., 11am-7pm Sun.). Inside this unique space, you'll find off-the-wall art, unusual clothing, and downright scary jewelry. Those who make an appointment in advance can also get a tattoo here, or purchase some keen body jewelry. A trip inside Five and Diamond can be an exciting adventure for the bold, but might be a bit much for the faint of heart. Decide for yourself whether you dare to take the plunge.

Author Dave Eggers's tongue-in-cheek storefront at **826 Valencia** (826 Valencia St., 415/642-5905, www.826valencia.org, noon-6pm daily) doubles as a pirate supply shop and youth literacy center. While you'll find plenty of pirate booty, you'll also find a good stock of literary magazines and books. Almost next door, **Paxton Gate** (824 Valencia St., 415/824-1872, www.paxtongate.com, 11am-7pm Sun.-Wed., and 11am-8pm Thurs.-Sat.) takes the typical gift shop to a new level with taxidermy. This quirky spot is surprisingly cheery, with garden supplies, books, and candles filling the cases in addition to the fossilized creatures.

THE HAIGHT

The **Haight-Ashbury shopping district** isn't what it used to be, but if you're willing to poke around a bit, you can still find a few bargains in the remaining thrift shops. One relic of the 1960s counterculture still thrives on the

Haight: head shops. However, all pipes, water pipes, and other paraphernalia are strictly for use in smoking tobacco.

Music has always been a part of the Haight. To this day you'll find homeless folks pounding out rhythms on *doumbeks* and congas on the sidewalks and on Hippy Hill in the park. Located in an old bowling alley, **Amoeba** (1855 Haight St., 415/831-1200, www.amoeba.com, 11am-8pm daily) is a larger-than-life record store that promotes every type of music imaginable. Amoeba's staff, many of whom are musicians themselves, are among the most knowledgeable in the business.

The award-winning **Booksmith** (1644 Haight St., 800/493-7323, www.booksmith.com, 10am-10pm Mon.-Sat., 10am-8pm Sun.) boasts a helpful and informed staff, a fabulous magazine collection, and Northern California's preeminent calendar of readings by internationally renowned authors.

The other specialty in the Haight is clothing. Join the countless bargain shoppers who prowl the racks for fabulous forgotten garments, but don't expect to pay $0.25 for that great 1930s bias-cut dress or $0.50 for a cast-off Dior blouse; the merchants in the Haight are experienced used clothiers who know what the good stuff is worth. This true at the **Buffalo Exchange** (1555 Haight St., 415/431-7733, www.buffaloexchange.com, 11am-8pm daily), another Haight institution filled with a mix of new and used über-hip clothes.

Originally a vaudeville theater, the capacious **Wasteland** (1660 Haight St., 415/863-3150, www.shopwasteland.com, 11am-8pm Mon.-Sat., noon-7pm Sun.) has a traffic-stopping art nouveau facade, a distinctive assortment of vintage hippie and rock-star threads, and a glamour-punk staff.

Make for the glam at **Piedmont Boutique** (1452 Haight St., 415/864-8075, www.piedmontsf.com, 11am-7pm daily). The narrow store is a riot of color, filled with feather boas, sequined shorts, fantastic wigs—and those who wear them. This is where San Francisco's drag queens shop.

Haight-Ashbury shopping district

Sports and Recreation

PARKS

Golden Gate Park

The largest park in San Francisco is **Golden Gate Park** (main entrance at Stanyan St. and Fell St., McLaren Lodge Visitors Center at John F. Kennedy Dr., 415/831-2700, www.golden-gate-park.com). In addition to housing popular sights like the Academy of Sciences, the de Young, and the Japanese Tea Garden, Golden Gate Park is San Francisco's unofficial playground. There are three botanical gardens, a children's playground (Martin Luther King Jr. Dr. and Bowling Green Dr.), tennis courts, and a golf course. Stow Lake offers paddleboats for rent (415/386-2531, http://stowlakeboathouse.com, 10am-5pm Mon.-Thurs., 10am-6pm Fri.-Sun., $20-34 per hour), and the park even has its own bison paddock. Weekends, find the park filled with locals inline skating, biking, hiking, and even Lindy Hopping. John F. Kennedy Drive east of Transverse Drive is closed to motorists every Saturday from April through September and Sunday year-round for pedestrian-friendly fun.

The park offers plenty of chances to go off-roading, with scores of paved and unpaved trails zigzagging through the park. The longest is the **Golden Gate Park and Ocean Beach Hike** (trailhead at Fell St. and Baker St., www.traillink.com), which runs from the Golden Gate Park panhandle all the way to the ocean, then down Ocean Beach to the San Francisco Zoo.

Presidio of San Francisco

Crissy Field (Marina Blvd. and Baker St., 415/561-4700, www.parksconservancy.org), with its beaches, restored wetlands, and wide promenade, is the playground of the **Presidio** (415/561-4323, www.nps.gov/prsf, free). It's part of the Golden Gate National Recreation Area and is dedicated to environmental education. At the **Crissy Field Center** (1199 E. Beach, 415/561-7690, 9am-5pm daily), you'll find a list of classes, seminars, and fun hands-on activities for all ages. Many of these include walks out into the marsh and the Presidio.

The rest of the Presidio offers the biggest and most diverse network of hiking trails in the city. (For trail descriptions, check out www.presidio.gov.) For an easy nature walk, try the **Lobos Creek Valley Trail** (Lincoln St. at Bowley St.). Less than a mile long (0.8 mile one-way), this flat boardwalk trail is wheelchair-accessible and shows off the beginning successes of the ecological restoration of the Presidio. Another easy Presidio hike goes way back into the region's history. The 0.6-mile (one-way) **Lover's Lane** (Funston Ave. and Presidio Blvd.) once served soldiers stationed at the Presidio who beat down the path into the city proper to visit their sweethearts. Today you'll have a peaceful tree-shaded walk on a flat semipaved path that passes the former homes of officers, crosses El Polin Creek, and ends at the Presidio Gate.

The **Bay Area Ridge Trail** (415/561-2595, www.ridgetrail.org) runs more than 325 miles around the San Francisco Bay Area. One of the prettiest San Francisco sections runs through the Presidio (Arguello Blvd. and Jackson St.). Extending from the Arguello Gate to the foot of the Golden Gate Bridge, it is 2.7 miles (one-way) of gently sloping dirt footpaths and passes through unpopulated forests and meadows. Another regional trail system running through the Presidio is the **California Coastal Trail** (Golden Gate National Recreation Area, www.californiacoastaltrail.info). Originating beneath the Golden Gate Bridge, the trail meanders all the way down the west side of the city and provides stunning views high above the Pacific.

The **Lands End Trail** (Merrie Way, 415/561-4700, www.nps.gov/goga) is also part of the Golden Gate National Recreation Area. Rising above rugged cliffs and beaches, Lands

End feels wild, but the three-mile trail, which runs from El Camino Del Mar near the Legion of Honor to the ruins of the Sutro Baths, is perfect for any hiking enthusiast. For a longer adventure, there are plenty of auxiliary trails to explore that lead down to little beaches. Be sure to look out for the remains of three shipwrecks on the rocks of Point Lobos at low tide. Grab a cup of hot chocolate at the stunning **Lands End Lookout visitor center** (680 Point Lobos Ave., 415/426-5240, www.parksconservancy.org, 9am-5pm daily) when your hike is finished.

Mission Dolores Park

If you're looking for a park where the most strenuous activity is people watching, then head to **Mission Dolores Park** (Dolores St. and 19th St., 415/554-9521, http://sfrecpark.org). Usually called Dolores Park, it's a favorite of Castro and Mission District denizens. Bring a beach blanket to sprawl on the lawn and a picnic lunch supplied by one of the excellent nearby eateries. On weekends, music festivals and cultural events often spring up at Dolores Park.

BEACHES

San Francisco boasts of being a city that has everything, and it certainly comes close. This massive urban wonderland even claims several genuine sand beaches within its city limits. No doubt the biggest and most famous of these is **Ocean Beach** (Great Hwy., parking at Sloat Blvd., Golden Gate Park, and the Cliff House, www.parksconservancy.org). This four-mile stretch of sand forms the breakwater for the Pacific Ocean along the whole west side of the city. Because it's so large, you're likely to find a spot to sit down and maybe even a parking place along the beach, except perhaps on that rarest of occasions in San Francisco—a sunny, warm day. Don't go out for an ocean swim at Ocean Beach: Extremely dangerous rip currents cause fatalities every year.

The beach at **Aquatic Park** (Beach St. and Hyde St., www.nps.gov/safr) sits at the west end of the Fisherman's Wharf tourist area. This makes Aquatic Park incredibly convenient for visitors who want to grab a picnic on the wharf to enjoy down on the beach. Aquatic Park was built in the late 1930s as a bathhouse catering to wealthy San Franciscans, and today one of the main attractions of Aquatic Park remains swimming: Triathletes and hard-core swimmers brave the frigid waters to swim for miles in the protected cove. More sedate visitors can find a seat and enjoy a cup of coffee, a newspaper, and some people watching.

Baker Beach (Golden Gate Point and the Presidio, www.parksconservancy.org) is best known for its scenery, and that doesn't just mean the lovely views of the Golden Gate Bridge. Baker is San Francisco's own clothing-optional (that is, nude) beach. But don't worry, plenty of the denizens of Baker Beach wear clothes while flying kites, playing volleyball and Frisbee, and even just strolling on the beach. Baker Beach was the original home of the Burning Man festival before it moved out to the Black Rock Desert of Nevada. Because Baker is much smaller than Ocean Beach, it gets crowded in the summer. Whether you choose to sunbathe nude or not, don't try to swim here. The currents get seriously strong and dangerous because it is so close to the Golden Gate.

BIKING

In other places, bicycling is a sport or a mode of transportation. In San Francisco, bicycling is a religion. Some might say that the high church of this religion is the **San Francisco Bike Coalition** (415/431-2453, www.sfbike.org). In addition to providing workshops and hosting events, the Bike Coalition is an excellent resource for anyone who wants to cycle through the city. Check out their website for tips, maps, and rules of the road.

As a newcomer to biking in the city, it may be wise to start off gently, perhaps with a guided tour that avoids areas with dangerous traffic. **Blazing Saddles** (2715 Hyde St., 415/202-8888, www.blazingsaddles.com, $8-15/hour) rents bikes and offers tips on where to go. If you prefer the safety of a group, take the guided tour (10am daily, 3 hours, adult $55, child $35, reservations required) through San Francisco and across the Golden Gate Bridge into Marin County. With five locations, most in the Fisherman's Wharf area, it's easy to find yourself a cruiser. One of the most popular treks is the easy and flat nine-mile ride across the **Golden Gate Bridge** and back. This is a great way to see the bridge and the bay for the first time, and it takes only an hour or two to complete. Another option is to ride across the bridge and into the town of Sausalito (8 miles) or Tiburon (16 miles), enjoy an afternoon and dinner, and then ride the ferry back into the city (bikes are allowed on board).

Another easy and low-stress option is the paved paths of **Golden Gate Park** (main entrance at Stanyan St. and Fell St., McLaren Lodge Visitors Center at John F. Kennedy Dr., 415/831-2700, www.golden-gate-park.com) and **The Presidio** (Montgomery St. and Lincoln Blvd., 415/561-4323, www.nps.gov/prsf). A bike makes a perfect mode of transportation to explore the various museums and attractions of these two large parks, and you can spend all day and never have to worry about finding parking. At the entrance of Golden Gate Park, **San Francisco Bike Rentals** (1816 Haight St., 415/922-4537, www.goldengateparkbikerental.com, 9:30am-6:30pm daily, $7-9/hour, $30-36/day) has a kiosk. Another option is **Golden Gate Park Bike and Skate** (3038 Fulton St., 415/668-1117, http://goldengateparkbikeandskate.com, 10am-6pm Mon.-Fri., 10am-7pm Sat.-Sun. summer, 10am-5pm Mon.-Fri., 10am-6pm Sat.-Sun. winter, bike rental $5/hour, $25/day) located just north of the park on Fulton near the de Young museum. You can also rent skates ($5/hour, $20/day) and in-line skates ($6/day, $24/day) here if that is more your style.

GOLF

A number of golf courses hide in the parks of San Francisco. One of the premier golf courses in the city, the **Presidio Golf Course** (400 Finley Rd., 415/561-4661, www.presidiogolf.com, $34-145) was once reserved for the exclusive use of military officers, government officials, and visiting dignitaries. Since 1995 the 18-hole, par-72 course, driving range, practice putting greens, and clubhouse have been available to the public. Reserve your tee time by phone or online.

Lincoln Park Golf Course (300 34th Ave., 415/221-9911, http://lincolnparkgolfcourse.com, $22-42) is a public, 18-hole, par-68 course in the Outer Richmond district near the Legion of Honor. It hosts the annual San Francisco City Golf Championships and is known for its spectacular setting abutting Lands End.

WHALE-WATCHING

With day-trip access to the marine sanctuary off the Farallon Islands, whale watching is a year-round activity in San Francisco. **San Francisco Whale Tours** (Pier 39, Dock B, 888/235-6450 or 415/448/7570, www.sanfranciscowhaletours.com, tours daily, $60-89, advance purchase required) offers six-hour trips out to the Farallons almost every Saturday and Sunday, with almost-guaranteed whale sightings on each trip. Shorter whale-watching trips along the coastline run on weekdays, and 90-minute quickie trips out to see slightly smaller local wildlife, including elephant seals and sea lions, also go out daily. Children ages 3-15 are welcome on boat tours (for reduced rates), and kids often love the chance to spot whales, sea lions, and pelicans. Children under age three are not permitted for safety reasons.

SPECTATOR SPORTS

Since 2000, baseball's **San Francisco Giants** have called the beautiful **AT&T Park** (24 Willie Mays Plaza, 3rd St. and King St., 415/972-2000) home, where the food and the views woo even non-baseball fans. Giants games take place March-September. As the Giants continue to win championships, tickets have gotten harder to come by, not to mention more expensive. Still, it's not impossible to snag last-minute tickets to a regular season game.

The NFL's **San Francisco 49ers** have moved into a shiny new stadium in Santa Clara, an hour away from the city where they dominated the NFL through the 1980s and 1990s.

Accommodations

San Francisco has plenty of accommodations to suit every taste and most budgets. Both the cheapest and most expensive places tend to be in Union Square, SoMa, and the Financial District. Consistently cheaper digs can be had in the neighborhoods surrounding Fisherman's Wharf. You'll find the most character in the smaller boutique hotels, but plenty of big chain hotels have at least one location in town if you prefer a known quantity. In fact, a number of chain motels have moved into historical San Francisco buildings, creating a more unusual experience than you might expect from the likes of a Days Inn. For the best rates, plan ahead and book a room at least a month in advance. Rates shoot up dramatically within the 30-day window.

Free hotel parking is rare in the city, existing mostly in chain motels down by the wharf. Overnight garage parking downtown can be excruciatingly expensive. Check with your hotel to see if they have a "parking package" that includes this expense (and possibly offers valet service as well). If you don't plan to leave the city on your trip, consider saving a bundle by skipping the rental car altogether and using public transit. To explore outside the city limits, a car is a necessity.

UNION SQUARE AND DOWNTOWN

In and around Union Square and Nob Hill, you'll find approximately a zillion hotels. As a rule, those closest to the top of the Hill or to Union Square proper are the most expensive. Within a one- or two-block walk, you get more personality and genuine San Francisco experience for less money and less prestige.

Top business execs stay near the towering offices of the Financial District, down by the water on the Embarcadero, or in SoMa. Thus, most of the lodgings in these areas cater to the expense-account set. The big-name chain hotels run expensive; book one if you're traveling on an unlimited company credit card. Otherwise, look for smaller boutique and indie accommodations that won't tear your wallet to bits or laugh at your checking account.

$100-150

Despite the prestigious pedigrees of Union Square and Nob Hill, there are quite a few very affordable hotels and even some B&Bs tucked into this old, noir-ish part of town. A local favorite is the **Baldwin Hotel** (321 Grant Ave., 415/781-2220, www.baldwinhotel.com, $119-240), right in the thick of Grant's high-end boutiques. There are few frills in the hotel's 50 rooms, except for the origami folded towels. Rooms are clean and retain the original charm (including claw-foot bathtubs) of the historical buildings in this part of town.

The B&B **Golden Gate Hotel** (775 Bush St., 415/392-3702 or 800/835-1118, $135-190) offers small, charming rooms with friendly, unpretentious hospitality. You'll find a continental breakfast every morning in the hotel lobby (should you overindulge the night before, breakfast can be brought to your room), along with an orange cat named Pip. Unlike most hotels, there are only two rates. The higher rate ($190) gets you a room with a private bathroom, while the lower rate ($135) gets you a room with a bathroom down the hall.

Should you find the need for a full-service professional recording studio in your hotel, head straight for **The Mosser** (54 4th St.,

415/986-4400, www.themosser.com, $99-189, parking $35). The Mosser's inexpensive rooms have European-style shared baths in the hallway and bright modern decor that nicely complements the century-old building. Pricier options include bigger rooms with private baths. With a rep for cleanliness and pleasant amenities, including morning coffee and comfy bathrobes, this hotel fulfills its goal—to provide visitors to the city with cheap crash space in a great location convenient to sights, shops, and public transportation.

$150-250

The **Hotel Bijou** (111 Mason St., 415/771-1200, www.hotelbijou.com, $140-220) is a fun spot. Whimsical decor mimics an old-fashioned movie theater, and a tiny "movie house" downstairs runs double features, free to guests, every night—with only movies shot in San Francisco. The rooms are small, clean, and nicely appointed.

The ★ **Hotel Monaco** (501 Geary St., 415/292-0100, www.monaco-sf.com, $179-389) shows the vibrant side of San Francisco. Big rooms are whimsically decorated with bright colors, while baths are luxurious and feature cushy animal-print bathrobes. Friendly service comes from purple-velour-coated staff, who know the hotel and the city and will cheerfully tell you all about both. Chair massage complements the free wine and cheese in the large open guest lounge.

Only half a block down from the square, the **Sir Francis Drake** (450 Powell St., 800/795-7129, www.sirfrancisdrake.com, $149-379) has its own history beginning in the late 1920s. Here at the Drake you'll find a bit less opulence in the lobby, compared to the St. Francis, and a bit more in the rooms. The Beefeater doorman (almost always available for a photo), the unique door overhang, and the red-and-gold interior all add to the character of this favorite.

The ★ **Hotel Triton** (342 Grant Ave., 800/800-1299, www.hoteltriton.com, $179-389) adds a bit of whimsy and eco chic to the stately aesthetic of Union Square. Jerry Garcia decorated a room here, and Haagen Dazs tailored its own suite, complete with an ice cream-stocked freezer case in the corner. You'll find the rooms tiny but comfortable and well stocked with ecofriendly amenities and bath products. The flat-panel TVs offer a 24-hour yoga channel, and complimentary yoga props can be delivered to your room on request.

Hotel Rex (562 Sutter St., 415/433-4434, www.jdvhotels.com, $195-300) channels San Francisco's literary side, evoking a hotel in the early 1900s when Bohemians such as Jack London, Ambrose Bierce, and even Mark Twain roamed and ruminated about the city. Rooms are comfortable and spacious, decorated with the work of local artists and artisans. The dimly lit lobby bar is famous in the city for its literary bent—you may find yourself engaged in a fascinating conversation as you enjoy your evening glass of wine.

Over $250

A San Francisco legend, the **Clift** (495 Geary St., 415/775-4700, www.clifthotel.com, $315-500) has a lobby worth walking into. The high-ceilinged industrial space is devoted to modern art. Yes, you really are supposed to sit on the antler sofa and the metal chairs. By contrast, the rooms are almost Spartan in their simplicity, with colors meant to mimic the city skyline. Stop in for a drink at the Redwood Room, done in brown leather and popular with a younger crowd. For dinner, a branch of Jeffrey Chodorow's Asia de Cuba restaurant is located inside the hotel.

Out of downtown fray and bordering the Embarcadero, the **Hotel Griffon** (155 Steuart St., 415/495-210, www.hotelgriffon.com, $250-360) is a posh boutique business hotel with a prime vacation locale. While the rooms are on the small side, the Griffon offers business and leisure packages to suit any traveler's needs. They're a bit pricier, but the best rooms overlook the bay, with views of the Bay Bridge and Treasure Island.

At the 1904-built **Westin St. Francis** (335 Powell St., 415/397-7000, www.

westinstfrancis.com, $295-595), the hotel's robber-baron and Jazz Age past is evident as soon as you walk into the immense lobby. The hotel's two wings are the original section, called the Landmark Building, and the 1972 renovation, The Tower. The hotel has 1,200 rooms, making it the largest hotel in the city. Rooms in the historical section are loaded with lavish charms like ornate woodwork and chandeliers, while the modern rooms are large and sport fantastic views of the city and the bay. A room in the new section grants you access to the glass elevators.

Certain names mean luxury in the hotel world. The **Fairmont San Francisco** (950 Mason St., 415/772-5000, www.fairmont.com, $329-529) is among the best of these. Opening shortly after the 1906 earthquake, it is designed in the Beaux-Arts style of the time, and like the Westin St. Francis, the Fairmont has a Tower addition. The Tower's rooms are large with marble baths and even more spectacular views than the historical rooms. Check online for package specials or to book a tee time or spa treatment. Some of the rooms actually allow smoking.

Another Nob Hill classically inspired contender with a top name, the **Ritz-Carlton** (600 Stockton St., 415/296-7465, www.ritzcarlton.com, $499-629) provides patrons with ultimate pampering. From the high-thread-count sheets to the hip new restaurant of celebrity chef Michael Rotondo and the full-service spa, guests at the Ritz all but drown in sumptuous amenities. Even the "standard" rooms are exceptional, but if you've got the bread, spring for the Club Floors, where they'll give you an iPod, a personal concierge, and possibly the kitchen sink if you ask for it.

Le Méridien San Francisco (333 Battery St., 415/296-2900, www.starwoodhotels.com, $249-570) stands tall in the Embarcadero Center, convenient to shopping, dining, and the streetcar and cable car lines to all the favorite downtown destinations. This expensive luxury hotel pampers guests with Frette sheets, plush robes, marble baths, and stellar views. Expect chic decor and nightly turndown service, free newspapers, and 24-hour room service.

Hotel Vitale (8 Mission St., 415/278-3700 or 888/890-8688, www.hotelvitale.com, $240-550) professes to restore guests' vitality with its lovely rooms and exclusive spa, complete with rooftop hot soaking tubs and a yoga studio. Many of the good-size rooms also have private deep soaking tubs and many have views of the Embarcadero and the bay.

The problem with staying at the ★ **Mandarin Oriental San Francisco** (222 Sansome St., 415/276-9888, www.mandarinoriental.com, $525-765) is that you may never want to leave. Rooms boast unparalleled views, top amenities and Asian-inspired decor. In the swank corner rooms and suites, raised bathtubs let bathers enjoy stunning sights (such as the Transamerica Pyramid, Alcatraz, and the Golden Gate Bridge) from the warmth of the bubbly water. You can find the best room rates on the hotel's website (the prices will make a budget-minded traveler's eyes bleed) along with various stay-and-play packages with an emphasis on golf and spa treatments.

For a unique San Francisco hotel experience, book a room at the famous **Hotel Palomar** (12 4th St., 415/348-1111 or 866/373-4941, www.hotelpalomar-sf.com, $250-575). You'll find every amenity imaginable, from extra-long beds for taller guests to in-room spa services and temporary pet goldfish. The overall decorative motif evokes M. C. Escher, and whimsical colorful touches accent each room. Be sure to make a stop at the Dirty Habit, a small bites bar. Check the website for special deals, some quite reasonably priced, that focus on shopping and spa-style relaxation.

The **Palace Hotel** (2 New Montgomery St., 415/512-1111, www.sfpalace.com, $329-600) enjoys its reputation as the grande dame of all San Francisco hotels. The rich history of the Palace began when its doors opened in 1875. It was gutted by fires following the 1906 earthquake, rebuilt and reopened in 1909, and refurbished for the new millennium during 1989-1991. In 1919 President Woodrow Wilson negotiated the terms of the Treaty of Versailles over lunch at the Garden Court. Today guests take pleasure in beautiful bedrooms, exercise and relax in the full-service spa and fitness center, and dine in the Palace's three restaurants. If you're staying at the Palace, having a meal in the exquisite Garden Court dining room is a must, though you may forget to eat as you gaze upward at the stained-glass domed ceiling.

NORTH BEACH AND CHINATOWN

Perhaps it's odd, but the tourist mecca of San Francisco is not a district of a zillion hotels. Most of the major hostelries sit down nearer to Union Square. But you can stay near the Wharf or in North Beach if you choose; you'll find some chain motels here, plus a few select boutique hotels in all price ranges.

$100-150

The **San Remo Hotel** (2237 Mason St., 415/776-8688 or 800/352-7366, www.sanremohotel.com, $99-139) is one of the best bargains in the city. The rooms boast the simplest of furnishings and decorations. None have telephones, or TVs, and the bathrooms are located down the hall. Couples on a romantic vacation can rent the Penthouse, a lovely room for two with lots of windows and a rooftop terrace boasting views of North Beach and the bay. Downstairs, Fior d'Italia is the oldest Italian restaurant in the country and has a generous happy hour seven days a week.

$150-250

Located in the thick of bustling North Beach, **Hotel Bohème** (444 Columbus Ave., 415/433-9111, www.hotelboheme.com, $195-245) aims to capture the neighborhood's literary past. The historical hotel has recently been refurbished, and the digs are small but extremely charming and decorated in modest midcentury decor. All rooms have their own bathrooms and free Wi-Fi. The double-queen rooms can sleep up to four people for an additional charge. Be aware that it can be extremely noisy outside, particularly on weekend nights.

The **Washington Square Inn** (1660 Stockton St., 800/388-0220, www.wsisf.com, $199-409) doesn't look like a typical California B&B, but more like a small, elegant hotel. The inn offers 16 rooms with queen or king beds, private baths, elegant appointments, and fine linens. Standard rooms are "cozy" in the European urban style, while some have spa bathtubs and others have views of Coit Tower and Saints Peter and Paul Church. A few of the amenities include a generous continental breakfast brought to your room daily, afternoon tea, a flat-screen TV in every room, and free Wi-Fi.

Over $250

In a district not known for its luxury, **The Argonaut** (495 Jefferson St., 415/563-0800 or 800/790-1415, www.argonauthotel.com, $309-579) in Fisherman's Wharf stands out. Housed in an exposed brick 1907 warehouse, the hotel embraces its nautical connections to the nines. Outlandishly decorated in bold patterns of blues and golds, with stars, sails, and ships, it may not be for everyone. But you can't argue with the service and amenities (including in-room spa treatments). Many rooms have great views of the bay, and its location is ideal, only steps away from Aquatic Park, Pier 45, Ghirardelli Square, and the excellent Maritime Museum.

MARINA AND PACIFIC HEIGHTS

Some of these areas are close enough to Fisherman's Wharf to walk there for dinner, but others in Pacific Heights are more central and far more affordable than downtown digs.

Under $100

For an unexpected, bucolic park hostel within walking and biking distance of frenetic downtown San Francisco, stop for a night at the **Fisherman's Wharf Hostel** (Fort Mason Bldg. 240, 415/771-7277, www.sfhostels.com/

fishermans-wharf, dorm $30-42, private room $75-109). The hostel sits on Golden Gate National Recreation Area land, pleasantly far from the problems that plague other SF hostels. The best amenities (aside from the free linens, breakfast, and no curfews or chores) are the views of the bay and Alcatraz and the sweeping lawns and mature trees all around the hostel.

$100-150

The rooms at the ★ **Marina Motel** (2576 Lombard St., 415/921-9406, www.marina-motel.com, $139-159) may be small, but the place is big on charm and character. This friendly little motel, decorated in French-country style, welcomes families with kids and dogs. Just ask for the room type that best suits your needs when you make your reservations. Rooms are pleasantly priced for budget travelers, and several vacation packages offer deep discounts on tours, spa treatments, and outdoor adventures.

The exterior and interior amenities of the **Hotel Majestic** (1500 Sutter St., 415/441-1100, www.thehotelmajestic.com, $120-200) evoke the grandeur of early 20th-century San Francisco. The Edwardian-style 1902 building boasts antique furnishings and decorative items from England and France. Cozy rooms, junior suites, and one-bedroom suites are available. The Cafe Majestic serves breakfast and dinner, with a focus on local healthful ingredients.

$150-250

Pack the car and bring the kids to the **Hotel del Sol** (3100 Webster St., 415/921-5520, www.thehoteldelsol.com, $175-320). This unique hotel-motel embraces its origins as a 1950s motor lodge, with the rooms decorated in bright, bold colors with whimsical accents, a heated courtyard pool, and the ever-popular free parking. Family suites and larger rooms have kitchenettes. The Marina locale offers trendy cafés, restaurants, bars, and shopping within walking distance as well as access to major attractions.

The stately **Queen Anne Hotel** (1590 Sutter St., 415/441-2828, www.queenanne.com, $150-250) is Victorian through and through. Sumptuous fabrics, ornate antiques, and rich colors in the rooms and common areas add to the feeling of decadence and luxury in this boutique bed and breakfast. Small, moderate rooms offer attractive accommodations on a budget, while superior rooms and suites are more upscale. Continental breakfast is included, as are a number of high-end services such as courtesy car service and afternoon tea and sherry.

The **Marina Inn** (3110 Octavia St., 415/928-1000, www.marinainn.com, $165-190), built in 1924, exudes old-fashioned San Francisco charm but boasts pleasant modern amenities. This small family-friendly hotel offers continental breakfast, concierge services, and free Wi-Fi. The Inn is within walking distance of major city attractions, including Fisherman's Wharf, Ghirardelli Square, and the cable cars. And if you're feeling a bit scruffy and want to freshen up before your big night on the town, visit the Inn's attached barbershop or salon.

Another Pacific Heights jewel, the **Jackson Court** (2198 Jackson St., 415/929-7670, www.jacksoncourt.com, $229) presents a lovely brick facade in the exclusive neighborhood. The 10-room inn offers comfortable, uniquely decorated queen rooms and a luscious continental breakfast each morning.

Over $250

The **Inn at Presidio** (42 Moraga Ave., 415/800-7356, www.innatthepresidio.com, $250-385) is inside historical Pershing Hall right in the center of The Presidio. Built in 1903, the large brick building was formerly home to single military officers. In the classic rooms and suites (some with fireplaces), subtle contemporary furnishings complement the framed photos and other Presidio memorabilia sprinkled throughout. On-site amenities include a breakfast buffet, wine and cheese reception, free Wi-Fi, a covered front porch with rocking chairs overlooking the Main Post, and an outdoor deck with fire pit. There is a $7 fee for self-parking, or take advantage of the PresidiGo shuttle.

Tucked in with the money-laden mansions of Pacific Heights, ★ **Hotel Drisco** (2901 Pacific Ave., 800/634-7277, www.hoteldrisco.com, $293-428) offers elegance to discerning visitors. Away from the frenzied pace and noise of downtown, at the Drisco you get quiet, comfy rooms that include a "pillow menu"; continental breakfast with a latte, smoked salmon, and brie; hors d'oeuvres and a glass of wine in the evening; and bicycles on loan.

CIVIC CENTER AND HAYES VALLEY

You'll find a few reasonably priced accommodations and classic inns in the Civic Center and Hayes Valley areas.

$100-150

Take a step back into an older San Francisco at the **Chateau Tivoli** (1057 Steiner St., 415/776-5462 or 800/228-1647, www.chateautivoli.com, $115-300). The over-the-top colorful exterior matches perfectly with the American Renaissance interior decor. Each unique room and suite showcases an exquisite style evocative of the Victorian era. Most rooms have private baths, though the two least expensive share a bath. With a reasonable price tag even for the most opulent suites, this B&B is perfect for families (though there are no TVs in any room) and for longer stays. Try to get a room for a weekend, so you can partake of the gourmet champagne brunch.

$150-250

Located in Hayes Valley a few blocks from the Opera House, the **Inn at the Opera** (333 Fulton St., 888/298-7198, www.shellhospitality.com, $225) promises to have guests ready for a swanky night of San Francisco culture. French interior styling in the rooms and suites once impressed visiting opera stars and now welcomes guests from all over the world.

It might seem strange to stay at an inn called **The Parsonage** (198 Haight St., 415/863-3699, www.theparsonage.com, from $220), but this classy Victorian bed-and-breakfast exemplifies elegance and fits in with the Civic Center and Hayes Valley chic. Rooms are decorated with antiques, and baths have stunning marble showers. Enjoy pampering, multicourse breakfasts, and brandy and chocolates when you come "home" each night.

MISSION AND CASTRO

Accommodations in these neighborhoods are few and tend to be modest B&Bs.

$100-150

For a romantic visit to the Castro with your partner, stay at the **Willows Inn Bed & Breakfast** (710 14th St., 415/ 431-4770 or 800/431-0277, www.willowssf.com, $120-180). The Willows has European-style shared baths and comfortable rooms with private sinks and bent willow furnishings, and serves a yummy continental breakfast each morning. Catering to the queer community, the innkeepers at the Willows can help you with nightclubs, restaurants, and festivals in the city and locally in the Castro. One of the best amenities is the camaraderie you'll find with the other guests and staff at this great Edwardian B&B.

At the **Inn on Castro** (321 Castro St., 415/861-0321, www.innoncastro.com, $125-185), you've got all kinds of choices. You can pick an economy room with a shared bath, a posh private suite, or a self-service apartment. Once ensconced, you can chill out on the cute patio, or go out into the Castro to take in the legendary entertainment and nightlife. The self-catering apartments can sleep up to four and have fully furnished and appointed kitchens and dining rooms. Amenities include LCD TVs with cable, DVD players, and colorful modern art.

GOLDEN GATE PARK AND THE HAIGHT

Accommodations around Golden Gate Park are surprisingly reasonable. Leaning toward Victorian and Edwardian inns, most lodgings are in the middle price range for well above average rooms and services. However, getting downtown from the quiet residential spots can be a trek; ask at your inn about car services, cabs, and the nearest bus lines.

Out on the ocean side of the park, motor inns of varying quality cluster on the Great Highway. They've got the advantages of more space, low rates, and free parking, but they range from drab all the way down to seedy; choose carefully.

$100-150

To say the **Seal Rock Inn** (545 Point Lobos Ave., 415/ 752-8000 or 888/732-5762, www.sealrockinn.com, $120-160, free parking) is near Golden Gate Park pushes neighborhood definitions. This pretty place perches near Lands End, a short walk from the Pacific Ocean. All rooms have ocean views, private baths, free Wi-Fi, and furnishings that create a pleasantly modern ambience. The Seal Rock offers rooms with kitchenettes (two-day minimum). Ask for a fireplace room that faces the Seal Rocks, so you can observe a popular mating spot for sea lions. The restaurant serves breakfast and lunch; for Sunday brunch you'll be competing with locals for a table.

$150-250

The **Stanyan Park Hotel** (750 Stanyan St., 415/751-1000, www.stanyanpark.com, $179-299) graces the Upper Haight area across the street from Golden Gate Park. This renovated 1904-1905 building, listed on the National Register of Historic Places, shows off its Victorian heritage both inside and out. Rooms can be small but are elegantly decorated, and a number of multiple-room suites are available. All 36 rooms include free Wi-Fi and flat screen TVs, but for a special treat, ask for a room overlooking the park.

SAN FRANCISCO AIRPORT

San Francisco Airport (SFO) is actually 13 miles south of San Francisco, situated on the peninsula. If you're hunting for an urban chic boutique hotel or a funky and unique hostel, the airport is *not* the place to motel-shop. SFO's hotel row, however, has many midpriced chain motels.

Don't expect ritzy accommodations at the **Ritz Inn** (151 El Camino Real, San Bruno, 800/799-7489, www.ritzinnsfo.com, $79-89). At this cheap plain Jane you'll get a bed with an uncomfortable mattress and a loud floral spread, a bathroom, a microwave, a fridge, and a TV. The **Villa Montes Hotel** (620 El Camino Real, San Bruno, 650/745-0111, www.ascendcollection.com, $139-189) offers mid-tier accommodations and amenities on a fairly nice block. Both the exterior and the interior are attractive and modern, complete with slightly wacky lobby decor and an indoor hot tub. **Millwood Inn & Suites** (1375 El Camino Real, Millbrae, 650/583-3935, www.millwoodinn.com, $145-305) offers big rooms and amenities that include free Wi-Fi, satellite TV with an attached DVD player, and a bigger-than-average free buffet breakfast. Perhaps best of all, the Millwood Inn offers a complimentary airport shuttle.

A generous step up in luxury is the **Bay Landing Hotel** (1550 Bayshore Hwy., Burlingame, 650/259-9000, www.baylandinghotel.com, $139-189). Updated rooms include pretty posted headboards, granite sinks in the baths, tub-shower combos, in-room safes, and free Wi-Fi. Free continental breakfast is served in the lobby, which has a lending library for guests.

Food

Some of the greatest culinary innovation in the world comes out of the kitchens in the city. The only real problem is how to choose which restaurant to eat dinner at tonight.

UNION SQUARE AND DOWNTOWN

Bakeries and Cafés

With a monopoly on cafés in Union Square, business is brisk at **Emporio Rulli** (350 Post St., www.rulli.com, 7am-7pm daily, $12-20). This local chain offers frothy coffee, pastries, and upscale sandwiches, plus beer and wine. Expect everything to be overpriced at Rulli. Often the only tables available are those outside, which in the summer can be pleasant. In the winter, heat lamps help ward off the chills and it feels quite festive watching the skaters wobble around the tiny rink in the square. Still pricey, but with loads more charm, is **Café de la Presse** (352 Grant Ave., 415/398-2680, www.cafedelapresse.com, 7:30am-9:30pm Mon.-Thurs., 7:30am-10pm Fri., 8am-10pm Sat.-Sun., $10). This 1930s-style French bistro serves breakfast, lunch, and dinner. Those in need of a relaxing espresso or glass of wine are welcome to take a table and drink in the atmosphere. If you need something to read to complete your experience, Café de la Presse sells international newspapers and magazines.

Asian

★ **Le Colonial** (20 Cosmo Pl., 415/931-3600, www.lecolonialsf.com, 5:30pm-10pm Sun.-Wed., 5:30pm-11pm Thurs.-Sat., $25-37) is tucked away in an alley in Nob Hill. It's exotic and exclusive, with a leafy, light-filled patio and cool, cavernous dining room. The decor invokes 1950s Saigon, with a tin-tiled ceiling and heavy Victorian woodwork. The Vietnamese dishes are as elegant as their surroundings. Standouts include the sea bass steamed in banana leaves and the crispy chili-glazed Brussels sprouts. The wine list is heavily French; the cocktails are big and tropical. For dessert, the huge banana split is meant to be shared.

You'll find all of Southeast Asia in the food at **E&O Trading Company** (314 Sutter St., 415/693-0303, www.eosanfrancisco.com, 11:30am-10pm Mon.-Wed., 11:30am-11pm Thurs.-Sat., 5pm-10pm Sun., $15-27). This fusion grill serves up small plates like Indonesian corn fritters, mixed in with larger grilled dishes such as black pepper shaking beef. Enjoy the wine list, full bar, and French colonial decor. Reservations are recommended.

New American

Nob Hill is a magnet for the city's power brokers, and no other restaurant speaks to this like **The Big 4** (1075 California, St., 415/771-1140, www.big4restaurant.com, 6:30am-10am, 11:30am-2pm, 5:30pm-10pm Mon.-Sat., 6:30am-2:30pm, 5:30pm-10pm Sun., $19-34). Ornate woodwork, green leather, and beveled glass partitions create a privileged and exclusive atmosphere. Dinner dishes are meat heavy and the cocktails are bourbon based. Established in 1976, the restaurant menu reflects the city's locavore sensibility while retaining its classic character with such throwbacks as the deviled eggs appetizer and oxtail and onion soup.

French

Tucked away in a tiny alley that looks like it might have been transported from Saint-Michel in Paris, ★ **Café Claude** (7 Claude Ln., 415/392-3505, www.cafeclaude.com, 11:30am-10:30pm Mon.-Sat., 5:30pm-10:30pm Sun., $21-28) serves classic brasserie cuisine to French expatriates and Americans alike. Much French is spoken here, but the simple food tastes fantastic in any language. Café Claude is open for lunch through dinner, serving an attractive post-lunch menu for weary shoppers looking for sustenance.

Seafood

Make reservations in advance if you want to dine at San Francisco legend ★ **Farallon** (450 Post St., 415/956-6969, www.farallonrestaurant.com, 5:30pm-9:30pm Mon., 11:30am-3pm, 5:30pm-9:30pm Tues.-Thurs. 11:30am-3pm, 5:30pm-10pm Fri.-Sat., 5pm-9:30pm Sun., $28-37). Dark, cave-like rooms are decorated in an underwater theme—complete with the unique Jellyfish Bar. Chef Mark Franz has made Farallon a 15-year icon that keeps gaining ground. Seafood dominates the pricey-but-worth-it menu. Desserts such as the Burnt Honey Goat Cheese Cake round out what many consider to be the perfect Californian meal.

FINANCIAL DISTRICT AND SOMA

Bakeries and Cafés

When ★ **Blue Bottle** began selling its handcrafted coffees at the Ferry Plaza Farmer's Market, they quickly set the gold standard for coffee in the city. The flagship location is the **Mint Plaza Café** (66 Mint St., 415/495-3394, www.bluebottlecoffee.net, 7am-7pm daily, $5-10). Choose from having Blue Bottle's coffee pulled into an espresso on a vintage San Marco lever espresso machine, brewed and iced on a "Kyoto style apparatus," or filtered on a $20,000 Japanese siphon bar. The prices may seem exorbitant and the lines painful, but the coffee is excellent. The café offers free newspapers and no Wi-Fi, a pleasant departure from the norm.

Classic American

Looking for an old-fashioned American breakfast? At **Dottie's True Blue Café** (28 6th St., 415/885-2767, http://dotties.biz, 7:30am-3pm Mon. and Thurs.-Fri., 7:30am-4pm Sat.-Sun., $9-14), the menu is simple: classic egg dishes, light fruit plates, and an honest-to-goodness blue-plate special for breakfast as well as salads, burgers, and sandwiches for lunch. The service is friendly, and the portions are huge. Everyone in San Francisco knows that there's a great breakfast to be had at Dottie's. Expect lines up to an hour long for a table at this locals' mecca, especially weekend mornings.

New American

Everything about **Boulevard** (1 Mission St., 415/543-6084, www.boulevardrestaurant.com, 11:30am-2:15pm, 5:30pm-10pm Mon.-Thurs., 11:30am-2:15pm, 5:30pm-10:30pm Fri., 5:30pm-10:30pm Sat., 5:30pm-10pm Sun., $31-49), from its historical 1889 building to the Belle Epoque interior and rich contemporary cuisine, is beautiful. Plates of roasted quail and line-caught swordfish are ferried around the intimate dining room, where patrons sip velvety wines and flutes of champagne. For years, chef and owner Nancy Oakes has set the standard for excellence in the city. In 2012, Boulevard was named Best Restaurant in America by the James Beard Foundation.

Handsome and sophisticated, Tyler Florence's **Wayfare Tavern** (558 Sacramento St., 415/772-9060, http://wayfaretavern.com, 11am-11pm Mon.-Fri., 11:30am-11pm Sat., 11:30am-10pm Sun., $20-49) serves hearty American comfort food with the rich twists befitting Florence's celebrity status. You'll find new takes on macaroni & cheese, poutine, and fried oysters, along with richly conceived desserts like chocolate cream pie and its house-made doughnuts. Dinner would not be complete without one of the restaurant's signature cocktails like the Tavern Sour or the Blood and Sand.

Chinese

It may not be in Chinatown, but the dim sum at **Yank Sing** (101 Spear St., 415/781-1111, www.yanksing.com, 11am-3pm Mon.-Fri., 10am-4pm Sat.-Sun., $20-60) is second to none. The family owns and operates both this restaurant and its sister location (49 Stevenson St., 415/541-4949), and now the third generation is training to take over. In addition to the traditional steamed pork buns, shrimp dumplings, egg custard tarts, and such, the "Creative Collection" offers unique bites you won't find elsewhere in the city. It's open for lunch only.

French

Believe it or not, **Crepes A Go-Go** (350 11th St., 415/503-1294, 6pm-midnight Wed. and Sun., 6pm-3am Thurs., 6pm-4am Fri.-Sat., $6), with its tiny, clean premises, lone employee working the crepes, and late-night hours is quite reminiscent of Paris. The cook can make you some quick and hearty nighttime sustenance or a fruity dessert. The house special is the turkey, egg, and cheese—a great way to fuel a full night of drinking and clubbing.

Japanese

Ame (St. Regis Hotel, 689 Mission St., 415/284-4040, www.amerestaurant.com, 6pm-9:30pm Mon.-Thurs., 5:30pm-10pm Fri.-Sat., 5:30pm-9:30pm Sun., $35-40) is a fancy fusion sushi restaurant. In stylish SoMa, this upscale Michelin-starred eatery serves a California-Japanese fusion style of seafood. Start with the offerings from the sashimi bar or check out the wealth of options in the appetizers and main courses. The blocky, attractively colored dining room has a modern flair that's in keeping with the up-to-date cuisine coming out of the kitchen.

Ozumo (161 Steuart St., 415/882-1333, www.ozumo.com, 11:30am-midnight Mon.-Fri., 5:30pm-midnight Sat.-Sun., $28-46) takes Japanese cuisine upscale. Inside the labyrinthine restaurant, partitioned with glass walls lined with sake bottles, is a lounge and a *robata* grill complete with bar seats. All dishes from the classic *nigiri* to the small-plate *izakaya* pub dishes are executed with panache. Wash down each artful dish with one of their high-quality sakes or choose from a selection of premium teas.

Seafood

One of the very first restaurants established in San Francisco during the Gold Rush in 1849, the ★ **Tadich Grill** (240 California St., 415/391-1849, www.tadichgrill.com, 11am-9:30pm Mon.-Fri., 11:30am-9:30pm Sat., $20-40) still serves fresh-caught fish and classic miner fare. The menu combines perfectly sautéed sand dabs, octopus salad, and the Hangtown Fry, an oyster and bacon frittata. Mix that with the business lunch crowd in suits, out-of-towners, and original dark wooden booths from the 1850s and you've got a fabulous San Francisco stew of a restaurant. Speaking of stew, the Tadich cioppino enjoys worldwide fame—and deserves it, even in a city that prides itself on the quality of its seafood concoctions.

Steak

How could you not love a steak house with a name like **Epic Roasthouse** (369 Embarcadero, 415/369-9955, www.epicroasthouse.com, 11:30am-9:30pm Mon.-Thurs., 11:30am-10pm Fri., 11am-10pm Sat., 11am-9:30pm Sun., $34-90)? Come for the wood-fired grass-fed beef; stay for the prime views over San Francisco Bay. The Epic Roasthouse sits almost underneath the Bay Bridge, where the lights sparkle and flash over the deep black water at night. On weekends, the steak house offers the hipster city crowd what it wants—an innovative prix fixe brunch menu complete with hair-of-the-dog cocktails.

Vietnamese

Probably the single most famous Asian restaurant in a city filled with eateries of all types is ★ **The Slanted Door** (1 Ferry Plaza, Suite 3, 415/861-8032, http://slanteddoor.com, 11am-2:30pm, 5:30pm-10pm Mon.-Sat., 11:30am-3pm, 5:30pm-10pm Sun., $19-45). Owner Charles Phan utilizes organic local ingredients in both traditional and innovative Vietnamese cuisine, creating a unique dining experience. Even experienced foodies remark that they've never had green papaya salad, glass noodles, or shaking beef like this before. The light afternoon tea menu (2:30pm-4:30pm daily) can be the perfect pick-me-up for weary travelers who need some sustenance to get them through the long afternoon until dinner, and Vietnamese coffee is the ultimate Southeast Asian caffeine experience.

Farmers Markets

Although farmers markets litter the landscape in just about every California town, the **Ferry Plaza Farmers Market** (1 Ferry Plaza, 415/291-3276, www.ferrybuildingmarketplace.com, 10am-2pm Tues. and Thurs., 8am-2pm Sat.) is special. At the granddaddy of Bay Area farmers markets, expect to see the freshest fruits and veggies from local growers, grass-fed beef from Marin County, and seasonal seafood pulled from the Pacific beyond the Golden Gate. You'll pay for the privilege of purchasing from this market—if you're seeking bargain produce, you'll be better served at one of the weekly neighborhood farmers markets. Even locals flock downtown to the Ferry Building on Saturday mornings, especially in the summer when the variety of California's agricultural bounty becomes staggering.

CHINATOWN

Chinese Banquets

The "banquet" style of Chinese restaurant may be a bit more familiar to American travelers. Banquet restaurants offer tasty meat, seafood, and veggie dishes along with rice, soups, and appetizers, all served family-style. Tables are often round, with a lazy Susan in the middle to facilitate the passing of communal serving bowls around the table. In the city, most banquet Chinese restaurants have at least a few dishes that will feel familiar to the American palate, and menus often have English translations.

The **R&G Lounge** (631 Kearny St., 415/982-7877, www.rnglounge.com, 11:30am-9:30pm daily, $12-40, reservations suggested) takes traditional Chinese American cuisine to the next level. The menu is divided by colors that represent the traditional elements. In addition to old favorites like moo shu pork and lemon chicken, you'll find spicy Szechuan and Mongolian dishes and house specialties. Salt-and-pepper Dungeness crab, served whole on a plate, is the R&G signature dish. Seafood comes right out of the tank in the dining room. This is a great place to enjoy Chinatown cuisine in a friendly setting.

Another great banquet house is the **Hunan Home's Restaurant** (622 Jackson St., 415/982-2844, http://hunanhome.ypguides.net, 11:30am-9:30pm Sun.-Thurs., 11:30am-10pm Fri.-Sat., $10-15). It is a bit more on the casual side, and it even has another location in suburban Los Altos. You'll find classic items on the menu such as broccoli beef and kung pao chicken, but do take care if something you plan to order has a "spicy" notation next to it. At Hunan Home's, they mean *really* spicy.

Dim Sum

The Chinese culinary tradition of dim sum is literally translated as "touch the heart," meaning "order to your heart's content" in Cantonese. In practical terms, it's a light meal—lunch or afternoon tea—composed of small bites of a wide range of dishes. Americans tend to eat dim sum at lunchtime, though it can just as easily be dinner or even Sunday brunch. In a proper dim sum restaurant, you do not order anything or see a menu. Instead, you sip your oolong and sit back as servers push loaded steam trays out of the kitchen one after the other. Servers and trays make their way around the tables; you pick out what you'd like to try as it passes, and enough of that dish for everyone at your table is placed before you.

One of the many great dim sum places in Chinatown is the ★ **Great Eastern** (649 Jackson St., 415/986-2500, www.greateasternsf.com, 10am-11pm Mon.-Fri., 9am-11pm Sat.-Sun., $15-25). Instead of steam carts, you'll get a menu and a list. Write down everything you want on your list and hand it to your waiter, and your choices will be brought out to you. Reservations are strongly recommended for diners who don't want to wait 30-60 minutes or more for a table. This restaurant jams up fast, right from the moment it opens, especially on weekends.

Dol Ho (808 Pacific Ave., 415/392-2828, 8am-3pm Thurs.-Tues., under $10) is another local favorite, but the hole-in-the-wall variety. The menu is in English, but it helps to have someone who is dim sum savvy at the table, particularly when then cart comes your way. The spare ribs over rice wins raves as do the deep-fried savory dumplings. What doesn't win rave reviews is the service (don't be afraid to be pushy) and the atmosphere (paper plates only), but eating here is an authentic Chinatown experience.

Tea Shops

Although oolong tea is the staple in California Chinese restaurants, you'll find an astonishing variety of teas in Chinatown's small tea shops. Enjoy a hot cup of tea or buy some loose tea to take home with you. Most tea shops also sell lovely imported teapots and other implements for proper tea making.

One option is **Blest Tea** (752 Grant Ave., 415/951-8516, http://blesttea.com, 11am-7pm Sun.-Fri., 10am-8pm Sat., tasting $3), which boasts of the healthful qualities of their many varieties of tea. You're welcome to taste what's available for a nominal fee to be sure you're purchasing something you'll really enjoy. If you're lucky enough to visit when the owner is minding the store, ask her lots of questions—she'll tell you everything you ever needed to know about tea.

NORTH BEACH AND FISHERMAN'S WHARF

Bakeries and Cafés

There is much talk about sourdough bread in San Francisco, but Boudin's version is the original. Started in 1849 by French immigrants, Boudin is such an institution that Herb Caen once claimed that a true San Francisco meal was cracked crab, a bottle of Chardonnay, and a hunk of Boudin. Today tourists at Boudin's **Bakers Hall** (160 Jefferson St., 415/928-1849, www.boudinbakery.com, 8am-9:30pm Sun.-Thurs., 8am-10pm Fri.-Sat., $8-12) can order a steaming bowl of clam chowder in a fresh bread bowl and watch how the bread is made in its demonstration bakery. If clam chowder is not for you, consider one of the many excellent sandwiches (including the superior grilled cheese) or a large and filling salad at the casual café. Upstairs, you can have a more formal dinner at **Bistro Boudin** (415/351-5561, 11:30am-9:30pm Sun.-Thurs., 11:30am-10pm Fri.-Sat., $16-38), which serves elegant American food and a whole host of oysters in its dark wood dining room overlooking the wharf. Boudin has another café location not far away at Pier 39 (Space 5 Q, 8am-8pm Sun.-Thurs., 8am-9pm Fri.-Sat., $8-12).

Widely recognized as the first espresso coffeehouse on the West Coast, family-owned **Caffé Trieste** (601 Vallejo St., 415/392-6739, www.caffetrieste.com, 6:30am-10pm Sun.-Thurs., 6:30am-11pm Fri.-Sat., cash only) first opened its doors in 1956 and is rumored to be where Francis Ford Coppola penned the original *Godfather* screenplay. Sip a cappuccino, munch on Italian pastries, and enjoy Saturday afternoon concerts by the Giotta family at this treasured North Beach institution.

Classic American

With its ultracasual vibe, large sunny windows, interior of country blue and yellow, bounty of freshly baked breads, hearty plates of omelets, huevos rancheros, French toast, and the indulgent crab Benedict, ★ **Mama's on Washington Square** (1701 Stockton St., 415/362-6421, www.mamas-sf.com, 8am-3pm Tues.-Sun., $9-14) is legendary for breakfast—and so is the line. Starting from down the block, the line flows through the heart of the restaurant to the counter where you place your order, then wait for a table to open up. The lunch options are also delicious. To minimize your wait, arrive at Mama's when they open or go after noon.

New American

San Francisco culinary celebrity Gary Danko has a number of restaurants around town, but perhaps the finest is the one that bears his name. **Gary Danko** (800 North Point St., 415/749-2060, www.garydanko.com,

5:30pm-10pm daily, prix fixe $76-111) offers the best of Danko's California cuisine, from the signature horseradish-crusted salmon medallions to an array of delectable fowl dishes. The herbs and veggies come from Danko's own farm in Napa. Make reservations in advance to get a table, and be prepared to dress up a little for your sojourn in the elegant white-tablecloth dining room.

A draw for the city's power brokers, **Park Tavern** (1652 Stockton St., 415/989-7300, http://parktavernsf.com, 5:30pm-10pm Mon.-Thurs., 11:30am-2:30pm, 5:30pm-11pm Fri., 10am-2:30pm, 5:30pm-11pm Sat., 10am-2:30pm, 5:30pm-10pm-Sun., $28-38) serves meat and fish dishes as well as exquisite appetizers such as venison carpaccio and braised pork cheeks in its elegant dining room. For a low-key meal at the bar, order off the "Jenn's Classics" menu, where the Marlowe burger is the best deal in the house.

Greek

In the Greek fishing village of Kokkari, wild game and seafood hold a special place in the local mythology. At **Kokkari Estiatorio** (200 Jackson St., 415/981-0983, www.kokkari.com, 11:30am-2:30pm, 5:30pm-10pm Mon.-Thurs., 11:30am-2:30pm, 5:30pm-11pm Fri., 5pm-11pm Sat., 5pm-10pm Sun., $17-29), patrons enjoy Mediterranean delicacies made with fresh California ingredients amid rustic elegance, feasting on such classic dishes as zucchini cakes and grilled lamb chops.

Italian

North Beach is San Francisco's version of Little Italy. Most of the family-style restaurants that once populated the neighborhood have now made way for more fashionable eateries, but you can still find excellent pizza and focaccia.

One of the last holdouts from North Beach's heyday is ★ **Mario's Bohemian Cigar Store** (566 Columbus Ave., 415/362-0536, 10am-11pm daily, $10-15). Not much has changed has changed in this slender café since it opened in 1972, except that it no longer sells tobacco. There are just a few tables and stools at the bar, where the bartender/server/cook pulls espresso, pours beer and wine, and prepares personal pizzas and focaccia sandwiches baked in a tiny oven. The meatball sandwich is a classic smeared with tomato sauce, and the breaded and grilled eggplant sandwiches satisfy vegetarians and meat eaters alike.

At busy **Caffe Delucchi** (500 Columbus Ave., 415/393-4515, www.caffedelucchi.com, 10am-10pm Mon.-Fri., 8am-11pm Sat.-Sun., $15-29), down-home Italian cooking meets fresh San Francisco produce to create affordable, excellent cuisine. You can get hand-tossed pizzas, salads, and entrées for lunch and dinner, plus tasty traditional American breakfast fare with an Italian twist on the weekends. Drinks run to *soju* cocktails and artisanal Italian and California wines.

Walk into **Tosca** (242 Columbus Ave., 415/986-9651, http://toscacafesf.com, 5pm-2am Tues.-Sun., $16-42) and step back in time to North Beach at its most romantic. Founded in 1919, Tosca spent much of its life as a bar, and until an ownership change in 2013, hadn't served food since the '60s. The fare is so good *Bon Appétit* rated it the fourth-best new restaurant in America in 2014. If there's a wait, take a seat at the bar and order the house cappuccino, a decadent concoction made of Armagnac, bourbon, chocolate ganache, and absolutely no coffee.

Want a genuine world-champion pizza while you're in town? Nine-time World Pizza Champion Tony Gemignani can hook you up. ★ **Tony's Pizza Napoletana** (1570 Stockton St., 415/835-9888, www.tonyspizzanapoletana.com, noon-10pm Mon., noon-11pm Wed.-Sun., $15-30) has four different pizza ovens that cook eight distinct styles of pizza. You can get a classic American pie loaded with pepperoni, a California-style pie with lamb and eucalyptus, or a Sicilian pizza smothered in meat and garlic. The chef's special Neapolitan-style pizza margherita is simple pizza made of perfection. The wood-fired atmosphere of this temple to the pie includes marble-topped tables, dark woods, and white

Delectable Dungeness

Dungeness crabs enjoy celebrity status in San Francisco. Although the crabs are named for a place on the Washington coast, the Dungeness came to fame in San Francisco. Dungeness season usually runs November-June, but the freshest crabs are caught and cooked from the start of the season (usually the second Tuesday of November) through New Year's.

Famed Italian seafood restaurant **Alioto's** (8 Fisherman's Wharf, 415/673-0183, www.aliotos.com, 11am-11pm daily, $17-48) serves whole cracked Dungeness in the traditional style. They've also got crab soups, salads, sandwiches, and stews. In Chinatown, **R&G Lounge** (631 Kearny St., 415/982-7877, http://rnglounge.com, 11:30am-9:30pm daily, $12-40, reservations suggested) offers deep-fried and salt-and-pepper crabs. In the Outer Sunset, **Thanh Long** (4101 Judah St., 415/665-1146, www.anfamily.com, 5pm-9:30pm Tues.-Thurs. and Sun., 5pm-10pm Fri.-Sat., $20-30) is famous for its roast crab soaked in garlic and butter.

linen napkins stuck into old tomato cans. The long full bar dominates the front dining room—grab a fancy bottle of wine or a cocktail to go with that pizza.

Over the years, and through two locations, **Quince** (470 Pacific Ave., 415/775-8500, www.quincerestaurant.com, 5:30pm-10pm Mon.-Thurs., 5pm-9:30pm Fri.-Sat., $190), a fine dining Italian restaurant spotlighting chef-owner Michael Tusk's celebrated pastas, has leapt to the upper stratosphere of Bay Area restaurants. In the exposed brick dining room where elegant Venetian chandeliers hang, two tasting menus feature such delicacies as caviar, white truffle, and abalone with black garlic. Expect impeccable service and specialty cocktails made tableside. If shelling out $190 (an additional $135 for wine pairing) is not in the cards, there are other options. At the swanky salon you can order from a limited menu that includes appetizers, pasta dishes, and a meat dish such as suckling pig. You can also book a table at neighboring **Cotogna** (490 Pacific Ave., 415/775-8508, www.cotognasf.com, 11:30am-10:30pm Mon.-Thurs., 11:30am-11pm Fri.-Sat., 5pm-9:30pm Sun., $17-28), also owned by Tusk. Dressed down, with a chic farm-table look, Cotogna offers excellent pizzas, classic meat dishes, and Tusk's signature pastas.

Seafood

It's tough to walk down the streets of the Wharf without tripping over seafood restaurants. You can pick just about any of the big ones and come up with a decent (if pricey and touristy) meal. A good way to choose is to stroll past the front doors and take a look at the menus.

It has the look of a big tourist trap, but at **McCormick and Kuleto's** (900 North Point St., 415/929-1730, www.mccormickandschmicks.com, 11:30am-10pm Sun.-Thurs., 11:30am-11pm Fri.-Sat., $20-35), the food, decor, views, and cocktail menu come together so nicely that it actually justifies the price. The menu is huge and offers mostly solid American surf and turf, but the most inventive stuff can be found on the bar menu, alongside its list of original cocktails.

Steak

5A5 Steak Lounge (244 Jackson St., 415/989-2539, http://5a5stk.com, 5pm-10pm Mon.-Thurs., 5pm-10:30pm Fri.-Sat., 5pm-9pm Sun., $22-49) has the swank of a 1960s steakhouse designed by Stanley Kubrick. White oversized booths, black snakeskin accents, and a perforated circular ceiling centerpiece put the *lounge* in "steak lounge." 5A5's menu is immense, with inventive takes on classic comfort foods, many Asian-inspired dishes, and a dozen different steak options, including the specialty Wagyu beef. The happy hour (5pm-7pm Mon.-Fri.) is considered one of the best around with eye-popping appetizers for only $5.

MARINA AND PACIFIC HEIGHTS

Bakeries and Cafés

For a café that is as chic as Pacific Heights, squeeze into the tightly packed **Jane** (2123 Fillmore St., 415/931-5263, http://janeonfillmore.com, 7am-6pm daily, $10). With high black wainscoting and black-and-white floral print wallpaper, the interior is a nod to the building's Victorian past that feels sleek and exclusive. The coffee is carefully poured, and the small open kitchen serves a selection of pastries, light breakfast dishes, a host of elegant salads, and hot pressed sandwiches.

Only looking for a quick snack to tide you over? Drop in at **The Chestnut Bakery** (2359 Chestnut St., 415/567-6777, www.chestnutbakery.com, 7am-noon Mon., 7am-6pm Tues.-Sat., 8am-5pm Sun.). A block and a half from Lombard Street, this small family-owned storefront is a perfect spot for weary travelers to take a load off and enjoy a cookie, pastry, or one of the bakery's famous cupcakes. In the morning, you'll find scones, croissants, and other favorite breakfast pastries. This is a favorite local spot, which means that some items sell out each day.

Sitting just east of Fort Point, the **Warming Hut** (983 Marine Dr., 415/561-3042, www.parksconservancy.org, 9am-5pm daily, $10) is the perfect destination after a stroll along Crissy Field. In an old army warehouse built in 1909, you'll find grilled sandwiches, a variety of salads, and steaming mugs of hot chocolate (along with the usual espresso drinks). Prices may not seem proportionate to the portions, but all ingredients are locally sourced and responsibly raised, and all proceeds go back to the park. Weekends can be packed. Although you can browse the cool little gift store that sells park related books and trinkets, you may want to make a stop at the Warming Hut's sister café, **Beach Hut Café** (1199 E. Beach St., 415/561-776, 9am-5pm daily, $10), at the east end of Crissy Field. With roughly the same menu, this little café also boasts stunning views of the Golden Gate in a sleek, sustainable new building.

New American

When famed chef Traci Des Jardins took over the 1895 mess hall in the Main Post, it became clear that there was no other place to eat in the Presidio. ★ **Commissary** (101 Montgomery St., 415/561-3600, www.thecommissarysf.com, 11:30am-2pm, 5:30pm-9pm Mon.-Thurs., 11:30am-2pm, 5:30pm-9:30pm Fri., 5:30pm-9:30pm Sat., $19-30) does more than give a nod to the building's past, it embraces it with modern panache. The cuisine is a blend of San Francisco and Spanish influences and utilizes such ingredients as cod, anchovies, chorizo, and peppers. Most of the seating is either at the bar looking into the open kitchen, where Des Jardins herself is at the helm, or at the long communal tables, reminding diners of the infantry men who ate here over one hundred years before.

Le Marais Bistro and Bakery (2066 Chestnut St., 415/359-9801, www.lemaraisbakery.com, 7am-7pm daily, $10) reflects the highly polished farm-to-table dining scene of the next generation. You'll find plenty of the buttery indulgences found in all good patisseries, plus soups, grilled sandwiches, and quiche that no self-respecting bistro would do without. Seating is tight, so consider taking your goodies to go and picnic at Fort Mason or the Marina Green.

Cajun

The unpretentious ★ **Elite Café** (2049 Fillmore St., 415/673-5483, www.theelitecafe.com, 5pm-10pm Mon.-Thurs., 5pm-10:30pm Fri., 10am-3pm, 5pm-10:30pm Sat., 10am-3pm, 5pm-9pm Sun., $22-31) has been around since 1928. Inside the art deco dining room, the restaurant serves big plates of Cajun food including jambalaya, ham hock gumbo, and shrimp and grits. For locals, this is a favorite brunch spot where you can order oysters, beignets, and the Elite's famed deviled eggs.

Italian

The name **A16** (2355 Chestnut St., 415/771-2216, www.a16sf.com, 5:30pm-10pm Mon.-Tues., 11:30am-2:30pm, 5:30pm-10pm Wed.-Thurs., 11:30am-2:30pm, 5:30pm-11pm Fri., 11:30am-2:30pm, 5pm-11pm Sat., 11:30am-2:30pm, 5pm-10pm Sun., $13-28) refers to the major road cutting through the Campania region of southern Italy. At A 16 in San Francisco, you'll find fabulous southern Italian food. Handmade artisanal pizzas, pastas, and entrées tempt the palate with a wealth of hearty flavors. Pasta dishes come in two sizes—a great thing for those with smaller appetites. A wonderful wine list complements the food.

Japanese

For a super-hip San Francisco sushi experience, strut on down to **Ace Wasabi's** (3339 Steiner St., 415/567-4903, http://acewasabisf.com, 5:30pm-10:30pm Mon.-Thurs., 5:30pm-11pm Fri.-Sat., 5pm-10pm Sun., $6-13). Advertising "rock 'n' roll sushi" and created with the atmosphere of an *izakaya* (a Japanese bar and grill), Ace Wasabi's appeals to a young, fun crowd. Be aware that the party can get loud on weekends.

If you're in Pacific Heights, give **Kiss Seafood** (1700 Laguna St., 415/474-2866, 5:30pm-9:30pm Tues.-Sat., $30-60) a try. This tiny restaurant (12 seats in total) boasts some of the freshest fish in town—no mean feat in San Francisco. The lone chef prepares all the fish himself, possibly because of the tiny size of the place. Reservations are a good idea. Anything seafood is recommended, but if you're up for sashimi, you'll be in raw-fish heaven. Round off your meal with a glass of chilled premium sake.

Food Trucks

Every culinary city worth its Himalayan sea salt has a fleet of food trucks. San Francisco is no exception and on various days of the week you can spot an idling armada handing out pizzas, pierogi, *papusas*, or crème brûlée. To get the very best food truck experience, plan a Sunday afternoon at the **Off the Grid Presidio Picnic** (Main Post Lawn, 415/339-5888, http://offthegridsf.com, 11am-4pm Sun. Apr.-Nov., $5-15), where 6 trucks, 17 tents, and 2 carts roving through the crowds sell everything from bloody Marys to Vietnamese soup. More than a food truck depot, the Presidio Picnic is in fact a party with live DJs and plenty of dogs, kids, hipsters, Frisbees, and picnic blankets. If you come, plan on spending most of the day.

CIVIC CENTER AND HAYES VALLEY

New American

Housed in a former bank, ★ **Nopa** (560 Divisadero St., 415/864-8643, http://nopasf.com, 5pm-1am Mon.-Fri., 11am-1am Sat.-Sun., $16-26) shepherded Divisadero's identity shift from the solidly African American Western Addition to the gentrified "NOPA" (North of the Panhandle). Suddenly, hip farm-to-table food was being served in the heart of San Francisco's barbecue country. The food served on the long communal table is comfort food made with the best ingredients, a global sensibility, and excellent execution. It is a quintessential San Francisco restaurant and impossible to get a table without a reservation.

French

Jardinière (300 Grove St., 415/861-5555, www.jardiniere.com, 5pm-10:30pm daily, $20-32) was the first restaurant opened by local celebrity chef Traci Des Jardins. The bar and dining room blend into one another and feature stunning exposed brick and art deco decor. The ever-changing menu is a masterpiece of French California cuisine, and Des Jardins has long supported the sustainable restaurant movement. Try the tasting menu ($110), or book a reservation before or after a show. No other place quite matches the elegance of a night at the opera, ballet, or symphony.

Absinthe (398 Hayes St., 415/551-1590, www.absinthe.com, 11:30am-midnight Mon.-Fri., 11am-midnight Sat., 11am-10pm Sun., $23-30) takes its name from the notorious "green fairy" drink made of liquor and wormwood. Absinthe indeed does serve absinthe—including locally made St. George Spirits Absinthe Verte. It also serves upscale French bistro fare, including what may be the best french fries in the city. The French theme carries on into the decor as well—expect the look of a Parisian brasserie or perhaps a café in Nice, with retro-modern furniture and classic prints on the walls. The bar is open until 2am Thursday through Saturday.

German

★ **Suppenküche** (525 Laguna St., 415/252-9289, www.suppenkuche.com, 5pm-10pm Mon.-Sat., 10am-2:30pm, 5pm-10pm Sun., $11-20) brings a taste of Bavaria to the Bay Area. The beer list is a great place to start, since you can enjoy a wealth of classic German brews on tap and in bottles, plus a few Belgians thrown in for variety. For dinner, expect German classics with a focus on Bavarian cuisine. Spaetzle, pork, sausage—you name it, they've got it, and it will harden your arteries right up. Suppenküche also has a Biergarten (424 Octavia St., http://biergartensf.com, 3pm-9pm Wed.-Sat., 1pm-7pm Sun.) two blocks away.

Seafood

Bar Crudo (655 Divisadero St., 415/409-0679, www.barcrudo.com, 5pm-10pm Tues.-Thurs., 5pm-11pm Fri.-Sat., 5pm-10pm Sun., $15-28) began its life above the grimy Stockton tunnel in Nob Hill. In 2009, it moved to the gentrifying Divisadero corridor, where its once dark and secret interior became light and airy, a perfect match for its carefully crafted menu of mostly raw seafood. Oysters, of course, can be found here, but so can delicate strips of raw scallops, yellow tail, and arctic char. To make the most of dinner, order items to share, particularly the Crudo Sampler and the San Sebastian Salad, Bar Crudo's take on the classic Nicoise. A bottle of crisp, minerally white wine is also not a bad idea.

MISSION AND CASTRO

Bakeries and Cafés

The Mission is ground zero for San Francisco's most recent culinary revolution. Expect to find everything here in abundance, including scores of cafes and delis hawking irresistible confections, coffee, and homey-yet-artisanal picnic grub.

Locals love the artful pastries and fresh breads at ★ **Tartine Bakery** (600 Guerrero St., 415/487-2600, www.tartinebakery.com, 8am-7pm Mon., 7:30am-7pm Tues.-Wed., 7:30am-8pm Thurs.-Fri., 8am-8pm Sat., 9am-8pm Sun., $4-13). Tartine's bakers use organic flour, sea salt, and locally sourced produce and cheeses to craft their culinary creations, and the French-Italian-California fusion pastries and panini have brought this bakery its word-of-mouth success. With hours that extend into early evening, Tartine makes an attractive alternative for a light dinner or fixings for an evening picnic.

Speaking of dinner, sister property **Bar Tartine** (561 Valencia St., 415/847-1600, www.bartartine.com, 6pm-10pm Mon.-Tues., 11am-3pm, 6pm-10pm Wed.-Thurs., 11am-3pm, 6pm-11pm Fri., 11am-2:30pm, 6pm-11pm Sat., 11am-2:30pm, 6pm-10pm Sun., $10-25) serves gourmet sandwiches, dinners, and weekend brunches.

If the line is too long at Tartine, head one block east to **Craftsman and Wolves** (746 Valencia, 415/913-7713, www.craftsman-wolves.com, 7am-8pm Mon.-Thurs., 7am-8pm Fri., 8am-8pm Sat., 8am-7pm Sun., $3-14).

This next generation of hipster bakery feels a bit like a piece of Los Angeles installation art with its spare industrial chic, ambience music, and slightly snobby customer service. But the food is for real. Behind the counter, you'll find all sorts of finely crafted pastries and the sandwiches, including the "haute dog," are excellent. For a quick breakfast, order the "rebel within." This "muffin" is everything rolled into one: cheese, green onion, and sausage, with a filling of soft poached egg.

Perhaps one of the hippest and least pretentious places to grab a sandwich is the tiny **Claire's Deli** (3505 17th St., 415/621-3505, http://claresdeli.com, 11am-7pm Tues.-Sat., 11am-6pm Sun.-Mon., $5-10). Fun, reasonably priced, and made with excellent ingredients, the sandwiches here are a clever (but not too clever) take on old favorites. The French dip is large and legendary, and the B.L.G.B.T. (bacon, lettuce, garlic mayo, brie, and tomato) will fill you up on a picnic at nearby Dolores Park. Keep a lookout for the Reuben special with house-cured corned beef and be sure to order a house-cured pickle as a side.

Around the corner, satisfy your sweet tooth at **Bi-Rite Creamery & Bakeshop** (3692 18th St., 415/626-5600, http://biritecreamery.com, 11am-10pm Sun.-Thurs., 11am-11pm Fri.-Sat.). The ice cream is made by hand with organic milk, cream, and eggs; inventive flavors include salted caramel, balsamic strawberry, and malted vanilla with peanut brittle and milk chocolate pieces.

Classic American

Sometimes all you want is a burger, and you want it fast, wrapped in paper, and paired with French fries in a place that smells like grease. **Super Duper Burger** (2304 Market St., 415/558-8123, www.superdupersf.com, 11am-11pm daily, $7) is San Francisco's answer to the all-American craving for fast food. The menu has only the basics—burgers, fries, and shakes—and the atmosphere—you order at the counter—is not fancy. The twist is that everything is made in house (buns, pickles, etc.) and is locally sourced, from your all-organic soft-served ice cream to your grass-fed burger.

New American

Range (842 Valencia St., 415/282-8283, 6pm-close Mon.-Thurs., 5:30pm-close Fri.-Sun., $23-28) may have lost its Michelin Guide star in 2011, but it's no less popular. Consistently rated one of the top Bay Area restaurants, Range serves up expertly crafted California cuisine such as coffee-rubbed pork shoulder and halibut cheeks à la nage. An inventive cocktail list doesn't hurt either.

Café Flore (2298 Market St., 415/621-8579, www.cafeflore.com, 10am-midnight Mon.-Fri., 8am-midnight Sat.-Sun., $7-22) has been a Castro mainstay since 1973. Its food is good, unfussy, and very reasonably priced. Order the eggs Benedict for brunch or the Wagyu steak and frites for dinner. Part of the place's charm is the somewhat ramshackle wood building and lush outside garden patio. It is the perfect place for an espresso and people watching or a no-frills cocktail late in the evening.

French

Frances (3870 17th St., 415/621-3870, 5pm-10:30pm daily, $21-32) has been winning rave reviews ever since it opened its doors. The California-inspired French cuisine is locavore friendly, with an emphasis on sustainable ingredients and local farms. The short-but-sweet menu changes daily and includes such temptations as caramelized Atlantic scallops and bacon beignets. Reservations are strongly advised, especially since Frances received its *Michelin Guide* star.

Italian

At times, even the most dedicated culinary explorer needs a break from the endless fancy food of San Francisco. When the time is right for a plain ol' pizza, head for **Little Star Pizza** (400 Valencia St., 415/551-7827, www.littlestarpizza.com, noon-10pm Sun.-Thurs., noon-11pm Fri.-Sat., $20). A jewel of the

Mission district, this pizzeria specializes in Chicago-style deep-dish pies, but also serves thin-crust pizzas for devotees of the New York style. Once you've found the all-black building and taken a seat inside the casual eatery, grab a beer or a cocktail from the bar if you have to wait for a table. Pick one of Little Star's specialty pizzas, or create your own variation from the toppings they offer. Can't get enough of Little Star? They've got a second location (846 Divisadero St., 415/441-1118).

★ **Delfina** (3621 18th St., 415/552-4055, www.delfinasf.com, 5pm-10pm Mon., 11:30am-10pm Tues.-Thurs., 11:30am-11pm Fri., noon-11pm Sat., 5pm-10pm Sun., $11-17) gives Italian cuisine a hearty California twist. From the antipasti to the entrées, the dishes speak of local farms and ranches, fresh seasonal produce, and the best Italian-American taste that money can buy. With both a charming, warm indoor dining room and an outdoor garden patio, there's plenty of seating at this lovely restaurant.

When cocktails began taking center stage at restaurants (and San Franciscans getting tipsy before the first course arrived), **Beretta** (1199 Valencia St., 415/695-1199, www.berettasf.com, 5:30pm-1am Mon.-Fri., 11am-1am Sat.-Sun.) led the charge. Its bar menu consistently wins rave reviews and is hard to pass up, particularly as the restaurant doesn't take reservations for parties under six and the only place to wait is at the bar. Order a Rattlesnake, and a pizza to suck up the venom of that bite.

Mexican

Much of the rich heritage of the Mission district is Hispanic, thus leading to the Mission being *the* place to find a good taco or burrito. It is generally agreed upon that **La Taqueria** (2889 Mission St., 415/285-7117, 11am-9pm Mon.-Sat., 11am-8pm Sun., $5-10) makes the best burrito in the city. Critics rave, as do locals grabbing dinner on their way home. Especially delicious are the fruit drinks and the carnitas tacos, which you can order crispy (but ask, as it is not on the menu).

Another authentic Mexican pick is **La Palma Mexicatessen** (2884 24th St., 415/647-1500, www.lapalmasf.com, 8am-6pm Mon.-Sat., 8am-5pm Sun., $6-10). While it is technically a Mexican deli, you can still get an outrageously large (and delicious) burrito, as well as tacos and tamales. After you place your order, browse the cramped market and pick up some picnic provisions and the best whole wheat tortillas in the city.

You could say that at **Tacolicious** (741 Valencia St., 415/626-1344, http://tacolicious.com, 11:30am-midnight daily, $8-14), the Mission's hipster and Mexican worlds collide. Relying on fresh ingredients and seasoned with bright and spicy flavors, the food at this epicurean taqueria doesn't compete with its older neighbors but offers something wholly different. There are no burritos, but instead you'll find a kale and quinoa salad, albacore tostadas, grilled squid Veracruz and plenty of unusual tacos. A large list of original cocktails makes this an eat-in taco joint, rather than a grab and go.

Seafood

For great seafood in a lower-key atmosphere, locals eschew the tourist traps on the Wharf and head for the ★ **Anchor Oyster Bar** (579 Castro St., 415/431-3990, www.anchoroysterbar.com, 11:30am-10pm Mon.-Sat., 4pm-9:30pm Sun., $19-28), an institution in the Castro since 1977. The raw bar features different varieties of oysters, but not so many as to be overwhelming or pretentious. The dining room serves seafood, including local favorite Dungeness crab. Service is friendly, as befits a neighborhood spot, and it sees fewer large crowds. This doesn't diminish its quality, and it makes for a great spot to get a delicious meal before heading out to the local clubs for a late night out.

GOLDEN GATE PARK AND THE HAIGHT

Bakeries and Cafés

Need to warm up after a stroll on Ocean Beach? Head over to the local hang out, **Java Beach Cafe** (1396 La Playa St., 415/665-5282, www.javabeachsf.com, 5:30am-11pm Mon.-Fri., 6am-11pm Sat.-Sun., $8-12). You may have to fight for a table, but the coffee, bagels and sandwiches make it worth it. If you are wearing the appropriate layers, take a table outside and get a taste of the local Sunset flavor. A good selection of beer and wine are also available, accounting for why some denizens never seem to want to leave.

New American

Adjacent to Golden Gate Park, **Park Chow** (1240 9th Ave., 415/665-9912, www.chowfoodbar.com, 8am-9:30pm Sun.-Thurs., 8am-10:30pm Fri.-Sat., $12-18) does a brisk business with locals and visitors alike. The cozy interior complements the organic comfort food menu featuring everything from wood-fired pizzas to steak frites. Opt for the rooftop garden on the rare sunny day.

Magnolia (1398 Haight St., 415/864-7468, http://magnoliapub.com, 11am-midnight Mon.-Thurs., 11am-1am Fri., 10am-1am Sat., 10am-midnight Sun., $14-26) began its life channeling the spirit of the Grateful Dead into its strong beer and laid-back pub fare. When the gastropub craze hit, Magnolia jumped on board. To match its muscular beers, the excellent menu is meat-heavy, with a whole section of sausages. The aesthetic is dark and brooding, tapping into the neighborhood's Victorian past. Selections include oysters, bread pudding, flat iron steak, and, for dessert, a stout ice cream float.

One of the most famous restaurant locations in San Francisco is the ★ **Cliff House.** The high-end eatery inhabiting the famed facade is **Sutro's** (1090 Point Lobos Ave., 415/386-3330, www.cliffhouse.com, 11:30am-3:30pm, 5pm-9:30pm Mon.-Sat., 11am-3:30pm, 5pm-9:30pm Sun., $26-46). Expensive plates of steak, rack of lamb, and bacon-crusted Scottish salmon are prepared with a San Francisco sensibility and are best with a hand-crafted cocktail or a glass of California wine. While you may get a better meal elsewhere in the city, you will never eat it with views such as these. The floor-to-ceiling windows overlooking the Sutro Baths and the Pacific Ocean and the beautiful, airy interior of white and sea-glass blue seem to make every plate taste more extravagant. To get the views without the price tag, take a table at the more casual **Bistro** (9am-3:30pm, 4:15pm-9:30pm Mon.-Sat., 8:30am-3:30pm, 4:15pm-9:30pm Sun., $15-30) and order a big bowl of cioppino or seafood Louie. The ornately carved zinc bar and leafy palms add a vintage touch to the modern atmosphere. The **Lounge** (9am-11pm Sun.-Thurs., 9am-midnight Fri.-Sat.) is the best deal in the house. Small tables line the plate glass windows, where you can sip coffee and drinks without all the fuss. You can also order appetizer-style bites from a select bar menu (11am-9:30pm daily), which includes some of the best dishes in the house at very reasonable prices.

French

One of the best places in the Haight is not really in the Haight, but in the pocket neighborhood of Cole Valley. Dripping with charm, ★ **Zazie** (941 Cole St., 415/564-5332, www.zaziesf.com, 8am-2pm, 5pm-9:30pm Mon.-Thurs., 8am-2pm, 5pm-10pm Fri.-Sat., $19-24), a tiny French bistro, is known mainly for brunch. To the joy of its fans, it has recently started to serve dinner. Benedict, croque monsieur, coq au vin, and boeuf Bourguignon go down perfectly with either a latte or Kir royale.

Japanese

Sushi restaurants are immensely popular in these residential neighborhoods. **Koo** (408 Irving St., 415/731-7077, www.sushikoo.com, 5:30pm-10pm Tues.-Thurs., 5:30pm-10:30pm Fri.-Sat., 5pm-9:30pm Sun., $30-50) is a favorite in the Sunset. While sushi purists are happy with the selection of *nigiri* and sashimi, lovers of fusion and experimentation will enjoy the small plates and unusual rolls created to delight diners. Complementing the Japanese cuisine is a small but scrumptious list of premium sakes. Only the cheap stuff is served hot, as high-quality sake is always chilled.

Vietnamese

Thanh Long (4101 Judah St., 415/665-1146, www.anfamily.com, 5pm-9:30pm Tues.-Thurs., Sun., 5pm-10pm Fri.-Sat., $20-30) was the first family-owned Vietnamese restaurant in San Francisco. Since the early 1970s, Thanh Long has been serving one of the best preparations of local Dungeness crab in the city—roasted crab with garlic noodles. This isn't a $5 pho joint—expect white tablecloths and higher prices at this stately small restaurant in the outer Sunset neighborhood.

Information and Services

VISITOR INFORMATION

The main San Francisco **Visitor Information Center** (900 Market St., 415/391-2000, www.sanfrancisco.travel, 9am-5pm Mon.-Fri., 9am-3pm Sat.-Sun. May-Oct., 9am-5pm Mon.-Fri., 9am-3pm Sat. Nov.-Apr.) can help you even before you arrive. See the website for information about attractions and hotels, and to order a visitors' kit and purchase discounted tickets for various museums and attractions. Once you're in town, you can get a San Francisco book at the Market Street location (just below Hallidie Plaza at Powell Street) as well as the usual brochures and a few useful coupons. There are materials at the Visitor Information Center in 14 different languages along with multilingual staff.

MEDICAL SERVICES

The **San Francisco Police Department** (766 Vallejo St., 415/315-2400, www.sf-police.org) is headquartered in Chinatown, on Vallejo Street between Powell and Stockton Streets.

San Francisco boasts a large number of full-service hospitals. The **UCSF Medical Center at Mount Zion** (1600 Divisadero St., 415/567-6600, www.ucsfhealth.org) is renowned for its research and advances in cancer treatments and other important medical breakthroughs. The main hospital is at the corner of Divisadero and Geary Streets. Right downtown, **St. Francis Memorial Hospital** (900 Hyde St., 415/353-6000, www.saintfrancismemorial.org), at the corner of Hyde and Bush Streets, has an emergency department.

Transportation

GETTING THERE

Air

San Francisco International Airport (SFO, 800/435-9736, www.flysfo.com) isn't within the City of San Francisco; it is actually about 13 miles south in the town of Millbrae, right on the bay. You can easily get a taxi ($35) or other ground transportation into the heart of the city from the airport. BART is available from SFO's international terminal, but Caltrain is only accessible via a BART connection from SFO. Some San Francisco hotels offer complimentary shuttles from the airport as well. You can also rent a car here.

As one of the 30 busiest airports in the world, SFO has long check-in and security lines much of the time and dreadful overcrowding on major travel holidays. On an average day, plan to arrive at the airport two hours before your domestic flight and three hours before an international flight.

Train and Bus

Amtrak does not run directly into San Francisco. You can ride into San Jose, Oakland, or Emeryville stations, and then take a connecting bus into San Francisco.

Greyhound (200 Folsom St., 415/495-1569,

www.greyhound.com, 5:30am-1am daily) offers bus service to San Francisco from all over the country.

GETTING AROUND

Car

The **Bay Bridge** (toll $6) links I-80 to San Francisco from the east, and the **Golden Gate Bridge** (toll $7) connects Highway 1 from the north. From the south, U.S. 101 and I-280 snake up the peninsula and into the city. Be sure to get a detailed map and good directions to drive into San Francisco—the freeway interchanges, especially surrounding the east side of the Bay Bridge, can be confusing, and the traffic congestion is legendary. For traffic updates and route planning, visit **511.org** (www.511.org).

A car of your own is not necessarily beneficial in San Francisco. The hills are daunting, traffic is excruciating, and parking prices are absurd. If you plan to spend all of your time in the city, consider dispensing with a car and using cabs and public transit options. Rent a car when you're ready to leave San Francisco, or turn your rental in early if the city is your last stop.

If you absolutely must have your car with you, try to get a room at a hotel with a parking lot and either free parking or a parking package for the length of your stay.

CAR RENTAL

All the major car rental agencies have a presence at the San Francisco Airport (SFO, 800/435-9736, www.flysfo.com). In addition, most reputable hotels can offer or recommend a car rental. Rates tend to run $50-100 per day and $200-550 per week (including taxes and fees), with discounts for weekly and longer rentals. If you're flying into Mineta San José Airport (SJC, www.flysanjose.com) or Oakland Airport (OAK, www.flyoakland.com), the cost can drop to $110-250 per week for budget agencies. Premium agencies like Hertz and Avis are much pricier—you'll pay $240-650 for the same car. Off-site locations may offer cheaper rates, in the range of about $250 per week.

PARKING

To call parking in San Francisco a nightmare is to insult nightmares. Every available scrap of land that can be built on has been built on, with little left over to create parking for the zillions of cars that pass through on a daily basis. Parking a car in San Francisco can easily cost $50 per day or more. Most downtown and Union Square hotels do not include free parking with your room. Expect to pay $35-45 per night for parking, which may not include in-and-out privileges.

If street parking seems like a better deal, keep in mind that meters cost up to $2 per hour, often go late into the night, and operate during the weekends. At least many now take credit cards (gulp). Unmetered street parking spots are as rare as unicorns and often require permits (which visitors cannot obtain) for stays longer than two hours during the day. Lots and garages fill up quickly, especially during special events. You're more likely to find parking included at the motels along the edge of the city—Fisherman's Wharf, the Marina, the Richmond, and the Sunset district have the most motor inns with parking included.

Muni

Local opinion about the Muni (www.sfmta.com, adults $2.25, youth and seniors $0.75, children under 4 free) transit system isn't printable in guidebooks. The truth is, Muni can get you where you want to go in San Francisco as long as time isn't a concern. A variety of lines snake through the city—those that go down to Fisherman's Wharf use vintage streetcars to heighten the fun for visitors, and the underground light rail system is relatively efficient. See the website for a route map, ticket information, and (ha ha) schedules.

Tickets can be purchased from any Muni driver, except for the underground trains, which have ticket machines at the entrance. Exact change is required, except on the cable cars, where drivers can make change for up to $20. See the website for more information about purchasing tickets. The multiday visitor passport ($15/1 day, $23/3 days, $29/week), which includes the cable cars, is a particularly good value.

BART

Bay Area Rapid Transit, or BART (www.bart.gov, one-way $1.85-7.50), is the Bay Area's latecoming answer to major metropolitan underground railways like Chicago's L trains and New York's subway system. Sadly, there's only one arterial line through the city. However, service directly from San Francisco Airport into the city runs daily, as does service to Oakland Airport, the cities of Oakland and Berkeley, and many other East Bay destinations. BART connects to the Caltrain system and San Francisco Airport in Millbrae. See the website for route maps, schedules (BART usually runs on time), and fare information.

To buy tickets, use the vending machines found in every BART station. If you plan to ride more than once, you can add money to a single ticket and then keep that ticket and reuse it for each ride.

Caltrain

This traditional commuter rail line runs along the peninsula into Silicon Valley, from San Francisco to San Jose, with limited continuing service to Gilroy. Caltrain (www.caltrain.com, one-way $3-13) Baby Bullet trains can get you from San Jose to San Francisco in an hour during commuting hours. Extra trains are often added for San Francisco Giants, San Francisco 49ers, and San Jose Sharks games.

You must purchase a ticket in advance at the vending machines found in all stations. The main Caltrain station in San Francisco is at the corner of 4th and King Streets, within walking distance of AT&T Park and Moscone Center.

Taxis and Ridesharing

You'll find some taxis scooting around all the major tourist areas of the city. If you have trouble hailing a cab, try **City Wide Dispatch** (415/920-0700).

Competing with the cabs are drivers for **Uber** (www.uber.com) and **Lyft** (www.lyft.com). By downloading either company's smartphone app, you can summon a driver quickly (and generally for less than the cost of a cab ride). Payment occurs through the app and is entirely electronic, but riders should beware surge pricing, when fares increase during high-demand times (rush hour, before or after popular events, or weekend nights downtown). To stay competitive, the city's taxis have their own app, **Flywheel** (www.flywheel.com).

San Francisco Bay Area

Look for ★ to find recommended sights, activities, dining, and lodging.

Highlights

★ **Angel Island State Park:** A visit to the largest island in the bay packs a lot into a short amount of time. Catch history, natural wonders, and unparalleled views at this rarely visited treasure (page 101).

★ **Muir Woods National Monument:** Stand among trees nearly 1,000 years old and 200 feet tall in one of the nation's earliest national monuments (page 104).

★ **Mount Tamalpais State Park:** The Bay Area's backyard is awash in hiking and biking trails and redwood groves—all topped by Mt. Tam's 2,571-foot peak (page 106).

★ **Point Reyes National Seashore:** Home to tule elk, desolate beaches, dairy and oyster farms, one of the oldest West Coast lighthouses, and scores of remote wilderness trails, Point Reyes is one of the most diverse parks in the Bay Area (page 110).

★ **Oakland Museum of California:** The East Bay's latest cultural institution takes a multidisciplinary approach to California's story. You'll see contemporary art, skeletons of long-extinct local fauna, and ephemera from California's early days (page 124).

★ **San Gregorio General Store:** Drinks, books, live music, and every type of houseware under the sun fill this local institution, frequented by cowboys, environmentalists, and farmers (page 136).

★ **Año Nuevo State Park:** Watch giant elephant seals, sea otters, endangered red-legged frogs, or any number of marine birds at this reserve's 4,000 acres (page 137).

★ **Filoli:** This Gregorian-style mansion is home to 16 acres of stunning gardens (page 139).

★ **Winchester Mystery House:** It may be touristy, but the creepiness of this sprawling manic mansion is no gimmick. Built by the heiress to the Winchester rifle fortune, it is a testament to the dark side of the Wild West (page 144).

San Francisco may steal the spotlight, but the rest of the Bay Area is home to nearly seven million people and is just as dynamic as the city it surrounds.

The Bay Area is home to captains of industry, towering redwoods, prestigious universities and their earnest and cantankerous college towns, ethnically diverse cities, and old Portuguese fishing and dairy communities. You can find some of the best minds, most spectacular scenery, and tastiest food. And much of it lies outside the perimeter of San Francisco.

Thanks to the foresight of previous generations, much of the land in the Bay Area has been preserved as open space. In the North Bay and the peninsula south of the city, you can hike to quiet beaches, stroll among ancient stands of redwoods, and enjoy the fruits of generations—old family farms that still operate on some of the most beautiful (and expensive) land in the world.

Across the bay, the cities of Berkeley and Oakland rival San Francisco in cultural diversity, radical thinking, and cutting-edge gastronomy. Built around the university and the war effort of the 1940s, the East Bay has grown to become as cosmopolitan as its neighbor to the west.

From the Campanile at the University of California, Berkeley, you can see the Hoover Tower at Stanford University, Cal's bitter rival. While undergraduates at Berkeley protest everything from nuclear power to tuition hikes, students at Stanford are busy trying to become the next Mark Zuckerberg. Planted firmly at the epicenter of the "new economy," Stanford and its home, Palo Alto, are saturated in entrepreneurial ethos, while Silicon Valley's work horse, San Jose, is home to some of the biggest names in the tech world.

PLANNING YOUR TIME

You can cross the Golden Gate Bridge and explore Marin County on a day trip, but you may spend more time in the car than strolling beaches and forests. To better enjoy the parks and hiking trails, plan an overnight stay. The East Bay is spread out and is often clogged by commuter traffic in the

Previous: Point Bonita Lighthouse; UC Berkeley's Campanile. **Above:** kayaks on Angel Island.

San Francisco Bay Area

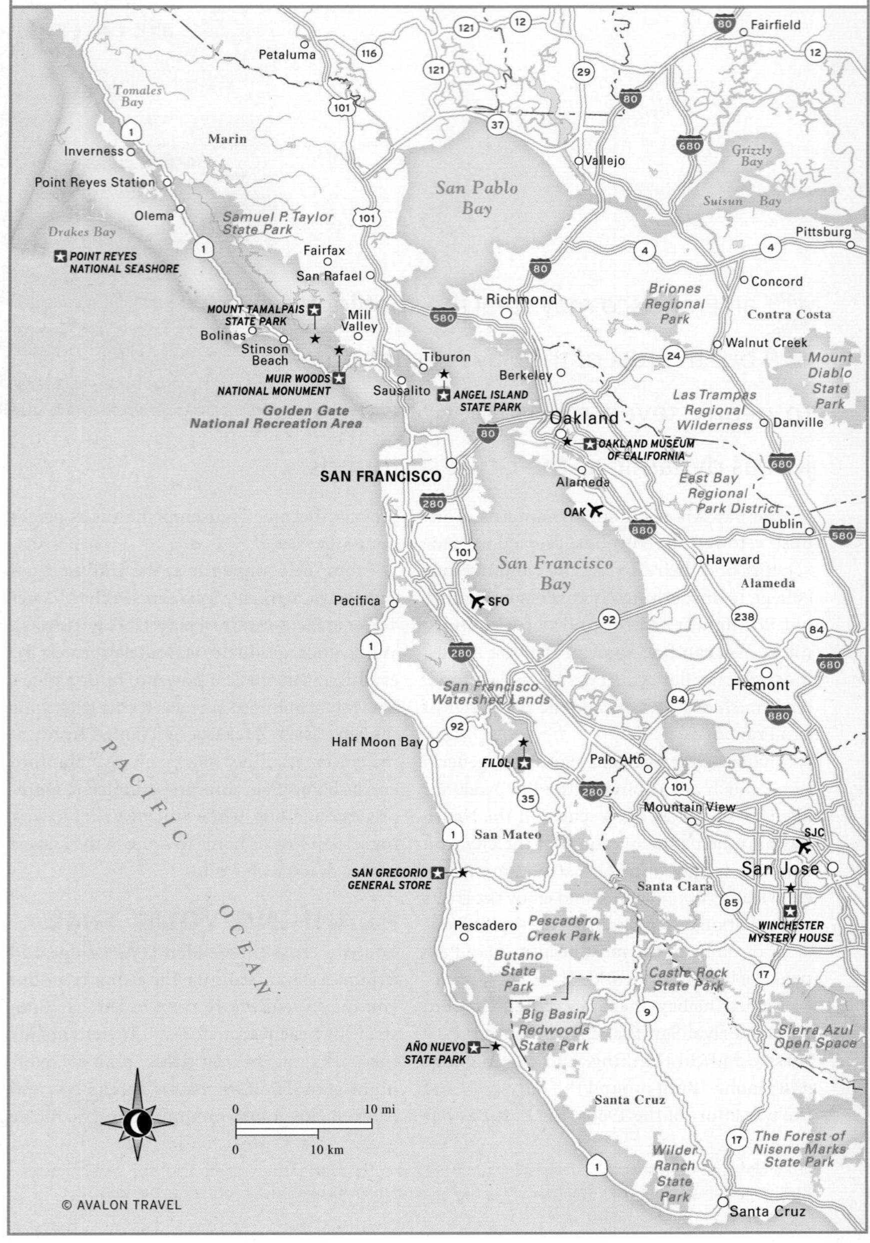

afternoon. Oakland and Berkeley offer easier access via the BART commuter rail system and have concentrated sights in their downtown areas. On the peninsula, Palo Alto is an easy drive from San Francisco. If all you have is an afternoon, take scenic Highway 1 to the beaches only 30 minutes from the city.

North Bay

Marin County, in the North Bay, is San Francisco's backyard. Beginning with the Marin Headlands at the terminus of the Golden Gate Bridge, there is a nearly unbroken expanse of wildlands from San Francisco Bay to Tomales Bay. Here you'll find rugged cliffs plunging into the Pacific, towering redwoods, the area's tallest mountain, and verdant pastures home to the Bay Area's celebrated grass-fed beef and award-winning, cheese-producing dairy cows.

MARIN HEADLANDS

The Marin Headlands lie north of San Francisco at the end of the Golden Gate Bridge. The land here encompasses a wide swath of virgin wilderness, former military structures, and a historical lighthouse.

Vista Point

At the north end of the Golden Gate Bridge, aptly named **Vista Point** offers views from the Marin Headlands toward San Francisco. If you dream of walking across the **Golden Gate Bridge** (gates 5am-9pm daily Apr.-Oct., 5am-6:30pm daily Nov.-Mar.), be sure to bring a warm coat as the wind and fog can really whip through. The bridge is 1.7 miles long, so a round-trip walk will turn into a 3.4-mile hike. Bikes are allowed daily 24 hours on the west side. Bicycle riders may also use the east side but must be careful to watch for pedestrians. Dogs are never allowed on either side.

To reach Vista Point, take U.S. 101 north across the Golden Gate Bridge. The first exit on the Marin County side is Vista Point; turn right into the parking lot. This small parking lot often fills early.

Fort Baker

Standing at Crissy Field in San Francisco, you may wonder about those charming white buildings across the bay. They are **Fort Baker** (435 Murray Circle, 415/331-1540, www.nps.gov/goga, sunrise-sunset daily), a 335-acre former Army Post established in 1905. With the transfer of many of the Bay Area's military outposts to parkland and civilian use, Fort Baker was handed over to the Golden Gate National Recreation Area. The location, just east of the Golden Gate Bridge, secluded in a shallow valley, makes it a great destination to enjoy city views and a wind-free beach. The fort is the best example of military architecture from the Endicott Period. It includes many elegant homes with large porches centered around the oval parade grounds. Fort Baker houses a hotel, Cavallo Point Lodge, and a nonprofit called the Institute at the Golden Gate. The Bay Area Discovery Museum is also nearby, along with the tiny Presidio Yacht Club, where all are welcome for a quick drink by the water.

Bay Area Discovery Museum

If you want to go somewhere kids will have fun, splurge on a trip to the **Bay Area Discovery Museum** (557 McReynolds Rd., Sausalito, 415/339-3900, www.baykids-museum.org, 9am-5pm Tues.-Sun., adults and children 1 and up $14, seniors and babies 6-12 months $13). The indoor-outdoor space is filled with the stuff that excites kids' imaginations. Most of the exhibits are directly related to the museum's location, encouraging kids to fish in the ports of San Francisco, build the Golden Gate Bridge, and travel with early explorers. There is also a train room, a

North Bay

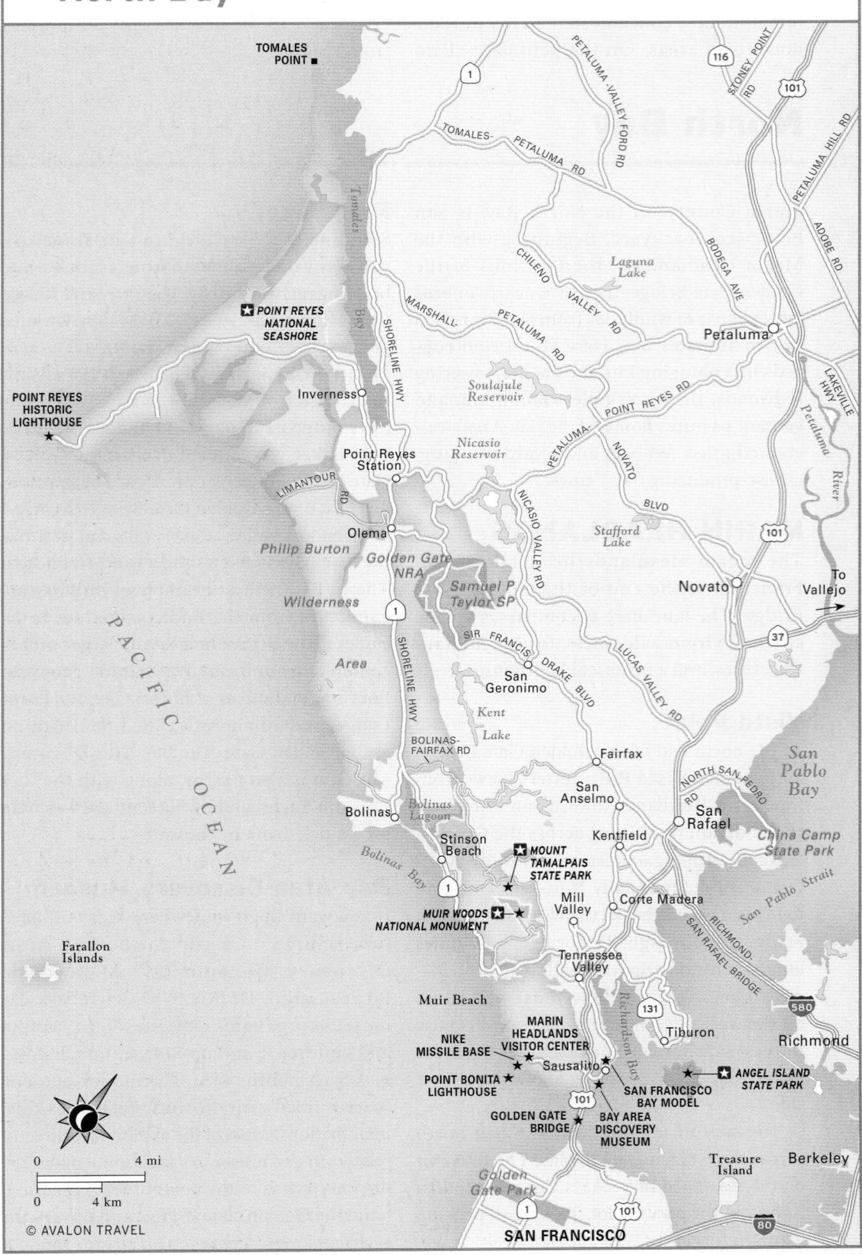
TOMALES POINT
POINT REYES NATIONAL SEASHORE
POINT REYES HISTORIC LIGHTHOUSE
Tomales Bay
SHORELINE HWY
Inverness
Point Reyes Station
LIMANTOUR RD
Olema
Philip Burton Wilderness Area
Golden Gate NRA
Samuel P Taylor SP
PACIFIC OCEAN
TOMALES-PETALUMA RD
PETALUMA-VALLEY FORD RD
STONEY POINT RD
PETALUMA HILL RD
ADOBE RD
BODEGA AVE
CHILENO VALLEY RD
MARSHALL-PETALUMA RD
Laguna Lake
Soulajule Reservoir
Nicasio Reservoir
PETALUMA-POINT REYES RD
NOVATO BLVD
NICASIO VALLEY RD
Stafford Lake
Petaluma
LAKEVILLE HWY
Petaluma River
Novato
To Vallejo
SIR FRANCIS DRAKE BLVD
LUCAS VALLEY RD
San Geronimo
Kent Lake
BOLINAS-FAIRFAX RD
Fairfax
San Anselmo
NORTH SAN PEDRO RD
San Rafael
San Pablo Bay
China Camp State Park
San Pablo Strait
Bolinas
Bolinas Lagoon
Stinson Beach
Bolinas Bay
MOUNT TAMALPAIS STATE PARK
Kentfield
Mill Valley
Corte Madera
MUIR WOODS NATIONAL MONUMENT
RICHMOND-SAN RAFAEL BRIDGE
Farallon Islands
Tennessee Valley
Muir Beach
MARIN HEADLANDS VISITOR CENTER
NIKE MISSILE BASE
POINT BONITA LIGHTHOUSE
Sausalito
Richardson Bay
Tiburon
Richmond
ANGEL ISLAND STATE PARK
SAN FRANCISCO BAY MODEL
GOLDEN GATE BRIDGE
BAY AREA DISCOVERY MUSEUM
Treasure Island
Berkeley
Golden Gate Park
SAN FRANCISCO
0 4 mi
0 4 km
© AVALON TRAVEL

tot room, an art studio, frequent story times, and a "construction site" where hard workers can don hard hats and dig to their heart's content.

Marin Headlands Visitors Center

A great place to start your exploration of the headlands is at the **Marin Headlands Visitors Center** (Field Rd. and Bunker Rd., 415/331-1540, www.nps.gov/goga, 9:30am-4:30pm daily), located in the old chapel at Fort Barry. The park rangers can give you the current lowdown on the best trails, beaches, and campgrounds in the Headlands. Grab a complimentary coffee and peruse the displays highlighting the park's human and natural history, as well as the small but well-stocked bookstore.

Point Bonita Lighthouse

The **Point Bonita Lighthouse** (415/331-1540, www.nps.gov/goga, 12:30pm-3:30pm Sat.-Mon.) has been protecting the Headlands for over 150 years. You need some dedication to visit Point Bonita, since it's only open a few days each week and there's no direct access by car. A 0.5-mile trail with steep sections leads from the trailhead on Field Road. Along the way, you'll pass through a hand-cut tunnel chiseled from the rock by the builders of the lighthouse, then over the bridge that leads to the building. Point Bonita was the third lighthouse built on the West Coast and is now the last staffed lighthouse in California. Today the squat hexagonal building shelters automatic lights, horns, and signals.

Marine Mammal Center

Inspired by the ocean's beauty and want to learn more about the animals that live in it? Visit the **Marine Mammal Center** (2000 Bunker Rd., 415/289-7325, www.marinemammalcenter.org, 10am-5pm daily, free) at Fort Cronkhite in the Marin Headlands. The center is a hospital for sick and injured seals and sea lions. Visitors are free to wander around and look at the educational displays to learn more about what the center does, but the one-hour docent-led tours (daily, times vary by season, adults $9, seniors and ages 5-17 $5, under age 5 free) explain the program in greater depth. Visitors will also get an education on the impact of human activity on marine mammals, and maybe a chance for close encounters with some of the center's patients.

Nike Missile Site

Military history buffs jump at the chance to tour a restored Cold War-era Nike missile base, known in military speak as SF-88. The **Nike Missile Site** (Field Rd. past the Headlands Visitors Center, 415/331-1453, www.nps.gov/goga, 12:30pm-3:30pm Thurs.-Sat.) is the only such restored Nike base in the United States. Volunteers continue the restoration and lead tours at 12:45pm, 1:45pm, and 2:30pm at the base, which is overseen by the Golden Gate National Recreation Area. On the tour, you'll get to see the fueling area, the testing and assembly building, and even take a ride on the missile elevator down into the pits that once stored missiles built to defend the United States from the Soviet Union. Because restoration work continues endlessly, the tour changes as new areas become available to visitors.

Hiking

Folks come from all over the world to hike the trails that thread through the Marin Headlands. The landscape is some of the most beautiful in the state, with unparalleled views of the Golden Gate Bridge and the Pacific Ocean.

From the Marin Headlands Visitors Center parking lot (Field Rd. and Bunker Rd.), the **Lagoon Trail** (1.75 miles, easy) encircles Rodeo Lagoon and gives bird-watchers an eagle's-eye view of the egrets, pelicans, and other seabirds that call the lagoon home. The trailhead is near the restrooms.

An easy spot to get to, **Rodeo Beach** draws many visitors on summer weekends—do not expect solitude on the beach or the trails, or even in the water. Locals come out

Marin Headlands

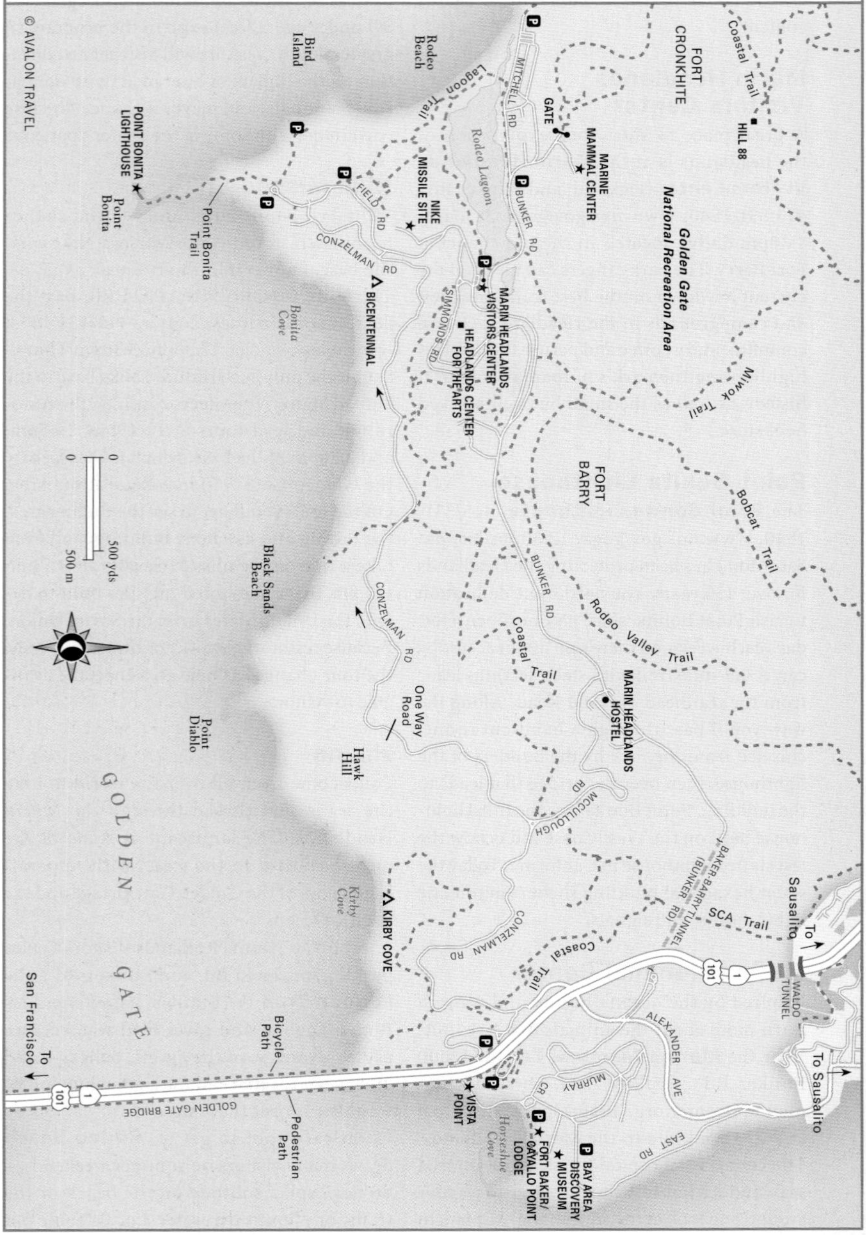

FORT CRONKHITE
Coastal Trail
HILL 88
Golden Gate National Recreation Area
Miwok Trail
FORT BARRY
Bobcat Trail
Rodeo Valley Trail
MARIN HEADLANDS HOSTEL
BAKER-BARRY TUNNEL (BUNKER RD)
SCA Trail
To Sausalito
WALDO TUNNEL
101
ALEXANDER AVE
EAST RD
To Sausalito
BAY AREA DISCOVERY MUSEUM
FORT BAKER/ CAVALLO POINT LODGE
Horseshoe Cove
MURRAY CR
VISTA POINT
GOLDEN GATE BRIDGE
Pedestrian Path
Bicycle Path
To San Francisco
GOLDEN GATE
KIRBY COVE
Kirby Cove
CONZELMAN RD
Coastal Trail
MCCULLOUGH RD
Hawk Hill
One Way Road
Point Diablo
Coastal Trail
BUNKER RD
CONZELMAN RD
Black Sands Beach
0 500 yds
0 500 m
BICENTENNIAL
Bonita Cove
HEADLANDS CENTER FOR THE ARTS
SIMMONDS RD
MARIN HEADLANDS VISITORS CENTER
BUNKER RD
CONZELMAN RD
NIKE MISSILE SITE
FIELD RD
Rodeo Lagoon
MARINE MAMMAL CENTER
GATE
MITCHELL RD
Lagoon Trail
Rodeo Beach
Bird Island
Point Bonita Trail
Point Bonita
POINT BONITA LIGHTHOUSE

to surf when the break is going while beachcombers watch from the shore. Note that the wind can really howl out here. The Lagoon Trail accesses the beach, but there is also a fairly large parking lot on Bunker Road that is much closer.

At Rodeo Beach is a trailhead for the **Coastal Trail.** To explore some of the battery ruins that pockmark these hills, follow the Coastal Trail (1.5 miles, easy) north to its intersection with Old Bunker Road Trail and return to Bunker Road near the Marine Mammal Center. Or extend this hike by continuing 2.3 miles up the Coastal Trail to the summit of **Hill 88** and stellar views. You can loop this trail by linking it with Wolf Ridge Trail to Miwok Trail for a moderate 3.8-mile round-trip hike.

To reach the trailheads and parking lots, follow Bunker Road west to either Rodeo Beach or the Marin Headlands Visitors Center and their adjoining parking lots.

Biking

If you prefer two wheels to two feet, you'll find the road and trail biking in the Marin Headlands both plentiful and spectacular. From the Tennessee Valley Trailhead, there are many multiuse trails designated for bikers as well as hikers. The **Valley Trail** (4 miles round-trip) takes you down the Tennessee Valley and all the way out to Tennessee Beach. A longer ride runs up the **Miwok Trail** (2 miles) northward, also accessed by Tennessee Valley Road. Turn southwest onto the **Coyote Ridge Trail** (0.7 mile); then catch the **Coastal Fire Road** (1.4 miles) the rest of the way west to Muir Beach. Another fun ride leads from just off U.S. 101 at the Rodeo Avenue exit. Park your car on the side of Rodeo Avenue, and then bike down the short **Rodeo Avenue Trail,** which ends in a T intersection after 0.7 mile at **Alta Trail.** Take a left, and access to **Bobcat Trail** is a few yards away. Continue on Bobcat Trail for 2.5 miles straight through the Headlands to the **Miwok Trail** for just 0.5 mile, and you'll find yourself out at Rodeo Beach.

Need to rent a bicycle for your travels? In San Francisco, **Bike and Roll** (899 Columbus Ave., 415/229-2000, www.bikeandroll.com/sanfrancisco, 8am-6pm daily) offers road ($58-110/day), mountain ($39-58/day), and hybrid ($32-39/day) bikes and loads of helpful advice.

Accommodations

Lodging options are fairly limited in the Marin Headlands. Many luxury-minded travelers choose to stay in Tiburon or Sausalito, while budget-motel seekers head for San Rafael.

Travelers who want budget accommodations indoors often choose the **Marin Headlands Hostel** (Bldg. 941, Fort Barry, 415/331-2777, www.norcalhostels.org/marin, dorm $28-35, private room $82-132). You'll find full kitchen facilities, Internet access, laundry rooms, and a rec room. Surprisingly cozy and romantic, the hostel is sheltered in the turn-of-the-20th-century buildings of Fort Barry, creating a unique atmosphere. With the headlands right outside your door, there is no lack of activities or exploration opportunities.

To stay in a national park with the luxury of a well-appointed hotel and spa, book a room at ★ **Cavallo Point Lodge** (601 Murray Circle, Fort Baker, Sausalito, 415/339-4700, www.cavallopoint.com, $500) at Fort Baker. Stay in beautiful historical homes that feature early 20th-century woodwork and wraparound porches, also boasting 21st-century amenities such as lush carpets, beds dressed in organic linens, flat-screen TVs, wireless Internet, gas fireplaces, and bathtubs so deep you can get lost. Cavallo Lodge also has eco-chic accommodations in its newer two-story buildings. You'll find floor-to-ceiling windows framing spectacular views, radiant floor heating, and private porches. The lodge has excellent environmental credentials and is dog friendly. The excellent Murray Circle Restaurant and Farley Bar are on-site.

Camping

Camping here requires some planning. You

must book a site in advance (up to 30 days for primitive sites, and six months for full-service sites). Bring warm camping gear, even during summer.

The most popular campground is **Kirby Cove** (877/444-6777, www.recreation.gov, Apr.-Oct., reservations required, $25). Secluded and shaded campsites provide a beautiful respite complete with bay views and a private beach. Make reservations well in advance for summer weekends since this popular campground fills up fast.

The **Bicentennial Campground** (Battery Wallace parking lot, 415/331-1540, reservations required, free) boasts three campsites easily accessible from the parking lot. Each site can accommodate a maximum of three people in one tent, and there's no water available or fires allowed on-site. A nearby picnic area has barbecue grills that campers can use to cook.

Food

Snag a blanket and a seat on the porch to watch the fog roll in over the Golden Gate Bridge at ★ **Farley Bar** (601 Murray Circle, Fort Baker, Sausalito, 415/339-4750, www.cavallopoint.com, 11am-11pm Sun.-Thurs., 11am-midnight Fri.-Sat., $20) at Cavallo Point Lodge. With cocktails, wine, and oysters, Farley is the perfect end to a day of hiking. After dinner, lounge in one of the lush leather chairs or sofas.

Upstairs from Farley, **Murray Circle Restaurant** (Cavallo Point Lodge, 601 Murray Circle, Fort Baker, Sausalito, 415/339-4750, www.cavallopoint.com, 7am-11am, 11:30am-2pm, 5:30pm-9pm Mon.-Thurs., 7am-11am, 11:30am-2pm, 5:30pm-10pm Fri., 7am-11am, 11:30am-2:30pm, 5:30pm-10pm Sat., 11:30am-2:30pm, 5:30pm-9pm Sun., $29-36) has a menu based on the best Marin produce, seafood, meat, and dairy, with touches from cuisines around the world, like Liberty duck with stinging nettle spaetzle and Alaskan salmon with hominy and poblano peppers.

Information and Services

Aside from the visitors centers and museums, there isn't much in the way of services in the headlands. Cell phone reception can be spotty.

Transportation

Fort Baker and the Marin Headlands are located just north of the Golden Gate Bridge on Highway 1 and U.S. 101.

Once over the bridge, the Alexander Avenue exit offers two options for exploring the headlands. Follow Alexander Avenue to Fort Baker and the Bay Area Discovery Museum, or turn left onto Bunker Road for the Marin Headlands Visitors Center and Nike Missile Site. If the Bonita Lighthouse is your first stop, follow Alexander Avenue right and travel under the highway to Conzelman Road, which leads up the hill along the edge of the Headlands. Keep in mind that many of the roads are very narrow and become one-way in places.

Traffic can be heavy on beautiful weekend days, particularly in the headlands, so plan to get here early. Another option is to take **Muni bus route 76** (415/701-2311, www.sfmta.com, 11am-7pm Sun., $2.25). Picking up throughout downtown and the north end of San Francisco, this Sunday-only Muni line crosses the Golden Gate and ventures as far as Rodeo Cove in the Headlands. It makes frequent trips, and you can even load bikes on the front.

SAUSALITO

The affluent town of Sausalito wraps around the north end of San Francisco Bay. A former commercial fishing town, Sausalito still has a few old cannery buildings and plenty of docks, most of which are now lined with pleasure boats. Bridgeway, the main drag, runs along the shore, and the concrete boardwalk is perfect for strolling and biking. Farther north is the heart of working Sausalito, where the lovely waterfront Dunphy Park is rarely crowded, and cool galleries, antique stores, and a few hip eateries fill the narrow streets.

San Francisco Bay Model

One of the odder attractions you'll find in the North Bay is the **San Francisco Bay Model** (2100 Bridgeway, 415/332-3871, www.spn.usace.army.mil, 9am-4pm Tues.-Fri., 10am-5pm Sat.-Sun. summer, 9am-4pm Tues.-Sat. winter, free). This scale hydraulic model demonstrates how the currents and tides of the bay and the Sacramento-San Joaquin River Delta affect the bay and estuary surrounding San Francisco.

Accommodations

The Gables Inn (62 Princess St., 415/289-1100, www.gablesinnsausalito.com, $199-495) opened in 1869 and is the oldest B&B in the area. Although this inn honors its long history, it has also kept up with the times, adding four rooms with panorama bay views and flat screen televisions, Internet access, and luxurious baths to all 13 rooms. Some also have fireplaces. Genial innkeepers serve a buffet breakfast each morning and host a wine and cheese soiree each evening.

With a checkered history dating back to 1915, the **Hotel Sausalito** (16 El Portal, 888/442-0700, www.hotelsausalito.com, $180-225) was a speakeasy, a bordello, and a home for the writers and artists of the Beat generation. Today this tiny boutique hotel, with its yellow walls and wrought iron beds, evokes the Mediterranean coast. Sink into your cozy room after a day spent walking or biking along the water and a scrumptious dinner out.

The **Casa Madrona Hotel and Spa** (801 Bridgeway, 800/288-0502, www.casamadrona.com, $280-390) is a sprawling collection of structures housing contemporary luxury hotel rooms and suites that satisfy even the pickiest celebrity guest. Poggio, the onsite restaurant, serves award-winning Italian food, and the full-service spa pampers guests with a full menu of body and salon treatments. If you're treating yourself to a room at Casa Madrona, be sure to ask for one with a view overlooking the bay or the harbor.

For a taste of the Marin good life, stay at Sausalito's **Inn Above Tide** (30 El Portal, 800/893-8433, www.innabovetide.com, $345-645). Billed as the only hotel in the Bay Area that's actually on the bay, the inn sits over the edge of the water looking out at the San Francisco skyline. Most rooms have private decks that show off sublime views. Guests love the smart upscale furnishings, the stand-alone fireplaces, and the rooms with oversized bathtubs set by windows.

The Sausalito boardwalk is perfect for a stroll or a bike ride.

Food

Sausalito's main drag is full of places to eat. Most are expensive, reflecting the quality of the view, not necessarily the food. Fortunately, there are some standouts. A sidewalk café across the street from the waterfront, **Copita Tequileria y Comida** (739 Bridgeway, 415/331-7400, www.copitarestaurant.com, 11:30am-10pm Mon.-Thurs., 11:30am-11pm Fri., 11am-11pm Sat., 11am-10pm Sun., $10-19) has earned a loyal following since opening its doors in 2012. It serves upscale Mexican food such as oyster tacos and slow-cooked carnitas alongside a variety of tangy ceviche. The bar pours 30 different tequilas and pitchers of sangria. The noise level and long wait on sunny summer or weekend days may beat out the restaurant's other charms.

Fish (350 Harbor Dr., 415/331-3474, www.331fish.com, 11:30am-4:30pm, 5:30pm-8:30pm daily, $10-25, cash only) can hook you up with some of the best sustainable seafood in the North Bay, in a charming, unpretentious café overlooking the water. No farmed salmon, overfished swordfish, or other more-harm-than-good seafood makes its way into the kitchen. Fresh wild fish prepared using a California-style mix of international cooking techniques results in amazing dishes you can't find anywhere else.

For a bite to go, continue down Bridgeway to **Cibo** (1201 Bridgeway, 415/331-2416, www.cibosausalito.com, 7am-5pm daily, $8-15), in the hip center of Sausalito. In crisp modern surroundings, this café serves a number of hot and cold panini, hearty salads with locally sourced ingredients, and a rich array of coffee drinks and boutique sodas. For a delicious no-nonsense breakfast, order the poached eggs on toast with avocado and heirloom tomatoes. Or simply order the divine oversized blackberry muffin dusted in sugar.

Information and Services

Used to store ice in the days before refrigeration, the Ice House is now home to the **Sausalito Visitors Center** (780 Bridgeway, 415/332-0505, www.sausalitohistoricalsociety.com, 11:30am-4pm Tues.-Sun.). Run by the Sausalito Historical Society, it also serves as a museum to the town's history. The Chamber of Commerce also has its own **Visitor Kiosk** (415/331-1093, www.sausalito.org, 10am-4pm daily) at the Ferry Terminal, where you can find helpful tips about activities around town.

Transportation

Sausalito is just over the Golden Gate Bridge from San Francisco and is easily accessible by bicycle on side roads or by car on U.S. 101. Once in town, navigating by car can be a challenge, as the narrow oceanfront main road gets very crowded on weekends. If you can, park and walk around town. Street parking is mostly metered.

If you have the time, a great way to get to Sausalito from San Francisco is by ferry. Two companies make the trip daily, which takes up to an hour. The scenery is beautiful, and it is a great chance to get out on the bay more cheaply than via tour boat. The **Blue and Gold Fleet** (415/705-8200, http://blueandgoldfleet.com, 11am-8:15pm Mon.-Fri., 9:45am-6pm Sat.-Sun., adults $11.50, children and seniors $6.75, under age 5 free) makes the trip from Pier 41. Largely serving commuters, the **Golden Gate Ferry** (415/455-2000, http://goldengate.org, 7:40am-7:20pm Mon.-Fri., 10:40am-6:50pm Sat.-Sun., adults $10.75, children and seniors $5.25, under age 5 free) leaves from the Ferry Building, closer to downtown San Francisco. The trip across the bay is cheaper and a bit faster than with Golden Gate.

TIBURON

Once the terminus of the North Pacific Railroad, Tiburon now has some of the most expensive waterfront real estate in the world. The small downtown area that backs onto the marina is popular with the young and affluent crowd as well as longtime yacht owners. Aside from the views, one of the greatest draws to Tiburon is its proximity to Angel Island, the largest island in the bay and one of the most unique state parks around.

★ Angel Island State Park

Angel Island (415/435-5390, www.parks.ca.gov, 8am-sunset daily, rates vary by ferry company) has a long history, beginning with regular visits (though no permanent settlements) by the Coastal Miwok people. During the Civil War the U.S. Army created a fort on the island in anticipation of Confederate attacks from the Pacific. The attacks never came, but the Army maintained a base here. Today many of the 19th-century military buildings remain and can be seen on the hour-long **tram tour** (415/435-3392, http://angelislandsf.com, daily Apr.-Sept., $10-15), on foot, or on a docent-led two-hour **Segway tour** (days and times vary, $68). Later, the Army built a Nike missile base on the island to protect San Francisco from possible Soviet attacks. The missile base is not open to the public but can be seen from roads and trails.

Angel Island's history also has a sobering side. From 1910 to 1940, it served as an immigration station for inbound ships and as a concentration camp for Chinese emigrants attempting to escape turmoil in their homeland. Europeans were waved through, but Chinese were herded into barracks as government officials scrutinized their papers. After months and sometimes years of waiting, many were sent back to China. Poetry lines the walls of the barracks, expressing the despair of the immigrants who had hoped for a better life. The **Immigration Station** (11am-3pm daily, adults $5, children 6-17 $3, under 6 free) is open to visitors and docent-led tours are also available (11am and 12:30pm daily, $7).

Angel Island is a destination for both casual and serious hikers. Multiuse trails of varying difficulty crisscross the island. Adventurous trekkers can scale Mount Livermore via either the **North Ridge Trail** or the **Sunset Trail.** Each runs about 4.5 miles round-trip for a moderate, reasonably steep hike. At the top, enjoy gorgeous bay views. For the best experience, make a loop, taking one trail up the mountain and the other back down. If you're up for a long paved-road hike, take the **Perimeter Road** (5 miles, moderate) all the way around the island.

Pick up a boxed lunch or take a table at the **Angel Island Café** (415/435-3392, www.angelisland.com, 11am-3pm Mon.-Fri., 11am-4pm Sat.-Sun., $9-14), which serves hot sandwiches, wraps, salad, soup, and ice cream. Open summer only, the nearby **Angel Island Cantina** (11:30am-4:30pm Fri.-Sun., $7-14) serves burgers, tacos, oysters, beer, wine, and pitchers of mimosas and sangria.

CAMPING

Camping is available at nine primitive campsites (800/444-7275 or www.reserveamerica.com, $30) that fill up quickly; successful campers reserve their campsites six months in advance. The campsites themselves are characterized as "environmental sites." Each is equipped with food lockers (a must), surprisingly nice outhouses, running water, and a barbecue. You must bring your own charcoal, as wood fires are strictly prohibited. Three of the sites, the **Ridge Sites**, sit on the southwest side of the island, known to be fairly windy. The other six sites, the **East Bay** and **Sunrise Sites**, face the East Bay. Wherever you end up, plan on walking up to 2.5 miles from the ferry to your campsite. Despite the dramatic urban views, camping here is a little like backpacking.

GETTING THERE

Angel Island State Park is located in the middle of San Francisco Bay. To get here, you must either boat in or take one of the ferries that serve the island. The harbor at Tiburon is the easiest place to access Angel Island. The private **Angel Island-Tiburon Ferry** (21 Main St., Tiburon, 415/435-2131, www.angelislandferry.com, adults $15, seniors $14, ages 6-12 $13, ages 3-5 $5, bicycles $1) can get you out to the island in about 10 minutes and runs several times a day. You can also take the **Blue and Gold Fleet** (415/705-8200, www.blueandgoldfleet.com, one-way $8.50) to Angel Island from San Francisco's Pier 41. Blue and Gold ferries leave once in the morning

(10am Mon.-Fri., 9:40am Sat.-Sun.) from San Francisco, and the last ferry back departs at 2:50pm Monday-Friday and 4:10pm Saturday-Sunday. Although the ferry out of Tiburon has more sailings during the day, the last ferry is still early (3pm-5pm daily), with very few sailings on weekdays during the winter.

Ferries have plenty of room for you to bring your own bicycle, or you can rent one at the **main visitors area** (415/435-3392, http://angelislandsf.com, Sat.-Sun. Mar.-Nov., daily Apr.-Oct., $13.50 per hour, $50 per day) near the ferry dock. Rentals must always be returned at 3pm. Grab a map from the gift shop. Not all trails are open to bikes, but those that are include the easy five-mile paved Perimeter Road around the island.

Accommodations

The lovely **Waters Edge Hotel** (25 Main St., 415/789-5999, www.marinhotels.com, $233-355) is a boutique lodging that lives up to its name, backing onto the marina and docks. You can stumble right out of your room onto the dock and over to the Angel Island ferry. Inside, you'll love the feather beds, cushy robes, a fireplace, and breakfast delivered to your room each morning.

Also wonderfully close to the water and attractions of downtown Tiburon, the **Lodge at Tiburon** (1651 Tiburon Blvd., 415/435-3133, www.thelodgeattiburon.com, $130-330) offers the comforts and conveniences of a larger hotel while providing the style and atmosphere of a boutique inn. For a special treat, book a table at the attached Tiburon Tavern, a favorite watering hole and gastro-pub for locals as well as guests.

Food

With only 40 tables (10 of which are located on the back patio, overlooking the marina), the small, husband-and-wife-owned **Luna Blu** (35 Main St., 415/789-5844, 11:30am-9:30pm Mon. and Wed.-Thurs., 11:30am-10:30pm Fri., 9:30am-10:30pm Sat., 9:30am-9:30pm Sun., $18-29) makes earthy Italian food. The menu changes daily and is heavy in seafood and pasta. For lunch there is a selection of sandwiches and egg dishes. Luna Blu is one of the few eateries in Northern California to offer a full English tea menu that includes tea sandwiches, fruit skewers, scones, and a unique selection of tea.

A Tiburon mainstay is **Sam's Anchor Café** (27 Main St., 415/435-4527, www.samscafe.com, 11am-9:30pm Mon.-Fri., 9:30am-9:30pm Sat.-Sun., $14-28). Sitting on the water with a large glassed-in deck, Sam's specializes in seafood and wine, perfect for lounging in the sun on beautiful afternoons. Locals and visitors catch some rays over oysters on the half shell, fish-and-chips, or a burger. At night, the place becomes a bit fancier, with white tablecloths and low lighting inside. You'll find more elegantly plated dishes, but seafood still reigns, as the does the good-time vibe.

Transportation

Tiburon is located on a peninsula about eight miles north of the Golden Gate Bridge. From San Francisco, take U.S. 101 north to the Tiburon Boulevard (CA 131) exit. Stay to the right and follow the road along the water for nearly six miles until you reach the small downtown area.

Like Sausalito, Tiburon is very walkable and is a great destination via ferry from San Francisco. The **Blue and Gold Fleet** (415/705-8200, http://blueandgoldfleet.com) runs daily trips (30-45 minutes, 10:10am-8pm Mon.-Fri., 9:45am-6:30pm Sat.-Sun., adults $11, children and seniors $6.75, under age 5 free) to Tiburon from San Francisco's Pier 41 and from the Ferry Building (6am-7:30pm).

MILL VALLEY

Although the population of Mill Valley is just shy of 14,000 people, the city covers a large swath of land, from the bayside marshlands to the slopes of Mount Tamalpais. Not surprisingly, it's a gateway to Marin's most breathtaking parkland. Continue past the turnoff to Highway 1 along Miller Avenue to reach the charming downtown, tucked in a redwood valley. The small square is filled with cute shops, galleries, and great food.

Tennessee Valley

After U.S. 101 enters Marin County, the Stinson Beach/Mill Valley exit leads through barely noticed and unincorporated Tamalpais Valley. One of the most popular—and crowded, especially on summer weekends—places to start hiking is the **Tennessee Valley Trailhead** (end of Tennessee Valley Rd.). A wealth of trails spring from this trailhead. A quick hike from the trailhead can take you out to the **Haypress Campground** (about 1 mile, moderate), which has picnic tables and pretty views. For a nice long hike, take the **Old Springs Trail** (1.3 miles) down to the **Miwok Trail.** Turn right and after 0.3 mile and take another right at **Wolf Ridge Trail** (0.7 mile) to the **Coastal Trail.** Taking a right, you'll intersect the **Tennessee Valley Trail** after 1.3 miles, which taking another right toward the east, takes you back to the trailhead (1.4 miles).

A nice 2.5-mile hike from the Tennessee Valley Trailhead leads to **Hawk Campground** (415/331-1540, reservations required, free) with three primitive sites. Your reward for the work of packing in all your gear and water is a near-solitary camping experience that lets you kick back and get to know the wilderness surrounding you. Amenities include chemical toilets but no water, and fires are not allowed.

To reach the Tennessee Valley Trailhead, take the Stinson Beach/Highway 1 exit off U.S. 101 and drive 0.6 mile, passing under the freeway and continuing straight. Turn left on Tennessee Valley Road and continue two miles to the trailhead.

Accommodations

Nestled amongst trees, the **Mill Valley Inn** (165 Throckmorton Ave., 415/389-6608, www.marinhotels.com, $246-340) is the only hotel in downtown Mill Valley. The inn offers 25 rooms, including private cottages. Rooms in the Creekhouse have a historical feel and overlook the creek, and all main building rooms have French doors that open onto private patios. Furnishings are classic yet contemporary, and some rooms have fireplaces. The list of services and amenities is extensive.

Food

Immediately after passing under U.S. 101, the **Buckeye Roadhouse** (15 Shoreline Hwy., 415/331-2600, www.buckeyeroadhouse.com, 11:30am-10:30pm Mon.-Thurs., 11:30am-11pm Fri.-Sat., 10:30am-10pm Sun., $20-34) hides off to the left. Dating from 1937, this classic building is the local go-to for steaks, barbecue, and classic cocktails, and it fills up every weekend. Valet parking is offered at the entrance, or park for free in the lot to the left (but you'll have to walk across the busy freeway entrance).

Venture downtown to find eateries with a decidedly hipster edge. The ★ **Mill Valley Beerworks** (173 Throckmorton Ave., 415/888-8218, http://millvalleybeerworks.com, 5:30pm-9:30pm Mon., 5:30pm-10:30pm Tues.-Fri., 11am-3pm, 5:30pm-10:30pm Sat., 11am-3pm, 5:30pm-9:30pm Sun., $17-26) tailors a local, seasonal menu to pair with their handcrafted beer. Eight beers are available, or try the flight of four ($12). The wine menu is small but exceptional, and everyone will enjoy what comes out of the kitchen, from the mushroom toast appetizer to the flat iron steak. Seating is at communal tables that still allow for an intimate dinner. There is a bar in the back overlooking the stainless steel fermentation tanks.

Molina (17 Madrona St., 415/383-4200, http://molinarestaurant.com, 5:30pm-10pm Sun.-Thurs., 5:30pm-11pm Fri.-Sat., $20-34) exudes Mill Valley's woodland charm. With only 42 seats in a Craftsman house, the restaurant uses a wood-fire oven to fill its earthenware plates with game hen, rabbit rillettes, and Manila clams cazuela. The wine list is small but perfectly paired to the menu, as is the restaurant's playlist: a stack of records next to a turntable, manned by the chef himself.

Funky, elegant, and wholly original, Molina is a standout.

Next door to Molina is the equally original and adored **Avatars Punjabi Burrito** (15 Madrona St., 415/381-8293, www.enjoyavatars.com, 11am-8pm daily, $7-10). Burritos are filled with garbanzo beans, basmati rice, herb salsa, fruit chutney, yogurt, and tamarind sauce. Additions include curried pumpkin, smoked eggplant, curried lamb, and blackened chicken. You can also opt for a more traditional rice plate. The small shop mostly caters to takeout orders, but there are a few tables with plastic chairs.

★ MUIR WOODS NATIONAL MONUMENT

Established in 1908 and named for naturalist and author John Muir, **Muir Woods National Monument** (1 Muir Woods Rd., 415/388-2596, www.nps.gov/muwo, 8am-sunset daily, adults $7, under 16 free) comprises acres of staggeringly beautiful redwood forest. More than six miles of trails wind through the redwoods and accompanying Mount Tamalpais area, crossing verdant creeks and the lush forest. These are some of the most stunning—and accessible—redwoods in the Bay Area.

If you're new to Muir Woods, the visitors center is a great place to begin your exploration. The **Muir Woods Visitors Center** (8am-sunset daily) abuts the main parking area and marks the entrance to Muir Woods. In addition to maps, information, and advice about hiking, you'll also find a few amenities. Inside the park, slightly past the visitors center, is the **Muir Woods Trading Company Gift Shop and Cafe** (415/388-7059, www.muirwoodstradingcompany.com, 9am-5:30pm daily, closing hours vary) where you can purchase souvenirs and sustenance made from high-quality local ingredients.

Hiking

Many lovely trails crisscross the gorgeous redwood forest. First-time visitors should follow the wheelchair- and stroller-accessible **Main Trail Loop** (1 mile, easy). Leading from the visitors center on an easy and flat walk through the beautiful redwoods, this trail has an interpretive brochure (pick one up at the visitors center) with numbers along the trail that describe the flora and fauna. Hikers can continue the loop on the **Hillside Trail** for an elevated view of the valley.

Muir Woods National Monument

One of the first side trails off the Main Trail, the **Ocean View Trail** (3.4 miles, moderate) soon appears to the left. Some advice: Either bring water, or pick up a bottle at the visitors center before starting up the trail. The trail climbs through the redwoods for 1.5 miles until its junction with **Lost Trail.** Turn right on Lost Trail and follow it downhill for 0.7 mile to **Fern Creek Trail.** Bear left onto the Fern Creek trail for a lush and verdant return to the Main Trail. Along the way you'll see the much-lauded Kent Tree, a 250-foot-tall Douglas fir.

Alternatively, you can continue on the Main Trail to where Fern Creek Trail starts and hike in the opposite direction up the **Camp Eastwood Trail.** At the campground, you can get a drink of water, use the restrooms, and even have a picnic in this developed area. To make it into a loop, take Lost Trail to Fern Creek Trail.

It's easier to avoid the crowds by following the Main Trail to its terminus with the **Bootjack Trail** (6.4 miles, moderate). The Bootjack Trail climbs uphill for 1.3 miles before its junction with the **TCC Trail.** Bear left for the TCC Trail and meander through the quiet Douglas firs. At 1.4 miles, the trail meets up with the **Stapleveldt Trail;** turn left again to follow this trail for 0.5 mile to **Ben Johnson Trail,** which continues downhill for 1 more mile to meet up with the Main Trail.

You may notice signs in this area for the **Dipsea Trail,** an out-and-back hike to Stinson Beach. This is a strenuous, unshaded 7.1-mile hike, and the only way back is the way you came—but uphill.

Getting There

Muir Woods is accessed via the long and winding Muir Woods Road. From U.S. 101, take the Stinson Beach/Highway 1 exit. On Highway 1, also named the Shoreline Highway, follow the road under the freeway and proceed until the road splits in a T junction at the light. Turn left, continuing on Shoreline Highway for 2.5 miles. At the intersection with Panoramic Highway, make a sharp right turn and continue climbing uphill. At the junction of Panoramic Highway and Muir Woods Road, turn left and follow the road 1.5 twisty miles down to the Muir Woods parking lots on the right.

If you're visiting on a holiday or a summer weekend, get to the Muir Woods parking areas early—they fill fast, and afternoon hopefuls often cannot find a spot. Lighted signs on U.S. 101 will alert you to parking conditions at the main parking lot. To avoid the traffic hassle, the **Muir Woods Shuttle** (415/455-2000, http://www.marintransit.org/routes/66.html, Sat.-Sun. summer, $5 round-trip, under 16 free) leaves from various points in southern Marin County, including the Sausalito ferry terminal.

MUIR BEACH

Few coves on the California coast can boast as much beauty as **Muir Beach** (just south of the town of Muir Beach, www.nps.gov/goga, sunrise-sunset daily). From the overlook above Highway 1 to the edge of the ocean beyond the dunes, Muir Beach is a haven for both wildlife and beachcombers. In the winter, beachgoers bundle up and walk the sands of the cove or along the many trails that lead from the beach. If you're lucky, you might find a Monterey pine tree filled with sleepy monarch butterflies. Spring brings rare sunshine to Muir Cove. As the air grows warmer in summer, the north end of the cove attracts another breed of beach life: nudists. The south side houses the brackish Redwood Creek lagoon and the windswept picnic grounds.

Muir Beach is directly off Highway 1. The most direct route is to take U.S. 101 to the Stinson Beach/Highway 1 exit and follow Highway 1 (also called Shoreline Highway) for 6.5 miles to Pacific Way (look for the Pelican Inn). Turn left onto Pacific Way and continue straight to the Muir Beach parking lot. If arriving from Muir Woods, simply continue on Muir Woods Road down to the junction with Highway 1 and turn right onto Pacific Way.

Accommodations and Food

The Pelican Inn (10 Pacific Way, Muir Beach, 415/383-6000, www.pelicaninn.com, $206-289) is one of the most beloved inns in Marin. Inside the Tudor structure, the historical ambience shines with big-beam construction, canopy beds, and lovely portrait prints. The seven mostly small rooms each come with private baths and full English-style breakfast, but no TVs or phones. The Pelican Inn is a perfect spot to unplug, disconnect, and truly get away from it all.

You can also get hearty food at the inn (11:30am-3pm, 5:30pm-9pm Mon.-Fri., 8am-11am, 11:30am-3pm, 5:30pm-9pm Sat.-Sun., $15-34). Dark wood and a long trestle table give the proper old English feeling to the dimly lit dining room. The cuisine brings home the flavors of old England, with dishes like beef Wellington, shepherd's pie, and fish-and-chips. Round off the meal with a pint of Guinness.

★ MOUNT TAMALPAIS STATE PARK

To see the whole Bay Area in a single day, go to **Mount Tamalpais State Park** (801 Panoramic Hwy., Mill Valley, 415/388-2070, www.parks.ca.gov, 7am-sunset daily, day-use parking $8). Known as Mount Tam, this park boasts stellar views of the San Francisco Bay Area—from Mount St. Helena in Napa down to San Francisco and across to the East Bay. The Pacific Ocean peeks from around the corner of the western peninsula, and on a clear day you can just make out the foothills of the Sierra Nevada Mountains to the east. This park is the Bay Area's backyard, with hiking, biking, and camping opportunities widely appreciated for both their beauty and easy access. Ample parking, interpretive walks, and friendly park rangers make a visit to Mount Tam a hit even for less outdoorsy travelers.

In addition to recreation, Mount Tam also provides the perfect setting for the arts. The **Mountain Theater** (E. Ridgecrest Blvd. at Pan Toll Rd.), also known as the Cushing Memorial Amphitheater, built in the 1930s, still hosts plays at its outdoor stone seating. Performances and dates vary; contact the Mountain Play Association (415/383-1100, www.mountainplay.org, May-June, $30-40) for information and tickets. Plan to arrive early, as both parking and seating fill completely well before the show starts. The Mountain Theater also serves as the meeting place for the **Mount Tam Astronomy Program** (415/289-6636, www.friendsofmt-tam.org). Held every Saturday from April to October near the new and first quarter moon, the group hosts a talk by an astronomer that lasts about 45 minutes, after which is a tour of the night sky and star viewing through telescopes. Bring flashlights.

The **East Peak Visitors Center** (end of East Ridgecrest Blvd., 11am-4pm Sat.-Sun.) is located at the top of Mount Tam, with a small museum and gift shop as well as a picnic area with tables and restrooms, and even a small refreshment stand. The on-site staff can assist with hiking tips or guided walks. The **Pantoll Ranger Station** (3801 Panoramic Hwy. at Pantoll Rd., 415/388-2070, 9am-5pm Fri.-Mon.), which anchors the western and

From the overlook on Mount Tamalpais, you can see much of the San Francisco Bay Area.

larger edge of the park, provides hikers with maps and camping information.

Enjoy the views without setting out on the trail at the **Bootjack Picnic Area** (Panoramic Hwy.), which has tables, grills, water, and restrooms. The small parking lot northeast of the Pantoll Ranger Station fills quickly and early in the day.

Hiking

Up on Mount Tam, you can try anything from a leisurely 30-minute interpretive stroll up to a strenuous hike up and down one of the many deep ravines. Mount Tam's hiking areas are divided into three major sections: the East Peak, the Pantoll area, and the Rock Springs area. Each of these regions offers a number of beautiful trails, so you'll want to grab a map from the visitors center or online to get a sense of the mountain and its hikes. For additional hikes, visit the Friends of Mount Tam website (www.friendsofmttam.org).

EAST PEAK

The charming, interpretive **Verna Dunshee Trail** (0.75 mile, easy) offers a short, mostly flat walk along a wheelchair-accessible trail. The views are fabulous, and you can get a leaflet at the visitors center that describes many of the things you'll see along the trail. Turn this into a loop hike by continuing on Verna Dunshee counterclockwise; once back at the visitors center, make the climb up to **Gardner Fire Lookout** for stellar views from the top of Mount Tam's East Peak (2,571 feet).

PANTOLL

The Pantoll Ranger Station is ground zero for some of the best and most challenging hikes in the park. The **Old Mine Trail** (0.5 miles, easy) is another accessible trail that leads to a lovely lookout bench and the Lone Tree Spring. Ambitious hikers can continue on the Dipsea Trail (1.4 miles, moderate), making it a loop by turning right on the **Steep Ravine Trail** (3.8 miles, moderate) as it ascends through lush Webb Creek and gorgeous redwoods back to the Pantoll parking lot.

The **Dipsea Trail** loop (7.3 miles round-trip, strenuous) is part of the famous Dipsea Race Course (second Sun. in June), a 7.4-mile course renowned for both its beauty and its challenging stairs. The trailhead that begins in Muir Woods, near the parking lot, leads through Mount Tam all the way to Stinson Beach. Hikers can pick up the Dipsea on the Old Mine Trail or at its intersection with the Steep Ravine Trail in Mount Tam, but a common loop is to take the **Matt Davis Trail** (across Panoramic Hwy. from the Pantoll parking area) west all the way to Stinson Beach and then return via the Dipsea Trail to Steep Ravine Trail. This is a long, challenging hike, especially on the way back, so bring water and endurance.

ROCK SPRINGS

Rock Springs is conveniently located near the Mountain Theater, and a variety of trails lead off from this historical venue. Cross Ridgecrest Boulevard and take the **Mountain Theater Fire Trail** to Mountain Theater. Along the top row of the stone seats, admire the vistas while looking for **Rock Springs Trail** (it's a bit hidden). Once you find it, follow Rock Springs Trail all the way to historical West Point Inn. The views here are stunning, and you'll see numerous cyclists flying downhill on Old Stage Road below. Cross this road to pick up Nora Trail, following it until it intersects with **Matt Davis Trail.** Turn right to reach the Bootjack day-use area. Follow the **Bootjack Trail** right (north) to return to the Mountain Theater for a 4.6-mile loop.

Here's your chance to see waterfalls via the lovely **Cataract Trail** (3 miles, easy-moderate). From the trailhead, follow Cataract Trail for a short bit before heading right on **Bernstein Trail.** Shortly, turn left onto **Simmons Trail** and continue to Barth's Retreat, site of a former camp that is now a small picnic area with restrooms. Turn left on **Mickey O'Brien Trail** (a map can be helpful here), returning to an intersection with the Cataract Trail. It's worth the short excursion to follow Cataract Trail to the right through the Laurel Dell picnic area and up to Cataract Falls. Enjoy a picnic at Laurel Dell before returning to Cataract Trail to follow it down to the Rock Springs trailhead.

Biking

To bike up to the peak of Mount Tam is a mark of local cyclists' strength and endurance. Rather than driving up to the East Peak or the Mountain Home Inn, sturdy cyclists pedal up the paved road to the East Peak. It's a long hard ride, but for an experienced cyclist the challenge and the views make it more than worthwhile. Just take care, since this road is open to cars, many of which may not realize that bikers frequent the area.

For mountain bikers, a hard but satisfying trip up the mountain begins at Phoenix Lake (Lagunitas Rd.,) in Ross. From here you take the **Eldridge Grade Fire Road** (15.8 miles, strenuous) all the way to East Peak. The scenery is as beautiful as the ride is challenging and technical. To make the trip into a loop, turn onto paved **Ridgecrest Boulevard** for a little over four miles. On the right is the **Rock Springs Lagunitas Fire Road.** Take it all the way back to the trailhead. To reach the peak when you are already up on the mountain, consider parking at the Pantoll Ranger Station and taking **Old Stage Grade**, then a sharp right on **Old Railroad Grade Fire Road** to East Peak (6 miles, moderate). Make the ride into a longer loop by jumping on **Eldridge Grade** at East Peak, taking it to **Wheeler Trail** (where you will have to walk your bike a short distance), and then turning right on **E-Koo Fire Road.** After a couple of miles it will intersect with **Old Railroad Grade** (stay right), which will then meet **Old Stage Grade.** Turn left and head down to the trailhead.

Accommodations and Food

When the **West Point Inn** (100 Old Railroad Grade Rd., Mill Valley, 415/388-9955, www.westpointinn.com, Tues.-Sat., $50) was built in 1904, guests would take the old train to its doorstep. Today it's a two-mile hike on a dirt road. The inn has no electricity; instead, it's lit by gaslights and warmed by fires in the large fireplaces in the downstairs lounge and parlor. There are seven rooms upstairs and five rustic cabins nearby. Guests must bring their own linens, flashlights, and food, which can be prepared in the communal kitchen. May-October, the inn hosts a monthly Sunday pancake breakfast (9am-1pm, adults $10, children $8) that draws local hikers. The wait can be long, but it's a lot of fun.

Boasting terrific views, **Mountain Home Inn** (810 Panoramic Hwy., 415/381-9000, www.mtnhomeinn.com, $195-345) was built during the heyday of the railroad. With 10 rooms, many with jetted tubs, wood-burning fireplaces, and private decks, the inn specializes in relaxation. You can opt for a massage, slip downstairs for a complimentary breakfast, or dine on a three-course prix fixe dinner ($38) in the cozy and warmly lit dining room.

The inn also opens its kitchen (11:30am-7pm Mon.-Fri., 8am-11am, 11:30am-7pm Sat.-Sun., prix fixe 5:30pm-8:30pm Wed.-Sun., $9-26) to the public, with an expansive menu that includes burgers, crab cakes, salads, ceviche, and ravioli. It's the perfect finish to a day on the mountain, especially when paired with a glass of wine on the patio. For something a little more fancy, opt for the three-course prix fixe dinner ($38).

Camping

With spectacular views of the Pacific Ocean, it's no wonder that the rustic accommodations at ★ **Steep Ravine** (800/444-7275, www.reserveamerica.com, cabins $100, campsites $25) stay fully booked. On the namesake ravine are six primitive campsites and nine cabins. The cabins are considered rustic, but each comes equipped with a small wood stove, a table, a sleeping platform, and a grill. The campsites are also spare but each has a table, a fire pit, and a food locker. Restrooms and drinking water are nearby. To reserve a cabin or campsite, you need to be on the phone at 8am six months before the date you intend to go.

If Steep Ravine is full or you want to camp within hiking distance of the top of the mountain, the **Pantoll Campground** (1393 Panoramic Hwy., 415/388-2070, www.parks.ca.gov, $25) has 16 sites with drinking water, firewood, and restrooms. Camping here is first-come, first-served, paid for at the ranger station, so get here early. The sites are removed from the parking lot, which means that you'll need to haul in all your gear; it also makes for a peaceful campground.

Information and Services

For more information, contact the volunteer-run **Friends of Mount Tam** (415/258-2410, www.friendsofmttam.org). The ongoing California state budget crisis has left the East Peak Visitor Center and ranger station with limited hours, but the state park did set up free Wi-Fi. If you arrive at the park and need information, you can access the Internet just 150-200 feet from the ranger station.

Transportation

Panoramic Highway is a long and winding two-lane road across the Mount Tamalpais area and extending all the way to Stinson Beach. Once upon a time, well-heeled visitors could take a scenic train ride up to and across Mount Tam. Today, visitors drive up to one of the parking lots and explore the trails from there. Take Highway 1 to the Stinson Beach exit, and then follow the fairly good signs up the mountain. Turn right at Panoramic Highway at the top of the hill. Follow the road for five winding miles until you reach the Pantoll Ranger Station. To get to the East Peak Visitors Center, take a right on Pantoll Road, and another right on East Ridgecrest Boulevard. To access the park from Stinson Beach, take a right on Panorama Highway at the T intersection with Highway 1 just south of town.

Bus access to the park is available via route 61 of the **West Marin Stagecoach** (415/526-3239, www.marintransit.org, daily, $2), providing public transit from Stinson Beach or Mill Valley to Mount Tam, dropping and picking visitors up at the Pantoll Ranger Station.

STINSON BEACH

The primary attraction at Stinson Beach is the tiny town's namesake: a broad 3.5-mile sandy stretch of coastline that's unusually congenial to visitors. Stinson Beach is the favorite destination for San Franciscans seeking some surf and sunshine.

To get out on the water, swing by **Stinson Beach Surf and Kayak** (3605 Hwy. 1, 415/868-2739, www.stinsonbeachsurfandkayak.com, weekdays by appointment, 9:30am-6pm Sat.-Sun., $20-40 per day). The owner, Bill, will set you up with a surfboard, kayak, boogie board, or stand-up paddleboard, plus a wetsuit, which you will certainly need. He also offers surf lessons and gives pointers on wildlife etiquette. During the week, Bill is "on call." You can call his cell phone (415/497-8260) and he'll be happy to help you out.

Accommodations

The **Sandpiper Inn** (1 Marine Way, 415/868-1632, www.sandpiperstinsonbeach.com, $130-245) has six rooms and four cabins. Two of the rooms have kitchenettes and all have gas fireplaces and comfortable queen beds. The individual redwood cabins offer additional privacy, bed space for families, and full kitchens.

Another nice spot is the **Stinson Beach Motel** (3416 Shoreline Hwy. 1, 415/868-1712, www.stinsonbeachmotel.com, $130-150). It features eight vintage-y beach bungalow-style rooms that sleep 2-4 guests each. Some of the blue-themed rooms have substantial kitchenettes; all have private baths, garden views, and TVs. The motel is a great spot to bring the family for a beach vacation.

Food

A few small restaurants dot the town, most of which serve seafood. Among the best is the **Sand Dollar Restaurant** (3458 Hwy. 1, 415/868-0434, www.stinsonbeachrestaurant.

com, 11am-9pm daily summer, 3pm-9pm Mon.-Fri., 11am-9pm Sat.-Sun. winter, $13-25). This so-called fish joint actually serves more land-based dishes than seafood, but the fact that the dining room is constructed out of three old barges makes up the difference. The Sand Dollar also serves a popular Sunday brunch.

A favorite in town is the **Parkside Café** (43 Arenal Ave., 415/868-1272, www.parksidecafe.com, 7:30am-9pm daily, $12-28). With the vibe of seaside hamburger joint, it is the perfect place to stop with your feet still sandy from the beach. Order the local rock cod tacos, the burger on a brioche bun, or a half dozen oysters on the half shell. Finish up with a root beer float made with local organic vanilla ice cream.

Getting There

Stinson Beach is an unbelievably beautiful destination. Take the Stinson Beach exit off U.S. 101 and follow Shoreline Highway (Hwy. 1) until it descends into Stinson Beach. Most of the town is strung along the highway, and signs make it easy to navigate to the beach.

Traffic can be a huge problem on weekend days. With only one lane in each direction and a couple of intersections with stop signs, traffic backups that stretch for miles are common. Your best bet is to drive in on a weekday or in the evening when everyone else is leaving.

An alternative to driving is **West Marin Stagecoach** (415/526-3239, www.marintransit.org, daily, $2), route 61, a daily bus that runs from Mill Valley into Stinson Beach.

★ POINT REYES NATIONAL SEASHORE

The Point Reyes area boasts acres of unspoiled grassland, forest, and beach. Cool weather presides even in the summer, but the result is lustrous green foliage and spectacular scenery. **Point Reyes National Seashore** (1 Bear Valley Rd., 415/464-5100, www.nps.gov/pore, dawn-midnight daily) stretches for miles between Tomales Bay and the Pacific, north from Stinson Beach to the tip of the land at the end of the bay. Dedicated hikers can trek from the bay to the ocean, or from the beach to land's end. The protected lands shelter a range of wildlife. In the marshes and lagoons, a wide variety of birds—including three different species of pelicans—make their nests. The pine forests shade shy deer and larger elk. A few ranches and dairy farms operate inside the park. Grandfathered in at the time the park was created, these sustainable, generations-old family farms give added character and historical depth to Point Reyes.

The Point Reyes area includes the tiny towns of Olema, Point Reyes Station, and Inverness.

Visitors Centers

The **Bear Valley Visitors Center** (1 Bear Valley Rd., 415/464-5100, 10am-5pm Mon.-Fri., 9am-5pm Sat.-Sun. May-Nov., 10am-4:30pm Mon.-Fri., 9am-4:30pm Sat.-Sun. Nov.-May) acts as the central visitors center for Point Reyes National Seashore. In addition to maps, fliers, and interpretive exhibits, the center houses a short video introducing the region. You can also talk to park rangers, either to ask advice or to obtain beach fire permits and backcountry camping permits.

The **Ken Patrick Visitors Center** (Drakes Beach, 415/669-1250, 9am-5pm daily summer, 9:30am-4:30pm Sat.-Sun. fall-spring) sits right on the beach in a building made of weathered redwood. Its small museum focuses on the maritime history of the region. It's also the location for the annual Sand Sculpture event.

Point Reyes Historic Lighthouse

The rocky shores of Point Reyes make for great sightseeing but incredibly dangerous maritime navigation. In 1870 the first lighthouse was constructed on the headlands. Its first-order Fresnel lens threw light far enough for ships to avoid the treacherous granite cliffs. Yet the danger remained, and soon after, a lifesaving station was constructed alongside the light station. It wasn't until the

Point Reyes National Seashore

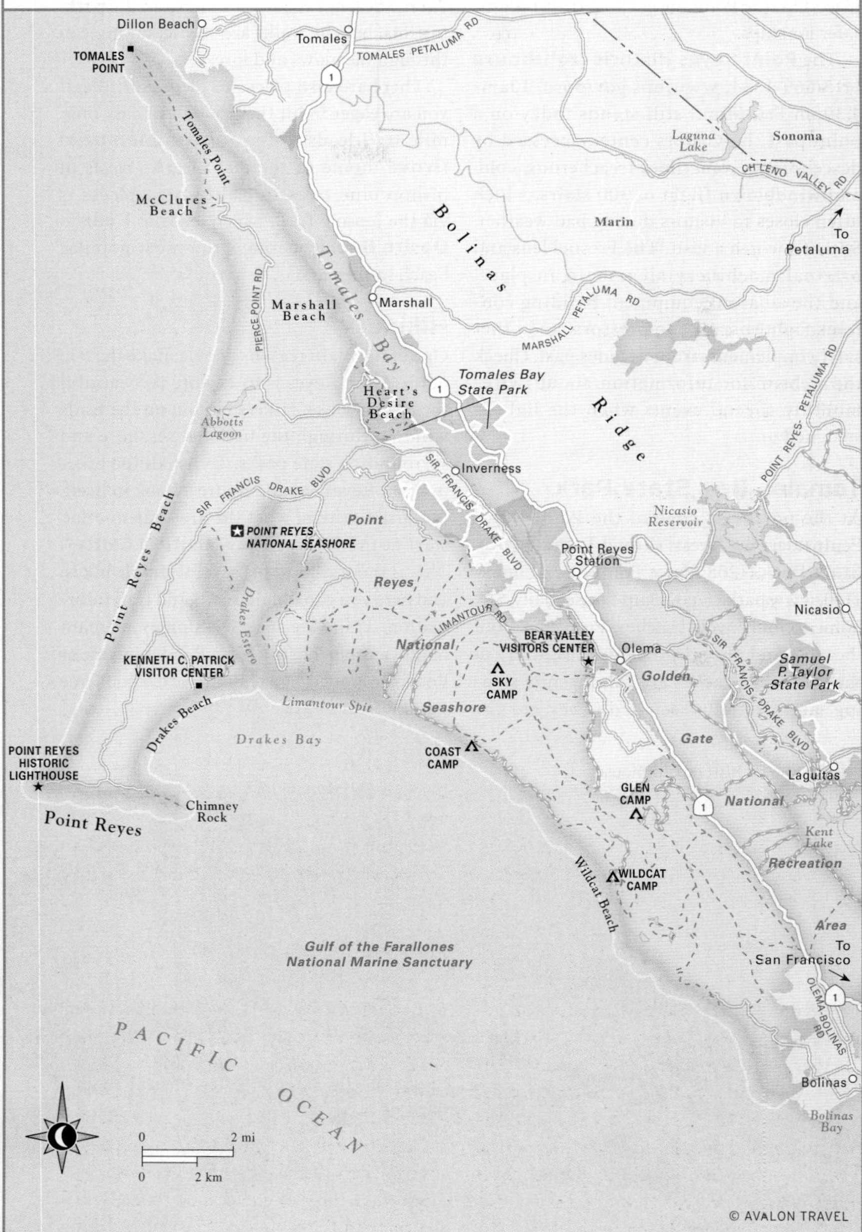

20th century, when a ship-to-shore radio station and newer lifesaving station were put in place, that the Point Reyes shore truly became safer for ships.

The **Point Reyes Historic Lighthouse** (415/669-1534, www.nps.gov/pore, 10am-4:30pm Fri.-Mon.) still stands today on a point past the visitors center, accessed by descending a sometimes treacherous, cold, and windblown flight of 300 stairs, which often closes to visitors during bad weather. Still, it's worth a visit. The Fresnel lens and original machinery all remain in place, and the adjacent equipment building contains foghorns, air compressors, and other safety implements from decades past. Check the website for information about twice-monthly special events when the light is switched on.

Tomales Bay State Park

At the northeast edge of the Point Reyes Peninsula, pine forests shroud **Tomales Bay State Park** (1208 Pierce Point Rd., 415/669-1140, www.park.ca.gov, 8am-sunset daily, $8), home to four lovely beaches. Protected from the wind and waves by the Inverness Ridge to the west, the beaches are calm, gently sloping, and partially secluded. They are the perfect place to read and sunbathe while the kids splash around in the gently lapping surf. All the beaches require a walk from the parking lots, but the walks are scenic, taking you through meadows and forest.

There are also places to picnic or hike, if you are eager to hit the woods. An easy one-mile trail leads to the **Jepson Memorial Grove**, home to the last virgin groves of bishop pine trees in California. Access is via the Jepson Trail, which leads to **Heart's Desire Beach**, perhaps the most popular beach in the park.

Hiking

One of the main reasons people make the trip out to Point Reyes is to explore its beautiful scenery up close. Hikers fan out on the trails winding through the national seashore and surrounding state parks. To list all the hikes in Point Reyes would require a book in itself. For just a taste of what the area has to offer, start at the **Bear Valley Visitors Center.** This is the trailhead for several simple hikes, and here you can obtain maps and trail information. Trails are accessed along four main roads (south to north): Mesa Road, Limantour Road, Sir Francis Drake Boulevard, and Pierce Point Road.

the Point Reyes Historic Lighthouse

MESA ROAD

At the very south end of Point Reyes, Olema-Bolinas Road leads to the Palomarin Trailhead. At the end of Mesa Road, the trailhead provides access to the **Coastal Trail**, which offers both day hikes and overnight backpacking trips to **Wildcat Camp** (5.5 miles one way, permit required). Day hikers can follow the trail out past Bass Lake, Pelican Lake, and Crystal Lake. To make the trip a loop, take a right on Old Out Road, another right on Alemea Trail, one on Ridge Trail, and on Lake Ranch Trail, which connects to Coast Trail only 2.2 miles from the trailhead. This is a good 11.7-mile trek with many ups and downs.

BEAR VALLEY VISITORS CENTER

From the visitors center, the **Bear Valley Trail** runs south all the way to the ocean and the dramatic perch above **Kelham Beach** (8.2 miles round-trip, moderate). For a shorter hike, follow Bear Valley Trail to **Divide Meadow** (3.2 miles round-trip, moderate) and then return to the visitors center.

Bear Valley Trail also provides access to **Mount Wittenberg** (2 miles, strenuous), though there is an easier trailhead off Limantour Road. This is the highest point in the park (1,407 feet), and you'll feel it on the climb up. From Bear Valley Trail, turn right at the intersection with Mount Wittenberg Trail and follow it to the top. Hikers can return via either the **Meadow Trail** (turn left on Sky Trail, then left again on Meadow Trail) or take **Z Ranch Trail** (left) to return via **Horse Trail** for a 5- or 6.1-mile loop.

LIMANTOUR ROAD

Limantour Road is north of the Bear Valley Visitors Center: Take Bear Valley Road north and turn west on Limantour Road. One of the first trailheads along this road is for the **Sky Trail** (moderate). The Sky Trail provides easier access to Mount Wittenberg with the bonus of passing by Sky Camp, one of the area's most popular hike-in campgrounds. Make it a 3.1-mile loop by taking Z Ranch Trail after Mount Wittenberg. Turn left on Horse Trail and after a short jog, you'll wind up back on Sky Trail heading to the trailhead.

Limantour Road eventually passes Point Reyes Hostel, where you'll find the trailhead for the **Coast-Laguna Loop** (5 miles, easy to moderate). Follow Coast Trail down to Drakes Bay, where it hugs the shoreline until reaching **Coast Camp**, another backpacking campsite. From Coast Camp, take **Fire Lane Trail** north to **Laguna Trail** and return to Limantour Road. You may have to walk along Limantour toward the Hostel to reach your car. Birders will want to make a beeline for the **Limantour Spit Trail** (2 miles, easy). From the parking lot at Limantour Beach, it's a quick hike to the beach; look for a spur trail headed west.

SIR FRANCIS DRAKE BOULEVARD

The Estero Trailhead is located off Sir France Drake Boulevard, shortly after the junction with Pierce Point Road. **Estero Trail** offers several options for hikers. For a short 2-mile hike, follow the trail to Home Bay and turn around there. You can extend the hike to **Sunset Beach** (7.8 miles round-trip, moderate), which overlooks Drakes Estero; or continue farther to **Drakes Head** (9.4 miles round-trip), via Estero Trail and **Drakes Head Trail,** with views overlooking Estero de Limantour and Drakes Bay.

Sir Francis Drake Boulevard continues rolling through pastures south and west until it ends at the Point Reyes Lighthouse. From the parking area on Chimney Rock Road, just south of the Point Reyes Lighthouse, follow the **Chimney Rock Trail** (1.6 miles, easy) through grassy cliffs to a wooden bench at the tip of the peninsula. The views of the Pacific and the Point Reyes coast are stunning even though the wind tends to whip mercilessly here. Return the way you came, but take the short spur trail left to the headlands overlook, where you may see and hear seals on the beach far below.

PIERCE POINT ROAD

Splitting off from Sir Francis Drake Boulevard at Tomales Bay State Park, Pierce Point Road extends to the northern end of the peninsula, where windswept sandy beaches, lagoons, and tule elk await. The trek to **Abbots Lagoon** (2 miles round-trip) is an easy hike that will be a hit with bird lovers. From there, Pierce Point Road continues north to another hiking option at **Kehoe Beach** (1 mile, easy), where a gravel trail descends to the beach. (Note that this is the only trail in Point Reyes where leashed dogs are permitted.)

Pierce Point Road runs almost to the tip of Tomales Point. From the trailhead at Pierce Point Ranch, there are two hiking options. For a short and easy hike to the beach, follow **McClures Beach Trail** (1 mile, easy) to explore tide pools bordered by granite cliffs. A bit longer, **Tomales Point Trail** is a wide smooth path through the middle of the Tule Elk Reserve to a viewpoint at Bird Rock. From Bird Rock, the "trail" to Tomales Point (9.5 miles round-trip, moderate) becomes trickier and less defined, but it is worth it for the views north to Bodega Bay.

Biking

Cyclists, sometimes in big packs, ply the area's many small roads. For a stout mountain-bike ride, take the **Bolinas Ridge Trail** (11 miles one-way, moderate), open to both bikers and hikers and offering stunning views down toward the Olema Valley. You'll find access to the trail off Sir Francis Drake Boulevard, east of Olema on the south side of the road. Bolinas-Fairfax Road, which intersects Highway 1 at the tip of Bolinas Lagoon, provides access from the south. The **Olema Valley Trail** (5.3 miles one-way, moderate) runs north-south and departs from the Five Brooks Trailhead off Highway 1, as does the **Stewart Trail** (6.1 one-way, strenuous), a more technical ride down to Wildcat Camp at the beach.

For road biking, most paved roads in Point Reyes are open to both bicycles and cars. Ask at one of the local bike shops for information about this year's hot biking spots and any trail closures.

You can find bike rentals in the heart of Point Reyes Station at **Point Reyes Outdoors** (11401 Hwy. 1, Point Reyes Station, 415/663-8192, www.pointreyesoutdoors.com, 9am-5pm daily, half day $35, full day $42). The small shop only offers mountain bikes, but they also rent child trailers and car racks if you don't want to start cycling right in the town. In addition to rentals, the staff will also point you to the best roads and trails for your skill level and mood.

Kayaking

The calm water of Tomales Bay practically calls out to be explored by kayak. **Blue Waters** (12944 Sir Francis Drake Blvd., Inverness and 19225 Shoreline Hwy., Marshall, 415/669-2600, www.bwkayak.com) offers both kayak tours ($68-98) and rentals (full day $70-110) with two launch sites, one in Inverness and one in Marshall, on the east side of the bay. In addition to paddles around the bay, tours include exploring Drake's Estero in Point Reyes, and some tours incorporate hikes into the afternoon. If you want to go it alone, Blue Waters rents stand-up paddleboards and single and double kayaks. Rates include all the gear you need plus a paddle lesson to make sure everyone is safe on the water.

In addition to renting out bikes, **Point Reyes Outdoors** (415/663-8192, www.pointreyesoutdoors.com) also provides the widest variety of kayak tours ($75-110) in the area. You can choose a day out in the wetlands of the southern part of the bay, where excellent birding awaits; a night paddling in water with bioluminescent creatures along Point Reyes Seashore; or a tour around Hog Island among the harbor seals and shorebirds. Tours last 3-6 hours and include a picnic of gourmet goodies from local businesses.

Horseback Riding

To tour the area on horseback, **Five Brook Ranch** (8001 Hwy. 1, 415/663-1570, www.fivebrooks.com, $40-180 per hour) can get you saddled up to ride through Point Reyes's forests and grasslands, up ridges and down to beaches on tours that last 1-6 hours. The most popular tour is up to an ospreys' nest along Inverness Ridge, then dropping down for a peaceful amble along Olema Creek. If you're up for an all-day adventure, opt for the Wildcat Beach Ride, which includes a picnic at the remote white-sand beach.

Accommodations

OLEMA

The **Point Reyes Seashore Lodge** (10021 Hwy. 1, 415/663-9000 or 800/404-5634, www.pointreyesseashorelodge.com, $155-245) offers both budget and luxury lodging in its 22 rooms. All rooms have private baths, some with whirlpool tubs and fireplaces. Larger suites offer kitchens and private patios. There are two cottages, which sleep four people, with outdoor hot tubs that are a relative bargain ($305). Enjoy the attractive gardens with winding brick pathways that roll out to Olema Creek. The Farm House Restaurant, Bar, and Deli adjoin the hotel, providing plenty of food and drink options.

To stay in one of the historical farmhouses dotting West Marin, book a room at the **Bear Valley Inn** (Hwy. 1 and Bear Valley Rd., 415/663-1777, www.bearvinn.com, $125-175). Built in 1910, this white Victorian farmhouse inn exudes charm. The three rooms upstairs are tiny, but each has its own bathroom and unique country furnishings. Larger groups can rent the Hummingbird Cottage ($180-250), which has a queen bed, a bunk bed, pull-out couches, and a full kitchen. Breakfast is continental and complimentary.

POINT REYES STATION

In Point Reyes Station, you can find a room and tasty board for a reasonable price at **One Mesa Bed & Breakfast** (1 Mesa Rd., 415/663-8866, www.onemesa.com, $147-189). All three rooms have private entrances, private baths, coffee makers, mini fridges, and microwaves. Most have fireplaces, and some have soaking tubs. Guests can make use of the inn's hot tub and enjoy a self-service breakfast on weekdays and a basket of goodies delivered to your door on weekends.

In the heart of Point Reyes Station is the **Point Reyes Station Inn** (11591 Hwy. 1, 415/663-9372, www.pointreyesstationinn.com, $125-225). The five-room inn drips with turn-of-the-20th-century charm with vaulted ceilings, large windows, and glass doors leading to private porches. All but one have fireplaces and private en suite baths. A communal hot tub is in the garden, and the continental breakfast features eggs from the inn's own chickens.

Lingonberry Farm B&B (12430 Hwy. 1, 415/663-1826, www.lingonberryfarm.com, $150) is outfitted in bright, simple Swedish style, and all rooms have private baths. Downstairs in the sunny dining area, guests are treated to a Swedish-style continental breakfast during the week and a full hot breakfast on weekends.

Choose **Point Reyes Hostel** (1390 Limantour Spit Rd., 415/663-8811, www.norcalhostels.org/reyes, $26-130) for what's outside the front door. Located just a few miles from the beach, the hostel is steps from fantastic hiking and lush natural scenery. The accommodations are spare but comfortable. Pick from the affordable dorm rooms ($26) or a private room ($87-130). The hostel has a communal kitchen, three lounge areas with furniture funky enough for any college-age apartment, and a place to lock up bicycles.

INVERNESS

Perhaps the most famous lodging around is ★ **Manka's Inverness Lodge** (30 Callendar Way, 415/669-1034, www.mankas.com, $215-615). Manka's is not so much a lodge as a compound dressed in an ethereal combination of hunting lodge and arts and crafts styles. Stay in the lodge or annex, where rooms are decked out with deep reading chairs, plush beds with tree-limb posts, and antique fixtures. Additional cabins are scattered, some overlooking the Inverness Ridge, others perched on the edge of Tomales Bay. All feature large sitting rooms with stone fireplaces. Some have private hot tubs or luxurious outdoor showers.

Located in the center of Inverness, **Ten Inverness Way** (10 Inverness Way, 415/669-1648, www.teninvernessway.com, $160-185) is a 1904 Craftsman building, and each of the five rooms is dressed in antiques and colorful quilts that border on country kitsch. All have a queen feather bed and a private bath and loads of cozy charm. In the morning, enjoy coffee, a newspaper, and a full breakfast. Evenings see complimentary wine and refreshments with the other guests.

Motel Inverness (12718 Sir Francis Drake Blvd., 415/236-1967, www.motelinverness.com, $99-195) sits handsomely on the bay. Constructed of natural wood with fanciful flourishes, Motel Inverness is more like a classic lodge than a typical motel. The parking lot abuts the entrance to each room, but the rooms open onto the serene wetlands bordering the bay. More spacious suites have full kitchens to accommodate families. Inside the main lodge is a grand lounge with an antique pool table and a great stone fireplace. Relax with a glass of wine on the expansive deck.

Camping

Although you would expect the Point Reyes area to abound in camping opportunities, finding a place to pitch a tent is a tall order. The only camping nearby is in the **Point Reyes National Seashore** (www.nps.gov/pore, 415/663-8522, reservations 877/444-6777 or www.recreation.gov, $20), and all are hike-in sites that require reservations months in advance. All campsites have a pit toilet, a water faucet, a picnic table, a charcoal grill, and a food locker.

Sky Camp is the closest to the Bear Valley Visitors Center and is accessed via a trail on Limantour Road. The hike is a moderate 1.4 miles uphill, and the campground includes 11 individual sites and a single group site. From its location, you'll get great views of the Pacific Ocean and Drake's Bay, provided it's not foggy.

Near the end of Limantour Road before the beach is the trailhead for the aptly named **Coast Camp.** Though not directly on the beach, the campground is in a quiet valley of coastal scrub and willow trees. There are 12 individual campsites and 2 group sites. There are two routes to get here: one that is 1.8 miles uphill along the Laguna and Firelane Trails, and the longer 2.7-mile Coast Trail route, which is flat and considerably easier for carrying camping gear.

The other coastal campground is **Wildcat Camp.** It has five individual sites and three group sites. Like Coast Camp, it is set away from the beach on an open bluff-top meadow. From Bear Valley it is a 6.3-mile hike, and from Palomarin it is a 5.5 mile hike along the Coastal Trail.

The most secluded campground is **Glen Camp.** Hidden deep within a valley and protected from ocean winds, the campground is a healthy 4.6 miles from the Bear Valley Trailhead. There are 12 individual sites and no group sites, keeping this a quiet getaway.

Food

OLEMA

Attached to the Point Reyes Seashore Lodge, the **Farm House Restaurant and Bar** (10021 Hwy. 1, 415/663-1264, www.pointreyesseashore.com, 11:30am-9pm daily, $18-29) is the oldest operating business in Olema. In the elegant, bright dining room enjoy a pleasant range of fresh California cuisine, with a heavy emphasis on ingredients grown, caught, and raised nearby. There is also a bar menu that features specialty cocktails, locally brewed beer, and oysters prepared half a dozen different ways.

The hottest restaurant in West Marin is the **Sir and Star at the Olema** (10000 Sir Francis Drake Blvd., 415/663-1034, http://sirandstar.com, 5pm-9pm Wed.-Sun., $20). Inside this soot-colored farmhouse in the heart of Olema are taxidermy animals, bouquets of dried kelp, and Shaker-esque furniture. The cuisine highlights the bounty of West Marin, from the cheese to the "faux gras," in style and execution. Saturday nights, a chef's five-course tasting menu ($75) is served.

POINT REYES STATION

If you're seeking a rarified organic California meal, you're in the right town. The star of the Point Reyes Station restaurant scene is the ★ **Station House Café** (11180 Hwy. 1, 415/663-1515, www.stationhousecafe.com, 8am-9pm Thurs.-Tues., $17-25), which is both casual and upscale. Since 1974, the Station House has been dedicated to serving food with ingredients that reflect the area's agrarian culture. More comfort food than haute cuisine, the restaurant offers fantastic takes on old classics. The oyster stew is not to be missed, nor are the popovers served with dinner. The dining room is open and unpretentious, with large multi-paned windows. At the full bar, bartenders deftly mix cocktails and pour beer and glasses of wine while the outside patio drips with wisteria.

For a drink and a bit of local color, slip through the swinging doors of the **Old Western Saloon** (11201 Hwy. 1, 415/663-1661, 10am-2am daily). At this crusty old West Marin haunt you'll see ranchers yukking it up with park rangers, longtime natives, and recent transplants. It's the place where everyone goes.

Traveling north from Point Reyes Station along the bay, a stop at **Nick's Cove** (23240 Hwy. 1, 415/663-1033, www.nickscove.com, 11am-9pm Mon.-Fri., 10am-9pm Sat.-Sun. $24-34) may be in order. Overlooking the bay in an expansive weathered redwood building, Nick's Cove has a well-designed menu, from light nibbles to a high-end meal. Oysters and other local seafood take center stage. Out back is a long deck and a boathouse, perfect to explore with the little ones.

There is no better place to stock a picnic basket than the **Bovine Bakery** (11315 Hwy. 1, 415/663-9420, 6:30am-5pm Mon.-Fri., 7am-5pm Sat.-Sun.), where you can pick up a cup of coffee, loaves of bread, and cookies. Then you'll need some cheese to go with your bread. Thankfully, **Cowgirl Creamery** (80 4th St., 415/663-9335, www.cowgirlcreamery.com, 10am-6pm Wed.-Sun.), which produces the best cheese in the Bay Area, is just around the corner. All of their cheese is made on-site in the French brie style. Tours of the facility are available Friday mornings (by appointment only). At the retail shop inside, pick up a stinky but oh-so-good round of Red Hawk, the milder Mount Tam and Pierce Point, or the subtle and seasonal St. Pat's. The store also sells other gourmet treats, from jams to crackers and even pasta and some sandwiches.

The **Tomales Bay Oyster Co.** (15479 Hwy. 1, 415/663-1242, http://tomalesbayoysters.com, 9am-5pm daily) is a low-key spot, where you can buy a wide selection of oysters, clams, and mussels in an open-air market feet from the bay from where they are harvested. The smaller oysters tend to be sweeter, but the bigger, meatier ones better lend themselves to barbecuing. Tomales Bay Oyster Company is set up with grills and picnic tables ready to host your oyster party. You can bring in whatever other food and drink you see fit.

While dining around the Bay Area, you may have seen **Hog Island** (20215 Hwy. 1, 415/663-9218, www.hogislandoysters.com, 9am-5pm daily, $5 table fee) oysters on many upscale menus. They have an open-air stand where you can buy and barbecue excellent oysters. Hog Island gets busy on weekends as many locals come to get their raw-oyster fix. Parking can be tricky, and unless you get here really early, you'll have to wait to get a grill and picnic table.

INVERNESS

Vladimir's Czechoslovakian Restaurant (12785 Sir Francis Drake Blvd., 415/669-1021, 4pm-8:30pm Tues., noon-8:30pm Wed.-Sun., prix fixe $27, cash only) is a favorite of both locals and visitors. Enter the dining room, complete with stuffed deer heads on the walls, and take a seat. The mugs of beer are generous, and the kitchen produces serious Czech food: borscht, rabbit, and duck. Vladimir's is very serious about its no-children policy, which makes it a perfect retreat for couples.

The sundrenched **Saltwater Oyster Depot** (12781 Sir Francis Drake Blvd., 415/669-1244, www.saltwateroysterdepot.com, 5pm-9pm Mon. and Thurs.-Fri., noon-9pm Sat.-Sun., $27) faces the bay and serves a variety of oysters prepared different ways. This charming seafood "shack," lit by skylights and warmed by long, rustic wood tables, is the ideal spot after a day of hiking in Point Reyes.

Information and Services

There's not much out in the wilderness here. You can get gas only in Point Reyes Station. There are full-service grocery stores in Point Reyes Station: **Palace Market** (11300 Highway 1, 415/663-1016, www.palacemarket.com, 7am-9pm Mon.-Sat., 8am-8pm Sun.) and in Inverness: **Inverness Store** (12784 Sir Francis Drake Blvd., 415/669-1041, 9am-7pm daily).

Cell phones don't work in most parts of Point Reyes National Seashore and the adjoining parklands. The closest hospital is **Novato Community Hospital** (180 Rowland Way, Novato, 415/209-1300, www.novatocommunity.sutterhealth.org).

Transportation

Point Reyes is only about an hour north of San Francisco by car, but getting here can be quite a drive. From the Golden Gate Bridge, take U.S. 101 north to just south of San Rafael. Take the Sir Francis Drake Boulevard exit toward San Anselmo. Follow Sir Francis Drake Boulevard west for 20 miles to the small town of Olema and Highway 1. At the intersection with Highway 1, turn right (north) to Point Reyes Station and the Bear Valley Visitors Center.

A slower but more scenic route follows Highway 1 into Point Reyes National Seashore and provides access to the trails near Bolinas in the southern portion of the park. From the Golden Gate Bridge, take U.S. 101 north to the Mill Valley/Stinson Beach exit. Follow Shoreline Highway for almost 30 miles through Stinson Beach and past Bolinas Lagoon to the coast. From the lagoon, it's 11 miles north to Point Reyes Station. Expect twists, turns, and slow going as you approach Point Reyes.

East Bay

The East Bay is unique not only because of its ethnic and economic diversity but for the way its divergent groups come together, making it feel like a true melting pot. In addition to the world-class University of California, Berkeley, the Oakland Museum of California gives the museums across the bay a run for their money. Big music names are drawn to Berkeley's Greek Theater and Oakland's Fox Theater, and nearly every old neighborhood has an erudite independent bookstore and multiple cafés where you can hear patrons arguing over ideas big and small.

BERKELEY

There's no place quite like Berkeley. The town has long been known for its radical, liberal, progressive activism. The youthful urban culture tends to revolve around the University of California, Berkeley. Yet well-heeled foodies also flock to town to sample some of the finest cuisine in Northern California.

University of California, Berkeley

Berkeley is a college town, and fittingly the **University of California, Berkeley** (www.berkeley.edu) offers the most interesting

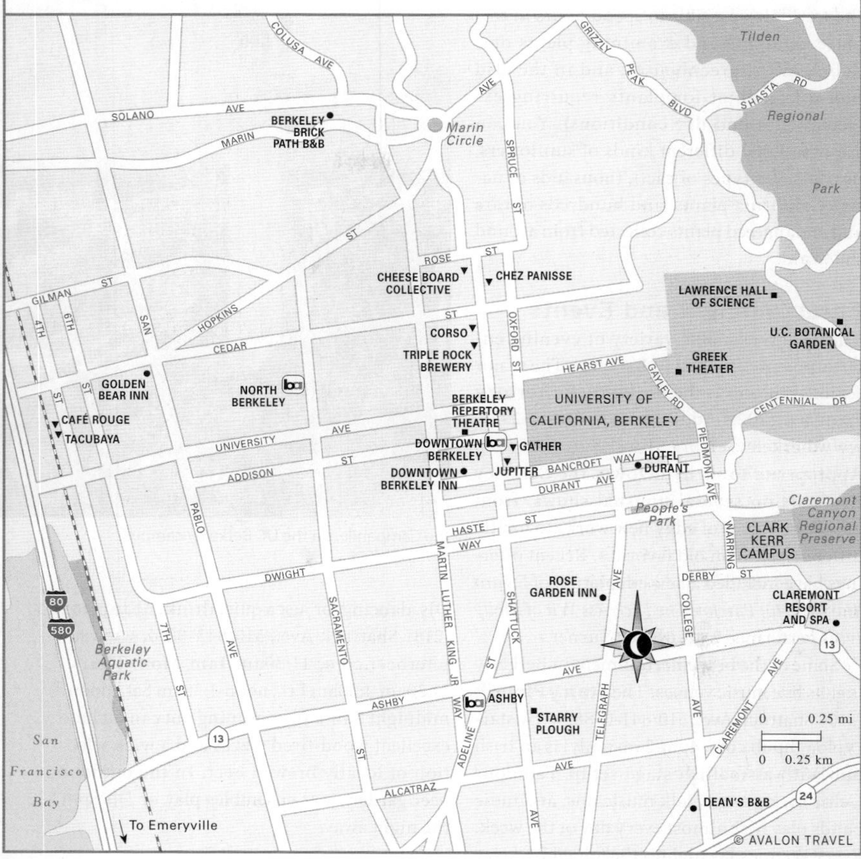

places to go and things to see. As an introduction to the school, take a guided **campus tour** (510/642-5215, www.berkeley.edu, 10am Mon.-Sat., 1pm Sun., by reservation only, free). To get a great view of the campus from above, take an elevator ride up the **Campanile** (10am-3:45pm Mon.-Fri., 10am-4:45pm Sat., 10am-1:30pm, 3pm-4:45pm Sun., adults $3, seniors and ages 4-17 $2, under age 4 free), formally called Sather Tower. Or wander around campus, discovering the halls where students live and learn; the California Memorial stadium, which is listed in the National Register of Historic Places; and architectural details such as Sather Gate and South Hall, built in 1873. Stop in at the **Lawrence Hall of Science** (1 Centennial Dr., 510/642-5132, www.lawrencehallofscience.org, 10am-5pm daily, adults $12, seniors and students $10, under age 3 free) for a look at the latest exhibits and interactive displays.

Also on campus is the **University of California Botanical Garden** (200 Centennial Dr., 510/643-2755, http://botanicalgarden.berkeley.edu, 9am-5pm daily, adults $10, seniors $8, ages 13-17 $5, ages 5-12 $2, free under age 5), an immense space with an astounding array of wild plants from around the world. It's possible to spend hours in this place, studying and examining plants outdoors, in the greenhouses, and in the arid house (a habitat for plants requiring extremely hot and dry conditions). You can see over 1,000 different kinds of sunflowers, nearly 2,500 types of cacti, thousands of native California plants, and hundreds of rare and endangered plants collected from around the world.

Entertainment and Events

There's a reasonable variety of evening entertainment to be had in Berkeley. The major regional theater is the **Berkeley Repertory Theatre** (2025 Addison St., 510/647-2949, www.berkeleyrep.org, Tues.-Sun., $25-87). Appropriate to its hometown, the Berkeley Rep puts on several unusual shows, from world premieres of edgy new works to totally different takes on old favorites. Recent offerings have included a new adaptation of *Figaro* and *Red Hot Patriot: The Kick Ass Wit of Molly Ivins* performed by Kathleen Turner.

Some of the best entertainment in Berkeley is at its live music venues. The **Starry Plough** (3101 Shattuck Ave., 510/841-0188, www.starryploughpub.com, 4pm-2am daily) is an Irish pub with a smallish stage setup. Fabulous Celtic rock groups, folk musicians, and indie bands play here almost every day of the week. Every Wednesday night is the famed Berkeley Poetry Slam—there's nothing like it. Order a full meal from the kitchen, or just quaff a pint or two of Guinness while you sit back and watch the stage.

The big-name acts come to the **Greek Theater** (2001 Gayley Rd., 510/548-3010, www.apeconcerts.com). This outdoor amphitheater, constructed in the classic Greek style, sits on the UC Berkeley campus. Expect to see top-tier performers playing the Greek, including artists such as The Decemberists, Lorde, and Dave Matthews Band.

For a slightly less formal outing, Berkeley has any number of bars and clubs that offer

the Campanile, on the UC Berkeley campus

DJs, dancing, or just a quiet drink. At **Jupiter** (2181 Shattuck Ave., 510/843-8277, www.jupiterbeer.com, 11:30am-1am Mon.-Thurs., 11:30am-1:30am Fri., noon-1:30am Sat., noon-midnight Sun.), your evening out can include excellent wood-fired pizzas and a wide selection of locally brewed beer. In the outdoor beer garden, jazz ensembles play or DJs spin the night away.

Shopping

A variety of funky independent shops live on the slightly grungy **Telegraph Avenue** (between the UC campus and Parker Ave.). In addition to several outstanding bookstores, there are a couple record stores where you can still find actual records and a smattering of import stores that harken back to the 1960s.

For a decidedly more tony shopping experience head east to College Avenue and follow it south to the **Elmwood District** (College Ave. between Garber and Prince Sts.). Just below the famed Claremont Hotel, College Avenue smartens up with chic clothiers, lovely home and garden shops, import stores, toy stores, and a few places to satisfy your sweet tooth.

In true Berkeley fashion, the best Berkeley shopping mall is the span of **Fourth Street** between Delaware Street and University Avenue. Here, scores of stores have created an upscale shopping district. Independent gems dominate, like stationary shops, an eclectic garden boutique, and an artisan chocolatier. Some national chains like Crate and Barrel and Apple are scattered amongst the smaller shops.

Sports and Recreation

TILDEN REGIONAL PARK

Tilden Regional Park (Grizzly Peak Blvd., 888/327-2757, www.ebparks.org, 5am-10pm daily) covers the ridge directly above Berkeley. Within its more than 2,000 acres, the park has a celebrated botanical garden, the swimmable Lake Anza and its sandy beaches, an antique carousel, and miniature steam trains, perfect to thrill the little ones. But aside from the attractions, Tilden also offers scores of hiking and mountain biking trails that almost convince you that you are in absolute wilderness, except for the breathtaking views of the Bay Area. This isn't really wilderness, but taking a trail map is advisable, as multiple trails crisscross one another, allowing for more adventure but also potential confusion.

For a simple stroll, take the **Jewel Lake Nature Trail** (1 mile, easy), located in the Nature Area of the park, a quiet area where no dogs are allowed. Park at the trailhead at the intersection of Central Park Drive and Canon Drive, near the Little Farm and Environmental Education Center. From the parking lot, the trail heads north along Wildcat Creek and out to Jewel Lake. You won't gain much elevation, and although there are exposed patches, the trail is mostly lush and leafy, surrounded by bay laurels, blackberries, and buckeye trees.

For a more rigorous climb, the **Wildcat Peak Loop** (3.5 miles, moderate) leaves from the same trailhead behind the Environmental Education Center. Take **Laurel Canyon Trail** through eucalypti and California bay laurels up through the canyon, which is a gentle grade most of the way. The trail then turns left toward the Rotary Peace Grove and on to Wildcat Peak (1,211 feet). From the stony vista, you'll be able to see the Golden Gate Bridge, San Pablo Bay, and Mount Diablo. To get back down the mountain, take **Wildcat Peak Trail** for about one mile. You'll hit **Jewel Lake Nature Trail.** Turn left, and it will take you back to the trailhead.

If you want to spend some time on the **Bay Area Ridge Trail** (3.5 miles, moderate), a pleasant loop starts at the Quarry Trailhead off Wildcat Canyon Road. Take **Wildcat Canyon Trail** to **Seaview Trail** and turn right. After some time, the trail changes names to **East Bay Skyline National Trail** and Bay Area Ridge Trail. At **Upper Big Springs Trail,** take a right back down the mountain. After nearly one mile, take a left on **Quarry Trail;** it will take you back to the parking lot.

Tilden offers many roads and trails for cyclists. The paved roads snaking through the park (Wildcat Canyon Rd., Grizzly Peak Blvd., and South Park Dr.) twist and turn while gaining and losing enough elevation to keep any cyclist busy. As for mountain biking, many of the big trails are shared with hikers. The **Bay Area Ridge, Meadows Canyon,** and **Big Springs Trails** are some of the most popular.

WILDCAT CANYON REGIONAL PARK

North of Tilden, the equally large Wildcat Canyon Regional Park (5755 McBryde Ave., Richmond, 510/544-3092, www.ebparks.org, sunrise-sunset daily) is filled with wide fire roads, all of which are open to cyclists. **Nimitz Way** is a paved trail along the ridgeline that is popular with cyclists young and old. **Harvey Canyon Trail** is a single-track trail also open to cyclists that descends from Nimitz Way down to Wildcat Creek. The only significant restriction for cyclists is that access via the south end of the park is only through the Tilden Nature Area, which allows limited bicycle access. The only route from the south starts at the Little Farm and Environmental Education Center. Bicycles are only permitted on Loop Road, which at Jewel Lake connects with Wildcat Creek Trail.

Wildcat Canyon has fewer trails than Tilden, but it is quieter, and the trails traverse a more challenging topography and allow for longer treks. A healthy loop (7 miles, moderate-strenuous) that allows you to see most of the park and some ridge-top views begins at the Alvarado Trailhead at the north end of the park. Start by taking **Wildcat Creek Trail** to **Harvey Canyon Trail,** which ascends sharply to the ridge. At the top you'll come to the paved **Nimitz Way.** After nearly one mile, continue straight (Nimitz Way veers slightly right) on **San Pablo Ridge Trail** until **Belgium Trail,** and turn left. This trail leads back down to the trailhead.

Accommodations

UNDER $100

Offering great value is the **Golden Bear Inn** (1620 San Pablo Ave., 510/525-6770, www.goldenbearinn.com, $80-99). At this family-friendly place, parents can rent an inexpensive room with two twin beds in a separate bedroom. There is even a cottage ($150) that has two bedrooms, a living room, and a full kitchen.

$100-150

Practically at the foot of campus, the **Downtown Berkeley Inn** (2001 Bancroft Way, 510/843-4043, www.downtownberkeleyinn.com, $110) offers inexpensive lodging with a chic urban vibe. Aside from the high-end beds and 42-inch plasma TVs, don't expect too many perks.

$150-250

Spend a weekend in the charming Claremont district by booking a room at **Mary's Bed and Breakfast** (47 Alvarado Rd., 510/848-1431, http://marysbedandbreakfast.com, weekend 2-day minimum, $175). The Craftsman-style home has been meticulously maintained and is elegantly decorated with antiques from the period. Three rooms with private baths are available, as is an apartment for longer stays. A deluxe continental breakfast is served daily in the dining room. Mary's is within walking distance of the Claremont Hotel's spa and restaurant as well as posh restaurants and shops.

The **Berkeley Brick Path Bed & Breakfast** (1805 Marin Ave., 510/524-4277, www.thebrickpath.com, $185-225) is a Craftsman B&B charmer. The garden is the pride of this inn. Stroll down the namesake path among the lush greenery and gorgeous flowers, take a seat out on the patio to enjoy your breakfast, or sip a glass of wine in the gazebo. Each of the three rooms has a unique style: one with a brick fireplace, one with a huge whirlpool tub, and the East-West cottage with a full kitchen and private entrance.

The **Rose Garden Inn** (2740 Telegraph Ave., 510/549-2145, www.rosegardeninn.com, Sat. 2-night minimum, $138-268) is a rambling structure with 40 rooms decorated in floral themes. All rooms have private baths, free Wi-Fi, and TVs, and some offer a refrigerator, microwave, fireplace, and sitting room. A hearty buffet breakfast is complimentary to all. In the spring, stroll in the lush gardens and smell the jasmine.

The **Hotel Durant** (2600 Durant St., 510/845-8981, www.hoteldurant.com, $189-220) has it all: location and views. Get a room on the upper floors for a view of Oakland, San Francisco, or the bay. Inside, you'll enjoy the high thread-count sheets, pet friendly options, and the pillow menu. From here, you can walk to the university, Telegraph Avenue, and the Elmwood shopping district.

Since 1915, the **Claremont Resort and Spa** (41 Tunnel Rd., 510/843-3000, www.claremontresort.com, $180-280) has catered to the rich and famous. No two of the 279 elegantly furnished rooms look quite the same, so you'll have a unique experience even in this large resort hotel. The real focus at the Claremont is fitness and pampering. A full-fledged health club, complete with yoga,

Pilates, and spinning classes, takes up part of the huge complex. And the full-service spa, which offers popular body treatments plus aesthetic services, finds favor with visitors and locals alike.

Food

CASUAL DINING

In a foodie cul de sac off Fourth Street, **Tacubaya** (1788 4th St., 510/525-5160, www.tacubaya.net, 10am-9pm Mon.-Fri., 9am-9pm Sat.-Sun., $10) is a taqueria as you will only find in Berkeley. Cesar Chavez, Diego Rivera, and Frieda Kahlo look down on patrons munching tacos made with Niman Ranch meat and locally sourced fruits and veggies. All the tortillas are freshly made from corn in house. There are plenty of offerings, scrawled on the blackboard above the register. The line is long, but worth the wait, especially if you indulge in a churro for dessert.

Two doors down from Tacubaya, oyster lovers will swoon over the $1.25 oysters at **Café Rouge** (1782 Fourth St., 510/525-1440, http://caferouge.net, 11:30am-3pm Mon., 11:30am-9:30pm Tues.-Thurs., 11:30am-10pm Fri.-Sat., 11am-9pm Sun., $14-32). The ample wine list, patio seating, and California-French bistro-style food rounds out the experience.

At **Triple Rock Brewery** (1920 Shattuck Ave., 510/843-2739, http://triplerock.com, 11:30am-1am Mon.-Wed., 11:30am-2am Thurs.-Sat., 11:30am-midnight Sun., $9-14), an ever-evolving menu of beer includes seasonal specialties and favorites, ranging from the Pinnacle Pale Ale to the Stonehenge Stout. The food is exceptional, made from local and organic ingredients. You'll find juicy free-range burgers, a great Reuben sandwich featuring beer-braised corned beef, and a variety of hand-cut fries. Triple Rock boasts a well-worn wood bar, large windows, and a rooftop beer garden.

Gather (2200 Oxford St., 510/809-0400, www.gatherrestaurant.com, 11:30am-2pm, 5pm-9:30pm Mon.-Fri., 10am-2:30pm, 5pm-9:30pm Sat.-Sun., $16-29) is where foodies gather. The food is all locally sourced. The menu is a thick binder containing details of each ingredient's former life in a field, out in the bay, or on a ranch. The décor stylishly employs reclaimed wine bottles, fishing nets, and old belts. Vegetarians and vegans will find many choices here, including vegetarian charcuterie, lentil ragout, and hearty pizzas.

A stop at the ★ **Cheese Board Collective** (1504 Shattuck Ave., 510/549-3183, http://cheeseboardcollective.coop, 7am-1pm Mon., 7am-6pm Tues.-Fri., 8am-5pm Sat., under $10) is a must. A worker owned co-op since 1971, the Cheese Board is filled with fresh bread, pastries, and cheese. At the counter are up to 400 different cheeses, which the clerks encourage customers to taste. Step next door to the Cheese Board's **pizzeria** (1512 Shattuck Ave., 11:30am-3pm, 4:30pm-8pm daily, $2.50-20). Only one type of pizza is made each day, but the crust is always a thin sourdough and the toppings are organic and vegetarian. Select from a slice ($2.50), half pizza ($10), or a whole pie ($20). The line is long but moves fairly quickly and live music softens the wait.

FINE DINING

The very best fine-dining venue is ★ **Chez Panisse** (1517 Shattuck Ave., 510/548-5525, www.chezpanisse.com, $65-100), where founder Alice Waters and her successors create French-California dishes at the cutting edge of current trends. Every dinner is prix-fixe, and there are two seatings per evening (5:30pm-6pm, 8pm-8:45pm Mon.-Thurs., 6pm-6:30pm, 8:30pm-9:15pm Fri.-Sat.). You'll need to make your reservations early. Reservations are made up to one month in advance (28 days when booked online) and require a deposit ($25 pp). Eating at the upstairs **café** (510/548-5049, 11:30am-2:45pm, 5pm-10:30pm Mon.-Thurs., 11:30am-3pm, 5pm-11:30pm Fri.-Sat., $19-25) is a bit more relaxed. The food is just as good and the casual atmosphere is less intimidating.

Corso (1788 Shattuck Ave., 510/704-8004, www.corsoberkeley.com, 5pm-9pm Sun.-Mon., 5pm-9:30pm Tues.-Thurs., 5pm-10pm

Fri.-Sat., $15-27) is devoted to sustainable cuisine, executed in traditional Italian dishes. Fresh house-made pastas and house-cured *salumi*, as well as classic meat and fish entrées fill the slim menu. The relaxed interior of exposed wood and warm lighting convey the feel of a traditional trattoria. Corso also has an inventive cocktail list.

Information and Services

Newcomers to Berkeley can start at the **Visitors Information Center** (2030 Addison St., 510/549-7040, http://visitberkeley.com, 9am-5pm Mon.-Fri., 10am-4pm Sat.).

For medical assistance, the **Alta Bates Summit Medical Center** (2450 Ashby Ave., 510/204-4444, www.altabatessummit.org) has a 24-hour emergency room.

Transportation

Berkeley is north of Oakland, along the east side of the San Francisco Bay. To drive into Berkeley, take the Bay Bridge from San Francisco, then merge onto I-80 East. Major roads in town include San Pablo, Ashby, Shattuck, Telegraph, and University Avenues. Parking in Berkeley can be frustrating. If you're visiting for the day or for an evening show, consider taking BART to avoid the parking hassle.

BART (www.bart.gov, one-way $1.85-7.50) is a major form of transit in the Bay Area. The Downtown Berkeley station is located underneath Shattuck Avenue. Other stations in the city include North Berkeley and Ashby. **AC Transit** (510/891-4706, www.actransit.org, adults $2.10, children and seniors $1.05) is the local bus service, offering routes that connect the East Bay and San Francisco (adults $4.20, children and seniors $2.10).

The closest airport is **Oakland International Airport** (OAK, 1 Airport Dr., Oakland, 510/563-3300, www.flyoakland.com). From the Oakland airport, you can rent a car, catch a cab, or take BART ($8-10) from the terminals to the BART Coliseum/Airport station. If you fly into San Francisco, you can take BART from SFO to Berkeley.

OAKLAND

Oakland is the biggest city in the East Bay. Although its reputation hasn't always been perfect (travelers should probably stay in the popular visitor areas), today a great deal of downtown urban renewal has made it a visitor-friendly place with plenty of attractions, accommodations, and exceptional food.

★ Oakland Museum of California

The **Oakland Museum of California** (1000 Oak St., 510/318-8400, www.museumca.org, 11am-5pm Wed.-Thurs., 11am-9pm Fri., 10am-6pm Sat.-Sun., adults $15, students and seniors $10, children 9-17 $6, parking $1 per hour) has launched itself into the stratosphere of must-see museums. Its multidisciplinary approach tells California's story through art, history, and science. Within its modernist concrete walls you'll be able to see Thiebaud's and Diebenkorn's take on the urban California landscape, a rare and authentic Ohlone basket, home furnishings from elite homes of California's early days, and a casting of a once-endemic mastodon. The museum also hosts special themed exhibits that complement its three-pronged approach. You may stumble into one celebrating the social consciousness of street art, a video installation exploring life as a black man in the United States, or retrospectives of local multimedia artists. The museum has a café, the Blue Oak, which serves wine, espresso, and a selection of salads and sandwiches.

Chabot Space and Science Center

One of the most spectacular sights in the East Bay, **Chabot Space and Science Center** (10000 Skyline Blvd., 510/336-7300, www.chabotspace.org, 10am-5pm Tues.-Thurs. and Sun., 10am-10pm Fri.-Sat., adults $16, students and seniors $13, youths 3-12 $12) makes science and space super cool. Up in the Oakland Hills, the Chabot complex includes observatories, a planetarium, a museum, and the Megadome theater, all open to the public (most

Bay Area observatory telescopes are private). Chabot focuses on the life of the earth and the rest of the universe. Create your own solar system in an interactive exhibit, ride a space shuttle at the Challenger Learning Center, and check out Saturn's rings through the telescopes. If your visit runs long, grab a bite to eat and a cup of coffee at the on-site café.

Entertainment and Events

Perhaps the best-known Oakland venue is **Yoshi's** (510 Embarcadero W., 510/238-9200, www.yoshis.com, 5:30pm-9pm Mon.-Wed., 5:30pm-10pm Fri.-Sat., 5pm-9pm Sun., shows 8pm, 10pm daily). With a sushi restaurant in one room and the legendary jazz club next door, it's possible to enjoy the sushi without attending the concert, or vice versa. If you're a dinner patron, make reservations for the show and claim a seat before you sit down for your meal. Performers at Yoshi's have included Diana Krall and Kurt Elling.

The renovated **Fox Theater** (1807 Telegraph Ave., 510/302-2250, www.thefoxoakland.com) attracts big names to this city landmark. Originally opened in 1928 and closed for nearly 40 years, it was designed in the Moorish style en vogue during the decade of the flapper. The theater is now in league with some of the more venerated venues across the Bay like the Filmore, Warfield, and Great American Music Hall. Past acts in this intimate venue have included Sufjan Stevens, the Pixies, and 2 Chainz. It also has a bar and café where you can get champagne with your fish tacos.

Luka's Taproom & Lounge (2221 Broadway, 510/451-4677, www.lukasoakland.com, 11:30am-midnight Mon.-Wed., 11:30am-2am Thurs.-Fri., 10:30am-2am Sat., 10:30am-midnight Sun.) is a restaurant during the day, then a lounge and dance club after the sun sets. With a separate room for DJs and dancing, another space reserved just for pool and a 45-playing jukebox, and the Taproom with its brasserie-style food, 16 beers on tap, and full bar, almost everyone can find something to enjoy at Luka's.

For truly diverse entertainment, **Plank** (98 Broadway, 510/817-0980, http://plankoakland.com, 11am-midnight Sun.-Thurs., 11am-midnight Fri.-Sat.) in Jack London Square is the place to go. Inside is a bowling alley, arcade, and pool tables. Outside, bocce ball courts and a beer garden overlook the Oakland harbor. There is a full bar and the menu is affordable and eclectic, offering burgers, noodles, and shareable snacks, like nachos and ceviche.

the Oakland Museum of California

With a big emphasis on style, **Era Art Bar** (19 Grand Ave., 510/832-4400, www.oaklandera.com, 4:30pm-1:30am Mon.-Sat., noon-1:30am Sun.) is carefully crafted with modern and antique furnishings, blown-glass chandeliers, and rotating art shows. Its cocktails employ unique spirits and fresh ingredients. Evenings are usually booked with DJs, live music, and unusual acts.

Head downtown to **The Trappist** (460 8th St., 510/238-8900, www.thetrappist.com, noon-12:30am Sun.-Thurs., noon-1:30am Fri.-Sat.) for excellent Belgian brews along with loads of local microbrews and fantastic gastropub fare.

Shopping

Most of Oakland's neighborhoods have thriving commercial corridors. For specialized shops with a neighborhood feel, head to **Rockridge** (College Ave. between Alcatraz Ave. and 51st St.). Inside the brick building of epicurean **Rockridge Market Hall** (5655 College Ave., 510/250-6000, http://rockridgemarkethall.com, 9am-8pm Mon.-Fri., 9am-7pm Sat., 10am-6pm Sun.) are a coffee roaster, a bakery, a fresh pasta shop, a fish market, a butcher, wine, and flowers. Every shop is known for its locavore ethos and its quality. The high-toned vibe continues along College Avenue with an independent bookstore and shops specializing in smart home décor and stylish threads.

Closer to the hills, the **Piedmont Avenue District** (between West Grand Ave. and Pleasant Valley Ave.) is an old Oakland neighborhood with a historical movie theater and mom-and-pop stores that cater to the tony denizens of the area. You'll find jewelry stores, fiber arts shops, and even an old school tobacconist.

Certainly the hippest place to shop is two tiny alleys off 49th Avenue in **Temescal** (between Telegraph Ave. and Clark St.). Temescal Alley and Alley 49 are lined in former horse stables that have been converted into pint-sized spaces selling cheap vintage treasures, handcrafted jewelry, gothic curios, and clothes from small scale clothing designers. You can even get a shave and a trim in the spirit of the 1890s, albeit with plenty of tattoos.

Sports and Recreation

The jewel of Oakland is **Lake Merritt** (650 Bellevue Ave., 510/238-7275). Here you can take a walk around the lake, play a few holes of golf, rent a kayak for a peaceful paddle, or even get in a set of tennis. For families, **Children's Fairyland** (699 Bellevue Ave., 510/452-2259, www.fairyland.org, 10am-4pm Mon.-Fri., 10am-5pm Sat.-Sun. summer, 10am-4pm Wed.-Sun. spring-fall, 10am-4pm Fri.-Sun. winter, $8) provides hours of entertainment and diversion on 10 acres at the edge of the lake.

If you're eager to get out on the water, the **Lake Merritt Boating Center** (568 Bellevue Ave., 510/238-2196, http://www2.oaklandnet.com, hours vary, $10-24 per hour, cash only) has everything from canoes to catamarans, kayaks, and sailboats. On the lake at Lakeside Park off Grand Avenue, it is run by the city, so the prices are fair; the only hitch is that it is cash only. You can also hit the water of the Oakland Estuary off Jack London Square at **California Canoe and Kayak** (CCK, 409 Water St., 510/893-7833, www.calkayak.com, 10am-6pm daily, $20-60 per hour). CCK has everything you'll need to explore the Oakland Estuary including single and double kayaks, canoes, and stand-up paddleboards.

If you'd rather watch than play, Oakland is home to several professional sports teams. The best consistent players are the Major League Baseball **Oakland A's** (510/538-5600, http://oakland.athletics.mlb.com). Part of the American League, the A's have seen their ups and downs, but they almost always put on a good show for their fans. Unstoppable action can always be found at a **Golden State Warriors** (888/479-4007, www.nba.com/warriors) game. In 2015, the NBA team won its first championship since 1975, igniting basketball fever throughout the Bay Area. The most notorious team in pro football, the

Oakland Raiders (510/864-5020, www.raiders.com) call the East Bay home. The home side of the stadium can get rowdy and rough.

All three teams play at the **Oracle Arena and O.co Coliseum** (7000 Coliseum Way, Oakland, 510/569-2121, www.coliseum.com). The Oakland Coliseum (as it's referred to by locals) is a complex with both a covered basketball arena and an open-air stadium that hosts both the A's and the Raiders. Though the vast majority of event and game goers are perfectly safe, the Coliseum isn't in the best neighborhood.

Accommodations

With all the amenities of a higher-priced chain motel, the **Bay Breeze Inn** (4919 Coliseum Way, 510/536-5972, www.baybreezeinnoakland.com, $56-150) offers both comfort and convenience. Located just down the street from the Oakland Coliseum and only a few miles from Oakland Airport, this is the perfect place to stay if you're into football, baseball, basketball, live concerts, or just need to be near the airport. The Coliseum area can be sketchy after dark, so take care if you're walking alone.

Located in the thick of Jack London Square, the **Inn at Jack London Square** (233 Broadway, 510/452-4565, www.innatthesquare.com, $129-159) offers comfortable digs for reasonable rates. In addition to its clean and modestly stylish decor, the hotel has standard amenities such as complimentary Wi-Fi plus an exercise room and an outdoor pool perfect for relaxing during summer days. The hotel is within easy walking distance of Oakland's waterfront.

The blue awnings and nautical theme of the **Waterfront Hotel** (10 Washington St., 510/836-3800, www.jdvhotels.com, $210-330) in Jack London Square are hard to miss. Compact, but packed with character and bright colors, the hotel boasts stellar views, an outdoor pool, and complimentary wine in the afternoons. Some of the more luxurious rooms have private balconies where you can sip your coffee in the morning.

★ **The Washington Inn** (495 10th St., Oakland, 510/452-1776, www.thewashingtoninn.com, $114-139) brings a hint of European elegance to Oakland. Rooms are smartly decorated in a refined style that highlights the 1913 landmark building while giving it a boutique hotel vibe. Downstairs, the white tablecloth Seison restaurant serves classic California fare and serious cocktails. Located in the heart of downtown, the inn offers a hip and convenient Oakland experience. **A Bed and Breakfast on Fairmount** (600 block Fairmount Ave., 510/653-7726, www.abedandbreakfastonfairmount.com, $120-160, two night minimum) pretty much says it all. Only blocks away from the affluent Piedmont shopping district, the three-room inn is a light-filled, beautifully maintained Craftsman home with ample gardens (and chickens!) on a quiet street. All rooms have private baths and one even boasts its own fireplace.

Food

In Jack London Square, you can't walk 10 yards without running into a restaurant, from the old-school and new-style seafood spots, wood fired pizza joints, and Korean barbecues. Many have expansive outdoor patios to take in the view. Perhaps the king is **Bocanova** (55 Webster St., 510/444-1233, www.bocanova.com, 11:30am-9:30pm Mon.-Wed., 11:30am-10:30pm Thurs.-Fri., 11am-10:30pm Sat., 11am-9:30pm Sun., $19-35). Billing itself as a "pan-American grill," Bocanova, though a bit pricey, boasts meat, fish, and vegetable dishes made with the spice and zest of the Americas. Slow cooked pork belly, duck tacos, ceviche, and crudos are a few examples. The full bar has a dizzying selection of spirits, perfect for the 1960s Bossa Nova vibe.

No matter how "Brooklyn by the Bay" Oakland becomes, there is no place more Oakland than the ★ **Home of Chicken and Waffles** (444 Embarcadero W., 510/836-4446, http://homeofchickenandwaffles.com, 10am-midnight Mon.-Thurs., 10am-4am Fri.-Sat.,

9am-midnight Sun., $7-17), which serves up good ol' Southern comfort food late into the night. Specialties of the house include the gooey mac and cheese, true Southern sides (lots of grits), and chicken and waffles—served together, if you please. After 11:30pm you must prepay for your meal.

Near Jack London Square, **Chop Bar** (247 4th St., 510/834-2467, www.oaklandchopbar.com, 8am-10pm Mon.-Thurs., 7am-11pm Fri., 9am-11pm Sat., 9am-10pm Sun., $15-24) serves food that is simple, affordable, and excellent, with an emphasis on artisanal ingredients. Whether you decide to go for a plate of charcuterie with a glass of wine or a sumptuous dinner of oxtail poutine or pan-seared trout, Chop Bar won't disappoint.

Mua (2442A Webster Ave., Oakland, 510/238-1100, http://muaoakland.com, 5:30pm-11:30pm Mon.-Thurs., 11:30am-midnight Fri., 5:30pm-midnight Sat., 5pm-10pm Sun., $12-32) is close to downtown and serves smart California fare and hip cocktails to the young urban set. Its interior is modern and industrial, and it is one of the few places in the Bay Area that serves food late into the evening. Although you'll find fresh offerings such as lamb cheeks and ahi sashimi, the burger is one of the best things on the menu.

If all you want is a burger and fries, stop by **True Burger** (146 Grand Ave., Oakland, 510/208-5678, http://trueburgeroakland.com, 11am-3pm Mon., 11am-9:30pm Tues.-Sat., noon-7pm Sun., $4-7), Oakland's answer to the all-American diner. The menu is small (a couple burgers, hot dogs, a few sides, and milkshakes) and inexpensive. Everything is made with care, from humanely raised and locally sourced ingredients. Best of all, it's all delicious.

At the foot of the Oakland Hills, the Piedmont district's main draw is the delightfully retro **Fenton's Creamery** (4226 Piedmont Ave., 510/658-7000, www.fentonscreamery.com, 11am-11pm Mon.-Thurs., 9am-midnight Fri.-Sat., 9am-11pm Sun., $10-15), which has been serving ice cream since 1894. The scores of flavors include Swiss milk chocolate, rum raisin, and pomegranate, which are sold by the scoop, in waffle cones, or made into a sundae. You can also opt for a burger, grilled ham and cheese, or breakfast, which is served all day.

Doña Tomas (5004 Telegraph Ave., Oakland, 510/450-0522, www.donatomas.com, 5:30pm-9:30pm Tues.-Thurs., 5:30pm-10pm Fri., 9:30am-2:30pm, 5:30pm-10pm Sat., 9:30am-2:30pm Sun., $20), in the Temescal neighborhood, retains a loyal following, and for good reason. The food is authentic, made from local handmade ingredients, and very affordable. The bar is stocked with a great selection of wine and tequilas, and the interior is bright and filled with Mexican textiles and heavy Mission-style tables and chairs. There can be a wait, particularly at dinner, but it's worth it.

Many believe that the best pizza in the Bay Area can be found in Temescal at ★ **Pizzaiolo** (5008 Telegraph Ave., Oakland, 510/652-4888, www.pizzaiolooakland.com, 8am-noon and 5:30pm-10pm Mon.-Thurs., 8am-noon and 5:30pm-10:30pm Fri.-Sat., $12-28) where the pies are always fire roasted, thin crusted, and topped with ingredients both traditional and inventive. Despite the fanfare, Pizzaiolo retains a casual vibe with simple wood tables, an open kitchen, and a cool patio. Pizzaiolo also doubles as a café, serving a light breakfast menu along with a rotating selection of unusual and delectable pastries.

Also in Temescal is **Hogs Apothecary** (375 40th Ave., Oakland, 510/338-3847, www.hogsapothecary.com, 5pm-11pm Mon.-Thurs., 5pm-midnight Fri., 10am-2:30pm, 5pm-midnight Sat., 10am-2:30pm, 5pm-11pm Sun., $14-25), the neighborhood's version of a German beer hall. Here you'll find lots of beer and lots of pork. Over 30 California microbrews crowd the changing chalkboard menu over the line of taps that also pour a few California wines. Order a pork chop, sausage sandwich, or a platter for three of smoked hock and trotter terrine.

In Rockridge, the place to go is **Wood**

Tavern (6317 College Ave., Oakland, 510/654-4607, www.woodtavern.net, 11:30am-10pm Mon.-Thurs., 11:30am-10:30pm Fri.-Sat., $26-32). With a cool, classy interior of dark wood, moss green, and picture windows overlooking the street, the restaurant serves sophisticated California fare. Mains include hanger steak, seafood stew, and a $15 burger. Come with enough room to start with either a cheese or charcuterie plate and one of the restaurant's famous cocktails.

For something a little lighter, Wood Tavern's sister restaurant **Southie** (6311 College Ave., Oakland, 510/654-0100, 9am-9pm Mon.-Sat., 9am-3pm Sun., $13-18) is a sandwich joint with an epicurean twist. Sandwiches of seared ahi, crab, and beef-pork meatballs are served on the white marble counter alongside poached egg and bacon salad and a coffee toffee ice cream sandwich. In the evening, the red-walled restaurant turns more upscale with such offerings as duck liver pâté, blue nose sea bass, and pork-shoulder confit. The beer and wine list are small but very carefully selected.

Information and Services

Start at the **Oakland Convention and Visitors Bureau** (481 Water St., Oakland, 510/839-9000, www.oaklandcvb.com, 9:30am-4pm Tues.-Sun.) to get good advice, maps, restaurant recommendations, and traffic tips. You'll find plenty of banks and ATMs scattered around Oakland. Stick to ATMs in well-lit areas. The same goes for gas stations and minimarts.

For medical attention, the **Alta Bates Summit Campus** (350 Hawthorne Ave., 510/655-4000, www.altabatessummit.org) has a 24-hour emergency room.

Transportation

Oakland is across the bay from San Francisco and slightly south of Berkeley. It's accessible by car from San Francisco via I-80 over the Bay Bridge. From I-80, I-580 borders Oakland to the east and north, and I-880 runs along the bay on the west. Try to avoid driving I-80, I-880, or I-580 during the commuting hours (7am-10am and 4pm-7pm).

The **Oakland International Airport** (OAK, 1 Airport Dr., Oakland, 510/563-3300, www.flyoakland.com) sees less traffic than San Francisco's airport and has shorter security lines and fewer delays. Major airlines include Alaska, Delta, JetBlue, Southwest, and Spirit.

BART (Bay Area Rapid Transit, www.bart.gov) is a good means of public transportation. The 12th Street/Oakland City Center station is convenient to downtown Oakland, but there are also trains out to 19th Street, Lake Merritt, Rockridge, and the Oakland Airport (via AirBART shuttle bus, $3). BART fares (most East Bay destinations $1.85-7.50 one-way) are based on distance, and ticket machines that accept cash and debit or credit cards are in every station.

Bus service in Oakland is run by **AC Transit** (510/891-4706, www.actransit.org, adults $2.10, children and seniors $1.05). Transbay routes connect the East Bay and San Francisco (adults $4.20, children and seniors $2.10).

The Peninsula

The San Francisco peninsula encompasses the coastal area from Pacifica down to Año Nuevo State Reserve and inland to Palo Alto. Many Bay Area locals escape to the coast for weekend vacations, enjoying the small-town atmosphere in Half Moon Bay and Pescadero along with the unspoiled beauty of the dozens of miles of undeveloped coastline. Peak seasons for major attractions include October's pumpkin season and winter, when elephant seals return to Año Nuevo.

The San Andreas Fault splits the coastal and inland peninsula, with dramatic views and curves from aptly named Skyline Boulevard (Hwy. 35). Nestled amid redwoods, quaint and beautiful Woodside sits midway between the coast and inland peninsula. Nearby Palo Alto provides eastern access via U.S. 101.

MOSS BEACH

Midway down the coast between San Francisco and Half Moon Bay on Highway 1, Moss Beach is one of several residential towns that line the coast south of the imposing Devil's Slide. There is little here besides stunning scenery, a few small businesses, and the Fitzgerald Marine Reserve. North of Moss Beach is the lovely Montara, and south is the Half Moon Bay Airport, El Granada, Princeton, and then Half Moon Bay.

Fitzgerald Marine Reserve

For tide pools, the **Fitzgerald Marine Reserve** (200 Nevada Ave., Moss Beach, 650/728-3584, http://parks.smcgov.org, 8am-sunset daily) is the place to go. The 32-acre reserve extends from the Montara Lighthouse south to Pillar Point and is considered one of the most diverse intertidal zones in the Bay Area. On its rocky reefs, you can hunt for sea anemones, starfish, eels, and crabs—there's even a small species of red octopus. The reserve is also home to egrets, herons, an endangered species of butterfly, and a slew of sea lions and harbor seals that enjoy sunning themselves on the beach's outer rocks. Rangers are available to answer any questions and, if need be, to remind you of tide pool etiquette. This includes a strict no-dog policy. Persistent ocean spray and blankets of seaweed can keep the reefs slick, so wear shoes with good traction. For the best viewing, come at low tide (tide logs are available at most local bookstores, but for a quick reference, check out www.protides.com). For a more leisurely and drier experience, numerous trails crisscross the windswept bluffs and through sheltering groves of cypress and eucalyptus trees.

Devil's Slide Trail

The moniker for the stretch of Highway 1 between Pacifica and Montara, Devil's Slide, is no joke. Starting in the 1940s, motorists white knuckled the thin asphalt strip hugging the sheer cliffs that plunged into the Pacific hundreds of feet below. The stretch was plagued by mudslides, accidents, and frequent closures. In 2013, the Tom Lantos Tunnel was completed and this once hellish road was converted to the 1.3 mile, multiuse **Devil's Slide Trail** (Hwy. 1 between Pacifica and Montara, 650/355-8289, http://parks.smcgov.org, 8am-sunset daily), one of the most spectacular in the Bay Area. The trail boasts views of the Farallon Islands on clear days, a healthy grade to get your heart pumping, lanes for cyclists and pedestrians, and two easily accessible parking lots, one at each end, complete with clean bathrooms.

Montara State Beach

Just north of Moss Beach is **Montara State Beach** (2nd St. and Hwy. 1, Montara, www.parks.ca.gov, 650/726-8819, 8am-sunset daily), one of the most beautiful beaches in this area. It is as popular with tide pool visitors, surfers, and anglers as it is with picnickers and beachcombers. In spite of this, the beach remains relatively uncrowded, but it does have a tendency to get windy.

For those who want a heart-pounding hike instead of a stroll on the beach, cross Highway 1 to the trailhead at **McNee Ranch.** Fire roads crisscross this eastern section of the state park, but the big hike is eight miles up **Montara Mountain** (1,900 feet), through California chaparral. The trail itself is dry and scrubby, but the sweeping views of the coast are breathtaking. On a clear day, you can see all the way across the Golden Gate, south past Half Moon Bay, and west out to the Farallon Islands. The trail is unmarked, but there are maps at the information board at the trailhead. It is also easy to wing it—just follow the roads uphill. With the crisscrossing trails, you won't have to come back the same way. Parking is in a small and poorly marked dirt lot directly across Highway 1 from the parking lot at Montara Beach. McNee Ranch is also a popular mountain biking area, and dogs are welcome on leash.

Accommodations

For an indulgent hideaway, make a reservation at the **Seal Cove Inn** (221 Cypress Ave., Moss Beach, 800/995-9987, www.sealcoveinn.com, $235-350). Tucked away in the cypress and pine forest of Moss Beach, this highly regarded 10-room B&B bills itself a "European sanctuary." Outside, the gabled roof, climbing ivy, and expansive gardens let guests know they have entered the inn's rarified world, as do the interior's warm colors, creamy soft linens, private decks and fireplaces, pre-breakfast coffee-and-newspaper room service, and complimentary wine stocked in the mini fridge.

In the neighboring community of Montara, the **Goose and Turrets** (835 George St., Montara, 650/728-5451, http://goose.montara.com, $175-230) is a local getaway favorite. A rambling old building houses the inn; inside, decor runs to the eclectic. The Clipper Room is perfect for aviation buffs, and guests who like their space will love the sweeping expanse of hardwood floor in the Hummingbird Room.

The **Point Montara Lighthouse Hostel** (16th St. and Hwy. 1, Montara, 650/728-7177, www.norcalhostels.org, dorm $27, private room $78, nonmembers add $3 per night) offers great views for a low price. Stay in the shared dorm rooms (either coed or gender-specific), each with 3-6 beds, or spring for a private room. Enjoy use of the shared kitchen, common areas with wood-burning fireplaces, the eclectic garden perched on the cliff, and the private cove beach. Other amenities include Wi-Fi, laundry facilities, an espresso bar, and complimentary linens.

Food

As many people come to the **Moss Beach Distillery** (140 Beach Way, Moss Beach, 650/728-5595, www.mossbeachdistillery.com, noon-8:30pm Mon.-Thurs., noon-9pm Fri.-Sat., 11am-8:30pm Sun., $13-38) for the ghost stories as for the hearty food and terrific ocean views. The restaurant operated as a speakeasy during Prohibition. The restaurant offers a cross between traditional American food and California cuisine. Portions are large, and service is friendly (if slow during peak times). To soak up the old-school speakeasy atmosphere, sit in the bar. Or on the terrace, stare out over the ocean, where plenty of blankets are on hand to ward off the Pacific chill as the sun goes down.

To pack a picnic lunch before you head out to the Fitzgerald Marine Reserve or Montara State Beach, swing by **Gherkin's Sandwich Shop** (171 8th St., Montara, 650/728-2211, 7am-7pm daily, $10). You'll find oddities like the Ooey Gooey, with peanut butter, Nutella, and marshmallows, and hallowed favorites like the BLT, burgers, and pastrami and swiss. Sides include garlic fries and macaroni salad. The sandwiches are huge and can easily be split between two people.

La Costanera (8150 Cabrillo Hwy., Montara, 888/294-0679, www.lacostanerarestaurant.com, 5pm-9pm Tues.-Thurs. and Sun., 5pm-10pm Fri.-Sat., $21-39), poised above Montara Beach, is about more than the view. Skillfully designed with grand sloping picture windows and sunken dining rooms, La Costanera is a sophisticated Peruvian restaurant and the only eatery on this part of the coast to earn a Michelin star three years in a row. There are a variety of ceviche options to choose from as well as slow-cooked pork shoulder and lobster. The bar menu offers hearty plates that could serve as a light dinner.

Transportation

Moss Beach is 23 miles south of San Francisco on Highway 1 (Cabrillo Hwy.). From San Francisco, the easiest and most direct route is to follow Highway 1 south all the way to Moss Beach. From I-280 on the peninsula, take Highway 92 west to Half Moon Bay and Highway 1. From Half Moon Bay, Moss Beach is seven miles north on Highway 1.

HALF MOON BAY

To this day, the coastal city of Half Moon Bay retains its character as an "ag" (agricultural) town. The locals all know each other, even though the majority of residents commute "over the hill" to peninsula- and Silicon Valley-based jobs. Strawberries, artichokes, and Brussels sprouts are the biggest crops, along with flowers, pumpkins, and Christmas trees, making the coast a destination for holiday festivities. Half Moon Bay enjoys a beautiful natural setting and earns significant income from tourism, especially during the world-famous Pumpkin Festival each October.

Four miles north are Pillar Point Harbor and the neighboring town of **Princeton-by-the-Sea,** the other workhorse on the coast. Here, anglers haul in crab, salmon, and herring, and local businesses cater to their needs. This is the place to rent kayaks, go on a chartered fishing trip, and buy fresh fish, sometimes straight off the boat (especially during crab season).

Beaches

The beaches of Half Moon Bay draw visitors from over the hill and farther afield all year long. As with most of the North Pacific region, summer can be a chilly, foggy time on the beaches. For the best beach weather, plan your Half Moon Bay trip for September-October. **Half Moon Bay State Beach** (www.parks.ca.gov, 650/726-8819, parking $10 per day) actually encompasses three discrete beaches stretching four miles down the coast, each with its own access point and parking lot.

beach at Half Moon Bay

A Festival of Pumpkins

The biggest annual event in this small agricultural town is the **Half Moon Bay Art & Pumpkin Festival** (www.miramarevents.com). Every October, nearly 250,000 people trek to Half Moon Bay to pay homage to the big orange squash. The festival includes live music, food, artists' booths, contests, activities for kids, an adults' lounge area, and a parade. Perhaps the best-publicized event is the pumpkin weigh-off, which takes place before the festivities begin. Farmers bring their tremendous squash in on flatbed trucks from all over the country to determine which is the biggest of all. The winner gets paid per pound, a significant prize when the biggest pumpkins weigh over 1,000 pounds.

Francis Beach (95 Kelly Ave.) has the most developed amenities, including a good-size campground with grassy areas to pitch tents and enjoy picnics, a visitors center, and indoor hot showers. **Venice Beach** (Venice Blvd., off Hwy. 1) offers outdoor showers and flush toilets. **Dunes Beach** (Young Ave., off Hwy. 1) is the northernmost major beach in the chain and the least developed.

Perhaps the most famous beach in the area is one that has no name. At the end of West Point Avenue in Princeton is the Pillar Point Marsh and a long stretch of beach that wraps around the edge of the point. This beach is the launch pad for surfers paddling out to tackle the infamous **Mavericks Break** (Pillar Point Marsh parking lot, past Pillar Point Harbor). Formed by unique underwater topography, the giant waves are the site of the legendary **Mavericks Surf Contest.** The competition is always held in winter, when the swells reach their peak, and left until the last minute to ensure that they are the biggest of the year. When perfect conditions present themselves, the best surfers in the world are given 48 hours' notice to make it to Mavericks to compete. Due to safety and environmental concerns, access to the beach and the cliffs above are closed during the competition. As of the time of research, organizers hadn't yet settled on a way to provide viewing access to spectators. Locals recommend watching the competition via live feed in one of the nearby bars or restaurants. Mavericks is not a beginner's break, especially in winter, and the giant breakers can be deadly.

Sports and Recreation

There are plenty of great trails around Half Moon Bay. A local favorite is **Purisima Creek Redwoods** (4.4 miles up Higgins Canyon Rd., 650/691-1200, www.openspace.org). There are a multitude of trails in this nearly 5,000-acre preserve, and many ascend to Skyline Boulevard for an elevation gain of 1,700 feet. You can take a leisurely stroll through the redwoods, complete with dripping ferns, flowering dogwood and wood sorrel, along **Purisima Creek Trail** (3.9 miles, easy-strenuous), until it turns steep and eventually takes you to its literally breathtaking Skyline terminus. If you don't want to crest the ridge of the Santa Cruz Mountains, you can opt for **Harkins Ridge Trail** (6 miles, moderate), which rises out of the canyon shortly past the trailhead. You'll hike through redwoods, then oaks and chaparral as you gain 800 feet in elevation over 2.5 miles. To make a loop, cut down **Craig Britton Trail,** which meets **Purisima Creek Trail.** To feel like you've conquered a mountain, make the climb to 2,102-foot **Bald Knob** (9.6 miles, strenuous) via the **Purisima Creek Trail, Borden Hatch Mill Trail,** and the **Bald Knob Trail.** You will be rewarded with terrific coastal views.

Fortunately for mountain bikers, nearly all the trails in the preserve are open to cyclists. As you can imagine, the trails are steep and knotted with rocks and trees roots, which makes for an exhausting, exhilarating, or terrifying ride, depending on your experience and attitude.

The most popular trail in Half Moon Bay is the **Coastside Trail** (www.parks.ca.gov). Extending five miles from Miramar Beach to Poplar Beach, this flat paved trail follows the coast and is filled with joggers, dog walkers, and bikes. There are a multitude of beach-access points along the way, and if you want to go downtown, jump off at Kelly Avenue and take it across Highway 1 to the heart of Half Moon Bay. Beyond the Poplar Beach parking lot, the trail crosses a wooden bridge and turns into a dirt trail. This area is known as the **Wavecrest Open Space** and goes all the way down to the Ritz Carlton. It is much less traveled than the paved Coastside Trail and is a great place to spot herons, egrets, and gray whales off the coast during their spring migration. Parking is plentiful at Poplar Beach ($2 per hour), at the end of Poplar Street on the south end of town.

For a sedate ocean adventure, book a spot on board the ***Queen of Hearts*** (Pillar Point Harbor, 510/581-2628, www.fishingboat.com). Depending on the time of year, you can select from whale-watching trips (Jan.-Apr., $40), deep-sea salmon fishing (Apr.-Nov., $98), shallow-water rock fishing (May-Dec., $68-82), Farallon Island rock fishing (call for season, $95), and deep-sea albacore fishing (July-Oct., call for rates). One of the coolest ways to see the coast is from the deck of a sea kayak. Many kayak tours with the **Half Moon Bay Kayaking Company** (2 Johnson Pier, 650/773-6101, www.hmbkayak.com) require no previous kayaking experience. For an easy first paddle, try the Pillar Point tour ($75), the full-moon tour ($80), or the sunset paddle ($75); all tours are roughly three hours. Rental kayaks are also available ($25-60 per hour) as are stand-up paddleboards ($25 per hour). The price of the rental includes a wetsuit, life jacket, and some basic instruction. **Sea Horse and Friendly Acres Ranches** (1828 Hwy. 1, 650/726-9903, www.seahorseranch.org, from 8am daily) offers one-hour ($60), 90-minute ($70), and two-hour guided tours ($80) that take you along the cliffs and down onto the sands at Half Moon Bay's state beaches. Children over the age of five are welcome, as are riders of all ability levels. The horses here are sedate rental nags who know the routes in their sleep, allowing riders to sit back and enjoy the stunning views and the company of fellow riders.

Accommodations

Half Moon Bay offers several lovely bed-and-breakfasts and one luxury resort hotel.

The **Ritz-Carlton Half Moon Bay** (1 Miramontes Point Rd., 650/712-7000, www.ritzcarlton.com, $500) resembles a castle looming over the ocean. The Ritz-Carlton has a top-tier restaurant, Navio; a world-class day spa; and posh rooms that are worth the rates. If you can, get a room facing the ocean. While you're here, enjoy free access to the spa's bathing rooms, an outdoor hot tub overlooking the ocean, tennis courts, and the basketball court. Golf at the Ritz is second to none in the Bay Area.

For a personal lodging experience, try the ★ **Old Thyme Inn** (779 Main St., 650/726-1616, www.oldthymeinn.com, $159-349), located downtown. Each uniquely decorated room has its own garden theme and luxurious amenities. Downstairs, guests can enjoy the common sitting rooms and the gorgeous garden. Each morning the owners serve up a sumptuous breakfast.

Built out of weathered redwood, the **Cypress Inn** (407 Mirada Rd., 650/726-6002, www.cypressinn.com, $229-459) is a neat compound where most of the rooms come with fireplaces, private decks, jetted tubs, and fridges. Adding to the luxury are a full-service breakfast and a cocktail hour offered in the Main House. The inn is an easy bike ride to downtown Half Moon Bay or a pleasant stroll to many beaches and the modest mix of galleries, restaurants, and cafés in the Miramar area.

Food

The quality of food in Half Moon Bay is superb. Open since 1987, ★ **Pasta Moon** (315 Main St., 650/726-5125, www.pastamoon.

com, 11:30am-2pm, 5:30pm-9pm Mon.-Thurs., 11:30am-2pm, 5:30pm-9:30pm Fri., noon-3pm, 5:30pm-9:30pm Sat., noon-3pm, 5:30pm-9pm Sun., $17-26) is the godmother of fine dining. While managing to be both casual and upscale at once, Pasta Moon serves updated Italian cuisine with an emphasis on fresh, light dishes. Their wood-fired pizzas are particularly good and affordable, as are any of the pasta dishes, made with house-made noodles. You can choose to sit in the elegant dining room, with a view of the creek below or at the bar and lounge, which hums with live jazz, offering a more urbane evening out.

It may not look like much, but the **Flying Fish Grill** (Hwy. 92, 650/712-1125, www.flyingfishgrill.net, 11am-8:30pm Wed.-Mon., $7-17) has some of the best fish tacos in the Bay Area. The grilled mahimahi with sweet mango salsa will make anyone swoon. Other hits are the crabby-cheesy bread, the delicate fish-and-chips, and the bright ceviche with chunks of avocado. The restaurant has a funky tropical ambience aided by a full bar pouring cocktails well matched to the food. It's a great way to wait out the late afternoon traffic of beachgoers heading back over the hill.

For seafood with atmosphere, come to **Sam's Chowder House** (4210 N. Cabrillo Hwy., Pillar Point Harbor, 650/712-0245, www.samschowderhouse.com, 11:30am-9pm Mon.-Thurs., 11:30am-9:30pm Fri., 11-9:30am Sat., 11am-9pm Sun., $12-35). The perpetually full parking lot out front points to Sam's golden touch. Inside, you can get everything from a stiff drink at the bar to light appetizers and champagne on the deck, steaming plates of whole lobster, seafood paella, and seared tuna served in the ample yet cozy dining room. Sam's is also known for its kid-friendly vibe and its $1 oyster nights.

When all you need is a quick bite or a casual lunch, the **Moonside Bakery & Cafe** (604 Main St., 650/726-9070, www.moonsidebakery.com, 7am-5pm daily) can fix you up. Stop in the morning for breakfast pastries and espresso. In the afternoon, expect sandwiches and hand-fired pizzas.

Information and Services

Visit the **Half Moon Bay Coastside Chamber of Commerce & Visitors' Bureau** (235 Main St., 650/726-8380, www.halfmoonbaychamber.org, 9am-5pm Mon.-Fri., 10am-3pm Sat.-Sun.), in the red house just after you turn on Main Street from Highway 92. Here you can find maps, brochures, and a schedule of events.

The only 24-hour emergency room on the coast between Daly City and Santa Cruz is at the **Seton Coastside Hospital** (600 Marine Blvd., Moss Beach, 650/563-7100, www.setoncoastside.org). For less serious health services, the **Coastside Clinic** (Shoreline Station, Suite 100A, 225 S. Hwy. 1, Half Moon Bay, 650/573-3941, www.sanmateomedicalcenter.org) is located just north of the intersection of Kelly Avenue and Highway 1.

Transportation

Half Moon Bay is on Highway 1 about 45 minutes south of San Francisco. From San Francisco, take I-280 south to Highway 92 west to Half Moon Bay and Highway 1. You can also take the scenic route by following Highway 1 directly south from San Francisco.

Parking in downtown Half Moon Bay is usually easy—except if you're in town during the Pumpkin Festival. Your best bet is to stay in town with your car safely stowed in a hotel parking lot before the festival.

PESCADERO

Pescadero is a tiny dot on the coastline, south of Half Moon Bay and well north of Santa Cruz, with one main street, one side street, and several smallish farms. Despite its tiny size, many Bay Area denizens visit Pescadero for the twisty roads that challenge motorcyclists and bicyclists, fresh produce, and the legendary Duarte's Tavern.

Pescadero State Beach

Pescadero State Beach (Hwy. 1, north of Pescadero Rd., 650/879-2170, www.parks.ca.gov, 8am-sunset daily) is the closest beach to the town of Pescadero. It's a great spot to walk in the sand and stare out at the Pacific, but near-constant winds make it less than ideal for picnics or sunbathing. It does have some facilities, including public restrooms.

Bird lovers flock to **Pescadero Marsh Natural Preserve** (Hwy. 1, www.smcnha.org), located on Highway 1 right across the highway from Pescadero State Beach. This protected wetland, part of Pescadero State Beach, is home to a variety of avian species, including great blue herons, snowy egrets, and northern harriers. For the best birding, visit the marsh early in the morning or in late fall or early spring, when migration is in full swing.

San Gregorio State Beach

North of Pescadero, at the intersection of Highway 84 and Highway 1, **San Gregorio State Beach** (650/726-8819, www.parks.ca.gov, 8am-sunset daily, $10) stretches farther than it seems. Once you're walking toward the ocean, the small-seeming cove stretches out beyond the cliffs to create a beach perfect for contemplative strolling. San Gregorio is clothing optional at the far north end and a local favorite in the summer, despite the regular appearance of thick, chilly fog over the sand. Brave beachgoers can even swim and bodysurf here, though you'll quickly get cold if you do so without a wetsuit. Picnic tables and restrooms cluster near the parking lot, but picnicking can be hampered by the wind.

★ San Gregorio General Store

San Gregorio is a tiny picturesque town of rolling rangeland, neat patches of colorful crops, and century-old homes, including a one-room schoolhouse and an old brothel. Its beating heart is the **San Gregorio General Store** (Hwy. 84 and Stage Rd., 650/726-0565, www.sangregoriostore.com, 10:30am-6pm Mon.-Thurs., 10:30am-7pm Fri., 10am-7pm Sat., 10am-6pm Sun.). Open since 1889, the store has an eclectic book section and a variety of cast-iron cookery, oil lamps, and raccoon traps. In the back of the store are coolers stocked with beverages and deli sandwiches made in the back kitchen. The real centerpiece is the bar, serving beer, wine, and spirits to ranchers and farmers out for a coffee break or just getting off work. On weekends the store is packed with out-of-towners, and live music keeps things moving. The deep picture windows out front make for a comfy place to watch the afternoon pass by.

driftwood structures on San Gregorio State Beach

Pigeon Point Lighthouse

South of Pescadero is **Pigeon Point Lighthouse** (210 Pigeon Point Rd., at Hwy. 1, 650/879-2120, www.parks.ca.gov, 8am-sunset daily). First lit in 1872, Pigeon Point is one of the most photographed lighthouses in the United States. Sadly, the lighthouse is in a state of disrepair, and past earthquakes have made climbing to the top unsafe. Yet the monument stands, its hostel still shelters travelers, and visitors still marvel at the incomparable views from the point. In winter, look for migrating whales from the rocks beyond the tower.

★ Año Nuevo State Park

Año Nuevo State Park (Hwy. 1, south of Pescadero, 650/879-2025, reservations 800/444-4445, www.parks.ca.gov, 8am-sunset daily, $10 per car) is world-famous as the winter home and breeding ground of once-endangered elephant seals. The reserve also has extensive dunes, marshland, and excellent bird habitat. The beaches and wilderness are open year-round. The elephant seals start showing up in late November and stay to breed, birth pups, and loll on the beach until early March. Visitors are not allowed down to the elephant seal habitats on their own and must sign up for a guided walking tour. Once you see two giant males crashing into one another in a fight for dominance, you won't want to get too close. Book your tour at least a day or two in advance since the seals are popular with both locals and travelers.

Accommodations

Pescadero has a small but surprisingly good array of lodging options.

If budget is a factor, try the **Pigeon Point Hostel** (210 Pigeon Point Rd., at Hwy. 1, 650/879-0633, http://norcalhostels.org/pigeon, dorm $26-28, private room $76). This Hostelling International spot has simple but comfortable accommodations, both private and dorm-style. Amenities include three kitchens, free Wi-Fi, and beach access. But the best amenity of all is the cliff-top hot tub.

At **Costanoa Lodge and Campground** (2001 Rossi Rd., at Hwy. 1, 650/879-1100, www.costanoa.com, campsite $31-45, rooms $80-245), pitch a tent in the campground or rent a whirlpool suite in the lodge. Other lodging options include log-style cabins with shared baths, small tent cabins with shared baths, and private rooms. Nature programs seek to educate visitors about the ecology of

two female elephant seals at Año Nuevo State Park

the coast. A small general store offers s'mores fixings and souvenirs while "comfort stations" provide outdoor fireplaces, private indoor-outdoor showers, baths with heated floors, and saunas that are open 24 hours to all guests.

For a truly Pescadero experience, book a room at the **Pescadero Creek Inn Bed & Breakfast** (393 Stage Rd., 650/879-1898, www.pescaderocreekinn.com, $150-185), an easy walk from Duarte's, the grocery stores, and the creek. The house isn't soundproof, but the rooms have high ceilings and are prettily appointed.

Camping

Most of the camping in Pescadero is inland, deep in the redwoods. **Butano State Park** (1500 Cloverdale Rd., Pescadero, 650/879-2040, reservations 800/444-7275, www.parks.ca.gov, Apr.-Nov., $35) offers 21 drive-in and 18 walk-in campsites. Although there are no showers, there are clean restrooms, fire pits, and drinking water. Perhaps the best amenity is the fantastic hiking in the park. There are quiet strolls through the canopy of redwoods or more athletic treks up dusty ridgelines. The most scenic is the **Butano Fire Road** that summits at an abandoned airstrip.

Farther inland, past the tiny town of Loma Mar, is **Memorial Park** (9500 Pescadero Creek Rd., 650/879-0238, www.co.sanmateo.ca.us, year-round, $30), with 158 campsites. Each site, which accommodates up to eight people, has a fire pit, picnic tables, and a metal locker to store food and sundries. There is also drinking water, baths with coin-operated showers, and a general store within the park that sells firewood, hot dog buns, ice cream, and soap. Despite having fewer hiking trails than at Butano, Memorial boasts an amphitheater and swimming holes.

Food

Once you walk through the doors of ★ **Duarte's Tavern** (202 Stage Rd., Pescadero, 650/879-0464, www.duartestavern.com, 7am-8pm daily, $15-28), you'll see why the restaurant has been honored with the James Beard Foundation's America's Classics award. The rambling building features sloping floors and dark wooden walls. Almost everybody in the Bay Area has been to Duarte's for a bowl of artichoke soup or a slice of olallieberry pie, but it is really the atmosphere that is the biggest draw. Here, locals of all stripes—farmers, farmhands, ranchers, and park rangers—sit shoulder to shoulder with travelers from "over the hill," sharing conversation and a bite to eat. The greatest assets are the outdated jukebox and excellent Bloody Marys, garnished with a pickled green bean.

The other Pescadero must-eat is inside the gas station across the street. **Mercado & Taqueria De Amigos** (1999 Pescadero Creek Rd., 650/879-0232, 9am-9pm daily, $7-12) has been written up by the *New York Times* and is rumored to be the best taqueria between San Francisco and Santa Cruz. Not that you can detect any of that notoriety inside. Squeezed in next to coolers of beer and energy drinks, the open kitchen prepares excellent shrimp burritos, *al pastor* tacos, and not-too sweet *horchata*. You'll find mainly locals here, most speaking Spanish, and the wait can be long. But the chips are free and salsa delicious. Cash only.

Transportation

Pescadero is 17 miles south of Half Moon Bay. At Pescadero State Beach, Highway 1 intersects Pescadero Road. Turn east on Pescadero Road and drive two miles to the stop sign (the only one in town). Turn left onto Stage Road to find the main drag. Parking is free and generally easy to find on Stage Road or in the Duarte's parking lot. On weekends, you might need to park down the road a ways.

WOODSIDE

Woodside, set among bucolic grasslands and oak groves, has been a moneyed area since its inception as a private club retreat at the turn of the 20th century, but it boomed with the dot-com millionaires of the 1990s. Huge mansions replaced more modest abodes, many of which can be seen through low fences in Woodside proper. The serene scenery, good food, and hiking and cycling options are the draw for visitors.

★ Filoli

Built in 1917, **Filoli** (86 Cañada Rd., Woodside, 650/364-8300, www.filoli.org, 10am-3:30pm Tues.-Sat., 11am-3:30pm Sun. June-Oct., adults $20, seniors $17, children 5-17 $10, 4 and under free, admission $2 lower June-Oct.) was the country manor of William Bowers Bourn II, one of San Francisco's richest people at the time. It is now owned by the National Trust for Historic Preservation and Filoli Center. Designed by Willis Polk in the modified Gregorian style, the house includes 17th- and 18th-century antiques, and many of the rooms reflect the truly rarefied world of the very wealthy.

The gardens are what Filoli is best known for. Of its nearly 700 acres, 16 acres are carefully cultivated plots that form the Formal Garden, which celebrates American horticultural style and botanical diversity. There are the manicured West Terraces, while botanists and epicureans marvel at the Gentleman's Orchard, which boasts the largest private collection of heirloom fruit in the United States. There is also the olive orchard, bonsai collection, camellia and citrus collection, and native plant garden. For the price of admission, you can wander the grounds on your own or join a docent-led tour. Some are a leisurely and informative stroll around the house and the gardens. Others take guests on robust orchard and nature hikes, many of which reach deep into Filoli's wilder corners.

Sports and Recreation

The official sport of Woodside is road cycling. There are no easy roads to bike in Woodside proper, except maybe Mountain Home and Whiskey Hill roads, but both have appreciable hills. True biking enthusiasts instead opt for the most perilous roads to peddle: Old La Honda, Alpine, King's Mountain, and Bear Gulch Roads. All are narrow, curvy, and sharply ascend through oaks and redwoods up to Highway 35. Many riders then come back

Filoli's Sunken Garden

down Highway 84, where they can cruise at the speed of traffic; it's a heart-stopping sight, so drivers beware.

Crystal Springs Trail (Canada Rd. at Raymundo Dr., 650/573-2592, http://parks.smcgov.org, 15 miles, easy), on the other hand, is the perfect fit for novice cyclists and those looking for a mellow afternoon bike ride. The trail starts in Woodside and follows Cañada Road past Filoli and the Pulgas Water Temple to the Crystal Springs Reservoir, where it skirts its eastern edge. Although the paved two-lane trail does not circumvent the reservoir, you can continue on to San Andreas Lake and ride alongside it to the lake's terminus in San Bruno. There are some gaps in the trail, meaning you have to jump onto Cañada Road or Skyline Boulevard, but thankfully both have wide bike lanes.

There are a number of open-space preserves in the Woodside area, but the most accessible, user-friendly, and diverse is **Huddart Park** (1100 Kings Mountain Rd., Woodside, 650/851-1210, www.smcgov.org). Crystal Springs Trail (9 miles, strenuous) starts at the eastern end of the park and zigzags its way west. To reach Skyline Boulevard, you can turn on either Richards Road or Summit Springs trails. The latter is longer, but it joins **Purisima Creek Trail** to descend down the western side of the mountains. Despite the 1,200-foot elevation gain, Crystal Springs Trail is wide, evenly graded, and a pleasant but invigorating hike. You certainly don't have to go all the way to Skyline Boulevard. For a shorter loop (4.5 miles, moderate), turn onto Dean Trail after 2.5 miles. The trail drops across McGarvey Gulch and hugs King's Mountain Road, but the heavily wooded trail is lovely despite the traffic noise. For those who simply want a taste of the outdoors, Huddart Park's 900 acres have a number of picnic areas, including covered spots, as well as a playground, group campsites, an archery range, and Chickadee Nature Trail (0.5 mile, easy), which crisscrosses a seasonal gorge.

Food

★ **Alice's Restaurant** (Hwy. 84 and Hwy. 35, 650/851-0303, www.alicesrestaurant.com, 8am-9pm daily, $10) has more than a whiff of counterculture to it. Located on Skyline Boulevard in the redwoods that were once home to Ken Kesey and the Merry Pranksters, it is still a hangout for bikers and locals. The menu features 20 different burgers, garlic fries, quesadillas, prime-rib sandwiches, and a slew of draft beers. The portions are big, and the outside deck is a favorite Bay Area spot on sunny weekend afternoons.

Opened in 1954, **The Village Pub** (2967 Woodside Rd., 650/851-9888, http://thevillagepub.net, 11:30am-2:30pm, 5pm-10pm Mon.-Fri., 5pm-10pm Sat., 10am-2pm, 5pm-10pm Sun., $28-39) is a longtime institution reinvented as a Michelin-starred restaurant. The inside carries a country-estate elegance, and the French-Mediterranean cuisine is based on the restaurant's partnership with a local farm. The pub menu (11:30am-10pm Mon.-Fri.) offers budget options.

The best place to stock up on picnic supplies is at **Robert's Market** (3015 Woodside Rd., 650/851-1511, www.robertsmarket.com, 6:30am-8pm daily), which boasts one of the best delis on the peninsula. There are also plenty of premade salads, along with grilled and marinated vegetables. Across the street, the **Woodside Bakery and Café** (3052 Woodside Rd., 650/851-7247, http://woodsidebakery.com, 6am-9pm daily, $15) is another Woodside institution and a great place to pick up pies, pastries, and pizzas. It also serves breakfast and lunch, along with an incongruously fancy dinner.

Transportation

Woodside is along Highway 84 between Highway 35 (Skyline Blvd.) and I-280. From San Francisco, take I-280 for 30 miles south to Highway 84 (Woodside Rd.) west. From the coast, take Highway 1 south to San Gregorio, about 14 miles south of Half Moon Bay. Turn onto Highway 84 east and follow it all the way to Woodside.

PALO ALTO

Palo Alto owes much of its prosperity and character to neighboring Stanford University. In the 1990s Palo Alto became a center for venture capitalists funding the emerging dot-com companies. Today Stanford retains its role as an incubator for some of Silicon Valley's great talents and entrepreneurs.

Stanford University

Stanford University (end of University Ave., Stanford, 650/723-2560, www.stanford.edu) is one of the top universities in the world, and fewer than 10 percent of the high school students who apply each year are accepted. The **visitors center** (295 Galvez St., www.stanford.edu, 8:30am-5pm Mon.-Fri., 10am-5pm Sat.-Sun.) is in a handsome one-story brick building; inside, well-trained staff can help you with campus maps and tours. Definitely download or procure a map of campus before getting started on your explorations, as Stanford is infamously hard for newcomers to navigate.

For a taste of the beauty that surrounds the students on a daily basis, begin your tour with **The Quad** (Oval at Palm Dr.) and **Memorial Church.** Located at the center of campus, these architectural gems are still in active use. Classes are held in the quad every day, and services take place in the church each Sunday. Almost next door to the Quad is **Hoover Tower** (650/723-2053, 10am-4pm daily, $2), the tall tower that's visible from up to 30 miles away. For great views of the Bay Area, head up to its observation platform.

On the other side of the Quad, just past the Oval, is the **Cantor Arts Center** (328 Lomita Dr. at Museum Way, 650/723-4177, www.museum.stanford.edu, 11am-5pm Wed.-Sun., 11am-8pm Thurs.). This free art museum features both permanent collections of classic paintings and sculpture donated by the Cantors and other philanthropists, along with traveling exhibitions. One of the center's highlights is the **Rodin Sculpture Garden,** pieces cast in France from Rodin's originals that include *The Burghers of Calais* and *The Gates of Hell.* The most famous member of this collection, *The Thinker,* can be found in the Susan and John Diekman Gallery inside the museum.

The second monument to science stretches for a full mile across Stanford land into the hills. The **Stanford Linear Accelerator Center** (SLAC, 2575 Sand Hill Rd., Menlo Park, 650/926-3300, www.slac.stanford.edu) is one of only a few research facilities of its

Stanford University

kind in the world. Here atoms are launched at one end of the building and reach high speeds before smashing into a barrier at the other end. Stanford researchers study the smashed pieces, increasing knowledge about the subatomic world. The work at SLAC is serious, and so is visiting. Unscheduled guests are promptly turned away at the gate. The only way to enter the facility is with an official tour, and unfortunately, as of this printing, those have been suspended. However, before your trip, check the website for any visitor updates.

Entertainment and Events

For a taste of local entertainment listings, check out the ***Daily Post*** (www.padailypost.com) or the ***Palo Alto Weekly*** (www.paloaltoonline.com), the older of the two and known for producing more in-depth features.

Palo Alto enjoys a vibrant entertainment scene. **Stanford Live** (650/724-2464, http://livelyarts.stanford.edu, prices and locations vary) puts on an array of concerts and live staged entertainment each season. Expect to see several jazz ensembles each year, some world music, a world premiere or two, and perhaps an unusual dance piece.

Many students and longtime residents of Palo Alto enjoy seeing classic black-and-white movies back up on the big screen where they belong. Old-school movie house **The Stanford Theatre** (221 University Ave., 650/324-3700, www.stanfordtheatre.org, $7) has plush red velvet seats, beautifully painted walls and ceiling, a Mighty Wurlitzer organ that plays before the evening show, and a year-round schedule of fabulous old films. The Stanford Theatre often hosts festivals to highlight a specific star or genre.

Shopping

Once populated by bookstores and boutiques, **University Avenue** is now dominated by restaurants of all stripes. For serious shopping, head across El Camino to the open-air **Stanford Shopping Center** (Sand Hill Rd. and El Camino Real, www.stanfordshop.com, 10am-9pm Mon.-Fri., 10am-7pm Sat., 11am-6pm Sun.), with upscale boutiques and top-tier department stores befitting the affluence of the area. Anchor stores include Bloomingdale's, Nordstrom, Macy's, and Neiman Marcus.

Sports and Recreation

Stanford University (www.gostanford.com) enjoys a reputation for athletics almost as great as its rep for academics. The women's basketball program is legendary, as is the men's baseball team. The golf team boasts Tiger Woods as an alumnus, and more than a few Olympians have swum in the pools and run on the tracks. Every fall, the Cardinals paint the town red as they strive to defeat Cal in "the Big Game."

After a long day of exploring the Stanford campus, a dip in the hot tub followed by a luxurious spa treatment makes the perfect end to the day. **Watercourse Way** (165 Channing Ave., 650/462-2000, www.watercourseway.com, 8:20am-11:30pm Sun.-Thurs., 8:20am-12:30am Fri.-Sat., hot tub rooms $20-30/hour, treatments $100-160) enjoys the title of the Silicon Valley's premier day spa. It stands out for its amazing tiled tub rooms, range of treatments, and array of top-tier products. Each rentable hot-tub room boasts unique and serene decor. The spa treatments are reasonably priced, and the pampering is second to none.

Accommodations

Cheap lodgings near Palo Alto can be found in the serene farm setting of **Hidden Villa Hostel** (26870 Moody Rd., Lost Altos Hills, 650/949-8648, www.hiddenvilla.org, Sept.-May, $27-60). Sustainably constructed, and with a private cabin that's perfect for families and romantic honeymooners, the hostel also provides access to hiking trails, the surrounding organic farm, and the small wealthy town of Los Altos Hills. Hidden Villa is the oldest operating youth hostel in the United States, and it's incredibly popular. The buildings are unique and attractive, created to showcase features such as the radiant floor heating and bale wall construction. Reservations are required on weekends and a good idea even on weekdays.

Down on El Camino Real, **Dinah's Garden Hotel** (4261 El Camino Real, 650/493-2844 or 800/227-8220, www.dinahshotel.com, $119-169) doesn't quite feel like a chain despite its location and basic shape. The cute koi ponds and gardens mix with the bright floral interior decor to create a tropical paradise theme. The basic rooms are the size and shape of a motel, but the high-priced suites are something to behold. Attached to the hotel are both a casual poolside grill and an upscale seafood restaurant with a decidedly Japanese bent. The **Creekside Inn** (3400 El Camino Real, 650/493-2411, www.creekside-inn.com, $115-250) provides garden accommodations set back a bit from the noisy road. The rooms are more upscale than many motels, with stylish fabrics and up-to-date amenities. This larger boutique hotel has more than 100 rooms, an outdoor heated pool, and an exercise room. All rooms have free Wi-Fi, fully stocked private baths, refrigerators, coffeemakers, in-room safes, and comfy bathrobes. You can get a package deal that includes breakfast with your room.

Much closer to the Stanford campus, the **Stanford Terrace Inn** (531 Stanford Ave., 650/857-0333, www.stanfordterraceinn.com, $259-309) provides appropriate luxury to visiting parents. The Terrace has eco-conscious rooms with all hypoallergenic and sustainable furnishings, linens, and toiletries. All rooms, even the standard ones, are huge and come with attractive furnishings and luxury amenities. There is even an outdoor heated saltwater pool.

Food

Palo Alto has a ton of restaurants. University Avenue feels a bit like a double-sided food court with every imaginable cuisine, fancy and casual, catering to starving students and wealthy venture capitalists alike. The downside of this abundance is the high turnover rate. The best Palo Alto restaurants have gone through the booms and busts, and though not the hippest, they certainly reward with an old-school peninsula experience.

For a cup of coffee, the place to go is the **Prolific Oven** (550 Waverly St., 650/326-8485, www.prolificoven.com, 7am-7pm Mon., 7am-10pm Tues.-Thurs., 7am-11pm Fri.-Sat., $4-10). Since 1980, the Prolific Oven has been making the best cakes around. It's impossible to pass by the glass case filled with cakes, cookies, and pastries without getting something. The Prolific Oven is at its best late in the evening. Sit in the unfussy café, surrounded by erudite locals discussing big and small ideas over a perfect slice of cake.

The **Rose and Crown** (457 Emerson Ave., 650/327-7673, www.roseandcrownpa.com, kitchen 11:30am-2pm, 6pm-9pm Mon.-Fri., 11:30am-9pm Sat.-Sun., $8-14) is a pub in every sense of the word, with a serious selection of beer and a menu of British food (including the to-die-for Stilton burger). The Rose and Crown is cozy, dark, and cluttered, perfect to while away an afternoon over a pitcher of beer or catch a soccer game with some noisy fans.

The kitschy decor at the **Palo Alto Creamery** (566 Emerson St., 650/323-3131, www.paloaltocreamery.com, 7am-10pm Mon.-Wed., 7am-11pm Thurs., 7am-midnight Fri., 8am-midnight Sat., 8am-10pm Sun., $8-20) feels like a genuine 1950s soda shop. Red vinyl, a black-and-white checked floor, and funky booths help complete the picture. The food runs to American classics, but what patrons really come for is the house-made ice cream. The Creamery gets crowded, especially on weekends. Late night begets locals looking for an after-show meal.

Information and Services

Inside the **Palo Alto Visitors Center** (355 Alma St., 650/324-3121, www.destinationpaloalto.com, 9am-5pm Mon.-Fri.) you'll find plenty of helpful tips on local sights, restaurants, and events. Grab a couple of maps of Stanford University.

Should an accident or illness befall you, you couldn't be in a better place. The nearest 24-hour emergency room is **Stanford University Hospital** (900 Quarry Rd., 650/723-5111, http://stanfordhospital.org), and for nonlife-threatening emergencies visit the **Palo Alto Medical Foundation Urgent Care Center** (795 El Camino Real, 650/321-4121, www.pamf.org, 7am-9pm daily).

Transportation

Palo Alto is easily accessed via U.S. 101 and I-280 and is equidistant between **Mineta San José International Airport** (SJC, 1701 Airport Blvd., 408/392-3600, www.flysanjose.com) and **San Francisco International Airport** (SFO, 800/435-9736, www.flysfo.com). **Caltrain** (95 University Ave., 800/660-4287, www.caltrain.com, $3.25-13.25) can get you here as well; the commuter rail line runs from Gilroy to San Francisco with a hub in San Jose.

SAN JOSE

Sprawled across the south end of Silicon Valley, San Jose proudly claims the title of biggest city in the Bay Area. It is the beating heart of the valley's high-tech industry and is home to eBay, Cisco, Adobe, IBM, and many others. Long considered a cultural wasteland, in the last decade San Jose has worked to change its image, supporting local art and attracting high-end restaurants.

Sights

SAN JOSE MUSEUM OF ART

The highly regarded **San Jose Museum of Art** (110 S. Market St., 408/271-6840, www.sjmusart.org, 11am-5pm Tues.-Sun., adults $8, students and seniors $5, under age 6 free) is right downtown. Housed in a historical sandstone building that was added on to in 1991, the beautiful light-filled museum features modern and contemporary art. Its permanent collection focuses largely on West Coast artists, but major retrospectives of works by the likes of Andy Warhol, Robert Mapplethorpe, and Alexander Calder come through often, giving the museum a broader scope. As a bonus, the Museum Store offers perhaps the best gift shopping in downtown San Jose. Likewise, the café, with both an indoor lounge and outside sidewalk tables, is a great place to grab a quick bite.

TECH MUSEUM OF INNOVATION

The **Tech Museum of Innovation** (201 S. Market St., 408/294-8324, www.thetech.org, 10am-5pm daily, adults $20, seniors and children 3-17 $15) brings technology of all kinds to kids, families, and science lovers. The interactive displays at the Tech invite touching and letting children explore and learn about medical technology, computers, biology, chemistry, physics, and more, using all their senses. The IMAX theater (additional $5) shows films dedicated to science, learning, technology, and adventure (and the occasional blockbuster).

ROSICRUCIAN EGYPTIAN MUSEUM

Perhaps San Jose's most unusual attraction is the imposing **Rosicrucian Egyptian Museum** (1660 Park Ave., 408/947-3635, www.egyptianmuseum.org, 9am-5pm Wed.-Fri., 10am-6pm Sat.-Sun., adults $9, students and seniors $7, children 5-10 $5, under 5 free). The museum was opened by the Rosicrucian Order in 1928 and has a wonderful collection of ancient Egyptian artifacts, including several mummies—partly unwrapped, a rarity today. Local children and adults love the Rosicrucian's jewels, tomb artifacts, tools, and textiles. The complex also boasts a planetarium, which has shows daily at 2pm Monday-Friday, and 2pm and 3:30pm Saturday-Sunday. Tickets are free with admission.

★ WINCHESTER MYSTERY HOUSE

For good old-fashioned haunted fun, stop in at the **Winchester Mystery House** (525 S. Winchester Blvd., 408/247-2101, www.winchestermysteryhouse.com, 9am-5pm daily). A San Jose attraction that predates the rise of Silicon Valley, the huge bizarre mansion was built by famous eccentric Sarah Winchester. Kids love the doors that open onto brick walls,

Downtown San Jose

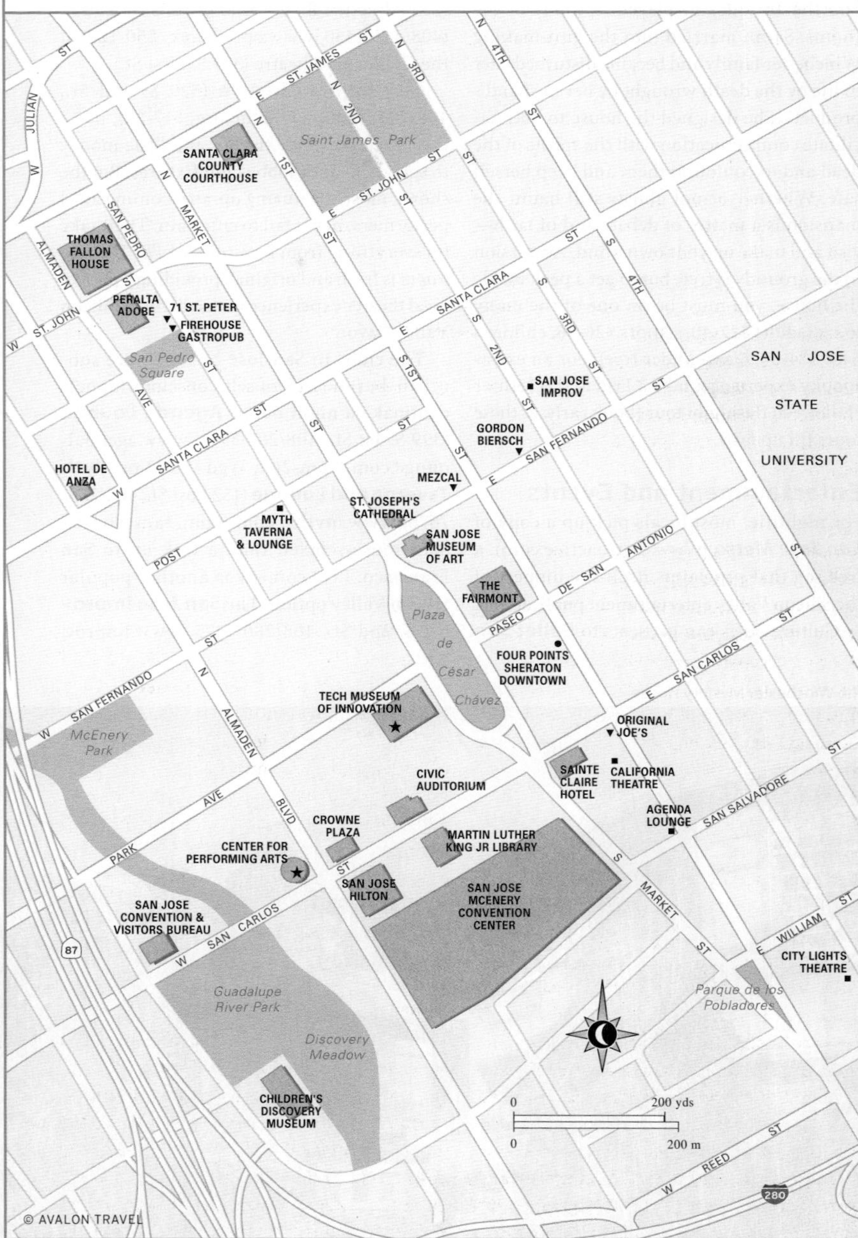

stairwells that go nowhere, and oddly shaped rooms, while adults enjoy the story of Sarah and the antiques displayed in many of the rooms. Sarah married into the gun-making Winchester family and became disturbed later in life by the death wrought by her husband's products. She designed the house to both facilitate communication with the spirits of the dead and to confound them and keep herself safe. Whether or not ghosts still haunt the mansion is a matter of debate and of faith—visit and make up your own mind. Admission to the grounds is free, but to get a peek inside the house, you must be on one of the many tours (adults $27-40, seniors $26-36, children 6-12 $24-30, 5 and under free). For an extra-spooky experience, take a Friday the 13th or Halloween flashlight tour (book early, as these tours fill up fast).

Entertainment and Events

For nightlife, most locals pick up a copy of ***San Jose Metro*** (www.metroactive.com), a free rag that proclaims itself the hippest of the Silicon Valley entertainment publications.

Culture buffs can get seats to **Ballet San Jose** (408/288-2800, www.balletsj.org, $25-80) at the Center for the Performing Arts (255 Almaden Blvd.) or to **Opera San Jose** (408/437-4450, www.operasj.org, $50-120) at the California Theatre (345 S. First St.).

City Lights Theatre (529 S. 2nd St., 408/295-4200, www.cltc.org, $17-30), has a tiny black box-style theater and little money to spend on fancy lobby light fixtures. But the shows, mostly featuring up-and-coming local performers, never fail to entertain. Their take on everything from *Lysistrata* to *The Waiting Room* is fresh and original, providing a perfect local theater experience with a definite Silicon Valley flavor.

The clubs in San Jose certainly are suburban, but the lack of self-conscious hipness can make a night out at **Agenda Lounge** (399 S. 1st St., 408/287-3991, www.agendallounge.com, 9pm-2am Wed.-Sun.) or **Myth Taverna and Lounge** (152 Post St., 408/286-7678, www.mythsj.com, 6pm-3am Thurs.-Sat.) more relaxed than a trek up to San Francisco. Live comedy is another popular Silicon Valley option. The **San Jose Improv** (62 S. 2nd St., 408/280-7475, www.improv.

the Winchester Mystery House

com, 6pm-midnight Mon.-Sat., 3:30pm-midnight Sun.), located in the historical San Jose Theatre, often hosts major-league headliners like Margaret Cho and Cedric the Entertainer while also granting stage time to local talent in showcases and contests.

Shopping

A variety of big shopping malls and an endless series of mini malls fan out over San Jose's miles of terrain. The top place to shop is **Santana Row** (377 Santana Row, 408/551-4611, www.santanarow.com, 10am-9pm Mon.-Sat., 11am-6pm Sun.). This upscale outdoor center dazzles the eye with its array of chic chain and one-off boutiques, shops, and restaurants. Shops include Sur La Table, Anthropologie, Brooks Brothers, and many more.

Sports and Recreation

For a straight-up thrill ride-heavy amusement park, go to **California's Great America** (4701 Great America Pkwy., Santa Clara, 408/988-1776, www.cagreatamerica.com, 10am-8pm Sun.-Fri., 10am-10pm Sat. June-Aug., $48, parking $15). With roller coasters from classic to leg-dangling, a vertical drop, water rides, a full-fledged water park, a slime-filled kid's zone, and much more, Great America makes for an energetic, often hot, all-day romp. To cool down, head to **Raging Waters** (2333 S. White Rd., 408/238-9900, www.rwsplash.com, 10:30am-6pm daily May-Aug., adults $30, children $22, parking $6). This sprawling water park features up-to-date slides and rides, plus a 350,000-gallon wave pool. For both parks, be sure to check out the website before you visit: Not only do hours vary, but significant deals on ticket prices can be had if purchased online.

San Jose boasts some serious professional sports. For a long time the big dog in the area was the **San Jose Sharks** (408/999-5757, http://sharks.nhl.com) National Hockey League team. They haven't won a Stanley Cup yet, but everyone gets into the games at the downtown SAP Center (525 W. Santa Clara St., 408/287-7070, www.sapcenter.com), making San Jose one of the loudest and liveliest places to watch a game in the league. In a move that caused a stir in the Bay Area sporting world, the National Football League's **San Francisco 49ers** (408/562-4949, www.49ers.com) left San Francisco and relocated to Santa Clara, just north of San Jose. The 2014-opened Levi's Stadium (4900 Marie P. DeBartolo Way, 415/464-9377, www.levisstadium.com) puts the 49ers into the luxury market. One side of the stadium is devoted to elite box suites, and even the nosebleed seats will hemorrhage your wallet at $135 a pop.

Accommodations

The **Arena Hotel** (817 The Alameda, 408/294-6500, www.pacifichotels.com, $140) is conveniently near SAP Center, making it perfect for hockey fans and concertgoers. It's more motel than hotel, since rooms tend toward the small and the decor toward chain-motel floral ticky-tacky. You do get the standard TV, mini fridge, coffeemaker, and a surprise whirlpool tub.

The Hotel Montgomery was promoted as San Jose's first luxury hotel when it opened in 1911. Now the **Four Points Sheraton Downtown San Jose** (211 S. 1st St., 408/282-8800, www.fourpoints.com, $119-234), it still prides itself on its old-school elegance and hospitality. Rooms add a touch of comfort with Egyptian cotton linens and cushy comforters on the beds, and are accented with local art. Amenities include a restaurant and bar, room service, and free Wi-Fi.

The **Sainte Claire Hotel** (302 S. Market St., 408/295-2000, www.thesainteclaire.com, $113-162) offers big city-style accommodations. Standard rooms are small but attractive, with carved wooden furniture and rich linens and draperies. The suites are more luxurious. Amenities include a flat-screen TV with a DVD player, a CD and MP3 player, free Wi-Fi, plush robes, and turndown service.

For a taste of Silicon Valley luxury, stay at **The Fairmont San Jose** (170 S. Market St., 408/998-1900, www.fairmont.com, $150-180), with a day spa and limousine service. Even the standard rooms at this 731-room hotel have plenty of space, elegant fabrics and appointments, and a marble-clad private bath with separate shower and bathtub. The hotel's South Tower has more luxurious rooms.

The top-tier **Hotel Valencia Santana Row** (355 Santana Row, 408/551-0010, www.hotelvalencia-santanarow.com, $219-319) is right in the middle of the prestigious shopping mall. Ultramodern elegance and convenience includes everything from an outdoor pool and hot tub to a slick lounge perched on the hotel's balcony and the complimentary continental breakfast at the swank Citrus Restaurant. Inside the rooms are Egyptian cotton sheets and lavish baths with upscale toiletries.

Food

Although often overlooked by Bay Area foodies, San Jose has an array of good restaurants that are as diverse as its population. The center of San Jose's hip restaurant scene is San Pedro Square, the long narrow block of North San Pedro Street, east of West Santa Clara Street. Anchoring the east end is enclosed **San Pablo Square Market** (87 N. San Pedro St., www.sanpedrosquaremarket.com, 7am-10pm daily), showcasing local eateries, including noodle shops, a burger joint, wine bar, a meat-centric bistro, and a bar serving artisan cocktails and local brews.

Longstanding **71 Saint Peter** (71 N. San Pedro St., 408/971-8523, www.71saintpeter.com, 11am-1pm, 5pm-8:30pm Mon.-Fri., 5pm-8:30pm Sat., $16-27) is the grandfather of this foodie district. Locals remain loyal to the restaurant's combination of solid Mediterranean classics and festive and romantic bistro atmosphere, dining out on the patio on San Jose's warm summer evenings.

Firehouse No.1 Gastropub (69 N. San Pedro St., 408/287-6969, http://firehouse1.com, 11:30am-midnight Mon.-Wed., 11:30am-2am Thurs.-Fri., 4pm-2am Sat., 11am-midnight Sun., $12-35) offers a hip experience. Exposed brick, reclaimed wood, and meat-heavy comfort food, much of which is plated to share, define the restaurant. A long elegant bar fills much of the small space, offering carefully selected wines, specialty beers, and original cocktails. Despite the upscale affectations, Firehouse can get rowdy on weekend nights, particularly when there is a Sharks game.

In Los Gatos, about 10 miles southwest of San Jose, ★ **Manresa** (320 Village Ln., Los Gatos, 408/354-4330, www.manresarestaurant.com, 5:30pm-9pm Wed.-Sun., tasting menu $198) is the Michelin-starred darling of the South Bay. The menu features such delicate oddities as panna cotta topped with abalone "petals," a "winter tidal pool" of shellfish, foie gras, and duck roasted in hay. Surprisingly, they do accept walk-ins, but if you're looking for a special Saturday night affair, don't wait until the last minute.

Gordon Biersch (33 E. San Fernando St., 408/294-6785, www.gordonbiersch.com, 11:30am-10pm Sun.-Mon., 11:30am-10:30pm Tues.-Wed., 11:30am-11pm Thurs., 11:30am-midnight Fri.-Sat., $12-28) is always busy, and the food and beer are tasty. Try the blackened ahi tacos or the Cajun pasta, but don't miss out on one of the handcrafted German-style beers brewed on-site. It has a lively happy hour, particularly if a local sports team is playing on the large overhead TVs in the bar.

Mezcal (25 W. San Fernando St., 408/283-9595, http://mezcalrestaurantsj.com, 11:30am-9pm Mon., 11:30am-10pm Tues.-Thurs., 11:30am-11:30pm Fri., 4pm-11:30pm Sat., 4pm-9pm Sun., $10-19) specializes in food from the Oaxaca region of Mexico. The menu is full of mole, pork cracklings, and fresh fish, fruit, and vegetables. The handmade corn tortillas win raves as do the *chapulines* (sautéed grasshoppers). High ceilings and exposed brick and beams give Mezcal a dynamic, urban touch.

A good reason to venture up to Japantown is **Gombei** (193 E. Jackson St., 408/279-4311, http://gombei.com, 11:30am-2:30pm, 5pm-9:30pm Mon.-Sat., $9) for traditional Japanese food at good prices. The menu is as minimal as the decor, with simple categories such as *udon*, tofu, and curry rice.

At **Original Joe's** (301 S. 1st St., 408/292-7030, www.originaljoes.com, 11am-11pm Sun.-Thurs., 11am-midnight Fri.-Sat., $18-40), little has changed—from the decor to the food—since it opened in 1937. Veal parmigiana and pot roast share the menu with calf's liver served four different ways. There is a variety of pasta and steaks as well as the midcentury bar, The Hideout.

Information and Services

Visit www.sanjose.org to get all the information you need about the Silicon Valley region and its attractions. Once in town, stop in at the **San Jose Convention and Visitors Bureau** (408 Almaden Blvd., 408/295-9600, 8am-5pm Mon.-Fri.) for maps, brochures, guidebooks, and local advice.

For medical attention, **Good Samaritan Hospital** (2425 Samaritan Dr., 408/559-2011, www.goodsamsj.org) has 24-hour emergency services.

Transportation

Travelers heading straight for Silicon Valley should skip San Francisco International Airport and fly into **Mineta San José International Airport** (SJC, 1701 Airport Blvd., 408/392-3600, www.flysanjose.com). This suburban commercial airport has shorter lines, has less parking and traffic congestion, and is convenient to downtown San Jose.

Amtrak (800/872-7245, www.amtrak.com) trains come into San Jose, and you can catch either the once-daily Seattle-Los Angeles *Coast Starlight* or the commuter *Capitol Corridor* to Sacramento at the **San Jose-Diridon Station** (65 Cahill St.).

San Jose-Diridon station is also a hub for **Caltrain** (800/660-4287, www.caltrain.com, $3.25-13.25), a commuter train that runs from Gilroy to San Francisco. If you'd like to spend a day in San Francisco but base yourself in Silicon Valley, taking Caltrain is an excellent way to go.

At Diridon station you can catch the **VTA Light Rail** (408/321-2300, www.vta.org, $2-4), a streetcar network that serves San Jose and some of Silicon Valley as far north as Mountain View. The VTA also operates Silicon Valley **buses**, which can get you almost anywhere you need to go if you're patient enough.

Avoid San Jose's freeways during **rush hour** (7am-9:30am and 4pm-7:30pm Mon.-Fri.). Arterial U.S. 101 is a dank stretch of road that's convenient to much of the peninsula. I-280 is much prettier but less convenient. It's the easiest, but not the shortest, route north to San Francisco. Highway 17 is the fast, treacherous route over the hills to the coast and Santa Cruz; it turns into I-880 in the middle of San Jose and runs along the east side of the bay to Oakland. Highway 87, sometimes called the Guadalupe Parkway, can provide convenient access to downtown San Jose and the airport.

Parking in San Jose isn't anywhere near as bad as in San Francisco, but be prepared to pay a premium for event parking and at enclosed lots at the fancier hotels.

Wine Country

Entering California's Wine Country is an incomparable experience. From the crest of the last hill, sunlight paints golden streaks on endless rows of grapevines that stretch in every direction for as far as the eye can see.

Trellises run alongside every road, with unpicked weeds beneath the vines and rose bushes capping each row. A heady aroma of earth and grapes permeates the area. Welcome to the Napa and Sonoma Valleys.

The area's beautiful grapevines are renowned worldwide for producing top-quality vintages and economical table wines. Foodies also know the area as a center for stellar cuisine. Yountville, a tiny upscale town in the middle of Napa Valley, is the favorite of celebrity chef Thomas Keller. The food served at his French Laundry restaurant is legendary, as are the prices. Keller's influence helped to usher in a culinary renaissance, and today the lush flavors of local sustainable produce are available throughout the region.

Sonoma Valley has long played second fiddle to Napa in terms of prestige, but the wines coming out of the area are second to none. Russian River Valley wineries are often friendlier and less crowded, while the wineries in the southern Carneros region are few and far between. Each offers a more personal experience than Napa and the chance to sample unique varietals.

PLANNING YOUR TIME

Napa and Sonoma are the epicenter of Wine Country. Many visitors plan a weekend in Napa, with another weekend to explore Sonoma and the Russian River. During summer and fall, you'll find a crush in almost every tasting room in the valley; even the smaller boutique labels do big business during the high season (May-Oct.).

Highway 29, which runs through the heart of Napa Valley, gets jammed up around St. Helena and can be very slow on weekends. U.S. 101 slows through Santa Rosa during the weekday rush hour and late in the day on sunny summer weekend afternoons. Downtown tasting rooms in the cities of Napa, Sonoma, and Santa Rosa are good alternatives to the slow trek up and down the wine roads.

Previous: vintage truck at Gundlach Bundschu Winery in Sonoma; picturesque building at Napa Valley winery. **Above:** Most wineries provide tastings.

Wine Country

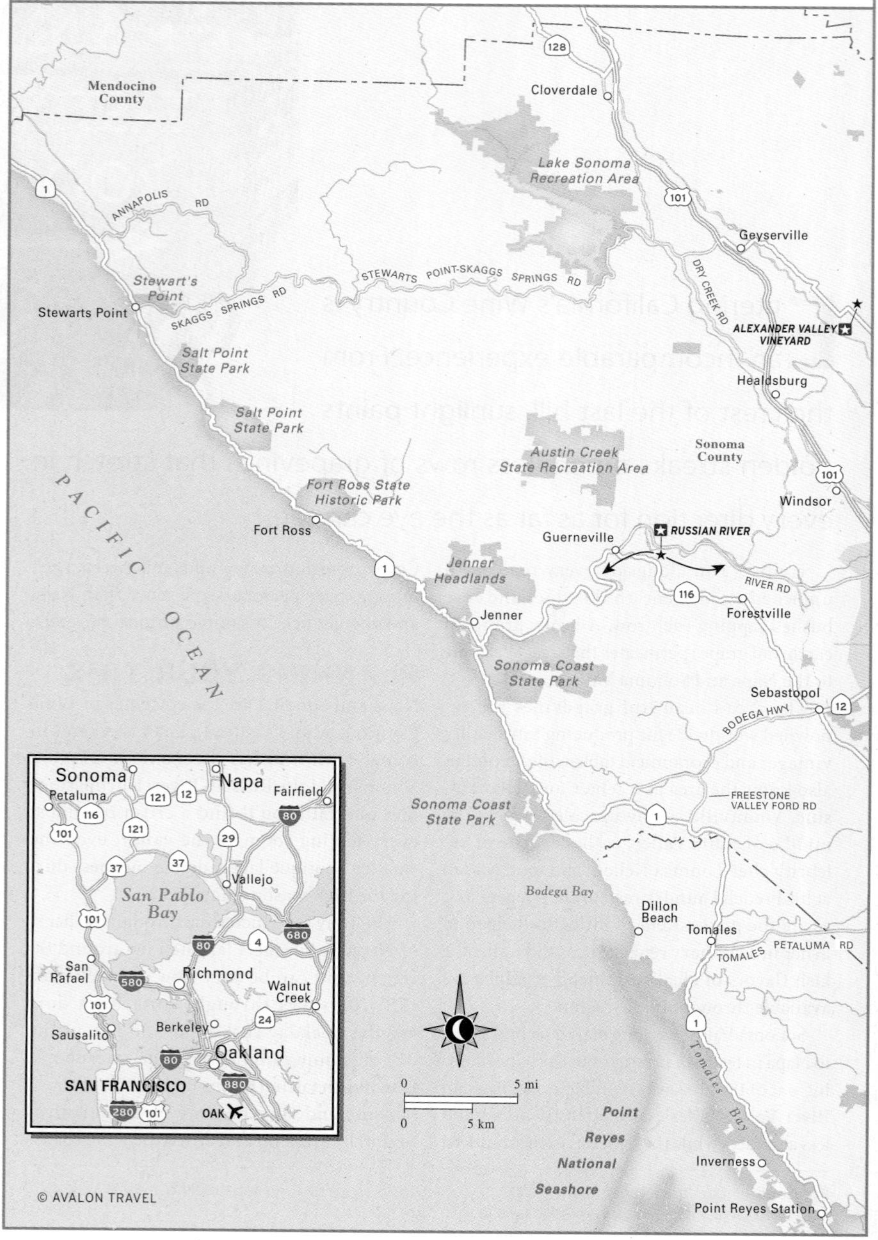

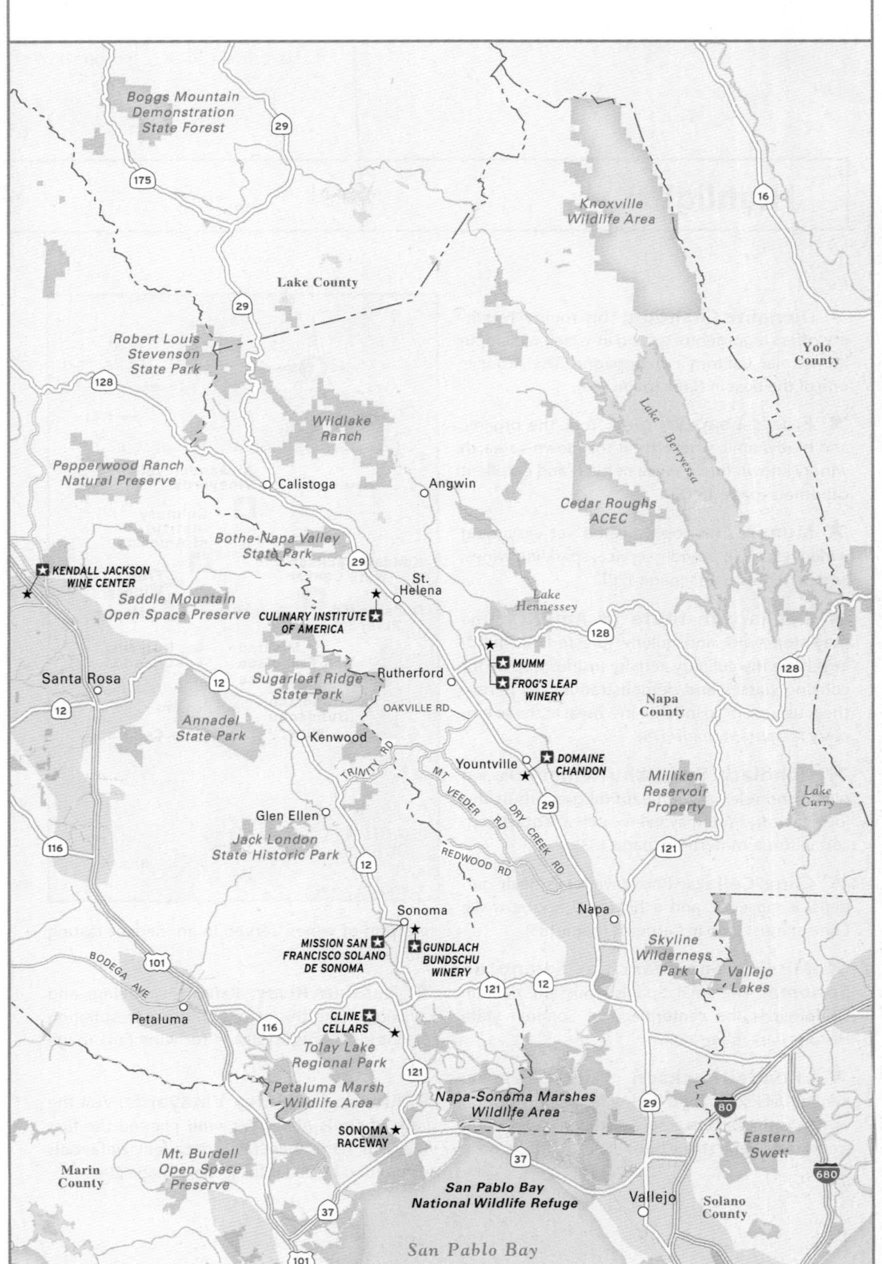

Boggs Mountain Demonstration State Forest
Knoxville Wildlife Area
Lake County
Yolo County
Robert Louis Stevenson State Park
Wildlake Ranch
Lake Berryessa
Pepperwood Ranch Natural Preserve
Calistoga
Angwin
Cedar Roughs ACEC
Bothe-Napa Valley State Park
KENDALL JACKSON WINE CENTER
St. Helena
Saddle Mountain Open Space Preserve
CULINARY INSTITUTE OF AMERICA
Lake Hennessey
MUMM
FROG'S LEAP WINERY
Santa Rosa
Sugarloaf Ridge State Park
Rutherford
Napa County
OAKVILLE RD
Annadel State Park
Kenwood
TRINITY RD
Yountville
DOMAINE CHANDON
Milliken Reservoir Property
Lake Curry
MT VEEDER RD
DRY CREEK RD
Glen Ellen
Jack London State Historic Park
REDWOOD RD
Sonoma
Napa
MISSION SAN FRANCISCO SOLANO DE SONOMA
GUNDLACH BUNDSCHU WINERY
Skyline Wilderness Park
Vallejo Lakes
BODEGA AVE
Petaluma
CLINE CELLARS
Tolay Lake Regional Park
Petaluma Marsh Wildlife Area
Napa-Sonoma Marshes Wildlife Area
SONOMA RACEWAY
Eastern Swett
Mt. Burdell Open Space Preserve
Marin County
San Pablo Bay National Wildlife Refuge
Vallejo
Solano County
San Pablo Bay

Look for ★ to find recommended sights, activities, dining, and lodging.

Highlights

★ **Domaine Chandon:** This Yountville winery offers a gorgeous setting in which to sample its premier California champagne. Their tour is one of the best in Napa (page 163).

★ **Frog's Leap Winery:** Tour the organic and biodynamic vineyards at this down-to-earth winery known for its sense of fun—and excellent cabernets (page 169).

★ **Mumm:** This sophisticated yet easygoing winery excels in friendly service, sparkling wines, and generous pours (page 170).

★ **Culinary Institute of America:** The gray stonework and quietly forested surroundings belie the culinary activity inside. Stop by for cooking classes and demonstrations, to peruse the museum, or to indulge in a meal at the exemplary restaurant (page 174).

★ **Gundlach Bundschu Winery:** Pack a picnic and relax at the beautiful grounds at this local favorite. You may even catch a Mozart concert in the summertime (page 183).

★ **Cline Cellars:** Rhone varietals, lush gardens, a museum, and a historical adobe make Cline at must stop in Carneros (page 185).

★ **Mission San Francisco Solano de Sonoma:** The final Spanish mission built in California is the centerpiece of Sonoma State Historic Park (page 186).

★ **Kendall-Jackson Wine Center:** Kendall-Jackson's food-and-wine pairing tasting option is the best example of this Wine Country trend: excellent small bites paired with a daily selection of wines, served in an elegant tasting room (page 198).

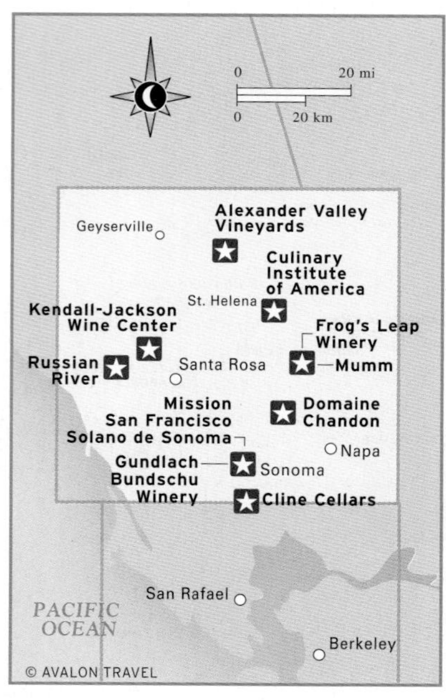

★ **Russian River:** Rafting, canoeing, and kayaking make this area as much a destination for outdoors enthusiasts as for wine fans (page 203).

★ **Alexander Valley Vineyards:** Visit the grave of Cyrus Alexander, who planted the first vineyards here, then taste decadent zinfandels surrounded by beautiful scenery (page 208).

Napa Valley

Napa Valley can feel like a wine theme park. Wineries cluster along Highway 29 and the Silverado Trail, each trying to outdo its neighbors to woo the thousands of weekend visitors. Tasting rooms are plentiful, tours sell out in advance, and special events draw hundreds. Then there's the food: As the wine industry in Napa exploded, top-tier chefs rose to the challenge, flocking to the area and opening amazing restaurants in the tiny towns that line the wine trails. Even if you don't love wine, a meal at one of the many high-end restaurants makes Napa worth a visit.

NAPA

The blue-collar heart of Napa Valley is the city of Napa, many of whose 80,000 residents work in banking, construction, the medical industry, and other businesses that serve the rest of the valley. The Napa River snakes through downtown, tempering the hot summer weather and providing recreation and natural beauty. Along the river, you'll find sparkling new structures with high-end clothiers and cutting-edge restaurants as well as the Oxbow Market—a one-of-a-kind culinary treat.

Wineries

The base of the valley has few wineries that host visitors without appointment. The best place to casually taste in Napa is in its downtown tasting rooms. The biggest is the **Vintner's Collective** (1245 Main St., 707/255-7150, www.vintnerscollective.com, 11am-6pm daily, $10-30) in the historical Pfeiffer Building. A house of ill repute during its Victorian youth, it is now the public face of 18 different wineries and winemakers. The standard tasting includes a flight of three everyday wines, and the premium tasting features six wines.

Next to Oxbow Market, **Mark Herold Wines** (710 1st St., 707/256-3111, www.markheroldwines.com, noon-7pm daily, $20-65) is a must stop for both the casual drinker and the oenophile. Known up and down the valley for his cabernets, Herold has a tasting room filled with beakers, test tubes, and other science-oriented knick-knacks.

Entertainment and Events

For current events, ***Wine Country This Week*** (www.winecountrythisweek.com) has the best up-to-date information.

For a night of entertainment, check out the lineup at the historical **Napa Valley Opera House** (1030 Main St., 707/226-7372, http://nvoh.org). This Napa institution hosts comedians, jazz ensembles, musical acts, theater performances, and even old-movie nights; you can count on something going on nearly every night of the week. Countless cultural icons, from Jack London to Steve Martin, have walked the stage over its long history, but the building itself is also a treat. With antique tile floors, curving banisters, a café, and two lounges, the 500-seat venue feels intimate for a romantic or elegant evening out.

The **Uptown Theatre** (1350 3rd St., Napa, 707/259-0123, www.uptowntheatrenapa.com) is another great place to see a show. Originally opened in 1937, this art deco theater hosts acts from Lindsey Buckingham to Hannibal Buress and Boz Scaggs.

At the Napa Mill complex, **Silo's** (530 Main St., 707/251-5833, www.silosnapa.com, cover charge up to $25) has become as popular for evening wine-tasting or a pre-dinner drink as it has for its live music. The eclectic mix includes everything from jazz to standup comedy and Johnny Cash tribute bands. The decent wine list has a far lower markup than at local restaurants, and there is also a small food menu.

Shopping

Downtown Napa strives to be a shopping destination, but it's not quite there. The north

Lower Napa Valley

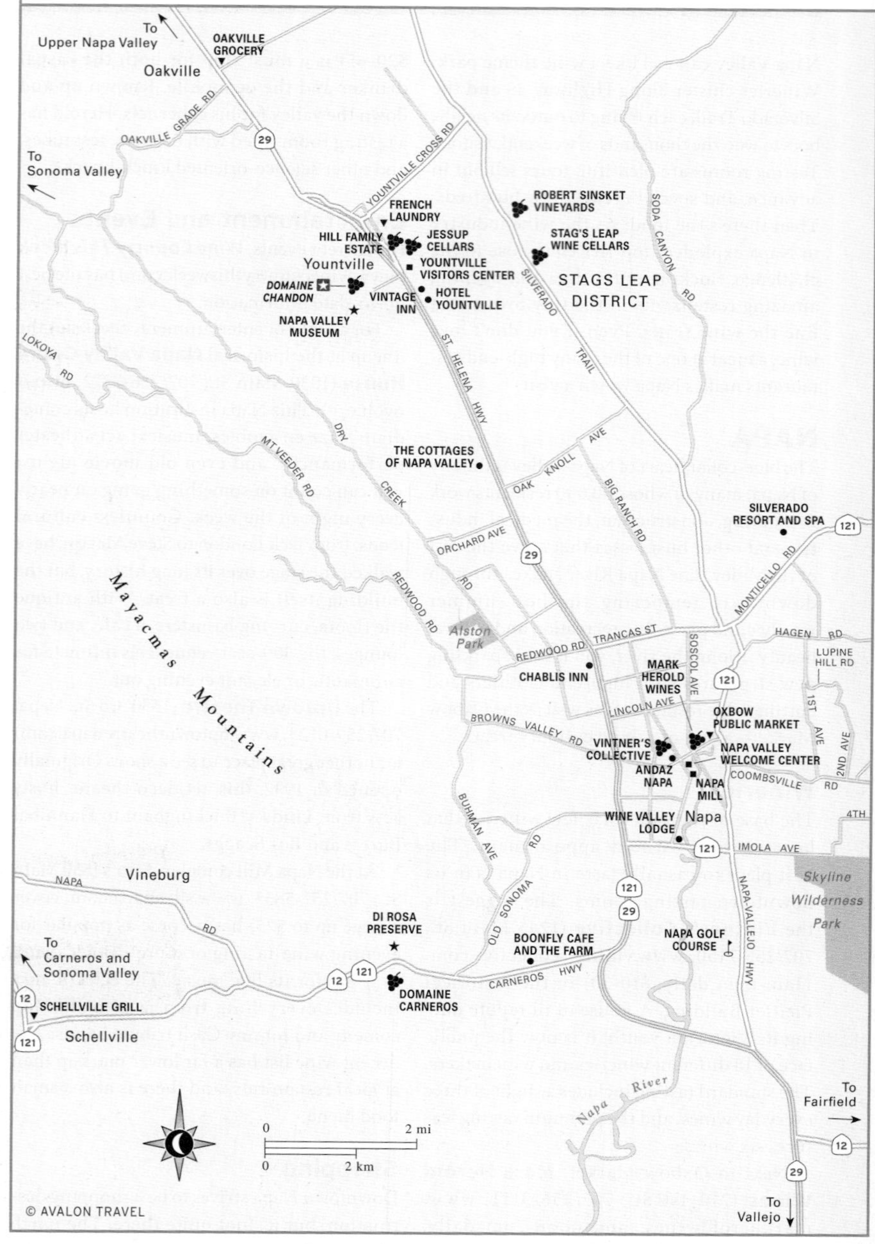

end of Main Street has some flashy buildings with equally flashy clothiers, but the place to go is the **Historic Napa Mill** (Main St., www.historicnapamill.com), one block down. Formerly the Hatt Warehouse, the mill was converted into a shopping and dining center, decorated with rustic touches—weathered redwood, trailing vines, and blooming planter boxes and hanging baskets. Here, the **Napa General Store** (540 Main St., 707/259-0762, www.napageneralstore.com, 8am-6pm daily) offers a bite to eat, a glass of wine, wine-related knickknacks, and other gifts. The store also sells local artwork, including leather crafts and fiber art, all of which has an ecological bent.

Across the river from downtown Napa, the **Oxbow Public Market** (610-644 1st St., 707/226-6529, www.oxbowpublicmarket.com, 9am-7pm daily) is a well-used piece of real estate. Located next to the defunct COPIA museum, the Oxbow Public Market has breathed life into this "across the tracks" section of Napa. Grab a cup of **Ritual Coffee** and browse through the epicurean wares. Pick through cooking- and kitchen-related knickknacks at the **Napastak.** Or get lost in the myriad spices and seasonings at the **Whole Spice Company.** There is also a chocolatier, an olive-oil company, and the in-house **Oxbow Wine and Cheese Market,** where you can pick up some vino, cheese, and other treats for the road.

Sports and Recreation

Once you're on the trails of **Skyline Wilderness Park** (2201 Imola Ave., 707/252-0481, www.skylinepark.org, 8am-5pm daily winter, 8am-7pm daily summer), you may forget you're in Wine Country. No vineyards encroach on the natural chaparral landscape of Napa's high country; instead you'll find the Martha Walker Garden—a botanical garden planted with California and Napa native plants in honor of a legendary figure in the local horticultural community. The rest of this 850-acre park is given over to multiple uses: a disc golf course, campgrounds, hiking

downtown Napa

Upper Napa Valley

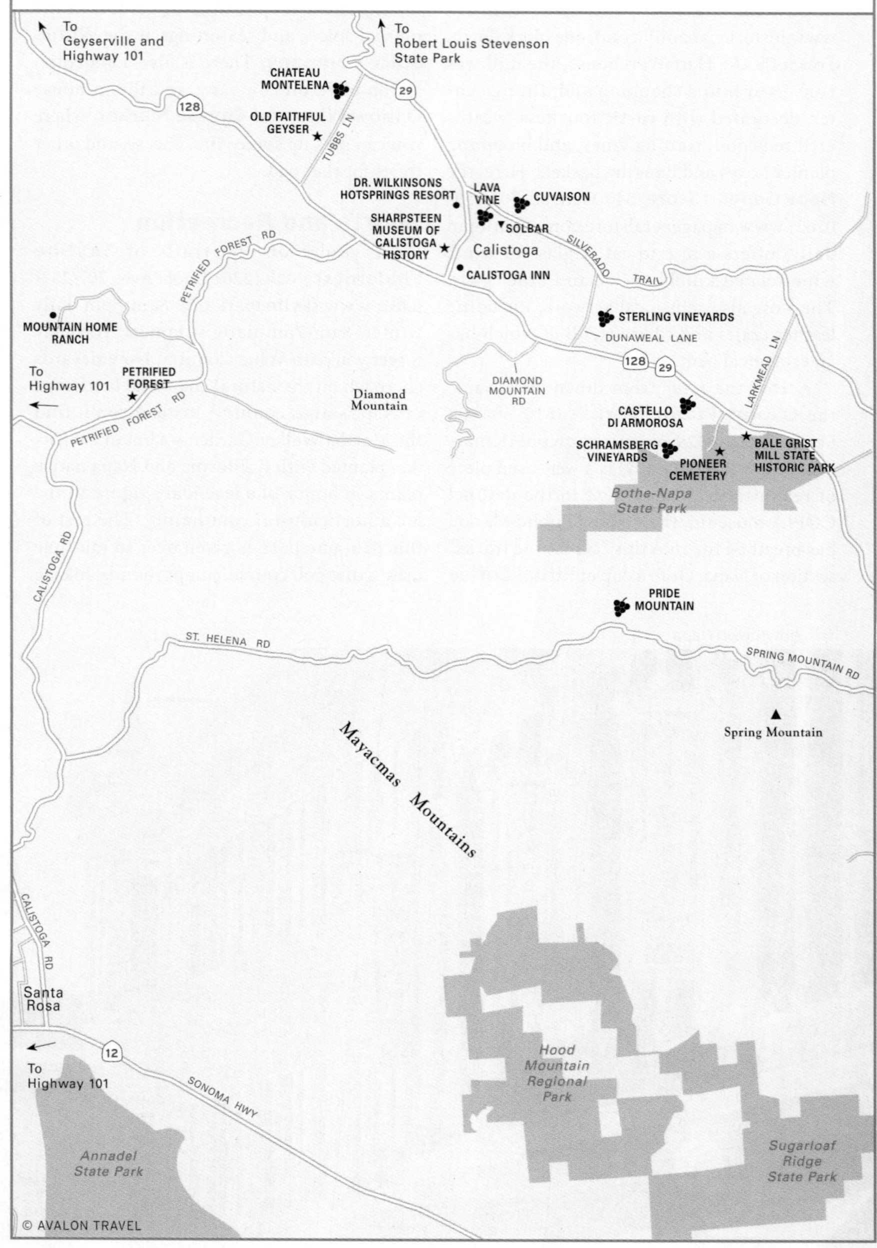

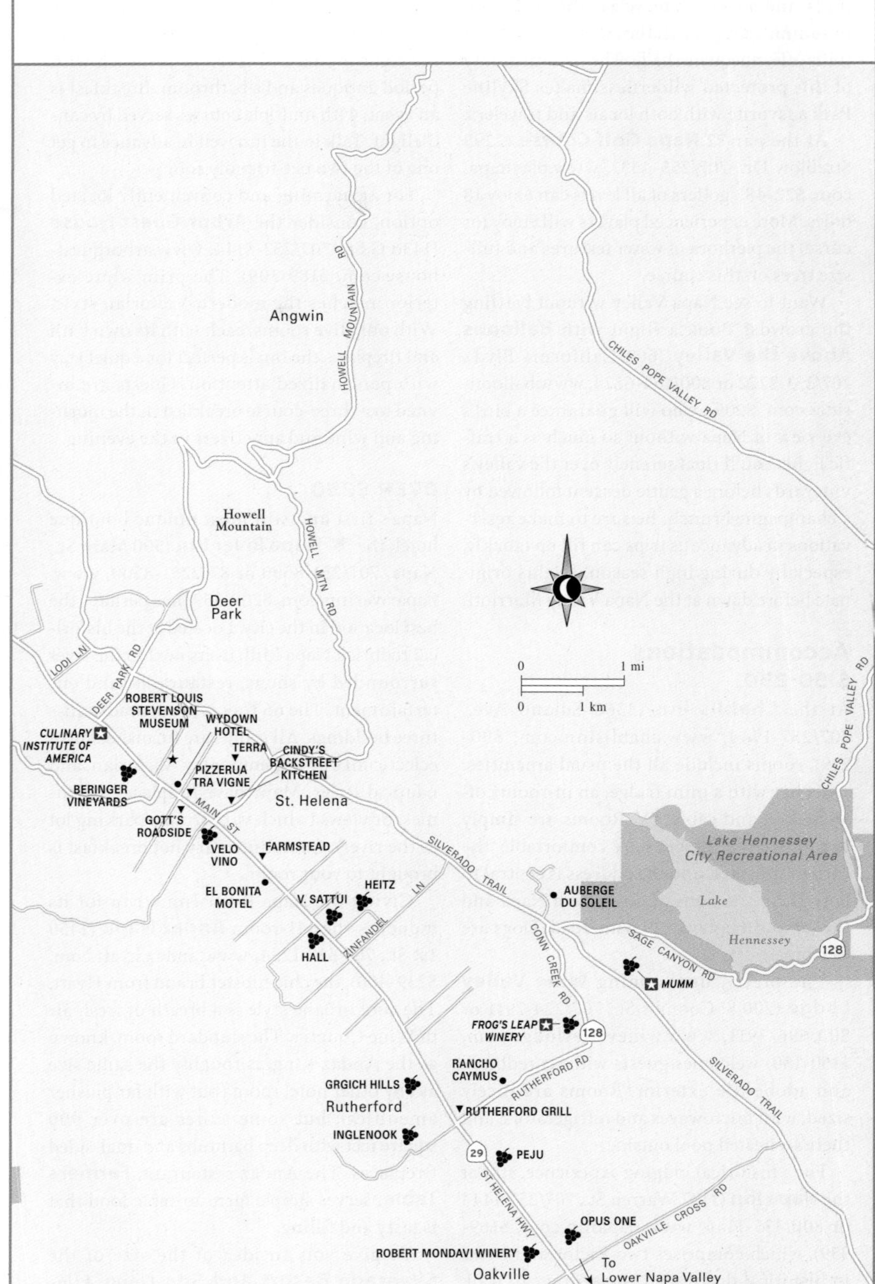

Angwin
HOWELL MOUNTAIN RD
CHILES POPE VALLEY RD
Howell Mountain
HOWELL MTN RD
Deer Park
LODI LN
DEER PARK RD
0
1 mi
0
1 km
ROBERT LOUIS STEVENSON MUSEUM
WYDOWN HOTEL
CULINARY INSTITUTE OF AMERICA
TERRA
CINDY'S BACKSTREET KITCHEN
PIZZERUA TRA VIGNE
BERINGER VINEYARDS
St. Helena
MAIN ST
GOTT'S ROADSIDE
VELO VINO
FARMSTEAD
SILVERADO TRAIL
EL BONITA MOTEL
HEITZ
V. SATTUI
ZINFANDEL LN
HALL
AUBERGE DU SOLEIL
CONN CREEK RD
CHILES POPE VALLEY RD
Lake Hennessey City Recreational Area
Lake
Hennessey
SAGE CANYON RD
128
MUMM
FROG'S LEAP WINERY
128
RANCHO CAYMUS
RUTHERFORD RD
SILVERADO TRAIL
GRGICH HILLS
Rutherford
RUTHERFORD GRILL
INGLENOOK
29
PEJU
ST HELENA HWY
OAKVILLE CROSS RD
OPUS ONE
ROBERT MONDAVI WINERY
Oakville
To Lower Napa Valley

trails, and horse and bicycle paths. It gets hot in summer, and not all the campgrounds and trails offer adequate shade. The natural beauty of this protected wilderness makes Skyline Park a favorite with both locals and travelers.

At the par-72 **Napa Golf Course** (2295 Streblow Dr., 707/255-4333, www.playnapa.com, $22-48), golfers of all levels can enjoy 18 holes. More experienced players will enjoy (or curse) the plethora of water features and full-size trees on this course.

Want to see Napa Valley without battling the crowds? Book a flight with **Balloons Above the Valley** (603 California Blvd., 707/253-2222 or 800/464-6824, www.balloonrides.com, $209), who will guarantee a bird's eye view of Napa without so much as a traffic light. You'll float serenely over the valley's vineyards before a gentle descent followed by a champagne brunch. Be sure to make reservations in advance as trips can fill up quickly, especially during high season. Flights originate before dawn at the Napa Valley Marriott.

Accommodations

$150-250

At the **Chablis Inn** (3360 Solano Ave., 707/257-1944, www.chablisinn.com, $90-219), rooms include all the usual amenities: a wet bar with a mini fridge, an in-room coffeemaker, and cable TV. Rooms are simply decorated, but the beds are comfortable, the carpets are dark, and the address is central to both the attractions of downtown Napa and the famous Highway 29 wine road. Dogs are welcome.

The pretty, unassuming **Wine Valley Lodge** (200 S. Coombs St., 707/224-7911 or 800/696-7911, www.winevalleylodge.com, $160-180) welcomes guests with its redbrick and adobe-tile exterior. Rooms are nicely sized, with microwaves and refrigerators, and there's a heated pool outside.

For a historical lodging experience, stay at the **Napa Inn** (1137 Warren St., 707/257-1444 or 800/435-1144, www.napainn.com, $169-339), which comprises two Victorian houses in historical downtown Napa. You can walk to downtown shops and restaurants, and the Wine Train depot is a very short drive. There are eight rooms and seven suites, each with period antiques and a bathroom. Breakfast is an event, with multiple courses served by candlelight. Talk to the inn well in advance to get one of the two pet-friendly rooms.

For a charming and conveniently located option, consider the **Arbor Guest House** (1436 G St., 707/252-8144, www.arborguesthouse.com, $189-309). The prim white exterior matches the modern-Victorian style. With only five rooms, each with its own bath and fireplace, the inn is perfect for a quiet stay with personalized attention. Guests are invited to a three-course breakfast in the morning and wine and appetizers in the evening.

OVER $250

Napa's first and still most unique boutique hotel, the ★ **Napa River Inn** (500 Main St., Napa, 707/251-8500 or 877/251-8500, www.napariverinn.com, $209-359) has perhaps the best location in the city. Located at the historical redbrick Napa Mill, it sits next to the river surrounded by shops, restaurants, and entertainment. The 66 rooms are spread across three buildings. All rooms are furnished in an eclectic mix of contemporary, Victorian, and nautical styles. Many have fireplaces, balconies, or views (which vary from a parking lot to the river). Complimentary hot breakfast is brought to your room.

Giving the Napa River Inn a run for its money is the 141-room **Andaz Napa** (1450 1st St., 707/687-1234, www.andaz.hyatt.com, $239-400), the chic hipster brand from Hyatt. The cool urbane style is a breath of fresh air in Wine Country. The standard room, known as the Andaz King, is roughly the same size as any other hotel room (but with far plusher amenities), but some suites are over 900 square feet with deep bathtubs and dual-sided fireplaces. The Andaz restaurant, **Farmers Table,** serves simple farm-to-table food that is tasty and filling.

To give you an idea of the size of the **Silverado Resort and Spa** (1600 Atlas

Peak Rd., 707/257-0200, www.silveradoresort.com, $290-339), accommodations are grouped into "neighborhoods." There are 370 rooms and suites, including cottages and vacation rentals, all boasting the finest modern amenities, including high thread-count linens, complimentary Wi-Fi, and a private patio or deck. Choose from the immense spa with full fitness and salon services, two 18-hole golf courses, two restaurants, 13 tennis courts, and 10 pools.

The **Meritage Inn** (875 Bordeaux Way, 707/251-1900, www.themeritageresort.com, $350-575) is an all-inclusive resort located near the small Napa Valley airport. The lush garden pool is the centerpiece of the property, which also includes the well-respected Trinitas winery tasting room, a fabulous spa, and a down-to-earth restaurant. The basic shape of the rooms remains true to the Meritage's motel roots, but the Tuscan-style decor and trimmings make a play for elegance, with comfortable beds, deep soaking tubs, and posh amenities. Expect a fridge stocked with free water and soda, a coffeemaker, and a complimentary bottle of wine.

Food

Napa's ultimate restaurant/tasting room is the sleek **1313 Main** (1313 Main St., 707/258-1313, www.1313main.com, 4pm-10pm Tues.-Thurs., 4pm-midnight Fri.-Sat., 10am-2pm, 4pm-10pm Sun., $20-32). This tasting room/wine bar/lounge/retail shop serves upscale dishes with haute cuisine flair. Escargot, oxtail ravioli, and Australian lamb chop are just a few of the selections. The menu is slim, particularly compared with 1,300 different wines available, of which 13 reds and 13 whites are sold by the glass. The atmosphere is more lounge than high-end restaurant, catering to the young, hip set.

Sake in Wine Country? Not a bad idea, if it's paired with dinner at **Morimoto's** (610 Main St., 707/252-1600, www.morimotonapa.com, 11:30am-2:30pm, 5pm-10pm Sun.-Thurs., 11:30am-2:30pm, 5pm-11pm Fri.-Sat., $14-65). This esoteric and sleek Japanese eatery is by celebrity chef Massaharu Morimoto. The food includes traditional Japanese dishes, all with a unique and modern twist—*gyoza* with bacon foam and duck confit-fried rice are just some of the menu items. Veterans of Tra Vigne in St. Helena, Michael and Christina Gyetvan opened **Azzurro Pizzeria** (1260 Main St., 707/255-5552, www.azzurropizzeria.com, 11:30am-9:30pm Sun.-Thurs., 11:30am-10pm Fri.-Sat., $15) with the intention of bringing their wood-fired pizzas to downtown Napa. The menu includes classic Italian starters, a handful of pasta dishes, and a dozen or so pizzas. The wine list is dominated by thoughtfully chosen Napa and Sonoma wines.

A completely original Napa joint is ★ **Bounty Hunter Wine Bar and Smokin' BBQ** (975 1st St., 707/226-3976, www.bountyhunterwinebar.com, 11am-10pm Sun.-Thurs., 11am-midnight Fri.-Sat., $13-28). This wine shop, tasting bar, and barbecue joint, housed in a historical brick-walled Victorian building with wine barrels for table bases, is as relaxed as the comfort food served. The menu includes gumbo, a beer-can chicken (a Cajun-spiced chicken impaled on a Tecate beer can), and big plates of barbecue pork, brisket, and ribs. There are 400 wines (40 by the glass) sold here or served as part of a tasting flight.

For a bit of this and a bit of that, venture across the Napa River to the ★ **Oxbow Public Market** (610-644 1st St., 707/226-6529, www.oxbowpublicmarket.com). Inside this large open space you can snack on oysters at the **Hog Island Oyster Company,** lunch on tacos from **C Casa,** or indulge at **Kara's Cupcakes.** Hamburgers are just out the side door at **Gott's Roadside,** and around the corner you can find some of the best charcuterie around in take-out sandwiches at the **Fatted Calf** or pizza by the slice at **The Model Bakery.** Head to the market's **Kitchen Door** (707/226-1560, www.kitchendoornapa.com, 11:30am-8pm Mon., 11:30am-9pm Tues.-Fri., 10am-9pm Sat., 10am-8pm Sun., $15-25) to escape the market's loud and congested interior, and order a big plate of global, gourmet comfort food. Most of what you'll get comes out of the white-tile wood oven, such as pizzas and roast chicken, but you'll also have your choice of noodle bowls, grilled fish, and ribs.

Information and Services

The **Napa Valley Welcome Center** (600 Main St., 707/251-5895 or 855/847-6272, www.visitnapavalley.com, 9am-5pm daily) in the middle of downtown Napa has complimentary maps, guidebooks, and wine-tasting passes. Chat with a friendly local who can direct you to the favorite wineries and restaurants.

For medical treatment (including alcohol poisoning), the **Queen of the Valley** (1000 Trancas St., 707/252-4411, www.thequeen.org) has both a 24-hour emergency room and a trauma center.

Transportation

Napa does not have infrastructure designed for the number of visitors it receives. The best way to experience the valley is to avoid the ever-popular autumn crush and summer weekend afternoons. November and early spring are beautiful seasons to see the valley. But if a summer Saturday spent wine-tasting is impossible to resist, hit the wineries early and stay off the roads from midafternoon to early evening.

BY CAR

Napa is not all that easy to get to. Most of the highways in this region are two lanes and frequently go by colloquial names. They are also susceptible to gridlocked traffic thanks to the numerous wine lovers and races at nearby Sonoma Raceway.

Highway 29 is the central conduit that runs north into the valley from the city of Napa. It is also known as the Napa-Vallejo Highway between those two cities, and as the St. Helena Highway from Napa to Calistoga, where it becomes Foothill Boulevard. To reach Highway 29 from San Francisco, take U.S. 101 north across the Golden Gate Bridge to Novato. In Novato, take the exit for Highway 37 East to Highway 121. Take Highway 121 until you reach Napa. From San Francisco, the trip is a little over 50 miles, taking about an hour.

If you're coming from I-80, Highways 121, 29, and 37 connect around Vallejo, making a quick jump over to the Napa Valley. Coming from Highway 121 in Sonoma, Highway 12 East leads directly to Napa. Highway 121 then picks up again at West Imola Avenue and leads east to the Silverado Trail, an alternate north-south route in the Napa Valley.

BY BUS

To avoid the potential headache of driving in Napa, take the **VINE bus** (707/251-2600 or 800/696-6443, http://nctpa.net, adults $1.50-5.50, children $1-2.50), which provides public transportation around Napa Valley, including Napa, Yountville, Oakville, Rutherford, St. Helena, and Calistoga. Route 10 makes stops along Highway 29 from Napa to Calistoga daily. If you don't want to drive at all, jump aboard the commuter VINE 29 Express, which runs all day Monday-Friday. The Express travels from the El Cerrito BART station in the East Bay and from the Vallejo Ferry Terminal into Napa Valley. Fares are cash-only and require exact change.

NAPA VALLEY WINE TRAIN

If trying to decide which wineries to visit, where to eat, and how best to avoid weekend traffic, consider taking the **Napa Valley Wine Train** (1275 McKinstry St., Napa, 800/427-4124, www.winetrain.com, $124-234). The Wine Train offers a relaxing sightseeing experience aboard vintage train cars, where you can sit back and enjoy the food, wine, and views. The train runs from Napa to St. Helena and back, a 36-mile three-hour round-trip. Add-ons include a gourmet three-course lunch or dinner, with the option of taking a winery tour along the way. Each package includes seating in a different historical railcar—you might lunch in the 1917 Pullman Car or aboard the 1952 Vista Dome Car. Advance reservations are strongly suggested.

YOUNTVILLE

Named for George Calvert Yount, who planted the first vineyard in Napa Valley, Yountville is the quintessential wine-loving town. There are not even 3,000 residents, but the town has earned widespread fame for its epicurean spirit. Although there are some prestigious wineries and champagneries, it is really restaurateur Thomas Keller who put this postage stamp-size town on the map. First came the French Laundry, then Bouchon and the Bouchon Bakery, and eventually Ad Hoc. But it's not just a Keller company town; other notable eateries have opened up and keep pace. Still, with so many fantastic dining options, you might wish there was more to do in Yountville to extend your stay in order to accommodate as many meals out as possible.

Wineries

★ DOMAINE CHANDON

One of the premier champagneries in Napa Valley, **Domaine Chandon** (1 California Dr., 888/242-6366, www.chandon.com, 10am-5pm daily, $20-40) offers one of the best tours in Napa. Walk out into the vineyards to look at the grapes, head down to the tank- and barrel-filled cellars to learn about the champagne-making process, then proceed into the aging rooms to see the racked bottles, tilted and dusty, aging to the point of drinkability. Finally, you'll adjourn to the tasting room. Chandon also makes still wines, which you can taste, and small bites are available should all the bubbly go to your head. Reservations are required for tours, and booking in advance is a good idea.

HILL FAMILY ESTATE

Right on Washington Street, the **Hill Family Estate** (6512 Washington St., 707/944-9580, www.hillfamilyestate.com, 10am-6pm daily, $20) tasting room and eclectic antiques shop offers an elegant tasting and shopping experience. Roam among the pricey French antiques as you sip, or stand at the bar to enjoy the company of the Hill family and a small selection of light, balanced red and white wines. The cabernet sauvignons are not made in the typical heavy-handed Napa style, so even tasters with delicate palates will find them drinkable.

JESSUP CELLARS

Also located in downtown Yountville, the tiny tasting room at **Jessup Cellars** (6740 Washington St., 707/944-8523, www.jessupcellars.com, 10am-6pm daily, $10-20) offers tastes of incredible boutique red wines that

Domaine Chandon

you'll have a hard time finding anyplace else. There are no tours here and no picnic grounds or fancy gardens, but you'll find lush, rich zinfandels and deep, smoky cabernets that are more than worth the sometimes-steep price tag. The tasting room boasts a cute little bar, a few shelves with items for purchase, and staff that love their jobs. If you chat them up, you may find yourself tasting rare Jessup vintages that are not on the usual list.

ROBERT SINSKEY VINEYARDS

Robert Sinskey Vineyards (6320 Silverado Tr., 707/944-9090, www.robertsinskey.com, 10am-4:30pm daily, $25-75) is best known for its pinot noir, but the winery itself is a feast for the senses. Fields of lavender greet guests on their way to the stone and redwood cathedral-like tasting area where a menu of small bites made with ingredients from the vineyard's organic garden is served alongside their list of wines. The appointment-only tour ($75) includes a look in the cave and cellar, and discussions about the art of winemaking make a visit worthwhile.

STAG'S LEAP WINE CELLARS

Perhaps the most famous winery near Yountville is **Stag's Leap Wine Cellars** (5766 Silverado Trail, Napa, 866/422-7523, www.cask23.com, 10am-4:30pm daily, $25-40), which made the cabernet sauvignon that beat out the best French Bordeaux in the now-famous 1976 blind tasting in Paris. It still makes outstanding single-vineyard cabernet. Such renowned wines command high prices, none more so than the Cask 23 cabernet, which retails at about $210. Although a magnet for serious wine enthusiasts, this family-run winery exudes an unassuming and friendly atmosphere, making it far less intimidating for the casual day-tripper than many of the valley's other big names.

Sights

More about the history of Napa and the entire valley can be found at the **Napa Valley Museum** (55 Presidents Circle, Yountville, 707/944-0500, www.napavalleymuseum.org, 10am-4pm Tues.-Sun., adults $5, seniors $3.50, 17 and under $2.50). It has a fascinating mix of exhibits exploring the valley's natural and cultural heritage. You'll learn about the modern wine industry with an interactive high-tech exhibit on the science of winemaking, as well as the local Native American tribes. The upstairs gallery houses rotating exhibitions featuring the work of local artists or art depicting food and wine.

Spas

An easy walk from anywhere in downtown Yountville, the **Spa Villagio** (6481 Washington St., 800/351-1133, http://villagio.com, 7:30am-9pm daily, nonguests $65-250) has a beautiful space in which to pamper its patrons. You don't need to be a guest at the Villagio Inn to book a treatment at the spa, though you may want to try one of the five Spa Suites—private spaces where singles, couples, and friends can relax before, during, and after their treatments. Show up an hour early for your massage, facial, or treatment package to take advantage of the saunas and hot tubs, relaxation rooms, and other chichi amenities. The spa recommends making reservations for your treatment at least three weeks in advance, especially during the high season.

A purely Napa Valley experience is the 50-minute "Uncorked" treatment at the **North Block Spa** (6757 Washington St., 707/944-8080, http://northblockhotel.com/spa, 8am-8pm daily, $120-300), in which masseurs rub patrons' feet with ground grape seeds and massage their pressure points with wine corks. The spa also offers acupuncture, facials, and dry exfoliation treatments in its modern and minimalist setting.

Entertainment and Events

At the **Lincoln Theater** (100 California Dr., 707/944-9900, www.lincolntheatre.com, $10-125), a packed year-round season brings top-end live entertainment of all kinds to Wine Country. See touring Broadway shows, locally produced plays, and stand-up comedy.

Although this large theater seats hundreds, purchase tickets in advance, especially for one-night-only performances.

A good excuse to walk off all that fine food and wine is the **Art Walk** (www.townofyountville.com), which stretches along Washington Street from California Street to Monroe Street. Forty works of modern art from local and internationally known artists dot the small town. Look for the 200 stone mushrooms outside of the post office or the elegant *Great Blue Heron* hidden by the Vintage Inn. The town website has a printable map of the Art Walk, or pick one up at the **Yountville Visitors Center** (6484 Washington St., 707/944-0904, http://yountville.com, 10am-5pm daily).

Shopping

You'll find plenty of shops lining Yountville's main drag, but most of the action is around the giant brick **V Marketplace** (6525 Washington St., Yountville, 707/944-2451, 10am-5:30pm daily). Once a winery and distillery built in 1870, the building lends an air of sophistication to the little boutique shops selling everything from clothes and accessories to toys, art, and the usual Wine Country gifts. **V Wine Cellar** (797/531-7053, 10am-7pm daily) occupies 4,000 square feet selling fine boutique wines. It has a lounge and a tasting area within the shop.

Arts and crafts lovers should cross Washington Street to **Beard Plaza,** where some of the town's galleries can be found. Another gallery hub is farther down Washington Street at the little plaza at the corner of Mulberry Street.

Sports and Recreation

Biking is a popular way to see the vineyards, forests, and wineries of Napa. You can get away from the highways and the endless traffic of the wine roads on two wheels. If you don't know the area, the best way to bike it is to take a tour. **Napa Valley Bike Tours** (6500 Washington St., 707/251-8687, www.napavalleybiketours.com, 8:30am-5pm daily, tours $99-159, bike rentals $45-90/day) offers guided and self-guided tours of the area in which you'll pedal through the vineyards, and a half-day or full-day tour that includes wine-tasting and meals. Bike rentals are also available if you want to explore on your own.

Accommodations

If you've come to Napa Valley to dine at the French Laundry or immerse yourself in the food scene, you'll want to stay in Yountville if you can. Several inns are within stumbling distance of the French Laundry, which is convenient for gourmands who want to experience a range of wines with the meal.

$150-250

A French-style inn, the **Maison Fleurie** (6529 Yount St., 800/788-0369, www.foursisters.com, $160-265) offers the best of small-inn style for a reasonable nightly rate. It is in a perfect location for walking to Bouchon, the Bouchon Bakery, and many other restaurants, boutiques, and tasting rooms in town. The 13 rooms in this "house of flowers" have an attractive but not overwhelming floral theme. All guests enjoy a full breakfast each morning as well as an afternoon wine reception, fresh cookies, and complimentary access to the inn's bicycles.

The **Napa Valley Railway Inn** (6503 Washington St., 707/944-2000, www.napavalleyrailwayinn.com, $125-260) is the only place in the valley where you can sleep on a train. The inn's nine railcars and cabooses took their last trip many decades ago and are fitted out with king or queen beds, air-conditioning, skylights, flat-screen TVs, and private bathrooms, making surprisingly comfortable accommodations right in the middle of Yountville. Some of the perks include the in-house Coffee Caboose, where you can start your day with pastries and coffee, access to the nearby Yountville Fitness Center, and a Napa Valley Travel Packet ($20), which includes tasting vouchers, maps, bottled water, and Advil.

Located next to Bouchon Bakery, wake up to mouthwatering smells at the cozy five-room

Petit Logis Inn (6527 Yount St., 877/944-2332, www.petitlogis.com, $145-310). Each room has a fireplace, a jetted tub, and a fridge and is decorated in warm colors with an occasional mural. Low key and unpretentious, the inn is best described as "the place to come to pretend you live in Yountville." Breakfast is not included but can be arranged for an additional charge.

OVER $250

At **The Cottages of Napa Valley** (1012 Darms Lane, 2 miles south of Yountville, 707/252-7810, www.napacottages.com, $305-575), you'll pay a princely sum to gain a home away from home in the heart of Wine Country. Each cottage has its own king bed, private garden, outdoor fireplace, and kitchenette. Every morning the quiet staff drops off a basket of fresh pastries from Bouchon Bakery and a pot of great coffee for breakfast, and a free shuttle will deliver you to your Yountville restaurant of choice for dinner.

Enjoy the location and luxury of the **Vintage Inn** (6541 Washington St., 707/944-1112, www.vintageinn.com, $337-650). Rooms in the elegant hexagonal buildings feature soft sheets and L'Occitane toiletries. The French country-meets-Wine Country decor extends to a private patio or deck overlooking the lush gardens. The dining room serves what might be the best complimentary hotel buffet breakfast in California, and at 3pm is a free full-fledged afternoon tea, complete with finger sandwiches, homemade scones, and organic teas—plus wine, of course. As a sister property of the nearby Villagio, Vintage Inn guests get use of the Villagio's fitness center, tennis courts, and spa.

The **Hotel Yountville** (6462 Washington St., 707/867-7900 or 888/944-2885, www.hotelyountville.com, $341-545) is another with a distinctively French farmhouse appeal. The 80-room hotel has a cobblestone exterior, exposed beams, and tons of natural light. The rooms have vaulted ceilings, a four-poster bed, white Italian linens, a fireplace, a spa tub, and French doors opening onto a private patio. Suites are also available with all the same amenities. There is a full-service spa, pool, and high-end restaurant.

Food

The tiny town of Yountville boasts perhaps the biggest reputation for culinary excellence in California—a big deal when you consider the offerings of San Francisco and Los Angeles. The reason for this reputation starts and ends with restaurateur Thomas Keller's indisputably amazing ★ **French Laundry** (6640 Washington St., 707/944-2380, www.frenchlaundry.com, 5:30pm-9pm Mon.-Fri., 11am-1pm, 5:30pm-9pm Sat.-Sun., by reservation only, $295). From the moment you walk in the door of the rambling Victorian, you're treated like royalty. You'll be led to your seat in one of the small dining rooms by one of the black-and-white-clad staff, who will make you feel more than welcome. The menu, which changes often, offers two main selections: the regular nine-course tasting menu and the vegetarian nine-course tasting menu. The sommelier is at your beck and call to assist with a wine list that weighs several pounds. Then the meal begins. From the start, waiters and footmen ply you with extras—an *amuse-bouche* here, an extra middle course there—and if you mention that someone else has something on their plate that you'd like to try, it appears in front of you as if by magic. Finally, the desserts come, and come, and come. All together, a meal at the French Laundry can run up to 13 courses and take four hours to eat.

If you can't get to the French Laundry, try another Thomas Keller option, **Bouchon** (6534 Washington St., 707/944-8037, www.bouchonbistro.com, 11am-midnight Mon.-Fri., 10am-midnight Sat.-Sun., $34). Reservations are still strongly recommended, but you should be able to get one just a week in advance. Bouchon's atmosphere and food scream Parisian bistro. Order traditional favorites such as the *croque monsieur* or steak frites, or opt for a California-influenced specialty salad or entrée made with local sustainable ingredients.

Reservations for French Laundry

Most people familiar with the world of high-end food know that the best restaurant in California, and possibly in the United States, is the **French Laundry.** Thomas Keller's culinary haven in tiny Yountville was the only restaurant in the greater Bay Area to earn the coveted three-star Michelin Guide rating in 2007. The restaurant is in a charming vintage house, and the kitchen garden is right across the street, where you can walk among the rows of vegetables and herbs. It may sound like a foodie paradise, but there's just one problem—getting a table.

The difficulty in getting reservations to the French Laundry is almost as legendary as the French Laundry itself. Rather than expecting to dine at the French Laundry during a planned trip to the Wine Country, savvy travelers expect to plan their whole trip around whatever French Laundry reservation they manage to get.

The bare facts: The French Laundry takes reservations *precisely* two months in advance by phone, online, and via local concierges. Reservations are accepted for parties of two, four, or six only. Diners can choose between lunch and dinner seatings that offer the same menu. It's easier to get a table for lunch than for dinner; both take 2.5-4 hours. Budget $500 per person for your meal if you plan to drink wine, and $300-350 if you don't.

The French Laundry starts taking **phone reservations** at 10am daily. Between 9:30am and 9:45am, program their number on your speed-dial and begin calling; continue calling until you get an answer. If you get a continuous busy signal past 11am, you'll probably need to try again the next day, and maybe the day after that.

Making **reservations online** works much the same way as on the phone, only it's harder. Each day the French Laundry offers only one table, for lunch, online. Visit OpenTable (www.opentable.com) at about 8:30am and start trying to snag that table. If you're still trying at 9:30am, it's probably already gone.

Hands down the least stressful way to get a coveted French Laundry table is to hire a concierge to do it for you. The French Laundry lets concierges walk downtown to the restaurant each day to put in bookings for their clients. Call or email a concierge and expect to pay a nominal fee ($20-30). Give your new best friend a range of dates and times that will suit you, and he or she will do their best to accommodate your request. Do not expect to get your first choice of times; flexible diners will find themselves with a remarkably trouble-free reservation experience.

So, is it really worth all this rigmarole just to get into one restaurant, and then pay a sizeable amount of money for a single meal? Yes. With the gracious welcome at the door, stunning service throughout, the meal, and the food that can be found nowhere else, dining at the French Laundry is worth both the hassle and the price tag.

If you're just looking for a breakfast pastry or a sandwich, walk from Bouchon next door to the **Bouchon Bakery** (6528 Washington St., 707/944-2253, www.bouchonbakery.com, 7am-7pm daily). This high-end bakery supplies both Bouchon and the French Laundry with pastries and breads and operates a retail storefront. Locals and visitors flock to the bakery at breakfast and lunchtime, so expect a line.

Ad Hoc (6476 Washington St., 707/944-2487, 5pm-10pm Mon. and Thurs.-Sat., 10am-1pm, 5pm-10pm Sun., prix fixe menu $52) is Thomas Keller's fourth adventure in Yountville. The four-course rustic menu changes nightly, and you'll get no choices, but considering the quality of the seasonal fare, that's not a bad thing. The only certainty is that there'll be either soup or salad followed by a meat or fish main course, a cheese course, and dessert. The wine list is endowed with moderately priced Californian and international wines. Reservations are not required, but don't expect to walk in and get a table.

If a visit to a Yountville restaurant is not complete without a celebrity chef sighting, make a reservation at **Bottega** (6525 Washington St., 707/945-1050, www.botteganapavalley.com, 5pm-9:30pm Mon.,

11:30am-2:30pm, 5pm-9:30pm Tues.-Sun., $17-36) in the V Marketplace, where celebrity chef Michael Chiarello frequently strolls out into the dining room. Aside from the finely executed Italian cuisine, the big draw here is the covered patio where two large fireplaces, ringed by couches, invite you to sip a cocktail or glass of wine late into the evening or on a rainy afternoon.

For a local favorite, **Bistro Jeanty** (6510 Washington St., 707/944-0103, www.bistro-jeanty.com, 11:30am-10:30pm daily, $15-39) may be the place for you. The menu is a single page devoted to Parisian bistro classics. Tomato bisque served with a puff pastry shell, cassoulet, and coq au vin are all crafted with joy. Service is friendly, and locals hang at the bar, watching the TV tuned to a sports channel. Jeanty has two dining rooms, making walk-in dining easy on off-season weeknights. Make a dinner reservation on the weekend or in high season.

Information and Services

Right in the thick of the epicurean madness is the Welcome Center at the **Yountville Chamber of Commerce** (6484 Washington St., 707/944-0904, www.yountville.com, 10am-5pm daily). They offer wine-tasting coupons for nearby wineries. There are also maps available, and the staff can offer helpful tips.

Transportation

CAR

Yountville is on Highway 29, nine miles north of Napa. Downtown Yountville is on the east side of Highway 29, and Washington Street is the main drag, connecting with Highway 29 at the south and north ends of town. To reach the heart of Yountville, exit on California Drive in the south and Madison Street in the north. The Yountville Cross Road will take you from the north end of town to the Silverado Trail.

BUS AND TROLLEY

To reach Yountville by bus, jump aboard the **VINE** (707/251-2600 or 800/696-6443, www.ridethevine.com, adults $1.50-5.50, children $1-2.50), which has routes running to Yountville daily.

Around town, take the **Yountville Trolley** (www.ridethevine.com, 10am-11pm Mon.-Sat., 10am-7pm Sun., free). The trolley runs on a fixed track from Yountville Park along Washington Street to California Drive, near Domaine Chandon. The trolley also offers free pickup service (707/944-1234, after 7pm 707/312-1509).

RUTHERFORD AND OAKVILLE

Driving north along Highway 29, you might not even notice the tiny hamlets of Oakville and Rutherford. Neither town has much in the way of a commercial or residential district, and both have tiny populations. Oakville earned a spot on the map in 1903 when the U.S. Department of Agriculture planted an experimental vineyard. Since then, it has garnered distinction as a unique American Viticultural Area (AVA) known for its Bordeaux-style varietals.

Rutherford was named for the 1,000 acres given to Thomas Rutherford by his father-in-law, George Yount. The region is a distinguished American Viticultural Area (AVA) known for growing some of the best cabernet grapes around.

Wineries

ROBERT MONDAVI WINERY

This sprawling mission-style complex, with its distinctive giant archway and bell tower, is considered the temple of modern Napa winemaking, with the late Robert Mondavi the high priest. The **Robert Mondavi Winery** (7801 Hwy. 29, Oakville, 888/766-6328, www.robertmondaviwinery.com, 10am-5pm daily, $20-45), started in the 1960s, has some very special wines (particularly the classic cabernet, chardonnay, and sauvignon blanc) that draw crowds. The impressive grounds and buildings are certainly highlights. There are a variety of tours ($20-50, reservations recommended) to choose from and all include a tasting.

OPUS ONE

That huge thing that looks like a missile silo really is a winery. **Opus One** (7900 Hwy. 29, Oakville, 707/944-9442 or 800/292-6787, www.opusonewinery.com, 10am-4pm daily, reservations required) boasts a reputation as one of the most prestigious and expensive vintners in Napa. The echoing halls inside the facility add to the grandeur of the place, as does the price of a tasting ($45 for a three-ounce pour of a single wine). It's rare to find a bottle of Opus One for under $250. Tours ($75-120, by appointment only) of the estate are also available.

PEJU

Peju (8466 Hwy. 29, Rutherford, 800/446-7358, www.peju.com, 10am-6pm daily, $25), with its manicured gardens, koi pond, and lofty tasting room (in a tower replete with a giant stained-glass window), has the feel of a French country estate viewed through a hallucinogenic haze. Owner Anthony Peju made his way to Napa Valley from his homeland of Azerbaijan by way of France, England, and Los Angeles. Peju is perhaps best known for its cabernet franc, but it's usually not available for tasting because of its cultlike status. Instead, visitors can taste the equally outstanding estate cabernet sauvignon and the unusual provence table wine, a dark rose blend of many varietals.

INGLENOOK WINERY

When a fabled Hollywood director buys a storied Napa Valley winery, it's inevitable that the result would be one of the most impressive in the valley. And so it is at **Inglenook Winery** (1991 St. Helena Hwy., Rutherford, 707/986-1100 or 800/782-4266, www.inglenook.com, 11am-5pm daily, reservations required, $50). The Inglenook Estate was established in 1871 and bought by Francis Ford Coppola in 1975. At the estate, a great effort is underway to recreate the style of wines made in the winery's heyday. To taste the wines, you must sign up for a tour and tasting, or a seated tasting paired with cheese or small bites. These generally last 1.5 hours and occur daily. Although the price is stiff, the tours are fascinating and the food pairings are significant enough to serve as lunch.

Another option is to stop by **The Bistro** (10am-5pm daily), a café space on the estate grounds. The menu offers French inspired food that pairs perfectly with wine served by the bottle or glass. If you want a casual tasting at Inglenook, buying a glass at The Bistro is the only option.

GRGICH HILLS WINERY

Some of the best wines in the valley are at **Grgich Hills Winery** (1829 St. Helena Hwy., Rutherford, 707/963-2784, www.grgich.com, 9:30am-4:30pm daily, $20-50), an entirely biodynamic winemaking operation. Grgich Hills established a rich history of California wine, taking its rightful place alongside or ahead of the great French vintages. When winemaker Mike Grgich (then working for Calistoga's Chateau Montelena) took his California chardonnay to the Paris Wine Tasting of 1976 and entered it in the white-burgundy blind tasting competition, it won. French winemakers were incensed. They demanded that the contest be held again; Grgich's chardonnay won for a second time.

The winery offers plenty of information about biodynamic farming, a process that takes organic practices to the next level. The best wine might be the descendants of Mike's legendary chardonnay—arguably the best chardonnay made in Napa or anywhere else. But don't ignore the reds; Grgich offers some lovely zinfandels and cabernets.

★ FROG'S LEAP WINERY

Frog's Leap Winery (8815 Conn Creek Rd., Rutherford, 707/963-4704, www.frogsleap.com, 10am-4pm daily, $25) is known for environmental stewardship and organic wine production. This understated winery is housed in a historical red barn and modest home, surrounded by vineyards and gardens. Tasting here is relaxing; sample a flight of four wines on the wraparound porch or inside the vineyard house, accompanied by cheese, crackers, and jam. The highly recommended tour (one hour, by appointment only, $25) also provides a tasting of four wines, and each pour is enjoyed somewhere different along the tour route.

★ MUMM

Even for genuine wine aficionados, it's worth spending an hour or two at **Mumm** (8445 Silverado Trail, Rutherford, 707/967-7700, http://mummnapa.com, 10am-5pm daily, $18-40), a friendly and surprisingly down-to-earth winery on the Silverado Trail. Tastings take place at tables, in restaurant fashion. The prices may look very Napa Valley, but you'll get more wine and service for your money at Mumm. Each pour is three ounces of wine—some of it high end—and you get three pours per tasting. Nonalcoholic gourmet grape sodas and bottled water are complimentary for designated drivers. Dogs are welcome in the tasting room, too.

For the best of the winery, join a tour (10am, 11am, 1pm, 3pm daily, no reservation necessary, $25) of the sample vineyard and the production facility. The knowledgeable and articulate tour guides describe the process of making sparkling wine in detail. All tours wind up at the only gallery showing original Ansel Adams prints outside Yosemite Valley. Tasting and a champagne flute are included in the price.

Frog's Leap Winery

Sports and Recreation

For a lake vacation 30 minutes from Wine Country, drive a few miles out to **Lake Berryessa** (Berryessa-Knoxville Rd., east of Rutherford, 916/989-7200, www.usbr.gov). On this largish lake you can ride powerboats, personal watercraft, kayaks, and canoes, and fish—or just sunbathe on the shore and splash around in the shallows with the family. If you've got your own boat, launch it at one of the marinas or the **Capell Cove Boat Ramp** (Knoxville Rd.), or rent one from one of the lakeside resorts. The **Markley Cove Resort** (7521 Hwy. 128, Napa, 707/966-4204, www.markleycoveresort.com) offers all kinds of boats, including patio cruisers, high-end ski-tow boats, personal watercraft, and kayaks. Make reservations well in advance to get the boat you want. You can also rent water skis, wakeboards, and ski tubes.

Lake Berryessa boasts some of the best fishing in California. Fish for cold- and warm-water fish, including bass, rainbow trout, and kokanee salmon. Rent a boat from one of the resorts, launch your own, or fish from the shore. The lakeside resorts sell California fishing licenses and bait and can advise you about the season's hottest fishing holes.

Accommodations

Courtyards dripping in wisteria, earth-tone stucco, tiled roofs, and rustic stonework draw guests back in time to **Rancho Caymus** (1140 Rutherford Rd., Rutherford, 707/963-1777 or 800/845-1777, www.ranchocaymus.com, $180-389) and Napa Valley's Spanish past. Each of the 26 suites is named for early Napa adventurers, and many include a separate sitting area, wood-burning fireplaces, Spanish tiled baths, a refrigerator, and a private outdoor area.

Perched above the valley, off the Silverado Trail, **Auberge du Soleil** (180 Rutherford Hill Rd., St. Helena, 707/963-1211 or 800/348-5406, www.aubergedusoleil.com, $700) is the ultimate in Wine Country luxury. The compound features multiple dining options in addition to a pool, a fitness room, a store, and well-kept gardens accented by modern art. The rooms are appointed with Italian sheets, private patios, fireplaces, and TVs in both the living room and the bath. Rooms range 500-1,800 square feet.

Food

For a special occasion, there's no better place in this part of the valley than ★ **Auberge du Soleil** (180 Rutherford Hill Rd., St. Helena, 800/348-5406, www.aubergedusoleil.com, 7am-11am, 11:30am-2:30pm, 5:30pm-9:30pm daily, $110-150). This resort restaurant has been wowing diners with its menu and stunning views of the valley since 1981. The set price menu buys a three-, four-, or six-course dinner with exquisitely prepared French-Californian food. Request a table on the terrace for the best views, especially at sunset. And casual as it might be, this is still a fancy restaurant, so don't turn up in baggy shorts and flip-flops. For a less indulgent affair, visit the adjacent **Bistro & Bar** (11am-11pm daily, $17-29). Choose from braised short ribs, a plate of charcuterie, or a light salad, accompanied by a rotating and wide selection of wines. Take in the wraparound deck and open fireplace without quite the pinch to your belt or wallet.

For down-to-earth dining, often without the need of a reservation, the **Rutherford Grill** (1180 Rutherford Rd., Rutherford, 707/963-1792, www.hillstone.com, 11:30am-9:30pm Mon.-Thurs., 11:30am-10:30pm Fri., 11am-10:30pm-Sat., 11am-9:30pm Sun., $15-40) offers traditional steakhouse fare in a slightly corporate setting. It has become one of the most popular steakhouses among Napa Valley residents and is a great place for a reliably cooked and aged steak paired with a Rutherford cabernet. There's also a shady patio, though it's too close to the road to be classified as peaceful.

For a picnic lunch or snacks for the road, stop by the **Oakville Grocery** (7856 St. Helena Hwy., Oakville, 707/944-8802, www.oakvillegrocery.com, 6:30am-5pm Mon.-Thurs., 6:30am-6pm Fri.-Sun., $12). A

vineyards at Mumm

long-standing Napa Valley institution, the Oakville Grocery has a reputation for stocking only the best food, wine, cheese, and other goodies. Browse the tightly packed shelves or order a hot lunch at the center counter; they have everything from crab cakes to chimichangas and boxed lunches. To find the building from the northbound highway, look for the large Coca-Cola sign painted on the south side of the building.

Transportation

Oakville is four miles north of Yountville on Highway 29; Rutherford is another two miles north. Both can be easy to miss because of their loose organization and rural character. The Silverado Trail runs parallel to Highway 29 along this stretch. To reach it from Oakville, take Oakville Road east; in Rutherford, take Rutherford Road (Hwy. 128) east.

ST. HELENA

There are few Northern California towns as picturesque and well groomed as St. Helena. Bolstered by the lucrative wine industry, St. Helena has the glossy sheen of a reinvented California farm town. It is filled with fine eateries and quaint shops housed in historical buildings and surrounded by well-maintained craftsman homes. The Napa campus of the Culinary Institute of America is a major employer in the area, as is the St. Helena Hospital. Highway 29 runs north-south through the center of town, which can give you a quick peek at the sights, but it's not so nice when sitting in traffic on a sunny weekend.

Wineries

V. SATTUI

A big winery that doesn't distribute to retailers, **V. Sattui** (1111 White Ln., 707/963-7774, www.vsattui.com, 9am-5pm Sun.-Fri., 9am-5:30pm Sat., $15) has won several Best Winery awards at the California State Fair. V. Sattui produces a wide selection of varietals—everything from light-bodied whites to full-flavored cabernet sauvignons. The dessert madeira is particularly fine—if it's not on the tasting menu, ask your pourer at the bar if they've got a bottle open.

The big tasting room boasts three spacious bar areas, a separate register, and a full deli. The surrounding gardens include picnic tables, making V. Sattui a popular lunchtime stop for all-day tasters. The tasting room fills on weekends in high season.

HEITZ

One of the oldest wineries in the valley, **Heitz** (436 St. Helena Hwy., 707/963-3542, www.heitzcellar.com, 11am-4:30pm daily, free) brings sincere elegance to the glitz and glamour of Napa. The high-ceilinged tasting room is dominated by a stone fireplace with comfy chairs. Heitz's cabernets are well balanced and easy to drink, and though costly, they approach affordable by Napa standards. Most of the grapes used for these wines grow right in the Napa Valley. In February, taste the current release of the Martha's Vineyard Cabernet—a vintage grown in the first wine-designated vineyard in the valley.

HALL WINES

At **HALL Wines** (401 St. Helena Hwy. S., St. Helena, 707/967-2626, www.hallwines.com, 10am-5:30pm daily, $30) you'll notice two things. One is that the Halls are big fans of modern art and design; the other is that their winery is the first LEED/Gold Certified winery in California. Hall's new "winery complex" and tasting room has an industrial chic different from the typical chateau aesthetic. Filled with art and surrounded by views of the mountains, HALL offers highly rated wines. Spend an extra $10 and book a spot on the HALLmark Tour and Tasting (daily, $40) or Wine and Art Exploration (Sun., $40). Both tour the grounds, discuss art, design, and the Halls' environmental mission, along with tasting several vintages.

VELO VINO

Velo Vino (709 Main St., St. Helena, 707/968-0625, www.cliffamilywinery.com,

Know Your Grapes

Chardonnay: Most of the white wine made and sold in California is chardonnay. The grapes grow best in a slightly cooler climate, such as the vineyards closer to the coast. Most California chardonnays taste smooth and buttery and a bit like fruit, and they often take on the oak flavor of the barrels they sit in. Chardonnay doesn't keep (age), so most chards are sold the year after they're bottled and consumed within a few months of purchase.

Sauvignon blanc: This pale-green grape is used to make both sauvignon blanc and fumé blanc wines. Sauvignon blanc grapes grow well in Napa, Sonoma, and other warm-hot parts of the state. The difference between a sauvignon blanc and a fumé blanc is in the winemaking more than in the grapes. Fumé blanc wines tend to have a strong odor and the taste of grapefruit; they pair well with fish dishes and spicy Asian cuisine. The California sauvignon blanc wine goes well with salads, fish, vegetarian cuisine, and even spicy international dishes.

Pinot noir: Pinot noir grapes do best in a cool coastal climate with limited exposure to high heat. The Anderson Valley and the Monterey coastal growing regions tend to specialize in pinot noir, though many Napa and Sonoma wineries buy grapes from the coast to make their own versions. California vintners make up single-varietal pinot noir wines that taste of cherries, strawberries, and smoke.

Zinfandel: These grapes grow best when tortured by their climate; a few grow near Napa, but most come from Dry Creek Valley, Gold Country, and the inland Central Coast. A true zinfandel is a hearty deep-red wine and boasts the flavors and smells of blackberry jam and the dusky hues of venous blood. Zinfandel often tastes wonderful on its own, but it's also good with beef, buffalo, and even venison.

Cabernet sauvignon: Cabernet sauvignon, a grape from the Bordeaux region of France, creates a deep, dark, strong red wine. The grapes that get intense summer heat make the best wine, which makes them a perfect fit for the scorching Napa Valley. In California, especially in Napa, winemakers use cabernet sauvignon on its own to brew some of the most intense single-grape wines in the world. A good dry cab might taste of leather, tobacco, and bing cherries. Cabs age well, often hitting their peak of flavor and smoothness more than a decade after bottling.

10am-6pm daily, $15-20) is the tasting room for Clif Family Winery. If the name rings a bell, you'll place it when you enter the tasting room where energy bars line the walls and just as much space is devoted to cycling as to wine. This is the enological endeavor of the man behind Clif Bar. Gary Erikson and his wife Kit moved to Napa Valley in 1999 and now make a variety of wines, from riesling to cabernet. The wines are good and the tasting is fun, but the best part is the bar itself. There, locals sip glasses of wine ($7 white, $10 red) and chat with the staff. Small bites are available and pours are generous. You can rent bikes here, too.

BERINGER VINEYARDS

The oldest continuously operating winery in Napa Valley, **Beringer Vineyards** (2000 Main St., 707/302-7592 or 866/708-9463, www.beringer.com, 10am-6pm daily June-late Oct., 10am-5pm daily late Oct.-May, $20-25) is a huge tourist attraction that often contributes to St. Helena's summer traffic jams. It is still worth a visit (ideally midweek, when it's a bit quieter) for its significance and for some outstanding reserve wines.

The winery was established in 1876 and the entire estate, including the lavish and ornate Rhine House built by German Frederick Beringer to remind him of home, was placed on the National Register of Historic Places in 2001. It is an impressive location to taste some of Beringer's reserve wines. The regular tasting is in the old winery building up the hill and offers several themed flights for less money (and atmosphere). Stroll in the beautiful estate gardens that stretch for acres on prime land. Tours (daily, reservation only, $25-40) show off the highlights of the vast estate and its winemaking facilities.

PRIDE MOUNTAIN VINEYARDS

Take advantage of some of Wine Country's scenic drives with a visit to **Pride Mountain Vineyards** (4026 Spring Mountain Rd., 707/963-4949, www.pridewines.com, 10am-3:45pm daily, reservations required, tour and tasting $25, tasting only $20), located at the top of a scenic winding road six miles from the turnoff on Highway 29. In addition to the wine, the views are the reward for the effort. Wine-tasting is by appointment only. It's worth it to take the tour, as you'll see the vineyard and the caves and will be able to taste wine straight out of the barrel. It's a great education in how wine matures with age.

Sights

Under the cool shade trees of the Napa hills, the gristmill at **Bale Grist Mill State Historic Park** (3369 N St./Hwy. 29, 3 miles north of St. Helena, 707/942-2236, www.parks.ca.gov, 10am-5pm Fri.-Mon. summer, 10am-5pm Sat.-Sun. fall-spring) is quiet. The huge water wheel no longer turns, and the vast network of elevated and ground-level wooden pipes and ducts have dried out. Visitors can take a pleasant nature walk to the site of Dr. Edward Bale's old wheel and mill structures. Take a tour inside the flour mill with a docent who will tell the story of the gristmill and show off the facility built from local stone, redwood, and fir. Afterward, hike farther into the woods along several shady trails.

The **Robert Louis Stevenson Museum** (1490 Library Ln., St. Helena, 707/963-3757, www.silveradomuseum.org, noon-4pm Tues.-Sat., free) is a rich collection honoring the celebrated 19th-century author. The museum boasts 9,000 items and is a draw for Stevenson scholars. In addition to original manuscripts, letters, and early and rare editions of his books, the museum houses the elegant wooden desk on which Stevenson wrote *Treasure Island*, his wedding ring, and the lead toy soldiers he played with as a boy. The museum takes up a wing of the St. Helena Library, which also has an impressive collection of 19th-century art adorning the walls.

★ CULINARY INSTITUTE OF AMERICA

Napa Valley takes food very seriously, so it's fitting that the West Coast outpost of the **Culinary Institute of America** (CIA, 2555 Main St., 707/967-1100, www.ciachef.edu, 10am-6pm daily) is housed in the fortresslike former Greystone Winery, one of the grandest winery buildings in California. Just north of downtown St. Helena, hour-long cooking demonstrations are open to the public. You can also pop into the **Bakery Café** (10:30am-5pm daily), take a seat at the highly celebrated **Wine Spectator Restaurant** (707/967-1010, 5:30pm-8:30pm Tues.-Sat., $22-29), or visit the slightly more casual farm-to-table **Conservatory Restaurant** (707/967-2300, 5:30pm-9pm Fri.-Sat.). The **Spice Islands Marketplace** (707/967-2309, 10:30am-6pm daily) is considered one of the best kitchen stores in the valley.

It's also possible to explore the historical building and grounds on your own. A small exhibit just beyond the carved redwood entry illustrates the history of the 1890 Greystone Winery with some of the original barrels, casks, and brandy-making stills. Most intriguing of all is a display of more than a thousand corkscrews, some of them hundreds of years old.

Shopping

Quaint and historical storefronts line Highway 29, housing galleries, clothiers, jewelers, kitchen stores, and wine shops (many of which offer tastings). The **St. Helena Olive Oil Company** (1351 Main St., 800/939-9880, www.sholiveoil.com, 10:30am-5pm daily), in the historical Bank of Italy building, will give you the opportunity to parse out notes of grass, citrus, or pepper in its Napa Valley olive oils. One temptation you might not be able to resist is a treat from **Woodhouse Chocolate**

(1367 Main St., 800/966-3468, www.woodhousechocolate.com, 10:30am-5:30pm daily). It's an old-fashioned chocolatier with a sumptuous interior decor.

In St. Helena, fine art eclipses the typical Wine Country kitsch. You'll find a number of galleries and tasting rooms with sophisticated (and sometimes kooky) installations. On Main street, a must stop is **Martin Showroom** (1350 Main St., 707/967-8787, www.martinshowroom.com, 10am-6pm Tues.-Sat.), a showcase for designer Erin Martin, who fashions contemporary pieces with a rustic or industrial chic from natural and reclaimed materials. Although you may not take home a $15,000 table or bronze statue as a souvenir of the Wine Country, there's plenty of inspiration, along with more affordable, whimsical items for sale, from jewelry to housewares.

Accommodations

St. Helena is right on Highway 29; its stop signs and traffic signals are often the cause of Wine Country traffic jams. Stay here to avoid the worst of the traffic and enjoy the wooded central Napa Valley area.

For the best rates, the **El Bonita Motel** (195 Main St./Hwy. 29, 707/963-3216 or 800/541-3284, www.elbonita.com, $109-309) can't be beat. It's within walking distance of downtown and has a 1950s motel charm. The low-slung 42-room hotel wraps around a patio shaded by oak trees and filled with tables, chairs, and umbrellas. In the center is a pool, a hot tub, and a sauna. The rooms may not match the indulgence of other Napa inns, but they are clean, comfortable, and pet-friendly, with refrigerators and microwaves; some even boast kitchenettes.

The **Hotel St. Helena** (1309 Main St., 707/963-4388, www.hotelsthelena.net, $115-275) is as central as can be, down a little alley off Main Street, right in the middle of town. The old Victorian building is full of original features and stuffed with knickknacks. The 18 rooms get some limited modern touches like air-conditioning, but you'll have to tolerate temperamental plumbing and poor sound insulation. The four smallest and cheapest rooms share a bathroom. The best deals are the North Wing rooms, which are small, but have private bathrooms.

In the thick of downtown St. Helena, the **Wydown Hotel** (1424 Main St., 707/963-5100, www.wydownhotel.com, $270-370) offers a break from Victorian excess. The 12 rooms are smartly decorated while the lobby downstairs outdoes itself in urban chic. If you want to saturate yourself if St. Helena's modern art scene, here is the place to stay. The small hotel has little in the way of luxury amenities, but it offers a convenient location and historical digs that are modern and stylish.

Food

For a taste of everything in St. Helena, have lunch at ★ **Farmstead** (738 Main St., 707/963-9181, 11:30am-9:30pm Mon.-Thurs., 11:30am-10pm Fri.-Sat., 11am-9:30pm Sun., $23-36). Run by the Rutherford-based Long Meadow Ranch, Farmstead takes the idea of farm fresh to a new level. The ranch supplies many of the vegetables, herbs, olive oil, eggs, and grass-fed beef served at the restaurant. The restaurant is housed in a former nursery, where farm equipment and tree stumps have found new life as fixtures, fittings, and furnishings. Even the booths are covered in leather sourced from the ranch's cattle. The food hits the right balance of sophistication and familiarity. To escape the noisy barn, ask for one of the tables on the tree-shaded patio. Visit the ranch's General Store (daily 11am-6pm) to taste their estate wines and olive oils, as well as shop for locally made gifts.

For Michelin-starred dining in St. Helena, make a reservation at romantic ★ **Terra** (1345 Railroad Ave., 707/963-8931, www.terrasrestaurant.com, 6pm-9:30pm Thurs.-Mon., $78-105) located in the historical stone Hatchery Building. The menu is French and Californian with Asian flourishes and might include such eclectic creations as sake-marinated Alaskan black cod with shrimp dumplings. Diners create their own prix fixe by selecting four ($78), five ($93), or six ($105) courses from the 17 savory dishes on the menu. For something more casual but with the same fusion flair, dine at adjacent ★ **Bar Terra** (5:30pm-9:30pm Thurs.-Mon., $15-29), with its full liquor license and à la carte menu. Nibble on any one of Terra's signature dishes for considerably less.

The Cindy of ★ **Cindy's Backstreet Kitchen** (1327 Railroad Ave., 707/963-1200, www.cindysbackstreetkitchen.com, 11:30am-9:30pm daily, $14-30) is Cindy Pawlcyn, who is credited with bringing casual-sophisticated dining to Napa Valley when she opened Yountville's Mustards Grill in 1983. Backstreet is a charming hole-in-the-wall with a side entrance that makes it feel like you're walking into someone's house. The menu goes for homey charm, with large plates including meatloaf, wood-oven duck, and steak frites. Lunch (small plates, sandwiches) can be ordered to go. The patio is a hive of activity at lunch and can require a wait.

Inside the relaxed **Pizzeria Tra Vigne** (1016 Main St., 707/967-9999, www.travignerestaurant.com, 11:30am-9pm Sun.-Thurs., 11:30am-9:30pm Fri.-Sat., $10-21) are long tables opposite the open kitchen, where a huge wood-fired oven sits center stage. The famous thin-crust Italian pizzas lure locals many weekend nights. Wash it all down with a pitcher of any number of beers on tap. If you're traveling with kids, Pizzeria Tra Vigne is a great place. There is even a pool table.

Until 2010, **Gott's Roadside** (933 Main St., 707/963-3486, http://gotts.com, 8am-9pm daily, $10-20) was known as Taylor's Refresher, which explains the wooden sign on Highway 29. This classic roadside diner has been around since 1949, but the burgers, fries, and milk shakes have been updated with local, organic ingredients. There is also some California-eclectic comfort food like fish tacos and smoked chicken po'boys. Gott's has earned three James Beard awards.

Fortunately for locals, the quick stop for a morning cup of joe also happens to be one of the most celebrated bakeries in the valley. Known chiefly for its bread, the **Model Bakery** (1357 Main St., 707/963-8192, www.themodelbakery.com, 7am-7pm daily, $5-12) has been around since 1920. There are shelves of flour-dusted bread and display cases full of pastries, scones, and croissants. Everything here can please even the most fickle sweet tooth, especially the divine espresso bundt cake, which goes perfectly with a cup of Blue Bottle Coffee. Sandwiches, wood-fired pizzas, and salads also make this an easy stop for lunch.

Information and Services

Pick up maps, information, and discounted wine-tasting vouchers at the **St. Helena Welcome Center** (657 Main St., 707/963-4456, www.sthelena.com, 9am-5pm Mon.-Fri., 10am-5pm Sat.-Sun.). There is parking in back; turn on Vidovich Lane just north of the visitors center.

For health concerns, the **St. Helena Hospital** (10 Woodland Rd., 707/963-6425, http://sthelenanowaiter.org) has a 24-hour emergency room for quick and reliable service.

Transportation

St. Helena is on Highway 29 in the middle of Napa Valley, eight miles south of Calistoga. To reach the Silverado Trail from St. Helena, take Zinfandel Lane or Pope Street east.

To avoid the headache of parking and driving around town, hop aboard **The VINE St. Helena Shuttle** (707/963-3007, http://nctpa.net, 7:45am-6pm Mon.-Thurs., 7:45am-11pm Fri., $0.50-1). During weekends, the shuttle runs on-demand (10am-11pm Sat., noon-7pm Sun.). The price is the same; call to schedule a pickup.

CALISTOGA

Despite their proximity, Calistoga and St. Helena couldn't be more different. Calistoga has a laid-back mountain-town crunchiness to it. Far from the city of Napa, it is one of the most economically diverse towns in the valley. Browse books, grab great barbecue, or sit at a sidewalk café to enjoy a cheap beer. Calistoga is also the land of great and affordable spas, where soaking is treated more as therapy than beauty treatment.

Wineries

CASTELLO DI AMOROSA

Driving up to **Castello di Amorosa** (4045 N. St. Helena Hwy., 707/967-6272, www.castellodiamorosa.com, 9:30am-6pm daily Mar.-Nov., 9:30am-5pm daily Dec.-Feb., general admission 21 and over $20, children 5-20 $10), it is difficult to remember that it is a winery. Everything from the parking attendant directing cars through the crowded parking lot to the admission prices (which include a tasting of five wines, and juice for the kids) screams "Disneyland." And then there is the castle itself, complete with 107 rooms, eight floors, and made from 8,000 tons of stone and 850,000 European bricks.

Admission includes access to the main floors of the castle. Tours (adults $35, children $25) include barrel tasting and take visitors to the armory and torture chamber.

STERLING VINEYARDS

Sterling Vineyards (1111 Dunaweal Ln., 800/726-6136, www.sterlingvineyards.com, 10:30am-4:30pm Mon.-Fri., 10am-5pm Sat.-Sun., general admission adults $29, under 21 $15, children 3 and under free) is more appealing for folks who are touring Wine Country for the first time than for serious wine aficionados. Once you've stood in line and bought your tickets, a gondola ride up the mountain shows off Napa Valley at its best. Admire the stellar views of forested hills and endless vineyards. The wine doesn't match the effort or the high price tag, but the estate has charm. Views from the deck match those from the gondola.

CUVAISON

The intimate tasting room at **Cuvaison** (4550 Silverado Trail N., 707/942-2468, www.cuvaison.com, 11am-4pm Sun.-Thurs., 10am-5pm Fri.-Sat., $15-20) doesn't hold busloads of visitors, and the bar might show a few scars, but the tasting room staff know quite a bit about the wine they're pouring, and they want to tell you all about it. The quaint building sits on the slope of the mountains bordering Napa Valley and shelters several friendly cats. A picnic area invites a longer stop to enjoy the vineyard views with your lunch and a bottle of Cuvaison chardonnay, or just to relax and sip one of their light tasty reds.

CHATEAU MONTELENA

The beautiful French- and Chinese-inspired **Chateau Montelena** (1429 Tubbs Ln., 707/942-5105, www.montelena.com, 9:30am-4pm daily, $25) will forever be remembered for putting Napa Valley on the map when its 1973-vintage chardonnay trounced the best French white burgundies at the famous 1976 Paris tasting. But if the wines aren't enough, the grounds are worth a visit. The stone chateau was built in 1882; the ornamental Chinese garden was added in 1965. It is centered around the lush five-acre Jade Lake, crisscrossed with lacquered bridges. Several tours (reservations required, $40) are available. Check the website for times and to book a spot.

LAVA VINE

Sitting on the Silverado Trail just outside of town, **Lava Vine** (965 Silverado Trail, 707/942-9500, www.lavavine.com, 10am-5pm daily, $10) is a winery that renounces the largess of Napa wineries. The tasting room is tiny, and the outside space is outfitted with rustic farm equipment and funky farm art. Lava Vine makes its wine on the premises. Tastings are comprised of five generous pours of whatever is on hand. The tasting menu deliberately lacks tasting notes, encouraging visitors to enjoy the wine rather than analyze it. Live music is common on Sunday afternoons as many pourers are also musicians.

Sights

OLD FAITHFUL GEYSER

No, you haven't accidentally driven to Yellowstone. The Napa Valley has its own **Old Faithful Geyser** (1299 Tubbs Ln.,

707/942-6463, www.oldfaithfulgeyser.com, 8:30am-8pm Sun.-Thurs., 8:30am-9pm Fri.-Sat. Mar.-Oct., 8:30am-6pm daily Nov.-Feb., adults $14, seniors $12, children ages 4-11 $8, under age 4 free). Unlike its more famous counterpart, this geothermal geyser is artificial. In the 19th and early 20th centuries, more than 100 wells were drilled into the geothermal springs of the Calistoga area, and many created geysers. Old Faithful is one of the few that wasn't eventually capped, and it's the only one that erupts with clockwork regularity. Expect no more than a 40-minute wait to see it erupt 60 feet or higher. A grassy area surrounds the geyser, with benches and chairs scattered around to allow an easy wait. A bamboo garden surrounds the grassy spot (bamboo is one of the few plants that can tolerate the hot mineral water of this area). Also at Old Faithful is an incongruous but cute petting zoo that houses several fainting goats, plus a few sheep and llamas. The water in the pool from which the geyser erupts as well as the geyser itself are very hot. It's not safe to wade in the water or to stand too close when the geyser goes off. Keep an eye on small children.

PETRIFIED FOREST

The namesake trees of the **Petrified Forest** (4100 Petrified Forest Rd., 707/942-6667, www.petrifiedforest.org, 10am-7pm daily summer, 10am-6pm daily spring and fall, 10am-5pm daily winter, adults $10, seniors and students 12-17 $9, children 6-11 $5, children under 6 free) no longer stand. The "forest" is an archaeological dig that uncovered a forest that existed more than three million years ago, when a volcano erupted, knocking over the trees and covering them with ash. Over hundreds of thousands of years, the minerals in the ash traded places with the contents of the trees' cells, petrifying them. Now these long-dead trees are made of stone.

Follow the trail map along a 0.5-mile loop to visit the various excavated petrified trees. You can touch some chunks of petrified wood, but most of the large stone trees are protected by fences. You'll get to see one rare petrified pine tree and a number of petrified coast redwoods. Inside the visitors center and gift shop are rocks and minerals, books on geology, and a few rare shards of the petrified trees from this forest.

SHARPSTEEN MUSEUM OF CALISTOGA HISTORY

The **Sharpsteen Museum of Calistoga History** (1311 Washington St., 707/942-5911, www.sharpsteen-museum.org, 11am-4pm daily, $3 donation) takes its name from its founder, Ben Sharpsteen, an Academy Award-winning animator for Disney who had a passion for dioramas. Go for the immense, exquisitely detailed dioramas depicting the 1860s Calistoga hot springs resort and life in 19th-century Calistoga. You'll also learn about the success and subsequent ruin of Sam Brannan, the Calistoga pioneer who was the first to build a hot-springs resort in the area. Other museum exhibits highlight daily life in 19th-century Napa, complete with artifacts and a nod to the Wappo people, the first residents of this area.

NAPA VALLEY PIONEER CEMETERY

You'll find the graves of many of Napa's earliest nonnative settlers and some of the prominent pioneer families at the **Napa Valley Pioneer Cemetery** (Bothe-Napa Valley State Park, 3801 St. Helena Hwy. N., www.parks.ca.gov, $8). The paths are kept clear and walkable, but many of the graves are overgrown with vines (some even have oak trees growing through them). Others are old wooden planks, their lettering worn away. The area is covered by a dense canopy of forest foliage, making it a pleasant place to visit on hot summer days. At the front entrance of the cemetery, a map and an alphabetical survey of the cemetery are posted. There's very little parking at the cemetery: enough room at the front for one small car. Otherwise, you have to park elsewhere and walk carefully along and across Highway 29 to the gate.

Spas

For an old-school Calistoga spa experience, head down the main drag to **Dr. Wilkinson's Hot Springs Resort** (1507 Lincoln Ave., 707/942-4102, www.drwilkinson.com, 8:30am-3:45pm daily, $89-179). The spa is part of the perfectly preserved midcentury compound rigorously dedicated to health and relaxation opened by "Doc" Wilkinson in 1952. Doc's proprietary blend of Calistoga mineral water and volcanic ash, Canadian peat, and lavender is still the gold standard for the Calistoga mud bath today. "The Works" includes the mud bath (complete with a soothing mud masque for your face), mineral bath, sauna, and a blanket wrap, and finished with a massage. A variety of facials are also available. The men's and women's spa areas are separated, and the whole experience is very down to earth, as are the prices. If you're a guest of the hotel, be sure to take a swim or a soak in one of the three mineral-water pools (there are two outdoor pools and one huge spa inside).

Couples and friends eager to soak together with privacy should book a treatment at **Golden Haven** (1713 Lake St., 707/942-8000, www.goldenhaven.com, 8am-11pm daily, $72-115). Here, rooms are designed for two or three people. Attendants leave the room once you are settled in to give you privacy not often found at other spas. A variety of massage and one-hour-long facials are also available.

At the **Calistoga Hot Springs Spa** (1006 Washington St., 707/942-6269, www.calistogaspa.com, 8:30am-4:30pm Tues.-Thurs., 8:30am-9pm Fri.-Mon.), indulge in a mud bath, a mineral bath, or other typical spa treatments. Also available to the public and guaranteed with a spa reservation is access to Calistoga Hot Springs's four outdoor mineral pools, each one catering to serious swimmers, families, and adults eager to relax and enjoy the serenity of spa country. **Indian Springs** (1712 Lincoln Ave., 707/942-4913, www.indianspringscalistoga.com, 9am-8pm daily, $85-125) also offers mud baths, spa services, and use of their pools, including the meditative Buddha pond.

If you want to get pampered without the muck, the **Lincoln Avenue Spa** (1339 Lincoln Ave., 707/942-2950, www.lincolnavenuespa.com, 10am-6pm Sun.-Thurs., 10am-7pm Fri.-Sat.) offers a wider array of spa and esthetic treatments, including a detoxifying body wrap. The spa also offers private rooms with an Ayurvedic steam table.

Indian Springs

Entertainment and Events

The **Napa County Fair** (1435 North Oak St., 707/942-5111, www.napacountyfair.org, adults $12, ages 7-12 $7, under age 7 free) is held every July 4th weekend at the Napa County Fairgrounds and is open to all. The annual fair features live music, a parade, carnival rides for the kids, and plenty of food and wine.

Sports and Recreation

Not every bit of open space in the Napa Valley is dedicated to grapes. There are several great state parks where you can indulge in the beauty of the valley. **Bothe-Napa State Park** (3801 St. Helena Hwy., 707/942-4575, www.parks.ca.gov, 8am-sunset daily) is south of Calistoga on the west side of Highway 29. The park's 2,000-foot elevation provides fantastic views of the valley below and the craggy Mayacamas Mountains beyond. The nearly 2,000 acres include oak woodlands, coastal redwoods, and occasional open grassland. There are a number of great hikes in the park. **Coyote Peak Trail** climbs to 1,170 feet and forms a 6.5-mile loop with **Upper Ritchey Canyon Trail,** providing great scenery and a backcountry feel.

Robert Louis Stevenson State Park (Hwy. 29, 7 miles north of Calistoga, 707/942-4575, www.parks.ca.gov, sunrise-sunset daily) is named for the author who spent his honeymoon in a tiny cabin here. The park offers fewer amenities than nearby Bothe-Napa State Park, but it does have a trail to the top of Mount St. Helena. The 11.2-mile round-trip hike is strenuous, especially when the trail rises above the lush canopy of bay, Douglas fir, and madrone trees to exposed chaparral. All that huffing and puffing is rewarded at the 4,300-foot summit, where great views of the valley unfold. If it's a clear day, you may even see the San Francisco skyline or Mount Shasta, 192 miles north. The park also has picnic tables for a lovely outdoor lunch.

Biking in Calistoga is a fun and scenic alternative to sitting in traffic. **Calistoga Bikeshop** (1318 Lincoln Ave., 707/942-9687, http://calistogabikeshop.com, 10am-6pm daily, $15-120 per day) offers guided tours, self-guided tours, and bike rentals. Hybrids run $39 per day, road bikes $60 per day, and mountain bikes $120 per day. On the self-guided "Calistoga Cool Wine Tour" ($90), the bike shop books your tastings, pays the fees, picks up any wine you buy, and provides roadside assistance.

The Napa County Fairgrounds in the heart of Calistoga has its own nine-hole golf course. The **Mount St. Helena Golf Course** (2025 Grant St., 707/942-9966, www.mtsthelena-golfcourse.org, 7am-sunset daily, $14-42) is a charming and inexpensive par-34 nine-hole course. It's the perfect spot for younger or less experienced golfers. The course is flat and straight, with easier lines than many other courses. The many trees along the fairways and the small greens make it interesting for intermediate players.

Take in Calistoga's dramatic scenery from the air with **Calistoga Balloons** (1458 Lincoln Ave., 707/942-5758 or 888/995-7700, www.calistogaballoons.com, $199-239), the only company offering regular flights in the north end of Napa Valley. In addition to the vineyards, wineries, spas, and the charming town of Calistoga, you'll also see Mount St. Helena and lush forested hills. The company provides a variety of packages that include winery tours and tastings, bicycle tours, and a post-flight champagne breakfast.

Accommodations

A plethora of places to stay cluster at the north end of Napa Valley, where you'll find most of the hotel-and-spa combos plus plenty of mineral-water pools and hot tubs. Calistoga also has some of the best lodging rates around.

$100-150

The **Calistoga Inn** (1250 Lincoln Ave., 707/942-4101, www.calistogainn.com, $119-169) has been in operation since 1882, giving guests an old-school hotel experience complete with shared baths and showers. The inn provides some of the best bargain accommodations in Napa Valley. Each of the 17 rooms is a cozy haven with a queen bed, simple but charming furnishings, and a view of the town. Amenities include a daily continental breakfast and an English pub downstairs that serves lunch and dinner. Make reservations in advance, especially in high season. The pub has live music four nights a week and gets loud on weekends.

Mountain Home Ranch (3400 Mountain Home Ranch Rd., 707/942-6616, www.mountainhomeranch.com, $71-156) almost feels like summer camp. Set deep in the forested mountains above Calistoga, it has an unpolished charm. Choose from a room with a full bath, a rustic cabin, or a cottage with a full bath, a fireplace, and a kitchen. There are two pools, a lake, volleyball and tennis courts, and a number of hiking trails on the property. The menagerie of barnyard animals will keep any kid happy. The main house serves a complimentary breakfast of eggs, waffles, and fresh fruit.

$150-250

Golden Haven Hot Springs (1713 Lake Street, 707/942-8000, www.goldenhaven.com, $149-199) began its life as a 1950s motel. Most of the rooms line the main drive, each with parking outside the door. The rooms are spacious, with lofted ceilings, king beds, and roomy bathrooms. Each has a smaller second bedroom with queen bed. There are three pools (one hot, one warm, and one cold), a sun deck, a lovely picnic area with bocce ball courts, and complimentary coffee and packaged pastries and granola bars in the morning.

Embracing its midcentury charm, ★ **Dr. Wilkinson's Hot Springs Resort** (1507 Lincoln Ave., 707/942-4102, www.drwilkinson.com, $165-270) has been meticulously maintained and feels as though it is frozen in the 1950s. Options range from the motel's main rooms to bungalows with kitchens and rooms in the adjacent restored Victorian. Guests are welcome to use the pools, including the indoor hot mineral pool with its Eichler-esque touches. In addition to complimentary bathrobes, all rooms have coffee makers, refrigerators, and hypoallergenic bedding. Dr. Wilkinson's even has bathing suits on loan.

The old-school **Hideaway Cottages** (1412 Fair Way, 707/942-4108, www.hideawaycottages.com, $164-315) is a collection of 1940s-era bungalows that retain their original details. Most have sitting rooms, full kitchens, and patios, all of which face the outdoor mineral pool and hot tub. In the interest of quiet, no pets or children under 18 are allowed. In the main house, built in 1877, guests pick up their complimentary "tote" breakfast, filled with fruit and pastries.

OVER $250

If you're looking for a traditional bed-and-breakfast experience, you can't miss **The Pink Mansion** (1415 Foothill Blvd., 707/942-0558 or 800/238-7465, www.pinkmansion.com, $225-375). The 1875 mansion is painted unmistakably bright pink, making it a local landmark. Each lush room features a unique theme suitable to romance and wine. The more economical rooms have queen beds and pretty antique furnishings. The larger suites are spacious enough to dwarf their king beds, and also house fireplaces, whirlpool tubs, and top-tier amenities. Enjoy the heated indoor pool and spa, and a full breakfast each morning.

One of the prettiest spa resorts in Calistoga is **Indian Springs** (1712 Lincoln Ave., Calistoga, 707/942-4913, www.indianspringscalistoga.com, $199-479). Located on the site of Sam Brannan's original Calistoga resort, Indian Springs is best known for its charming cottages, but rooms in the two-story mission-style lodge are far more affordable. Cottages and bungalows have kitchenettes and patios, but you're really paying for the pools. Both are spring fed and kept between 82-102°F. The Olympic-sized pool is one of the biggest in California; the smaller pool is quieter and adults only.

On Calistoga's charming main drag is the **Mount View Hotel and Spa** (1457 Lincoln Ave., 707/942-6877, www.mountviewhotel.com, $199-399). All 29 rooms and suites have an eclectic mix of modern furnishings with Victorian antique and art deco touches that harken back to the hotel's 1920s and 1930s heyday. The list of standard features includes espresso machines, breakfast in bed, and an outdoor pool.

Food

The beauty of Calistoga is how well the locals rub shoulders with the tourists. Just take a booth at the **Café Sarafornia** (1413 Lincoln Ave., 707/942-0555, http://cafesarafornia.com, 7am-2:30pm daily, $9-15) and see. Farmers and tradespeople sidle up next to out-of-towners for a down-home breakfast and bottomless coffee refills. The huevos rancheros stand up to their claim of being the best and the Brannon Benedict is one-of-a-kind. Breakfast here may be the most expensive meal of the day in the otherwise quite affordable Calistoga.

Pacifico Mexican Restaurant (1237 Lincoln Ave., 707/942-4400, 11am-9pm Sun.-Thurs., 11am-10pm Fri., 10am-10pm Sat., $11-19), on the corner of Lincoln Avenue and Cedar Street, is just the place for a margarita. The food may not be hole-in-the-wall authentic, but it makes up for it in atmosphere, particularly at the sidewalk tables lining Cedar Street.

For a fancy dinner out, locals go to **JoLe** (1457 Lincoln Ave., 707/942-5938, www.jolerestaurant.com, 5pm-9pm Sun.-Thurs., 5pm-11pm Fri.-Sat., $18-32) in the Mount View Hotel. The emphasis is on small plates of locally sourced, Mediterranean-inspired food in a contemporary setting. Select two or three dishes per person, such as sea scallops and sweetbreads or roasted quail with fingerling potatoes. Another option is the tasting menu: Pick from four ($55), five ($70), or six ($80) courses. The desserts are just as sophisticated but a bit more playful, like the Campfire Cake, with house-made marshmallow and graham crackers. The wine list is exceptional, but the cocktails steal some of the spotlight, loaded with fresh ingredients and artisanal spirits.

Perhaps the hottest restaurant is the trendy **Solbar** (755 Silverado Trail, 877/684-6146, www.solagecalistoga.com, 7am-3pm, 5:30pm-9pm Sun.-Thurs., 7am-3pm, 5:30pm-9:30pm Fri.-Sat., $26-33). Part of the luxurious Solage Calistoga resort at the eastern edge of town, the sleek dining room is a fine backdrop for the innovative cuisine that gives farm fresh a modern twist. The result has garnered the restaurant a Michelin star from 2009 to 2014. The biggest draw in the summer and fall is the spacious patio with its floating fireplace.

Information and Services

For discounted wine-tasting vouchers, maps, or tips for the best mud bath, swing by the **Calistoga Visitors Center** (1133 Washington St., 707/942-6333, http://visitcalistoga.com, 9am-5pm daily), located in the heart of downtown Calistoga.

The **Vermeil House Clinic** (913 Washington St., 707/942-6233, 9am-5pm Mon.-Fri.) is affiliated with the St. Helena Hospital and treats nonemergency health concerns. For something more serious, the **St. Helena Hospital** (10 Woodland Rd., 707/963-6425, http://sthelenanowaiter.org) has a 24-hour emergency room.

Transportation

Calistoga is eight miles north of St. Helena on Highway 29. In Calistoga, Highway 29 turns east, becoming Lincoln Avenue. It intersects with the Silverado Trail at the east end of town.

Highway 128 also runs through Calistoga, connecting to U.S. 101 north near Healdsburg. To reach Calistoga from U.S. 101 in Santa Rosa, take Exit 494 off U.S. 101 labeled "River Rd./Guerneville." Turn right on Mark West Springs Road and continue up the mountain. The road name changes to Porter Creek Road in the process. At the T intersection with Petrified Forest Road, turn left and travel a few miles until Highway 128. Turn right and follow Highway 128 south for one mile to Lincoln Avenue, Calistoga's main drag.

Sonoma Valley

The Sonoma and Carneros wine regions are in the southeast part of Sonoma Valley. The scenery features oak forests, vineyard-covered open spaces, and pristine wetlands bordering San Pablo Bay. The terminus of El Camino Real is in the small city of Sonoma, which includes the famed Sonoma Mission Inn, historical sights, and a charming town square with plenty of shopping and great places to grab a bite.

SONOMA AND CARNEROS

Sonoma Wineries

Sonoma wineries produce award-winning wine and are some of the oldest in the state.

★ GUNDLACH BUNDSCHU WINERY

Not many wineries in California can boast that they won awards for their wines 100 years ago, but **Gundlach Bundschu Winery** (2000 Denmark St., 707/938-5277, www.gunbun.com, 11am-4:30pm daily, $10), or GunBun, as it's known, is one of them. The 19 Gundlach Bundschu wines entered into the 1915 Panama-Pacific International Exhibition all won medals. Today the winery focuses on red bordeaux- and burgundy-style wines, and the cabernets and merlots tend to have plenty of tannic backbone. The tasting room is housed in one of the original stone winery buildings, which can feel cramped when full of visitors—but the fun atmosphere makes it bearable. Browse the historical memorabilia. Nearby is the hillside cave, which is often part of the winery tour. GunBun is most loved for its picnicking area at the top of Towles' Hill. It boasts one of the nicest outdoor winery spaces in the valley.

RAVENSWOOD WINERY

Ravenswood Winery (18701 Gehricke Rd., Sonoma, 707/933-2332 or 888/669-4679, www.ravenswood-wine.com, 10am-4:30pm

Gundlach Bundschu has some of the best picnic grounds in Wine Country.

Sonoma Valley

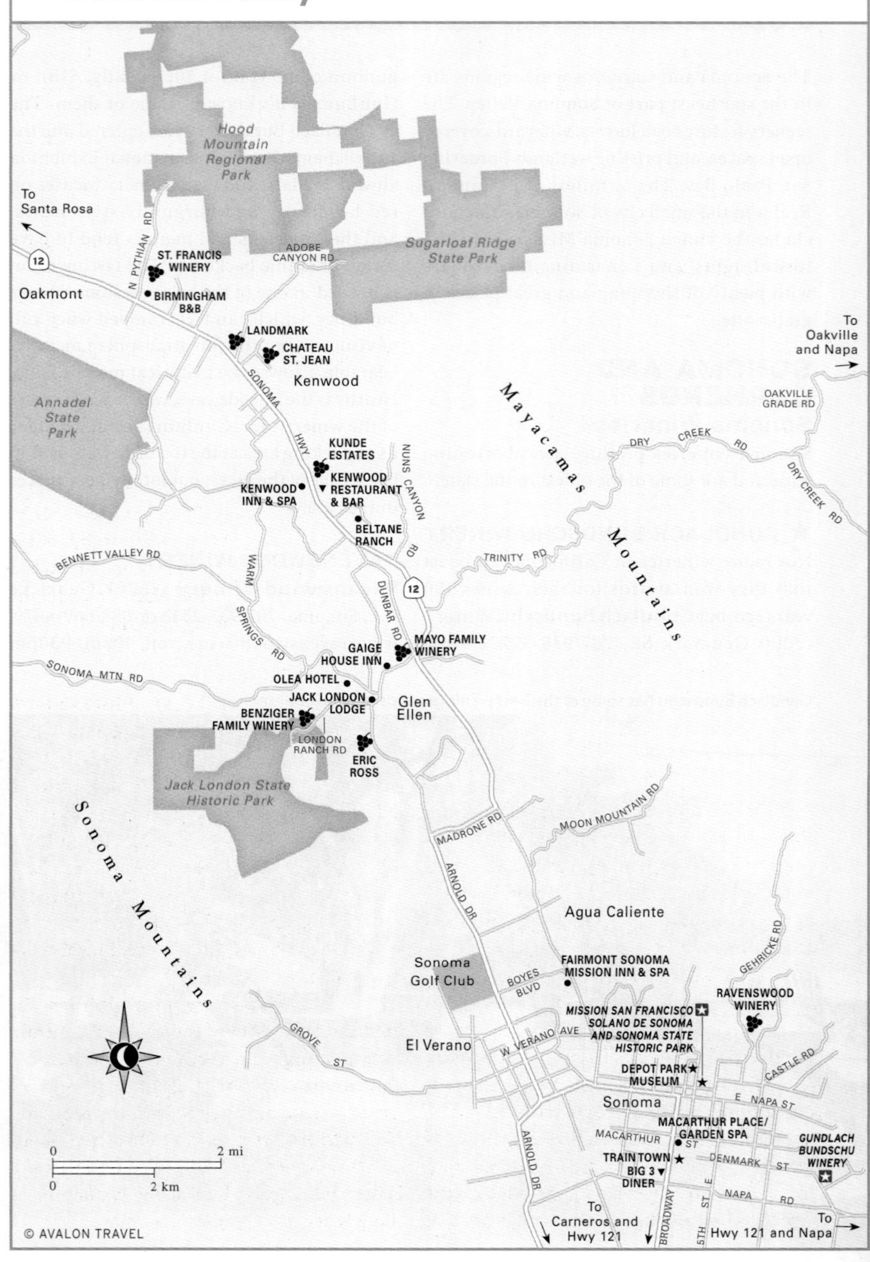

daily, $18) prides itself on making "no wimpy wines." Although the company is now owned by a large corporation, Ravenswood wines are still overseen by the original winemaker, Joel Peterson, who began making California zinfandel in 1976. Zinfandel remains Ravenswood's signature varietal. The winery strives to make tasters of all types feel at home. Tours and barrel tastings (daily 10am, $25, reservations required) teach newcomers the process of winemaking, but "blend your own" seminars beckon to serious wine connoisseurs. Ravenswood wines range $15-60 per bottle.

ROCHE WINERY & VINEYARDS

The homey 1940s craftsman-style cottage kitty-corner from Sonoma's main square is the tasting room for the Carneros-based winery **Roche Winery & Vineyards** (122 W. Spain St., Sonoma, 707/935-7115, www.rochewinery.com, 11am-7pm daily, $10-15). You can taste chardonnays, pinots, merlots, and a variety of dessert wines indoors or on the sun-dappled patio. Buy a bottle to accompany the selections from the light tasting menu provided by the nearby Sunflower Caffe. The laid-back winery also encourages patrons to bring along their own brown bags.

Carneros Wineries

The Carneros region might be described as the "lost" area of Wine Country. This former grazing land bordering San Pablo Bay looks much as it did 100 years ago. In this vast expanse are a handful of hearty vintners and several large champagne houses, rather than boutique resorts or fabulous eats.

DOMAINE CARNEROS

On the road to Napa is **Domaine Carneros** (1240 Duhig Rd., Napa, 800/716-2788, www.domaine.com, 10am-5:45pm daily, $30). The grand estate structure is styled in both architecture and garden setting like the great châteaux of France. Even more impressive are the finely crafted sparkling wines and a few still pinot noirs using grapes from the Carneros region. The Art of Sparkling Wine Tour ($40) is an excellent opportunity to sample the best wines, tour the grounds, and see how bubbly is made. Domaine Carneros also offers a seated tasting. To nibble on something while sipping, select from a cheese or charcuterie plate or caviar and smoked salmon.

GLORIA FERRER

For a taste of some of Sonoma's upscale sparkling wines, visit the Spanish farmhouse-style tasting room at **Gloria Ferrer** (23555 Hwy. 121/Arnold Dr., Sonoma, 707/933-1917, www.gloriaferrer.com, 10am-5pm daily, $18-33). The champagnerie now has the largest selection of sparkling wine in Carneros, from the classic Brut to the lively and aromatic Va de Vi and the flagship Carneros Cuvee in a distinctly curvaceous bottle. Gloria Ferrer also makes still wines. You can taste either by flight or by glass. It can get crowded, but if you can snag a terrace table and it's not too foggy, there are few better places in Carneros to enjoy an early evening aperitif.

★ CLINE CELLARS

For a departure from bubbly, **Cline Cellars** (24737Arnold Dr., Sonoma, 707/940-4030, www.clinecellars.com, 10am-6pm daily, free) specializes in rhone-style wines. Tasting is free and takes place in a modest farmhouse with wraparound porch that dates from 1850. Natural springs feed the three ponds and help sustain the giant willow trees, magnolias, and colorful flower beds. The tasting room contains a small deli, and the wines include several picnic-friendly options.

The area was also the site of a Miwok village and later used by Father Altimira while investigating a site for what would become the Sonoma mission. Celebrating the site's history as a temporary Spanish mission, the **California Missions Museum** (10am-4pm daily) is located in a barn behind the tasting room and displays intricately detailed scale models of every California mission.

Find a little history at the California Missions Museum at Cline Cellars.

Sights

★ MISSION SAN FRANCISCO SOLANO DE SONOMA AND SONOMA STATE HISTORIC PARK

Mission San Francisco Solano de Sonoma (114 E. Spain St., 707/938-9560, www.parks.ca.gov, 10am-5pm daily), also called simply the Sonoma Mission, is the northernmost of Spanish missions in California. It is at the corner of the historical plaza in downtown Sonoma. The last mission established (in 1823), and one of the first restored as a historical landmark (in 1926), the Sonoma Mission isn't the prettiest or most elaborate of the missions. Visitors can see exhibits depicting the life of the missionaries and indigenous people who lived here. Outdoors is the Native American mortuary

Mission San Francisco Solano de Sonoma

monument and a cactus "wall" that has been growing on the property since the mission era.

The mission is a central piece of **Sonoma State Historic Park,** which consists of five other historical attractions. The majority of the sights were built in the heyday of General Mariano Vallejo, the Mexican army commander who became a key figure in California's transition from Mexican province to statehood. The sites include the two-story adobe **Sonoma Barracks**, the old **Toscano Hotel**, and Vallejo's opulent home, **Lachryma Montis.** Tours for both Lachryma Montis and the Toscano Hotel are free with the park's $3 admission fee and are available Saturday and Sunday.

DEPOT PARK MUSEUM

If you haven't had enough history in Sonoma, stop by the **Depot Park Museum** (270 1st St. W., 707/938-1762, http://depotparkmuseum.org, 1pm-4pm Fri.-Sun., free) right down the street from the plaza and around the corner from the mission. The museum, set inside a reproduction of the historical Northwestern Pacific Railroad depot, features exhibits about the Bear Flag Rebellion, the indigenous Miwok people, and memorabilia from Sonoma life in the late 1800s.

TRAIN TOWN

Riding the only trains left in town requires a visit to the brightly painted station of **Train Town** (20264 Broadway, 707/938-3912, www.traintown.com, 10am-5pm daily June-Aug., 10am-5pm Fri.-Sun. Sept.-May, $2.75-6.25). The often-crowded amusement park, model railway, and petting zoo is a treat for little ones. Ride the 15-inch scale railroad that winds through 10 forested acres, take a spin on the roller coasters, or ride the vintage carousel and Ferris wheel. Rides are paid for with coupons, which add up quickly, so buy a Family Pack (six for $12.75).

DI ROSA PRESERVE

As Sonoma Valley yields to the open spaces of Carneros, history gives way to modern art. To visit the 217-acre **di Rosa Preserve** (5200 Sonoma Hwy., 707/226-5991, www.dirosapreserve.org, 10am-4pm Wed.-Sun., $5-15) is to enter an eclectic, artistic wonderland, where giant sculptures march up into the hills, a car hangs from a tree, and every indoor space is crammed with photographs, paintings, and video installations. Even nature seems to do its part to maintain the sense of whimsy as di Rosa's 85 peacocks (including two albinos) strut, screech, and occasionally crash-land around the galleries.

The preserve is on the north side of the Carneros Highway (Highway 121) almost opposite the Domaine Carneros winery. Look for the two-dimensional sheep on the hillside. A $5 donation will get you into the Gatehouse Gallery, which displays rotating exhibits along with some pieces from the permanent collection. To wander around the property or explore other indoor gallery space, you have to join one of the three or four daily tours (1.5-2 hours, $12-15). During the dry summer months, the Nature Hike takes visitors up Milliken Peak, a 2.5-mile round trip to the highest peak in Carneros. Chances are you'll need a reservation for tours, especially on weekends.

CORNERSTONE SONOMA

Find outdoor art and design at **Cornerstone Sonoma** (23570 Hwy. 121, 707/933-3010, www.cornerstonegardens.com, 10am-5pm daily). This unique installation combines an art gallery with the work of the foremost landscape and garden designers in the world. Stroll the unusual gardens, which range from traditional plantings to postmodern multimedia installations, and then finish up your excursion by visiting the boutiques, upscale food shops, and wine bars that populate the garden complex.

Spas

The most famous spa in the area is the **Willow Stream Spa** (100 Boyes Blvd., Sonoma, 877/289-7354, www.fairmont.com/sonoma, 7:30am-8pm daily, $89-200). A natural mineral hot spring provides warm water for the indoor and outdoor pools and whirlpools. The spa offers massages, scrubs, wraps, facials, and more rarified treatments to pamper even the most discerning spa-goer. The famous pools are open to non-guests for $89, but it's best to call in advance.

At the **Garden Spa at MacArthur Place** (29 E. MacArthur St., Sonoma, 707/933-3193, www.macarthurplace.com, 9am-8pm daily, $125-250), take in the serene beauty of the inn's lush garden as you are rejuvenated and beautified. All of the spa's signature treatments are made from the flowers, herbs, and fruit found in the garden, distilled into such creations as pomegranate body polish, golden passionflower body wrap, peppermint foot soak, and the red-wine grape-seed bath. The spa also offers a mud-bath soak, massages, and facial and waxing treatments. Book treatments at least two weeks in advance as space fills up fast.

Entertainment and Events

For upcoming events, turn to the Do and Shop sections of the ***Sonoma Index-Tribune*** (www.sonomanews.com), one of the local papers in the Sonoma Valley.

For a fun evening of drinking and live entertainment, head to **Murphy's Irish Pub** (464 1st St. E., Sonoma, 707/935-0660, www.sonomapub.com, 11am-11pm Sun.-Thurs., 11am-midnight Fri.-Sat.) on the Sonoma Plaza. Grab an imported Irish pint or a glass of local wine, some barbecued oysters or down-home pub fare, and enjoy an evening of live music or literary entertainment. Murphy's welcomes kids in its dining room, so bring the whole family.

Shopping

There's no more pleasant place to window shop than in Sonoma. Around its leafy square are famous structures and state parks, cafés and eateries, and lots of shops. Many are on **1st Street West, 1st Street East, Spain Street,** and **Napa Street,** the main streets bordering the square, but some are inside the historical buildings and down tiny retail alleys. With its eclectic mix of dusty bookstores, touristy galleries, Fair Trade import shops, general store emporiums, bath and body stores, and old-school men's shoe and clothing stores, Sonoma is a fun place to shop.

Sports and Recreation

Not every inch of ground in Sonoma County grows grapes. One huge plot of invaluable dirt has long been given over to the **Sonoma Raceway** (29355 Arnold Dr., Sonoma, 800/870-7223, www.racesonoma.com), known locally as Sears Point. This massive motorsports complex hosts every sort of vehicular race possible, with several NASCAR events each year, various American Motorcyclist Association motorcycle races, an Indy car race, and a National Hot Rod Association drag race. Sonoma sees more action than many of the country's most popular racetracks, with events scheduled 340 days per year, though many of these are local track days and small-time club races. Ticket prices vary widely, so check the website for event prices. The turnoff to Sonoma Raceway is near the intersection of Highways 37 and 121, and wretched traffic jams can last for hours as people exit the racetrack into the non-signaled intersection. Check the race schedule online to avoid this area for at least four hours after the end of a big race.

To take a fabulous hike from the heart of downtown Sonoma, hop on the three-mile **Overlook Trail,** which winds through woods and meadows to the top of Schocken Hill, with fine views over the town below. Find the trailhead near the entrance to the Mountain Cemetery on First Street West about a half mile north of the plaza. Within an hour you'll feel like you're in the middle of nowhere. Dogs, bikes, and smoking are not allowed on the trail.

The area around downtown Sonoma is perfect for exploring by bike. The **Sonoma Valley Visitors Bureau** (453 1st St. E., 866/996-1090, www.sonomaplaza.com, 9am-5pm Mon.-Sat., 10am-5pm Sun.) has a helpful map that gives the best bike routes, including one that hits all the historical downtown sites as well as the Ravenswood and Gundlach Bundschu Wineries. The **Sonoma Valley Cyclery** (20091 Broadway, Sonoma, 707/935-3377, 10am-6pm Mon.-Sat., 10am-4pm Sun., $7-15/hour, $30-75/day) rents bikes, including mountain and tandem bikes, as well as bike trailers for kids. For an extra $25, you can have your bike delivered and picked up from your hotel. Maps and advice come at no extra charge.

Accommodations

In 1840, General Vallejo's brother built a home for his family on the town square. In the 1890s, it became a hotel, which would eventually become the **Swiss Hotel** (18 W. Spain St., 707/938-2884, www.swisshotelsonoma.com, $110-240). The rooms have plenty of modern amenities, though the exterior and the public spaces retain the feel of the original adobe building. Enjoy a meal at the restaurant or have a drink at the historical bar.

For price and character, the **Sonoma Hotel** (110 W. Spain St., Sonoma, 707/996-2996 or 800/468-6016, www.sonomahotel.com, $150-210) can't be beat. Built in 1880, the hotel is one of Sonoma's landmark buildings. The interior is decorated in the fashion of the era, with high wood wainscoting, cream-colored walls, polished antiques, and elegant light fixtures. The rooms, all with private baths, are similarly outfitted in trim Victorian fixtures, and many have sloped ceilings, creating a cozy, intimate atmosphere.

Not nearly as historical but located just a few blocks from the square is **El Pueblo Inn** (896 W. Napa St., 707/996-3651, www.elpuebloinn.com, $189-249). All rooms face a lush central courtyard with a pool and hot tub. Some of the rooms boast adobe brick walls or lounge areas with fireplaces, but many are standard hotel accommodations—clean and modestly decorated. For the price, location, and views of the garden, it's a good deal. The inn also offers a fitness room, complimentary breakfast, and an in-room safe.

The **Fairmont Sonoma Mission Inn & Spa** (100 Boyes Blvd., 707/938-9000 or 800/257-7544, www.fairmont.com/sonoma, $600) has luxury appeal. There's the spa, an 18-hole golf course, and the Michelin-starred restaurant, but the rooms themselves are the kind of place you'll want to return to after a long day. Decorated in Provençal yellows and featuring four-poster beds with deep mattresses covered in down comforters, some rooms have fireplaces, and others feature marble bathtubs. Many overlook gardens.

South of Sonoma, **The Carneros Inn** (4048 Sonoma Hwy., 707/299-4900, www.thecarnerosinn.com, $350-600) is an expansive cottage resort. The immense property, which backs onto the countryside, has three restaurants, a spa, two pools, and even a small market. Unpretentious cottages spread out in small clusters for acres, each group surrounding its own garden paths and water features. Inside, the cozy cottages sparkle with white linens, tile floors, and windows overlooking sizeable private backyards with decks and comfy chaises.

Food

SONOMA

★ **the girl and the fig** (110 W. Spain St., 707/938-3634, www.thegirlandthefig.com, 11:30am-11pm Fri.-Sat., 11:30am-10pm Sun.-Mon., $20-28), right on Sonoma Plaza, is a valley institution. The French country menu includes main courses like free-range chicken and duck confit, Sonoma rabbit, and steak frites. The Thursday evening Plat du Jour menu is a bargain at $38 for three courses. The wine list focuses on rhone varietals, with many from local Sonoma producers. Thirsty patrons can also opt for a shot of pernod or an aperitif of absinthe.

It's rare when locals and travelers agree on the best restaurant. Traditional Portuguese eatery ★ **LaSalette** (452 1st St. E., 707/938-1927, www.lasalette-restaurant.com, 11:30am-9pm daily, $19-28) has a simple, charming atmosphere with a wood-fired oven facing a bar and a large outdoor patio. The menu features fresh fish and hearty meat dishes plus some good meatless options, or make an easy choice with the Tasca Tasting Plates: three, five, or seven plates ($16-34) sampling a range of dishes.

Tired of looking at wine menus? Pull up a bar stool at **Maya** (101 E. Napa St., 707/935-3500, www.mayarestaurant.com, 11:45am-9pm Sun.-Thurs., 11:45am-11pm Fri.-Sat., $12-19) and pick from one of the 60-plus tequilas on the menu. Opt for a cool margarita on the rocks, or sip it straight with lime and salt. The food, especially the addictive spicy roasted pumpkin seeds, will help wash it down. Influenced by the cuisine of the Yucatan Peninsula, the menu relies heavily on fresh fish and locally grown fruits and vegetables. Ceviche, fish tacos, and slow-roasted carnitas are offered alongside taquitos, nachos, and enchiladas.

For a cup of coffee or a quick pastry, swing by the **Basque Boulangerie Cafe** (460 1st St. E., 707/935-7687, http://basqueboulangerie.com, 6am-6pm daily, $5-12). The line often snakes out the door on weekend mornings, but it usually moves fast. The wide selection of soups, salads, and sandwiches can also be bought to go, handy since table space inside and out is scarce. Pay attention after ordering: Customer names are only called once when food is ready.

At the colorful **Sunflower Caffe** (421 1st St. W., 707/996-6645, 7am-4pm daily, $5-15), the wait can be long. It sells basic breakfast selections and upscale salads and sandwiches, but the real gem is a big patio hidden down the side passageway of the El Dorado Hotel, an oasis of greenery with plenty of tables. Later in the day, swap your espresso for a beer or a glass of wine during the café's daily happy hour (3pm-4pm).

CARNEROS

For breakfast, make a trip to the Carneros Inn's ★ **Boon Fly Cafe** (707/299-4870, www.boonflycafe.com, 7am-9pm daily, $16-27). At this industrial chic spot, gourmet takes on hearty egg favorites fill the menu. Wash one down with the signature bacon Bloody Mary. Lunch and dinner are just as good, with decadent salads and fried chicken.

Book a table at Carneros Inn's **The FARM** (707/299-4880, www.thecarnerosinn.com, 5:30pm-10pm Wed.-Sun., $32-49). It serves upscale California cuisine, complete with a chef's tasting menu and big white plates topped with tiny artistic piles of food. Dress up a little—despite its name, The FARM has an upscale vibe. More casual, but still with a whiff of luxury, the bar (4pm-11pm daily) serves lighter fare like burgers, flatbreads, and lobster risotto.

The **Schellville Grill** (22900 Broadway, Sonoma, 707/996-5151, www.schellvillegrill.com, 8am-2pm Mon., 8am-3pm, 5:30pm-8:30pm Thurs.-Sat., 8am-3pm Sun., $12-25), at the intersection of Highways 12 and 121, represents the blue-collar side of Carneros. Hearty plates of comfort food are delivered by a crew of relaxed locals. If the weather is nice, take a table on the covered back patio. This is primarily a sandwich joint with plenty of burgers, pulled pork, and fish sandwiches. The real standout is the Hot Matty's Smoked Tri-Tip Sandy that bursts with strips of tender, flavorful meat.

Information and Services

Before you begin your Sonoma and Carneros wine-tasting adventure, stop in at the **Sonoma Valley Visitors Bureau** (453 1st St. E., Sonoma, 866/996-1090, www.sonomavalley.com, 9am-5pm Mon.-Sat., 10am-5pm Sun.) in the Carnegie Library building in the middle of the plaza. Ask the volunteers for advice on which wineries to visit, and be sure to pick up some complimentary tasting passes. In Carneros, the visitors bureau has an outpost at the **Cornerstone Sonoma** (23570 Arnold Dr./Hwy 121, 10am-4pm daily).

For medical attention, head for the **Sonoma Valley Hospital** (347 Andrieux St., Sonoma, 707/935-5000, www.svh.com), which has a full-service emergency room.

Transportation

The town of Sonoma is over the mountains west of the Napa Valley. The main route through the valley is Highway 12, also called the Sonoma Highway. From the Bay Area, take U.S. 101 north to Highway 37 east. At the light near Sonoma Raceway, turn left on Highway 121, the central conduit through Carneros. To reach Sonoma, turn left on Highway 12 midway through Carneros.

For public transit, use the buses run by **Sonoma County Transit** (SCT, 707/576-7433, www.sctransit.com, $1.25-3.65). Several routes serve the Sonoma Valley daily. It's also possible to use SCT to get from Sonoma Valley to Santa Rosa, Guerneville, and other parts of the Russian River Valley.

GLEN ELLEN

North of the town of Sonoma, the valley becomes more rural. The next hamlet on Highway 12 is Glen Ellen (pop. 784), surrounded by a couple of regional parks and Jack London State Historic Park. Despite having some excellent wineries, downtown Glen Ellen has not caught the Wine County bug; instead, it feels like a historical farm town.

Wineries

MAYO FAMILY WINERY

The **Mayo Family Winery** (13101 Arnold Dr., at Hwy. 12, 707/938-9401, www.mayofamilywinery.com, 10:30am-6:30pm daily, $8-12) breaks from the chardonnay-cab-merlot juggernaut of Sonoma and produces an array of interesting Italian-style varietals. Here you might taste smoky rich carignane or barbera, enjoy a fruity white viognier, or savor the chianti-based sangiovese. Mayo Family boasts a big presence in the region: the Glen Ellen tasting room, with picnic-friendly grounds, and five miles north in Kenwood, the prized **reserve tasting room** (9200 Sonoma Hwy., Kenwood, 10:30am-6:30pm Thurs.-Mon., reservations recommended, $40). At the reserve tasting room, your experience includes seven pours of Mayo's best wines, each paired with a small bite of gourmet California cuisine created by chefs on-site.

ERIC ROSS WINERY

You can almost imagine author Jack London relaxing with a book in the cozy tasting room of the **Eric Ross Winery** (14300 Arnold Dr., 707/939-8525, www.ericross.com, 11am-5pm daily, $10), across the street from the Jack London Village complex. The bright red rustic building is thronged with visitors on summer weekends, but during the week you'll likely have the comfy leather sofa inside to yourself. The metal-topped corner tasting bar almost seems like an afterthought. The pinots in particular are worth trying, and there are usually two or three available to taste, each featuring classic Russian River complexity and smoothness. The syrah and zinfandel also offer some of the same cool-climate elegance and a refreshing alternative to the warmer Sonoma Valley wines.

BENZIGER FAMILY WINERY

With vines poking out from the hillside grass, free-range cockerels crowing, and rustic wooden buildings hidden among the trees, the mountainside **Benziger Family Winery** (1883 London Ranch Rd., Glen Ellen, 707/935-3000, www.benziger.com, 10am-5pm daily, $10) seems like an old family farm rather than a business. Started in the 1980s, Benziger is a family-run operation and the valley's only biodynamic winery.

To get a better understanding of biodynamic methods, hop aboard a 45-minute tractor drawn-wine tram tour ($25, under 21 $10). You'll wind through the gorgeous and slightly wild-looking estate while learning about biodynamic principles, the natural environment, and winemaking in general. The tour concludes with stops at the winemaking facility and hillside storage cave, a special tasting of biodynamic wines, and a tasting back at the large commercial tasting room. It's the best tour in the valley for the money. Tours are offered every half hour 11am-3:30pm. Tram space is limited, so in the summer you should buy a ticket in advance. If you miss the tour, check out the Biodynamic Discovery Trail just off the parking lot. The short walking tour guides you through the basics while providing a shady place to take in the scenery.

Jack London State Historic Park

Travelers come to Sonoma not just for the fine food and abundant wine but for the chance to visit **Jack London State Historic Park** (2400 London Ranch Rd., 707/938-5216, www.parks.ca.gov or http://jacklondonpark.com, 10am-5pm daily Mar.-Nov., 10am-5pm Thurs.-Mon. Dec.-Feb., $10). Author Jack London lived and wrote in rural Sonoma County at the beginning of the 20th century. Docents offer tours of the park, which include talks on London's life and history. Explore the surviving buildings on London's prized Beauty Ranch or hike up Sonoma Mountain and check out the artificial lake and bathhouse. The pretty stone House of Happy Walls, a creation of London's wife, houses a small museum. There's no camping at the park.

The **Triple Creek Horse Outfit** (707/887-8700, www.triplecreekhorseoutfit.com, $75-220) offers guided horseback rides at Jack London State Historic Park that last from one hour up to half a day. Tours take you through the writer's life in Sonoma County and the literary history of the region. At the conclusion of your ride, you'll be given complimentary tasting passes to Benziger and Imagery Estate wineries.

Accommodations

Attached to the redbrick Jack London Saloon and Wolf House Restaurant, the **Jack London Lodge** (13740 Arnold Dr., 707/938-8510, www.jacklondonlodge.com, $95-185) anchors central Glen Ellen. The 22-room lodge is modern, with a broad patio, a kidney-shaped pool, and groomed lawns. The interior offers a Victorian feel with dark wood furniture, rich linens, and low lighting, but the relative newness of the building shines through. Vines draping the balcony add to the ambience, as do the hot tub and the creek running through the back of the property.

For historical lodgings, book a room, suite, or cottage at the ★ **Olea Hotel** (5131 Warm Springs Rd., 707/996-5131, www.oleahotel.com, $235-415), a B&B tucked away behind Glen Ellen. Built at the turn of the 20th century to accommodate railroad travelers, the property has since received a sleek update. Spare, modern furnishings grace the rooms, all equipped with flat screen TVs and Internet access. Some rooms come with a stone fireplace, and others boast an expansive porch overlooking the well-maintained grounds. For more privacy, 300 square foot cottages dot the property. Guests receive a hot two-course breakfast, and can soak in the outdoor hot tub or partake in the complimentary wine-tasting in the lobby. The hotel also offers massage services ($110-210) and accommodations for your pooch (extra $25) that include a welcome basket full of treats, doggie bags, bowls, and towels.

For a bit of Asian-infused relaxation, stay at one of the best-reviewed inns in Wine Country: the **Gaige House Inn** (13540 Arnold Dr., 800/935-0237, www.gaige.com, $275-425), which offers comfort and luxury. Special attention is paid to every detail, and each of the 23 rooms and suites resemble a spread in an interior-design magazine. Suites have baths the size of bedrooms and their own gardens. The complimentary breakfast helps to soften the financial blow, but the numerous spa treatments (extra fee) are almost too dreamy to refuse.

Food

Glen Ellen has a small, but distinguished collection of eateries. One of the oldest is the **Glen Ellen Inn Restaurant** (13670 Arnold Dr., 707/996-6409, www.glenelleninn.com, 11:30am-9pm Thurs.-Tues., 5pm-9pm Wed., $13-26), where French bistro cuisine meets California gastropub. This self-described oyster grill and martini bar seats 80, but it is broken up into various dining rooms, patios, and porches, giving it an intimate feel. In addition to the seafood-heavy gourmet menu, the restaurant boasts a full bar and a wine list worthy of its location.

Since it opened in 2012, the ★ **Glen Ellen Star** (13648 Arnold Dr., 707/343-1384, www.glenellenstar.com, 5:30pm-9pm Sun.-Thurs., 5:30pm-9:30pm Fri.-Sat., $14-32) has been a favorite, representing the newest wave of California and Wine Country cuisine. It serves locally sourced, wood-oven fare (pizzas, roasted meats and vegetables, iron skillet quickbreads) that leans toward comfort food with an urban sensibility. The wood and brushed metal interior is spare, with a gleaming, stainless steel kitchen. Reservations are encouraged, but patio and bar seating are open for walk-ins.

Aventine Glen Ellen (14301 Arnold Dr., 707/934-8911, http://glenellen.aventinehospitality.com, 4pm-10pm Tues.-Sun., $13-46), located in an old gristmill, features revamped classic Italian dishes. With the 40-foot water wheel and the surrounding evergreen forest, the restaurant has an earthy, historical feel.

Transportation

Glen Ellen is located just off Highway 12, seven miles north of Sonoma. Arnold Drive is the main street through town, and it runs south to Sonoma. To reach Glen Ellen from Santa Rosa, take Highway 12 east through Kenwood for about 15 miles.

It is also possible to jump over to Glen Ellen from Highway 29 in Oakville via the Oakville Grade. After about three miles, Oakville Grade becomes Dry Creek Road; the name changes again to Trinity Road in about three miles. Keep to the right on Trinity Road, and in another three miles you'll reach Sonoma Highway (Hwy. 12); turn left toward Glen Ellen.

KENWOOD

At Kenwood, the Sonoma Valley widens to accommodate more rolling vineyards and more tasting rooms. Kenwood offers little in the way of food and accommodations, but does have plenty of hiking opportunities because of its proximity to Sugarloaf Ridge State Park.

Wineries

KUNDE ESTATES

One of the largest wineries in the West, **Kunde Estates** (9825 Hwy. 12, 707/833-5501, www.kunde.com, 10:30am-5pm daily, $10) has wines that are well worth the price, if not quite spectacular. The variety of tours makes the most of the large estate.

The spacious tasting room rarely seems crowded, and in summer the patio of 202 Lounge is the place to be. The best tasting option is in the Kinneybrook Room, where you can taste the more expensive Grand Estate reserve wines ($25) while relaxing in a leather club chair. Free tours of the aging caves under the hillside occur almost daily (inquire with staff). Other tours, which are more like hikes, go up the mountain every Saturday (reservations required, $40) to explore the caves and vineyards and learn about the winery's sustainable practices, culminating with a tasting at the mountaintop tasting room 1,400 feet above the valley floor. To get to the mountaintop tasting room without the hike, jump aboard one of the winery's passenger vans ($10, two-day advance reservations required).

CHATEAU ST. JEAN

True to its name, **Chateau St. Jean** (8555 Hwy. 12, 707/833-4134, www.chateaustjean.com, 10am-5pm daily, $15-25) is built in the style of a French château, with flat graveled walks through formal gardens. Stroll under the arbors to reach both tasting rooms—the regular one (on the right) and the one for reserve wines (on the left). In the regular (and cheaper) tasting room you'll find the story of the first winemaker to come to Sonoma along with a selection of traditional California wines—chardonnay, cabernet, pinot noir, and the like. Although Chateau St. Jean wines are sold in stores and at restaurants, the single-vineyard varietals poured here can't be purchased anywhere else.

LANDMARK

Owned and operated by descendants of John Deere, **Landmark** (101 Adobe Canyon Rd., 707/833-0053, www.landmarkwine.com, 10am-5pm daily, $25) continues the agricultural tradition while producing top wines. In the tasting room are premium chardonnays and pinot noirs. Outside, walk in some of the most spectacular gardens in the region. In the summer, take a horse-drawn wagon ride through the vineyards. Or bring a picnic and enjoy a game of bocce ball on the grassy court surrounded by flowers, fountains, and grapes. You can arrange in advance to stay in either the guest suite or the cottage on the estate grounds.

ST. FRANCIS WINERY

Named to honor the Franciscan monks who are widely credited with planting California's first wine grapes, **St. Francis Winery** (100 Pythian Rd., 707/538-9463 or 888/675-9463, www.stfranciswine.com, 10am-5pm daily, $15) is a place for red-wine lovers, particularly merlot, and fans of Spanish architecture. The spacious tasting room is one of the best-designed in the valley. Windows running the length of the room look out onto vineyards and mountains; escape into the garden if it gets too crowded.

Picnickers are welcome on the sun-drenched patio across from the tasting room, but the tables just outside the picture windows are reserved for indulging in the charcuterie and wine pairing ($35, 11am-4pm daily, no reservation required). Want to make it into a lunch? For $60, you can get five courses that highlight the diversity of the wine selection. Call or check the website for the current seating schedule and to make a reservation.

Sports and Recreation

Waterfalls, hilly grassland bordered by oak trees, exposed rock outcroppings, and even Sonoma Creek's headwaters can be found at **Sugarloaf Ridge State Park** (2605 Adobe Canyon Rd., 707/833-5712, www.parks.ca.gov, sunrise-sunset daily, $8), just outside Kenwood. Despite its beauty, Sugarloaf is rarely visited. There are plenty of trails to suit your mood and hiking ability. Meander down **Creekside Nature Trail** (1 mile, easy) or take **Canyon Trail** (1.6 miles, easy) to the waterfall, which descends 25 feet through mossy boulders beneath a canopy of redwoods. More athletic hikers can take **Vista Trail Loop** (4.1 miles, moderate-difficult) to the Indian Rock outcropping, which has a lovely view of the canyon below. To hike this trail, take Stern Trail to Bald Mountain Trail and turn right. Take another right on Vista Trail and cross the mountain; then take yet another right on Grey Pine Trail. Turn right once more on Meadow Trail to return to the parking lot.

The crown jewel of the park is **Bald Mountain.** Although only 2,729 feet high, the mountain boasts views of nearly all of Wine Country as well as the Golden Gate and Sierra Nevada on clear days. The hike to the summit is not that challenging: **Bald Mountain Loop** (6.6 miles, moderate-difficult) begins at Stern Trail. Take a right turn onto Bald Mountain Trail and follow it to the top. To descend, turn right on Grey Pine Trail, and then make another right onto Meadow Trail.

Although the lower part of the park has a lush, heavy canopy, the upper trails are quite exposed and can get hot in the summer and early fall. Be sure to bring sunscreen, a hat, plenty of water, and a map, as the trails can be confusing.

Accommodations

The Tuscan-style villa that is the **Kenwood Inn & Spa** (10400 Hwy. 12, 707/833-1293 or 800/353-6999, www.kenwoodinn.com, no children under 18, $350-525) has 29 plush rooms, a world-renowned spa, and a rustic-elegant Italian restaurant. Every room has a private patio, fireplace, and luxurious bathroom (which, for an extra $95, can be your own private spa with the hotel's Bath Butler Service). Massages run $140-225, body wraps $125-175, and Hollywood-esque facial treatments $150-300. You will be relaxed and beautiful, even if you never manage to leave the hotel.

Built in 1915 and now a National Historic Landmark, the five-room **Birmingham Bed and Breakfast** (8790 Hwy. 12, 707/833-6996, www.birminghambb.com, $199-275) exudes charm. Each room is warm, light, and has a private bath. Enjoy a two-course hot breakfast served on china and crystal and a gift card for free wine-tastings at 30 wineries in the Sonoma Valley. The Inn also has an attached cottage that has a full kitchen and living room.

If you're pinching pennies or just want to sleep beneath the stars, **Sugarloaf Ridge State Park** (2605 Adobe Canyon Rd., 707/833-5712, www.parks.ca.gov or www.sugarloafpark.org, reservations 800/274-7275 or www.reserveamerica.com, $35) has 47 campsites with showers and free Wi-Fi at the park's visitor center.

Food

Eating outdoors right next to the vineyards is one of the attractions of the **Kenwood Restaurant and Bar** (9900 Sonoma Hwy., 707/833-6326, 11:30am-8:30pm Wed.-Sun., $11-35). The small plates and main courses are simple, unpretentious combinations of local ingredients. You'll find rabbit sausage, grilled artichokes, and the "Spaghetti Western" with pork belly and fava beans on the menu. The wine list includes wines from almost every Sonoma Valley winery, plus a few bottles from Napa, France, and Italy for good measure.

Information and Services

Kenwood has few services for visitors. Cellphone reception is better here than in Glen Ellen, but don't count on finding reliable wireless Internet access.

Transportation

Kenwood is located about 10 miles east of downtown Santa Rosa on Highway 12, and about five miles north of Glen Ellen. To reach Kenwood from U.S. 101 in Santa Rosa, take the exit for Highway 12 east.

Russian River Valley

The Russian River Valley may be the prettiest part of Wine Country. The Russian River runs through it, providing ample water for forests and meadows as well as wide calm spots with sandy banks. Rafting, canoeing, and kayaking opportunities abound on the zippier stretches of the river. The area called the Russian River Valley actually encompasses several prestigious American Viticultural Areas, including Dry Creek, Alexander Valley, and Russian River. Wineries are clustered along three main roads: the Gravenstein Highway (Hwy. 116), River Road, and Dry Creek Road.

To the west of the area's concentrated wine region, you'll reach the river in Guerneville, a noted gay and lesbian resort destination. A general sense of friendliness and fun permeates the area, including its kitschy downtown and the clothing-optional resorts.

SANTA ROSA

Santa Rosa is the biggest city in Wine Country and the largest in the North Bay. As such, it functions as a gateway to Wine Country and its transportation hub. It's a convenient place to stay as you venture out to Napa and Sonoma, or as a stopover on your way there.

Wineries

HANNA WINERY

The specialty at **Hanna Winery** (5353 Occidental Rd., 707/575-3371, www.hannawinery.com, 10am-4pm daily, $10-25) is crisp, steel-fermented sauvignon blanc. A hit with critics, it's exactly what you want to drink while soaking in the Russian River sun, either on the winery's wraparound front porch or beneath the great live oak out front. Inside, the tasting room makes the most out of the

Russian River Valley

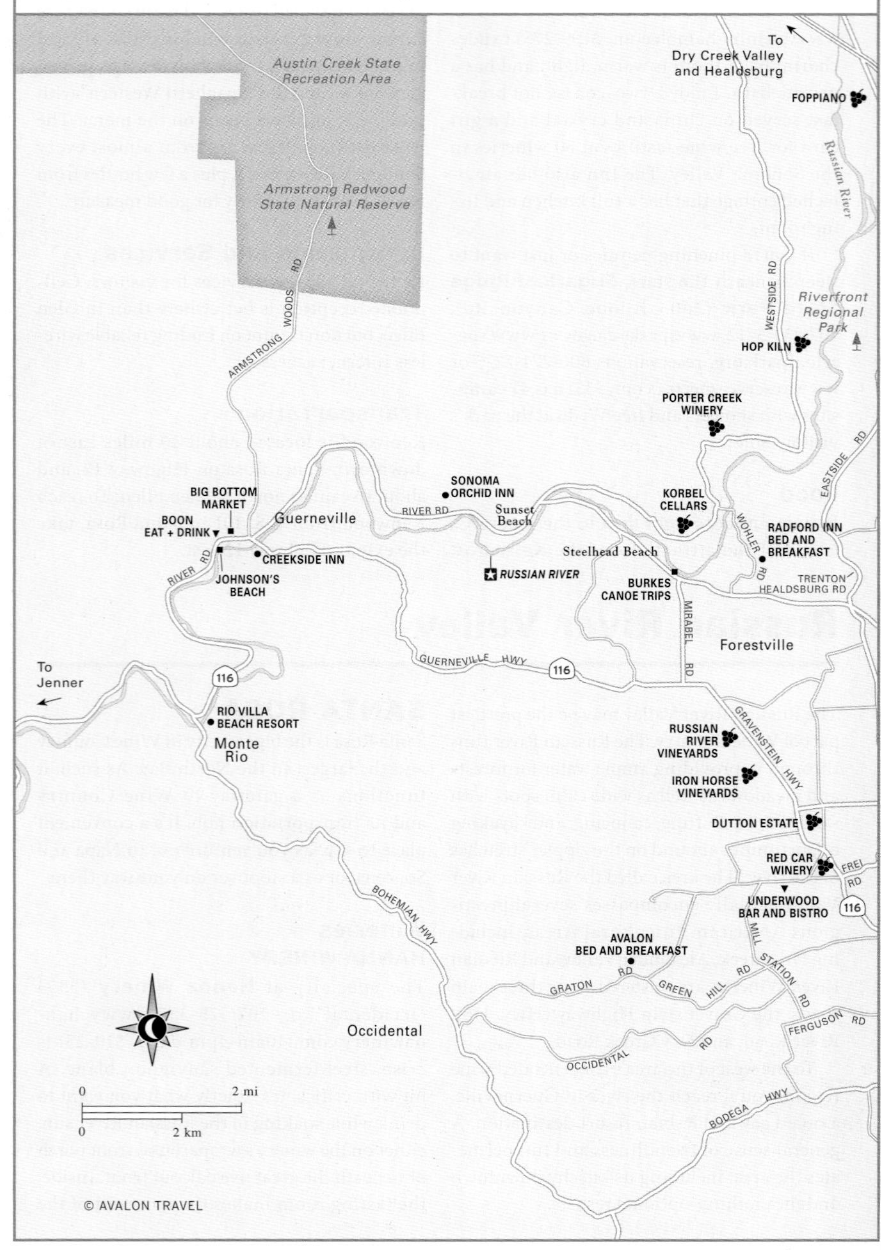

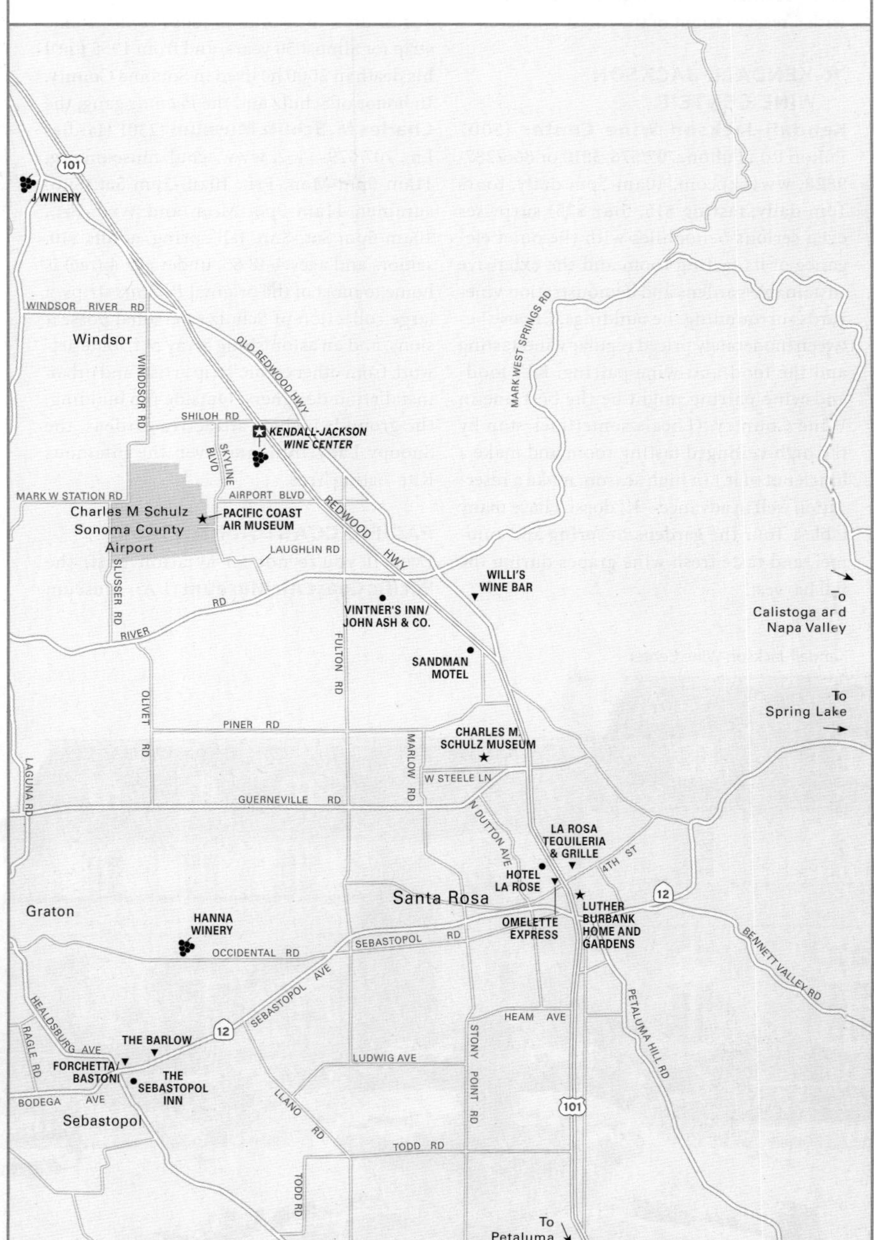
101
J WINERY
WINDSOR RIVER RD
Windsor
OLD REDWOOD HWY
WINDSOR RD
SHILOH RD
KENDALL-JACKSON WINE CENTER
SKYLINE BLVD
MARK W STATION RD
AIRPORT BLVD
Charles M Schulz Sonoma County Airport
PACIFIC COAST AIR MUSEUM
REDWOOD HWY
LAUGHLIN RD
SLUSSER RD
MARK WEST SPRINGS RD
WILLI'S WINE BAR
RIVER RD
VINTNER'S INN/ JOHN ASH & CO.
FULTON RD
SANDMAN MOTEL
To Calistoga and Napa Valley
To Spring Lake
OLIVET RD
PINER RD
MARLOW RD
CHARLES M. SCHULZ MUSEUM
W STEELE LN
LAGUNA RD
GUERNEVILLE RD
N DUTTON AVE
LA ROSA TEQUILERIA & GRILLE
4TH ST
HOTEL LA ROSE
Santa Rosa
12
Graton
HANNA WINERY
OMELETTE EXPRESS
LUTHER BURBANK HOME AND GARDENS
SEBASTOPOL RD
OCCIDENTAL RD
SEBASTOPOL AVE
BENNETT VALLEY RD
HEALDSBURG AVE
RAGLE RD
THE BARLOW
FORCHETTA/ BASTONI
THE SEBASTOPOL INN
HEAM AVE
PETALUMA HILL RD
STONY POINT RD
LUDWIG AVE
BODEGA AVE
Sebastopol
LLANO RD
TODD RD
To Petaluma

views and sunlight with large picture windows. Hanna offers a large tasting list, along with a reserve flight of the finest vintages.

★ KENDALL-JACKSON WINE CENTER

Kendall-Jackson Wine Center (5007 Fulton Rd., Fulton, 707/576-3810 or 866/287-9828, www.kj.com, 10am-5pm daily, tours 1pm daily, tasting $15, tour $25) surprises even serious oenophiles with the quiet elegance of its tasting room and the extensive sustainable gardens and demonstration vineyards surrounding the buildings. Choose between moderately priced regular wine-tasting and the food-and-wine pairing. KJ's food-and-wine pairing might be the best one in Wine Country. (Locals sometimes stop by the high-ceilinged tasting room and make a lunch out of it.) In high season, make a reservation well in advance—KJ doesn't have many tables. Tour the gardens in spring and summer, and taste fresh wine grapes during the fall harvest.

Sights

CHARLES M. SCHULZ MUSEUM

Schulz drew the world-famous *Peanuts* comic strip for almost 50 years, and from 1958 until his death in 2000 he lived in Sonoma County. In honor of Schulz and the *Peanuts* gang, the **Charles M. Schulz Museum** (2301 Hardies Ln., 707/579-4452, www.schulzmuseum.org, 11am-5pm Mon.-Fri., 10am-5pm Sat.-Sun. summer, 11am-5pm Mon. and Wed.-Fri., 10am-5pm Sat.-Sun. fall-spring, adults $10, seniors and ages 4-18 $5, under age 4 free) is home to most of the original *Peanuts* strips, a large collection of Schulz's personal possessions, and an astonishing array of tribute artwork from other comic-strip artists and urban installation designers. Outside the building, the grounds include attractive gardens, the Snoopy Labyrinth, and even the infamous Kite-Eating Tree.

PACIFIC COAST AIR MUSEUM

Even if you're not an aviation buff, the **Pacific Coast Air Museum** (1 Air Museum

Kendall-Jackson Wine Center

Way., 707/575-7900, www.pacificcoastair-museum.org, 10am-4pm Tues., Thurs. and Sat.-Sun., adults $10, seniors $7, ages 6-17 $5, under age 6 free) is worth a visit. Learn about the history of aviation in the United States through interpretive and photographic exhibits. Many of the planes are examples of ones that can be found on aircraft carriers today. Check out the funky Pitts aerobatic plane, the likes of which you'll see doing impossible-looking tricks during the museum's annual **Wings Over Wine Country Air Show,** held each September.

LUTHER BURBANK HOME AND GARDENS

If you love plants and gardening, don't miss the **Luther Burbank Home and Gardens** (204 Santa Rosa Ave., 707/524-5445, www.lutherburbank.org, gardens 8am-dusk daily year-round, free; museum and tours 10am-4pm Tues.-Sun. Apr.-Oct., $7). Using hybridization techniques, Luther Burbank personally created some of the most popular plants grown in California gardens and landscapes today. Burbank's own house, where he lived until 1906, is preserved along with a small greenhouse and the gardens as part of the 1.6-acre National and State Historic Landmark. Check the website for a list of what's in bloom during your visit, as something is sure to be showing its finest flowers every month of the year.

Entertainment and Events

One of the biggest annual events in this agricultural region is the **Sonoma County Fair** (Sonoma County Fairgrounds, 1350 Bennett Valley Rd., 707/545-4200, www.sonomacountyfair.com, 13 and up $11, children 7-12 $5, children 6 and younger free), held during two weeks at the end July through the beginning of August. Even the biggest Sonoma wineries prize the awards they win here. At the fair you'll find live entertainment, amusement rides, and an amazing array of contests and exhibitions featuring the work of folks from all over the Sonoma region.

Sports and Recreation

A popular way to get a great view of the Russian River Valley is from the basket of a hot-air balloon. **Wine Country Balloons** (707/538-7359 or 800/759-5638, www.balloon-tours.com, adults $225, children $195) gets you up in the air to start the day high above Wine Country. This big company maintains a fleet of balloons that can carry 2-16 passengers. Expect the total time to be 3-4 hours, with 1-1.5 hours in the air. You'll end your flight with brunch and a handful of wine-tasting coupons. Groups meet at Kal's Kaffe Mocha (397 Aviation Blvd.).

Accommodations

In the city of Santa Rosa, you'll find all the familiar chain motels. You'll also see a few charming inns and upper-tier hotels that show off the unique aspects of the region.

In the Historic Railroad Square, **Hotel la Rose** (308 Wilson St., 707/579-3200, www.hotellarose.com, $119-189) offers historical and modern accommodations for very reasonable prices. In the stone-clad main building guests will enjoy antique furniture and floral wallpaper, but across the street the carriage house offers modern decor and amenities, and each large room and suite feels light and bright. There's an attention to detail and a level of service that's missing in the larger motels and hotels in the area.

Food

Get in line for breakfast, brunch, or lunch at the ★ **Omelette Express** (112 4th St., 707/525-1690, http://omeletteexpress.com, 6:30am-3pm Mon.-Fri., 7am-4pm Sat.-Sun., $7-11), a spot favored by locals. The very casual dining rooms are decorated with the front ends of classic cars, and the menu involves lots of omelets. Portions are huge and come with a side of toast made with homemade bread, so consider splitting with a friend.

The cavernous ★ **La Rosa Tequileria & Grille** (500 4th St., 707/523-3663, http://larosasantarosa.com, 11:30am-9pm Sun.-Thurs., 11:30am-2am Fri.-Sat., $10-19) is the place to go for a casual lunch downtown or a late night out with friends. The large restaurant has multiple dining rooms and a large back patio, each done up in a Mexican Gothic style with deep booths, luscious murals of roses, and collections of crucifixes. The classic south-of-the-border cuisine is excellent and delivered with artistic panache. La Rosa also specializes in tequila, so try a flight or several rounds of margaritas.

Information and Services

In downtown Santa Rosa, the **Santa Rosa Convention & Visitors Bureau** (9 4th St., Santa Rosa, 707/577-8674 or 800/404-7673, www.tastesantarosa.com, 9am-5pm Mon.-Sat., 10am-5pm Sun.) offers countless maps and brochures about accommodations, food and wine, and activities in the city and surrounding region.

Santa Rosa has plenty of available medical services. If you need help, try to get to **Santa Rosa Memorial Hospital** (1165 Montgomery Ave., 707/546-3210, www.stjosephhealth.org), which includes an emergency room.

Transportation

Santa Rosa is 50 miles north of San Francisco on U.S. 101. Traffic on this major corridor gets congested, particularly during the morning and evening commutes and sunny summer afternoons. The side roads that lead to various tasting rooms and recreation spots are seldom crowded.

From U.S. 101, take exit 489. West of the freeway is the historical Railroad Square, and downtown is on the east side. Wineries are on the west side of town and can be accessed by taking Highway 12 west as well as the U.S. 101 exits for River Road and Guerneville.

Golden Gate Transit (415/455-2000, http://goldengatetransit.org, $11.75) runs buses between San Francisco and Santa Rosa. These routes are geared toward commuters who work in San Francisco, so the southbound buses run in the morning and those going north run in the afternoon. Once you're in the North Bay, **Sonoma County Transit** (707/576-7433 or 800/345-7433, $1.25-3.65) runs buses throughout Santa Rosa and out to Guerneville, Sebastopol, and Healdsburg.

SEBASTOPOL

Low-key and alternative Sebastopol is undoubtedly the artistic heart of Sonoma County. The relatively low cost of living, liberal politics, natural beauty, and small-town vibe have attracted artists that include heavyweights like Tom Waits and Jerry Garcia. Downtown Sebastopol contains shops where local artists sell their work, along with bookstores, record stores, and tie-dyed T-shirt shops. The surrounding farmland was once devoted to orchards, particularly apples, but grapes now dominate. The remaining orchards give fragrance and beauty to the already scenic country roads, especially during the spring bloom.

Wineries

DUTTON ESTATE

A small winery along the Gravenstein Highway, **Dutton Estate** (8757 Green Valley Rd., 707/829-9463, www.duttonestate.com, 10am-4:30pm daily, $10) is in the middle of its own vineyards. Tasters enjoy personal attention from pourers, along with a small list of white and rosé wines, red pinots, and syrahs. Dutton's syrahs stand out among the offerings.

RED CAR WINERY

Vintage Hollywood meets the Sonoma coast at **Red Car Winery** (8400 Graton Road, 707/829-8500, 10am-5pm daily, $15). The winery's name is homage to the red electric trolley cars that crisscrossed Los Angeles during the early 1900s, and the hip tasting room has a rustic-chic appeal, with comfortable couches, antique store memorabilia and vinyl spinning on a turntable. Tastings are comprised of six generous pours, including their well-balanced artisan blends and burgundy varietals of pinot noir and chardonnay that have received wide recognition.

IRON HORSE VINEYARDS

Iron Horse Vineyards (9786 Ross Station Rd., 707/887-1507, www.ironhorsevineyards.com, 10am-4:30pm daily, $20) is down a one-lane road that winds through orchards, over a creek, and past some wild turkeys before climbing up the palm-lined driveway to the winery. The rustic simplicity of the barnlike building and its indoor-outdoor tasting bar belies the pedigree of the sparkling wines made here—they have been served to presidents and won accolades from wine critics since the 1970s. On Friday, tours (10am Mon.-Fri. by appointment only, $25) are led by the winemaker, David Muskgard.

Accommodations

There are not that many places to stay in Sebastopol. The very best is the expensive but lovely **Avalon Bed and Breakfast** (11910 Graton Rd., 707/824-0880, www.avalonluxury-inn.com, $239-355). With only three rooms, the inn seeks to channel the woodsy charm of its mystical island namesake, complete with high-end decor. All rooms (which are suite sized) have king beds, fireplaces, and access to the garden hot tub. At breakfast, you'll be served an organic feast made with local produce.

At **The Sebastopol Inn** (6751 Sebastopol Ave., 707/829-2500, www.sebastopolinn.com, $119-249), rooms are a cut above standard hotel accommodations, with homey furnishings. Most rooms have a refrigerator and microwave, and guests can enjoy the heated pool and hot tub. The on-site coffeehouse hosts live music on weekend afternoons. The inn's location is an easy stroll to Sebastopol's shops and eateries.

Food

For years Sebastopol was not known for its food, with its many eateries catering to commuting locals. My, how things have changed: In 2013, the town's own version of Napa's Oxbow Market, **The Barlow** (6770 McKinley St., 707/824-5600, http://thebarlow.net), opened downtown and aims to be the focal point of Russian River foodie crowd.

One of the restaurants anchoring The Barlow is the area's hippest farm-to-table restaurant, **ZaZu** (6770 McKinley St., 707/523-4814, http://zazukitchen.com, 5pm-10pm Mon., 11:30am-10pm Wed.-Thurs., 11:30am-midnight Fri.-Sat., 9am-10pm Sun., $18-33), known for its house-cured bacon and *salumi* made by the chefs' Black Pig Meat Co. The pork-heavy menu changes daily and is infused with such twists as eggplant with cocoa nibs or lamb with preserved meyer lemon. The wine list is also locally sourced, and there is always an affordable option for a glass.

At The Barlow is the ultra casual **Ultra Crepes** (6760 McKinley St., 707/827-6187, http://ultracrepes.com, 8:30am-10pm daily, $6-9), which serves sweet and savory crepes. You'll find classics like the ham and cheese and the Monte Cristo, and more unique options, like one with bacon and maple syrup. The menu is on the slim side, but for the price, size, and variety, Ultra Crepes is the place to go for an affordable meal out.

Walking into downtown's ★ **Forchetta/Bastoni** (6948 Sebastopol Ave., 707/829-9500, http://forchettabastoni.com, $12-30) presents a difficult decision. On one side is Southeast Asian street food (*bánh mì* sandwiches, noodle bowls, and curry plates). On the other side is rustic Italian fare in the form of wood-fired pizzas and pasta, all with a California twist. The twin restaurants are both smartly decorated. Pan-Asian Bastoni (11:30am-10pm Mon.-Sat., 11am-4pm Sun.) features skinny communal tables, colorfully worn stools, and cans of chopsticks. Forchetta (5pm-9pm Thurs.-Mon., 11:30am-2pm Sun.) is a bit more urbane with exposed vents, simple glass chandeliers, and reclaimed wood accents. Bastoni is frequently less busy and has a full bar, but both sides often have space at counters that face the open kitchens.

The **Underwood Bar and Bistro** (9113 Graton Rd., Graton, 707/823-7023, www.underwoodgraton.com, 11:30am-10pm Tues.-Sat., 5pm-10pm Sun., $23-35) is filled with plush red velvet and dark wood tables and is considered by many locals to be the best spot in the region for a serious dinner. The menu leans French, with a Catalan dish here and an Italian dish there, with oyster menu and cheese plates that perfectly accompany the decor and vibe. On Friday and Saturday nights, the bar stays open late (10pm-11pm), serving elegant small bites.

Information and Services

For maps of the area, souvenirs, newspapers, and wine-tasting coupons, swing by the **Sebastopol Chamber of Commerce Visitors Center** (265 S. Main St., 707/823-3032, www.sebastopol.org, 10am-5pm Mon.-Fri., 10am-3pm Sat.). If you arrive after hours, they have a 24-hour information kiosk outside.

Transportation

Sebastopol is west of Santa Rosa, accessed by Highways 116 and 12. The heart of downtown Sebastopol is at the intersection of Sebastopol Avenue (Hwy. 12) and Main Street (Hwy. 116). Sebastopol Avenue becomes the Bodega Highway once it hits downtown Sebastopol and extends all the way to Bodega Bay.

To reach Sebastopol from U.S. 101, take either the exit for Highway 12 west in Santa Rosa or the exit for Highway 116 west at Cotati, eight miles south of Santa Rosa. Highway 116 is the most direct route to continue to the Russian River from Sebastopol.

GUERNEVILLE AND VICINITY

There are a number of wineries in the Guerneville area, but most people come here to float, canoe, or kayak the gorgeous Russian River that winds from Healdsburg all the way to the Pacific Ocean at Jenner. In addition to its busy summertime tourist trade, Guerneville is also a very popular gay and lesbian resort area. The rainbow flag flies proudly here, and the friendly community welcomes all.

Wineries

FOPPIANO

One of the oldest wineries in the Russian River Valley, **Foppiano** (12707 Old Redwood Hwy., 707/433-7272, www.foppiano.com, 11am-5pm daily, $5) dates from 1896. Foppiano makes a small list of premium red wines, of which their signature is a legendary petit sirah. Inside the farmhouse-style tasting room, enjoy sips of the various vintages. Make it an afternoon with a picnic at one of the tables out front.

downtown Guerneville

HOP KILN

Hop Kiln (6050 Westside Rd., Healdsburg, 707/433-6491, www.hopkilnwinery.com, 10am-5pm daily, $7), true to its name, is housed in an old hop kiln. The Russian River Valley once grew more beer-making ingredients than grapes, and this distinctively shaped kiln dried the valley's crop of hops each year. Inside the main kiln is an extensive wine-tasting bar with typical Wine Country varietals including their award-winning pinot noir. Tastings are comprised of six wines.

J WINERY

J Winery (11447 Old Redwood Hwy., 888/594-6326, www.jwine.com, 11am-5pm daily, $20-75) loves the cutting edge of the California wine scene. J specializes in California-style sparkling wines, and its tasting room is a triumph of modern design. Make a reservation at the Bubble Lounge, where there are tables and waitstaff, to enjoy wines specially paired with small bites of high-end California cuisine prepared in J's kitchen by their team of gourmet chefs. You'll get the chance to taste the sparkly vintages as they are meant to be enjoyed—with an array of often-spicy foods. Or just sidle up to the stylish tasting bar and enjoy a tasting flight ($20).

KORBEL CELLARS

Korbel Cellars (13250 River Rd., Guerneville, 707/824-7316, www.korbel.com, 10am-4:30pm daily, free) is the leading producer of California champagne-style sparkling wines. The large, lush estate welcomes visitors with elaborate landscaping and attractive buildings, including a small area serving as a visitors center. Tours of the estate are offered several times daily. Korbel makes and sells a wide variety of high-end California champagnes, plus a few boutique still wines and brandies. Brandy tastings are not offered, but you can purchase a bottle from the winery store. The facility also has a full-service gourmet deli and picnic grounds.

PORTER CREEK WINERY

Serious cork dorks recommend the tiny tasting room at **Porter Creek Winery** (8735 Westside Rd., Healdsburg, 707/433-6321, www.portercreekvineyards.com, 10:30am-4:30pm daily, $10), which casual tasters might otherwise miss. Turn onto the dirt driveway, pass the farm-style house (the owner's family home), and park in front of a small converted shed—the tasting room. Porter Creek has been making its precious few cases of rich red wine since the 1980s. Porter Creek's wines are almost all reds, made from grapes grown organically within sight of the tasting room.

RUSSIAN RIVER VINEYARDS

At **Russian River Vineyards** (5700 Gravenstein Hwy., Forestville, 707/887-3344, www.russianrivervineyards.com, 11am-5pm daily, $10), the friendly staff create a classy small-winery experience, and the small list of wines reflects the locale. You'll enjoy full-bodied, fruity pinot noirs, pinot noir rosés, and a couple Sonoma Coast chardonnays. Stick around for lunch or dinner at the winery's **Cork Restaurant** (11:30am-4pm, 5pm-8pm Mon.-Fri., 10am-4pm, 5pm-8pm Sat.-Sun., $25), which serves earthy plates of locally sourced gourmet food in an 1890s farmhouse.

★ Russian River

Guerneville and its surrounding forest are the center for fun on the river. In summer the water is usually warm and dotted with folks swimming, canoeing, or simply floating tubes serenely downriver amid forested riverbanks. **Burke's Canoe Trips** (8600 River Rd., Forestville, 707/887-1222, www.burkescanoetrips.com, Memorial Day-mid-Oct., $65) rents canoes and kayaks on the Russian River. The put-in is at Burke's beach in Forestville; paddlers then canoe downriver 10 miles to Guerneville, where a courtesy shuttle picks them up. Burkes also offers overnight campsites for tents, trailers, and RVs.

On the north bank, **Johnsons Beach & Resort** (16241 1st St., Guerneville, 707/869-2022, www.johnsonsbeach.com, 10am-6pm daily May-Oct., $35) rents canoes, kayaks, pedal boats, and inner tubes for floating the river. There is a safe kid-friendly section of the

the Russian River

riverbank that is roped off for small children; parents and beachcombers can rent beach chairs and umbrellas for use on the small beach. The boathouse sells beer and snacks.

Fly fishers can cast their lines nearby off **Wohler Bridge** (9765 Wohler Rd., Forestville) and **Steelhead Beach** (9000 River Rd., Forestville).

Armstrong Redwoods

Armstrong Redwoods (17000 Armstrong Woods Rd., Guerneville, 707/869-2015, www.parks.ca.gov, 8am-sunset daily, $8 per vehicle) is an easy five-minute drive from Guerneville. This little redwoods park often gets overlooked, which makes it less crowded than some of the popular North Coast and Sierra redwood forests. Take a fabulous hike—either a short stroll in the shade of the trees or a multiple-day backcountry adventure. The easiest walk to a big tree is the 0.1 mile from the visitors center to the tallest tree in the park, named the **Parson Jones Tree.** If you saunter another 0.5 mile, you'll reach the **Colonel Armstrong Tree,** which grows next to the Armstrong Pack Station—your first stop if you're doing heavy-duty hiking. From the Pack Station, another 0.25 mile of moderate hiking leads to the **Icicle Tree.**

The more adventurous can choose from any number of longer hikes up out of the redwoods to the oak and madrone forests on the ridges higher up. One such hike is a quick 2.3-mile **Pool Ridge Trail Loop,** which climbs 500 feet up a series of switchbacks before looping back down into the forest.

Right next to Armstrong is the **Austin Creek State Recreation Area** (17000 Armstrong Woods Rd., Guerneville, 707/869-2015, www.parks.ca.gov, 8am-sunset daily, $8 per vehicle). It's rough going on 2.5 miles of steep, narrow, treacherous dirt road to get to the main entrance and parking area; no vehicles over 20 feet long and no trailers of any kind are permitted. But once you're in, some great—and very difficult—hiking awaits you. The eponymous **Austin Creek Trail** (4.7 miles one-way) leads down from the hot meadows into the cool forest fed by Austin Creek. To avoid monotony on this challenging route, create a loop by taking the turn onto **Gilliam Creek Trail** (4 miles one-way). This way you get to see another of the park's cute little creeks as you walk back to the starting point.

Entertainment and Events

Guerneville wouldn't be a proper gay resort town without at least a couple of good gay bars that create proper nightlife for visitors and locals. The most visible and funky-looking of these is the **Rainbow Cattle Company** (16220 Main St., Guerneville, 707/869-0206, www.queersteer.com, noon-2am daily). Mixing the vibes of a down-home country saloon with a happening San Francisco nightspot, the Rainbow has cold drinks and hot men with equal abandon. Think cocktails in Mason jars, wood paneling, and leather nights. This is just the kind of queer bar where you can bring your mom or your straight-but-not-narrow friends, and they'll have just as much fun as you will.

It may not look like much from the road, but the **Stumptown Brewery** (15045 River Rd., 707/869-0705, www.stumptown.com, 11am-midnight Sun.-Thurs., 11am-2am Fri.-Sat.) is *the* place to hang out on the river. Inside this atypical dive bar are a pool table, Naugahyde barstools, and a worn wooden bar crowded with locals. Out back is a second bar and an outdoor deck with tables overlooking the river. The brewery only makes a few of the beers sold on tap, but they are all great and perfect to enjoy by the pitcher. If you are feeling a little woozy from the beer and sunshine, Stumptown also serves a menu of burgers and grilled sandwiches; the food is a perfect excuse to stay put.

Held at Johnson's Beach in Guerneville, the **Russian River Jazz and Blues Festival** (www.omegaevents.com, 707/869-1595, $50-60 each day, Sept.) is a two-day affair with jazz one day and blues the next. The main stage has some pretty big acts, including Buddy Guy, Al Green, and Taj Mahal, but there is plenty of music to groove to throughout the festival grounds. In addition to live acts, food vendors showcase regional fare, local artists hawk their wares, and tents serve glass after glass of wine while sunburned devotees splash around in the river. Much more than just a music festival, this event is the last big bash of the summer season; it takes place at the end of September, just before the weather reliably turns cold. If you plan to stay both days, consider camping here. **Johnson's Beach** (707/869-2022, http://johnsonsbeach.com) has designated campsites available on a first-come, first-served basis.

Accommodations and Camping

You'll find a few dozen bed-and-breakfasts and cabin resorts in town. Many of these spots are gay friendly, some with clothing-optional hot tubs.

The **Creekside Inn & Lodge** (16180 Neeley Rd., 707/776-6586 or 800/776-6586, www.creeksideinn.com, $98-300) is right beside the Russian River and just a few minutes' stroll to Guerneville's main street. Rooms with a shared bath in the main house are cheapest, and the suites, which boast a small sitting area, balcony, and private bathroom, go for only $175. The several acres of grounds include a pool and eight cottages, from studios to two-bedrooms, none of which cost above $300. The rooms at the high end of the price range are solar-powered suites with fully equipped kitchens and can sleep four.

The experience at the ★ **Sonoma Orchid Inn** (12850 River Rd., Guerneville, 707/869-4466 or 888/877-4466, www.sonomaorchidinn.com, pets welcome, $149-249) is made by its amazing owners, who can not only recommend restaurants and spas, they'll make reservations for you. They've got knowledge about the local wineries, hikes, river spots, and just about everything else in the region. The best rooms have microwaves and small fridges, while the budget rooms are tiny but cute, with private baths and pretty decorations. The Orchid is perfect for visitors who've never been to the area—they're dog and kid friendly, clothing mandatory in the communal hot tub, and welcoming.

Riverfront balconies, a private beach, and

beautifully landscaped grounds combine to make **Rio Villa Beach Resort** (20292 Hwy. 116, Monte Rio, 877/746-8455, www.riovilla.com, $119-245) an ideal Russian River getaway. With only 11 rooms—including some with kitchens—you're guaranteed privacy. A generous continental breakfast is available in the morning, and the Russian River is mere steps away.

On the road to Armstrong Redwoods, **boon hotel + spa** (14711 Armstrong Woods Rd., Guerneville, 707/869-2721, www.boonhotels.com, $155-265) is the antithesis of Guerneville's woodsy funkiness. It's minimal in the extreme, with a palette of white, slate, and chrome. Many of the 14 rooms have freestanding cast-iron fireplaces, private patios, and fridges, and all have large beds with fair trade organic cotton sheets. There is a pool and hot tub (both saltwater) and plenty of facial and massage options. In the morning, wake up to a pressed pot of locally roasted coffee; in the evening, chill out with a cocktail by the pool.

About 10 miles east of Guerneville proper, **Raford Inn Bed and Breakfast** (10630 Wohler Rd., Healdsburg, 707/887-9573 or 800/887-9503, www.rafordinn.com, $170-270) offers Healdsburg-level luxury at slightly-less-than-stratospheric prices. Each of the five rooms has a queen bed, air-conditioning, and a private bath. Some have fireplaces, oversize showers, and other luxury amenities. All rooms have been decorated in minimalist Victorian style. Every morning, the Raford serves up a hearty country breakfast.

CAMPGROUNDS

There are plenty of resort campgrounds along the Russian River. Catering to summer crowds and RVs, they usually charge a premium price for the extensive services and facilities they offer. Reservations are essential during the busy summer months. One of the more reasonably priced is **Burkes Canoe Trips** (8600 River Rd., Forestville, 707/887-1222, $10 pp/day), hidden in the redwoods right next to the river (and the road) just north of Forestville. The full-service campground, open May-October, has 60 sites for tents or RVs.

The more serene campgrounds are generally off the beaten track, as is the case for the primitive and scenic creekside campgrounds in the **Austin Creek State Recreation Area** (17000 Armstrong Woods Rd., Guerneville, 707/869-2015, www.parks.ca.gov, $25). The road into the park through Armstrong Redwoods State Reserve ends at the **Bullfrog Pond Campground**, with 23 sites, toilets, and drinking water. No vehicles over 20 feet long are allowed into the park, so the camping experience here is free of humming RVs. The park does not take reservations; camping is first-come, first-served. To register for a campsite, stop by the Armstrong Redwoods park office (17000 Armstrong Woods Rd., Guerneville, 707/869-2958, 11am-3pm daily) on the way into Austin Creek. You can also inquire about (or get permits for) the three backcountry sites ($25) that are roughly four miles from the parking lot. If you arrive after hours, register for the Bullfrog Pond sites at the self-pay kiosk at the campground.

Food

A focal point of downtown Guerneville, **Main Street Bistro** (16280 Main St., 707/869-0501, www.mainststation.com, 4pm-10pm daily, $16-30) offers a big menu filled with homey, casual grub. The mainstay is handmade pizza, by the slice or pie. In the evenings, locals and visitors come to eat pizza, drink beer, and listen to live entertainment on the small stage.

Pat's Restaurant (16236 Main St., 707/869-9905, www.pats-restaurant.com, 7am-3pm daily, $10) is the kind of diner that travelers love to find. It's homey, casual, and where locals come to sit at the counter and have breakfast. At night Pat's is another restaurant entirely, and that's not speaking figuratively. The diner is home to **Dick Blomster's Korean Diner** (5pm-9pm Sun.-Thurs., 5pm-10pm Fri.-Sat., $15-25) where comfort food (short ribs, hamburgers, fried chicken) is served up Korean style with twists such as deep-fried pickles, kimchi aioli, sake ice cream, and hash browns with a seafood medley. The specialty is a peanut butter sandwich, dipped in pancake batter, and fried with Pop-Rocks. Dick Blomster's is easily the hippest restaurant in Wine Country.

Big Bottom Market (16228 Main St., 707/604-7295, www.bigbottommarket.com, 8am-5pm Sun.-Mon. and Wed.-Thurs., 8am-6pm Fri.-Sat., $8-12) is a café that serves its coffee via French press and has a small but select local wine list. The food includes excellent cold and hot-pressed sandwiches, savory bread pudding, and a wide assortment of biscuits so dense and satisfying, they can be a meal on their own. The atmosphere, with touches of brushed metal on beautiful wood topped tables, will make you want to linger.

It was ★ **boon eat + drink** (16248 Main St., 707/869-0780, http://eatatboon.com, 11am-3pm, 5pm-9pm Mon.-Tues. and Thurs., 5pm-9pm Wed., 11am-3pm, 5pm-10pm Fri., 10am-3pm, 5pm-10pm Sat., 10am-3pm, 5pm-9pm Sun., $16-26) that first got Guerneville on the culinary map. Light and airy with splashes of metal and bright colors, this bistro is related to the nearby boon hotel + spa, where some of the vegetables are grown. Lunch usually consists of panini, small plates, and the grass-fed Boon burger ($14). For dinner, hearty mains combine lamb shank with mint pesto or flat iron steak with truffle fries.

Information and Services

There isn't much in the way of services in Guerneville. Off the beaten wine path is the **Russian River Chamber of Commerce and Visitors Center** (16209 1st St., Guerneville, 707/869-9000, http://russianriver.com, 10am-4:45pm Mon.-Sat., 10am-3pm Sun. May-Oct., 10am-4:45pm Mon.-Sat. Nov.-Apr.) in downtown Guerneville, where the staff will give you serious local recommendations not only for wineries but for river recreation, restaurants, and other less-traveled attractions. There's also an outpost at Korbel Winery (13250 River Rd., 10am-4pm daily May-Oct., 10am-3:15pm daily Nov.-Apr.).

Transportation

Guerneville is on Highway 116, alternately named River Road. In downtown Guerneville, Highway 116 is briefly called Main Street. The most direct access is via U.S. 101 north of Santa Rosa; take the River Road/Guerneville exit and follow River Road west for 15 miles to downtown Guerneville.

Alternately, a more scenic and often less crowded route is to take U.S. 101 to Highway 116 near Cotati, south of Santa Rosa. Also called the Gravenstein Highway, Highway 116 winds about 22 twisty miles through Sebastopol, Graton, and Forestville to emerge onto River Road in Guerneville.

HEALDSBURG AND VICINITY

Healdsburg, a small city of 11,000, is so charming it's easy to forget that people live and work here. The plaza anchors downtown and the wide and slow Russian River, creating the town's natural southern border. Boutiques, chic restaurants, and galleries dot the town, and fresh paint brightens the historical storefronts and planters filled with flowers and trailing vines. Healdsburg is also the nexus of three American Viticulture Areas (AVAs): Russian River Valley, best known for producing pinot noir and chardonnay; Dry Creek, famous for its zinfandel and sauvignon blanc; and the Alexander Valley, which produces predominantly cabernet sauvignon and merlot.

Wineries

DRY CREEK VINEYARD

The midsize **Dry Creek Vineyard** (3770 Lambert Bridge Rd., 800/864-9463, www.drycreekvineyard.com, 10:30am-4:30pm daily, $10-15) focuses much effort within its own AVA (Dry Creek), producing many single-vineyard wines from grapes grown within a few miles of the estate. Other wines include grapes from the Russian River Valley AVA. Dry Creek prides itself on both its classic California varietals such as chardonnay, fume blanc, zinfandel, cabernet, and merlot.

It occasionally produces something unusual, like a chenin blanc, or a sauterne-style dessert wine. Try as many as you can in the ivy-covered tasting room, styled after a French château.

PRESTON VINEYARDS

At Lou Preston's idiosyncratic establishment, **Preston Vineyards** (9282 W. Dry Creek Rd., Healdsburg, 707/433-3372, www.prestonvineyards.com, 11am-4:30pm daily, $10), homemade bread, organic vegetables, and olive oil get nearly equal attention as the wine. Inside the homespun tasting room, you'll taste some organic wine from its small portfolio dominated by rhone varietals. The selection of locally produced foods makes this an ideal place to buy everything you need for an impromptu picnic next to the bocce courts.

FERRARI-CARANO

One of the best large wineries in Dry Creek Valley, **Ferrari-Carano** (8761 Dry Creek Rd., 707/433-6700 or 800/831-0381, www.ferrari-carano.com, 10am-5pm daily, $5-15) provides great standard and reserve wines in an upscale tasting room and winery facility. Upstairs you'll get to taste from Ferrari-Carano's extensive menu of large-production, moderately priced whites and reds. Downstairs, enjoy the elegant lounge area, which includes comfortable seating and a video describing the wine-making process, from grape to glass. Look down into one of the major barrel storage areas, where wines age right before your eyes. And finally, open the glass doors and enter the reserve tasting room, where for an additional fee you can taste the best of Ferrari-Carano's vintages—smaller runs that are mostly bold, assertive reds.

★ ALEXANDER VALLEY VINEYARDS

Alexander Valley Vineyards (8644 Hwy. 128, Healdsburg, 707/433-7209 or 800/888-7209, www.avvwine.com, 10am-5pm daily, free) shares a name with the historical valley for good reason. In the 1960s the founders of the winery bought a chunk of the homestead once owned by Cyrus Alexander, the man credited with planting the valley's first vineyards in 1846.

The winery's vineyards provide the grapes for two decadent blends, Temptation Zin and Redemption Zin, and the Bordeaux-style Cyrus flagship wine. Historical sites pepper the estate, including a wooden schoolhouse built by Alexander in 1853 and the Alexander family gravesite, up the hill. Complimentary tours of the expansive wine caves are available daily at 11am and 2pm.

PORTALUPI

There are a number of tasting rooms in downtown Healdsburg, but if you go to one, make it **Portalupi** (107 North St., 707/395-0960, www.portalupiwine.com, 11am-7pm daily, $5-10). You'll find Russian River pinot noirs and zinfandel, as well as Italian barbera, a port made from carignane, and the Vaso di Marina, a blend of pinot noir, zinfandel, and cabernet sauvignon. As a nod to Jane Portalupi's grandmother, who used to make wine in her native village in Italy, the wine comes in a liter ($28) or half-gallon glass jug ($48). The sole white is the bianco blend of sauvignon blanc, chardonnay, and muscat canelli.

The lush, inky quality of Portalupi's wines is perfectly matched by its sophisticated tasting room filled with two large couches. Taste a flight or order by the glass. Cheese and salami plates are also available ($15), and a small deli case offers local cheese, charcuterie, and other snacks. Despite the tasting room's small size, this is a great place to hang out, particularly when the large glass doors are open.

Sights

If you're a serious student of wine, don't miss out on the **Sonoma County Wine Library** (Healdsburg Regional Library, 139 Piper St., 707/433-3772, www.sonomalibrary.org/wine, 10am-6pm Tues. and Thurs.-Fri., 10am-8pm Wed., 10am-4pm Sat.). This public library extension contains a collection of over 5,000

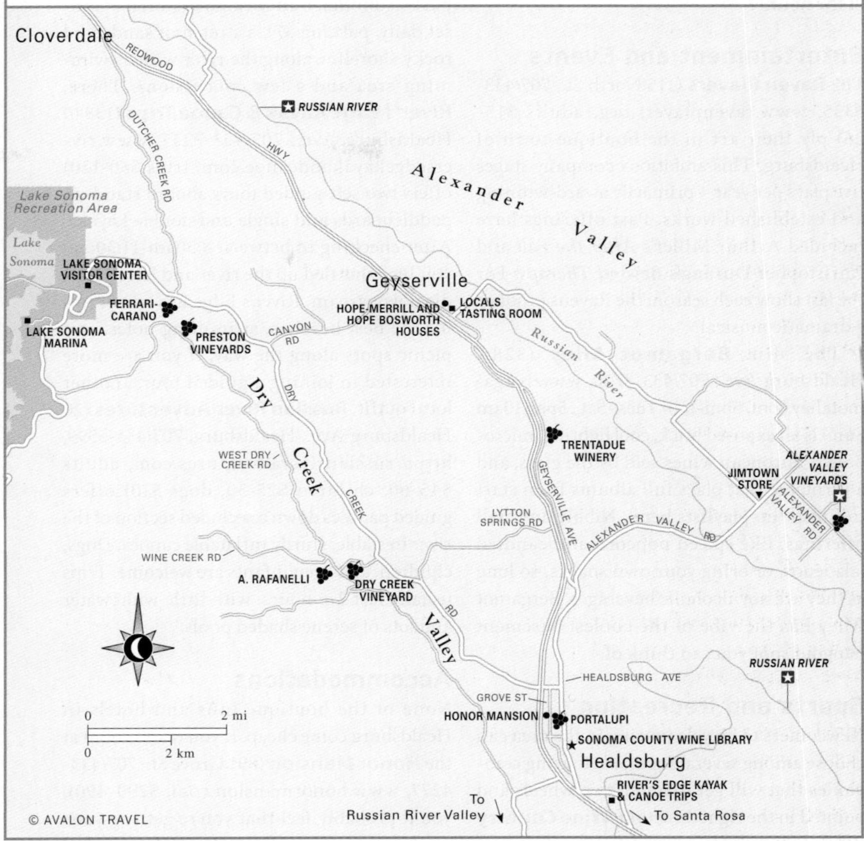

books on wine and subscriptions to more than 80 wine periodicals, along with photos, prints, and wine labels. Among the 1,000 or so rare wine books, you'll find treatises on the history, business, and art of wine from as far back as 1512. The library is a perfect place for wine drinkers who want to take their habit or hobby to the next level.

The **Healdsburg Plaza** is one of the town's most treasured features. Shaded benches are scattered throughout the large square, perfect for resting during summer afternoons. Most of the trees in the plaza were planted between 1897 and 1900, and include Canary date palms, orange and lemon trees, and a rare dawn redwood from China.

The tiny **Hand Fan Museum of Healdsburg** (Healdsburg Hotel, 219 Healdsburg Ave., 707/431-2500, www.handfanmuseum.com, 11am-4pm Wed.-Sun.) seeks to tell the cultural histories of Europe, America, and Asia through the creation, decoration, and use of fans. It doesn't take long to view both the permanent collection and seasonal exhibits at this fun museum. You'll learn about how fans were and are used in various societies: The 17th-19th-century courting practices and sexual invitations in some

European countries included intricate movements of a woman's fan, directed at the man of the hour.

Entertainment and Events

The **Raven Players** (115 North St., 707/433-6335, www.ravenplayers.org, adults $15-26) ply their art in the boutique town of Healdsburg. This ambitious company stages five plays per year—primarily award-winning and established works. Past offerings have included Arthur Miller's *After the Fall* and Christopher Durang's *Beyond Therapy*. For the last show each season, the Ravens produce a dramatic musical.

The slim **Bergamot Alley** (328A Healdsburg Ave., 707/433-8720, www.bergamotalley.com, 5pm-1am Tues.-Sat., 5pm-10am Sun.) is all exposed brick, cool lighting, microbrews, European wines sold by the glass, and a turntable that plays full albums from start to finish (no playlists here). Nibble on small offerings, like spiced popcorn and candied jalapenos, or bring your own snacks, so long as they are not alcoholic beverages. Bergamot Alley has the vibe of the coolest basement hangout spot you can think of.

Sports and Recreation

Newcomers to bicycle touring in the area can choose among several reputable touring companies that will get them on two wheels and pointed in the right direction. **Wine Country Bikes** (61 Front St., 707/473-0610, www.winecountrybikes.com, 9am-5pm daily, tours $139) is on the square in downtown Healdsburg. Its Classic Wine Tour pedals through the Dry Creek region, where you'll stop and taste wine, take walks in vineyards, and learn more about the history of wine. A gourmet picnic lunch is included with the tour. For independent souls who prefer to carve their own routes, Wine Country Bikes also rents road bikes, tandem bikes, and hybrids ($39-145 per day) that you can also take on park trails where biking is permitted.

The Russian River provides water-related recreation opportunities. On the south side of town is **Memorial Beach** (13839 Old Redwood Hwy., 707/433-1625, http://parks.sonomacounty.ca.gov, sunrise-sunset daily, parking $7), a stretch of sandy and rocky shoreline along the river with a swimming area and a few concessions. There, **River's Edge Kayak & Canoe Trips** (13840 Healdsburg Ave., 707/433-7247, www.riversedgekayakandcanoe.com, trips $50-120) offers two self-guided tours aboard stand-up paddleboards and single and double kayaks. After checking in between 8:30am-11:30am, you'll be shuttled up the river and left to paddle downstream. River's Edge has lots of tips for the best beaches, swimming holes, and picnic spots along the way. If you are more interested in joining a guided tour, another local outfit, **Russian River Adventures** (20 Healdsburg Ave., Healdsburg, 707/433-5599, http://russianriveradventures.com, adults $45-60, children $25-30, dogs $10) offers guided paddles down a secluded section of the river in stable, sturdy inflatable canoes. Dogs, children, and even infants are welcome. Trips usually last 2-6 hours, with little whitewater and lots of serene shaded pools.

Accommodations

None of the boutique inns and hotels in Healdsburg come cheap. If you take a room at the **Honor Mansion** (891 Grove St., 707/433-4277, www.honormansion.com, $290-490), you'll probably feel that you're getting your money's worth. Each of the 13 rooms and suites has been furnished and decorated with exquisite attention, including private baths stocked with high-end toiletries. Many also have fireplaces and private patios. All rooms come with a full gourmet breakfast each morning. The Honor Mansion also has a lap pool, a tennis court, a croquet lawn, a bocce pit, a putting area, and outdoor professional massage service.

The **Haydon Street Inn** (321 Haydon St., Healdsburg, 707/433-5228 or 800/528-3703, www.haydon.com, $195-450) is a small inn on a quiet residential street about a 10-minute walk from the plaza. The Queen Anne-style house was built in 1912 and is perfectly maintained with original detailing and period antiques. The six rooms in the main house all have private baths, with the exception of the Blue Room, whose bathroom is across the hall. Two additional deluxe rooms ($400 and up) are in a separate cottage on the manicured grounds. Expect a sumptuous three-course breakfast, and wonderful hors d'oeuvres at the inn's nightly wine hour.

On the town plaza, the **Hotel Healdsburg** (25 Matheson St., 707/431-2800, www.hotel-healdsburg.com, $309-509) is a local icon. The 55-room boutique hotel offers the most upscale amenities, including Frette towels and linens, soaking tubs, walk-in showers, and beautiful modern decor. Rooms include free Wi-Fi and a gourmet breakfast, and guests can enjoy the outdoor pool, fitness center, and full-service day spa. Downstairs, grab a cocktail at the chic **Spirit Bar** (5pm-11:30pm Mon.-Thurs., noon-11:30pm Fri.-Sun.), or a table on the leafy patio at the renowned **Dry Creek Kitchen** (707/431-0330, www.charliepalmer.com, 5:30pm-9:30pm Sun.-Thurs., 5:30pm-10pm Fri.-Sat., $27-39).

Food

The high-ceilinged, concrete, wood, and glass dining room of ★ **Spoonbar** (219 Healdsburg Ave., 707/433-7222, http://spoonbar.com, 5pm-9pm Sun.-Thurs., 5pm-9pm Fri.-Sat., $21-33) excels at minimalism. The warehouse-like space opens out to bustling Healdsburg Avenue. Servers carry out plates of slow-cooked pork belly, braised clams and mussels, and Cornish game hen roulade. Small plates of raw and cured fish, snacks such as chicken cracklings, a wine list that ranges from local to European, and an artisanal cocktail menu polish off the experience.

The large barn housing **Barndiva** (231 Center St., Healdsburg, 707/431-0100, www.barndiva.com, noon-3pm, 5:30pm-9pm Wed.-Thurs., noon-3pm, 5:30pm-10pm Fri.-Sat., 11am-1:45pm, 5:30pm-9pm Sun., $24-38) looks very Wine Country from the outside, but inside is more Manhattan. The menu has 10 items (a $20 filet mignon burger is one), all French-inspired and Sonoma County sourced. Barndiva also has an impressive, retro-fresh cocktail menu.

Unpretentious and delicious Italian small plates, pizza, and pastas, along with an energetic yet intimate vibe have made **Scopa** (109A Plaza St., 707/433-5282, www.scopahealdsburg.com, 5:30pm-10pm daily, $14-18) wildly popular. Antipasti dishes like grilled calamari and Venetian-style sardines have won accolades for perfect execution and very reasonable prices.

If you can't get a table at Scopa's, head around the corner to Scopa's sister restaurant, the casual **Campo Fina** (330 Healdsburg Ave., 707395-4640, www.campo-fina.com, 11:30am-10pm daily, $15-23). You'll find everything from oysters on the half shell to antipasti plates and main courses like breaded pork loin. The semi-covered patio has plenty of tables, plus bocce ball courts.

At **Mateo's Cocina Latina** (214 Healdsburg Ave., 707/433-1520, www.mateoscocinalatina.com, 11:30am-9pm Wed.-Mon., $13-25) the flavors of the Yucatan are served surrounded by colorful textiles and wood furniture. It's a pleasant reprieve from Wine Country haute style, but the menu will no doubt impress. Order several of the finger food *tacones* or the *cochinita pibil*, a slow-roasted suckling pig, the signature dish. There is a well-balanced drink menu of a dozen microbrews, local wines, and a host of tequila cocktails. Aficionados will swoon over the range of tequilas, reserve *anejo* tequilas, and mezcals.

For an independent cup of coffee in Healdsburg, **Flying Goat Coffee** (324 Center St., 707/433-3599, www.flyinggoatcoffee.com, 7am-7pm daily) sits opposite the square. The place to go for picnic supplies is **Oakville Grocery** (124 Matheson St., 707/433-3200, www.oakvillegrocery.com, 9am-5pm daily, $7-12), a block away. Like its cousin in the Napa Valley, it sells a great selection of cheeses, fresh local breads, and wine, plus fresh eats from its upscale deli counter.

The **Jimtown Store** (6706 Hwy. 128, 707/433-1212, www.jimtown.com, 7am-4pm Mon.-Thurs., 7am-5pm Fri.-Sun. May-Dec., 7am-3pm Mon. and Wed.-Fri., 7:30am-5pm Sat., 7:30am-3pm Sun. Jan.-Apr., $6-12), six miles out of town on a country road, has been in operation since 1895. At this combination of old-fashioned country store and gourmet sensibility, you'll find house-made gourmet jams, jellies, and condiments; penny toys; housewares; and best of all, hot lunches. The chalkboard menu presents a tasty assortment of smoked-brisket sandwiches, chili, buttermilk coleslaw, and chorizo and provolone grilled-cheese sandwiches. Enjoy table service in the back, unwrap your sandwich on benches outside, or pick up one of their prepared box lunches to go.

Information and Services

The **Healdsburg Chamber of Commerce and Visitors Bureau** (217 Healdsburg Ave., 707/433-6935, www.healdsburg.com, 10am-4pm Mon.-Fri., 11am-2pm Sat.-Sun.) is centrally located off U.S. 101, just as you come into town on Healdsburg Avenue. The friendly staff is happy to load you up with maps, brochures, and helpful tips. If arriving after hours, the chamber has a 24-hour visitor kiosk.

The **Healdsburg District Hospital** (1375 University Ave., 707/431-6500, http://healdsburgdistricthospital.org) has a 24-hour emergency room.

Transportation

Healdsburg is an easy destination, as it is about 15 miles north of Santa Rosa on U.S. 101. To reach downtown Healdsburg from U.S. 101, take exit 503 for Central Healdsburg. Healdsburg can also be accessed from Calistoga. Drive north of Calistoga on the beautiful Highway 128 for almost 20 miles. At Jimtown, Highway 128 intersects Alexander Valley Road. Continue straight on Alexander Valley Road as Highway 128 turns right, heading north to Geyserville. In about three miles, turn left onto Healdsburg Avenue, which runs to downtown Healdsburg.

GEYSERVILLE

At the tip of Wine Country, Geyserville is also at the edge of California's great northern redwood forest and has a small mountain-town feel. Fewer than 900 people call Geyserville home, and despite its name, which inspires images of healing waters, you won't find any big spas or rejuvenating fountains. The town got its name for the Geysers,

Jimtown Store

a series of hot springs and fumaroles deep in the Mayacamas Mountains east of town. It became a tourist attraction at the turn of the 20th century, and Geyserville sprang up as a result. Now the Geysers is a complex of geothermal power plants, the largest in the world, but Geyserville retains its Old West charm. The downtown is tiny, with a few shops and restaurants and a number of historical buildings. In many ways, Geyserville feels like a snapshot of an earlier time.

Wineries

TRENTADUE

As you walk up to the magnificent Italianate tasting room at **Trentadue** (19170 Geyserville Ave., 707/433-3104, www.trentadue.com, 10am-5pm daily, $5-10), the first thing you'll notice is how the gardens sweep out toward the vineyards. Many of Trentadue's vintages are made from estate-grown grapes, including Italian varietals. Inside the narrow tasting room is a tasting bar that pours still wines and a couple of sparkling varieties. The stars of the show are the ports, of which Trentadue makes an array of different styles and flavors. To take in the beautiful estate, book a seat on the gondola tour ($25) offered every day by appointment. This is a particular treat during harvest time.

LOCALS TASTING ROOM

The tiny town of Geyserville boasts more than its fair share of great tasting rooms, but if you can only pick one, make it **Locals Tasting Room** (Geyserville Ave. at Hwy. 128, 707/857-4900, www.tastelocalwine.com, 11am-6pm daily, free), the first wine cooperative in the state. With over 40 wines available, tasting is complimentary as Locals is confident you'll find something you'll want to take home. Most of the wines cost $20-40 and hail from northern Sonoma's boutique wineries. The overall mix of wineries is broad ranging, from the Central Coast up to Mendocino.

Sports and Recreation

At the north end of the Dry Creek Valley, the 17,000 acres of hot, oak-studded hills of the **Lake Sonoma Recreation Area** (3333 Skaggs Springs Rd., 707/433-9483, www.parks.sonoma.net) have more than 40 miles of trails for hikers, bikers, and riders, the region's best bass fishing, and plenty of open water (about 2,700 surface acres, to be precise) for swimming and boating.

The main access points to the lake and trails are Stewarts Point Road just south of the bridge, Rockpile Road north of the bridge, and the grassy **Yorty Creek Recreation Area** (at the end of Shady Ln./Hot Springs Rd.) on the eastern side of the lake and accessible from Cloverdale. A public boat launch at Warm Springs Bridge lets you launch your own ski or fishing boat for a $3 fee, and the marina off Stewarts Point Road (707/433-2200, www.lakesonoma.com) offers boat and slip rentals.

The easiest, most accessible hiking trails start at the **South Lake Trailhead** (on Stewarts Point Rd. about 0.5 miles south from its junction with Skaggs Springs Rd., just before the marina turnoff). From there it's a quick jaunt up the hill to the **Overlook**, with great views of the lake, or take the **South Lake Trail** for a longer hike. Pick up information at the **Milt Brandt Visitor Center** (3333 Skaggs Springs Rd., Geyserville, 707/433-5433, 8:30am-3:30pm Wed.-Sun.), right at the end of Dry Creek Road.

Accommodations and Camping

In Geyserville, the bed-and-breakfast to visit is the ★ **Hope-Merrill and Hope-Bosworth Houses** (21253 Geyserville Ave., 707/857-3356 or 800/825-4233, www.hope-inns.com, $153-309). This Victorian charmer comprises two historical houses across the street from one another. Aficionados of the Victorian style will love the flowers, lace, frills, and gewgaws that fill the rooms. Each room has its own private bath—most in the same room, and amenities include a saltwater pool, two hot tubs, and a homemade breakfast each morning.

There are plenty of places to pitch your

tent at the **Lake Sonoma Recreation Area** (3333 Skaggs Springs Rd., 707/433-9483, www.parks.sonoma.net). Hike-in or boat-in primitive campsites dot the 50 miles of shoreline. These require backcountry permits, available at the **Milt Brandt Visitor Center** (3333 Skaggs Springs Rd., Geyserville, 707/431-4533). Car campers can pull into the **Liberty Glen Campground** (877/444-6777, www.reserveusa.com), where 113 campsites abut the lake. The campground is rustic, with chemical toilets and no potable water.

Food

Geyserville may not have a huge selection of places to eat, but what is here is excellent. **Catelli's** (21047 Geyserville Ave., 707/857-3471, www.mycatellis.com, 11:30am-8pm Tues.-Thurs., 11:30am-9pm Fri., noon-9pm Sat., noon-8pm Sun., $15-21) is helmed by the eponymous family, one of whom is a celebrity chef who has appeared on *Iron Chef* and *Oprah*. Honoring her family's roots, but with an added dedication to healthy local food, Domenica Catelli and her brother Nick have created an earthy, high-quality Italian eatery geared toward sophisticated comfort food.

Diavola Restaurant (21021 Geyserville Ave., 707/814-0111, www.diavolapizzeria.com, 11:30am-9pm daily, $15-26) is a great Italian joint in a historical brick building. Centered around a wood-burning oven, this small restaurant is all about pizzas and its house-made *salumi* and sausages. Even traditional pasta dishes will be accented with crispy pork belly or pork cheek. Expect many of the thin-crust pizzas to be topped with various sausages. Diavola has a well-stocked deli case if you are eager to take some cured meats home with you.

Information and Services

Tiny Geyserville has little in the way of services. Even the small **Geyserville Chamber of Commerce** (21060 Geyserville Ave., 707/276-6076, www.geyservillecc.com, 12:30pm-4:30pm Fri.-Sun.) opens only a few days a week.

Transportation

Geyserville is located about 10 miles north of Healdsburg at the junction of U.S. 101 and Highway 128. It is also 25 miles north of Calistoga via Highway 128.

North Coast

Look for ★ to find recommended sights, activities, dining, and lodging.

Highlights

★ **Whale-Watching:** Bodega Bay offers the perfect coastal setting for spying Pacific gray whales during their migration to Alaska (page 219).

★ **Fort Ross State Historic Park:** For a taste of California history, explore this fortified outpost that served as a waypoint for 19th-century traders (page 223).

★ **Mendocino Coast Botanical Gardens:** Stretching out to the sea, 47 acres of botanical gardens offer a vast variety of flowers and plants and the butterflies who love them (page 235).

★ **Avenue of the Giants:** This aptly named scenic drive parallels U.S. 101 for 31 miles through Humboldt Redwoods State Park and the last remaining stands of virgin redwoods (page 254).

★ **Blue Ox Millworks and Historic Park:** This working lumber mill, park, and school are filled with 19th-century tools used to customize historical homes—you can even make a piece of your own (page 259).

★ **Redwood National and State Parks:** Northern California's legendary redwoods stretch along the coast from Garberville to Crescent City, offering unlimited photo ops of redwood giants (page 269).

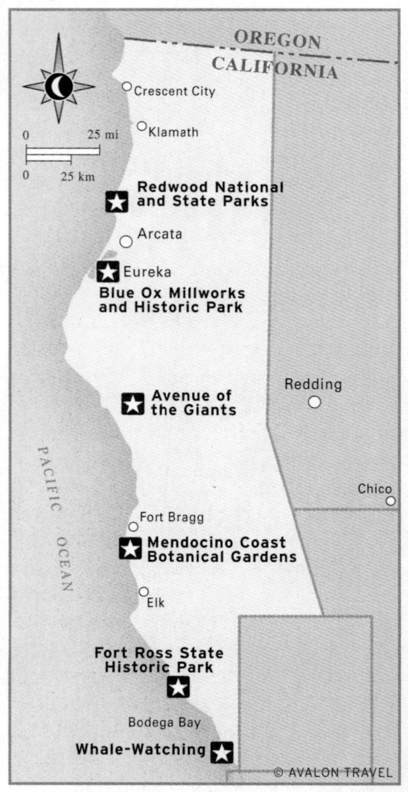

The rugged North Coast is a spectacular place. Its wild beauty is unspoiled and almost desolate. The cliffs are forbidding, the beaches are rocky and windswept, and the surf thunders in with formidable authority.

This is not the California coast of surfer movies. Hardy souls do ride the chilly Pacific waves as far north as Crescent City.

From Bodega Bay, Highway 1 twists and turns north along hairpin curves that will take your breath away. The Sonoma and Mendocino coasts offer lovely beaches and forests, top-notch cuisine, and a friendly, uncrowded wine region. Along the way, tiny coastal towns—Jenner, Gualala, Mendocino, Fort Bragg—dot the hills and valleys, beckoning travelers with bed-and-breakfasts, organic farms, and relaxing respites from the road. Inland, Mendocino's hidden wine region offers the rural and relaxed pace missing from that other famous wine district. Anderson Valley and Hopland can quench your thirst, while nearby Clear Lake—California's largest natural freshwater lake—provides more than 100 miles of sunny shoreline to cool off. Where Highway 1 merges with U.S. 101 is the famous Lost Coast, accessed only via steep narrow roads and on foot along the scenic California Coastal Trail that runs 64 miles over mountains and across beaches.

For most travelers, the North Coast means redwood country, and U.S. 101 marks the gateway to those redwoods beginning south of the small town of Willits. A plethora of state and national parks lure travelers with numerous hiking trails, forested campgrounds, kitschy redwood tourist traps, and some of the tallest and oldest trees on the continent. Pitch a tent in Humboldt Redwoods State Park, cruise the Avenue of the Giants, and gaze in wonder at the primordial Founders Grove. Towns like Eureka made their fortune in the logging industry and are filled with ornate redwood Victorians. Crescent City marks the northern terminus of the North Coast, a coastal seaside town known for fishing, seafood, and for surviving a tsunami.

Previous: the Mendocino coast; giant coastal redwoods at Jedediah Smith State Park. **Above:** Trinidad Memorial Lighthouse.

North Coast

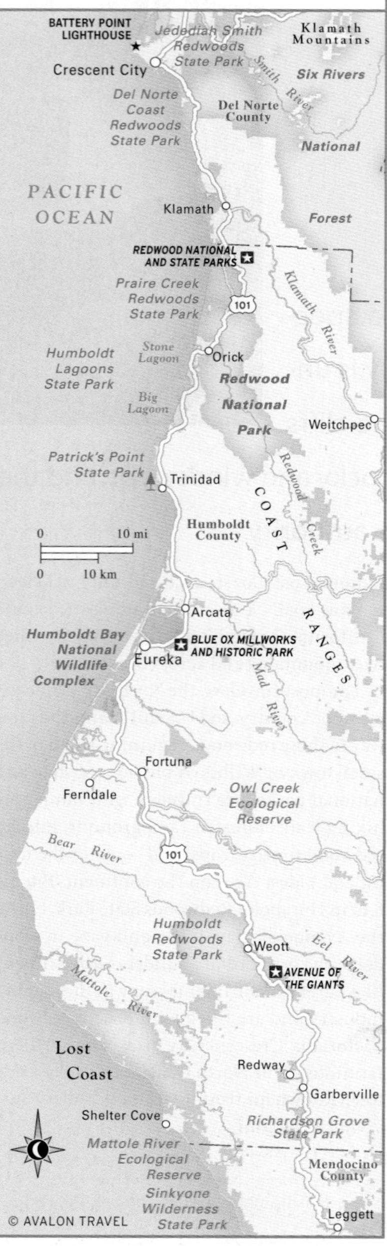
BATTERY POINT LIGHTHOUSE
Jedediah Smith Redwoods State Park
Klamath Mountains
Crescent City
Smith River
Six Rivers
Del Norte Coast Redwoods State Park
Del Norte County
National
PACIFIC OCEAN
Klamath
Forest
REDWOOD NATIONAL AND STATE PARKS
Praire Creek Redwoods State Park
101
Klamath River
Humboldt Lagoons State Park
Stone Lagoon
Orick
Redwood National Park
Big Lagoon
Weitchpec
Patrick's Point State Park
Trinidad
Redwood Creek
COAST RANGES
Humboldt County
0 10 mi
0 10 km
Arcata
Humboldt Bay National Wildlife Complex
Eureka
BLUE OX MILLWORKS AND HISTORIC PARK
Mad River
Fortuna
Ferndale
Owl Creek Ecological Reserve
Bear River
101
Humboldt Redwoods State Park
Weott
Eel River
AVENUE OF THE GIANTS
Mattole River
Lost Coast
Redway
Garberville
Shelter Cove
Richardson Grove State Park
Mattole River Ecological Reserve
Mendocino County
Sinkyone Wilderness State Park
Leggett
© AVALON TRAVEL

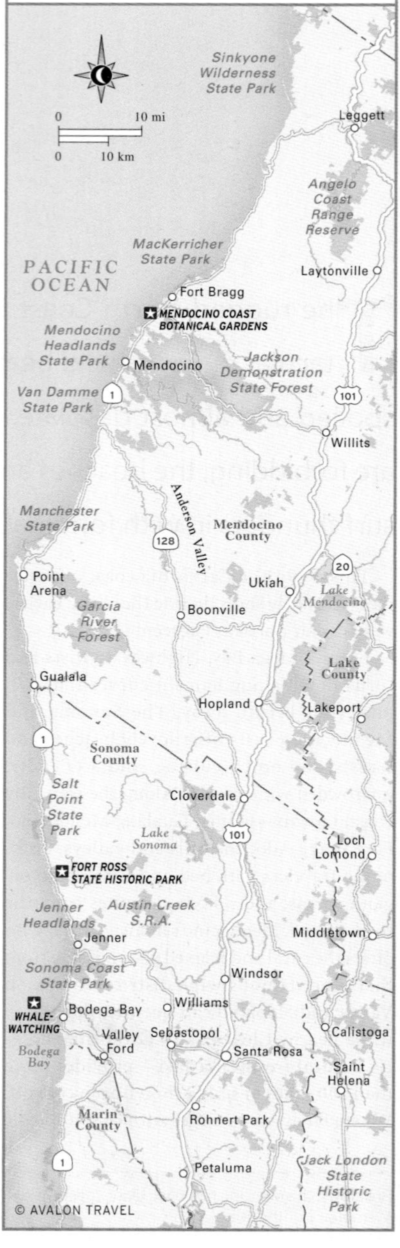

Sinkyone Wilderness State Park
0 10 mi
0 10 km
Leggett
Angelo Coast Range Reserve
MacKerricher State Park
PACIFIC OCEAN
Laytonville
Fort Bragg
MENDOCINO COAST BOTANICAL GARDENS
Mendocino Headlands State Park
Mendocino
Jackson Demonstration State Forest
Van Damme State Park
1
101
Willits
Anderson Valley
Manchester State Park
Mendocino County
128
20
Point Arena
Ukiah
Lake Mendocino
Garcia River Forest
Boonville
Lake County
Gualala
Hopland
Lakeport
1
Sonoma County
Salt Point State Park
Cloverdale
Lake Sonoma
101
Loch Lomond
FORT ROSS STATE HISTORIC PARK
Jenner Headlands
Austin Creek S.R.A.
Jenner
Middletown
Sonoma Coast State Park
Windsor
WHALE-WATCHING
Bodega Bay
Williams
Valley Ford
Sebastopol
Calistoga
Bodega Bay
Santa Rosa
Saint Helena
Marin County
Rohnert Park
1
Petaluma
Jack London State Historic Park
© AVALON TRAVEL

PLANNING YOUR TIME

The outdoors is the primary attraction in this region. Driving is the way to get from place to place, unless you're a hard-core backpacker. Make time to explore the redwoods in the parks and spend time on the rugged beaches (in warm waterproof clothes) as well. Hiking is the one don't-miss activity. Close seconds are fishing, whale-watching, and watching the fog roll in as you sit in a cozy café.

Sonoma Coast

One good way to begin your meander up the coast is to take U.S. 101 out of San Francisco as far as Petaluma, and then head west toward Highway 1, on this stretch also called the Shoreline Highway. As you travel toward the coast, you'll leave urban areas behind for a while, passing through some of the most bucolic farmland in California.

BODEGA BAY

Bodega Bay is popular for its coastal views, whale-watching, and seafood—but it's most famous as the filming locale of Alfred Hitchcock's *The Birds.*

★ Whale-Watching

The best sight you could hope to see is a close-up view of Pacific gray whales migrating home to Alaska with their newborn calves. The whales head past January-May on their way from their summer home off Mexico. If you're lucky, you can see them from the shore. **Bodega Head,** a promontory just north of the bay, is a place to get close to the migration route. To get to this prime spot, travel north on Highway 1 about one mile past the visitors center and turn left onto Eastshore Road; make a right at the stop sign, and then drive three more miles to the parking lot. To get out on the water, book a tour with **Bodega Bay Charters** (707/875-3495, www.bodegacharters.com, adults $50, children under 13 $35). Tours are offered twice daily December through April and last three hours. The **Bodega Bay Sport Fishing Center** (707/875-3344, www.bodegabaysportfishing.com, adults $55, children $35) is another outfit that has tours during the spring migration. These are three to four hours long and available December through May.

Doran Regional Park

When you arrive in Bodega Bay, you'll see a sign pointing left for **Doran Regional Park** (201 Doran Beach Rd., 707/875-3540, www.sonoma-county.org, 7am-sunset daily, day use $7 per vehicle, camping $26-32). It is less than one mile down the road and worth the trip. You can even swim at Doran Beach; although it's cold, it's protected from the open ocean waves, so it's much safer than most of the beaches along the coast.

Sonoma Coast State Park

Seventeen miles of coast are within **Sonoma Coast State Park** (707/875-3483, www.parks.ca.gov, day use $8 per vehicle). The park's boundaries extend from Bodega Head at the south up to the Vista Trailhead, four miles north of Jenner. As you drive up Highway 1, you'll see signs for various beaches. Although they're lovely places to walk, fish, and maybe sunbathe on the odd hot day, it is not advisable to swim here. If you go down to the water, bring your binoculars and your camera. The cliffs, crags, inlets, whitecaps, mini islands, and rock outcroppings are fascinating in any weather, and their looks change with the shifting tides and fog.

Accommodations

Sandwiched between the golf course and the dunes, **Bodega Bay Lodge** (103 Hwy. 1, 707/875-4212 or 888/875-2250, www.bodegabaylodge.com, $239-450) is one of the more luxurious places to stay in the area. It is a large

Sonoma and Mendocino Coasts

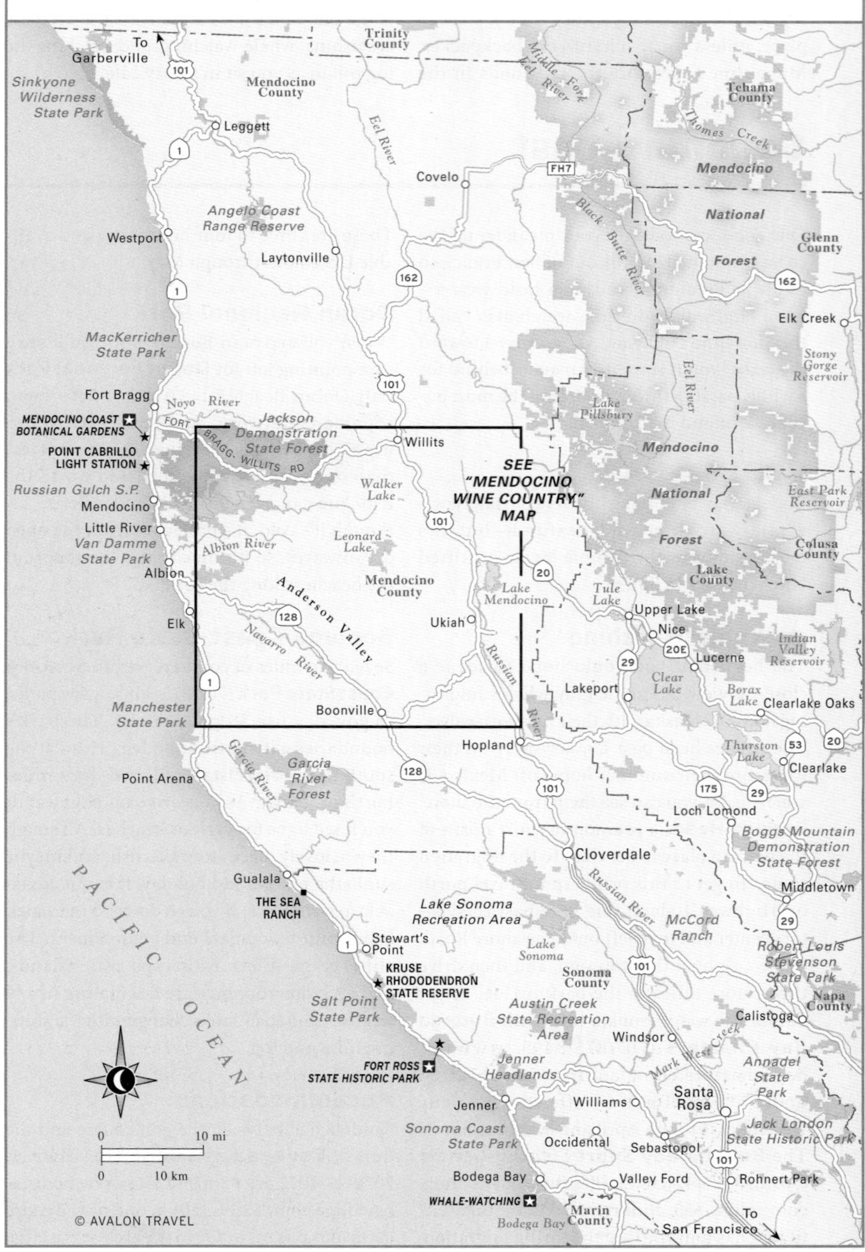

resort with long rows of semidetached cabins. All the rooms have unobstructed views of the dunes and the ocean, and many feature fireplaces, private patios, and whirlpool tubs. The facility also has a spa, a pool, a fitness center, two fine restaurants, and a library.

The **Inn at the Tides** (800 Hwy. 1, 707/875-2751, www.innatthetides.com, $159-250) takes full advantage of its location. Settled on a hill, the inn's collection of redwood shingle buildings provides lovely views of the harbor and the surrounding hills. A complimentary full breakfast and a bottle of wine upon arrival are included, as is access to the pool, fitness room, and sauna. Massages are extra as are lunch and dinner at the inn's two restaurants, one of which was a backdrop for the film *The Birds*.

Doran Regional Park (201 Doran Beach Rd., 707/875-3540, www.sonoma-county.org, reservations 707/565-2267 or http://sonomacountycamping.org, $32, plus a $9.50 reservation fee) has 130 campsites along the jetty separating the bay from the harbor.

Sonoma Coast State Park (707/875-3483, www.parks.ca.gov, $35) encompasses several campgrounds along its 17-mile expanse. Get a lovely sandy spot in the trees in **Bodega Dunes Campground** (2585 Hwy. 1), complete with hot showers and flush toilets. Another option is the smaller **Wrights Beach Campground** (7095 Hwy. 1). There are no hot showers here, but campers may use those at Bodega Dunes a few miles south on Highway 1. However, what you may lose in convenience you gain in quiet: Wrights Beach has only 27 campsites to the 98 sites at Bodega Dunes.

Food

Any fishing village worth its salt has a good place to get a basket of fish-and-chips. Bodega Bay's is named **The Birds Café** (1407 N. Hwy. 1, 707/875-2900, 11:30am-6pm Mon.-Thurs., 11:30am-7pm Fri.-Sat., $10). From its perch on the west side of Highway 1, the exposed patio overlooks the harbor as patrons chow down on oysters, fish tacos, and artichoke fritters while drinking Lagunitas IPA. Orders are taken and food is made in the no-frills stand where a couple of stools offer indoor seating.

Bodega Bay Lodge's **Duck Club Restaurant** (103 Hwy. 1, 707/875-3525, www.bodegabaylodge.com, 7:30am-11am, 6pm-9pm daily, $19-34) offers a warm and elegant dining experience featuring hearty American entrées like steak, chicken, and halibut with seasonal vegetables. There's a fireside lounge overlooking the bay, and outdoor seating for warmer days.

One of the best restaurants in the area is **Terrapin Creek** (1580 Eastshore Dr., 707/875-2700, www.terrapincreekcafe.com, 4:30pm-9pm Thurs.-Sun., $23-32), where they make creative use of fresh seafood. Billing itself as a "casual neighborhood spot," Terrapin Creek serves elegant food in a refurbished old farmhouse.

Information and Services

The **Sonoma Coast Visitors Center** (850 Hwy. 1, 707/875-3866, www.visitbodegabayca.com, 9am-5pm Mon.-Sat., 10am-5pm Sun.) in Bodega Bay may look small, but it's chock-full of maps, brochures, trail guides, event schedules, and even a map of shooting locations for *The Birds*.

Transportation

Bodega Bay is located on Highway 1 north of Point Reyes National Seashore and west of Petaluma. It's a beautiful drive north, hugging the coast, but the cliffs and the road's twists and turns mean a slow 1.5-hour trek from San Francisco. A faster way to get here is to take U.S. 101 to Petaluma. Exit at East Washington Street and follow Bodega Avenue to Valley Ford Road, cutting across to the coast. You'll hit Bodega Bay just about two miles after you pass through Valley Ford. This route takes about an hour and 15 minutes.

JENNER

Jenner is on Highway 1 at the Russian River. It's a beautiful spot for a quiet honeymoon or a walk along the coast. **Goat Rock Beach** (Goat Rock Rd., 707/875-3483, www.parks.

ca.gov, day use $8) is the northernmost tip of **Sonoma Coast State Park** at the mouth of the Russian River. With a lovely boardwalk, abundant wildlife, and an impressive hunk of serpentine rock, it is a lovely place to spend the afternoon. You'll likely see gray whales, sea otters, elephant seals, shore birds and, if you arrive March-August, harbor seal pups. Pets are not allowed, and swimming is prohibited. Access to the beach is on the south side of the river, off Highway 1.

To get out on the water, rent a kayak or join a tour at **WaterTreks** (10438 Hwy. 1, 707/865-2249, rentals $30-70). Next to the Jenner boat ramp, the folks here will get you set up on a single or double kayak and suggested routes around the estuary or along the river. The company also offers shuttle drop-off farther up river for a longer paddle, and guided tours around the estuary.

Accommodations and Food

Tiny Jenner is blessed with both great food and digs. The ★ **River's End** (11048 Hwy. 1, 707/865-2484, www.ilovesunsets.com, noon-3:30pm, 5pm-8:30pm Sun.-Tues. and Thurs., noon-3:30pm, 5pm-9pm Fri.-Sat. winter, noon-3:30pm, 5pm-8:30pm Sun.-Thurs., noon-3:30pm, 5pm-9pm Fri.-Sat. summer, $25-45) is perched above the spot where the Russian River flows into the Pacific, and it's a beautiful sight to behold. Prices are high, but if you get a window table at sunset, you may forget to think about it. If you can't get enough, rent one of the five two-person cabins ($239-279) down the hill from the restaurant. The cabins have excellent views and a romantic atmosphere. Children under 12 are "not recommended."

Stellar accommodations can be found at the **Jenner Inn** (10400 Hwy. 1, 707/865-2377 or 800/732-2377, www.jennerinn.com, $118-268). You'll find a variety of options, including gingerbread cottages nestled in tea roses, charming economy rooms in the main lodge, and waterfront suites that make you feel like you are hovering just above the river. Luxurious perks such as hot tubs and private decks can be found in many of the rooms, and all feel like a great deal for the price. The inn also operates a café, **Eatery by the Sea** (8am-3pm Wed.-Mon., $11-16) in a window-filled dining room built by Swedish boat builders. The café serves burgers, soups, and salads and some killer desserts, all with local ingredients.

Fourteen miles north of Jenner, Bene Bufano's "Peace Obelisk" rises 93 feet from its high rocky perch to survey the coast and send its message of transcendence out across the sea. This is the totem of the 1960s-era **Timber Cove Inn** (21780 N. Hwy. 1, 707/847-3231 or 800/987-8319, www.timbercoveinn.com, $195-310). Large and luxurious, the wood-framed lodge has a capacious bar and lounge, an oceanfront patio, rooms with spa tubs and fireplaces, and hiking trails nearby. The decor of the swinging sixties and seventies has been perfectly preserved, adding a bit of kitsch to the spectacular setting. Take a seat in the sunken dining room or out on the patio with a personal fire pit blazing before you. At the lodge's **Alexander's Restaurant** (8am-11:30am, 5pm-9pm daily, $21-36) and the **Sequoia Lounge** (noon-5pm daily, $10-16) you can savor the vibe over a stiff drink and a plate of farm-to-fork food.

Information and Services

The small but friendly **Jenner Visitors Center** (10439 Hwy. 1, 707/865-9757, www.stewardsofthecoastandredwoods.org, 11am-3pm Mon.-Fri., 11am-4pm Sat.-Sun.) is located across the street from the Jenner Inn. The center is staffed by volunteers, so hours can be unpredictable.

Transportation

Jenner is located on Highway 1, right along the ocean. The fastest route from San Francisco (about 1.75 hours) is to drive up U.S. 101, make a left onto Washington Street in Petaluma, and continue north on Highway 1. You can also reach Jenner by following the Russian River from the River Road exit off U.S. 101 in Santa Rosa, a little over 20 miles.

NORTH OF JENNER

★ Fort Ross State Historic Park

The "Ross" in **Fort Ross State Park** (19005 Hwy. 1, Jenner, 707/847-3286, www.parks.ca.gov, grounds sunrise-sunset daily, fort and visitor center 10am-4:30pm Fri.-Tues., parking $8) is short for "Russian." The park commemorates the history of Russian settlement on the North Coast. Stretching from Tomales Bay to Point Arena, the network of fortified settlements lasted less than 50 years. In addition to plundering the seas for seal fur, the Russians also grew food for the more lucrative Alaskan trade. Learn more at the park's large visitors center, which provides a continuous film and a roomful of exhibits.

You can also walk into the reconstructed fort buildings and see how the settlers lived. The only original building still standing is the captain's quarters—a large, luxurious house for the time. The other buildings, including the large bunkhouse, the chapel, and the two cannon-filled blockhouses, were rebuilt using much of the original lumber. A visit to the whole fort and the beach beyond takes some time as the park is fairly spread out. Wear comfortable shoes and bring a bottle of water.

Salt Point State Park

Stretching for miles along the Sonoma coastline, **Salt Point State Park** (25050 Hwy. 1, Jenner, 707/847-3221, www.parks.ca.gov, visitors center 10am-3pm Sat.-Sun., day use $8) provides easy access from U.S. 101 to more than a dozen sandy state beaches. You don't have to visit the visitors center to enjoy this park and its many beaches—just follow the signs along the highway to the turnoffs and parking lots.

If you're looking to scuba dive or free dive, head for **Gerstle Cove,** accessible from the visitors center just south of Salt Point proper. The cove was designated one of California's first underwater parks, and divers who can deal with the chilly water have a wonderful time exploring the diverse undersea wildlife.

The park has plenty of camping options. **Gerstle Cove Campground** has 30 sites near the visitor center, and just across Highway 1 on the east side, **Woodside Campground** has a total of 79 sites. Both have flush toilets, but no showers, and must be reserved by phone (800/444-7275, $35). Near the Woodside Campground, 10 hike- or bike-in sites ($6) are available on a first-come, first-served basis.

historic Fort Ross

Kruse Rhododendron State Reserve

Tucked above the northeast corner of Salt Point State Park, **Kruse Rhododendron State Reserve** (707/847-3221, www.parks.ca.gov, sunrise-sunset daily, free) offers a chance to meander along the **Chinese Gulch Trail** in the spring, admiring the profusion of pink rhododendron flowers blooming beneath the second-growth redwood forest. If you prefer a picnic, snag a table and enjoy this quiet, exquisite little park.

Stewart's Point

Stewart's Point is home to a post office, a small store, and a restaurant—and that's it. **Stewart's Point Store** (32000 S. Hwy. 1, 707/785-2406, www.stewartspoint.net, 8am-6pm daily, hours vary by season) sells groceries, wine, collectible dishes, and hand-knitted hats. They've also got a deli and a bakery on-site.

The Sea Ranch

Developed in the mid-1960s for Bay Area residents seeking a personal getaway, the planned community of vacation homes known as The Sea Ranch seeks to blend in, rather than "subdue" the landscape. Naturally weathered wood and few architectural frills dominate the style. The mountain trails and facilities are reserved for guests of The Sea Ranch, but the beaches are open to the public, and parking is $7.

The **Sea Ranch Lodge** (60 Sea Walk Dr., 707/785-2371 or 800/732-7262, http://searanchlodge.com, $279-409) offers 19 rooms right along the bluffs, all sporting unobstructed ocean views, and many featuring 1970s Malm fireplaces. The lodge is dog friendly.

Food and drinks can be found in the **Lodge at the Black Point Grill** (707/785-2371, http://searanchlodge.com, 7am-9pm daily, $16-28), which is surprisingly casual. In addition to breakfast, the restaurant serves "tavern fare" (steak, fish-and-chips, burgers). There is also a kids menu, 150 wines to choose from, and lovely views outside the picture windows. Off the beaten path (and Annapolis Rd.) is the much loved **Two Fish Bakery** (35590 Verdant View, 707/785-2443, www.twofishbaking.com, 8am-3pm Thurs.-Sat., 8am-1:30pm Sun.). You'll find loaves of bread, pastries, salads and sandwiches to go, and even homemade energy bars, plus rich mochas to warm you after a morning stroll on the beach.

Mendocino Coast

The Mendocino coast is a popular retreat. On weekends, Bay Area residents flock north to their favorite hideaways to enjoy windswept beaches, secret coves, and luscious cuisine. This area is ideal for deep-sea anglers, wine aficionados, and fans of luxury spas. Art is especially prominent in the culture; from the 1960s onward, aspiring artists have found supportive communities, sales opportunities, and homes in Mendocino County, and a number of small galleries display local artworks.

The most popular inns fill up fast many weekends year-round. Fall-winter can be high season, with the Crab Festival, the Mushroom Festival, and the various harvest and after-harvest wine celebrations. If you want to stay someplace specific on the Mendocino coast, book your room at least a month in advance for weekday stays and six months or more in advance for major festival weekends.

GUALALA

Across the river and county line from The Sea Ranch, Gualala ("wa-LA-la") was once a lumber town, but now largely caters to The Sea Ranch and coastal tourists. Despite its size, you will find the greatest variety of services between Jenner and the Mendocino Village here.

Sweatpants, Parkas, and North Coast Beaches

The Hollywood view of California beaches is all about long stretches of sugary-white sand drenched in warm sunshine, populated by sun worshippers lounging on the sand and surfers riding the photogenic waves. Nothing could be further from the reality of the Northern California coast. Make no mistake—you'll find gorgeous beaches, but it's a different kind of beauty. Craggy cliffs tower over narrow, rocky sand spits teeming with tide pools and backing into ever-changing sea caves. Wide swaths of beach are covered with driftwood, semiprecious minerals, polished sea glass, and ancient fossils. Nonetheless, hardy beachgoers bring their folding chairs, umbrellas, coolers, wetsuits, and surfboards to these beaches to enjoy a day on the sand and surf. Here are some tips to help you prepare for your North Coast beach trip:

- **Dress in layers:** North Coast beach temperatures can hover in the 50s even in the middle of summer. Wear a sweatshirt and warm pants over shorts and a T-shirt, and wear all that over your swimsuit.
- **Prepare for dampness:** Fog and drizzle are ubiquitous on the coast, even when it's sunny and hot only a few miles inland. Bring a wool or fleece cap in addition to your optimistic sunhat. And toss a warm synthetic jacket in your pack (not a down jacket, as down doesn't keep you warm when it's wet).
- **Bring appropriate footwear:** Most North Coast beaches are not barefoot friendly. Exploration of rocky beaches and tide pools demands either specialized water shoes or good broken-in hiking boots. Jellyfish sometimes wash ashore on California's northern beaches, making bare feet or even beach sandals a painful proposition. And on beaches where fires are allowed, some people just cover over an abandoned fire with a little sand, which could give a hot foot to the next beachcomber to walk by. Even if you choose to go barefoot on the sand, carry a pair of closed-toed shoes with you, just in case the going gets tough farther down the beach.
- **The water is cold:** Going swimming or surfing? Wear a wetsuit and booties if you don't want to chance hypothermia or needing to be rescued by the Coast Guard.
- **Learn about fire restrictions:** Fires are illegal on many California beaches. Check restrictions for the beach you are visiting before lighting a driftwood bonfire to keep warm.
- **Wear sunscreen:** Even if a layer of fog covers the sun, you are still at risk of sunburn; locals call it a "fog burn."
- **Prepare your kids:** Bring plenty of beach toys and talk up tide pool walks, but don't promise the little ones a swim in the ocean. The reality is that it is likely too cold, too rough, or otherwise unsafe to swim.

Gualala is home to a strong arts organization. Since 1961, **Gualala Arts** (46501 Old State Hwy., 707/884-1138, www.gualalaarts.org, 9am-4pm Mon.-Fri., noon-4pm Sat.-Sun., free) has been going strong. In addition to rotating art exhibits, the organization runs the **Art in the Redwoods Festival** (adults $6, under age 18 free) where artists from all over the country display their work beneath the redwoods on the Gualala Ridge during a long weekend mid-August. The organization also manages the annual **Whale and Jazz Festival,** which takes place along the Sonoma and Mendocino Coast throughout April and into May each year. Some of the nation's finest jazz performers play in a variety of venues while the whales put on their own show out in the Pacific.

For a walk along the bluffs, visit **Gualala Point Regional Park** (42401 Hwy. 1, 707/785-2377, camping reservations 707/565-2267, www.sonoma-county.org, sunrise-sunset daily, day use $7 per vehicle), one mile south of the town of Gualala. There are plenty of easy, accessible trails along the bluffs above the mouth of the river as well as access to the beach below. The park also has 19 campsites ($32 per night), as well as six bike-/hike-in sites ($5), right along the river, with flush toilets and showers. Another camping option is the private **Gualala River Redwood Park** (46001 Gualala Rd., 707/884-3533, www.gualalapark.com, May-Sept., day use $5 pp, camping $42-49 for 2 people), which has 235 sites, most of which are on the river.

Accommodations

For the budget-conscious, a good option is **The Surf Motel** (39170 Hwy. 1, 707/884-3571 or 888/451-7873, www.surfinngualala.com, $129-249). Only a few of the more expensive rooms have ocean views, but a full hot breakfast and wireless Internet access are included.

The **Breakers Inn** (39300 Hwy. 1, 707/884-3200, www.breakersinn.com, $135-265) resembles a series of large seaside cottages, each with flower boxes in the windows and a private deck overlooking the ocean. All rooms are individually decorated with ocean views. Many have refrigerators and microwaves.

Food

If you're hungry when you hit town, try **Bones Roadhouse** (39080 Hwy. 1, 707/884-1188, www.bonesroadhouse.com, 8am-9pm daily, $15-25) for barbecue and pulled pork in giant portions, served in a casual atmosphere with ocean views.

The **Surf Market** (39250 Hwy. 1, 707/884-4184, http://surfsuper.com, 7:30am-8pm daily) has everything you need for a gourmet picnic, such as a great wine selection, full service deli, local cheese, and fresh artisan bread. You can also pick up camping essentials like firewood and ice, and you can get a cheap cup of Peet's coffee at the coffee station.

Transportation

Gualala is located 115 miles north of San Francisco on Highway 1, and 60 miles south of Fort Bragg.

POINT ARENA

With less than 450 residents, Point Arena, surrounded by bucolic dairy land, boasts one

the rocky Mendocino coast

of the quaintest main streets on this stretch of the Mendocino coast.

Point Arena Lighthouse

The biggest draw in town is the **Point Arena Lighthouse** (45500 Lighthouse Rd., 707/882-2777 or 877/725-4448, www.pointarenalighthouse.com, 10am-4:30pm daily summer, 10am-3:30pm daily winter, adults $7.50, children $1), which offers stunning views of the windswept coast as well as a fantastic place to spot migrating whales. The location is notable as the point where the San Andreas Fault runs into the Pacific Ocean. The 1906 earthquake, whose epicenter was over 120 miles away, so badly damaged the original 1870 lighthouse that it had to be rebuilt. Consequently, engineers devised the aboveground foundation that gives the lighthouse its distinctive shape and additional structural stability.

The extensive interpretive museum is housed in the fog station beyond the gift shop. Docent-led tours up to the top of the lighthouse are well worth the trip, both for the views and for the fascinating story of its destruction and rebirth through the 1906 earthquake as told by the knowledgeable staff. Tour groups also have the opportunity to climb right up to the Fresnel lens, taking a rare close look at an invention that reflected pre-electric light far enough out to sea to protect passing ships.

Accommodations

The attractive yet plain **Coast Guard House** (695 Arena Cove, 707/882-2442, www.coastguardhouse.com, $145-265) was originally built in 1901 as housing for the U.S. Life-Saving Service, which later became part of the Coast Guard. It was decommissioned in 1957. Now it's an appealing bed-and-breakfast, with four rooms in the main building and two cottages. Some rooms have ocean views. Check online for last-minute specials—you may get a deal if they're not booked up.

The **Wharf Masters Inn** (785 Port Rd., 707/882-3171 or 800/932-4031, www.wharfmasters.com, $135-200) offers historical lodging at reasonable prices. The Victorian building retains its original charm, including elaborate porches to take in the views. Each of the 10 rooms is decorated in antiques, and many have a whirlpool tub, fireplace, and refrigerator.

the Point Arena Lighthouse

Food

The **Uneda Eat Café** (206 Main St., 707/882-3800, http://unedaeat.com, 5:30pm-8:30pm Wed.-Sun., $9-20) brings some hipster locavorism to tiny Point Arena. The storefront says "Uneda Meat Market," a holdover from the former owner, an Italian butcher. A family-run operation, this small restaurant serves a limited menu, which changes daily. Expect to find house-made sausage, pork confit, rabbit, and oysters served up in a dining room lined in reclaimed wood.

Blue on the outside, pink on the inside, **Franny's Cup and Saucer** (213 Main St., 707/882-2500, www.frannyscupandsaucer.com, 8am-4pm Wed.-Sat.) is whimsical and welcoming. The small store is filled with pastries, cakes, candies, truffles, and savory treats, and everything is made here from scratch. It's takeout only.

Arena Market & Café (185 Main St., 707/882-3663, www.arenaorganics.org, 7am-7pm Mon.-Sat., 8am-6pm Sun.) is a co-op committed to a philosophy of local, sustainable, and organic food. At this medium-size grocery store, you can stock up on staples or sit at one of the tables in the front of the store and enjoy a bowl of homemade soup.

Transportation

Point Arena is located 10 miles north of Gualala on Highway 1 and about 120 miles north of San Francisco.

ELK

The town of Elk used to be called Greenwood, after the family of Caleb Greenwood, who settled here in about 1850. Details of the story vary, but it is widely believed that Caleb was part of a mission to rescue survivors of the Donner Party after their rough winter near Truckee.

Greenwood State Beach

From the mid-19th century until the 1920s, the stretch of shore that comprises **Greenwood State Beach** (Hwy. 1, 707/937-5804, www.parks.ca.gov, visitors center 11am-1pm Sat.-Sun. Memorial Day-Labor Day) was a stop for large ships carrying timber to San Francisco and China. The visitors center displays photographs and exhibits about Elk's past in the lumber business. It also casts light on the Native American heritage of the area and the natural resources that are still abundant.

The short walk down to the cliffs demonstrates what makes this area so special. In less than a mile, you'll experience lush woods, sandy cliffs, and dramatic ocean overlooks. In winter, the walk can be dark and blustery.

Accommodations and Food

The ★ **Elk Cove Inn** (6300 S. Hwy. 1, 707/877-3321 or 800/275-2967, www.elkcoveinn.com, $100-305) is the perfect spot for a secluded getaway. Choose from antique-furnished rooms in the historical main building or plush spa cabins overlooking the lawn. The tiny restaurant serves a sumptuous champagne breakfast. Take a hike down to Elk Cove, the secluded beach beside the inn, or simply relax with the in-room fireplace roaring and order a spa treatment.

Elk is home to the luxurious **Griffin House Inn** (5910 S. Hwy. 1, 707/877-3422, www.griffinn.com, $145-220). There are no TVs or phones in these lovely cottages with oceanfront decks. A full breakfast is delivered to your room. Attached is **Bridget Dolan's Pub** (707/877-1820, 4:30pm-8pm daily, $12-22) where you'll find both visitors and locals sharing casual pub food and a pint, or two.

For breakfast and lunch, join the locals at **Queenie's Roadhouse Café** (6061 Hwy. 1, 707/877-3285, http://queeniesroadhousecafe.com, 8am-3pm Thurs.-Mon.). A classic small-town diner, Queenie's serves excellent, inexpensive American food with a dash of the hippie ethos that pervades this part of the coast. Don't pass up the burger or Reuben sandwich.

Not only is the **Beacon Light by the Sea** (7401 S. Hwy. 1, south of Elk, 707/877-3311, 5pm-11pm Fri.-Sat.) the best bar in the area, its colorful owner, R. D. Beacon, claims it's the only place you can get hard liquor for 14 miles in any direction. With 54 different brands of vodka, 20 whiskeys, and 15 tequilas on offer, there's something for every sort of drinker. On a clear day, the views stretch all the way to the Point Arena Lighthouse.

Transportation

From San Francisco, Elk is 150 miles north on Highway 1 and about 23 miles south of Fort Bragg. Elk is also just south of the junction with Highway 128, which connects with U.S. 101 north of Santa Rosa in Cloverdale.

ALBION AND LITTLE RIVER

You could say that the tiny communities of Albion and Little River are the "suburbs" of picturesque Mendocino. Aside from a state park, there's little else beyond the post office, clusters of residential and vacation homes, and quaint and luxurious lodges tucked in the hillsides or perched over the rugged Pacific.

Van Damme State Park

At **Van Damme State Park** (Hwy. 1, 3 miles south of Mendocino, 707/937-5804 or 707/937-4016 summer only, www.parks.ca.gov, sunrise-sunset daily, free), take a walk to the park's centerpiece, the **Pygmy Forest.** Here you'll see a true biological rarity: mature yet tiny cypress and pine trees perpetually stunted by a combination of always-wet ground and poor soil-nutrient conditions. You can get to the Pygmy Forest from the **Fern Canyon Trail** (6 miles one-way, difficult), or drive Airport Road to the trail parking lot (opposite the county airport) directly to a wheelchair-accessible loop trail (0.25 mile, easy).

Kayak Mendocino (707/813-7117, www.kayakmendocino.com) launches four Sea Cave Nature Tours (9am, 11:30am, 2pm, and sunset daily, $60 pp, $40 children 12 and under) from Van Damme State Park. No previous experience is necessary, as the expert guides provide all the equipment you need and teach you how to paddle your way through the sea caves and around the harbor seals.

Accommodations and Food

Ledford House Restaurant (3000 N. Hwy. 1, Albion, 707/937-0282, www.ledfordhouse.com, 5pm-close Wed.-Sun., $19-30) adds a French café vibe to the wild coast of Mendocino. With colorful fabric murals, excellent French bistro fare, and nightly jazz performances, you'll get a dose of culture while looking over the expansive Pacific. The **Albion River Inn** (3790 N. Hwy. 1, Albion, 707/937-1919 or 800/479-7944, www.albionriverinn.com, $195-325) is a gorgeous and serene setting for an away-from-it-all vacation. A full breakfast is included in the room rates, but pets and smoking are not allowed, and there are no TVs.

To take in the forest, the cliffs, the ocean, and the sky, there is no better place than the ★ **Heritage House Resort** (5200 N. Hwy. 1, Little River, 707/202-9000, http://heritagehouseresort.com, $200-310). This 37-acre compound is a collection of duplexes and triplexes, in which stylish rooms have private decks, fireplaces, giant soaking tubs, and excellent views. Perched at the edge of a private cove where the ocean booms, Heritage House is one of the oldest resorts on the Mendocino Coast.

If staying at Heritage House is not in the cards, consider making a stop for breakfast, dinner, or drinks. The **5200 Restaurant** (8am-10:30am, 5pm-9pm Mon.-Fri., 8am-11am, 5pm-9pm Sat.-Sun., $17-35) is unpretentious (it even has a kids' menu), with excellent service and "farm to fork" fare. At the rear of the restaurant, the **5200 Lounge** (4pm-9pm daily) overlooks the water in a bar that is cozy and a little salty. For more room, take a comfy seat in the lounge, where a roaring fireplace, board games, and a healthy selection of bar bites and high-end cocktails will keep you happy all evening.

The **Little River Inn** (7901 N. Hwy. 1, Little River, 707/937-5942 or 888/466-5683, www.littleriverinn.com, $189-375) appeals to vacationers who like a little luxury. It has a nine-hole golf course and two lighted tennis courts, and all its recreation areas overlook the Pacific, just across the highway from the inn. The sprawling white Victorian house hides the sprawl of the grounds, which also has a great restaurant and a charming sea-themed bar. Relax at the in-house Day Spa.

One of the more luxurious B&Bs around is the **Glendeven Inn** (8205 N. Hwy. 1, 707/937-0083 or 800/822-4536, www.glendeven.com, $175-315), situated in a historical farmhouse with ocean views. The hosts will help you settle in with a complimentary wine and hors d'oeuvres hour in the late afternoon, and they wake you in the morning with a three-course made-to-order breakfast, delivered to your room exactly when you want it.

Camping is available in **Van Damme State Park** (Hwy. 1, 3 miles south of Mendocino, 800/444-7275, www.parks.ca.gov, $35). There are 74 sites, in addition to a handful of hike-/bike-in sites. The campground offers picnic tables, fire rings, and food lockers, as well as restrooms and hot showers and a communal campfire. Reservations are strongly encouraged, especially during the summer and early fall.

Transportation

Tiny Albion is along Highway 1 almost 30 miles north of Point Arena and about 10 miles south of Mendocino. Little River is about five miles farther north, also on Highway 1. From Santa Rosa, it's a two-hour drive along U.S. 101 north for about 30 miles to Highway 128 north before reaching Highway 1 after about 60 miles.

MENDOCINO

The town of Mendocino has long been an inspiration and a gathering place for artists of many varieties, and the **Mendocino Art Center** (45200 Little Lake St., 707/937-5818 or 800/653-3328, www.mendocinoartcenter.org, 10am-5pm daily, donation) is the main institution that gives these diverse artists a community, provides them with opportunities for teaching and learning, and displays their work. Founded in 1959, the center now has a flourishing schedule of events and classes, five galleries, and a sculpture garden. You can even drop in and make some art of your own. Supervised "open studios" in ceramics, jewelry making, watercolor, sculpture, and drawing take place throughout the year (call for specific schedules, $5-20 per session).

Kelley House Museum

The mission of the lovely, stately **Kelley House Museum** (45007 Albion St., 707/937-5791, www.kelleyhousemuseum.org, 11am-3pm Fri.-Mon., free, tours 11am Sat.-Sun., $10) is to preserve the history of Mendocino for future generations. In the museum, antique furniture and fixtures grace the rooms. A collection of Victorian clothing, photos, and documents illuminate Mendocino history, and knowledgeable docents are available to offer more information. Ask about the town's water-rights issues for a lesson in the untold history of the Mendocino coast.

Point Cabrillo Light Station

Whether you're into scenery or history, you won't want to miss a visit to the **Point Cabrillo Light Station Historic Park** (12301 N. Hwy. 1, 707/937-6122, www.parks.ca.gov, sunrise-sunset daily, lighthouse 10am-4pm daily, $5), about five miles north of Mendocino. This beautiful lighthouse has been functioning for more than 100 years since it was built in 1908. Take a tour to see the famous Fresnel lens, learn about the infamous *Frolic* shipwreck of 1850, and explore the tide pool aquarium.

Entertainment and Events

For a place to hunker down over a pint in Mendocino, saunter over to **Patterson's Pub** (10485 Lansing St., 707/937-4782, www.pattersonspub.com, bar 10am-midnight daily, restaurant 11am-11pm daily). This traditional Irish-style pub is in the former rectory of a 19th-century Catholic church. It nods to the 21st century with six plasma TVs that screen current games. Order a simple and filling meal at the tables or at the bar, and choose from the dozen beers on tap, a full-fledged

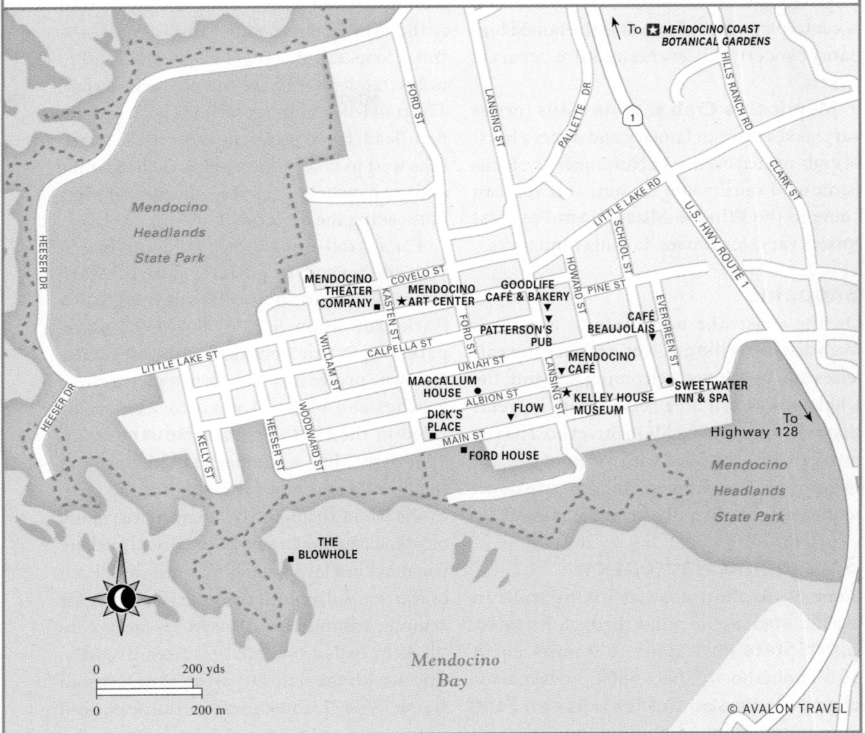

wine list, or hard liquor imported from around the world.

Locals drink at **Dick's Place** (45080 Main St., 707/937-6010, until 2am daily), sometimes called Richard's by the Sea. The crowd is a little younger than at Patterson's, and they're always having a good time. Dick's is easy to find, as it's next to the hotel with the only neon sign on Main Street, in the shape of a martini glass.

The **Mendocino Theater Company** (45200 Little Lake St., 707/937-4477, www.mendocinotheatre.org, shows 8pm Thurs.-Sat., 2pm Sun., $12-25) offers a genuine small community-theater experience. All plays are staged in the 81-seat Helen Schoeni Theater for an intimate night of live drama or comedy. The small, weathered old building exudes just the right kind of charm to draw in lovers of quirky community theater. This little theater company tends to take on thought-provoking work by contemporary playwrights.

For two weekends every March, the Point Cabrillo Light Station is host to the annual **Whale Festival** (707/937-6123, www.pointcabrillo.org, $5), a chance to get expert guidance as you scan the sea for migrating gray whales headed north for the summer.

For two weeks in July, musicians of all types descend on the temporarily warmish coast for the **Mendocino Music Festival** (707/937-2044, www.mendocinomusic.com, performances $12-49). At venues around the area, there are live performances of chamber music, orchestral concerts, opera, jazz, and bluegrass, and usually world music, blues, singer-songwriters, and dance performances. A centerpiece of the festival is the famed big-band concert. All events require separate tickets.

Mendocino Crab & Wine Days (prices vary) takes place in January and offers a burst of crab-related events. In November, the focus is on wild mushroom season, and you can come to the **Wine & Mushroom Festival** (prices vary) for classes, tastings, and tours.

Shopping

On the coast, the best place to browse is **Mendocino Village.** Not only are the galleries and boutiques welcoming and fun, the whole downtown area is beautiful. It seems that every shop in the Main Street area has its own garden, each filled with a riotous cascade of flowers in the summer. Make the trip down to the village to literally smell the roses.

Sports and Recreation

Some of the most popular hiking trails in coastal Mendocino wind through **Russian Gulch State Park** (Hwy. 1, 2 miles north of Mendocino, 707/937-5804, www.parks.ca.gov, $8). Russian Gulch has its own **Fern Canyon Trail** (3 miles round-trip), winding into the second-growth redwood forest filled with lush green ferns. At the end of the trail is the ever-popular waterfall. To make the trek a loop, take a left at **Loop Falls Trail** (2 miles, moderate) to the top of the waterfall. The trail will continue and hook back up with Fern Trail. If you prefer the shore to the forest, hike west to take in the lovely wild headlands and see blowholes, grasses, and even trawlers out seeking the day's catch.

For a stroll along protected ocean bluffs, you don't need to go farther than Main Street. The **Mendocino Headlands State Park** (735 Main St., 707/937-5397, www.parks.ca.gov) anchors the southwest corner of town, protecting the town's picturesque beaches and bluffs. The visitor center, located in the **Historic Ford House** (11am-4pm daily), has a number of exhibits about the human and natural history of the area. Trails wend through the open space, many of which lead down **Big River Beach,** where you may find locals catching some rays. Even braver souls dive into the water and look for abalone around **The Blowhole,** or explore the kelp beds populated by friendly seals. Check with the state Department of Fish and Game (888/773-8450, www.wildlife.ca.gov)

Mendocino Village at sunset

for abalone regulations; most species are endangered and can't be harvested. Game wardens can explain the abalone season opening and closing dates, catch limits, licensing information, and the best spots to dive each year.

Kayak and canoe trips are a popular summer activity on the coast. To explore the sedate waters of the Big River estuary, rent an outrigger or a sailing canoe from **Catch a Canoe & Bicycles Too** (Hwy. 1 and Comptche Ukiah Rd., 707/937-0273, www.catchacanoe.com, 9am-5pm daily, boat rentals adults $28-40, ages 6-17 $14-20, guided tours June-Sept. $65-85) at the Stanford Inn. For an adventurous day on the ocean, consider taking a sea-cave tour by kayak.

Of all the reasons people choose to vacation on the Mendocino coast, the main one seems to be plain old relaxation. The perfect way to do so is to seek out one of the many nearby spas. The **Sweetwater Eco Spa** (955 Ukiah St., 707/937-4140, www.sweetwaterspa.com, 1pm-9pm Mon.-Fri., noon-9pm Sat.-Sun.) rents indoor hot tubs by the hour ($10-28/hour) and offers a range of massage services ($90-155) at reasonable rates. The rustic buildings and garden setting complete the experience. Appointments are required for massage and private tubs, but walk-ins are welcome to use the communal tub and sauna.

Accommodations

The warm and welcoming ★ **Blackberry Inn** (44951 Larkin Rd., 707/937-5281 or 800/950-7806, www.blackberryinn.biz, $125-225) is in the hills, beyond the center of Mendocino. The inn looks like a perfectly styled town from the Old West. Each of the 16 rooms has a different storefront outside, including the bank, the saloon, and the barber shop, and each is charmingly decorated and beautifully maintained with plush, comfortable bedding cozied up with colonial-style quilts, along with the modern convenience of microwaves, fridges, sunken bathtubs, and free wireless Internet.

★ **Sweetwater Inn and Spa** (44840 Main St., 800/300-4140, www.sweetwaterspa.com, $125-275) harks back to the days when Mendocino was a colony of starving artists. A redwood water tower was converted into a room, joined by cottages that guarantee privacy. Every room and cottage has its own style—you'll find a spiral staircase in the water tower, a two-person tub set in a windowed alcove in the Zen Room, and fireplaces in many of the cottages. Thick gardens surround the building complex, with a path leading back to the Garden Spa. The location is perfect for dining, shopping, and art walks.

For luxurious lodging at a great value, book a room at **MacCallum House** (45020 Albion St., 707/937-0289 or 800/609-0492, www.maccallumhouse.com, $145-275). The facility includes several properties in addition to the main 1882 inn building in Mendocino Village, and you can choose from private cottages with hot tubs, suites with jetted tubs, and regular rooms with opulent antiques. The woodwork gleams, and the service pleases. A two-night minimum is required on weekends, and a three-night minimum goes into effect for most holidays. Full breakfast at the Grey Whale Restaurant is included in the room rates.

The **Stanford Inn** (44850 Comptche Ukiah Rd., 707/937-5615 or 800/331-8884, www.stanfordinn.com, $211-335) is one of the largest accommodations in the Mendocino area. This resort hotel sits away from the beaches in a redwood forest and is surrounded by gardens. Accommodations range from economy rooms to larger suites, but all have a wood-burning fireplace and a TV. Also included in the price is access to the indoor pool, sauna, and hot tub, use of mountain bikes, and breakfast at Ravens (8am-10:30am, 5:30pm-9pm Mon.-Fri., 8am-11pm, 5:30pm-9pm Sat.-Sun., $23-27), the onsite vegan restaurant. The place prides itself on its exceptional cell phone service and its pro-environmental practices.

After you check in at the **Sea Rock Bed & Breakfast Inn** (11101 Lansing St., 707/937-0926 or 800/906-0926, www.searock.com, $185-395), sit outside on the Adirondack chairs to watch the sunset, or take it all in from the viewing platform across the street, right above the beach. The breakfast room, where quiche and fresh fruit, included in the room rates, is served every morning, is also perfectly situated for optimal ocean views. This little village of cottages, junior suites, and suites sleeps 2-4 people each. The Sea Rock has been around in its current incarnation since the late '90s, but the site has a long history—it was a brewery before Prohibition.

Food

One of the most appealing and dependable places to get a good meal any day of the week is the **Mendocino Café** (10451 Lansing St., 707/937-6141, www.mendocinocafe.com, 11am-4pm, 5pm-8:30pm daily, $14-33). The café has simple, well-prepared food, a small kids' menu, a wine list, and a beer list. Enjoy a Thai burrito, a fresh salmon fillet, or a steak in the warm, well-lit dining room. Or sit outside: The café is in the gardens of Mendocino Village, and thanks to a heated patio, you can enjoy outdoor dining any time of day.

★ **Café Beaujolais** (961 Ukiah St., 707/937-5614, www.cafebeaujolais.com, 5:30pm-close Mon.-Tues., 11:30am-2:30pm, 5:30pm-close Wed.-Sun., $23-35) is a standout French-California restaurant. This charming out-of-the-way spot is a few blocks from the center of Mendocino Village in a quaint Victorian home. Despite the white tablecloths and fancy crystal, the atmosphere is casual at lunch and gets only slightly more formal at dinner. The giant salads and delectable entrées are made with organic produce, humanely raised meats, and locally caught seafood. The portions can be enormous, but you can get them half-size just by asking.

There is no better place in Mendocino to dine on a cold stormy night than the ★ **MacCallum House Restaurant** (45020 Albion St., 707/937-6759, www.maccallumhouse.com, 8am-10am, 5:30pm-close Mon.-Fri., 8am-11am, 5:30pm-close Sat.-Sun., $28-39) The cozy dining room makes the most of the historical house's charm with dark wood paneling, two huge fireplaces that roar on chilly evenings, and windows overlooking the garden. The food encapsulates Mendocino, from the Pacific Rim oysters to the venison with wild boar sausage. For a pre-dinner drink, stop by the friendly Grey Whale Bar located in the house parlor.

Something more casual can be found on top of Main Street's water tower at **Flow** (45040 Main St., 707/937-3569, 8am-10pm daily, $14-20). With fantastic ocean views from the large porch and picture-window-framed dining room, this restaurant serves omelets, burgers, pasta, and small pizzas. There is a focus on local seafood, as well as wild mushrooms in the fall.

Locals grab their coffee and pastries at the **GoodLife Café and Bakery** (10483 Lansing St., 707/937-0836, http://goodlifecafemendo.com, 8am-5pm Mon.-Sat., 8am-4pm Sun., $7). In addition to the organic lattes and slew of sweets, there are bagels, hot breakfast items, grilled panini, and pizza by the slice. Snag a table in the café, or take your order to go and find a quiet perch in the Mendocino Headlands.

Information and Services

The **Ford House** (735 Main St., 707/937-5397, www.parks.ca.gov, 11am-4pm daily) doubles as the visitor center for Mendocino Headlands State Park and the town itself. Get helpful tips from the knowledgeable staff, then browse the historical displays in the house's museum.

The **Mendocino Coast District Hospital** (700 River Dr., Fort Bragg, 707/961-1234, www.mcdh.org) in Fort Bragg has the nearest full-service emergency room.

Transportation

To get to Mendocino from U.S. 101 near Cloverdale, take Highway 128 northwest for 60 miles. Highway 128 becomes Highway 1 on the coast; Mendocino is another 10 miles north. You can also jump over to the coast on Highway 20. In only 30 (albeit slow) miles it connects Fort Bragg with Willits along U.S. 101, about 3 hours north of San Francisco. Mendocino is 10 miles south of

Fort Bragg. A slower, more scenic alternative is to take Highway 1; from San Francisco to Mendocino via Highway 1 takes at least 4.5 hours. Mendocino has a fairly compact downtown area, Mendocino Village, with a concentration of restaurants, shops, and inns a block away from the beach. Turn off at Main Street, park the car and explore by foot.

The **Mendocino Transit Authority** (800/696-4682, http://mendocinotransit.org) operates a dozen bus routes that connect Mendocino and Fort Bragg with larger cities like Santa Rosa and Ukiah, where you can make connections to Amtrak, Greyhound, and airports.

FORT BRAGG

The village of Mendocino may be where folks savor the scenery, but Fort Bragg is where the work gets done. This blue-collar town is home to lumber mills, fishing boats, and scores of working train tracks. It is rougher around the edges than its gentle cousin down the coast, but it has some great attractions, beautiful scenery, and tons of local color.

★ Mendocino Coast Botanical Gardens

Mendocino Coast Botanical Gardens (18220 N. Hwy. 1, Fort Bragg, 707/964-4352, www.gardenbythesea.org, 9am-5pm daily Mar.-Oct., 9am-4pm daily Nov.-Feb., adults $14, seniors $10, ages 6-17 $5) is an expanse of land with an astonishing variety of vegetation. Stretching 47 acres down to the sea, these gardens offer miles of paths through careful plantings and wild landscapes. The garden map is also a guide that shows visitors what's in season. Informative labels show plant names clearly. Children can pick up their own brochure and enjoy an exploratory adventure designed just for them.

Skunk Train

One of the famed attractions in Mendocino County is the California Western Railroad, popularly called the **Skunk Train** (depot at end of Laurel St., 707/964-6371, www.skunktrain.com, departure 10am daily, adults $54, children 2-12 $34), named for the pungent early locomotives. The restored steam locomotives pull trains from the coast at Fort Bragg 40 miles through the redwood forest to the town of Willits and back. The ride lets passengers see the majesty of the redwoods while giving insight into life in Northern California before the era of highways. The gaily painted trains appeal to children, and the historical aspects and scenery call to adults.

Guest House Museum

The **Guest House Museum** (343 N. Main St., 707/964-4251, www.fortbragghistory.org, 1pm-3pm Mon., 11am-2pm Tues.-Fri., 10am-4pm Sat.-Sun. May-Oct., 11am-2pm Thurs.-Sun. Nov.-May) is a pleasant trip down Fort Bragg's memory lane. Perched just above the train yard, the large 1892 Victorian is filled with artifacts from Fort Bragg's lumber heyday, including antique logging and woodworking tools.

MacKerricher State Park

Stretching nearly 10 miles from the northern tip of Fort Bragg, **MacKerricher State Park** (Hwy. 1, 707/964-9112, visitors center 707/964-8898, www.parks.ca.gov, sunrise-sunset daily, free) offers the small duck-filled Cleone Lake, six miles of sandy ocean beaches, four miles of cliffs and crags, and camping (reservations 800/444-7275, www.reserveamerica.com, $35). The main attraction is a gigantic, almost complete skeleton of a whale near the park entrance. Stop in to see the whale even if you don't have time to hang out at the park. If you're lucky, you can also spot live whales and harbor seals frolicking in the ocean.

At the park's southern end in Fort Bragg, **Glass Beach** (Elm St. and Glass Beach Dr.) is the most famous beach in the area. The unpleasant origin of this fascinating beach strewn with sea glass was the Fort Bragg city dump. As the ocean rose over the landfill, the heavy glass that had been dumped there stayed put. Years of pounding surf polished and smoothed the broken edges. Beachcombers used to collect the smooth coated shards of green, blue, brown, and clear glass. Now that the beach is under the management of the state park, it's against the rules to remove the glass.

The coast can be rough here, so don't swim or even wade unless it's what the locals call a "flat day"—no big waves and undertow. If the kids want to play in the water, take them to **Pudding Creek Beach** in the park just north of Glass Beach, where they can play in the relatively sheltered area under the trestle bridge.

Triangle Tattoo Museum

This is not your grandmother's art museum, so enter at your own risk. The **Triangle Tattoo Museum** (356B N. Main St., 707/964-8814, www.triangletattoo.com, noon-6pm daily, free) displays the implements of the trade and photos of their results. All forms of the art are represented, from those done by indigenous people to those done at carnivals and in prisons. The street-side rooms house a working tattoo parlor, and you can find intrepid artists working late into the evening on their "canvases."

Pacific Star Winery

The only winery on the Mendocino coast, **Pacific Star Winery** (33000 N. Hwy. 1, 707/964-1155, www.pacificstarwinery.com, 11am-5pm daily, free) makes the most of its location. Barrels of wine are left out in the salt air to age. Wines are tasty and reasonably priced. You can also visit their downtown tasting room (401 N. Main St., 707/962-9463, noon-5pm Fri.-Tues.) in the Skunk Train Depot Mall.

Entertainment and Events

Beer lovers will not want to miss **North Coast Brewing Company Taproom & Grill** (444 N. Main St., 707/964-3400, www.northcoastbrewing.com, 2pm-9pm Sun.-Thurs., 2pm-10pm Fri.-Sat., $14-30). Opened in 1988 and marketing to the artisanal beer market, the North Coast Brewing Company has since become one of the country's most respected microbreweries. Just across the street from the brewery, the taproom pours the beloved Red Seal Ale, Old Rasputin Russian Imperial Stout, and the resurrected Acme beer, first introduced in the 1860s. At 4pm, the kitchen opens, serving top-notch pub food, including half Dungeness crabs when in season.

Glass Beach

The **Gloriana Opera Company** (210 N. Corry St., 707/964-7469, www.gloriana.org, adults $18, children under 13 $8) focuses more on musicals than operas, and their shows delight young and old theatergoers alike. Gloriana seeks to bring music and theater to young people, so they produce major musicals that appeal to kids, such as *The Aristocats* and *Charlotte's Web.*

Sports and Recreation

The Mendocino coast is an ideal location to watch whales dance, or try to land the big one (salmon, halibut, rock cod, or tuna). During Dungeness crab season, you can even go out on a crab boat, learn to set pots, and catch your own delectable delicacy.

Many charters leave out of Noyo Harbor in Fort Bragg. The ***Trek II*** (Noyo Harbor, 707/964-4550, www.anchorcharterboats.com, 7am-8pm daily) offers five-hour fishing trips ($80-125) and two-hour whale-watching jaunts (Dec.-May, $35). They'll take you rock fishing in summer, crabbing in winter, and chasing after salmon and tuna in season.

The **Noyo Fishing Center** (32440 N. Harbor Dr., Noyo Harbor, 707/964-3000, www.fortbraggfishing.com, fishing $65-100, whale-watching $35) will take you out on its boat, the *Profish'nt,* where you can watch a demonstration of crab fishing or look for whales in the winter from the comfort of the heated cabin. They'll help you fish for cod and various deep-sea dwellers in season (May 15-Aug. 15). The crew can even clean and vacuum-pack your catch on the dock before you leave.

The best hike to take in **MacKerricher State Park** (Hwy. 1, 707/964-9112, www.parks.ca.gov, visitors center sunrise-sunset daily, free), three miles north of Fort Bragg, is the **Ten Mile Beach Trail** (14 miles round-trip, moderate), starting at the Beachcomber Motel at the north end of Fort Bragg and running seven miles up to the Ten Mile River. Most of the path is fairly level and paved. It's an easy walk you can take at your own pace. Street bikes and inline skates are also allowed on this trail.

What better way to enjoy the rugged cliffs, windy beaches, and quiet forests of the coast than on horseback? **Ricochet Ridge Ranch** (24201 N. Hwy. 1, 707/964-7669, www.horse-vacation.com, private guided rides $90-310) has beach trail rides ($50) departing four times a day. They also offer longer beach and trail rides, sunset beach rides, and full-fledged riding vacations by reservation.

Accommodations

Fort Bragg may not boast the type of luxurious accommodations found in Mendocino, but many of the options are a quarter of the price.

One budget option is the **Surf Motel** (1220 S. Main St., 707/964-5361 or 800/339-5361, www.surfmotelfb.com, $69-169). The rooms are nothing to write home about, but the hotel has a variety of outdoor amenities. There is a bike-washing station, a fish-cleaning station, an outdoor shower for divers, a garden to stroll through, and an area set aside for horseshoes and barbecues. Included in the room rate are breakfast, free wireless Internet, a microwave, a fridge, and a shuttle to nearby attractions. The two apartments have kitchens and room for four people.

★ **Weller House** (524 Stewart St., 707/964-4415, www.wellerhouse.com, $110-320) is a picture-perfect B&B with elegantly restored Victorian-style rooms, ocean views, and sumptuous home-cooked meals. There are even a few rooms in the old water tower, which is the highest point in the city. The third floor of the main building—a gorgeous 1886 mansion listed on the National Register of Historic Places—is a ballroom. The virgin redwood floor, the outstanding acoustics, and the spacious porch where dancers can step out for a breath of air make it a marvelous place for a *milonga.* Weller House is one block west of Main Street, in view of the Skunk Train depot, and an easy walk to good restaurants and shopping.

The stately **Grey Whale Inn** (615 N. Main St., 707/964-0640 or 800/382-7244, www.greywhaleinn.com, $135-195) was once a community hospital. The blocky craftsman-style building was erected by the Union Lumber Company in 1915. Today 13 spacious, simple rooms welcome travelers. Rooms, with water views or city views, are individually decorated, with a private bath and queen or king bed, perhaps covered by an old-fashioned quilt. The inn prides itself on simplicity and friendliness, and its location in downtown Fort Bragg makes for an easy walk to dinner or the beach.

CAMPING

MacKerricher State Park (Hwy. 1, 707/964-9112, www.parks.ca.gov, reservations 800/444-7275, www.reserveamerica.com, $35), three miles north of Fort Bragg, is a fine place to spend a night or two. Reservations are recommended April 1-October 15, and they're site specific. In winter, camping is available on a first-come, first-served basis. The park has three different camping loops, but as of 2015, Surfwood and Eastwood have been closed because of budget cuts. Restrooms with flush toilets as well as hot showers are provided, and each site has a fire ring, picnic table, and food storage locker.

Food

It used to be that you had to go to the village of Mendocino for a meal, but Fort Bragg has developed a more-than-respectable culinary scene of its own. Many excellent restaurants are available within a few blocks of the town center and beach. Despite this renaissance, the king in Fort Bragg remains the ★ **Mendo Bistro** (301 N. Main St., 707/964-4974, www.mendobistro.com, 5pm-9pm daily, $15-28). Located in the top floor of the old Company Store building, tables look out over downtown. The bistro is unassuming and casual. Everything is excellent and made in-house. Seafood fills the menu. During crab season, don't pass up the crab and linguine, or simply order a whole crab.

With the small fishing and crabbing fleet of Fort Bragg's Noyo Harbor, it's natural that lots of seafood restaurants are clustered nearby. For the most authentic, freshest, and simplest fish preparations, head down to the harbor to any one of the casual restaurants and fish markets. This harbor deals in salmon, mussels, and Dungeness crab in season. Locals rave about the fish-and-chips at the **Sea Pal Cove** (32390 N. Harbor Dr., 707/964-1300, 11am-9pm Sun.-Thurs., 11am-11pm Fri.-Sat., $8-32). With big portions of fried fish and bowls of fresh clam chowder, outdoor seating perfect for dogs and kids, and reasonable prices, the Sea Pal fits the bill.

Egghead's (362 N. Main St., 707/964-5005, www.eggheadsrestaurant.com, 7am-2pm daily, $7.50-24) serves an enormous menu of breakfast, lunch, and brunch items. The menu includes every imaginable omelet combination, Reuben sandwiches, and "flying-monkey potatoes," derived from the *Wizard of Oz* decor.

The most popular burger in town is at **Jenny's Giant Burger** (940 N. Main St., 707/964-2235, 10:30am-9pm daily, $5-8). This little place has a 1950s hamburger-stand feel, but there's nothing stale about it. The food is good, simple, and cheap. Devoted followers tend to fill the place, but there are a few outdoor tables, and you can always get your order to go.

If it's coffee and a pastry you want, the **Headlands Coffeehouse** (120 Laurel St., 707/964-1987, www.headlandscoffeehouse.com, 7am-10pm Mon.-Sat., 7am-7pm Sun.) is unquestionably the place to go. The big windows give it a cheerful atmosphere, and the blueberry Danishes from the nearby Mendo Bakery may be the biggest and best you'll ever have. For something savory, opt for a breakfast burrito or a grilled panini. There's live music in the evenings and free Internet access.

Cowlick's Ice Cream (250 N. Main St., 707/962-9271, www.cowlicksicecream.com, 11am-9pm daily) serves delectable handmade ice cream in a variety of flavors. They even serve mushroom ice cream during the famous fall mushroom season. You can get the perennial favorites such as vanilla, chocolate, coffee, and strawberry, but you could also choose a seasonal flavor like banana daiquiri, cinnamon, or green tea.

Information and Services

The **Mendocino Coast Chamber of Commerce and Visitors Center** (217 S. Main St., 707/961-6300, www.mendocinocoast.com, 9am-5pm Mon.-Fri., 10am-5pm Sat.-Sun.) has attentive and well-trained staff in addition to maps, brochures, and information. This operation also serves as the Mendocino coast film office. Come in to find where to see some famous filming locations.

The **Mendocino Coast District Hospital** (700 River Dr., 707/961-1234, www.mcdh.org) boasts a full-service emergency room.

Transportation

Fort Bragg is located on Highway 1, 10 miles north of Mendocino. Driving here from San Francisco or Sacramento takes about 4 hours; from Ukiah it's about 1.5 hours. There is no "fast" way to reach Fort Bragg. The most expeditious way from the Bay Area is up U.S. 101. At Willits, take Highway 20 (Fort Bragg-Willits Rd.) west for 30 miles.

As one of the largest towns in the region, Fort Bragg has access to more public transportation. In the spring and summer the **Skunk Train** (707/964-6371, www.skunktrain.com) runs overnight trips from Willits. Check the website for more details. The **Mendocino Transit Authority** (707/462-1422 or 800/696-4682, http://mendocinotransit.org) has a number of bus lines that pass through Fort Bragg, and it also offers Dial-a-Ride Curb-to-Curb Service (707/964-1800, 8am-6pm Mon.-Fri., 10am-5pm Sat., $6).

Mendocino Wine Country

Mendocino's interior valley might not be quite as glamorous as the coast, but it is home to history, art, and booze. The Anderson Valley is the apex of Mendocino's wine region, though the tiny town of Hopland also has its share of tasting rooms. Ukiah, the county seat, is home to microbreweries, hot springs, and counterculture spirituality. Up in funky Willits, a late-1960s art vibe thrives in the 21st century.

Unlike the windy coast, the interior valleys of Mendocino get hot in the summer. Bring shorts, a swimsuit, and an air-conditioned car if you plan to visit June-September.

ANDERSON VALLEY

The Anderson Valley wine trail, also known as Highway 128, begins in Boonville and continues northwest toward the coast, with most of the wineries clustered between Boonville and Navarro.

Wineries

A big name in the Anderson Valley, **Scharffenberger Cellars** (8501 Hwy. 128, Philo, 707/895-2957, www.scharffenbergercellars.com, 11am-5pm daily, $3) makes highly rated sparkling wine. The tasting room is elegant and child friendly.

A broad-ranging winery with a large estate vineyard and event center, **Navarro Vineyards** (5601 Hwy. 128, Philo, 707/895-3686 or 800/537-9463, www.navarrowine.com, 10am-6pm daily May-Oct., 10am-5pm daily Nov.-Apr., free) offers a range of tasty wines as well as some interesting specialty products, like verjuice (sour grape juice).

In a valley full of great wineries, **Roederer Estate** (4501 Hwy. 128, 707/895-2288, www.roedererestate.com, 11am-5pm daily, $6) sparkles. Its California sparkling wines are some of the best you'll taste. The large tasting room features sweeping views of vineyards and display cases filled with Roederer's well-deserved awards. Pourers are knowledgeable, and you'll get to taste from magnum bottles—a rarity at any winery. Ask for a taste of Roederer's rarely seen still wines.

Husch Vineyards (4400 Hwy. 128,

Mendocino Wine Country

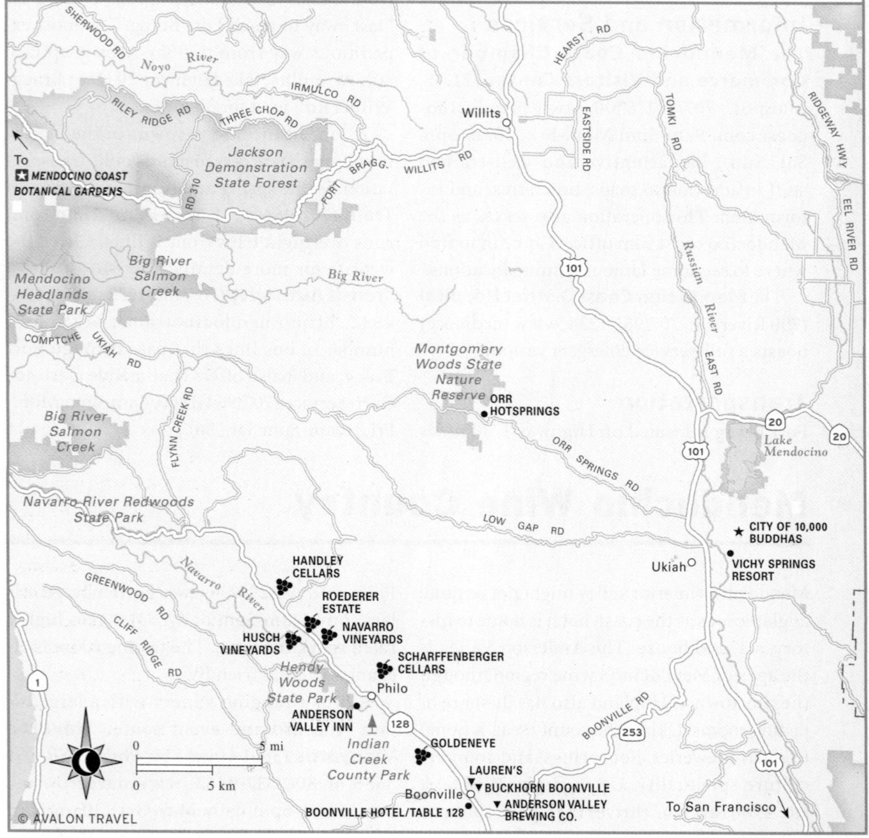

800/554-8724, www.huschvineyards.com, 10am-6pm daily May-Oct., 10am-5pm daily Nov.-Apr.) pours excellent wine in a rustic, flower-filled barn with a friendly atmosphere. Husch has perhaps the best sauvignon blanc in the valley and is the perfect place to relax.

Handley Cellars (3151 Hwy. 128, Philo, 707/895-3876 or 800/733-3151, www.handleycellars.com, 10am-6pm daily May-Oct., 10am-5pm daily Nov.-Apr., free) offers a complimentary tasting of handcrafted wines you probably won't see in grocery stores. The intriguing tasting room features folk art from around the world for sale. Well-behaved dogs are welcome in the tasting room and are given special Handley treats while their owners sip Chardonnay.

Goldeneye (9200 Hwy. 128, Philo, 800/208-0438, www.goldeneyewinery.com, 10:30am-4:30pm daily, $15) is a must stop for any pinot lover. Served at President Obama's inaugural lunch in 2009, Goldeneye's pinots have garnered much acclaim.

For visitors who prefer a cold beer to a glass of wine, **Anderson Valley Brewing Company** (17700 Hwy. 253, Boonville, 707/895-2337 or 800/207-2337, www.avbc.com, 11am-6pm Sat.-Thurs., 11am-7pm Fri.

chickens, vines, and redwoods in the Anderson Valley

spring-fall, 11am-6pm Thurs. and Sat.-Mon., 11am-7pm Fri. winter) serves an array of microbrews that changes each season. The warehouse-size beer hall has a bar, tables, and a gift shop. The beer garden out back is comfortable in spring and fall, and a disc golf course is popular with travelers and locals alike. Tours of the brewery are available at 1:30pm and 3pm daily.

Sports and Recreation

To hike in the redwoods, visit **Hendy Redwoods State Park** (18599 Philo-Greenwood Rd., 707/895-3557 or 707/895-3141 in summer, www.parks.ca.gov, $8). The trail to **Big Hendy Grove** is wheelchair accessible and perfect for a sedate forest walk. Another good short hike with just a little slope is the moderate **Hermit's Hut Trail,** which leads to a structure made out of a tree stump. Fit hikers who want a longer trek can weave around the whole park: **Big Hendy Loop** connects to the fire road, which joins Hermit's Hut Trail, which then intersects the Azalea Loop and runs down to the **Little Hendy Loop** for a complete survey of the park's best regions.

For a picnic, there is no better place than **Navarro River Redwoods State Park** (Hwy. 128, 2 miles east of Hwy. 1, www.parks.ca.gov, 707/937-5804). The slender park snakes along the highway and the river from about 10 miles west of Philo to 2 miles east of the junction with Highway 1. Picnic sites along the way are tucked in lush redwood groves overlooking the peaceful, winding river.

Accommodations

The **Anderson Valley Inn** (8480 Hwy. 128, Philo, 707/895-3325, www.avinn.com, $95-180, two-night minimum Sat.-Sun.), between Boonville and Philo, makes the perfect spot from which to visit both the Anderson Valley and the Mendocino coast. Eight small rooms are done up in bright colors and homey bedspreads in this small multi-building inn. The two suites have full kitchens and are perfect for travelers with dogs or children in tow. The inn often fills quickly on summer weekends.

In the middle of Boonville, the **Boonville Hotel** (14050 Hwy. 128, 707/895-2210, www.boonvillehotel.com, $125-375) balances a modern sensibility with its quirky, rural location. There are 15 rooms available, ranging from an economy queen to a studio with a private entrance through the garden. All rooms are charming and many an extremely good value. The upstairs rooms facing the highway can be loud. Amenities include a bookshop and gift shop, a good-size bar, and a dining room. Book one of the rooms with a balcony, which comes with a hammock.

Camping

For wine and nature lovers on a budget, the campgrounds at **Indian Creek County Park** (Hwy. 128 at mile marker 23.48, 1 mile east of Philo, 707/234-6050, www.co.mendocino.ca.us, $20) and **Hendy Woods State Park** (18599 Philo-Greenwood Rd., 707/895-3557, www.parks.ca.gov, reservations 800/444-7275 and www.reserveamerica.gov, $35) provide woodsy, shady campsites.

Food

A picnic makes a perfect lunch in the Anderson Valley, and farmers markets and farm stands can supply fresh local ingredients. The **Boonville Farmers Market** (14050 Hwy. 128, Boonville, www.mcfarm.org, 10am-12:30pm Sat. May-Oct.) draws a crowd, so be prepared to hunt for parking. For fresh fruit and vegetables every day, try **Gowan's Oak Tree Farm Stand** (6600 Hwy. 128, Philo, 707/895-3353, 8am-7pm daily summer, 8:30am-5:30pm daily winter). The stand belongs to the local Gowan's Oak Tree Farm and sells in-season produce and homemade products.

For an elegant full-service dining experience, enjoy **Table 128** (14050 Hwy. 128, Boonville, 707/895-2210, www.boonvillehotel.com, by reservation only Thurs.-Mon. Apr.-Nov., Fri.-Sun. Dec.-Mar., $38-58), the restaurant at the Boonville Hotel. The food at this family style, prix fixe spot is so fresh and seasonal that the chef won't commit to a menu more than a week in advance.

A nice dinner can be found at **Lauren's** (14211 Hwy. 128, Boonville, 707/895-3869, http://laurensgoodfood.com, 11:30am-2:30pm, 5pm-9pm Thurs.-Sun. May-Oct., 5pm-9pm Tues.-Sat. Nov.-Apr., $11-17), the cheerful yellow restaurant in the heart of town. The unpretentious menu is filled with burgers, pot pies, and meat loaf, all of which have made Lauren's a local favorite for years.

Get lunch and a pint of Boonville's famous brews at **Buckhorn Boonville** (14081 Hwy. 128, Boonville, 707/895-9378, www.thebuckhornboonville.com, 11am-9pm Mon. and Wed.-Fri., 10am-9pm Sat.-Sun., $11-20). The redwood pub has hot sandwiches, steaks, and a slew of sides, plus local-centric beer and wine menus.

Transportation

You can see pretty much all of Anderson Valley from the wine trail, Highway 128. The highway intersects just north of Cloverdale on U.S. 101 and is a scenic, if twisty, 27 miles to Boonville. You also can get to Highway 128 directly out of Ukiah on Highway 253. From San Francisco, the trip is 115 miles and takes a little over two hours.

HOPLAND

Hopland is a great bend in U.S. 101 as it races up toward Ukiah and the Redwood Coast. Here the freeway slows down, turns into a highway, and gives travelers a taste of the small, Victorian, and hippie-ish towns of the North Coast. With less than 800 people, its quirky character, ecofriendly shops, and tasting rooms earn it a stop on a northern itinerary.

Solar Living Center

The Solar Living Center (13771 S. U.S. 101, 707/472-2450, http://solarliving.org, 10am-5pm daily) is a "12-acre sustainable living demonstration site," showing, among other things, what life might be like without petroleum. The center has exhibits on permaculture, an organic garden, and a demonstration of solar-powered water systems. The **Real Goods** store on-site is also a draw for visitors, and the completely recycled restrooms are worth a look. If your vehicle runs on biodiesel, you can fill your tank here.

Wineries

To get to the best wineries in Hopland, you don't even need to leave U.S. 101. The highway runs through the center of town, and almost all the tasting rooms are located along it. The tiny wineries and tasting rooms in Hopland are the perfect place to relax and chat with the pourer, who just might be the winemaker and owner.

In the "downtown" tasting room of **Graziano** (13275 S. U.S. 101, 707/744-8466, www.grazianofamilyofwines.com, 10am-5pm daily, free), have fun comparing old and new world wines. Graziano pours varietals from different wineries: two from Mendocino and two from Italy. The staff is friendly and extremely knowledgeable. The small tasting room small makes for a personalized experience.

The star of the region is **Brutocao Cellars** (13500 S. U.S. 101, 800/433-3689, www.brutocaocellars.com, 10am-5pm daily, free), whose vineyards surround the town. Brutocao took over the old high school to create its tasting room and restaurant complex. The wide stone-tiled tasting room houses exceptional wines poured by knowledgeable staff. A sizeable gift shop offers gourmet goodies. If you can't get enough of Brutocao, there is another tasting room in the Anderson Valley (7000 Hwy. 128, Philo, 800/661-2103, www.brutocaocellars.com, 10am-5pm daily, free).

Heading north, the highway passes through acres of vineyards. Many of these grapes belong to **Jeriko** (12141 Hewlett and Sturtevant Rd., 707/744-1140, www.jerikoestate.com, 10am-5pm daily Apr.-Dec., 11am-4pm daily Jan.-Mar., $8.50). Visitors drive between the chardonnay and the cabernet to get to the immense Napa-style tasting room. A glass wall exposes the barrel room with aging wines stacked high.

Food

At the **Bluebird Café & Catering Company** (13340 S. U.S. 101, 707/744-1633, 7am-2pm Mon.-Fri., 7am-3pm Sat.-Sun., $17-20), you'll get hearty plates of American food, the perfect fuel for wine-tasting.

Transportation

Hopland is inland on U.S. 101 about 100 miles north of San Francisco and 15 miles south of Ukiah. Navigating town is a snap, as all of it lines U.S. 101.

UKIAH

City of 10,000 Buddhas

There's plenty to interest the spiritually curious at the **City of 10,000 Buddhas** (2001 Talmage Rd., 707/462-0939, www.cttbusa.org, 8am-6pm daily). The showpiece of this active Buddhist college and monastery is the temple, which really does contain 10,000 golden Buddha statues. An extensive gift- and bookshop provides slightly silly souvenirs as well as serious scholarly texts on Buddhism. The community asks that guests wear modest clothing (avoid short shorts and short skirts, bare chests, and skimpy tank tops) and keep their voices down out of respect for the nuns and monks who make their lives here. For a treat, stop in for lunch at the **Jyun Kang Vegetarian Restaurant** (707/468-7966, 11:30am-3pm Wed.-Mon., $7).

Grace Hudson Museum and Sun House

One of the few cultural offerings in Ukiah is the **Grace Hudson Museum** (431 S. Main St., 707/467-2836, www.gracehudsonmuseum.org, 10am-4:30pm Wed.-Sat., noon-4:30pm Sun., adults $4, seniors and students $3). This small set of galleries focuses on the life and work of the artist Grace Hudson and her husband, Dr. John Hudson, who studied the Pomo people and other indigenous groups. The museum's permanent collection includes many of Grace's paintings, Pomo baskets, and the works of dozens of other California artists. The 1911 craftsman-style **Sun House,** adjacent to the main museum building, was the Hudsons' home, and docent-guided tours are available.

Entertainment and Events

Ukiah Brewing Company (102 S. State St., 707/468-5898, www.ukiahbrewing.com, 11am-11pm Mon.-Thurs., 11am-1am Fri.-Sun., $8-11) offers good beer and good entertainment several nights each week. There is also a long list of organic wines available, specialty cocktails, and a menu full of delicious pub food (under $13).

To taste a bit of microbrew history, stop in at the **Mendocino Brewing Company's Ale House** (1252 Airport Park Blvd., 707/467-2337, http://mendobrew.com, noon-8pm Mon.-Thurs., noon-9pm Fri.-Sat., noon-6pm Sun.). Opened in 1983 in its original Hopland location, the Ale House was the first brewpub in California, and the second in the United States. Today its expanded location has scores of beers on tap, including its famous Red Tail Ale. Pool, darts, and flat screen TVs playing the game keep the atmosphere fun, and a limited menu of sausages and bar snacks keeps stomachs full.

Wine lovers won't want to miss **Parducci** (501 Parducci Rd., 707/463-5357, www.parducci.com, 10am-5pm daily, $5). Mendocino's oldest winery is as dedicated to sustainable farming as it is to its fabulous flagship petite syrah. Surrounding the winery, organic gardens and vineyards are nurtured by chickens, grazing sheep, and cover crops. The Spanish-style tasting room, with its thick walls and low ceilings, is the perfect place to cool off on a hot Ukiah day, and a bottle taken out to the patio overlooking the vineyards extends your stay.

Sports and Recreation

A great place to take a shaded hike is **Montgomery Woods State Nature Reserve** (Orr Springs Rd., 707/937-5804, www.parks.ca.gov, free), about 10 miles west of Ukiah. This remote redwood park is less crowded than its more accessible brethren. The quintessential hike at Montgomery runs along **Montgomery Creek** (3 miles, moderate), where both coastal redwoods and giant sequoia grow in the same area, a rare occurrence. Montgomery's location and climate make it hospitable to both types, which usually grow hundreds of miles apart.

The most famous hot spring in the area is **Vichy Springs** (2605 Vichy Springs Rd., 707/462-9515, www.vichysprings.com, treatments $115-155 per hour, baths $50 per day). Since its establishment in 1854, Vichy has been patronized by the likes of Mark Twain, Jack London, Ulysses S. Grant, and Teddy Roosevelt. The springs, mineral-heavy and naturally carbonated, resemble the world-famous waters of their namesake at Vichy in France. Services include the baths, a hot pool, and an Olympic-size swimming pool as well as a day spa.

Hot springs aficionados swear by **Orr Hot Springs** (13201 Orr Springs Rd., Ukiah, 707/462-6277, 10am-10pm daily, $30). Only two miles outside Montgomery Woods, Orr is nestled in a deep forest of redwood, cedar, buckeye, and bay laurel. The retreat's tubs are either in claw foot tubs, or carved into the rock hillside. No chemicals are added, and the hot springs are rich in minerals, reaching 106 degrees, while the cold tub is spring fed and provides a bracing reprieve. The resort is small, so day use is limited. Advanced reservations are recommended.

Accommodations

There are plenty of lodgings in Ukiah, although they tend to be standard chain motels. Out by the airport, the **Fairfield Inn** (1140 Airport Park Blvd., 707/463-3600, www.marriott.com, $115-165) is a good choice, with an elegant lobby, an indoor pool and spa, a small exercise room, and a generous complimentary continental breakfast.

For a peaceful retreat, the best choice may be **Vichy Springs Resort** (2605 Vichy Springs Rd., 707/462-9515, www.vichysprings.com, $195-390). The rooms, in a genteel and rustic old inn and cottages, are small but comfortable, with private baths, and many have views of the mountains or creek. Use of all the pools and hiking trails on the 700-acre grounds, along with Internet access and a buffet breakfast, are included.

Deep in the mountains, ★ **Orr Hot Springs** (13201 Orr Springs Rd., Ukiah, 707/462-6277, $60-260) provides a variety of accommodations. There are six very primitive campsites ($60). All the rooms are simply decorated, and many have private baths and decks. The six yurts ($180-190) offer complete privacy, "living roofs," and unparalleled charm (but no bathrooms), tucked into the forest. Three higher-occupancy cottages have kitchenettes and private bathrooms. The rates for all accommodations include access to the lodge, all pools, and the communal kitchen.

Food

A local favorite, the **Maple Restaurant** (295 S. State St., 707/462-5221, 7am-2pm daily, $10) serves excellent and inexpensive breakfasts and lunches. Excellent service complements uncomplicated, classic American food and shockingly good coffee.

For a breather on a hot Ukiah day, stop in at **Schat's Bakery Café** (113 W. Perkins St., 707/462-1670, www.schats.com, 5:30am-6pm Mon.-Fri., 5:30am-5pm Sat., $5-12). They'll make you a filling sandwich on fresh-baked bread, and you can hang out as long as you want in the large airy dining room or at the sidewalk tables.

Downtown, **Saucy Ukiah** (108 W. Standley St., 707/462-7007, http://saucyukiah.com, 11:30am-9pm Mon.-Thurs., 11:30am-10pm Fri., noon-10pm Sat., $12-19) is a joint venture from several Wine Country veterans. The down-home menu features wood-fired pizzas, pasta, and hot sandwiches, including the Triple Bypass Burger. The atmosphere is casual, but the food and wine selection shows off the restaurant's Napa pedigree.

For a fancy dinner out, the best option is **Patrona** (130 W. Standley St., 707/462-9181, www.patronarestaurant.com, 11am-9pm Sun.-Thurs., 11am-10pm Fri.-Sat., $9-28), where the attentive waitstaff serves innovative California cuisine in a bistro-casual atmosphere. Portions are a good size but not enormous, and the kitchen's attention to detail is impressive. The wine list features Mendocino County vintages, plus a good range of European wines. The dining room and lounge are modern and stylish, but on a warm night there's no better spot than at a table outside.

Information and Services

If you need assistance with local lodging, dining, or wine-tasting, try the **Visit Ukiah Visitors Center** (200 S. School St., 707/467-5766, 9am-5pm Mon.-Fri.). You can also find information here about Mendocino County.

The **Ukiah Valley Medical Center** (275 Hospital Dr., 707/462-3111, www.uvmc.org) has a 24-hour emergency room as part of its full-service facility.

Transportation

Ukiah is about 110 miles north of San Francisco (2 hours), a straight shot on U.S. 101. It's about 60 miles north of Santa Rosa (1 hour) on U.S. 101.

CLEAR LAKE

The centerpiece of scenic and sunny Lake County is **Clear Lake,** a natural freshwater lake. With 68 square miles of surface area, it is the largest natural freshwater lake in California. Clear Lake is filled with bass and catfish, making it popular with anglers as well as swimmers and boaters, who flock to its shores to cool off in summer. Clear Lake is shallow, which means sunlight easily reaches the bottom of the lake and it's easy for plants to grow in the water.

Towns both large and small line the lake. The large **Lakeport** anchors the northern part of the lake, as does historical **Upper Lake.** The smaller lakefront villages of **Nice, Lucerne**, and **Clearlake Oaks** follow the shore south. Working-class **Kelseyville** is west of Clear Lake and seven miles south of Lakeport. The largest town in Lake County, **Clearlake** is located on the southeast arm of the lake. **Lower Lake** is four miles south of Clearlake. **Middletown** is one of the larger settlements of Lake County, located south of the lake, where Harbin Hot Springs lures visitors for relaxing and dining.

The Clear Lake area was devastated by multiple wildfires in summer 2015. Middletown was particularly affected. Many businesses have expressed determination to rebuild.

Harbin Hot Springs

Harbin Hot Springs (18424 Harbin Springs Rd., Middletown, 707/987-2477 or 800/622-2477, www.harbin.org) is a clothing-optional resort and spiritual retreat. Harbin's 5,000-acres of wooded property include rolling hills, hiking trails, and a series of spring-fed pools. The largest pool is warm and about five feet deep. Behind it are two smaller pools—one very cold and the other very hot. There is also a large lap pool, a small kid-friendly heart-shaped pool, a sauna, a steam room, and multiple sundecks. Free movies are shown every evening in a comfy, intimate theater with floor pillows and a few old couches. Massages and other bodywork treatments are also available, including Watsu (aquatic massage). Yoga classes, chanting sessions, and sweat lodges are frequently offered.

Membership ($10 per month or $30 per year) is required. A six-hour pass (Mon.-Thurs. $20, Fri.-Sun. and holidays $30) includes use of all the pools and facilities. The 24-hour pass (Mon.-Thurs. $30, Fri.-Sun. $40) is a better deal as it allows guests to camp overnight. Accommodations ($80-260) in a private room or cabin, or in a dome up on the mountain, can be reserved by phone. The resort also has a café, full-service restaurant, and small health-food store, as well as a large communal kitchen.

Sports and Recreation

PARKS

Clear Lake State Park (5300 Soda Bay Rd., Kelseyville, 707/279-2267, www.parks.ca.gov, day use $8, boat launch $5) is on the shore of Clear Lake, about 3.5 miles northeast of Kelseyville. In addition to superior fishing, the park provides opportunities for swimming, boating, picnicking, and birdwatching. There is a visitors center and a boat launch, and several hiking trails, including the **Dorn Nature Trail** (2 miles, moderate) and the **Indian Nature Trail** (0.5 mile, moderate). The park has 138 campsites ($30) in four campgrounds, plus eight lakeside cabins ($60, reservations strongly recommended). Amenities include restrooms, showers, and fire rings.

Nearby, **Anderson Marsh State Historic Park** (8225 Hwy. 53, Lower Lake, 707/279-2267, www.parks.ca.gov, sunrise-sunset daily, $4) offers a taste of this region's history in a beautiful natural setting. The park was named for John Still Anderson, whose family had a cattle ranch here from 1885 until the 1960s. Today it is a nature preserve that protects the tule marsh, which provides a habitat for many fish, birds, and mammals. Highlights of the park include ancient Pomo petroglyphs, a reconstructed Pomo village, and the Cache Creek, Ridge, and Anderson Flats Trails.

HIKING

Just to the south of Clear Lake looms the 4,300-foot **Mount Konocti,** a mountain that is actually a volcano. The mountain and the surrounding environs (which include five peaks and numerous caves) were turned into **Mount Konocti County Park** (end of Konocti Rd., Kelseyville, 707/262-1618, http://www.co.lake.ca.us). The **Wright Peak Summit Trail** (6 miles round trip, strenuous) climbs nearly 1,650 feet to the summit. Along the way, you'll pass the tiny homestead of Mary Downen, a widow who made her home here in 1903.

BOATING AND WATER SPORTS

Clear Lake is a major destination for boaters and water-skiers. There are a number of free public boat launches:

- **Keeling Park** (1000 Lakeshore Blvd., Nice, 707/262-1618)
- **Library Park** (222 Park St., Lakeport, 707/263-5615)
- **Lucerne Harbor Park** (6225 E. Hwy. 20, Lucerne, 707/262-1618)
- **Redbud Park** (14655 Lakeshore Dr., Clearlake, 707/994-8201)
- **Rodman Slough Park** (small boats only, Hwy. 20, Nice-Lucerne cutoff, 707/262-1618)

If you don't have a boat, **Disney's Watersports** (401 S. Main St., Lakeport, 707/263-0969, www.disneyswatersports.com, 9am-6pm daily June-Aug., hours vary Apr.-May and Sept.-Oct.) rents all sorts of watercraft, including Jet Skis and WaveRunners ($85/hr., $375/day), kayaks, pedal boats, and stand-up paddleboards ($25/hr., $75/day), and patio boats (2 hours $195, $435/day). If you prefer to have someone else pilot the boat, take a pontoon-boat tour of the lake with **Indian**

Beach Resort (9945 E. Hwy. 20, Clearlake Oaks, 707/998-3760, www.theindianbeachresort.com, daily year-round, 1st hour $195, additional $90/hr. for up to 10 people).

Eyes of the Wild (Lakeport, 707/262-2401, www.eyesofthewild.us, $45-150 based on group size) offers customized 2-hour pontoon-boat tours and specializes in wildlife-viewing. You'll see an astounding array of birds from nesting great blue herons to pelicans and bald eagles.

FISHING

There's no sport pursued with more enthusiasm in Lake County than fishing. Clear Lake is often called the "bass capital of the West." Bass aren't the only fish in the lake, though—it's also well stocked with catfish, crappie, trout, sunfish, bluegill, and carp. If you're thinking of trying a little fishing but want some help, call a fishing guide. They'll provide the boat, tackle, and expertise; you can just relax and reel them in.

If it's bass you're after, contact **Bassin' with Bob** (Bob Myskey, Nice, 707/274-0373, www.fishclearlake.com, 5-hour trip $275-375 for 1-3 people), who fishes Clear Lake year-round, or Bob Thein of **Bob Thein's Fishing Guide Service** (Clearlake, 707/994-4886, www.bobtheinguide.com, Mar.-Oct., $40-60/hr. for up to three people, 5-hour minimum). Thein guarantees you will catch something. Catfish specialist Tommy Wheeler of **Gut Buckets Catfish'n Guide Service** (530/300-3336, www.gutbucketsclearlakecatfishn.com, 5-hour trip $120-300 for 1-4 people) will take you out day or night and provides instruction, bait, and tackle.

Accommodations

CLEARLAKE

Clearlake has some of the most affordable hotels on the lake, though many lack the charm of the historical digs in Lakeport and Upper Lake. The **Best Western El Grande Inn** (15135 Lakeshore Dr., Clearlake, 707/994-2000, www.bestwestern.com, $99-159) is a Spanish-style hotel with 68 rooms, a lounge with a pool table and a bar, and an atrium with a fountain. It fills up occasionally with tournament participants and business travelers at conferences, so plan ahead to be sure of getting a room.

A locally run budget option, the **Lamplighter Motel** (14165 Lakeshore Dr., Clearlake, 707/995-9700, www.lamplighterclearlake.com, $60-90), has a private fishing dock and pier on the lake as well as a small outdoor pool.

CLEARLAKE OAKS

You won't get closer to the water than at **Indian Beach Resort** (9945 E. Hwy. 20, Clearlake Oaks, 707/998-3760, www.theindianbeachresort.com, $83-206). With 300 feet of lakefront, the resort is the ideal place to fish, swim, and paddle without ever having to get in the car. Ten cabins line the lake, each with a full bathroom and kitchen. Most sleep three or more, making them a bargain for large groups and families. The little resort also has its own convenience store with ice, groceries, beer, and bait.

The **Lake Point Lodge** (13470 E. Hwy. 20, Clearlake Oaks, 707/998-4350, www.lakepointlodge.net, $80-150) sits across the highway from the lake on a large, well-groomed campus, close enough to offer outstanding views of the lake but removed enough that you won't be bothered by roaring motorboats. Amenities include free continental breakfast and a juice bar, free wireless Internet access, a microwave, fridge, pool, and spa.

LAKEPORT

One of the most popular places to stay is the lovely ★ **Lakeport English Inn** (675 N. Main St., 707/263-4317, www.lakeportenglishinn.com, $175-200). You can choose from the Robin Hood Room, the Prince of Wales, the Langtry Room, or even the Roll in the Hay. Or rent the two-room Schilling Cottage, which comes with its own gardens, porch, and fireplace. In addition to a full English breakfast, guests are served tea and scones at 4pm.

MIDDLETOWN

Hotel rooms in the **Twin Pine Casino** (2223 Hwy. 29, 707/987-0297 or 800/564-4872, www.twinpine.com, $100-280) are large, smoke-free, and have all the amenities—refrigerators, microwaves, blow-dryers, Internet access, and flat-screen TVs. There aren't a lot of places to stay in Middletown apart from the casino and **Harbin Hot Springs** (18424 Harbin Springs Rd., 707/987-2477 or 800/622-2477, www.harbin.org, camping $30-40, rooms, tent cabins, and cottages $80-260). If you're looking for a simple motel, your best bet may be the **Eagle & Rose Inn** (21299 Calistoga St., 707/987-7330, www.eagleandroseinn.com, $70-125). Its 22 renovated rooms are basic but serviceable; some have microwaves and fridges.

UPPER LAKE

The historical **Tallman Hotel** (9550 Main St., Upper Lake, 707/275-2245, www.tallmanhotel.com, $159-219), built in 1896, offers elegant features, including high ceilings and period-style fixtures. Select a garden or verandah room, or a suite in the Farmhouse or the Caretaker's Bungalow. The Tallman is also ecofriendly, with an electric-car charging station, solar panels, and organic cleaning products. Most rooms do not accommodate children and pets are not allowed.

Food

CLEARLAKE

One of the most popular restaurants in Clearlake is the **Main Street Bar & Grill** (14084 Lakeshore Dr., Clearlake, 707/994-6450, http://mainstreetbarandgrillclearlake.com, 6am-9pm daily, $10-23), a casual family place. Burgers, fish-and-chips, and chicken-fried steak are favorites, but those in the know are enthusiastic about the steak and prawns with fried mushrooms. Breakfast is served all day, and there's a large selection of local wines and a variety of beers.

CLEARLAKE OAKS

Happy Garden Restaurant & Bar (13440 E. Hwy. 20, Clearlake Oaks, 707/998-0398, 11am-9:30pm Sun.-Thurs., 11am-10pm Fri.-Sat., $11-25) is one of the few places to eat in the Clearlake Oaks area, and their Chinese and Thai cuisine is quite good. Both the food and the service get consistently positive reviews. It's conveniently located next door to the Lake Point Lodge.

LAKEPORT

Angelina's Bakery (365 N. Main St., Lakeport, 707/263-0391, 7am-5pm Mon.-Fri., 8am-2pm Sat.) has the best home-baked muffins in the county (try the blackberry-cream cheese). Angelina's also serves pressed panini and specialty sandwiches, salads, and wraps for a day out on the water.

LOWER LAKE

It may not look like much, but when you start smelling what's coming out of the smoker on the side of the road, you'll know it's time to pull over. ★ **Danny's Roadside Kitchen** (9800 Hwy. 53, Lower Lake, 707/701-6025, 10am-7:30pm Mon.-Sat., $10) sits at the edge of small strip mall that has seen better days, but this mostly one-man operation is a labor of love. Not only does Danny make outstanding BBQ chicken, tri tip, ribs, and pulled pork, but all the buns are made fresh, the fries hand cut, and the even the tomatoes are flavorful. Plus, everything is under $10. Aside from a few outside tables, there aren't many places to sit.

MIDDLETOWN

Middletown has its fair share of eateries. The cheerful **La Parrilla Mexican Grill** (21389 Stewart St., Middletown, 707/987-4663, noon-8pm Wed.-Mon., $8-12) is a family-run business offering reasonably priced burritos and southern Mexican dishes. La Parrilla has ample seating indoors, but on a nice day the picnic tables on the patio are even more attractive.

The **Little Cowpoke Café** (21118 Calistoga Rd., Middletown, 707/987-0661, 6am-2pm daily, $8-20) has been around forever and remains a local favorite. Expect grass-fed Black Angus cheeseburgers served at red vinyl booths and counter stools, friendly staff, a convenient location, and breakfast served all day.

UPPER LAKE

The excellent ★ **Blue Wing Saloon** (9520 Main St., 707/275-2233, www.bluewingsaloon.com, 11:30am-3pm, 4pm-9pm Mon.-Sat., 10:30am-3pm, 4pm-9pm Sun., $11-24) serves down-home cuisine on the site of the town's first saloon, built in the 1880s and torn down during Prohibition, with modern touches like solar panels, geoexchange heating and cooling systems, and an ultramodern kitchen. The outstanding menu features seasonal ingredients served with beef tenderloin medallions, chicken cordon bleu, and risotto with white truffle oil. This restaurant is quite popular, so reservations are recommended, especially for dinner.

Information and Services

Lake County maintains an **information line** (707/274-5652 or 800/525-3743, 8an Tues.-Sat.) staffed with knowledgeabl enthusiasts.

There are two hospitals in Lake Cou **Helena Hospital** (15630 18th Ave., Cle 707/994-6486, www.adventisthealth.org/clear-lake) and **Sutter Lakeside Hospital** (5176 Hill Rd. East, Lakeport, 707/262-5000, www.sutterlakeside.org). St. Helena Hospital also operates family health centers in Middletown (21337 Bush St., 707/987-3311) and Kelseyville (5290 St. 707/279-8813).

Transportation

Clear Lake is east of U.S. 101, about 40 miles east of Ukiah via Highway 20 and 20 miles east of Hopland via Highway 175. Highways 29, 20, and 53 circumnavigate the lake. The lake is large—jumping from town to town takes time. To drive all the way around, expect to be in the car for nearly 1.5 hours.

It takes an hour and 40 minutes to reach Clearlake from San Francisco.

The Redwood Coast

Of all the natural wonders California has to offer, the one that seems to inspire the purest awe is the giant redwood. *Sequoia sempervirens,* also called coast redwood, grows along the California coast from around Big Sur in the south and into southern Oregon in the north. Coast redwoods hold the records for the tallest trees ever recorded, and they also include some fine examples of the world's oldest and all-around most massive living things. The two best places to experience extensive wild groves of these gargantuan treasures are Humboldt Redwoods State Park, in Humboldt County, and Redwood National and State Parks, near the north end of California around Eureka and Crescent City.

Most of the major park areas along the Redwood Coast can be accessed via U.S. 101 and U.S. 199. To get to the redwood parks from the south, drive up U.S. 101 or the much slower but prettier Highway 1. The two roads merge at Leggett, north of Fort Bragg, and continue north as U.S. 101.

GARBERVILLE

Richardson Grove State Park

The drive north of Willits on U.S. 101 frequently feels like you're in a green tunnel of redwoods, but once you hit **Richardson Grove State Park** (1600 U.S. 101, 707/247-3318, www.parks.ca.gov, $8), the road narrows and traffic slows as the highway weaves through old-growth redwoods, seemingly inches away. Even if your sights are set for the great parks to the north, pull over and stretch your legs. The Eel River flows through the park, so there's good fishing as well as camping, swimming, and hiking. The **visitors center** (May-Sept.) in the 1930s Richardson

Grove Lodge has cool exhibits and a nature store. Richardson Grove State Park is seven miles south of Garberville.

Accommodations

The luxurious and charming ★ **Benbow Inn** (445 Lake Benbow Dr., 707/923-2124 or 800/355-3301, www.benbowinn.com, $85-450), a swank resort dating back to the 1920s, has it all: a gourmet restaurant, an 18-hole golf course, and a woodsy atmosphere that blends perfectly with the ancient redwood forest surrounding it. Rooms glow with dark polished woods and jewel-toned carpets. The rooms below the restaurant's terrace offer the most space and even private balconies, but the historical rooms, though smaller, have the most charm, best views, and the best price. The entire hotel was refurbished in 2013.

Several small motels offer reasonable rooms, and many have outdoor pools. The best of these is the **Best Western Humboldt House Inn** (701 Redwood Dr., 707/923-2771 or 800/862-7756, www.humboldthouseinn.com, $140-200). Rooms are clean and comfortable, the pool is sparkling and cool, and the location is convenient to restaurants and shops in Garberville. Most rooms have two queen beds.

Camping

Richardson Grove State Park (1600 U.S. 101, 800/444-7275, www.parks.ca.gov, reservations www.reserveamerica.com, camping $35) has 169 campsites in three campground areas surrounded by redwoods and the Eel River. Oak Flat, the largest campground area, is across the river and farther away from the highway, but it is only open mid-June through mid-September.

You can pitch a tent or park your RV year-round at the Benbow Inn's **KOA Kampground** (7000 Benbow Dr., 707/923-2777, http://koa.com, $34-54). The KOA also offers cottages with full kitchens ($124-450), plus a pool, splash park, and plenty of other activities that will keep the kids happy.

Walk through an ancient redwood tree.

Food

The restaurant at the ★ **Benbow Inn** (445 Lake Benbow Dr., 707/923-2124 or 800/355-3301, www.benbowinn.com, 7am-3pm, 5pm-9:30pm Sun.-Thurs., 7am-3pm, 5pm-10pm Fri.-Sat. $18-45) serves upscale California cuisine (vegan menu available on request), and its extensive wine list features many regional wineries. The white-tablecloth dining room is exquisite, and the expansive outdoor patio is the perfect place to sit as the temperature cools. Prices are expensive, particularly for breakfast, but the quality justifies the cost. At the daily happy hour (4pm-6pm), all drinks are half price. Make reservations (even if you're a guest of the inn), as the restaurant can fill up.

Garberville has several modest eateries that appeal to weary travelers and families with kids. One of these is the **Woodrose Café** (911 Redwood Dr., 707/923-3191, www.thewoodrosecafe.com, 8am-2pm daily, $9-14). This small, independent spot serves a traditional American-style breakfast and lunch. A lot of the food is organic, local, and healthy, but it doesn't come cheap.

Sicilito's (445 Conger St., 707/923-2814, www.asis.com/sicilitos, 4:30pm-10pm daily, $16-21) has some decent examples of Italian and Mexican food. The pizzas and taco salads are tasty, and the beer and wine selection pair well with the food. The small dining room's walls are crowded with patriotic memorabilia. The establishment sometimes fills with bikers making their way north on U.S. 101.

You won't find too many Starbucks around here, so enjoy a taste of local Humboldt-roasted coffee instead. The **Signature Coffee** (3455 Redwood Dr., Redway, 707/923-2661, www.signaturecoffeecompany.com, 7am-5pm Mon.-Fri.) takes pride in its organic product and sustainable practices. They sell beans, too, so you can stock up for the campsite.

Information and Services

The nearest hospital with an emergency room is **Redwood Memorial Hospital** (3300 Renner Dr., Fortuna, 707/725-3361, www.redwoodmemorial.org).

The little towns of the Humboldt redwoods region can be short on necessary services such as gas stations. There is a **Shell** (860 Redwood Dr.) and a **Chevron** (830 Redwood Dr.) on the main drag.

Transportation

Garberville is located 65 miles south of Eureka and 200 miles north of San Francisco on U.S. 101. The best way to get to Humboldt Redwoods State Park from either direction is via U.S. 101.

THE LOST COAST

From Shelter Cove to Mattole is the Lost Coast, the remote rugged coastline accessible by few roads and no highways. People make the arduous trek out to the Lost Coast to hike the miles of wilderness trails. Even GPS navigators lose connectivity with the trees out here, so bring an old-fashioned map to explore this unspoiled wilderness.

Mattole Road

One of the few drivable routes from which to view the Lost Coast is **Mattole Road,** a narrow, mostly paved two-lane road that affords views of remote ranchland, unspoiled forests, and a few short miles of barely accessible cliffs and beaches. In sunny weather, the vistas along Mattole Road are spectacular. It stretches 28 long miles from Ferndale in the north, out to Cape Mendocino, before heading inland through Humboldt Redwoods State Park, reaching U.S. 101 just north of Weott.

Big Black Sands Beach

Big Black Sands Beach (King Range National Conservation Area, end of Beach Rd., Shelter Cove, 707/986-5400, www.blm.gov) is one of the most beautiful and accessible features of the Lost Coast. Just north of the town of Shelter Cove, the long walk across the dark sands of Big Black Sands Beach to either Horse Creek or Gitchell Creek is relatively easy. This beach also serves as the south end of the Lost Coast Trail.

Cape Mendocino Lighthouse

At Mal Coombs Park in Shelter Cove, the 43-foot tower of the **Cape Mendocino Lighthouse** is quiet and dark. It began life on Cape Mendocino—a 400-foot cliff that marks the westernmost point of California—in 1868. In 1951 the tower was abandoned in favor of a light on a pole, and in 1998 the tower was moved to Shelter Cove. The original first-order Fresnel lens is now on display in nearby Ferndale.

Hiking and Backpacking

Mattole Beach (end of Lighthouse Rd., Mattole, 707/986-5400, www.blm.gov) is a broad sandy beach that's perfect for an easy stroll of any length. At the south end of the Lost Coast, the **Chemise Mountain Trail** (1.5 miles, moderate to strenuous) leaves from the Wailaki Campground (Chemise Mountain Rd.) and gives hikers beautiful views of beaches and mountains from the top of Chemise Mountain. For a schedule of guided day hikes, contact the **Sanctuary Forest** (707/986-1087, sanctuaryforest.org).

For a great but challenging hike, take the **King Crest Trail** (11.6 miles, strenuous), a mountainous trek from the southern Saddle Mountain Trailhead to stunning King Peak and on to the North Slide Peak Trailhead. A challenging one-day round-trip can be done from either trailhead. An arduous but gorgeous loop trail, the **Hidden Valley-Chinquapin-Lost Coast Loop Trail** (8.3 miles, strenuous) can be done in one day, or in two days with a stop at water-accessible Nick's Camp.

Serious Lost Coasters bring their backpacks and spend days on the trail. The ultimate Lost Coast experience is the 26-mile **Lost Coast Trail,** which takes about three days. The trail is within the King Range National Conservation Area, and there are trailheads at Usal Campground, Big Black Sands Beach, and Mattole Beach. Pack water and a current tide table, since the beach areas of the trail dwindle and disappear in some spots at high tide. Campsites, many with restroom facilities and small usage fees, are clustered along the trail. You need a backcountry permit, but they are free as long as you're not an organized group or a commercial enterprise, and they double as fire permits. You can get a permit at a self-service box at one of the trailheads, at the King Range office in Whitethorn (768 Shelter Cove Rd., Whitehorn, 707/986-5400, www.blm.gov, 8am-4:30pm Mon.-Fri.), or at the field office in Arcata (1695 Heindon Rd., Arcata, 707/825-2300, www.blm.gov, 7:45am-4:30pm Mon.-Fri.). Bear canisters are mandatory, but you can rent one ($5) with a major credit card at the Petrolia General Store (40 Sherman Rd., Petrolia, 707/629-3455, 9am-5pm Mon.-Sat., 11am-4:30pm Sun.).

Fishing and Whale-Watching

The Lost Coast is a natural fishing haven. The harbor at Shelter Cove offers charter services for ocean fishing. **Shelter Cove Sport Fishing** (707/923-1668, www.codking.com, half day $175, full day $250), offers excursions to fish for crab, halibut, albacore, rockfish, and lingcod. Prices include bait and tackle. They also offer whale-watching trips.

Come to the Shelter Cove area in the spring to enjoy the Northern California **abalone season.** Ask locally for the best diving spots, and be sure to obtain a license. The California Department of Fish and Wildlife (916/928-5805, www.dfg.ca.gov) can explain the rules about taking abalone, which is strictly regulated.

Surfing

Big Flat is a legendary surf spot about 10 miles north of Shelter Cove. Although the hike in is challenging, hard-core surfers will find it worth the effort. Other surf breaks along the Lost Coast are **Deadman's, No Pass,** and **Gale Point.**

Accommodations

Shelter Cove offers several nice motels for those who aren't up for roughing it in the wilderness. At the **Shelter Cove Beachcomber Inn** (412 Machi Rd., 707/986-7551 or 800/718-4789, $75-115), each room has its own character along with views of the coast or the woods. The inn is an easy stroll to the airstrip and downtown.

The Tides Inn of Shelter Cove (59 Surf Point, 707/986-7900 or 888/998-4337, www.sheltercovetidesinn.com, $150-205) has standard rooms and luxurious suites with fireplaces and full kitchens. Most rooms face the sea, only steps from the inn. The inn is located within walking distance of the airstrip, local shops, and restaurants.

The **Inn of the Lost Coast** (205 Wave Dr., 707/986-7521 or 888/570-9676, www.innofthelostcoast.com, $160-275) has an array of large and airy rooms and suites with stellar views to suit even luxurious tastes. The relatively large hotel has laundry services and is one of the few pet-friendly hotels here. A coffeehouse and a pizzeria are on-site for added convenience. The **Cliff House at Shelter Cove** (141 Wave Dr., 707/986-7344, www.cliffhousesheltercove.com, $180-200) is perched atop the bluffs overlooking the black-sand beaches. Only two suites are available; each has a full kitchen, living room, bedroom, gas fireplace, and satellite TV. This is a perfect spot for a romantic vacation or family getaway.

Camping

For many, staying on the Lost Coast means camping in the wilderness near the trails. To camp in the backcountry, you need a permit. Permits are free and can be obtained from self-service boxes at the trailheads, or by visiting the local office of the Bureau of Land Management (BLM, 768 Shelter Cove Rd., Whitethorn, 707/986-5400, www.ca.blm.gov, 8am-4:30pm Mon.-Fri.) or at the field office in Arcata (1695 Heindon Rd., Arcata, 707/825-2300, www.blm.gov, 7:45am-4:30pm Mon.-Fri.). Bear canisters are mandatory. You can rent one ($5) with a major credit card at the Petrolia General Store (40 Sherman Rd., Petrolia, 707/629-3455, 9am-5pm Mon.-Sat., 11am-4:30pm Sun.).

If you prefer a developed campground with amenities like restrooms, grills, fire rings, picnic tables, bear boxes, and potable water, there are a number of sites in the King Range National Conservation Area (no permit required). Campgrounds are open year-round, and are first-come, first-served. The odds of getting a site are good, given the small number of people who come here, even in high season. Some of the larger BLM camping areas in the King Range are **Wailaki** (Chemise Mountain Rd., 13 sites, $8), **Nadelos** (Chemise Mountain Rd., tents only, 8 sites, $8), **Tolkan** (King Peak Rd., 5 RV sites, 4 tent sites, $8), **Horse Mountain** (King Peak Rd., 9 sites, no water, $5), and **Mattole Campground** (end of Lighthouse Rd., 14 sites, $8). Trailers and RVs (up to 24 feet) are allowed at most sites except Nadelos, though it's wise to check road conditions beforehand.

In **Sinkyone Wilderness State Park** (707/986-7711, www.parks.ca.gov), there are a number of trail camps along the Lost Coast Trail. The only drive-in campground is at **Usal Beach** (Usal Rd., no reservations, $35). The campground is open year-round but is only intermittently staffed; self-register in the park.

For more developed camping, the nearby **Shelter Cove RV Campground** (492 Machi Rd., Shelter Cove, 707/986-7474, tents $33, RVs $43) is attractive. They've even got a deli and store (8am-6pm daily summer, 10am-5pm daily winter, grill 8am-5pm daily summer, 10am-4pm daily winter) on-site so you don't have to bring all your own food.

Food

Most Lost Coast dining options are around Shelter Cove. For delicious seafood, visit the glass-fronted A-frame **Chart Room** (210 Wave Dr., 707/986-9696, www.chartroom.cc, 5pm-8:30pm Mon.-Wed., 5pm-9pm Sat., $20-25). In addition to seafood, hearty meat and pasta dishes are available along with vegetarian fare. Be sure to check out the nautical and aeronautical gift shop.

At **The Cove Restaurant** (10 Seal Court, 707/986-1197, www.thesheltercoverestaurant.com, 5pm-9pm Thurs.-Sun., $15-32), a hearty American menu, heavy on the seafood, is perfect after a hard day of hiking, fishing, or beachcombing. If you'd rather have a slice, the Inn of the Lost Coast is home to the **Delgada Pizzeria and Bakery** (205 Wave Dr., 707/986-7672, 1pm-9pm daily, $15-20). Also in the hotel, the **Fish Tank Café** (707/986-7850, 7am-2pm Mon.-Thurs., 7am-2pm, 5pm-9pm Fri.-Sat.) serves espresso, pastries, sandwiches, and sushi.

Information and Services

If you plan on spending time on the Lost Coast, the best place to start is at the local office of the **Bureau of Land Management** (BLM, 768 Shelter Cove Rd., Whitethorn, 707/986-5400, www.ca.blm.gov, 8am-4:30pm Mon.-Fri.) or at the field office in Arcata (1695 Heindon Rd., Arcata, 707/825-2300, www.blm.gov, 7:45am-4:30pm Mon.-Fri.). There, someone will answer your questions, provide road and trail conditions, and help navigate this large track of wilderness.

The **Sinkyone Wilderness State Park Visitors Center** (Needle Rock Campground, Usal Rd., www.parks.ca.gov, hours vary on staff availability) is the largest information center in the area, but it's run by volunteers, so its schedule is unpredictable. For regional information, call the Sinkyone Wilderness State Park information line (707/986-7711).

Emergency services are coordinated through the **Shelter Cove Fire Department** (9126 Shelter Cove Rd., Whitethorn, 707/986-7447, www.sheltercove-ca.gov).

For a one-way journey through the Lost Coast Wilderness, you can take a shuttle from one of the trailheads back to your car. Both **Lost Coast Shuttle** (707/98607437, www.lostcoastshuttle.com) and **Lost Coast Adventure Tours** (707/986-9895, http://lostcoastadventures.com) have special permits to operate in the King Range BLM land. The cost for this service can be upward of $400 for two people, depending how far you want to go.

Transportation

You can get to the Lost Coast via Highway 1 or U.S. 101. From the south, Usal Road connects to Highway 1, just as the highway turns east toward Leggett. Usal Road is a rough dirt road that eventually reaches the Sinkyone Wilderness State Park in less than 10 miles. Outside of Garberville, the Briceland Thorn-Shelter Cove Road takes 20 miles to reach the coast. Mattole Road out of Ferndale is one of the most popular routes from the north.

Expect rough terrain on many of the roads here, especially in wet weather, which can make the roads impassable. Be sure to keep a physical map and compass with you before you start exploring on your own.

HUMBOLDT REDWOODS STATE PARK

Surprisingly, the largest stand of unlogged redwood trees isn't on the coast, and it isn't in the Sierras; it's here in Humboldt, bisected by U.S. 101. Come to this park to hike beneath 300-foot-plus old-growth trees that began their lives centuries before Europeans knew California existed. Start your visit at the **Humboldt Redwoods State Park Visitors Center** (707/946-2263, www.parks.ca.gov or www.humboldtredwoods.org, 9am-5pm daily Apr.-Oct., 10am-4pm daily Nov.-Mar.), located along the Avenue of the Giants (Hwy. 254), between the towns of Weott and Myers Flat and next to the Burlington Campground. It's a nice visitors center, with plenty of information for anyone new to the region or looking for hiking or camping information. You can also enjoy the theater, interpretive museum, and gift shop. There is no entrance fee for Humboldt Redwoods State Park. The only fee in the park is for the Williams Grove Day Use Area ($8 per vehicle).

★ Avenue of the Giants

The most famous stretch of redwood trees is the **Avenue of the Giants,** paralleling U.S. 101 and the Eel River for about 31 miles between Garberville and Scotia (look for signs on U.S. 101). Visitors come from all over the world to drive this stretch of road and gaze in wonder at the sky-high old-growth redwoods along the way. Campgrounds and hiking trails sprout among the trees off the road. Park your car at various points along the way and get out to walk among the giants.

Much of the Avenue of the Giants meanders through Humboldt Redwoods State Park, but it also passes through grassland and quirky little towns, appearing more like a country road than a world-renowned scenic drive. If you're just looking for the big trees, jump on at Myers Flat and continue on through Pepperwood.

Hiking and Biking

Stop at the Humboldt Redwoods State Park Visitors Center (707/946-2263, www.parks.ca.gov or www.humboldtredwoods.org, daily 9am-5pm Apr.-Oct., daily 10am-4pm Nov.-Mar.) to pick up a trail map showing the number of hikes accessible on or near the Avenue of the Giants. Many are very short, so you can make a nice day of combined driving and walking.

Many visitors start with the **Founder's Grove Nature Loop Trail** (0.6 mile, easy), at mile marker 20.5 on the Avenue of the Giants. This sedate, flat nature trail gives walkers a taste of the big old-growth trees in the park. The onetime tallest tree in the world, the Dyerville Giant, fell in 1991 at the age of about 1,600. But it's still doing its part in this astounding ecosystem, decomposing on the forest floor and feeding new life in the forest.

Right at the visitors center, you can enjoy the **Gould Grove Nature Trail** (0.6 mile, easy)—a wheelchair-accessible interpretive nature walk with helpful signs describing the denizens of the forest.

If you're looking for a longer walk in the woods, try the lovely **River Trail** (Mattole Rd., 1.1 miles west of Ave. of the Giants, 7 miles round-trip, moderate). It follows the South Fork Eel River, allowing access to yet another ecosystem. Check with the visitors center to be sure that the summer bridges have been installed before trying to hike this trail.

Hard-core hikers can get their exercise at Humboldt Redwoods State Park. Start at the **Grasshopper Multiuse Trailhead** (Mattole Rd., 5.1 miles west of Ave. of the Giants) to access the **Johnson Camp Trail** (10.5 miles round-trip, difficult) that takes you to the abandoned cabins of railroad tie makers. Or pick another fork from the same trailhead to climb more than 3,000 feet to **Grasshopper Peak** (13.5 miles, difficult). From the peak, you can see 100 miles in any direction, overlooking the whole of the park and beyond.

You can bring your street bike to the park and ride the Avenue of the Giants or Mattole Road. A number of the trails around Humboldt Redwoods State Park are designated multiuse, which means that mountain bikers can make the rigorous climbs and then rip their way back down.

Swimming and Kayaking

The Eel River's forks meander through the Humboldt redwoods, creating lots of great opportunities for cooling off on hot summer days. Check with the park's visitors center for this year's best swimming holes, but you can reliably find good spots at **Eagle Point,** near Hidden Valley Campground; **Gould Bar;** and **Garden Club of America Grove.** In addition to the usual precautions for river swimming, a poisonous (if ingested) blue-green algae can bloom late in the summer (Aug.-Sept.), making swimming in certain parts of the river hazardous. Before canoeing or kayaking, check in with the visitors center. They will let you know if there has been sufficient rain to assure a good ride.

Camping

Few lodging options are close to the park. Fortunately, the camping at Humboldt Redwoods State Park (800/4447275, www.reserveamerica.com) is good, with three developed car-accessible campgrounds ($35) and primitive backcountry campsites ($5). Each developed campground has its own entrance station. Reservations are strongly recommended, as the park is quite popular with weekend campers.

Burlington Campground (707/946-1811, year-round) is adjacent to the visitors center and is a convenient starting point for the marathons and other races that traverse the park in May and October. It's dark and comfortable, engulfed in trees, and has ample restroom facilities and hot showers. **Albee Creek** (Mattole Rd., 5 miles west of Ave. of the Giants, 707/946-2472, May-mid-Oct.) offers some redwood-shaded sites and others in open meadows. ★ **Hidden Springs Campground** (Ave. of the Giants, 5 miles south of the visitors center, 707/943-3177, Memorial Day-Labor Day) is large and popular. Minimalist campers will enjoy the seclusion of hike-in trail camps at **Johnson** and **Grasshopper Peak.**

Equestrians can also make use of the multiuse trails, and the **Cuneo Creek Horse Camp** (old homestead on Mattole Rd., 8 miles west of Ave. of the Giants, mid-April-mid-Oct., 1 vehicle and 2 horses $35) provides a place for riders who want to spend more than just a day exploring the thousands of acres of forest and meadowland.

FERNDALE

Ferndale was built in the 19th century by Scandinavian immigrants who came to California to farm. Dairy pastures and farmland still surround the town today, and many cows munch grass near Ferndale. In town little has changed since the immigrants constructed their fanciful gingerbread Victorian homes and shops.

The main sight in Ferndale is the town itself—it's a designated historical landmark. Ferndale is all Victorian, all the time—just ask about the building you're in and you'll be told all about its specific architectural style, its construction date, and its original occupants. Even the public restrooms are housed in a small Victorianesque structure, surrounded by Main Street's shops, galleries, inns, and restaurants, all set into scrupulously maintained and restored late-19th-century buildings.

Sights

The **Ferndale History Museum** (515 Shaw St., 707/786-4466, www.ferndale-museum.org, 11am-4pm Tues.-Sat., 1pm-4pm Sun. June-Sept., 11am-4pm Wed.-Sat., 1pm-4pm Sun. Oct.-Dec. and Feb.-May, $1) is a block off Main Street and tells the story of the town. Life-size dioramas depict period life in a Victorian home, and an array of antique artifacts brings history to life. Downstairs, the implements of rural coast history vividly display the reality that farmers and craftspeople faced in the preindustrial era.

To cruise further back into the town's history, wander out into the **Ferndale Cemetery** on Bluff Street in the east end of town. Well-tended tombstones and mausoleums wend up the hillside behind the town. Genealogists will love reading the scrupulously maintained epitaphs that tell the human history of the region.

To get a true taste of the region, make a trip out to the **Loleta Cheese Factory** (252 Loleta Dr., 707/733-5470 or 800/995-0453, www.loletacheese.com, 9am-5pm daily), where the cheese is handmade with local milk. Inside the small, unpretentious shop, you'll find shelves of local goodies, 34 flavors of cheese available to taste, and a friendly

Ferndale

staff who will walk you through their process aided by plate glass windows looking into the tiny factory. Besides a smattering of old farmhouses, the cheese factory is the only thing in Loleta. It's on the road to the Humboldt Bay National Wildlife Reserve trailhead, making it an easy stop between Ferndale and a walk through the Eel River wetlands.

Festivals and Events

Ferndale has hosted the **Humboldt County Fair** (1250 5th St., 707/786-9511, www.humboldtcountyfair.org, adults $8, seniors $6, children 6-12 $4, under 6 free) each August since 1896. For 10 days people from all around the county come to celebrate at the old-fashioned fair, complete with livestock exhibits and horse racing, competitions, a carnival, musical entertainment each night, and a variety of shows for kids and adults on the fairground stages. If you're in the area, come join the fun.

Shopping

A tour of Ferndale's Main Street shops makes for an idyllic morning stroll. The Victorian storefronts house antiques stores, jewelry shops, clothing boutiques, and art galleries. Ferndale is also a surprisingly good place to buy a hat.

The **Golden Gait Mercantile** (421 Main St., 707/786-4891, 10am-5pm Mon.-Sat., 11am-4pm Sun.) has it all: antiques, candies, gourmet foodstuffs, clothing, hats, souvenirs, and more. Antiques and collectibles tend to be small and reasonably priced. **Silva's Fine Jewelry** (400 Ocean Ave., 707/786-4425 or 888/589-1011, www.silvasjewelry.com, 8:30am-9pm daily), on the bottom floor of the Victorian Inn, is not a place for the faint of wallet. But the jewels, both contemporary and antique, are classically gorgeous. The **Blacksmith Shop** (455 Main St. and 491 Main St., 707/786-4216, www.ferndaleblacksmith.com, 10am-5:30pm or later daily) displays a striking collection of jewelry, furniture, kitchen implements, and fireplace tools made by top blacksmiths and glassblowers from around the country. A section of the store is a real blacksmith shop, where you can look at all the tools of the trade. **Antiques & More** (580 Main St., 707/502-8005, 10am-5pm Fri.-Mon., 11am-6pm Tues.-Wed. summer, winter hours vary), in a rambling historical storefront, features a collection of antiques, upcycled materials made into lamps and other decorative items, new things fashioned after old things, vintage clothing, and a milliner who wears her hats with aplomb.

Sports and Recreation

Just north of Loleta is the largest reserve in the **Humboldt Bay National Wildlife Complex** (1020 Ranch Rd., Loleta, 707/733-5406, www.fws.gov), which encompasses several wildlife refuges stretching up to Samoa and Arcata. At the Salmon Creek Unit, you'll find the **Richard J. Guadagno Headquarters and Visitors Center** (8am-5pm daily), which is an excellent starting place for a number of wildlife walks. Keep a look out for river otter, mink, coyotes, and even black bears. The estuary is also a great place for bird watching; just be sure to keep your dog at home. To get to the visitors center from U.S. 101, take the exit for Hookton heading north and turn left onto Eel River Drive. Take the first right onto Ranch Road, and you'll find the visitors center parking lot.

If Fido is in tow, head west on Centerville Road from downtown Ferndale. **Centerville Beach County Park** (707/445-7651, http://co.humboldt.ca.us) is only five miles down the road, but feels completely secluded. Dogs are welcome on all of its nine miles of shoreline, and the bluffs on the south end of the beach are a great place to look for migrating whales in the spring.

Accommodations

In Ferndale, lodgings tend to be Victorian-style inns, mostly bed-and-breakfasts. The queen of the B&Bs is **Shaw House Inn** (703 Main St., 707/786-9958, www.shawhouse.com, $125-275). Its eight rooms are festooned with lace, quilts, and floral wallpaper accenting the pop-out windows and Victorian woodwork of this historical home. A delightful continental breakfast is served in the morning. Out back, huge shade trees and perfectly positioned garden benches make a lovely spot to sit and read a book, hold a quiet conversation, or just enjoy the serene beauty.

The **Victorian Inn** (400 Ocean Ave., 707/786-4949 or 888/589-1808, www.victorianvillageinn.com, $135-255) is an imposing structure at the corner of Ocean Avenue and Main Street that also houses Silva's Jewelry. The inn comprises 13 rooms, all decorated with antique furnishings, luxurious linens, and pretty knickknacks. Package deals are available, and rates include a full breakfast downstairs.

Hotel Ivanhoe (315 Main St., 707/786-9000, http://hotel-ivanhoe.com, $95-145) is kitty-corner across from the Victorian Inn. In a town full of history, the Ivanhoe is the oldest extant hostelry. Plaques on the building's exterior describe its rich legacy. Fully refurbished in 2001, the four rooms are done in rich colors that revive the Western Victorian atmosphere of the original hotel.

An inexpensive non-inn lodging option in Ferndale is the **Redwood Suites** (332 Ocean Ave., 707/786-5000 or 888/589-1863, www.redwoodsuites.com, $115-145). Only a block off Main Street, the property has rooms that are simple but comfortable, complete with modern amenities like flat-screen TVs. Family suites with full kitchens are available, and rates include a full breakfast.

Food

The restaurant and saloon at the **Hotel Ivanhoe** (315 Main St., 707/786-9000, http://hotel-ivanhoe.com, 5pm-9pm Wed.-Sun., $14-20) is a favorite for diners from as far away as Eureka. It's all about the hearty homemade Italian dishes and friendly personal service. **VI Restaurant** (400 Ocean Ave., 707/786-4950, http://virestaurant.com, 8am-9pm daily, $24-38), on the bottom floor of the Victorian Inn, aims to be high end and contemporary. Expect to find oysters, artisan mac and cheese, steak, and lobster on the menu while the bar pours chic cocktails and a respectable wine list.

Stop in at the local favorite **Poppa Joe's** (409 Main St., 707/786-4180, 6am-2pm Mon.-Fri., 6am-noon Sat.-Sun., $6-12) for a hearty breakfast, or a hamburger at lunch. At ★ **Curley's Full Circle** (460 Main St., 707/876-9696, 11:30am-9pm Fri.-Tues., $14-30), find an eclectic, locally sourced menu in a charming, cozy atmosphere. On sunny days, opt to eat on the postage-sized back patio. Standouts include the coconut prawn appetizer, the fish-and-chips, and the braised lamb shanks.

Information and Services

There is a **US Bank** (330 Ocean Ave., www.usbank.com) at the corner of Main St. and Ocean Avenue.

Transportation

Ferndale is not directly accessible from U.S. 101. Exit at Fernbridge and follow Highway 211 to Ferndale. Main Street will guide you into the center of town. Walking provides the best views and feel of the town. To sally forth from town, the long and windy Mattole Road leads out of town south toward the Sinkyone Wilderness area, and Centerville Road at the south end of town heads out to the beach. To get to Loleta and the Humboldt Bay National Wildlife Refuge, take 211 and cross Fernbridge, and then take Eel River Drive north.

EUREKA

The town of Eureka began as an access point to the remote gold mines of the Trinity area. Almost immediately, settlers realized that the real gold lay in the trees covering the hills. By the late 19th century, logging became a chief industry. Today lumber remains a major industry in Eureka, but hard times have fallen on this boom town. Still, tourism continues to grow as people come to enjoy the waterfront boardwalk, shopping and dining in its charming downtown, and the Victorian lumber-baron history that pervades the town.

Outdoors enthusiasts can fish, go whale-watching, and hike. History buffs can explore museums, Victorian mansions, and even a working historical mill.

★ Blue Ox Millworks and Historic Park

Even in a town that thrives on the history of lumber, the **Blue Ox Millworks and Historic Park** (1 X St., 707/444-3437 or 800/248-4259, www.blueoxmill.com, tours 9am-5pm Mon.-Fri., 9am-4pm Sat. Apr.-Oct., 9am-5pm Mon.-Fri. Nov.-Mar., adults $10, seniors $9, ages 6-12 $5, under 6 free) is special. Inside the rambling complex of old buildings, there is a working lumber mill, upscale wood and cabinetry shop, ceramics studio, blacksmith forge, shipbuilding yard, and a historical park. All the tools date back to the 1800s and are still used to create ornate custom items for historical buildings nationwide. Arrive at least an hour before closing time to give yourself plenty of time for the self-guided tour and an opportunity to peruse the gift shop—a converted lumberjack barracks—stocked with wares made by students of the Blue Ox. If you want to try your hand at one of the Blue Ox's crafts, book a Full Workshop Package ($30/person, 6 person minimum). In addition to the self-guided tour, you'll attend two workshops in which you can forge your own nail, spin yarn, or make a bowl on a human-powered lathe.

Clarke Historical Museum

The privately owned **Clarke Historical Museum** (240 E St., 707/443-1947, www.clarkemuseum.org, 11am-4pm Wed.-Sat., suggested donation $3/person or $5/family) is dedicated to preserving the history of Eureka and the surrounding area. Visitors get a view of changing exhibitions that illuminate the Native American history of the area as well as the gold rush and logging eras. The Nealis Hall annex displays one of the best collections of Northern California Native American artifacts in the state.

Fort Humboldt State Historic Park

Established in 1853 to protect white settlers—particularly gold miners—from the local Native Americans, the original Fort Humboldt lasted only 17 years as a military installation. Today **Fort Humboldt State Historic Park** (3431 Fort Ave., 707/445-6567, www.parks.ca.gov, 8am-5pm daily) gives visitors a glimpse into the lives of 19th-century soldiers and loggers. The original fort hospital now serves as a museum. A sedate but fairly long walking tour takes you through re-creations of historical fort buildings, then out to the logging display, where you'll find several "steam donkeys," a piece of equipment that revolutionized the logging industry, along with examples of the type and size of redwood trees loggers were cutting and removing from 19th-century forests. Finally you can spend a few minutes enjoying the tranquil historical garden, where master gardeners maintain the type of garden fort residents kept here 150 years ago.

Sequoia Park Zoo

Sitting far away from downtown, the **Sequoia Park Zoo** (3414 W St., 707/442-6552, www.sequoiaparkzoo.net, 10am-5pm daily summer, 10am-5pm Tues.-Sun. winter, adults $6.75, seniors $5.75, ages 3-12 $4.75, under 3 free) is the perfect activity for road-weary kids. The oldest zoo in California, it seeks not only to entertain visitors but also to preserve local species and educate the public about their needs. The "Secrets of the Forest" exhibit recreates the ecology of the Northern California forest while allowing visitors to see the multifarious species that live there. At the red panda exhibit visitors are frequently treated with an up-close look at one of the nearly extinct red panda cubs. Kids will also enjoy the zoo's watershed play area; their parents will undoubtedly love the 67 acres that surround the zoo, the largest stand of redwoods (including 40 acres of old growth) in the city strangely devoid of any trees.

Humboldt Botanical Gardens

To see Humboldt's best flora, make a trip out to the **Humboldt Botanical Gardens** (College of the Redwoods, 7351 Tompkins Hill Rd., 707/442-5139, www.hbgf.org, 10am-2pm Wed.-Sat., 11am-3pm Sun., adults $5, under age 13 free), where a patchwork of gardens celebrate the ecosystems of Humboldt County. Give yourself an hour and a half to make the most of your trip. Be sure to hike up to the Oliver Eitzen Lookout Point for some of the best views of the bucolic Eel River Valley.

Entertainment and Events

Music lovers flock to Eureka each year for a number of big music festivals, including the **Redwood Coast Music Festival** (707/445-3378, www.redwoodjazz.org, all-event pass $75-85, individual events $10-50). For four days in March, music lovers can enjoy every style of jazz imaginable, including Dixieland, zydeco, and big band. The festival also features dance contests and silent-movie screenings.

Shopping

For an afternoon of shopping in Eureka, head down toward the water to **Old Town** (between C and I Streets and 6th Street and the waterfront). Most of the buildings here are historical, and you might find the unassuming brass plaque describing the former famous brothel that is now a toy store. Literature lovers have a nice selection of independent bookstores: **Eureka Books** (426 2nd St., 707/444-9593, www.eurekabooksellers.com, 10am-6pm daily) has a big airy room in which to browse new and used books. **Booklegger** (402 2nd St., 707/445-1344, 10am-5:30pm Mon.-Sat., 11am-4pm Sun.), just down the street, is a small but well-organized new-and-used bookshop that specializes in antique books.

Eureka is the largest California antiques market north of the Bay Area. In Old Town and downtown, seekers find treasures from lumber-baron-era and Victorian delights, from tiny porcelain figurines to huge pieces of furniture. **Annex 39** (610 F St., 707/443-1323, noon-5:30pm Mon.-Fri.) specializes in vintage linens and laundry products, and has a great selection of art deco and midcentury modern pieces. Root through the huge **Antiques and Goodies** (1128 3rd St., 707/442-0445, www.antiquesandgoodies.com, 10am-5pm Wed.-Sat. and by appointment).

You'll also find plenty of galleries and gift shops highlighting local artists. Run by the Northern California Indian Development Council, the **American Indian Art & Gift Shop** (517 5th St., 707/445-8451, http://ncidc.org, 10am-6pm Mon.-Sat.) sells jewelry, ceramics, and art from over 40 local Indian artists. For stunning local woodworking, stop by **Humboldt Hardware** (531 2nd St., 707/444-2717, http://humboldthardware.com, 11am-6pm Tues.-Wed and Fri.-Sat., 1pm-8pm Thurs., noon-4pm Sun.), which carries home goods, including furniture, kitchen utensils, and garden doodads. Occupying a huge storefront on the corner of 2nd and F Streets, **Many Hands Gallery** (438 2nd St., 707/445-0455, www.manyhandsgallery.net, 10am-9pm Mon.-Sat., 10am-6pm Sun.) displays work from national and international artists cooperatives, fair-trade organizations, and commercial importers. The offerings are eclectic, with merchandise representative of many cultural, spiritual, and religious traditions.

Sports and Recreation

FISHING

Eureka is a serious fishing destination. Oodles of both ocean and river fishing opportunities abound all over the region, and several fishing tournaments are held each year. You must have a valid state fishing license to fish in either the ocean or the rivers surrounding Eureka. Be sure to check with your charter service or guide to be sure they provide a day license with your trip. If they don't, you will have to get your own.

For deep-sea fishing, **Celtic Charter**

Tour Eureka's Old Town in style.

Service (Woodley Island Marina, Dock D, 707/442-7115, fishing mid-May-Sept., crabbing Nov.) offers excursions including salmon and rockfish ($170 pp), halibut ($220 pp), albacore ($280 pp), and crabbing ($60 pp). All trips leave daily at 6:30am and return at 2pm-3pm. **Full Throttle Sportfishing** (Woodley Island Marina, 707/498-7473, www.fullthrottlesportfishing.com, $175-275) supplies all needed tackle and can take you out to fish for salmon, rockfish, tuna, or halibut. Trips last all day, and most leave at 6:30am.

If you're launching your own boat, public launches are the **Samoa Boat Ramp** (New Navy Base Rd., 5am-midnight daily) and the **Fields Landing Boat Ramp** (Railroad Ave.), both managed by Humboldt County Public Works (1106 2nd St., 707/445-7651, 8am-noon and 1pm-5pm Mon.-Fri.).

Eureka also has good spots for pier fishing. In town, try the **K Street Pier, F Street Dock,** or the pier at the end of **Del Norte Street.** Farther north, the **north jetty** (Hwy. 255, across Samoa Bridge) also has a public pier open for fishing.

KAYAKING AND RAFTING

If you're new to kayaking or just want a guided trip of the area, guided paddles, lessons, rentals, and whale-watching trips are available through **Humboats Kayak Adventures** (Woodley Island Marina, 707/443-5157, www.humboats.com, canoe and kayak rentals $25-80, 2-hour full-moon kayak tour $50). Guides lead a huge variety of tours, from serene paddles in the harbor suitable for children to 30-mile-plus trips designed for experienced kayakers.

River rafters and kayakers have great opportunities for rapids fun on the Klamath and Trinity Rivers. **Bigfoot Rafting Company** (40630 Highway 299, Willow Creek, 530/629-2263, www.bigfootrafting.com, $69-89) leads half-day, full-day, and multiday trips on both rivers as well as on the Cal-Salmon and the Smith Rivers. Experts can take inflatable kayaks down the Class IV rapids, and newcomers can find a gentle paddle with just enough white water to make things interesting.

Accommodations

There are plenty of chain motels in Eureka, but the historical inns are much more interesting. Consider staying in nearby Arcata, where the accommodations, while limited, are more tourist-friendly and feel safer.

The ★ **Carter House Inns** (301 L St., 800/404-1390, www.carterhouse.com, $179-595), a compound of historical inns and cottages at the east end of Old Town, offers a wide variety of accommodations, from charming cottages ($595/night) to suites with soaking tubs set in windowed alcoves ($350/night) and the economical "really nice rooms" ($179). All are clean and stylish, with nods to the Victorian era. The best values are found in the standard rooms at the Hotel Carter, and at the Bell Cottage ($179-250), which also offers a full communal kitchen and sitting room. The rooms and suites of the stately Carter House ($312-412) are the most lovely. Enjoy a magnificent dinner at the attached Restaurant 301, book an in-room massage, or go for a wine-tasting package that delves into the inn's remarkable cellars.

In the heart of Old Town is **Eagle House Victorian Inn** (139 2nd St., 707/444-3344, www.eaglehouseinn.com, $105-205). Built at the end of the 19th century as a grand hotel, the four-story inn's grander days have passed, but the rates, location, and historical flavor make it a decent option. It is full of dark antiques and often-clashing floral prints. Most rooms have a private bath and some suites are available.

Food

The Eureka institution ★ **Samoa Cookhouse** (511 Vance Rd., Samoa, 707/442-1659, www.samoacookhouse.net, 7am-9pm daily summer, 7am-8pm daily winter, $14-17) has been around since 1890. Red-checked tablecloths cover long rough tables to recreate the atmosphere of the logging-camp dining hall it once was. The all-you-can-eat meals are served family-style from huge serving platters. Think big hunks of roast beef, mountains of mashed potatoes, and piles of vegetables. This is the place to bring your biggest appetite.

Oenophiles flock to **Restaurant 301** (301 L St., 707/444-8062, www.carterhouse.com, 6pm-9pm daily, $22-29), not only for the 3,400-plus vintages on the wine list, but also for the food. The sophisticated menu relies heavily on local ingredients (including from its own kitchen garden). Must tries are the ahi tuna tartare and the simple yet unbelievably moist pan-roasted chicken breast. Order the divine chocolate and white chocolate bread pudding. You can also opt for bites at the bar (4pm-11pm daily, $7-16). Don't miss a tasting of the Carter House wines and the small-batch Kentucky Owl bourbon.

Some of the best barbecue in the county can be found at **Humboldt Smokehouse** (310 5th St., 707/497-6261, http://humboldtsmokehouse.com, 11am-9pm Mon.-Sat., $10-12). This is a no-frills joint with walk-up counter service, limited seating, and extremely reasonable prices. Choose from big plates of meat, burritos, or sandwiches and sides like deviled eggs topped with pork belly. Most items are spicy, but are cooled down with a healthy slathering of smoked cream cheese.

For a dining experience like no other, plan a night at **Shamus T Bones** (1911 Truesdale St., 707/407-3550, 11:30am-9:30pm daily, $12-24). The menu is straightforward, with tasty Southern pit-style barbecue along with steak, seafood, and pasta, but the atmosphere is pure Humboldt. The wacky interior aims for the hunting lodge aesthetic, but a Tesla coil randomly emits violet rays and a fountain shoots water. Plenty of microbrews are on tap at the full bar. The location right on the edge of the bay has great views.

For a quick breakfast or a quiet cup of coffee, Old Town has a couple of options. **Ramone's Bakery & Café** (209 E St., 707/442-2923, www.ramonesbakery.com, 7am-6pm Mon.-Fri., 8am-5pm Sat., 8am-4pm Sun.) is a local North Coast chain selling from-scratch baked goods, premade sandwiches, and a variety of coffee drinks. The Old Town location is charming, with exposed brick walls, outdoor seating, and plenty of space to spread out. Another excellent North Coast chain, **Los Bagels** (403 2nd St., 707/442-8525, http://losbagels.com, 6:30am-5pm Mon.-Fri., 7am-5pm Sat., 7am-4pm Sun.) is just down the street and sells house-made bagels, spreads, and sandwiches at very reasonable prices.

Information and Services

Eureka may have the coolest visitor center in Northern California. The **Humboldt Bay Tourism Center** (205 G St., 707/672-3850, http://humboldtbaytourismcenter.com, noon-9pm Wed.-Sun.) anchors the corner of 2nd and G Streets, and offers everything from booking tours and lodging to buying tickets for local attractions and activities. The multitude of iPads and laptops help with planning, but an in-person concierge is usually there after 3pm on weekends to answer any additional questions. The historical space, filled with reclaimed Humboldt lumber, is also a tasting bar and gift shop. Sample any number of local wines and brews over freshly shucked Humboldt Bay oysters and platters of local cheese.

As the big urban area on the North Coast, Eureka has the major services travelers may need. Eureka has a full-service hospital, **St. Joseph Hospital** (2700 Dolbeer St., 707/445-8121, www.stjosepheureka.org), with an emergency room and an urgent care center.

Transportation

Eureka is on U.S. 101, easily accessed by car from north or south. From San Francisco, Eureka is a five-hour drive north on U.S. 101, and an hour and a half south of Crescent City.

Driving is the only option if you're not staying downtown, especially if you want to venture out to any of the nearby parks and wilderness areas. You can easily visit the 2nd Street shops and restaurants on foot. Parking downtown is metered or free on the streets, and not too difficult to find.

Bus service around Eureka is operated by the **Humboldt Transit Authority** (HTA, www.hta.org, adults $1.40-1.70, children and seniors $.95-1.30, all-day passes adult $3.95, children and seniors $3). The HTA's **Eureka Transit System** (ETS) runs within town limits, and the **Redwood Transit System** (RTS, www.redwoodtransit.org, adults $3, children and seniors $2.75) travels north to Crescent City, south to Ferndale, and east to Willow Creek.

Eureka has a small commercial airport, **Arcata-Eureka Airport** (3561 Boeing Ave., McKinleyville, 707/839-5401, http://co.humboldt.ca.us/aviation), which serves the North Coast. United Airlines offers direct flights to Portland, San Francisco, and Sacramento. Flights are expensive but convenient.

ARCATA

If Eureka is the working-class brawn of Humboldt County, then Arcata is its hippie heart. Located about 10 miles north of Eureka on U.S. 101, this small college town is largely populated by Humboldt State University students and alumni. Although Arcata lacks the Victorian splendor of Eureka, the attractive little town centers around a main plaza filled with benches and is surrounded by lovely places to eat and shop.

Arcata Marsh and Wildlife Sanctuary

When you ask a local about the **Arcata Marsh and Wildlife Sanctuary** (569 S. G St., 707/826-2359, www.cityofarcata.org), they may refer to it as the sewage station. The marsh was created by reclaiming wetlands once lost to the processing of municipal sewage. It is still part of the municipal water treatment facility but is also a modern victory for habitat restoration. With over 300 acres and five miles of trails, the marsh has a wide diversity of wetland habitat and sits on the Pacific Flyway, making it a great place to bird watch, particularly in the spring and fall. Check out the exhibits at the **Interpretive Center** (1pm-5pm Mon., 9am-5pm Tues.-Sun.), or join one of the guided hikes every Saturday at 2pm (www.arcatamarshfriends.org). Early birds can join the hike organized by the Redwood Regional Audubon Society (www.rras.org) at 8:30am on Saturdays at the South I Street entrance.

Entertainment and Events

Arcata has a pretty happening nightlife. A number of bars cater to the college crowd, but the best by far is **The Alibi** (744 9th St., 707/822-3731, 8am-2am daily). A dive bar par excellence, The Alibi pours 42 different beers, mean martinis, and the best Bloody Mary on the Redwood Coast. There is a full kitchen serving breakfast, lunch, and dinner. Kids are welcome here.

In Arcata, the place to go for North Coast microbrews is the **Redwood Curtain Brewing Company** (550 S. G St., 707/826-7222, www.redwoodcurtainbrewing.com, 3pm-11pm Mon.-Tues., 3pm-midnight Wed.-Fri., noon-midnight Sat., noon-11pm Sun.). The funky tasting room overlooks steel fermentation tanks and has over 10 German- and Belgian-style beers on tap. If you can't decide, order the generous 11-beer sampler tray ($13). The red and golden ales win rave reviews, as does the Belgian-style porter and the hoppy IPAs. The brewery is a walk from downtown Arcata, but there is often a food truck out front to help stave off hunger, and toys and games for kids and adults.

An unusual event is the **Kinetic Grand Championship sculpture race** (707/733-3841, www.kineticgrandchampionship.com), a three-day, 42-mile race from Arcata to Ferndale, held each year on Memorial Day weekend. If creating your own colorful human-powered locomotive sculpture isn't your thing, it's worth taking a spot along the course to see what the artists have come up with. Be prepared for dinosaurs, donkeys, dung beetles, and other sublimely silly things. The sculptures traverse pavement, sand, water, and mud over the course of the three-day race. Other towns have their own kinetic sculpture races, but the North Coast claims the original event, and this remains the grand championship of them all. For a great view, try to get a spot to watch Dead Man's Drop or the Water Entry.

Shopping

Lining Arcata's plaza are scores of shops that cater to the local community. You'll find stores selling futons, books, outdoor gear, and garden trinkets. The best assortment of local art can be found at **Natural Selection** (708 9th St., 707/822-6720, 10am-6pm Mon.-Sat., noon-5pm Sun.), on the first floor of the Hotel Arcata, where local potters, jewelers, and haberdashers hawk their wares. Look out for **Fire & Light Glassware** (www.fireand-light.com). These handmade dishes, bowls, cups, and glasses are all blown from recycled glass in brilliant colors. This small company is one of Arcata's standouts. Across the plaza, step back in time to the scratchy bliss of vinyl. **People's Records** (725 8th St., www.peoples-records.org, 11am-6pm Mon.-Sat., 11am-4pm Sun.) was established in 1981. Punk sensibility dominates here, but they offer every genre, and even some CDs and DVDs.

Swing by **The Rocking Horse** (791 8th St., 707/822-3509, 10am-6pm Mon.-Sat., 11am-5pm Sun), a great little toy store/baby boutique, with tie-dyed onesies, natural fiber baby clothes, and wooden toys.

Accommodations

Arcata is an attractive place to stay, but the digs are extremely limited. On the outskirts of town, there are plenty of chain hotels that fill up on graduation weekend. This leaves the historical **Hotel Arcata** (708 9th St., 707/826-0217 or 800/344-1221, http://hotelarcata.com, $89-115) as the only game in town, where service is subpar and rooms are rather small and grungy (despite the claw foot bathtub in every room). Still, it's cheap and perfectly located on the plaza and you can get room service from the delicious Tomo sushi restaurant downstairs. Ask for a room away from the bar next door. The quieter rooms are mostly the smoking rooms, but given enough notice, the hotel will air out the room for you.

For a clean, quiet, and charming place to stay, the **Lady Anne Victorian Inn** (902 14th St., 707/822-2797, http://ladyanneinn.com, $115-220) is the place for you. One of

Arcata

the more stately Victorians in Arcata, the inn has five rooms that are all appointed in antiques, floral wallpaper, and handmade quilts. All rooms have private bathrooms, some with claw foot tubs, and two have their own sitting rooms.

Food

Arcata is rich in great places to grab a relaxed bite. A local favorite is **Tomo** (708 9th St., 707/822-1414, www.tomoarcata.com, 11:30am-2pm, 4pm-9pm Mon.-Sat., 4pm-9pm Sun., $18-21), a Japanese restaurant and sushi bar at the base of the Arcata Hotel. The celebrated restaurant, both large and welcoming, attracts every walk of life.

At quiet **Folie Douce** (1551 G St., 707/822-1042, www.foliedoucearcata.com, 5:30pm-9pm Tues.-Thurs., 5:30pm-10pm Fri.-Sat., $16-30), the food is French inspired with plenty of Humboldt twists, such as local oysters presented in a "Japanese" style and the artichoke heart pancetta cheesecake. Most fans come for pizzas baked in the wood-fired oven, but keep an eye out for the fish specials, which are expertly executed. You can add duck confit to just about any dish, and the servers let you taste any wine before ordering.

There are plenty of breakfast joints in Arcata, but the place to go is **Renata's Creperie** (1030 G St., 707/825-8783, 8am-3pm Tues.-Thurs. and Sun., 8am-3pm, 5pm-9pm Fri.-Sat., $8-14). In one of Arcata's older buildings, popular Renata's has tin-tiled ceilings and colorful local art. It has plenty of sweet and savory crepes to choose from, and you can even opt to have yours topped with salad. The savory crepes are large enough for lunch, particularly hearty ones like the bacon, avocado, tomato, and gorgonzola. Renata's famously decadent mochas, heavily dolloped with freshly whipped cream, are delivered in soup bowls. No brunch here is complete without one.

For coffee, beeline to **Café Brio** (791 G St., 707/822-5922, 7am-5pm Mon.-Wed., 7am-5pm, 6pm-9pm Thurs.-Fri., 8am-4pm Sat.-Sun., $6-25), where you'll find baristas pouring cups and pulling shots of Blue Bottle Coffee. All coffee goes down better with one of their wicked French pastries, or a bistro-style breakfast, served on the patio overlooking the plaza. You can also grab a loaf of artisanal bread.

Arcata is a great place to pick up provisions for outings along the Redwood Coast. The **Arcata North Coast Co-op** (811 I St., 707/822-5947, 6am-9pm daily) is full of local, organic, and natural foods, in addition to a full-service deli and a counter brimming with premade food. If you're in town on a Saturday, don't miss the Arcata **Farmers Market** (Arcata Plaza, 707/441-9999, www.humfarm.org, 9am-2pm Sat. Apr.-Nov., 10am-2pm Sat. Dec.-Mar.). Scores of booths sell local produce and locally raised and harvested meats and fish. Live music adds to the festivities and strolling the market will make you feel like a real local.

Information and Services

The **Arcata Welcome Center** (1635 Heindon Rd., 707/822-3619, www.arcatachamber.com) is inconveniently located several miles north on U.S. 101 from downtown Arcata. It's one of the state's California Welcome Centers, jointly run with the Arcata Chamber of Commerce. It provides plenty of information about the area, including the surrounding parks and beaches.

Transportation

Arcata is about 10 miles north of Eureka on U.S. 101. For an alternate scenic route, take Highway 255 at the north end of Eureka. It crosses the bay over Woodley Island and travels along the bay's northern peninsula through wetlands and farmland to downtown Arcata.

TRINIDAD

Perhaps the most spectacular real estate in Humboldt is in Trinidad, a tiny peninsula that juts out from the ragged coastline. Strolling through town, you won't find any Victorians, but plenty of beautiful midcentury homes, most of which are vacation rentals.

Sports and Recreation

BEACHES

Trinidad is the place to go for beaches. Once you pass through McKinleyville and U.S 101 is reunited with the coast, you'll see why. Miles of sand, scores of coves, and clusters of rock punctuate the shoreline providing great opportunities for strolling, surfing, kayaking, and even rock climbing. **Clam Beach** (7.5 miles north of Arcata, 707/445-7651, http://co.humboldt.ca.us) is the largest beach, with a huge expanse of sand hugging the coastline. It is a popular spot for surfers, horseback riders, dog lovers, and the occasional drum circle. At low tide you can dig for razor clams and even cook them at one of nine campsites situated close to the beach.

Moonstone Beach (12.5 miles north of Arcata, 707/445-7651, http://co.humboldt.ca.us) is a county park, and what it lacks in size, it makes up for in perks. Cradled between the terminus of Little River and the redwoods, Moonstone has tide pools, sea caves, and plenty of large rocks for bouldering and rock climbing. The setting is spectacular; don't be surprised if you see a wedding take place around sunset.

In the heart of Trinidad, **Trinidad State Beach** (Stagecoach and State Park Rd., 707/677-3570, www.parks.ca.gov, sunrise-sunset daily) covers the coast on the north side of town. **College Cove** is one of its most popular beaches, with plenty of shelter from the wind. It's known as a clothing-optional spot. The park also offers picnic areas and easy to moderate hikes through the grassy bluffs and spruce forests.

KAYAKING

To get on the water, book a two-hour tour with **Kayak Zak's** (115336 Hwy. 101, Trinidad, 707/498-1130, tour $100) and look for wildlife on one of the most pristine sections of California's northern coast. The company only rents kayaks ($25-35/hour, $40-70/half day, and $65-100/24 hours) out of its main location at Stone Lagoon, and seasonally at Big Lagoon. Both lagoons are a part of **Humboldt Lagoons State Park** (15336 Hwy. 101, Trinidad, 707/677-3570, sunrise-sunset daily) about 15 miles north of Trinidad proper, and have great (and calm) kayaking opportunities. If you have your heart set on kayaking on Trinidad Bay, **Humboats Kayak Adventures** (Woodley Island Marina, 707/443-5157, www.humboats.com), out of Eureka, offers a three-hour tour of Trinidad Bay for only $75. During whale migration, you can also book a whale and wildlife tour for $95.

Accommodations

Along Patrick's Point Drive, several small, family-owned motels and lodges seem to date back to the 1950s. Many include RV parking and camping or offer affordable cottages. For a room for a night or two, the **Trinidad Inn** (1170 Patrick's Point Dr., 707/677-3349, www.trinidadinn.com, $75-195) has clean, comfortable rooms for excellent prices. Many rooms come with a full kitchen, and a couple of suites accommodate larger groups.

B&Bs are popular in Trinidad. In the heart of downtown, overlooking the bay, the **Trinidad Bay Bed & Breakfast** (560 Edwards St., 707/677-0840, www.trinidadbaybnb.com, $200-350) has only four rooms and has a coastal New England feel. Each room has wonderful views of the bay and is decorated in a contemporary and charming style. Families are happily accommodated, and the filling three-course breakfast is pleasant. The inn never has a minimum stay and has a generous check-out time (1pm), so guests can take their time reading and lounging in their room's cozy window chairs.

Though billed as a B&B, the **Lost Whale Inn** (3452 Patrick's Point Dr., 707/677-3425 or 800/677-7859, http://lostwhaleinn.com, $199-325) feels more like a resort. Tucked deep in the forest, the inn has eight rooms that overlook the ocean and its private beach just below a manicured lawn and lush gardens. Breakfast is served buffet style and includes several different breakfast meats, egg dishes, and freshly prepared pastries. There's a cocktail hour each evening, and you can also book a massage ($120/1 hour and $145/1.5 hours) or have a soak and a steam with views of the Pacific. Plan ahead: The inn has a two-night minimum stay, and you are advised to book spa services two weeks in advance.

Food

Like something out of a fairy tale, ★ **The Larrupin' Café** (1658 Patrick's Point Dr., 707/677-0230, www.larrupin.com, 5pm-9pm daily, $23-36) is the warm hearth in the middle of the fog-enshrouded forest. The two-story house sits on an empty stretch of road, and the restaurant is by turns baroque, whimsical, and earthy. Red high-backed chairs, white tablecloths, and low lighting invite diners to dine on Cornish game hen, Creole prawns, and filet mignon. The wine list lines up Northern California boutique wines alongside those of France and Italy. Live jazz is played here every Wednesday and Sunday. Larrupin' is the best, most magical restaurant on the Redwood Coast.

At **Seascapes Restaurant and Pier** (1 Bay St., 707/677-3762, 7am-8pm daily spring-fall, 7am-9:30pm daily summer, $15), you'll find lots of burgers, seafood, hearty breakfasts, and no-frills desserts. Located at the pier, nearly every table has an excellent view of the bay.

Transportation

Trinidad is 24 miles north of Eureka. To get to downtown, take Exit 728 and follow the signs pointing toward the coast. Main Street runs through the heart of town, and Patrick's Point Drive shoots north parallel to U.S. 101 on the west side.

PATRICK'S POINT STATE PARK

Patrick's Point State Park (4150 Patrick's Point Dr., Trinidad, 707/677-3570, www.parks.ca.gov, $8) is a rambling coastal park 25 miles north of Eureka replete with campgrounds, trails, beaches, and landmarks. It's not the biggest of the many parks along the North Coast, but it is one of the best and can feel remarkably empty even on busy holiday weekends. The climate remains cool year-round, making it perfect for hiking and exploring.

Patrick's Point State Park

There's a native plant garden, a visitors center, and three campgrounds ($35), plus a recreated Yurok Village. Because Patrick's Point is small, it's easy to get around. Request a map at the gate and follow the signs along the tiny and often unnamed park roads.

Sights

Prominent among the local landmarks is the place the park was named after: **Patrick's Point,** which offers panoramic Pacific views and can be reached by a brief hike from a convenient parking lot. Another popular spot is **Wedding Rock,** adjacent to Patrick's Point in a picturesque cove. People really do hike the narrow trail out to the rock to get married, and you might even see a bride and groom on their way back from a ceremony.

The most fascinating area in the park is **Sumeg Village,** a re-creation of a native Yurok village based on an archaeological find east of here. Visitors can look through the perfectly round hole-doors into semi-subterranean homes, meeting places, and storage buildings. Or check out the native plant garden, a collection of local plants the Yurok people used for food, basketry, and medicine. Today the local Yurok people use Sumeg Village as a gathering place for education and celebrations, and they request that visitors tread lightly and do not disturb this tranquil area.

Patrick's Point has a number of accessible beaches. The steep trail leading down to **Agate Beach** deters few visitors. This wide stretch of coarse sand bordered by cliffs shot through with shining quartz veins is perfect for lounging, playing, and beachcombing. The semiprecious stones for which it is named really do appear here. The best time to find good agates is in the winter, after a storm. People are welcome to take home the agates they find.

Hiking

Six miles of trails thread their way through Patrick's Point. Choose from the **Rim Trail,** which will take you along the cliffs for a view of the sea and migrating whales (Sept.-Jan, Mar.-June). **Penn Creek** and **Ceremonial Rock Trails** both cut through the heart of the park.

Camping

The three campgrounds at Patrick's Point (information 707/677-3570, reservations 800/444-7275, www.reserveamerica.com, $35) have a total of 120 sites. It can be difficult to determine the location of **Agate Beach, Abalone,** and **Penn Creek,** so be sure to get good directions from the park rangers when you arrive. Most campsites are pleasantly shaded by the groves of trees. All include a picnic table, a grill, and a food storage cupboard, and you'll find running water, restrooms, and showers nearby.

Information and Services

You can get a map and information at the **Patrick's Point State Park Visitors Center** (707/677-1945, generally 9am-4:30pm daily), immediately to the right of the entry gate. Information about nature walks and campfire programs is posted on the bulletin board, and the small bookstore in back is worth a browse.

Transportation

Patrick's Point State Park is located on the coast 30 miles north of Eureka and 15 miles south of Orick on U.S. 101.

★ REDWOOD NATIONAL AND STATE PARKS

The lands of **Redwood National and State Parks** (www.nps.gov/redw, day use and camping free for the national park, fees vary for state parks) meander along the coast and include three state parks—Prairie Creek Redwoods, Del Norte Coast Redwoods, and Jedediah Smith. This complex of parkland encompasses most of California's northern redwood forests. The main landmass of Redwood National Park is just south of Prairie Creek State Park along U.S. 101, stretching east from the coast and the highway.

Redwood National Park

THOMAS H. KUCHEL VISITOR CENTER

If you're new to the Redwood National and State Parks, the **Thomas H. Kuchel Visitor Center** (U.S. 101, south of Orick, 707/465-7765, 9am-5pm daily spring-fall, 9am-4pm daily winter) is a large facility with a ranger station, clean restrooms, and a path to the shore. You can get maps, advice, permits for backcountry camping, and books. In the summer, rangers run patio talks and coast walks that provide a great introduction to the area. You can also have a picnic at one of the tables outside the visitors center, or you can walk a short distance to Redwood Creek.

HIKING

One of the easiest, most popular ways to get close to the trees is to walk the **Lady Bird Johnson Trail** (Bald Hills Rd., 1.4 miles, easy). This nearly level loop provides an intimate view of the redwood and fir forests that define this region. It's not far from the visitors center, and the staff there can direct you to the trailhead and provide a simple map. Another easy-access trail is **Trillium Falls** (Davison Rd. at Elk Meadow, 2.5 miles, easy-moderate). The redwood trees along this cool, dark trail are striking, and the small waterfall is a nice treasure in the woods. This little hike is lovely any time of year but best in spring, when the water volume over the falls is at its peak.

The **Lost Man Creek Trail** (east of Elk Meadow, 1 mile off U.S. 101, up to 22 miles, easy-difficult) has it all. The first half mile is perfect for wheelchair users and families with small children. But as the trail rolls along, the grades get steeper and more challenging. You can customize the length of this out-and-back trail by turning around at any time. If you reach the Lost Man Creek picnic grounds, your total round-trip distance is 22 miles with more than 3,000 feet of elevation gain and several stream crossings. Bikes are permitted on this trail.

Another fabulous long hike is the **Redwood Creek Trail** (Bald Hills Rd. spur off U.S. 101, 8-14 miles, moderate-difficult), which follows Redwood Creek for eight miles to the **Tall Trees Grove.** If you have someone willing to act as a shuttle driver, you can pick up the **Tall Trees Trail** and walk another 6 miles (a total of 14 miles) to the **Dolason Prairie Trail,** which takes you back out to Bald Hills Road. During the winter, many of the foot bridges crossing the Redwood Creek are removed to prevent damage by the high waters. If hiking during the rainy season, be sure to ask a ranger about the condition of the trail before venturing out.

ACCOMMODATIONS AND CAMPING

If you want to sleep indoors but still stay close to the national park, your best bet is the **Palm Café & Motel** (121130 U.S. 101, Orick, 707/488-3381, $60-90). It's a far cry from fancy, but it's a great location, and the food in the attached café (6am-8pm daily summer, $10-12) is good, and service is friendly at both.

Redwood National Park has no designated campgrounds, but free backcountry camping is allowed; permits may be necessary in certain areas. **Elam Camp** and **44 Camp** are both hike-in primitive campgrounds along the Redwood Creek and Tall Trees Trails, respectively.

Contact either the **Thomas H. Kuchel Visitor Center** (U.S. 101, south of Orick, 707/465-7765, 9am-5pm daily spring-fall, 9am-4pm daily winter) or the **Crescent City Information Center** (1111 2nd St., Crescent City, 707/465-7335, 9am-5pm daily spring-fall, 9am-4pm daily winter) if you're planning a backcountry camping trip. Someone will help you determine whether you need a permit and issue one if you do. Permits are free.

TRANSPORTATION

The Thomas H. Kuchel Visitor Center, at the south end of the park, is 40 miles (45-min. drive) north of Eureka on U.S. 101.

Prairie Creek Redwoods State Park

At the junction of the south end of the

Newton B. Drury Scenic Parkway and U.S. 101, **Prairie Creek Redwoods State Park** (Newton B. Drury Scenic Pkwy., 25 miles south of Crescent City, 707/488-2039, www.parks.ca.gov, $8) offers 14,000 acres of lush and shady hiking trails through redwoods as well as several large campgrounds ($35).

One of the things that makes a drive to Prairie Creek worth the effort is the herd of **Roosevelt elk.** These big guys hang out at the Elk Prairie, a stretch of open grassland along the highway. To find the viewing platform, watch for the road signs. The best times to see the elk out grazing in the field are early morning and around sunset. Stay in the viewing area and let the elk enjoy their meals in peace.

PRAIRIE CREEK VISITOR CENTER

Just beyond the entrance off U.S. 101, the **Prairie Creek Visitor Center** (Newton B. Drury Scenic Pkwy., 707/488-2171, 9am-5pm daily summer, 9am-4pm Thurs.-Mon. fall-spring) includes a small interpretive museum describing the history of the California redwood forests. A tiny bookshop adjoins the museum, well stocked with books describing the history, nature, and culture of the area.

NEWTON B. DRURY SCENIC PARKWAY

A gorgeous scenic road through the redwoods, **Newton B. Drury Scenic Parkway,** off U.S. 101 about halfway between Orick and Klamath, features old-growth trees lining the roads, a close-up view of the redwood forest ecosystem, and a grove or trailhead every hundred yards or so. A great place to turn off is at the **Big Tree Wayside.** The eponymous tree is only a short walk from the parking area, and several trails radiate from the little grove.

HIKING

Perhaps the single most famous hiking trail along the redwood coast is **Fern Canyon** (Davison Rd.), near Gold Bluffs Beach. This hike runs through a narrow canyon carved by Home Creek. Ferns, mosses, and other water-loving plants grow thick up the sides of the canyon, creating a beautiful vertical carpet of greenery. It's so unusual, in fact, that scenes from both *Jurassic Park 2* and *Return of the Jedi* were filmed here. This area is home to the very large and relatively rare Roosevelt elk. Look for them especially around Gold Bluffs Beach. Take an easy one-mile loop here to experience Fern Canyon. You can extend this hike into a longer (6.2 miles, moderate) loop by starting at the same place. When the trail intersects with **Friendship Ridge Trail**, bear left, then left again onto **West Ridge Trail**, which will cross and then follow Butler Creek to the beach. Walk two miles along Gold Bluffs Beach to complete the loop. To get to the Fern Canyon trailhead, take U.S. 101 three miles north of Orick, and then at Elk Meadow, turn west onto Davison Road (no trailers allowed) and travel two more miles. This rough dirt road takes you through the campground and ends at the trailhead 1.5 miles later.

To avoid the rough terrain of Davison Road, the **Miners Ridge** and **James Irvine Loop** (12 miles, moderate) starts from the visitors center and reaches the beach. From the trailhead, start out on **James Irvine Trail** and bear right when you can, following the trail all the way until it joins Fern Canyon Trail. Turn left when you get to the coast and walk along Gold Bluffs Beach for 1.5 miles. Then make a left onto the **Clintonia Trail** and head back toward the visitors center. If you're starting at the visitors center but don't want to do the entire 12-mile loop, you can cut this hike roughly in half. When you get to the Clintonia Trail on your way out to the coast, make a left instead of continuing on the James Irvine Trail. This will take you over to Miners Ridge, where you make another left to loop back to the starting point, for a total of about six miles. This is a pleasant hike with plenty of great trees; the drawback is that you don't get to see Fern Canyon.

If you're hiking the **California Coastal Trail** (www.californiacoastaltrail.info), you can do a leg here at Prairie Creek. The Coastal Trail runs along the entire coast of this park.

It can be accessed by taking Davison Road to the coast in the south and by Newton B. Drury Scenic Parkway in the north, via the one-mile, moderate **Ossagon Creek Trail.**

CAMPING

The **Elk Prairie Campground** (127011 Newton B. Drury Scenic Pkwy., campground 707/488-2171, reservations 800/444-7275, www.reserveamerica.com, vehicles $35, hikers and cyclists $5) has 75 sites for tents (and some RVs) and a full range of comfortable camping amenities. You can get a shower and purchase wood for your fire ring. Several campsites are wheelchair-accessible (make request at reservation). A big campfire area is north of the campground, an easy walk for campers interested in the evening programs put on by rangers and volunteers.

For beach camping, head out to **Gold Bluffs Beach Campground** (Davison Rd., www.parks.ca.gov, no reservations, $35). There are about 26 sites for tents or RVs. Amenities include flush toilets, water, solar showers, and wide ocean views. The surf can be quite dangerous here, so be extremely careful if you go in the water.

Prairie Creek has no designated backcountry campsites, and backcountry camping is not allowed.

GETTING THERE

Prairie Creek Redwoods is located 50 miles north of Eureka and 25 miles south of Crescent City on U.S. 101. Newton B. Drury Scenic Parkway traverses the park and can be accessed from U.S. 101 north or south.

Del Norte Coast Redwoods State Park

South of Crescent City, **Del Norte Coast Redwoods State Park** (Mill Creek Campground Rd., off U.S. 101, 707/465-5128, www.parks.ca.gov, $8) encompasses a variety of ecosystems, including eight miles of wild coastline, second-growth redwood forest, and virgin old-growth forests. One of the largest in this system of parks, Del Norte is a great place to get lost in the backcountry with just your knapsack and your fishing rod, exploring the meandering branches of Mill Creek.

Del Norte State Park has no visitors center, but you can get information from the **Crescent City Information Center** (1111 2nd St., Crescent City, 707/465-7335, 9am-5pm daily spring-fall, 9am-4pm daily winter).

HIKING

Nature trails and wheelchair-accessible trails are available at Del Norte. You'll want to dress in layers to hike as it can get down into the 40s even in summer. Several rewarding yet gentle and short excursions start and end in the Mill Creek Campground.

The **Trestle Loop Trail** (1 mile, easy) begins across from the campfire center in the campground. Notice the trestles and other artifacts along the way; the loop follows the route of a defunct railroad from the logging era. If you want more after this brief walk, take the nearby **Nature Loop Trail** (1 mile, easy), which begins near the campground entrance gate. This trail features interpretive signage to help you learn about the varieties of impressive trees you'll be passing.

The northern section of the great **California Coastal Trail** (CCT, www.californiacoastaltrail.info) runs right through Del Norte Coast Redwoods State Park. The Coastal Trail is reasonably well marked; look for signs with the CCT logo.

The "last chance" section of the California Coastal Trail (Enderts Beach-Damnation Creek, 14 miles, strenuous) makes a challenging day hike. To reach the trailhead, turn west from U.S. 101 onto Enderts Beach Road, three miles south of Crescent City. Drive 2.3 miles to the end of the road, where the trail begins. The trail follows the historical route of U.S. 101 south to Enderts Beach. You'll walk through fields of wildflowers and groves of trees twisted by the wind. The trail climbs about 900 feet to an overlook with a great view of Enderts Beach. At just over two miles, the trail enters Del Norte Coast Redwoods State Park, where it meanders through Anson

Grove's redwood, fir, and Sitka spruce trees. At 4.5 miles, cross Damnation Creek on a footbridge, and at 6.1 miles, cross the Damnation Creek Trail. (For a longer hike, take the four-mile round-trip side excursion down to the beach and back.) After seven miles, a flight of steps leads up to milepost 15.6 on U.S. 101. At this point, you can turn around and return the way you came, making for a day hike of about 14 miles round-trip.

CAMPING

The **Mill Creek Campground** (U.S. 101, 7 miles south of Crescent City, 800/444-7275, www.reserveamerica.com, mid-May-Oct., vehicles $35, hikers and cyclists $5) is in an attractive setting along Mill Creek. There are 145 sites for RVs and tents, and facilities include restrooms and fire pits. Feel free to bring your camper to the Mill Creek campground; it has spots for RVs and a dump station on-site. Call in advance to reserve a spot and to confirm the camper-length limit. On the website, the campsite is referred to as the Del Norte Coast Redwoods SP, not Mill Creek. Del Norte has no designated backcountry campsites, and backcountry camping is not allowed.

GETTING THERE

Del Norte Coast Redwoods is located seven miles south of Crescent City on U.S. 101. The park entrance is on Hamilton Road and at the Mill Creek Campground, both east of U.S. 101.

Jedediah Smith Redwoods State Park

The best redwood grove in the old growth of **Jedediah Smith Redwoods State Park** (U.S. 199, 9 miles east of Crescent City, 707/465-7335, www.parks.ca.gov) is **Stout Memorial Grove.** These are some of the biggest and oldest trees on the North Coast and were somehow spared the loggers' saws. This grove is very quiet and less populated than others, since its far-north latitude makes it harder to reach than some of the other big redwood groves in California.

VISITORS CENTERS

Jedediah Smith has two visitors centers, about five minutes apart. Both offer similar information and include materials about all of the nearby parks. One is the **Jedediah Smith Visitor Center** (U.S. 101, Hiouchi, 707/458-3496, noon-8pm daily summer) and the other is the **Hiouchi Information Center** (U.S. 199, Hiouchi, 707/458-3294, 9am-5pm daily summer).

HIKING

The trails running through the trees make for cool and shady summer hiking. Many trails run along the river and the creeks, offering a variety of ecosystems and plenty of lush scenery to enjoy. Avoid damaging the delicate and shallow redwood root systems by staying on established trails.

The **Simpson Reed Trail** (U.S. 199, 6 miles east of Crescent City, 1 mile, easy) takes you from U.S. 199 down to the banks of the Smith River.

To get a good view of the Smith River, hike the **Hiouchi Trail** (2 miles, moderate). From the Hiouchi Information Center and campgrounds on U.S. 199, cross the Summer Footbridge and then follow the river north. The Hiouchi Trail then meets the Hatton Loop Trail and leads away from the river and into the forest.

If you're looking for a longer and more aggressive trek, try the **Mill Creek Trail** (7.5 miles round-trip, difficult). A good place to start is at the Summer Footbridge. The trail then follows the creek down to the unpaved Howland Hill Road.

If it's redwoods you're looking for, take the **Boy Scout Tree Trail** (5.2 miles, moderate). The trail is usually quiet, with few hikers, and the gargantuan forest will make you feel truly tiny. About three miles into the trail, you'll come to a fork. If you've got time, take both forks: first the left, which takes you to the small, mossy, and very green Fern Falls, and then the right, which takes you to the eponymous Boy Scout Tree, one of the impressively huge redwoods.

BOATING AND SWIMMING

You'll find two boat launches in the park: one at Society Hole and one adjacent to the Summer Footbridge that's only open in winter. Down by the River Beach Trail, you'll find **River Beach** (immediately west of the Hiouchi Information Center), a popular spot for swimming in the river. Swimming is allowed throughout the park, but be very careful—rivers and creeks move unpredictably, and you might not notice deep spots until you're over them. Keep a close eye on children.

CAMPING

The ★ **Jedediah Smith Campground** (U.S. 199, Hiouchi, 800/444-7275, www.reserveamerica.com) is beautifully situated on the banks of Smith River, with most sites near the River Beach Trail (immediately west of the Hiouchi Information Center). There are 86 RV and tent sites (vehicles $35, hike/bike in primitive sites $5). Facilities include plenty of restrooms, fire pits, and coin-operated showers. Reservations are advised, especially for summer and holiday weekends. The campground is open year-round, but reservations are accepted only Memorial Day-Labor Day. Jedediah Smith has no designated backcountry campsites, and camping outside the developed campgrounds is not allowed.

GETTING THERE

Jedediah Smith Redwoods State Park is north of Crescent City along the Smith River, next to the immense Smith River National Recreation Area.

CRESCENT CITY

The northernmost city on the coast of California perches on the bay whose shape gave the town its name. Cool and windswept, Crescent City is a tough town and sees little of the boom brought by tourist dollars. Still, its proximity to fabulous state and national parks, deep-sea fishing, and the best surfing beaches on the Redwood Coast make it a good destination. Its surrounding underwater geography and its position extending out into the Pacific make Crescent City vulnerable to tsunamis. In fact, the city harbor suffered extensive damage in 2011 from a tsunami triggered by an earthquake off Japan.

Point St. George

The wild, lonely, beautiful **Point St. George** (end of Washington Blvd.) epitomizes the glory of the North Coast and is one of the most pristine coastal prairies in the state. Walk out onto the cliffs to take in the deep blue sea, salt- and flower-scented air, and craggy cliffs and beaches. Short, steep trails lead across wild beach prairie land down to broad, flat, nearly deserted beaches. Spring through summer, wildflowers bloom on the cliffs, and swallows nest in the cluster of buildings on the point. On rare and special clear days, you can almost make out the St. George Reef Lighthouse alone on its perch far out in the Pacific.

Battery Point Lighthouse Park

West of downtown Crescent City, past the visitors center, is **Battery Point Lighthouse Park** (end of A St., 707/464-3089, www.delnortehistory.org/lighthouse, tides permitting daily Apr.-Sept., tides permitting Sat.-Sun. Oct.-Mar.). Plan carefully and pick up a recent tide schedule because the lighthouse is not always accessible. Access may be possible for as little as a couple of hours on any given day. At high tide, the causeway that connects the city to the lighthouse is underwater. But if you catch the tide when it's lower, you'll get a treat as you walk out to the lighthouse: tide pools. The Battery Point tide pools are rife with sea stars, anemones, worm colonies, and barnacle clusters. Small fish trapped by the receding tides hunt for food in the pools until the waters rise again. Up in the lighthouse, built in 1856, a tiny bookstore features local- and lighthouse-themed books and souvenirs. There's a free self-guided tour of the lighthouse, which is now both a museum and a working private light station.

Ocean World

A great family respite is **Ocean World** (304 U.S. 101 S., 707/464-4900, www.oceanworldonline.com, 9am-9pm daily summer, 10am-6pm daily winter, adults and children 12 and up $12.95, children 4-11 $7.95, children 3 and under free). Tours of the small sea park depart about every 20 minutes and last about 45 minutes. Featured attractions are the shark petting tank, the 500,000-gallon aquarium, and the sea lion show. After the tour, take a stroll through the immense souvenir shop, which sells gifts of all sizes, shapes, and descriptions, many with nautical themes.

Del Norte County Historical Society Museum

The **Del Norte County Historical Society Museum** (577 H St., 707/464-3922, www.delnortehistory.org/museum, 10am-4pm Mon.-Sat. May-Sept., 10am-4pm Mon. and Sat. Oct.-Apr., free) provides an educational reprieve from the chilly sea breezes. The Historical Society maintains this small museum that features the local history of both the Native Americans, once the only inhabitants of Del Norte County, and the encroaching white settlers. Featured exhibits include the wreck of the *Brother Jonathan* at Point St. George, the story of the 1964 tsunami, and artifacts of the local Yurok and Tolowa people.

Sports and Recreation

BEACHES

The sands of Crescent City are a beachcomber's paradise. Wide, flat, sandy expanses invite strolling, running, and just sitting to contemplate the broad crashing Pacific. **South Beach** is located at the south end of town. Long, wide, and flat, it's perfect for a romantic stroll, as long as you're bundled up. The adventurous and chill-resistant can try surfing and boogie boarding. Farther south, **Crescent Beach** and **Enderts Beach** (Enderts Rd.) offer picnic spots, tide pools, and acres of sand to walk and play on. The sand is dark, soft, and perfect for families. The trails down to the beach are steep and rocky, so take care. Hikers enjoy the trails that lead away from the beach into the national forest.

Swimming from the beaches of Crescent City is not for the faint of heart. The water is icy cold, the shores are rocky, and undertow and rip currents can be dangerous. No lifeguards patrol these beaches.

BIRD-WATCHING

Birders flock to Crescent City because the diverse climates and habitats nourish a huge variety of avian residents. The parks and preserves have become destinations for enthusiasts looking for species hard to find anyplace else. Right in town, check out **Battery Point Lighthouse Park** and **Point St. George.** For a rare view of an Aleutian goose or a peregrine falcon, journey to **Tolowa Dunes State Park** (Kellogg Rd. off Lower Lake Road, 707/465-7335, www.parks.ca.gov, sunrise-sunset daily, free), specifically the shores of **Lake Earl** and **Kellogg Beach.** The dunes are a part of the **Lake Earl Wildlife Area** (2591 Old Mill Rd., 707/445-6493), perfectly situated on the Pacific Flyway. Visit the information center on Old Mill Road for tips on hikes and the best bird-watching opportunities.

FISHING AND WHALE-WATCHING

Anglers on the North Coast can choose between excellent deep-sea fishing and exciting river trips. The Pacific yields lingcod, snapper, and salmon, while the rivers are famous for chinook (king) salmon, steelhead, and cutthroat trout. Mammal-loving travelers can go on whale-watching tours. The ***Tally Ho II*** (Doc D-29 at the harbor, 707/464-1236) is available for a variety of deep-sea fishing trips (May-Oct., half-day trip $110), whale-watching (Feb.-Mar., 3-hour trip $60), or a combination of the two.

River fishers have a wealth of guides to choose from. **Ken Cunningham Guide Service** (50 Hunter Creek, Klamath, 707/391-7144, www.salmonslayer.net, $200-250 pp) will take you on a full-day fishing trip; the price includes bait, tackle, and the boat. **North Coast Fishing Adventures** (1657

Childrens Ave., McKinleyville, 707/498-4087 or 707/839-8127, www.norcalriverfishing.com, $225 pp, minimum $400 per day) covers the Klamath and Smith Rivers as well as smaller waterways.

HORSEBACK RIDING

The rugged land surrounding Crescent City looks even prettier from the back of a horse. Casual riders enjoy a guided riding adventure through redwoods or along the ocean with **Crescent Trail Rides** (2002 Moorehead Rd., 707/951-5407, www.crescenttrailrides.com, 1.5 hours $60, 4 hours $160). You can opt for a coastal ride through the dunes and wetlands of **Tolowa Dunes State Park** or through the redwoods in **Del Norte Coast Redwoods State Park**.

SURFING

For surfers and bodysurfers willing to don heavy wetsuits and brave the cold North Coast waters, some great waves can be found at **South Beach.** Don't worry if you forgot your board or booties: Rentals (and plenty of free advice) can be found at **South Beach Outfitters** (128 Anchor Way, 707/464-2963, http://southbeachoutfitters.com, 10am-5pm Wed.-Sun.) conveniently located between the harbor and South Beach.

River rafters and kayakers have great opportunities for rapids fun on the Klamath and Trinity Rivers. **Bigfoot Rafting Company** (40630 Highway 299, Willow Creek, 530/629-2263, www.bigfootrafting.com, $69-89) leads half-day, full-day, and multiday trips on both rivers as well as on the Cal-Salmon and the Smith Rivers. Experts can take inflatable kayaks down the Class IV rapids, and newcomers can find a gentle paddle with just enough white water to make things interesting.

Accommodations

Accommodations in Crescent City are affordable, even during midsummer high season, and can be surprisingly comfortable.

The aptly named **Curly Redwood Lodge** (701 U.S. 101 S., 707/464-2137, www.curlyredwoodlodge.com, $56-98) is constructed of a single rare curly redwood tree. You'll get to see the lovely color and grain of the tree in your large, simply decorated room. A 1950s feel pervades this friendly unpretentious motel, conveniently located right on U.S. 101 near the area's best restaurants.

The **Lighthouse Inn** (681 U.S. 101 S., 707/464-3993 or 877/464-3993, www.lighthouse101.com, $89-145) has an elegant but whimsical lobby filled with dolphins and dollhouses to welcome guests, and the enthusiastic staff can help with restaurant recommendations and sights. Every room has a refrigerator, a microwave, and a coffee maker. Corner suites with oversize whirlpool tubs and fireplaces make a perfect romantic retreat for couples at a reasonable nightly rate, but standard double rooms are downright cheap and comfortable.

Food

Standard fare in Crescent City tends to be seafood, but family restaurants and even one or two ethnic eateries offer some appealing variety as well.

If you ask a local where to eat, chances are they will direct you to **The Chart Room** (130 Anchor Way, 707/464-5993, www.chartroom-crescentcity.com, 11am-4pm Tues., 7am-8pm Wed.-Sun., $10-28). It's very casual, the food is excellent, and it's right on the ocean, so you can watch sea lions cavort on the pier while you eat. If anyone in your party is not a seafood lover, the lasagna is excellent.

The Good Harvest Cafe (575 U.S. 101 S., 707/465-6028, 7:30am-9pm Mon.-Sat., 8am-9pm Sun., $10-27) offers plenty of hearty breakfast, lunch, and dinner options. Everything is made from scratch with wholesome ingredients. Even though the atmosphere is casual, this comfortable airy restaurant feels upscale. With fruit salad, yogurt, and fresh oatmeal, this is the best place around for a light healthy breakfast. For dinner, the steak-and-lobster entrée is at the high end of the menu, but there are also burgers, pasta, and vegetarian entrées.

Winning raves is **Hensel's Seafood and Deli** (191 Citizens Dock Rd., 707/951-8011, 11am-3:30pm Tues.-Sat., $8). The small eatery sells take-out style sandwiches, sliders, and tacos. Although the pulled pork and the gooey caramel brownies have big followings, the specialty here is seafood. Fish tacos draped in avocado, Asian-style fish and rice bowls, and grilled rock cod sandwiches are favorites. Most likely you'll be served at the tiny counter by a family member, or the owner himself, who will tell you how he caught the fish you are about to eat that morning.

Crescent City runs a **farmers market** (Del Norte County Fairgrounds, 421 U.S. 101 N., 707/464-7441, 9am-1pm Sat. June-Oct.). The harvest season is more restricted here than points south, but veggie lovers can choose from an array of fresh local produce all summer long.

Information and Services

The **Crescent City and Del Norte County Chamber of Commerce Visitors Center** (1001 Front St., 707/464-3174 or 800/343-8300, www.delnorte.org, 10am-4pm Tues.-Sat.) is a good place to visit when you arrive. You'll find knowledgeable staffers who can advise you on "secret" local sights as well as the bigger attractions advertised in the myriad brochures lining the walls.

Nearby is the **Crescent City Information Center** (1111 2nd St., 707/465-7335, 9am-5pm daily spring-fall, 9am-4pm daily winter), run by Redwood National and State Parks. This friendly place has maps, souvenirs, and rangers who can chat about hiking, camping, and exploring the parks. Pick up a Del Norte County Map and a copy of *101 Things to Do in Del Norte/Southern Oregon* (www.101things.com) at the visitors center and many local businesses.

Any aches and pains can be attended to at the emergency room of **Sutter Coast Hospital** (800 E. Washington Blvd., 707/464-8511, www.suttercoast.org).

Transportation

The main routes in and out of town are U.S. 101 and U.S. 199. Both are well maintained but are twisty in spots, so take care, especially at night. From San Francisco, the drive to Crescent City is about 350 miles (6.5 hours). It is 85 miles (under 2 hours) from Eureka north to Crescent City on U.S. 101. Traffic isn't a big issue in Crescent City, and parking is free and easy to find throughout town.

Jack McNamara Field (CEC, 3 miles northwest of town, 707/464-7311http://flycrescentcity.com) is also called Del Norte County Airport and is the only airport in Crescent City. United has daily nonstop flights to San Francisco and Sacramento.

Shasta and Lassen

The mountains in the far northern reaches of California are some of the most unspoiled areas in the state, protected by a wealth of national and state parks and forest-lands.

The most prominent features of this region are two iconic mountains: Shasta and Lassen. The stunning snow-capped peak of Mount Shasta may look familiar—it often graces calendars, postcards, and photography books. Shasta is a dormant volcano, which means it's not extinct—it will erupt again—but unlike an active volcano, it probably won't do so soon. Mount Shasta, and the town and lake that share its name, are easy to get to. The mountain itself, though, is daunting to climb and should be attempted only by experienced climbers.

South of Mount Shasta is the major resort area of Shasta Lake, which attracts boaters and water enthusiasts from far and wide.

Mount Lassen, about 150 miles southeast of Shasta, is classified as an active volcano, and the national park that surrounds it includes many volcanic features—boiling mud pots, steam vents, and sulfur springs. Both mountains make great vacation destinations, beautiful to behold and surrounded by recreation opportunities. Not quite as many visitors flock to Lassen as they do to Shasta, yet scaling Mount Lassen's peak is only a moderate day hike, accessible to almost anyone who is fit and game to try it.

As you drive up into this remote area, you'll discover a number of quirky places worth a visit of their own. Go underground at Lava Beds National Monument, scale the cliffs at Castle Crags, feel the spray of waterfalls at McArthur-Burney Falls, and discover the sad and shameful history of a World War II Japanese "segregation center" at Tulelake.

PLANNING YOUR TIME

Either Shasta or Lassen make a fabulous weekend getaway—particularly if you've got a three-day weekend. Mount Shasta offers fairly easy and reliable year-round access along I-5 with both winter and summer outdoor recreation. The weather on and near Shasta can get

Previous: Mount Shasta; Bumpass Hell. **Above:** Lassen Volcanic National Park.

Shasta and Lassen

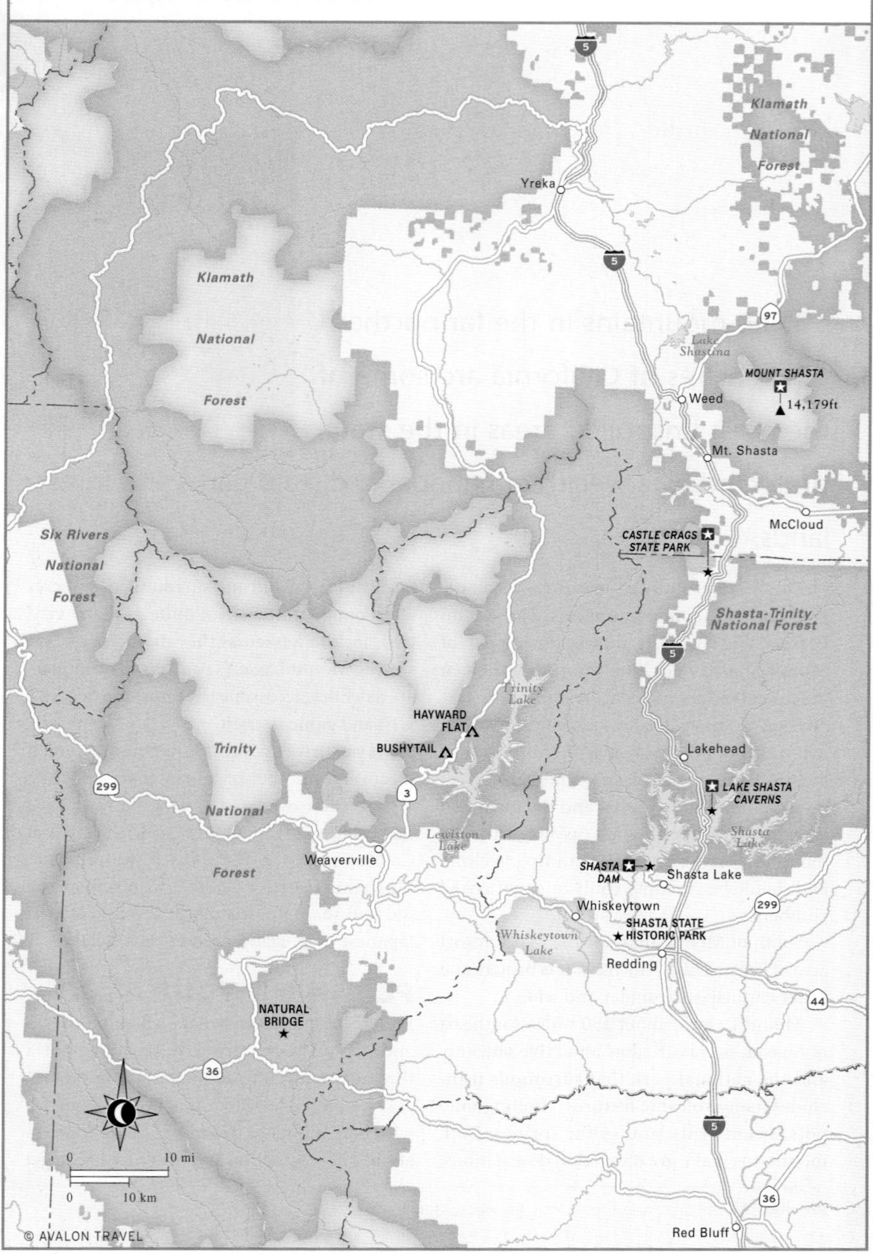

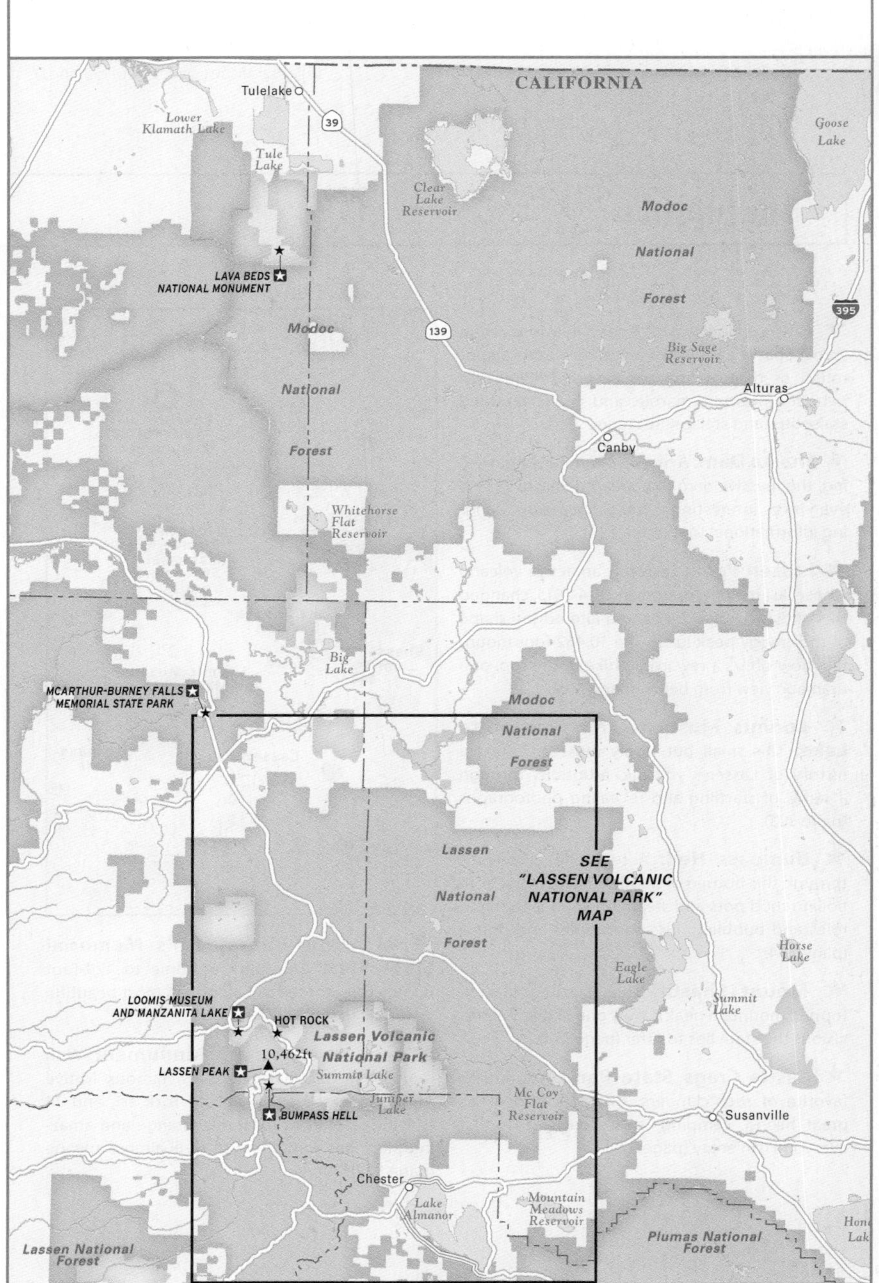
CALIFORNIA
Tulelake
39
Lower Klamath Lake
Tule Lake
Clear Lake Reservoir
Goose Lake
Modoc National Forest
LAVA BEDS NATIONAL MONUMENT
Modoc National Forest
139
395
Big Sage Reservoir
Alturas
Canby
Whitehorse Flat Reservoir
Big Lake
MCARTHUR-BURNEY FALLS MEMORIAL STATE PARK
Modoc National Forest
Lassen National Forest
SEE "LASSEN VOLCANIC NATIONAL PARK" MAP
Horse Lake
Eagle Lake
Summit Lake
LOOMIS MUSEUM AND MANZANITA LAKE
HOT ROCK
Lassen Volcanic National Park
10,462ft
LASSEN PEAK
Summit Lake
Juniper Lake
Mc Coy Flat Reservoir
BUMPASS HELL
Susanville
Chester
Lake Almanor
Mountain Meadows Reservoir
Plumas National Forest
Lassen National Forest

Look for ★ to find recommended sights, activities, dining, and lodging.

Highlights

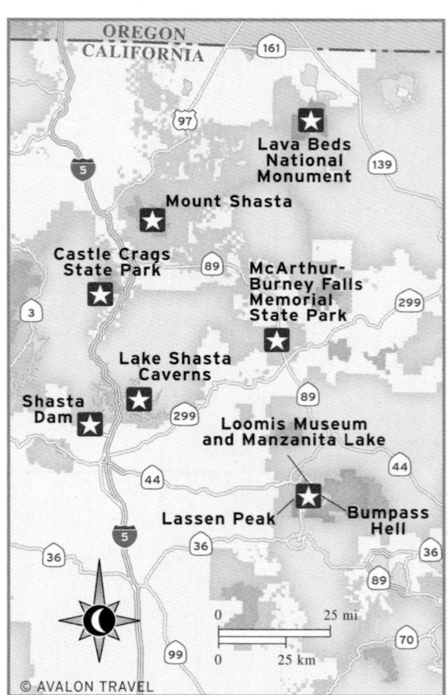

★ **Lake Shasta Caverns:** A lovely cruise across Shasta Lake is just a prelude to the exploration of these wondrous caverns, filled with natural limestone, marble, and crystal-studded stalactites and stalagmites (page 292).

★ **Shasta Dam:** A marvel of human engineering, the massive dam that created Shasta Lake is even more interesting if you catch the outstanding informational tour (page 294).

★ **Lassen Peak:** Lassen is an active volcano whose last major eruption, in 1914-1915, changed the landscape of the area and altered the shape of the craggy peak itself. The 10,462-foot mountain now offers a rewarding hike to the top, or a dramatic view from below (page 303).

★ **Loomis Museum and Manzanita Lake:** This small but lovely museum offers a history of Lassen's volcanic eruptions through a series of startling and revealing photographs (page 303).

★ **Bumpass Hell:** A two-mile hike leads through this hotbed of geothermal activity, from boiling mud pots and steaming springs to fumaroles and bubbling, hissing puddles and ponds (page 304).

★ **Mount Shasta:** This dazzling glacier-topped mountain peak is truly one of the greatest visions the state has to offer (page 314).

★ **Castle Crags State Park:** A longtime favorite of rock climbers, this park also offers great hiking, camping, and scenic views that everyone can enjoy (page 324).

★ **McArthur-Burney Falls Memorial State Park:** This park is home to 129-foot Burney Falls, touted as California's most beautiful waterfall (page 326).

★ **Lava Beds National Monument:** With more than 700 natural caves, famous Native American battle sites, ancient rock art, and 14 thriving species of bats, this strange and amazing place has something to thrill almost anyone (page 328).

extreme; expect winter storms half the year and occasionally brutally high temperatures in the summer months. Check the weather reports so you can pack the right clothes for your trip. If you're planning to climb even part of Mount Shasta, be aware that it's high enough to create its own weather.

The best time to visit Mount Lassen is mid to late summer. Lassen is in the remote eastern part of the state, where the weather gets extreme; it can still be snowy on Lassen as late as June, so keep that in mind when you make your camping plans. During winter the main road through the park closes, making a visit to the region far less interesting—unless you've brought snowshoes or skis to explore the backcountry.

Redding and Vicinity

The biggest city in the region, Redding has all the amenities you might need on your journey. The town has a lot of turnover, so establishments that were here last time might have moved or been replaced. If you just want to get off I-5 for some quick food, skip the Market Street exit; the largest concentration of food and shops is west of the Lake Boulevard exit.

SIGHTS

The best-known sight in the Redding region is undoubtedly the magnificent **Sundial Bridge** (800/887-8532, daily 24 hours, free). Part of the Turtle Bay Exploration Park, the Sundial Bridge crosses the Sacramento River. This beautiful bit of architecture was designed by Santiago Calatrava and opened in 2004. For pedestrians only, the bridge features a single large pylon structure that anchors suspension cables that fan out over the bridge. Most people get to the bridge from Turtle Bay and walk north across its 200 tons of green glass, strips of granite, and ceramic tiles from Spain.

ACCOMMODATIONS

Under $100

The **Motel 6 Redding South** (2385 Bechelli Lane, 530/221-0562, www.motel6.com, $55-66) is known to regular travelers as one of the best examples of a Motel 6 anywhere—it's definitely better than the other two in the Redding area. What you will get is a clean room with a clean bath and a comfortable bed for the night, and an outdoor pool that is clean and totally swimmable.

One tier up in the hierarchy of chain motels, the **Redding Travelodge** (540 N. Market St., 530/243-5291, reservations 800/243-1106, www.travelodge.com, $80-130) offers a few more amenities for a little more money. Rooms have queen or king beds, flowery comforters, dark carpets, white walls, and plenty of space; some rooms include fridges and partial kitchens, and all have free Internet access. Take a dip in the heated outdoor pool or soak in the indoor whirlpool tub (year-round). A hot breakfast at the nearby restaurant **Lumberjacks** (501 E. Cypress Ave., 530/223-2820, www.lumberjacksrestaurant.com, 6am-10pm daily winter, 6am-11pm daily summer) is included.

$100-150

For something more than a standard-issue motel, stay at the **Tiffany House B&B** (1510 Barbara Rd., 530/244-3225, www.tiffanyhousebb.com, $125-170). High on a hill in a quiet residential neighborhood, the Tiffany House shows off the best of Redding's views, accommodations, and people. All the rooms offer charm and comfort as well as views all the way to Mount Lassen on a clear day. The inn's spacious cottage has a huge spa tub, separate bath, and private porch. Common spaces include shady gardens and an outdoor pool, a music room, a parlor, and plenty of cozy nooks to sit and read a book. A two-course gourmet breakfast is included.

Another lovely little inn is the **Bridge House Bed and Breakfast** (1455 Riverside Dr., 530/247-7177, www.bridgehousebb.com, $119-$189). The distinctive yellow house with a steeply pitched roof is along the Sacramento River just a few blocks from historical downtown Redding. Inside, you'll find a tranquil haven in one of four rooms; the Sundial Bridge room has a view of the Sacramento River. Each room is named after a bridge and is decorated with prints of its namesake and attractive furniture. All rooms have TVs, spa bathrobes, and lots of amenities—the two largest rooms boast upscale "massage tubs." The Bridge House acts primarily as a romantic retreat for couples; babies and small children are not allowed. Four additional (and just as comfy) rooms next door in the Puente are owned by the same innkeepers as the Bridge House.

FOOD

If you're planning to camp on Lassen or Shasta, or houseboat on the lake, the cheapest options for groceries are in Redding. For a generous array of groceries, head for one of two **Safeways** (2275 Pine St., 530/247-3030, 6am-midnight daily; 1070 E. Cypress Ave., 530/226-5871, 24 hours daily). For local produce, visit the **Redding Certified Farmers Market** (behind Redding City Hall, 777 Cypress Ave., 530/226-7100, www.shastagrowersassociation.com, 7:30am-noon Sat. early Apr.-mid-Dec.).

Bakeries and Cafés

From the Hearth Artisan Bakery (1292 College View Dr., 530/245-0555, http://fromthehearth.wix.com, 7am-9pm Mon.-Sat., 7am-6pm Sun., $3.75-10) offers homemade sourdough bread, chocolate croissants, and other baked goods as well as smoothies and sandwiches. From the Hearth also has a location on Churn Creek Road (2650 Churn Creek Rd., 530/646-4315, 7am-9pm Mon.-Sat., 7am-6pm Sun.) with the same yummy menu.

Sweetspot (1675 Hilltop Dr., 530/226-8086, 7am-9:30pm Sun.-Thurs., 7am-10pm Fri., $5-10) bakes some of the prettiest cupcakes this side of a Wayne Thiebaud exhibit. The bakery usually hosts an open mic night for local bands on Fridays. They also have a wine bar and serve espresso.

Classic American

Bartel's Giant Burger (18509 Lake Blvd. E., 530/243-7313, www.bartelsgiantburger.com, 10am-9pm Mon.-Sat., 11:30am-9pm Sun. summer, 10am-8pm Mon.-Sat., 11:30am-8pm Sun. winter, $4-7.50) has plenty of raving fans, and a sprinkling of disappointed customers who think the burgers aren't as fresh or as big as they recall. If you're extra hungry, ask for double or triple—rumor has it they'll even make you a stack with six patties on one bun. Enjoy it with lots of onions and the highly recommended special sauce.

Take I-5's Cypress Avenue exit east and proceed to Hilltop Drive, where you'll find the local iteration of the **Black Bear Diner** (2605 Hilltop Dr., 530/221-7600, www.blackbeardiner.com, 6am-11pm Sun.-Thurs., 6am-midnight Fri.-Sat.). This Northern California chain began in the mountains and offers classic American dishes made fresh with better ingredients than at similar chains. The menu includes American breakfast classics, salads, sandwiches, and chicken. Breakfast is served all day, as are the thick, real-ice-cream milkshakes (try the huckleberry). Service is friendly, and it can get crowded on weekends.

Steak and Seafood

Fancy restaurants are hard to come by in Redding, but a couple fill the void. After a day outdoors, sometimes you just need a big ol' steak. **Jack's Grill** (1743 California St., 530/241-9705, www.jacksgrillredding.com, 5pm-11pm Mon.-Sat., $16-38) can hook you up. This locally owned favorite has been serving steaks for more than 70 years. Don't expect the high-end cuts and preparations of big-city steakhouses; instead, look for tasty and less expensive steaks, ground steak, and skewers. All meals come with soup or salad and a baked potato or fries. Jack's has a full bar that serves beer, wine, and cocktails.

With slick décor and roomy booths, **Clearie's Restaurant and Lounge** (1325 Eureka Way, 530/241-4535, http://cleariesrestaurant.com, 11am-3pm, 5pm-9pm Mon.-Fri., 11am-3pm, 5pm-10pm Sat., $20-75) feels like a throwback to the swanky eateries of the 1950s and '60s. It's also one of the only restaurants in Northern California serving abalone. If splurging $75 is too steep, the rest of the menu has more standard American fare such as steaks and fresh fish. The lounge stays open late on Friday and Saturday evenings, and serves food that's less pricey than in the dining room.

Italian

For a hearty Italian meal, **Gironda's Restaurant** (1100 Center St., 530/244-7663, www.2girondas.com, 4:30pm-9pm Sun.-Thurs., 4:30pm-10pm Fri.-Sat., $16-30) serves ravioli and other pasta as well as big Italian-style dinner entrées. Dine in the casually elegant dining room, or order takeout to enjoy elsewhere—even at your campsite.

INFORMATION AND SERVICES

For visitors camping at Shasta Lake or Mount Lassen, Redding is the last serious outpost of civilization before trekking to the more remote reaches of the state. The **Redding Convention & Visitors Bureau** (Turtle Bay Exploration Park, 840 Sundial Bridge Dr., 530/243-8850 or 800/887-8532, www.visitredding.com, 9am-5pm daily summer, 9am-4pm Wed.-Sat., 10am-4pm Sun. winter) is a good first stop.

The best place to find ATMs and bank branches is Redding. A **Bank of America** (1300 Hilltop Dr., 530/226-6172, www.bankofamerica.com, 9am-5pm Mon.-Thurs., 9am-6pm Fri., 9am-1pm Sat.) and a **Wells Fargo** (830 E. Cypress Ave., 530/221-6835, 9am-6pm Mon.-Sat.) are near I-5 for easy access.

Redding has the only major medical services available in the entire Shasta-Lassen region. **Mercy Medical Center Redding** (2175 Rosaline Ave., 530/225-6000, www.redding.mercy.org) has a 24-hour emergency room with a full trauma center for major medical problems.

TRANSPORTATION

Redding is on I-5 about 160 miles (3 hours) north of Sacramento and acts as the gateway to the Shasta and Lassen region. Redding is easy to navigate by car and parking is plentiful and free.

The **Redding Municipal Airport** (RDD, 6751 Woodrum Circle, 530/224-4320, http://ci.redding.ca.us) offers flights on United Express, which runs multiple daily nonstop trips to and from San Francisco. Flying in and out of the small airport isn't cheap, but ticketing and security lines are short.

Most visitors to the region will need a car to explore farther. Outside of the nearby airports, the best opportunities to rent a car are in Redding at **Hertz** (773 N. Market St., 530/241-2257; 6751 Woodrum Circle in the airport, 530/221-4620, www.hertz.com, $250-550 per week) and **Budget** (2945 Churn Creek Rd., 530/225-8652; 6751 Woodrum Circle, 530/722-9122, www.budget.com, $182-1,245 per week). **Avis** (6751 Woodrum Circle, 530/221-2855, www.avis.com, $204-1,235 per week) has an office at the airport. **Enterprise** (217 Cypress Ave., 530/223-0700, www.enterprise.com, $172-387 per week) has a full range of cars in stock. With advance notice, they can often accommodate special requests for trucks, vans, and large SUVs.

SHASTA STATE HISTORIC PARK

Believe it or not, the Shasta region was once more populous than it is now; the area was once crowded with 19th-century gold miners and the people providing goods and services to them. Today **Shasta State Historic Park** (Hwy. 299, 5 miles west of I-5, 530/243-8194, www.parks.ca.gov, 10am-5pm Thurs.-Sun.) honors that regional history. Two on-site museums, the **Litsch Store Museum** (11am-2pm Sat., hours vary Sun.-Fri., free) and the **Courthouse Museum** (530/243-8194, 10am-5pm Thurs.-Sun., adults $3, ages 6-17 $2) allow history buffs to dig deeper into the life and times of early Shasta residents. See everything from an extensive collection of California landscape paintings to the area's original gallows. Outdoors, you'll get the chance to wander through the remains of cottages and read the history of Shasta through the grave markers in the cemeteries. The park also features the brick ruins of a former town.

WHISKEYTOWN

Whiskeytown National Recreation Area comprises 39,000 acres of wilderness for hiking, biking, and water sports just 10 miles west of Redding.

Whiskeytown Visitors Center

Exhibits at the **Whiskeytown Visitors Center** (Hwy. 299 and John F. Kennedy Memorial Dr., 530/246-1225, www.nps.gov/whis, 9am-5pm daily Memorial Day-Labor Day, 10am-4pm daily Labor Day-Memorial Day, $5 day use fee per vehicle for recreation area) illuminate the area's history as a gold-mining destination. It's also a good place to get maps, advice, and information about camping, hiking, and tours in the park.

Whiskeytown Lake

Whiskeytown Lake is the centerpiece of this delightfully uncrowded outdoor playground in Northern California. The lake, formed by the Whiskeytown Dam on Clear Creek, has 30 miles of shoreline. Its capacity is 241,100 acre-feet, plenty of room for fish, and the lake is stocked with rainbow and brown trout; largemouth, smallmouth, and spotted bass; and kokanee salmon. Bald eagles nest and breed nearby. Personal watercraft are prohibited on the lake, but nearly every other kind of water activity is encouraged—feel free to kayak, canoe, swim, sail, water-ski, fish, or scuba dive.

One of the coolest features on the lake are the free 2.5-hour ranger-led **kayak tours** (reservations 530/242-3462, 9:30am Mon.-Sun. spring-fall, 5:30pm Thurs.-Sun. summer). "Summer" is defined by the weather and other conditions, but it's usually at least mid-June-Labor Day. Call ahead to check availability and reserve space. The park service provides kayaks, paddles, and life jackets. Ask about the handful of moonlight kayak trips scattered throughout the summer, usually

Whiskeytown Lake

starting in July, and the family kayak trips (1 hour, 1:30pm Mon. and Thurs.) for younger children.

On Whiskeytown Lake, the National Park Service concessionaire, Forever Resorts, runs two marinas. **Oak Bottom Marina** (12485 Hwy. 299 W., Whiskeytown, 530/359-2671, www.whiskeytownmarinas.com, year-round) is the larger of the two. Rentals include kayaks and canoes (4 hours $20-40, 8 hours $30-60); a 16-foot fishing boat suitable for five people (4 hours $100, 8 hours $175); and tubes, wakeboards, ski boats, water skis, and other conveyances. It also has a small campground store (530/359-2269, 8am-7pm daily late May-mid-Oct., 8am-4pm Wed.-Sun. mid-Oct.-late May). Hours can vary at the store during winter. **Brandy Creek Marina** (530/359-2671, www.whiskeytownmarinas.com, 1 month $220, mid-Apr.-mid-Oct. season $960, annually $1,750) is located on the south side of the lake. Boat-slip rental is the only service provided; no watercraft rentals are available.

Steve Huber (530/623-1918, www.stevehuberguideservice.com, $200-$225 pp) uses a drift boat or powerboat to take anglers out on Whiskeytown Lake. He'll supply the gear and assist with fly-fishing, bait casting, or trolling.

Hiking

Park rangers lead a number of hikes in Whiskeytown National Recreation Area. A helpful list of hikes for a variety of fitness levels is available online (www.nps.gov/whis). An unusual hike is the ranger-led **Walk in Time Tour** (visitors center, Hwy. 299 and John F. Kennedy Memorial Dr., 530/246-1225, 3pm Wed. and Sat.). You can even pan for gold.

The hike to **Whiskeytown Falls** (3.4 miles, moderate) is one of four great waterfall hikes in the park (and if you do them all, you can pick up a free "I Walked the Falls" bandana at the visitors center starting in spring until the visitors center runs out). Oddly enough, this beautiful 220-foot waterfall was "lost" for about 40 years. It was recently rediscovered, and park officials developed and reopened the access trail, called the James K. Carr Trail; it has become one of the most popular in the area. It's steep in places and not an easy hike. Group hikes are sometimes offered, beginning with a carpool to the trailhead from the visitors center; call 530/242-3451 to check the schedule.

Biking

Nearly all of the trails in the Whiskeytown National Recreation Area are open for mountain biking. Pick up free trail maps at the visitors center (Hwy. 299 and John F. Kennedy Memorial Dr., 530/246-1225, www.nps.gov/whis, 9am-5pm daily Memorial Day-Labor Day, 10am-4pm daily Labor Day-Memorial Day, $5). One of the most scenic rides is **The Chimney** (8.3 miles, moderate-challenging), which is difficult and steep in places but worth it. The hilly trail leads over bridges, along Brandy Creek, and up to some great views. Though technically an out-and-back ride, the trail includes two loops along the way, so you don't have to retrace your path. The Chimney is very popular with intermediate and skilled riders.

The **Oak Bottom Water Ditch Trail** (5.5 miles, easy) is ideal for beginners. It's both flat and attractive and runs along Whiskeytown Lake with lots of good spots to pull over and take a break—or even swim—if you get tired of riding. Parking is available at the trailhead, about five miles west of the Whiskeytown visitors center, near the Oak Bottom Campground.

Accommodations and Camping

The **Oak Bottom Campground** (530/359-2269 or 800/365-2267, www.whiskeytownmarinas.com) is located within Whiskeytown National Recreation Area but managed by a for-profit concessionaire called Forever Resorts. This is the only campground on the shores of Whiskeytown Lake, and it offers 94 tent sites and 22 RV sites. The sites right on the lake—where you can tether a boat at your campsite—are $25; the other tent sites are $23, and RV sites are $20 in summer.

October-April all sites are $11, and reservations usually aren't needed. A beach for swimming and shower facilities are available. Cold showers are free, but hot ones cost a little.

Getting There

Whiskeytown is 10 miles (15 minutes) directly west of I-5 in Redding on Highway 299.

WEAVERVILLE

Located about 50 miles west of Redding, Weaverville is the county seat of Trinity County and is listed on the National Register of Historic Places. Weaverville is on the south side of the Trinity Alps Wilderness Area in the Klamath Mountains. A charming little town in its own right, it is also a good starting point for hikes and other adventures in the Trinity Alps.

Sights

Weaverville Joss House State Historic Park (southwest corner of Hwy. 299 and Oregon St., 530/623-5284, www.parks.ca.gov, 10am-4pm Thurs.-Sun., adults $4, ages 6-17 $2) has been part of California's state park system since 1956, but the temple it preserves and celebrates has been around much longer. The Temple of the Forest beneath the Clouds, also known as Joss House, is California's oldest Chinese temple in continual use. A Taoist house of worship, it is now a museum as well. The current building was erected in 1874 as a replacement for a previous incarnation that was lost in a fire. Through displays of Chinese art, mining tools, and weapons used in the 1854 Tong War, this museum tells some of the Chinese immigrant history in California. Admission includes a tour of the temple (hourly 10am-4pm).

Accommodations

Southwest of Weaverville near the small town of Hayfork is an unusual lodging. The **Forest Glen Guard Station** (Hwy. 36, Forest Glen, 877/444-6777 or 530/628-5227, www.recreation.gov, mid-Apr.-Dec., $35-75) was built in 1916 and is the oldest Forest Service building in the Shasta-Trinity National Forest. The two-story building has an indoor kitchen and bath, a large porch, and sleeps up to eight. It's near the South Fork of the Trinity River, so both the swimming and hiking nearby are excellent.

Food

Red House Coffee (86 S. Miner St., 530/623-1635, 6:30am-6pm Mon.-Fri., 7:30am-6pm Sat. summer., 6:30am-5:30pm Mon.-Fri., 7:30am-6pm Sat. winter, $5-12) is a cute, friendly diner in a historical 1930s building, serving breakfast, lunch, and the gamut of coffee beverages, including a few house specialties.

Beckett's Trail End Steakhouse (1324 Nugget Ln., 530/623-2900, noon-3pm, 4:30pm-7pm Mon., 4:30pm-9pm Tues. and Thurs., 11am-3pm, 4:30pm-9pm Wed. and Fri.-Sat. summer, shorter winter hours, $10-30) doesn't let diners go home hungry. The plate-busting portions come with two generous sides like the sweet potato fries or crunchy onion rings; a big hit is the Black and Blue Steak, which comes slathered in a Cajun rub and bleu cheese.

Information and Services

The U.S. Forest Service maintains **Weaverville Ranger Station** (360 Main St., 530/623-2121, www.fs.usda.gov, 8am-4:30pm Mon.-Fri.). The Forest Service offers free recreation maps and boating safety maps for Shasta Lake and Trinity Lake if you come to the office in person. And if you get here after hours, don't despair: They have a self-service center in front of the office where you can get a campfire permit or a Trinity Alps Wilderness permit.

Getting There

Weaverville is due west of Shasta Lake. The nearest airport is in Redding, and the drive from Redding to Weaverville, west on Highway 299, takes about an hour. If you're driving from San Francisco's airport or elsewhere in the Bay Area, take I-80 east to I-505 north to I-5 north. At Redding get onto Highway 44 west, and then follow signs for Highway 299 west to Weaverville. From Sacramento, the trip is just over 200 miles (3.5 hours).

TRINITY ALPS

The **Trinity Alps Wilderness** (530/226-2500, www.fs.usda.gov) is one of the five federally designated wilderness areas within the Shasta-Trinity National Forest. At 517,000 acres, it's the second-largest wilderness area in California. The Alps themselves are part of the Klamath Mountain Range, and their highest point is Thompson Peak (8,994-9,002 feet, depending on who you ask). This area seems somewhat resistant to climate change, and the Alps encompass various small glaciers and permanent snowfields, including a 15-acre glacier on the north side of Thompson Peak. The forest is noted for its wide variety of conifers: subalpine fir, ponderosa pine, foxtail pine, and incense cedar are just a few of the trees you'll find. Wildflower enthusiasts will find the rare Trinity penstemon (*Penstemon tracyi*)—almost worth a trip on its own. Naturally enough, given the minimal human use of this area, birds, fish, and wildlife abound as well. You're likely to encounter black bears as well as deer, California newts, and maybe even the Trinity Alps giant salamander, an elusive alligator-size creature that may or may not exist but holds a place in the annals of cryptozoology—our own Loch Ness Monster of the woods.

Natural Bridge

The striking **Natural Bridge** of Trinity-Shasta National Forest has both geological and historical significance. This natural limestone arch spans a 200-foot ravine near Hayfork. Names and dates engraved in the limestone attest to the fact that early pioneers used this as a picnic site. This is also the site of the infamous Bridge Gulch Massacre of 1852, in which a conflict between a band of Wintu people and some prominent Weaverville settlers ended with the deaths of most of the Wintu people living in the area. Striking to behold, this limestone phenomenon is worth a side trip—but be respectful. Descendants of the Wintu still consider this a place of cultural significance. Water, wind, and other forces alter the bridge's natural formation, but the more gently we treat it, the longer it will be around for others to marvel at.

Natural Bridge is about 30 miles southwest of Weaverville. From Weaverville, follow Highway 3 south for 26 miles. Turn left onto Wildwood Road, and in another five miles the road transitions onto Bridge Gulch Road. Natural Bridge is 1.2 miles south on Bridge Gulch Road.

Lewiston Lake

Lewiston Lake is an artificial reservoir created by a dam on the Trinity River. Located less than two miles north of the town of Lewiston, east of Weaverville, Lewiston Lake has a surface area of 750 acres. It's a popular spot for water sports and is particularly celebrated as a fly-fishing destination.

Trinity Lake

In an area rife with clear blue mountain lakes, **Trinity Lake** still manages to stand out. Formed by Trinity Dam, the lake is one of California's largest reservoirs, with 145 miles of shoreline and a capacity of about 2.5 million acre-feet. Trinity Lake was formerly called Clair Engle Lake, in honor of U.S. senator Clair Engle of California, who died in office in 1964. That name never really caught on, and it's easiest to refer to it as Trinity Lake.

Most people value this large lake as an aquatic playground, and it's particularly popular with water-skiers and houseboaters. If you're interested in renting or docking a houseboat, the lake has three marinas: **Trinity Alps Marina** (530/286-2282, www.trinityalpsmarina.com, 8am-5pm daily May-mid-Oct., $357-767 per day, ski boats and pontoon boats $40-375) in the south offers 50-foot houseboat rentals in midsummer; **Cedar Stock Marina** (530/286-2225 or 800/255-5561, www.trinitylakeresort.com, 8am-6pm daily Apr.-Oct., $560-1,200 per day) in the west also has 50-foot houseboat rentals; and **Trinity Center Marina** (530/286-2225 or 800/255-5561, www.trinitylakeresort.com, 8am-6pm daily May-Oct.), near the north end, offers private moorings (full season $1,000) but no boat rentals.

For technical data about reservoirs, storage capacity, precipitation, and climate, check http://cdec.water.ca.gov/reservoir.html. Trinity Lake is located along Highway 3 at the eastern edge of the Trinity Alps, north of the also-large Lewiston Lake and west of Shasta Lake.

Hiking

Hiking opportunities in the Trinity Alps abound. However, this is not the place to go for short, easy hikes; it is largely a backpacking destination, and if your interest in hiking is more about communing with nature, you can go for days in the wilderness without seeing anyone else. That said, a couple hikes start near Weaverville that can get you into the Trinity Alps.

One of the most popular hikes in the Trinity Alps is the **Granite Peak Trail** (9 miles round-trip). This trek to the summit of Granite Peak gains more than 4,000 feet of elevation in a fairly short distance—if you're into views, this is the way to get them. From the summit, you can survey vast areas of the Trinity Alps plus Trinity Lake, Mount Shasta, and Mount Lassen. To reach the trailhead from Weaverville, drive north on Highway 3 and look for the signed Stoney Ridge Trailhead. Shortly after the sign, turn left onto Granite Peak Road (Forest Rd. 35N28Y) and continue approximately three miles until you reach a spacious turnaround area; park here to start the hike.

For a particularly rewarding backcountry hike, head for the **Rush Creek Lakes Trail** (8 miles, moderate-strenuous). The trail passes Lower, Middle, and Upper Rush Creek Lakes along its route. Each of the three lakes provides enough fish (especially brook trout) for a good supper if you're a patient angler and don't mind cleaning and cooking a bunch of little ones instead of one big one. Much of the terrain along this hike is rocky, uphill, or both, but it's well worth the trouble if you like cool mountain lakes and a serious break from civilization. This trail is great for an overnight backpacking trip but is good as a challenging day hike as well. To reach the trailhead from Weaverville, follow Highway 3 north for about eight miles. Turn right onto unmarked Kenney Camp Road, a dirt road about one mile north of Rush Creek Camp Road.

The **Stuart Fork Trail** leads to beautiful Emerald and Sapphire Lakes; this is a good trail into the heart of the Trinity Alps. The whole trail is approximately 30 miles out and back (2-4 days) with 3,000-4,000 feet of elevation gain. However, you can opt for just a short day hike and turn around when you've had enough of the mountains, valleys, and forest. The trailhead is north of Weaverville; take Highway 3 north for 13 miles until it becomes Trinity Lake Boulevard, and then turn left onto Trinity Alps Road.

Fishing

Trinity and Lewiston Lakes are good places to catch rainbow trout, brown trout, and smallmouth bass. The McCloud, Upper Sacramento, and Trinity Rivers are also rife with trout. Fishing licenses are required and are available for a day or for life; prices and requirements vary. For more information, contact the California Department of Fish and Game (601 Locust St., Redding, 530/225-2300, www.dfg.ca.gov, 8am-4:30pm Mon.-Fri.).

John Gray, who calls himself **The Maine Guide** (530/739-0242, www.snowcrest.net/themaineguide, $360 per day for 2 people including lunch), takes visitors on fishing trips to Lewiston Lake and Trinity Lakes. Gray will also help design a personal fishing adventure, which might include hiking to nearby alpine lakes instead of going out on his boat.

Scott Stratton at **Trinity River Adventures** (361 Ponderosa Pines Rd., Lewiston, 530/623-4179, www.trinityriveradventures.com, $450-550 per day for 1-2 people including lunch) takes anglers out on his 16-foot Lowe jet boat on Lewiston Lake or the Trinity River. Trips include a gourmet lunch as well as fly-fishing instruction.

Helpful and knowledgeable Liam Gogan of **Trinity River Outfitters** (1 Steiner Flat Rd., 530/623-6224, Douglas City, http://trinityriveoutfitters.com, $465 per day for two people) has 35 years of fishing experience. He will take you out in a drift boat on the Trinity River and supply top-quality gear for your trip; all you need is a fishing license, a steelhead punch card, and your own waders.

Travis Michel from **Sweet Trinity Fishing Guide Service** (Weaverville, 530/623-4695 or 530/623-7654, http://www.sweet-trinity.com, $300-$325 per 4 hours for 1-2 people, $375-425 per day for 1-2 people) is known among locals as the "long-haired guide who likes to have fun," and indeed, the man has a glorious mullet. He's also a friendly and innovative resource for rookie anglers looking to bag their first steelhead or salmon on either the Trinity or Lower Sacramento Rivers while also respecting the local ecology.

Versatile **Steve Huber** (530/623-1918, www.stevehuberguideservice.com, $200-225 pp) takes anglers out on the Trinity River in a drift boat or powerboat, as well as on the Rogue, Oregon, Klamath, and Sacramento Rivers. Huber supplies the gear and assists with fly-fishing, bait casting, or trolling—you name it. Plan to bring your own lunch.

Camping

A good campground near Trinity Lake, with easy access to the boat dock, is the U.S. Forest Service's **Bushytail Campground** (near Hwy. 3, 16 miles north of Weaverville, 877/444-6777, www.recreation.gov, May 15-Sept., tents $10, RVs $12-22.50). Of Bushytail's 12 large wooded sites, nine have electrical hookups. Amenities include flush toilets, drinking water, and showers. It has a two-night minimum on weekends and a three-night minimum on holidays.

Also located near Trinity Lake is the larger **Hayward Flat Campground** (near Hwy. 3, 15 miles north of Weaverville, 877/444-6777, www.recreation.gov, mid-May-mid-Sept., $18-30). Amenities at the 98 sites include flush toilets and drinking water, and there is an amphitheater and ranger programs. It is popular because of its proximity to Trinity Lake, which makes it a great spot for swimming, fishing, and family vacations.

Information and Services

In Lewiston, stock up on supplies at the **Lewiston Mini Mart** (4789 Trinity Dam Blvd., Lewiston, 530/778-3268, 6:30am-9pm Mon.-Sat., 7am-9pm Sun.).

Getting There

The Trinity River Scenic Byway (Hwy. 299) stretches from Redding west through Whiskeytown, Weaverville, and all the way to Arcata on the coast. In Weaverville, Highway 3 runs north-south through the Trinity Alps region, past Trinity and Lewiston Lakes, and as far north as Yreka, where it connects with I-5.

Shasta Lake

Shasta Lake doesn't look like most lakes. Rather than a bowl shape, the lake is fed by three major rivers—the Sacramento, the Pit, and the McCloud—plus Squaw Creek, and each of these has an arm of the lake named after it. To create this sprawling artificial lake, five towns were drowned. The remains are still down there, most sunk so deep that even scuba divers cannot explore them. Altogether, the lake has 29,500 acres of surface area, and it's 517 feet deep when it's full. It also has 369 miles of shoreline, which means lots of great places for camping in a tent or an RV as well as hiking and wildlife-viewing. The unusual layout of this lake makes it all the more interesting for houseboats, waterskiing, fishing, swimming, canoeing, and wakeboarding.

The lake's four main arms and its many inlets all have their own characters, shapes, and surprises. Surrounding many fingers of the lake and some of the bigger pools are marinas, campgrounds, resorts, cabins, and restaurants for lakeside vacations. Marinas dot the shores of the lake's fingers, offering boat rentals, gas, snacks, water, ice, and more. For those few who don't want to spend all day every day on the water, hiking trails and 4WD roads thread through the forested wilderness areas surrounding the lake.

There are several very small towns close to Shasta Lake and Shasta Dam. At the south side of the lake is the tiny City of Shasta Lake. You won't find much besides a couple of motels and a pizza parlor. At the north side of the lake is Lakehead, right on I-5 midway between Redding to the south and the City of Mount Shasta to the north.

SIGHTS

★ Lake Shasta Caverns

Summer lake visitors can find themselves longing for cool air—hard to come by at Shasta in August. The best natural air-conditioning in the region is inside the **Lake**

Shasta Lake

Shasta Caverns (20359 Shasta Caverns Rd., Lakehead, 530/238-2752 or 800/795-2283, www.lakeshastacaverns.com, 9am-4pm daily Memorial Day-Labor Day, 9am-3pm daily Apr.-May and Sept., tours 10am, noon, 2pm daily Oct.-Mar., adults $24, ages 3-15 $14). Tours begin across the lake from the caverns at the Caverns Park and gift shop. In summer, tours leave every 30 minutes 9am-4pm. When your tour is called, you walk down to the boat launch and board a broad flat-bottomed ferry with plenty of bench seats and a canopy. On the quick ride across a narrow section of the lake, the pilot regales you with tales of the caverns. At the dock, where boaters can meet their tour groups, if they prefer, you board a bus and take a staggeringly steep drive 800 feet up to the cavern entrance. The road has some fabulous views out over the lake and all the way to Mount Shasta.

Your cavern tour guide meets you at the entrance and leads you into an artificial tunnel. You'll head up a bunch of stairs and into a series of natural limestone and marble caverns. The guide describes the amazing formations that spring from the walls, the ceiling, and the floor. The cathedral size of most of the cavern areas and the railed walkways help to remind visitors not to touch the delicate stalactites, drapes, pancakes, and ribbons of "cave bacon" that decorate each space. You're welcome to bring a camera to record the marvels here, but memories may provide better lighting.

Both kids and adults enjoy the tour of the Lake Shasta Caverns, but you'll want to keep an eye on younger children throughout the trip for their safety. No matter how hot it is outside, bring a jacket or sweater for your tour; the caverns remain cold year-round. The tour isn't extremely strenuous, but you need to be able to walk and to climb 100 stairs at a time. To get to Shasta Caverns, take the exit for O'Brien Road on I-5 north of Redding.

Shasta Caverns also offers a **Lake Shasta Dinner Cruise** (530/238-2752 or 800/795-2283, www.lakeshastadinnercruises.com, 6pm-8pm Fri.-Sat. Memorial Day-Labor Day, adults $65, under age 12 $33). The cruises depart from the Lake Shasta Caverns' Gift Store, the same location as the regular cavern boat trips, 17 miles north of Redding, near I-5 exit 695. Dinner cruises may also be available at

Lake Shasta Caverns

a slightly earlier time for a few weeks after Labor Day; call for reservations.

★ Shasta Dam

Completed in 1945 and operated by the U.S. Bureau of Reclamation, **Shasta Dam** is a massive concrete dam that is second in size only to Hoover Dam. At 60 stories high and weighing 30 billion pounds, it is an impressive sight, and the water it stores is one of the reasons California has such fertile farmland.

Even if you're not fascinated by engineering statistics and superlatives, the one-hour **tour** (9am, 10:15am, 11:30am, 1pm, 2:15pm, and 3:30pm daily Memorial Day-Labor Day, 9am, 11am, 1pm, and 3pm daily Labor Day-Memorial Day, free) is a great experience, and it offers one of the best ways to get a broad view of Shasta Lake. Tours are limited to 40 people; it's recommended to arrive 45 minutes before start time. The tours begin at the **visitors center** (530/275-4463, 8am-5pm daily). It's a bit of a walk from the parking lot. To explore the area yourself, you can walk across Shasta Dam daily 6am-10pm to take in the views of the lake and Mount Shasta. This is a beautiful walk, especially at sunset, and one of many wonderful vantage points to see and photograph the mountain.

Shasta Dam is officially located at 16349 Shasta Dam Boulevard. To get here, take I-5 exit 685 onto Shasta Dam Boulevard. Drive west six miles on Highway 151 to the Shasta Dam visitors center.

SPORTS AND RECREATION

Houseboating and Marinas

Most of the marinas along the shores of Shasta Lake provide all the rentals and services you'll need. If you've got a vacation rental or a campsite on or near the lake, you'll probably want to pick one of the marinas near your lodgings for convenience; Shasta Lake really is that big and definitely that spread out. But not all marinas offer public gas docks or public launch facilities, and one or two of them are maintained for the owners of private slips.

SHASTA MARINA RESORT

One of the nearest marinas to the Shasta Caverns gift shop and loading dock is the **Shasta Marina Resort** (18390 O'Brien

Shasta Dam

Houseboating on Shasta Lake

Shasta Lake PR agencies have named the lake "the houseboating capital of the world." That bold statement may or may not be true, but Shasta Lake certainly is California's most popular houseboating destination. It's quite difficult to find a houseboat that sleeps fewer than 10 people (most sleep 14-18) and a few true leviathans can hold more than 20 partiers. The beds aren't big, and private bedrooms are few, so for true comfort it's best to pile in no more than half to two-thirds the recommended number of overnight guests.

You can rent a houseboat at almost any marina on the lake. No special boating knowledge is required to rent a houseboat, though you may be required to provide a valid driver's license. Most marina websites post photos and price lists; for example, **Houseboats.com** (877/468-7326, www.houseboats.com), which works with the Jones Valley Resort at Shasta Lake, includes blogs, photos, and information about the lake while you shop online. Whichever marina you rent from, expect to pay anywhere from $2,000 per weekend for a small minimal craft to $9,100 per weekend for a huge luxury boat. Weekly rates, which include one weekend, are often a bargain at double or less the cost of a single weekend.

Expect to find a fair amount of luxury; many Shasta houseboats come with upper-deck hot tubs, waterslides, barbecues, satellite TV, and high-end entertainment systems. Your houseboat will also come with some necessities—most have fully equipped kitchens, basic cleaning supplies, and basic sanitary supplies (meaning toilet paper). But you'll need to bring a bunch of your own stuff too, such as pillows, towels, sheets, paper towels, folding chairs, ski-quality life jackets, and first-aid kits—as well as food and booze, of course. Talk to your rental company about the full list of supplies they recommend to bring.

Piloting a mammoth houseboat on the waters of Shasta Lake is a bit like driving a big RV up I-5. Take it slow, carefully follow all the instructions you're given at the marina, and you'll do fine. Most Shasta houseboaters pull their craft into small inlets and moor them for the night. Your marina staff can advise you on how to maneuver your houseboat safely toward shore in the evening and back out again the next morning.

Many Shasta houseboats have the equipment to tow smaller watercraft along behind them. If you choose, you can rent a ski boat, personal watercraft, or fishing boat and bring it along with you as you explore Shasta Lake.

Inlet Rd., Lakehead, 800/959-3359, www.shastalake.net, Apr.-Oct.). Easily accessed from I-5 toward the south end of the lake, this marina offers midsize houseboats and SeaSwirl BowRider ski boats with wakeboard towers. A 56-foot houseboat, which sleeps 14 people and has a hot tub, satellite TV, gas fireplace, and swim slide, rents for $3,600 for three nights; there's a three-night minimum in summer. Marina facilities include a gas dock, a convenience store with ice and swimsuits, and a boat launch (free with moorage or houseboat rental). This middle-of-the road rental spot definitely offers friendly service, so be sure to ask about good houseboating spots if you're new to Shasta Lake.

PACKERS BAY MARINA

The **Packers Bay Marina** (16814 Packers Bay Rd., Lakehead, 530/275-5570 or 800/331-3137, www.packersbay.com, 8am-6pm Mon.-Sat., weekly houseboat rentals $1,365-7,135) is located in Packers Bay, a couple of miles west of I-5 near the big bridge. Getting to the marina from Redding is tricky; you must get off northbound I-5 at the exit for Shasta Caverns and O'Brien Road, then get back on I-5 southbound to reach the Packers Bay Road exit. A small independent operator, this marina offers some of the rare honest-to-goodness modest houseboats on Shasta Lake. These can sleep 10 people but are really comfortable for groups of 4-6 and are less expensive than the bigger models. Packers Bay Marina offers only houseboats and fewer services than the larger places. But houseboat renters can expect more personal service and nicer boats than at the big marinas. No pets are allowed on any boats.

BRIDGE BAY RESORT MARINA

You can see the **Bridge Bay Resort Marina** (10300 Bridge Bay Rd., Redding, 530/275-3021 or 800/752-9669, www.bridgebayhouseboats.com, patio boat $110-840, ski boat $190-1,250, houseboat $1,050-3,500) from the big bridge on I-5. This huge marina, the largest on the lake, is part of a full-scale resort that sees some real crowds in the summer. Bridge Bay Marina has a large rental fleet, which includes small-medium houseboats, closed-bow speedboats, patio boats, and ski boats with or without a tower, most of which can be rented by the day or by the week, as well as for two-hour or four-hour periods. Fishing boat rentals, for example, start at $55 for a half-day. If you bring your own boat, it's $15 per day to launch it here, but you get one free launch with any room or other rental. You can also moor your boat temporarily. Three docks are available for service of various kinds: the Gas Dock, where you can also get ice, propane, and pump-outs of your holding tank; the Load-out Dock, for houseboat customers of Bridge Bay only; and the Courtesy Dock, which is open to the public and located next to the launch ramp. If you pull up and park your boat at the Courtesy Dock, it's just a short walk to the store (7am-7pm daily May-Aug.) where you can get groceries, bathing suits, bait and tackle, and souvenirs. You can also walk to the marina's restaurant, the **Tail O' the Whale** (10300 Bridge Bay Rd., Redding, 800/752-9669, www.sevencrown.com, $12-20). There's good fishing all year; around Bridge Bay, anglers hook catfish, trout, sturgeon, and bass. In winter Bridge Bay hosts bass-fishing tournaments.

JONES VALLEY MARINA

One of the few year-round marinas on Shasta Lake, the **Jones Valley Marina** (22300 Jones Valley Marina Dr., Redding, 530/275-7950 or 877/468-7326, www.houseboats.com, houseboats $3,533-15,965) is situated on the secluded Pit River Arm, away from the higher-traffic areas near the bridge, but it is still easily accessible from Redding and I-5. The McCloud Arm and the Squaw Creek Arm adjoin this marina, which is one of the few that sells gas in this part of the lake. Jones Valley Marina is part of a larger resort and includes a floating recreation area in addition to wheelchair-accessible docks and houseboats. Should you find yourself needing a three-deck houseboat that sleeps 22 people with eight flat-screen TVs, you can rent it—it's called *The Titan*—at Jones Valley. They've also got more modest houseboats, plus the usual array of patio party boats and smaller craft, including a top-tier wakeboard-ready speedboat.

SUGARLOAF RESORT

If you have your own boat and need a place to dock it for the summer, contact **Sugarloaf Resort** (19761 Lakeshore Dr., Lakehead, 877/468-7326, www.houseboats.com, May-Oct., full season $1,095) on the Sacramento River Arm. Formerly a full-service marina, Sugarloaf now operates only as a moorage for small private boats. Their modern wheelchair-accessible concrete docks are an appealing starting point for boating adventures, and the docks are a little distance from the busier boating areas on the lake, making it a quiet place to get used to the water before you have to contend with serious traffic.

Fishing and Patio Boating

If you just want to go out and putter on the lake for a day or host a sunset cocktail party, and all those beds and kitchens in the houseboats seem like overkill, what you want is a patio boat. These flat-bottomed pontoon-style boats rent by the hour and by the day and are much cheaper than houseboats. Most come with plenty of seating and canopies for shade. Larger patio boats might have barbecues and storage chests as well. You're free to bring your own coolers, fishing gear, stereo, and friends.

Bridge Bay Resort (10300 Bridge Bay

Rd., Redding, 530/275-3021 or 800/752-9669, www.bridgebayhouseboats.com) rents patio boats ($190 per day) and fishing boats ($89 per day). At **Jones Valley Marina** (22300 Jones Valley Marina Dr., Redding, 503/275-7950 or 877/468-7326, www.houseboats.com), you can rent a 30-foot patio boat ($230-295 per day), and choose from two options with capacity for 10 people; one boat is slightly larger and has a shower on board. Jones Valley also rents 14-foot aluminum fishing boats ($65 per day).

Waterskiing and Wakeboarding

Shasta Lake is an ideal place to water-ski and wakeboard; even on crowded weekends, chances are good that you'll find a place to water-ski. Most marinas rent recreation equipment for waterskiing and wakeboarding. **Bridge Bay Resort** (10300 Bridge Bay Rd., Redding, 530/275-3021 or 800/752-9669, www.bridgebayhouseboats.com) rents wakeboards ($37-205), ski boats ($290-310), and water skis ($30 per day). **Jones Valley Marina** (22300 Jones Valley Marina Dr., Redding, 503/275-7950 or 877/468-7326, www.houseboats.com) rents wakeboards, water skis, tubes, and other water play equipment. Ski boat rentals include a 21-foot Malibu Wakesetter ($550 per day), a 22-foot Centurion Wakeboard ($750 per day), and a 19-foot Sea Ray Bowrider ($375 per day). **Shasta Marina Resort** (18390 O'Brien Inlet Rd., Lakehead, 800/959-3359, www.shastalake.net) rents wakeboards ($20 per day) and water skis ($15 per day). Ski boat rentals (3 nights $1,000-1,150) include one pair of water skis. They also rent personal watercraft ($350-1,500). Houseboat renters usually get first dibs on renting ski boats and personal watercraft, so the marina usually doesn't offer reservations for that equipment, but sometimes will rent them out on a walk-up basis.

You can put your own boat in at any number of public launches and rent a slip from one of the marinas. If you don't, you'll find that most of the marinas around the lake rent both speedboats and personal watercraft; a wide selection is available. Personal watercraft are mostly WaveRunners and the occasional Sea-Doo (get a Sea-Doo if you can; they're better machines). Prices run about $70-130 per hour, with good half-day, full-day, and full-week rates available at most marinas. Be aware that no matter what marina you work with, these are high-performance rental boats, and problems sometimes crop up.

If you'd like a guided boating adventure on a 22-foot professional series Sanger wakeboard boat, check with the **Fun Factory** (Weed, 530/925-1465 or 530/926-5387, www.funfactoryrentals.com, $140-550, reservations required). The same friendly people who bring you snowmobile rentals and tours in winter will take you out on their boats in summer. They operate on five lakes: Shasta, Shastina, Siskiyou, McCloud Reservoir, and Iron Gate Reservoir, so you can take your pick. Training in water and boat safety is included.

ENTERTAINMENT AND EVENTS

The main entertainment in the Shasta Lake area centers on the lake itself. The cool thing to do is to rent a patio boat or houseboat and throw your own party on the water. The major festival at Shasta Lake each year is the annual **Shasta Damboree** (530/949-2759, www.shastadamboree.org). The first Friday and Saturday in May is devoted to family-friendly events that bring out the community and draw visitors to the region. The events are typical of a good small-town celebration, with spaghetti feeds, pancake breakfasts, an arts-and-crafts area, and a parade and evening party with fireworks and live music.

Some of the best drinking, pool playing, and occasional live music happens up on the northern Sacramento River Arm, just off the I-5 at **The Basshole** (20725 Lakeshore Dr., Lakehead, 530/238-2170, www.bassholebarandgrill.com). This bar, restaurant, and pool hall are all in one large hall, with the bait shop hiding in a tiny room just off the dining area. The food is nothing special, though for dinner they put out an array of slightly fancier entrées. Locals come for the beer.

Another option for a little nightlife is the

Wonderland Tavern (15041 Wonderland Blvd., Redding, 530/275-5669, noon-10pm Mon.-Sat., $4) just off I-5, where they serve drinks and inexpensive appetizers. Wonderland has karaoke on Friday night and often stays open until 11:30pm if it's going strong—but there is no guarantee about the business hours. The owner makes the decision depending on the crowd.

You could try the **Idle Hour Bar & Grill** (14961 Bear Mountain Rd., Redding, 530/275-0230, 11am-8:30pm daily, $5-16), south of the Silverthorn Resort, close to the intersection of Bear Mountain Road and Silverthorn Road, for beer, wine, burgers, and a rotating menu of dinner specials—Friday is prime-rib night.

ACCOMMODATIONS

Lakehead's cutest motel is the bright-yellow **Lakehead Lodge** (21417 Main St., Lakehead, 530/238-9688, www.lakeheadlodge.com, summer $70-95, fall-spring $50-75), which offers small but adequate rooms with free wireless Internet access. The distinctive hand-painted tables help make this a cheerful oasis in a quiet woodsy area, and the motel has the advantage of being very close to the lake. It's a good alternative if you're visiting Mount Shasta but you can't find lodging there. The city of Mount Shasta can get crowded on holiday weekends, and Lakehead is quite close.

If your main purpose is to visit Shasta Dam, a good place to stay is the **Shasta Dam Motel** (1529 Cascade Blvd., Shasta Lake, 530/275-1065, www.shastadammotel.com, $50-75). Just four miles from the dam, this is a simple little motel without many amenities, but it does have an outdoor pool. Free Internet access is also on the menu, though management does not guarantee that it's always working.

In the woods one mile south of the lakeshore, the **Fawndale Lodge & RV Park** (15215 Fawndale Rd., 530/275-8000 or 800/38-0941, www.fawndale.com, $73-123) offers comfortable lodge rooms and cabins at bargain prices. You can't see the lake from the lodge, but the surrounding forest has charm, and the garden and pool offer beauty. Rooms include a fridge, a microwave, and a private bath. Suites have full kitchens, sleeping space for six, and air-conditioning. The decor is rustic wood walls and furniture. Tent campers are welcome at Fawndale ($18-21); full-hookup RV spots ($30) are available, though you may need a reservation to guarantee a spot.

Toward the north end of the lake, the **Shasta Lake Motel** (20714 Lakeshore Dr., Lakehead, 530/238-2545 or 886/355-8189, www.shastalakemotel.com, $80-140) is a favorite for regular visitors. For low rates you'll get air-conditioning, cable TV, and microwaves. Each room glows softly with wood-paneled walls and furniture, and the decor is rustic prints and artifacts. All the twin and double beds are extra-long, making them a treat for people over six feet tall. Enjoy the motel pool or walk down to the shores of the lake. The motel is only a few minutes off I-5, close enough for convenience but not so near that you'll be listening to the trucks all night.

The ★ **Bridge Bay Resort** (10300 Bridge Bay Rd., Redding, 800/752-9669, www.sevencrown.com, $115-190) has one of the best locations of any resort here, right where the big I-5 bridge crosses the lake. It's close to the center of the lake's arms, making its full-service marina a perfect spot from which to launch a boat. Bridge Bay also includes a restaurant and a store with groceries, souvenirs, and bait and tackle. The lodgings aren't terribly stylish; rooms are decorated with particle-board furniture and generic prints. But this is a cheerful, family-friendly place—many of the rooms sleep 4-6, and some have full kitchens.

Well east of I-5, on the tip of a small peninsula in the Pit River Arm, the **Silverthorn Resort** (16250 Silverthorn Rd., Redding, 530/275-1571, www.silverthornresort.com, $594-1,194 per week, houseboats $4,990-8,490 for 7 nights) has the advantage of a location right on the water. The views from the common areas and guest cabins are phenomenal, and the resort has its own full-service marina with houseboats for rent. Cabins rent only by the week in summer and require a three-day minimum the rest of the year. Each cabin sleeps 4-6 people (the large family cabin can handle eight). Inside, you'll find wood-paneled interior walls and simple but attractive lodge-style decor. All cabins include a full kitchen with a full-size fridge. Bedrooms are small but cute, and the atmosphere is woodsy and restful. Book your boat rentals with the marina at the same time you book your cabin to ensure that you get what you want. A small grocery store and a "Pizza and Pub" room offer easy shopping and dining on-site.

CAMPING

For a nominal fee, the U.S. Forest Service rents ★ **Hirz Mountain Lookout Tower** (information 530/275-8113, reservations 877/444-6777, www.recreation.gov, late Apr.-mid-Oct., up to 4 people $75). Located in the Shasta-Trinity National Forest, this 20-foot tower is on top of a 3,540-foot peak, so the views are phenomenal. In addition to the vast overview of the McCloud Arm, you can see both Mount Lassen and Mount Shasta. Getting here is a little tricky. Drive 5 miles down a dirt road (Forest Rd. 35N04) in a high-clearance 4WD vehicle, then walk the last 0.25 miles, and climb a couple of flights of metal steps to the tower.

For more traditional camping in the vicinity of Shasta Lake, one of the best places around is the **Hirz Bay Campground** (Gilman Rd., 20 miles northeast of Redding, 530/275-1589, www.fs.usda.gov, reservations 877/444-6777, www.recreation.gov, reservations accepted mid-May-mid-September, walk-ups only mid-Sept.-mid-May, $20-35). This 42-site U.S. Forest Service family campground has nice amenities such as flush toilets, picnic tables, and paved parking. It also offers easy access to the lake via the Hirz Bay boat ramp.

FOOD

The **Tail O' the Whale** (10300 Bridge Bay Rd., Redding, 530/275-3021, www.sevencrown.com, breakfast, lunch, and dinner daily, $8-20) at the Bridge Bay Resort has a casual dining room that's perfect for lakeside vacationers. The lengthy menu has plenty of American favorites. Breakfast is ordinary but hearty, with a bit of a Southern accent: Biscuits and gravy are served along with the usual eggs and pancakes. Lunch is the usual burgers, BLTs, and chicken salad with the addition of a Pacific Northwest salmon entrée. Dinner has the full range of surf-and-turf, from calamari and salmon to prime rib and pork loin. Seating is on the porch or inside with views of Shasta Lake through the large windows. Upstairs is the **Pelican's Perch Cocktail Lounge** (4pm-close Thurs.-Sun.), with its own share of views.

On the east side of the lake, the Silverthorn Resort has the best (and only) pizza at the **Silverthorn Pizza and Pub** (16250 Silverthorn Rd., Redding, 530/275-1571 or 800/332-3044, www.silverthornresort.com, 4pm-9pm Thurs., 2pm-midnight Fri., noon-midnight Sat., noon-9pm Sun. late May-early Sept., $6-29). This casual eatery offers ice-cold beer and piping-hot pizzas. A huge deck overlooking the lake lures people out for cocktails.

In the little town of Shasta Lake, you'll find fast food as well as one local place with a little character, the **Old Mill Eatery** (4132 Shasta Dam Blvd., Shasta Lake, 530/275-0515, 7am-3pm Wed. and Fri.-Sun., 8am-2pm Thurs. $11-16), noted for its large portions of basic fare such as hamburgers, omelets, and pancakes, its low prices, and its friendly hometown atmosphere.

The **Lakeshore Village Market** (20750 Lakeshore Dr., Lakehead, 530/238-8615, 7am-8pm daily winter, 7am-9pm Sun.-Thurs., 7am-10pm Fri.-Sat. Memorial Day-Oct.) has plenty of food plus basic camping, fishing, and outdoor recreation supplies for visitors staying at the north end of the lake. The market often stays open until 10pm during the summer if business permits.

INFORMATION AND SERVICES

Stop in at the **Shasta Lake Visitors Center** (14250 Holiday Rd., Mountain Gate,

530/275-1589, www.fs.usda.gov, 9am-5pm Thurs.-Mon. Memorial Day-Labor Day), a U.S. Forest Service facility set up specifically to provide information for visitors. During the off-season (Labor Day-Memorial Day), when the visitors center is closed, go across the street to the **Shasta Lake Ranger Station** (530/275-1587, www.fs.usda.gov, 8am-4:30pm Mon.-Fri. year-round) for campfire permits and permits to enter the Trinity Alps Wilderness. These are not just backcountry camping permits. In a few wilderness areas, including Trinity Alps, you need a permit to enter. For the Shasta Wilderness, go to the **Mount Shasta Ranger Station** (204 W. Alma St., Mount Shasta, 530/926-4511, 8am-4:30pm Mon.-Sat. Memorial Day-Labor Day, 8am-4:30pm Mon.-Fri. Labor Day-Memorial Day). The nearest major medical facilities are in Redding.

TRANSPORTATION

Most people come to Shasta Lake by car via I-5, which runs over the lake in two different places. Bridge Bay is one of the more popular spots on the lake because of its proximity and easy access to I-5. The Sacramento Arm to the north is also easily accessible from I-5.

Many people bring their own boats to Shasta Lake rather than paying the high fees to rent from the marinas. Check local maps to find the public launch nearest to your accommodations, and expect to pay a small launching fee. Before you launch, your boat may be inspected both for proper state licensing and for pernicious mussels. A special license is not required to pilot a boat in California. All drivers of boats over 15 horsepower (that includes personal watercraft) must be age 16 or older. Children ages 12-15 can drive if directly supervised by an adult. All children under age 13 must wear a life jacket at all times when on board a boat. For more information about boating rules, visit www.dbw.ca.gov.

The nearest full-service airport is **Redding Municipal Airport** (RDD, 6751 Woodrum Circle, Redding, 530/224-4320), where you can rent a car to drive out to the lake.

Lassen Volcanic National Park

Lassen Volcanic National Park (www.nps.gov/lavo, 530/595-4480, 9am-5pm daily, visitors center 530/595-4480, 9am-5pm daily Apr.-Oct., 9am-5pm Wed.-Sun. Nov.-Mar., $10 per vehicle, $5 pp for visitors on bike, motorcycle, foot, or visiting as part of a large group) resulted from the merger of two National Monuments—**Cinder Cone** and **Lassen Peak**—in 1916. As such, it is one of the oldest national parks in the United States; it is also one of the remotest and most primitive. A paved road runs through the middle of the park, making it easy in summer for visitors to enjoy many of the major attractions—including the park's active volcanic features. The rugged weather and isolated location mean that a visit to Lassen Volcanic National Park is a trip to a largely unspoiled wilderness rather than an overdeveloped amusement park with rocks. A good half of the park has only minimal dirt-road access and offers its rugged beauty only to those travelers willing to hike for miles into the backcountry. Even the trails and campgrounds accessible by the paved main road maintain a kind of charm that's hard to find in the more popular California parks.

Mount Lassen itself is an active volcano with a long recorded history of eruptions, the last of which took place in 1914-1917. The mountain is a beautiful sight, and it's only accessible to most people during the short summer months when the temperatures rise and the snow melts.

SIGHTS

Lassen Volcanic National Park has ample hiking trails, lovely little ponds scattered

Lassen Volcanic National Park

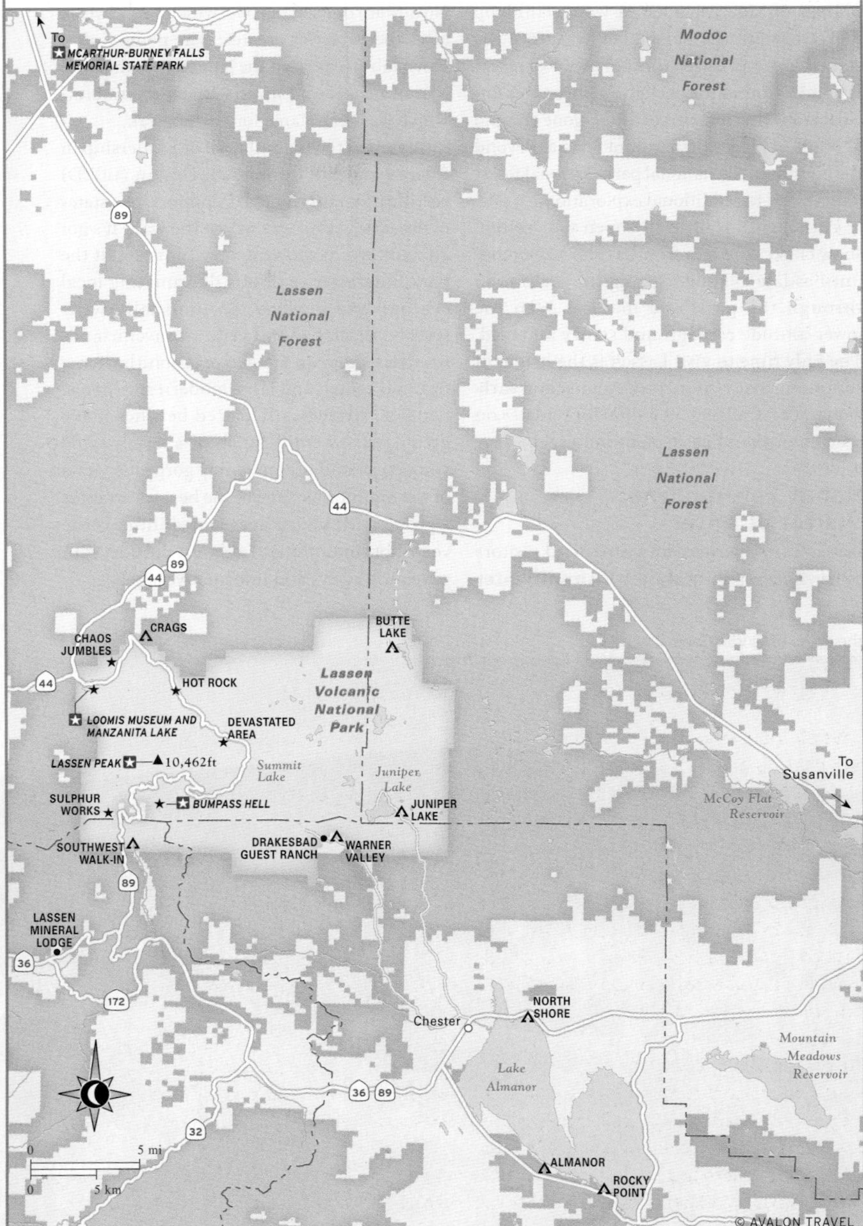

throughout, and many campsites that let visitors settle in and really enjoy the amazing panoramas of Mount Lassen. A wonderful loop drive through the park takes you from the stark slopes and jagged rocks of the most recent eruption around the back to an enormous ancient crater, the remains of a long-gone volcano as big as or bigger than Mount Shasta. Beyond the bounds of the national park, national forest lands allow for additional exploration.

Although it is officially open year-round, snow chokes the area from as early as October until as late as June, closing the main road through the park and making even the lower-altitude campground snowy and cold. The only time to visit Lassen is the height of summer; most visitors pick August and early September. Call 530/595-4480 for updates on road conditions before planning a trip.

Kohm Yah-mah-nee Visitors Center

Lassen's first permanent year-round visitors center, **Kohm Yah-mah-nee Visitors Center** (530/595-4480, www.nps.gov/lavo, 9am-5pm daily Apr.-Oct., 9am-5pm daily Wed.-Sun. Nov.-Mar.) opened in 2008, which was 92 years after the park was created. The name Kohm Yah-mah-nee is from the language of the local Maidu people and means "snow mountain," which was their name for Lassen Peak.

Awarded the highest level of Leadership in Energy and Environmental Design (LEED) certification, this modern, comfortable, state-of-the-art facility was worth the wait. It's got an auditorium showing new films about the park, interactive exhibits illuminating local geology and ecology, an unusually well-stocked snack bar and grill, a souvenir-and-sundries shop, an attractive amphitheater, a first-aid center, and large modern restrooms. Outside, strategically placed benches make great spots to enjoy lunch or a snack while you take a load off and enjoy gorgeous views of the mountains. One of the best features for a group with mixed ages and abilities is the very short interpretive trails just outside, with paved walkways and informative signage.

the crater of Cinder Cone

Located near the southwest entrance to the park on Highway 89, the visitors center is open every day except Thanksgiving and Christmas, and it's accessible even when other roads in the park are closed because of snow (which is common). It's convenient to the Sulphur Works and to the trailheads for Brokeoff Mountain and Ridge Lakes.

★ Lassen Peak

It's not as tall as it used to be, but **Lassen Peak** still reaches 10,457 feet into the sky. Even if you're not up to climbing it, it's worth stopping at the parking lot at the trailhead to crane your neck and enjoy the view. The craggy broken mountain peak is what's left after the most recent eruption—hence the lack of vegetation. The starting elevation for the summit trail is 8,000 feet, which means the Lassen Peak trailhead tends to be cool even in the heat of summer. You may need to break out a windbreaker or light sweater if you plan to explore at length. The **Lassen Peak Trail** (5 miles, difficult) leads to the highest point on Mount Lassen.

★ Loomis Museum and Manzanita Lake

As you enter the northwestern edge of the park on Highway 89, almost immediately you'll find **Loomis Museum** (530/595-6140, 9am-5pm Fri.-Sun. mid-May-mid-June, 9am-5pm daily mid-June-Oct., free) and **Manzanita Lake.** Inside the museum is a wonderful opportunity to learn about the known history of Mount Lassen, focusing heavily on the 1914-1915 eruptions photographed by Mr. B. F. Loomis. Prints of those rare and stunning photos have been enlarged and captioned to create these exhibits; the museum was named for the photographer, who later became a major player in the push to make Mount Lassen a national park. This interpretive museum offers a rare chance to see, through photos, the devastation and following stages of regrowth of the ecosystem on the volcanic slopes.

Chaos Jumbles

The broken and decimated area known as

view of Lassen Peak

Chaos Jumbles may seem like another spot that was splashed with rocks and lava during the 1915 eruption of Mount Lassen, but rather than a volcanic eruption, this interesting formation was actually caused by a massive avalanche about 300 years ago. The results look similar to the regions affected by volcanoes, with devastation of the living ecosystem, displacement of massive rocks, and the general disorder of the landscape. The avalanche that occurred here was so big and came down so fast that it actually trapped a pocket of air underneath it, adding to the destruction. Now visitors can enjoy a wealth of new life, including a broader-than-average variety of coniferous trees. The newness of the living landscape has allowed a greater variety of competing types of plants to get a foothold.

Hot Rock

No, it's not hot anymore, but this huge boulder, called **Hot Rock,** was untouchable back when the Loomises explored the eruption zone soon after the 1915 blast. Frankly, the site isn't all that amazing now, except when you think that that big rock remained warm to the touch for months. The Hot Rock turnout also offers more great views of the Devastated Area.

Devastated Area

It seems like an odd name for a point of interest, but in fact the **Devastated Area** is one of the most fascinating geological and ecological sites in California. When Mount Lassen blew its top in 1915 after nearly a year of sporadic eruptions, a tremendous part of the mountain and all the life on its slopes was destroyed. Boiling mud and exploding gases tore off the side of Lassen's peak and killed all the vegetation in the area. A hail of lava rained down, creating brand-new rocks, in sizes from gravel to boulders, across the north side of the mountain.

Today visitors can easily see how a volcano's surface ecosystem recovers after an eruption. First, park at the Devastated Area lot and take the interpretive walk through a small part of the recently disrupted mountainside. You'll see everything from some of the world's youngest rocks to grasses and shrubs through tall pine trees. Be sure to check out the photos in the Loomis Museum that depict the area during and immediately after the eruption for a great comparison to the spot as it looks now.

The Devastated Area offers ample parking, and the interpretive walk is flat and wheelchair accessible. Don't pick up any of the red and black volcanic rocks; they are part of the redeveloping ecosystem and necessary to the area's recovery.

Summit Lake

Lassen National Park is dotted with tiny lakes, though many might better be called ponds or puddles. One of the most popular and most easily accessible of these is **Summit Lake,** along the main road. The bright and shining small lake attracts many campers to its two forest-shaded campgrounds. There's an easy walk around the lake that lets you see its waters and the plants that proliferate nearby. You can also find one of the small trails down to the edge of the water to eke out a spot on the miniscule beach with all the other visitors who come to escape the heat. You can swim and fish in Summit Lake, and even take rafts and canoes out to paddle around. No power boats are permitted on any lake in Lassen Volcanic National Park.

★ Bumpass Hell

The best and most varied area of volcanic geothermal activity on Lassen is at a location called **Bumpass Hell** (6 miles from the southwest entrance). The region was named for Kendall Vanhook Bumpass, who, during his explorations, stepped through a thin crust over a boiling mud pot and severely burned his leg, ultimately losing the limb. In fact, the tale of the unfortunate Bumpass illustrates a good point for travelers visiting the mud pots and fumaroles: Stay on the paths! The dangers at Bumpass Hell are real, and if you step off the boardwalks or let your children run wild, you are risking serious injury.

Still, a hike down to Bumpass Hell on the

Bumpass Nature Trail is fun. As long as you're careful, it's worth the risk. You'll need to walk about two miles from the parking lot and trailhead out to the interesting stuff—boiling mud pots, fumaroles, steaming springs, and pools of steaming boiling water cluster here. Prepare for the strong smell of sulfur, more evidence that this volcano is anything but extinct. Boardwalks are strategically placed through the area, creating safe walking paths for visitors.

The spacious parking lot at Bumpass offers stunning views to the east and south, giving you a hint at the scope of the ancient volcano that once stood here. Right at the parking lot you can see a famous "glacial erratic," a boulder carried along by a glacier; this one is about 10 feet high, demonstrating the colossal forces of nature that have been at work in this park over the millennia. There are also primitive toilet facilities in the parking lot.

Sulphur Works

For visitors who can't quite manage the trek out to Bumpass Hell, the **Sulphur Works** offers a peek at the geothermal features of Lassen from the main road. A boardwalk runs along the road, and a parking area is nearby, making it easy for visitors to get out of the car and examine the loud boiling mud pots and small steaming stream. The mud pots both look and sound like a washing machine, sending up steam and occasional bursts of boiling water. Keep hold of your children.

Starting from the Sulphur Works is a two-mile round-trip trail to Ridge Lakes. It's a fairly steep climb, but the payoff at the top is a view of two alpine lakes between Brokeoff Mountain and Mount Diller. Along the way, you'll walk through beautiful green meadows dotted with bright yellow wildflowers and then into a forest before reaching the lakes.

RECREATION

Hiking

Most of the easy interpretive walks and short day hikes run out to the sights of Mount Lassen Volcanic National Park. For hikers who want to get out and away from the more heavily visited areas but still make it back to the car before dark, several moderate-difficult hiking trails offer adventure, challenge, and maybe even a touch of solitude.

Be aware that the lower elevations of Mount Lassen's trails are still more than 7,000 feet above sea level. If you're planning to do

Bumpass Hell

serious hiking, it's good to come a day early, if you can, to acclimate to the elevation.

LASSEN PEAK TRAIL

The must-do hike for any serious hiker is **Lassen Peak Trail** (5 miles, difficult, 3-5 hours round-trip). A large parking lot with chemical-toilet facilities is at the trailhead, and you're likely to see a lot of other cars here. This path not only takes you to the highest point on Mount Lassen, it's also a starkly beautiful, unusual trail that offers long views of the rest of the park and beyond.

The climb to the top is dramatic, challenging, and worth it. It's not actually a long hike—only 5 miles round-trip—but the trail gains more than 2,000 vertical feet in only 2.5 miles on the way up. The trail is well graded and has many switchbacks, which help manage the steepness. And some good news: Exhibits along the way explain some of the fascinating views of volcanic remains, lakes, wildlife, and rock formations.

The recent (by geologic standards) eruption and prevailing weather conditions leave this peak without much plant life, which means nothing blocks your views downward and outward, and the rocky terrain is visually interesting. Only the last 0.25 mile or so actually involves any scrambling over large rocks; most of the trail is just a steady upward walk. When you get to the top, ooh la la! Be sure to turn all the way around to get 360-degree views back down to the newest volcanic landscape, across to the remains of the giant caldera of a huge extinct volcano, and then out west toward the Cascade Range, where you'll see Mount Shasta shining in the distance.

KINGS CREEK FALLS TRAIL

The **Kings Creek Falls Trail** (Hwy. 89, road marker 32, 3 miles round-trip, moderate) starts out easy. The initial walk begins downhill to the falls. Be sure to stop to admire the small cascade and pool and maybe sit down and have a snack as you prepare for the 700-foot climb back up to the trailhead. This is a good hike for fit day-hikers who've already been on the mountain for a few hours.

SUMMIT LAKE TO ECHO AND TWIN LAKES

It's the length of the trail that runs from **Summit Lake to Echo and Twin Lakes** (east side of Summit Lake, 8 miles round-trip, moderate-difficult) that makes it challenging. But you can choose how many little lakes you really want to see if you run short of breath. The elevation gain over the course of this long trail is only 500 feet in total—a gentle slope in these mountainous reaches. A pleasant and sedate four-mile walk is out to Echo Lake. It's another two miles to get to Upper Twin Lake and back, and two more miles to reach Lower Twin Lake. You might want to wear a swimsuit under your hiking clothes on hot summer days to cool off in one of the lakes before trekking back to base.

BROKEOFF MOUNTAIN

For a good solid all-day hike with some invigorating uphill stretches, climb **Brokeoff Mountain** (Hwy. 89, road marker 2, 7.5 miles round-trip, difficult). Brokeoff makes a good second- or third-day Lassen hike, after you've seen the sights and climbed Mount Lassen. It's near the Kohm Yah-mah-nee Visitors Center and the southern entrance to the park along Highway 89, so it can serve as a last big adventure before you head back to the Bay Area or points south. Brokeoff involves a 2,600-foot ascent from a mile-high starting point, so the thin air and rigorous climb can be quite difficult for hikers who are unused to altitude or are out of shape. On the other hand, if you're ready for it, this is one of the prettiest and most serene hikes in the more visited section of the park. Enjoy the pretty mountain streams and stellar views out over the mountains and valleys of Northern California.

Backpacking

Some of the most beautiful and interesting remote hiking in California can be found in Lassen's expanse of backcountry. Check with the ranger station when you enter the park to obtain any necessary backcountry permits and get the season's scoop on trail conditions. Although you might not be the only backpacker out here, you'll definitely leave the crowds on the main road behind and find yourself with more trees, birds, and other mountain critters than people. You might even get lucky enough to have a pristine lake or mountain stream to yourself.

No major park in California would be complete without a hunk of the **Pacific Crest Trail** (www.pcta.org) running through it. This high-altitude stretch (17 miles, difficult) of the continent-spanning trail offers lots of challenge and solitude and a fairly short window in which you can traverse this part of California. If you're doing the California leg of the Pacific Crest Trail, try to hit Lassen June-September, and be prepared for extreme weather conditions from blistering heat to snowstorms.

For a radical change of scenery, take the **Cinder Cone Trail** from Butte Lake (west end of Butte Lake Campground, 4-5 miles, moderate). Be sure to wear your sturdiest ankle-covering hiking boots on this adventure, since the ground on the Cinder Cone is . . . well . . . cinders. Watch your footing so you don't slide down; even cold cinders can cut you up. The trail rises 800 vertical feet over two miles; to lengthen the hike, walk down the south side of the cone. Geology and photography buffs particularly like this hike, which is accessible by dirt road and shows off some of the more interesting and less-seen volcanic history of Mount Lassen.

If you can't get enough of Lassen's geothermal features, enter the park from Warner Valley Road and take a hike to **Boiling Springs Lake** (Warner Campground parking lot, 3 miles, easy-moderate). You'll get to see bubbling mud pots and check out the boiling springs from a safe distance. The walk out and back is reasonably short and nonstrenuous. Just be very careful once you reach the geothermal area; unlike Bumpass Hell, this region has no nice safe boardwalks encircling the mud pots and fumaroles. These features,

Brokeoff Mountain

along with the hot springs, can be extremely dangerous. This might not be a hike for young spirited children, but it's heaven for serious nature lovers who want to see what volcanic geothermal features look like in their wild state. Needless to say, trying to swim in sulfurous, acidic, 125°F Boiling Springs Lake is a very bad idea.

Looking for a more serious, multiday backcountry trek? Check the park website for maps and feel free to call the park to get advice on route planning and necessary equipment before you come. Once you're in the park, the visitors centers can issue a free wilderness permit for backcountry hiking and camping and provide last-minute pointers and current trail information.

Boating and Fishing

If you've got a canoe, a kayak, or a rowboat, bring it to Lassen in the summer. Many of the small to midsize lakes on the mountain allow unpowered boating and fishing. Although most of the lakes on the west side of the park near the road are too small to boat, in the east part of the park, Juniper, Snag, and Butte Lakes have plenty of space to row or paddle out and enjoy the serenity of the water. No boat rentals are available inside Lassen Volcanic National Park.

Several varieties of trout inhabit the larger Lassen lakes. All you need is a pole, some bait, and a valid California fishing license. Manzanita Lake offers catch-and-release fishing only, but at all the other fishable lakes you're welcome to take a state limit of rainbows and browns. Fishing at several of the campgrounds makes it easy to enjoy the freshest dinner possible.

Fishing licenses are available online (www.dfg.ca.gov) and at the Redding office of the California Department of Fish and Game (601 Locust St., Redding, 530/225-2300, 8am-4:30pm Mon.-Fri.).

ACCOMMODATIONS

Accommodations near Lassen Volcanic National Park are few and far between. Plan to camp in the park, or stay near Redding or Chester and take day trips into the park. The nearest lodgings are about nine miles south in Mineral.

Lassen Mineral Lodge (Hwy. 36, Mineral, 530/595-4422, www.minerallodge.com, May-early Nov., $85-115) is on Highway 36 near the southwest entrance to the park. The lodge offers 20 small motel-style rooms with private baths and few frills; pets are not allowed. The lack of TVs and telephones encourages visitors to get out and enjoy the park and its surrounding landscape. Hiking and fishing are favorite pastimes of lodge guests. The on-site **Mineral Lodge Restaurant** (daily 8am-8pm summer, 8am-7pm Sat. 8am-6pm Sun. winter, $12-21) has a bar and is open to nonguests.

Located near the southern entrance station is the ★ **Drakesbad Guest Ranch** (end of Warner Valley Rd., Chester, 866/999-0914, www.drakesbad.com, June-mid-Oct., $189-209, $119 and up spring and fall). This all-inclusive ranch includes three meals per day, though the national park entrance fee is not included. Spend anywhere from a couple of hours to a full day taking guided trail rides through the national park ($75-190) on one of the ranch's horses. Guests can board their own horses ($37.50 per day, includes feed). You're also within easy reach of hiking trails. Bring your tackle along on a walk or a ride to take advantage of the fishing available in the local lakes and streams; the ranch can also connect you with local guides from the Lake Almanor Fly-Fishing Company (530/258-3944, http://almanorflyfishing.com). The ranch even has a wonderful pool that's fed by the water from a local hot spring.

CAMPING

Lassen has eight campgrounds, four of which are accessible via the paved park road. The remaining four campgrounds offer primitive facilities or are accessible via a short hike.

Backcountry camping is permitted at Lassen; several hike-in campgrounds offer some minimal facilities and a way to lessen your impact on the landscape. You need a wilderness permit to camp in the backcountry, but the permit is free, and there are no quotas. To apply for a backcountry permit, download an application from www.nps.gov/lavo and mail or fax it prior to your trip. Permits are also available in the park from the Loomis Museum (530/595-6140, 9am-5pm Fri.-Sun. mid-May-mid-June, daily 9am-5pm mid-June-Oct. 31) and Kohm Yah-mah-nee Visitors Center (530/595-4480, www.nps.gov/lavo, daily 9am-5pm Apr. 1-Oct. 31, 9am-5pm Wed.-Sun. Nov. 1-Mar. 31); self-registration is possible at the Loomis, Butte Lake, Warner Valley Ranch, and Juniper Lake Ranger Stations.

MANZANITA LAKE

Closest to the park entrance along Highway 89 is the pleasant and serene **Manzanita Lake Campground** (179 sites, 877/444-6777, www.recreation.gov, May-Oct. or first snowfall, $18). By far the largest campground in Lassen, Manzanita Lake has a full slate of amenities, including flush toilets, potable running water, fire rings or pits, picnic tables in all campsites, and an RV dump station, and it's the only place in the park where showers are available, in the nearby camp store (quarters required). Trailers and campers up to 35 feet are allowed. Advance reservations are recommended at this popular campground.

CRAGS

Five miles south of Manzanita Lake, the more primitive **Crags Campground** (45 sites, first-come, first-served, June-Sept., $12) offers an out-in-the-woods style of camping. Crags has potable running water and pit toilets but no showers. Each site has a picnic table, a metal food locker, and a fire pit.

SUMMIT LAKE NORTH AND SOUTH

Farther south along Highway 89 at Summit Lake, ★ **Summit Lake North** (46 sites, 877/444-6777, www.recreation.gov, late June-Sept., $18) and ★ **Summit Lake South** (48 sites, 877/444-6777, www.recreation.gov, late June-late Sept., $16) campgrounds are some of the most popular spots in the park, so reservations are recommended. Visitors can swim in Summit Lake, easily accessing its banks from trails and campsites. These two developed campgrounds have flush toilets, fire pits, and tables, but to be safe bring enough potable water for the length of your trip for drinking and washing. At 6,650 feet elevation, the Summit Lake campgrounds are among the highest in the park. Be sure to take it easy setting up camp on your first day so that you can get used to the thin air.

BUTTE LAKE

Out in the backcountry, well away from the main road, the **Butte Lake Campground** (101 sites, 877/444-6777, www.recreation.gov, June-Oct., $16) shows off the beauty of Lassen to its best advantage. Despite its remote location at the northeast corner of the park, you'll find this to be a fairly well-developed campground, with pit toilets and running water. Check with the National Park Service to be sure the water at this campground is drinkable. Each site has a fire pit and a table. Trailers and RVs up to 35 feet that can negotiate the road can camp at Butte Lake. To reach the campground, take Highway 44 to the dirt road, and then drive six miles to the campground. Reservations are recommended.

JUNIPER LAKE

The **Juniper Lake Campground** (18 sites, June-Oct., $10) takes campers farther off the beaten path. Since the campground is located on the east side of the park, at the end of a rough dirt road near Chester, you'll do much better if you're a tent camper rather than if you have an RV or trailer. This small campground beside beautiful Juniper Lake has pit toilets, fire pits, and tables, but the water isn't drinkable. Either bring purifying agents or your own drinking water in containers. Because it is at almost 7,000 feet elevation, definitely take it easy during your first day.

If you're bringing horses with you, you can reserve the only campsite at the Juniper

Lake Stock Corral (late June-mid-Oct., $28 per day). The site is pretty rugged. Water is available for livestock, but there's no potable water for campers. No showers, either, but there's a vault toilet on-site. Two corrals can hold a total of 10 animals and the campsite can accommodate groups up to 10. The campsite and corral are located directly behind the Juniper Lake Ranger Station.

WARNER VALLEY

Warner Valley (18 sites, June-Sept., $14) is along the south edge of the park. Another small gem of a semi-developed campground, Warner Valley has pit toilets and drinking water as well as tables and fire pits at each site. Trailers are not allowed: Although the dirt road is only one mile long, it's too rough for large campers and RVs to navigate.

SOUTHWEST WALK-IN

The only campground open year-round is the **Southwest Walk-In Campground** (21 sites, tents only, first-come, first-served, $14). Plumbing is turned off in this campground when the snows come, so don't expect flush toilets and drinking water unless it's summer. However, you won't be far from the Kohm Yah-mah-nee Visitors Center, so you can use the facilities and get water there. The restrooms are located outside the main building, so they're accessible all night. "Walk-in," by the way, doesn't mean this is for backpackers only. The parking lot for this campground is quite close to the campsites; you just can't park right beside your tent.

FOOD

Mount Lassen offers little in the way of dining options. If you're camping, shop in Redding and bring in lots of food. Don't expect to get to a restaurant during your stay unless you're willing to drive a long way. The best food available in the park is at **Kohm Yah-mah-nee Visitors Center** (Hwy. 89, 530/595-4480, www.nps.gov/lavo, 9am-5pm daily Apr.-Oct., 9am-5pm Wed.-Sun. Nov.-Mar.), where the snack bar sells burgers, slices of pizza, hot coffee, and ice cream. Hours can vary during the winter.

Part of the year, a small **camp store** (9am-5pm daily late spring and early fall, 8am-8pm daily summer) opens near Manzanita Lake. The store sells gifts, camping supplies, hot food, snacks (including s'mores for campfires), and ice cream. The park's only gas station is located right behind the camp store and is available 24 hours per day.

INFORMATION AND SERVICES

The **Kohm Yah-mah-nee Visitors Center** (Hwy. 89, 530/595-4480, www.nps.gov/lavo, 9am-5pm daily Apr.-Oct., 9am-5pm Wed.-Sun. Nov.-Mar.) is located at the south entrance station of the park, and there's a ranger station at the Highway 44/89 entrance. At either station you can get wilderness permits for backcountry camping, any other necessary permits, and advice about where you can and cannot hike, ride, swim, fish, and camp in Lassen.

Park rangers can provide first aid and help you get phone access to emergency services in Redding.

TRANSPORTATION

By Air

The nearest major airport to Lassen is the **Reno-Tahoe International Airport** (RNO, 2001 E. Plumb Lane, Reno, NV, 775/328-6400, www.renoairport.com). You can also fly into **San Francisco International Airport** (SFO, Hwy. 101, San Francisco, 650/821-8211 or 800/435-9736, www.flysfo.com), or **Sacramento International Airport** (SMF, 6900 Airport Blvd., Sacramento, 916/929-5411, www.sacramento.aero), either of which involves a somewhat longer but still fairly easy drive to Lassen.

By Car

Lassen Volcanic National Park is about a four-hour drive from the Bay Area and three hours from Sacramento, most of it spent traveling north on I-5. At the town of **Red Bluff**, exit

I-5 onto Highway 36 and head east for about 43 miles before making a left onto Highway 89, which leads into the park.

On Mount Lassen, winter usually begins in November and continues through May. Highway 89 through the park closes from about October until May, June, or July depending on the weather and snowfall in any given year. Highway 89 serves as the main road through the park, and the visitors center, campgrounds, trailheads, and lakes cluster along it. You can get a good feel for Lassen by taking a day trip along Highway 89.

South of Lassen, roads run from the tiny town of **Chester** to the park. Warner Valley Road is paved, but other roads from the town to the park are good old-fashioned dirt. On the northeast side of the park, Highway 44 leads from the remote town of **Susanville.** Dirt roads lead from Highway 44 into the park.

However you get to Lassen, be sure to bring a good map and possibly a GPS device as well. The only gas station in the park is located by the Manzanita Lake Campground store. It's available 24 hours per day and accepts credit cards. Gas up in Red Bluff, Chester, or Susanville before driving up to Mount Lassen.

RED BLUFF

Red Bluff is just one hour west of the entrance to Lassen Volcanic National Park, and it's also a good stopping place on the way to Shasta. The town has a quaint and lively Main Street, good for shopping, and multiple parks and recreation opportunities for fishing, hiking, and camping.

Sports and Recreation

About one mile south of Red Bluff is the **Red Bluff Recreation Area** (530/527-2813, www.fs.usda.gov), within Mendocino National Forest. Volunteers help develop and maintain the trails here so that hikers can enjoy the wildlife and views while getting some exercise. The visitors center doubles as the **Sacramento River Discovery Center** (1000 Sale Lane, 530/527-1196, www.srdc.tehama.k12.ca.us, 9am-3pm Tues.-Sat. winter, 8am-4pm Tues.-Sat. summer). Soon after entering the recreation area, you'll come to the trailhead for the **Shasta View Trail** (2 miles, easy), a mostly flat loop that delivers the views it promises. You can even see the Yolla Bolly Mountains from some places, worth it just so you can say it. The trail is a great leg-stretcher for people passing through town.

Bird-watching is a big attraction in the Red Bluff Recreation Area, and the park is home to great blue herons, great egrets, great horned owls, wood ducks, Anna's hummingbirds, and many other species. It also features bobcats, western pond turtles, Pacific tree frogs, opossums, woodchucks, and more. Various short nature trails, some of which are paved, make for easy forays into the best wildlife-viewing spots.

Accommodations and Camping

Red Bluff offers the standard hotel chains such as **Super 8** (30 Gilmore Rd., 530/529-2028, www.super8.com, $51-61) and **Comfort Inn** (90 Sale Lane, 877/287-4809, www.comfortinn.com, $100-120). For something more specific to the area, try the **Sportsman Lodge** (768 Antelope Blvd., 530/527-2888, www.redbluffsportsmanlodge.com, $70-80). It's nothing fancy, but it has an outdoor pool, free wireless Internet access, and friendly local owners.

If you've got your own bed on wheels, the place to park it is the upscale **Durango RV Resort** (100 Lake Ave., 530/527-5300 or 866/770-7001, www.durangorvresorts.com, $45-58), which offers a lap pool, a sauna, free wireless Internet access, paddle tennis, bocce ball courts, two laundries, a lodge and concession center, and facilities to wash your dog *and* your vehicle. The resort is on the Sacramento River and is surrounded by woods. Because of underground watering, this is not a place for tents.

Within the Red Bluff Recreation Area, **Sycamore Grove Campground** (Sale Ln., 2 miles southeast of Red Bluff, 530/934-3316, www.fs.usda.gov, reservations 877/444-6777, www.recreation.gov, $16-30, with electricity $25, year-round) offers 30 sites for tents and trailers with up to eight people allowed per site; it also has a large group site that accommodates 16 people. Coin-operated showers are available in the modern restrooms.

Food

The Green Barn (5 Chestnut Ave., 530/527-3161, 11:30am-8pm Mon.-Thurs., 11:30am-9pm Fri., 4pm-9pm Sat., $9-32), with its aged steaks and divine homemade sticky buns, has been satisfying locals since 1959. It is located at the corner of Chestnut and Antelope Avenues, and you can see Mount Shasta as you arrive. Inside is a warm, mellow, and comfortable atmosphere.

For ranch-style barbecue and baked beans, **2 Buds BBQ** (592 Antelope Blvd., 530/528-0799, 11am-6pm Mon.-Fri., 11am-3pm Sat., $7-12) is a hole-in-the-wall that earns raves from locals. Grab a table beneath the glowering elk's head mounted on the wall and order the house tri-tip or pulled pork sandwich; the short ribs are also a good choice.

Los Mariachis (604 Main St., 530/529-5154, 9am-9pm Mon.-Fri., 9am-9:30pm Sat.-Sun., $10-15) serves traditional Mexican fare like burritos and quesadillas, along with American-style burgers and sandwiches. They also serve huevos rancheros and Spanish omelets for breakfast. **Casa Ramos** (2001 Main St., 530/527-2684, www.casaramos.net, 11am-9pm Sun.-Thurs., 11am-10pm Fri.-Sat., $7-18) is part of a small family-owned chain.

Information and Services

The **Sacramento River Discovery Center** (1000 Sale Lane, Red Bluff, 530/527-1196, www.srdc.tehama.k12.ca.us, 9am-3pm Tues.-Sat. winter, 8am-4pm Tues.-Sat. summer) is the go-to spot for information about the river and wildlife in the area.

Transportation

Red Bluff is 130 miles north of Sacramento, right on I-5. It is about 30 miles south of Redding and 50 miles west of the southern entrance to Lassen Volcanic National Park.

CHESTER

The tiny town of Chester is 25 miles east of the southwest entrance to Lassen Volcanic National Park on Highway 89/36. From Red Bluff, the 70-mile drive takes about one hour. The primary interest is Chester's proximity to the southwest entrance station of the national park and activities on nearby Lake Almanor.

Drakesbad Guest Ranch (Chester Warner Valley Rd., 866/999-0914, www.drakesbad.com, June-mid-Oct., $189-209 summer) offers the closest lodging to Lassen Volcanic National Park. The all-inclusive rates include meals, and stables, hiking trails, and fishing opportunities are nearby. Drakesbad is 17 miles north of Chester on Chester Warner Valley Road.

North Shore Campground (Hwy. 36/89, 530/258-3376, www.northshorecampground.com, Apr.-Oct., tents $26-36, RVs $40-56) is two miles east of Chester with 130 sites for tents and RVs. Facilities include picnic tables, fire rings, drinking water, restrooms with flush toilets and showers, and a small store.

Rocky Point Campground (916/386-5164 or 530/284-1785, www.pge.com, May-Oct., $23-46) is at the southwest end of Lake Almanor, with 131 sites for tents and RVs. Facilities include picnic tables, fire rings, drinking water, and vault toilets. You can reserve most of those sites online starting in early March; 24 sites are first-come, first-served only.

Almanor North and South Campgrounds (877/444-6777, www.recreation.gov, May-Sept., $15-100) are operated by the Almanor Ranger District (530/258-2141, www.fs.fed.us). Situated directly on the lake, the 104 campsites offer great views of Lassen as well as biking, hiking, and fishing. Facilities include picnic tables, fire rings, drinking water, vault toilets, and a boat ramp. To reach the campgrounds, turn right on Highway 89 two miles west of Chester and drive six miles to County Road 310; turn left for the campground.

SUSANVILLE

The small town of Susanville is the seat of Lassen County, and you're likely to pass through it if you're approaching Lassen Volcanic National Park from the east. The town is located on the Susan River, and although it's the home of two large prisons, Susanville has a certain Old West charm.

Susanville is the main trailhead for the famous 25.4-mile **Bizz Johnson National Recreation Trail** (530/257-0456, www.blm.gov), a favorite with hikers and cyclists that winds along the Susan River, following the Fernley and Lassen Branch Line of the former Southern Pacific Railroad route. The trail begins at the **Susanville Depot Trailhead Visitors Center and Museum** (601 Richmond Rd., 530/257-3252, Mon.-Sat. 9am-5pm, free), and winds its way toward the small community of Westwood. At the depot visitors center you'll find trail maps, exhibits about the trail and the area, and a bookstore.

Accommodations and Food

The River Inn (1710 Main St., 530/257-6051, $59-77) was built in the 1970s. It's a simple motel without many frills, but it's a locally owned business with an unusually helpful and pleasant staff. The location is good, too—right on Main Street beside several restaurants. The beds don't sag, the rooms are clean, and you can get the senior citizen rate and AAA discount whether you qualify or not.

The **Diamond Mountain Casino Café** (900 Skyline Rd., 877/319-8514 or 530/252-1100, www.diamondmountaincasino.com, $10-20) inside the Diamond Mountain Casino has rotating specials throughout the week such as carved tri-tip steak, Indian tacos, turkey dinners with gravy, and prime rib, as well as a regular menu of steaks and other American comfort food. They're open from breakfast until late at night.

The **Lassen Steakhouse** (1700 Main St., 530/257-7220, 4:30pm-9pm Mon.-Sat., $17-32) is popular, with favorites like the flat-iron and the porterhouse; this lively place can please nearly any carnivore. Although they don't have any vegetarian entrées, the same owner—self-professed workaholic Esther Faustino—also runs **El Tepeyac Grille** (1700 Main St., 530/257-7220, 7am-9pm daily, $5-15), a coffee shop and Mexican restaurant next door.

Transportation

Susanville is on Highway 36, just a few miles east of where Highways 36 and 44 split and begin making a loop around Lassen. The fastest way to get to the national park from here is to stay on Highway 36, called Main Street as it passes through Susanville, and travel 60 miles to Highway 89. Make a right and the park entrance is just over five miles. To get to Susanville from the Bay Area, take I-80 east to I-505 north to Highway 36 east. The trip is about 290 miles (5 hours). Susanville is about 90 miles east of Red Bluff and 90 miles north of Reno, Nevada.

Mount Shasta and Vicinity

> When I first caught sight of Mount Shasta, over the braided folds of the Sacramento Valley, I was fifty miles away and afoot, alone and weary. Yet all my blood turned to wine, and I have not been weary since.
>
> John Muir, 1874

One of the most iconic natural formations in the United States, Mount Shasta is stunning from every angle at any time of day. Like Utah's Delicate Arch or the Grand Canyon, Shasta is immediately recognizable from calendars, book covers, and photographs on the walls of hotels and restaurants—but you need to see it with your own eyes. Once you experience it in person, you'll never forget it, and you'll find yourself longing to see it again.

The gorgeous sunny village known as the City of Mount Shasta is a shining jewel of Northern California. A visit is a must for hikers, boaters, skiers, anglers, and others who revel in the outdoors.

★ MOUNT SHASTA

Mount Shasta is a tremendous dormant volcano that last erupted in 1786. Although it may someday erupt again, for now it's a delightful playground and a magnetic attraction. At 14,162 feet, Mount Shasta is the 49th highest peak in the country, the fifth highest in California, and the second tallest volcano in the Cascade Range. It has a 17-mile perimeter and stands pretty much alone, with no close neighbors of anywhere near similar stature. In winter, snow covers much of the mountain; in summer a series of glaciers make the mountain appear white and glistening.

Mount Shasta is covered with snow, at least in places, year-round. This makes it an appealing, if not always accessible, destination for skiers of all kinds. Some people like to go to the back side of the mountain (the "bowl"), climb as high as they can with skis strapped to their backpacks, and then ski down. Families with children can bring plastic sleds, hike a little less far up the mountain, and then let everyone sled down. The **Bunny Flat Trailhead** (6,900 feet) is recommended for this kind of activity.

Hiking

Some of the best hiking in California can be found on and around Mount Shasta. This beautiful region abounds with waterfalls, pine forests, rivers, streams, and fascinating geology. Informal camping and backpacking (wilderness permits required) can create a wonderful multiday hiking trip. Day hikes offer everything from easy strolls great for kids to strenuous miles that can take you up to minor mountain peaks for tremendous views of the whole southern Cascade mountain region.

If you want to hike on Mount Shasta but don't have the time or the training to go all

Mount Shasta

the way to the top, try a nice day hike to **Gray Butte** (3.4 miles, moderate), an intermediate peak on the south slope of the mountain. The trail runs east across Panther Meadow, which is quite beautiful and full of heather and other wildflowers, and into the nearby forest. At the first fork in the trail (just past 0.5 miles), choose the fork to the right. In 1.5 miles, you'll come to a saddle—a good place for views, but there are more to come. From the saddle, bear right again to reach the peak of Gray Butte in less than 0.25 miles. Not only can you see the peak of Mount Shasta, but on a clear day you can see all the way to Castle Crags, Mount Eddy, and even Lassen Peak. Return the same way. To reach the trailhead, take I-5 to the Central Mount Shasta exit. Turn east onto Lake Street, which becomes Everitt Memorial Highway. In 13.5 miles, you'll reach Panther Meadows Campground, which has extensive trail signage and plenty of information about the ecology and wildlife of the area.

For an unexpected connection to the Hearst family, take a walk along the **Ah-Di-Na Historic Trail** (0.25 miles, easy). Follow the signs from Squaw Valley Creek Road at the reservoir to this odd little resort area along the McCloud River. The William Randolph Hearst family built a retreat here, and you'll see photos of their property on the interpretive signs marking the short, flat trail. It's a bit of a drive out to Ah-Di-Na on slow dirt roads. It is possible to get there in a passenger car, but not an RV or towing a trailer; expect the drive to take some time.

The name of the **Sims Flat Historic Trail** (Sims Rd., south of the river, 1 mile, easy) refers to the name of a former logging town, but the trail itself is flat too. Sims Flat was once a bustling town with the railroad running through it to carry products from the busy sawmill to the big cities that needed lumber. Nearly a century later, a few signs tell the history of this diverse former town. Take in the up-close views of Mount Shasta, which looms over Sims Flat.

On the other end of the hiking spectrum is the **Sisson-Callahan National Recreation Trail** (North Shore Rd., 18 miles round-trip, difficult). Just past Deer Creek Bridge, take the left fork and park off the road. Starting near Lake Siskiyou, this trail gains almost one mile in elevation, peaking at over 8,000 feet at Deadfall Summit, and then dropping 1,000 feet to Deadfall Lakes. Be sure to dress in layers, since you might start out in the intense summer heat of the lower elevations and end up making snowballs on the summit. Because it is long, steep, and challenging, many hikers prefer to do this trail over more than one day. A number of campsites are along the North Fork of the Sacramento River and beyond, welcoming weary travelers with a spot to pitch a tent and enjoy a night's rest. In fact, the Sisson-Callahan links up with the Pacific Crest Trail (www.pcta.org) near Deadfall Lakes, so backpackers can keep going if they choose to.

If you like hikes that are big on views and not so much about climbing, the place for you is the **Lake Siskiyou Trail.** This mostly flat seven-mile loop circumnavigates the spectacular lake and offers changing perspectives on the nearby mountains, bridges, and shorelines. You can start from any one of several well-marked parking areas and enjoy four rest stops with pit toilets and helpful signage along the way. This gently undulating, easy-to-follow trail is also a great place for a run. To get to one of the main trailheads, start from the town of Mount Shasta and head west on W. A. Barr Road until you see signs for Lake Siskiyou Trail.

For a lovely long hike that takes you up to views of the whole of the Far North mountain region and into Oregon, trek up **Mount Eddy** (Forest Rd. 17, Mount Shasta Ranger Station 530/926-4511, 10 miles round-trip, difficult). This steep trail takes you up to the 9,000-foot peak, where you can turn around and check out the various highlights of the Cascade range: Mount Shasta, Mount Lassen, the Trinity Alps, and even Mount McLoughlin in Oregon. Bring plenty of water as there's none at the Deadfall Lake trailhead, where the hike starts. Along the way, Deadfall Lake and

Deadfall Creek both offer what appears to be very clear, clean water, but, as always, it's best to treat it before you drink it. The early part of the trail is mostly mild climbing, and there's some shade to keep you cool as you do it. The last 0.8 miles is the hard part: It's a serious of steep exposed switchbacks, guaranteed to give you a workout no matter how fit you are. The reward is worth it, though: You'll soon be on a truly exceptional mountaintop with views you'll remember for a long time. If you're not up for such a long day hike, consider an overnight camping trip; the lake makes a great informal primitive campground.

For serious hikers, **Black Butte** is a great half-day adventure. This odd cinder-cone peak stands at 6,325 feet and looks like a giant cone of black pepper. (The U.S. Forest Service says it's actually made of hornblende andesite.) From some angles, the butte looks almost as impressive as its neighbor, the famous Mount Shasta, but the climb is not nearly as daunting; no ice axes or other special equipment is needed. Still, the hike up Black Butte is rocky, steep, and mostly unshaded. And although it's only 2.56 miles to the top, you gain 1,845 feet in elevation in that short distance. Take sunscreen, plenty of water, binoculars, and a camera. And if you're on a schedule, leave a little more time than you think you'll need, since finding the trailhead can be a little confusing. To get here from Mount Shasta Boulevard in the center of the city of Mount Shasta, turn east onto Lake Street, which soon becomes Everitt Memorial Highway. Drive a total of just under three miles and look for a small sign that says "Black Butte Trail." Make a left onto the gravel road (Forest Rd. 41N18). From here, the road winds through the forest (go slowly, if you value your car's undercarriage and windshield) on narrow, uneven, rocky roads. If someone has given you detailed instructions about turning left and right and bearing north and so on, feel free to try to follow them, but it's easy to make a mistake if you're overthinking the twists and turns. The best advice is to stick to the main narrow gravel road all the way to the trailhead. Don't be distracted by forks off to the sides, and you will eventually get there.

Climbing

Climbers come from all over the world come to tackle Shasta's majestic 14,162-foot peak. Be sure to pack your sturdiest hiking boots and your strongest leg muscles; fewer than one-third of the 15,000 intrepid mountaineers who try to conquer Mount Shasta each

Black Butte

year actually make it to the top. Shasta's steep and rocky slopes, its long-lasting snowfields, and the icy glaciers that persist year-round all contribute to making this one of the most difficult climbs in the country. On top of all that, the thin air at this altitude makes breathing a challenge. If you're serious about doing the climb, you can get plenty of help from the locals.

Bagging this peak is not for everyone, but for healthy, well-trained, and well-equipped climbers, this can be the adventure of a lifetime; you'll see Mount Shasta up close in ways that most casual visitors could never imagine. The main climbing season is June-August, but do not expect sunny weather and easy footing. Casual visitors should exercise care accessing even the trailheads that lead to Shasta's peak. Some of the dirt roads around the base of the mountain require a 4WD vehicle, and weather conditions can have severe effects on the roads. Contact the **Mount Shasta Climbing Advisory** (530/926-4511, www.shastaavalanche.org) before your trip for current weather and climbing conditions.

More than a dozen routes lead to the top. You can pick a quick, hard-core climb that takes you from the base camp up to the top in a single day, or choose a longer and more leisurely trail and spend two days making the trek, camping overnight in the wilderness. The most popular route begins near the Mount Shasta **Alpine Lodge** (www.alpinelodgeca.com) at Horse Camp and runs along Avalanche Gulch. The Alpine Lodge is a lovely 1923 building made of local volcanic rock and wood from the Shasta forest. It is owned by the Sierra Club Foundation (www.sierraclub.org) and is sometimes called the Sierra Club hut, but it's much more solid than the word "hut" implies. Located at an altitude of 7,900 feet on the mountain's southwest side, this is a great destination for a modest day hike on the mountain or a good base camp for a mountaineer heading toward the summit.

Mountaineering and glacier classes are available, and several guides and outfitters can provide equipment and even lead you up the mountain. Private mountain guide Robin Kohn (530/926-3250, www.mountshastaguide.com) maintains a comprehensive website with up-to-date information and helpful advice. Contact her for help hiring a guide or arranging trip plans. **Shasta Mountain Guides** (Mount Shasta, 530/926-3117, www.shastaguides.com, $550-750 pp) has been taking climbers to the top for decades. Join one of their scheduled group trips along various routes up the mountain, or call to arrange a custom expedition. Snowboard and backcountry ski tours ($129-650 pp, minimum 2 people) are also available. **Sierra Wilderness Seminars** (210 E. Lake St., 888/797-6867, www.swsmtns.com, Jan.-Sept., $525-695 pp) leads groups of up to eight people up Mount Shasta. If you want to learn as well as climb, check out the Ice & Snow Expedition Course (June-Sept., 5 days $995). The rigorous training on the use of ice axes and crampons, and what to do if someone falls into a crevasse, may come in handy during the climb to Shasta's summit along a "glaciated north-side route." If you're new to this, start with one of the company's one-day courses, such as the Ice Ax Clinic (Jan.-Aug., $135), which teaches basic snow-climbing techniques. Or make a weekend of it by combining this with the Basic Mountaineering Clinic (1 day $150). All clinics and climbs take place on Mount Shasta. **Alpine Skills International** (530/582-9170, www.alpineskills.com, $495-980 pp) provides training and guides for climbers of various skill levels. The founder, Bela Vadasz, has earned a lifetime achievement award from the American Mountain Guides Association and was instrumental in establishing certification programs for mountain guides in the United States. His company still takes training as seriously as adventure. One of their challenging courses on Mount Shasta is the four-day Glacial Ice Seminar (July-Aug., $725), which takes place on the Hotlum or Whitney Glaciers near the top of the mountain.

Fishing

Almost all the major rivers and feeder streams

running through the Mount Shasta region are open for fishing. You can tie your fly on and cast into the McCloud, Sacramento, and Trinity Rivers, among many others. These rivers carry salmon, steelhead, and trout. If you want a guide to help you navigate these waters, contact one of the many services that can take you out to the perfect fishing holes. For fly-fishing or scenic rafting tours, call **Jack Trout International Fly Fishing Guide Service** (530/926-4540, www.jacktrout.com, year-round, $325-400 for 2 people, gear rentals $25). Jack will take you out on the McCloud, Klamath, Upper and Lower Sacramento, Pit, or Trinity Rivers, or to Hat Creek. Jack supplies all the gear and brings a gourmet lunch complete with wine and homemade strawberry shortcake for you to enjoy by the side of the river. It you're an expert fly-fisher who wants to improve your technique, he can help you. If you've never done it before but think you might like to try, give him a call—he loves beginners and says they always catch something. See his blog, complete with great photos, at www.mtshasta.com to help you visualize your fishing trip. You have to bring a California fishing license, available online at www.dfg.ca.gov.

Outdoor Adventures Sport Fishing (530/221-6151 or 800/670-4448, www.sacriverguide.com, year-round by appointment only, $175-600 pp/day) takes anglers on fly-fishing drift trips on the Sacramento and Trinity Rivers, where they specialize in salmon, trout, and steelhead; they'll also guide you on a jet-boat trip on Shasta Lake, where you can catch salmon and trout.

Rafting and Kayaking

In the Cascades, the best white-water rafting is definitely on the Trinity River. A good guide service to take you out onto this river is **Trinity River Rafting** (530/623-3033 or 800/307-4837, www.trinityriverrafting.com, guided trips $65-180 per day, kayak rental $40 per day). In addition to its flagship runs on the Trinity, this major rafting company runs on the Klamath, Salmon, and Upper Fork Sacramento Rivers as well as Canyon Creek. Depending on where you're staying and what level of rafting you can handle, you can choose the river to paddle. Half-day to three-day trips ($65-375) are available, and you can choose from a placid Class I-II float suitable for the whole family to a Class IV-V run for fit, experienced rafters only. Trinity Rafting also rents rafts and 1-2-person inflatable kayaks for paddlers who want to go off on their own.

Another major player in the northern mountains rafting scene is the **Bigfoot Rafting Company** (530/629-2263, www.bigfootrafting.com, $69-410). With day trips on the Trinity and Salmon Rivers, and multiday rafting campouts on the Trinity and Klamath Rivers, Bigfoot presents a depth of knowledge of the rivers it runs. Your guide will know a great deal about the history and natural surroundings of your chosen river, and as a bonus can cook you up fabulous meals on the full-day and multiday trips. Bigfoot also rents equipment.

Skiing and Snowboarding

The snowpack on Mount Shasta each winter creates a haven for downhill skiers, cross-country skiers, snowboarders, and snowshoers. The place to go for all this is the **Mount Shasta Ski Park** (Ski Park Hwy., off Hwy. 89 between McCloud and Mount Shasta, 530/926-8600 or 530/926-8619, www.skipark.com, 9am-4pm daily mid-Dec.-mid-Apr., night skiing 3pm-8pm Thurs.-Sat., adults $20-55, ages 8-12 and seniors $12-33, under age 8 $7-13). This small but exciting downhill park has 425 skiable acres, three chairlifts, and two carpet lifts. Nearly half the runs are open for night skiing (if there's enough snow) and the Marmot lift in the beginner area makes a perfect spot for beginners of all ages to gain their snow legs (at a fraction of the cost of the resorts at Lake Tahoe). Half-day discount lift tickets and night-skiing-only lift tickets make skiing here even more attractive for snow-loving bargain hunters. Call ahead if you're interested in night skiing (adults $20, youth and seniors $12, children $7); the park offers extended night skiing until 9pm on some holiday weekends, but sometimes doesn't offer night skiing at all if snow conditions aren't favorable.

Cross-country skiers can also get their fix at the **Mount Shasta Nordic Center** (Ski Park Hwy., 1 mile before downhill park, 530/925-3495, www.mtshastanordic.org, 9am-4pm daily winter, adults $15, youth and seniors $8). Since 2006 this lovely ski center has been a not-for-profit organization dedicated to the promulgation of physical and mental health through cross-country skiing. It's open for the winter season, as determined by when the snow comes, usually in late December, and closes in mid-April; the center is closed Tuesdays after Jan. 1. The center has about 16 miles of groomed trails for cross-country skiing, and there's ample backcountry where you're welcome to explore off-trail. Snowshoers are allowed on the groomed trails as long as they stay to the side. Call the hotline (530/925-3495) for conditions and grooming updates. If you plan to come often, you can buy an annual membership, priced from $75 (individual) to $250 (family). Memberships and other donations are tax-deductible. The organization sponsors clinics, demos, races, and other events. Ski and snowshoe rentals and lessons are available.

Horseback Riding

The wilderness around Mount Shasta beckons to anyone with a penchant for trail rides. One good outfit that serves the area is the **Rockin Maddy Ranch** (11921 Cram Gulch Rd., Yreka, 530/340-2100, www.rockinmaddyranch.com, year-round, by reservation only, 1-2 hours $55-75 pp, full day $175 pp). Choose from rides like the popular 90-minute Shasta View ride, featuring grand vistas of the mountain, or a full-day excursion into the Marble Mountains. Rockin Maddy allows smaller children to ride double on the same horse. You can even book a pony party for your children, a horse-drawn carriage ride for a wedding or special event, or a hayride led by a team of powerful Percherons.

Camping

The Shasta-Trinity National Forest (Shasta Ranger District, 530/926-4511, www.fs.usda.gov, 8am-4:30pm Mon.-Fri.) manages three campgrounds on Mount Shasta. All are popular and fill quickly on summer weekends. Reservations are not accepted; weekdays are when it's easiest to find space. **McBride Springs** (12 sites, first-come, first-served, late May-Oct., $10) is conveniently located on the mountain at 5,000 feet, just four miles from Mount Shasta city. Facilities include drinking water, vault toilets, and picnic tables. ★ **Panther Meadows** (Everitt Memorial Hwy., 1.7 miles past Bunny Flat, 15 sites, first-come, first-served, mid-July-Nov., free) is 14 miles northeast of Mount Shasta city at an elevation of 7,500 feet on the slopes of Mount Shasta. Because of the high elevation, it can be cold at night and snowed-in well into summer. Although this is a walk-in campground, it is only 100-500 feet from the parking lot to the campsites. Facilities include picnic tables, fire rings, and vault toilets; bring your own water. Because this is the most popular campground on Mount Shasta, the maximum stay is three nights. The third campground is **Red Fir Flat** (530/926-4511, $12), a group site (8-75 people) available by reservation. Facilities include picnic tables, fire rings, and vault toilets, but not drinking water.

Dispersed camping is allowed throughout the Shasta-Trinity National Forest. A wilderness permit is required on Mount Shasta itself. Otherwise, anywhere you want to sleep is fair game, though you do need a campfire permit, available for free at any ranger station. For permits and information, contact the **Mount Shasta Ranger Station** (204 W. Alma St., 530/926-4511, www.fs.usda.gov, 8am-4:30pm Mon.-Fri. fall-spring, 8am-4:30pm Mon.-Sat. summer).

MOUNT SHASTA CITY

The main street of Mount Shasta city is Mount Shasta Boulevard, and nearly every business in town includes "Shasta" in its name. A plaque outside the Mount Shasta Police Department

(303 N. Mt. Shasta Blvd.) proclaims "Mount Shasta—Where Heaven and Earth Meet," and in the town center, near a coin-operated telescope aimed at the mountain, is an inscription of a quote from Joaquin Miller that reads "Lonely as God and white as a winter moon."

Nightlife

The Gold Room (903 S. Mt. Shasta Blvd., 530/926-4125, 11am-2am daily, cash only) is Mount Shasta's most authentic old-time locals bar, with two pool tables in the back, a couple of old-fashioned pinball and video games, and comfy vinyl-covered chairs at the bar so you can settle in. The jukebox often plays loud country music during the daytime hours for what the bartender describes as her "professional drinkers," but the atmosphere changes in the evening, as the crowd gets younger and more varied and includes visitors to the area.

The Goat Tavern (107 Chestnut St., 530/926-0209, 11:30am-7:30pm Mon.-Wed.) offers 8 beers on tap at any given time. The service often resembles Mt. Shasta's craggy terrain, but there's a relaxing patio where guests can slurp their beers after a long day on local trails.

Accommodations

UNDER $100

One of the first lodgings you'll come across as you arrive from the south is the **Finlandia Hotel and Lodge** (1621 S. Mt. Shasta Blvd., 530/926-5596, www.finlandiamotelandlodge.com, $65-125), offering comfortable rooms from a single with a queen bed at the low end to a suite with king bed and a kitchen at the top. The hotel is pet-friendly, and you can book online. The lodge ($200-$250) can sleep up to eight people; amenities include three bedrooms, a fully equipped kitchen, a sauna, an outdoor spa, and wood-burning fireplace crafted out of lava rock.

One of the friendliest of the cheap motels on the south end of town is the **Evergreen Lodge** (1312 S. Mt. Shasta Blvd., 530/926-2143, $49-99 winter, $89-109 summer). The hosts are warm and welcoming, and the place is more than adequate. There are a table and chairs even in the smaller rooms, free Internet service, and large TVs. The lodge has a small pool outside. The no-pets and no-smoking policies help keep the place clean and pleasant.

One of the most pleasant inexpensive lodging options is the ★ **Mount Shasta Ranch Bed & Breakfast** (1008 W. A. Barr Rd., 530/926-3870 or 877/926-3870, www.stayinshasta.com, $45-125), offering homey luxury just slightly out of town. The budget-friendly rooms in the Carriage House offer small spaces, queen beds, and shared baths. The separate Cottage ($150-180) is the largest option, with two bedrooms that can comfortably sleep up to six. The four rooms in the Ranch House are spacious and furnished with country-Victorian antiques and tchotchkes, and each has its own big private bath. All rooms include a full country breakfast.

Another bargain spot on the outskirts of the village is the **A-1 Choice Inn** (1340 S. Mt. Shasta Blvd., 530/926-4811, www.mtshastamotel.com, $79-119), with the motel standard pink-and-green polyester bedspreads and cheesy framed prints on the walls. With a coffeemaker, fridge, and microwave in each room, a small pool and a hot tub beside the highway, and views of the top of Mount Shasta, it has everything you need, as long as you don't need anything fancy.

As you progress toward the town center, you'll eventually come to the **Travel Inn** (504 S. Mt. Shasta Blvd., 530/926-4617, $59-69), one of the budget motels closest to the restaurants and shopping.

The cute **Dream Inn** (326 Chestnut St., 530/926-1536 or 877/375-4744, www.dreaminnmtshastacity.com, $80-160) offers bed-and-breakfast accommodations at the base of the magnificent mountain. The four small inexpensive upstairs rooms have shared hallway baths. Downstairs, a bigger white antique bedroom has its own private bath and a view of Mount Eddy out the lace-curtained window. Next door, two large suites share space in a Spanish adobe-style home; each has its own living space, bath, and truly homelike cluttered decor. Rooms at the Dream Inn include a daily full breakfast.

The **Alpine Lodge** (908 S. Mt. Shasta Blvd. 530/926-3145, www.alpinelodgeca.com, $69-159) is on the not-so-fancy end of the spectrum, but it does offer Internet access, in-room coffeemakers, and a small outdoor pool and hot tub. The higher-end option ($159) is a two-bedroom unit with three beds and a kitchenette.

If you drive north through the center of town to the other side, you'll find the **Cold Creek Inn** (724 N. Mt. Shasta Blvd., 530/926-9851 or 800/292-9421, www.coldcreekinn.com, $92-155 summer), a small motel with 19 simple but comfortable rooms and suites, some with mountain views. Amenities include free wireless Internet access, continental breakfast with organic coffee, and a sundeck for those who want to get out of the room for a while. The inn prides itself on using environmentally friendly cleaning products. All rooms are nonsmoking, and pets are welcome. Cold Creek offers discounts for travelers who stay more than four nights.

$100-150

For something more upscale than a budget motel, there's the **Mount Shasta Inn & Suites** (710 S. Mt. Shasta Blvd., 530/918-9292, www.mtshastainn.com, $89-209). This place was built in 2000, making it one of the newer facilities in the area. All rooms of the sparkling clean inn are nonsmoking and pet-free. Amenities include an outdoor hot tub, a complimentary light breakfast, and free wireless Internet access.

To get a sense of life in this region, book one of the rooms at the ★ **Shasta MountInn Retreat & Spa** (203 Birch St., 530/926-1810, www.shastamountinn.com, $150-175). The white farmhouse exterior fits perfectly into its semi-alpine setting, while the rooms ooze country charm and modern comforts. Each of the four rooms has its own private bath and memory-foam mattress. In the morning, head downstairs for a healthy continental breakfast and a cup of organic coffee. There are also on-site massage services and a barrel-shaped redwood sauna. The retreat's hosts can guide you to the sacred spots that dot this area.

The **Strawberry Valley Inn** (1142 S. Mt. Shasta Blvd., 530/926-2052, http://strawberryvalleyinn.net, $129-159) is an attractive property with a large green lawn and well-kept garden beside the Native Grounds Nursery and Mount Shasta Florist. The inn has an English feel to it, encouraging you to sit among the flowers and have tea before retiring to your charming, smallish, but lovely room. Continental breakfast is included in the room rates; the breakfast room can get crowded, so try to get here early and consider taking your breakfast out to the lawn.

$150-250

In a location and a class by itself is the **Tree House** (111 Morgan Way, 530/926-3101, www.bestwesterncalifornia.com, $162-230), a Best Western Plus hotel. It is slightly off the main drag near the Mount Shasta Shopping Center. Best Western hotels are individually owned and operated, but most of them tend to be at the upper-middle end of the chain hotel spectrum, and the ones designated "Plus" are a little nicer than average. The Mount Shasta version is a large, full-service hotel with an indoor pool, a hot tub, and a fitness center; full hot breakfast included; microwaves, fridges, and blow-dryers in the rooms; wireless Internet access; and a computer station in the lobby. The on-site **Tree House Restaurant** (6:30am-10:30am and 5pm-9pm daily, $13-24) serves breakfast and dinner, and **Cooper's Bar and Grill** (11am-10pm Mon.-Thurs., 11am-11pm Fri.-Sun., $6-10) serves tacos, burgers, pasta, cocktails, wine, and beer.

Off the boulevard are a few more elegant and more pricey places to stay, often with spacious grounds and lots of beautiful scenery. One of the nicest of these is **Mount Shasta Resort** (1000 Siskiyou Lake Blvd., 530/926-3030, reservations 800/958-3363, www.mtshastaresort.com, summer $159-339, winter $169-289). If you're looking for a spa treatment or a golf course (530/926-3030, 18 holes

$30-75) in addition to a beautiful suite to sleep in, this is the place for you. The staff from **Sacred Mountain Spa** (530/926-2331, http://sacredmountainresortspa.com, by appointment 10am-5pm daily, 1-hour massage $90) offer massages, facials, waxing, and hair and nail care on the resort premises. Every room is special at the Mount Shasta Resort. If you want a lakeside deck, a fireplace, a jetted tub, two TVs, or a kitchenette or full kitchen, just ask, and the resort can probably accommodate you. All rooms come with free wireless Internet access, ironing boards and irons, blow-dryers, and all the other amenities expected from upscale lodgings.

CAMPING

If the campgrounds on Mount Shasta are full, there are several options on the west side of I-5. The McCloud area also has developed camping.

Lake Siskiyou Beach and Camp (4239 W. A. Barr Rd., 530/926-2618 or 888/926-2618, www.lakesiskiyouresort.com, Apr.-Oct.) is located on the shore of glacier-fed Lake Siskiyou, just three miles west of Mount Shasta city. It has hundreds of tent sites ($20) and RV sites ($26-29) with partial and full hookups as well as cabins ($65-250). Plentiful amenities include a beach, boat and equipment rentals, a Splash Zone water park for kids ($8 per hour, $15 per 4 hours), a Snack Shack (10am-6pm daily Memorial Day-Labor Day), and the on-site Lake Sis Grille & Brew (530/926-1865, 8am-9pm Sun.-Thurs., 8am-10pm Fri.-Sat. Memorial Day-Labor Day, $10-15).

Castle Lake Campground (Castle Lake Rd., 6 sites, first-come, first-served, May-Nov., free) is about nine miles southwest of Mount Shasta city on beautiful Castle Lake. Facilities include picnic tables, fire rings, and vault toilets, but not drinking water. A stay at this campground has a three-night limit.

In addition to Lake Siskiyou Camp & Resort, **Chateau Shasta Mobile Home & RV Park** (704 S. Old Stage Rd., 530/926-3279, year-round, $25) offers a great location to park your vehicle and enjoy the area. Some of the spots are a bit crowded and exposed, but they all have great views.

Gumboot Lake (Forest Rd. 26, 6 sites, first-come, first-served, June-Oct., free) is an undeveloped campground located on Gumboot Lake about 12 miles west of Mount Shasta city. Facilities include fire rings and a vault toilet but no picnic tables or drinking water. A campfire permit is required.

Food

To stock up on groceries for camping and picnics, stop by the **Berryvale Grocery** (305 S. Mt. Shasta Blvd., 530/926-1576, www.berryvale.com, store 8am-8pm daily, café 8am-7pm daily). You can pick up high-quality international foods and then enjoy a cup of coffee at the café. From their attractive storefront in the center of town, **Mountain Song Natural Foods** (314 N. Mt. Shasta Blvd., 530/926-3391, www.mountainsong.biz, 10am-5pm Mon.-Sat., noon-4pm Sun.) offers health-food groceries, including a large selection of trail mix, homemade bread from the Oven Bakery, and local beans from Northbound Coffee Roasters, along with the best dried mango. The regular Monday **farmers market** (N. Mt. Shasta Blvd. between E. Castle and E. Alma Sts., 530/436-2532, www.mtshastafarmersmarket.com, 3:30pm-6pm Mon. early June-mid-Oct.) is a treat.

BAKERIES AND CAFÉS

Seven Suns Coffee and Café (1011 S. Mt. Shasta Blvd., 530/926-9701 or 530/926-9700, 6am-4pm daily, $7-12) is very pleasant. Breakfast and lunch are available in the form of local baked goods, burritos, wraps, and salads. They make all sorts of coffee and espresso drinks and sell beans by the pound. There's a spacious porch on the south side with umbrella-shaded tables, but the prime spot is the front sidewalk, with two small tables. During the summer, visit their small coffee outpost across the street with drive-through and walk-up windows.

The best baked goods in town come from the ★ **Oven Bakery** (214 N. Mt. Shasta

Blvd., 530/926-0960, www.theoven-bakery.com, 7:30am-noon Mon. and Wed., 7:30am-5pm Tues. and Thurs., 7:30am-noon, 5pm-7pm Fri., 2pm-5pm Sun.), which not only supplies the local coffee shops and grocery stores but also has its own storefront where you can come in, sit down, and enjoy a hot scone and a cup of coffee while you smell the baking in the background. The bakery also serves mouthwatering pizzas every Friday night ($24).

CLASSIC AMERICAN

As you drive through California, you'll see lots of signs for Black Bear Diners. Since its founding in 1995, it has grown into a chain of nearly 50 franchises concentrated in the Western states. The Mount Shasta **Black Bear Diner** (401 W. Lake St., 530/926-4669, www.blackbeardiner.com, 5:30am-10pm Sun.-Thurs., 5:30am-10:30pm Fri.-Sat., $7-17), was the original Black Bear, and sure enough, it has the feel of a local joint. The food is the usual diner fare, served up fast to guests in oversize red vinyl booths. The staff is helpful and willing to make good recommendations, and best of all, it's open late.

★ **The Goat Tavern** (107 Chestnut St., 530/926-0209, 11:30am-7:30pm Mon.-Wed., $9-15) offers microbrews, burgers, sandwiches, and vegetarian specialties. The laughter from the outdoor deck will let you know just how much fun everyone is having. Popular especially with the young and active crowd, it's recommended as part of an after-fishing or after-hiking recovery.

At the south end of town is the ★ **Wayside Grill** (2217 S. Mt. Shasta Blvd., 530/918-9234, www.waysidegrill.com, 4pm-10pm daily summer, 4:30pm-9pm Wed.-Sun. winter, $10-30) a big casual place that's so popular there's sometimes a wait in spite of its size. Reservations at busy times of year are a good idea. It has lots of brick-oven pizza plus burgers, sandwiches, pasta, steak, tacos, 12 beers on tap, and wine. All menu items are also available to take out, there's an outdoor patio with mountain views, and there's live music on weekends.

At the north edge of the town center is the retro **Burger Express Frosty & Grill** (415 N. Mt. Shasta Blvd., 530/926-3950, 11am-6pm Mon.-Fri., 11am-5pm Sat., $5-22). With great 1950s-style red stools and tables, a cheerful red-and-white counter, and a checkerboard floor, the place feels up-to-the-minute and delightfully old-fashioned at the same time. It serves basic burgers and hotdogs, shakes, sundaes, and soft-serve ice cream in cones. Eat in or take your food out to the small patio and enjoy the sun and the community. Either way, the eating and the nostalgia are good.

MEXICAN

Casa Ramos (1136 S. Mt. Shasta Blvd., 530/926-0250, www.casaramos.net, 11am-9pm daily, $8-15) is a small chain of 11 authentic Mexican family restaurants in Northern California. The local incarnation is particularly cheerful and welcoming. "It's Taco Time!" says the sign out front, and when you see the place, you'll probably agree. Prices are reasonable, portions are ample, and the whole family is welcome. It has specials for kids and lots of choices, including steak, chicken, and cheeseburgers, to satisfy anyone who isn't in the mood for Mexican.

FINE DINING

At the white-tablecloth end of the dining spectrum in Mount Shasta is **Lily's** (1013 S. Mt. Shasta Blvd., 530/962-3372, www.lilysrestaurant.com, 8am-2pm, 5pm-9pm daily, $12-24), a lovely spacious place with a white picket fence. Breakfast is a full selection of omelets, pancakes, and other American favorites, plus huevos rancheros, biscuits and gravy, and healthier choices like tofu and fruit. Lunch is usually burgers, salads, and choices like the eggplant hoagie and the walnut dal burger. Dinner entrées might include char-grilled filet mignon au poivre flambéed with brandy, finished in a green peppercorn sauce, and wrapped in bacon, or a tofu vegetable curry.

Information and Services

At the **Mount Shasta Visitors Bureau** (300 Pine St., 530/926-4865, ext. 203, http://visitmtshasta.com) you'll find information about hotels, restaurants, and local recreation; the staff is also helpful with driving directions to nearby sites.

For wilderness permits and trail advice, head for one of the local ranger stations. The **Mount Shasta Ranger Station** (204 W. Alma St., 530/926-4511, www.fs.usda.gov, 8am-4:30pm Mon.-Fri. fall-spring, 8am-4:30pm Mon.-Sat. summer) can supply wilderness and summit passes, plus park maps and information about current mountain conditions. A summit pass ($20 for three days, $30 for yearly pass) is required when hiking above 10,000 on Mount Shasta, and it allows you to climb to the summit; you can buy one at the ranger station during business hours. A free wilderness pass is also necessary. You have the option of self-registering at the trailhead and leaving payment in an envelope as long as you have a check or cash. In person at the ranger station you can use a credit card as well. California campfire permits are free, but you must get them in person, so plan to come to the ranger station during business hours. The Shasta Wilderness requires you to have a permit just to enter, even if you're not spending the night. Those permits are also available here for free, and you can get them inside or from a self-service station out front.

The town of Mount Shasta has a full-service hospital, **Mercy Medical Center Mount Shasta** (914 Pine St., 530/926-6111, www.mercymtshasta.org), with a 24-hour emergency room.

Transportation

Mount Shasta is on I-5; from Sacramento it's 220 miles (3.5 hours). Parking in the town is usually easy, except during local events that draw numerous visitors. The nearest commercial airport is 60 miles (1 hour) away. **Redding Municipal Airport** (RDD, 6751 Woodrum Circle, 530/224-4320, http://ci.redding.ca.us) is served by United Express.

VICINITY OF MOUNT SHASTA

★ Castle Crags State Park

Castle Crags State Park (20022 Castle Creek Rd., Castella, 530/235-2684, www.

Castle Crags State Park

parks.ca.gov, $8 per vehicle) is one of the greats in California's extensive network of state parks. With 4,350 acres of land, 28 miles of hiking trails, and some very dramatic granite peaks and cliffs, it is a wonderful destination or a convenient place to camp while you enjoy Mount Shasta to the north or Shasta Lake to the south. You can fish and swim in the Sacramento River, rock-climb the spectacular 6,000-foot crags, take a variety of hikes, or just enjoy stunning views of Shasta and other nearby mountains and ranges.

If you don't have much time, you can still have a nice little walk and a great Castle Crags experience. After you enter at the gate, drive through the park following the signs for "Vista Point." A paved walk of no more than 0.25 mile from the Vista Point parking lot leads to a spectacular overlook with views all around. Bring your binoculars and your camera.

If you can stay longer, drive to the Vista Point parking lot and use it as access to the Crags Trailhead. The **Crags Trail to Castle Dome** (5.5 miles round-trip) is strenuous and worth every step. If you're a strong hiker with a brisk pace, it will take about 2 hours on the way up and 1-1.5 hours on the way down. Feel free to go slower, though—it's a steep climb with memorable views all along the way. Pull out your camera for an excuse to take lots of breaks. About 2 miles up the trail is a sign for Indian Springs, a 0.25-mile jaunt off the main trail.

Castle Crags has more than 40 established **rock climbing** routes plus plenty of wide, open formations for explorers who prefer to make their own paths. You'll get to tackle domes, spires, and walls of granite that reach 6,000 feet into the sky. The crags first thrust upward and then broke off and were scrubbed by glaciers into the fascinating climbable formations visible today. Some favorite climbs at Castle Crags are the Cosmic Wall on Mount Hubris, Castle Dome, and Six Toe Crack.

The park also has a **campground** (www.reserveamerica.com, reservations May-Sept., first-come, first-served Oct.-Apr., $25) with 64 sites as well as 12 environmental sites ($15) available year-round on a first-come, first-served basis. Some sites are close to the freeway and can be loud, but others are tucked deep enough in the pines to feel miles away from civilization.

Castle Crags is easy to find. Take I-5 north toward the city of Mount Shasta and follow signs for the park. From the Bay Area, it's a 170-mile trip on I-5 north to exit 724 at Castella. Turn left onto Castle Creek Road, and the park is less than 0.5 mile. If you're coming from the north, the park is just 6 miles south of Dunsmuir and about 13 miles (15 minutes) south of the city of Mount Shasta.

McCloud

A wonderful waterfall to visit is **McCloud Falls** (McCloud Ranger Station, 530/964-2184, www.shastacascade.com) on the McCloud River. At Lower McCloud Falls you'll see roiling white water pouring over a 30-foot rock wall into an aerated river pool below. Middle McCloud Falls resembles a tiny Niagara, a level fall of water that's wider than it is tall. Upper McCloud Falls cascades powerfully but briefly down into a chilly pool that can double as a swimming hole if you're feeling brave. The loop trail that takes you past all three is about 3.5 miles long. To get here, take the McCloud exit from I-5 onto Highway 89 east. After about five miles, look for a sign on the left directing you to Fowler's Camp and Lower McCloud Falls. After another mile is the Lower Falls picnic area, where you can park.

Little Mount Hoffman Lookout Tower (Hwy. 89, east of McCloud, McCloud District Office 530/964-2184, reservations 877/444-6777, www.recreation.gov, July-mid-Oct., $75) is in the northeast corner of the Shasta-Trinity National Forest near Medicine Lake. This 1920s-era lookout tower was used regularly until 1978 and is sometimes still employed in fire emergencies. Meanwhile, you can rent it for a romantic vacation, writer's retreat, or hiking base camp. The views are outstanding—from the tower's height of more than

7,300 feet, you can see Mount Shasta, Mount Lassen, Mount McLoughlin, and more.

The McCloud area has several campgrounds with access to the McCloud River as well as to nearby Mount Shasta. Popular **Fowlers Camp** (39 sites, first-come, first-served, Apr.-Nov., $15) is at 3,400 feet elevation on the Upper McCloud River. Facilities include picnic tables, fire rings, vault toilets, and drinking water. Fowlers Camp is five miles east of McCloud on Highway 89.

At 3,700 feet elevation, **Cattle Camp** (27 sites, first-come, first-served, Apr.-Nov., $15) is the second campground on the Upper McCloud River. Facilities include picnic tables, fire rings, vault toilets, and drinking water. Cattle Camp is 10 miles east of McCloud on Highway 89.

Ah-Di-Na (16 sites, first-come, first-served, Apr.-Nov., $10) is a remote campground located at 2,300 feet elevation on the Lower McCloud River. Facilities include picnic tables, flush toilets, and drinking water. The campground is located 10 miles south of McCloud. Access is via a rough dirt road.

★ McArthur-Burney Falls Memorial State Park

Often billed as the most beautiful waterfall in California, even by regular visitors to Yosemite, Burney Falls in **McArthur-Burney Falls Memorial State Park** (24898 Hwy. 89, Burney, 530/335-2777, www.parks.ca.gov, $8) has been thrilling viewers for generations. No less a naturalist than Theodore Roosevelt declared these falls one of the wonders of the world. The park is the second oldest in the California State Park system and is about halfway between Mount Lassen and Mount Shasta.

Burney Falls flows strong and true year-round and is just as beautiful in September as in April. More good news: You don't have to hike to reach the falls; they're right by the parking lot. Still, it's more than worth your time to get out of your car and take a walk around the wide sheets of water that almost look like a miniature Niagara; it's only a quick walk to the pool at the base of the falls. For the best views, take the one-mile hike around the 129-foot waterfall.

spectacular Burney Falls

The McArthur-Burney Falls campground (Hwy. 89, 530/335-2777, reservations May-Sept. 800/444-7275, www.reserveamerica.com, year-round, $35) has 102 reservable campsites and three primitive hike-in/bike-in sites. It also has 24 cabins ($105) with heaters and platform beds. Facilities include restrooms with flush toilets, showers, picnic tables, and fire rings.

McArthur-Burney Falls Memorial State Park is on Highway 89 near Burney; from Redding, take Highway 299 east to Burney, and then head north on Highway 89 for six miles.

Weed

★ **Stewart Mineral Springs** (4617 Stewart Springs Rd., Weed, 530/938-2222, www.stewartmineralsprings.com, $70-160) is a rustic resort nestled in the woods about 20 minutes north of the town of Mount Shasta. Secluded

Tule Lake

Near the very tip of California, north of Lava Beds National Monument, is large and lovely Tule Lake, visible from a long distance across the high desert landscape. Although the lake you see today is still beautiful, blue, and deep, it is much smaller than it used to be. One of the early projects of the U.S. Bureau of Reclamation was to "reclaim" the land beneath Tule Lake and Lower Klamath Lake and make it available for homesteading. What was once underwater, and later homestead land, is now mostly farmland.

You can still see some striking evidence of the lake's original size from **Petroglyph Point,** a section of Lava Beds National Monument located east of the lake and separate from the main lava beds area. Along **Petroglyph Point Trail,** you may wonder how the ancient markings on the rock walls high above got up there. Tule Lake was much bigger 5,000-6,000 years ago, and what is now hot dry land was all underwater. The Modoc artists simply steered their boats to the edge of the lake and worked on the lakeshore rock face—now far out of reach.

and peaceful yet close to local attractions, Stewart Mineral Springs offers a variety of sleeping options. Four private cabins ($90-110) each have a queen bed, full bath, woodstove, and kitchenette. Campers can choose among tent sites ($35), RV sites with electrical hookups ($55), or one of the five tepees ($45, optional cot rental $5). Other options include rooms in a small motel ($70), apartments of various sizes with kitchenettes ($80-160), and a whole A-frame house that sleeps up to 15 ($460 plus $20 pp beyond 10). No phones, TVs, or wireless Internet are on the premises, and cell-phone coverage is spotty. Overnight guests can enjoy the clothing-optional sundeck and the "last dry-wood sauna in Northern California." Massages and indoor mineral baths are available for an additional fee, and members of the local Karuk Tribe lead traditional Sweat Lodge Purification Ceremonies (1pm, 3pm, or 6pm Sat., donation $30) on the premises every week during warmer months, and usually monthly during the winter. The **Glorified Roots Juice Bar** (noon-4pm Sat.-Sun. May-Sept., $4-12) offers smoothies and vegetarian wraps on the patio between the creek and the bathhouse. For more formal dining, the **Creekside Café** offers lunch and dinner indoors or out (530/938-2221, noon-9pm Thurs.-Sun. Memorial Day-Sept., $10-24). The fare is carefully prepared vegetarian, vegan, pasta, and seafood with beer and wine. Visitors to Stewart Mineral Springs are advised to bring their own coffee, breakfast, and lunch.

Tulelake

From 1942 to 1946 Tule Lake was the name of one of the 10 internment camps where Japanese Americans were held during World War II. In commemoration of the events that went on here and in the other camps, in December 2008 a total of nine sites were made into one national monument, collectively called the **World War II Valor in the Pacific National Monument Tule Lake Unit** (530/260-0537, www.nps.gov/tule). This is the site of the largest and most controversial of the internment locations, where a "segregation center" stayed open even after the war, incarcerating Japanese Americans who had given unsatisfactory answers to the infamous loyalty questionnaire.

The temporary **visitors center** (800 Main St., 530/260-0537, 8:30am-5pm daily late May-early Sept.) is in the Tulelake-Butte Valley Fairgrounds Museum (530/667-5312, 9:30am-4:30pm Mon.-Fri.). Take a tour (530/260-0537, 1pm Sat. late May-early Sept., hours vary early Sept.-late May) of the very interesting **Tule Lake Segregation Center Jail** and **Camp Tulelake.** The visitors center at Lava Beds National Monument (530/667-8113) can arrange tours during the off-season.

The five rooms in the simple, homey **Winema Lodge** (5215 Hill Rd., 530/667-5158, www.winemalodge.com, $85-110) sleep up to five people each and have access to a bath down the hall. Ten motel rooms with private baths are available, and there are RV sites with full hookups ($25). Family-style meals ($13-30) are also available.

Captain Jack's Stronghold (45650 Hwy. 139, 530/664-5566, www.cjstronghold.com, 9am-8pm Tues.-Sun., $9-22) is a popular spot in Tulelake. The menu includes brisket and chicken-fried steak, but there's also a salad bar and some vegetarian options. If you like Americana, stop in at **Jolly Kone Burgers** (223 Main St., 530/667-2622, 8am-6pm Mon.-Fri., 10am-5pm Sat., 11am-4pm Sun., open until 7pm or 8pm late-Mar.-late Oct., $6.25-10) for hamburgers, ice cream, and homemade pies and cakes.

★ Lava Beds National Monument

One of the best places to see the results of volcanic activity is at **Lava Beds National Monument** (Hill Rd., 530/667-8113, www.nps.gov/labe, sunrise-sunset daily, visitors center 8am-6pm daily late May-early Sept., 8:30am-5pm daily early Sept.-late May, $10). This fascinating 47,000-acre park is delightfully undervisited, no doubt owing to its remote location. With ancient Native American petroglyphs, an unrivalled series of deep and twisting "tube" caves, primordial piles of lava, and an abundance of desert wildlife, it is a mother lode of history, nature, and awe-inspiring sights.

Over the course of about 500,000 years, Medicine Lake Volcano has created an amazing landscape. Among the hiking trails, Modoc battle sites, and scrubby high-desert wilderness are more than 700 caves created by underground lava flows. Some of the caves have been developed for fairly easy access—outfitted with ladders, walkways, and lights—but others remain in their original condition. All are home to whole ecosystems that thrive in the damp darkness.

In summer about 200,000 bats live in the park; two of the 14 species represented here live in trees, and the other 12 live in caves. Park officials monitor where and when bats

a cave in Lava Beds National Monument

are likely to be concentrated, and they'll steer you away from those places, mainly for the safety of the bats.

HIKING AND CAVING

The **visitors center** (530/667-8113, 8am-6pm daily late May-early Sept., 8:30am-5pm daily early Sept.-late May) recommends bringing up to three flashlights per person to explore the caves, as well as caving or bicycle helmets (it's easy to hit your head on the low ceilings of the caves). The visitors center will lend you a large flashlight and sells a simple helmet ($8.15). For the more challenging caves, gloves, knee pads, a cave map, and a compass are also recommended.

However, you don't necessarily need a lot of equipment to visit the caves here. The short, paved **Cave Loop Trail** (2.25 miles) outside the visitors center leads past 16 different caves—their cool rocky entrances are fascinating in themselves. Three more caves are accessible via a short hiker-only trail beside the visitors center. The park recommends **Mushpot Cave** (770 feet) as an introductory cave; it's well-lit and easy to get into.

In addition to the numerous caves are 12 hiking trails. One of the best-known trails is **Captain Jack's Stronghold** (1.5 miles, moderate); the interpretive signage will help you understand the contentious history of this area. Start at the visitors center and take the park's main road seven miles north.

The wide, easy **Schonchin Butte Trail** (1.4 miles round-trip, moderate) leads to a working fire tower, along with the trail built by the Civilian Conservation Corps between 1939 and 1941. If a ranger is present when you get to the top, you may be able to go up to the fire tower's lookout deck. To get to the Schonchin Butte Trail from the visitors center, turn left onto the main park road and drive 3.2 miles to the trail sign on the right. From here, it's a 0.5-mile drive on a gravel road to the parking area.

CAMPING

Lava Beds National Monument (Hill Rd., 530/667-8113, www.nps.gov/labe) features one campground, **Indian Well** (43 sites, first-come, first-served, $10), close to the visitors center. The campground has ample potable water, modern restrooms with flush toilets (no showers), and an amphitheater; don't expect much shade at the campsites, however. One of the best features for history buffs are the picnic tables, built by hand out of local lava stone by the Civilian Conservation Corps in the 1930s.

GETTING THERE

Lava Beds National Monument is in the remote northeastern corner of the state about 70 miles from Mount Shasta city. To get here from I-5, take U.S. 97 north at Weed. Drive 50 miles north, and at the state line just north of Dorris, turn east onto Highway 161. Continue 16 miles east on Highway 161 to Hill Road, then turn right (south), and drive 9 miles to the park entrance. Plan at least two hours for the drive from Weed, and note that U.S. 97 gets snow at high elevations.

Lake Tahoe

The San Francisco Bay Area is a top vacation destination for people from all over the world. So where do people who live there take their vacations? Tahoe.

Sparkling blue Lake Tahoe and its surrounding mountains, lakes, ski resorts, hiking trails, hot springs, charming mountain towns, casinos, and varied wilderness areas say "vacation" to just about anyone. Lake Tahoe is 22 miles long, 12 miles wide, and 1,645 feet deep at its deepest point, with a surface elevation of 6,225 feet. It's the 10th-deepest lake in the world and the second-deepest in the United States, after Crater Lake in Oregon. Sixty-three streams flow into the lake, and the Truckee River flows out, carrying Lake Tahoe's waters to Pyramid Lake. Even though Lake Tahoe's water temperature ranges 41-68°F, the lake is a great place for all sorts of water activities.

The Tahoe area has an international reputation as a skiing paradise, with some of the finest ski resorts in the nation—second only to the Rockies for vertical drop, quality of snow, and the number of resorts. It offers many opportunities for skiers, snowboarders, cross-country skiers, and snowshoers, as well as for playing in the snow with the kids.

Tahoe is slightly less crowded in the summer months than during ski season, and the weather is gorgeous every day. Between the pristine lake and the unspoiled wilderness areas, it is a delight for wakeboarders, waterskiers, campers, hikers, and families to swim, sun, play in the sand, rent kayaks, or just be in a beautiful place.

Californians often refer to Lake Tahoe simply as Tahoe, but the locals get more specific—it's all about the North Shore, with ski resorts, the South Shore, with its sprawling town, and East Shore, with glittering casinos just across the state line in Nevada.

It's possible to drive all the way around the lake, stopping at both the South and North Shores and enjoying the eastern and western perspectives as well as the attractions and natural beauty of both California and Nevada. Whether you're looking for radical recreation or traditional relaxation of the more restful kind, you can find it at Tahoe year-round.

Previous: Heavenly Gondola; Lake Tahoe's unique boulders. **Above:** bear crossing.

Look for ★ to find recommended sights, activities, dining, and lodging.

Highlights

★ **Heavenly Gondola:** Winter or summer, a ride up the gondola at Heavenly ski resort rewards with views from 9,163 feet (page 334).

★ **Emerald Bay:** The most beautiful section of the "Most Beautiful Drive in America," Emerald Bay sparkles year-round. Whether you hike the trails of the state park of the same name, or just stop to gaze down at it from a highway overlook, the bay is Tahoe at its best (page 336).

★ **Ed Z'berg Sugar Pine Point State Park:** Visit one of the state's best parks and ski on trails from the 1960 Olympics (page 353).

★ **The Village at Squaw Valley:** This adorable mountainside village is the perfect place to while away a winter day amid boutiques, galleries, and restaurants (page 355).

★ **Donner Memorial State Park:** Donner offers a lake that's perfect for recreation, along with interpretive trails and monuments illuminating one of the most compelling stories about the settlement of the West (page 374).

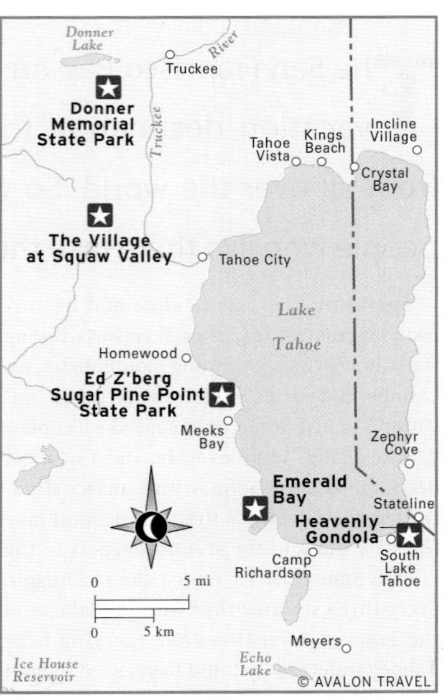

Lake Tahoe

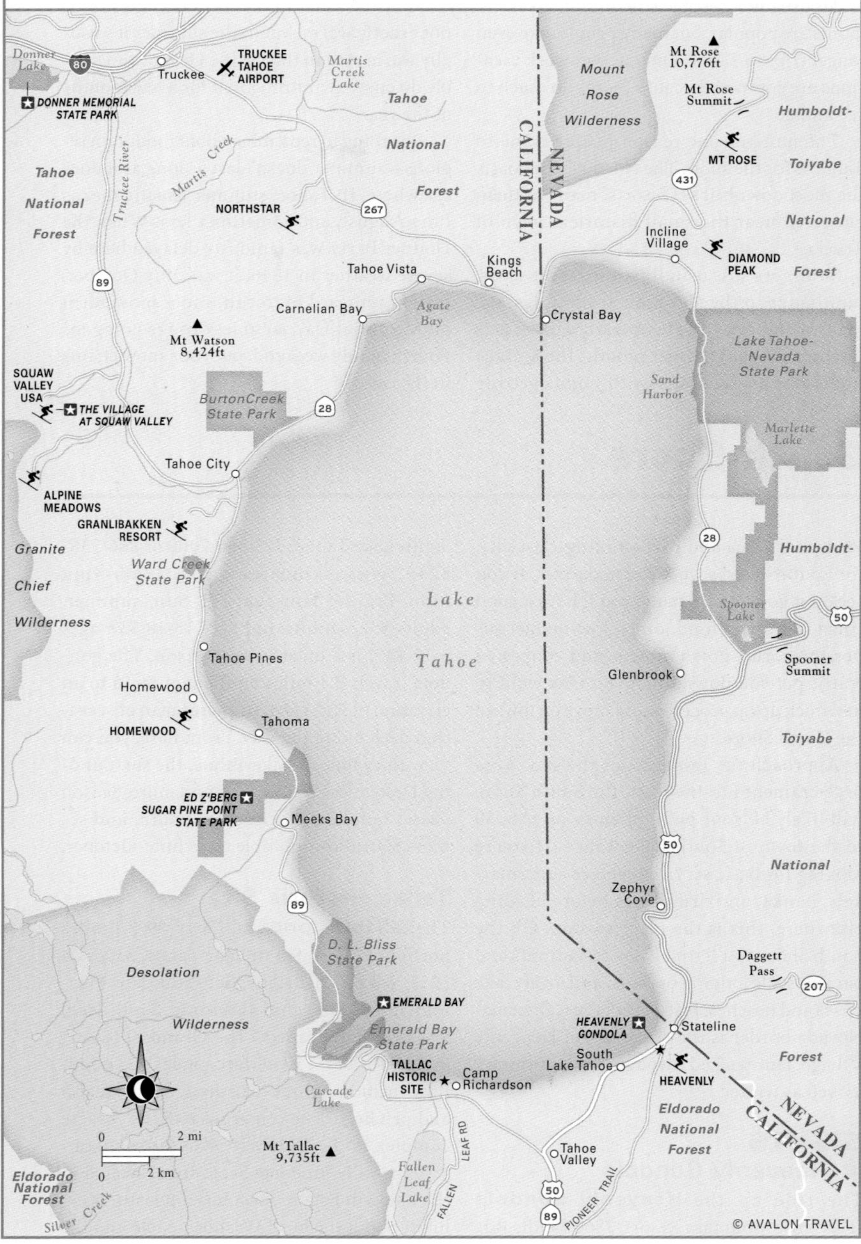
Donner Lake
80
Truckee
TRUCKEE TAHOE AIRPORT
Martis Creek Lake
DONNER MEMORIAL STATE PARK
Tahoe National Forest
Martis Creek
Truckee River
NORTHSTAR
267
Tahoe Vista
Kings Beach
89
Carnelian Bay
Agate Bay
Mt Watson 8,424ft
SQUAW VALLEY USA
THE VILLAGE AT SQUAW VALLEY
BurtonCreek State Park
28
Tahoe City
ALPINE MEADOWS
GRANLIBAKKEN RESORT
Granite Chief Wilderness
Ward Creek State Park
Tahoe Pines
Homewood
HOMEWOOD
Tahoma
ED Z'BERG SUGAR PINE POINT STATE PARK
Meeks Bay
D. L. Bliss State Park
Desolation Wilderness
EMERALD BAY
Emerald Bay State Park
TALLAC HISTORIC SITE
Camp Richardson
Cascade Lake
0
2 mi
2 km
Mt Tallac 9,735ft
Eldorado National Forest
Silver Creek
Fallen Leaf Lake
LEAF RD
FALLEN
50
PIONEER TRAIL
Tahoe Valley
Mount Rose Wilderness
CALIFORNIA
NEVADA
Mt Rose 10,776ft
Mt Rose Summit
MT ROSE
431
Humboldt-Toiyabe National Forest
Incline Village
DIAMOND PEAK
Crystal Bay
Lake Tahoe-Nevada State Park
Sand Harbor
Marlette Lake
Lake Tahoe
Spooner Lake
Spooner Summit
Glenbrook
Zephyr Cove
Daggett Pass
207
HEAVENLY GONDOLA
Stateline
South Lake Tahoe
HEAVENLY
Eldorado National Forest
© AVALON TRAVEL

PLANNING YOUR TIME

Lake Tahoe has numerous recreation options and is usually accessible year-round. Weekend jaunts are popular, but many people take even longer trips to Tahoe. One- to two-week vacations are common because there's so much to see and do.

The number-one reason people come to Tahoe is for the snow. The North Shore boasts the most downhill ski resorts, many of them clustered near the small historical town of Truckee.

Summers are usually sunny and clear, but thanks to the elevation around the lake (5,000-7,000 feet), the temperature never gets too high. In the summer months the average highs stay around 80°F with nights getting down to the 40s. The South Shore offers great lakeshore parks with numerous opportunities to enjoy the water in the summer. The lake is not exactly warm, but in the summer it's usually warmer than the Pacific Ocean, and people do enjoy swimming in it for a few months of the year.

One thing to remember about mountain regions—summer doesn't last as long as it does elsewhere. In Tahoe, summer usually means June-August, and sometimes less. When the Donner Party was famously delayed here by severe weather in 1846, it was only October. It's not unheard of to run into a snowstorm on Memorial Day, so unless you're going for Fourth of July weekend, put your snow chains in the car.

South Shore

Part resort area and part working-class city, the South Shore is what you make of it. If you seek out good restaurants, you'll have a good time. But if fast food joints, low-budget superstores, run-down motels, and congested traffic get you down, then you may want to just stock up on groceries and move on toward the North Shore.

Approaching Tahoe from the Bay Area or Sacramento to the west, the South Shore will likely be your point of entry on U.S. 50 to the town of South Lake Tahoe. If you're looking for basic services such as supermarkets, banks, and drugstores before heading elsewhere, this is the place to stop. On the South Shore you'll find lively restaurants and bars, upscale lodging options, and lovely lake views and beaches. Just west of the California-Nevada border is the ski resort of Heavenly Village, jam-packed throughout the summer as well as winter.

SIGHTS

★ Heavenly Gondola

The ride up the **Heavenly Gondola** (Heavenly Mountain Resort, 3860 Saddle Rd., South Lake Tahoe, 775/586-7000 or 866/736-8245, www.skiheavenly.com, 9am-4pm Mon.-Fri., 8:30am-4am Fri.-Sun. summer, adults $52, seniors and ages 13-18 $37, ages 5-12 $27) is a must in any season. The gondola travels 2.4 miles up the mountain to an elevation of 9,123 feet, stopping at an observation deck along the way. From here, you can view the whole of Lake Tahoe, the surrounding Desolation Wilderness, and more. Season passes (adults $70, children, youth, and seniors $50) allow multiple rides June-October.

Tallac Historic Site

The **Tallac Historic Site** (Hwy. 89, 3.1 miles north of U.S. 50, South Lake Tahoe, 530/541-5227, www.fs.usda.gov, Sat.-Sun. late May-mid-June, daily mid-June-mid-Sept., free) was originally called "The Grandest Resort in the World." Most of the complex's 33 buildings, including three mansions, exude wealth and privilege. The centerpiece of the 74-acre complex is the **Baldwin Museum** (10am-4:30pm daily June-late Sept., free), located in the Baldwin Estate. The museum features exhibits about the local Washoe people and the

South Shore

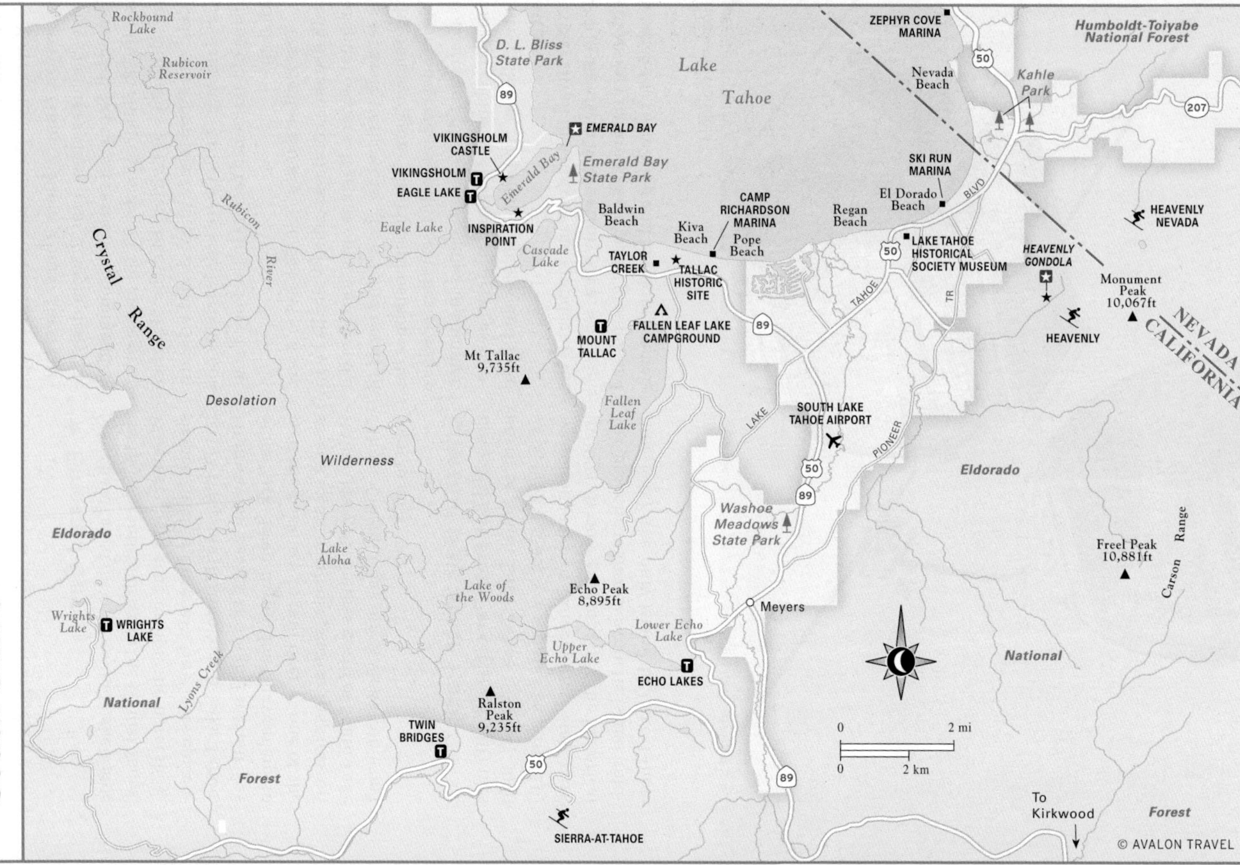
Rockbound Lake
Rubicon Reservoir
D. L. Bliss State Park
Lake
Tahoe
ZEPHYR COVE MARINA
Humboldt-Toiyabe National Forest
50
Nevada Beach
Kahle Park
207
89
EMERALD BAY
VIKINGSHOLM CASTLE
Emerald Bay
Emerald Bay State Park
VIKINGSHOLM
EAGLE LAKE
SKI RUN MARINA
Rubicon
Eagle Lake
INSPIRATION POINT
Baldwin Beach
CAMP RICHARDSON MARINA
Regan Beach
El Dorado Beach
BLVD
HEAVENLY NEVADA
Crystal
Range
River
Cascade Lake
Kiva Beach
Pope Beach
TAYLOR CREEK
TALLAC HISTORIC SITE
LAKE TAHOE HISTORICAL SOCIETY MUSEUM
HEAVENLY GONDOLA
Monument Peak 10,067ft
TAHOE
TR
MOUNT TALLAC
FALLEN LEAF LAKE CAMPGROUND
HEAVENLY
NEVADA
CALIFORNIA
Mt Tallac 9,735ft
Desolation
Fallen Leaf Lake
LAKE
SOUTH LAKE TAHOE AIRPORT
PIONEER
Wilderness
Eldorado
Washoe Meadows State Park
Eldorado
Lake Aloha
Freel Peak 10,881ft
Carson Range
Lake of the Woods
Echo Peak 8,895ft
Meyers
Wrights Lake
WRIGHTS LAKE
Lower Echo Lake
Upper Echo Lake
ECHO LAKES
National
Lyons Creek
National
Ralston Peak 9,235ft
TWIN BRIDGES
0
2 mi
0
2 km
Forest
SIERRA-AT-TAHOE
To Kirkwood
Forest
© AVALON TRAVEL

importance of Lucky Baldwin to the history of California.

You can tour the interior of the 1894 **Pope Mansion** (1pm, 2:30pm Thurs.-Tues. late-May-late June, 11am, 1pm, 2:30pm daily late June-early Sept., reservations recommended, adults $8, children under 13 $3) and sign up for children's activities, like the "Kitchen Kids" workshop (age 6-12, Wed. and Fri. early July-late Aug., $10), where kids learn to cook using old-fashioned recipes in the Pope Estate kitchen.

The **Heller Estate** (530/541-4975, www.valhallatahoe.com) was called Valhalla by its original owners. It is not open for tours but is set aside to showcase the art and music of the Tahoe region. The Heller boathouse has been converted into a 164-seat theater where concerts and plays are presented in summer. Smaller cabins on the grounds serve as summer galleries for photographers and local artists.

Next to all that history and grandeur is the **Pope-Baldwin Recreation Area,** which includes easy nature trails, a picnic ground, and a beach for swimming and kayaking (rentals are available). In winter, the Tallac buildings are closed, but the grounds are a great spot for cross-country skiing and snowshoeing.

★ Emerald Bay

Some have called the road around Lake Tahoe the most beautiful drive in the United States. Whether that's true or not, the horseshoe-shaped inlet of **Emerald Bay** is its epicenter. Driving north from South Lake Tahoe, Highway 89 passes through Emerald Bay State Park. Even if you don't have plans to visit the park, try to pull over at one of the several scenic overlooks, such as **Inspiration Point** (Hwy. 89, 8 miles north of South Lake Tahoe). Emerald Bay offers views you won't want to miss.

Emerald Bay State Park

Emerald Bay State Park (Hwy. 89, 10 miles north of South Lake Tahoe, 530/541-3030 or 530/525-3345, www.parks.ca.gov, $10) was designated an "underwater" state park in 1994. It now encompasses the historical Vikingsholm mansion; Fannette Island (mid-June-Feb.), the only island in Lake Tahoe;

Heavenly Gondola

the Eagle Point Campground; and a boat-in campground on the north side of the bay. In addition, there are miles of hiking trails, including the **Rubicon Trail,** from Emerald Bay State Park to nearby D. L. Bliss State Park. Some visitors still enjoy the underwater aspect—scuba divers can see the remains of boats, cars, and some artifacts that date back to the turn of the 20th century.

Vikingsholm Castle

Wealthy benefactor Lora Josephine Knight had summered on the North Shore for 16 years when she decided to build her dream home on Emerald Bay. The result was the elegant Scandinavian-style mansion **Vikingsholm Castle** (Emerald Bay State Park, Hwy. 89, 530/525-9530, www.vikingsholm.org or www.parks.ca.gov, tours 10:30am-3:30pm daily late May-late Sept., grounds free, tours adults $10, ages 7-17 $8, cash or check only). This architectural gem is an intriguing reminder of a world gone by. Built by a Swedish architect in 1929, the castle-like structure is composed of granite boulders and includes towers, hand-cut timbers, and sod roofs green with growing grass. The interior is furnished with authentic Scandinavian period reproductions.

Visitors are welcome to enjoy the beach, the grounds, and the exterior of Vikingsholm at no charge; the mansion is only accessible on the tours. Access is via a steep one-mile trail from the Harvey West parking lot at the **Emerald Bay Overlook** (Hwy. 89, $10). You can also reach Vikingsholm via the Rubicon Trail (1.7 miles one-way) from Eagle Point Campground in Emerald Bay State Park ($8).

D. L. Bliss State Park

D. L. Bliss State Park (Hwy. 89, 2 miles north of Emerald Bay, 530/525-3345 or 530/525-7277, www.parks.ca.gov, spring-fall, $10) has some of the best views in Tahoe. The park is directly north of Emerald Bay State Park, and the two are sometimes considered one unit. Hiking is a popular activity; trails include the **Rubicon-Lighthouse Trail** to Rubicon Point's lighthouse, built in 1919 and restored and stabilized in 2001; it was once the highest-elevation lighthouse on a navigable body of water in the world. Swimming is great at the Lester and Calawee Cove Beaches,

Emerald Bay

and trout and salmon fishing are also popular from D. L. Bliss's shores. Three campgrounds are within the park.

SPORTS AND RECREATION

Ski Resorts

Skiing can be an expensive hobby, and the cost of lift tickets may be a key factor in your vacation planning. The prices listed are subject to change, and the cost of lift tickets sometimes changes substantially and more often than other expenses. Check with the resort directly to confirm prices and availability before planning a trip.

HEAVENLY

On the less-skied South Shore, the queen bee of the few resorts is undoubtedly **Heavenly** (Wildwood Rd. and Saddle Rd., South Lake Tahoe, 775/586-7000, www.skiheavenly.com, 9am-4pm Mon.-Fri., 8:30am-4pm Sat.-Sun. Dec.-Apr., adults $98-125, youth $90-103, children $58-69, seniors $90-103). At 10,067 feet, Heavenly offers the highest elevation of any mountain at Tahoe, along with the longest tubing hill on the West Coast and one ski run that's five miles long.

Heavenly sprawls more than most resorts. Skiers can choose from four lodge and village access points up to the ski area: Heavenly Village down by the lake, California Lodge in the South Shore downtown area, and Boulder Lodge and Stagecoach Lodge inland. Ninety-seven runs snake down the mountainside, taking advantage of the more than 3,500 vertical feet. Beware: Even the lowland ski area near the California Lodge has mostly black-diamond runs. Approach the Killebrew and Mott Canyons carefully—gates at the head of these runs underscore the fact that only expert skiers should take them on. About 20 percent of Heavenly's runs are for beginners, and most of the beginner area is served by the gondola and the Powderbowl Express Six Chair. Freestylers have four terrain parks—High Roller, Groove, Ante Up, and Player's. In the works is a new adventure zone just for newbies and youngsters, called Black Bear Hollow, as well as a ski school lodge for children.

Heavenly is an intensely popular resort, so prepare to find parking a challenge at whichever lodge you choose. Crowding and lines at the lifts, especially at the bottom of the mountain, can get bad on weekends and holidays. On the other hand, once you're out of your car and on the mountain, you'll have access to nearly every service and amenity you need. Even better, take the **BlueGo Shuttle** (530/541-7149, www.bluego.org, free), which picks up at all the major lodging areas around town and drops skiers off at any of Heavenly's four lodges.

KIRKWOOD

The South Shore's mid-tier resort is **Kirkwood** (1501 Kirkwood Meadows Dr., off Hwy. 88, Kirkwood, 209/258-6000, www.kirkwood.com, 9am-4pm daily Dec.-Apr., adults $86-102, seniors $77-92, ages 13-18 $77-92, ages 6-12 $63-74). Kirkwood offers dozens of downhill runs, plus everything from pipes to a cross-country space. Lift-ticket prices change seasonally, and the pricing scheme is complex, with special rates for military personnel and college students, multiday packages, and more.

Both the easiest runs and the ski school **Tahoe Learning Center** (209/258-7754) are located near the Timber Creek Day Lodge. The Kirkwood Mountain Lodge lifts lead to more intermediate and advanced runs. The back of the mountain is devoted to double-black-diamond runs. Kirkwood features terrain parks for skiers and boarders, including a boarder-skier cross course, half-pipes, beginner terrain, and areas with sound systems and music to complete the atmosphere. For a more sedate adventure, check out the snowshoe and cross-country park; you can rent equipment at the **Cross Country and Snowshoe Center** (Hwy. 88 before Kirkwood, 209/258-7248, 9am-4pm daily winter, adults $26, youth and seniors $22, children $14).

You'll find plenty of sustenance in and

around Kirkwood. The resort includes three restaurants: **Off the Wall Bar & Grill** (209/258-7365) is in the Lodge at Kirkwood; **Cornice Grill** (209/258-7225) is in the Kirkwood Village; and the **Kirkwood Inn** (209/258-7304) is at the entrance to Kirkwood, next to the Nordic Center. The **Red Cliffs Day Lodge** at the Nordic Center also has a café and a deli. If you prefer to stay where you ski, look into Kirkwood's array of lodges and vacation rentals.

Kirkwood also offers backcountry snowcat tours beyond the resort's northwest boundary near Martin Point. The tours (209/258-7360, 3.5-4.5 hours, $250 pp, includes four runs per group) are available by reservation and depend on snow conditions. Avalanche beacons, probes, 30-minute safety briefing, and backpacks are included.

SIERRA-AT-TAHOE

For a smaller and less crowded South Shore ski experience, check out **Sierra-at-Tahoe** (1111 Sierra-at-Tahoe Rd., Twin Bridges, 530/659-7453, www.sierraattahoe.com, 9am-4pm Mon.-Fri., 8:30am-4pm Sat.-Sun. late Nov.-Apr., rates vary), with plenty of long sweeping advanced runs as well as many good intermediate tracks. The "Easy Street" area is 100 acres of beginner-only terrain; slightly advanced beginners can enjoy the Sugar 'n Spice Trail, which runs all the way from the top. The Grandview Express quad chairs take skiers to the very top, the Nob Hill double chair lands midway up the mountain and also provides access to the backside, and the Rock Garden and Easy Rider Express lifts handle those who want to stay lower on the mountain. It's all black-diamond runs on the east side of the big quads, and mostly blues with a few black diamonds for spice in the west, coming off the West Bowl Express quad or the Puma triple chair. A few more beginning and intermediate runs go down the back of the mountain. Sierra-at-Tahoe prides itself on being "the most affordable mountain in Lake Tahoe," so check the website for rates and discounts.

Eight different eateries are on the mountain. The Main Lodge has five dining options, from **Mama's Kitchen,** with its hearty breakfasts and hot soups, to the **Golden Bear Terrace,** where you can sit outside on sunny days. The **Solstice Eatery** in the Solstice Plaza serves up healthy wraps, salads, and gluten-free pizzas, which you can wash down with an organic cocktail. The Grandview Lodge features the **360 Smokehouse BBQ.** One of the most popular eateries is the **Baja Grill,** located at the West Bowl.

Cross-Country Skiing and Snowshoeing

In some places, cross-country skiers feel like the poor cousins of downhillers, noodling around the edges of the "main" resorts and trails. Not so in Tahoe: Deep snow and ample wildlands make for a variety of cross-country options. You can find groomed and maintained trails at numerous cross-country centers, easy trails for a glide through the woods, or opportunities for some serious backcountry adventures.

A **Sno-Park** parking pass (recording 916/324-1222, information 916/324-4442, www.ohv.parks.ca.gov, $5 per day, all-season $25) is required for many forest ski trailheads November-May. You can pick up the pass at the Placerville Ranger Station (4260 Eight Mile Rd., Camino, 530/644-2324, 8am-4:30pm Mon.-Fri.), the Kyburz Silverfork Store (13200 U.S. 50, Kyburz, 530/293-3172), and the Tahoe Roadrunner gas station (2933 U.S. 50, South Lake Tahoe, 530/577-6946). The website lists additional vendors, and you can buy Sno-Park passes online (www.ohv.parks.ca.gov).

There's also **Adventure Mountain** (21200 U.S. 50, Echo Summit, 530/577-4352 or 530/659-7217, http://adventuremountaintahoe.com, 10am-4:30pm Mon.-Fri., 9am-4:30pm Sat.-Sun., $25 per vehicle) a privately operated sno-park on Echo Summit with snowshoe trails, six groomed sledding runs, and a lodge with fireplace and café.

Equipment rentals include two-person sleds ($10 per day), inner tubes ($20 for 2 hours, $25 all day), and snowshoes with poles ($18 per day). Cash only at the entrance gate, but the lodge does take credit cards.

Those planning overnight ski-camping trips must first get a **wilderness permit** from the Placerville Ranger District's El Dorado Information Center (4260 Eight Mile Rd., Camino, 530/644-2324, 8am-4:30pm Mon.-Fri.). While snow conditions tend to be best in the morning, moonlight skiing is allowed in some areas.

Sections of the beautiful **Tahoe Rim Trail** (775/298-4485, www.tahoerimtrail.org) can be ideal for snowshoeing, depending on conditions, which are never predictable. The west side of the lake gets a lot more snow than the east. The first snowfall usually hits the trail sometime in November, and some places will still have a little snow as late as July. The Rim Trail office suggests calling close to your planned trip dates for an updated report on conditions and specific advice on where to go. In the heart of winter (Jan.-Mar.), the Tahoe Rim Trail Association (775/298-4485, www.tahoerimtrail.org) offers guided snowshoe hikes on Saturday.

A number of cross-country trails that really do cross some country are maintained by the U.S. Forest Service. Some of these trails offer short single-day excursions, while others lead miles back into the ominously named Desolation Wilderness and may appeal to hard-core ski-campers who want a multiday adventure. Beginner explorers can have the safest backcountry fun at **Taylor Creek** (Hwy. 89, just west of Camp Richardson, 530/543-2600, www.fs.usda.gov or www.parks.ca.gov), an uncongested but reasonably populous area with many flat marked trails to help newcomers get a feel for the forest. Lots of trails for skiers of all levels run along the South and West Shores of Lake Tahoe. If you're planning to camp in Desolation Wilderness, the most popular trailhead takes you past **Echo Lakes** (U.S. 50 at Echo Lake Rd.) and then into the backcountry along the Pacific Crest Trail.

Snowmobiling

Operating from the town of Meyers on the South Shore, **Lake Tahoe Adventures** (3071 U.S. 50, Meyers, 530/577-2940 or 800/865-4679, www.laketahoeadventures.com, 8am-5pm daily, $50-220) specializes in snowmobile tours of all kinds—for groups, individuals, and even children (drivers must be at least eight years old). Snowmobile tours are usually available November-April, depending on snow conditions. The company also offers Jeep and ATV tours. A shuttle will take riders from the tour center up to the base camp in Hope Valley, where a fleet of Arctic Cat snowmobiles awaits to explore the high-elevation backcountry Sierra terrain. First-time drivers and families with children can pick one of the more sedate trail tours or practice on the snowmobile track at the company's home base in Meyers. Expert snowmobile enthusiasts prefer the "ultimate" off-trail tours that go deep into the backcountry and offer rougher riding. Reservations are required for all tours; drop-ins are welcome at the snowmobile track.

Sledding and Snow Play

Just a couple of miles from Heavenly Valley in a cute residential area is the **Tube & Saucer Hill at Hansen's Resort** (1360 Ski Run Blvd., South Lake Tahoe, 530/544-3361, www.hansensresort.com, 9am-5pm daily mid-Dec.-Mar., $20 for first hour, $15 per additional hour, cash only). An annual favorite, Hansen's offers more features than many impromptu snow-play spots. Don't bother stacking a bunch of equipment in the car, since the hourly cost includes the use of a Hansen's saucer or tube. With constructed runs, you'll definitely get some thrills as you slip down the hill through the scattered pine trees. The resort also has a snack bar and a redwood hot tub available to customers. Note that hours depend on snow conditions and may be reduced if Mother Nature isn't cooperating.

In the South Shore area past Meyers, **Adventure Mountain Lake Tahoe** (21200 U.S. 50, Echo Summit, 530/577-4352, http://adventuremountaintahoe.com, 10am-4:30pm Mon.-Fri., 9am-4:30pm Sat.-Sun., $25 per vehicle) has the best groomed sledding area in Tahoe. With 40 acres of sled runs and play areas, plus restrooms and a concession stand that sells hot coffee and new sleds, Adventure Mountain also has access to the Pacific Crest Trail as well as a few other cross-country skiing and snowshoeing trails for those who want a quieter but more labor-intensive day in the snow. Feel free to bring your own sled and tubes.

Sleigh Rides

Catch a ride with **Wilderness Sleigh Rides at the Camp Richardson Corral** (Hwy. 89, between Camp Richardson Resort and Fallen Leaf Rd., 530/541-3113 or 877/541-3113, www.camprichardsoncorral.com, hours vary Dec.-Feb., adults $30, children under 4 free). Rides are about 45 minutes long, and it's best to call ahead for reservations.

Ice-Skating

Each year at the South Shore, **Heavenly Gardens** (1021 Heavenly Village Way, South Lake Tahoe, 530/542-4230, www.theshopsatheavenly.com/skating, 10am-8pm daily mid-Nov.-early Apr., adults $20, children under 13 $15) turns part of its landscape into a winter wonderland. The outdoor rink appeals especially to kids, newbies, and those more serious about having fun than being great skaters. As Tahoe attractions go, this is an entertainment bargain, since your pass includes skate rental and in-and-out access all day long. They turn off the phones in the summer, but that doesn't mean things won't be ready to go as soon as the season arrives.

For serious skaters and hockey players who want to indulge while vacationing in Tahoe, the **Tahoe Ice Sports Center** (1176 Rufus Allen Blvd., South Lake Tahoe, 530/544-7465, www.tahoese.com, generally 11am-7pm daily, adults $15, children under 6 $8) can hook you up. This year-round center offers drop-in hockey, public skating, and a skate school (drop-in lessons $20 per half hour); admission prices include skate rental.

Tours and Cruises

If exploring on your own isn't enough, take one of any number of cruises and tours offered all around Lake Tahoe. To get out on the water in a big boat, book a cruise with **Lake Tahoe Cruises** (800/238-2463, www.laketahoecruises.com or www.zephyrcove.com). Two honest-to-goodness paddle-wheel riverboats cruise Lake Tahoe on a near-daily basis—even in winter. The first boat, ***Tahoe Queen,*** sails from Ski Run Marina (900 Ski Run Blvd., South Lake Tahoe, 530/543-6191) and offers a 2.5-hour sightseeing cruise (adults $51, children $15) around Emerald Bay. If you're lucky, Mark Twain may even be your narrator. This is a beautiful way to see the lake, with photo opportunities that never end. If you really want to luxuriate, try the *Tahoe Queen*'s sunset cruise (6:30pm daily Sat. May-Oct., adults $83, children $35), which lasts 2.5 hours. It includes a gourmet dinner onboard followed by dancing to live music.

The other boat is the **MS *Dixie II,*** a rear paddle wheeler that was imported from the Mississippi River. It sails from the Zephyr Cove Marina (760 U.S. 50, Zephyr Cove, NV, 775/589-4907, www.zephyrcove.com) and offers a 2.5-hour-long morning or afternoon cruise (adults $51, ages 3-11 $15). The Dinner Dance Cruise (adults $83, children $35) includes an on-board narrator, a live band, and a four-course meal. As with most things in Tahoe, weather can affect the cruise schedules, so be sure to check in advance.

A company that can take you to see the lovely Emerald Bay is **Bleu Wave** (866/413-0985, www.tahoebleuwave.com, adults

$55-65, children $27-32), which operates from the Round Hill Pines Resort Beach & Marina (300 U.S. 50, Zephyr Cove, NV, 775/588-3055, www.roundhillpinesresort.com). You'll see many popular sights on the lake during this two-hour lunch cruise with an all-you-can-eat buffet, drinks included. For winter cruises, enjoy the onboard fireplace and spacious heated cabin.

Boating, Waterskiing, and Wakeboarding

Once the summer sunshine has warmed the air—if not the waters of the lake—thoughts turn to other kinds of skiing and boarding. The vast clear waters of Lake Tahoe are irresistible to water-skiers, wakeboarders, Jet Skiers, and powerboaters. There are miles of open water to cross, a number of docks and marinas, and a lovely coastline to explore. Dive deeper than 18 inches into the lake and you'll find that the water is ice-cold—in the 40s—even in the height of summer. But that's no matter if you're sunning yourself on the bow of a speedboat or flying along on a wakeboard.

Be aware that the communities and the governments around Tahoe take water quality very seriously—not only that of Lake Tahoe but also of Falling Leaf, Echo, and the other small lakes nearby. If you plan to bring your own powered watercraft, it's wise to familiarize yourself with the rules and restrictions governing all waterways in the Tahoe Basin (regulations online at http://boattahoe.com/trparegs.htm).

Full-service **Tahoe Keys Marina** (2435 Venice Dr. E., South Lake Tahoe, 530/541-2155, www.tahoekeysmarina.net) is one of the largest marinas, selling gas, providing launch access, and renting slips as well as offering boat rentals and charter fishing trips. You can also dock your boat ($3.45 per foot per day plus $3.70 per day water quality and dredging fee, $14.50 per foot per week plus $25.90 in fees).

Tahoe Keys Boat & Charter Rentals (2435 Venice Dr. E., South Lake Tahoe, 530/544-8888, www.tahoesports.com) operates out of the Tahoe Keys Marina and offers boat rentals of various kinds: a 49-passenger 52-foot yacht, pontoon boats, powerboats, kayaks, and Yamaha Jet Skis. Powerboats rent for $145-234 per hour, $435-702 per four hours, and $870-1,404 for eight hours.

The **Ski Run Boat Company** (Ski Run Marina, 900 Ski Run Blvd., South Lake Tahoe, 530/544-0200, www.tahoesports.com)

the *MS Dixie II*

is a sister company to the Tahoe Keys Boat & Charter Rental, operating out of a different location with even more variety. In addition to Jet Skis, pontoon boats, and 18- to 24-foot Reinell powerboats, you can rent canoes, ocean kayaks, stand-up paddleboards, a Catalina sailboat, and even a double hydrobike ($25 per hour) or a water tricycle ($25 per hour). At this location you can also get a parasail ride ($65-95 pp).

The marina at **Camp Richardson** (1900 Jameson Beach Rd., South Lake Tahoe, 530/542-6570, www.camprichardson.com, 9am-5pm daily late May-late June and mid-Sept.-mid-Oct., 8am-8pm daily mid-June-mid-Sept.) rents kayaks ($20-30 per hour), pontoon boats ($180 per hour, $1,080 per day), paddleboards ($30 per hour), Sea-Doos ($125 per hour), and more. You can also take the 1.5-hour Rum Runner Emerald Bay Cruise (530/542-6570, 1pm, 3:30pm daily, late May-mid-Oct., adults $49, children $19).

For a guided kayak tour of Emerald Bay, contact **Kayak Tahoe** (Timber Cove Marina, 3411 Lake Tahoe Blvd., South Lake Tahoe, 530/544-2011, www.kayaktahoe.com, 9am-2:30pm daily, by reservation only, $70-95 pp, minimum 6 people). You'll paddle the entire perimeter of the bay with a knowledgeable guide, stopping at Vikingsholm and Fannette Island. The company has four tour locations, including the Upper Truckee River (9am-noon daily, $45 pp), Sand Harbor (9am-2pm daily, $80 pp), and a sunset tour at Timber Cove (6:30pm-8:30pm daily, $40 pp). Beginners are welcome, but the minimum age is 12 for most tours. There's usually an $8-10 parking fee at each location, though parking is free at the Timber Cove Marina. The company also rents kayaks ($20-32 per hour, $30-50 per 2 hours, $65-85 per day) and stand-up paddleboards ($20 per hour, $30 per 2 hours, $65 per day) at Timber Cove Marina.

Fishing

Several companies offer charter trips on Lake Tahoe for anglers looking to score mackinaw, rainbow, and brown trout or kokanee salmon. Operating out of the Ski Run Marina (900 Ski Run Blvd., South Lake Tahoe, 530/541-5448, www.skirunmarina.com) and the Zephyr Cove Marina (760 U.S. 50, Zephyr Cove, NV, 775/586-9338, www.zephyrcove.com), **Tahoe Sport Fishing** (530/541-5448 or 800/696-7797, www.tahoesportfishing.com, $110-120) offers half-day and full-day fishing trips tailored to suit all styles of lake fishing. The fishing boats have heated cabins and modest

boat anchored near Camp Richardson

restroom facilities, and trips include all the trimmings: bait and tackle, cleaning and bagging services, cold beer and soda on board, and a choice of morning or afternoon half-day trips.

With the proliferation of rivers and streams surrounding Lake Tahoe, it's easy to find a good place to cast if you prefer fly-fishing to lake fishing. **Tahoe Fly Fishing Outfitters** (2705 Lake Tahoe Blvd., South Lake Tahoe, 530/541-8208, www.tahoeflyfishing.com, $225-400) can take you on an expert-guided fly-fishing or spin-fishing trip on one of the smaller lakes, Walker River, Carson River, Truckee and Little Truckee Rivers, or the Pleasant Valley Fly Fishing Preserve.

Hiking

TALLAC HISTORIC SITE

Along the South Shore, hikes range from easy walks along the shore at the Tallac Historic Site to hard-core treks up the **Mount Tallac Trail** (Hwy. 89 at Baldwin Beach, South Lake Tahoe, 10 miles round-trip, difficult, wilderness permit required, $5 for overnight hiking). This long hike starts out easy, taking casual strollers past the Floating Island and Cathedral Lakes, and then gets steeper and harsher as it ascends the front face of the mountain. To access the trail, turn off Highway 89 away from the beach toward a dirt road to the trailhead parking lot. For a more moderate but equally beautiful hike, choose the **Echo Lakes Trail** (Johnson Pass Rd. at Lower Echo Lake, 5-12 miles, moderate-strenuous, wilderness permit required). You can pick your distance on this route, depending on how many small alpine lakes you want to see. Start with a short walk to Upper Echo Lake, where you have the option to catch a water taxi rather than continuing on the trail along the lake. If you keep going, you'll see Tamarack Lake, Lucille and Margery Lakes, Lake in the Woods, and maybe even Aloha Lake.

EMERALD BAY STATE PARK

Emerald Bay State Park is a treasure trove of easy-moderate hiking trails. Near campsite 28 in Eagle Point Campground is the beginning of the **Overlook Trail,** a short (0.5 mile) walking trail to a camera-ready spot. Near campsite 34 and the campfire center amphitheater you can park in a lot and take one of two trails. The first is another short walk to an overlook. The second is the **Rubicon Trail** (1.7 miles), which takes you to Vikingsholm. This is the longer route, as opposed to the steep 0.5-mile trail to Vikingsholm that you can pick up from the Harvey West Parking Lot. The well-marked trail features undulating terrain, shade, and gorgeous views. The first mile is a gentle downhill slope, overlooking the lake on the right. The water at the edge is so shallow and clear that you can see the lake bottom from your perch on the trail. If it's been a wet year, some sections may be muddy, so wear boots. From the bridge, take a brief (0.2-mile) detour to your left to visit Lower Eagle Falls, or turn right to reach the visitors center in less than a mile. At the visitors center, you can buy tickets for a Vikingsholm tour or just walk another 0.2 mile to explore the Vikingsholm grounds on your own. Bring food, water, money for the tour, and a bathing suit to take a dip in the very cold water near the sandy beach beside Vikingsholm. Eagle Point Campground was scheduled for repairs through the 2015-2016 seasons. Call ahead to check on trail access.

Altogether, the Rubicon Trail runs 4.5 miles along the shoreline of Emerald Bay. Hikers who complete it will see osprey nests and an old wooden lighthouse in addition to the many other highlights.

D. L. BLISS STATE PARK

Hiking trails within D. L. Bliss State Park include the **Rubicon-Lighthouse Trail** to Rubicon Point's lighthouse, which was built in 1919 and restored and stabilized in 2001. You can take a short portion of this trail, from Calawee Cove Beach to the lookout at Rubicon Point, or walk a little farther to see the lighthouse. For a longer adventure, follow the Rubicon Trail all the way down around the bay, past Vikingsholm, and on to its end point at Upper Eagle Point Campground in Emerald Bay State Park. The complete trail has a total distance of about 4.5 miles one-way, but the terrain is mostly easy.

On the west side of D. L. Bliss is a short (0.5-mile) self-guided **nature trail** to Balancing Rock that nearly anyone can enjoy. Nineteen numbered signs along the way illuminate the history and geology of the area.

TAHOE RIM TRAIL

If you're in good shape and like a challenge, you will definitely want to experience the 165-mile **Tahoe Rim Trail** (775/298-4485, www.tahoerimtrail.org). This beautiful and varied trail, built between 1984 and 2001, encircles the entire lake through six counties in California and Nevada, one state park, three national forests, and three wilderness areas. About a third of it overlaps the Pacific Crest Trail. You can hike the trail in segments, or if you're up for a little planning, do it in a multiday loop. Casual day-hikers can pick one portion of the trail and tackle it, either doing an out-and-back or using a shuttle service to get back at the end of the day.

The Tahoe Rim Trail is managed and maintained by the nonprofit Tahoe Rim Trail Association (TRTA, 128 Market St., Stateline, NV, info@tahoerimtrail.org). The TRTA organizes a number of events, including trail maintenance work parties, workshops on backcountry skills, and informative Trail Talks. They're the people to contact if you want to volunteer, become an official member of the 165-Mile Club, or get information about the trail. Note that horseback riding is permitted on the Tahoe Rim Trail, and mountain biking is permitted on certain sections. For details, check the website (www.tahoerimtrail.org), which includes regular updates and specifics.

In summer, the TRTA runs several 14-day through-hikes (775/298-4491, $1,725), during which participants cover all 165 miles and bag elevation gains and losses totaling 27,500 feet. The cost includes food, trip leaders, transportation to and from the trail, and delivery of meals and supplies to key locations along the way by a group of "Trail Angels"—which greatly reduces the weight of your backpack on a trek of this length. These trips fill up fast, so call early to get on the list.

If you're not up for hiking the whole trail in one bite, you might love the TRTA's Segment Hiking Program (membership fee $550), where you can join the expert guides as they hike the whole trail over the course of 10-13 weeks through the summer. The program fills quickly; register through the website or contact the trail-use director (775/298-4491, lindseys@tahoerimtrail.org).

Biking

A great place to get out and cycle in summer is **Kirkwood** (1501 Kirkwood Meadows Dr., off Hwy. 88, Kirkwood, www.kirkwood.com, 209/258-7277, early July-early Sept.). When there's no snow, the slopes of this ski resort become great mountain biking tracks. Two lifts run on weekends in the summer (10am-4pm Sat., 10am-3pm Sun., adults $36), and a third lift operates occasionally on holidays. At the Red Cliffs Lodge base area (9am-4pm Sat.-Sun. summer) at Kirkwood, you can rent high-end mountain bikes (adults $45-80, children $19-25, includes helmets, gloves, and protective gear). Kirkwood also offers several mountain-bike clinics through the season to help hone your skills.

Much of the **Tahoe Rim Trail** on the California side is not open to bicycles, because the trail is in the Desolation Wilderness and along the Pacific Crest Trail. The one segment that's accessible is the five miles from Big Meadow to Echo Summit and Echo Lake. To reach the trailhead from South Lake Tahoe, drive south on U.S. 50 to Highway 89. Continue south on Highway 89 for about five miles, until the Tahoe Rim Trail crosses the road at Big Meadow, where you can park. The trail starts out heading south but soon turns northwest up to Echo Summit and then Echo Lake. When you near the lake, you'll see a sign warning that the trail is about to join the Pacific Crest Trail and cyclists must turn around. This round-trip is a scenic and invigorating 10-mile ride.

Horseback Riding

For travelers who prefer to explore the forests and trails on horseback, a few stables offer guided rides. On the west side of the South Shore, find the **Camp Richardson Corral** (Emerald Bay Rd. between Fallen Leaf Rd. and Valhalla Rd., 530/541-3113 or 877/541-3113, www.camprichardsoncorral.com, $43-83). Choose a one- or two-hour trail ride to explore the meadows and the forest, or a ride with a meal included. Camp Richardson offers an early-morning ride that culminates in a hearty, hot cowboy-style breakfast and a two-hour evening ride with a steak barbecue. Riders must be at least six years old and weigh 225 pounds or less. Camp Richardson also offers horse boarding by the day, week, and month.

To get out and see the Sierra foothills and mountains from the back of a horse, check **Kirkwood Corrals** (51965 Hwy. 88, 775/315-1932 or 775/315-6222, 30-90-minute rides $35-95). Kids will especially love the Little Buckaroo Day Camp (9am-noon Tues.-Wed. early July, ages 7-12, $160) if you're around during the middle of summer. If you're more advanced and want a gorgeous guided trail ride out into the Mokelumne Wilderness, join **Kirkwood Sierra Outfitters** (209/258-7433, www.kirkwoodsierraoutfitters.com) for a ride of half a day or more.

Golf

For golfers looking to play a few holes on the cheap, **Tahoe Paradise Golf Course** (3021 U.S. 50, South Lake Tahoe, 530/577-2121, www.tahoeparadisegc.com, 8am-7pm daily May-Oct., $20-55) offers a pleasant course as well as pleasantly low greens fees. Conveniently located on U.S. 50 on the South Shore, this course has pretty mountain views and plenty of lovely pine trees along with 18 holes of moderate golf that provides a good game for beginners and intermediates. It also has a pro shop, a practice area, and a modest snack bar with hot dogs and beer.

The **Lake Tahoe Golf Course** (2500 Emerald Bay Rd., South Lake Tahoe, 530/577-0788, www.laketahoegc.com, sunrise-sunset daily spring-fall, 18 holes and cart $87) offers a full-service restaurant and bar, cart service on the course, a grass driving range, pros and a pro shop, and—the main selling point—gorgeous views, but the greens fees are higher. If you want to save a little money, go later for the "super twilight" (from 4pm, $39) price for 18 holes and a cart. The course closes for the winter around November 1.

Spas

The welcoming and soothing **BioSpirit Day Spa** (1116 Ski Run Blvd., South Lake Tahoe, 530/542-4095, www.massagetahoe.com, 10am-2pm Mon., 9am-6pm Tues.-Sat.) is a stand-out in the area. With a full menu of massages, facials, waxing, wrapping, and more, you're sure to find something to make you feel good. BioSpirit is one of the only places in the area that does eyelash tinting and extensions, and use of their eucalyptus steam room is included with any service. It offers special facials just for men and teens; you can also get a discount on services if you schedule a Pamper Party for a small group of friends or if you book in advance. In addition to their regular hours, BioSpirit is usually open on Sunday holiday weekends. Fans of the defunct Shannon's Day Spa will be pleased to find that BioSpirit is of similar quality and welcomes former Shannon's clients.

ENTERTAINMENT AND EVENTS

Nightlife

The casinos over the Nevada border in Stateline are nearby, but the South Shore has its own entertainment. The **Brewery at Lake Tahoe** (3542 Lake Tahoe Blvd., South Lake Tahoe, 530/544-2739, www.brewerylaketahoe.com, 11am-9pm daily, $12-28) is a casual, comfortable bar with a menu of local microbrews, including the signature Bad Ass Ale and the popular Washoe Wheat Ale, as well as a selection of seasonal brews. The food includes pizza, pasta, salads, salmon, steaks, and barbecued ribs. The Brewery is across the street from the lake; the outdoor picnic tables are a great place to watch the scenery.

A happening place is **Whiskey Dick's Saloon** (2660 Lake Tahoe Blvd., South Lake Tahoe, 530/544-3425, 1pm-2am daily), with a full bar and live bands several times a week. Cover charges range from free to $20, depending on the band.

Festivals and Events

Late September, the Lake Tahoe Airport (TVL, 1901 Airport Rd., South Lake Tahoe) is the site of the annual **Lake in the Sky Air Show** (www.lakeintheskyairshow.com, free), with aerobatic performers, a search-and-rescue aircraft demonstration, some vintage war birds and World War II fighter planes, a CALSTAR helicopter flight simulator, a 5K run, and a pancake breakfast. Parking is free but limited at the airport, so use the free bus transportation (8am-4pm) from the transit station at the South Y shopping center.

If you enjoy costumes and want to dive into the living history of the early-20th-century wealth and privilege that surrounded Lake Tahoe, hit the **Great Gatsby Festival** (530/544-7383, www.tahoeheritage.org, 2nd weekend in Aug.) at the Tallac Historic Site. In the heat of summer each year, actors and volunteers dress in period attire and stroll the grounds of the estates as 1920s vacationers. The most popular event of this two-day festival is the Gatsby Tea ($65) on Sunday afternoon, a sumptuous high tea spiced up by entertainment that culminates in a vintage fashion show.

SHOPPING

You won't find a lot of high-fashion boutiques or glittering malls, but South Lake Tahoe is a good place to stock up on batteries and basic foodstuffs before heading out. Many of the region's small quaint towns don't have much in the way of practical services. If you're in need of basic necessities, head to the **Factory Outlet Stores at the Y** (2014-2062 Lake Tahoe Blvd., at Hwy. 89 and U.S. 50, South Lake Tahoe). For athletic equipment and apparel, check out the **Tahoe Sports Limited** (4000 Lake Tahoe Blvd., South Lake Tahoe, 530/542-4000, www.tahoesportsltd.com, 9am-7pm Mon.-Thurs., 8am-8pm Fri.-Sun. winter, 9am-7pm daily summer).

You can rent or buy a wide array of winter equipment at **Powder House Ski & Snowboard** (4045 Lake Tahoe Blvd., 530/542-6222, www.tahoepowderhouse.com, 7am-8pm Mon.-Fri., 7am-9pm Sat.-Sun.), with eight locations in South Lake Tahoe, including one at Heavenly Village (1001 Heavenly Village Way, Heavenly Village, 530/541-6422, 7am-8pm Mon.-Fri., 7am-9pm Sat.-Sun.) right next to the gondola.

At the upscale **Shops at Heavenly Village** (1001 Heavenly Village Way, www.theshopsatheavenly.com) you'll find a **Patagonia** (530/542-3385, www.patagonia.com, 8:30am-7pm Mon.-Thurs., 8:30am-8pm Fri., 8am-8pm Sat., 8am-7pm Sun. winter, 8:30am-8pm Mon.-Thurs., 8:30am-9pm Fri., 8am-9pm Sat., 8am-8pm Sun. summer) and a **Quiksilver** (530/542-4857, www.quiksilver.com, 10am-6pm Mon.-Fri., 9:30am-7pm Sat.-Sun.). You'll pay a premium for equipment here, but the atmosphere is fun, and food, gift shops, and other attractions are all around.

At Heavenly Mountain Village, the good-size **North Face** (4118 Lake Tahoe Blvd., 530/544-9062, www.skiheavenly.com, 8am-8pm daily) is where you can rent recreational gear as well as buy it. Whether you're planning to hit the slopes or just hang around looking cool, you may want to check out the selection of goggles and sunglasses available at **Heavenly Eyes** (4080 Lake Tahoe Blvd., 775/586-6116, www.skiheavenly.com, 9am-7pm Mon.-Fri., 9am-8pm Sat.-Sun. summer, 8am-7pm Mon.-Fri., 8am-8pm Sat.-Sun. winter).

ACCOMMODATIONS

Under $100

South Lake Tahoe has quite a few basic motels that offer a room for the night without breaking the bank. Midsummer rates, however, can rival resort prices. One of the nicer ones is the **Matterhorn Motel** (2187 Lake Tahoe Blvd., South Lake Tahoe, 530/541-0367, $69-199). The rooms are clean and adequate, with free Internet access, and it has a small outdoor pool. It's family-owned, and the proprietors are warm and helpful beyond expectations.

For inexpensive rooms year-round, check in to the **Ambassador Motor Lodge** (4130 Manzanita Ave., South Lake Tahoe, 530/544-6461, www.laketahoeambassador.com, $50-157, under age 16 free with adult), with private beach access and water-recreation options. Rooms have a basic motel feel, but a few soft touches make them prettier than the average bargain chain. The Honeymoon Suite ($250-292) is a modestly decorated step up for couples celebrating a special weekend. Amenities are reminiscent of most chains. The Ambassador is right on the lake and only a short walk to the Heavenly Gondola.

The **Apex Inn** (1171 Emerald Bay Rd., South Lake Tahoe, 530/541-2940, reservations 800/755-8246, www.apexinntahoe.com, $65-249) offers the winning combination of a good location and rates almost on par with camping. It has a small outdoor hot tub and free Internet access. Breakfast is included.

Another reasonable option is the **High Country Lodge** (1227 Emerald Bay Rd., 530/541-0508, $60). The yellow standard-issue motel could use some paint, but the gardens and lawn are well-kept, and the new owners have plans for hot tubs and picnic tables, with the goal of becoming a choice family destination. The place is pet-friendly for cats and small dogs only, and conveniently located.

$100-150

The small rustic **Lazy S Lodge** (609 Emerald Bay Rd., South Lake Tahoe, 530/600-3721, www.lazyslodge.com, $59-263) is in a great location away from the center of town and has some of the most reasonable rates in the region. The 21 rooms all have microwaves, wet bars, and private baths. Choose a studio room with a nice bed or a two-room cabin with room for several people, a kitchenette, and a fireplace. Facilities include a year-round hot tub, a summer-only swimming pool, barbecue grills and picnic tables, and easy access to hiking and biking trails, swimming, and Heavenly.

$150-250

The most famous place to stay in the area is ★ **Camp Richardson** (1900 Jameson Beach Rd., South Lake Tahoe, 530/541-1801 or 800/544-1801, www.camprichardson.com, $95-262). This full-spectrum resort has 33 rooms and suites, which feature rustic furnishings and luxurious fabrics. Rooms in the hotel are comfortable and quaint, with private baths and upscale amenities. The 38 individual cabins offer full kitchens and linens but no TVs or phones. It also has an RV Village (late May-Oct., $40-45) with 100 sites. Accommodations include use of the beach, the lounge, and the marina. Facilities include the excellent **Beacon Bar and Grill,** the **Mountain Sports Center,** and a coffee shop. Cross-country ski and snowshoe rentals are available in winter, and paddleboats in summer. All this development has not interfered with the ambience of the surrounding nature.

The **Beach Retreat and Lodge at Tahoe** (3411 Lake Tahoe Blvd., 530/541-6722, www.tahoebeachretreat.com, $129-269) has the advantage of being right on the lake. It has more than 200 rooms and a complicated pricing structure that varies with the week; midsummer stays usually require at least two nights. One thing stays constant: You pay an extra $20 for a room with a partial view of the lake and $40 per night for a full lake view.

The **Pine Cone Acre Motel** (735 Emerald Bay Rd., South Lake Tahoe, 530/541-0375, www.pineconeacremotel.com, rooms $150-175, cabin $300) has a great location on Highway 89 (Emerald Bay Rd.), just north of where Highway 89 crosses U.S. 50—which means the motel is very close to the center of South Lake Tahoe, but it's also out of the traffic in the attractive rustic vicinity of Emerald

Bay. Rooms have microwaves and fridges, and a pool and picnic tables are on the grounds.

Over $250

On the road to Heavenly, the lovely large ★ **Black Bear Inn** (1202 Ski Run Blvd., South Lake Tahoe, 530/544-4451 or 877/232-7466, www.tahoeblackbear.com, $235-315) features lodgepole pine and river rock, which blend in with the surrounding nature. A giant fireplace dominates the great room, and smaller but equally cozy river-rock fireplaces are in each of the upstairs lodge rooms. The 10 rooms feature king beds, plush private baths, free Internet access, and an energy-building full breakfast. Appointments are luxurious, with cushy comforters and rustic-elegant furnishings. Take a few moments to stroll along the tree-lined paths and serene green lawns.

Cabin and Condo Rentals

South Lake Tahoe's Marriott Grand Residence (1001 Heavenly Village Way) has about 40 condos available for rent through **Condos at Tahoe** (775/586-1587 or 888/666-0773, www.condosattahoe.com). All units here have full kitchens and provide easy access to the Heavenly Gondola. Studios run $260-525, and three-bedroom units—which are huge and sleep up to 14 people—are $400-675.

Spruce Grove Cabins (3599-3605 Spruce Ave., South Lake Tahoe, 530/802-2343, www.sprucegrovetahoe.com, $99-235) offers a gay-friendly and dog-friendly Tahoe vacation experience. With only seven cabins, you're guaranteed peace and privacy. The one- and two-bedroom cabins all have full kitchens, dining rooms, and living rooms. Each cabin has its own wilderness-based theme, including Snowshoe, Steamboat, and Washoe Native American. As one of the closest resorts to the Heavenly ski resort, Spruce Grove gets its heaviest traffic in the winter.

For homey cabin living on the West Shore, you can't beat **The Tahoma Lodge** (7018 Westlake Blvd., Tahoma, 866/819-2226, www.tahomalodge.com, $170-240), a series of 11 distinctive cabins, including studios and one- and two-bedroom units. Each cabin has a modern kitchen, and the picnic tables, barbecues, and heated swimming pool outside help you enjoy your stay in summer. In winter, you'll appreciate the fireplace in each unit and the year-round outdoor hot tub.

For a condo on the South Shore, head on over to **The Lodge at Lake Tahoe** (3840 Pioneer Trail, South Lake Tahoe, 530/541-6226 or 800/469-8222, www.lodgeatlaketahoe.com, $120-230). The rooms have the elegant look of proper vacation condos, with colorful furnishings and tasteful prints on the walls. The smallest studios have only kitchenettes, but the larger condos offer fully equipped kitchens as well as a nice table and chairs. Complex amenities include a summertime pool and spa, a swing set, a horseshoe pit, and outdoor barbecues near the pool area. Skiers will have easy access to Heavenly, and gamblers can get to the Stateline casinos in Nevada in a few minutes.

CAMPING

Camping at Lake Tahoe in the summer is so easy and gorgeous that you almost wonder why anyone would sleep indoors. June-August, the weather is usually perfect and the prices are reasonable, with campsites just minutes from mountain-bike trails or beaches.

The two great state parks of the South Shore both have gorgeous campgrounds. **Emerald Bay State Park** (Hwy. 89, north of South Lake Tahoe, 22 miles south of Tahoe City, 800/444-7275, www.reserveamerica.com, $35) has the 100-site Eagle Point Campground and a Boat-in Campground (July-Sept.) on the north side of the bay. Campsites include fire rings, and restrooms and showers are available in the park. Note: Eagle Point Campground was tentatively scheduled for repairs during 2015 and 2016, so make sure to call ahead and check availability. ★ **D. L. Bliss State Park** (Hwy. 89, 800/444-7275, www.parks.ca.gov, May-Sept., $35-45) has some of the best campsites around. Of the 150 sites, beachfront campsites have a premium price of $45, and they're worth it. All campsites have picnic tables, bear-proof food lockers, and grills. Hot showers, flush toilets, and potable water are available in the park. **Camp Richardson Resort** (530/541-1801 or 800/544-1801, www.camprichardson.com, $35-45) offers sites for tents, campers, and RVs. Amenities include a beach, a group recreation area, and a marina. On-site facilities include the Beacon Bar and Grill and the Mountain Sports Center.

The U.S. Forest Service runs 206 sites at **Fallen Leaf Lake Campground** (Fallen Leaf Lake Rd., off Hwy. 89, 3 miles north of U.S. 50, 530/543-2600 or 877/444-6777, www.recreation.gov, mid-May-mid-Oct., $32-34). RVs up to 40 feet are welcome, though there are no hookups or dump stations. Each campsite has a barbecue grill, a picnic table, and a fire ring. And not only are there modern baths with flush toilets, but some restrooms even have free showers. The campground is just 0.25 mile north of Fallen Leaf Lake, where you can swim at your own risk.

The **Tahoe Valley RV Resort** (1175 Melba Dr., South Lake Tahoe, 530/541-2222 or 877/570-2267, www.rvonthego.com, May-Sept. $41-74, weekly $258-354, Oct.-Apr. $29, weekly $196, monthly $500-1,407) has 439 sites that can accommodate everything from small tents to big-rig RVs with water, electric, and cable TV hookups. Tall pine trees give each site some shade and privacy. Amenities include tennis courts, a swimming pool, an ice cream parlor serving Tahoe Creamery products, activities for children and families, a dog run, and free wireless Internet access.

FOOD

Breakfast and Cafés

For a classic American breakfast, it's tough to do better than the ★ **Original Red Hut Café** (2723 Lake Tahoe Blvd., South Lake Tahoe, 530/541-9024, www.redhutcafe.com, 6am-2pm daily, $6-10). This down-home waffle spot serves classic crispy-thin waffles, plus biscuits and gravy, omelets, and plenty more. Locals recommend the waffle sandwich, a complete breakfast in a single dish. Expect to wait for a table or a seat at the counter on weekend mornings, as this spot is very popular with visitors and locals. If you can't get in, try the **New Red Hut Café** (3660 Lake Tahoe Blvd., 530/544-1595, 6am-8pm daily).

Rude Brothers Bagel & Coffee (3117 Harrison Ave., Suite B, www.rudebrothers-bagels.com, 530/541-8195) looks and feels just right for an indie coffee shop and sandwich bar. It has a big open room for hanging out, outstanding breakfast burritos, and plenty of lunch goodies. All the usual espresso drinks are available at the counter.

One of the most pleasant spots for a light breakfast is **Camp Richardson's Coffee & Confectionery** (1900 James Beach Rd., South Lake Tahoe, 530/542-6555, 7am-5pm daily late May-early Sept.). This small friendly spot, right across Highway 89 from the main lodge at Camp Richardson, has been around since 2009, and it fills a need for good coffee, good pastries, and a no-hassle Internet connection outside of town.

Casual Dining

For a great combination of delicious healthy food and budget dining, check out ★ **Sprouts Café** (3123 Harrison Ave., South Lake Tahoe, 530/541-6969, 8am-9pm daily, $8-10). This cute, casual walk-up eatery offers ultra-healthy dishes made with fresh, mostly organic ingredients. Breakfast is served all day, and the lunch and dinner menus run to several pages. Choose among salads, burritos, rice bowls, and tasty vegetarian and vegan desserts.

An unassuming local joint with great food and veggie options is **Freshies Restaurant & Bar** (3330 Lake Tahoe Blvd., South Lake Tahoe, http://freshiestahoe.com, 530/542-3630, www.freshiestahoe.com, 11:30am-9pm daily, $10-22). This small, popular Hawaiian-themed restaurant has been voted the "Best Place for Dinner" and "Best Place for Lunch" by the *Tahoe Daily Tribune*. The main dining room is accessed through a mall, but the best way to experience Freshies is to go to the side entrance and add your name to the list for a rooftop table, where you can see the lake.

Blue Angel Café (1132 Ski Run Blvd., South Lake Tahoe, 530/544-6544, www.blueangelcafe.com, 11am-9pm daily summer, 11am-9pm Tues.-Sun. winter, $14-18) has a globetrotting menu with a distinct West Coast flavor. The pizzas are amazing; try the Thai chili chicken with goat cheese and gluten-free dough. If you're thinking of chowing down on something lighter for dinner, try the salmon with smoked paprika, mango coulis, quinoa, and veggies.

If you're hungry and approaching South Lake Tahoe from the west, you can get a decent pizza next door to the visitors center in Meyers at **Bob Dog Pizza** (3160 U.S. 50, Meyers, 530/577-2364, www.bobdogpizza.com, 10am-9pm daily, $7-19).

New American

Boasting a *Wine Spectator* Award of Excellence and a creative California cuisine menu that includes wild boar chops, Asian chicken mandarin orange stir-fry, and summer *ragu* bolognese, **Nepheles** (1169 Ski Run Blvd., South Lake Tahoe, 530/544-8130, www.nepheles.com, daily by reservation, $26-38) is the perfect place for a romantic dinner or a celebration of any kind.

Italian

If the crowds at Heavenly have you longing for a more intimate evening, book one of the seven tables at **Café Fiore** (1169 Ski Run Blvd., South Lake Tahoe, 530/541-2908, www.cafefiore.com, 5:30pm-10pm daily, $18-35). This tiny bistro serves upscale Italian fare with a fabulous wine list. The exterior charms with its alpine-chalet look while the interior is the definition of a romantic restaurant. Located on Ski Run Boulevard, Café Fiore is convenient to both the Heavenly ski resort and the lakeshore resorts of South Lake Tahoe.

For delicious, dependable Italian food at family-friendly prices, **Passaretti's** (1181 Emerald Bay Rd., South Lake Tahoe, 530/541-3433, www.passarettis.com, 11am-9pm Sun.-Thurs., 11am-9:30pm Fri.-Sat., $13-21) is a good bet. Extensive choices include hand-tossed pasta in a fresh homemade sauce, a children's menu, and daily lunch specials ($8). The back dining room seats 40, but if you're bringing a large party, call first.

Seafood

Serious sushi aficionados might be concerned about eating raw ocean fish so far from the Pacific, but **Off the Hook** (2660 Lake Tahoe Blvd., 530/544-5599, www.offthehooksushi.com, 4:30pm-9:30pm Mon.-Fri., 5pm-9:30pm Sat.-Sun fall-spring, 4:30pm-9pm Mon.-Thurs., 4:30pm-9:30pm Fri., 5pm-9:30pm Sat., 5pm-9pm Sun. summer, $6-23) offers good rolls and fresh *nigiri* for reasonable prices. Don't expect too much of some of the traditional Japanese dishes and you'll have an enjoyable dining experience.

For an all-around fine dining experience and some of the best fish ever, try **Kalani's** (1001 Heavenly Village Way, South Lake Tahoe, 530/544-6100, www.kalanis.com, noon-close daily, $18-65). Serving Pacific Rim fusion cuisine, Kalani's offers subtly spiced salmon, mahimahi, sushi, barbecued ribs, and house specialties like the *kalua* smoked pork quesadilla and Portuguese bean soup. The sushi bar is open all day, as is Kalani's Puka Lounge, which serves wine, sake, and cocktails. Kalani's is located in the Shops at Heavenly Village complex.

Good fish, good views, and entertainment too: That would be **Fresh Ketch** (2435 Venice Dr., South Lake Tahoe, 530/541-5683, www.thefreshketch.com, 11:30am-close daily, $8-38), located in the Tahoe Keys. Prices are somewhat reasonable, from fish tacos ($16) to pan-seared fresh fish ($21-32). The salads, sandwiches, and other light fare are good too, so you don't have to save this place for a fancy-dinner night. The Seafood Bar and Lounge is open for lunch (11:30am-close daily summer, 11:30am-close Tues.-Sat. winter). Check the website for details on live music evenings (Fri.-Sat.).

One of the area's best restaurants, the ★ **Beacon Bar & Grill** (1900 Jameson Beach Rd., South Lake Tahoe, 530/541-0630, www.camprichardson.com, brunch, lunch, and dinner daily, $19-40) is located inside Camp Richardson, a just a few miles north of South Lake Tahoe on Highway 89. If you're driving Highway 89 from the north, look for the entrance on the left, seven miles south of Emerald Bay State Park. In addition to excellent food (filet mignon, fresh seafood, and a great spinach salad), the Beacon offers a beachfront patio and live music (Wed.-Sun. summer, Fri.-Sat. winter).

INFORMATION AND SERVICES

The Lake Tahoe Visitors Authority (LTVA) maintains the spacious, welcoming, and well-staffed **LTVA Visitors Center** (3066 Lake Tahoe Blvd., South Lake Tahoe, 530/544-5050, www.tahoesouth.com, 9am-5pm daily), across from the *Tahoe Daily Tribune* office.

For medical attention off-slope, go to **Barton Memorial Hospital** (2170 South Ave., South Lake Tahoe, 530/541-3420, www.bartonhealth.org) or the **Tahoe Urgent Care Center** (2130 Lake Tahoe Blvd., South Lake Tahoe, 530/541-3277, www.tahoeurgentcare.com, 8am-5:30pm daily). A local drugstore is **Rite Aid** (1020 Al Tahoe Blvd., South Lake Tahoe, 530/541-2530).

TRANSPORTATION

Air

South Lake Tahoe has its own airport (1901 Airport Rd., www.laketahoeairport.com), but it has no commercial flights. So if you don't have a private plane, the nearest commercial airport is the **Reno-Tahoe International Airport** (RNO, 2001 E. Plumb Lane, Reno, NV, 775/328-6400, www.renoairport.com) or the **Sacramento International Airport** (SMF, 6900 Airport Blvd., Sacramento, 916/929-5411, www.sacramento.aero).

Bus and Train

The *Capital Corridor* route on **Amtrak** (800/872-7245, www.amtrak.com, $34 one-way) will take you to South Lake Tahoe from Sacramento by bus in about two hours and 20 minutes. From San Francisco, you must take a bus to Emeryville, then a train to Sacramento, and then a bus to South Lake Tahoe ($55 one-way). The bus will drop you off at one of two unstaffed curbside locations in South Lake Tahoe: the South Y Transit Center (1000 Emerald Bay Rd.) and the South Lake Tahoe Transit Center (4114 Lake Tahoe Blvd.).

Car

U.S. 50 provides the quickest access to South Lake Tahoe. From the San Francisco Bay Area, the drive takes about five hours in good weather without traffic; from Sacramento it's only about two hours. However, don't expect good weather or light traffic if you plan to drive to Tahoe on a Friday in winter. Everybody else will be on the road with you, significantly slowing down the routes. Be sure to check traffic reports before you hit the road.

In winter, carry snow chains that fit your vehicle (unless you have a 4WD vehicle and you know how to navigate in snow). Chains are often required near and around Tahoe in winter. You can pull off the road to attach your chains at many spots on I-80 and U.S. 50. You can also buy chains on the road, but the closer you get to Tahoe, the more expensive they are.

In winter, highways can close during major storms, and smaller roads surrounding the lake can shut down for weeks at a time. Traffic reports both on the radio and online offer information about road closures and alternate routes. If you're planning a winter trip, be aware of the weather and plan for some uncertainty.

CAR RENTALS

Avis (4130 Lake Tahoe Blvd., South Lake Tahoe, 530/544-5289, www.avis.com, 8am-5pm Mon.-Fri., 8am-3pm Sat.-Sun.) and **Budget** (4130 Lake Tahoe Blvd., 530/544-3439, www.budget.com, 8am-5pm Mon.-Fri., 8am-3pm Sat.-Sun.) are next door to the Stateline Transit Center bus station. You can also try **Enterprise** (2281 Lake Tahoe Blvd., 530/544-8844, www.enterprise.com, 9am-5pm

Mon.-Fri., 9am-noon Sat.), which has a full range of cars and small-midsize SUVs.

Public Transportation

In the South Lake Tahoe area, local public transportation is provided by **BlueGO** (530/541-7149, www.bluego.org, adults $2-5), which runs buses, trolleys, and ski shuttles. The cheerful-looking trolley can help you get around the South Shore without driving. Routes and schedules vary, so consult the website for details.

Ski Resort Shuttles

Parking at the ski resorts, especially on weekends, can be a serious hassle. A much better option is a ski-resort shuttle. Most of the major ski resorts maintain shuttles that bring skiers and their equipment up to the mountains in the morning and back down to their hotels in the late afternoon. Look for seasonal brochures in major hotels and resorts or check online for the shuttles for Heavenly (www.skiheavenly.com) and Kirkwood (www.kirkwood.com), among others.

North and West Shores

The North and West Shores are often considered the most desirable areas of Lake Tahoe, filled with ski resorts, beachfront property, and tall pines. One of the larger towns on the West Shore is Tahoe City, a lively happening place with good restaurants, bars, and entertainment and a sparkling waterfront. The smaller communities of Lake Forest, Sunnyside, Tahoe Pines, Homewood, and Tahoma are close by and easy to access.

SIGHTS

★ Ed Z'berg Sugar Pine Point State Park

The Tahoe area has more than its share of outstanding state parks, and **Ed Z'berg Sugar Pine Point State Park** (Hwy. 89, Tahoma, 530/525-7982, www.parks.ca.gov, $10) is one of the greats. Located on the West Shore, north of Emerald Bay and a few miles south of the town of Homewood, the park features tours of the historical Ehrman Mansion, ski trails from the 1960 Winter Olympics, and great camping, among other attractions.

The park is split into two sections. Sugar Pine Point includes the General Creek Campground, the Ehrman Mansion, and the visitors center and gift shop. The smaller Edwin L. Z'berg Natural Preserve features the Sugar Pine Point Lighthouse. You can camp in both sections for just the day-use fee. Note that if you can't find "Sugar Pine Point" on the state park website, try a search for "Ed Z'berg."

EHRMAN MANSION

A fine example of a former home of the wealthy turned tourist attraction, the **Ehrman Mansion** (Hwy. 89, 1 mile south of Tahoma, 530/525-7232, www.parks.ca.gov) is located within the day-use area of Sugar Pine Point State Park. This beautifully preserved 12,000-square foot house was built in 1903 and is now owned by the State of California. You can take a tour (530/583-9911, www.sierrastateparks.org, on the hour 11:30am-3:30pm daily late May-late Sept., adults $10, ages 7-17 $8, under age 7 free).

Tahoe Maritime Museum

The **Tahoe Maritime Museum** (5205 W. Lake Blvd., Homewood, 530/525-9253, www.tahoemaritimemuseum.org, 10am-4:30pm Thurs.-Tues. late May-Oct., 10am-4:30pm Fri.-Sun. Oct.-late May, adults $5, children under 13 free) seeks to illuminate the significant marine history of Lake Tahoe. Located on the West Shore, the museum resembles a big old boathouse and has a great collection of historical boats that share the history of the lake; some of them still run on the lake each summer. It also has photos and artifacts related to the lake's history. You'll learn about

North and West Shores

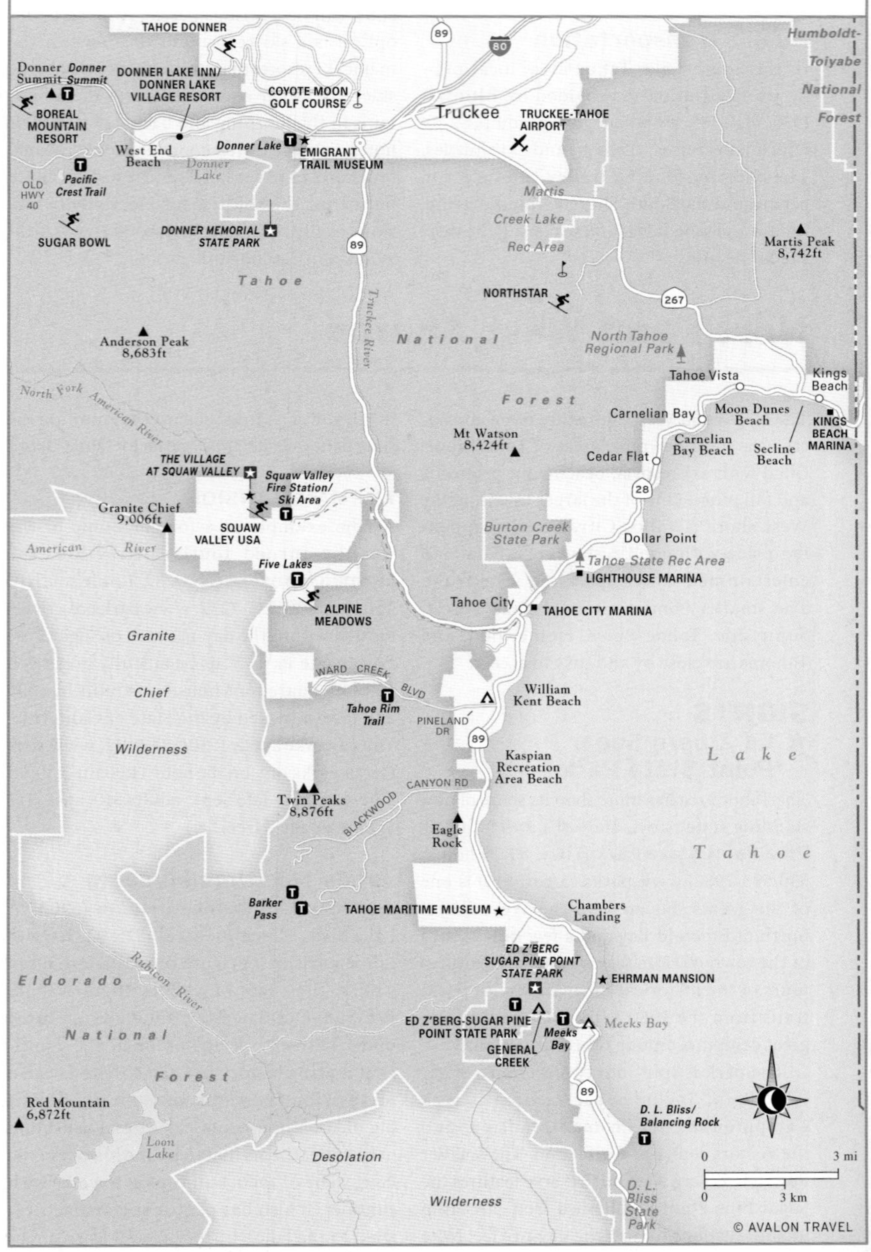

"gentlemen's racing"; steam ferries, like the 1896 *Tahoe,* which used to take people around the lake in the days before roads circumnavigated it; and fishing, which has been part of the lake's culture for more than a century. Young visitors will enjoy a children's learning area with exhibits about small and midsize boats and activities designed just for them.

Gatekeeper's Museum and Marion Steinbach Indian Basket Museum

Together, the **Gatekeeper's Museum and Marion Steinbach Indian Basket Museum** (130 West Lake Blvd., Tahoe City, 530/583-1762, www.northtahoemuseums.org, 10am-5pm daily early June-Sept., noon-4pm Wed.-Sun. Oct.-late May, adults $5, seniors $4, under age 13 free accompanied by an adult) offer an in-depth history of society around the lake. You'll find transcribed oral histories, photographs, dolls, costumes, and many other artifacts displayed in attractive and unusual pine-and-glass cases that match the wooden floors of the galleries. The authentic Native American artifacts include a large collection of baskets and caps made of willow, tule, and pine needles, among other things.

Watson Cabin

Visit an authentic early-20th-century log cabin at **Watson Cabin** (560 North Lake Blvd., Tahoe City, 530/583-8717, www.northtahoemuseums.org, noon-4pm Thurs.-Sun. mid-June-mid-Sept., donation). Built by Robert Watson as a private family residence for his son and daughter-in-law, the cabin opened for use in 1909 and became a museum in the early 1970s, still on the original site. Inside, you'll find diorama displays of pioneer life in early modern Lake Tahoe.

★ The Village at Squaw Valley

You might think of **The Village at Squaw Valley** (1750 Village East Rd., Olympic Valley, 530/584-1000, www.squawalpine.com) as a ski area, but it's actually a small upscale town designed to mimic a European Alpine village. There's no need to hit the slopes to enjoy what the village has to offer. Spend hours rambling around the colorfully painted clusters of buildings or strolling the cute exclusive boutiques and galleries. Souvenir seekers can go straight to **Squaw One Logo Company** (530/584-6250, www.squawalpine.com, 9am-6pm daily). Those craving more outdoor gear and clothing can stop in at **North Face**

The Village at Squaw Valley

(530/452-4365, www.northface.com, 9am-5pm Mon.-Fri., 8am-6pm Sat.-Sun.). For something local, visit the aromatic **Lather & Fizz Bath Boutique** (530/584-6001, www.latherandfizz.com, 10am-6pm daily) for soaps, lotions, and face products made in nearby Truckee as well as luxurious signature pajamas, among other great gifts.

More than half a dozen restaurants, snack bars, and coffee shops offer sushi, pizza, high-end wine, and more. Entertainment options include skiing and ice-skating in the winter, hiking in summer, and the **Aerial Tram** (hours vary, daily winter and summer, Sat.-Sun. spring and fall, adults $39, youth and seniors $25, children under 13 $10) up to **High Camp** (1960 Squaw Valley Rd., Olympic Valley, 530/584-1000, www.squawalpine.com) at 8,200 feet elevation. At High Camp, you can play tennis or paintball, roller-skate, soak in a hot tub, browse the **Olympic Museum** (www.squawalpine.com/olympic-museum, free with Aerial Tram ride), or just stand outside and enjoy the tremendous views. In summer there's often live music at the base of the mountain; various other special events offer year-round fun for adults and kids.

SPORTS AND RECREATION

Ski Resorts

SQUAW VALLEY

Squaw Valley (1960 Squaw Valley Rd., Olympic Valley, 530/583-6985, www.squawalpine.com, adults $95-119, youth $82-98, children under 12 $55-68) was the headquarters for alpine sports during the 1960 Winter Olympics. Today it is perhaps the most popular ski resort in California, with practically every amenity and plenty of activities, from geocaching to ziplining, but skiing and snowboarding remain the most important pursuits. Squaw Valley has a great ski school with plenty of fun for new skiers and boarders of all ages along with a wide selection of intermediate slopes. Some slopes are long, such as those served by the Squaw Creek, Red Dog, and Squaw One Express lifts—perfect for skiers who want to spend more time on the snow than on the lifts. But the jewels of Squaw are the many black-diamond and double-black-diamond slopes and the two terrain parks. Whether you prefer trees, moguls, narrow ridges, or wide-open vertical bowls, you'll find your favorite at Squaw. The slopes off KT-22 are legendary with skiers around the world. If you want to try freestyle for the first time, head for Belmont Park. During the day, especially weekends and holidays, expect long lines at the lifts, crowds in the nice big locker rooms, and still more crowds at the numerous restaurants and cafés.

ALPINE MEADOWS

Just one ridge over from Squaw Valley is the other grand ski resort at Tahoe, **Alpine Meadows** (2600 Alpine Meadows Rd., Tahoe City, 530/583-4232 or 800/441-4423, www.squawalpine.com, mid-Nov.-mid-May). This sprawling resort encompasses both sides of its two Sierra peaks, Scott and Ward. With a full range of trails, an all-day every-day ski school, and brand-new state-of-the-art rental equipment, Alpine is ideal for all levels of skiers. Beginners will particularly enjoy their new "rocker" skis, which make steering easier than ever, and the scenic network of green trails. An intermediate skier can have a great time at Alpine, especially coming off the Summit Six or the Roundhouse Express chairlifts. On the south side, from Scott Peak off the Lakeview Chair, all ski runs are blue. Alpine devotes considerable space to what it refers to as "Adventure Ski Zones." These are large clusters of black-diamond and double-black-diamond bowls and runs intended for expert skiers only. Thirteen lifts serve the mountains, including three high-speed chairs. If you're an expert, take just about any chair up the mountain, and you'll find exhilarating ways down. The Scott Chair leads to a bunch of single black-diamond runs on the front of the mountain, as does the Summit Express six-passenger chair at the back of Ward Peak. You can get to Art's Knob from the Sherwood Express. Alpine has two terrain parks: Tiegel, with a few small snow features for beginners and young adventurers, and Howard's Hollow, which usually has more features for medium-level skiers and snowboarders.

GRANLIBAKKEN

Many large, famous, and modern ski resorts around Tahoe overshadow each other in their own ways. But in the history of Tahoe, none is more venerable than **Granlibakken** (725 Granlibakken Rd., Tahoe City, 530/583-4242 or 800/543-3221, www.granlibakken.com, lift tickets $16-30, lodging $165-665). Actually called the Granlibakken Conference Center and Lodge, this lovely, historical resort dates to the turn of the 20th century, when the original Tahoe Tavern was built on this site. In 1928 the Tavern stayed open through winter for the first time for vacationers who wanted to play in the snow, and the facilities grew quickly afterward. Soon there was an ice rink and a toboggan run, and then a ski jump used for demonstrations by traveling Norwegian ski jumpers entertaining the local community. The Tahoe Tavern was the site of the 1932 and 1936 U.S. Olympic trials, and over the years it has hosted various national championships, Junior Olympics, and other competitions. After World War II the famous Norwegian ski jumper Kjell "Rusty" Rustad moved here, renamed the place Granlibakken after a ski area from his youth, and developed a mountain for skiers. Later, Rusty helped the developers of Squaw Valley get started and lived to see other resorts become grander than his own.

Today, Granlibakken is unable to compete as a major downhill ski destination, but it still has much to offer. With a large outdoor pool and hot tub, the on-site **Granlibakken Spa** (530/583-8111), a ropes course, bicycles, hiking and cross-country ski trails, and one of the best groomed sledding hills anywhere (saucer-sled provided, $14 per day), this is an ideal spot for family vacations, retreats, and corporate events. Most of the 84 condos on the site are managed by the company and are available for rent year-round. Granlibakken still offers some downhill skiing, but those who crave the excitement of bigger mountains should sleep here and take advantage of the package deals with other resorts, which include discount lift tickets and shuttle transportation to one of seven other ski areas.

Granlibakken's **Cedar House Pub** (530/583-4242 or 800/543-3221, 5pm-9pm Fri.-Sat. mid-Dec.-Apr. 1, $10-23) serves German and American comfort food, and the **Ski Hut Snack Bar** (10am-4:30pm Fri.-Mon. winter) offers Mexican food and hot dogs. A lavish buffet breakfast is included for overnight guests.

Cross-Country Skiing and Snowshoeing

One of the best cross-country ski trails for beginners is the **General Creek Trail,** also known as the 1960 Winter Olympiad X-C Ski Trail. A lot of the Olympic facilities in the area were neglected or forgotten for many years, but some of the ski trails were rediscovered and restored in connection with the 50th anniversary celebration in 2010. The first-ever Olympic biathlon competition was held on this trail, a 20K course designed by the former U.S. Olympian Wendall "Chummy" Broomhall and Allison "Al" Merrill, who was the head coach of the U.S. Ski Team 1963-1968. The trailhead is located inside Sugar Pine Point State Park (Hwy. 89, Tahoma, 530/525-7982, www.parks.ca.gov, $10) just a few miles south of the town of Tahoma. On entering the park, drive through the campground to campsite 148. Signs and a trail map are posted and explain a little about the trail's Olympic history. The trail is largely flat, so it's not too challenging for skiers at most levels—it's also amazingly beautiful. It's an out-and-back trip, so you can glide silently through the woods for as long as you like then turn around before you get too tired. Snowshoers are welcome but must stay out of the ski tracks.

Snowshoeing enthusiasts will be happy to hear that rangers in Sugar Pine Point State Park (Hwy. 89, Tahoma, 530/525-7982, www.parks.ca.gov, $10) lead **full-moon snowshoe tours** (West Shore Sports, reservations 530/525-9920, $25, under age 12 free, includes snowshoe rental) on specific dates in winter; call for details.

Snowmobiling

If you're up on the North Shore, check out **Lake Tahoe Snowmobile Tours** (Hwy. 267, south of Northstar Resort, 530/546-4280, www.laketahoesnowmobiling.com, $150-390). With a fleet of Ski-Doo snowmobiles and more than 20 years of guided touring experience, this outfit offers everything from easy two-hour tours with gorgeous lake views through private three- to four-hour adventures for expert riders who want to tackle ungroomed backcountry terrain. You'll see sweeping North Shore views and drive through miles of unspoiled forest. Reservations are strongly recommended. Drivers must be age 16 or older and have a valid driver's license; children under age five may not ride.

Sledding and Snow Play

Granlibakken (725 Granlibakken Rd., Tahoe City, 877/552-6301 or 800/543-3221, www.granlibakken.com, 9am-4pm daily, $14 per day, resort guests $7) is a great place for the whole family to spend a day sledding down the machine-groomed mountain on saucers (included). You may also want to join the Granlibakken staff and longtime Tahoe residents when they build their community of snow people each year.

Fishing

Mickey's Big Mack Charters (530/546-4444 or 800/877-1462, www.mickeysbigmack.com, 5-hour trip $90 pp) operates out of the Sierra Boat Company on Highway 28 in Carnelian Bay. The 43-foot fishing boat goes out twice daily, in the early morning and for a late-afternoon cruise that includes spectacular sunset views. The cabin and restroom on board add to the comforts of the trip as you fish for mackinaw, rainbow, and brown trout.

Hiking

Sugar Pine Point State Park (Hwy. 89, Tahoma, 530/525-7982, www.parks.ca.gov, $10) offers trails suitable for all levels of hikers. One simple and pleasant hike is the **Edward F. Dolder Nature Trail** (1.5 miles, easy). To reach the trailhead, enter the northeast section of the park—the Edwin L. Z'Berg Natural Preserve—and begin hiking the paved Rod Beaudry trail. The Dolder Trail circles the Z'berg Preserve, with views of the subalpine meadow and wildlife habitats. Along the way you'll pass through trees, a sandy beach, and the world's highest-elevation operating navigational lighthouse, the Sugar Pine Point Lighthouse.

A good hike in the southwestern section of Sugar Pine Point State Park is along the 1960 Olympic Ski Trails out to **Lily Pond** (3-6 miles, easy-moderate). Start in General Creek Campground, near site 148, and take the **General Creek Trail,** also known as the 1960 Winter Olympiad X-C Ski Trail. This sunny wooded path is wide enough that it almost feels like an unpaved forest road. After about 1.5 miles, you'll come to a wooden bridge curving off to the left across General Creek. If you're ready to turn around, take the bridge to complete the loop back to the trailhead for a total of three miles.

If you're up for a few more miles, bear right; at this point, the path becomes more trail-like, narrow and winding through the woods. In 0.5 mile you'll come to a trail marker directing you to Lily Pond on the right. The next 0.75 mile are a bit of climbing, but then you're at Lily Pond, a small lake that actually has lily pads. You can walk around the pond or just turn around and head back, rejoining the General Creek Trail for a total of 5-6 miles.

If you like easy terrain and great views, the **Lakeside Trail,** a kind of paved boardwalk, is a great place for a stroll or a hike. The 1-mile boardwalk is actually part of a larger 19-mile trail network that links the North Shore, West Shore, Truckee River, and Squaw Valley. Access the trail from Heritage Plaza in the center of Tahoe City.

The 165-mile **Tahoe Rim Trail** (775/298-4485, www.tahoerimtrail.org) runs along the shore of the entire lake, including the north and west sides. There are two good trailheads where you can gain access and do a segment of the trail. The northern trailhead is at Brockway Summit. To get to the Brockway trailhead, start in Kings Beach at the junction of Highways 28 and 267. Travel north on Highway 267 for four miles. Look for a "Tahoe Rim Trail" sign on the right, and then park on the nearby dirt road or on the roadside pullout. This trailhead has no restrooms, water, or other services.

The southern trailhead is Barker Pass. To get to the Barker Pass trailhead from Tahoe City, travel about 4.25 miles south on Highway 89. Make a right (west) onto Blackwood Canyon Road. When the road splits, take the left fork. Drive 7 miles to the crest of the hill and then another 0.2 mile on a dirt road. Park at the pullout to the right. Pit toilets are available at this trailhead, but there's no water. The famous **Pacific Crest Trail** (916/285-1846, www.pcta.org) joins the Tahoe Rim Trail here at Barker Pass and runs concurrent with it for the next 50 miles into the Desolation Wilderness.

Spas

One of the most popular day spas on the North Shore is the **Lighthouse Spa** (850 N. Lake Blvd., Suite 20A, Tahoe City, 530/583-8100, www.lighthousespa.com, 9am-7pm daily, massage $60-175). Look for it behind the Safeway, even if it seems like an unlikely spot for a spa. Once inside, choose a Swedish, deep-tissue, or hot-stone massage; expectant moms can get a special prenatal massage. Lighthouse also offers facials, body wraps, luxurious foot treatments, and aesthetic services that include manicures, pedicures, and waxing. Late appointments (until 8pm) are available for those in desperate need of après-ski TLC. To make its pampering more convenient, Lighthouse Spa has a second location at the **Granlibakken Resort** (725 Granlibakken Rd., Tahoe City, 530/583-8111, www.granlibakken.com). If you're anywhere in the North Shore or Truckee areas, they'll also come to you for an extra fee ($100-200).

FESTIVALS AND EVENTS

For the annual **Weavers Market** (Marion Steinbach Indian Basket Museum, 130 West Lake Blvd., Tahoe City, 530/583-1762, www.northtahoemuseums.org), which takes place early in September, the Indian Basket Museum hosts members of California and Nevada indigenous groups (Washoe, Miwok, Yurok, and Northern Paiute) who make baskets for exhibit and for sale while demonstrating the craft of basket-making. The event also has basket appraisers on hand who will identify pieces of your Native American art for free. Entry to the market is usually free with museum admission.

ACCOMMODATIONS

Under $100

Mother Nature's Inn (551 N. Lake Blvd., Tahoe City, 530/581-4278 or 800/558-4278, www.mothernaturesinn.com, $65-145) brings the Tahoe camping experience inside while still providing creature comforts. Rooms are themed based on a distinct wild creature, and you can expect plenty of decorative tchotchkes in keeping with your room's animal totem. You'll also find lodge-style furnishings in cozy if somewhat cluttered arrangements. All rooms have private baths, fridges, and coffeemakers. Pets are welcome for a small additional fee. The inn is only a few steps from the shores of the lake and downtown Tahoe City.

$100-150

If you want to stay in town, Tahoe City's **Pepper Tree Inn** (645 N. Lake Blvd., Tahoe City, 530/583-3711 or 800/624-8590, www.peppertreetahoe.com, summer $96-213, winter $105-175) is a reasonable choice. With whirlpool tubs, blow-dryers, and coffee grinders in each room, plus an outdoor swimming pool and free wireless Internet access, Pepper Tree is an above-average hotel. It also has the advantage of a great location across the street from the lake, the Lakeside Trail, and some of the best restaurants in Tahoe City. This is a great base for local adventures.

$150-250

The exclusive and beautiful ★ **Stanford Alpine Chalet** (1980 Chalet Rd., Tahoe City, 530/583-1550, www.stanfordalpinechalet.com, $120-309) is situated at the base of Alpine Meadow's mountain. With only 14 rooms, each is special enough to make you feel like a rock star during your stay. Rooms are decorated in a simple yet elegant style with wood, private baths, and striking mountain views. Meals are served family-style at communal tables. In summer the chalet offers a heated swimming pool, sports courts, and horseshoe pits. Winter guests enjoy a private ski shuttle and a giant great-room fireplace. An outdoor hot tub lures guests with its bubbling year-round warmth.

Over $250

For that special vacation when you're willing to spend a little more to make everything perfect, try the **West Shore Inn** (5160 W. Lake Blvd., Homewood, 530/525-5200, www.skihomewood.com, $149-1,699, as low as $99 spring and fall). Each of the four suites, one room, and two villas has distinctive luxury, with balconies, lake views, leather sofas, fireplaces, and flat-screen TVs. A freshly baked continental breakfast is included in the suites and room, as is use of the inn's fleet of bicycles, kayaks, and paddleboards.

Condo Rentals

For the ultimate convenience in ski vacations, get a condo at **The Village at Squaw Valley** (1750 Village East Rd., Olympic Valley, 866/818-6963, www.squawalpine.com, 1-bedroom condo $99-700, 3-bedroom $299-1,300) and never leave the vicinity of the lifts. Elegant, modern condos range from compact studios perfect for singles or couples to three-bedroom homes that sleep up to eight. Condos have full kitchens—some even have granite countertops—as well as a living room with a TV and maybe a fireplace, and a dining table. The skiers' favorite condo has heated tile floors in the kitchen and bath. Included in the price is use of the Village's eight outdoor hot tubs, five saunas, five fitness rooms, and heated underground parking garage. Stay in Building 5; it has the clearest view of the mountain and the most comfortable amenities.

CAMPING

Sugar Pine Point State Park's ★ **General Creek Campground** (Hwy. 89, Tahoma, 800/444-7275, www.reserveamerica.com, mid-May-mid-Sept., $25-35) is a great place to stay on a family vacation or an overnight trip while exploring West Shore attractions. Every campsite in this wooded wildlife-filled park has a picnic table, a charcoal grill, and ample space for a tent or camper. Some sites are ADA-compliant. It has clean showers, and you can get a hot five-minute shower for $0.50 (bring quarters). The campground can get crowded in midsummer, so make reservations in advance. The campground offers 16 sites for off-season camping on a first-come, first-served basis.

Not far from Sugar Pine Point State Park, the Washoe Tribe runs the **Meeks Bay Resort** (7941 Hwy. 89, Tahoma, 530/525-6946 or 877/326-3357, www.meeksbayresort.com, May-Oct., tent sites $20-30, RV sites $30-50). The 14 tent sites and 23 RV sites all have a two-night minimum; pets are not allowed. The resort features a sandy beach and a marina (530/525-5588) where you can rent single kayaks and pedal boats ($20 per hour) and double kayaks, canoes, and paddleboards ($30 per hour). You can also launch your own boat ($15 one-way, $25 round-trip) or rent a slip ($60 per night, weekly $360).

For great tree-lined campsites with easy beach access, the **William Kent Beach and Campground** (Hwy. 89, 2 miles south of Tahoe City, 877/444-6777, www.recreation.gov, mid-May-mid-Oct., $27-29) is a good choice. The 95 sites are suitable for tents or campers, but have no showers or electrical hookups. There are restrooms with flush toilets and bear lockers for your food. The facility is operated by the state's Lake Tahoe Basin Management Unit.

If you don't mind giving up a woodsy camping experience, the **Tahoe State Recreation Area** (Hwy. 28, east of Tahoe City, 530/583-3074 or 800/444-7275, www.reserveamerica.com, late May-early Sept., $35) is a good choice with 23 sites and coin-operated showers, and you can walk to the lake or to the shops of Tahoe City. A utilitarian place to sleep is the **Lake Forest Campground** (Lake Forest Rd., 1.5 miles east of Tahoe City on Hwy. 28, 530/583-3796, www.tahoecitypud.com, mid-May-early Oct., $20), run by the Tahoe City Public Utilities District. The 20 sites are first-come, first-served; RVs up to 25 feet are welcome, though there are no hookups. Facilities include drinking water, flush toilets but no showers, and picnic tables, and the campground is next to the public **Lake Forest Boat Ramp** (530/583-3796, www.tahoecitypud.com, 5am-7pm daily Apr.-Oct., 6am-4pm daily Oct.-Apr., $15/day), also run by the Public Utilities District.

FOOD

More than half a dozen restaurants, snack bars, and coffee shops at **The Village at Squaw Valley** (1750 Village East Rd., Olympic Valley, 530/584-1000, www.squawalpine.com) offer sushi, pizza, high-end wine, and more. Numbering among them are **Mamasake Sushi** (1850 Village South Rd., 530/584-0110, www.mamasake.com, 11:30am-9pm Mon.-Thurs., 11:30am-10pm Fri.-Sun., $6-76) and **Fireside Pizza Co.** (1985 Squaw Valley Rd., 530/584-6150, www.firesidepizza.com, $13-26), plus several other eateries.

Bakeries and Cafés

To fuel up for a day out on the lake or in the mountains, head over to the **Fire Sign Café** (1785 W. Lake Blvd., Tahoe City, 530/583-0871, 7am-3pm daily, $8-12). This breakfast-and-lunch spot is a favorite with locals, serving up an enormous menu of hearty fare. Choose whole-grain waffles with fruit, a kielbasa omelet, crepes, or blueberry coffee cake. Expect a wait for a table on weekend mornings.

If you want to relax with some fine caffeine and really soak in the vacation vibe, you'll revel in **Syd's Bagelry & Espresso** (550 N. Lake Blvd., Tahoe City, 7am-5pm daily). Syd's offers free wireless Internet access, and one of its best features is the location next door to Heritage Plaza, so you can take your latte outdoors while you watch the sunrise over the water.

A good choice for casual, inexpensive dining and drinking in Tahoe City is **Fat Cat Café** (599 N. Lake Blvd., Tahoe City, 530/583-3355, www.fatcattahoe.com, 11am-9pm Mon.-Thurs., 9am-10pm Fri.-Sat., 9am-9pm Sun., $9-14), especially if you like entertainment with your food. Thursday is karaoke night, and Friday and Saturday have live music starting around 10pm. The food includes decent sandwiches, salads, and burgers. The café also has free wireless Internet access.

Casual Dining

The Blue Agave (425 N. Lake Blvd., Sunnyside-Tahoe City, 530/583-8113, www.tahoeblueagave.com, 11:30am-9pm daily, $10-30) is the place to go for Mexican food on the West Shore. It's located in the Tahoe Inn, built circa 1934, which has a long history involving gold miners, bootleggers, and film stars. The ample and delicious food is absolutely current and draws loyal patrons from all over.

Fine Dining

Wolfdale's (640 N. Lake Blvd., Tahoe City, 530/583-5700, www.wolfdales.com, 5:30pm-10pm Wed.-Mon., $15-35) has been serving "cuisine unique" dishes that fuse Asian and Western ingredients since 1978. The small seasonal menu is heavy on seafood, but also includes tasty beef and game meats in season. Save room for the delicious desserts, most made in a light California style.

An ideal spot for a delicious dinner and some lake-watching is ★ **Christy Hill Lakeside Bistro** (115 Grove St., Tahoe City, 530/583-8551, www.christyhill.com, 5pm-9:30pm daily summer, 5pm-9pm daily winter, $21-33) and its outdoor Sand Bar (beer and wine only) on the back deck. Entrées range from fresh cannelloni with homemade lemon ricotta to Moroccan spiced lamb loin.

For a light meal and a fabulous sunset, end your day at the Mountain Grill at the **Sunnyside Resort** (1850 West Lake Blvd., Sunnyside, 2 miles south of Tahoe City, 530/583-7200 or 800/822-2754, www.sunnysidetahoe.com, 4pm-9pm Sun.-Thurs., 4pm-9:30pm Fri.-Sat., $12-22). The patio has an expansive view of the lake and the mountains beyond; it also has plenty of room. The menu is brief—mostly appetizers, salads, and burgers—and the food is good, though not great. For a relaxing drink and a chance to mellow out by the water, this place is hard to beat.

At the ★ **West Shore Café & Inn** (5160 West Lake Blvd., Homewood, 530/525-5200, www.skihomewood.com, 11am-9pm daily winter, 11am-3pm, 5pm-9pm daily summer, 5pm-9pm daily spring and fall, $16-34), the atmosphere is classy, with white tablecloths and well-dressed patrons. On the back patio, you can watch the sun go down over the lake, or grab a table out on the pier, illuminated by strings of lights. The West Shore Burger ($16) is the dish you'll be talking about when you get home, and the service is both professional and friendly. Try one of the signature cocktails, such as the West Shore Margarita or the Mango Zombie.

The **River Grill** (River Rd. at Hwy. 89 and Hwy. 28, 530/581-2644, www.rivergrilltahoe.com, 5pm-close daily, $19-45) is located where the Truckee River meets Tahoe City. Eat outside on the rustic heated wooden porch, enjoying the river view while listening to live music, or sit indoors in the casually elegant dining room, complete with a fireplace. Happy hour (5pm-6:30pm daily) features discounted drinks and food in the bar and at the outdoor fire pit.

INFORMATION AND SERVICES

The Lake Tahoe Visitors Bureau maintains the **North Lake Tahoe Visitors Information Center and Chamber of Commerce** (100 N. Lake Blvd., Tahoe City, 530/581-6900, www.gotahoenorth.com, 9am-5pm daily). For medical attention, the **Tahoe Forest Hospital** (10121 Pine Ave., Truckee, 530/587-6011, www.tfhd.com) and its affiliate, **Incline Village Community Hospital** (880 Alder Ave., Incline Village, NV, 775/833-4100 or 800/419-2627, www.tfhd.com), are the nearest options for full-service emergency rooms.

TRANSPORTATION

Air

The nearest airports are **Reno-Tahoe International Airport** (RNO, 2001 E. Plumb Lane, Reno, NV, 775/328-6400, www.renoairport.com) and **Sacramento International Airport** (SMF, 6900 Airport Blvd., Sacramento, 916/929-5411, www.sacramento.aero). Both are served by several major airlines.

Car

I-80 leads near the North Shore from Sacramento or the San Francisco Bay Area. From I-80, take Highway 89 south for 14 miles to Tahoe City. U.S. 50 runs along the West Shore from the south. From U.S. 50 in South Lake Tahoe, take Highway 89 north for 25 miles along the West Shore, passing Meeks Bay, Tahoma, and Tahoe Pines on the way to Tahoe City on the North Shore.

Bus

Tahoe Area Regional Transit (TART, 530/550-1212 or 800/736-6365, www.laketahoetransit.com) is the North Shore's public bus system. Buses (adults $1.75 one-way, 24-hour pass $3.50) run from Tahoma on the West Shore to Incline Village, Nevada, with many stops along the way. Seniors, youth, and travelers with disabilities get discounted fares.

Ski Resort Shuttles

Many ski resorts maintain shuttles to bring skiers up to the mountains in the morning and back to their hotels in the late afternoon. Contact the transportation office for **Squaw Valley** and **Alpine Meadows** (530/452-7181, www.squawalpine.com) for shuttle schedules between the two mountains.

In a few places a free **Night Rider bus service** (866/216-5222, http://northlake-tahoeexpress.com, 7pm-midnight daily, as late as 2am in some areas, free) is provided by North Lake Tahoe Express. The winter service goes to Squaw Valley, Tahoe City, Northstar, and the Biltmore in Crystal Bay, Nevada. In summer, the West Shore Night Rider offers service from the Tahoe City Y to Granlibakken, Sunnyside, Homewood, and Tahoma.

East Shore

Lake Tahoe straddles California and Nevada, and so do visitors to the area. Heading east on U.S. 50 from the South Shore, the town of South Lake Tahoe becomes Stateline, Nevada, with barely a sign announcing the transition. On the North Shore, shortly west of the intersection of Highways 28 and 267, Crystal Bay marks the California-Nevada border crossing. The drive along the Nevada side of Lake Tahoe is beautiful, woodsy, and quiet, with fewer towns and stopping points along the way. You'll often find yourself deep in the pines with fewer lake views, though they certainly exist.

If you're driving the perimeter of the lake, many locals recommend driving the route clockwise, northbound on the west side and southbound on the east. The obvious advantage is that your car stays on the lake side, making it easier to admire the views and to pull over at beaches and scenic overlooks. But either direction provides a lovely excursion.

THUNDERBIRD LODGE

On the Nevada side of the lake is the **Thunderbird Lodge** (5000 Hwy. 28, Incline Village, NV, 775/832-8750 or 800/468-2463, www.thunderbirdlodge.org, tours Tues.-Sat. late May-mid-Oct., adults $39, children $19), built in 1936 by a Tahoe resident called the Captain who intended to create a luxury hotel and casino on his vast lakeside acreage. It was one of the last great upscale residential mansions constructed beside the lake and includes several outbuildings.

You won't be able to drive directly to Thunderbird Lodge. Instead, park at the **Crystal Bay Visitors Center** (969 Tahoe Blvd., Incline Village, NV, 775/832-1606 or 800/468-2463, 8am-5pm Mon.-Fri., 10am-4pm Sat.-Sun.) to meet the tour guide and bus. You'll be driven out to the lodge for a two-hour walking tour of the grounds and several of the buildings. The 600-foot underground tunnel from the mansion to the boathouse and card house is one of the tour highlights, especially for kids. Another highlight is the unbelievable 1930s-era mahogany yacht ***Thunderbird,*** which still floats in the boathouse.

If you're staying on the west side of the lake, book a **boat tour** (Zephyr Cove Marina, 775/230-8907, www.tahoeboatcruises.com, 10am Tues.-Sat. summer, reservations required, adults $139, ages 6-11 $59) on a historical wooden powerboat across the lake and along the eastern shore. The boat docks at the Thunderbird Lodge, and the walking tour continues from there. A continental breakfast is served on board the ship, and a buffet lunch at Thunderbird is included with the five-hour tour. Children under age six are not permitted. Both tours operate in summer only, with exact dates set by the lodge.

SPORTS AND RECREATION

Ski Resorts

MT. ROSE

Mt. Rose (22222 Mt. Rose Hwy., Reno, NV, 775/849-0704 or 800/754-7673, www.mtrose.com, lift 9am-4pm daily winter, adults $79-89,

East Shore

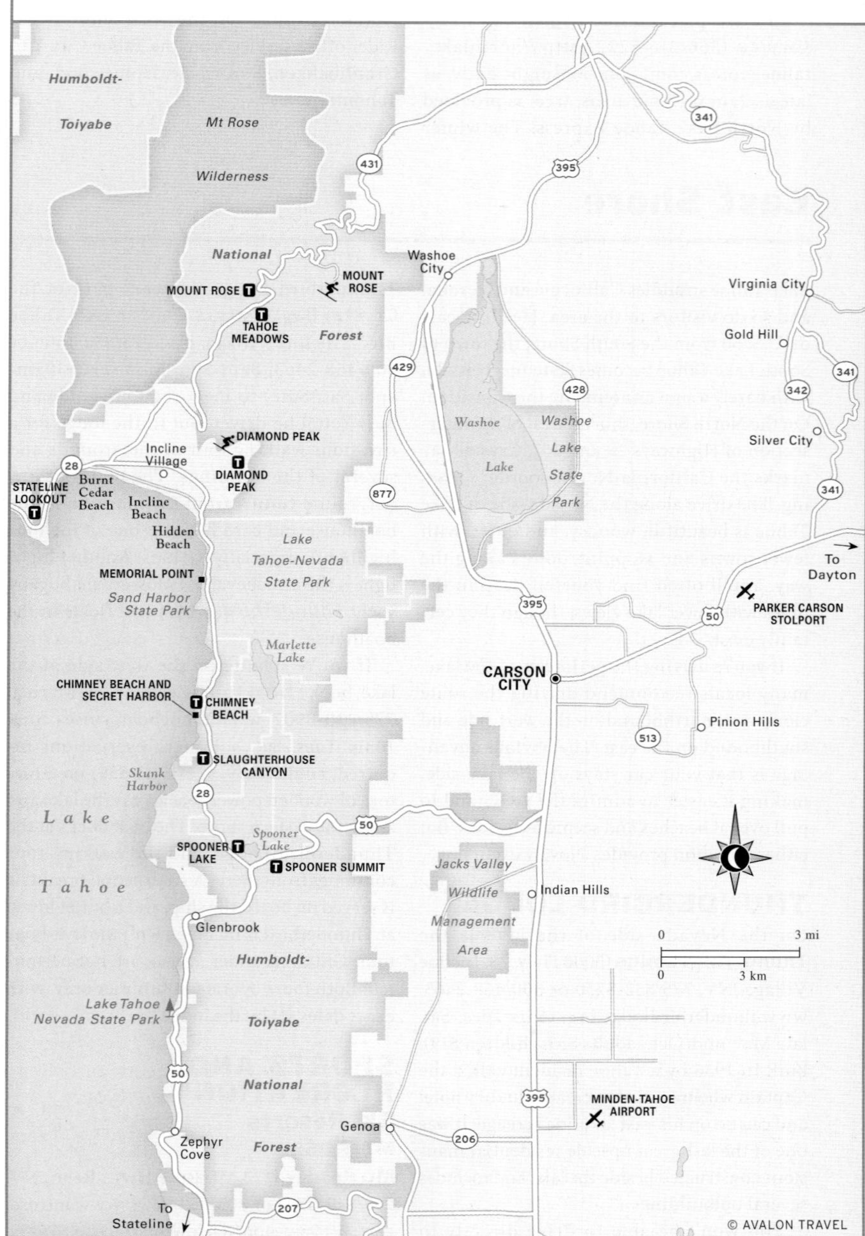
Humboldt-
Toiyabe
Mt Rose
Wilderness
National
Forest
431
395
341
Washoe City
MOUNT ROSE
MOUNT ROSE
TAHOE MEADOWS
Virginia City
Gold Hill
341
342
429
428
Washoe
Washoe
Lake
Lake
State
Park
Silver City
DIAMOND PEAK
Incline Village
DIAMOND PEAK
28
STATELINE LOOKOUT
Burnt Cedar Beach
Incline Beach
Hidden Beach
877
341
Lake
Tahoe-Nevada
State Park
To Dayton
MEMORIAL POINT
Sand Harbor State Park
395
50
PARKER CARSON STOLPORT
Marlette Lake
CARSON CITY
CHIMNEY BEACH AND SECRET HARBOR
CHIMNEY BEACH
Pinion Hills
513
SLAUGHTERHOUSE CANYON
Skunk Harbor
28
Lake
50
Spooner Lake
SPOONER LAKE
SPOONER SUMMIT
Jacks Valley
Wildlife
Management
Area
Tahoe
Indian Hills
Glenbrook
Humboldt-
0
3 mi
0
3 km
Lake Tahoe Nevada State Park
Toiyabe
50
National
395
MINDEN-TAHOE AIRPORT
Genoa
206
Zephyr Cove
Forest
207
To Stateline
© AVALON TRAVEL

seniors $69, ages 13-17 $69, ages 6-12 $47, ages under 6 $15) offers the most choice in terms of both variety and beginner routes. Many different ski school packages and private-lesson options are available for children ages three and older as well as seniors who want to cut it up on a snowboard. Sign the kids up for ski or snowboard camps, where they will have a great time, learn lots, and make ski buddies their own age.

Novices should avoid the center of Mt. Rose, an area called Chutes, with a morass of double-black-diamond runs and names like Detonator and Yellow Jacket. If you're looking for green runs, park at the Main Lodge and take the Ponderosa or the Galena Chairs up to beginner territory. For lots of great long intermediate tracks, start at Winters Creek Lodge (the second access point for the Mt. Rose resort) and take the Blazing Zephyrs Six-Chair almost to the top of the mountain. You can enjoy a hot cocoa and a meal or use restrooms at either lodge.

DIAMOND PEAK

Smaller **Diamond Peak** (1210 Ski Way, Incline Village, NV, 775/832-1177, www.diamondpeak.com, lift 9am-4pm daily winter, adults $59-69, seniors and youth $44-59, ages 7-12 $22-33, children under 7 free) is easy to access from Incline Village and has two—count 'em, two—green runs at the bottom of the hill. It's probably not the best place to bring young children or beginners as there isn't much variety. However, if you're an intermediate skier or boarder, take the Crystal Express quad up to the top of the peak. Stop for a moment and enjoy the amazing vistas before taking a wonderfully long run down the blue Crystal Ridge, or cut into one of the black-diamond chutes that branch off through the forest. You'll start your day down at the Base Lodge, where you can also eat, drink, and make merry. In the middle of the day, the Snowflake Lodge on the ridge is the perfect setting for looking out onto the lake as you sip a drink or just sit with your feet up.

Snowmobiling

It's hard to miss the presence of the **Zephyr Cove Snowmobile Center** (Zephyr Cove Resort, 760 U.S. 50, 775/589-4906, www.zephyrcove.com, $135) in Zephyr Cove. A free shuttle runs along the highway for all reserved riders to use at their convenience. Zephyr Cove offers several different tour options on a new Ski-Doo snowmobile, including a Lakeview tour for riders of all skills, or an "Ultimate Experience" tour for experienced riders; both tours include breathtaking views, easy riding on groomed trails, and plenty of stops to take pictures. Advanced riders can work with the guides to create a challenging personal tour.

Sledding and Sleigh Rides

Take an old-school sleigh ride at several locations around Tahoe. Just across the street from the Harrah's and MontBleu casinos in Stateline is **Borges Family Sleigh Rides** (110 Lake Parkway, Stateline, NV, 775/588-2953, www.sleighride.com, 60-minute ride adults $45-50, ages 1-11 $25). The Borges have been giving sleigh rides on the South Shore for more than 30 years. They've got sleighs seating 2-20 passengers and lovely blond Belgian draft horses; rides on Sand Harbor are also available. Cuddle under blankets as you listen to stories and songs—but bring a thermos of cocoa. In summer, check out the carriage tours and hayrides.

Cruises

Bleu Wave (775/588-9283 or 866/413-0985, www.tahoebleuwave.com, adults $50-65, children $25-32) operates from the Round Hill Pine Beach & Marina (300 U.S. 50, Zephyr Cove, NV, 775/588-3055, www.roundhillpinesresort.com) in Stateline. Their Emerald Bay cruise lasts two hours with an all-you-can-eat lunch buffet, drinks included.

Waterskiing and Wakeboarding

Zephyr Cove Marina (750 U.S. 50, Zephyr Cove, NV, 775/589-4901, www.zephyrcove.com, ski boats $149-189, WaveRunners

$110-135) offers a full complement of services and watercraft rentals. For skiers and wakeboarders, Zephyr Cove has a small fleet of 22- to 24-foot Sea Ray open-bow ski boats, plus skis, boards, and toys. Personal watercraft riders can rent one of the marina's three-person WaveRunners. Truly adventurous visitors can also sign up for a parasailing session with professional drivers.

Sand Harbor Beach

Beaches

Sand Harbor Beach (Hwy. 28, 3 miles south of Incline Village, NV, 775/831-0494, www.parks.nv.gov, 8am-7pm daily May, 8am-9pm daily June-Aug., 8am-7pm Sept., 8am-5pm daily Oct.-Apr., $12 per vehicle Apr. 15-Oct. 15, $7 per vehicle Oct. 16-Apr. 14, walk-in $1 pp) is part of the Lake Tahoe-Nevada State Park, but people often refer to it as Sand Harbor State Park. The 55-acre sandy beach is one of the most popular places to swim at Lake Tahoe. Big boulders make great destinations to swim out to, dive off, and perch on top of to rest and take in the views. There's a large picnic area, and the on-site restaurant-snack bar **Char-Pit Sand Harbor** (530/546-3171, www.charpit.com, 11am-9pm daily, $4-23) specializes in burgers and ice cream—the ample barbecue ribs are popular with hungry families. If it's boating you're interested in, see **Sand Harbor Rentals** (530/581-4336, www.sandharborrentals.com, single kayak or paddleboard $25 per hour, $75 per day, double kayak $40 per hour, $95 per day), the only officially sanctioned boat concessionaire in the park. Sand Harbor Rentals is right on the beach next to the boat ramp; you can walk up and try your luck at getting a rental, but reservations are recommended. The company also offers a morning East Shore kayak tour ($95 pp) and a sunset kayak tour ($65 pp), for which reservations are also required; the Get-Up, Stand-Up program (daily 8am-9am, $40, 2-person minimum, summer only) teaches the basics of stand-up paddleboarding to novice paddlers.

Fishing

At Zephyr Cove you can book a fishing trip with **O'Malley's Fishing Charters** (775/588-4102, www.omalleysfishingcharters.com, Apr.-Oct., $115 pp). You need your own fishing license, but O'Malley's supplies the bait, tackle, and equipment. A cozy 22-foot boat and lots of personal attention from your guide make for an intimate angling experience.

At **Spooner Lake** (Lake Tahoe-Nevada State Park, U.S. 50 and Hwy. 28, 775/831-0494, www.parks.nv.gov, park 24 hours daily, fishing allowed dawn-until 2 hours after sunset, $10, Oct. 16-Apr. 14 $7) you can fish year-round and experience ice fishing in winter. You can keep up to five trout. A Nevada state fishing license is required.

Nearby **Marlette Lake** (Lake Tahoe-Nevada State Park, summer $10) is full of brook, rainbow, and cutthroat trout. Marlette fishing is catch-and-release only, and the season runs July 15-September 30. For more information, visit the Nevada Department of Wildlife (www.ndow.org).

Golf

The championship George Fazio course at **Edgewood Tahoe** (180 Lake Pkwy., Stateline, NV, 775/588-3566, www.edgewood-tahoe.com, daily June-Oct., $170-220) has been called better than the Pebble Beach Golf Links. Not everyone agrees with that bold assessment, but the consensus is that Edgewood is one of the top courses in the West if not the nation. Walking the course, you'll enjoy views of the lake and mountains so wonderful that you may forget all about that pesky putting for a moment or two. Several holes are right on the shores of Lake Tahoe—the biggest water hazard around. The rather hefty greens fees include a golf cart; you can also rent clubs and hire a caddie. After your game, enjoy lunch and a stiff drink at the **Brooks' Golf Bar & Deck** (11:30am-8:30pm daily).

Hiking

For a serious lake-to-lake hike, try the **Marlette Lake Trail** (10 miles, moderate). The Spooner Lake trailhead is located in Lake Tahoe-Nevada State Park (775/831-0494, www.parks.nv.gov, $10) at the junction of U.S. 50 and Highway 28. The hike slopes uphill for five miles to the Marlette Dam, but you're on a fire road much of the way, so the trail is easy to follow and the terrain never gets too rough.

For a shorter hike with less climbing and even more shoreline, try the **Spooner Lake Trail** (2 miles) from the Spooner Lake trailhead in Lake Tahoe-Nevada State Park. The level trail features interpretive signage and gets you some close-up views of birds and other wildlife, including—if you're lucky—eagles and ospreys.

The **Sand Harbor** (Apr. 15-Oct. 15 $12, Oct. 16-Apr. 14 $7) area of Lake Tahoe-Nevada State Park has additional pleasant hiking. The **Sandy Point Trail** starts near the visitors center and takes you down a paved-and-boardwalk path for 0.3 mile, with interpretive signs along the way.

Farther north, the scenic hiking continues. For a quick easy walk near Crystal Bay, Nevada, head up to the **State Lookout** (iron-pipe gate on Forest Rd. 1601, 1 mile, easy). At the lookout, you'll find summer volunteers who can give you information about the region, including the short self-guided nature trail that surrounds the lookout.

Horseback Riding

Equestrians can sign up for a ride with **Zephyr Cove Resort Stables** (U.S. 50, Zephyr Cove, 775/588-5664, www.zephyrcovestable.com, 9am-5pm daily summer, daily 10am-4pm spring and fall, 1 hour $43-45, 2 hours $80-83). Enjoy a lovely scenic trail ride complete with panoramic views of the lake. Zephyr Cove also offers "food rides" (2-2.5 hours, $55-68) at breakfast (8am), lunch (11am), and dinner (5pm). If you have dietary restrictions, call ahead to make arrangements in advance. As at many stables, restrictions include a weight limit (225 pounds) and a minimum age (7 years) for riders.

Mountain Biking

You can rent a mountain bike from **Flume Trail Mountain Bikes** (1115 Tunnel Creek Rd., Incline Village, 775/298-2501, http://flumetrailtahoe.com, 8am-6pm daily May-Oct., $35-85 per day), inside the Spooner Lake State Park day-use area in the Toiyabe National Forest in Zephyr Cove. The company, owned by Patti McMullan and Mountain Bike Hall of Fame member Max Jones, provides shuttle services to certain trailheads and offers knowledgeable advice about mountain biking in the area. Reservations are recommended and can be made by phone or online.

The spectacular **Tahoe Rim Trail** (www.tahoerimtrail.org) provides mountain bikers access to about half of the 165 miles of rugged and varied terrain. You can't bike where the trail enters the Desolation or Mount Rose Wilderness Areas, or where it joins the Pacific Crest Trail. These areas are usually well signed. If you'd like to bike the particularly beautiful section from the Tahoe Meadows trailhead to Spooner Lake, a private shuttle service (775/749-5349, www.theflumetrail.com, mid-June-Nov., $10-15) is available. The shuttle, with a trailer for your bike, leaves from the parking lot at Spooner Lake State Park and delivers you to the Tahoe Meadows Rim Trail trailhead on the Mount Rose Highway. Signs at the trailhead indicate that this section of the trail—between Tahoe Meadows and beyond Spooner Lake to Spooner Summit—is bikable only on even-numbered days of the month.

CASINOS

If you think casinos are smoke-filled holes sheltering lonely souls pouring their savings into slot machines, think again: On the South Shore, just over the Nevada state line, various casinos attract a young crowd looking for a lively, hip night out. Note that the casinos sometimes call the town Lake Tahoe, Nevada, though it's legally Stateline.

MontBleu Resort Casino and Spa

The gaming floor of the **MontBleu Resort Casino and Spa** (55 U.S. 50, Stateline, NV, 775/588-3515 or 800/648-3353, www.montbleuresort.com) is great fun on weekend evenings, with go-go dancers and youthful gamblers enjoying free drinks as they hammer the slots. As with other casinos here, you'll find full-fledged table games of the Vegas variety: craps, roulette, blackjack, and Texas hold 'em, among others. The Zone contains the sports book and the poker room, but slots and video poker machines are everywhere. MontBleu's casino is better lit and less smoky than many others, making it easy to stay and play late into the night. If you get tired of gambling, wander around to the full-service salon and spa, pool, lingerie shop, art gallery, ski-rental shop, nightclub, or several restaurants.

Harrah's Lake Tahoe

Gambling fans should definitely bring their frequent-player cards to the casino floor at **Harrah's Lake Tahoe** (15 U.S. 50, Stateline, NV, 775/588-6611 or 800/427-7247, www.caesars.com/harrahs-tahoe), which has all the Vegas gaming favorites—classic craps, rapid roulette, and Keno pads and monitors scattered all over the place. The atmosphere is a bit more classic casino, with dim lights in the evening and a warren of slot machines that make it easy to get lost. Now that Caesars Entertainment has absorbed Harrah's and its neighbor, Harvey's, it has a solid lock on its block. When you've had enough gaming, check out the live entertainment or the popular nightclub.

Harvey's Lake Tahoe

Harvey's Lake Tahoe

For those who can't get enough, Harrah's affiliated casino **Harvey's Lake Tahoe** (18 U.S. 50, Stateline, 775/588-2411 or 800/427-8397, www.caesars.com/harveys-tahoe) is nearby. At Harvey's, you can play all the usual games of chance or enjoy state-of-the-art video screens while betting on football, NASCAR, and horse races in The Book, the nonsmoking racing and sports site. Harvey's also boasts a fitness center, a pool, and entertainment, from improv comedy to headliner musical acts (Tues.-Sun.) and concerts in the outdoor arena in summer.

Lakeside Inn and Casino

Smaller and less flashy, **Lakeside Inn and Casino** (168 U.S. 50, Stateline, NV, 775/588-7777 or 800/624-7980, www.lakesideinn.com) is a local favorite. Lakeside looks more like a mountain lodge than a high-rise gaming emporium, and it has won the most votes for Best Casino, Loosest Slots, and Friendliest Casino Employees. The casino offers all the usual games and machines, and it is particularly welcoming for beginners, who may want to attend the "University of Lakeside" (6pm Wed.), a free seminar in the Poker Room where Lakeside employees teach the basics of blackjack, craps, and more. In a way, they pay you to come, with a free cocktail, souvenirs, and $5 worth of free play at the slots.

ENTERTAINMENT AND EVENTS

Nightlife

Since the youthful snowboarding crowd packs Tahoe in winter and the wakeboarders fill the summer, it's no surprise that some noticeable nightlife crops up around the lake. The favorite clubs tend to be inside the Stateline casino resorts. Often the hip dancing crew spills out of the clubs and onto the casino floor throughout the evening.

A favorite nightclub for many locals is **PEEK at Harrah's** (15 U.S. 50, Stateline, NV, 775/586-6705, www.caesars.com/peek, 10:30pm-4am Fri.-Sat., cover $10-20 men, $5-10 women). This late-night watering hole features in-house and guest DJs like DJ Skribble and DJ Spider; the tunes are mostly house music, with some hip-hop sprinkled into the mix. Grab a cocktail at the bar, or for additional cost, enjoy table service by the lovely cocktail staff in a plush VIP booth.

For late-night entertainment, **The Opal Ultralounge at MontBleu** (55 U.S. 50, Stateline, NV, 775/586-2000 or 888/829-7630, www.montbleuresort.com, 10pm-dawn Thurs.-Sat., cover $10-20) is one of the most happening places around. Entertainment includes expert mash-up DJs, resident body painters (midnight Thurs.-Sat.), and go-go dancers (11:30pm Thurs.-Sat.). If you'd like to be painted, you can have it done in private at no charge, though gratuities are accepted. All drinks are $1 on Thursday, women drink for free until 2am on Friday, and women pay no cover before midnight on Saturday.

Comedy

For an evening of laughter, get tickets to **The Improv at Harveys** (18 U.S. 50, Stateline, NV, 800/786-8208, www.caesars.com/harrahs-tahoe, 9pm Wed.-Sun., $25-30). Each evening an old-school Budd Friedman comic showcase goes up. Howie Nave is the host and emcee. This is the place where many of today's major comedy stars honed their acts—come see who'll be famous next.

Festivals and Events

California theater-lovers have been known to drive for hours to see a show at the **Lake Tahoe Shakespeare Festival** (800/747-4697, www.laketahoeshakespeare.com, July-Aug., $15-89). A new stage facility was built in 1995 at the classic Sand Harbor State Park beach location (Hwy. 28, 3 miles south of Incline Village). Shuttle service used to be offered from Incline Village but has stopped transporting festivalgoers; check the web site in case that info changes in the future. Expensive sections of the theater have reserved seating and chairs, but in the cheap seats you can bring your own chair or lie on a blanket in the sand. Gates open at 5pm and performances begin at 7:30pm. Come early to enjoy food and drinks from Shakespeare's Kitchen.

ACCOMMODATIONS

Casinos

Tahoe's casino resorts are some of the spiffiest places to stay on the Nevada side, offering upscale attractive hotel rooms often at lower than expected rates. You'll also find the occasional noncasino lakeshore resort that focuses more on recreation than the slots.

The most popular casino resort is **Harrah's** (15 U.S. 50, Stateline, NV, 775/588-2411 or 800/427-7247, www.caesars.com/harrahs-tahoe, $99-589), with upscale accommodations, all the nightlife and entertainment you need, and easy access to Heavenly and other South Shore ski resorts in winter and the lakeshore in summer. The high-rise hotel has more than 500 upscale rooms; even the lower-end rooms have ample space, a California king or two double beds, two baths, Wi-Fi, cable TV, and minibars. Premium rooms provide excellent views of the lake and the mountains. The decor is upscale and contemporary, with bright colorful accents and sleek furnishings and art.

Harvey's Casino (18 U.S. 50, Stateline, NV, 775/588-2411 or 800/427-8397, www.caesars.com/harveys-tahoe, $89-289 plus $35 in fees), now under the same ownership as Harrah's, has rooms that tend to be a little less plush and a little less expensive than those at Harrah's. At Harvey's, midweek off-season rates can run as low as $79 plus $35 in booking fees.

MontBleu Casino (55 U.S. 50, Stateline, NV, 775/588-3515 or 800/648-3353, www.montbleuresort.com, $115-335 summer) definitely shines when it comes to attractive hotel rooms with top amenities. With 437 rooms, MontBleu is prepared to offer a range of affordable choices. Tower rooms include a comfortable bed, loud decor and fabrics, private baths, and all the conveniences. For luxury, try a spa room, which includes a pink-marble bath, walk-in shower, and two-person hot tub in the bedroom. MontBleu used to be a Caesar's, and though they renovated beautifully, the walls remain paper-thin—bring earplugs. Free wireless Internet access is also available.

Condo Rentals

Club Tahoe (914 Northwood Blvd., Incline Village, NV, 775/831-5750 or 800/527-5154, www.clubtahoe.com, $149-250) is a great place to rent a condo on the Nevada shore. Each three-story unit includes two bedrooms and a loft with twin beds. The decor isn't the most contemporary—expect 1970s-1980s-era sofas, bargain-basement wood furniture, and paneling on the walls—but the full-size kitchens are stocked with appliances and utensils, and a second bath makes sharing the condo easy. Amenities include an outdoor pool and spa, a tennis court, a racquetball court, an arcade, and a full bar with pool table.

Resorts

If you prefer a Nevada ski resort to a casino, try the **Parkside Inn at Incline** (1003 Tahoe Blvd., Incline Village, NV, 775/831-1052 or 800/824-6391, www.innatincline.com, $114-199, two-night minimum on weekends), with 38 rooms in a modest midcentury-style motel. The rooms are reminiscent of a low-end motel, with slightly shabby furniture, but they are clean, and the private baths are adequate. Amenities include an indoor pool and a hot tub available year-round, flat-screen TVs, and free wireless Internet access in all rooms.

Perhaps the best non-casino is ★ **Zephyr Cove Resort** (760 U.S. 50, Zephyr Cove, NV, 888/896-3830, www.zephyrcove.com, $179-339 summer, $119-219 winter). This resort has it all: lakefront property, lodge rooms and individual cabins, full-service marina, winter snowmobile park, and restaurants. The four lodge rooms all have private baths and attractive modern appointments. For a special treat, ask for the room with the spa tub. The 28 cabins run from cozy studios to multistory chalets that sleep up to 10 people ($319-600 with two-night minimum on weekends). Although they look rustic from the outside, inside you'll find modern furniture, phones, TVs, and wireless Internet access. Pets are welcome; when making reservations, let them know which furry friends you'll bring.

CAMPING

Within the Spooner Lake area of Lake Tahoe-Nevada State Park, **Spooner Summit** (775/749-1120 or 775/589-4957, www.zephyrcove.com, $141, two-night minimum required) offers two log cabins for foot travelers: Spooner Cabin and Wild Cat Cabin. Accessible only by snowshoe, cross-country skiing, or hiking, these backwoods cabins are basic. Each cabin can sleep at least four guests with a queen bed upstairs and a futon downstairs, and the Spooner Cabin also has two foam mattresses. Both cabins have a kitchen stove, a wood stove for heat, and five gallons of drinking water every other day. Both cabins have compostable toilets; the commode for the Wild Cat is located inside the attached outhouse.

Nevada Beach Campground (Elks Point Rd., 3 miles north of Stateline, NV, 0.25 mile northwest of U.S. 50, summer 775/588-5562, www.fs.usda.gov; reservations 877/444-6777, www.recreation.gov, mid-May-mid-Oct., $32-34) is a U.S. Forest Service campground offering 54 lakefront sites on the Nevada side of Lake Tahoe. RVs up to 45 feet are welcome, although no hookups are available. Drinking water, flush toilets, and convenience to both Lake Tahoe and the nightlife of Stateline are all attractions here.

FOOD

Stateline

The popular **Red Hut Café Nevada** (229 Kingsbury Grade, Stateline, NV, 775/588-7488, www.redhutcafe, 6am-2pm daily, $6-11) opened an outpost in Stateline. **Starbucks** is served inside Harrah's (15 U.S. 50, Stateline, NV, 775/588-2411 or 800/427-7247, www.caesars.com/harrahs-tahoe, 24 hours).

The **Ciera Steakhouse at the MontBleu** (55 U.S. 50, Stateline, NV, 775/588-3515 or 800/648-3353, www.montbleuresort.com, 5:30pm-10pm Wed.-Sun., $28-56) provides plenty of steak and nonsteak options, with preparations designed to appeal to visitors from around the country. The coolest part of the Ciera dining experience is the coffee ($6), complete with a fabulous tray of fixings, including delicious flavored whipped creams. Finally, you'll be presented with a complimentary dish of chocolate-covered strawberries resting atop a frothing container of dry ice.

With decor as cute as its name, **Thai One On** (292 Kingsbury Grade, Suite 33, Stateline, NV, 775/586-8424, www.thaioneontahoe.com, 11am-9pm Mon.-Fri., 2pm-9:45pm Sat.-Sun., $11-15) serves delicious food at reasonable prices. The menu is eclectic: french toast, tacos, egg rolls, and curry in addition to traditional Thai favorites such as pad thai. Most of the food is prepared on the premises with fresh ingredients, and the results are tantalizing.

The best French food in the area is at **Mirabelle's** (290 Kingsbury Grade, Stateline, NV, 775/586-1007, www.mirabelleatlaketahoe.com, 5:30pm-9:30pm Tues.-Sun., $21.50-32.50). Mirabelle's offers a three-course Epicurean Menu ($35) or an á la carte dinner menu with entrées such as venison, lobster, and ostrich.

One of the best dining experiences is at ★ **Edgewood Tahoe Restaurant** (100 Lake Pkwy., Stateline, NV, 775/588-2787, www.edgewoodtahoe.com, 5:30pm-9pm daily summer, 5:30pm-9pm Wed.-Sun. winter, $28-40). Located on the world-famous Edgewood golf course, the restaurant features elk chops, sea bass, and rack of spring lamb. The prices are reasonable considering the quality of the food. For dessert, try the nightly crème brûlée.

Incline Village

Jack Rabbit Moon (893 Tahoe Blvd., Suite 600, Incline Village, NV, 775/833-3900, 5:30pm-close Tues.-Sun. late May-Oct., $14-36) is a small but popular fine-dining establishment noted for its extensive wine list, fresh contemporary menu, and seafood specialties such as lobster tamales and wild salmon. Hours can fluctuate and reservations are a must, so call ahead to confirm.

If your tastes run to the creative and pleasantly surprising, you'll enjoy **Fredrick's Fusion Bistro** (907 Tahoe Blvd., Incline Village, NV, 775/832-3007, www.fredricksbistro.com, 5pm-9:30pm Tues.-Sat., $11-32), where lobster dogs share a table with surf-and-turf sushi rolls. The fusion is mostly French and Asian, but the seasonal menus have a definite California feeling, as they make good use of fresh and local ingredients.

A good place to splurge on a meal with an exceptional lake view is the **Lone Eagle Grille** (111 Country Club Dr., Incline Village, NV, 775/886-6899, www.loneeaglegrille.com, 5:30pm-9pm Mon.-Thurs., 5:30pm-10pm Fri., 11:30am-3pm, 5:30pm-10pm Sat., 11:30am-3pm, 5:30pm-9pm Sun., $34-59). Entrées include steak, lamb, and Dungeness crab, but a special menu just for vegetarians has several choices for every course; fresh creative soups, salads, and vegetables are prominent on both.

INFORMATION AND SERVICES

The **Lake Tahoe Visitors Authority Visitors Center** (169 U.S. 50, Stateline, NV, 775/588-4591, www.tahoesouth.com) is across from the Lakeside Inn and Casino. It's a big spacious place with maps, brochures, and clean restrooms. The **Incline Village Crystal Bay Visitors Bureau** (969 Tahoe Blvd., Incline Village, NV, 775/832-1606 or 800/468-2463, www.gotahoenorth.com, 8am-5pm Mon.-Fri., 10am-4pm Sat.-Sun.) is another source of information.

To get cash, hit the ATMs in Stateline; the towns on the Nevada side of the lake are small and far apart. The casinos have plenty of cash machines too.

Incline Village Community Hospital (880 Alder Ave., Incline Village, NV, 775/833-4100 or 800/419-2627, www.tfhd.com) is the place to go for help on the Nevada side. The hospital has a 24-hour emergency room.

TRANSPORTATION

Air

The closest commercial airport to Lake Tahoe is in Reno, the **Reno-Tahoe International Airport** (RNO, 2001 E. Plumb Lane, Reno, NV, 775/328-6400, www.renoairport.com). It is particularly convenient for travelers heading to the Nevada side of the lake. To get to Incline Village from the airport, take U.S. 395 south for 8 miles to Highway 431 south for another 24 miles. The airport is open year-round, but be sure to check on your flights in advance in the winter since storms delay and sometimes cancel flights.

Car

I-80 and U.S. 50 are the main roads to the Nevada side of Lake Tahoe from points west. To reach the North Shore on the Nevada side, take I-80 to Truckee, and then follow Highway 267 south to Kings Beach (still in California). Take Highway 28 east, which quickly enters Nevada, toward Incline Village. Highway 28 continues south along the lake, meeting U.S. 50 at the Spooner Lake area; continue south on U.S. 50 to reach Stateline, Nevada, in about 12 miles.

From South Lake Tahoe, follow U.S. 50 east for about three miles into Stateline, Nevada. U.S. 50 runs to Carson City, Nevada in another 12 miles. To continue circumnavigating the lake, bear left onto Highway 28 toward Incline Village and Highway 431 in about 12 miles.

From Reno, you can reach the North Shore on the Nevada side in 45-60 minutes, depending on the weather. Always check road conditions before attempting any route in winter, as storms may cause chain requirements or even road closures.

Truckee-Donner

Gateway to the Tahoe ski world, Truckee is a historical Old West town that really has no off-season. Storefronts line the main street, Donner Pass Road, offering ski rentals, a bite to eat, and places to stay. Parking is hard to find and expensive, and both the prices and the lines at restaurants can resemble those in San Francisco. But this bustling small mountain town has its charms.

SIGHTS

Old Jail Museum

The **Old Jail Museum** (10142 Jibboom St., Truckee, 530/582-0893, www.truckeehistory.org, 10am-4pm Sat.-Sun. late May-Sept., donation $2) is such a cute little building that it's hard to believe it was an Old West jail in use until recently. Built in 1875, it housed prisoners continually until 1964. "Baby Face" Nelson and "Machine Gun" Kelly are among the notorious outlaws believed to have spent time here. Today, it has historical exhibits, cool information, and docents from the local Truckee-Donner Historical Society. In addition to the sometimes erratic weekend schedule, the museum is often open on Thursday evenings (5pm-9pm) in summer during the citywide "Truckee Thursdays" events.

Donner Camp Picnic Ground Historical Site

If you want to learn more about what really happened to the infamous Donner party, visit the **Donner Camp Picnic Ground Historical Site** (Hwy. 89, 2.5 miles north of Truckee, www.fs.usda.gov/tahoe, free). The site is in the Tahoe National Forest, and it's a good place to stop for a picnic, a hike, or a mountain-bike ride. This is also where 25 members of the Donner party, who had left Springfield, Illinois, in April 1846 on their way to new lives in California, stopped to repair their wagons in the fall after being slowed down by an ill-fated shortcut through Hastings Cutoff. It was only October when they got here, but a blizzard hit hard. Some of the party ended up staying the whole winter, and some, as you may know, never left.

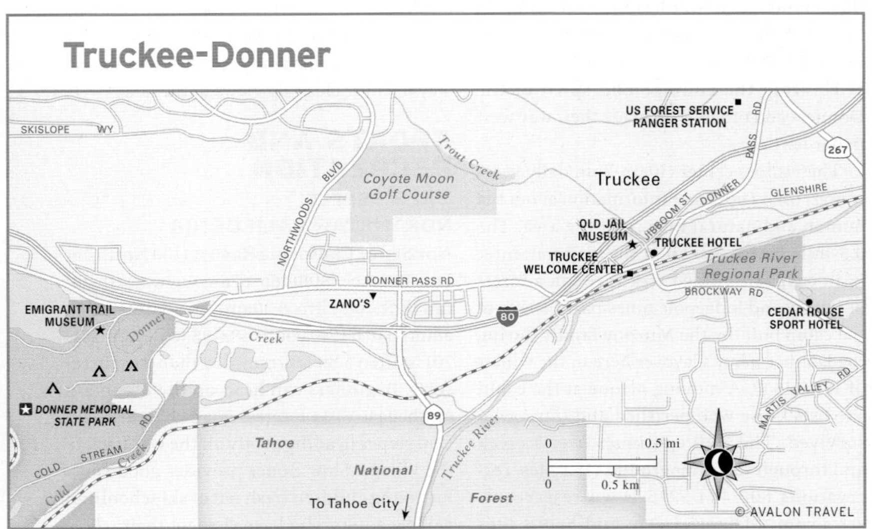

The interpretive **loop trail** that begins and ends here is short and pretty flat, with signs along the way that illuminate the Donner Party's history.

Donner Summit

Just west of Truckee, **Donner Summit** (I-80, 530/587-3558, www.exploredonnersummit.com or www.donnersummithistoricalsociety.org) is one of the legendary natural landmarks of the North Tahoe region. Come to see the Native American petroglyphs, to climb the varied rock faces, to ski the summit's snowy paths, or to watch the trains below, descendants of the first transcontinental railroad that went through here. Make sure to check out the stunning view of Donner Lake and the surrounding area from the Donner Summit Bridge on Donner Pass Road, which used to be U.S. Route 40 before the federal Interstate Highway System was built.

Donner Memorial State Park

★ Donner Memorial State Park

Donner Memorial State Park (12593 Donner Pass Rd., off I-80, 530/582-7892, www.parks.ca.gov, daily year-round, $8) is a great place to experience the lush beauty that the Donner party was heading to California to find. Near the entrance to the park is the **Pioneer Monument,** a massive structure celebrating the courage and spirit of the Donners and others who made their way west in harder times.

The visitors center (10am-5pm daily year-round) offers uplifting information about the human and natural history of the area. The 0.5-mile **Nature Trail** at the visitors center is an easy self-guided trek through a forest of Jeffrey and lodgepole pines past the site of the cabin built by the Murphy family during the Donner party's layover here in the winter of 1846-1847. A moving plaque at the cabin site lists those who perished and those who survived. The trail continues over a creek and through the campground (152 sites, reservations 800/444-7275, www.reserveamerica.com, Memorial Day-mid-Sept., sites first-come, first-served rest of the year, $35). Guided nature hikes are offered from the museum starting daily at 10am during summer.

Donner Lake is a paradise for children and adults alike, offering swimming, boating, fishing, and hiking. Walking the Lakeside Interpretive Trail along the shore is a great way to enjoy close-up views of the lake.

SPORTS AND RECREATION

Ski Resorts

NORTHSTAR CALIFORNIA

Northstar California Resort (100 Northstar Dr., Truckee, 800/466-6784, www.northstarattahoe.com, lifts 8:30am-4pm daily winter, adults $102-120, youth $93-98, children $61-70) is often a bit less crowded than the big resorts. Beginners can head up the mountain on the fast Vista Express quad chair and still find slopes heading gently all the way back to the village. Slow Zones provides good spots for young children fresh out of ski school and wobbly adults who haven't spent their whole lives on the slopes. Intermediate runs crisscross the front of the mountain, starting at the very peak off Comstock and running all the way down the mountain. The Backside, reachable via the Comstock Express quad chair and served by the Backside Express, is reserved for black-diamond skiers, although adventurous intermediates can test their ski legs here. Freestylers will find the most terrain right off the Vista Express quad, although a couple of other small areas dot the mountain elsewhere.

SUGAR BOWL

A great mid-tier ski area is **Sugar Bowl** (629 Sugar Bowl Rd., Norden, 530/426-9000, www.sugarbowl.com, lifts 9am-4pm daily Nov.-May, adults $80-95, seniors $63-78, ages 13-22 $63-78, ages 6-12 $40-55, under age 5 free). With lots of skiable snow spread across a wide area and plenty of vertical drop, Sugar Bowl can satisfy skiers and boarders of all abilities. Blue and black-diamond runs toward the top of the peaks offer intense variety, with a smattering of double-black-diamond runs out toward the edges and down the ridges. At the base, green and blue runs make it easy for younger and less experienced athletes to have a good time in the mountains. A gondola ferries visitors from the remote parking lot up to the village. The resort's Summit Chairlift brings visitors to the top of Judah Peak for easy access to backcountry trails. The resort offers two base lodges: a day lodge at Judah and the Lodge at Sugar Bowl, located in the village. The on-site **Lodge at Sugar Bowl** (750 Mule Ears Dr., Truckee, 530/426-6742, www.sugarbowl.com, $210-698) allows you to ski right up to your room door.

BOREAL MOUNTAIN RESORT

Boreal Mountain Resort (19749 Boreal Ridge Rd., Soda Springs, 530/426-3666, www.rideboreal.com, 9am-9pm daily winter, adults $34-64, ages 13-18 $34-54, ages 5-12 $24-34) may not feel as fabulous as Squaw or Alpine, but many Californians find their snow legs here. The Accelerator Chair serves Boreal's Superpipe, its Core terrain park, and a night-skiing area; the 49er Chair serves the intermediate and advanced terrain. Even on weekends, the lines at Boreal seem pleasingly short compared to the bigger resorts. In 2012 a new 33,000-square-foot complex, the **Woodward Tahoe Action Sports Training Facility** (530/426-3666, www.woodwardtahoe.com), opened to offer weeklong summer camps for skiers, snowboarders, bicycle motocross riders, cheerleaders, skateboarders, and gymnasts. Trampolines, foam pits, an indoor skate park, and a digital-media learning center make it training heaven. Boreal is very family-friendly, with ski and snowboard lessons for beginners and a lodge where parents can relax with a cup of coffee or a drink at the Upper Deck bar and watch their children ski; the cafeteria (8am-7pm daily) offers limited service after 4pm.

SODA SPRINGS

Small **Soda Springs** (10244 Soda Springs Rd., Soda Springs, 530/426-3901, www.skisodasprings.com, 10am-4pm Thurs.-Mon., adults $44, under age 18 $34) is a great family resort. Its claim to fame is tubing, included with every lift ticket, or you can buy a $34 tubing-only package. The Planet Kids area for young athletes (under age 9, $34) offers a safe place for the little ones to practice tubing, skiing, and snowboarding. Rentals and instruction are included in the price, and there are even two tubing carousels to add to the thrills. Soda Springs has no on-site lodging but does have an adequate cafeteria.

TAHOE DONNER SKI AREA

Tahoe Donner Ski Area (11603 Snowpeak Way, Truckee, 530/587-9444, www.tahoedonner.com/downhill-ski, hours vary Dec.-May, adults $39-47, youth $34-42, children $16-22) prides itself on being "a great place to begin." With only five lifts, including two conveyor belts and one carpet, 15 runs, and 120 skiable acres, Donner will seem miniscule to skiers used to the big resorts. It's a great spot to bring your family, however, to get a feel for snowboarding or skiing, take lessons, and enjoy

Exploring Tahoe's Backcountry

Lake Tahoe is surrounded by national forests. To the west of the lake is **Eldorado National Forest.** To the northwest is **Tahoe National Forest.** Farther north is **Plumas National Forest.** For more information, visit www.fs.fed.us. To make reservations or apply for permits, visit www.recreation.gov.

ELDORADO NATIONAL FOREST

Here you'll find beautiful lakes and abundant hiking and cycling trails. A scenic trail on the border between the Tahoe and Eldorado National Forests is the **Hell Hole Trail** (4.3 miles, easy-moderate).

Desolation Wilderness

The Desolation has 125 alpine lakes and 120 miles of trails, including segments of the Tahoe Rim Trail and the Pacific Crest Trail. Permits are required for day hikers as well as for backpackers. Before venturing into the Desolation Wilderness, stop at the **Taylor Creek Visitors Center** (Hwy. 89, 3 miles north of South Lake Tahoe, 530/543-2674, www.fs.usda.gov, hours vary, Memorial Day-Oct.) to get wilderness and campfire permits and up-to-date information on conditions in the Desolation. You can also reserve a permit (877/444-6777, www.recreation.gov, $6) before you arrive. One of the most popular hikes is **Twin Lakes Trail** (7 miles round-trip, 1,200 feet elevation gain, moderate).

Backcountry camping in the Desolation Wilderness requires a permit ($5-10). For information, call the U.S. Forest Service supervisor's office in South Lake Tahoe (530/543-2694) or the Taylor Creek Visitors Center; for reservations call 877/444-6777.

Loon Lake

One of the most popular and beautiful places to visit in the Eldorado National Forest is the 76,000-acre **Loon Lake,** a reservoir created in 1963 with the damming of Gerle Creek. It's a delightful place to camp, swim, sail, or kayak.

Accommodations and Food

The **Ice House Resort** (9199 Ice House Rd./Forest Rd. 3, Pollock Pines, 23 miles east of Placerville, 15 miles north of U.S. 50, 530/293-3221, late Apr.-Oct., $88-98) has rooms, RV sites ($45), a campground ($20), a restaurant (7am-9pm Thurs.-Mon. Apr.-Oct.), and a small grocery store (9am-8pm Mon.-Fri., 7am-9pm Sat.-Sun.).

More than 60 campgrounds dot Eldorado. One of the most attractive is the **Loon Lake Campground** (Ice House Rd./Forest Rd. 3, 23 miles east of Placerville, 15 miles north of U.S. 50, 877/444-6777, www.recreation.gov, mid-June-Sept., $25-50).

Getting There

To reach Eldorado and Desolation Wilderness from Sacramento or San Francisco, travel east on U.S. 50. About 20 miles past Placerville, turn left (north) onto Forest Road 3 (Ice House Rd.). Coming from Tahoe, travel west on U.S. 50 and make a right turn onto Ice House Road.

TAHOE NATIONAL FOREST

The Tahoe National Forest contains 800,000 acres of public land interspersed with 400,000 acres of privately owned land.

Sierraville

At **Sierra Hot Springs** (521 Campbell Hot Springs Rd., Sierraville, 530/994-3773, www.sierrahotsprings.org, 3 hours $15, until midnight $20, ages 5-15 $7.50), natural hot springs feed a large outdoor swimming pool and the small Temple Dome Hot Pool. A membership fee ($5 monthly, $20 yearly, lifetime $300) is charged.

Accommodations and Food

Around Sierra Hot Springs and Sierraville are two basic choices. The **Main Lodge** (521 Campbell Hot Springs Rd., Sierraville, 530/994-3773, www.sierrahotsprings.org, private rooms $88 Sun.-Thurs., $110 Fri.-Sat. and holidays, dormitory $39 Sun.-Thurs., $50 Fri.-Sat. and holidays, two-night minimum required on the weekends) is on the resort premises. The historical **Globe Hotel** (530/994-3773, www.sierrahotsprings.org, $88 Sun.-Thurs., $110 Fri.-Sat. and holidays) is in Sierraville.

The campgrounds at **Sierra Hot Springs** (521 Campbell Hot Springs Rd., Sierraville, 530/994-3773, www.sierrahotsprings.org, $27.50) have no designated campsites. The nearest U.S. Forest Service campground is **Lower Little Truckee Campground** (Hwy. 89, 11 miles north of Truckee, 877/444-6777, www.recreation.gov or www.fs.usda.gov, May-Oct., $18-20). For an unusual option, consider the **Calpine Lookout** (3 miles northwest of Calpine, near Hwy. 89, 877/444-6777, www.recreation.gov or www.fs.usda.gov, $45), used as a forest-fire lookout until 1975.

The **Philosophy Café** (521 Campbell Hot Springs Rd., Sierraville, 530/994-3773, www.sierrahotsprings.org, 6:30pm-8:30pm Fri.-Mon., $7-17) is located in the Main Lodge at the Sierra Hot Springs Resort. In Sierraville are **Sierraville Kitchen** (101 E. Main St., Sierraville, 530/994-3400, daily 8am-2pm, $7-14) and **Los Hermanos** (100 S. Lincoln St., Sierraville, 530/994-1058, 11am-8pm Tues.-Sun., $9-15).

Transportation

From Truckee, the main roads form a loop that roughly surrounds much of the Tahoe National Forest area. Highway 89 heads northwest from Truckee toward Sierraville (24 miles).

PLUMAS NATIONAL FOREST

Plumas National Forest features alpine lakes and streams, challenging trails, and memorable vistas. Go to Plumas to boat, snowshoe, mountain bike, or horseback ride.

Gold Lake Stables (7000 Gold Lake Rd., Lakes Basin Recreation Area, 530/836-0940, www.reidhorse.com) offers guided trail rides, including overnight trips. Kid-friendly **Graeagle Stables** (Hwy. 89, Graeagle, 530/836-0430, www.reidhorse.com, reservations required) offers private lessons, pony rides, and guided trail rides for adults.

Plumas-Eureka State Park

In the middle of **Plumas-Eureka State Park** (310 Johnsonville Rd., Blairsden, 530/836-2380, www.parks.ca.gov, free) is a **museum** (daily 9am-4:30pm Memorial Day-Labor Day, 9am-4:30pm Fri.-Sun. Labor Day-late Sept., donation) in a former bunkhouse for gold miners. Outside is the former mining area, two historical stamp mills, and a blacksmith shop.

Accommodations and Food

Chalet View Lodge (72056 Hwy. 70, Graeagle, 530/832-5528 or 800/510-8439, www.chaletviewlodge.com, $95-255) is a lovely place to stay in the Plumas area.

As many as 50 different campgrounds are scattered throughout Plumas. One of the most scenic and peaceful is **Gold Lake Campground** (9 miles southwest of Graeagle, June-Sept. $10, Oct.-May free). Camp in one of 67 sites at **Plumas-Eureka State Park** (310 Johnsonville Rd., Blairsden, 800/444-7275, www.reserveamerica.com, $35). One of the more unusual places to stay in Plumas is the **Black Mountain Lookout** (Beckwourth Ranger District, 530/836-2575, reservations 877/444-6777, www.recreation.gov, up to 8 people $60).

Restaurants are rare, but include the **Grizzly Grill** (250 Bonta St., Blairsden, 530/836-1300, www.grizzlygrill.com, daily 5pm-9pm summer, hours vary fall and spring, $20-27), **Mountain Cuisine** (250 Bonta St., Blairsden, 530/836-4646, www.mountaincuisine.com, 11:30am-3pm Tues.-Sun., $4-9), and **Coffee Tree Express** (196 E. Sierra Ave., Portola, 530/832-4563, 6am-2:30pm Mon.-Sat.).

Getting There

Highways 89 and 70 are the main routes into the Plumas National Forest.

the snow in the beautiful Tahoe forest. To be truly family-friendly, Tahoe Donner offers lessons for children as young as age three, interchangeable lift tickets for parents, and even kid-friendly items on the snack-bar menu.

Cross-Country Skiing and Snowshoeing

The granddaddy of Tahoe cross-country ski areas, the **Royal Gorge Cross Country Ski Resort** (Summit Station, Soda Springs, 530/426-3871 or 800/500-3871, www.royalgorge.com, 8:30am-4pm daily winter, adults $27-35, ages 13-22 $21-30, up to age 12 free) has a truly tremendous chunk of the Sierra—6,000 acres—within its boundaries. Striving to provide a luxurious ski experience comparable to what downhillers expect, the Royal Gorge offers lodging, food, drink, a ski school, equipment rentals, equipment care facilities and services, and much more. With the most miles of groomed trails anywhere in the Tahoe area, Royal Gorge offers two stride tracks and a skate track on every trail to allow easy passing. They even have a surface lift for skiers who want to practice downhill technique or try telemarking.

The Rainbow Lodge (50080 Hampshire Rocks Rd., 530/562-5061, www.therainbowlodge.com, $79-159) has nine warming huts dotting the cross-country wonderland. At the lodge is a restaurant and a ski-in snack bar. A café can also be found near Kilbourn Lake. Pick up a map before you head out for the day; patches of the mountains are off-limits because of avalanche danger.

Tahoe Donner Cross Country (15275 Alder Creek Rd., Truckee, 530/587-9484, www.tahoedonner.com/cross-country, hours vary, adults $19-29, ages 60-69 $14-21, ages 7-12 $11, under age 7 free) offers some of the better cross-country ski action in the area. Tahoe Donner has almost 3,500 acres crisscrossed with trails ranging from easy greens all the way up through double-black-diamond trails, and has four trails set aside just for snowshoers. A cross-country ski school introduces newcomers to the sport and helps more experienced skiers expand their skills. A separate day lodge just for cross-country skiers and a snack bar are halfway up the mountain in Euer Valley. Tahoe Donner is scheduled to open a new central lodge in late 2015 with additional food and beverage services, upgraded locker room, a new grand deck with fire pits, and a larger parking lot.

Snowmobiling

Several snowmobile outfits operate west of Truckee along the main roads—you'll see the tracks as you drive in and out of town. **Cold Stream Adventures** (11760 Donner Pass Rd., Truckee, 530/582-9090, www.coldstreamadventures.com, hours vary daily, 2-hour tour $150-175) also offers tours into the mountains, promising climbs up to 2,000 feet higher than the starting point. These guided tours run through private forest, so you'll see forested landscapes available no other way. Make reservations and grab your sunglasses.

Hiking

The **Donner Camp Picnic Ground Historical Site** (Hwy. 89, 2.5 miles north of Truckee, www.fs.usda.gov/tahoe, free) has two hikes, each excellent in its own way. A short educational interpretive loop trail begins in the picnic-area parking lot. The trail is very well maintained, with raised wooden planks above the grasslands in the sections that occasionally get wet. Six trailside signs explain the history. If you're a fast reader, you can do the whole trail in about 15 minutes.

Follow the coast of Donner Lake for an easy and scenic hike within **Donner Memorial State Park** (12593 Donner Pass Rd., 530/582-7892, www.parks.ca.gov, sunrise-sunset daily year-round); about 1.75 miles, or one-third, of the lake's coastline is within the park's boundaries. Start at the Lagoon parking area near the park entrance and follow the lakeshore to China Cove. Turn around and come back the same way for a 3.5-mile hike. Note that you can't hike all the way around the lake; some of the shore is located on private land outside the park. For a more physically strenuous hike, try the excellent Commemorative Emigrant Trail (15 miles round-trip), also accessible from the parking lot at the Donner Picnic Ground. This mostly flat trail leads to Prosser Creek and the Stampede Reservoir and is popular with mountain bikers and equestrians as well as pedestrians.

For serious hikers, an outstanding day trip is the hike from Sugar Bowl to Squaw Valley along the **Pacific Crest Trail** (18 miles one-way, challenging). To begin, take Donner Pass Road to the Sugar Bowl Ski Academy (19195 Donner Pass Rd., Norden, 530/426-1844) and park in the free lot on the right side of the highway. Find the Pacific Crest Trail (PCT) trailhead and start walking south. The trail's middle name is "Crest," so expect some magnificent high places with great views, varied terrain, and often chilly conditions. Snow as late as July is not uncommon. In midwinter, this trail section is best done as a cross-country ski adventure. This is a good hike to do as a car shuttle: Have someone in your party leave a car at Squaw Valley in the morning to ferry you, or arrange for a ride.

Golf

Coyote Moon (10685 Northwoods Blvd., Truckee, 530/587-0886, www.coyotemoon-golf.com, $100-160) is not inexpensive, but according to expert golfers, it's more than worth it. Coyote Moon offers fairways dotted with granite boulders and lined by dense natural forest. No, the builders didn't make it that way; the designer created a layout that takes advantage of the natural features of this locale. While Coyote Moon tends to beckon advanced golfers, even beginners can play an enjoyable round here.

ENTERTAINMENT AND EVENTS

Nightlife

Truckee's **Pastime Club** (10096 Donner Pass Rd., 530/582-9219, 2pm-2am Mon.-Thurs., noon-2am Fri.-Sat.) is open year-round with drinks every night and live music Thursday-Saturday, and occasionally Sunday. There's usually no cover unless the music is for a special event. The **Bar of America** (10040 Donner Pass Rd., Truckee, 530/587-2626, www.barofamerica.com, 11am-11:30pm Mon.-Thurs., 11am-12:30am Fri., 10am-12:30am Sat., 10am-11:30pm Sun., $9-17), in the Pacific Crest restaurant, offers an upscale atmosphere along with local beers, cocktails, food, and music. Bands tend to play here Thursday-Saturday, usually without charging a cover.

Festivals and Events

Lake Tahoe hosts a number of festivals every year in both summer and winter, though undoubtedly summer has more. One of the biggest is the **Lake Tahoe Music Festival** (530/583-3101, www.tahoemusic.org). Performers such as Michael Bolton, Blues Traveler, and Big Bad Voodoo Daddy perform alongside symphony orchestras over a three-week stretch in late July-early August. Festival concerts are spread around at various venues such as the Village at Northstar in the Northstar-at-Tahoe Resort (5001 Northstar Dr., Truckee, 530/562-2267) and the Ehrman Mansion at Sugar Pine Point State Park (Hwy. 89, Tahoma, 530/525-7982, www.parks.ca.gov, year-round, $10).

SHOPPING

Donner Pass Road is the center of Truckee's historical district, and lots of little shops line both sides of the street. For summertime sports, the **Cycle Paths Bike Shop** (10095 West River St., 530/582-1890, www.cyclepaths.com, 9am-6pm daily summer, 10am-5pm Fri.-Mon. winter) can hook you up with bike rentals, sales, equipment, and repairs.

For women's clothing, gifts, and handmade jewelry, the woman-run family business **Mo Jo & Zoe** (10076 Donner Pass Rd., Truckee, 530/587-3495, www.mojozoe.com, 10am-6pm daily) is a pleasant and friendly spot with reasonably priced goods. If your clothing tastes run to the more dramatic, you will enjoy the **Unique Boutique-Viviane's Vintage &**

Vogue (10925 W. River St., Truckee, 530/582-8484, 11:30am-6pm Tues.-Sat.). Viviane has been in business for roughly two decades, dressing partygoers, Burning Man attendees, and anyone else who's in or around Truckee looking for a little flair.

ACCOMMODATIONS

Under $100

In Norden, a few miles west of Truckee, is an unusual lodging option. Since 1934, the Sierra Club has run the **Clair Tappaan Lodge** (19940 Donner Pass Rd., Norden, 530/426-3632 or 800/679-6775, www.ctl.sierraclub.org, $65-75). The lodge is a great starting point for cross-country skiing or hiking day trips. Accommodations are pretty basic: Most travelers sleep in the men's or women's dormitories, though a few small rooms are for couples and larger rooms for families. Bring your own bedding, and expect to share a bathroom. Overnight lodging includes three home-cooked meals (Sierra Club members $65; nonmembers $70, ages 4-13 $50, under age 4 free). Rates in winter and on weekends and holidays are usually $5 more. Communal spaces include a toasty library with a wood-burning stove, hot tub, recreation room, and extensive grounds.

$100-150

The **Truckee Hotel** (10007 Bridge St., at Donner Pass Rd., Truckee, 530/587-4444, www.truckeehotel.com, $79-229) offers fabulous period ambience for reasonable rates. The hotel has welcomed guests to the North Shore since 1873. Rooms show their age with high ceilings, claw-foot tubs, and little Victorian touches. Part of the historical charm includes third- and fourth-floor rooms without an elevator. Most of the 36 rooms have shared baths in the hall that are clean and comfortable, with either a shower or a bathtub and a privacy lock. Breakfast is included, and the hotel also houses Moody's, the best restaurant in town.

Low-priced accommodations around Truckee are not easy to come by, especially in ski season. A decent basic hotel with affordable rates is the **Inn at Truckee** (11506 Deerfield Dr., Truckee, 530/587-8888 or 888/773-6888, www.innattruckee.com, $90-195). It's pet-friendly ($25 per night) and offers a spa and sauna, included continental breakfast, and free wireless Internet access. The rooms are nothing special, but the convenience to major ski areas and other attractions makes it a good buy.

the Truckee Hotel

$150-250

If you prefer a longer stay, call the **Donner Lake Village Resort** (15695 Donner Pass Rd., Truckee, 855/979-0402 or 530/587-6081, www.donnerlakevillage.com, $110-297), on the shores of Donner Lake. Choose from regular motel rooms without kitchens or studio, one-bedroom, and two-bedroom condos with full kitchen facilities. Guest rooms include all the amenities of a nicer motel. Donner Lake Village has its own marina with rental ski boats, fishing boats, and slips if you've brought your own watercraft; a bait and tackle shop is across the street. The nearby North Shore ski resorts are an easy drive. A two-night minimum is sometimes required in summer.

The **Donner Lake Inn** (10070 Gregory Place, Truckee, 530/587-5574, www.donnerlakeinn.com, $164-189) is an intimate five-room B&B offering rustic charm beside Donner Lake. Each room has its own simple homey decorating scheme, private bath with a shower, private entrance, queen bed, large-screen TV with a DVD player, and free wireless Internet access. Each morning, the friendly and hospitable owners serve up a delicious full breakfast in the dining room.

The ★ **Cedar House Sport Hotel** (10918 Brockway Rd., Truckee, 866/582-5655, www.cedarhousesporthotel.com, $170-270) sports an exposed wood exterior and is landscaped with trees, fallen stumps, and a rusty steel girder. Rooms are all about luxury, with wood platform beds, designer leather chairs and sofas, and shining stainless-steel fixtures in the private baths. Choose comfortable rooms with queen or king beds or fancy suites with flat-screen TVs and every possible amenity. The expert staff can put together guided hikes, bike rides, and rafting or kayaking trips.

CAMPING

Donner Memorial State Park (12593 Donner Pass Rd., off I-80 west of downtown Truckee, 800/444-7275, www.reserveamerica.com, reservations late May-mid-Sept., first-come, first-served early Sept.-late May, $35) offers a spacious tree-filled campground with easy access to the lake, the new visitors center, and the trails in the park. It has 152 sites spread across three campgrounds: Ridge Campground (May-Oct.), Creek Campground (June-Sept.), and Splitrock (June-Sept.). Sites include fire rings and picnic tables, and there are restrooms with showers.

The Forest Service (877/444-6777, www.fs.usda.gov or www.recreation.gov) maintains three campgrounds along Highway 89 between Truckee and Tahoe City: **Granite Flat** (74 sites, Hwy. 89, 1.5 miles south of Truckee, mid-May-mid-Oct., $22-44) and **Goose Meadow** (24 sites, Hwy. 89, 4 miles south of Truckee, mid-May-Sept., $20) offer potable water and vault toilets; **Silver Creek** (27 sites, Hwy. 89, 6 miles south of Truckee, mid-May-Sept., $20) offers potable water and both flush and vault toilets. All three campgrounds get noise from the highway as well as the gentler sounds of the nearby Truckee River.

FOOD

Bakeries and Cafés

For a cool crisp salad or a relaxing espresso, you can't beat the simply named ★ **CoffeeBar** (10120 Jibboom St., Truckee, 530/587-2000, www.coffeebartruckee.com, 6am-7pm daily, $5-9). Although it's located just one block from the main drag, Donner Pass Road, CoffeeBar feels calm and peaceful even when the nearby resorts emphatically do not. Expect lots of space, free wireless Internet access, and good food—homemade baked goods, crepes, panini, salads, and breakfast calzones.

New American

Jax at the Tracks (10144 W. River St., Truckee, 530/550-7450, www.jaxtruckee.com, 7am-10pm daily, $10-19) looks authentic inside and out. Housed in an actual 1940s diner, it has been thoroughly fixed up to be clean, fresh, and original. Jax has a creative California-style chef who puts his own stamp on comfort food, with homemade English muffins, Kobe beef meatloaf with root-beer raisin glaze, and a mean hollandaise.

Italian

Zano's Pizza (11401 Donner Pass Rd., Truckee, 530/587-7411, www.zanos.net, 4pm-9pm Mon.-Wed., 11:30am-9pm Thurs.-Sun., $14-24) serves huge pizzas and tremendous salads in a big casual dining room with sports playing on TV. The full menu includes pastas and Italian entrées; at lunch, the hot crisp panini tastes great. But it's the thin-crust pizzas that rule here; pick one of Zano's interesting combinations, or build your own from the list of fresh ingredients.

Fine Dining

The best restaurant in Truckee is ★ **Moody's Bistro and Lounge** (10007 Bridge St., Truckee, 530/587-8688, www.moodysbistro.com, 11:30am-9pm daily, $16-40). This casual yet elegant eatery adjoins the historical Truckee Hotel, just off the main drag. A wooden bar and booths give the main lounge an old-time feel, but the white-tablecloth dining room in the back feels more classically elegant. The chef promises ingredients that are "fresh, local, seasonal, and simple" and then jazzes them up with creative preparations. You might find antelope or local fish on the menu with do-it-yourself s'mores for dessert (the hands-down favorite), with a burner and skewers brought to your table. For weekend evenings, make a reservation.

The food at **Bar of America** (10040 Donner Pass Rd., Truckee, 530/587-2626, www.barofamerica.com, 11:30am-9:30pm Mon.-Thurs., 11:30am-10:30pm Fri., 10:30am-10:30pm Sat., 10:30am-9:30pm Sun., $11-42) is worth the extra few bucks. The menu offers fresh organic ingredients and daily specials, as well as local beers and creative cocktails with professional service; the wood-fired pizzas are especially a hit. Reservations are recommended.

Dessert

Bud's Sporting Goods & Fountain (10108 Donner Pass Rd., Truckee, 530/214-0599, www.truckeeicecream.com, noon-5pm daily winter, 10am-8pm daily summer) delivers what its name promises—a counter, lots of ice cream, 1950s-era decor, and plenty of coffee drinks. At **Sweets** (10118 Donner Pass Rd., Truckee, 530/587-6556, 888/248-8840, www.sweetshandmadecandies.com, 10am-close daily, hours vary), you can watch the experts make fudge or come inside for a free sample. Sweets also offers hand-dipped chocolates and sundaes and cones made with Häagen-Dazs ice cream.

INFORMATION AND SERVICES

Truckee has a good comprehensive **California Welcome Center** (10065 Donner Pass Rd., 530/587-8808, www.visitcalifornia.com, 8:45am-6pm Mon., 9am-6pm Tues.-Sun.) featuring free Internet access on your computer or theirs, public baths, huge brochure racks, and friendly personal advice. The center is attached to the town's Amtrak station, perfect if you're coming from Reno or San Francisco.

If you need medical attention, the **Tahoe Forest Hospital** (10121 Pine Ave., Truckee, 530/587-6011, www.tfhd.com) has a full-service emergency room, among other services.

TRANSPORTATION

Air

The closest commercial airport is **Reno-Tahoe International Airport** (RNO, 2001 E. Plumb Lane, Reno, NV, 775/328-6400, www.renoairport.com), about 32 miles east of Truckee via I-80. **Sacramento International Airport** (SMF, 6900 Airport Blvd., Sacramento, 916/929-5411, www.sacramento.aero) is about 105 miles west of Truckee, also via I-80. Both airports are served by several major airlines.

Train

The **Amtrak *California Zephyr*** (800/872-7245, www.amtrak.com, reservations required) departs Emeryville in the Bay Area daily at 9:10am and Sacramento at 11:09am, arriving in Truckee at 2:38pm. It leaves Truckee daily at 9:37am to arrive in Sacramento at 2:13pm and Emeryville at 4:10pm—at least when all goes according to plan. This is a long-distance train covering a lot of ground, so delays are common. Fares from Truckee to Sacramento are $41 one-way, and to Emeryville $44 one-way.

Amtrak's ***Capitol Corridor*** (877/974-3322, www.capitolcorridor.org or www.amtrak.com) originates in San Jose, stopping at Oakland, Emeryville, Berkeley, Davis, and Sacramento before connecting via bus from Auburn to Truckee and Reno, Nevada, at the eastern end of the route. Reservations are not available; the one-way fare from Emeryville to Truckee is $49.

Car

Truckee is located on I-80. From San Francisco to Truckee is 185 miles, 3.25 hours' drive in good weather. From Sacramento, the trip is about 105 miles and (1.75 hours). If you're driving to Truckee from Reno, follow I-80 west for 32 miles (35 minutes).

Public Transit and Ski Shuttles

Truckee Transit (530/550-7451, www.townoftruckee.com or www.laketahoetransit.com, adults $2.50 one-way, day pass $5, seniors $1, under age 12 $1.50) handles routes between the Truckee Tahoe Airport, downtown Truckee, and the Donner Memorial State Park and Donner Lake.

The free **Night Rider bus service** (866/216-5222, www.laketahoetransit.com, 7pm-midnight daily, some routes until 2am) runs in winter to Squaw Valley, Tahoe City, North Star, and the Biltmore in Crystal Bay, Nevada. In summer, the West Shore Night Rider offers service from the Tahoe City Y to Granlibakken, Sunnyside, Homewood, and Tahoma. Your ski resort may also run a shuttle service of its own, making it possible to enjoy a low-stress Truckee-area ski vacation without a car.

Sacramento and Gold Country

The capital of California, Sacramento is a cosmopolitan city with a friendly vibe and a newly energized entertainment scene. The city grew along the Sacramento and American Rivers during the Gold Rush era.

It provided a vital transit link between the mining country and the port of San Francisco. Today Sacramento has become one of the most diverse cities in the country, known for its multicultural population, politics, outdoor recreation, and a thriving foodie movement sprouting amidst a new generation of gourmet restaurants and the region's 8,000 acres of boutique farms. It's no wonder that Sacramento is the Farm-to-Fork Capital of America.

In the city's historical Midtown, Downtown, and East Sacramento neighborhoods, an urban renaissance has remade this storied city into a vibrant, multicultural metropolis with cutting-edge art museums and packed bistros. More than ever, Sacramento is a place of brilliant contrasts, a town always caught in the crucible of compelling styles and personalities. On any day, you might see politicians in tailored suits pedaling their beach cruisers alongside shaggy-haired hipsters in pegged jeans. Where else could flamboyant movie stars like Ronald Reagan and Arnold Schwarzenegger begin a second life as governors of the country's most populous state?

The fun continues in the Gold Country, a gorgeous 130-mile-long belt of award-winning wineries and rugged outdoor scenery deep in the Sierra Nevada foothills. After prospectors first discovered precious metal here in 1848, California was forever changed by the Gold Rush and the pioneers who poured into the new state searching for riches. These days, modern-day Gold Country prospectors search for antiques, explore caves, find hole-in-the-wall eateries, try river rafting, and discover luxurious inns in renovated farmhouses. From the foothills to Sacramento's farmland, this diverse region of California has something for every traveler.

Previous: the covered bridge at Bridgeport; Gold Country is also horse country. **Above:** the town of Auburn.

Look for ★ to find recommended sights, activities, dining, and lodging.

Highlights

★ **Capitol Building:** This building is the epicenter for the city's political history, past and present. Be sure to check out the museum's impressive collection of art and antiques (page 388).

★ **Old Sacramento:** Stroll the wooden sidewalk and cobblestone streets to get a sense of the state's origins 150 years ago (page 389).

★ **Empire Mine State Historic Park:** The best example of Gold Country mining is this living history museum and park (page 406).

★ **Marshall Gold Discovery State Historic Park:** This is the place that started it all—the spot where gold was discovered in 1848. The rest is literally history (page 416).

★ **Apple Hill:** This 20-mile swath of grower heaven includes dozens of orchards, vineyards, and pit stops for dining and relaxing along the way (page 416).

★ **Rafting the American River:** Both rookie and expert rafters will find opportunities to hit the water on the American River (page 419).

★ **Daffodil Hill:** This private ranch is carpeted in golden color every March, when visitors can explore the more than 300 species of daffodils on display (page 431).

★ **Columbia State Historic Park:** Former Gold Rush town Columbia is now an indoor-outdoor museum, with exhibits, shops, and even a saloon—all preserved in homage to the area's mining history (page 439).

Sacramento and Gold Country

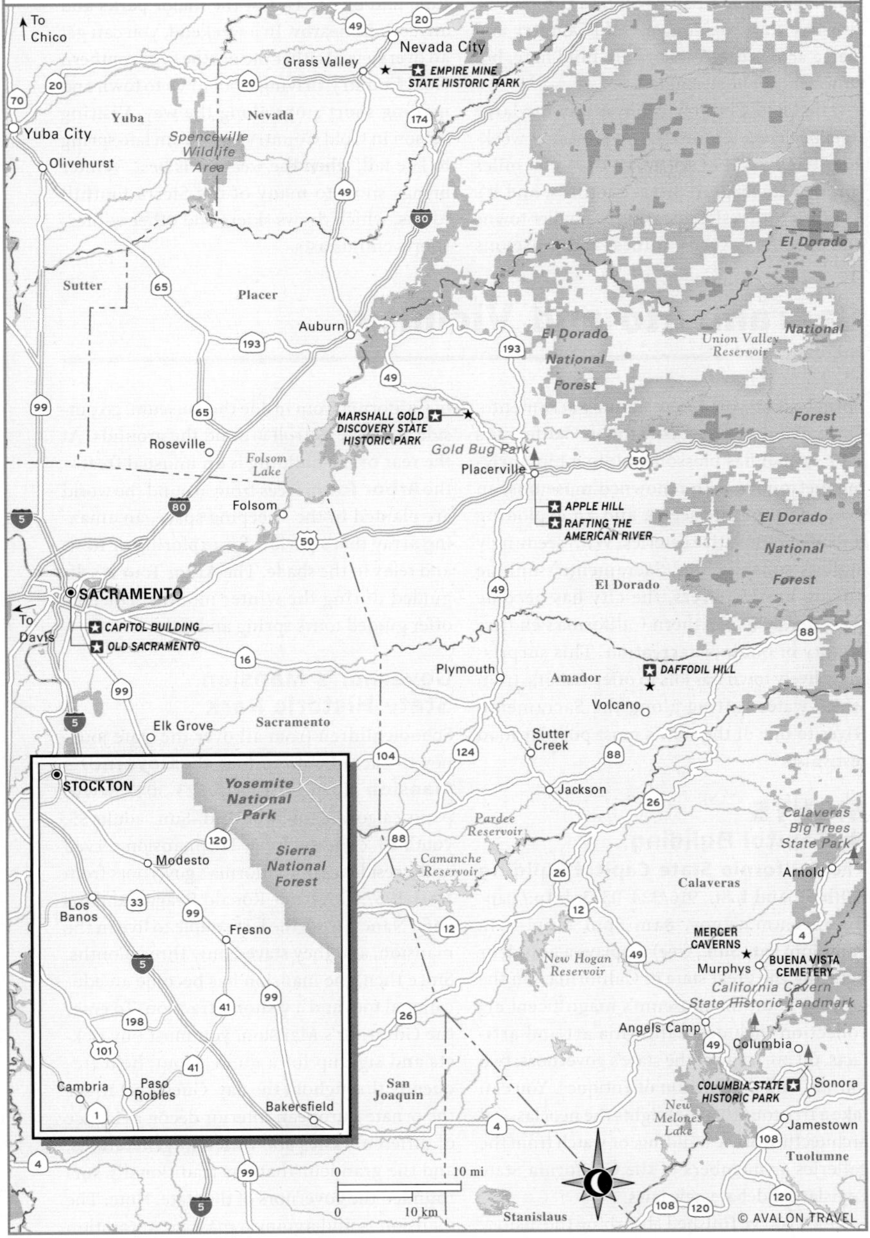

To Chico
Nevada City
Grass Valley
EMPIRE MINE STATE HISTORIC PARK
Yuba
Nevada
Yuba City
Spenceville Wildlife Area
Olivehurst
El Dorado
Sutter
Placer
Auburn
El Dorado National Forest
Union Valley Reservoir
National
Forest
MARSHALL GOLD DISCOVERY STATE HISTORIC PARK
Gold Bug Park
Roseville
Folsom Lake
Placerville
Folsom
APPLE HILL
RAFTING THE AMERICAN RIVER
El Dorado National Forest
SACRAMENTO
El Dorado
To Davis
CAPITOL BUILDING
OLD SACRAMENTO
Plymouth
Amador
DAFFODIL HILL
Volcano
Elk Grove
Sacramento
Sutter Creek
STOCKTON
Yosemite National Park
Jackson
Modesto
Sierra National Forest
Pardee Reservoir
Camanche Reservoir
Calaveras Big Trees State Park
Arnold
Los Banos
Calaveras
Fresno
MERCER CAVERNS
New Hogan Reservoir
Murphys
BUENA VISTA CEMETERY
California Cavern State Historic Landmark
Angels Camp
Columbia
Cambria
Paso Robles
San Joaquin
Bakersfield
COLUMBIA STATE HISTORIC PARK
Sonora
New Melones Lake
Jamestown
Tuolumne
0 10 mi
0 10 km
Stanislaus

PLANNING YOUR TIME

Sacramento makes a nice day trip or weekend getaway from the Bay Area, or a fun one- to two-day start to a longer Gold Country and Sierra adventure. Winters are mild here, but summers get blisteringly hot.

The Gold Country is physically too large to experience in one day, or even in a weekend. Highway 49 runs more than 100 miles through the rugged Sierra foothills, and it's impossible to resist side trips to smaller towns and specific caverns, mines, and museums along the way. If you've got one day, pick a specific Gold Country town as your destination, and one or two of the major parks and attractions nearby. In a weekend, you can get an overview of either the northern or southern Gold Country, driving from town to town and making short stops along the way. Visiting season in Gold Country runs from late spring to late fall, when the weather is best. Winter brings snow to many of the Sierra foothill towns, which draws skiers and other winter-sports enthusiasts.

Sacramento and Vicinity

Forget what you know about Sacramento. Once dismissed as a cow town, California's state capital has blossomed into a hip, thriving metropolis with renowned museums, an evolving nightlife scene, and an exploding lineup of innovative eateries. With seemingly endless sunshine and Sacramento's unique setting on two rivers, the city has become the gateway to Northern California's endless bounty of outdoor recreation. This surprisingly lively town has lots to offer visitors, from white-water rafting along the Sacramento River to one of the state's most popular food festivals.

SIGHTS

★ Capitol Building

The **California State Capitol Building** (10th St. and L St., 916/324-0333, http://capitolmuseum.ca.gov, 8am-5pm Mon.-Fri., 9am-5pm Sat.-Sun., free) displays a grandeur befitting the great state of California. On the ground floor, the museum's magnificent art collection includes California art and artifacts, oil portraits of the state's governors, two murals, and a collection of antiques. You can take a free tour that highlights the neoclassical architecture of the building, or watch from the galleries as members of the California State Legislature debate new laws.

Once you've finished absorbing the history of California from inside the museum, go outside and take a stroll around the grounds. At the rear of the building is an unusual treat—the **Arbor Tour.** Trees from around the world are planted in the sweeping space, an amazing array that's perfect for exploring or to sit and relax in the shade. The Arbor Tour is self-guided during the winter months. Docents offer guided tours spring and fall.

Governor's Mansion State Historic Park

Schoolchildren from all over the state journey to Sacramento to tour the **Governor's Mansion** (1526 H St., 916/323-3047, www.parks.ca.gov, 10am-5pm Wed.-Sun., adults $5, youth $3, children free). The mansion served as the residence of California's governors from 1903-1967. Governor Ronald Reagan and his wife, Nancy, were the last couple to live in the mansion, and they stayed only three months. Since then, the mansion has become an educational tool and a visitor attraction. To enter the Governor's Mansion, you must buy tickets and sign up for a guided tour, held frequently throughout the day. Guests get to see the ornate European interior decor, evidence of different tastes and different generations, and the grandeur that has traditionally surrounded the governors of the state. Note: The mansion is undergoing a massive restoration as of 2015, and some exhibits may be altered during this time. All admission prices will be half-off while restoration is completed, but do call ahead to verify tour availability.

★ Old Sacramento

Sacramento became an important town as the Gold Rush progressed and supplies were sent up the Sacramento River from San Francisco. The most important part of the early town was the embarcadero along the river, and that's still where **Old Sacramento** (visitors center, 1002 2nd St., 916/442-7644, 10am-5pm daily, www.discovergold.org) is today. The charming cobblestone streets and clattery wooden sidewalks pass old-time shops, restaurants, and attractions. You can take a carriage ride through the streets or walk the wharf along the river and wander the decks of the ***Delta King*** **steamboat.** Check out the tiny **Wells Fargo History Museum** (1000 2nd St., 916/440-4263, 10am-5pm daily, www.wellsfargohistory.com) and **Old Sacramento Schoolhouse Museum** (1200 Front St., 916/483-8818, www.oldsacschoolhouse.org), or lighten your wallet in the shops and boutiques. To really get into the spirit of the location, look for the Old Sacramento Living History activities (916/808-6896, www.oslhp.net) that take place every month, when costumed actors conjure characters from the city's storied past and ramble throughout the cobbled streets to interact with visitors. You can also join one of two guided walks (Sat.-Sun. June-Aug., www.historicoldsac.org, $5 general admission) to hear tales of Sacramento's place in Gold Rush history or learn more about the capital's architectural history. Both walks begin at the Sacramento History Museum (101 I St., 916/808-7059, 10am-5pm daily). The fun continues beneath the city's bustling streets with **Old Sacramento Underground Tours** (916/808-7059, www.historicoldsac.org, hours vary Apr.-Dec., adults $15, youth $10, children free but not recommended). Back in the 1860s, Sacramento was repeatedly inundated by catastrophic floods, so officials raised the city

the California State Capitol Building

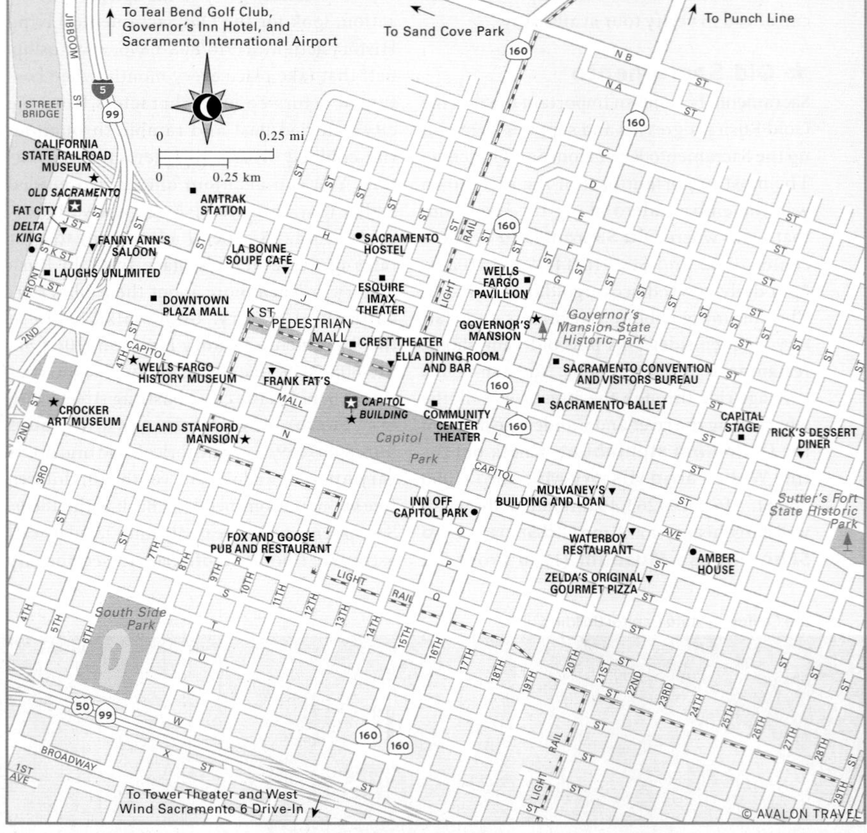

one story to escape the ravaging waters of the Sacramento River. Underground tours reveal the hidden corridors and passageways that were buried when the city was elevated. The tour schedule frequently changes; check the website for current times. The evening tour ($20) has racier details on the city's more scandalous history.

California State Railroad Museum

If you've ever felt a lick of romance for the rails, stop at the **California State Railroad Museum** (125 I St., 916/323-9280, www.csrmf.org, 10am-5pm daily, adults $10, youth $5, children free). Inside the mammoth museum buildings are artifacts and models that illustrate the building of the railroads to the West, especially the all-important Transcontinental Railroad. The main floor plays host to the museum's fabulous collection of rolling stock—locomotives, freight and passenger cars, and cabooses. It's strange to see mammoth locomotives standing still inside these walls; machines that made so much industry possible seem to belong outdoors. The museum occasionally lends its stock for photography and films.

You can look in on the stylish appointments of the private rail cars of the wealthy and stand next to the immense wheels of mighty steam locomotives. Climb aboard the open cars and locomotives for a look inside the railroad that made the growth and expansion of California possible. Along the edges of the room are memorabilia from the heyday of the railroads, including timetables and fine china. A gift shop offers souvenirs for visitors of all ages, including Thomas the Tank Engine toys for young kids, replica china for collectors, and thick tomes of railroad history for history buffs.

Cross the plaza to board the steam-powered **Excursion Train** (916/445-6645, 11am-5pm Sat.-Sun. Apr.-Sept., adults $10, youth $5, children free) for a 40-minute ride along the riverfront. The museum also offers family-friendly rides around certain holidays, including the Spookomotive ride in October and the Polar Express during December.

Sutter's Fort State Historic Park

Sutter's Fort State Historic Park (2701 L St., 916/445-4422, www.parks.ca.gov, 10am-5pm daily, adults $5, youth $3, children free), situated in the middle of downtown Sacramento, was originally the center of John Sutter's "New Helvetia" settlement. A tour of the park begins with the mazelike museum at the entrance. Inside the fort structure, the story of John Sutter is told in photos, artifacts, and placards. After perusing the interpretive area, wander outside into the sunlight and into the fort's inner courtyard to see how the early settlers lived—from dragging their luggage from the East to their bedrooms at the settlement. Denizens of the park, dressed in 19th-century costumes, engage in the activities that filled the days of California's settlers. With their help, you can try your hand at making rope, baking bread, and doing all sorts of pioneer activities. Afterward, stop at the gift shop, which evokes a small 1800s store, filled with historical costume patterns, books, and period toys. Admission prices increase (adults $7, youth $5) on special interpretive days that occur occasionally between Monday and Friday.

Leland Stanford Mansion

Railroad baron, former California governor, and Stanford University founder Leland Stanford and his family spent a number of years living in the capital city at what is now the **Leland Stanford Mansion State**

the *Delta King* steamboat

Historic Park (800 N St., 916/324-9266, http://www.parks.ca.gov, 10am-5pm Wed.-Sun., free). Some years after Leland Stanford's death, his wife, Jane Stanford, donated the family mansion to the Catholic Church for use as a children's home. It was eventually purchased by the state, and the current museum was constructed in the 1990s. Tours begin in the visitors center, next to the museum store outside the mansion. From here you'll journey inside the lavish main building, where you can admire the lovingly restored furnishings, carpets, walls, and antiques. Visitors get a hint of what it might have been like to live as one of the wealthiest people in the country in some of the most exciting years of California's history.

Mansion tours are wheelchair accessible, and assistive listening devices and other aids are available on request. You must be part of a tour to explore the mansion; the last tour each day starts at 4pm. The museum may cancel tours during official state events held by California's governor and legislature, so call ahead.

Crocker Art Museum

The **Crocker Art Museum** (216 O St., 916/808-7000, www.crockerartmuseum.org, 10am-5pm Tues.-Wed. and Fri.-Sun., 10am-9am Thurs., adults $10, seniors and students $8, youth $5, children free) hosts centuries of fine art and historical exhibits. Donated to the city in 1885 by Margaret Crocker, sister-in-law of Big Four railroad magnate Charles Crocker, this museum hosts an incredible collection of Californian art. Notable Californian artists include Thomas Hill, Joan Brown, and Guy Rose; the museum also boasts quite a few works by Sacramento State alumnus Wayne Thiebaud. You might also catch traveling exhibits from artists like Andy Warhol, Georgia O'Keeffe, or Norman Rockwell. The Crocker also has stunning exhibits of international art, including 16th- and 17th-century Dutch and Flemish masters, African and Oceanic art, and Asian artifacts that include Japanese armor and Chinese ceramics. When you arrive, stand outside and appreciate the contrast between the museum's stately Victorian mansion (and former Crocker residence) and the brilliant contemporary expansion that opened next door in 2010.

Sacramento Zoo

You can visit more than 600 animals from 140 different species at the **Sacramento Zoo** (Sutterville Rd. and Land Park Dr., 916/808-5888, www.saczoo.org, 9am-4pm daily Feb.-Oct., 10am-4pm daily Nov.-Jan., adults $11.25, seniors $10.50, children $7.25). A fabulous array of animals awaits, including shy lemurs, regal lions, mighty grizzly bears, slithering reptiles, sleepy-eyed giraffes, and many other creatures. No matter how you feel about zoos, it's hard to beat the feeling of locking eyes with a Sumatran tiger for the first time. For just $3, visit the new **Giraffe Encounter** (11:45am and 2pm daily) to help feed the long-necked animals. It's some of the most fun you can have in 30 minutes. To mix things up, download the zoo's Art Tour map from their web site and keep an eye out for sculptures depicting different animal species throughout the compound.

Tours

Enjoy sightseeing as you dine aboard the **Sacramento RiverTrain** (400 N. Harbor Blvd., West Sacramento, 800/866-1690, www.sacramentorivertrain.com, $30-72). Outside the window or on the open-air observation deck, look down at the river and the stunning Fremont Trestle. Choose from a variety of rides, including a standard weekday lunch trip, an upscale weekend dinner party, or even a reenactment of the Great Train Robbery, complete with costumed robbers and a Western-style barbecue lunch. Most rides last 2-4 hours. Check the website for departure times, ride lengths, and special-event rides that happen several times each year.

If you're looking for a laugh, try one of the three **Hysterical Walks & Rides** (916/441-2527, www.hystericalwalks.com, $20-120). On the historical walking tour (10:30am

Sat. June-Oct), a standup comedian guide gives visitors the sidesplitting story of Old Sacramento as the tour winds past the city's historical riverfront. Need more drama with your laughs? Sign up for a ghost walk (8:30pm Fri.-Sat.). These sometimes spooky and always silly walks take adult visitors through the back alleys of Old Sacramento as your guide relates all the best ghost stories from this area. If you prefer a smooth ride to using your own feet, sign up for the Segway tour (10am-1pm daily) that takes you through Old Town, to the Capitol Building and gardens, the city's historical riverfront, and other historical Sacramento sights. Your standup comedian will share the history of the city as you glide along the sidewalk. This tour lasts two hours, and all riders must be at least age 16. Call ahead for exact times and reservations. Walking tours are offered June through late October.

ENTERTAINMENT AND EVENTS

Bars and Clubs

The sleek, urbane interior of **Harlow's** (2708 J St., 916/441-4693, www.harlows.com, tickets $10-70, shows age 21 and over) has a big-city feel and a moneyed vibe; make sure to spiff up before rubbing elbows with the swanky crowd. The live acts range from local favorites like Tainted Love and Irish rockers Young Dubliners to up-and-coming local DJs. Harlow's often has a line to get in, especially if there's a show.

Mix (1525 L St., 916/442-8899, www.mix-downtown.net, hours vary Tues.-Sun.) is the destination for Sacramento's elite. Lobbyists and lawmakers come after office hours. It's also a great spot to meet friends for a night on the town. Polished wooden ceilings and wall panels give a minimalist European feel with California flair. A rooftop patio with fire pits and comfy chairs invites relaxing with a glass of wine or a beer. Mix is popular on weekends and will have a line later in the evening.

De Vere's Irish Pub (1521 L St., 916/231-9947, http://deverespub.com, 11am-2am Mon.-Fri., 9am-2am Sat., 9am-midnight Sun.) oozes Irish history—most of the vintage photographs and mementos adorning the walls belong to the owners. All of the furniture and fixtures were designed and imported from Ireland, including the towering wooden bar that spans two rooms. The 20-ounce pints of Guinness are popular, but you can also order from a sizable cocktail list. The pub also has a full menu of Irish and British cuisine. De Vere's is one of the busier stops for Sacramento's singles scene.

There's no secret password, but the **Shady Lady Saloon** (1409 R St., 916/231-9121, http://shadyladybar.com, 11am-2am Mon.-Fri., 9am-2am Sat.-Sun.) feels like a speakeasy with a Gold Rush vibe in the heart of Midtown's up-and-coming R Street Historic Corridor. Bartenders don vintage vests and wear garters on their sleeves, all while serving up libations like the White Linen or the Horse Neck. The bar decor is stylish and decadent, and you can catch a variety of live acts nightly. The bar also serves dinner and weekend brunch with a Southern-inspired menu.

58 Degrees and Holding (1217 18th St., 916/442-5858, www.58degrees.com, 11am-10pm Sun.-Thurs., 11am-11pm Fri., 10am-11pm Sat.) is a wine bar and upscale eatery in Midtown's Handle District. The wine list is stacked with European and Californian wines, including a few from Amador County, and the wait staff is knowledgeable about the vino. With a good balance here between busy and chill, it's a great place for couples and small groups.

If a Seattle coffeehouse married a Vegas lounge, their baby would look like **Capitol Garage** (1500 K St., 916/444-3633, www.capitolgarage.com, 6am-midnight Mon.-Thurs., 6am-2am Fri., 8am-2am Sat.-Sun.). This espresso bar-nightclub serves coffee and cocktails all day long. Stop by for karaoke every Thursday and Sunday. Capitol Garage also serves a killer brunch.

Live Music

For a night of impeccable classical music,

buy tickets for a concert by the **Sacramento Philharmonic Orchestra** (916/808-2000, http://2intune.org, $21-117). The Philharmonic performs all over the area, most often in the Community Center Theater (1301 L St., 916/808-5181) and the Harris Center for the Arts (10 College Parkway, Folsom, 916/608-6888). The Philharmonic's concerts occur about one Saturday a month during their October-May season.

Each May, music lovers from around the state flock to the capital for the **Sacramento Music Festival and Jubilee** (www.sacmusicfest.com). Every Memorial Day Weekend, more than 100 acts—representing musical genres like New Orleans-style jazz, zydeco, bluegrass, western swing, Latin, and American roots rock—descend on Sacramento to perform in venues ranging from the sprawling Convention Center stage to the wooden planks of Old Sacramento's sidewalks. Festival organizers also book blues, country, rockabilly, and R&B bands, giving the event an inclusive feel. Be sure to get tickets in advance; this is one of the best events that Sacramento has to offer.

Comedy

Sacramento has three major comedy clubs waiting to bust your funny bone. The **Punch Line** (2100 Arden Way, 916/925-5500, www.punchlinesac.com, Wed.-Sun., tickets $14-38), a sister club to the San Francisco Punch Line, brings in top national talent. You might see the likes of Dana Carvey and Wayne Brady live and in person. Shows run nightly Wednesday-Sunday, with hot local and up-and-coming national acts such as Gabriel Iglesias, Jo Koy, and Amy Schumer. All tickets are general admission.

In the middle of Old Sacramento, **Laughs Unlimited** (1207 Front St., 916/446-8128, www.laughsunlimited.com, Wed.-Sun., tickets $5-20) brings hilarity to the waterfront with comics such as Todd Paul and Chris Titus doing multiple-night engagements every week and occasional shows by comedy legends such as Shawn Wayans, Alonzo Bodden, and local resident Jack Gallagher. There's a two-drink minimum, and a reasonable appetizer and dessert menu.

If you're a sucker for improv comedy, head to the **Sacramento Comedy Spot** (1050 20th St., 916/444-3137, http://saccomedyspot.com, shows daily, tickets $5-12). Attend an improv class to sharpen your comedic skills or watch the mostly local acts run through their skits. The Comedy Spot is open to all ages, though shows can sometimes get a little salty. The Spot also hosts the annual **Sac Comedy Fest** (www.saccomedyfest.com) every September.

Theater

Live theater is an important part of the nightlife of Sacramento. **Capital Stage** (2215 J St., 916/995-5464, http://capstage.org, $26-40) takes regional theater to the next level. This professional company has a small space to perform works by up-and-coming playwrights such as Aaron Loeb and Nina Raine, and classic, less-often-produced plays by heavy hitters like Sam Shepard and Harold Pinter. All the plays Capital Stage puts on are geared for the over-18 set.

On board the *Delta King,* **Suspects Murder Mystery Dinner Theater** (1000 Front St., 916/443-3600, www.suspectstheater.com, $40-43) combines dinner and a fun show. As dinner begins, gunshots ring out, and you'll spend the rest of your meal laughing as you participate in an Agatha Christie-style murder mystery. You might find yourself a suspect, or possibly a victim. However the story plays out, you'll enjoy the comedy, the mystery, and the tasty food and drink at this fun, kitschy night.

For musical theater, catch the latest show at **California Musical Theater** (CMT, 916/557-1999, www.calmt.com, $22-153). CMT uses the Wells Fargo Pavilion (1419 H St.) and the Community Center Theater (1301 L St.) for its productions. The Broadway Series features iconic Broadway classics like *Phantom of the Opera* and *Mamma Mia.* The Music Circus series at the Wells Fargo Pavilion puts on beloved musicals such as *South Pacific, Spamalot, Annie,* and *Wicked.* Purchase tickets online or over the phone.

Dance

Classical dance lovers can enjoy a night out at the **Sacramento Ballet** (1631 K St., 916/552-5800, www.sacballet.org, Thurs.-Sun., adults $19-90, children $17-76). Since 1954, this company has brought high-level dance spectacles to the capital. It has produced famous ballets such as *Sleeping Beauty* and *The Nutcracker,* as well several new and interpreted works, including an acclaimed production of *The Great Gatsby.* Purchase tickets directly from the box office, by phone, or on the website. Most performances are held at the Sacramento Community Center theater.

Festivals and Events

The highlight of each year at the mammoth **California Exposition & State Fair Center** (Cal Expo, 1600 Exposition Blvd., 916/263-3000, www.calexpo.com) is the **California State Fair** (www.bigfun.org). The fair lasts for two weeks every July. During that period, nearly one million people pass through the gates. There are concerts performed by national acts, horse races at the Miller Lite Racetrack Grandstand, a carnival, exhibitions, and contests. A major wine competition is held at the fair each year, and the biggest and most impressive wineries from around the state take it very seriously.

SHOPPING

If you prefer the old to the new, come to the **57th Street Antiques Mall** (855 57th St., www.57thstreetantiquerow.com, 10am-5pm Tues.-Sun.). With seven shops selling their wares, you're likely to find whatever antique or collectible you're looking for. Between H Street and Capitol Avenue are a number of **art galleries** displaying works of local and worldwide artists in a variety of media. The best way to explore these is through **2nd Saturdays** (5:30pm-9pm every second Sat. of the month, free), an art walk when galleries stay open late and residents crowd the streets filled with vendors, live music, and food. Finally, the revitalized **Midtown** (www.midtowngrid.com) offers an array of boutiques, galleries, and shops that please shoppers.

SPORTS AND RECREATION

Amusement Parks

Kids and adults alike can escape the summer's heat at **Raging Waters** (1600 Exposition Blvd., 916/924-3747, www.rwsac.com, $22-31). With rides like Shark Attack, Hurricane, and Cliffhanger, thrill-seekers can get a full day of excitement. For a more sedate day at the water park, ride a slow tube down the Calypso Cooler River, play in Hook's Lagoon, or catch a wave at Breakers Beach.

Golf

With mostly sunny weather and a dry Mediterranean climate, Sacramento is a bona fide golfing paradise that has plenty of great, affordable courses. January and February can be a bit wet and summer is scorching, but really, that's just being picky.

When most weekend duffers hit the links in Sacramento, they're usually teeing off at **Haggin Oaks** (3645 Fulton Ave., 916/481-4653, www.hagginoaks.com, $16-60). Golfing magic lurks under the 100-year-old heritage oaks on these fairways. Famed course architect Alistair MacKenzie (the brains behind Augusta National) designed the 18-hole championship layout here, and golfing legends like Sam Snead and Walter Hagen have putted the greens. Haggin is actually two golf courses: the more esteemed MacKenzie course (18 holes, 6,991 yards) for low handicappers and the neighboring **Arcade Creek Golf Course** (18 holes, 6,552 yards, $12.50-19) for beginners. Get warmed up at the driving range, named by Range Magazine as one of the top 100 in the country; it stays open almost all night (closed 3am-5am for maintenance) and boasts 100 stalls.

In town, perhaps the most beloved public course is the **Bing Maloney Golf Course**

(6801 Freeport Blvd., 916/808-2283, www.bingmaloney.com, $16-49), with two courses: the 18-hole course that's been on the property since 1952, and the newer par-29 nine-hole executive course ($8.50-13), a bargain on weekdays and perfect for beginners. Make reservations for a tee time up to eight days in advance online or by phone. The par-72 18-hole course has been described as "what you see is what you get"—a straightforward course that will challenge your game with sloping greens and huge heritage oak trees, but not frustrate you with gimmicks or unwelcome surprises.

Cherry Island (2360 Elverta Rd., 916/991-7293, www.golfcherryisland.com, $15-43) seems to fly under the radar for most golfers. Maybe it's the location just beyond the northern city limits that keeps some duffers away, but you should make the trip. The course is beautiful and fairly tough. The layout is 18 holes, a modest 6,494 yards, shaded by towering heritage oak trees. Walking all 18 holes at twilight is usually only $15 if you book online.

The **Teal Bend Golf Club** (7200 Garden Hwy., 916/922-5209, www.tealbendgolf.com, $20-65) has been around since 1997. It's conveniently located near the airport and the river, and you can slip in a quick round of golf no matter how little time you have. As you walk and play, look out for the teal duck—the course's namesake—as well as deer, geese, and hawks. This course, a local favorite, is famous for its many water features. Make tee time reservations by phone or online up to eight days in advance, or enroll in one of the club's many annual tournaments. After the game, relax at the Bar and Grille, enjoying a casual meal of a burger or a salad and a cold beer.

Hiking

A trip to Sacramento wouldn't be complete without a hike along the **American River Parkway** (www.regionalparks.saccounty.net, 23 miles, easy-moderate). The parkway is actually a series of paved trails that run through wetlands, oak woodlands, and several regional parks along the American River. The trails start at **Discovery Park,** a grassy 302-acre park at the confluence of the Sacramento and American Rivers, and end 23 miles away in the city of Folsom. Along the way, you'll pass cyclists pedaling along river levees, families pushing strollers by the water, and plenty of dog owners taking their pets for a walk. If you're hiking on the trail near Folsom, stop by the **Nimbus Fish Hatchery** (2001 Nimbus Rd., Gold River, 916/358-2820, www.dfg.ca.gov), where the hatchery raises fingerling steelhead trout and salmon in dozens of tanks. The parkway has more than just hiking and biking trails; anglers will find plenty of fishing opportunities along the river, and boating enthusiasts can launch from various points.

Swimming and Fishing

The heat of Sacramento's summers can make anyone want to jump in a lake—or the river, as the case may be. For a fun and refreshing day out on the banks of the Sacramento River, head for **Sand Cove Park** (2005 Garden Hwy., 916/808-6060). Walk from the parking lot down the trail to the sandy river beach, a perfect spot to swim or fish. The park also has a grassy lawn area, shade trees, hiking trails, and a boat dock at the north end, though no launch. Bring a picnic and while away the day alternately swimming in the water, sunning yourself, and fishing for dinner. The river shelters bass, sturgeon, and salmon; you'll need a California fishing license. Amenities at this municipal park are minimal—portable toilets and no food vendors.

Spectator Sports

Sacramento is the home of professional sports teams at all levels. It's easy to take in a game while you're visiting. Basketball is a local favorite, and the NBA's **Sacramento Kings** (www.nba.com/kings, $19-216) play at **Sleep Train Arena** (1 Sports Pkwy., 916/928-6900, www.sleeptrainarena.com). A fast-paced basketball game can be a great way to unwind after a long day of historical sights and museums. You can get cheaper seats if you're willing to sit in the nosebleeds. Tickets are available online or at the arena box office. The arena has ample parking ($10, cash only). The Kings plan to move by October 2016 into a brand-new arena in downtown Sacramento. Call or visit the team's web site to confirm the moving schedule.

ACCOMMODATIONS

Sacramento tends to be a working town, with folks coming in for meetings and conventions and staying at big-box chain motels and hotels. The best bets for cheap-and-easy rooms are the various Holiday Inns, Quality Inns, and Sheratons. Most Sacramento hotels don't provide airport shuttles, so you'll have to take a taxi or make other plans for transportation.

Under $100

For budget accommodations, you can't beat the **Sacramento Hostel** (925 H St., 916/443-1691, www.norcalhostels.org/sac, $30-99), in a grand old Victorian home downtown. The parlor, drawing room, and recreation room all have high ceilings and period-style moldings. A full shared kitchen boasts all the equipment needed to create tasty meals. On warm evenings, take your dinner out to the wraparound porch. Lodgings include coed and single-sex dorms, plus a few private rooms. Only one private room includes a private bath—all the other hall baths are shared. The attractive wooden bunks do not include linens, so bring your own. The hostel has free wireless Internet access, laundry, on-site parking, and 24-hour guest access.

The **Governors Inn** (210 Richards Blvd., 916/448-7224, www.governorsinnhotel.com, $80-139), with classic motel styling, is near everything. Walk to the Capitol, or take a five-minute drive to Old Sacramento or Midtown. Whether you book a standard room or a two-room suite, you'll enjoy the understated elegance of this motel. Kids enjoy the outdoor pool in the hot summer months, and adults take advantage of the fitness center, free Wi-Fi, and continental breakfast. Check the website or ask at the desk for local recommendations for shopping, restaurants, golf courses, and sights around town. The inn offers free shuttle service to Sacramento International Airport.

$100-150

The **Inn off Capitol Park** (1530 N St., 916/447-8100, www.innoffcapitolpark.com, $100-179) offers luxury at moderate prices. The inn is within easy walking distance of the Capitol and the Sacramento Convention

Sacramento Hostel

Center. The furniture and lighting feel more like home than a motel. Amenities include free Wi-Fi and a continental breakfast. With only 36 rooms, this friendly boutique hotel can fill up fast during conventions. The Inn off Capitol Park does not allow smoking.

$150-250

For a touch of luxury near the Capitol, stay at the **Inn and Spa at Parkside** (2116 6th St., 916/658-1818, www.innatparkside.com, $200-280). Each of the dozen rooms features unique decorations with vibrant colors and sumptuous fabrics, feeling like a cross between a small B&B and a luxury hotel. Many rooms have spa tubs, flat-screen TVs, balconies, and fireplaces. For extra pampering, book a treatment at the attached luxury spa. Some rooms at the inn are set up for in-room massage; check when you book. This inn is set up for couples, so consider choosing a different lodging if you're traveling with children.

An integral part of the Old Town neighborhood, the ***Delta King*** (1000 Front St., 916/444-5464, www.deltaking.com, $150-230) is a hotel, restaurant, theater, and gathering space. To stay on the *Delta King* means stepping back into the Prohibition era, when the riverboat plied the Sacramento River. Of the modern, elegant staterooms, the less expensive ones can be quite small, but all have private bathrooms. The Captain's Quarters ($550) is a two-story suite with stunning river views and wrap-around balcony.

The best B&B in Sacramento has long been the ★ **Amber House** (1315 22nd St., 916/444-8085, www.amberhouse.com, $180-280), located on a quiet residential street in Midtown within walking distance of shopping, restaurants, and nightlife. Consisting of 10 rooms between two houses, Amber House has a level of service similar to upscale hotel chains. The innkeepers will see to your every need from the moment you enter the front door. Every room at the inn has either a jetted tub or a deep-soaking bathtub, a very comfortable bed, and top-end amenities. The stellar comfort and service extend to the food as well.

The majestic art deco brownstone ★ **Citizen Hotel** (926 J St., 916/447-2700, www.jdvhotels.com, $127-250) is one of downtown's most recognizable landmarks. Inside, the retro decor has a 1960s vibe, with a marble foyer and rooms with vintage pin-striped wallpaper and upholstered headboards. Amenities include a minibar, flat screen TV, and Italian linens. Other services include same-day laundry, a fitness center, and valet parking ($25 per day).

Over $250

The **Hyatt Regency** (1209 L St., 916/443-1234, http://sacramento.hyatt.com, $145-265) looks out over the State Capitol across the street. The Hyatt is probably Sacramento's classiest chain hotel, and all rooms have a sleek Euro design with hip ultramodern linens and furniture. Amenities include HDTVs, opening windows, and free Wi-Fi in the lobby. Downstairs is an indoor-outdoor lounge and sparkling outdoor pool, lined with awnings and comfortable lounge chairs.

FOOD

Sacramento is experiencing a foodie revolution. The city recently became the Farm-to-Fork Capital of America, which means local restaurants are serving fresh produce harvested the very same day from farms just a short drive from town. Sacramento's culinary boom is even attracting top chefs from nearby San Francisco and the Napa Valley who dig the city's location and hip, urban vibe. Make sure to check out the hugely popular **Farm-to-Fork Festival** (September, 916/808-7777, www.farmtofork.com), which throws a month-long party in downtown; events have included a cattle drive to the California State Capitol, a tractor parade, a gourmet dinner for 700 guests on the Tower Bridge over the Sacramento River, a sprawling farmers market on Capital Avenue, and plenty of smaller events around town.

Classic American

At Old Sacramento's **Fat City Bar and Cafe**

(1001 Front St., 916/446-6768, www.fats-restaurants.com, 11:30am-9pm Mon.-Fri., 10:30am-10pm Sat.-Sun., $11-29), you'll imagine you've walked into an Old West saloon from the gold-mining heyday. Award-winning stained glass graces the windows, the lamps, and almost anything else it could be affixed to. From the eclectic menu, you can get chow mein, tacos, meatloaf, pot pie, or an enormous cheeseburger (the bourbon barbecue burger is the best of these). On weekends, enjoy a mixed brunch menu that includes the best of the lunch menu, plus breakfast specialties.

A good Old Sac burger joint is in **Fanny Ann's Saloon** (1023 2nd St., 916/441-0505, www.fannyannsaloon.com, 11:30am-midnight Sun.-Thurs., 11:30am-2am Fri.-Sat., $9). Fanny's has four floors of cozy booths and vintage Americana decor serving greasy diner food. The hamburgers are awesome with an order of curly fries, and you can't go wrong with the sandwiches.

Holy blue cheese and bacon! As seen on the Food Network's *Diners, Drive-Ins and Dives*, **Dad's Kitchen** (2968 Freeport Blvd., 916/447-3237, http://ilovedadskitchen.com, 11am-9pm Tues.-Thurs., 11am-10pm Fri., 9am-10pm Sat., 9am-8pm Sun., $8-13) is a tiny hole in the wall. The Dad's Burger is legendary: bacon and blue cheese seared onto a grass-fed beef patty with house-made garlic and paprika oil. Make sure to start with an order of deep-fried garbanzo beans. Stop by for the weekend brunch to venture beyond the burgers.

Pangaea Bier Café (2743 Franklin Blvd., 916/454-4942, http://pangaeatwobrews.com, 11am-10pm Tues.-Sun., $8-19) pours around 20 Belgian or Belgian-style beers in this hip little eatery. The sandwiches are as good as anything you'll find in Midtown. Try the Apri-hopped Chicken with apricot marmalade, cream cheese, and pepper jack; for dinner, the grass-fed Pangaea burger with cheddar and bacon will make your heart race in more ways than one.

Asian

For American-style sushi and an upbeat atmosphere, try **Mikuni Japanese Restaurant and Sushi Bar** (1530 J St., 916/447-2112, www.mikunisushi.com, 11:30am-10pm Mon.-Thurs., 11:30-midnight Fri., noon-midnight Sat., noon-9pm Sun., $5-17). The crowd skews young on weekends, as bar-hoppers start their

The Tower Bridge hosts a gourmet feast during the Farm-to-Fork Festival in September.

evenings. Expect to wait on busier nights unless you have a reservation. Make sure to try the spicy sushi rolls packed with stuff like fried tempura, seared ahi, and salmon roe.

Frank Fat's (806 L St., 916/442-7092, www.fatsrestaurants.com, 11am-10pm Mon.-Fri., 5pm-10pm Sat.-Sun., $9-27) is a legendary Sacramento institution, opened by Frank Fat in 1939, serving authentic upscale Chinese food. For years, Frank's has been a favorite among local politicos for power lunches. The interior has a hip, cosmopolitan vibe with classy leather booths, a long shiny bar, and modern furniture. Typical plates include mango ginger chicken, chow mein, and pineapple sweet and sour pork.

Kru (2516 J St., 916/551-1559, http://krurestaurant.com, 11:30am-9:30pm Mon., 11:30am-10pm Tues.-Thurs., 11:30am-11pm Fri., noon-11pm Sat., 4pm-9:30pm Sun., $5-18) wraps a mean sushi roll with top-notch fish. Grab a bar seat for quicker service. The vibe here is best described as chill lounge. Rolls are slightly more expensive than average, but they use organic rice in everything.

New American

The hottest restaurant in Sacramento is **Mother** (1023 K St., 916/594-9812, http://mothersacramento.com, 11am-2:30pm Mon., 11am-4pm, 5pm-9pm Tues.-Thurs., 11am-4pm, 5pm-10pm Fri.-Sat., $12). The menu is Southern-themed but vegetarian, the decor hip yet friendly. The food is Michelin-worthy and simple at the same time. Mother's menu changes seasonally, but a few standbys include the mouthwatering nut burger smothered with agave mustard, and the fried green tomato sandwich with mozzarella and cashew pesto. Check the restaurant's live web feed to see the line before arriving.

Magpie Café (1409 R St., 916/452-7594, www.magpiecafe.com, 10:30am-9pm Mon.-Wed., 10:30am-10pm Thurs.-Fri., 8am-10pm Sat., 8am-2pm Sun., $10-29) only serves what's in season on local farms, so the menu changes all the time. Veggie fans dig this place for the gourmet meat-free options like baked polenta squares or the Caprese sandwich. Locals flock here on weekend evenings. Get here early; they don't take reservations.

★ **Mulvaney's Building & Loan** (1215 19th St., 916/441-6022, www.mulvaneysbl.com, 11:30am-2:30pm, 5pm-10pm Tues.-Fri., 5pm-10pm Sat., $14-38) is a product of Midtown's renaissance, an upscale eatery showcasing the best of California cuisine. The menu changes often to take advantage of local seasonal produce. Go for a standard appetizer and main dish, or order small plates. The wine list offers a reasonable number of tastings and interesting vintages. Pick a seat in the lively and loud dining room or a quieter table on the garden-like back patio.

Without a doubt, ★ **Ella Dining Room and Bar** (1131 K St., 916/443-3772, www.elladiningroomandbar.com, 11:30am-9pm Mon.-Thurs., 11:30am-10pm Fri., 5:30pm-10pm Sun., $10-40) is downtown Sacramento's culinary superstar. This swanky eatery dishes up local, sustainably farmed fare. Typical plates might be Scottish salmon with succotash, juniper-braised oxtail, or naturally raised trout from a nearby fish farm. Call ahead on weekends to secure a table.

Breakfast

Simple yet tasty fare is king at **Orphan** (3440 C St., 916/442-7370, http://orphanbreakfast.com, 7am-2pm, 11am-2pm Mon.-Fri., 7am-2pm Sat.-Sun., $5-14), where they serve the best pancakes in town. Try the buttermilk Naked Cakes or the cornmeal flapjacks. The menu is a Californian take on Latin-Mediterranean fusion, heavy on soy products (tofu, soy chorizo), rosemary, pesto, avocado, and black beans. Orphan is cash only but has an ATM inside.

★ **Fox and Goose Pub and Restaurant** (1001 R St., 916/443-8825, www.foxandgoose.com, 6:30am-9:30pm Mon.-Sat., 6:30am-3pm Sun., $10) might just dish up Sacramento's best breakfast. Whether you're jonesing for fresh pastries, delicious pancakes, or killer omelets, make sure to come here. Show up early: A line starts forming around 9am on weekends.

French

For a fancy French restaurant experience, dine at the **Waterboy Restaurant** (2000 Capitol Ave., 916/498-9891, www.waterboyrestaurant.com, 11:30am-2:30pm, 5pm-9pm Mon., 11:30am-2:30pm, 5pm-9:30pm Tues.-Thurs., 11:30am-2:30pm, 5pm-10:30pm Fri., 5pm-10:30pm Sat., 5pm-9pm Sun., $10-29). The light, bright dining room feels like the south coast of France, and the cuisine takes much from the culinary traditions of Provence (as well as Tuscany and California). If you've got a serious appetite, go for the full three courses: appetizer, first, and main.

★ **Café Rolle** (5357 H St., 916/455-9140, www.caferolle.com, 11am-3pm Tues. and Sat., 11am-3pm, 5:30pm-7:30pm Wed.-Fri., $5-16) is about as French as they come. The owners greet visitors with a "bonjour!" every time the door opens. Choices range from gourmet sandwiches, salads, and finger food to salmon or chicken plates for dinner. The portions are filling and rich. Lunch is pretty busy and a line usually runs out the door, so arrive early if you can.

For a tasty and inexpensive French lunch near the Capitol Building, head for **La Bonne Soupe Café** (920 8th St., 11am-3pm Mon.-Fri., $8). La Bonne Soupe serves hot soups—from classics such as French onion to tasty treats made with in-season produce—while sandwiches are made with fresh ingredients. If you usually eat a smaller lunch, consider splitting an order of soup and a sandwich—portions are pretty hefty. If you come at noon, you'll likely wait in line with local businesspeople who come from miles around to have lunch here.

Mexican

Both the atmosphere and the mole are authentic at ★ **Tres Hermanas** (2416 K St., 916/443-6919, www.treshermanasonk.com, 11am-9pm Mon.-Thurs., 11am-10pm Fri., 7am-10pm Sat., 7am-8pm Sun., $10-14). The food is influenced by northern Mexican cuisine, so expect quesadillas, tacos, and enchiladas heavy on herbs and veggies, lots of pork and fish, and enchiladas smothered in one of three amazing sauces. This Midtown spot gets busy. Between 7pm and 9pm, figure on waiting 30 minutes for a table.

Midtown Taqueria (3754 J St., 916/452-7551, 8am-11pm daily, $3-8) serves basic burritos and tacos like you'd expect from a roadside stand. This place even serves breakfast. On a balmy evening it's fun to sit on the patio and watch locals ride cruisers down J Street, unless your favorite *fútbol* team is playing on the inside TV.

Italian

Owned since 1986 by celebrity food guru Biba Caggiano, the elegant Italian-themed ★ **Biba Restaurant** (2801 Capitol Ave., 916/455-2422, www.biba-restaurant.com, 11:30am-2pm, 5:30pm-9pm Mon.-Thurs., 5:30pm-10pm Fri.-Sat., $16-38) still dominates Sacramento's dining scene. The fare is ultra-upscale Bolognese served both prix fixe and à la carte in a country club atmosphere. Valet parking is available, and Biba is usually around to greet guests.

Though it's billed as "California Mediterranean cuisine," you'll recognize the food at **Lucca Restaurant and Bar** (1615 J St., 916/669-5300, www.luccarestaurant.com, 11:30am-10pm Mon.-Thurs., 11:30am-11pm Fri., noon-11pm Sat., 4pm-9pm Sun., $14-20) simply as darn good Italian grub. The California influence comes from fresh veggies like squash, baby artichokes, green beans, and olives. Order the zucchini chips for an appetizer. Call ahead; you'll need reservations at this fashionable eatery.

Zelda's Original Gourmet Pizza (1415 21st St., 916/447-1400, www.zeldasgourmetpizza.com, 11:30am-10pm Mon.-Thurs., 11:30am-11pm Fri., 5pm-11pm Sat., 5pm-9:30pm Sun., $6.50-27) serves deep-dish Chicago-style pies that locals just can't resist. You won't find much health food here, but a Zelda's pizza might just be the perfect answer to your pizza craving. The pizzeria closes about a half-hour earlier on Sundays during the winter.

Quick Bites

By far the healthiest deli in town is **Sacramento Natural Foods Co-op** (1900 Alhambra Blvd., 916/455-2667, www.sacfoodcoop.com, 7am-10pm daily, $5-10). This place is a full-sized organic foods store, with produce and meats supplied from sustainable, local sources. The deli serves wraps, smoothies, casseroles, and vegan baked goods. Lunch is very busy and parking is limited.

Hot Italian (1627 16th St., 916/444-3000, www.hotitalian.net, 11:30am-9:30pm Mon.-Thurs., 10:30am-10:30pm Fri.-Sat., 10:30am-9:30am Sun., $15) is sleek yet unpretentious, and feels like a traditional urban deli in Milan or Rome. The interior's simple black-and-white decor is spare yet trendy. They're known for pizza and panini made with seasonal ingredients, but the pasta is also pretty darn good.

Bakeries and Cafés

Sacramento coffeehouses are roasting some of the best beans this side of Seattle. Downtown has the most indie coffee joints per capita in the United States, with several earning accolades from *Coffee Review*. If you're in town, check out the city's **Specialty Coffee Week** (http://specialtycoffeeweek.com, Oct.) to really feel the buzz.

Start by grabbing a latte at **Temple Coffee** (1010 9th St., 916/443-4960, www.templecoffee.com, 6am-11pm daily, $4), where beans are roasted daily. Grab a Mexican mocha or pick your own beans and watch the barista brew up a single cup just for you at the pour-over bar.

One of the city's caffeine pioneers is **Naked Lounge** (1500 Q St., 916/442-0174, www.nakedcoffee.net, 6am-11pm daily, $4). This café has a neo-grungy vibe that's manifested in edgy artwork on the wall and overstuffed couches where folks sip drinks like the Bowl of Soul (chamomile tea steamed with condensed milk and honey) and the Kerouac, billed as the "martini of coffee drinks."

Insight Coffee Roasters (1901 8th St., 916/642-9555, http://insightcoffee.com, 6:30am-7pm Mon.-Fri., 7am-7pm Sat.-Sun., $4) serves basics like lattes, mochas, Americanos, and house coffee. This place has a beautiful copper espresso machine and postmodern grungy decor, and the brew is consistently rated among the best in town by local newspapers.

The best of the best may just be ★ **Old Soul** (1716 L St., 916/443-7685, www.oldsoulco.com, 6am-9pm daily, $2-5), perhaps the purest Seattle-style coffeehouse in town. Choices are simple here: just tea, house coffee, basic lattes and mochas, and one of the best breakfasts in town.

Consider skipping dessert elsewhere in order to hit ★ **Rick's Dessert Diner** (2401 J St., 916/444-0969, http://ricksdessertdiner.com, 10am-11pm Mon., 10am-midnight Tues.-Thurs., 10am-1am Fri.-Sat., noon-11pm Sun., $6), a 1950s-style diner serving all desserts, all the time. Open late, Rick's is popular with local teenagers as well as older patrons and often has a line out the door on weekends after 10pm. The pies are nothing special, but the impossibly high layer cakes have wonderful flavor and texture. They also offer hot fudge sundaes and banana splits. Take it out or eat at one of the small booths clad in sparkling red vinyl.

INFORMATION AND SERVICES

Need help from local experts for your time in Sacramento? Visit the **Sacramento Convention and Visitors Bureau** (1608 I St., 916/808-7777, www.visitsacramento.org, 8am-5pm Mon.-Fri.). Call or check the website in advance for deals on hotels, advance reservations for attractions, and information about what's going on in and around the city.

Sutter General Hospital (2801 L St., 916/454-2222, http://suttermedicalcenter.org) is right downtown and has an emergency room. Another local emergency center is run by **UC Davis Medical Center** (2315 Stockton Blvd., 916/734-5010).

TRANSPORTATION

Air

Major carriers fly into **Sacramento International Airport** (SMF, 6900 Airport

Blvd., 916/929-5411, www.sacairports.org), a great starting point for trips into the Gold Country.

Train

If you're coming into Sacramento from the San Francisco Bay Area, one of the best ways is on the *Capitol Corridor* train run by **Amtrak** (www.amtrak.com, 800/872-7245). Serving the centrally located Amtrak station (401 I St.), this train runs from Sacramento to Oakland and on to San Jose and back several times each day. The Oakland-Sacramento trip takes two hours, and San Jose-Sacramento is just over three hours. You can also get to Sacramento on the *California Zephyr,* which crosses the country from Chicago to Emeryville, in the Bay Area, once daily in each direction, or the *Coast Starlight,* which runs from Seattle to Los Angeles, also once daily in each direction. The *San Joaquin* route runs several times daily up the middle of California's Central Valley, from Sacramento to Bakersfield.

Bus

Sacramento has a busy and reasonably extensive public transit system that includes both buses and a light-rail train system, **Sacramento Regional Transit** (SACRT, www.sacrt.com, single ride $2.50, day pass $6). Including the downtown trolley and the light rail lines, SACRT has nearly 100 routes; check the website for schedules and maps.

It's easy to catch a bus to and from Sacramento. **Megabus** (877/462-6342, http://us.megabus.com, 65th St. and Q St., one way $1-24) operates routes to San Francisco, Reno, and Sparks. The best fares are usually offered early in the morning, but you can sometimes get $1 fares in the middle of the day. Megabus doesn't have a station in Sacramento; you'll get picked up or dropped off in the SACRT light rail parking lot on 65th Street. **Greyhound** (420 Richards Blvd., 916/444-6858 or 800/231-2222, www.greyhound.com, $7.50-48) sells cheap tickets to San Francisco ($7.50-13), Modesto ($7-13), Redding ($30-46.50), and Los Angeles ($24-48).

Car

I-80 runs through Sacramento roughly east-west, and the I-80 Business adjunct goes into downtown on a slightly different route. I-5 splits the city on its north-south route. U.S. 50 runs east to Lake Tahoe, and Highway 99 runs south to Los Angeles and north to Chico.

Parking in town can get difficult during major events, but otherwise spots aren't hard to come by. Near the Capitol Building, bring change to feed the meters; some meters also take credit cards. In Old Sacramento, spots right in the middle of the action can be at a premium during high season—you may have to walk a few blocks to get to Front Street, but there are pay lots at the north and south ends of Old Sacramento. The theaters and arenas tend to have ample parking lots, though you'll pay at many of those. Most hotels offer parking free with your room.

DAVIS

Davis is a bustling town with a lively nightlife and restaurant scene. It's also home to the region's agricultural brainpower—the University of California, Davis, home of the "Aggies." The town is among rice fields and orchards in the fertile valley between Sacramento and California's coastal mountains. Most of the region's organic and community-supported farms are just northwest of Davis, and much of this bounty can be found twice a week at the town's renowned farmers market.

Known for its progressive vibe and left-leaning politics, Davis also consistently earns national recognition as a top-notch cycling town with some of the country's most prolific and well-maintained bike paths. Downtown, you'll find plenty of arty boutiques and antiques stores scattered throughout the town's shady streets, a perfect place for avoiding the hot valley sun.

University of California, Davis

One of the country's most esteemed educational institutions is the **University of California, Davis** (1 Shields Ave.,

530/752-1011, www.ucdavis.edu). Students at UC Davis are known as Aggies, a nod to the school's storied agricultural background. First opened in 1905 as a farm school, the expansive campus, California's largest at 5,300 acres, has an on-site dairy and a working farm. Today UC Davis is renowned for its biological and political science programs, along with one of the nation's biggest engineering schools. Sports are also an important part of Aggie life, and the UC Davis athletic program has rivalries with other NCAA Division I schools like Stanford, UC Berkeley, and nearby Sacramento State. If you visit Davis, make sure to visit the beautiful campus for a stroll or to catch an Aggies game.

How many universities teach students how to brew their own beer? At the **Robert Mondavi Institute for Wine and Food Science** (392 Old Davis Rd., 530/754-6349, http://robertmondaviinstitute.ucdavis.edu, tours $5), the on-campus brewery is just one of the world-class research facilities dedicated to food and beverage-making at UC Davis. Completed in 2008 and named for the famed Napa winemaker who donated $25 million to build it, the sprawling agricultural complex also boasts a green-certified winery and an organic vegetable garden on-site. Many of the cutting-edge techniques developed here have been applied at California's top wineries. Foodies will love the institute's olive oil center, which offers courses in how to produce artisanal olive oils. Stop by for a student-led tour or pay a little more for a faculty member to guide you around the institute. Tours are available Monday-Friday.

If you love bugs, check out the **Bohart Museum of Entomology** (1124 Academic Surge, 530/752-0493, http://bohart.ucdavis.edu, 9am-noon and 1pm-5pm Mon.-Thurs., free, parking $9). With more than seven million insects, the museum has one of the largest collections in North America, and 50,000 new specimens are added every year. Kids will especially love checking out the museum's trove of wasps, bees, and California's native insects. If you're coming with a group, call ahead and book a special guided tour. The museum does offer special weekend hours during the school year; call ahead or check the Bohart web site before visiting.

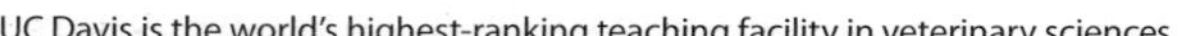
UC Davis is the world's highest-ranking teaching facility in veterinary sciences.

Transportation

Davis is 14 miles west of Sacramento on I-80. The Richards Boulevard exit provides easy access to downtown.

The closest airport is **Sacramento International Airport** (SMF, 6900 Airport Blvd., Sacramento, 916/929-5411, www.sacairports.org). The **Davis Airporter** (530/756-6715, www.davisairporter.com, $21) provides door-to-door shuttle service to the airport.

The *Capitol Corridor* train run by **Amtrak** (840 2nd St., 530/758-4220 or 800/872-7245, www.amtrak.com) stops several times daily in downtown Davis on the way to Oakland, San Jose, and Sacramento. **Unitrans** (1 Shields Ave., Davis, 530/752-2877, http://unitrans.ucdavis.edu, $1) provides student-run public transit around Davis and the university campus.

Davis Pedicab (410/829-0249, noon-3am Fri., 11am-3am Sat.) is a fun and reliable human-powered option for getting around Davis. Hours change during warmer months, and service can sometimes be irregular; if you have a special request, Davis Pedicab can usually make arrangements ahead of time. Bring cash and a generous spirit; the cabs don't charge a regular fare but do accept tips.

CHICO

The Sacramento Valley community of Chico is a thriving college town with outstanding urban parks, lush agricultural surroundings, and a living connection to its history. California State University, Chico, tends to dominate local culture.

Bidwell Mansion State Historic Park

Chico prides itself on having one of the largest and most diverse urban parks in the country. The original land for **Bidwell Mansion State Historic Park** (525 Esplanade, 530/891-4671, www.bidwellpark.org or www.friendsofbidwellpark.org) was donated by John and Annie Bidwell, the town's first and most prominent citizens. Their **Bidwell Mansion** (525 Esplanade, 530/895-6144, www.parks.ca.gov, visitors center 11am-5pm Sat.-Mon., tours hourly 11am-4pm Sat.-Mon., adults $6, ages 5-17 $3), a preserved 26-room Victorian house, is available for tours. Completed in 1868, this beautiful home features prime examples of 19th-century furnishings and decor.

The park boasts 3,670 acres in two sections. The undeveloped Upper Park is a sprawling canyon in the Sierra Nevada foothills that includes Big Chico Creek and Horseshoe Lake. This area of the park is great for hiking or horseback riding. It is also the location of the 18-hole par 72-73 **Bidwell Park Golf Course** (3199 Golf Course Rd., 530/891-8417, www.golfbidwellpark.com, sunrise-sunset daily, Mon.-Fri. $13-40, Sat.-Sun. $17-48). Amenities at the Lower Park include the **Sycamore Pool** (9am-9pm daily April-Sept., 9am-9pm daily Oct.-Mar., free); **Caper Acres** (9am-sunset Tues.-Sun., free), a special play area for children under age 12; the **Chico Creek Nature Center** (1968 E. 8th St., 530/891-4671, 11am-4pm Wed.-Sat.); the **Living Animal Museum** (11am-4pm Wed.-Sat., adults $4, children $2); and the **Howard Tucker Exhibit Hall** (11am-4pm Fri., 11am-1:30pm Sat.). The entrance fee for the Living Animal Museum also includes admission to the exhibit hall.

Sierra Nevada Brewing Company

The **Sierra Nevada Brewing Company** (1075 E. 20th St., 530/893-3520, www.sierranevada.com, tours 11am-4pm Sun.-Thurs., 11am-5:30pm Fri.-Sat., free) was founded in 1980. Sierra Nevada was at the forefront of the microbrew movement, and its original creation, Sierra Nevada Pale Ale, is still a star. The company continues to develop innovative new beers that win awards and fans. Sign up for the free tour or pay $25 for the three-hour Beer Geek Tour to immerse yourself in hops. Make sure to reserve a spot online or by calling ahead.

Transportation

Chico is 90 miles north of Sacramento on

Highway 99. It can be accessed from I-5: From Orland, exit I-5 onto Highway 32 east for about 20 miles to Chico. The *Coast Starlight* train, run by **Amtrak** (www.amtrak.com, 800/872-7245), runs from Seattle to Los Angeles once daily in each direction with a stop at the Chico platform (450 Orange St., no services).

Northern Gold Country

California's Gold Country is a great sprawling network of small towns and roads crisscrossing the Sierra Nevada foothills where much of California's modern history began. It was the gold in these hills that drew migrants from the East Coast and around the world to come to work the fields, build the railroads, and drag the wild lands of California into the modern era.

When visiting, it's easiest to traverse the Gold Country from north to south. The northern Gold Country extends from Nevada City down into the Shenandoah Valley. Interstate 80 can get you from Sacramento or the Bay Area to the northern Gold Country town of Auburn. Here you can pick up Highway 49 north to Grass Valley and Nevada City. On Highway 49 south of Auburn, head east to Placerville, Coloma, and Fair Play, and south down into the Shenandoah Valley, where small highways and roads lead to other tiny dots on the map.

NEVADA CITY AND GRASS VALLEY

★ Empire Mine State Historic Park

Arguably the best mining museum in the Gold Country is the **Empire Mine State Historic Park** (10791 E. Empire St., Grass Valley, 530/273-8522, www.empiremine.org, 10am-5pm daily, adults $7, children $3, tour included). Walking into the yard, you can see and feel the life of the 19th- and 20th-century miners who extracted tons of gold from the earth below your feet. Kids can run and shout in the yard, enjoying the open spaces and strange tools and machines. Keep a close eye on children; the museum contains many dangers both obvious and hidden. Adults can

Empire Mine State Historic Park

Northern Gold Country

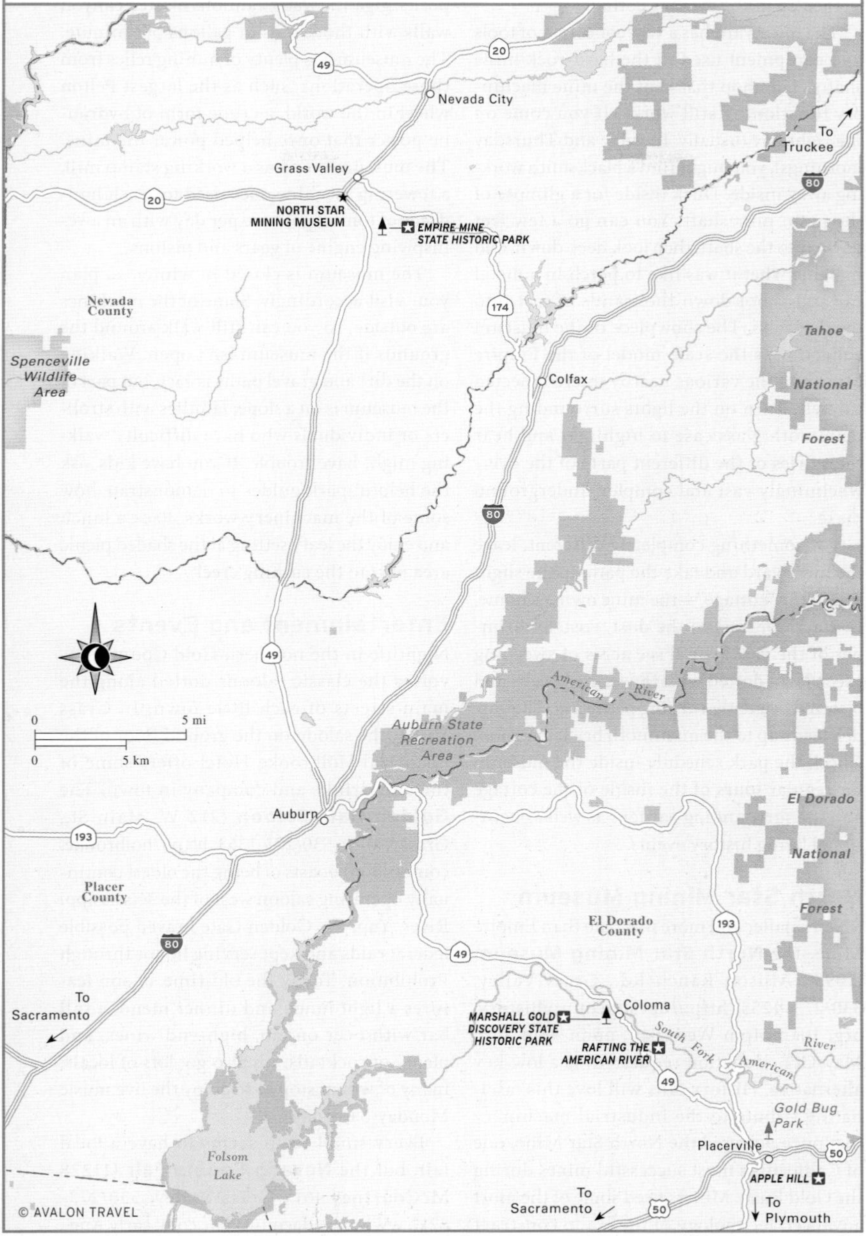

Nevada City
To Truckee
Grass Valley
NORTH STAR MINING MUSEUM
EMPIRE MINE STATE HISTORIC PARK
Nevada County
Spenceville Wildlife Area
Colfax
Tahoe National Forest
American River
Auburn State Recreation Area
Auburn
Placer County
El Dorado County
El Dorado National Forest
To Sacramento
Coloma
MARSHALL GOLD DISCOVERY STATE HISTORIC PARK
RAFTING THE AMERICAN RIVER
South Fork American River
Gold Bug Park
Placerville
APPLE HILL
Folsom Lake
To Sacramento
To Plymouth
20
49
80
174
193
50
0 5 mi
0 5 km

enjoy the history of the place and imagine a hard-rock life in the mine or a privileged existence up in the owner's cottage.

The mine yard has a vast collection of tools and equipment used in the hard-rock mine shafts. The shop that kept the mine machinery functioning still works. If you come on the right day (usually Tuesday and Thursday mornings), you might find a blacksmith working away inside. Duck inside for a glimpse of the main mineshaft. You can go a few feet down into the shaft, then look deep down, and imagine what it was like to perch in a metal car and shoot down thousands of feet into the darkness. The showpiece of the museum collection is the scale model of the Empire Mine and the various nearby interconnected tunnels. Turn on the lights surrounding the mammoth glass case to highlight and hear the stories of the different parts of the overwhelmingly vast and complex underground maze.

For something completely different, leave the mine yard and take the path up the slight rise to the "cottage"—the mine owner's home. In stark contrast to the dust, rust, and timber of the yard, you'll see acres of sweeping green lawn dotted with flowering shrubs and bisected by gently curving pathways. The garden leads up to the mammoth brick mansion. Check the park schedule inside the museum for regular tours of the inside of the cottage and the surrounding gardens as well as occasional living history events.

North Star Mining Museum

Much smaller and more intimate than Empire Mine, the **North Star Mining Museum** (10933 Allison Ranch Rd., Grass Valley, 530/273-4255, http://nevadacountyhistory.org, 10am-4pm Wed.-Sat., noon-4pm Sun. May-Oct., donation requested) is a low-key alternative. History fans will love this fascinating tribute to the industrial machinery that once powered the North Star Mine, one of California's most successful mines during the Gold Rush. Miners used some of the most advanced technology of the era to construct sprawling hydraulic operations or burrow deep into the hillsides to find the quartz deposits; gigantic water cannons blasted canyon walls with thousands of gallons per minute. The museum has plenty of mining relics from those operations, such as the largest Pelton wheel in the world, a crude form of hydraulic power that once helped power the mine. The museum even has a working stamp mill, a towering machine once used to crush hundreds of tons of gold ore per day with an awe-inspiring engine of gears and pistons.

The museum is closed in winter, so plan your visit accordingly. Some of the machines are outside, so you can still walk around the grounds if the museum isn't open. Walking on the dirt and gravel paths is easy, but part of the museum is on a slope; families with strollers or individuals who have difficulty walking might have trouble. If you have kids, ask the helpful park guides to demonstrate how some of the machinery works. Pack a lunch and enjoy the leafy setting at the shaded picnic area next to the rushing creek.

Entertainment and Events

Nightlife in the northern Gold Country involves the classic saloons dotted along the main streets of each little town. In Grass Valley, the saloon on the ground floor of the historical Holbrooke Hotel offers some of the best drinks and company in town. The **Golden Gate Saloon** (212 W. Main St., Grass Valley, 530/273-1353, http://holbrooke.com/saloon) boasts of being the oldest continually operating saloon west of the Mississippi River. Yup, the Golden Gate braved possible federal raids and kept serving liquor through Prohibition. Today the old-time saloon features a light lunch and dinner menu, a full bar with beer on tap, high-end wines, and plenty of cocktails. It's also got lots of locals, many of whom stop in to enjoy the live music Monday-Saturday.

Every small town seems to have a local fair, but the **Nevada County Fair** (11228 McCourtney Rd., Grass Valley, 530/273-6217, www.nevadacountyfair.com, early Aug., adults $9, seniors $6, children $4) stands out for its atmosphere. For one week every August, this rustic and charming little fair takes place under a shady canopy of towering evergreens. Attractions include the usual assortment of carnival games for kids, plus crafts, musical acts, art exhibitions, a rodeo, and appearances by the Budweiser draft horses. Stop by the food court and grab a homemade corn dog at a booth run by the local chapter of Job's Daughters. Don't miss the livestock exhibits from the Nevada County farms and the local high school FFA clubs, many of whom earn top prizes at the California State Fair later in the year. Pets are not allowed. If you visit the fair in the evening, pack a light jacket—even in August the foothills can be slightly chilly. Children under age five get in free.

Shopping

Both Nevada City and Grass Valley are chock-full of tiny boutiques, art galleries, and quirky gift stores. In Nevada City, most shopping is on Broad and Commercial Streets; in Grass Valley, head for Main and Mill Streets. Parking in either town can be a challenge and is mostly on the street, so be patient and check side streets for empty spaces.

If you've always dreamed of surrounding yourself in leather and fur, **Nevada City Fur Traders** (233 Broad St., Nevada City, 530/265-2000, www.furtraders.com, 10am-6pm daily) will satisfy that craving. From the fringed to the furry, Fur Traders definitely has something to catch your eye. Apparently, one store wasn't enough; there are three Fur Traders on Broad Street within a block of each other, and each store has slightly different merchandise.

At **Utopian Stone** (301 Broad St., Nevada City, 530/265-6209, www.utopianstone.com, 10am-5:30pm daily), the jewelers divide their work into two categories: one-of-a-kind pieces and everything else. The shop's master goldsmiths produce some of the most luminous fine jewelry you'll ever see—and if you don't see it, they'll build anything on commission. Some of the gold comes from nuggets found in the nearby Yuba River and quartz from Nevada County mines. Utopian Stone's superb gemstone carvings are also quite lovely.

For a unique gift for any occasion, stop by **Yuba Blue** (116 Mill St., Grass Valley, 530/273-9620, www.yubablueonline.com, 10am-6pm daily). Part boutique and part novelty shop, this store is a little pricey, but it has everything from exquisite jewelry and clothing to housewares and decorations.

Booktown Books (107 Bank St., Grass Valley, 530/272-4655, http://booktownbooks.com, 10am-6pm Mon.-Sat., 11am-5pm Sun.) is truly the mother lode for rare and used tomes. More co-op than store, 11 independent booksellers share the same open space. Every genre is represented, from science fiction to romance and comic book art. If you're pressed for time, grab a store directory at the front counter to find each bookseller; nothing separates them from each other, so the different sections blend together.

Sports and Recreation

In addition to its fabulous park and museum, the **Empire Mine State Historic Park** (10791 E. Empire St., Grass Valley, 530/273-8522, www.empiremine.org) doubles as an outdoor hiking park. With 800 acres of former mining lands and 14 miles of trails, this park offers both natural beauty and views of abandoned mines that are being overgrown as nature reestablishes dominance. The Hardrock Trails can run 1-3.5 miles, depending on how far you want to hike. Loop from the visitors center around to see the remains of the Pennsylvania, WYOD, and Orleans Mines before heading out to the Osborn Hill Loop or back to the parking lot. The Hardrock Trails and their offshoots are reasonably flat and easy to hike, but have some rocky stretches. Along the trail you'll see the remains of the major hard-rock mines that once produced gold. From the Hardrock Trails Area, you can head farther afield on the Osborn Hill Loop Trail to check out several more abandoned mines and their detritus. This loop runs about one mile and is a bit steeper and more challenging than the Hardrock Trails. The trails don't have restrooms.

Looking to cool off after traipsing through the foothills? Head to the **South Yuba River State Park** (17660 Pleasant Valley Rd., Penn Valley, 530/273-3884, sunrise-sunset daily, visitors center 11am-4pm Thurs.-Sun., free). This 20-mile stretch of the Yuba River winds all the way from Malakoff Diggins State Historic Park to the picturesque covered bridge at Bridgeport. There are plenty of Gold Rush ruins on the river, including an old mining camp and several sections of the Virginia Turnpike, a 14-mile-long toll road. A short nature walk leads through oak woodlands and wildflowers that include California poppies and purple lupine; during spring, the visitors center offers guided wildflower walks on weekends. Come on the last Sunday in April and October, when the park offers wagon rides and exhibits on pioneer life and the indigenous Maidu people that lived in the canyon before gold was discovered. In summer, explore a small gravel beach just a short hike east of the covered bridge and the nearby rocks, where more adventurous visitors can jump into the river. Parking is provided in a fenced lot ($5); street parking on Pleasant Valley Road is not allowed. The visitors center is open every day during summer.

One of the most beautiful hikes in South Yuba River State Park is the **Independence Trail** (Hwy. 49, 5.5 miles north of Nevada City, 10 miles round-trip, easy), which was used as an old mining flume during the Gold Rush era; it has since been converted into a flat stroll along the river canyon. The best time to visit is in spring, when live oaks cover the path in a lime-green canopy and wildflowers bloom. It's also the best time to spot California newts crawling on their orange bellies through puddles beside the trail. The trail is actually two separate hikes that both start from Highway 49; each is roughly five miles round-trip. The eastern section ends near a bucolic picnic area with a creek and plenty of shade. Parking is permitted in turnouts along the highway, so keep an eye on traffic.

Hike through the eerie but colorful canyon at **Malakoff Diggins State Historic Park** (Tyler Foote Rd., 26 miles north of Nevada City, 530/265-2740, www.parks.ca.gov, sunrise-sunset daily, $8 per vehicle), once the site of California's largest hydraulic mine. During the Gold Rush, miners blasted the hillsides with water to find gold buried deep in the ground, leaving behind strange land formations streaked with red and orange mineral deposits. The best way to explore the park is by hiking the **Diggins Loop Trail** (3 miles round-trip). This is also the easiest route if you have kids; several other more challenging hikes let you explore farther. The park includes the ghost town of **North Bloomfield,** which has several notable structures, including a one-room schoolhouse, an old cemetery, St. Columncille's Church, and a small museum. Malakoff Diggins is about 25 miles north of Nevada City, but it can take almost an hour to drive. To reach the park from Nevada City, take Highway 49 north for about 10 miles toward the small town of Downieville. Turn right onto Tyler-Foote Road and follow the road into the park.

Accommodations

Built in 1862, the **Holbrooke Hotel** (212 W. Main St., 530/273-1353, www.holbrooke.com, $75-239), in downtown Grass Valley, is one of the oldest lodgings in California. A host of famous 19th-century figures stayed here, including U.S. presidents Ulysses S. Grant and Grover Cleveland, writer Mark Twain, and entertainers Lotta Crabtree and Lola Montez. Expect updated amenities in all 28 rooms, which are fully stocked with modern conveniences like a private bath with antique claw-foot tub, cable TV, and free Wi-Fi; some rooms also have balconies or fireplaces.

For elegance in the land of gold, you can't beat the **Emma Nevada House** (528 E. Broad St., Nevada City, 530/265-4415, www.emmanevadahouse.com, $170-250). History permeates this large Victorian house, which once belonged to the family of noted opera singer Emma Nevada. You'll see real antiques in the front rooms and charming collectibles in the six uniquely styled rooms, all with comfortable beds and plush baths, some with claw-foot tubs. A multi-course gourmet breakfast is served each morning—come out early to get a seat in the sunroom, the best seat in the house. Prices are $30 cheaper if you forgo breakfast.

A short stroll from downtown Nevada City is the **Outside Inn** (575 E. Broad St., Nevada City, 530/265-2233, www.outsideinn.com, $85-165). Converted from a 1930s motel, each room has a different outdoor theme, including the Single Track Room and the romantic Creekside Hideaway cabin. A natural creek runs through the laid-back patio area, which includes a pool and a brick fire pit. The inn is pet-friendly; for kids, ask about the quirky scavenger hunt for lawn trolls hiding on the neatly tended hotel grounds.

Just minutes from downtown Grass Valley, the charming motel-style accommodations at **Sierra Mountain Inn** (816 W. Main St., Grass Valley, 530/273-8133, www.sierramountaininn.com, $110-185) offer a romantic and relaxing option to get away from it all. The rooms combine rustic decor with luxurious touches like marble baths and vaulted ceilings for a quirky farmhouse feel. Most rooms offer kitchenettes with mini fridges, sinks, and microwaves. The inn usually requires a two-night minimum, but single-night stays can be arranged over the phone. Dogs are at least $25 extra, depending on the room.

Food

Any trip to Grass Valley would be incomplete without visiting ★ **Cousin Jack Pasties** (100 S. Auburn St., Grass Valley, 530/272-9230, www.historichwy49.com, 10:30am-6pm Mon.-Sat., 11am-5pm Sun., $6). Open since 1989, this adorable café serves up delicious pasties, a hearty meat pie filled with piping-hot ingredients. Try the turkey pasty or one of the specials; the Greek pasties are amazingly good. You can also order traditional British fare like fish-and-chips and English tea.

Unpretentious and unassuming, the ★ **Flour Garden Café and Bakery** (999 Sutton Way, Grass Valley, 530/272-2043, www.flourgarden.com, 6am-6pm Mon.-Sat., 6am-5pm Sun., $5) serves homemade pastries, soups, sandwiches, and cakes to a mostly local crowd. This Gold Country mini chain uses local, natural ingredients. Order a flaky and delicious pastry plus an espresso drink or a cup of Fair Trade coffee. For lunch, pick up any number of prepared items, have a sandwich made, or order the fresh homemade soup of the day. There's often a line at

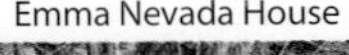
Emma Nevada House

mealtime. The Flour Garden has two other locations, in downtown Grass Valley (109 Neal St., Grass Valley) and Auburn (340C Elm Ave., Auburn).

The relaxed vibe at **Diego's Restaurant** (217 Colfax Ave., Grass Valley, 530/477-1460, http://diegosrestaurant.com, 11am-9pm daily, $14-21) will make you feel right at home. This eatery leans heavily to the local crowd and has an eclectic funky interior. The cuisine is Chilean with a California flair. Try the *panqueque especial,* a tasty mix of pineapple, chorizo, cheese sauce, and rice rolled in a crepe and slathered with tomatillo sauce. The menu has a few vegetarian options besides salads, like the stuffed portobello with tofu and quinoa, but most entrées are meat-heavy.

Call **Tofanelli's** (302 W. Main St., Grass Valley, 530/272-1468, www.tofanellis.com, 8am-9pm daily, $13-28) an "Italian-inspired" restaurant because it refuses to be pigeonholed. This place serves lamb shanks, different cuts of beef, seared ahi, meatloaf and, yes, lots of pasta dishes. The claim to fame is the omelet menu, which features 101 variations. Sit on the patio during busy hours, where it's a little quieter.

The last thing you might expect in Nevada City is high-quality sushi. But before opening **Sushi in the Raw** (315 Spring St., Nevada City, 530/478-9503, 5:30pm-9pm Tues.-Sat., $6-15) in 2002, owner Ru Suzuki already had a dedicated following as one of Gold Country's premier sushi chefs, and he's topped himself with this cozy authentic location. Start with the scallop shooters and then order Ru's white-truffled sashimi—your taste buds will swear they're in Tokyo. Call several days ahead for a reservation; the restaurant is small and very popular with locals.

Lefty's Grill (101 Broad St., Nevada City, 530/265-5838, www.leftysgrill.com, 11:30am-9:30pm daily, $15-28) has some of the best upscale bar food. The restaurant is located in a handsome brick building, a historical landmark that was once a bank. Inside, cheerful lighting and spotless white tablecloths give the restaurant a hip urban feel. For starters, order a side of sweet-potato fries slathered in apricot chipotle sauce. Leave room for the Napa pizza (named Best in the West at the International Pizza Expo).

Café Mekka (237 Commercial St., Nevada City, 530/478-1517, 8am-midnight daily, $5) is more than a coffee shop; it's an eye-opening coffee experience. Beverage concoctions such as the Café Borgia (mocha steamed with orange peel) and the Fairy Tea (steamed rice milk with white chocolate and cinnamon) are typical. Some of the amazing pastries are made locally.

South Pine Café (110 S. Pine St., Nevada City, 530/265-0260, http://southpinecafe.com, 8am-3pm daily, $8-12) is a homey little breakfast spot serving healthy grub made from local produce. Some dishes favor a Southwestern theme and others are more international. The Southwestern corn cakes come highly recommended. South Pine also boasts a fantastic lunch menu with a similar international theme as breakfast.

Information and Services

The major hospital with an emergency room is **Sierra Nevada Memorial Hospital** (155 Glasson Way, Grass Valley, 530/274-6000, www.snmh.org).

Transportation

Grass Valley and Nevada City are on Highway 49, north of I-80 and Auburn. To reach the area by car, take I-80 to Auburn and follow Highway 49 (Golden Chain Hwy.) northwest. Grass Valley is 25 miles from Auburn, and Nevada City is 4 miles farther north. Weekend traffic on I-80 between San Francisco and Tahoe can be quite congested, and the area can receive heavy snowfall in winter. Check on the weather, road conditions, and traffic reports with **Caltrans** (http://dot.ca.gov) before heading out.

The local **Nevada County Airport** (13083 John Bauer Ave., Grass Valley, 530/273-3374, www.nevadacountyairport.com) has no scheduled commercial flights. The closest airports served by the airlines are **Sacramento International Airport** (SMF, 6900 Airport Blvd., Sacramento, 916/929-5411, www.sacairports.org), 60 miles south, and **Reno-Tahoe International Airport** (RNO, 2001 E. Plumb Lane, Reno, NV, 775/328-6400, www.renoairport.com), about 90 miles east.

Car rentals are available with **Hertz** (10069 Joerschke Dr., Grass Valley, 530/272-7730) and **Enterprise** (470 Idaho-Maryland Rd., Grass Valley, 530/274-7400).

Gold Country Stage (www.mynevadacounty.com, adults $1.50, day pass $4.50, under age 5 free) runs buses and minibuses through Nevada City, Grass Valley, Auburn, and points north of the Gold Country.

AUBURN

Placer County Museum

Located on the first floor of the historical Placer County courthouse, the **Placer County Museum** (101 Maple St., 530/889-6500, www.placer.ca.gov, 10am-4pm daily, free) offers a glimpse into the town's rustic past. While small, the museum is a worthwhile stop before heading farther into the Gold Country to visit other historical sites. The exhibits span different themes and time periods in Placer County history, such as the women's jail, a recreated sheriff's office, and the stagecoach that ran from Auburn up into the mountains. Watch a video about the history of I-80, the transcontinental highway through Auburn, plus see different art pieces depicting the indigenous Maidu and Miwok people who lived in the Auburn area before the pioneers arrived. Outside the museum, views from the courthouse are photo worthy, and it's just a short walk to the restaurants and bars in Auburn's Old Town. A free guided tour of Old Town is offered every Saturday (rain or shine!) at 10am.

Gold Country Museum

Auburn was one of California's first mining settlements, built after gold was discovered in 1848. Learn more about the area's history at the newly restored railroad depot **Gold Country Museum** (601 Lincoln Way, 530/889-6500, www.placer.ca.gov, 10:30am-4pm Tues.-Sun., free). Many standard Gold Country exhibits are on display, including a reconstructed mine, a stamp mill, and a miner's tent. Kids can pan for gold in the museum's indoor stream ($3). You might be underwhelmed by the displays after visiting some of the region's larger historical sites, but the attentive docents are knowledgeable about Auburn's place in Gold Rush lore.

Sports and Recreation

Tucked inside the stunning American River canyon, **Auburn State Recreation Area** (www.parks.ca.gov, 7am-sunset daily, $10) should be a priority for outdoors enthusiasts. More than 100 miles of trails wind through leafy oak woodlands amid California poppies in spring and past seasonal waterfalls like Codfish Falls. The area is used by hikers, joggers, mountain bikers, dirt bikers, and horseback riders. Parking is easiest at the confluence of the American River's North and Middle Forks, and it's also where most of the trails begin. This area is arguably one of the best local places for water sports: rafting, kayaking, and boating are all available along various stretches of the river. Pack a swimsuit in summer and enjoy the cooling waters of the river confluence, which has plenty of swimming holes and jumping rocks. Keep your eyes peeled for wildlife; white-tailed deer, bald eagles, river otters, black bears, and even the occasional mountain lion roam the park.

History buffs will enjoy exploring the Gold Rush sights, such as the ancient railroad bridge spanning the lower Middle Fork. Farther upriver at **Upper Lake Clementine** (Apr. 15-Oct. 15), look for a jagged rock formation named Robber's Roost—local outlaws once used it for a hideout. The **Lower Clementine Trail** (10.5 miles, moderate) is an exhilarating way for mountain bikers to check out the canyon's scenery. Part of the trail plunges down an old stagecoach road, providing unrivaled views of the canyon. A word of caution: Beaches south of the Highway 49 bridge, about 0.5 mile downstream from the river confluence, are unofficially clothing optional. Parking in the area is limited, so arrive early in the summer to find a spot close to the confluence.

Hidden Falls Regional Park (7587 Mears Place, Auburn, 530/889-6808, www.placer.ca.gov, sunrise-sunset daily) has seven miles of easy to moderate trails that meander through blue oak woodlands to the bottom of a deep creek canyon. Once you reach the 30-foot falls, rest on the large wooden overlook clinging to the cliffside and watch the water plunge down a series of small drops into a glistening emerald pool. Just below the falls, a fork in the creek has decent-sized swimming holes. Walk farther upstream on Coon Creek for several places to fish. Many of the trails are open to horseback riders or cyclists; hikers just need to yield the trail if they happen upon equestrians in the park. To reach the park, take Grass Valley Highway to Atwood Road and head west for 1.7 miles. Atwood Road becomes Mt. Vernon Road. Continue going straight on Mt. Vernon for another 2.7 miles and turn right on Mears Road. Stay on Mears for 0.5 mile and take the first right. The turnoff for the park is another 1,000 feet down the road.

RAFTING

From Auburn, it's a 15- to 20-minute drive to either the Middle Fork or the North Fork of the mighty American River; the South Fork is about 30 minutes away. Most guided trips in the area are run by companies based near Placerville or in Calaveras County, and they usually meet just east of Auburn for river excursions. If guided tours aren't your thing, it's possible to rent rafts and kayaks from outfitters in Auburn sans guides, though it's best to steer clear of more dangerous Class IV-V rapids, especially on the North Fork, on your own. The season usually runs April-October, and outfitters can advise about the best spots to put in on the river.

If you'd rather hit the rapids without a guide, **Canyon Raft Rental** (133 Borland Ave., 530/823-0931, www.canyonraftrentals.com, rafts $42-250, kayaks $35-70) offers inflatable kayak and raft rentals. It's certainly much cheaper to go guideless, but this option is best for rafters with some experience. Canyon Raft has a shuttle service providing transport to the Middle Fork and back to Auburn, but make sure to reserve it beforehand; occasionally, you can arrange shuttle pickup on the North Fork. If you're not using the shuttle, it's easy to pack a raft into your trunk and inflate it at the river; air pumps are included with all rentals.

Accommodations

The **Best Western Golden Key** (13450 Lincoln Way, 530/885-8611, www.bestwesterngoldenkey.com, $78-150) has tidy and comfortable accommodations in a location perfect for exploring nearby Gold Country attractions. It has a hot tub and a heated outdoor pool that's enclosed during winter. Wi-Fi is included, and a hearty continental breakfast with hubcap-size waffles is another perk. The hotel is pet-friendly but charges an additional $15 per night.

The slightly more upscale **Auburn Holiday Inn** (120 Grass Valley Hwy., 530/887-8787, www.auburnhi.com, $139-179) has an outdoor pool and large, well-equipped rooms with flat-screen TVs and king beds. The hotel is comfortable without being lavish. The convenient location is less than a mile from the historical town center and offers a decent view of the courthouse. Amenities include free Wi-Fi, on-site laundry pickup, room service, and a fitness center. Pets are welcome for a $30 surcharge.

Food

Located inside a former Gold Rush saloon in Old Town Auburn, ★ **Carpe Vino** (1568 Lincoln Way, 530/823-0320, www.carpevinoauburn.com, 5pm-10pm Tues.-Sun., $10-31) feels like a place John Wayne might have enjoyed. The building dates to 1855, with restored rustic vaulted ceilings and aged brick walls. On the menu, you'll find only sustainably grown ingredients from local farms and vendors. The red-wine braised beef, Muscovy duck breast, and roasted Angus strip loin are all standout dishes. The gleaming mahogany bar is a replica of the original. Carpe Vino opens at noon Tuesday through Sunday for wine-tasting.

For delicious fast food with an Asian twist, head to **Ikeda's California Country Market** (13500 Lincoln Way, 530/885-4243, www.ikedas.com, 11am-7pm Mon.-Thurs., 10am-8pm Fri.-Sun., $10; fruit stand 8am-7pm Mon.-Thurs., 8am-8pm Fri.-Sun.). This roadside burger joint and fruit stand has become a de facto rest stop for travelers headed to Lake Tahoe. The food is a culinary mash-up of traditional diner fare and Japanese cuisine; menu options include everything from pot pies to teriyaki bacon burgers. The turkey burger—showered with secret spices—is delicious. Lunch and dinner hours can bring a crowd, so expect a short wait for your food.

Katrina's Cafe (456 Grass Valley Highway, 530/888-1166, www.katrinas-cafe.com, 7am-2:30pm Wed.-Sat., 7am-2pm Sun., $6-11) serves arguably the most delicious home-cooked breakfast in the Gold Country. Famous for their awesome pancakes and mouthwatering eggs Benedict, this place is legendary for whipping up belt-busting meals. Even though it's packed on weekends, the friendly staff always keep their cool. A secret item that's not on the menu is the delicious orange-oat flapjacks. Katrina's doesn't take credit cards.

Family-owned **Machado Orchards** (100 Apple Ln., 530/823-1393, 8am-7pm daily May-Dec., $16) has been selling fresh produce and baked goodies for several generations. Their small grocery store rarely has a crowd, even during harvest time, when the family cranks out the most delicious apple cider you'll ever drink. During summer, Machado's is an indoor produce stand selling fresh fruit and vegetables. Most of the produce is offered in dried snack packs, which make perfect treats for the road. But everything comes back to the pies—oozing with fresh fruit from the Machados' orchards. Look for the small white blimp soaring above the orchards. The store closes one hour earlier in autumn.

Auburn Alehouse Brewery and Restaurant (289 Washington St., 530/885-2537, http://auburnalehouse.com, 11am-9pm Mon.-Tues., 11am-10pm Wed.-Thurs., 11am-11pm Fri., 10am-11pm Sat., 10am-9pm Sun., $9-22) is a local microbrewery and bustling sports bar, where every pint is brewed in the gleaming silver tanks in the back. Try the beer sampler—for less than $15, you can sample every beer on tap. The cuisine is typical bar food, with burgers, sandwiches, and sides like sweet potato fries. During summer, live blues bands play on the back patio.

Information and Services

A great website for local visitor information is the **Placer County Visitors Bureau** (www.visitplacer.com). There's a **visitors center** (1103 High St., 530/887-2111, 9:30am-4:30pm Mon.-Sat., 11am-4pm Sun.) on High Street.

For medical assistance, **Sutter Auburn Faith Hospital** (11815 Education St., 530/888-4500, www.sutterauburnfaith.org)

offers an emergency room and a full range of hospital services.

Transportation

Auburn is located on I-80 and provides access to Highway 49 north and south. As such, it experiences heavy weekend traffic as well as snow in winter. Check weather, road conditions, and traffic reports online with **Caltrans** (http://dot.ca.gov) before traveling in winter.

The closest major airport is **Sacramento International Airport** (SMF, 6900 Airport Blvd., Sacramento, 916/929-5411, www.sacairports.org), 30 miles south. The local **Auburn Municipal Airport** (13626 New Airport Rd., 530/823-4211) has no scheduled commercial flights.

The **Amtrak** *Capitol Corridor* train (www.amtrak.com, 800/872-7245) departs several times a day on its way to Sacramento, Oakland, and San Jose at Auburn Station (277 Nevada St.), but there are no ticket services. The **Gold Country Stage** (www.mynevadacounty.com, adults $1.50, day pass $3, under age 5 free) runs buses and minibuses through Nevada City, Grass Valley, Auburn, and to points north of the Gold Country.

PLACERVILLE AND VICINITY

★ Marshall Gold Discovery State Historic Park

One day in 1848, a carpenter named James W. Marshall took a fateful stroll by the sawmill he was building for John Sutter on the American River and found gold specks shining in the water. Marshall's discovery sparked the California Gold Rush and one of the greatest migrations in history. See where it all began at **Marshall Gold Discovery State Historic Park** (310 Back St., Coloma, 530/622-3470, www.parks.ca.gov, 8am-7pm daily summer, 8am-5pm daily fall-spring, $8 per vehicle). Start inside the visitors center (10am-5pm daily Mar.-Nov., 10am-4pm daily Nov.-Mar.) for a quick lesson on the park's storied past, complete with artifacts from the indigenous Nisenan and Miwok people who lived in the area before the Gold Rush. Outside the visitors center, history buffs will love the park's interactive exhibits—catch a live pioneer cooking demonstration, or help load a real wagon with mining supplies like a true forty-niner.

Feel like recreating Marshall's discovery for yourself? Take a gold-panning lesson at the park's Eureka Experience Center, and then try your luck by the river. Kids will especially love getting elbow-deep in the mud for a chance to strike it rich. The park also provides nature walks and hikes through the scenic American River canyon; the **Gold Discovery Loop Trail** (3.6 miles) takes you to the very spot where Marshall made his discovery. Surrounded by beautiful wildflowers in spring, a full-size replica of **Sutter's Mill** stands near several immaculately restored historical buildings, like the tiny one-bedroom Mormon cabin, the Chinese-operated Wah Hop and Man Lee stores, the old blacksmith shop, and the Price-Thomas home. The park is undergoing renovations but is open during the construction.

Gold Bug Park

If you're traveling with kids and want them to experience a gold-mining museum, don't miss **Gold Bug Park** (Bedford Ave., 530/642-5207, www.goldbugpark.org, 10am-4pm daily Apr.-Oct., noon-4pm Sat.-Sun. Nov.-Mar., adults $6, youth $4, children $3). This smaller mine, originally called the Hattie, dates from the 1850s. Today the museum offers lessons in history, including tours of the mine, an interpretive museum, and a gift shop. For a small fee, you can pan for gold in a manufactured sluice. Many of the tour features and exhibits are designed for children, combining education and entertainment as kids don their hard hats, check out the mine shaft, and learn the function of a stamp mill.

★ Apple Hill

The farms of **Apple Hill** (Apple Hill Dr./Carson Rd., north of U.S. 50, between Placerville and Pollack Pines, 530/644-7692,

an orchard in Apple Hill

www.applehill.com), east of Placerville, produce many of the apples grown in California. You'll find dozens of family-owned orchards, vineyards, and Christmas tree farms clustered near the quaint community of Camino. For a scenic tour, download a map from the website or visit in person by taking exit 48 or 54 from U.S. 50 onto Apple Hill Drive (also known as Carson Road). Charming country roads and cute farm buildings fronted by orchards fill the landscape. At some orchards you can pick your own apples in season. At others you'll find a large shop stuffed with homemade pies frozen and ready to be baked, as well as preserves, cookbooks, and every type of apple product you can imagine. Come in the middle of summer to enjoy the raspberry, blackberry, and blueberry crops, and in summer-fall for the dozens of apples varieties grown in the region. Check the website for information about events and festivals that draw crowds out to Apple Hill, including country fair-style activities, arts and crafts shows, food and drink tastings, and more.

Wineries

CAMINO

The Apple Hill farms near Camino grow more than just Fujis and Granny Smiths. The region, just northeast of Placerville, is also home to vineyards and award-winning wineries.

Among the largest of the Apple Hill wineries is **Boeger Winery** (1709 Carson Rd., 800/655-2634, www.boegerwinery.com, 10am-5pm daily, free). Visit the elegant tasting room for a regular or reserve tasting of Boeger's best current-release wines. Better yet, bring a picnic to enjoy in the redwood grove. Boeger's specialties tend to be big hearty reds (the Barbera is quite possibly California's best), though you can taste the occasional delicate white wine here too.

At the opposite end of the spectrum, tiny **Fenton Herriott Vineyards** (120 Jacquier Court, 530/642-2021, www.fentonherriott.com, 11am-5pm daily, free) makes only a few hundred cases of wine each year. When visiting the little tasting room off the main drag, you'll get to try a small variety of tasty and reasonably priced red wines that you won't find in retail shops. The tasting staff knows a lot about the wines they're pouring and can tell you the story of each one.

Named for the distinctive tree that grows abundantly at higher elevations, **Madroña Vineyards** (2560 High Hill Rd., Camino, 530/644-5948, www.madronavineyards.com, 11am-5pm daily, free) is an old-school El Dorado County winery. The Bush family was among the first Apple Hill winemakers to produce Rhône and Bordeaux varietals, such as Barbera, Cabernet Franc, and a well-balanced Zinfandel with raspberry, black pepper, and spice—typical for the El Dorado varietal.

Wofford Acres Vineyards (1900 Hidden Valley Lane, Camino, 530/626-6858, www.wavwines.com, 11am-5pm daily, free), another red specialist, exemplifies the new era of small family wineries in California. Open since 2003, Wofford Acres is owned and operated by the Wofford family, and you're likely to run into one or more Woffords when you visit the small tasting room. Look for low-priced but high-flavored red table wines, red varietals, and possibly even a yummy dessert port to finish off your tasting experience.

FAIR PLAY

The Fair Play appellation is still fairly new, but this rugged area south of Placerville boasts some of the best vino in the Gold Country. Start by visiting **Fitzpatrick Winery & Lodge** (7740 Fairplay Rd., 800/245-9166, www.fitzpatrickwinery.com, 11am-5pm Thurs.-Sun., free), Fair Play's first winery, opened in 1980. Fitzpatrick focuses on "earth-friendly" wines, using organically grown grapes and producing wines in small lots to preserve the essence of the *terroir* where the grapes were grown. The wine is bottled in recycled glass with untreated cork, and then stored in a warehouse running almost entirely on solar energy on land maintained with tractors running 90 percent vegetable oil. The lengthy wine list features some California classics in the way of zinfandels, chardonnays, and merlots. To get into this winery properly, try some of the less common vintages, which can range from Irish-themed white and red blended wines to a surprisingly complete array of ports in both red and white. The estate also operates a bed-and-breakfast inn. Stay for the Ploughman's Lunch (noon-4pm or until sold out Sat.-Sun.), hearty hot fare that will set you up for an afternoon of tasting elsewhere in Fair Play and the northern Gold Country.

Charles B. Mitchell Vineyards (8221 Stoney Creek Rd., 530/620-3467, http://charlesbmitchell.com, 11am-5pm Thurs.-Sun., free) is one of the more recognizable names in the Fair Play American Viticultural Area. In the tasting room, you'll get a chance to try a wide variety of wines, including sparkling, white, Amador County-grown reds, and lush dessert ports. You can take a tour of the winery as well, but for a special treat, book ahead to bottle your own wine.

The winemakers at **Skinner Vineyards** (8054 Fairplay Rd., 530/620-2220, www.skinnervineyards.com, 11am-5pm Thurs.-Mon., $10) have deep roots in Fair Play. Their ancestor, a Scottish immigrant named James Skinner, planted one of the area's first vineyards in 1860. Those family roots inspired the current generation of Skinner winemakers to produce well-balanced Rhône varietals with complex aromas, including Syrah, Mourvèdre, and Grenache.

The reds at **Miraflores** (2120 Four Springs Trail, Placerville, 530/647-8505, www.mirafloreswinery.com, 10am-5pm daily, free) have quite the reputation; *Wine Spectator* has consistently scored the zinfandel over 90 points. They produce muscular, focused reds from small lots of syrah and petite syrah. Whites include viognier and pinot grigio, both typical for the Fair Play terroir.

Entertainment and Events

For something in the old-school biker-bar department, try **PJ's Roadhouse** (5641 Mother Lode Dr., Placerville, 530/626-0336, 11am-2am Mon.-Sat., 9am-2am Sun.). Off the main drag, PJ's features cheap beer and shots, a small dance floor, and the occasional DJ or live band designed to drag drinkers off their barstools. Expect lots of Harleys out front, precious little light inside, and perhaps a whiff of marijuana emanating from the back porch.

A stuffed buffalo looks down from the wall as you walk into **Buford's** (835 Lotus Rd., Coloma, 530/626-8096, www.sierranevadahouse.com, 4pm-2am Thurs.-Mon.), the bar at Sierra Nevada House. Remodeled to resemble an Old West saloon, the gleaming wooden interior and immaculate bar give Buford's an upscale vibe. Still, it's a lively place to spend an evening after a day on the river, especially if you're staying in the adjoining hotel. The bar offers an extensive list of local wines and beer along with reasonably priced cocktails. Coloma's nightlife isn't exactly hopping, so Buford's is probably your best bet for evening fun. The bar closes earlier on slow nights.

Shopping

Good retail opportunities abound on

Main Street in **Old Hangtown** (central Placerville). The main shopping blocks run from Center Street to Cedar Ravine Road and are easily walkable. Placerville is a great place to look for antiques and vintage collectibles. Several antiques shops are clustered on Main Street—start at **Empire Antiques** (432 Main St., Placerville, 530/642-1025, 10am-5pm daily) or **Placerville Antiques and Collectibles** (448 Main St., 530/626-3425, 10am-6pm daily).

Placerville has a smattering of art galleries that appeal to a variety of shoppers. **Volution Gallery** (434 Main St., 530/748-7675, www.volutiongallery.com, 11am-6pm Sun.-Thurs., 11am-8pm Fri.-Sat.) displays surrealist art with distinct flashes of pop culture and fantasy influences. Only local artists show and sell their work at the **Gold Country Artist's Gallery** (379 Main St., Placerville, 530/642-2944, www.goldcountryartistsgallery.com, 10am-5pm daily).

The bookstores of Placerville are unique to the town; make sure to stop by **The Bookery** (326 Main St., 530/626-6454, 10am-5:30pm Mon.-Thurs., 10am-7pm Fri.-Sat., 10am-4pm Sun.) if you need a new read.

You won't find any big chain clothing stores in the Gold Country. Instead, shop in cute one-of-a-kind boutiques like **Lighthouse** (451 Main St., Suite 1, 530/626-5515, 9am-6pm Sat.-Thurs., 9am-9pm Fri.), **Treehouse** (327 Main St., 530/295-0102, 10am-6pm Mon.-Sat., 11am-5pm Sun.), or **Winterhill** (321 Main St., 530/626-6369, www.winterhillfarms.com, 10am-6pm Mon.-Sat., 11am-5pm Sun.).

Head to **CandyStrike: Old Tyme Candy & More** (398 Main St., 530/295-1007, www.candystrike.com, 11am-5pm Mon.-Thurs., 11am-7pm Fri., 10am-7pm Sat., 10am-5pm Sun.) for goodies like black licorice, saltwater taffy, and fudge. For something heartier, get some great cheese and artisanal bread from **Dedrick's Main Street Cheese** (312 Main St., 530/344-8282, www.dedrickscheese.com, 10am-6pm Mon.-Fri., 9am-6pm Sat., 11am-6pm Sun.).

Sports and Recreation

★ RAFTING THE AMERICAN RIVER

For guided river trips, Placerville is the whitewater capital of the Gold Country. From here, outfitters can take you to all three forks of the American River, including the rugged Class IV-V rapids of the North Fork and the more moderate Class III-IV white water of the Middle Fork. Rafting trips are designed for all experience levels, and you can even book overnight excursions; if you're a rookie rafter, try a more leisurely half-day trip down the lower section of the South Fork. The season usually runs April-October, except for trips on the North Fork, which usually run April-May or June, depending on weather and water levels. Check online for specific dates.

All-Outdoors Whitewater Rafting (925/932-8993, www.aorafting.com, $100-495) offers half-day, full-day, and multiday trips on the North, Middle, and South Forks of the American River. If you have time, take a two- to three-day jaunt and camp deep in the stunningly beautiful river canyons. Guides prepare all your meals, and it's an excellent way to experience a different side of the Gold Country. You can also book full-day trips on any of the three forks if a multiday expedition isn't feasible. If you have small kids or just want to calmly drift down the river, consider the full-day Tom Sawyer Float Trips along the rapids-free section of the South Fork.

Beyond Limits Adventures (530/622-0553, www.rivertrip.com, $100-300) offers mostly half-day and one-day excursions to the North, Middle, and South Forks; you can also take two-day trips on the South Fork with complimentary wine and beer served at dinner. Two-day trips also include a stop at a riverside resort where you can fish, play basketball, and try your hand at panning gold.

American Whitewater Expeditions (800/825-3205, www.americanwhitewater.com, $50-288) offers half-day, full-day, and multiday trips to all three forks of the American River. All expeditions come with delicious meals, friendly guides, and jaw-dropping Sierra Nevada scenery.

O.A.R.S. (800/346-6277, www.oars.com, $110-320) offers trips to all three forks of the American River. They are one of the most experienced rafting companies in the West, and the guides are extremely knowledgeable. O.A.R.S. offers full-day trips with a picnic on the Middle and North Forks; you can also take half-day, full-day, and two-day trips on the South Fork with meals included. Or enjoy a two-day wine-and-raft tour that includes side trips to several El Dorado County wineries.

Whitewater Connection (530/622-6446, www.whitewaterconnection.com, $95-421) offers the standard full-day trips to the North, Middle, and South Forks, along with multiday expeditions. You can also book half-day trips on the South Fork if time is an issue. Whitewater Connection also offers two-day trips combining one day on the North Fork with another day on either the Middle or South Fork.

Accommodations

PLACERVILLE

More safari resort than bed-and-breakfast, the renovated hay barn of **Eden Vale Inn** (1780 Springvale Rd., 530/621-0901, http://edenvale-inn.com, $170-400) combines a rustic foothill vibe with Napa-style luxury. Inside are seven rooms, each named after native California trees, with gas fireplaces and lavish amenities. Five rooms have private hot tubs and enclosed patios. If that's not decadent enough, book a relaxing massage or a facial at the on-site spa. Don't miss the homemade breakfast buffet made from locally grown ingredients and herbs from the inn's garden. The inn is only a 10-minute drive from Coloma.

The 1857 **Historic Cary House Hotel** (300 Main St., 530/622-4271, www.caryhouse.com, $109-169) is an imposing brick building in downtown Placerville. The rooms are small but bristle with character, with period antiques and old tintype photographs on the walls. From the elaborately decorated lobby, complete with wooden paneling and plush furniture, a 1920s-style elevator lifts visitors to the rooms. Amenities include Wi-Fi, continental breakfast, and cable TV. Guests frequently report ghost sightings and other strange activity—the second floor is supposedly the most haunted. Live bands play most weekends, so noise may be a factor.

Step back into the Gilded Age at the **Albert Shafsky House** (2942 Coloma St., 530/642-2776, www.shafsky.com, $135-185), a cozy Victorian bed-and-breakfast built in 1902. Each room boasts luxurious antiques from the late 19th century. The mouthwatering breakfasts are fixed with local gourmet ingredients. Guests are treated to a complimentary bottle of El Dorado wine and an artisanal cheese plate. The house was originally built for a wealthy Placerville man whose friendly ghost supposedly still haunts the rooms. The Shafsky House has only three rooms, so call well ahead to reserve.

The **Mother Lode Motel** (1940 Broadway, 530/622-0895, www.placervillemotherlode-motel.com, $60-80) has clean and reasonably priced accommodations halfway between Placerville and Apple Hill. Don't be discouraged by the motel's cheap-looking sign; inside, the rooms are comfortable and tastefully decorated. You'll find modern amenities like included Wi-Fi, microwaves, mini fridges, and private hot tubs, as well as a decent-size pool and lounge area that offers relief during the sweltering foothill summers.

COLOMA

The **Sierra Nevada House** (835 Lotus Rd., 530/626-8096, www.sierranevadahouse.com, $130-150) is just a stone's throw from the South Fork of the American River and offers charming and romantic accommodations. The six rooms each have a different Gold Rush theme. This roadside inn is actually more of a couples' retreat—families with children might do better to stay elsewhere. The hotel is right on Highway 49 and can be somewhat noisy, and the Bordello Room is right above the bar. The location is convenient to the area's historical and recreational attractions, and the room rates are quite reasonable for the area.

For casual accommodations, camp at the

American River Resort (6019 New River Rd., 530/622-6700, http://americanriverresort.com, cabins $160-280, campsites $35-55, RV hookup sites $45). The resort is located on the South Fork of the American River and gives visitors the chance to feel closer to nature. Restrooms and showers are available near all 85 campsites (35 spots have RV hookups), along with a swimming pool. The riverside cabins have kitchens fully stocked with appliances and utensils, though bed linens are not provided.

FAIR PLAY

For an up-to-date bed-and-breakfast experience plus great access to a fabulous wine region, book a room at **Lucinda's Country Inn** (6701 Perry Creek Rd., 530/409-4169, www.lucindascountryinn.com, $180-230). Each of the five rooms welcomes visitors with the style of a luxury hotel. You'll find classy understated decor, a fireplace, a fridge, a microwave, a coffeemaker, plush robes to relax in, and a two-person spa tub in some rooms. Outside the inn is the Fair Play wine region, and not too far away is the Shenandoah Valley.

The **Fitzpatrick Winery and Lodge** (7740 Fairplay Rd., Somerset, 530/620-3248, www.fitzpatrickwinery.com, $170-350) takes its Irish roots seriously—down to the green eggs and ham served at breakfast. Two of the five rooms feature Celtic-themed decor with patterned cushions and Fitzpatrick family photos, and most rooms include a claw-foot tub and a woodstove. The log-cabin theme continues inside the Great Room, which has a vaulted log ceiling and plush sofa set before a fireplace. Breakfast is homemade with local ingredients. Take a dip in the Olympic-length lap pool or ease into the lodge's hot tub for a relaxing soak.

Food

PLACERVILLE

The Shoestring (1320 Broadway, 530/622-7125, 11am-8pm daily summer, 11am-7pm daily fall, 11am-6pm daily winter, $10) is a roadside hole-in-the-wall serving burgers, hot dogs, and chili cheese fries. It also has a small children's menu, but most of the food is already kid friendly. The restaurant is conveniently located near the northern tip of downtown Placerville, making it easy to swing by on the way to Apple Hill. The Shoestring doesn't have restrooms.

★ **The Heyday Café** (325 Main St., 530/626-9700, www.heydaycafe.com, 11am-3pm Mon., 11am-9pm Tues.-Thurs., 11am-10pm Fri.-Sat., 11am-8pm Sun., $12-26) has gained a reputation as one of the best eateries in Placerville. The stripped-brick interior and rough-hewn wooden ceiling gives the café a rugged yet hip vibe. The California bistro-style food is fused with Asian, Italian, and Mediterranean influences. Try the bacon-artichoke-pesto pizza or the lemon salsa skewers; pair with a crisp riesling from Apple Hill to sample the extensive wine list.

For upscale Mexican food in the heart of Gold Country, grab a table at **Cascada** (384 Main St., 530/344-7757, 11am-8pm Sun.-Thurs., 11am-9pm Fri.-Sat., $12-18). In downtown Placerville, Cascada is Mexican with a California-bistro twist. You'll find familiar Mexican favorites like burritos, tacos, and enchiladas. If you're feeling adventurous, try the pork medallions with raspberry chipotle sauce. Since the restaurant is elegant-casual, you might want to freshen up before arriving, and reservations are a good idea.

COLOMA

The ★ **Café Mahjaic** (1006 Lotus Rd., 530/622-9587, www.cafemahjaic.com, 5pm-8pm Wed.-Sun., $17-26), housed inside a historical brick building, offers fine dining near the banks of the American River. The New American fare, made with natural and organic ingredients, includes subtle Mediterranean touches—the Hillbilly salad is a delicious twist on a traditional Greek favorite, and the grilled flatbread with *tzatziki* sauce and hummus is wonderful. The white tablecloths and cosmopolitan interior will make you want to spiff up before dinner. The last reservation is

Apple Hill Eateries

There's plenty of good healthy food to be had in the Apple Hill region. But what if you need more than a nice fresh apple to keep hunger away? Stop at one of the orchard-based restaurants along the meandering trails, where the food ranges from sandwiches to hot handmade apple pies. The area maps available at almost every orchard point out which establishments offer a restaurant.

For a fresh slice of pie, some of the best is sold at the **Apple Pantry Farm** (2310 Hidden Valley Lane, Camino, 530/318-2834, www.applepantryfarm.com, 9am-4pm Thurs.-Sun. Sept.-Nov., pies $16-18). The farm's attractive small store sells apples and an array of frozen uncooked pies ready to be baked in your home oven. To the right of the main store, a small trailer exudes aromas that draw visitors as if by magic. You can buy just a slice or a whole apple, apple-blackberry, or other seasonal fruit pie. Every from-scratch Apple Pantry pie is sold hot out of the industrial ovens in the trailer. The frozen ready-bake pies in the shop are made by the same team. The farm also sells other goodies like turnovers, crisps, and apple butter.

For more filling grub, try the **Forester Pub and Grill** (4110 Carson Rd., Camino, www.foresterpubandgrill.com, 530/644-1818, 11:30am-9pm daily, $8-19). This English-style pub serves German-themed food like stroganoff and schnitzel, along with good ol' American comfort food such as meatloaf. Sides include red cabbage kraut and spätzle, which is a pile of pea-sized dumplings with gravy. **Apple Blossom Coffee House** (4077 Carson Rd., 530/644-0284, http://appleblossomcoffeehouse.com, 7am-2pm Mon.-Sat., $2-10) serves espresso and pastries for breakfast. At lunch, power up for a busy day of hayrides and pumpkin patches with an order of soup, salad, or one of this joint's famous empanadas.

Once you've picked out pumpkins, scarfed some pie, and braved Apple Hill's crowds, head to **Jack Russell Brewery** (2380 Larsen Dr., Camino, 530/647-9420, 11am-6pm Mon.-Thurs., 11am-7pm Fri., 10am-6pm Sat.-Sun.) for a pint of English-style beer. Located behind an apple orchard, Jack Russell has handicraft vendors and live music on weekends. But the best things about this place are the beer and the cider. The sampler comes with taster cups filled with every Jack Russell brew. The brewery sometimes stays open right up until sunset during the summer.

at 8pm; make sure to reserve a table, as this restaurant is very popular.

You can't go wrong at the **Sierra Nevada House** (835 Lotus Rd., 530/626-8096, www.sierranevadahouse.com, 5pm-8pm Thurs. and Sun., 5pm-9pm Fri.-Sat., $19-34). The mostly steak house cuisine is surprisingly good. The menu has plenty of vegetarian options. Try the wild mushroom ravioli, the stuffed acorn squash, or the baby back ribs rubbed in garlic and rosemary.

The ★ **Argonaut** (331 Hwy. 49, 530/626-7345, http://argonautcafe.com, 8am-4pm daily, $8) is a tiny shack steps from where James Marshall discovered gold in 1848. The food—homemade sandwiches, soups, chili, and pie made nearby in Apple Hill—is reasonably priced. Grab a picnic table behind the Argonaut, or just sit at one of the small tables on the patio with views of the South Fork of the American River. The Argonaut is conveniently located across Highway 49 from the visitors center at the Marshall Gold Discovery State Park.

FAIR PLAY

From the outside, the **Gold Vine Grill** (6028 Grizzly Flat Rd., 530/626-4042, www.goldvinegrill.com, 5pm-9pm Wed.-Thurs., 11am-3pm, 5pm-9pm Fri.-Sun., $17-24) looks like a run-of-the-mill roadside café. Inside, the gleaming wooden tables and exquisite artwork give this restaurant a stylish feel. The mostly California cuisine—blackened salmon with Cajun cream sauce, pork chops with jalapeño and honey, and macadamia-crusted mahimahi—is mouthwateringly good. And if you're staying at any of Fair Play's bed-and-breakfasts, there's no need to drive into Placerville for dinner.

For a quick espresso or a sandwich, stop by

Crossroads Coffee and Cafe (6032 Grizzly Flat Rd., 530/344-0591, 7am-3pm daily, $9), serving breakfast and lunch along with excellent espresso drinks. Choose from about 20 different sandwiches on the menu; almost all of the sandwiches include meat, so vegetarians will have to stick to salads.

Information and Services

For medical assistance, **Marshall Hospital** (1100 Marshall Way, 530/622-1441, www.marshallmedical.org) offers an emergency room and a full range of hospital services in Placerville.

If you're low on fuel and deep in the countryside, **Riverside Mini Mart** (7215 Hwy. 49, Lotus, 530/642-9715) provides gas for travelers in Coloma, but **Gray's Mart** (6711 Mount Aukum Rd., Melsons Corners, 530/620-5510) is the place to stop near Fair Play.

Transportation

Placerville is 45 miles east of Sacramento at the intersection of U.S. 50 and Highway 49. Stoplights on U.S. 50 can cause traffic to back up on weekends; winter snows can close the roads in the winter. To reach Apple Hill, take U.S. 50 two exits east of Placerville. Coloma is almost nine miles north of Placerville on Highway 49; the Marshall Gold Discovery State Historic Park is the easiest landmark. It snows in Coloma November-April, and sometimes even into May, so check road conditions with Caltrans (http://dot.ca.gov) before driving.

Fair Play is up in the Sierra foothills well off Highway 49. Have a full tank of gas before you take the winding country roads into this mountainous area. To reach Fair Play from Placerville, take Highway 49 south to Pleasant Valley Road. Follow Pleasant Valley Road east for about 10 miles to Pleasant Valley, and then head south on County Road 16 (Plymouth-Shenandoah Rd.). County Road 16 winds almost 30 miles up to Omo Ranch Road; turn east and then left onto Fair Play Road.

Shenandoah Valley

The best-known wine region in the Gold Country is the Shenandoah Valley. Dozens of wineries are near the towns of Plymouth, Amador City, Sutter Creek, Jackson, and even tiny Volcano, and most use locally grown grapes that show the best of what the Sierra foothills can produce.

PLYMOUTH

Amador Flower Farm

Nearly 1,000 different kinds of daylilies grow at the **Amador Flower Farm** (22001 Shenandoah School Rd., 209/245-6660, www.amadorflowerfarm.com, 9am-4pm daily Mar.-Nov., 9am-4pm Thurs.-Sun. Dec.-Feb.). Take a serene and colorful walk through the eight acres of farmland and four acres of demonstration gardens, flowers, and perennials. If you brought a picnic, enjoy it in the gardens shaded by heritage oak trees. In the gift shop, get a single lily for your sweetheart, or pick up a bundle of bulbs to take home.

Shenandoah Valley Museum

If you're a history buff with a few extra minutes on your hands, you can find a wealth of 15-minute museums in northern Gold Country. In these tiny galleries, learn about little-explored aspects of California pioneer life. The **Shenandoah Valley Museum** (14430 Shenandoah Rd., 209/245-6554, www.sobonwine.com, 10am-5:30pm daily, free) describes the winemaking process that began in Gold Country almost as soon as the first miners arrived. It's part of the Sobon Estate—a winery that has been in continuous operation in the Shenandoah Valley since 1856.

Wineries

Arguably the best of the small-medium

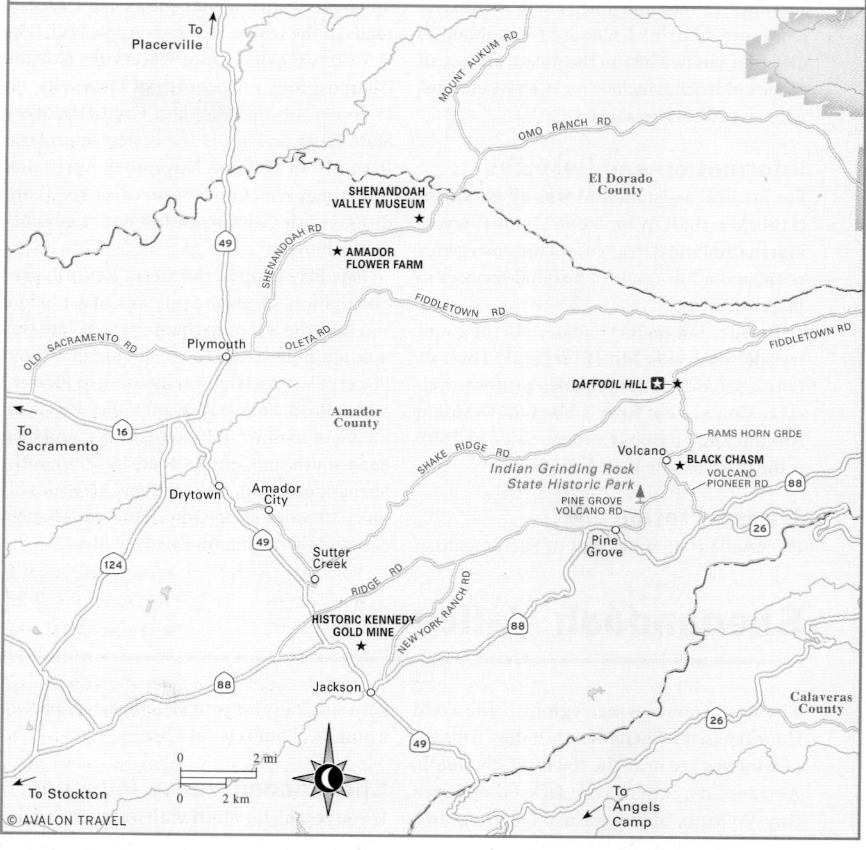

Shenandoah wineries is **Story Winery** (10525 Bell Rd., 800/713-6390, www.zin.com, noon-4pm Mon.-Thurs., 11am-5pm Fri.-Sun. winter, 11am-5pm daily summer, free), where you can taste the true history of Amador County wines. Some of the Story vineyards have been around for nearly 100 years and still produce grapes for wines made today. The specialty of the house is zinfandel—check out the amazing selection of old-vine single-vineyard zins. Tastings takes place in a charming, casual environment where you'll feel at home even if you're new to high-end wine. Walk outside to admire the estate vineyards ranging down the hills.

With only the barest of nods to California favorite varietals, the friendly folks at **Bray Vineyards** (10590 Shenandoah Rd., 209/245-6023, www.brayvineyards.com, 10am-5pm Wed.-Mon., $5) go their own way, pouring wines made from grapes even savvy wine lovers won't find familiar. Taste a wine made from verdelho, tempranillo, alicante bouschet, or an intriguing blend of Portuguese grapes. To get a feel for what Bray does, go outside the tasting room and into the vineyards; Bray grows its own grapes, plus olives for estate olive oil, and has a number of native oak trees.

One of the biggest names in the Shenandoah Valley, **Montevina** (20680 Shenandoah School Rd., 209/245-6942, www.montevina.com, 10am-4:30pm daily, free) prides itself on its zinfandels, boasting that it makes "the best in the world." That's a bold claim in Amador County, which is the zinfandel heartland, but Montevina doesn't box itself in—you can taste white wines, light red wines, medium red wines, blends, and more at this fun tasting room. Check out something from each of the three labels: the standard Montevina, reserve Terra d'Oro, and the fun, inexpensive Wild Bunch blends.

For a small winery experience, stop by the charming barn at **Deaver Vineyards** (12455 Steiner Rd., 290/245-4099, www.deavervineyard.com, 10:30am-5pm daily, $5). Deaver produces a couple of white and rosé wines and some flavored sparklers, but reds are unquestionably the mainstay. At the tasting bar you can sip a range of intense layered zins and syrahs or get bold with a carignan or a barbera. Even if you're not a wine fan, you can't help but be charmed by the farm-style atmosphere, complete with decrepit outbuildings and sweeping green fields.

Wilderotter Vineyard (19890 Shenandoah School Rd., 209/245-6016, www.wilderottervineyard.com, 10:30am-5pm daily, $5) started as a vineyard that sold all its grapes to various winemakers and only transformed into a winery in 2002. The production is limited both in quantity and in scope. Zinfandel, grenache, viognier, and barbera are what's planted in the vineyards, so that's what's available in the bottles.

Accommodations

The ★ **Amador Harvest Inn** (12455 Steiner Rd., 800/217-2304, www.amadorharvestinn.com, $164-186) brings a bit of uptown Napa to the Shenandoah Valley while retaining the down-home feel of Amador County. The exterior of the inn is unpretentious—a simple farmhouse set on a green lawn surrounded by trees and water. Inside you'll find four rooms named after wine grapes, each decorated in a charming country style. The dining room continues the farmhouse charm, with kitchen-style tables and chairs and a home-cooked breakfast each morning. The Amador Harvest Inn makes a perfect base from which to explore the Shenandoah Valley wine country.

The romantic **Plymouth House Inn** (9525 Main St., 209/245-3298, www.plymouthhouseinn.com, $115-180) blends Amador wine culture with a dash of Gold Rush past. Underneath the building is an old mineshaft where gold was discovered in the late 1800s. The seven Victorian-style rooms feature quaint wood stoves, handmade antique furniture, quilted linens, and air-conditioning. The inn has a full breakfast in the morning, a complimentary wine hour, and plenty of country charm in the plush but understated common room. The ambience is perfect for couples, but less so for families.

For a Californian experience, book a cabin at **Rancho Cicada Retreat** (10001 Bell Rd, 209/245-4841, www.ranchocicadaretreat.com, $85-159) in the backwoods of the foothills. The retreat offers both tent cabins and wood-sided cabins, most of which share gender-divided restrooms. The main attraction, the Cosumnes River, runs along the tent cabins. Visitors can swim, inner-tube, and fish in the river. Or visit the riverside hot tubs, perhaps after a trip to the Mi-Wok sweat lodge. Rancho Cicada offers primitive lodgings—bring your own sleeping bags or bedding, pillows, towels, and food to cook, plus ice chests for drinks.

For casual accommodations at the right price, consider the **49er Village** (18265 Hwy. 49, 800/339-6981, www.49ervillage.com, cottages $130-210, RV sites $58-80). Primarily an asphalt-covered RV park, the 49er Village also rents studio and one-bedroom vacation cabins at reasonable rates. Cottages include private baths, private decks, full kitchens with utensils, and full access to the park's pools and amenities. One-bedroom cottages sleep 5-6 people; studio cottages can comfortably fit two people. Pets are allowed with a $100 deposit.

Food

Set in a modest building off Plymouth's main drag, ★ **Taste Restaurant** (9402 Main St., 209/245-3463, http://restauranttaste.com, 5pm-9pm Mon. and Thurs.-Fri., 11:30am-2pm, 4:30pm-9pm Sat.-Sun., $21-44) has an upscale vibe. Chef Mark Berkner's menu is stocked with gourmet food made from seasonal healthy ingredients, and the entrées are meat-heavy fare done to perfection. The wine list is a balanced selection of Amador wines and California varietals with some international labels thrown in. If you're vegan or have gluten sensitivities, make sure to call ahead and the restaurant will create a special menu.

The **Amador Vintage Market** (9393 Main St., 209/245-3663, www.amadorvintagemarket.com, 10am-6pm Wed.-Sun., $8) whips up gourmet sandwiches and take-out cuisine in this downtown Plymouth eatery. For lunch, try the Miner's Reuben with pastrami and pepper-jack cheese on grilled focaccia. Locals recommend the half-pound balsamic pork tenderloin along with the potato of the day.

If you're craving burgers, pop into **Marlene and Glen's Diner** (18726 Hwy. 49, 209/245-5778, 7am-2:30pm Wed.-Sun., $4-14). This quirky roadside stop has polished chrome and red leather seats at the counter, homey curios on the wall, and heaping portions of American diner food. For breakfast choose from nine different eggs Benedict, including the steak Benedict with Cajun hollandaise sauce. The menu has plenty of greasy but tasty lunch choices—the Kelly Blue Cheese Burger is a standout. The service can slow down considerably on weekends.

Information and Services

Plymouth is a small town without many of the services found in larger cities, so the best place for news and events is online (http://plymouthcalifornia.com). If you're planning to visit local wineries, a good place to start is the **Amador Vintner's Association visitor center** (9310 Pacific St., 209/245-6992, 10am-2pm Mon.-Fri., 10:30am-2:30pm Sat.-Sun.) to pick up brochures and directions. The **Amador 360 Wine Collective** (18590 Hwy. 49, 209/245-6600, www.amador360.com, 11am-6pm daily) offers tasting and advice about smaller boutique wineries that can be hard to find.

Plymouth has few bank branches, but you can find an ATM at the **El Dorado Savings Bank** (18726 Hwy. 49, 209/245-3000, www.eldoradosavingsbank.com, 9am-5pm Mon.-Thurs., 9am-6pm Fri.). To fill up your tank before heading into the wine country, go to Shell **gas station** (17699 Village Dr., 209/245-4026) just south of town on Highway 49.

Transportation

Plymouth is just off Highway 49, north of Jackson and Sutter Creek. If you're driving from the north, follow Highway 49 south from Placerville for about 20 miles. From Sacramento, take Highway 16 southeast to Highway 49 and then head northeast. These highways are all two-lane roads and can become packed on weekends, so adjust your travel time accordingly.

Amador Transit (209/267-9395, http://amadortransit.com, $2) runs buses between Plymouth and Sutter Creek, where you can catch connections to Jackson and other towns in the region.

SUTTER CREEK

Monteverde Store Museum

Miners, their wives, and everybody else who came to live in the bustling boomtowns of Gold Country needed supplies: food, cloth, tools, and medicines. In 19th-century California, many of those supplies were sold at the general store. The **Monteverde Store Museum** (11A Randolph St., 209/267-1344, www.suttercreek.org, by appointment) sold staples to Sutter Creek residents for 75 years. After its last shopkeepers, Mary and Rose Monteverde, died, the city took over the building. The sisters had stipulated that it was to become a museum, and so it is—a look into the hub of town life in the 19th century.

Shopping

To shop Sutter Creek, simply take a stroll down historic **Main Street.** You'll find cluttered antiques shops filled with treasures great and small. For something fun to spruce up the house, walk into **Water Street Antiques** (33 C Main St., 209/267-0585, www.waterstreetantiques.com, 10am-4pm Mon. and Wed.-Fri., 10am-5pm Sat., 11am-5pm Sun.). Peruse imported furniture, housewares, and hundreds of decorative items.

At **Chaos Glassworks** (121 A Hanford St., 209/267-9317, www.chaosglassworks.com, 11am-5pm Wed.-Fri., 10am-7pm Sat., 10am-6pm Sun.), you can purchase handmade works of glass art and watch the glassblower create new pieces before your very eyes.

Accommodations

With the ethos of a classic B&B and the fun touches of a hostel, the perfect mix is at **Hanford House** (61 Hanford St., 209/267-0747, www.hanfordhouse.com, $135-295), a brick manor house with nine rooms, each decorated in a floral country style with unique furnishings and textiles. Beds are large and comfy, and baths squeak with cleanliness and feel like home. Enjoy the hearty breakfast and pass the morning reading the walls and ceiling of the inn. Guests have signed and commented on the plain white walls over the years. They're almost full now, so you'll have to hunt for a bare spot to add your own.

The **Imperial Hotel** (14202 Hwy. 49, Amador City, 209/267-9172, www.imperialamador.com, $105-195) shows off the brick facade and narrow-column architecture of a classic Old West hotel. You'll get a true mining town hotel experience in one of six rooms on the second floor, or in one of three rooms in the cottage out back, which include private baths and are done in a simple antique style. Each room is a haven of peace and quiet, without a TV or phone. You can take all your meals downstairs, including the full hot breakfast that's included in the room rate. Dinner is a special time, featuring gourmet California cuisine made with local organic produce, natural meats, and sustainable seafood.

Food

Pizza Plus (20 Eureka St., Sutter Creek, 209/267-1900, 11am-9pm daily, $16) serves the best pies in Amador in one of the best

downtown Sutter Creek

settings. The pizza is great, but the cheese-covered breadsticks are just as famous. Vegetarians will be pleasantly surprised by the small mountain of tomatoes, olives, yellow onions, mushrooms, artichoke hearts, and green bell peppers on the veggie pizza. There are no big-screen TVs on the walls. An old Wells Fargo bank vault is even available for banquets.

★ **Andrae's Bakery** (14141 Hwy. 49, Amador City, 209/267-1352, www.andraesbakery.com, 7:30am-4pm Thurs.-Sun., $8) feels like eating at grandmother's house. Locals order the gourmet sandwiches—the turkey is a standout, made with locally raised meat, cheese, and veggies on house-baked focaccia bread. For dessert, you must have one of the pastries. The cookies are dangerously good, but the seasonal scones (strawberry and peach in summer, cranberry in winter) are worth the trip. You can order to go, but a better alternative is to sit outside on the back patio. There's a fair number of old-fashioned sodas in the drink case to wash down your meal.

Locals swear that **Susan's Place** (15 Eureka St., 209/267-0945, www.susansplace.com, 11:30am-2:30pm, 5pm-8pm Thurs.-Sun., $14-28) is the best restaurant in town, with its relaxing patio shaded by wisteria. The menu advertises itself as Mediterranean fare, but other than a Greek salad and the lamb shanks, most of the dishes are mainstream California cuisine. Susan's is the only fine dining option in Sutter's Creek. If you're in town for a romantic weekend, this restaurant should be on your itinerary.

Information and Services

The **Sutter Creek Visitors Center** (71A Main St., 209/267-1344, www.suttercreek.org, 11am-5pm daily) has a helpful website with loads of travel advice and tips on local sights, along with an events list for upcoming cultural happenings. The visitors center is staffed by volunteers, so the daily hours often fluctuate; call ahead to make sure someone is there. There are ATMs and several bank branches in Sutter Creek.

Transportation

Sutter Creek is 10 miles south of Plymouth and roughly 5 miles north of Jackson on Highway 49. From Placerville, head south on Highway 49 for about 30 miles to reach Sutter Creek. From the Central Valley, take Highway 88 northeast from Stockton and drive 42 miles to Highway 49; turn north for 2.5 miles to Sutter Creek.

The local **Westover Field-Amador County Airport** (12380 Airport Rd., Jackson, 209/223-2376, www.co.amador.ca.us) is between Jackson and Sutter Creek, but it has no scheduled commercial flights. The closest airport served by the airlines is **Sacramento International Airport** (SMF, 6900 Airport Blvd., Sacramento, 916/929-5411, www.sacairports.org), 55 miles west.

If you're interested in the exploring the mines, drive along the **Sutter Creek Gold Mine Trail** (209/267-1344, www.suttercreek.org). Highways 49 and 88 are the main thoroughfares through the Amador County gold-mining district—a commercial map of the

Indian Grinding Rock State Historic Park

area makes a good companion to the hand-drawn map in the official brochure.

Amador Transit (115 Valley View Way, 209/267-9395, http://amadortransit.com, $2 most routes, $1 to Jackson) runs several bus routes all over Amador County and to Sacramento from its station.

JACKSON

Historic Kennedy Gold Mine

The **Historic Kennedy Gold Mine** (12594 Kennedy Mine Rd., 209/223-9542, www.kennedygoldmine.com, guided tours 10am-3pm Sat.-Sun. Mar.-Oct., adults $10, children $6) is a great place to learn about life in a California gold mine. The Kennedy Mine was one of the deepest hard-rock gold mines in the state, extending more than a mile into the earth. Tour the stately Mine House, marvel at the size of the head frame, and learn how a stamp mill worked to free the gold from the rocks. For the best experience, take a guided tour and learn the true stories of the mine.

Indian Grinding Rock State Historic Park

Indian Grinding Rock State Historic Park (14881 Pine Grove-Volcano Rd., 209/296-7488, www.parks.ca.gov, sunrise-sunset daily, $8 per vehicle) focuses on the history of the state before the European influx. This park, 12 miles east of Jackson, celebrates the life and culture of the Miwok people, specifically the Northern Sierra Miwok who inhabited the foothills for centuries. One of the central aspects of Miwok life was grinding acorns, their principal food. Women came to the grinding rock to grind and then soak their acorns for the day's meals. The park's focal point is a huge grinding rock, one used by all the women of the group who lived in the adjacent meadow and forest. The dozens of divots in the rock, plus the fading petroglyphs drawn over generations, attest to the lengthy use of this chunk of marble. The grinding rock's marble is frail, so don't walk on it.

Follow the pathways past the grinding rock to the reconstructed roundhouse, a sacred space in current use by local Miwoks, implying that visitors should be respectful. Walk farther toward the **Miwok village,** where you can enter the dwellings to see how these native Californians once lived. If you're up for a longer hike, the **North Trail** winds around most of the park. For a deeper look into Miwok history, spend some time in the visitors center and museum (11am-2:30pm Fri.-Mon).

Sports and Recreation

Golf addicts can find plenty to keep themselves busy at the highly rated public **Castle Oaks Golf Club** (1000 Castle Oaks Dr., Ione, 209/274-0167, www.castleoaksgolf.com, $14-53). This 18-hole par-71 championship course offers five different levels of tee, making it fun for golfers of any skill level. Lots of water features keep the game interesting, and the relatively flat terrain makes for a lovely walk. Located in Ione, west of Jackson and Plymouth, Castle Oaks makes a perfect diversion from the endless museums, mines, and wineries of the area. If you're just looking for practice, Castle Oaks has a driving range, chipping green, and putting green. The club recommends that you book your tee time at least one week in advance.

At **Lake Camanche** (2000 Camanche Rd., Ione, 209/763-5121, www.camancherecreation.com), you can zip around the lake on a personal watercraft, try your skills at waterskiing or wakeboarding, or enjoy a relaxing afternoon or evening of fishing. You can fish at Camanche all year. Beautiful scenery and plentiful fishing combine at **Pardee Lake Recreation Area** (4900 Stony Creek Rd., Ione, 209/772-1472, www.pardeelakerecreation.com).

Accommodations

El Campo Casa (12548 Kennedy Flat Rd., Jackson, 209/223-0100, http://elcampocasa.com, $50-110) is a throwback motel with Old World character. The 15 simple rooms evoke a midcentury motel feel, and have ceiling fans, air-conditioning, and TVs. There's also an outdoor pool and a shady patio area. It makes a perfect base for excursions to the Shenandoah Valley. The rooms are somewhat Spartan, and the baths are a little too cozy. All rooms are nonsmoking.

For a place with modern conveniences, stay at the **Best Western Amador Inn** (200 S. Hwy. 49, 209/223-0211, www.bestwestern.com, $85-160), a homey place to crash after touring the area's wineries. During the scorching summer months, take a dip in the outdoor pool and enjoy the patio area. Amenities include coffeemakers, air-conditioning, fridges, and cable TV; some rooms have gas fireplaces. The continental breakfast is included, and you can even make decent-size waffles. Make sure to ask for a nonsmoking room.

The **Holiday Inn Express** (101 Clinton Rd., 209/257-1500, $125-250) is a modern and comfortable hotel just off Highway 49. Rooms are well stocked, with microwaves, fridges, cable TV, and blow-dryers. It also has a business center and a fitness room. A breakfast buffet is included.

Food

The **Mother Lode Market and Deli** (36 Main St., 209/223-0652, 8am-3pm Mon.-Sat., $5) is a local institution that serves down-home meals and some local history. This quaint rustic café is in downtown Jackson and makes a perfect stop for coffee or a bite to eat. The menu is filled with standard sandwiches, deli items, salads, and soups—it's nothing fancy, but everything is prepared from scratch. Order a sandwich with freshly baked bread and a heaping pile of homemade potato salad; the tri-tip beef and the Italian sausage sandwiches are excellent choices.

Thomi's Café (627 S. Hwy. 49, 209/257-0800, www.thomiscafe.com, 8am-9pm Mon.-Sat., 8am-8pm Sun., $10-25) is an old-fashioned family restaurant. Meals are served pretty much any time of the day, but make sure to come hungry—to say the portions are hearty is an understatement. The menu is American surf-and-turf, though Thomi also has an astonishingly good stir-fry menu. Locals like the breakfasts here, especially the California Benedict with eggs, tomato, bacon, and avocado. There aren't many vegetarian options, other than some salads and a few pasta dishes.

Information and Services

The **Amador Chamber of Commerce & Visitors Bureau** (115 Main St., 209/223-0350, http://amadorcountychamber.com, 8am-4pm Mon.-Fri., 10am-2pm Sat.-Sun.) is the best place to learn about what's happening in town.

For medical emergencies and health needs, visit **Sutter Amador Hospital** (200 Mission Blvd., 209/223-7500, www.sutteramador.org).

Transportation

Jackson is near the intersection of Highways 49 and 88 and is fairly easy to reach by car. From the north or south, take Highway 49; from the Bay Area or the Central Valley, Highway 88 is the best bet. Both highways are two-lane roads that become congested during summer and on weekends. Jackson can also receive snowfall, which can complicate travel plans; check weather and traffic reports with Caltrans (http://dot.ca.gov) before traveling.

The local **Westover Field-Amador County Airport** (12380 Airport Rd., 209/223-2376, www.co.amador.ca.us) is between Jackson and Sutter Creek, but it has no scheduled commercial flights. The closest airport served by the airlines is **Sacramento International Airport** (SMF, 6900 Airport Blvd., Sacramento, 916/929-5411, www.sacairports.org), 60 miles west.

Public transit options are limited in the area, but **Amador Transit** (209/267-9395, http://amadortransit.com, $2 for most fares, $1 to Sutter Creek) runs several bus routes between Sutter Creek and Jackson Monday-Friday.

VOLCANO

Black Chasm Caverns

For an underground experience in nature, take an easy one-hour tour of the **Black Chasm Caverns** (Volcano-Pioneer Rd., 866/762-2837, www.caverntours.com, 9am-5pm daily Apr.-Aug., 10am-4pm daily Sept.-Mar., adults $15, children $8). Enjoy a sedate stroll into the immense chasm filled with amazing calcite formations. In the Landmark Room, you'll get a chance to check out the rare helictite formations (a crystalline cave formation) that made Black Chasm famous. Enjoy the visitors center on the way out or as you wait for your tour. Many visitors enjoy the video that describes how the creators of *The Matrix* used the look and feeling of Black Chasm in their films. You can even see some of the immense stalagmite props made for the movie. Tour schedules can fluctuate during holidays. Tours aren't accessible to strollers or wheelchairs.

★ Daffodil Hill

Spring is the time to visit the famed **Daffodil Hill** (18310 Rams Horn Grade, 209/296-7048, http://suttercreek.org, daily mid-Mar.-mid-Apr., free). Perfect for travelers who love the greenery aboveground as much as the minerals beneath it, Daffodil Hill explodes each March into a profusion of sunny yellow that lasts for about a month. Daffodil Hill is actually the private working ranch of the McLaughlin family, which has been planting daffodil bulbs on their property since they first acquired the land in 1887. Today you'll see more than 300,000 flowers blooming, and more are planted each year. In addition to the more than 300 different species of daffodils, other bulb flowers and plants help create carpets of color across the meadows and hills. Even among the many fabulous landscapes and gardens of California, Daffodil Hill is special; out here, you can't help but feel the joy and promise of spring.

Daffodil Hill opens to the public only during daffodil season. Exact opening and closing dates vary each year; call ahead to get the latest information. Parking can be scarce during busier times, so prepare to park a distance from the farm.

Accommodations and Food

For a budget hotel deep in northern Gold Country, head for the **Union Inn and Pub** (21375 Consolation St., 209/296-7711, www.volcanounion.com, $85-140). It has only four rooms, but each one is decorated with a different luxurious theme. Modern amenities include flat-screen TVs and radios with iPod docks; some rooms have sunken porcelain tubs. A gourmet breakfast is served each day. The Union is best for couples looking for a romantic getaway. Children and pets are not allowed. Some of the best food in Amador County is served in the hotel's restaurant (5pm-8pm Mon. and Thurs., 5pm-9pm Fri., noon-9pm Sat., noon-8pm Sun., $11-24).

The venerable **St. George Hotel** (16104 Main St., Volcano, 209/296-4458, www.stgeorgevolcano.com, $55-200) has affordable rooms with vintage Gold Country charm. This attractive, plain building houses a hodgepodge of 14 second- and third-floor rooms, some that peer out onto Volcano's main drag, and a bungalow in the back. Only two of the rooms in the main building and the bungalow have private baths. Rooms have polished wood floors and antique-styled bedsteads. Take your coffee out onto the wraparound verandah each morning to enjoy the cool early hours. The hotel has a restaurant (5pm-9pm Thurs.-Fri., noon-9pm Sat., 9am-8pm Sun., $15-30), but the food is uninspiring.

Information and Services

In Volcano you won't find much in the way of services. The closest bank branches and gas stations are located four miles southwest in Pine Grove or eight miles east in Pioneer, both on Highway 88.

Transportation

Volcano is on the eastern edge of Gold Country, where the elevation starts to climb among towering pine trees that blanket the hillsides. By car, take Highway 88 northeast from Jackson for about nine miles; turn left on Pine Grove-Volcano Road. Volcano will appear in about three miles. Because of the higher elevation, Volcano often has heavy snowfall in winter, and chains may be required. Check weather and traffic reports with Caltrans (http://dot.ca.gov) before planning your trip.

Southern Gold Country

The southern Gold Country runs from the town of Jackson down almost to Yosemite Valley. Every few miles along Highway 49 and on the roads through Sonora and Jamestown are historical plaques commemorating everything from the local hanging tree to the prostitutes who made life more, um, bearable for the rough men working the mines. You'll also find museums, caverns, mines, parks, wineries, great restaurants, and quirky hotels.

Southern Gold Country runs south from Jackson and includes the towns of Murphys, Angels Camp, Sonora, Columbia, Jamestown, and Arnold. Highway 49 can take you north-south through the region. Highway 4 runs northeast-southwest, intersecting Highway 49 at Angels Camp and running east to Murphys. Highway 4 also runs south from Vallecito to Columbia and then south to Sonora. You can also drive Highway 49 all the way to Jamestown and pick up Highway 108 east to Sonora.

ANGELS CAMP

California Caverns

California Caverns (9565 Cave City Rd., Mountain Ranch, 866/762-2837, www.caverntours.com, 9am-5pm daily Apr.-Aug., 10am-4pm Sat.-Sun Sept.-Mar., adults $15, children $8) has been welcoming underground explorers for more than 150 years. An Army captain discovered the caves in 1850 when he noticed a strange breeze blowing from a rocky outcropping; since then, visitors such as Mark Twain and John Muir have wondered at the bizarre and beautiful formations in these caverns. The basic tour is geared toward families and lasts just over an hour; a knowledgeable guide leads you through a wonderland of subterranean chambers while describing the cavern's history and geology. Kids will especially love gazing at the numerous forms of stalactites, especially the vine-like formations in the **Jungle Room** cavern. If you're not claustrophobic, you can also do some serious spelunking, spending hours with a guide as you plunge into murky depths and raft across underground pools on the **Middle Earth Expedition** (4 hours, $130), or wriggle through 13 natural chambers on the **Mammoth Expedition** (2-3 hours, $99). Make sure to bring hiking shoes or boots, since the underground paths can be quite slippery, and wear clothes you won't mind getting muddy—some of the tours involve crawling through damp wormholes and crevices. Many of the tours can't be accessed in certain seasons, especially in late spring and early summer, so call the cavern visitors center or check the website for more information.

Southern Gold Country

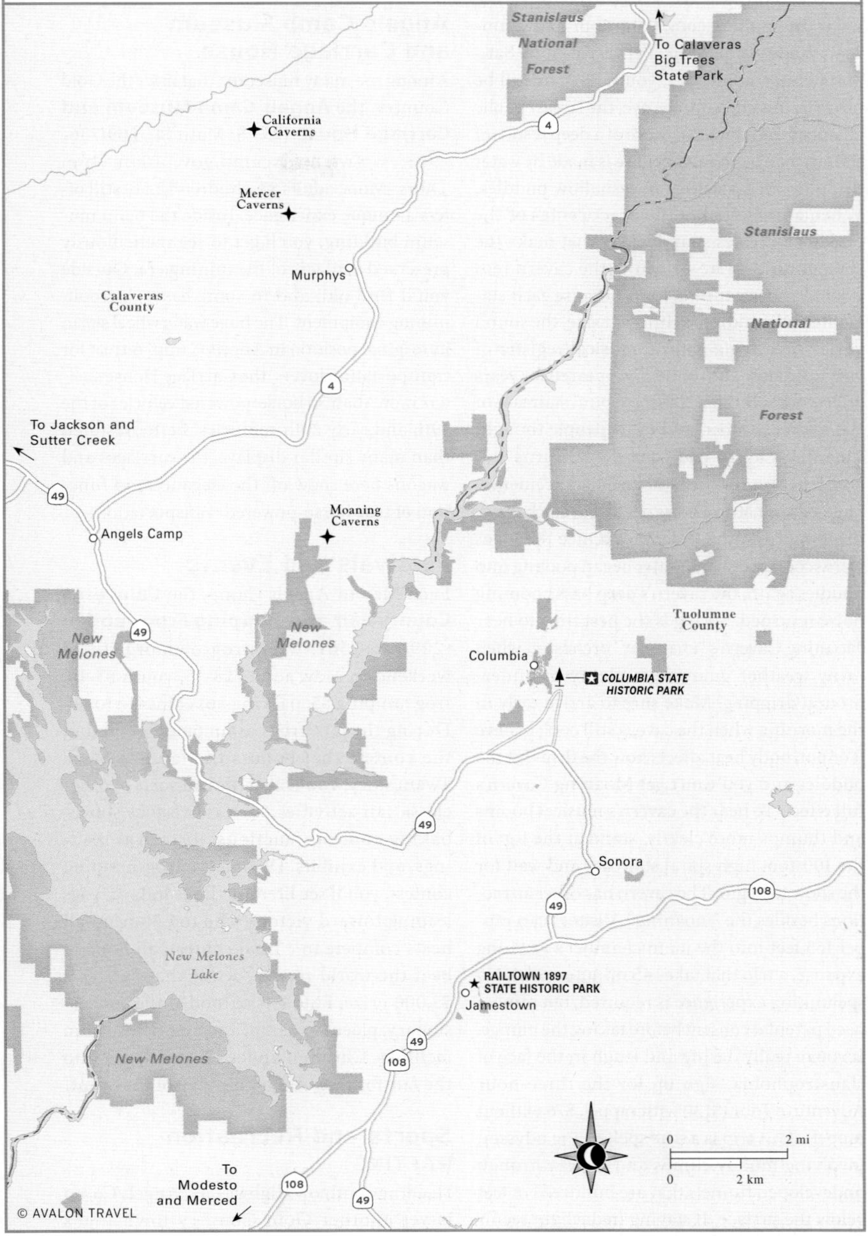
Stanislaus
National
Forest
To Calaveras
Big Trees
State Park
4
California
Caverns
Mercer
Caverns
Murphys
Calaveras
County
Stanislaus
National
Forest
4
To Jackson and
Sutter Creek
49
Moaning
Caverns
Angels Camp
49
New
Melones
New
Melones
Tuolumne
County
Columbia
COLUMBIA STATE
HISTORIC PARK
49
Sonora
108
49
New Melones
Lake
RAILTOWN 1897
STATE HISTORIC PARK
Jamestown
49
108
New Melones
0
2 mi
0
2 km
To
Modesto
and Merced
108
49
© AVALON TRAVEL

Moaning Cavern

The haunting sounds of **Moaning Cavern** (5350 Moaning Cave Road, 209/736-2708, www.caverntours.com, 9am-6pm daily summer, 10am-4pm Mon.-Fri., 9am-5pm Sat.-Sun. winter, adults $15, youth $8) can still be heard in this enchanting cave, the largest public chamber in California. More of a deep resonant thump than a moan, the noise is made by water dripping off stalactites into shallow puddles. When a drop strikes the exact center of the puddle, it creates sound waves that make the stalagmites vibrate—turning the cavern into a subterranean tuning fork. Because each stalactite and puddle is a different size, the sound varies, creating a natural musical register of varying tones. The sound disappeared for years after workers built a 235-step spiral staircase in the main chamber, and most people thought Moaning Cavern had gone silent. Turns out, construction on the staircase had accidently plugged the natural holes needed to catch water dripping from the stalactites. Once the holes were scooped out and water began pooling into puddles again, the cavern's deep bass booming noise returned. Spring is the best time to hear Moaning Cavern's "chamber" orchestra, when rainy weather guarantees plenty of underground dripping. Make sure to arrive early in the morning when the cave is still cool; believe it or not, body heat affects how the drips hit the puddles and you won't get Moaning Cavern's full effect. To hear the cavern's musical booms and thumps more clearly, stand at the top of the 100-foot high spiral staircase and wait for the show to begin. The cavern has other attractions besides the "moaning." Visitors can rappel 165 feet into the main chamber's yawning expanse, a trip that takes 45 minutes ($72). No spelunking experience is required, but minors need parental consent before taking the plunge. If you're really daring and laugh in the face of claustrophobia, sign up for the three-hour Adventure Tour ($130 with rappel, $76 without rappel). This trip is a true spelunking odyssey, involving muddy climbs and crawls through undeveloped tunnels that are hundreds of feet below the surface. If staying in daylight seems more fun, try the 1,500-foot-long zip line ($44) along the ridge by the cave's visitors center.

Angels Camp Museum and Carriage House

Among the many museums that litter the Gold Country, the **Angels Camp Museum and Carriage House** (753 S. Main St., 209/736-2963, www.angelscamp.gov, 10am-4pm Thurs.-Mon., adults $5, children $2.50) still offers a unique experience. Inside the main museum building, you'll get to see meticulously preserved artifacts of the mining era. Outside you'll find old, and in some cases decrepit, mining equipment. The huge waterwheel sits in its original position in Angels Camp. A treat for transportation lovers, the Carriage House shelters more than 30 horse-powered vehicles of the 19th and early 20th centuries. Better restored than many similar displays, the carriages and wagons here show off the elegance and function of true horse-powered transportation.

Festivals and Events

Each May in Angels Camp, the **Calaveras County Fair and Jumping Frog Jubilee** (209/736-2561, www.frogtown.org, third weekend in May, adults $8-15, youth $5-10, frog jumping $5, parking $6) comes to town. During the fair, frogs jump on command in the contest that honors the famous Mark Twain story. You'll also find all sorts of other classic fair activities, such as livestock shows, baking contests, auctions, historical readings, and exhibits. During the frog-jumping contest, you'll see literally thousands of frogs leaping toward victory. The top 50 from all heats compete in a final contest; all hope to beat the world record, a feat that carries a $5,000 prize. Find lots of food at the concessionary, places to camp, and ample restroom facilities. Children under 13 usually get into the fair for free on the first day of the event.

Sports and Recreation

RAFTING

Heading south on Highway 49, Angels Camp is yet another Gold Country town that's within a short shuttle ride of churning white water. Here the options change slightly from the excursions offered farther north. You can still take guided tours on the South Fork of the American River with local outfitters, but the North Fork of the Stanislaus River is closer to Angels Camp and offers more intermediate-advanced trips through roaring Class III-IV rapids. The season is shorter on the Stanislaus and runs mid-April-May, weather and river conditions permitting; be sure to call ahead.

All-Outdoors (925/932-8993, www.aorafting.com, mid-Apr.-late May, $164-184 pp) runs full-day trips to the North Fork of the Stanislaus. You can plunge through Class IV rapids with hair-raising names like Beginner's Luck, Rattlesnake, and Maycheck's Mayhem; the last rapid is a partial Class V drop. You can also take full-day and two-day trips on the calmer South Fork of the American River if the Stanislaus is beyond your experience level.

O.A.R.S. (209/736-4677, www.oars.com, Apr.-June, $144-170) also offers trips to the mighty North Fork of the Stanislaus River where it churns through Calaveras Big Trees State Park. The guides are knowledgeable and friendly, and lunch is provided. If you'd rather raft the South Fork of the American River, O.A.R.S. offers half-day, full-day, and two-day excursions.

Accommodations

If you're traveling with family or a group of friends, stay at the **Greenhorn Creek Resort** (711 McCauley Ranch Rd., 209/736-9372, www.greenhorncreekvacationcottages.com, $125-260), where you can rent a condo or a two- or three-bedroom cottage. Cottages have full kitchens, dining areas, and living rooms decorated in light, bright styles. Each bedroom has its own separate bath; most bedrooms have king beds, but some have two twins. These cottages are perfect for a longer stay in the region. The property offers amenities that include an on-site restaurant, 18-hole golf course, and tennis courts. The resort has a shallow family pool, a large main pool, and a hot whirlpool tub.

It's impossible not to feel spoiled at the **Cooper House Inn** (1184 Church St., 888/330-3764, www.cooperhouseinn.com, $190-260), a renovated Victorian-era country home. The three rooms feature locally made linens, biodegradable bath kits, and private showers, plus 21st-century conveniences like free wireless Internet and flat-panel TVs. The Chardonnay suite is the only room with a king bed; the others have either a queen or a double. None have en suite bathrooms. Downstairs take a complimentary bottle of wine onto the patio and relax in the padded lounge chairs. Breakfast is made with organic and local ingredients.

Food

Locals say **Mike's Pizza** (294 S. Main St., 209/736-9246, www.mikespizzaangelscamp.com, 11am-9pm Sun.-Thurs., 11am-10 pm Fri.-Sat., $6-40) whips up the finest pies in town. The Pesto Californian (with pesto, chicken, marinated artichoke hearts, olives, and mushrooms) is especially tasty. The interior oozes an old-fashioned pizza parlor vibe with dark-paneled walls, arcade games, and glowing neon signs. If you don't feel like pizza, there's plenty of other pub grub like burgers, pasta, and ribs. Mike's also has a salad bar and offers gluten-free crust.

Crusco's (1240 S. Main St., 209/736-1440, www.cruscos.com, 11:30am-3pm, 5pm-9pm Thurs.-Mon., $18-27) serves hearty homemade Italian food with a Californian flair, serving dishes like wild salmon with orange madeira cream sauce and New York steak topped with crab and butter sauce. Save room for the chocolate truffle torte for dessert. The best part about this restaurant is the Old World hospitality and attentive service from the owner, who is usually on hand to greet customers.

Information and Services

Begin your trip at the **Calaveras County Visitors Bureau** (1192 S. Main St., 800/225-3764, www.gocalaveras.com, 9:30am-4:30pm Mon.-Fri., 11am-4pm Sat.). **U.S. Bank** (580

S. Main St.) has a 24-hour ATM just north of downtown Angels Camp.

For urgent medical needs and health issues, go to **Angels Camp Prompt Care** (23 N. Main St., 209/736-9130, 8am-6pm daily). They can treat medical conditions such as broken bones or infections, but it is not equipped to handle major emergencies.

Transportation

Angels Camp is in the heart of Gold Country, on Highway 49 about 28 miles south of Jackson. From Stockton, take Highway 4 east for 50 miles and turn south on Highway 49; Angels Camp is another 2 miles. Sacramento is 75 miles away, and Placerville is 60 miles north.

If you have your own plane, or have access to one, you can fly into the **Calaveras County Airport** (3600 Carol Kennedy Dr., San Andreas, 209/736-2501). There's isn't much public transportation in Angels Camp, but **Calaveras Transit** (209/754-4450, www.calaverastransit.com, $2) runs three bus routes to the surrounding area Monday-Friday, including trips to Arnold and Murphys.

MURPHYS AND VICINITY

Mercer Cavern

One of the fascinating caverns that pock the Sierra foothills, **Mercer Cavern** (1665 Sheep Ranch Rd., 209/728-2101, www.mercercaverns.com, 10am-4:30pm daily early Sept.-late May, 9am-5pm daily late May-early Sept., adults $15, children $8.50) winds into the mountains just outside of Murphys. Mercer Caverns has been in continuous operation as an attraction for more than 125 years. Visitors descend 172 steps into the narrow cavern, crowding the numerous walkways that run 162 feet down from the surface entrance. The 45-minute standard tour is a fun family activity, provided that everyone is reasonably fit and mobile. Kids love "seeing" objects like fruit, vegetables, and people's faces in the myriad limestone formations that populate the various rooms of the cavern.

Buena Vista Cemetery

Overlooking a small hill outside downtown Murphys, the **Buena Vista Cemetery** (Cemetery Ln., 209/728-2387, http://murphyscemetery.com) has been in continuous use since the 1850s. The cemetery is adjacent to an old schoolhouse museum; visitors can drive through many parts of the graveyard, or spend hours wandering the plots. Despite its size and regular maintenance, Buena Vista has plenty of ghostly atmosphere. A parade of slightly crooked marble and granite markers meander across the acres, and a few elderly oak trees provide light shade. You can piece together the Gold Rush history of Murphys by reading the town's collection of tombstones; you'll find the graves of war veterans, Masons, miners, immigrants, wives, mothers, and children. Locals whose time in Murphys has ended are still buried here, and the modern markers stand out in stark contrast to the softened lines of the older stones.

Calaveras Big Trees State Park

Take some time away from mining history to visit **Calaveras Big Trees State Park** (Hwy. 4, 3 miles east of Arnold, 209/795-2334, www.bigtrees.org, sunrise-sunset daily, $10). Highlights of the park include the North and South Groves of rare giant sequoia trees; be sure to take a walk in both groves to check out the landmark trees and stumps. Beyond the sequoias, you can hike and bike in 6,000 acres of pine forest crisscrossed with trails and scattered with campgrounds (reservations 800/444-7275) and pretty groves set up for picnicking. Feel free to take a dip in the cool refreshing Stanislaus River running through the trees, or cast a line out to try to catch a rainbow trout. In the winter, break out the snowshoes and cross-country skis—the trails are marked for winter sports as well as summer.

Start your day at the visitors center, where you can talk to rangers about the best hikes for you and pick up trail maps for several of the major hiking areas in the park. In winter, many of the roads through the park are closed, but drive in as far as you can and snowshoe or ski from there. The visitors center (209/795-3840, 10am-4pm daily) has a gaggle of exhibits and artifacts depicting different periods in California history.

Wineries

Downtown Murphys has a number of tasting rooms. Out in the countryside, a few vineyards boast major estates. The largest estate belongs to **Ironstone Vineyards** (1894 Six Mile Rd., 209/728-1251, www.ironstonevineyards.com, 10am-5pm daily, $5). This huge complex of vineyards, winery buildings, a museum, an amphitheater, and gardens can draw hundreds of visitors in a single day. Inside the vast tasting room are three bars and a pleasant surprise. The complimentary regular tasting includes any number of wines, most priced at $10 per bottle. The reserve tasting bar shows off the higher-end vintages.

The tiny but elegant tasting room of **Black Sheep Winery** (221 Main St., 209/728-2157, www.blacksheepwinery.com, 11am-5pm daily, free) offers higher-end red wines at a bar that could fit maybe six people—if they're friendly. Black Sheep's specialty is zinfandel made from Calaveras County and Amador County grapes, but they also make cabernet sauvignon, cabernet franc, and more unusual varietals like cinsault.

With a focus on Spanish and Rhône varietals and an unlikely rubber-chicken mascot, **Twisted Oak Winery** (363 Main St., 209/736-9080, www.twistedoak.com, 11:30am-5:30pm Mon.-Fri., 10:30am-5:30pm Sat.-Sun., $5) makes award-winning wines. The tasting fee buys the option to try 15 different wines.

Shopping

The bustling shopping district in the heart of this old mining town has antiques shops, small boutiques, and a few surprises. Most shops are between the parallel Church and Main Streets, with a few stores farther out along Highway 4. On weekends, parking can be a frustrating challenge, so arrive earlier in the day if you can.

Tea an'Tiques (419 Main St., 209/728-8240, 11am-5pm Mon.-Fri., 10:30am-6pm Sat., 11am-5:30pm Sun.) serves tea while you browse their wonderful selection of old knickknacks and curios. Stepping through the bright yellow door is like stepping into an English country cottage—only with a self-serve tea bar stocked with 100 different varieties of fine tea.

At the **Sierra Nevada Adventure Company General Store** (448 Main St., 209/728-9133, www.snacattack.com, 10am-6pm daily), you'll find gear for any kind of trek, climb, or walkabout imaginable. It's the perfect place to pick up hiking shoes, a new backpack, or cool-weather fleece before heading into the foothills.

If you need a summer reading book or travel journal, stop by **Sustenance Books** (416 Main St., 209/728-2200, 11:11am-5:30pm Sun.-Mon., Wed.-Thurs., 11:11am-6pm Fri.-Sat.). Yes, you read that right—the bookstore opens at 11 minutes past 11 o'clock. You can find new and used tomes from every genre on the shelves here. Sustenance specializes in children's books. They also have a wide selection of books on nature and sustainability.

At **Marisolio Tasting Bar** (488 Main St., 209/728-8853, www.marisolio.com, noon-5pm Tues., 10am-5pm Wed.-Mon.), you can belly up to a different kind of bar—one that serves tastings of artisanal olive oils and vinegars. The oils and vinegars are mostly from California, but the shop also has imported products made with fair-trade and sustainable ingredients from all over the world. Try either the white or the black truffle extra virgin olive oil, and if you taste the vinegars, don't miss the delicious black cherry.

Your nose will have no trouble finding **The Spice Tin** (457 N. Algiers St., 209/728-8225, www.thespicetin.com, 11am-5pm daily). Spices aren't the only goods—sauces, salts, dips, and rubs also line the tangy shelves.

Sports and Recreation

When winter snows come to the southern Gold Country, the skiers and boarders come out to play. Only a few miles past Arnold, **Bear Valley ski resort** (2280 Hwy. 207, Bear Valley, 209/753-2301, www.bearvalley.com, 9am-4pm daily, adults $67-72, youth $50-55, children $20-25) lures snow lovers with a big mountain filled with great runs and tracks. You can take lessons on the wide gentle beginner slopes near the lodge. If you prefer to take your chances, head up the hill to the array of intermediate and advanced trails that make up 75 percent of the skiable terrain at Bear Valley. Ten different lifts make lines short on weekdays. If you're looking for something edgier, take your snowboard out to the "Cub" terrain parks.

In summer, Bear Valley turns its runs into tracks and its slopes into trails. Everyone from the most sedate walkers and road bikers to the most dedicated backpackers and off-road vehicle riders will find fun at Bear Valley. Check the website for maps of the acres of road-biking areas, mountain-biking tracks, and hiking trails.

Accommodations and Camping

Murphys Inn Motel (76 Main St., 888/796-1800, www.murphysinnmotel.com, $130-180), centrally located in downtown Murphys, makes a perfect base of operations for Gold Country. Most of the 37 rooms have two queen beds, furnished and decorated in traditional motel style. Outside your room, you can take a cooling dunk in the pool or enjoy a hard workout in the small fitness room.

From the outside, the blocky **Dunbar House 1880** (271 Jones St., 209/728-2897, www.dunbarhouse.com, $190-280) evokes a Dickensian air. Inside are modern comforts and Victorian decor. In the bath you might find an antique claw-foot tub and vintage shower, or the most modern of whirlpool tubs. All rooms have English towel warmers. For breakfast, feast on homemade baked goods, a delicious hot entrée, coffee, tea, and specially blended hot chocolate. Eat in the dining room, the garden, or, if you're in one of the suites, in the privacy of your own room.

Calaveras Big Trees State Park (Hwy. 4, 3 miles east of Arnold, 800/444-7275, www.parks.ca.gov or www.reserveamerica.com, reservations Memorial Day-Labor Day, reservation fee $8, sites $35) has two seasonal campgrounds for tents and RVs. The North Grove Campground (Apr.-Nov.) lies closest to the park entrance on Highway 4 and has 74 sites. Oak Hollow Campground (May-Oct.) is four miles inside the park and two miles from the Stanislaus River. The 55 sites are set on a hill and are a bit quieter. All campsites include a fire ring, a picnic table, and parking. Flush toilets, coin-operated showers, and drinking water are available in the campgrounds. Reservations are accepted up to seven months in advance and are strongly recommended in summer. Off-season, campsites are first-come, first-served.

Food

Grounds (402 Main St., 209/728-8663, www.groundsrestaurant.com, 7am-3pm Mon.-Tues., 7am-3pm, 5pm-8pm Wed.-Thurs., 7am-3pm, 5pm-9pm Fri.-Sat., 8am-3pm, 5pm-9pm Sun., $16-29) was one of Murphys' first gourmet restaurants, and it's still one of the best places to eat in town. The food is modern California cuisine, with standard dishes like a grilled eggplant sandwich and seared swordfish steak over linguini. For breakfast, make your own omelet from ingredients like sweet Italian sausage, black olives, gouda, and cheddar. This restaurant is one of the busiest in town, so reservations are recommended.

At **Firewood** (420 Main St., 209/728-3248, www.firewoodeats.com, 11am-9pm Sun.-Thurs., 11am-9:30pm Fri.-Sat., $12), housed in a former fire station, everything has a fiery theme, from wood-fired pizzas to the ax handles that grace the front doors. You can't go wrong with the chicken pesto with basil and parmesan pizza; or try the gorgonzola burger or the fish tacos. There's also a children's menu.

For fancy steak dinners in Murphys go to **V Restaurant** (402 Main St., 209/728-0107, http://vrestaurantandbar-murphys.com, bistro 11am-8 p.m. Mon.-Thurs., 11am-9pm Fri.-Sun.; dining room 11am-8 p.m. Wed.-Thurs., 11am-9pm Fri.-Sun., $18-32). This small but elegant dining room dishes upscale American fare with plates like bacon-wrapped filet mignon and lamb T-bone. Call ahead on busy weekends to nab a table.

Information and Services

Murphys doesn't have much in the way of visitor services, so the best place for information is online (www.visitmurphys.com). Try **El Dorado Savings** (245 Tom Bell Rd., 209/728-2003, www.eldoradosavingsbank.com) for an ATM and banking services.

Several gas stations in Murphys are along Highway 4, the main thoroughfare in town.

Transportation

Reach Murphys by taking Highway 4 northeast from Angels Camp for 10 miles. It is a fair drive from any major city; you'll have to drive about 80 miles from Sacramento and about 60 miles from Modesto. If you need public transportation, **Calaveras Transit** (209/754-4450, www.calaverastransit.com, $2) runs round-trip bus routes between Murphys and Angels Camp Monday-Friday.

SONORA AND COLUMBIA

★ Columbia State Historic Park

A stroll down Main Street in **Columbia State Historic Park** (11255 Jackson St., Columbia, 209/588-9128, www.parks.ca.gov, daily year-round, most businesses 10am-5pm daily, free) is a stroll into California's boomtown past. Start with the **Columbia Museum** (Main St. and State St., 209/532-3184, 10am-4pm daily, free) to discover the history of this fascinating place, one of the early California mining towns. Gold was discovered here in the spring of 1850, and the town sprang up as miners flowed in, growing to become one of California's largest cities for a short time. It inevitably declined as the gold ran out, and in 1945 the state took it over and created the State Historic Park. In the museum, you'll

Columbia State Historic Park

see artifacts of the mining period, from miners' equipment and clothing to the household objects used by women who lived in the bustling city. After the museum, walk the streets, poking your head into the exhibits and shops selling an array of period and modern items. Examine the contents of the Dry Goods Store, imagine the multiculturalism of another age in the Chinese Store Exhibit, or grab a bite to eat in the City Hotel Saloon.

This large indoor-outdoor museum experience is an easy flat walk, with plenty of wheelchair-accessible areas. The horses, carriages, and staff in pioneer costumes delight children. It can get hot in the summer and cold in winter, and you'll be on your feet a lot, so dress accordingly and wear sensible shoes. Docent-led tours happen at 11am Saturday-Sunday.

Tuolumne County Museum

If you can hit only one local museum in your journey through southern Gold Country, make it the **Tuolumne County Museum** (158 Bradford St., Sonora, 209/532-1317, www.tchistory.org, 10am-4pm Mon.-Fri., 10am-3:30pm Sat., donations only). The county leaders took entertaining advantage of the museum's location in the old Sonora jailhouse; a number of exhibits are inside cells, and one cell has been recreated as an exhibit of what incarceration might have been like in 19th-century Tuolumne County (hint: unpleasant). Appropriate homage is paid to Tom Horn, a prisoner who died in a jailhouse fire—one that he set himself in an ill-conceived escape attempt.

Throughout the rest of the museum, you'll find plenty of artifacts from the mines, shops, and homes of the county. Interpretive areas describe the process of hard-rock mining, the arduous journey the would-be gold miners took to get from the East to California, and the history of the county.

Entertainment and Events

It's only fitting that the land where thousands gambled their futures on finding a fortune in gold should play host to a casino or two. If you're already in Sonora, take a detour to the **Black Oak Casino** (19400 Tuolumne Rd. N., Sonora, 877/747-8777, www.blackoakcasino.com) in Tuolumne County. This full-service family-friendly casino features games for kids and adults alike. While the under-21 crowd bowls at the Black Oak Lanes or spends their quarters in the Underground Arcade, the grown-ups can play over 1,000 slots and video poker machines plus a small array of table games. When you're ready for a break, you can eat and drink at any one of Black Oak's nine restaurants and bars, take in some live weekend entertainment at the Willow Creek Lounge, or even spin a few more slots in the smoke-free Jumping Coyote Espresso and Coffee Bar on the second floor.

Shopping

Looking for some Wild West mementos straight from the Gold Country? You won't find anywhere better than the gift shops in Columbia's old buildings. Hard-core travelers might pick up a tourist-trap vibe, but families traveling with children will get a kick out of the old-timey shops staffed by their costumed clerks. If Columbia is too kitschy for you, head for Sonora's more refined downtown to browse the abundant boutiques and antiques shops along Highway 49. Be careful while driving through the city's narrow streets or finding parking downtown; on crowded weekends, the two-lane main drag often feels like all of California is visiting.

Need some fixings for the homestead? At the **Fancy Dry Goods and Clothing Store** (22733 Main St., Columbia, 209/532-1066, 10am-5pm Tues.-Sun. summer, 10am-4pm Wed.-Sun. winter), you can browse the "supplies" on hand like a true forty-niner. Everything here would have been in style 150 years ago, including the bonnets, calico dresses, and men's hats on the store's shelves. You can also check out the mock weapons and mining tools. Still, this isn't a museum; you can buy gifts for men, women, and kids, including sewing kits for quilting or knitting your very own Wild West wardrobe.

The next best thing to stepping back in time is visiting **Kamice's Photographic Establishment** (22729 Main St., Columbia, 209/532-4861, www.photosincolumbia.com, 10am-5pm daily summer, 10am-5pm Thurs.-Sun., by appointment Tues.-Wed. winter). Bring the family and snap a sepia-toned portrait like true pioneers. Kids will love posing in fake miner's outfits or with a replica six-shooter. You can even bring along the family dog.

You can't leave town without visiting **Nelson's Columbia Candy Kitchen** (22726 Main St., Columbia, 209/532-7886, www.columbiacandykitchen.com, 9am-5pm Mon.-Fri., 9am-6pm Sat.-Sun.). The store has been serving candy for more than 100 years, and they've just about perfected the recipes. Everything here is diet-busting, finger-licking good; make sure to try the homemade marshmallow bars or a piece of whipping cream fudge. Luckily, Nelson's also has a few sugar-free candies if your sweet tooth can't indulge in the other goodies.

You'll quickly find that **Legends** (131 S. Washington St., Sonora, 209/532-8120, 11am-5pm daily) is a different kind of bookstore. Instead of just books and a coffee bar, this fun little shop also has an old-fashioned soda fountain. Grab some ice cream or a hot dog while browsing the rare books and antiques, or settle into the comfy bar stools for a sandwich.

If you've toured the Gold Country from top to bottom, you've probably breezed through quite a few antiques stores, but **Mother Lode Trading Post** (163 S. Washington St., Sonora, 209/533-1012, 9am-6pm Thurs.-Tues.) is one of the best. It's actually a collective of several antiques dealers, many specializing in vintage American and European furniture. For collectors, this place will yield all sorts of finds, like a German gun cabinet or a Victorian kerosene chandelier. Besides furniture, the collective has the standard lineup of antique glassware, porcelain, jewelry, and clocks. The store often stays open later during warmer months, especially on busier days.

Sports and Recreation

For a peaceful fishing trip in the Gold Country, go to **Pinecrest Lake** (Hwy. 108, 30 miles east of Sonora, www.fs.fed.us). The Stanislaus National Forest permits boating, and a launch is available for your convenience. Bring your pole and bait to the pier and fish in peace from dry land. The U.S. Forest Service stocks the lake with rainbow trout. As long as you have a California fishing license, you're good to go.

Fishing and boating are also allowed on a number of other lakes. **New Melones Lake** (6850 Studhorse Flat Rd., Sonora, 209/536-9094, www.usbr.gov) has beautiful hiking and biking trails along its edges. Dive in for a swim, go out on your boat, or cast a line to catch your dinner.

Many native Californians cut their first turns in the snow at **Dodge Ridge** (1 Dodge Ridge Rd., Pinecrest, 209/965-3474, www.dodgeridge.com, 9am-4pm daily winter, adults $58-68, youth $48-55, children $15-20). Only a few miles from Sonora, Dodge Ridge is a reasonable drive from the Bay Area, and an easy drive from Gold Country towns. A major bowl served by three different chairlifts has all beginner and advanced-beginner runs. The pee-wee area is reserved for kids learning to ski, and Ego Alley offers a chance for adventurous new skiers to try a slightly steeper slope. The rest of the mountain beckons to intermediate and advanced skiers and boarders. Intermediates love this resort, since you can get all the way down the mountain on blue slopes from almost every lift in the park. For experts, a few double-black-diamond runs nestle at the top of Chair 3. Freestylers have fun on the five terrain parks scattered throughout the park.

Adjacent to Dodge Ridge, the **Gooseberry** area calls to hard-core cross-country skiers. Trails range from "more difficult" to "most difficult" at this park. The tiny parking lot fits only about eight cars, but there is a restroom for weary skiers needing a break.

Accommodations

For history in your hotel room, you can't beat

the **Gunn House Hotel** (286 S. Washington St., Sonora, 209/532-3421, http://gunnhouse-hotel.com, $84-125). The original home of Dr. Lewis Gunn—a gold prospector and newspaper owner—the building has been a home, a hospital, and a hotel in its more than 150 years. A dozen rooms are done up in elegant jewel tones and rich fabrics, each with a king or queen bed with a teddy bear to welcome you. The Gunn House offers cable TV in every room, plus full heating and air-conditioning. Each morning, partake in the included sumptuous Innkeeper's Breakfast.

Barretta Gardens Inn (700 S. Barretta St., Sonora, 209/532-6039, www.barrettagardens.com, $150-325) is a restored farmhouse with some of the most lavish digs in the Gold Country. The eight rooms feature serious luxury—Persian carpets, mahogany bed frames, and polished antique furnishings. Enjoy a glass of wine outside into the sprawling one-acre garden or play croquet on the lawns.

The **Bradford Place Inn** (56 W. Bradford St., Sonora, 209/536-6075, www.bradfordplaceinn.com, $145-265) feels like an authentic Gold Rush home. First built in 1889 for a Wells Fargo agent, the house has been a bed-and-breakfast since the 1980s. Four rooms are decorated with Victorian-style floral wallpaper, plush furniture, and vintage wooden headboards. Each room has private heating and air-conditioning, a flat-screen TV, Wi-Fi, and a phone. Breakfast is included. There are only four rooms, so call well in advance to book your stay.

The two authentic Wild West hotels in town have been restored in similar fashion. The **Columbia City Hotel** (22768 Main St., Columbia, 209/532-1479, http://reserveamerica.com, $75-126) is located near the north end of the state park. The **Fallon Hotel** (11175 Washington St., Columbia, 209/532-1470, http://reserveamerica.com, $75-126) is near the park's southern boundary on the county road. The cozy rooms in each hotel have been faithfully restored with Victorian-style wallpaper, handmade furniture, Gold Rush-era photos, and double beds. Both hotels have a strict no-pets policy, so leave your furry friends at home. Cottages ($126-170) with complete kitchens and bathrooms are also available near the Columbia City Hotel.

Food

One of the top picks in the region, the ★ **Diamondback Grill** (93 S. Washington St., Sonora, 209/532-6661, www.thediamondbackgrill.com, 11am-9pm Mon.-Thurs., 11am-9:30pm Fri.-Sat., 11am-8pm Sun., $10) serves good grill food at extremely reasonable prices. Everyone loves the burgers and the sweet-potato fries, and the garlic fries are a treat. Fresh salads feed lighter appetites, and you can enjoy a glass of wine with your meal. Expect a wait, especially on weekends.

With costumed bartenders, old-time piano music, and a fully restored bar from the 1800s, the **Jack Douglass Saloon** (22718 Main St., 209/533-4176, 10am-6pm daily, $5-10) feels like a place where duels might happen. These days, the only conflict comes from deciding between the homemade sarsaparilla or the wild cherry soda. For lunch, choose from sandwiches, salads, and the gigantic nachos, a specialty. The saloon stays open until midnight on Saturdays if there's a band playing.

Talulah's (13 S. Washington St., Sonora, 209/532-7278, www.talulahs.com, 11:30am-2:30pm, 5:30pm-8pm Tues.- Thurs., 11:30am-2:30pm, 5pm-9pm Friday, noon-3pm, 5pm-9pm Sat., $14-20) serves up piping-hot pastas like the ravioli sampler and the homemade veggie lasagna stuffed with portabella mushrooms and eggplant; other entrees include gorgonzola chicken breast and meatloaf. Most of the ingredients are local and organic, and the kitchen serves mostly seasonal dishes. Gluten-free diners can substitute rice pasta for most items on the menu.

Columbia Kate's (22727 Columbia St., Columbia, 209/532-1885, www.columbiakates.com, bakery 8am-4pm daily, teahouse 11am-4pm daily, $12-16) is a cozy English-style tea house with plenty of country hospitality. You can eat lunch here or stop by for a full afternoon tea. Order the chicken pot pie with a raspberry green salad, along with the thirst-quenching lavender lemonade.

Information and Services

Sonora is one of the largest towns in the southern Gold Country and has plenty of services. For the central municipal visitors center, head for the **Tuolumne County Visitors Bureau** (542 Stockton St., Sonora, 209/533-4420, www.tcvb.com, 9am-6pm Mon.-Fri., 10am-6pm Sat., 10am-5pm Sun. summer, 9am-5pm Mon.-Sat. winter).

Sonora Regional Medical Center (1000 Greenley Rd., Sonora, 209/532-5000, www.adventisthealth.org) has an emergency room.

Transportation

Sonora is at the tip of the southern Gold Country. By car, it's about 15 miles south of Angels Camp on Highway 49. South of Sonora, it's 55 miles to Mariposa. From the Central Valley, take Highway 108 from Modesto for 48 miles and then head north on Highway 49 for another 2 miles to reach Sonora. If you need to rent a car, **Enterprise** (14860 Mono Way, Sonora, 209/533-0500) and **Hertz** (13413 Mono Way, Sonora, 209/588-1575) have rentals available.

Sonora has several public transit options. Don't miss a ride on the **Historic 49 Trolley** (209/532-0404, www.tuolumnecountytransit.com, Sat.-Sun. early Apr.-Labor Day, adults $1.50, day pass $4, under age 13 free), an old-fashioned (but air-conditioned) way to see local sights in Sonora, Columbia, and Jamestown. For bus rides during the week, **Tuolumne County Transit** (209/532-0404, www.tuolumnecountytransit.com, Mon.-Fri., adults $1.50, day pass $4, under age 13 free) runs six bus routes in Sonora and the immediate vicinity.

JAMESTOWN

Railtown 1897 State Historic Park

Start your tour of **Railtown 1897** (Hwy. 108, 209/984-3953, www.railtown1897.org, 9:30am-4:30pm daily Apr.-Oct., 10am-3pm daily Nov.-Mar., adults $5, youth $3) inside. The old depot waiting room includes artifacts, a video describing the filmography of the Railtown trains, and locomotives used in films and TV shows. Prize locomotives sit in the century-old roundhouse. Train fans, history lovers, film buffs, and children all love this unusual indoor-outdoor museum. Behind the roundhouse you can check out the functioning turntable, then wander out

Locomotives sit on the turntable at Railtown 1897 State Historic Park.

to the rolling stock (some of it in fairly decrepit condition) and poke around a little. You can take a six-mile, 40-minute ride in a car of a steam locomotive into the Sierra foothills. Trains depart on the hour (11am-3pm Sat.-Sun. Apr.-Oct., adults $15, youth $8, fares include admission to the park).

Accommodations

The at-times infamous ★ **National Hotel** (18183 Main St., 209/984-3446, www.national-hotel.com, $140) has operated almost continuously since 1859—either as a hotel, a brothel, a small casino, or as a Prohibition-era bar. Each of the nine rooms features antique furniture and comfy linens and comforters on the one queen bed. All rooms have their own baths with a shower and access to the soaking room, which the hotel describes as its "1800s Jacuzzi." An upscale gourmet restaurant is downstairs, and the Gold Rush Saloon serves up signature cocktails and wines.

The **Victorian Gold B&B** (10382 Willow St., 888/551-1851, www.victoriangoldbb.com, $115-185) is a stunningly renovated Gilded Age mansion built in the 1890s. The eight rooms are charmingly decorated with modern amenities and include a private bath with either a shower or a claw-foot tub; some rooms have both. The inn is fully air-conditioned, with Wi-Fi in every room. Don't miss the homemade breakfast with fresh fruit and made-to-order omelets.

Food

In a town thick with Gold Rush atmosphere, Jamestown's ★ **Willow Steakhouse and Saloon** (Willow St. and Main St., 209/984-3998, www.willowsteakjamestown.com, 11am-9pm daily, $11-41) fits right in. The steaks are good rather than great, but the baked potatoes and the bucket of fixings make up for it. For an after-dinner cocktail, head into the Saloon and have a drink with the locals. You might have to wait for a table on weekend evenings.

One of the best Mexican spots in the area is **Morelia** (18148 Main St., 209/984-1432, 11am-9pm daily, $10), for enchiladas, Mexican grilled meat dishes, good beans and guacamole, and plenty of other tasty classic fare.

Information and Services

Jamestown doesn't have a visitors center, but you can find travel advice and maps online (www.jamestown-ca.com). To fill up your car, stop by **Chip's Chevron Mini Mart and Car Wash** (18151 Hwy. 108, 209/984-5245) on the main drag. **Umqua Bank** (18281 Main St., 209/984-3971) has a 24-hour ATM.

Transportation

By car, Jamestown is less than four miles south of Sonora on Highway 49. If you're driving from Modesto, take Highway 108 northeast for 43 miles and then head north on Highway 49 for 3 more miles to reach Jamestown. **Enterprise** (209/533-0500) and **Hertz** (209/588-1575) rent cars.

Two bus routes operate between Jamestown and Sonora. For a more whimsical ride that families will especially love, hop on the **Historic 49 Trolley** (209/532-0404, www.tuolumnecountytransit.com, Sat.-Sun. early Apr.-Labor Day, adults $1.50, day pass $4, under age 13 free). **Tuolumne County Transit** (209/532-0404, www.tuolumnecountytransit.com, adults $1.50, day pass $4) runs Monday-Friday.

Yosemite and the Eastern Sierra

Look for ★ to find recommended sights, activities, dining, and lodging.

Highlights

★ **Half Dome:** Even in a park filled with iconic monuments, Half Dome towers over all others. Whether you come to scale its peak or just to see the real-life model for all those wonderful photographs, Half Dome lives up to the hype (page 450).

★ **Bridalveil Fall:** It's the most monumental—and the most accessible—of Yosemite's marvelous collection of waterfalls (page 451).

★ **Mist Trail:** The best way to experience Yosemite Valley's grandeur is on one of its many scenic trails. A hike along the Mist Trail to the top of Vernal Fall brings the valley views alive (page 455).

★ **Badger Pass Ski Area:** California's first downhill ski area is as popular as ever, with affordable downhill and cross-country skiing, sledding hills for the kids, and full-moon snowshoe walks (page 462).

★ **Tuolumne Meadows:** Explore the wonders of the park's high elevations at this rare alpine meadow, where numerous hiking trails thread through Yosemite's backcountry (page 470).

★ **Mono Lake Tufa State Natural Reserve:** Freestanding calcite towers, knobs, and spires dot the alien landscape of Mono Lake. Several interpretive trails provide history and access to what is undoubtedly the most unusual lake you will ever see (page 496).

★ **Bodie State Historic Park:** A state of "arrested decay" has preserved this 1877 gold-mining ghost town. Tours of the abandoned mine provide background on the settlement's sordid history (page 500).

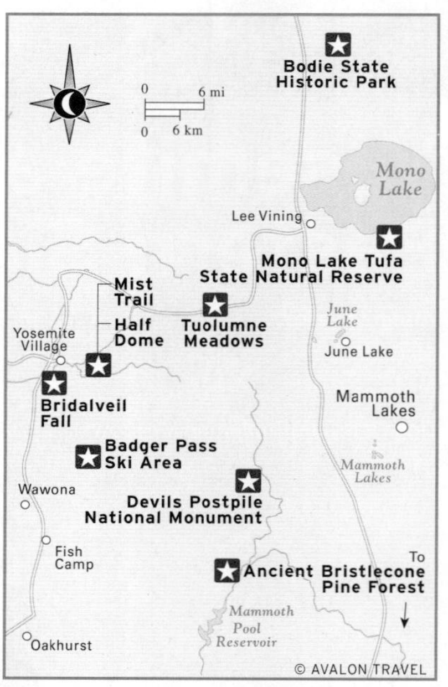

★ **Devils Postpile National Monument:** One visit to these strange natural rock formations and you'll understand how they got their name. A mix of volcanic heat and pressure created near-perfect, straight-sided hexagonal posts that have to be seen to be believed (page 506).

★ **Ancient Bristlecone Pine Forest:** The oldest trees on earth are on view in this quiet section of the Inyo National Forest. Take a self-guided nature trail past Methuselah, a 4,750-year-old tree (page 514).

Of all the wondrous sights, natural and otherwise, that Northern California has to offer, few are more iconic than the 1,200-square-mile Yosemite National Park.

This natural playground has been immortalized in the photographs of Ansel Adams and in the words of the naturalist John Muir, who called it "the grandest of all the special temples of Nature I was ever permitted to enter." It was Muir who introduced Yosemite to President Theodore Roosevelt, an event that eventually resulted in its national park designation in 1890.

No one seems to visit Yosemite without being profoundly affected by it. If this is your first visit, prepare to be overwhelmed. If you're a regular visitor, then you already know you're going to see something new this time that will knock your polar-fleece socks off. Whether you scale a legendary granite precipice, wake at dawn to watch bear cubs frolic in a glistening meadow, hike under a crashing waterfall, or sit by the fire in one of the park's rustic lodges and watch the snow fall in the moonlight, you'll be different by the time you leave; enjoy the transformation.

East of the great park, Mono Lake greets visitors with an eerie stillness. This treeless, alkaline, and salt-filled lake is home to odd calcite (tufa) formations—mute testament to the extraordinary mineral content of the water. The rough High Sierra climate, with its deep winter snows and summer heat, attracts few year-round residents, though the mining town of Bodie—now California's biggest ghost town—once sheltered 10,000 gold-hungry adventurers.

South of Mono Lake, the picturesque town of Mammoth Lakes supports the Mammoth Mountain ski area. Winter tourism plays a big part in the local economy, but there's much more to do around Mammoth than just skiing and snowboarding. Hiking, mountain biking, fishing, backpacking, and sightseeing are great in this part of the Eastern Sierra, and you can find bargains on lodging in the summertime "off-season."

PLANNING YOUR TIME

Yosemite National Park (209/372-0200, www.nps.gove/yose, $30 per vehicle Apr.-Oct., $25 Nov.-Mar., $15 pedestrians, $15 bicycles,

Previous: Half Dome; the ghost town of Bodie. **Above:** El Capitan.

Yosemite National Park

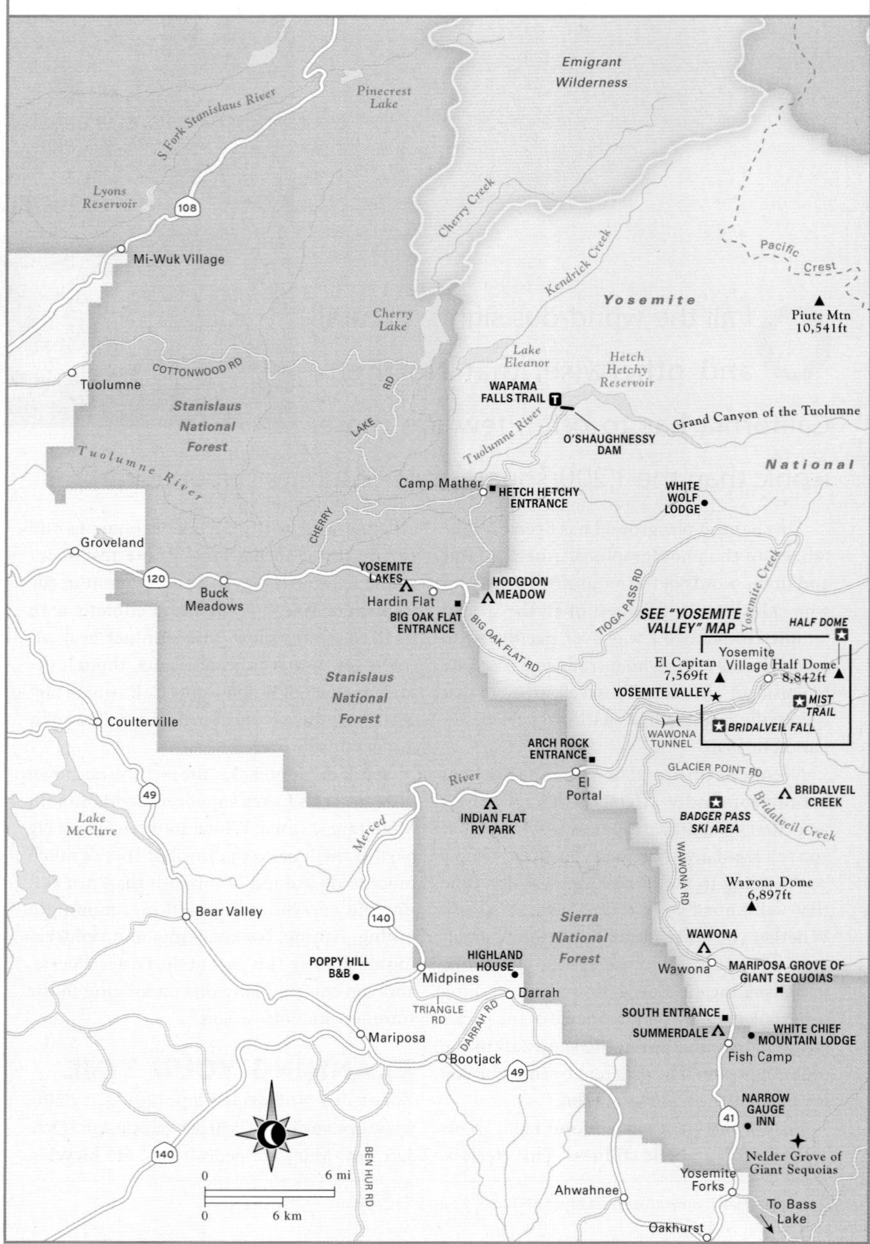

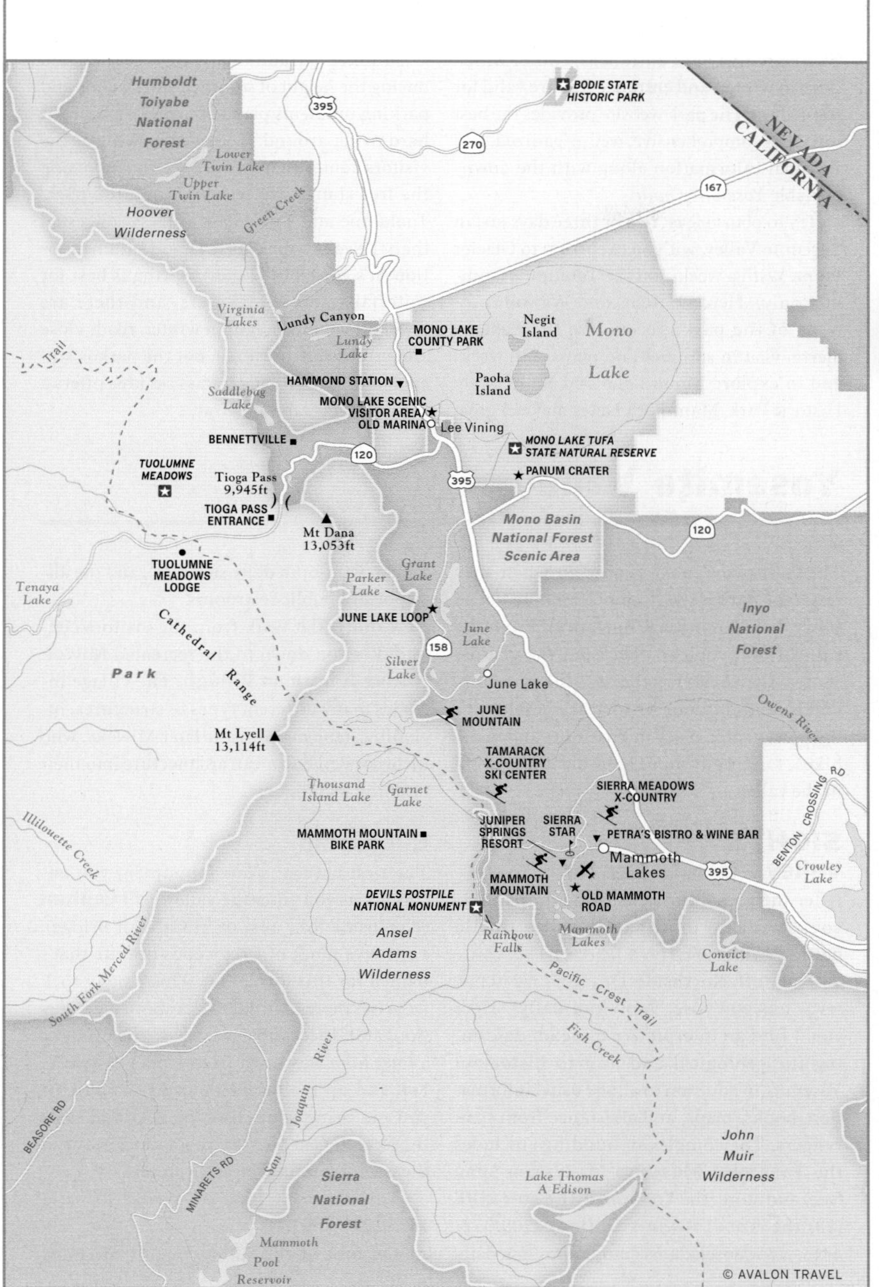
Humboldt Toiyabe National Forest
Lower Twin Lake
Upper Twin Lake
Hoover Wilderness
Green Creek
395
270
BODIE STATE HISTORIC PARK
NEVADA
CALIFORNIA
167
Virginia Lakes
Lundy Canyon
Lundy Lake
MONO LAKE COUNTY PARK
Negit Island
Mono Lake
Paoha Island
Trail
HAMMOND STATION
Saddlebag Lake
MONO LAKE SCENIC VISITOR AREA/ OLD MARINA
Lee Vining
BENNETTVILLE
MONO LAKE TUFA STATE NATURAL RESERVE
120
TUOLUMNE MEADOWS
Tioga Pass 9,945ft
PANUM CRATER
TIOGA PASS ENTRANCE
Mt Dana 13,053ft
Mono Basin National Forest Scenic Area
TUOLUMNE MEADOWS LODGE
Grant Lake
Parker Lake
Tenaya Lake
JUNE LAKE LOOP
Cathedral Range
June Lake
158
Inyo National Forest
Park
Silver Lake
June Lake
JUNE MOUNTAIN
Owens River
Mt Lyell 13,114ft
TAMARACK X-COUNTRY SKI CENTER
Thousand Island Lake
Garnet Lake
SIERRA MEADOWS X-COUNTRY
BENTON CROSSING RD
Illilouette Creek
MAMMOTH MOUNTAIN BIKE PARK
JUNIPER SPRINGS RESORT
SIERRA STAR
PETRA'S BISTRO & WINE BAR
Mammoth Lakes
MAMMOTH MOUNTAIN
OLD MAMMOTH ROAD
Crowley Lake
DEVILS POSTPILE NATIONAL MONUMENT
Ansel Adams Wilderness
Rainbow Falls
Mammoth Lakes
Convict Lake
South Fork Merced River
Pacific Crest Trail
Fish Creek
San Joaquin River
BEASORE RD
MINARETS RD
John Muir Wilderness
Sierra National Forest
Lake Thomas A Edison
Mammoth Pool Reservoir
© AVALON TRAVEL

motorcycles, noncommercial buses Apr.-Oct., $20 Nov.-Mar.) is open daily year-round. There are five park entrances, two of which close in winter, and entrance fees are valid for seven days. The park website provides the best source of comprehensive, well-organized, and seasonal information along with the downloadable *Yosemite Guide*.

Try to plan at least two or three days just in Yosemite Valley, with an excursion to Glacier Point. With a week, add the Tuolumne (summer only), Hetch Hetchy, and Wawona sections of the park. To explore the Eastern Sierra, visit in summer and plan a full weekend to explore Mono Lake and Bodie State Historic Park. Mammoth Lakes makes a great ski getaway in winter, but you'll need a three-day weekend here at the very least.

Summer is traditionally high season, and during the height of summer, traffic jams and parking problems plague the park, making it hard to get around. Consider parking at the visitors center in Yosemite Valley and using the free shuttles to travel around the park. Tuolumne and Tioga Pass are less congested than the valley, making it a good summer option (it's closed in winter). Spring is best for waterfalls and wildflowers, and there are fewer crowds, as in fall. In winter, roads close and crowds are minimal, but the park is still enchanting. The Badger Pass ski area offers a fun and affordable getaway.

Yosemite Valley

The first place most people go when they reach the park is the floor of Yosemite Valley (Hwy. 140, Arch Rock Entrance). From the valley floor, you can check out the visitors center, the theater, galleries, the museum, hotels, and outdoor historical exhibits. It's the most visited place in Yosemite, and many hikes, ranging from easy to difficult, begin in the valley.

SIGHTS

Valley Visitors Center

After the scenic turnouts through the park, your first stop in Yosemite Valley should be the **Valley Visitors Center** (Yosemite Village, off Northside Dr., 209/372-0299, www.nps.gov/yose, 9am-5pm daily). Here you'll find an interpretive museum describing the geological and human history of Yosemite in addition to all the usual information, books, maps, and assistance from park rangers. The complex of buildings includes the **Yosemite Museum** (daily 9am-5pm, free) and store, the **Yosemite Theater LIVE** ($8) the **Ansel Adams Gallery** (209/372-4413, www.anseladams.com, 10am-5pm daily winter, 9am-6pm daily summer), and the all-important public restrooms.

A short, flat walk from the visitors center takes you down to the recreated **Miwok Native American Village.** The village includes many different types of structures, including some made by the later Miwoks, who incorporated European architecture into their building techniques.

El Capitan

The first natural stone monument you encounter as you enter the valley is **El Capitan** (Northside Rd., west of El Capitan Bridge), a massive hunk of Cretaceous granite that's named for this formation. This craggy rock face rises more than 3,000 feet above the valley floor and is accessible two ways: You can take a long hike westward from Upper Yosemite Fall and up the back side of El Capitan, or you can bring your climbing gear and scale the face. El Cap boasts a reputation as one of the world's seminal big-face climbs.

★ Half Dome

At the foot of the valley, one of the most

Bridalveil Fall

recognizable features in all of Yosemite rises high above the valley floor. Ansel Adams's famed photographs of **Half Dome,** visible from most of the valley floor, made it known to hikers and photography lovers all over the world. Scientists believe that Half Dome was never a whole dome—the way it appears to us now is actually its original formation. This piece of a narrow granite ridge was polished to its smooth dome-like shape tens of millions of years ago by glaciers, giving it the appearance of half a dome.

★ Bridalveil Fall

Bridalveil Fall (Southside Dr., past the Hwy. 41 turnoff) is many visitors' first introduction to Yosemite's famed collection of waterfalls. The **Bridalveil Fall Trail** (0.5 mile, 20 minutes) is a pleasantly sedate walk up to the fall. Although the 620-foot waterfall runs year-round, its fine mist sprays most powerfully in the spring—expect to get wet!

The trailhead has its own parking area, which is west of the main lodge and visitors center complex, so it's one of the first major sights people come to upon entering the park. It's a great first stop as you travel up the valley.

Yosemite Falls

Spring and early summer are the best times to view the many waterfalls that cascade

El Capitan

Yosemite Valley

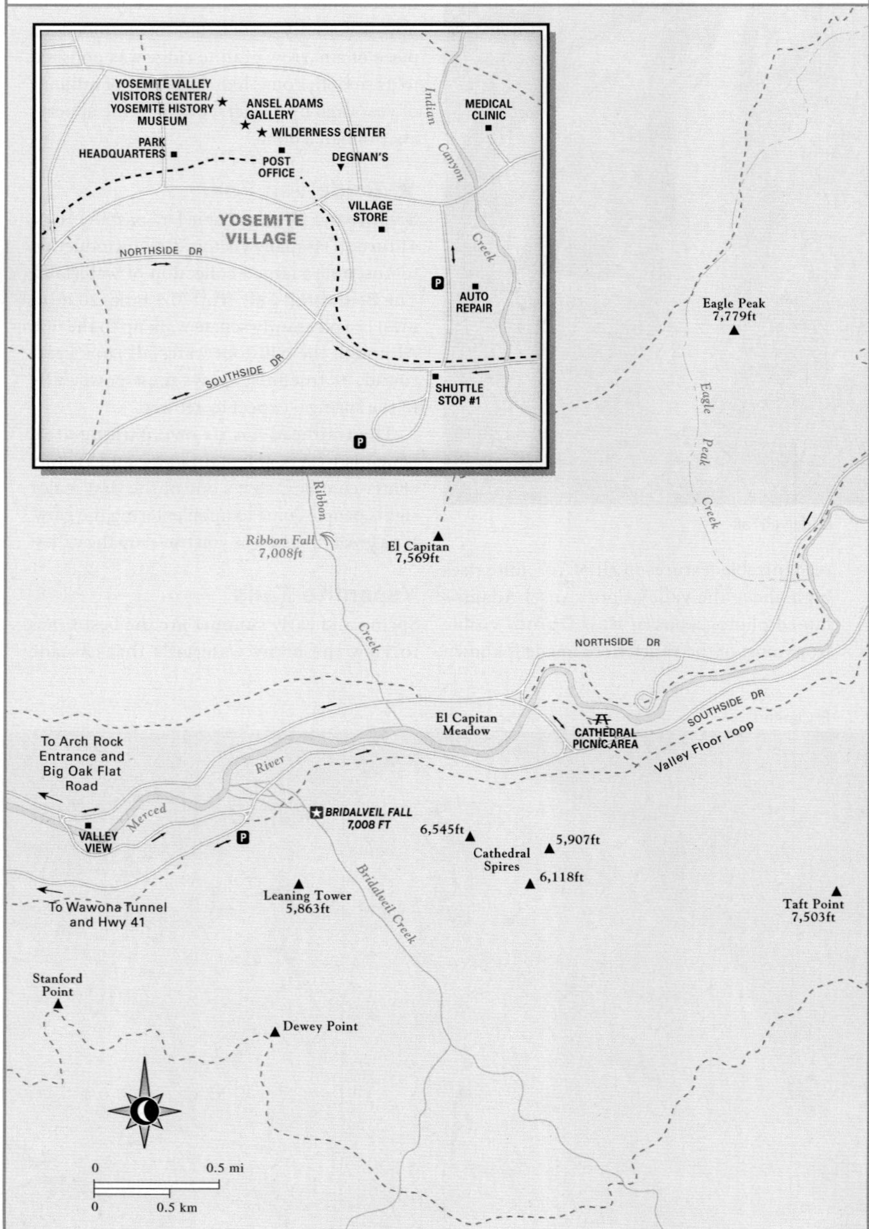

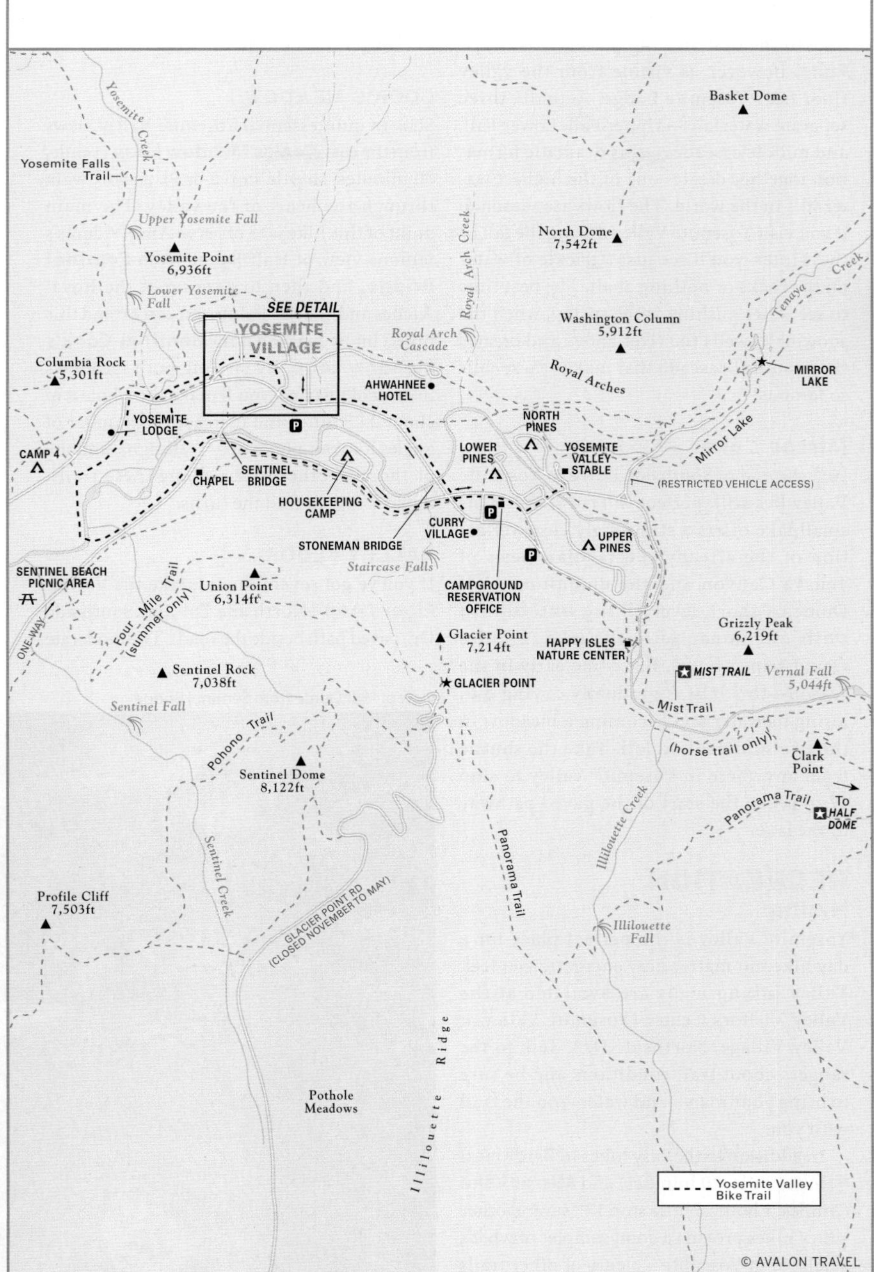
Basket Dome
Yosemite Creek
Yosemite Falls Trail
Upper Yosemite Fall
Yosemite Point
6,936ft
Lower Yosemite Fall
SEE DETAIL
YOSEMITE VILLAGE
Royal Arch Creek
Royal Arch Cascade
North Dome
7,542ft
Washington Column
5,912ft
Royal Arches
Tenaya Creek
MIRROR LAKE
Mirror Lake
Columbia Rock
5,301ft
AHWAHNEE HOTEL
YOSEMITE LODGE
CAMP 4
NORTH PINES
LOWER PINES
YOSEMITE VALLEY STABLE
(RESTRICTED VEHICLE ACCESS)
SENTINEL BRIDGE
CHAPEL
HOUSEKEEPING CAMP
CURRY VILLAGE
STONEMAN BRIDGE
UPPER PINES
SENTINEL BEACH PICNIC AREA
Union Point
6,314ft
Staircase Falls
CAMPGROUND RESERVATION OFFICE
Four Mile Trail (summer only)
ONE-WAY
Glacier Point
7,214ft
HAPPY ISLES NATURE CENTER
Grizzly Peak
6,219ft
Sentinel Rock
7,038ft
GLACIER POINT
MIST TRAIL
Vernal Fall
5,044ft
Sentinel Fall
Mist Trail
Pohono Trail
(horse trail only)
Clark Point
Sentinel Dome
8,122ft
To HALF DOME
Panorama Trail
Illilouette Creek
Sentinel Creek
Profile Cliff
7,503ft
GLACIER POINT RD (CLOSED NOVEMBER TO MAY)
Illilouette Fall
Illilouette Ridge
Pothole Meadows
Yosemite Valley Bike Trail
© AVALON TRAVEL

down the granite walls of Yosemite. Most of the major waterfalls require at least a short hike to the best viewing points. **Yosemite Falls,** however, is visible from the valley floor near Yosemite Lodge. Actually three separate waterfalls—Upper Fall, Lower Fall, and middle cascades—this dramatic formation together creates one of the highest waterfalls in the world. The flows are seasonal; if you visit Yosemite Valley during the fall or the winter, you'll see just a trickle of water on the rocks or nothing at all. The best time to see water gushing is the spring, when the snowmelt swells the river above and creates the beautiful cascade that makes these falls so famous.

Mirror Lake

Past the end of Southside Drive in Yosemite Valley lies still, perfect **Mirror Lake.** This small lake offers a stunningly clear reflection of the already spectacular views of Tenaya Canyon and the ubiquitous Half Dome. A short, level **hiking and biking path** circumnavigates the lake (2 miles round-trip, 1 hour). But come early in the season—this lake is gradually drying out, losing its water and becoming a meadow in the late summer and fall. Take the shuttle from anywhere in Yosemite Valley to stop 17 to get to the start of the paved pathway to the lake.

RECREATION

Hiking

Yosemite Valley is the perfect place for a day hike, no matter how energetic you feel. Valley hiking maps are available at the Valley Visitors Center (Yosemite Valley at Valley Village, Northside Dr.). Talk to the rangers about trail conditions and be sure to bring your map—and water—on the trail with you.

In addition to the easy hikes to **Bridalveil Fall** (0.5 mile, 20 minutes) and **Mirror Lake** (2 miles, 1 hour, shuttle stop 17), several other valley hikes provide a good sampler of what's available in Yosemite—plenty of other trails wind through this gorgeous area. Be aware that many people love the valley trails, so you likely won't be alone in the wilderness.

COOK'S MEADOW

Soak in quintessential Yosemite Valley views from the easy **Cook's Meadow Loop** (1 mile, 30 minutes, shuttle stop 5 or 9), a short walk through the heart of the valley. The main point of this hike is to observe Ansel Adams's famous view of Half Dome from **Sentinel Bridge,** and then to gaze up at the Royal Arches and Glacier Point. You can extend this hike a bit by making it the **Sentinel-Cook's Meadow Loop.** By circling both meadows instead of just one, you'll make the whole trip about 2.25 miles and increase the number of angles for your photo ops. Trail signs, and the plethora of other hikers doing these trails, make it easy to find the turns.

VALLEY FLOOR

If you've got several hours, take the **Valley Floor Loop** (Northside Dr. and Southside Dr., paved path beside the road). The moderate

view of Half Dome from Sentinel Bridge

half loop (6.5 miles, 3 hours, shuttle stop 6) traverses the El Capitan Bridge, following the path of many old wagon roads and historical trails. The **full loop** is 13 miles long and takes about six hours to hike. It's a great moderate day hike, and you'll see the most beautiful parts of the valley while escaping the crowds on the roads. If you want to hike the Valley Floor Loop, talk to the rangers at the visitors center; the route is not entirely clear on the trail map, and getting lost in the meadows or forests is a distinct possibility.

LOWER YOSEMITE FALL

If you're staying at Yosemite Lodge and want an easy, gentle walk with a great view, take the **Lower Yosemite Fall Loop** (1.1 miles, 30 minutes, shuttle stop 6). Enjoy the wondrous views of both Upper and Lower Yosemite Falls, complete with lots of cooling spray. If you can, hike this trail in the spring or early summer, when the flow of the falls is at its peak. This easy trail works well for families with children who love the water.

UPPER YOSEMITE FALL

Naturally, some of the more challenging hikes in Yosemite Valley are also the most rewarding. One of these is the strenuous trek up to **Upper Yosemite Fall** (7.2 miles, 6-8 hours, shuttle stop 7). You can start this hike from the Upper Yosemite Fall trailhead or walk from Lower Yosemite Fall. The trail starts getting steep right away—you'll climb 2,700 vertical feet in three miles to reach the top of America's tallest waterfall. Your reward will be some of the most astonishing views to be had anywhere in the world. You can look down over the fall and out over the valley, with its grassy meadows far below. Plan all day for this hike, and bring plenty of water and snacks to replenish your energy for the potentially tricky climb down. This trail is well marked and much used, and the steep parts are made passable with stone steps, switchbacks, and occasional railings. But much of the trail tends to be wet and slippery, so hold on and take it slow.

★ MIST TRAIL

Starting at the Happy Isles Nature Center (shuttle stop 16), the moderate-strenuous Mist Trail leads first to **Vernal Fall** (3 miles, 3 hours) over much steep, slick granite—including more than 600 stairs—up to the top of Vernal Fall. Your reward is the stellar view of the valley below while relaxing on the flat granite boulders that abut the Merced River. If you packed a lunch, stop and eat here before returning back the same way. Hardier souls should continue another steep and strenuous 1.5-2 miles of switchbacks to the top of **Nevada Fall** (5.4 miles, 5-6 hours) and return via the John Muir Trail. Plan six hours for this hike, with a 2,000-foot elevation gain, and consider taking a lightweight rain jacket since this aptly named trail gives hikers a shower in the spring and early summer months.

The Mist Trail is closed in winter because of ice and snow and can be dangerous in the spring months when the river is at its peak; hikers have been lost in the waters here. Exercise caution in extreme conditions, and obey all trail signage.

view of Vernal Fall from the Mist Trail

HALF DOME

The most famous climb in Yosemite Valley takes you to the top of monumental **Half Dome** (14-16 miles, 10-12 hours, May-Oct. only, shuttle stop 16). But before you start, a word of warning: This hike can be dangerous. With a round-trip distance of 14 miles by the Mist Trail or 16 miles by the John Muir Trail, and with a very strenuous 4,800-foot elevation gain, this arduous, all-day hike is not for small children, the elderly, or anyone remotely out of shape. The trek is significantly riskier in rain, snow, high wind, or other adverse conditions, and rangers will not be able to rescue you should you become stranded at the top. Attempt this hike only in the summer (Memorial Day-Columbus Day) when the cables are up (you must hold onto cables to help pull yourself up the last 400 feet of steep granite to the top of the dome). Most importantly, obey all signage on the trail. If the park posts that the trail is closed or unsafe, heed the conditions and turn back. Continuing when conditions deem otherwise risks your life and others, including those who will try to rescue you.

Before you commit to Half Dome, make sure you're ready, mentally and physically, for a long and sometimes treacherous challenge. Check weather conditions and sunrise and sunset times before you hike, and establish a turn-around point so that you aren't hiking back in darkness. Take a well-organized pack with water (1 gallon pp), food, a topo map and compass, a headlamp or flashlight (with batteries), and other safety essentials. Wear hiking shoes that have been broken in and bring a hat.

From the Happy Isles shuttle stop, follow the Mist Trail to Nevada Fall (or, alternately, take the John Muir Trail instead), and then follow the signs for Half Dome. Once you stagger to the top, you'll find a restful expanse of stone on which to sit and rest and enjoy the scenery.

Yosemite requires all hikers to have a permit (877/444-6777, www.recreation.gov, $12.50-14.50 pp) to climb Half Dome. There are 300 permits issued per day; 225 permits are allotted for day hikers, and the rest are for backpackers. The park distributes permits through an online lottery starting in March. Permits are not available on a same-day basis. However, a few almost-last-minute options exist: Check the website starting at midnight two days before you want to climb and enter the last-minute lottery by 1pm the same day. You will be notified the following morning of the lottery results. The park's public information office (209/372-0826) can answer questions about the lottery process.

Biking

Biking is a great way to get out of the car, off the crowded roads, and explore Yosemite at a quicker-than-walking (and sometimes even quicker than driving) pace. Twelve miles of paved trails are mostly flat. You can bring your own bike, or rent one in Yosemite Village from the in-park concessionaire, Delaware North Companies (209/372-4386, www.yosemitepark.com, 9am-6pm daily, $11.50 per hour, $32.00 per day). Check at Yosemite Lodge (801/559-5000, shuttle stop 8) for more information about rentals and to get a bike trail map.

Horseback Riding

Two different rides begin at the **Yosemite Valley Stable** (end of Southside Dr., 209/372-8348, www.yosemitepark.com, 8am-5pm daily April-Oct., $65-88.50). The sedate two-hour trek to Mirror Lake works well for children and beginning riders. Along the way, your guide will explain the geologic forces that are slowly drying out the lake. A half-day ride takes you out to Clark Point, from where you can admire Vernal Fall, Nevada Fall, and the valley floor. This ride takes about four hours but isn't terribly difficult.

Ice-Skating

Curry Village (end of Southside Dr., 209/372-8319, www.yosemitepark.com, 3:30pm-6pm, 7pm-9:30pm Mon.-Fri., 8:30am-11am, noon-2:30pm, 3:30pm-6pm, 7pm-9:30pm Sat.-Sun.

Yosemite at Night

Yosemite National Park does not roll up its meadows and trails at sunset. In fact, some aspects of the park come alive only at nightfall. Many of the animals that live in the park are crepuscular by nature—they're most active in the twilight hours of dawn and dusk. Take a quiet stroll in the park early in the morning or just as darkness is falling and you're likely to see more wildlife than you'll run into during the day.

If you prefer a guided tour, join the **Night Prowl** (209/372-4386, www.yosemitepark.com, 90 minutes, $7.50 pp, $30 per family). This guided tour takes you along easy trails near Yosemite Lodge at the Falls and explains the nightlife of the valley floor's inhabitants. Night Prowl takes place once or twice a week, starting at various times and places, and is good for both children and adults. Purchase your tickets at any activity desk in Yosemite, or call 209/372-4386, and you'll get all the information on where and when to meet. The Prowl is offered year-round but is a bit more comfortable during warmer months.

If astronomy is your interest, join experienced guides for the **Starry Skies** (209/372-4386, http://www.yosemitepark.com, $7.50 pp, $30 per family) program. Equally well suited for beginners and more experienced stargazers, this 90-minute program takes you out to the meadows to look at the stars and the moon free of light pollution. You'll learn about constellations, comets, and meteors and enjoy the myths and legends about the night sky. Starry Skies happens several times each week in Yosemite Valley and once a week in Wawona.

For families tired after a long day of running around the park, more sedentary evening programs are available. **Fireside Storytelling** (fall-spring, free) focuses on, well, telling stories around the big fire inside the Ahwahnee Great Lounge. Take refuge from the bugs and the cold and listen to great tales in a comfortable indoor environment during the off-season. Check the *Yosemite Guide* for more information about these and other programs.

The **Yosemite Valley Auditorium and Yosemite Theater** (Northside Dr.) share a building behind the visitors center in the heart of Yosemite Village. Check the copy of *Yosemite Guide* you received at the gate for a list of what shows are playing during your visit. The John Muir Performances (209/372-0731, 7pm Sun.-Thurs. May-Sept., adults $8, children $4), starring Yosemite's resident actor Lee Stetson, have been running for roughly 30 years. Other programs in the theater and auditorium include presentations by Shelton Johnson (who appeared in the Ken Burns documentary *The National Parks: America's Best Idea*) about the Buffalo Soldiers, films about climbing, and extreme filmmaking.

mid-Nov.-Mar., adults $10.50, children $10, rentals $4) has an ice-skating rink in winter.

Rock Climbing

The rock climbing at Yosemite is some of the best in the world. **El Capitan,** the face of **Half Dome,** and **Sentinel Dome** in the high country are challenges that draw climbers from all over. If you plan to climb one of these monuments, check with the Yosemite park rangers and the Mountaineering School well in advance for necessary information and permits.

Many of the spectacular ascents are not beginners' climbs. The right place to start climbing in Yosemite is the **Yosemite Mountaineering School** (209/372-8344, www.yosemitepark.com). Here you'll find "Go Climb a Rock" classes for beginners, perfect for older kids or adult team-building groups. You'll also find guided climbs out of Yosemite Valley and Tuolumne Meadows, and if you're looking for a one-on-one guided climb experience, you can get it through the school. Also available are guided hikes and backpacking trips as well as cross-country skiing lessons and treks in winter.

ACCOMMODATIONS

All lodgings, including campsites, fill up quickly—up to months in advance. In Yosemite Valley, **Delaware North Companies**

(801/559-5000, www.yosemitepark.com) handles reservations for the lodgings at Curry Village, Housekeeping Camp, Yosemite Lodge at the Falls, and the Ahwahnee Hotel.

Curry Village

Curry Village (801/559-5000, www.yosemitepark.com) offers some of the oldest lodgings in the park. Often called Camp Curry, this sprawling array of wood-sided and canvas-tent cabins was originally created in 1899 to provide affordable lodgings so that people of modest means could visit and enjoy the wonders of Yosemite. At Curry Village, you can rent a tent cabin or a wood cabin, with or without heat and with or without a private bath. You can also reserve a motel room. Curry Village has showers ($5) and several eateries. The Curry Village breakfast buffet (7am-10am) is included in some special "hiker's packages"; it can also be added to any accommodations option for $12. You won't find any TVs or telephones in the Curry Village lodgings.

The 60 **Yosemite cabins** (year-round, $152-203) are hard to come by, and they're usually booked far in advance. These wood structures include one or two double beds (some have a double and a single) that sleep up to five. Cabins have private baths, electricity, decks or patios, and maid service. There are 14 cabins without private baths; these share a central bathhouse instead.

In addition, there are 319 **canvas tent cabins** ($79-125), the most affordable option. These are small, wood-frame, canvas-covered structures that sleep 2-4 in a combination of single and double cot beds. A small dresser, sheets, blankets, and pillows are provided, but no electricity or heat. Bear-proof lockers are available outside each tent cabin. Shared showers and restrooms are found within Curry Village. A few **heated tent cabins** (801/559-4884, late Sept.-mid-May, $125) are available on a limited basis.

The 18 rooms in the **Stoneman Motel** ($198) sleep 2-6 and have heat, private baths, and daily maid service. An extra charge of $10-12 applies for each person beyond the first two.

Housekeeping Camp

Want to camp, but don't want to schlep all the gear? On the banks of the Merced River, the tent cabins at **Housekeeping Camp** (801/559-5000, www.yosemitepark.com, mid-Apr.-mid-Oct., $109) have their own sandy river beach for playing and sunbathing. Cabins have cement walls, white canvas roofs, and a white canvas curtain that separates the bedroom from the covered patio that doubles as a dining room. Every cabin has a double bed plus two bunks (with room for two additional cots), a bear-proof food container, and an outdoor fire ring. You can bring your own linens, or rent a "bed pack" (no towels, $3). No maid service is provided, but you won't miss it as you sit outside watching the sunset over Yosemite Valley.

Yosemite Lodge at the Falls

★ **Yosemite Lodge at the Falls** (209/372-1274, www.yosemitepark.com, $199-250), situated near Yosemite Village on the valley floor, has a location perfect for touring the park. The motel-style rooms are light and pretty, with polished wood furniture, bright bed linens, and Native American design details. Lodge rooms with king beds offer romantic escapes for couples, complete with balconies overlooking the valley. Enjoy the heated pool in the summer and free shuttle transportation up to the Badger Pass ski area in winter. The amphitheater runs nature programs and movies. The lodge is central to the Yosemite shuttle system and has a post office, an ATM, the on-site **Mountain Room Restaurant** (209/372-1499, 5:30pm-8:30pm daily May-Oct., 5pm-8pm Sun.-Thurs., 5pm-8:30pm Fri.-Sat. Oct.-May), the **Mountain Room Lounge** (4:30pm-11pm Mon.-Fri., noon-11pm Sat.-Sun.), and a food court (6:30am-9pm daily summer, 6:30am-8pm daily winter).

Ahwahnee Hotel

Built as a luxury hotel in the early 1900s, the

★ **Ahwahnee Hotel** (209/372-1407, www.yosemitepark.com, $490-544) lives up to its reputation with a gorgeous stone facade, striking stone fireplaces, and soaring ceilings in the common rooms. The rooms, in both the hotel and the cottages, drip with sumptuous appointments. The decor is Native American, with intricate geometric and zoomorphic designs on linens, furniture, and pillows. The Ahwahnee includes 24 cottages and 99 hotel rooms in the main building. All bedrooms come with either one king bed or two doubles; rooms in the main hotel may be combined with a parlor to make a suite. The cottages come with small stone patios as well as TVs, telephones, small refrigerators, and private baths.

A bonus is the on-site **Ahwahnee Dining Room** (Ahwahnee Hotel, 209/372-1489, www.yosemitepark.com, 7am-10am, 11:30am-2pm, 5pm-9pm Mon.-Sat., 7am-2pm, 5pm-9pm Sun., $31-50).

CAMPING

There are four campgrounds in Yosemite Valley, and they are deservedly popular. Upper Pines, Lower Pines, and North Pines require **reservations** (877/444-6777, www.recreation.gov), sometimes up to five months in advance; leashed pets are permitted at these three campgrounds. Campground reservations in Yosemite Valley are very competitive. At 7am (Eastern time) on the 15th of each month, campsites become available for a period up to five months in advance. A few minutes after 7am, choice sites and dates—maybe even all of them—will be gone. If you need a reservation for a specific day, get up early and call or check online diligently starting at 7am.

If you're in the valley and don't have a campsite reservation, call the **campground status line** (209/372-0266) for a recording of what's available that day. Or try one of the first-come, first-served campgrounds (but get there early).

the Ahwahnee Hotel

Lower Pines

The **Lower Pines campground** (60 sites, Mar.-late Oct., $26) is across from Curry Village. Sites accommodate tents and RVs up to 40 feet and include fire rings, picnic tables, a bear-proof food locker, water, flush toilets—and very little privacy. Supplies and showers ($5) are available in Curry Village. Reservations are required and are available up to five months in advance.

Upper Pines

Upper Pines campground (238 sites, year-round, $26) is the largest campground in the valley. It lies immediately southwest of Lower Pines and is encircled by the park road. Sites accommodate tents and RVs up to 35 feet and include fire rings, picnic tables, a bear-proof food locker, water, and flush toilets. Supplies and showers ($5) are available in Curry Village. Reservations are required March 15-November and are available up to five months in advance. Sites are available first-come, first-served December-March 15.

North Pines

Set along the Merced River and Tenaya Creek, **North Pines** (81 sites, Apr.-Sept., $26) offers slightly more privacy than its Upper and Lower Pines siblings. Sites accommodate tents and RVs up to 40 feet and include fire rings, picnic tables, a bear-proof food locker, water, and flush toilets. Supplies and showers ($5) are available in Curry Village, and the Yosemite Valley Stables are right nearby. Reservations are required and are available up to five months in advance.

Camp 4

Camp 4 (35 campsites, first-come, first-served, $6) stays open year-round. Yes, you can camp in the snow! Bring a tent—no RVs or trailers are allowed. You'll find showers nearby at Curry Village, and food and groceries at Yosemite Lodge. Sites include fire pits, picnic tables, and a shared bear-proof food locker. Restrooms with water and flush toilets are nearby. Pets are not permitted.

Reservations are not accepted. Spring-fall, hopeful campers must register with a park ranger. Plan to wait in line at the campground kiosk well before the ranger arrives at 8:30am. Sites are available first-come, first-served and hold six people each, so you may end up sharing with another party.

FOOD

Casual Dining

For casual food options, head to Yosemite Village for **Degnan's Loft** (209/372-8381, noon-9pm daily June-Aug., 5pm-9pm Mon.-Fri., noon-9pm Sat.-Sun. Apr.-May and Sept.-Oct., $8-20) for hot pizza, soups, and appetizers. **Degnan's Deli** (209/372-8454, 7am-5pm daily year-round, $7-8) offers an array of sandwiches, salads, and other take-out munchies, and **Degnan's Cafe** (Apr.-Sept.) has coffee and baked goods. The **Village Grill** (11am-5pm daily Apr.-Oct., $5-15) offers standard burgers and grilled food.

Curry Village is where to go for relatively cheap fast food. Hiking clothes are expected! The **Curry Village Pavilion** (209/372-8303, 7am-10am, 5:30pm-8pm daily Mar.-Nov., $10-12) serves breakfast and dinner. There is also **Coffee Corner** (6am-10pm daily summer, 7am-11am Sat.-Sun. spring and fall), the **Curry Village Bar** (noon-10pm daily summer), **Pizza Deck** (noon-10pm daily summer, 5pm-9pm Fri., noon-9pm Sat. Jan.-May and Oct.-Nov.), the **Meadow Grill** (11am-5pm daily summer), and the **Happy Isles Snack Stand** (11am-7pm daily summer) at shuttle stop 16.

The **Yosemite Lodge Food Court** (Yosemite Lodge, 6:30am-9pm daily summer, 6:30am-8pm daily winter, $5-15) offers basic meals in a cafeteria-style setting. A casual bar menu is available at the **Mountain Room Lounge** (4:30pm-11pm Mon.-Fri., noon-11pm Sat.-Sun., $5-21), immediately across from the Mountain Room Restaurant.

Fine Dining

The ★ **Ahwahnee Dining Room** (Ahwahnee Hotel, 209/372-1489, www.

The Bears of Yosemite

Although grizzlies have not been seen in California since 1922, the smaller but still impressive black bears (*Ursus americanus californiensis*) are plentiful, especially in Yosemite. Black bears do not seek out humans and they're usually not looking for trouble. They are, however, looking for food, and this often leads them into campgrounds and other places frequented by humans.

To protect both people and bears, national and state park rangers are very strict about enforcing rules to minimize contact between the species. Yosemite is particularly vigilant about its bear rules. The park provides metal bear-proof storage lockers in which all visitors must store any food, ice chests, or anything that looks or smells like food. Remember that garbage, toothpaste, shampoo, deodorant, beer, and soda all smell like food even if they don't seem like it to you—don't ever put any of these items in a tent. Even if you're only in a park for the day, you must use these lockers or at least put all your food in the trunk of your vehicle, out of sight. If it looks like food to a bear, it can lead to trouble and visitors have been known to get expensive tickets for having even an empty grocery sack within view inside a locked car. Bears do not hibernate in Yosemite during the winter; the visitors center and lodge display disturbing videos of bears tearing apart car doors and rooftops in winter to get at food inside.

If you see a bear at least 50 yards away, be quiet and keep your distance. If the bear approaches you or your campsite, actively discourage it by banging on pots and pans, yelling, and waving your arms. If you're carrying food or a backpack or other parcel, drop it and move slowly away. The bear will probably switch its attention to the pack and leave you alone. For backpacking, Yosemite requires the use of approved bear-resistant canisters; these can be bought at any outdoor supply store, and sometimes you can borrow or rent one at a trailhead or visitors center. Bear spray and pepper spray are not permitted in the park.

yosemitepark.com, 7am-10am, 11:30am-2pm, 5pm-9pm Mon.-Sat., 7am-2pm, 5pm-9pm Sun., $31-50) enjoys a reputation for fine cuisine that stretches back to 1927. The grand dining room features expansive ceilings, wrought-iron chandeliers, and a stellar valley view. The restaurant serves three meals daily, with dinner the highlight. The California cuisine mirrors that of top-tier San Francisco restaurants (with a price tag to match). Reservations are recommended for all meals, though it's possible to walk in for breakfast and lunch. For dinner, "resort casual" attire is requested, which is similar to semiformal. The dress code says no shorts on anyone, and men should wear collared shirts with long pants, but some people dress up quite a bit more than that, and it's fun to join in and make an elegant evening of it.

At the other side of the valley, you can enjoy a spectacular view of Yosemite Falls at the **Mountain Room Restaurant** (209/372-1499, 5:30pm-8:30pm daily May-Oct., 5pm-8pm Sun.-Thurs., 5pm-8:30pm Fri.-Sat. Oct.-May, $22-40), part of Yosemite Lodge at the Falls. The glass atrium lets every table take in the view. The menu runs to American food, and there is a full bar.

TRANSPORTATION

Car

From the San Francisco Bay Area, Yosemite Valley is about 195 miles, and the drive takes about 4.5 hours. The most efficient way to get to the valley from the Bay Area is to take I-580 east to I-205 to I-5 to Highway 120, and enter through Groveland and the **Big Oak Flat Entrance** on the west side of the park. After you enter the park, it's 25 miles to the valley, which takes about 45 minutes.

If you plan to drive to most places in Yosemite Valley, be aware that in summer—especially on weekends—traffic and parking can be slow and stressful. If possible, leave your car parked somewhere during those busy times and use the free shuttle buses to get around.

Bus

The **Yosemite Area Regional Transportation System** (YARTS, 877/989-2787, www.yarts.com) runs daily buses from Mariposa ($8-12 round-trip, $4-6 one-way) and Merced ($18-25 round-trip, $9-13 one-way) to Yosemite Valley. If you enter the park on one of these buses, you won't have to pay the entrance fee ($20). You can buy tickets on the bus, as well as from several businesses in the area. No reservations are necessary, and children under 12 ride free. You can also take your bicycle on the bus, making a complete no-car vacation a real possibility. Buses run more frequently in summer. Check the YARTS website for current schedules.

Shuttle Services

The free Yosemite Shuttle is particularly active in Yosemite Valley. The **Yosemite Valley shuttle** (7am-10pm daily year-round) runs every 10-20 minutes, stopping at Yosemite Lodge, the Valley Visitors Center, Curry Village, all campgrounds, and the Happy Isles trailhead. Check the map in the *Yosemite Guide* for a list of numbered shuttle stops.

Glacier Point

The best view of Yosemite Valley may not be from the valley floor. To get a different look at the familiar formations and falls, drive up Glacier Point Road to Glacier Point (16 miles from Chinquapin junction). The trail from the end of the road to the actual point is an easy one—paved and wheelchair accessible—but the vista down into Yosemite Valley is anything but common. The first part of Glacier Point Road stays open all year, except when storms make it temporarily impassable, to allow access to the Badger Pass ski area, but chains may be required.

In summer, park rangers host evening programs at Glacier Point. Check the *Yosemite Guide* for specific listings.

BADGER PASS

Five miles east of Wawona Road on the way toward Glacier Point is Badger Pass, a beautiful section of Yosemite and probably the only one that's actually busier in winter than in summer. This is the site of the Badger Pass Ski Area, which was California's first-ever downhill ski hill; it is one of only three areas with ski lifts in any national park. In winter, Badger Pass is bustling with downhill skiers, cross-country skiers, ice skaters, sledders, and people drinking hot chocolate. In summer, it's a good starting place for hikes to Glacier Point and nearby.

RECREATION

★ Badger Pass Ski Area

Downhill skiing at **Badger Pass** (Glacier Point Rd., 5 miles from Chinquapin turnoff and 15 miles from Wawona, www.yosemitepark.com, 9am-4pm daily mid-Dec.-mid-Mar. or early Apr.) is a favorite wintertime activity at Yosemite. Badger Pass was the first downhill ski area created in California, and today it's the perfect resort for families and groups who want a relaxed day or three of moderate skiing. With plenty of beginner runs and classes, Yosemite has helped thousands of children and adults learn to ski and snowboard as friends and family look on from the sundecks at the lodge. Enough intermediate runs make it interesting for mid-level skiers as well. Double black-diamond skiers may find Badger Pass too tame for their tastes since it has just a few advanced runs. But the prices are more reasonable than at Tahoe's big resorts, and the focus is on friendliness and learning rather than extreme skiing. Downhill ski lessons are available (1 lesson $47-87, private lessons available). Lift tickets run $25-48.50 for a full day and $22-40 for a half-day. Season passes are also available ($99-461). Ski or snowboard rentals (adults $28.50-37, ages 12 and under $21-27) are available.

And here's a snowshoe adventure to remember: If you're lucky enough to be in Yosemite during a full moon, or the four days leading up to one, do your best to reserve a spot on one of the **Full Moon Snowshoe Walks** (Badger Pass Day Lodge, reservations 209/372-1240, weather 209/372-1000, Jan.-Mar., tickets $15, $5 for snowshoe rentals, reservations required). These two-hour treks into the snowy forest, not recommended for children under 10, include an expert guide who can help you with your snowshoes and also discuss survival techniques, winter wildlife, folklore about full moons, and more.

Cross-Country Ski School

Glacier Point Road is the only place in Yosemite with groomed tracks for cross-country skiing, but the park has more than 800 miles of trails, and nearly all of them are skiable when the snow gets deep enough. In fact, many places in Yosemite are accessible in winter only on cross-country skis or snowshoes. The **Cross-Country Ski School** (www.yosemitepark.com) has classes, rentals (adults $21-25, under age 13 $11-14.50), and guided cross-country ski tours. Skiers of any level can have a good day out in the snow on the groomed trails from Badger Pass to Glacier Point. This 21-mile run is wide and well maintained; much of it is flat, so beginners can enjoy it slowly while experts fly past at top speed on skating skis or carry backpacks for overnight hut-to-hut ski trips. Many tributary trails branch off into the backcountry from this main trail; they're much less crowded and can be very beautiful. Just make sure you have a trail map if you decide to explore them, and don't go alone. Conditions can change rapidly in the woods, and things can get hazardous when frozen streams start melting, tree branches block a trail, or darkness falls faster than expected.

Cross-country skiing lessons ($35.50, with rental $46) are available, and tours and packages ($146-550 pp) include an overnight trip to **Glacier Point Hut.** The school also offers guided hikes and winter camping trips. In winter, guides from the Cross-Country Center at Badger Pass lead group snowshoe walks to **Dewey Point** (9am-3pm Wed. and Sun., $50, with snowshoe rental $60).

Hiking

If you love the thrill of heights, head up Glacier Point Road and take a hike up to or along one of the spectacular and slightly scary granite cliffs. Hikes in this area run from quite easy to rigorous, but many of the cliffside trails aren't appropriate for rambunctious children.

PANORAMA TRAIL

The very difficult **Panorama Trail** (17 miles) runs all the way from Glacier Point to Yosemite Valley with 3,000-4,000 feet of elevation change each way, and can be impassable in winter when snows are heavy. But if you like a challenge, and the views that go with it, you may want to give it a try. The Panorama Trailhead is located at Glacier Point; the road is usually open late May-October. Two miles into the hike, you'll see Illilouette Fall, cross Illiloutte Creek, and begin walking along Panorama Cliff. In about 0.5 mile an unmarked turn-off leads out to Panorama Point. (The sheer drop-off at the Point and no guardrails mean this detour is not for everyone!) Those who brave it will be rewarded with views of Half Dome, the Mist Trail, Upper and Lower Yosemite Falls, and a sweeping vista of the valley. Return to the main trail and continue until mile six, where you turn left to join the Mist Trail. Follow the Mist Trail down to the Happy Isles trailhead in Yosemite Valley.

If this sounds like a bit much, you can park a car at one end of the trail and then take the **Glacier Point Tours shuttle** (209/372-4386, www.yosemitepark.com, 8:30am, 10am, and 1:30pm daily spring-fall, adults $25 one-way, $41 round-trip, ages 5-12 $15 one-way, $23 round-trip, seniors $23 one-way, $35 round-trip, children under 5 free) to the other end and hike back.

SENTINEL DOME

The two-mile round-trip hike up **Sentinel Dome** starts at the trailhead just southwest of the end of Glacier Point Road. It is a surprisingly easy walk; the only steep part is climbing the dome at the end of the trail. You can do this hike in 2-3 hours, and you'll find views at the top to make the effort and the high elevation (over 8,000 feet at the top) more than worthwhile. On a clear day, you can see from Yosemite Valley to the High Sierras and all the way to Mount Diablo in the Bay Area to the west. Be sure to bring a camera! Be aware that there are no guardrails or walls to protect you from the long drops along the side of the trail and at the top of the dome.

TAFT POINT AND THE FISSURES

Another not-too-long walk to a magnificent vista point is the hike to **Taft Point and the Fissures.** To get here, park 1-2 miles southwest of Glacier Point on Glacier Point Road. This two-mile round-trip hike takes you along unusual rock formations called the Fissures, through the always lovely woods, and out to Taft Point. This precarious precipice does not have any walls, only a rickety set of guardrails to keep visitors from plummeting off the point down 2,000 feet to the nearest patch of flat ground. Thrill seekers enjoy challenging themselves to get right up to the edge of the cliff to peer down. Happily for more sedate hikers, the elevation gain from the trailhead to the point is only about 200 feet.

FOUR MILE TRAIL

If you're looking for a mid-level or challenging hike, plus the most spectacular view of all of Yosemite Falls in the park, take the misnamed **Four Mile Trail** (9.6 miles round-trip) that connects Glacier Point to Southside Drive in Yosemite Valley. It's actually 4.8 miles each way, but who's counting? In summer, the easiest way to take this hike is to start from Glacier Point and hike down to the valley. You can then catch a ride back up to your car on the **Glacier Point Tours shuttle** (209/372-4386, www.yosemitepark.com, 8:30am, 10am, and 1:30pm daily spring-fall, adults $25 one-way, $41 round-trip, ages 5-12 $15 one-way, $23 round-trip, seniors $23 one-way, $35 round-trip, children under 5 free), but be sure to buy tickets in advance. The steep climb up the trail from the valley can be much harder on the legs and the lungs, but it affords an ascending series of views of Yosemite Falls and Yosemite Valley that grow more spectacular with each switchback.

Taft Point

OSTRANDER LAKE

For a longer high-elevation hike, take the 12.5-mile walk to **Ostrander Lake** and back. The trailhead is approximately two miles past Bridalveil Creek Road on Glacier Point Road. You can also cross-country ski to the lake in the winter and stay overnight at the local ski hut (209/379-5161, www.yosemiteconservancy.org, Dec.-Mar., reservations required, $35-55). This trek can take all day if you're going at a relaxed pace—especially if you're visiting during June-July and stopping to admire the wildflowers in bloom all along the trail. The lake itself is a lovely patch of shining clear water surrounded by granite boulders and picturesque pine trees. Consider starting up the trail in the morning and packing a picnic lunch to enjoy beside the serene water. And remember to bring bug repellent since the still waters of the lake and nearby streams are mosquito breeding grounds during hiking season.

ACCOMMODATIONS AND FOOD

If you're planning an extended stay at Yosemite with friends or family, it might be convenient and economical to rent a condo or house through the **Yosemite West Condominiums** (Yosemite West Community, 7519 Henness Circle, 800/669-9300, www.yosemitelodging.com, $125-199), off Glacier Park Road. Modular buildings can be divided into a number of separate units—or not, if you want to rent a large space for a big group. The studio and loft condos sleep 2-6 and have full kitchens and access to all complex amenities. Luxury suites are actually one-bedroom apartments with full kitchens, pool tables, hot tubs, four-poster beds, and all sorts of other amenities. Two- and three-bedroom apartments sleep 6-8. And a duplex house ($200-450) can actually fit up to 22 guests, so you could fit an entire family reunion or college ski party into one huge house. All units also have free wireless Internet.

The **Glacier Point Snack Stand** (9am-5pm daily late May-Oct., $5-10) sells snacks and hot chocolate.

CAMPING

Bridalveil Creek (110 sites, first-come, first-served, mid-July-early Sept., $18) is halfway up Glacier Point Road, eight miles from Chinquapin junction and 45 minutes south of the valley. Its season is fairly short because of the snow that blankets this area, but its location along Bridalveil Creek makes it an appealing spot. Sites permit tents and RVs up to 35 feet and include fire pits, picnic tables, a shared bear-proof food locker, and a bathroom with water and flush toilets nearby. In addition, there are three equestrian campsites (877/444-6777, $25, reservations required) and two group sites (www.recreation.gov, $40, reservations required).

GETTING THERE

Car

Glacier Point is in the southwestern quadrant of the park, about an hour's drive from Yosemite Valley. From the Valley Visitors Center, drive 14 miles south to Chinquapin junction, and then make a left turn onto Glacier Point Road. Drive another 16 miles to the end of the road, and park in the lot on the left.

If you're driving from San Francisco directly to Glacier Point, allow at least five hours; it's 213 miles. The most efficient route is to enter through Big Oak Flat, and once you're inside the park, turn right (south) onto Wawona Road (Hwy. 41). In 9.2 miles, you'll come to Glacier Point Road. Turn left and take it 16 miles to the point itself.

If you enter through the South Entrance (Hwy. 41), drive 20 miles to Chinquapin junction, make a right turn onto Glacier Point Road, and take it all the way to the end, about 16 miles.

Glacier Point Road is closed approximately November-May. You can get as far as Badger Pass Ski Area (5 miles) on the road whenever the ski area is open, which is usually December-March; chains may be required.

Bus

The Yosemite shuttle system does not serve Glacier Point, but during the season when conditions allow, the park's official concessionaire, Delaware North Companies, operates four-hour trips from Yosemite Valley to Glacier Point and back: **Glacier Point Tours shuttle** (209/372-4386, www.yosemitepark.com, 8:30am, 10am, and 1:30pm daily spring-fall, adults $41 round-trip, $25 one-way). Tickets can be purchased by telephone (209/372-4386) or in person at the tour desks in Yosemite Lodge, Curry Village, or the Yosemite Village Grocery Store.

The **Badger Pass to Glacier Point shuttle** (July-early Sept., free) leaves from the Badger Pass parking lot to Glacier Point.

Wawona

The small town of Wawona is only four miles from the South Entrance of Yosemite. The historical Wawona Hotel was opened in 1879 and also houses a popular restaurant and a store.

SIGHTS

Wawona Visitors Center at Hill's Studio

The **Wawona Visitors Center at Hill's Studio** (209/375-9531, 8:30am-5pm daily mid-May-mid-Oct.) is right next to the Wawona Hotel, in the former studio and gallery of Thomas Hill, a famous landscape painter from the 1800s. The visitors center is perfect for information gathering; you can also get free wilderness permits (self-register outside in the off-season) and rent bear-proof canisters ($5 for 2 weeks).

Pioneer Yosemite History Center

Wawona is home to the **Pioneer Yosemite History Center** (near Wawona Store parking lot, 209/375-6502, daily year-round). The first thing you'll see as you enter this outdoor display area is a big open barn housing an array of vehicles used over a century ago in Yosemite, including big cushiony carriages for wealthy tourists and oil wagons once used in an ill-conceived attempt to control mosquitoes on the ponds. Farther along, walk under the Vermont-style covered bridge to

Pioneer Yosemite History Center

the main museum area. This rambling, uncrowded stretch of land contains many of the original structures built in the park. Most were moved here from various remote locations. Informative placards describe the history of Yosemite National Park through its structures, from the military shacks used by the soldiers who were the first park rangers through homes lived in by early settlers in the area presided over by stoic pioneer women.

In summer, take a 10-minute tour by **horse-drawn carriage** (adults $5, ages 3-12 $4), or buy a self-guided tour brochure ($0.50). Check the *Yosemite Guide* for listings of living history programs and live demonstrations held during the summer.

Mariposa Grove of Giant Sequoias

One of three groves of rare giant sequoia trees in Yosemite, the **Mariposa Grove** (Wawona Rd./Hwy. 41, dogs and bicycles not permitted) offers a view of these majestic trees. During high season, a one-hour open-air tram ride meanders through the grove, complete with an audio tour describing the botany and history of this area. You can also walk throughout the grove, taking your time to admire the ecology of the giant sequoia forest. The **Wawona to Mariposa Grove Trail** entails a moderate walk of about six miles from the Wawona Hotel; also shorter loop walks allow you to see some of the most impressive trees in a mile or less. The **Mariposa Grove Museum** (Upper Mariposa Grove) is another good place for visitors interested in sequoias. The museum building is a replica of the cabin of Galen Clark, a former guardian of Yosemite National Park who is credited as the first non-native to see Mariposa Grove.

As of the time of publication, the Mariposa Grove is set to be closed to vehicle traffic until spring 2017. The Mariposa Grove-Wawona shuttle will not offer service through this time. The only access is by foot or horseback on the Outer Loop Trail.

RECREATION

Hiking

It's not quite as popular (or crowded) as Yosemite Valley, but the hikes near Wawona in southern Yosemite can be just as scenic and lovely. In addition to the numerous trails that weave throughout the **Mariposa Grove of Giant Sequoias,** there are easy walks along the **Swinging Bridge Loop** (4.8 miles, 2 hours), from the trailhead at the Wawona Store, and up to the more strenuous **Alder**

Mariposa Grove of Giant Sequoias

Creek Trail (12 miles, 6-8 hours) from the trailhead on Chilnualna Falls Road.

WAWONA MEADOW LOOP

From the trailhead at the Pioneer Yosemite History Center, start with the easy **Wawona Meadow Loop** (3.5 miles, 2 hours), a flat and shockingly uncrowded sweep around the lovely Wawona meadow and a somewhat incongruous nine-hole golf course. This wide trail was once fully paved and is still bikeable, but the pavement has eroded over the years, and you'll find much dirt and tree detritus. It is best in late spring because the wildflowers bloom in profusion. For a longer trip, you can extend this walk to five miles, with about 500 feet of elevation gain, by taking the detour at the south end of the meadow.

CHILNUALNA FALLS

If you're up for a hard-core hike and a waterfall experience few who visit Yosemite ever see, take the difficult 8.5-mile trail to **Chilnualna Falls,** with a 2,300-foot elevation gain. The trailhead is near the Pioneer Yosemite History Center. Plan for 4-6 hours and bring water, snacks, and a trail map. You'll see a few fellow hikers and many tantalizing views of the cascades. Sadly, there's no viewing area, so you'll need to peek through the trees to get the best looks and photos of the falls. The trail runs all the way up to the top of the falls, but be careful to avoid the stream during spring and summer high flow—it's dangerous, what with the waterfall and everything!

Horseback Riding

You'll find more horses than mules at **Wawona Stable** (Pioneer Yosemite History Center, Wawona Rd., 209/375-6502, www.yosemitepark.com, 7am-5pm daily May-Sept., $65-88.50), and more travelers too—reservations for the rides out of Wawona are strongly recommended. From Wawona you can take a sedate two-hour ride around the historical wagon trail running into the area. Or try the five-hour trip out to Chilnualna Falls. Both of these rides are fine for less experienced riders, and the wagon-trail ride welcomes children with its easy, flat terrain.

Snowshoeing and Cross-Country Skiing

Mariposa Grove maintains winter trails for snowshoeing and cross-country skiing in winter. A popular trail is the **Loop Road** (8 miles round-trip) from the South Entrance to the Mariposa Grove of Sequoias. Pick up a copy of the *Mariposa Grove Winter Trails* guide ($0.50) at the visitors center, or download a copy from the park's website (www.nps.gov/yose).

ENTERTAINMENT AND EVENTS

Listen to the delightful piano music and singing of the legendary Tom Bopp in the **Piano Lounge at the Wawona Hotel** (209/375-1425, Tues.-Sat. Apr.-Dec.) five nights a week throughout Wawona's season. Older visitors especially love his old-style performance and familiar songs, but everyone enjoys the music and entertainment he provides. **Ranger Programs** include "Coffee with a Ranger" (8am Sat. summer) at the Wawona Campground Amphitheater and a nightly campfire. Check the *Yosemite Guide* for specific listings.

ACCOMMODATIONS AND FOOD

The charming **Wawona Hotel** (801/559-5000, www.yosemitepark.com, Apr.-Nov. and mid-Dec.-early Jan., $235, $159 shared bath) opened in 1879 and has been a Yosemite institution ever since. The black-and-white exterior of the hotel complex may remind visitors of a 19th-century Mississippi riverboat. The interior matches the outside well, complete with Victorian wallpaper, antique furniture, and a noticeable lack of in-room TVs and telephones. The Wawona feels more like a huge European pension than an American motel, including rooms with shared baths for the more economically minded traveler.

The ★ **Wawona Dining Room** (Wawona

Hotel, 209/375-1425, 7am-10am, 11:30am-1:30pm, 5:30pm-9pm daily Apr.-Dec., $22-27) serves upscale California cuisine for reasonable prices. All seating is first-come, first-served. The large white dining room is family friendly, and the menu offers options for vegetarians; breakfast is always a lavish buffet. You'll probably have to wait for a table on high-season weekends, but the large common area offers seating, drinks, and live piano music (Tues.-Sat.). The dining room is only open when the hotel is operating, and hours for each meal may be slightly shorter in the off-season (late Oct.-Dec). Call ahead to make sure they're open.

The **Wawona Golf Shop & Snack Stand** (9am-5pm daily in season) and the **Wawona Store & Pioneer Gift Shop** (8am-8pm daily summer, 8am-6pm Sat., 8am-5pm Sun.-Fri. winter) fills the gap when the Wawona Dining Room is closed.

CAMPING

Camp at the lovely and forested **Wawona Campground** (877/444-6777, www.recreation.gov, 93 sites, reservations required Apr.-Sept., $26; first-come, first-served Oct.-mid-Apr., $18), one mile north of Wawona. RVs are welcome, but there are no hookups. If you want to camp with your horse, Wawona offers two equestrian sites. The small grocery store in town can provide a few basics, but most services (including showers) can't be found closer than Yosemite Valley.

GETTING THERE

Enter the park at the **South Entrance** (year-round) and continue four miles up Highway 41 (Wawona Rd.) to Wawona. From Wawona, it's another 1.5 hours to Yosemite Valley. Wawona is well served by the Yosemite Shuttle bus system. The **Wawona to Yosemite Valley** shuttle (daily Memorial Day-Labor Day, free) leaves the Wawona Hotel at 8:30am and the Wawona Store at 8:35am, delivering passengers to Yosemite Valley. It returns to Wawona in the afternoon, leaving Yosemite Lodge at 3:30pm.

The **Mariposa Grove-Wawona shuttle** (9am-6pm daily spring-fall, free) takes passengers to the Wawona Store, the South Entrance, and the Mariposa Grove of Giant Sequoias. The shuttle will not run for most of 2016.

the Wawona Hotel

Tioga Pass and Tuolumne Meadows

Tioga Road (Hwy. 120), Yosemite's own "road less traveled," crosses Yosemite from west to east, leading from the more visited west edge of the park out toward Mono Lake in the eastern Sierra. Along the road, you'll find a number of developed campgrounds, plus a few natural wonders that many visitors to Yosemite never see.

SIGHTS

In the spring, walk out to view the wildflowers at **White Wolf,** about 15 miles east of the Tioga Road junction (turn north on a dirt road to get to the parking lot). Another 12 miles east along Tioga Road, bring out your camera to take in the vista at **Olmsted Point.** Stroll along the sandy beach at **Tenaya Lake,** two miles east of Olmsted, while staring up toward **Clouds Rest.** Nearby Tuolumne Meadows is bracketed by **Pothole Dome** on its west end and **Lembert Dome** to the east.

Tuolumne Meadows Visitors Center

The **Tuolumne Meadows Visitors Center** (209/372-0263, 9am-6pm daily summer, 9am-5pm daily early fall) is in a rustic building not far from the campground and the Tuolumne Meadows Store. Frequent ranger talks are held in the parking lot throughout the summer; details on upcoming programs are available in the *Yosemite Guide.* Wilderness permits are available year-round, and a separate structure across the parking lot houses large handicapped-accessible restrooms.

Soon after entering the park through the west entrance, you'll come to the **Big Oak Flat Information Station** (209/379-1899, 8am-5pm daily May-Sept.) on the right. You can get a free wilderness permit here in the summer when it's open; in winter you can self-register for a permit right outside.

★ Tuolumne Meadows

Tuolumne Meadows lies along Tioga Road (summer only), about 40 miles from the Crane Flat junction. After miles of soaring rugged mountains, it's almost surprising to come upon these serene grassy High Sierra alpine meadows. In tones of brilliant green, and dotted with

Tuolumne Meadows

wildflowers in spring, the waving grasses support a variety of wildlife. Stop the car and get out for a quiet, contemplative view of the meadows. Or if you prefer a long trek, Tuolumne Meadows serves as a good base camp for high-country backpacking. The short, easy trail to **Soda Springs** and **Parsons Lodge** (1.5 miles, 1 hour), from the trailhead at Lembert Dome, leads past a carbonated spring to the historical Parsons Lodge (10am-4pm daily in season) before leading to the Tuolumne Meadows Visitors Center.

RECREATION

Hiking

For smaller crowds along the trails, take one or more of the many scenic hikes along Tioga Road. Just be aware that they don't call it "high country" for nothing; the elevation starts at 8,500 feet and goes higher on many trails. If you're not in great shape, or if you have breathing problems, take the elevation into account when deciding which trails to explore.

Trailheads are listed in west-to-east order along Tioga Road.

TUOLUMNE GROVE OF GIANT SEQUOIAS

If you're aching to see some giant trees but were put off by the parking problems at Mariposa Grove, try the **Tuolumne Grove of Giant Sequoias.** Parking and the trailhead are at the junction of Tioga Road and Old Big Oak Flat Road. This 2.5-mile round-trip hike takes you down about 400 vertical feet into the grove, which contains more than 20 mature giant sequoias. (You do have to climb back up the hill to get to your car.) While you'll likely see other visitors, the smaller crowds make this grove an attractive alternative to Mariposa, especially in the high season.

OLMSTED POINT

For nonathletes who just want a short walk to an amazing view, **Olmsted Point** (Tioga Rd., 1-2 miles west of Tenaya Lake, shuttle stop 12) may be the perfect destination. The trail is only 0.5 mile round-trip from the parking lot to the point, and it exists to show off Clouds Rest in all its grandeur. Half Dome peeks out behind Clouds Rest, and right at the trail parking lot, a number of large glacial erratic boulders draw almost as many visitors as the point itself.

TENAYA LAKE

A great place to start your high-country exploration, the loop trail to **Tenaya Lake** (Tioga Rd., 12 miles west of the east

Tenaya Lake

Tioga Pass

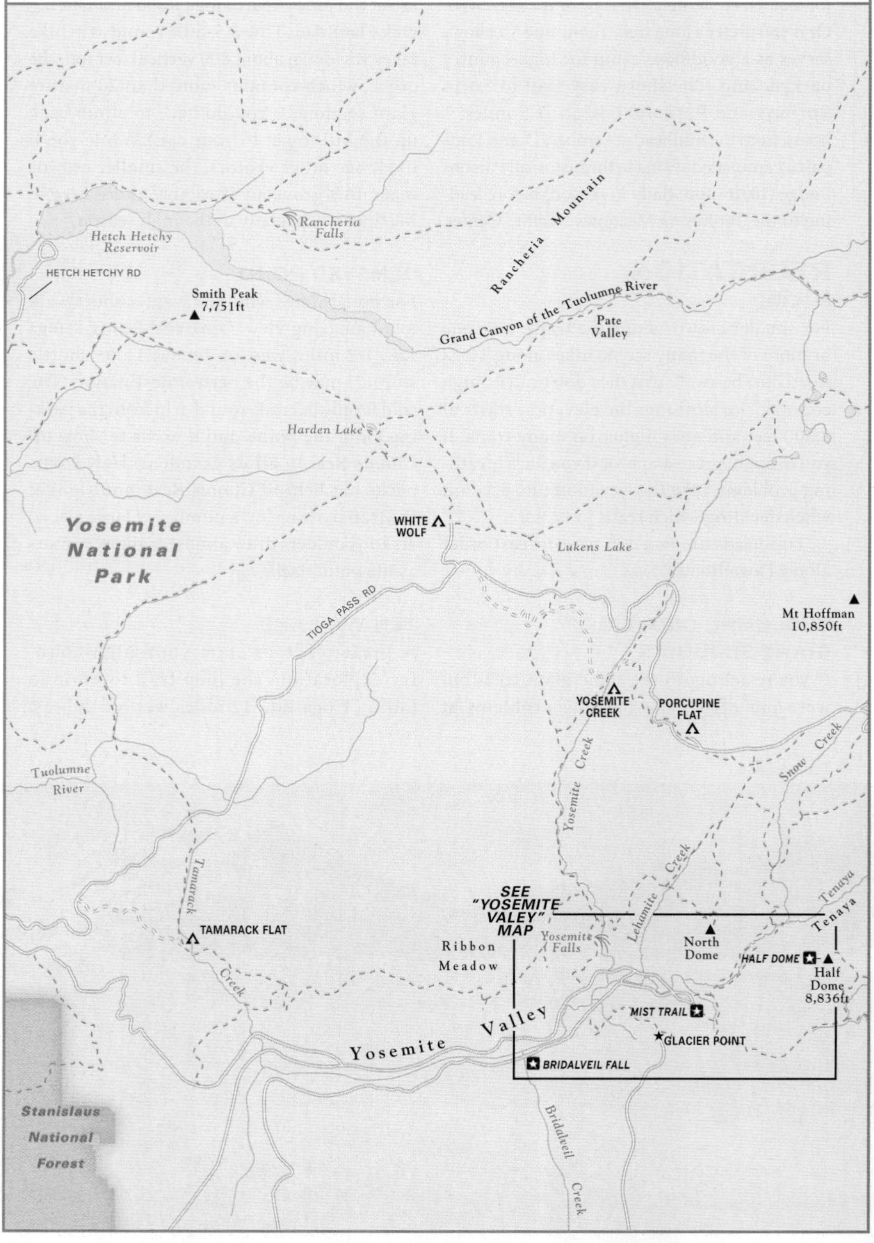

Rancheria Falls
Hetch Hetchy Reservoir
HETCH HETCHY RD
Rancheria Mountain
Smith Peak 7,751ft
Grand Canyon of the Tuolumne River
Pate Valley
Harden Lake
Yosemite National Park
WHITE WOLF
Lukens Lake
TIOGA PASS RD
Mt Hoffman 10,850ft
YOSEMITE CREEK
PORCUPINE FLAT
Snow Creek
Tuolumne River
Yosemite Creek
Tamarack
Lehamite Creek
SEE "YOSEMITE VALLEY" MAP
Tenaya
TAMARACK FLAT
Ribbon Meadow
Yosemite Falls
North Dome
HALF DOME
Half Dome 8,836ft
Creek
MIST TRAIL
GLACIER POINT
Yosemite Valley
BRIDALVEIL FALL
Stanislaus National Forest
Bridalveil Creek

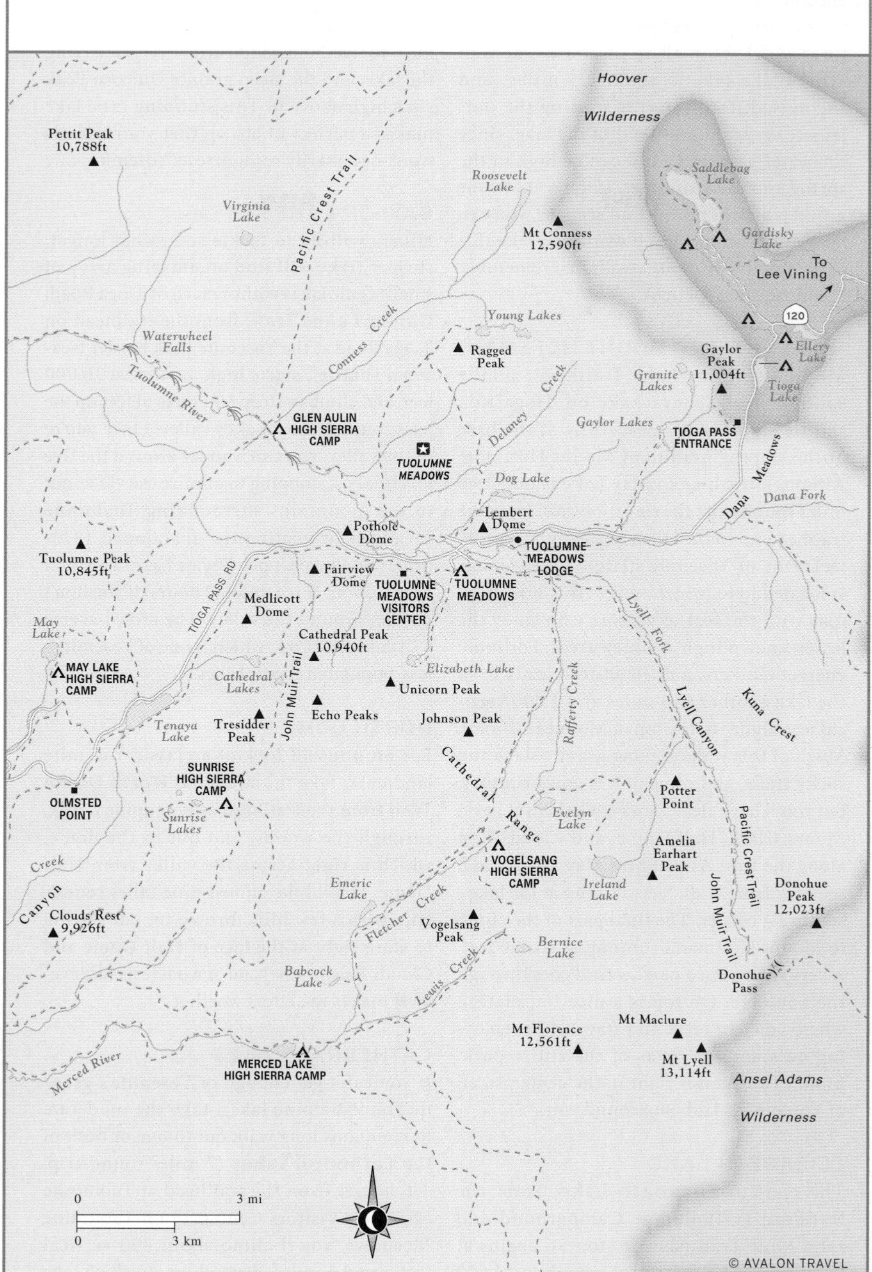
Hoover
Wilderness
Pettit Peak
10,788ft
Pacific Crest Trail
Roosevelt Lake
Virginia Lake
Saddlebag Lake
Mt Conness
12,590ft
Gardisky Lake
To Lee Vining
120
Young Lakes
Conness Creek
Waterwheel Falls
Ragged Peak
Ellery Lake
Gaylor Peak
11,004ft
Tuolumne River
Granite Lakes
Delaney Creek
Tioga Lake
GLEN AULIN HIGH SIERRA CAMP
Gaylor Lakes
TIOGA PASS ENTRANCE
TUOLUMNE MEADOWS
Dana Meadows
Dog Lake
Dana Fork
Lembert Dome
Pothole Dome
Tuolumne Peak
10,845ft
TUOLUMNE MEADOWS LODGE
Fairview Dome
TUOLUMNE MEADOWS VISITORS CENTER
TUOLUMNE MEADOWS
TIOGA PASS RD
Medlicott Dome
Lyell Fork
May Lake
Cathedral Peak
10,940ft
MAY LAKE HIGH SIERRA CAMP
Elizabeth Lake
Cathedral Lakes
John Muir Trail
Unicorn Peak
Rafferty Creek
Lyell Canyon
Kuna Crest
Tenaya Lake
Tresidder Peak
Echo Peaks
Johnson Peak
Cathedral Range
SUNRISE HIGH SIERRA CAMP
Potter Point
OLMSTED POINT
Sunrise Lakes
Evelyn Lake
Pacific Crest Trail
Amelia Earhart Peak
Creek
VOGELSANG HIGH SIERRA CAMP
Canyon
Emeric Lake
Fletcher Creek
Ireland Lake
John Muir Trail
Donohue Peak
12,023ft
Clouds Rest
9,926ft
Vogelsang Peak
Bernice Lake
Babcock Lake
Lewis Creek
Donohue Pass
Mt Maclure
Mt Florence
12,561ft
Mt Lyell
13,114ft
Merced River
MERCED LAKE HIGH SIERRA CAMP
Ansel Adams
Wilderness
0
3 mi
0
3 km
© AVALON TRAVEL

entrance, shuttle stop 9) offers an easy walk, sunny beaches, and possibly the most picturesque views in all of Yosemite. The trail around the lake is about 2.5 miles, and the only difficult part is fording the outlet stream at the west end of the lake, since the water gets chilly and can be high in the spring and early summer. If the rest of your group is sick of hiking and scenery, you can leave them on the beach while you take this easy one- to two-hour stroll. Just remember the mosquito repellent.

MAY LAKE AND MOUNT HOFFMAN

May Lake (May Lake Trailhead, 1 mile southwest of Tenaya Lake on Tioga Rd., shuttle stop 11) sits peacefully at the base of the sloping granite of Mount Hoffman. Although the hike to May Lake is only two miles round-trip, the elevation gain from the trailhead up to the lake is a steady, steep 500 feet. One of Yosemite's High Sierra camps is located here, which makes this hike popular with the sort of visitors who enjoy the lesser-known high-country areas. For more energetic hikers, a difficult trail leads from the lake another two miles and 2,000 vertical feet higher to the top of Mount Hoffman. Much of this walk is along granite slabs and rocky trails, and some of it is cross-country, but you'll have clear views of Cathedral Peak, Mount Clark, Half Dome, and Clouds Rest along the way. As you pass May Lake, you'll see May Lake High Sierra Camp at the lake's southeast corner. The final part of the climb to Mount Hoffman's summit, at 10,850 feet, is very rocky, but a narrow trail goes through the boulders. On top is a nice flat plateau where you can relax and stay awhile, enjoying outstanding vistas of the entire park. Mount Hoffman is right in the center, so all of Yosemite is laid out around you.

ELIZABETH LAKE

The trail to **Elizabeth Lake,** from the trailhead at Tuolumne Campground and John Muir Trail (shuttle stop 5), begins at Tuolumne Meadows and climbs almost 1,000 vertical feet up to the lake, with most of the climb during the first mile of the 4.8-mile, four- to five-hour round-trip. Evergreens ring the lake, and the steep granite Unicorn Peak rises high above it. This stunning little lake makes a perfect photo op that your friends won't necessarily recognize as Yosemite.

GAYLOR LAKES

Hikers willing to tackle somewhat longer, steeper treks will find an amazing array of small scenic lakes within reach of Tioga Road. **Gaylor Lakes Trail,** from the trailhead on Tioga Road at the Yosemite Park border (seasonal shuttle), starts high, at almost 10,000 feet, and climbs a steep 600 vertical feet up the pass to the Gaylor Lakes valley. Once you're in the valley, you can wander around the five lovely lakes, stopping to admire the views out to the mountains surrounding Tuolumne Meadows or visiting the abandoned 1870s mine site above Upper Gaylor Lake. The total hike is about three miles (2 hours) if you don't wander around the valley. The crowd-averse will enjoy this trek, which is one of Yosemite's less-populated scenic hikes.

NORTH DOME

For an unusual look at a classic Yosemite landmark, take the strenuous **North Dome Trail** from the trailhead at Porcupine Creek, through the woods, and out to the dome, which is right across the valley from Half Dome. You'll hike almost nine miles round-trip, with a few hills thrown in, but getting to stare right at the face of Half Dome and Clouds Rest just beyond at what feels like eye-level makes the effort worth it.

CATHEDRAL LAKES

If you can't get enough of Yosemite's granite-framed alpine lakes, take the moderate to strenuous long walk out to one or both of the **Cathedral Lakes** (7 miles round-trip, 4-6 hours) from the trailhead at Tuolumne Meadows Visitors Center. From Tuolumne Meadows, you'll climb about 800 vertical feet over 3.5 miles, depending on which lake you choose. These picture-perfect lakes show off the dramatic alpine peaks, surrounding lodgepole pines, and crystalline waters of Yosemite to their best advantage. Be sure to bring your camera, water, and food for a lovely picnic.

GLEN AULIN TRAIL

The strenuous **Glen Aulin Trail,** from the trailhead at Tuolumne Meadows Stable to Tuolumne Fall and White Cascade, is part of the John Muir Trail, and several of its forks branch off to pretty little lakes and other nice spots in the area. From Tuolumne Meadows to Tuolumne Fall and back is 11 miles round-trip (6-8 hours), with some steep and rocky areas. But if you've got the lungs for it, you'll be rewarded by fabulous views of the Tuolumne River alternately pooling and cascading right beside the trail. This hike may get a bit crowded in the high season. In the summer, many trekkers trade their dusty hiking clothes for swimsuits and cool off in the pools at the base of both White Cascade and Tuolumne Fall. A great way to do this hike is to enter the High Sierra Camp lottery, and if you win, arrange to stay the night at the Glen Aulin camp. If you do this, you can take your hike a few miles farther, downstream to California Fall, Le Conte Fall, and finally Waterwheel Fall.

Horseback Riding

The **Tuolumne Meadows Stable** (209/372-8427, www.yosemitepark.com, 7am-4pm daily May-Sept., $65-88.50) is accessible on a short dirt road on the north side of Tioga Road past the Tuolumne Visitors Center. You can get the perfect overview of the Yosemite high country by taking the introductory-level two-hour ride. For a longer ride deeper into the landscape, do the four-hour trip that passes Twin Bridges and Tuolumne Falls. An all-day ride with a variable route beckons the adventurous traveler, but you need to be in good shape and be an experienced rider for this one. To customize a longer pack trip, call 209/372-8348.

Snowshoeing and Cross-Country Skiing

Crane Flat has a variety of ungroomed winter trails for snowshoeing and cross-country skiing. Pick up a copy of the *Crane Flat Winter Trails* guide ($0.50) at the visitors center or download a copy from the park's website (www.nps.gov/yose).

ACCOMMODATIONS AND FOOD

Tuolumne Meadows Lodge (801/559-5000, www.yosemitepark.com, early June-mid-Sept., $126) offers rustic lodgings and good food in a gorgeous subalpine meadow setting. Expect no electricity, no private baths, and no other plush amenities. What you will find are small, charming wood-frame tent cabins that sleep up to four, with wood stoves for heat and candles for light. Central facilities here include restrooms, hot showers, and a dining room. The location is perfect for starting or finishing a backcountry trip through the high-elevation areas of the park.

The **Tuolumne Meadows Lodge Restaurant** (7am-9am, 5:45pm-8pm daily early June-mid-Sept., $11-29) serves dinner nightly in a rustic central building near the tent cabins. The quality of the food is better than you'd expect in what feels like a mess hall. Order the Sierra flatiron steak, wild salmon linguine, or the chef's specialty. Seafood is selected in accordance with the Monterey Bay Aquarium's recommendations for health and sustainability, and the vegetables are locally grown and organic. The "Lighter Eaters" menu has small portions of hot dogs, hamburgers, and macaroni and cheese.

Right next to Tuolumne Meadows campground, **Tuolumne Meadows Grill** (209/372-8426, 8am-5pm daily June-Sept., $10) offers sustenance for hungry campers. Breakfasts include filling egg and biscuit sandwiches and pancakes, and lunch offers burgers and chili. Eat outside on the accompanying picnic benches with views of Tuolumne Meadows across the road.

Another rustic high-country lodging option, the **White Wolf Lodge** (801/559-5000, www.yosemitepark.com, mid-June-Sept.) sits back in the trees off Tioga Road. Rent either the standard wood-platform, wood stove-heated tent cabin with use of central restroom and shower facilities, or a solid-wall cabin with a private bath, limited electricity, and daily maid service. All cabins and tent cabins at White Wolf include linens and towels. Breakfast and dinner ($30, reservations required) are served family-style in the White Wolf dining room; they'll also make you a box lunch to take along on your day hikes. Amenities are few, but the scenery is breathtaking. White Wolf has only 24 tents and four cabins. White Wolf Lodge is closed for restoration work in 2015 and is scheduled to reopen in 2016; call the lodge for more information and updates.

CAMPING

Yosemite visitors who favor the high country tend to prefer to camp rather than to stay in a lodge. Accordingly, most of Yosemite's campgrounds are north of the valley, away from the largest crowds (excluding the High Sierra Camps, which are also up north).

If you're entering the park from the west on Highway 120, the first campground you'll come to is **Hodgdon Meadow** (877/444-6777, www.recreation.gov, 105 sites, reservations required mid-Apr.-mid-Oct., $26; first-come, first-served late Oct.-early Apr., $18). This can be an excellent choice for people who drive up Friday night, since you can set up camp right after entering the park and won't have to drive in the dark. At 4,900 feet, Hodgdon Meadow can accommodate tents or RVs, though it has no hookups. Sites include fire rings and picnic tables, and there are bear-proof food lockers, water, and flush toilets. Supplies are available at Crane Flat, and the closest showers are in Yosemite Valley. Pets are permitted.

At the intersection of Big Oak Flat Road and Tioga Road is **Crane Flat** (877/444-6777, www.recreation.gov, 166 sites, reservations required, mid-July-Sept., $26). Crane Flat is 17 miles from Yosemite Valley at 6,200 feet elevation. Although it does allow RVs up to 35 feet as well as tents, it has no hookups. Sites include fire pits and picnic tables, and there are bear-proof food lockers, water, and flush toilets. Pets are permitted. A small grocery store is down the road at Crane Flat gas station; the closest showers are in Yosemite Valley.

Heading east along Tioga Road, **Tamarack Flat** (Tioga Rd., 52 sites, first-come, first-served, late June-early Oct., $12) keeps you reasonably close to Yosemite Valley, but still in a fairly primitive environment. Tamarack Flat is at 6,300 feet elevation and is a tent-only

Hodgdon Meadow campground

campground. Although it has picnic tables and bear-proof food lockers, there are no restroom facilities except pit toilets, and you must bring your own water or be prepared to treat the water you find.

Serene **White Wolf** (74 sites, first-come, first-served, July-early Sept., $18) is at 8,000 feet elevation on Tioga Road. The turnoff is on the left down a narrow side road. Sites accommodate tents and RVs up to 27 feet and include fire pits and picnic tables, and there are bear-proof food lockers, water, and flush toilets; pets are permitted. Crane Flat is the closest place for supplies.

Ditch the traffic and the crowded central visitor areas and head for **Yosemite Creek** (75 sites, first-come, first-served, late July-mid-Sept., $12). Yosemite Creek flows right through this tent-only campground, a perfect spot for cooling off on a hot day. Yosemite Creek offers few amenities—fire pits, picnic tables, and bear-proof food lockers but no groceries, showers, or water, and only vault toilets. In the same vicinity is **Porcupine Flat** (52 sites, first-come, first-served, July-Oct. 15, $12) at 8,100 feet with some limited RV sites, but no water.

★ **Tuolumne Meadows** (Tioga Rd. at Tuolumne Meadows, 877/444-6777, www.recreation.gov, 304 sites, July-late Sept., reservations strongly advised, tents and RVs $26, equestrian sites $25) has one of the largest campgrounds in the park, with more than 300 sites, including four horse sites. Half of the sites are available by reservation; the remaining half are first-come, first-served. Tuolumne can be crowded for the whole of its season, and the campground tends to fill up every night. Tuolumne is accessible for RVs up to 35 feet, though it does not have hookups. Sites include fire rings and picnic tables, and there are bear-proof food lockers, water, and flush toilets. Leashed pets are permitted. Food is available at nearby Tuolumne Meadows Lodge and the Tuolumne Grill, and the closest showers are in Yosemite Valley. Tuolumne Meadows is at about 8,600 feet elevation, so nights can get quite chilly even in midsummer.

The ★ **High Sierra Camps** (801/559-5000, www.yosemitepark.com, June or July-Sept., lodging, dinner, and breakfast adults $180, ages 7-12 $109, sack lunches adults $15.75, children $7.75) at Yosemite offer far more than your average backcountry campground. High Sierra provides tent cabins with amenities, breakfast and dinner in camp, and a sack lunch. Choose from Merced Lake, Vogelsang, Glen Aulin, May Lake, and Sunrise Camp—or hike from one to another if you're lucky enough to get a spot. Starting September 1, a lottery takes place for spots at High Sierra Camps through the following summer. You must submit an application to join the lottery; even if you get a spot, there's no guarantee you'll get your preferred dates. Check the website during the high season (June-Sept.) to see if any dates are available. The High Sierra Camps have a limited number of spaces available for hikers looking for dinner and breakfast (801/559-4909, adults $68.25, ages 7-12 $31.50), but not for overnight campers.

TRANSPORTATION

Car

Tuolumne Meadows is located along Tioga Road (Hwy. 120), which runs all the way across the park to the eastern boundary. At Tioga Pass, the east entrance, Highway 120 becomes Tioga Pass Road. Although you'll sometimes hear it referred to as Tioga Pass Road, technically that name does not apply within Yosemite.

From the west, Highway 120 becomes Big Oak Flat Road at the Big Oak Flat park entrance. In nine miles, at Crane Flat junction, the left fork becomes Tioga Road. The Tuolumne Meadows Visitors Center is 38 miles from the west entrance. To get to Tioga Road from Yosemite Valley, take Northside Road to Big Oak Flat Road. At the Tioga Road junction, turn east.

Tioga Road is always closed in winter, and remember that "winter" can come at almost any time at this elevation. To check weather conditions and road closures, call 209/372-0200.

Shuttle and Bus

In summer, the free **Tuolumne Meadows shuttle** (7am-7pm daily June-mid-Sept., weather permitting) runs along Tioga Road between Olmsted Point and the Tuolumne Meadows Lodge. Trips begin at 7am at Tuolumne Meadows Lodge and run every half hour, stopping at the Dog Lake Parking area, the Tuolumne Meadows Wilderness Center, Lembert Dome, Tuolumne Meadows Campground and Store, Tuolumne Meadows Visitors Center, Cathedral Lakes Trailhead, Pothole Dome, the east end of Tenaya Lake, Sunrise Lakes Trailhead at the west end of Tenaya Lake, May Lake Trailhead, and Olmsted Point. Going the other direction, the first bus leaves Olmsted Point at 7:30am daily. Limited service is available to the Mono Pass Trailhead and Tioga Road-Gaylor Lakes Trailhead, on the east end of this route.

July-September, Delaware North Companies offers a **guided bus tour** (209/372-4386, www.yosemitepark.com, adults $5-14.50 one-way, $9.50-23 round-trip, children half price) between Yosemite Valley and Tuolumne Meadows. The coach makes multiple stops, starting from Curry Village (8am) and ending at Tuolumne Meadows Lodge (arriving at 10:35am). It departs Tuolumne Meadows again at 2:05pm for the return trip. Fares are prorated if you only want to travel part of the way.

Hetch Hetchy

One of the most politically controversial areas in California, Hetch Hetchy (Hetch Hetchy Rd. past the Hetch Hetchy park entrance), about 30 minutes north of Highway 120, was once a valley similar to Yosemite Valley. It is now Hetch Hetchy Reservoir, with 1,972 acres of surface area, a maximum depth of 312 feet, and a capacity of 117 billion gallons. Hetch Hetchy supplies famously clean, clear water (plus some hydroelectric power) to the city of San Francisco and other parts of the Bay Area. But many environmental activists—beginning with the patron saint of Yosemite himself, John Muir, who opposed the project before it had even begun—see the reservoir's existence as an affront, and lobby to have O'Shaughnessy Dam torn down and the valley returned to its former state of natural beauty. For those of us who didn't have the privilege of seeing this spot before the dam was built,

Hetch Hetchy

Hetch Hetchy

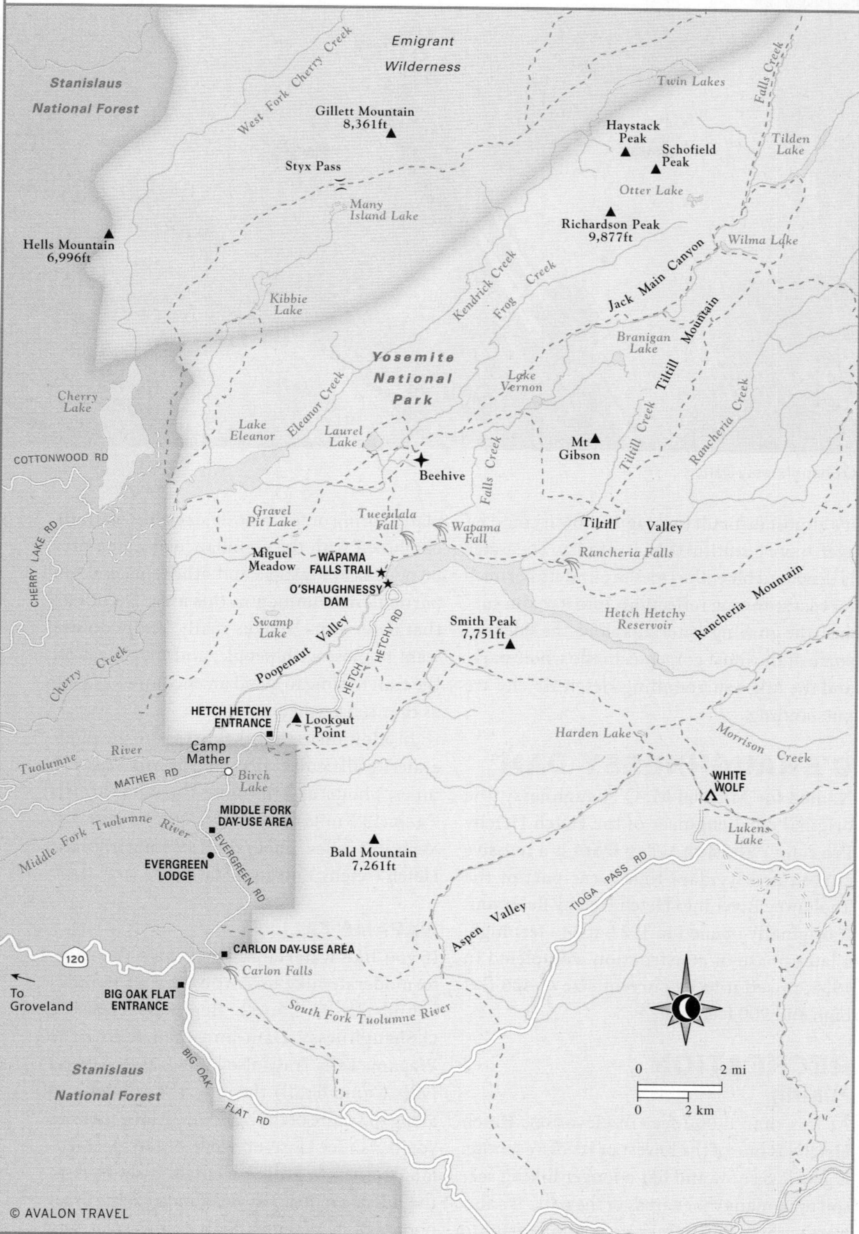

O'Shaughnessy Dam

it's almost difficult to imagine how it could be even more beautiful than it is today. The water is deep and blue, the trees around its perimeter cast stunning reflections into its calm surface, the gushing waterfalls along the sides are some of the most gorgeous in the whole park, and the hikes surrounding Hetch Hetchy are outstanding.

O'SHAUGHNESSY DAM

Named for Michael M. O'Shaughnessy, the original chief engineer of the Hetch Hetchy Project, **O'Shaughnessy Dam** is a massive curved gravity dam that turns part of the Tuolumne River into Hetch Hetchy Reservoir. It originally opened in 1923 at 344 feet high; a later phase of construction, completed in 1938, raised it to its current size of 426 feet high and 900 feet long.

RECREATION

Hiking

At less than 4,000 feet in elevation, Hetch Hetchy is one of the lowest parts of Yosemite; it gets less snow and has a longer hiking season than many other areas of the park. It's also warmer here in summer, so you may want to plan a spring or fall visit. The relative warmth, combined with the abundance of water, may be one reason rattlers and other snakes seem particularly common in this area. Do not let that deter you—snakes really, really do not want to mess with people, and they'll get off the trail in time to avoid an encounter as long as they sense you coming.

In addition to the hikes listed are the moderate-to-difficult trails to **Lookout Point** (2 miles, 1 hour) and the more strenuous **Smith Peak** (13.5 miles, 6-8 hours) and **Poopenaut Valley** (3 miles, 2 hours), all starting from the Hetch Hetchy Entrance Station.

WAPAMA FALL

If you like waterfalls, you'll love the easy-to-moderate hike to **Wapama Fall** (5 miles round-trip, 2 hours). Begin by crossing O'Shaughnessy Dam and then follow the Wapama Falls Trail (also known as Rancheria Falls Camp Trail) through the tunnel and along the shore of the reservoir. Along the way, you'll also see close-up views of the spectacular **Tueeulala Fall.** Tueeulala is set back in the hillside a little, so you can get some great photos of it. Wapama Falls comes splashing

Wapama Fall

down right onto the trail, so you'll experience it in a whole different way—and you'll probably want to keep your camera safely packed away. For a longer hike, bring a large poncho or rain gear to protect yourself and your pack before stepping onto the wooden bridge that crosses under these falls. On a hot day, the shower could be a very welcome treat.

A word of warning: The amount of water flowing over Tueeulala and Wapama Falls varies greatly with the season and recent precipitation in the park. In spring, water can be especially abundant and powerful. Although thousands of hikers have passed through here safely over the years, and many families with young children enjoy playing in the falls, they can be quite dangerous at times. In June 2011 two experienced male backpackers were killed when they tried to cross under the falls during an unusually high runoff. If you go, follow any posted restrictions and use good judgment to stay safe.

RANCHERIA FALLS

A longer day hike, also a recommended backpacking trip, is the 13.4-mile round-trip (6-8 hours) **Rancheria Falls Camp Trail,** which begins at O'Shaughnessy Dam and continues past Wapama Falls along the shore of Hetch Hetchy Reservoir. This trail can be done comfortably in one day by fit hikers. The terrain is rolling, with some up and some down each way, and the total elevation gain is less than 700 feet. Along the way, you'll pass Tueeulala Fall and become one with Wapama Falls (remember to bring your rain gear). You'll continue along the same path, but with far fewer people around as you complete the journey to Rancheria Falls. Beautiful views of Hetch Hetchy Reservoir continue most of the way. You'll walk through pine forests, on stone stairs, across creeks, and past sunny overlooks. Large flat granite slabs beside Rancheria Falls make a great place for lunch before you turn around to return the same way.

CARLON FALLS

For a short, easy hike that still includes a nice waterfall at the end, try the hike to **Carlon Falls** (4 miles, easy). The trail actually begins outside the Yosemite park boundaries, in the Stanislaus National Forest, but enters the park soon after. The trail follows the South Fork of the Tuolumne River and blooms with wildflowers in the spring. The payoff at the end, after one brief uphill climb, is the lovely Carlon Falls. This year-round waterfall is much smaller than dazzling superstars like Bridalveil Fall, but it's no less attractive in its own way and much more approachable. You may even want to play in the river nearby or have a picnic on the rocks. To get to the trailhead from the Big Oak Flat Entrance, drive north on Highway 120 for one mile. Bear right onto Evergreen Road, toward Mather and Hetch Hetchy, and continue another mile. Just past the Carlon Day Use Area is a pullout on the right with room for a few cars.

Backpacking

A great backpacking destination from Hetch Hetchy is Rancheria Falls. This 6.5-mile (one-way) trek along the **Rancheria Falls Camp Trail** begins at O'Shaughnessy Dam and continues past Wapama Falls along the shore of Hetch Hetchy Reservoir. The terrain is rolling, meaning there's some up and some down each way, but no major mountains to climb on the way to your destination. The total elevation gain is less than 700 feet. When you get to Rancheria Falls, you'll find a beautiful woodsy area with plenty of space for multiple visitors to set up tents and enjoy some peace. The sense of privacy and seclusion here is enhanced by the sound of the nearby falls, which muffles the noise of human activity. Rancheria Falls isn't the kind of waterfall that crashes down from high atop a mountain; it's a wide expanse with water flowing gradually over massive rocks. You can wade in and fill your water bottle as long as you treat the water before drinking it. This area makes a good base camp for challenging day hikes.

ACCOMMODATIONS

The **Evergreen Lodge** (33160 Evergreen Rd., Groveland, 209/379-2606, www.evergreenlodge.com, $180-415) has 88 cabins in a variety of styles and sizes available for rent. The location on Evergreen Road is only one mile from the Hetch Hetchy Entrance to the park and seven miles from the Big Oak Flat Entrance. Although most visitors to Evergreen Lodge are here for the easy access to Yosemite, it is almost a destination in itself with a summer camp atmosphere and organized activities like campfire singalongs, bingo, and s'mores-making. The largest accommodation onsite is the 2,500-square foot John Muir House ($875-1,175 per night, sleeps 10), which has three bedrooms and a loft, plus a private deck with a hot tub.

CAMPING

There are no developed campgrounds in the Hetch Hetchy region of the park. The **Hetch Hetchy Backpackers Campground** is next to the overnight parking lot at the end of Hetch Hetchy Road. To backpack overnight in the Hetch Hetchy area, you need a bear canister ($5) for your food and a wilderness permit (free) from the Hetch Hetchy Entrance Station (209/372-0200, 7am-9pm daily May-Labor Day, 8am-7pm daily Apr. and Labor Day-Oct., 8am-5pm daily Nov.-Mar.).

GETTING THERE

Hetch Hetchy is in the northwest corner of Yosemite National Park. The Hetch Hetchy Entrance is about 10 miles north of the Big Oak Flat Entrance on Highway 120. From Highway 120, take the Hetch Hetchy turnoff onto Evergreen Road, and then follow Evergreen Road north for 7.2 miles. At the town of Mather, turn onto Hetch Hetchy Road and proceed another 16 miles through the gate and to the parking lot near O'Shaughnessy Dam.

If you're already in the park, you have to leave through the Big Oak Flat Entrance and onto Highway 120 before reentering at the Hetch Hetchy Entrance. It takes about 1.25-1.5 hours to get to Hetch Hetchy from Yosemite Valley, a distance of about 40 miles.

Hetch Hetchy Reservoir is about 185 miles from San Francisco, and the drive takes about four hours. The road to Hetch Hetchy is open year-round, except in extreme weather conditions, but the park gate is only open during daylight hours.

Practicalities

RESERVATIONS

If you plan to spend the night in the park, advance reservations for overnight accommodations are essential. All lodgings, including campsites, fill up quickly—up to months in advance. For reservations and details on lodging in the park, you must contact Yosemite's concessionaire, **Delaware North Companies** (DNC, 801/559-5000, www.yosemitepark.com). DNC books reservations for Yosemite as well as many other national parks, but they are not located near Yosemite and cannot answer park-specific questions. The website lists lodging rates, but always confirm prices and other details with a reservation agent.

Yosemite has 13 campgrounds, seven of which are available by reservation. Campground reservations are required March 15-November and are absolutely necessary April-September. Yosemite National Park campgrounds are managed by **Recreation.gov** (877/444-6777, www.recreation.gov, 7am-9pm daily Mar.-Oct., 7am-7pm daily Nov.-Feb.). Campsite availability is released in one-month blocks, and you can book up to five months in advance. Only two site reservations at a time are permitted per booking.

When reservations become available in the campgrounds, booking can become competitive. You'll want to be online, or to start calling, first thing in the morning the day sites become available. The reservation system works on Eastern time.

INFORMATION AND SERVICES

Banks and Post Offices

ATMs are available throughout Yosemite. **Citizens Bank** (www.citizensbank.com) maintains cash machines inside the park at the Village Store, Degnan's Deli, the lobby of Yosemite Lodge at the Falls, the Curry Village Gift and Grocery Store, the Wawona Pioneer Gift & Grocery, the Crane Flat Store, the Ahwahnee Lodge, the Tuolumne Meadows store (seasonal), and the Badger Pass Ski Area (seasonal). In addition, a **Valley First Credit Union** ATM is in Yosemite Village at the Yosemite Art & Education Center.

Yosemite has several **post offices:** in Yosemite Village (8:30am-5pm Mon.-Fri., 10am-noon Sat.), inside Yosemite Lodge (12:30pm-2:45pm Mon.-Fri.), in El Portal (8:30am-1pm, 1:30pm-3pm Mon.-Fri.), and in Wawona (9am-5pm Mon.-Fri., 9am-noon Sat.).

Gas and Automotive Services

There is no gas available anywhere in Yosemite Valley. The nearest gas stations in the park are at **El Portal, Wawona,** and **Crane Flat,** and at **Tuolumne Meadows** (late spring-early fall). All gas stations are open 24 hours and are pay-at-the-pump with debit or credit cards. Gas is in Mariposa at **Pioneer Texaco** (5177 Hwy. 140, Mariposa, 209/966-2136), which also has a minimart.

If your car breaks down, you can take it to the **Yosemite Village Garage** (9002 Village Dr., off Northside Dr., Yosemite Village, 209/372-8320, 8am-5pm daily, towing 24 hours daily). Because it's the only game in town, expect to pay a high premium for towing and repairs.

Laundry, Groceries, and Showers

Laundry facilities are available at the **Housekeeping Camp** (8am-10pm daily Apr.-Oct.) inside the Curry Village complex. Several expensive, crowded, and limited-stock grocery stores are located in the park: the Yosemite **Village Store** (8am-8pm daily), the **Curry Village Gift and Grocery** (9am-7pm daily), the **Yosemite Lodge Gift Shop** (8am-7pm daily), the **Crane Flat Store** (10am-4pm daily May-Oct.), and the **Wawona Store and Pioneer Gift Shop** (8am-6pm daily). In summer, you can also get groceries in the **Housekeeping Camp Grocery Store** (8am-8pm daily May-Oct.) and the **Tuolumne Meadows Store** (8am-8pm daily spring-late Sept.).

Showers are available at **Curry Village** (24 hours daily year-round, $5) and **Housekeeping Camp** (7am-10pm daily Apr.-Oct., $5).

Media and Communications

The official *Yosemite Guide* is published several times a year by the park. This paper provides general information about the park and its services. More important, it has a detailed schedule of all classes, events, programs, and so on for the upcoming weeks. You'll receive a copy when you enter the park at one of the entrance stations; you can also download it (www.nps.gov/yose) ahead of time.

Internet access is available in a few spots in Yosemite Valley. Guests of the lodge can use the wireless service at no extra charge; nonguests are charged $5.95. In Curry Village, wireless Internet access is available in the lounge for Curry Village guests only. Guests of the Ahwahnee Hotel have access to wireless Internet service. Internet kiosks are available in Degnan's Deli (209/372-8454, 7am-5pm daily year-round, $1 for 3 minutes, summer only); wireless Internet is also available ($2.95 for 4 hours, $5.95 for 12 hours, $9.95 for 24 hours). Free Internet access is available at the **Yosemite Valley Branch Library** (Girls Club Bldg., 9000 Cedar Ct., 209/372-4552, www.mariposalibrary.org/yosemite, 9am-noon Mon.-Tues., 9am-1pm Wed.-Thurs.) in Yosemite Valley.

Medical Services

The park maintains its own clinic, the **Yosemite Medical Clinic** (9000 Ahwahnee Dr., 209/372-4637) in Yosemite Village at the floor of the valley. It's got a 24-hour emergency room, other services available 9am-7pm, and a domestic violence crisis center.

Wilderness Permits

There is a wilderness center near each of the visitors centers (at Big Oak Flat, both are in the same building). The Tuolumne wilderness center closes at the end of September, and the others close at the end of October; they all reopen in April or May. In summer, you can get a free wilderness permit in any of the wilderness offices. The permit allows access to backcountry trails anywhere in the park. When the wilderness centers are closed, you can get permits in the visitors centers. And when the visitors centers are closed, you can self-register for permits right outside each visitors center. To self-register during the off-season, you need to go to the office in the district where you plan to hike. When wilderness offices and visitors centers are open, they rent bear-proof canisters ($5 for up to 2 weeks, $95 security deposit required), which are required in the backcountry. Separate campfire permits are not necessary in Yosemite, but no fires are allowed above the tree line.

GETTING THERE

Yosemite's regions are accessible via five park entrances: Big Oak Flat, Arch Rock, South, Tioga Pass, and Hetch Hetchy. The **Arch Rock** Entrance (Hwy. 140) and the **Big Oak Flat** Entrance (Hwy. 120 west) are usually open year-round. The **Tioga Pass** (Hwy. 120 east) Entrance is just a few miles from Tuolumne Meadows and is the eastern access to Yosemite from U.S. 395. Tioga Road closes in November or December each year and reopens in the spring, usually in May or June. The **Hetch Hetchy** Entrance is to the northwest of the park and also closes in winter. The **South** Entrance is open year-round.

In winter it is always possible that roads can close unexpectedly and chains may be required on any road at any time. Check the park website (www.nps.gov/yose) or call 209/372-0200 for current road conditions.

Car

BIG OAK FLAT ENTRANCE

The most popular route into the park, particularly for those coming from the Bay Area, is through the Big Oak Flat Entrance. **Highway**

120 leads through Modesto, Manteca, and Groveland. Inside the park, Highway 120 becomes Big Oak Flat Road; if you follow it to the right (southeast), it will lead you into the famed **Yosemite Valley.** The trip from the entrance to the valley is only about 25 miles, but allow at least 45 minutes. Speed limits in the park are set low to protect animals and people, and they are strictly enforced.

The drive to Big Oak Flat is about 170 miles from San Francisco and takes at least four hours; however, traffic, especially in summer and on weekends, has the potential to make it much longer. Try to time your drive for weekdays or early mornings to avoid the biggest crowds. For the most efficient route to Yosemite from San Francisco, take I-580 east to I-205 east. In Manteca, take I-5 to Highway 120 and follow it south to Big Oak Flat Road.

If you're headed for **Tioga Road** or Tuolumne Meadows, the Big Oak Flat Entrance is a good way to get there. About nine miles into the park, take the left fork east off Big Oak Flat Road onto Tioga Road (closed in winter). **Tuolumne Meadows** is 38 miles from the Big Oak Flat Entrance, and it will take about 1.5 hours to reach (maybe a little less if traffic is light). If you continue on Tioga Road another eight miles past Tuolumne, you'll get all the way to Tioga Pass, the east entrance to the park.

ARCH ROCK ENTRANCE

The most direct route into **Yosemite Valley** is through the Arch Rock Entrance. This gateway, south of the Big Oak Flat Entrance, is reached via **Highway 140** from Merced and Mariposa. From San Francisco, take I-580 east to I-205 east. In Manteca, take Highway 99 south for 56 miles to Merced. In Merced, turn right onto Highway 140 east. Highway 140 will take you right to the Arch Rock Entrance. After you enter the park you're on El Portal Road, which follows the Merced River.

TIOGA PASS ENTRANCE

The Tioga Pass Entrance is on the east side of Yosemite, 12 miles west of **U.S. 395.** The entrance road is **Tioga Road** west of the entrance and **Tioga Pass Road** to the east. The town of Lee Vining is near the east entrance. Tioga Pass is closed in winter (usually Oct.-May or early June), but closing dates can vary depending on the weather. To check on weather and road closings in Yosemite, call 209/372-0200.

SOUTH ENTRANCE

Yosemite's South Entrance is accessed from **Highway 41,** coming north from Fresno and Oakhurst. Inside the park, Highway 41 becomes Wawona Road. The road is open year-round, though chains may be required in winter. The smaller Mariposa Grove Road, which leads off to a giant sequoia grove to the east, is closed to vehicles in winter (but you can walk it); the road will also be temporarily closed 2015-late 2016.

You can take Wawona Road farther north to Yosemite Valley (from the South Entrance to the Yosemite Valley Visitors Center is about 35 miles, or 1.25 hours); or you can make a right turn from Wawona Road onto Glacier Point Road and reach the Badger Pass Ski Area (about 17 miles from the South Entrance). At the end of that road is Glacier Point.

HETCH HETCHY ENTRANCE

The northernmost route on the west side of Yosemite is the Hetch Hetchy Entrance. This is the entrance for Hetch Hetchy Reservoir, and it accesses much of the vast backcountry in the less developed section of the park. To get here from **Highway 120,** make a left (north) onto Evergreen Road before the Big Oak Flat Entrance. After about seven miles, Evergreen Road passes through the tiny town of Mather and becomes Hetch Hetchy Road, which leads right through the entrance and on to O'Shaughnessy Dam, Hetch Hetchy Reservoir, and the Hetch Hetchy Backpackers Camp. This entrance, and Hetch Hetchy Road, are open year-round but only at limited times. The road tends to be open sunrise-sunset; in summer (May 1-Labor Day) that translates to 7am-9pm.

Train

It is possible to reach Yosemite via **Amtrak** (800/872-7245, www.amtrak.com, $38-64 one-way from San Francisco, $58-94 from Los Angeles). From San Francisco (6.5 hours), you must take a bus to the Amtrak station in the East Bay (5885 Horton St., Emeryville, 45 minutes) and connect to the San Joaquin line to Merced. From Los Angeles (9 hours), take the bus from Union Station downtown (800 N. Alameda St., Los Angeles, 3 hours) to Bakersfield and then the Amtrak San Joaquin line to Merced.

All trains terminate at the Merced Amtrak station (324 W. 24th St. at K St., Merced, www.amtrak.com, 7:15am-9:45pm daily). From Merced, the YARTS bus takes passengers into Yosemite (2.5 hours), making stops at Curry Village, the Ahwahnee Lodge, the Yosemite Valley Visitors Center, and Yosemite Lodge (year-round); as well as Crane Flat, White Wolf Lodge, and Tuolumne Meadows (summer only).

Bus

Greyhound (Merced Transportation Center, 710 W. 16th St., 209/722-2121, reservations 800/231-2222, www.greyhound.com, Merced station 8am-5:30pm Mon.-Fri., 8am-3pm Sat., $19-52 from San Francisco, $31-60 from Los Angeles) can get you as close as Merced. From Merced, you must then catch the YARTS bus into Yosemite.

The **Yosemite Area Regional Transportation System** (YARTS, 877/989-2787, www.yarts.com) runs daily buses into Yosemite. The Highway 140 bus ($13-25) picks up passengers in Merced, Mariposa, Midpines, and El Portal on the way into Yosemite. The Highway 120 bus (daily July-Aug., Sat.-Sun. June and Sept., $4-36) runs in summer only, picking up passengers at Mammoth Lakes, June Lake, and Lee Vining on the way to Tuolumne and Yosemite Valley. Schedules vary and change often. Check the YARTS website for the most up-to-date information before your trip.

GETTING AROUND

Once you've reached Yosemite, most of the popular sights, attractions, and trailheads are accessible by road, at least in the summer. However, summer traffic and parking in Yosemite can be every bit as frustrating as it is in a big city. Preserve your good mood and help save the air by leaving your car behind and relaxing on one of Yosemite's free, comfortable, and efficient shuttle buses.

In winter (Nov.-May), Tioga Road, Glacier Point Road, and Mariposa Grove Road are closed, and chains may be required on any park road at any time. Check the park website (www.nps.gov/yose) or call 209/372-0200 for current road conditions.

Shuttle Services

Yosemite runs an extensive network of free shuttle buses in various areas of the park. The system works extremely well and frees up visitors to enjoy the park and decrease the traffic.

- **Yosemite Valley** shuttle (7am-10pm daily year-round, free) provides access to numbered shuttle stops in the valley, including Yosemite Lodge, the Valley Visitors Center, Curry Village, all campgrounds, and the Happy Isles trailhead. Shuttles run about every 10-20 minutes; check the map in the *Yosemite Guide* for stops.
- **El Capitan** shuttle (9am-6pm daily mid-June-early Oct., free) runs during the summer season and stops at the Valley Visitors Center, El Capitan, and the trailhead for Four Mile.
- **Wawona-Mariposa Grove** shuttle (spring-fall, free) transports travelers between Wawona and the Mariposa Grove, picking up passengers at the South Entrance, the Wawona Store, and the Mariposa Grove gift shop. Note: This route may experience temporary closures during road construction through late 2016.
- **Wawona to Yosemite Valley** shuttle (Memorial Day-Labor Day, free) leaves the Wawona Hotel at 8:30am for Yosemite

Valley. The shuttle picks up passengers at Yosemite Lodge at 3:30pm for the return trip to Wawona.

- **Badger Pass to Yosemite Valley** shuttle (Dec.-Mar., free) runs twice daily between Yosemite Valley and the Badger Pass ski area during the winter ski season.
- **Badger Pass to Glacier Point** shuttle (July-early Sept., free) goes from the Badger Pass Ski Area parking lot to Glacier Point, stopping by request at the Sentinel Dome/ Taft Point trailhead, Washburn Point, and McGurk Meadow, as well as the Ostrander Lake and Mono Meadow trailheads.
- **Tuolumne Meadows** shuttle (7am-7pm daily June-mid-Sept., free) runs along Tioga Road, making multiple stops between Olmsted Point and the Tuolumne Meadows Lodge.

In-Park Bus Tours

Separate from the Yosemite shuttle system, a few commercial operators provide bus services in the park for a fee. **Glacier Point Tours** (209/372-4386, www.yosemitepark.com, 8:30am, 10am, and 1:30pm daily spring-fall, adults $25 one-way, $41 round-trip, discounts for children, seniors, and groups) runs daily trips from Yosemite Valley Lodge to Glacier Point (4 hours round-trip). A popular choice for the hardy is to take the bus one way and then hike back to the valley.

July-September, Glacier Point Tours offers a luxurious guided bus tour between Yosemite Valley and Tuolumne Meadows. The coach makes multiple stops from Curry Village (8am) all the way to Tuolumne Meadows Lodge (arriving at 10:35am). It departs Tuolumne Meadows again at 2:05pm and heads back. You don't have to take the whole journey; you can travel any segment and get off when you like. Round-trip fares range $5-23 for adults, depending on the distance traveled, and children ages 5-12 are half price.

GATEWAYS TO YOSEMITE

Groveland

The little town of Groveland, 26 miles outside the north entrance to Yosemite National Park on Highway 120, is the perfect place to stop for a last fill-up of gas, food, coffee, and anything else you may need. If you're trying to avoid rush hour traffic or getting a jump on your weekend trip to Yosemite by driving up late the night before, it can be a great idea to sleep in Groveland and enter the park the next morning, rested and ready to go.

The most elegant option in Groveland is the historical ★ **Groveland Hotel** (18767 Main St., 800/273-3314, www.groveland.com, $131-257), built in 1849 and located in the center of town. The proprietor, Peggy A. Mosley, oversees a blend of historical intrigue, which includes gold miners, gambling, and ghosts, with the modern comfort of the hotel's 17 rooms, each furnished with down comforters, feather beds, and large flat-screen HDTVs. Amenities include fresh coffee beans, chocolate chip cookies, and an open-door policy for dogs and cats.

The best feature of the **Yosemite Riverside Inn** (11399 Cherry Lake Rd., Groveland, 209/962-7408 or 800/626-7408, www.yosemiteriversideinn.com, $69-295) is its proximity to Yosemite—it's located just 11 miles west of the Big Oak Flat Entrance. Rooms range from simple ($69-149) to deluxe ($99-160), with kitchenettes and river or courtyard views. One- and two-bedroom suites ($225-275) and cabins with full kitchens ($99-160) are also available. Yosemite Riverside Inn offers a woodsy setting and a free continental breakfast; wireless Internet is available for a fee ($5).

The modern **Yosemite Westgate Lodge** (7633 Hwy. 120, Groveland, 800/253-9673 or 209/962-5281, www.yosemitewestgate.com, $185-235) is a convenient overnight spot, just 13 miles from the Big Oak Flat Entrance. This independently owned lodge is part of the America's Best Value Inn network, and its 45 rooms are all non-smoking and pet-free. A heated pool, spa, and playground are some of the notable amenities.

Camp in Big Oak Flat along Highway 120 at the Thousand Trails Campground at **Yosemite Lakes** (31191 Harden Flat Rd., 800/533-1001, ranger station 209/962-0103, www.thousandtrails.com, RVs $58, tents $41). This sprawling wooded campground beside the Tuolumne River has more than 250 RV sites with full hookups, 130 tent sites, a few dozen cabins, tent cabins, yurts, and a 12-bed hostel. It's only five miles from the park entrance, and it has a full slate of recreational amenities, laundry facilities, and Internet service.

The **Iron Door Saloon** (18761 Main St., 209/962-6244, www.iron-door-saloon.com, bar 11am-2am daily year-round, grill 7am-9pm daily summer, 7am-9pm Thurs.-Sat., 7am-3pm Sun.-Mon. and Wed. winter, $9-25) claims to be the oldest bar in California. It served gold prospectors sometime in the 1850s, and through the early 20th century it was the saloon of choice for the engineers who built the O'Shaughnessy Dam at Hetch Hetchy. With live music every weekend, it's still arguably the center of nightlife for many miles around. The food is about what you'd expect, but the drinks are strong. The bar stays open until 2am, but may close earlier in the off-season.

Stop in at **Dori's Tea Cottage** (18744 Main St., 209/962-5300, www.doristeacottage.com, English tea 11am-3pm Thurs.-Mon., café 8am-5pm daily, $8-17), which serves a "traditional English tea luncheon in a quaint and comfortable atmosphere." Wine, champagne, and dessert are always available, as well as vegetarian options. Reservations are recommended for lunch in the summer. The café is open until 7pm Friday-Saturday during the summer.

The **Priest Station Café** (16756 Old Priest Grade, Big Oak Flat, 209/962-1888, http://prieststation.com, 8am-8pm daily summer, 8am-3pm Mon.-Thurs., 8am-8pm Fri.-Sun. fall and spring, $13-22) goes way back. Six generations of the Priest-Anker family have operated this joint since 1850s. This tiny roadside eatery serves up hearty dishes like

The Iron Door Saloon is California's oldest drinking establishment.

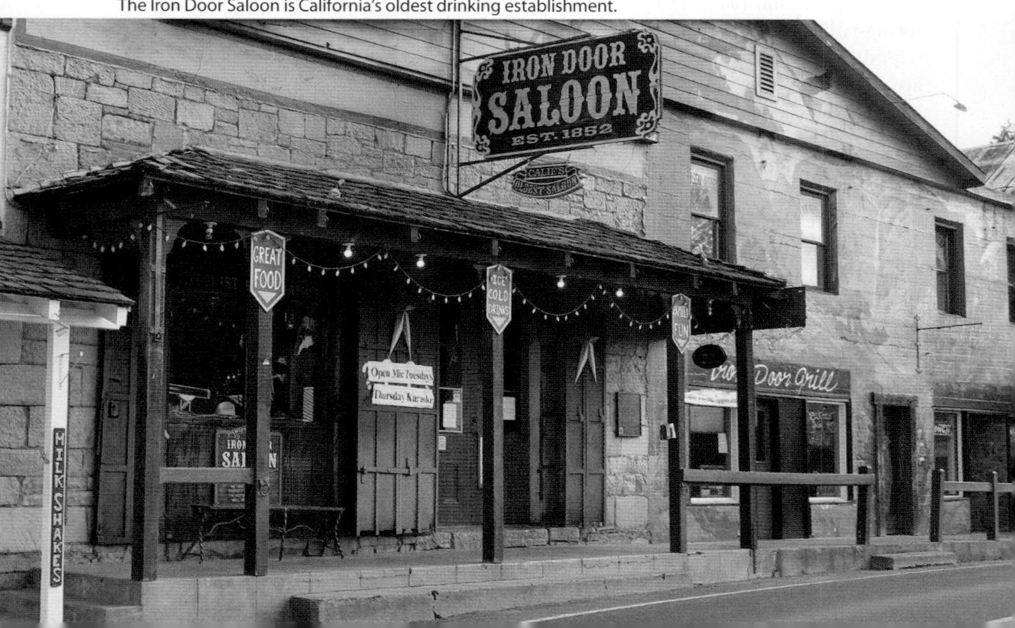

jambalaya, ribs, and roasted turkey. The station also has two cabins built in the 1940s ($119) available for families or couples seeking cozy confines.

The **Cellar Door** (18767 Main St., 800/273-3314, www.groveland.com, 8am-10am, 5:30pm-9:30pm daily spring-fall, 8am-10am, 5:30pm-9:30pm Thurs.-Mon. winter, $19-27, reservations suggested in summer) is the excellent restaurant at the Groveland Hotel. Outdoor tables are equipped with sun umbrellas and surrounded by lush gardens of roses and local flora. On cool evenings, propane heaters ensure that the patio stays comfortable, and indoor tables are also available in the hotel's oak-paneled dining room.

Mariposa

Mariposa lies about 30 miles from the Arch Rock Entrance and about 40 miles from Yosemite Valley. You can't miss the **River Rock Inn and Deli Garden Café** (4993 7th St., 209/966-5793, www.riverrockmariposa.com, $135-149), with its vivid orange-and-purple exterior in the heart of Mariposa. What was once a rundown 1940s motor lodge is now a quirky, whimsical motel with unusually decorated rooms. Two suites provide enough space for families, and the other five rooms sleep couples in comfort. The River Rock is a 45-minute drive from the west entrance to Yosemite.

For cozy seclusion, stay at the **Highland House** (3125 Wild Dove Ln., 559/250-0059, www.highlandhouseinn.com, $130-165), outside Mariposa. The house is set deep in the forest far from town, providing endless peace and quiet away from civilization. This tiny B&B has only three rooms, each decorated in soft colors and warm, inviting styles. All rooms have down comforters, sparkling clean bathtubs and showers, free wireless Internet access, and TVs with DVD players.

Another lovely small B&B, **Poppy Hill Bed and Breakfast** (5218 Crystal Aire Dr., 209/742-6273 or 800/587-6779, www.poppyhill.com, $150-160) is 27 miles from the west entrance to the park. The four airy rooms are done in bright white linens, white walls, lacy curtains, and antique furniture. No TVs mar the sounds of birds from the expansive gardens surrounding the old farmhouse, but you can take a dip in the modern hot tub any time. A full gourmet breakfast is served on your schedule.

Several campgrounds surround the Arch Rock Entrance near Mariposa. The **Yosemite Bug Rustic Mountain Resort** (6979 Hwy. 140, Midpines, 209/966-6666 or 866/826-7108, www.yosemitebug.com, dorm $23-30, tent cabin $30-70, private room $50-95, private cabin $65-155) is part hostel, part rustic lodge. This facility includes five hostel dormitories, attractively appointed tent cabins with real beds (bring your own sleeping bag), and a few cabins with private rooms, some with private baths. Solo travelers and families on tight budgets favor Yosemite Bug for its comfortable and cheap accommodations. The Bug is part of the Hostelling International network; HI members get discounted rates for dorm rooms.

El Portal

El Portal is less than 4 miles from the Arch Rock Entrance and just 15 miles from Yosemite Valley, making it one of the closest places for a final overnight on the way to the park. With a population of fewer than 500 people, it's smaller than Mariposa, so don't expect too much in the way of services.

RVers aiming for the Arch Rock Entrance flock to the **Indian Flat RV Park** (9988 Hwy. 140, 209/379-2339, www.indianflatrvpark.com, tents $20-30, RVs $42-48, tent cabins $79, cottages $129, pet fee $5). This park is a full-service low-end resort, with everything from RV sites (with water and electricity; some with sewer hookups) to tent cabins and full-fledged cottages. Showers are available ($3), and you can stop in for a shower even if you're not spending the night. The lodge next door allows Indian Flat campers to use of their outdoor pool. Because Indian Flat is relatively small (25 RV sites, 25 tent sites), reservations are strongly recommended for May-September. You can book up to a year in advance.

Oakhurst

Oakhurst lies less than 15 miles from the South Entrance of Yosemite National Park. The **Best Western Plus Yosemite Gateway Inn** (40530 Hwy. 41, Oakhurst, www.yosemitegatewayinn.com, 559/683-2378 or 888/256-8042, www.yosemitegatewayinn.com, $149-159) offers both indoor and outdoor pools and spas, free wireless Internet, and better-than-your-average-chain rooms. If you're bringing a group, consider one of their two-room "family suites," which feature four queen beds ($200/night in summer). The on-site **Yosemite Gateway Restaurant** (6:30am-11am, 5pm-9pm Mon.-Sat., 6:30am-1pm, 5pm-9pm Sun., $8-20) serves breakfast and dinner daily with brunch on Sunday. Dinner features steaks and a full salad and soup bar.

The family-owned **Oakhurst Lodge** (40302 Hwy. 41, Oakhurst, 559/683-4417 or 800/655-6343, www.theoakhurstlodge.com, $155-165) is within walking distance of the shops and restaurants of Oakhurst. Wireless Internet service and a continental breakfast are included, and the unheated outdoor pool is open year-round.

Chateau du Sureau (48688 Victoria Ln., Oakhurst, 559/683-6800, www.chateausureau.com, $385-585) is a breathtakingly beautiful lodge with just 10 rooms, each spectacularly appointed. Request a canopy bed, a French balcony, a Jacuzzi tub, a garden view—whatever your fantasy of luxury is, you can probably find it here. This Forbes five-star property was built in 1991 and has all the modern conveniences, but with the charm of a country house. Free wireless Internet is available, and rates include an elegant European-style breakfast. A two-night minimum is required for Friday and Saturday arrivals.

The best restaurant in the Oakhurst area is **Erna's Elderberry House** (48688 Victoria Ln., Oakhurst, 559/683-6800, www.elderberryhouse.com, 5:30pm-8:30pm Mon.-Sat., 11am-1pm, 5:30pm-8:30pm Sun., $45-108) on the grounds of the Chateau du Sureau. This astonishingly chic establishment features classical French cuisine and the farm-to-table sensibility that's becoming increasingly en vogue among California's dining establishments. The five-course prix fixe dinner features a different menu nightly ($108), and the four-course Sunday brunch ($64) includes a glass of wine.

Fish Camp

Fish Camp is 40 miles from Yosemite Valley via the South Entrance, a little over an hour's drive. The **Narrow Gauge Inn** (48571 Hwy. 41, 559/683-7720 or 888/644-9050, www.narrowgaugeinn.com, $149-248) is a charming 26-room mountain inn offering one- and two-bed nonsmoking rooms done in wood paneling, light colors, white linens, and vintage-style quilts. Each room has its own outdoor table and chairs to encourage relaxing outside with a drink on gorgeous summer days and evenings. The restaurant and common rooms feature antique oil lamps, stonework, and crackling fireplaces. Step outside your door and you're in the magnificent High Sierra pine forest.

For inexpensive lodge-style accommodations east of Fish Camp, check in to the **White Chief Mountain Lodge** (7776 White Chief Mountain Rd., 559/683-5444, www.whitechiefmountainlodge.com, Apr.-Dec., $159-179). The basic rooms feature light wood paneling, tribal-design textiles, small TVs, and wireless Internet access.

The **Tenaya Lodge** (1122 Hwy. 41, 559/683-6555 or 888/514-2167, www.tenayalodge.com, $305-540) offers plush lodge-style accommodations. Rooms in the lodge are styled with rich fabrics in bright colors; the three dozen cottages have a Native American-themed decor. The modern wall art evokes the woods and vistas of Yosemite. The beds are comfortable, the baths attractive, and the views forest-filled. Tenaya Lodge focuses on guest care, offering five dining venues on-site, from pizza and deli to fine dining; a full-service spa that specializes in facials; and daily guided nature walks.

The **Pines Resort** (54432 Rd. 432, Bass Lake, 559/642-3121 or 800/350-7463, www.basslake.com, June-Aug. $209-399) is perfectly located for your angling convenience right on the shores of Bass Lake. You can choose a suite, a split-level king room with dark floors, light walls, fireplaces, some with spa tubs; or rent a chalet, a two-story cabin in rustic mountain style that sleeps six, with a full kitchen, a deck, and a grill. The Pines is a full-service resort, with a lake-view restaurant, **Ducey's on the Lake** (7am-11am, 4pm-8pm Sun.-Thurs., 7am-11am, 4pm-9pm Fri., 7am-noon, 4pm-9pm Sat. winter, 7am-noon, 4pm-11pm daily summer, $25-40), a grocery store (7am-9pm Sun.-Thurs., 7am-10pm Fri.-Sat. summer., 7am-8pm Sun.-Thurs., 7am-9pm Fri.-Sat. winter), tennis courts, a swimming pool, hot tubs, and massage services.

A mile south of the South Entrance is the small, attractive **Summerdale Campground** (Hwy. 41, northeast of Fish Camp, 877/444-6777, www.recreation.gov, May-Sept., $28-30). This lovely spot has a two-night minimum on weekends and a three-night minimum on holiday weekends, only 26 campsites, and a strict limit on RV size (24 feet), making it a bit quieter and less city-like than the mega-campgrounds. You'll have a fire ring and a grill at your site, plenty of room under mature shade trees, and maybe even a water spigot (boiling the water before drinking is recommended).

The Eastern Sierra

LEE VINING AND VICINITY

Whether you've been camping out in the backcountry for weeks or you've just driven across it, you'll be glad to come upon the lively town of Lee Vining on the eastern edge of the park. Although it's not large (pop. 222) and some of its services close down in the winter months, Lee Vining couldn't be a more welcoming place for travelers. Set right on the southwest edge of Mono Lake, convenient to the ghost town of Bodie and the recreational paradise of June Lake, and a good stopover for travelers heading south to Mammoth Lakes and Bishop, Lee Vining takes tourism seriously, offering a variety of restaurants and lodgings, and two top-quality visitors centers.

Accommodations

Soon after exiting the Tioga Pass Entrance on the east side of the park, you'll come to the rustic ★ **Tioga Pass Resort** (85 Hwy. 120 W., Lee Vining, www.tiogapassresort.com, summer only, $195-520, cash or check only), which offers both charm and convenience. Whether your plan is to visit Yosemite, the Eastern Sierra like Bodie and Mono Lake, or do some of both, this is a great spot. The resort offers 10 cabins and four rooms. The rooms don't have kitchens or showers but do have access to shared showers. The cabins require a two-night stay. The resort doesn't have reliable telephone and Internet access, which means they cannot accept credit cards at the resort, but you can use them to book online. To contact the resort, send an email to tiogapassresortllc@gmail.com.

For clean, comfortable, affordable lodgings, try **Murphey's Motel** (51493 U.S. 395, 760/647-6316 or 800/334-6316, www.murpheysyosemite.com, $63-143). Open all year, this motel provides double-queen and king beds with cozy comforters, TVs, tables and chairs, and everything you need for a pleasant

The Eastern Sierra

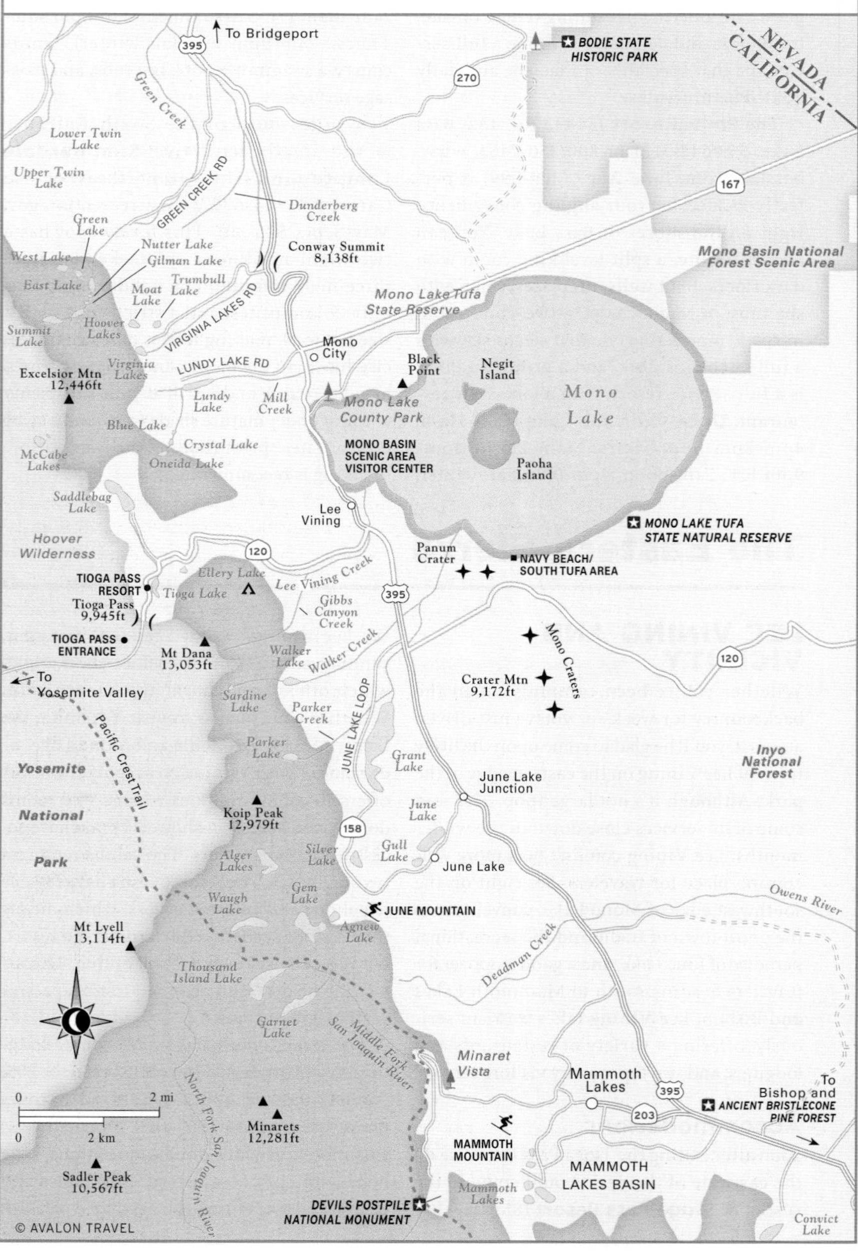

stay in the Mono Lake area. Its central location in downtown Lee Vining makes dining and shopping convenient.

El Mono Motel (1 3rd St. at U.S. 395, 760/647-6310, www.elmonomotel.com, late May-Oct., depending on weather, $69-95 shared bath, $89-99 private bath) offers comfy beds and clean rooms at very reasonable prices. Enjoy the location in downtown Lee Vining, and start each morning with a fresh cup of organic coffee from the on-site café (7am-8pm daily summer).

At the junction of Highway 120 and U.S. 395, stay at the comfortable and affordable **Lake View Lodge** (51285 U.S. 395, 760/647-6543 or 800/990-6614, www.bwlakeview-lodge.com, $59-269). This aptly named lodge offers cottages, which can be rented in summer only, and motel rooms, available year-round. Whether you choose a basic room for a night or two or a larger option with a kitchen for more than three days, you'll enjoy the simple country-style decor, the outdoor porches, and the views of Mono Lake. All rooms have TVs with cable, and Internet access is available in the motel rooms but spotty in the cottages.

Named for its main claim to fame—its proximity to the park, only 14 miles from Yosemite's east gate—the **Yosemite Gateway Motel** (51340 U.S. 395, 760/647-6467, www.yosemitegatewaymotel.com, $89-259) offers a charming rustic experience for travelers to the Eastern Sierra. The red and white exterior is echoed in the decoration of the rooms, which are supplemented with gleaming wood, new furnishings, and clean baths. TVs and Internet access provide entertainment on chilly evenings, and the wonderful outdoor recreation opportunities of the Eastern Sierra are just outside the door.

Camping

There are campgrounds in the Inyo National Forest on the east side of Yosemite, near U.S. 395 and Tioga Pass. You can stay at **Ellery Lake Campground** (Hwy. 120, Upper Lee Vining Canyon, ranger station 760/873-2400, www.fs.fed.us/r5/inyo, $21), which has 12 campsites at an elevation of 9,500 feet with drinking water, pit toilets, and garbage cans. It's not possible to reserve these sites, so get here at dawn if you want a site on a weekend. Another option is **Sawmill Walk-In** (Saddlebag Rd., on Forest Rd. 04, 1.6 miles north of Hwy. 120, ranger station 760/873-2400, www.fs.fed.us/r5/inyo, June-Oct., $16). This primitive hike-in campground, at an elevation of 9,800 feet, has 12 sites and no water, so walk in slowly. It's not possible to reserve these sites.

Food

Tioga Pass Resort's simple diner-restaurant, the **Tioga Pass Resort Café** (85 Hwy. 120 W., Lee Vining, www.tiogapassresort.com, 8am-8pm Mon.-Fri., 7am-9pm Sat.-Sun. summer, $20), offers breakfast, lunch, and dinner, served with plenty of good cheer.

The best way to kick off any vacation in the Eastern Sierra is with a memorable meal (and a tank of gas) at the ★ **Whoa Nellie Deli** (Hwy. 120 and U.S. 395, 760/647-1088, www.whoanelliedeli.com, 6:45am-9pm daily late Apr.-Oct., $8-14) at the Tioga Gas Mart. The deli is right at the east entrance to Yosemite, so it's the perfect place to stop when leaving the park or heading in. You'll get a hearty meal of fish tacos, buffalo meatloaf, or pizza; a pleasant place to eat it all; and a friendly, festive atmosphere. Expect to wait in line at the counter to order, as Whoa Nellie is popular. Seating is available both inside and out, so there are usually enough tables to go around. There's a fairly large grocery store and souvenir shop, and the restrooms are large and clean. The place is closed in winter, since Tioga Pass tends to be closed.

Lee Vining has several charming independent coffee shops. The **Latte Da Coffee Café** (1 3rd St. at U.S. 395, 760/647-6310, 7am-8pm daily summer) uses organic coffee and local fresh water to create delicious coffee drinks at the El Mono Motel. Over at the Lake View Lodge, enjoy a cup of joe at the **Garden House Coffee Shop** (51285 U.S. 395, 760/647-6543, www.bwlakeviewlodge.

com, 7am-11am daily June-Sept.). To get a great start to your day, you can pick up a smoothie or a fresh pastry in addition to your favorite espresso drinks.

A classic American diner, **Nicely's** (U.S. 395 and 4th St., Lee Vining, 760/647-6477, 7am-9pm daily summer, 7am-8pm Thurs.-Mon. winter, $15-25) offers friendly service and familiar food. Inside, you'll find a large dining room with half-circle booths upholstered in cheerful red vinyl. The cuisine includes eggs and pancakes in the morning; salads and sandwiches for lunch; and steak, trout, and salmon in the evening. Portions are more than generous. Nicely's has longer hours and a longer season than most places in the area. This is a good place for comfort foods like burgers, fries, and macaroni and cheese.

If you're looking for a Wild West atmosphere and a good spicy sauce, have lunch or dinner at **Bodie Mike's Barbecue** (51357 U.S. 395 at 4th St., Lee Vining, 760/647-6432, 11:30am-10pm daily June-Sept.). Use your fingers to dig into barbecued ribs, chicken, beef, brisket, and more. A rustic atmosphere with rough-looking wood, red-checked tablecloths, and local patrons in cowboy boots completes your dining experience. Don't expect the fastest service in the world. At the back of the dining room is the entrance to a small, dark bar populated by locals.

Pop into **Mono Cone** (51508 Highway 395, 760/647-6606, 11am-8pm daily summer, $5, cash only), where you can get mouthwatering burgers, fries, and soft-serve ice cream, but figure on waiting in line at this popular little roadside shack. Indoor and outdoor seating is available.

Information and Services

A fine visitors center sits in the middle of Lee Vining, the **Mono Lake Committee Information Center & Bookstore** (U.S. 395, 760/647-6595, 8am-9pm daily summer, 9am-5pm daily winter) with a big selection of free maps and brochures and helpful staff. The **Mono Basin National Forest Scenic Area Visitor Center** (U.S. 395, 0.5 mile north of Lee Vining, 760/647-3044, www.monolake.org, 8am-5pm daily summer, 9am-4:30pm Thurs.-Mon. spring-fall) is nearby at Mono Lake.

Lee Vining has few ATMs, but you can find one or two places to get cash (which you'll need, because many places out here don't take plastic). Try the gas stations, the Mono Lake visitors center, and the grocery-minimart.

Getting There

AIR

The nearest airport to Lee Vining is the **Mammoth Yosemite Airport** (MMH, 1200 Airport Rd., Mammoth Lakes, 760/934-3813, www.ci.mammoth-lakes.ca.us). Alaska Airlines serves this airport year-round. United offers flights December 15-April. For more options at a major hub, book a flight to **Reno-Tahoe International Airport** (RNO, 2001 E. Plumb Lane, Reno, NV, 775/328-6400, www.renoairport.com). From Reno, drive south on U.S. 395; Lee Vining in about 137 miles (3 hours).

From the **Sacramento International Airport** (SMF, 6900 Airport Blvd., Sacramento, 916/929-5411, www.sacramento.aero) you can get to Lee Vining in about four hours. From the **San Francisco International Airport** (SFO, U.S. 101, San Francisco, 650/821-8211 or 800/435-9736, www.flysfo.com) it takes approximately 5.5 hours.

CAR

Lee Vining is located just north of the junction of Highway 120 (also known as Tioga Pass Rd.) and U.S. 395. In summer the drive is quite beautiful, if not always fast. From the Bay Area, take I-580 east to I-205 east to Highway 120. Follow Highway 120 east as it becomes Tioga Road and across Yosemite National Park. When you reach U.S. 395, turn left, and you'll find yourself in Lee Vining. Expect the trip to take about 5.5 hours, but don't be surprised if it's longer. Traffic near and through Yosemite can be intense—especially on summer weekends—and many of the other travelers are enjoying the scenery, stopping to take photos along the way. When the snow comes, Tioga Road is closed.

From the Bay Area or Sacramento, you can take an alternate route to avoid Tioga Road, which is closed in winter. Take I-80 east for about 80 miles before turning onto U.S. 50 east for about 100 miles. Turn right onto Highway 89/88 and drive about 30 miles until you reach U.S. 395. Turn right (south) onto U.S. 395, and you'll arrive in Lee Vining in another 93 miles. The total distance is about 300 miles, a travel time of about six hours, depending on traffic and weather.

MONO LAKE

Mono Lake, eerie in its stillness, is the main attraction in the northern part of the Eastern Sierra, just east of Yosemite. This unusual and beautiful lake is 2.5 times as salty as the ocean and is 1,000 times more alkaline.

The reason for Mono Lake's odd appearance? It is fed by only about seven inches' worth of rain and snowfall each year; the rest of the water inflow is from various streams. No streams or tributaries flow out of Mono Lake, but it loses about 45 inches of water each year to evaporation. Meanwhile, any salt and minerals that have been carried into the lake stay in the lake as water evaporates. Over time, the lake has collected huge stores of calcium carbonate, which solidifies into strange-looking tufa towers.

The lake surrounds two large islands: **Negit Island,** a volcanic cinder cone and nesting area for California gulls, and **Paoha Island,** which was created when volcanic activity pushed sediment from the bottom of the lake up above the surface. Mono Basin, where the lake is located, is part of the Inyo National Forest. In 1984 the U.S. Congress designated Mono Basin a National Forest Scenic Area, which gives it additional protections.

If you're visiting the Eastern Sierra, you won't want to miss this natural wonder. It's large enough that you can see it from a distance—in fact, you can get a pretty good view just by driving by on U.S. 395, but stop to take

Mono Lake

a closer look if you can. One of the best viewpoints is on the grounds of the Mono Basin National Forest Scenic Area Visitors Center (U.S. 395, 0.5 mile north of Lee Vining, 760/647-3044, www.monolake.org, closed winter). Another good spot for looking through binoculars and taking photos is the lookout area on the east side of U.S. 395 near the junction with Highway 120, right across from the Whoa Nellie Deli. Look for a grassy hill with a parking lot, a large American flag, and a "Mono Lake" sign with a big hunk of volcanic rock hanging from it. If you want to do more than just look, come in summer and enjoy an oddly buoyant swim in its heavily salted waters or a boat trip around the silent, uninhabited islands.

Mono Basin National Forest Scenic Area Visitors Center

The large building that houses the visitors center for Mono Lake is only a short drive from the highway. The **Mono Basin National Forest Scenic Area Visitors Center** (U.S. 395, 0.5 mile north of Lee Vining, 760/647-3044, www.monolake.org, 8am-5pm daily summer, 9am-4:30pm Thurs.-Mon. spring-fall) is the perfect place to learn about Mono Lake, to take a walk around the lake, and to photograph the landscape. The interpretive museum inside details the natural and human history of the lake, from the way tufa towers form to the endless litigation involving the lake. Original films, interactive exhibits, a bookstore, and friendly staff are all available to help get you up to speed on this beautiful and unusual area. Walk out the back of the building to take one of several brief interpretive walks through the landscape or to sit on a bench and gaze down at the lake for a while. Talk to the staff to learn about the best hikes and spots to visit, swim, launch a boat, or even cross-country ski.

At the visitors center, you can also learn about various guided walks and hikes at Mono Lake, which can give you a more in-depth look at the wonders of the area.

★ Mono Lake Tufa State Natural Reserve

The tufa formations—freestanding calcite towers, knobs, and spires—make Mono Lake one of the most unusual lakes you'll ever see. The **Mono Lake Tufa State Natural Reserve** (U.S. 395, just north of Lee Vining, 760/647-6331, www.parks.ca.gov, 24 hours daily, free) educates and amazes visitors. Free tours are offered daily at 10am, 1pm, and 6pm in summer. Among other reasons to visit, the California State Parks service has declared it the "best place to watch gulls in the state." About 85 percent of the entire population of California gulls nests here in the spring.

A boardwalk trail provides access to the North Tufa area. Enjoy wandering through the different chunks of this preserve, which appear along the shore all the way around the lake. Be aware that much of the land adjacent to the state reserve areas is restricted—help take care of this delicate terrain by not venturing out of the designated visiting areas. Also, to access some of the reserve at the east side of the lake, you'll need either a boat or a 4WD vehicle, since no paved roads circle Mono Lake.

South Tufa

The **South Tufa area** (off Hwy. 120, 11 miles east of Lee Vining, $3 pp, free with Federal Parks Pass) on the—where else?—south shore of Mono Lake is one of the best places to view the spectacular tufa towers and a good place for newcomers to start exploring. This area is managed by the U.S. Forest Service, which charges a fee even though most of the state-run areas around here do not. But the good news is that all summer long, naturalists lead a one-mile, one-hour **walking tour** (10am, 1pm, and 6pm daily summer) around South Tufa, and it's free.

If you're hiking on your own, a good place to start is the one-mile **interpretive trail** (southeast of the visitors center, adjacent to Navy Beach) that winds through the South

Tufa area and describes the natural history of the area and the formations.

Old Marina

Years ago, the stillness of Mono Lake was broken by quite a bit of boat traffic. Private boats and small tour operators still travel the lake in the summer, but no major commercial water traffic remains. The hub of this activity was the marina north of Lee Vining. Today the **Old Marina** (1 mile north of Lee Vining, off U.S. 395, www.monolake.org, $3 per car) is a good spot to take a short stroll down to the edge of the lake and to enjoy outstanding views of the lake's two large islands and several nearby tufa towers. A 1.5-mile trail leads from the Mono Basin Scenic Area Visitors Center to the Old Marina, and an even shorter boardwalk trail is wheelchair-accessible.

Panum Crater

Even if you aren't a professional geologist, the volcanic **Panum Crater** (Hwy. 120, 3 miles east of U.S. 395) is worth visiting. This rhyolite crater, accessed from a parking area down a short dirt road off Highway 120, is less than 700 years old—a mere baby on geologic time scales. Take a hike around the rim of the crater, and if you're feeling up to it, climb the trail to the top of the plug dome. Be sure to slather on the sunscreen, since no trees shade these trails and it gets quite warm in the summer. Check the Mono Lake website (www.monolake.org) for occasional guided tours of Panum Crater.

Hiking

Mono Lake is not like Yosemite and its clusters of trailheads everywhere. But the hiking near Mono Lake is usually quieter, with fewer other travelers around, and the scenery is unlike anything you'll find anywhere else. The trails around the Mono Basin National Forest Scenic Area Visitors Center and the South Tufa area are open year-round, even when the visitors centers are closed.

You can get a quick and informative introduction to the ecosystem around the lake by taking the 0.25-mile **Secrets of Survival Nature Trail** right outside the Mono Basin National Forest Scenic Area Visitors Center (U.S. 395, 0.5 mile north of Lee Vining, 760/647-3044, www.monolake.org). This trail offers interpretive signage and long views of the lake.

For an easy walk along the lake, go to the **Mono Lake County Park** (Cemetery Rd.), where the trailhead is 0.5 mile east of Cemetery Road, and take the boardwalk trail 0.25 mile down to the tufa formations. Wandering through the tufa will add distance to your walk, but the ground is flat and the scenery is diverting.

A lovely interpretive trail, the **Nunatak Tioga Tarns Nature Walk** (Hwy. 120, east of Tioga Lake) is about 0.5 mile long and includes numerous signs describing the flora, fauna, and geology of the area.

A nature walk that offers both gentle exercise and increased knowledge is the **Lee Vining Creek Trail.** This easy-to-moderate 1.6-mile (one-way) walk stretches from the Mono Basin National Forest Scenic Area Visitors Center (U.S. 395, 0.5 mile north of Lee Vining, 760/647-3044, www.monolake.org) to the south end of Lee Vining, following Lee Vining Creek, which is currently under restoration to return it to its natural state after decades of diversion. If you start at the visitors center, you can pick up a free trail guide. The total round-trip walk is just over three miles and takes an hour or two, depending on how much time you spend admiring the revitalized ecosystem.

You can find any number of moderate hikes in the Mono Lake vicinity. The **Lundy Canyon Trail** (Lundy Lake Rd.), from the trailhead at the dirt lot, can be anywhere from 0.5 mile of fairly easy walking through Lundy Canyon to a strenuous 7-mile hike all the way out to Saddlebag Lake. Another trail leads out to **Parker Lake** or **Parker Bench** (Parker Lake Rd., off Hwy. 158). This hike is a minimum of 4 miles round-trip, and it can be 10 miles if you take the left fork of the trail out to Silver Lake and Parker Bench. Steep sections make this trek a bit demanding, but you'll love the scenic, shady trail that follows Parker Creek along the shorter right fork to Parker Lake. If one or two lakes just aren't enough, take the longish but only moderately tough **20-Lakes Basin Trail** (Saddlebag Lake Rd.) from the parking area across from the dam. This six-mile loop trail will take you out past many of the lakes for which the basin is named. If you're tired of all that water, take a moderate two-mile round-trip pilgrimage out to the remains of the mining town at **Bennettville** (Junction Campground Rd.). You can prowl around the abandoned mine, but be careful—old mine shafts and abandoned buildings can be extremely hazardous.

Boating and Swimming

Go ahead and bring your powerboat, canoe, kayak, or even a sailboat out to Mono Lake. You can launch from **Navy Beach** (0.5 mile east of South Tufa), though there's no direct access to the water from the parking lot, so you'll have to carry your canoe or kayak about 30 yards to get it into the water. If you're putting a heavier boat into the lake, check with the staff at the Mono Basin National Forest Scenic Area Visitors Center (U.S. 395, 0.5 mile north of Lee Vining, 760/647-3044, www.monolake.org, daily 8am-5pm summer, 9am-4:30pm Thurs.-Mon. spring-fall, closed winter) for directions to the launch ramp near Lee Vining Creek. For the protection of nesting California gulls, you cannot beach any kind of boat on the islands April 1-August 1. Outside that time frame, the islands of Mono Lake can be a great destination for boaters.

Swimming is allowed (and even encouraged) in Mono Lake in the summer. You can swim from your boat or from any of the unrestricted shore access points. You'll find yourself floating easily since the salt content of Mono Lake is several times higher than that of the ocean. But take care and watch kids closely: No lifeguards patrol the area, and you're swimming at your own risk.

Bird-Watching

The birds of the Eastern Sierra are so varied and abundant that three organizations—the Eastern Sierra Audubon Society (www.esaudubon.org), the Mono Lake Committee (760/647-6595, www.monolake.org), and the Owens Valley Committee (760/876-1845, www.ovcweb.org)—got together to produce the wonderful ***Eastern Sierra Birding Trail Map.*** The map covers 200 miles of territory from **Bridgeport Reservoir** (near the junction of U.S. 395 and Hwy. 182) in the north to **Cactus Flat** and the **Haiwee Reservoir** in the south (near Olancha and the junction of U.S. 395 and Hwy. 190). Along the way, 38 stops identify good birding habitats, and callouts provide details on the natural habitat of each area and the species to look out for. For an online version of the map, visit www.easternsierrabirdingtrail.org. To get your own free hard copy, contact the Mono Lake Committee (707/647-6595, info@monolake.org).

Entertainment and Events

It's called the **Ghosts of the Sagebrush Tour** (760/647-6461, www.monobasinhs.org, late Sept., $25 per day), but this annual education-and-entertainment weekend event, produced by the Mono Basin Historical Society, is much more than just a tour. Friday evenings, the **Lee Vining community center** (U.S. 395, Lee Vining, 760/647-6581, www.monoinn.com, $25) has a catered dinner with a presentation by a living history interpreter. Saturday is a full day of activities, which change from year to year, but usually include walks, talks, special exhibits, and lunch. The tour starts at the Historical Society museum and old schoolhouse (by Hess Park, Mattly Ave., 10am-4pm Mon., Thurs.-Sat., noon-4pm Sun. mid-May-early Oct.).

Accommodations and Food

Just across the freeway from Mono Lake, the **Tioga Lodge at Mono Lake** (54411 U.S. 395, Lee Vining, reservations 619/320-8868, 760/647-6423, www.tiogalodgeatmonolake.com, late May-mid-Oct., $99-159) offers a view of the lake from every room. This old lodge offers the perfect location for sightseeing and outdoor adventures, plus heated rooms and comfortable beds. Rooms are simple and appealingly decorated, each with tile floors and a full private bath. Some rooms sleep two, and others have room for up to four. The two-bedroom suites are perfect for families. Don't expect to find TVs or other digital entertainment.

The **Hammond Station Restaurant** (54411 U.S. 395, Lee Vining, reservations 619/320-8868, 760/647-6423, www.tiogalodgeatmonolake.com, 7:30am-10am, 5pm-9:30pm daily mid-June-early Oct., $10-24), at the Tioga Lodge, offers an excellent variety of good food. Choose from the health-conscious vegetarian/spa menu, which includes vegan, gluten-free, and dairy-free options; the California Casual menu; or the Drinks & Desserts menu. The small dining room has attractive wrought-iron furniture plus an ample outdoor seating area perfect for warm summer evenings. The food is tasty, and the service makes you feel like a local even if you're from out of town.

A great place to get a to-go breakfast or lunch is the **Mono Market** (51303 U.S. 395, 760/647-1010, 7am-9pm daily summer, 7:30am-6pm Thurs., 7:30am-8pm Fri.-Wed. winter). Breakfast sandwiches and pastries are made fresh daily, as are the sandwiches, wraps, and larger entrées you can carry out for lunch or dinner.

Information and Services

The **Mono Basin National Forest Scenic Area Visitors Center** (U.S. 395, 0.5 mile north of Lee Vining, 760/647-3044, www.monolake.org, 8am-5pm daily summer, 9am-4:30pm Thurs.-Mon. spring-fall) is an excellent resource for information about the area. It includes an interpretive museum that describes the creation of Mono Lake and the strange tufa formations that define it. This visitors center also has a ranger station with knowledgeable staff who can help you with the best seasonal trail and lake advice.

Right in the center of Lee Vining is another fine visitors center that's about much more than just the lake. The **Mono Lake Committee Information Center & Bookstore** (U.S. 395, Lee Vining, 760/647-6595, 8am-9pm daily summer, 9am-5pm daily winter) is a pleasant and welcoming place, with endless free maps and brochures, helpful staff, and souvenirs available for purchase.

The nearest medical facility to Mono Lake is to the south in Mammoth Lakes at **Mammoth Hospital** (85 Sierra Park Rd., Mammoth Lakes, 760/934-3311, emergency services 760/924-4076, www.mammothhospital.com), which has a 24-hour emergency room.

Transportation

Mono Lake is very close to the junction of Tioga Pass Road and U.S. 395. Getting here from San Francisco, Los Angeles, or anyplace else in California with a major airport usually requires a long drive.

Tioga Road is closed November-May each year, sometimes longer if snows are heavy. Check the Yosemite National Park website (www.nps.gov/yose) or call 209/372-0200 for updates on road closings in and around Yosemite. U.S. 395 remains open all year, though storms can close it briefly until the plows do their work. But accessing U.S. 395 from the north or south involves long drives from most places. You might want to consider flying into Reno or even Las Vegas and approaching Mono Lake from the north or east. From the **Reno-Tahoe International Airport** (RNO, 2001 E. Plumb Lane, Reno, NV, 775/328-6400, www.renoairport.com), you can drive 140 miles south on U.S. 395 and get to Mono Lake in about three hours.

From **McCarran International Airport** (LAS, 5757 Wayne Newton Blvd., Las Vegas, 702/261-5211, www.mccarran.com), the 350-mile trip takes about six hours, mostly on U.S. 95 north.

Very little public transit of any kind gets as far as Lee Vining and Mono Lake. To adequately explore this region, you need a vehicle of your own. On the bright side, parking in Lee Vining and around the lake tends to be both easy and free.

★ BODIE STATE HISTORIC PARK

Bodie State Historic Park (end of Hwy. 270, 13 miles east of U.S. 395, 760/647-6445, www.parks.ca.gov, 9am-6pm daily Apr. 15-Oct, 9am-4pm daily Nov.-Apr. 14, adults $5, ages 1-17 $3) is the largest ghost town in California and possibly the best-preserved in the whole country. Its preservation in a state of "arrested decay" means you get to see each house and public building just as it was when it was abandoned. What you see is not a bright shiny museum display; you get the real thing: dust and broken furniture and trash and all. It would take all day to explore the town on foot, and even then you might not see it all. If you take a tour, you can go into the abandoned mine and gain a deeper understanding of the history of the buildings and the town.

The town of Bodie sprang up around a gold mine in 1877. It was never a nice place to live at all. The weather, the work, the scenery, and, some say, the people all tended toward the bleak or the foul. By the 1940s mining had dried up, and the remote location and lack of other viable industry in the area led to Bodie's desertion.

A visit to Bodie takes you back in time to a harsh lifestyle in an extreme climate, miles from the middle of nowhere. As you stroll down the dusty streets, imagine the whole town blanketed in 20 feet of snow in winter and scorched by 100°F temperatures in summer, with precious few trees around to provide shade. In a town filled with rough men working the mines, you'd hear the funeral bells tolling at the church every single day—the only honor bestowed on the many murder victims Bodie saw during its existence. Few families came to Bodie (though a few hardy

Bodie State Historic Park

souls did raise children in the hellish town), and most of Bodie's women earned their keep the old-fashioned way: The prostitution business boomed while mining did.

Today most of the brothels, stores, and houses of Bodie aren't habitable or even tourable. Structures have been loosely propped up, but it's dangerous to go inside, so doors remain locked. You can peer in the windows at the remains of the lives lived in Bodie, however, and get a sense of hard-core California history.

To reach Bodie, take U.S. 395 to Highway 270 and turn east. Drive 10 miles to the end of the paved road, and then continue another 3 miles on a rough dirt-and-gravel road to the ghost town.

HOOVER WILDERNESS

The **Hoover Wilderness** (Bridgeport Ranger District, 760/932-7070, www.fs.usda.gov) is a 128,421-acre section of Mono County within the Inyo and Humboldt-Toiyabe National Forests with plenty of room for hiking and camping, and with some sweet mountain lakes to help you enjoy it all. It's a narrow strip of land east of Yosemite and west of Mono Lake that runs into the Ansel Adams Wilderness and Tioga Pass to the south, near the Emigrant Wilderness and Sonora Pass to the north.

Travertine Hot Springs

A delightful treasure in the Eastern Sierra, **Travertine Hot Springs** (www.monocounty.org) is a naturally occurring series of spring-fed pools hidden in the hills. Only one of the pools has a concrete bottom, added by human hands. The rest are pretty much the way nature made them, with uneven rocky sides. They can be slippery with moss or smelly from sulfur, but if you like to relax outdoors in a peaceful setting, especially under a full moon, you'll find a visit a memorable experience. Temperatures in the small pools vary from warm to extremely hot, so explore the area until you find one that's just right for you. The population varies too: It's not uncommon to have the whole isolated backcountry spot to yourself, but around sunset on a summer weekend you might find the pools crowded with people.

Steam rises at Travertine Hot Springs.

And not everyone who visits here wears a bathing suit.

The pools are accessible by car, though finding them can be tricky. To reach Travertine Hot Springs, drive north from Lee Vining on U.S. 395. In about 24 miles, just south of the town of Bridgeport, you'll see a ranger station on the right-hand side, and then a sign that says "Animal Shelter." Turn right at that sign onto Jack Sawyer Road. After a few hundred yards, make a left onto a dirt road and follow it for about a mile until you come to the springs.

Hiking

The strenuous hike from **Glines Canyon to Virginia Pass** (10 miles) starts at an elevation over 8,000 feet and climbs more than 2,500 vertical feet, making it a pretty serious workout among wildflowers, waterfalls, and mountain lakes. Start by walking alongside Green Creek for about 2.5 miles to Green Lake. On the north side of the lake, begin climbing Glines Canyon all the way to Virginia Pass (about 10,500 feet), which is between Yosemite National Park and Hoover Wilderness. From here, you can see Twin Peaks, Matterhorn Peak, and Camiaca Peak, the two small Par Value Lakes, and Soldier Lake, all spread out in various directions far below.

Another strenuous hike that's not quite as long is **Lundy Canyon Trail** (7 miles), though it still gains more than 2,000 feet of elevation. The trail begins by crossing Mill Creek and continues up above Lundy Lake. From here, continue climbing alongside Mill Creek until you reach Blue Lake, then Crystal Lake, and then Oneida Lake. Along the way, you'll see remains of the May Lundy Mine as well as a beaver pond, two waterfalls, and plenty of alpine lakes. This is an out-and-back hike, so turn around when you start to get tired. The trailhead is at the end of Lundy Lake Road; to get here, drive 7 miles north of Tioga Pass on U.S. 395. Turn right on Lundy Lake Road and go 6.3 miles, passing the Lundy Lake Resort along the way.

Camping

There's plenty of room for camping throughout the Hoover Wilderness, but you do need a wilderness permit ($3 reservation fee). Pick one up in either of the two national forests (Humboldt-Toiyabe and Inyo) that share management of the Hoover. Closest to Lee Vining, and much of the rest of this area, is the **Bridgeport Ranger Station** (U.S. 395, Bridgeport, 760/932-7070, www.fs.usda.gov, 8am-4:30pm Mon.-Fri.). If the Bridgeport Ranger Station is closed, you can self-register there. You can also order a permit by mail up to three weeks in advance of your trip. Permits can be scarce between the last Friday in June and September 15, when the Forest Service enforces quotas in the part of the Hoover Wilderness that's in the Humboldt-Toiyabe National Forest; half of those permits are available on a first-come, first-served basis at the Bridgeport Ranger Station when quotas are in effect. There are no quotas for the parts of the wilderness that overlap with the Inyo National Forest, so reservations are not required and visitors can obtain a permit upon arriving. Contact the Inyo National Forest Permit Reservation line (760/873-2483, 8am-4:30pm daily summer, 8am-4:30pm Mon.-Fri. winter) for information about wilderness permits.

Food

The **Bridgeport Inn** (205 Main St., Bridgeport, 760/932-7380, www.thebridgeportinn.com, 8am-9pm Thurs.-Tues. mid-Mar.-mid-Nov., $10-30) offers the most genteel dining experience around here, with steaks, fish, and salads in a historical-inn sort of atmosphere. For something more youthful and budget friendly, the place to go is **Rhinos Bar & Grille** (226 Main St., Bridgeport, 760/932-7345, 6am-10pm daily summer, 8am-8pm Mon.-Tues., 7am-8pm Fri.-Sun. winter, $10-23), where the bar is usually open until 2am.

Information and Services

In this northern section of the Eastern

Sierra, the best place for information is the **Bridgeport Ranger Station** (U.S. 395, Bridgeport, 760/932-7070, www.fs.usda.gov, 8am-4:30pm Mon.-Fri.). The small **Mono County Museum** (123 Emigrant St., 760/932-7500, www.bridgeportcalifornia.com, 9am-4pm Tues.-Sat. late May-Sept., adults $2, seniors $1.50, children $1) is in downtown Bridgeport, run by the local chamber of commerce.

Transportation

Green Lakes, Bodie, and the Hoover Wilderness are all on the east side of Yosemite National Park. If you're traveling from the Bay Area in summer, you have a choice of routes. You can cut through Yosemite on Tioga Road (closed in winter); or you can take the northern route along Sonora Pass, also known as Highway 108 (closed in winter). The route along Tioga Road takes about six hours. From San Francisco, take I-580 east to I-205 east to Highway 120 east. Enter the park through the Big Oak Flat Entrance and drive south to the junction with Tioga Road. Take Tioga Road east for almost 60 miles to U.S. 395. Drive north on U.S 395, and in 26 miles you'll come to the town of Bridgeport, the most significant town of any size near the Hoover Wilderness.

To travel via the Sonora Pass, when Highway 108 splits from Highway 120, east of Oakdale, stick with Highway 108 and head north. When you get to U.S. 395, turn right and drive south. After a total of about 228 miles (5 hours), you'll reach Bridgeport. To get from Bridgeport to Bodie, take U.S 395 south another seven miles, and then make a left onto Highway 270, also known as Bodie Road. Bodie lies 12.8 miles down this partly unpaved road.

In winter, when Tioga Road and Highway 108 are closed, take I-80 east from the Bay Area for about 80 miles before turning onto U.S. 50 east for about 100 miles. Turn right onto Highway 89/88 and drive about 30 miles until you reach U.S. 395. Turn right (south) onto U.S. 395, and you'll arrive in Lee Vining in another 93 miles. The total distance is about 300 miles, a travel time of about six hours, depending on traffic and weather.

JUNE LAKE

The small community of June Lake lies east of Yosemite, just 15 minutes south of Mono Lake and Lee Vining. Although less famous than Mammoth Lakes, June Lake is a popular ski destination, thanks to June Mountain, which offers everything you need in a ski resort, yet manages to hold onto the feeling of an unspoiled outdoor wonderland. Even though the town is named for just one of the alpine lakes nearby, there are actually three others: Gull Lake, Silver Lake, and Grant Lake. Each has its own style of beauty. If you don't have time to stop by for a swim, you can still enjoy driving the scenic 15-mile June Lake Loop.

June Lake Loop

The 15-mile scenic **June Lake Loop** (Hwy. 158), accessible from U.S. 395 south of Lee Vining, takes you away from the high-traffic, heavily visited areas of the Eastern Sierra. Along the way, you get the full-fledged alpine experience. Once you get out of the car, the loop's namesake—June Lake—offers good recreation. You can take a hike, go fishing, or even plan to stay overnight at one of the campgrounds. Next you'll come to Gull Lake, and then to Silver Lake, two other popular boating and angling waterways. As you drive north on the loop, stop at least once to admire Reversed Peak, a 9,500-foot Sierra mountain. Finally, you'll come to Grant Lake. Though no resorts or major trailheads are here, you'll find a boat launch and some spectacular alpine trout fishing. Finally, take a break at the Mono Craters Monument before heading back out to U.S. 395 toward Lee Vining or Mammoth Mountain.

June Mountain

Like so many other parts of the Eastern Sierra, June Lake as a vacation destination is largely about skiing. Although the lake and the others nearby make lovely summer recreation spots, most people who come here are headed for the snow. One of the most popular places to hit the slopes in this area is the **June Mountain Ski Resort** (3819 Hwy. 158, 760/648-7733, www.junemountain.com, lifts 8:30am-4pm daily, adults $72, seniors $48, ages 13-18 $48, up to age 12 free). About 20 miles north of Mammoth Lakes, June Mountain offers seven lifts (two quads, four doubles, and a carpet) and more than 2,500 feet of vertical drops on 1,400 skiable acres. The resort caters to beginners and intermediate skiers, and 80 percent of its trails are green or blue. Beginners can even take a lift up to the top of Rainbow Summit and enjoy a long run down the Silverado Trail. However, a number of black and double black-diamond slopes make a trip to June Mountain fun for more advanced skiers and boarders as well. Thrill-seeking experts and adventurous intermediates head up to the top of June Mountain Summit and then plummet down the bowl (double black diamond) or slide along the ridgeline (blue). Be sure to check your trail map before going up this way unless you're very sure of your abilities. For a cup of coffee or hot chocolate, stop at the June Meadows Chalet (top of Chair J1, breakfast and lunch from 8am daily) at the center of the ski area.

Accommodations and Food

June Lake has plenty of cabins and lodges available. One particularly nice one is the **Double Eagle Resort and Spa** (5587 Hwy. 158, June Lake, 760/648-7004, www.doubleeagle.com, year-round, $169-649). Its 15 two-bedroom cabins ($249-349) sleep six, and all come complete with decks and fully equipped kitchens. The 16 luxurious lodge rooms ($169-229) come with coffee service, free Internet access, a refrigerator, and whirlpool tubs. There's also a sprawling guest house ($599-649) that sleeps 12, with three bedrooms, a full kitchen, laundry room, grill, and wood-burning fireplace. The on-site Creekside Spa includes an indoor pool and a fitness center, and the resort's **Eagle's Landing Restaurant** (7:30am-9pm daily, $16-36) helps make this an everything-you-need destination.

A little more rustic but also very pleasant is **The Four Seasons** (24 Venice St., 760/648-7476, www.junelakesfourseasons.com, late Apr.-Oct., $135-195), which, ironically, is only open in summer. The five A-frame cabins each sleep up to six, with a master bedroom and a sleeping loft as well as a full kitchen, a living room, and a large deck. The resort is just two miles from the town of June Lake and a short drive to all the lakes.

Camping

The U.S. Forest Service maintains several campgrounds near June Lake in the Inyo National Forest. A particularly good one is **Silver Lake Campground** (Hwy. 158, 7 miles west of U.S. 395, reservations www.recreation.gov, mid-Apr.-mid-Nov., $22, $5 for each additional vehicle). Each of the 39 sites has a bear-proof food locker, a picnic table, and a fire ring; the campground has flush toilets, drinking water, and even a small store. The best part is that the campground is right on the shore of lovely Silver Lake, which is a good place to fish, watch for wildlife, or just sit and enjoy the view.

Information and Services

The small **June Lake Visitors Kiosk** (U.S. 395 and Hwy. 158, summer only) is staffed by volunteers, so there's no guarantee of when it is open.

Getting There

June Lake is located east of Yosemite, west of U.S. 395, south of Lee Vining, and north of Mammoth Lakes. To get to June Lake, take U.S. 395 and turn west onto Highway 158 at the June Lake Loop. June Mountain Ski Resort is about four miles west of U.S. 395.

Mammoth Lakes

The town of Mammoth Lakes, located east of Yosemite and about 28 miles south of Tioga Pass, started out as a gold mining settlement and then became a logging site. The gorgeous mountain scenery, however, along with multiple alpine lakes, natural hot springs, and dependable snowfall, soon helped to establish Mammoth Lakes as a prime tourist destination. Today outdoor sports—and skiing in particular—are the town's main reason for existing. Ski and snowboard season can last up to 11 months, so don't be surprised if you come for hiking in July and see lifts running and skiers gliding down the hills. Even when the snow stops, this idyllic town and its surrounding nature do not grind to a halt. In winter, the roads are subject to the whims of weather, though they rarely close. It's best to carry chains and to check weather reports before starting out.

SIGHTS

The Village at Mammoth Lakes

Like many large ski resort areas, **The Village at Mammoth Lakes** (www.villageatmammoth.com) is a hybrid of a real town, an overly planned shopping mall, and a clean, upscale amusement park. Its central purpose is to provide support services for people who come to enjoy Mammoth Mountain, most of whom are skiers. To that end, the Village offers lodging, dining (the standard chains plus a few local places), and shopping—all organized around a central pedestrian plaza. In summer, the plaza is sprinkled with outdoor benches, tables with umbrellas, and recently planted greenery as it tries to impersonate an actual village square. Concerts and outdoor movies are presented here in the warmer months.

Gondola Rides

Mammoth Mountain, like all ski resorts, has plenty of gondolas, chairlifts, and other ways to get up to the mountain while relaxing and enjoying the view. Of the two main gondolas, one is open only in winter: **Village Gondola** (7:45am-5pm, free) takes you from The Village at Mammoth Lakes to Canyon Lodge. The other gondola, **Panorama Gondola** (8:30am-4pm, last ride to top at 3:30pm), sometimes called the Scenic Gondola Ride, operates in summer and winter. Panorama runs from the Main Lodge at Mammoth to McCoy Station and then, after a stop there, goes all the way to the top of the mountain. In winter, the gondola is extremely popular with skiers: Intermediate-level skiers get off at McCoy to access the trails there; the top of the mountain is for experts only. In summer (9am-4:30pm daily June-Sept., adults $21, ages 13-18 $17, under age 13 free with an adult) it serves sightseers, mountain bikers, hikers, and anyone else who wants to get to the top of the 11,053-foot mountain. From the top, you can see as far as 400 miles on a clear day.

The ride all the way to the top takes about 20 minutes. Some people do it just for the thrill of the ride; others stop for a meal or a snack at the **Top of the Sierra Café** (9:30am-4pm daily summer, 11am-2pm daily winter, $8-20), open when the gondola is running.

One of the most popular reasons to ride up is to ride down—on your mountain bike. In summer, 70 miles of trails are open for biking and 25 miles of hiking trails are available. You can buy a day pass (over age 12 $43, under age 13 $22) to bike the trails, which includes all-day access to both the Panorama Gondola and the shuttle. Hikers only pay to ride the gondola, and then they're free to walk down. If you're not a skier, you can still ride the Panorama Gondola to the top and back in winter (ages 18-64 $24, over age 64 $20, ages 13-17 $19, ages 7-12 $8).

The Panorama Gondola is sometimes closed

in October for maintenance between the two big seasons. The Village Gondola sometimes operates in summer for special events.

Inyo Craters

California is full of volcanic action, and some of the most interesting results to behold are the three **Inyo Craters** (www.fs.usda.gov). These phreatic craters on and near Deer Mountain were created by explosions of steam. Scientists believe that all three craters came into being at about the same time, around AD 1350. Two of the three craters are about 200 feet deep and large enough that they actually have lakes inside them. The third crater is smaller, but all are worth seeing. If you can, make time for this geologic side trip.

To reach Inyo Craters, drive five miles north of Mammoth Lakes on Highway 203. Turn right (east) onto the Mammoth Scenic Route (Dry Creek Rd.) and continue about 3.2 miles until you see the sign for the Inyo Craters. Turn right at the sign and drive about 1.3 more miles on a dirt road (not plowed, or advised, in winter). Park in the lot and walk 0.3 mile to the crater site.

★ Devils Postpile National Monument

Compared to the area's other national parks, **Devils Postpile National Monument** (Minaret Vista Rd., 760/934-2289, www.nps.gov/depo, mid-June-mid-Oct., 24 hours daily, ranger station 9am-5pm daily late June-Labor Day, adults $7, ages 3-15 $4) is small, but what you'll see is worth a visit. The park is named for the strange natural rock formation called the Devils Postpile. It's hard to fathom that the near-perfect, straight-sided hexagonal posts are a natural phenomenon created by volcanic heat and pressure. Less heavily traveled than many other parks, Devils Postpile has hikes to serene meadows and unspoiled streams, and you're likely to see the occasional deer or maybe even a bear meandering through the woods. Free guided ranger walks are held at 11am most days throughout the summer, starting from the ranger station.

Devils Postpile National Monument

Also part of the monument is the beautiful crystalline **Rainbow Falls.** The thick sheet of water cascades 101 feet down to a pool, throwing up stunning rainbows of mist. For the best rainbows at the waterfall, hike the three miles (round-trip) from Red Meadow near the middle of the day when the sun is high in the sky.

The $7 park entry fee includes the Reds Meadow-Devils Postpile Shuttle. During summer, visitors must access the park via shuttle, which runs hourly 7am-10am every day from the Village at Mammoth Lakes and every 15-30 minutes from 7am-7pm every day mid-June-early September from the Mammoth Mountain Adventure Center and Main Lodge area. When the shuttle isn't running, visitors may drive their cars into the park, but will need to pay a $10 vehicle fee.

Old Mammoth Road

Like most of the Eastern Sierra region, Mammoth Lakes became of interest to miners in the 19th century after the gold rush began—miners got out this far in 1877. Along **Old Mammoth Road** (south off Hwy. 203/ Main St.) you'll find a number of old mining sites. At the height of the short-lived boom, about 20 different small mines operated in the area. Along this road, you can see the grave of a miner's wife, a stamp mill's flywheel, and then the meager remains of Mammoth City and the nearby Mammoth Mine. The highlight of this summertime half-day trip is the ruins of the Mammoth Consolidated Mine. You can still see some bits of the camp and its housing buildings, the assay office, the mill, and mining equipment. The mine shaft is also visible, but do not attempt to get around the security features to head down there. Old mine shafts are unbelievably dangerous and should not be entered for any reason.

SPORTS AND RECREATION

Skiing

MAMMOTH MOUNTAIN

The premier downhill ski and snowboard mountain is, aptly, **Mammoth Mountain** (1 Minaret Rd., information 760/934-2571, lodging and lift tickets 800/626-6684, snow report 888/766-9778, www.mammothmountain.com, lifts 8:30am-4pm daily, 2014-2015 rates adults $95, seniors $89, ages 13-18 $82, ages 5-12 $35). Whether you're completely new to downhill thrills or a seasoned expert looking for different terrain, you'll find something great on Mammoth Mountain. More than two dozen lifts, including three gondolas and 10 express quads, take you up 3,100 vertical feet to the 3,500 acres of skiable and boardable terrain; there are also three pipes. If you're staying at Eagle Lodge, Canyon Lodge, Mammoth Mountain Inn, the Main Lodge, or The Village at Mammoth Lakes, enjoy the convenience of a lift or gondola right outside your door. All these, plus the Mill Café and McCoy Station halfway up the mountain, offer hot drinks, tasty snacks, and a welcome spot to rest during a long day of skiing.

The easiest runs on the mountain mostly cluster around the ski school and the lower area near the Mammoth Mountain Inn; they are recognizable by their cute nursery-school names. If you're an intermediate skier, runs swing down all over the mountain just for you. Build your confidence by taking the Panorama Gondola up to Panorama Lookout at the top of the mountain then skiing all the way down the east side of the mountain along the intermediate-to-harder ridge runs. Advanced skiers favor the bowls and chutes at the front of the mountain, and hard-core experts go west from Panorama Lookout to chase the dragon.

TAMARACK CROSS-COUNTRY SKI CENTER

Here's your chance to explore the snow-covered Mammoth Lakes Basin in winter. **Tamarack Cross-Country Ski Center** (163 Twin Lakes Rd., 760/934-2442, www.tamaracklodge.com, 8:30am-5pm daily mid-Nov.-Apr., adults $16-28, youths and seniors $13-22, children $5) offers 19 miles of groomed cross-country ski tracks, some with groomed skating lanes, for all abilities and levels. This lovely resort also has a restaurant, a lounge, and a bar where you can enjoy a nice cup of hot chocolate and good book if you get tired of skiing. And getting here from Mammoth Lakes is free: Just take the Orange shuttle line from Mammoth Village hourly on the half-hour (8:30am-5:15pm daily late Jan.-mid-Apr.).

BLUE DIAMOND TRAILS

The **Blue Diamond Trails** (www.mammothlakes.us) system starts just behind the Mammoth Lakes Welcome Center (Hwy. 203, 3 miles west of U.S. 395, 760/924-5500, www.visitmammoth.com, daily 8am-5pm), at the entrance to Mammoth Lakes, and winds through 25 miles of Inyo National Forest, marked by signs bearing a blue diamond on the trees. Pick up a free trail map in the Welcome Center before you set out. Some trails are not groomed, so be prepared to deal with varying snow conditions and unbroken trails. There's plenty of relatively flat land here for beginners, however. The **Shady Rest Trails** (Hwy. 203, just before the Welcome Center) might sound like a cemetery, but in fact it's a group of beginner loops with plenty of shade trees to keep skiers cool through their exertions. The **Knolls Trail** (Mammoth Scenic Loop, 1.5 miles north of Hwy. 203) makes a good intermediate day out, passing through lovely stands of lodgepole and Jeffrey pines. Beginners beware of the deceptively named **Scenic Loop Trail** (Mammoth Scenic Loop, across from Knolls Trail). This reasonably short trail—about four miles long—includes steep descents and some difficult terrain.

Hiking

Hikers will find plenty of worthwhile terrain around Mammoth Lakes for both short day hikes and longer backpacking adventures. The **Mammoth Mountain Bike Park** (1 Minaret Rd., 800/626-6684, www.mammothmountain.com, 8am-6pm daily summer, adults $16-49, ages under 13 $5-23) includes a number of great hiking trails. For an all-downhill walk, take the Panorama Gondola (9am-4:30pm daily June-Sept., adults $21, ages 13-18 $17, under age 13 free with an adult) up to the Panorama Overlook and hike back down to town. Just be sure to get a trail map at the **Mammoth Adventure Center** (1 Minaret Rd., 800/626-6684, www.mammothmountain.com, 8am-6pm daily June-Sept.) so you can keep to the hiking areas and avoid being flattened by fast-moving mountain bikers.

Mammoth Lakes also acts as a jumping-off point for adventurers who want to take on the **John Muir Wilderness** (south of Mammoth Lakes to Mount Whitney, www.sierrawild.gov). John Muir pioneered the preservation of the Sierra Nevadas, and more than 500,000 acres in the area have been designated national wilderness areas in his honor. Day hikers are welcome, and there's plenty to see. Check with the Inyo and Sierra National Forests (www.fs.usda.gov) for trail maps of the area. The main attractions to the John Muir, as it's called locally, are the **John Muir Trail** (JMT, 215 miles Yosemite-Mount Whitney, www.johnmuirtrail.org) and the **Pacific Crest National Scenic Trail** (PCT, 2,650 miles, www.pcta.org), both among the holiest of grails for backpacking enthusiasts from around the world.

If you're planning an overnight camping trip in the John Muir, Ansel Adams, Dinkey Lakes, or Kaiser Wilderness areas of the Sierra National Forest, you must first obtain a wilderness permit. You can apply for these up to one year in advance by downloading an application (www.fs.usda.gov/sierra) or by calling 559/297-0706. If you reserve in advance, there is a charge of $5 pp for the permit. On the other hand, if you're willing to be flexible, you can just show up at a ranger station no more than 24 hours before your trip begins and apply in person. There is no charge for these "walk-up" permits, though their availability is not guaranteed. The main office is the **High Sierra Ranger District Office** (29688 Auberry Rd., Prather, 559/855-5355, 8am-4:30pm daily Apr.-Nov., 8am-4:30pm Mon.-Fri. Nov.-Apr.).

If you're planning an overnight in the Inyo National Forest, you can apply for your permit in person at the **Mammoth Lakes Welcome Center** (Hwy. 203, 3 miles west of U.S. 395, 760/924-5500, www.visitmammoth.com, 8am-5pm daily), at the entrance to Mammoth Lakes, or apply online (www.fs.usda.gov/inyo).

Biking

Come summertime and melting snow, Mammoth Mountain transforms from a ski resort to a mountain bike mecca. The **Mammoth Mountain Bike Park** (1 Minaret Rd., 800/626-6684, www.mammothmountain.com, 8am-6pm daily, $16 for trail access, $49 for trail, gondola, and shuttle access) spans much of the same terrain as the ski areas, with almost 90 miles of trails that suit all levels of biking ability. The park headquarters is at the **Mammoth Adventure Center** (Main Lodge, 1 Minaret Rd., 760/934-0706 or 800/626-6684, 8am-6pm daily June-Sept.), at the Main Lodge at Mammoth Mountain. You can also buy bike park tickets at the Mountain Center at the Village (760/924-7057).

You can take your bike onto the Panorama Gondola and ride all the way to the top of Mammoth Mountain, then all the way down (3,000-plus vertical feet) on the single tracks. Be sure to pick the trails that best suit your fitness and experience level. Several other major lodges and mountain cafés offer rider services, including the Mountain Center at The Village at Mammoth Lakes and Juniper Springs. If you value scenery as much as extreme adventure, pack your camera and plan to rest at the various scenic overlooks throughout the trail system.

If you need to rent a bike or buy park tickets, go to the **Mammoth Adventure Center** (Main Lodge, 1 Minaret Rd., 760/934-0706) or to **Mammoth Sports at Mountain Center** (6201 Minaret Rd., inside the Village, 760/934-2571, ext. 2078). Both locations offer new high-end bikes for adults and kids. These shops can also help with parts and repairs for bikes you've brought up with you, and they sell accessories.

Horseback Riding

Perhaps the most traditional way to explore the Eastern Sierra is on the back of a horse or mule. Early pioneers to the area came on horseback, and you can follow their example from several locations near Mammoth Lakes. From the **McGee Creek Pack Station** (2990 McGee Creek Rd., Crowley Lake, June-Sept. 760/935-4324, Oct.-May 760/878-2207, www.mcgeecreekpackstation.com, $40 per hour, $140 full day), 10 miles south of Mammoth Lakes on U.S. 395, you can ride into McGee Canyon, a little-visited wilderness area. Other day-trip destinations include Baldwin Canyon and Hilton Lakes. Standard rides range from one hour to a full day, but McGee's specialty is multiday and pack trips that let you really get out beyond the reach of paved roads to camp for a number of days by one of the many pristine lakes dotting the mountains. If you love the outdoors and really want a vacation as far away from it all as you can get, consider a few days' camping in Convict Basin or near Upper Fish Creek in the John Muir Wilderness. The McGee Creek guides will help you pack your gear and guide you through the incredible backcountry of the Eastern Sierra.

Snowshoeing

If you prefer walking to all that sliding around on planks, rent or bring your own snowshoes to Mammoth and enjoy a snowy hike through the mountains and meadows. Check the cross-country ski areas first—many have specifically designated snowshoe trails. Or head out to the backcountry and explore Mammoth Lakes Basin or the Sherwin Range. Groomed trails start right behind the Mammoth Lakes Welcome Center.

ENTERTAINMENT AND EVENTS

Bars and Clubs

For possibly the best evening in Mammoth, try the **Clocktower Cellar Pub** (Alpenhof

Lodge, 6080 Minaret Rd., 760/934-2725, www.clocktowercellar.com, 4pm-11pm daily winter, 5pm-11pm daily summer). This happening nightspot offers a full bar with more than 160 whiskeys, 26 brews on tap, and 50 different bottled beers. They also provide glasses of fine wine from Petra's Bistro and Wine Bar next door, and a casual atmosphere complete with sports on TV, vintage video games, and a pool table. The location is perfect—in the basement of the Alpenhof just across the street from the Village.

For a French-style wine bar experience, try the vintages at the **Side Door Bistro** (100 Canyon Blvd., 760/934-5200, www.sidedoormammoth.com, 11am-9pm Mon.-Thurs., 9am-11pm Fri.-Sat., 9am-9pm Sun. winter, 11am-9pm daily summer). Not only can you enjoy glasses of California's top wines in the evening, you can order up a delicious dinner or dessert crepe to go with your favorite varietal. The wine list is often called the best in the Village. They're open until 9pm or later in summer and winter, and they often close a few weekdays during spring and fall.

Sports bar **Grumpy's** (361 Old Mammoth Rd., 760/934-8587, www.grumpysmammoth.com, 11:30am-2:30am daily) has the usual array of TVs showing major sporting events, along with pool tables and an arcade. Grumpy's has a full bar and serves up a lunch and dinner menu of Mexican and American specialties; sometimes they close early on slower evenings, especially during the week.

The **Lakanuki Tiki Bar** (6201 Minaret Rd., 760/934-7447, www.lakanuki.net, noon-2am Tues.-Sun., 3pm-2am Mon. winter, 3pm-2am daily summer) is a popular tiki bar, especially on weekends, and especially with the young male snowboarding crowd. Stop by for happy hour (3pm-6pm) when drinks are $4 and some menu items are discounted. Hours may vary and the bar is usually closed Monday-Tuesday in spring and fall, so call ahead.

Festivals and Events

If music is your thing, check out the **Sierra Summer Festival** (760/935-3837, www.sierrasummerfestival.org, $20-35, free for K-12 students) in mid-August. The Eastern Sierra Symphony Orchestra, under musical director emeritus Bogidar Avramov and assorted guest conductors, performs during this weeklong festival, along with special guests. For art enthusiasts, the **Labor Day Festival of the Arts and Music** (760/914-3752, www.monoarts.org) has been going on for more than 40 years, showcasing both fine artists and craftspeople to the soundtrack of the Eastern Sierra's finest live musicians.

And what's a festival roundup without beer? In early August, the annual **Mammoth Festival of Beers and Bluespalooza** (888/992-7397, www.mammothbluesbrewsfest.com, $35-75 individual events, $155-180 weekend pass) gives attendees the chance to sample the work of more than 60 craft breweries and listen to major performers like Buddy Guy, Robert Cray, and Blues Traveler.

ACCOMMODATIONS

Under $100

Want to ski the slopes of Mammoth, but can't afford the hoity-toity condo resorts? Stay at the **Innsbruck Lodge** (Forest Trail between Hwy. 203 and Sierra Blvd., 760/934-3035, www.innsbrucklodge.com, $85-295). Economy rooms offer twin beds, a table and chairs, and access to the motel whirlpool tub and lobby with a stone fireplace at very reasonable nightly rates. Other rooms have queen or king beds, some sleep up to six, and some include kitchenettes. The quiet North Village location is on the ski area shuttle route for easy access to the local slopes. It's also an easy walk to most restaurants and other Village attractions. The inn requires a two-night stay on weekends during ski season.

The inexpensive **Boulder Lodge** (2282 Hwy. 158, 760/648-7533 or 800/458-6355, www.boulderlodgejunelake.com, $88-375) provides an array of options, from simple motel rooms to multiple-bedroom apartments and even a five-bedroom lake house. The Boulder Lodge goes back a few decades with its decor—the browns, wood paneling, and faux leather furniture recall the 1950s. But the views of June Lake and the recreation area surrounding the lodge are timeless.

$100-150

The **Sierra Lodge** (3540 Main St., 760/934-8881 or 800/356-5711, www.sierralodge.com, $109-199) offers reasonably priced nonsmoking rooms right on the ski shuttle line, and only 1.5 miles from the Juniper Ridge chair lift. Rooms have either a king or two double beds, a kitchenette, and plenty of space for gear. The decor is simple motel styling in cool, relaxing blues. Breakfast, cable TV, and Internet access are included. This small motel's rates are rock-bottom in the off-season and on weekdays in winter.

One of the best things about the **Tamarack Lodge & Resort** (163 Twin Lakes Rd., Mammoth Lakes, 760/934-2442, www.tamaracklodge.com) is that you can cross-country ski right up to your door. The 11 lodge rooms ($100-269) and 35 cabins ($179-749) range from studios to three-bedroom units that sleep up to nine. Lodge rooms sometimes go for as low as $89 per night on weeknights. Tamarack prides itself on its rustic atmosphere, so accommodations have fireplaces or wood stoves, but no televisions.

$150-250

From the outside, the ornate, carved-wood, fringed **Austria Hof** (924 Canyon Blvd., 760/934-2764 or 866/662-6668, www.austriahof.com, $150-188) might be a ski hotel tucked into a crevice of the Alps. But on the inside, you'll find the most stylish American appointments. These motel rooms, some with king beds and spa tubs, are peaceful. Austria Hof's location adjacent to the Canyon Lodge and the free gondola to the Village make it a great base camp for winter skiing or summer mountain biking. In the evening, head down to the Austria Hof Restaurant ($25-30) for some hearty German fare. The Hof also boasts several lavish condos ($245-395) with anywhere from one to three bedrooms during winter.

Across the street from Mammoth Mountain's Main Lodge and right beside the Panorama Gondola is the **Mammoth Mountain Inn** (10400 Minaret Rd., Mammoth Lakes, 760/934-2581 or 800/626-6684, www.themammothmountaininn.com). The main building at the inn features standard hotel rooms ($169-299). The nearby East-West Building features condos that range from studios ($249) to one-bedrooms ($329) to deluxe two-bedrooms with lofts that can sleep up to 11 people ($769/night in ski season). All rooms and condos have flat-screen TVs in addition to all the amenities you'd expect in an upscale ski lodge.

Over $250

It's not cheap, but the ★ **Juniper Springs Resort** (4000 Meridian Blvd., reservations 760/924-1102 or 800/626-6684, www.juniperspringsmammoth.com, $249-1,100) has absolutely every luxury amenity to make your ski vacation complete. Condos come in studios, one- to three-bedrooms, and townhouses. The interiors have stunning appointments, from granite-topped kitchen counters and 60-inch flat-screen TVs. Baths include deep soaking tubs. The resort also features heated pools year-round and six outdoor heated spas. The on-site **Talons Diner** (760/934-0797 or 760/934-2571, ext. 3797, 7:30am-4:30pm daily Nov.-Apr., hours can fluctuate during the week) serves breakfast and lunch, and the **Daily Grind** (7am-1pm daily summer, 7am-11pm daily winter) provides coffee, snacks, breakfast, and lunch year-round. Juniper Springs is located next door to the Eagle Lodge, which serves as one of the Mammoth Mountain base lodges, complete with a six-seat express chairlift up to the main ski area.

The company that owns Juniper Springs also owns the luxury condo complex at **The Village Lodge** (1111 Forest Trail, 760/934-1982 or 800/626-6684, www.mammothmountain.com, $239-1,200), which is even a little closer to the ski mountain. Check them out if you can't get the condo of your dreams at Juniper.

For another fine condo rental, check out **Mountainback** (435 Lakeview Blvd., 800/468-6225, www.mountainbackrentals.com, $200-500, two-night minimum, $60-85 booking fee). This complex has an array of all-two-bedroom units, some that sleep up to 10. Every individual building has its own outdoor spa, and the complex has a heated pool and a sauna. Every condo is decorated differently. Check the website for photos—big stones everywhere, wood paneling, gentle cream walls, or even red-and-green holiday-themed furniture.

FOOD

Petra's Bistro and Wine Bar (6080 Minaret Rd., 760/934-3500, www.petrasbistro.com, 5:30pm-close Tues.-Sun.) offers a seasonal menu that's designed to please the palate and a wine list that's worth a visit itself. The by-the-glass offerings change each night, and your server will happily cork your unfinished bottle to take home. Two dining rooms and a wine bar divide the seating, and the atmosphere feels romantic without being too dark. Petra's stays open all year. Reservations are a good idea during ski season.

The popular gourmet establishment **Skadi** (587 Old Mammoth Rd., 760/934-3902, www.skadirestaurant.com, 5:30pm-9:30pm Wed.-Sun., $24-32) describes its menu as "alpine cuisine." The restaurant, co-owned by a chef and a rancher, offers a creative menu of fresh local meat and plants to their best advantage. Consider ordering a couple of items from the ample selection of appetizers for a "small plates" experience. Don't skip dessert!

Even Californians who eat Mexican food on a regular basis tend to agree that **Roberto's Mexican Café** (271 Old Mammoth Rd., 760/934-3667, www.robertoscafe.com, 11am-close daily, $7-15) is special. This casual spot serves classic California-Mexican food in great quantities but includes specialty items like lobster burritos and duck tacos. It's perfect for skiers and boarders famished after a long day on the slopes. For a quiet meal, stay downstairs in the main dining room. To join a lively younger crowd, head upstairs to the bar, which has tables and serves the full restaurant menu.

Hopheads will love the **Eatery By Bleu at Mammoth Brewing Company** (18 Lake Mary Rd., 760/934-7141, www.mammothbrewingco.com, 10am-10:30pm Wed.-Sun., hours can fluctuate during summer, $8-24). The beer is legendary in these parts, but the restaurant is just as worthy. Standard pub grub gets a new twist with dishes like flatbread pizzas, lobster corn dogs, and Irish Caesar salad. Look for offerings like the pan-roasted salmon with kale and chipotle guava vinaigrette. Order a pitcher of suds, like the crisp and malty Golden Trout Pilsner, or go for the hoppy Epic IPA.

Look for the best steaks in town at **The Mogul Restaurant** (1528 Tavern Rd., 760/934-3039, www.themogul.com, 5:30pm-close daily, $20-40). The menu is chock-full of standard surf-and-turf entrées like crab legs, pork tenderloin, rack of lamb, and ribs. Consider the house chicken dish, dripping in a marinade of red wine, honey, soy sauce, Worcestershire, brown sugar, and a whole rack of spices. Stop by for the happy hour (5:30pm-6:30pm), when bottled beer starts at only $2.50—a steal in this town during the ski season.

INFORMATION AND SERVICES

Visitor Information

The town of Mammoth Lakes has an awesome visitors center at the entrance to Mammoth Lakes, the **Mammoth Lakes Welcome Center** (Hwy. 203, 3 miles west of U.S. 395, 760/924-5500, www.visitmammoth.com or www.fs.usda.gov/inyo, hours vary). The facility is jointly run by the U.S. Forest Service, the town of Mammoth Lakes tourism bureau, the Eastern Sierra Interpretive Association, and the National Parks Service, so they can help you with everything from condo rentals and restaurant reservations before you arrive to the latest bar openings and best seasonal recreation options when you get here. They're also your best resource for camping information, weather travel advisories, updates on snowmobile trails, and even backcountry passes for your backpacking trip.

Medical Services

Need medical service beyond that offered at the ski resorts? You can get it at **Mammoth Hospital** (85 Sierra Park Rd., 760/934-3311, www.mammothhospital.com), which has a 24-hour emergency room.

TRANSPORTATION

Air

The nearest airport to Mammoth Lakes is the **Mammoth Yosemite Airport** (MMH, 1200 Airport Rd., 760/934-3813, www.ci.mammoth-lakes.ca.us). Alaska Airlines serves this airport year-round; United Express also flies December 15-April 30. In winter, nonstop flights run to Mammoth from Los Angeles, San Francisco, Denver, Las Vegas, and San Diego. For a major transportation hub, fly to the **Reno-Tahoe International Airport** (RNO, 2001 E. Plumb Ln., Reno, NV, 775/328-6400, www.renoairport.com). From there, you can drive 166 miles south on U.S. 395 and get to Mammoth Lakes in about 3.5 hours.

Car

U.S. 395 is the main access road to the Mammoth Lakes area. To get to the town of Mammoth Lakes from U.S. 395, turn onto Highway 203, which will take you right into town. Expect a seven-hour drive from San Francisco if the traffic and weather cooperate. If you fly into Reno, the drive out to Mammoth takes about 3.5 hours.

In the winter, be aware that it snows at Mammoth Lakes more than it does in almost any other place in California. Carry chains! Even if the weather is predicted to be clear for your visit, having chains can prevent a world of hurt and the need to turn back in a sudden storm. The longer you plan to stay, the more you should stock your car with items such as ice scrapers, blankets, water, food, and a full tank of gas whenever possible. For the latest traffic information, including chain control areas and weather conditions, call Caltrans (800/427-7623).

Parking in Mammoth Lakes in the off-season is a breeze. In the winter, it can get a bit more complicated, as constant snow removal means that parking on the street is illegal throughout town. Most of the major resorts and hotels offer heated parking structures, and many of the restaurants, bars, and ski resorts have plenty of parking in their outdoor lots.

Shuttles and Buses

The **Eastern Sierra Transit Authority** (ESTA, 760/920-3359 or 760/914-1315, www.estransit.com) runs a number of bus lines, including the CREST line, which takes passengers from Lone Pine through Bishop, Mammoth, Lee Vining, and other stops on the way to the Reno Greyhound station and the Reno-Tahoe International Airport. The trip from the Reno Airport to Mammoth Lakes takes 3.5 hours (adults $46, children and seniors $42). The ESTA also operates local bus routes around Mammoth Lakes, including the **June Mountain Shuttle** ($14.50 round-trip), which takes skiers from Mammoth Lakes to the June Lake ski area. Some routes only run on certain days of the week, so check the schedule ahead of time for updated info.

The **Mammoth Transit System** (www.visitmammoth.com, Nov.-May, free) offers complimentary rides all over town in the winter, freeing visitors from their own cars most of the time. You can download a copy of the transit map from the website.

Devils Postpile National Monument (760/934-2289, www.nps.gov/depo, adults $7, children $4) runs a shuttle that's mandatory for all visitors during high season (except for vehicles with handicap placards). During summer, visitors must access the park via shuttle, which runs hourly 7am-10am daily from the Village at Mammoth Lakes and every 15-30 minutes from 7am-7pm daily mid-June to early September from the Mammoth Mountain Adventure Center and Main Lodge area.

BISHOP

Bishop is located west of the Inyo and White Mountains, southeast of Yosemite, and northeast of Kings Canyon, and is a great jumping-off point for travelers to explore some of the natural wonders of this area. Bishop is the largest city in Inyo County. Its quaint western main street offers some low-key hotels and restaurants and ample places to rent equipment for a variety of active sports. Additional local color—including nightlife—is provided by the Paiute and Shoshone peoples, who have a large reservation nearby and operate a casino in Bishop. With an elevation of just over 4,000 feet, Bishop doesn't get as cold, or anywhere near as snowy, as nearby Mammoth Lakes, which is twice its elevation. Still, the area is pretty remote, so it's best to be prepared for emergencies. Carry chains, food, and water in your car, and don't pass up a chance to fill the gas tank on the way.

Ancient Bristlecone Pine Forest

Laws Railroad Museum and Historic Site

If you've got a railroad buff in the family, make time to visit the **Laws Railroad Museum and Historic Site** (Silver Canyon Rd., off U.S. 6, 760/873-5950, www.lawsmuseum.org, 10am-4pm daily, sometimes opening a half-hour earlier during summer, donation), 4.5 miles north of Bishop. There's more here than just trains—in fact, it has a whole historical village with artifacts from the area's history well preserved and on display. But the center of the village is the railroad depot, which is pretty much how towns were organized back when residents depended on the railroads not only for transportation but also for commerce and communication with the outside world. Come and see the self-propelled Death Valley Car from 1927, a caboose from 1883, model railroad displays, and more.

★ Ancient Bristlecone Pine Forest

Directly to the east of Bishop near the Nevada border is yet another amazing California wilderness area. Little visited but worth a trip on its own, **Ancient Bristlecone Pine Forest** is a section of the Inyo National Forest in the White Mountains where the world's oldest trees reside. The bristlecone pines can be even older than the coastal redwoods and sequoias. The most famous bristlecone pine, **Methuselah,** at the ripe age of about 4,750, is believed to be 1,000 years older than any other tree in the world. To protect the tree, the Forest Service has chosen not to mark it or produce maps directing people to it, but don't worry—almost all the trees around here are beautiful to behold.

There are two main groves of trees that you won't want to miss. The **Schulman Grove** is where you'll find the **Bristlecone Pine Forest Visitors Center** (Hwy. 168, 23 miles east of Big Pine, 760/873-2500, www.fs.usda.gov/inyo, 10am-4pm Fri.-Mon. mid-May-early Nov., $3 pp or $6 per car).

The second notable grove, 12 miles north of Schulman on a dirt road, is the **Patriarch Grove.** Here you'll see the Patriarch Tree, which is the world's largest bristlecone pine.

A self-guided nature trail in the Patriarch Grove enables you to get out among the trees and learn more about them. Note that the road from the visitors center to the Patriarch Grove isn't paved and can be treacherous for light passenger vehicles. At 11,000 feet, the grove's elevation can also be difficult for visitors with health issues.

Three hiking trails begin right outside the Bristlecone Pine Forest Visitors Center. The **Discovery Trail** is an easy one-mile loop with helpful signs along the way. The **Methuselah Trail** is a roughly five-mile loop that's also easy. Yes, you will see the world's oldest tree if you take this walk—you just won't know exactly which tree it is. Its secret identity is protected, but you can have fun admiring *all* the noble specimens here and guessing which gnarled tree is most ancient. Finally, the **Mexican Mine Trail** is an out-and-back hike of about five miles in total that leads past some abandoned mine buildings made out of tough bristlecone pine wood, of course, in addition to still more living trees.

You can get to the Ancient Bristlecone Pine Forest by car from the town of Bishop in about an hour. Take U.S. 395 south to Big Pine and turn left (east) onto Highway 168. Take Highway 168 for 13 miles to White Mountain Road. Turn left (north) and drive 10 miles to the visitors center in Schulman Grove.

Horseback Riding

Operating out of Bishop, **Rainbow Pack Outfitters** (off Hwy. 168, west of Bishop, 760/873-8877, http://rainbow.zb-net.com) offers a wide range of options for horse lovers. At the stables, small children can enjoy their "Li'l Cowpoke" ride ($20) on a pony or horse with an expert leading. Options for bigger kids and adults include the Rainbow Meadow Ride (1 hour, $35), the South Lake Vista Ride (2 hours, $50), the Long Lake Scenic Ride (4 hours, $75), the All-day Ride (9am-5pm, $105), and the All-day Fishing Ride (9am-5pm, $125), which is a mini-pack trip. If you're looking for a longer horseback vacation, check into Rainbow's options for full-service multiday riding trips, with hunting, fishing, photography, birding, and more. Rainbow provides service into the John Muir Wilderness, the Inyo National Forest, and Sequoia and Kings Canyon National Parks. Another part of Rainbow's business is displaying the historical side of packing. Free facility tours are available during the summer season when the pack station is open. Reservations are recommended for all rides. The best way to reach Rainbow is by telephone.

Snowmobiling

Given the heavy snows, great scenery, and wide-open spaces, snowmobiling in Bishop is a given. To rent equipment and get some help getting started, stop into **Bishop Motosports** (205 Grove St., 760/934-0347, www.snomobiles.com, $275-300 for 3 hours, $325-395 for 6 hours, $400-525 full day). Maps, helmets, and trailers (for off-road vehicles) are included with all rentals. Bishop Motosports makes themselves available to customers from early in the morning till late at night every day of the week. If you make an appointment, they'll be there. Another location in Mammoth offers similar services.

Entertainment and Events

Each September for more than 20 years, the Inyo Council for the Arts has put on the sort of music festival you'd expect to find in a much larger metropolitan center. The **Millpond Music Festival** (Millpond Park, Sawmill Rd., 5 miles northwest of Bishop, 760/873-8014, www.inyo.org, mid-Sept., day pass adults $25-35, students $15, weekend pass $75-90 adults, K-12 students $25) has performers as varied as Los Lobos, Ray Bonneville, and the Marc Atkinson Trio. In addition to amazing music in a beautiful mountain setting, you'll find work by local artists, arts and crafts activities for children, food and drink booths, and musician workshops. You can usually buy tickets starting in early spring.

If an hour or three at the slots or the blackjack tables sounds like a good way to unwind, go to the **Paiute Palace Casino** (2742 N.

Sierra Hwy., 888/372-4883, www.paiutepalace.com, 24 hours daily), owned by the Bishop Paiute Tribe. You can play more than 300 slots plus table blackjack and poker. Look for Texas hold 'em tournaments Wednesday-Sunday.

Camping

A nice place to stay near Bishop is **Keough's Hot Springs** (800 Keough Hot Springs Rd., 760/872-4670, www.keoughshotsprings.com, adults $10-75, children $7-55). The 100- by 30-foot swimming pool is heated by natural hot springs, so it's open year-round, as is the campground and other facilities. Lodging options include "dry" tent or RV sites ($23), campsites with water and electricity ($28), four tent cabins ($85-100), and a mobile home ($125-135). To get to Keough's, travel six miles south of Bishop on U.S. 395. When you see the big blue sign on your left, turn right. You'll be there in less than 10 minutes.

Campgrounds are available in the Inyo National Forest near Bishop. One of the most popular is **Bishop Park** (Hwy. 168, 12 miles west of Bishop, 760/873-2400, www.fs.usda.gov, 21 sites, first-come, first-served, Apr.-Oct., $23). It's right on the banks of Bishop Creek, with flush toilets and space for RVs. Another nice option is **Intake Two** (Hwy. 168, 16 miles west of Bishop, 8 sites, first-come, first-served, Apr.-Oct., $23), located near Intake Two Lake. Swimming is not advised because the water is so cold, but you can catch trout here. **Sabrina Campground** (Hwy. 168, 18 miles west of Bishop, 18 sites, first-come, first-served, late May-Sept., $23) is at 9,300 feet elevation, making it low on oxygen but high on views. Lake Sabrina is nearby, and it's a good trout-fishing destination. Showers are not available at any of the national forest campgrounds, but you can buy a shower at a couple of places nearby: **Bishop Creek Lodge** (2100 S. Lake Rd., 760/873-4484, www.bishopcreekresort.com, Apr.-Oct., $6 for a 10-minute token, $1 for soap and towel) and **Parchers Resort** (5001 S. Lake Dr., 760/873-4177, www.parchersresort.net, resort mid-May-late Oct., showers year-round, $6 for a 10-minute shower, $1 for soap and $1 for towel).

Food

Even if you don't usually like casinos, consider having a meal at **TuKaNovie** (2742 N. Sierra Hwy./U.S. 395, 888/372-4883, www.paiutepalace.com, 7am-9pm Sun.-Thurs., 7am-11pm Fri.-Sat., $10-16), the restaurant at the Paiute Palace Casino. The food, service, and prices are all better than you might expect, and the restaurant is smoke-free. Expect basic American food, with a prime rib special on Friday and Saturday nights starting at 5pm. The absence of sales tax on Native American land makes the place even more affordable.

Bishop doesn't have many options for dining, but a couple of eateries in town will satisfy the mightiest of hunger pangs. **Holy Smoke Texas Style BBQ** (772 N. Main St., 760/872-4227, www.holysmoketexasstylebbq.com, 11am-9pm Wed.-Mon., $10-15) grills meats that might rival the Lone Star State itself. Come hungry; entrées include the Longhorn, a dry-rubbed and hickory-smoked brisket with more flavor than an Austin blues band, and the Big Bubba smoked tri-tip steak. The *Inyo Register* says **Bishop Burger Barn** (2675 W. Line St, 760/920-6567, www.bishopburgerbarn.com, 10:30am-8pm Mon., Wed.-Fri., 10:30am-3pm Tues., 10am-9pm Sat.-Sun. winter, 10am-9pm daily summer, hours can vary by season, $5-10) serves the best burger in town. The price is tough to beat—you can get a patty here for less than $5. Make sure to try the mouthwatering local grass-fed beef burger—it's definitely worth every penny. The Burger Barn also serves breakfast burritos, coffee, smoothies, and ice cream.

Information and Services

The **Bishop Chamber of Commerce and Visitors Bureau** (690 N. Main St., Bishop, 888/395-3952, www.bishopvisitor.com, 10am-5pm Mon.-Fri., 10am-4pm Sat. winter, 10am-5pm Mon.-Fri., 10am-4pm Sat.-Sun. summer) offers friendly advice on lodgings, local attractions, and more.

Getting There

The nearest airport to Bishop is the **Mammoth Yosemite Airport** (MMH, 1200 Airport Rd., Mammoth Lakes, 760/934-3813, www.ci.mammoth-lakes.ca.us). Alaska Airlines serves this airport year-round, and United Express also offers flights from December 15-April.

Bishop is not located near a major city, so expect it to take a while to get here from almost anywhere else. Bishop is located at the junction of U.S. 395 and U.S. 6, west of Sequoia National Forest and east of the Inyo National Forest's Ancient Bristlecone Pine Forest. From the San Francisco Bay Area, in summer, cross through Yosemite on Highway 120 (Tioga Rd., closed in winter), or drive north and cross on Highway 108 via the Sonora Pass (closed in winter). Once you get to U.S. 395, follow it south to Bishop, about 64 miles from Tioga Pass or 107 miles from Sonora Pass. Plan on at least 6.5 hours to drive the 300-320 miles. Since both mountain passes are closed in winter (usually Nov.-May), the only way to get here during those months is to take I-80 to U.S. 50 all the way to Lake Tahoe, then cross over into Nevada on Highway 88/89, and connect with U.S. 395. From this point, the trip south to Bishop is 157 miles. Altogether, this winter route is about 370 miles and will take at least seven hours.

The route from Sacramento to Bishop is shorter than the winter route from San Francisco. Take U.S. 50 to Lake Tahoe, and turn onto Highway 88/89. Go south on U.S. 395 for the final 157 miles. The total trip is 285 miles and takes about 5.5 hours.

Sequoia and Kings Canyon

Sequoia and Kings Canyon National Parks offer some of the tallest and oldest trees on earth, numerous hiking trails, thriving wildlife, and far smaller crowds than their famous neighbor.

Among other wonders, these two parks showcase the largest tree in the world, the deepest canyon in the country, and the highest peak in the continental United States.The area actually encompasses two distinct parks, a forest, and a monument: Kings Canyon National Park to the north, Sequoia National Park to the south, Sequoia National Forest surrounding much of the parkland, and Giant Sequoia National Monument, a subset of the national forest to the south and west of the parks.

In Sequoia National Park, the trees are the main attraction. Groves of giant sequoias, including the largest known tree on earth—General Sherman—soar out of the fertile Sierra soil. These *Sequoiadendron giganteum* grow only in a narrow 60-mile band on the western slope of the Sierra Nevada range between roughly 3,000 and 9,000 feet elevation. The species is distinct from the magnificent coast redwoods (*Sequoia sempervirens*) that grow along the Pacific Coast. The giant sequoias are truly massive, from stalwart trunk to hefty branches to towering top.

Kings Canyon National Park is characterized by rough granite slabs and dramatic canyons—in fact, Kings Canyon is deeper than the Grand Canyon. In both parks, expect marble caverns, rushing rivers, and an astounding variety of ecosystems, from chaparral to alpine meadow.

Sequoia National Park was California's first national park, dating to 1890. The same year, the small General Grant National Park was born with the goal of preserving the giant sequoia known as the General Grant Tree. Kings Canyon National Park was established in 1940, encompassing a large tract of land north of Sequoia. At that point, the small General Grant Park, though separated from the main body of Kings Canyon by forestland, was absorbed into it. Today Sequoia and Kings Canyon are jointly administered by the National Park Service, and together they encompass more than 864,000 acres.

Previous: Kings Canyon; black bear in Sequoia National Park. **Above:** giant sequoias in Sequoia National Park.

Look for ★ to find recommended sights, activities, dining, and lodging.

Highlights

★ **General Grant Grove:** A paved walkway leads to the General Grant Tree, the world's second-largest tree and the country's only living war memorial. Other natural wonders include the Fallen Monarch, a tree you can walk through (page 522).

★ **General Sherman Tree:** The biggest tree on the face of the earth is here in Sequoia National Park (page 534).

★ **Giant Forest Museum:** It's great to wander outside and see all the big trees, but if you want to learn more about what you're seeing, this is the place to be (page 534).

★ **Crystal Cave:** Well-lit tunnels lead into the grand chambers of this cavern, filled with dramatic calcite formations and polished marble (page 535).

★ **Moro Rock:** An invigorating climb up the stairs to the top of Moro Rock leads to some of the best views in the park (page 535).

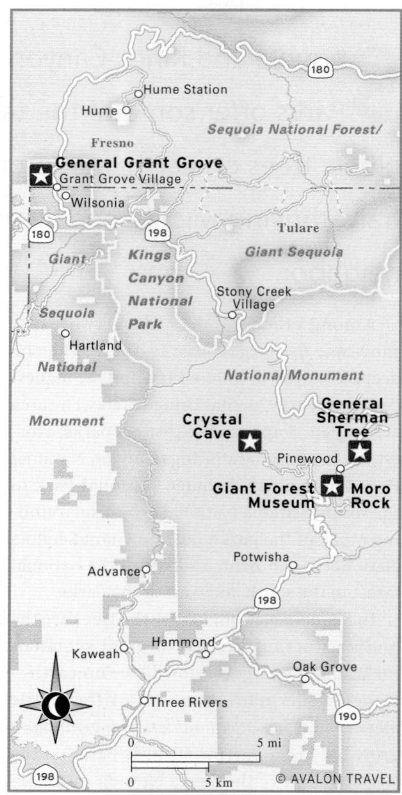

Sequoia and Kings Canyon

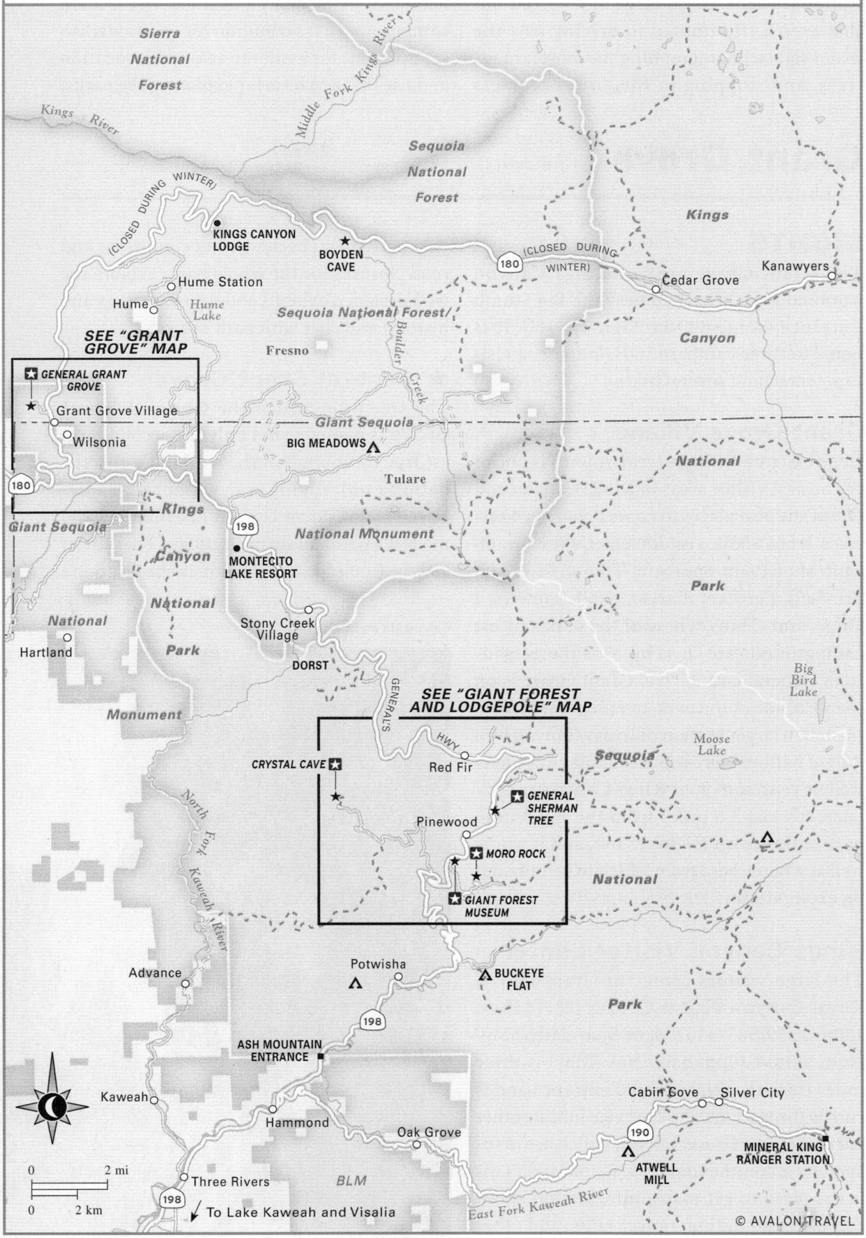

Sierra National Forest
Kings River
Middle Fork Kings River
Sequoia National Forest
(CLOSED DURING WINTER)
KINGS CANYON LODGE
BOYDEN CAVE
180 (CLOSED DURING WINTER)
Kings Canyon
Cedar Grove
Kanawyers
Hume Station
Hume
Hume Lake
Sequoia National Forest/
Boulder Creek
Fresno
SEE "GRANT GROVE" MAP
GENERAL GRANT GROVE
Grant Grove Village
Wilsonia
180
Giant Sequoia
BIG MEADOWS
Tulare
National Monument
National
Park
Kings Canyon National Park
Giant Sequoia National Monument
198
MONTECITO LAKE RESORT
Stony Creek Village
Hartland
DORST
GENERALS HWY
Big Bird Lake
SEE "GIANT FOREST AND LODGEPOLE" MAP
CRYSTAL CAVE
Red Fir
Moose Lake
Sequoia National Park
GENERAL SHERMAN TREE
Pinewood
MORO ROCK
GIANT FOREST MUSEUM
North Fork Kaweah River
Potwisha
BUCKEYE FLAT
Advance
198
ASH MOUNTAIN ENTRANCE
Kaweah
Hammond
Oak Grove
Cabin Cove
Silver City
190
ATWELL MILL
MINERAL KING RANGER STATION
0 2 mi
0 2 km
Three Rivers
BLM
198
To Lake Kaweah and Visalia
East Fork Kaweah River

PLANNING YOUR TIME

Together, Sequoia and Kings Canyon National Parks are so large and spread out that even a trip limited to driving past the major sights, photographing the most famous trees, and stopping in the visitors centers could easily occupy several days. To explore the parks in depth plan to stay 3-4 days and take some of the many long hikes. In the main campgrounds, it's common for vacationers to set up a tent for a one- to two-week vacation and use that as a base for exploring the parks.

Grant Grove

SIGHTS

The Grant Grove area of Kings Canyon National Park is located near the Big Stump Entrance, accessed via Highway 180. It is home to three campgrounds, lodging, a visitors center, and several hikes.

Grant Grove Village

Grant Grove Village (year-round) is one of the busiest visitor areas in Kings Canyon and one of the best places to come if you need services. It has a large visitors center, a restaurant, a gift shop (9am-6pm Sun.-Thurs., 9am-7pm Fri.-Sat.), a grocery market, public showers, a lodge, and cabins. Three of the park's nicest campgrounds are close by, as is the gargantuan General Grant Tree. Grant Grove is on the west side of the park area, separated from the much larger section of Kings Canyon by a gulf of national forest. Still, Grant Grove may well be central to your Kings Canyon experience. It's just 3.5 miles from the Big Stump park entrance on Highway 180, and it works well as a home base from which to venture out on explorations.

Kings Canyon Visitor Center

The large visitors center in Grant Grove, **Kings Canyon Visitor Center** (83918 Hwy. 180 E., 559/565-4307, 8am-5pm daily May-Nov., 9am-4:30pm daily Nov.-May) is three miles from the Highway 180 entrance and is run by the National Park Service (unlike other parts of Grant Grove Village, which are managed by a commercial concessionaire). This is the place to get maps, information about camping and hiking, ranger talks, and other park activities; check weather conditions and road closures for the whole park; explore the well-designed exhibits about park ecology and history; and chat with park rangers.

★ General Grant Grove

The tree after which the **General Grant Grove** is named is not only the second-largest tree by volume in the world, it's also the nation's only living war memorial, as declared by President Dwight Eisenhower, who made it a national shrine in 1956. (That's after Calvin Coolidge ennobled it as the "Nation's

General Grant Grove

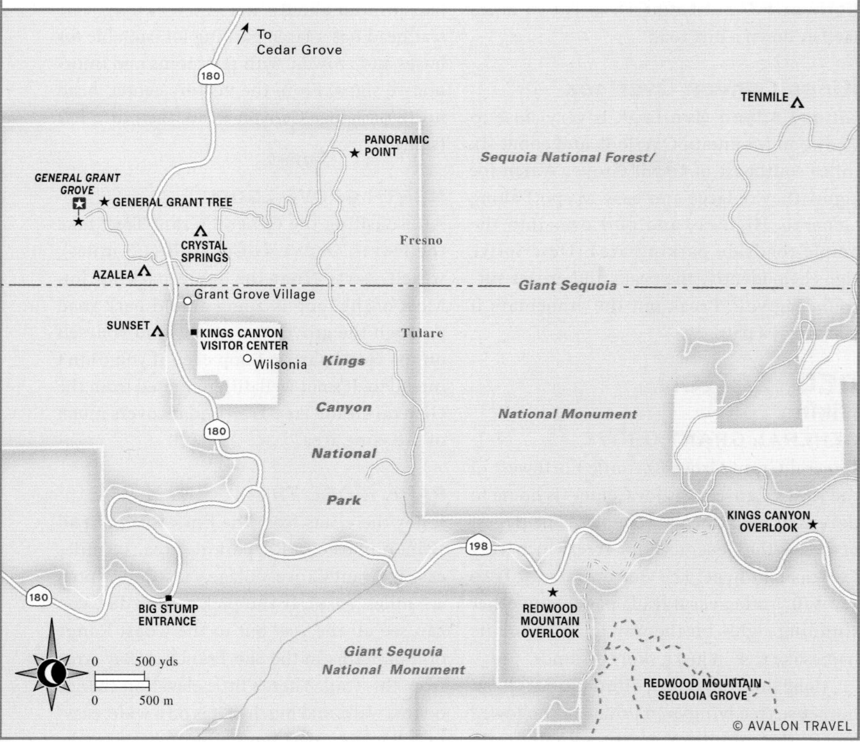

Christmas Tree" in 1926.) This 1,700-year-old tree is about 268 feet tall, with a diameter of 40 feet and a volume of 46,608 cubic feet. Of all the giant sequoias that have been discovered and studied, this is the widest. You'll still see some references to General Grant as the third-largest tree on earth, but its ranking improved in 2005, when the Washington tree lost some of its stature in a fire. Now Grant is second only to General Sherman, its compatriot at the other end of the Generals Highway. From the visitors center, head north on Kings Canyon Road then turn left (signed).

Panoramic Point

Panoramic Point is one of the best viewpoints in the parks. To get here, drive east through the Kings Canyon Visitor Center parking lot, turn left at the meadow, and then turn right onto the steep and winding road marked Panoramic Point. (This route is closed in winter and is not appropriate for trailers.) In 2.3 miles you'll reach the parking lot and the 0.25-mile walk to the ridge. From your perch at more than 7,500 feet you'll see Hume Lake, Kings Canyon, and mountains and trees galore. The **Park Ridge Trail** also starts here and leads to a fire lookout.

Redwood Mountain Overlook

From Grant Grove, travel south on Generals Highway for six miles and look for the signed **Redwood Mountain Overlook.** Pull over to look out over one of the world's largest groves of giant sequoias. It's fun to see them from above for once. The trailhead for the **Redwood Mountain Grove** is two miles farther down a dirt road.

Kings Canyon Overlook

Kings Canyon Overlook is very close to Redwood Mountain Overlook and about six miles southeast of Grant Grove. Watch for signs (they're large and easy to spot) along Generals Highway and pull over into the ample roadside parking area. Descriptive signs help identify the peaks and groves surrounding you. Break out the binoculars if you've got a pair.

RECREATION

Hiking

GENERAL GRANT GROVE

General Grant Grove (0.1 mile northwest of the Kings Canyon Visitor Center) is home to dozens of monumental sequoias. The largest of these is the General Grant Tree, which truly lives up to its hype. The **General Grant Tree Trail** (0.3 mile, easy) leads past many other stunning sights on the way to and from its namesake tree in just a short distance.

Along this trail is the **Fallen Monarch,** an immense tree lying on its side and hollowed out in the middle. You can actually walk lengthwise through the tree, and no matter how tall you are it's unlikely you'll have to duck. If ever you wanted to feel like a Keebler elf, this is your chance—it's amazing.

You'll also pass the **Gamlin Cabin,** built in 1872 and later used as the living quarters for the first ranger stationed here back when this was General Grant National Park. Farther along the trail lies **Centennial Stump,** so large that whole Sunday school classes have been held on top of it.

The General Grant Tree Trail is a paved, short, and easy walk and is accessible for wheelchairs. It's not always easy to follow, though, since a few turns, side trails, and distractions can pull you off the main thoroughfare if you're not careful. Trail guides ($1.50) are available at the trailhead and can help keep you on track as well as give you more background about what you're seeing. The trailhead has a large parking lot, suitable for buses and crowds, with restrooms and informative signs. From the visitors center, head north on Kings Canyon Road, then turn left (signed).

NORTH GROVE LOOP

After visiting the General Grant Tree, take the **North Grove Loop Trail** (1.5 miles), which starts from the same parking lot. Most of the loop is along an old park road through the grove. You might find yourself on the North Grove Loop even if you didn't intend to. It's not well differentiated from the General Grant Tree Trail and it covers much of the same area.

PARK RIDGE TRAIL

Enjoy the vistas from the **Park Ridge Trail** (Panoramic Point Rd. parking area, 2.5 miles east of Grant Grove Village, closed in winter, 4.7 miles, easy). If you pick a clear day, you can see all the way out to the Coast Range of mountains in the San Francisco Bay Area from this trail. There's little elevation change on this walk, and much of it is on a wide, easy-to-follow fire road, but the altitude can make it a little challenging. To reach the trailhead, drive east through the Kings Canyon Visitor Center parking lot; turn left at the meadow and then turn right onto the steep and winding road marked Panoramic Point.

SEQUOIA LAKE OVERLOOK-DEAD GIANT LOOP

For a different view on the life and death of the giant sequoias and human intervention in this area, hike the **Sequoia Lake Overlook-Dead Giant Loop** (lower end of General Grant Tree parking area, 2.2 miles, easy). This trail takes you to the Dead Giant, a first-growth giant sequoia that was mostly likely killed by loggers who tried and failed to cut it for lumber. The trail continues to an overlook of Sequoia Lake, actually an old mill pond from the logging days.

SUNSET TRAIL

For a longer, more demanding day hike, check out the **Sunset Trail** (across the street from Kings Canyon Visitor Center, 6 miles, strenuous). From the visitors center, cross Kings Canyon Road entering the Sunset Campground (the trail leaves the campground at site 118) After 1.25 miles, follow the South Boundary Trail for 0.25 mile to Voila Falls. Then, on the Sunset Trail, hike downhill to Ella Falls. Altogether, you'll climb about 1,400 vertical feet round-trip through magnificent mixed forests. To return to the trailhead, either return the way you came or follow the fire road north to the General Grant Tree trailhead.

BIG STUMP TRAIL

Immediately outside the Big Stump Entrance (three miles south of Grant Grove Village), take the **Big Stump Trail** (2 miles round-trip) through a grove that was heavily logged in the late 19th century, but is now reclaiming its true nature as a sequoia grove. One of the sights along here is the Mark Twain stump, the remains of a 26-foot-wide tree that was cut in 1891.

REDWOOD MOUNTAIN SEQUOIA GROVE

Redwood Canyon is home to the largest grove of giant sequoias in the world. The 16 miles of trails within the canyon make it a good place to wander around and see the trees up close. At the trailhead, turn left to begin the **Hart Tree and Fallen Goliath Loop.** This easy 6.5-mile trek leads across Redwood Creek and past the former logging site of Barton's Post Camp. About halfway around the loop, you'll come to a short spur trail that takes you to the Hart Tree, the largest in the grove and the 25th largest known in the world. Fallen Goliath, a little farther along, is another impressive site, even lying down.

To get here, take Generals Highway seven miles south of Grant Grove Village. When you see the sign for Redwood Canyon, turn right onto the dirt road and travel another two miles along Quail Flat. At the end of this road, you'll find ample room for parking, since this area is rarely crowded.

BUENA VISTA PEAK

Buena Vista Peak is an ideal spot for gazing out at the Western Divide, Mineral King, and Farewell Gap and pondering the regrowth of a sequoia forest after a fire. (This area had a prescribed burn in 2004.) The hike to reach the peak is a fairly easy two miles. Park at the Buena Vista trailhead, which is near the Kings Canyon Overlook, three miles north of Montecito Sequoia Lodge on Generals Highway and six miles south of Grant Grove.

BIG BALDY TRAIL

The **Big Baldy Trail** (4 miles, easy-moderate) is a popular out-and-back hike with only 600 feet of elevation gain. It's one of the most rewarding hikes in the park, considering the relatively small effort you have to expend for the major views. From the granite summit of Big Baldy, you'll be able to see far into Redwood Canyon. The trailhead and parking area are along the Generals Highway, eight miles south of Grant Grove.

Horseback Riding

If you love horses, the place to go is **Grant Grove Stables** (Hwy. 180, 0.25 mile north of Grant Grove Village, summer 559/335-9292, winter 559/799-7247, www.nps.gov/seki, early June-Sept., $40 per hour). Expert equestrians lead one- to two-hour trail rides to the General Grant Tree or deep into the sequoia forests. If you're up for a multiday trip, ask about the affiliated pack station in Cedar Grove.

ACCOMMODATIONS

Although reservations at Grant Grove lodgings are not as competitive as those in

Yosemite, the popular rooms fill up 4-6 months in advance. This includes the camp cabins (which are economical) and the bath cabins (which are warm, private, and very nice). Tent cabins and the John Muir Lodge usually need to be reserved about three months in advance. Only the bath cabins are open during winter.

Grant Grove Cabins

The **Grant Grove Cabins** (877/436-9615 or 866/807-3598, www.visitsequoia.com) offer an array of lodging styles at a variety of prices. Many of these cabins have been around awhile—some since the early days of what was then the General Grant National Park. The economy option is the **tent cabins** (17 cabins, May-Sept., $62), which are short on amenities, with no electricity or heat and with shared central baths. They have a great location, however, right in Grant Grove Village, with easy access to the Grant Grove Restaurant and all the other services and attractions in the neighborhood, making these a fine option for travelers on a budget.

The so-called **camp cabins** (May-Nov., $89-103) are at the low end of the fully enclosed cabins. They have solid walls, unlike the tent cabins, plus electricity, a propane heater, and daily maid service, but they do not have private baths. Each camp cabin comes with 2-3 double beds. **Rustic cabins** (May-Nov., $99) also come with at least two double beds and are a step up from camp cabins—they have carpets and insulation, which makes them considerably warmer during the chilly seasons. The **bath cabins** (8 duplex cabins, 1 single, year-round, $129-140) have all of the amenities of the other cabins, plus private baths with a tub and shower.

John Muir Lodge

The attractive, simple, and sturdy **John Muir Lodge** (Grant Grove Village, 866/565-6343, www.jmlodge.com, 36 rooms, year-round, summer $201-211, winter as low as $101) is both a comfortable motel and a classic woodsy lodge. Big timber poles combine form and function in the large common room, which has a fireplace, wireless Internet access, tables, sofas, and board games. Rooms are simply decorated in an alpine theme, with comfortable beds, private baths, and good views out into the forest. Soda machines, free ice, and clean baths are available inside the building, making this a comfortable place to hang out. You don't have to be a guest of the lodge to enjoy it; campers in the area are welcome to use the Internet access or relax by the fire. Since you're up at the edge of Grant Grove Village, you'll find plenty of nearby food and services, including the Grant Grove Restaurant, a market, gift shop, and the Kings Canyon Visitor Center. The lodge is convenient to hiking and to Generals Highway. John Muir Lodge is two stories with no elevator. If anyone in your party has a problem with stairs, be sure to mention that when you book.

The check-in desk at John Muir Lodge (24 hours daily) is located inside the building that houses the gift shop and restaurant, near the entrance to Grant Grove Village. John Muir Lodge and cabins are managed by a park concessionaire, Delaware North Companies, and it's their helpful staff who run the check-in desk. They know a lot about the parks, but they're not the source for camping information; contact the park-run visitors center across the way.

CAMPING

The **Sunset** (159 sites, summer only, $18-40) and ★ **Azalea** (110 sites, year-round, summer $18) campgrounds are both located 3.5 miles from the Kings Canyon park entrance and are close to the visitors center and Grant Grove Village. Only slightly farther, on the east side of Highway 180, is **Crystal Springs** (49 sites, summer only, $18-35). All campgrounds are supplied with picnic tables, fire

campfire in Azalea campground

rings, bear lockers, drinking water, and restrooms with flush toilets; they are all beautifully decorated in top-of-the-line national park scenery, with towering trees, artistically jumbled boulders, and winding paths. There are no showers in the campgrounds, but showers are available at Grant Grove Village nearby.

Campgrounds are first-come, first-served and fill up on weekends in July-August. To confirm campground opening and closing dates, call 559/565-3341 prior to your visit.

FOOD

Grant Grove Restaurant (Hwy. 180 at Generals Hwy., 559/335-5500, 7am-10am, 11:30am-4pm, 5pm-9pm daily summer, 7:30am-10:30am, 11:30am-3pm, 5pm-8pm daily winter, $13-25) serves three meals each day. The basic dining room offers standard American fare (hamburgers, pasta, steak) with prime rib on Friday and Saturday at pretty high resort prices. The food is nothing special, but it's a good place for a decent meal and a glass of wine or beer.

You'll find a minimart at **Grant Grove Village** (86728 Hwy. 180, 8am-8pm Sun.-Thurs., 8am-9pm Fri.-Sat. summer, 9am-6pm Sun.-Thurs., 9am-7pm Fri.-Sat. fall and spring, 9am-5:30pm Fri.-Sun. winter) selling a few staples, soda, beer, s'mores fixings, and some packaged food suitable for reheating over a campfire. You can also get some non-food supplies like batteries, flashlights, and moleskin.

GETTING THERE

Grant Grove is located in Kings Canyon National Park, four miles east of the Big Stump Entrance on Highway 180.

Cedar Grove

Cedar Grove Village (May-Oct., weather permitting) is located within Kings Canyon National Park, 30 miles northeast of Grant Grove on Highway 180. In mid- to late October, the eastern part of Highway 180 closes past the junction of Highway 180 with Generals Highway, near the Princess Campground in Sequoia National Forest. If you visit when the road is open, the drive out to Cedar Grove is a treat in itself. This section of Highway 180 is known as the **Kings Canyon Scenic Byway,** and it offers tremendous views of the vast canyons that give the park its name. The drive starts at 6,600 feet at Grant Grove, weaving down as far as 3,000 feet around Convict Flat before climbing back up to 5,000 feet before its terminus at Road's End. Though curvy, the road is not treacherous; it is wide with shoulders most of the way, and most vehicles maintain a reasonable-to-slow speed. Ample roadside pullouts are available on both sides of the highway, so you'll find it easy to stop for photos along the way.

SIGHTS

Cedar Grove Visitor Center

Located next to the Sentinel Campground near Cedar Grove Village, the **Cedar Grove Visitor Center** (559/565-3793, 9am-5pm daily mid-May-late Sept.) has books, maps, first aid, and park rangers.

Cedar Grove Village

The centerpiece of **Cedar Grove Village** (8am-9pm daily summer, 8am-8pm daily spring and fall) is the **Cedar Grove Lodge** (559/565-0100, May-Oct.). Other services in the village include a snack bar (7:30am-10:30am, 11:30am-2:30pm, 5pm-8pm daily), gift shop, small grocery market, laundry, showers, and an ATM.

Canyon View

On Kings Canyon Road, approximately one mile east of Cedar Grove Village, pull off the road and really take in the shape of this stunning canyon at **Canyon View.** The U-shaped canyon was carved through these soaring peaks by glaciers; the Kings River now flows through its dramatic descent.

Knapp's Cabin

Small but picturesque **Knapp's Cabin** was built in the 1920s by George Knapp, a Santa Barbara businessman who stored the extensive gear he used on fishing expeditions here. To get there, take the Kings Canyon Scenic Byway and pull over two miles east of the Cedar Grove Village turnoff. The cabin is just a short walk from the road.

Zumwalt Meadow

The largest in Kings Canyon, **Zumwalt Meadow** is one of the most beautiful areas to view native grasses, colorful wildflowers, and the birds and animals that live here. Zumwalt Meadow is also the best vantage point for Grand Sentinel and North Dome, two of the canyon's most impressive granite formations.

Roads End

Roads End is really is the end of Highway 180 (E. Kings Canyon Rd.). Roads End is located deep in the middle of Kings Canyon, a few miles past Cedar Grove Village and about 35 miles from Grant Grove. Beyond Roads End, the park is trails, canyons, forests, and lakes.

What you will find at the end of the road is the **Roads End Permit Station** (7am-3:45pm daily late May-late Sept.). This small wooden building is the place to get your permit and to talk to the rangers about trail conditions, recommended routes, and food storage and bear management regulations before you begin your backcountry adventure. A wilderness permit ($15) is required for any overnight camping outside of the official campgrounds. During high season (May-Sept.), there's a quota for permits, and you must obtain your permit at the station nearest to the trailhead you plan to use. You can reserve a permit up to two weeks in advance by downloading the application form online (www.nps.gov/seki) and sending it in with payment, or you can stand in line at 1pm the day before your hike for a first-come, first-served permit. When the quota season ends in late September, permits are free and you can self-register at the permit station.

There is no way to cross the Sierra through Kings Canyon by car. To reach points east of the park, you need to take the long way around or hike.

RECREATION

Cedar Grove Pack Station

Cedar Grove Pack Station (1 mile east of Cedar Grove Village, summer 559/565-3464, www.nps.gov/seki, May-Oct., weather permitting) offers customized backcountry horseback riding trips for up to two weeks. They will provide the food and do the cooking, bring all the gear (except your sleeping bag), and will take care of the horses along the way. Backcountry pack trips are $250 per day for each person, and the minimum trip is three days for four people. Short trips in the Cedar Grove area are also possible, provided horses are still available after the pack trips have left. Day trips include one-hour ($40) and two-hour ($70) excursions along the Kings River, a half-day ride to Mist Falls or the Kings Canyon Overlook ($100), and an all-day trip ($150).

Day trips are first-come, first-served. You can show up at the stable or call one day in advance. Reservations are required for multi-day trips, which can go anywhere in the High Sierra, and you can help design the itinerary. For information in the off-season, contact Tim and Maggie Loverin (559/337-2413).

Hiking

SHEEP CREEK CASCADE

Moderate hikes abound in this area. A good place to bring a picnic is Sheep Creek Cascade. The hike to **Sheep Creek** (2 miles, 1.5 hours) ascends 600 vertical feet to a picturesque shaded glen that's perfect for taking a load off your feet and enjoying the serene surroundings.

DON CECIL-LOOKOUT PEAK

One of the more challenging day hikes in the Cedar Grove area is **Don Cecil Trail to Lookout Peak** (13 miles round-trip, strenuous). As you climb 4,000 feet to the top, you'll see long distances into the wild parts of Sequoia. The Don Cecil trailhead is well marked with a large sign along Highway 180 near Sheep Creek, 0.2 mile east of Cedar Grove Village.

HOTEL CREEK-LEWIS CREEK LOOP

The **Hotel Creek-Lewis Creek Loop** (8 miles, moderate) has only 1,200 feet of elevation gain and offers a variety of forest and mountain scenery in addition to two creeks. You'll still be able to discern effects of a major 1980 forest fire and the rejuvenated forest that's grown since. Expect to pop in and out of the woods along the way and be prepared for sun, as significant portions of the trail are exposed. Enjoy long views of the canyon, and look for Monarch Divide in the distance. The hike starts from the Lewis Creek Trailhead on the north side of Kings Canyon Scenic Byway, just before you get to Cedar Grove.

ROARING RIVER FALLS

Even if you're not really a hiker, you'll want to get out of the car and stroll the negligible distance (less than 0.25 mile) from the parking area three miles east of Cedar Grove Village to the **Roaring River Falls.** The whole tiny trail is under a canopy of trees, making it cool even in the hottest parts of summer, and just looking at the falls feels refreshing after driving the Generals Highway.

ZUMWALT MEADOW TRAIL

The **Zumwalt Meadow Trail** (1.5 miles, easy) leads through the meadow for optimal viewing and continues through a grove of heavenly smelling incense cedar and pine trees along the Kings River. The trailhead parking lot is one mile west of Roads End.

MIST FALLS

The **Mist Falls Trail** (park at the Roads End trailhead) is a popular jumping-off point for backpackers destined for the Kings Canyon backcountry. You can hike to Mist Falls (8 miles round-trip, moderate-strenuous) or keep going all the way to Paradise Valley (14 miles, strenuous). Plan for dust and heat on the first couple of miles of the trail, and then steep switchbacks that take you up 1,500 vertical feet to the falls. If you're passing through on your way to the John Muir Trail, keep going past the falls all the way to Paradise Valley and then on to the trail crossing at Upper Woods Creek.

Backpacking

Without a doubt, the most famous backpacking trip in this region is to Mount Whitney. Whitney's not for everyone, though. For more moderate backpackers, the premier trip in these parks is the **Rae Lakes Loop** in Kings Canyon. This is a 46-mile loop trail with more than 5,000 feet of elevation gain. How difficult it is depends largely on how quickly you try to complete it. Ten days or more is ideal. The trail is shady and beautiful, with terrain that varies from flat and pleasant to rolling to some mettle-testing rock-scrambling and stream-crossing. If you don't have the time or the stamina to do it all, don't think you can't still enjoy Rae Lakes. Hiking in for a day or two and turning around to return the same way makes for a very good short trip.

Backcountry permits ($15) are required and are available at the permit station at Roads End. There's a quota for permits during high season (May-Sept.). You can reserve a permit up to two weeks in advance by downloading the application form online (www.nps.gov/seki) and sending it in with payment, or you can stand in line at 1pm the day before your hike for a first-come, first-served permit. When the quota season ends in late September, permits are free and you can self-register at the permit station. Bear canisters are required, but you can rent one from the ranger station if you don't have your own.

ACCOMMODATIONS AND FOOD

Cedar Grove Lodge (559/565-0100, reservations 866/522-6966, May-Oct., $119-135) has 21 rooms in the main building, each with two

Mist Falls

Mount Whitney

One of the most famous climbing or backpacking trips in Northern California is Mount Whitney (www.nps.gov/seki). At 14,500 feet, Whitney is the highest peak in the continental United States, and this must-do trek draws intrepid hikers and climbers from around the world. Whitney also marks the southern end of the John Muir Trail and makes for a dramatic end or beginning for through-hikers doing the whole trail.

hiker on Mount Whitney

Mount Whitney is located at the far eastern edge of Sequoia National Park, just west of the town of Lone Pine. You can see the impressive peak from a few places in the backcountry of Sequoia and Kings Canyon, but you can't get there from within the parks. There is no road that crosses the parks all the way from west to east. If you're coming from the west, you have to circle around the parks and enter from the eastern side.

Although Mount Whitney is a very challenging climb, it need not be a technical one. You can climb all the way to the top of Mount Whitney and back in one day if you're in good shape and prepared properly for the journey. Very fit hikers can walk the trail to the top, even without ropes and carabiners. The climbs up the steep East Face of the mountain or up the Needles are not beginners' journeys, but the East Face isn't out of reach for intermediate climbers. Most of the East Face is rated a Class 3, with the toughest bits rated 5.4. It's important to plan ahead, start early, bring all the right safety gear, and prepare for extreme weather.

Permits are required for anyone entering the Mount Whitney Zone—even day hikers. May-October, there's a quota for hikers; those who want to hike must enter the February lottery in order to have a good chance of getting a permit for the following summer. For more information about the lottery, and to download an application, visit www.fs.fed.us/r5/inyo or call the wilderness permit information and reservation line for Inyo National Forest (760/873-2483, recreation.gov). November to April, hikers still need a permit, but there are no quotas in place. Pick up a permit in person at the **Mount Whitney Ranger Station** within the **Interagency Visitors Center** (U.S. 395 and Hwy. 136, 1 mile south of Lone Pine, 760/876-6200, www.fs.fed.us/r5/inyo, 8am-6pm daily Apr.-Oct., 8am-5pm daily Nov.-Apr.). During the off-season, you can self-register for a permit if the visitors center is closed.

Hikers should plan to stay nearby and get an early start in the morning—very early if you're planning to summit. The nearest campground is **Whitney Portal** (end of Whitney Portal Rd., 6 miles west of Lone Pine, 877/444-6777, www.recreation.gov, 47 sites, late April-late Oct., $21) in the Inyo National Forest; it's seven miles from the trailhead. If you're planning to climb the summit, you'll want to stay even closer to wake up in the wee hours and start your ascent. Twenty-five walk-in sites are located near the **Mount Whitney Trailhead** (first-come, first-served, one-night limit, $12).

queen beds, private baths, telephones, and air-conditioning. It also offers three patio rooms, each with one queen bed, a private bath, a phone, and a patio looking directly on the Kings River.

The snack bar at Cedar Grove (559/565-0100, 7:30am-10:30am, 11:30am-2:30pm, 5pm-8pm daily in season, $10-20) is a no-frills place. Diners walk up to a window to place their orders and then take their food on a tray out to a group table in the casual dining room, or out onto the porch. In addition to simple hamburgers and other items, they occasionally have fresh trout and other specials in season.

The lodge and snack bar at Cedar Grove are run by Delaware North Companies (866/807-3598 or 559/335-3096, www.visitsequoia.com), the same company that runs the facilities at Grant Grove.

CAMPING

Several attractive campgrounds are available within a short distance of Cedar Grove Village, making food, showers, and access to ranger programs a breeze. In order, the campgrounds are **Sheep Creek** (111 sites, May-Nov., $18), **Sentinel** (82 sites, Apr.-Sept., $18), **Canyon View** (12 group sites, no RVs or trailers, May-Sept., $35-40), and **Moraine** (120 sites, May-Sept., $18). Campgrounds are first-come, first-served and have drinking water, flush toilets, and food lockers. Most are open in summer only, as this section of the park is inaccessible once the snows come. To confirm seasonal opening and closing dates, call 559/565-3341 prior to visiting.

GETTING THERE

Cedar Grove is 30 miles northeast of Grant Grove on Highway 180, less than 35 miles from the Big Stump Entrance to Kings Canyon. Only the first six miles of the road are open in winter, so this section of the park is unreachable October-April. Exact opening and closing dates depend on snowfall, and chains can be required at any time. Call the park (559/565-3341) to confirm road conditions and seasonal status.

Giant Forest and Lodgepole

If you have limited time to spend in Sequoia, the first place to visit is the Lodgepole and Giant Forest area. Here you can see and learn about some of the most impressive living things on earth, all within a fairly small geographical area. The Giant Forest contains some of the best natural attractions, and the Lodgepole complex provides support services and human comforts to help you enjoy and appreciate it all.

The Giant Forest was named by the patron saint of California wilderness, John Muir. The childlike simplicity of his description reflects the way many people feel when they encounter this extraordinary grove of giant sequoias. The General Sherman Tree, believed to be the largest tree on earth, is the star here—but it is by no means the only impressive sight. The sheer abundance of awe-inspiring trees all in one place makes visiting an amazing experience. Many of the trees are named for people and even the groups of trees are personified—one grove is called "Congress" and another is "The Senate," as if they've gathered together for meetings. To understand more about the natural history of these trees, start your visit with a trip to the Giant Forest Museum. But whatever you do, make sure to save time for one of several short trails that make it easy to see an enormous amount in a short time.

SIGHTS

Wuksachi Village

Wuksachi Village (year-round, weather permitting) is located near Generals Highway, about two miles north of Lodgepole. Of all

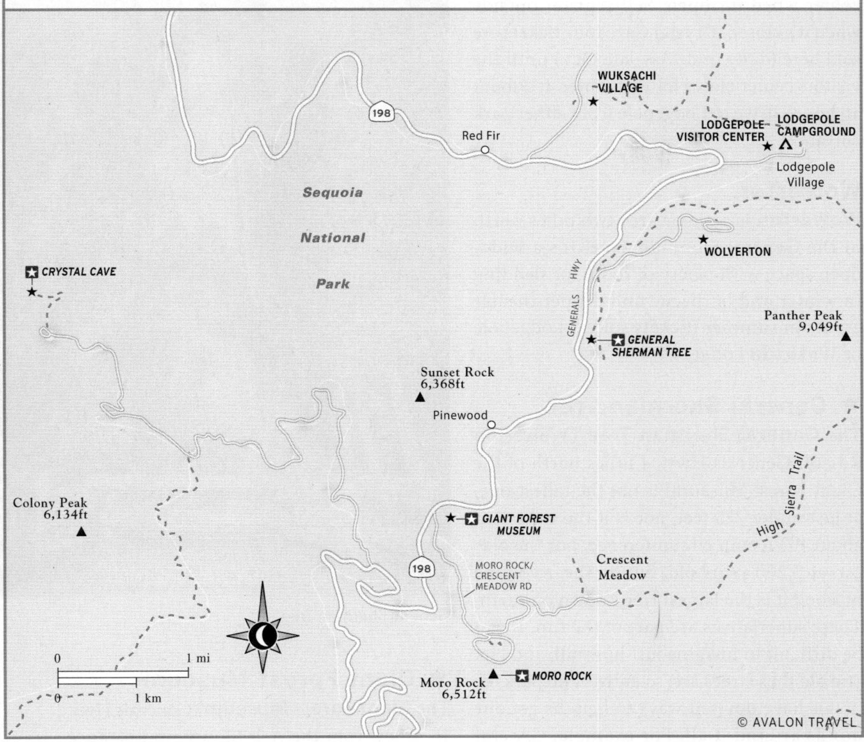

the accommodations and restaurants in the parks, those at Wuksachi Village are the most upscale and elegant, and the drive here (1 hour from Grant Grove) may well be worth it for at least one really nice meal. Other services at Wuksachi include a luxurious lodge, a gift shop (daily 8am-8pm), wireless Internet access, and an ATM.

Lodgepole Village

Lodgepole Village (559/565-3301) contains the major visitor services for Sequoia National Park, including a large visitors center, market, the Watchtower Deli (9am-6pm daily early Mar.-early May, 8am-8pm early May-late Oct.), gift shop, coin laundry, ATM, shuttle services, and a post office. The market, gift shop, and laundry stay open spring through fall (8am-9pm daily early May-late Oct., 9am-6pm daily late Mar.-early May). Showers are also available (9am-1pm, 3pm-5pm daily Apr.-May, 8am-1pm, 3pm-8pm daily early May-late Oct., $1 for 3 minutes).

Many of the facilities here are closed in winter, so check the website before you come.

Lodgepole Visitor Center

The **Lodgepole Visitor Center** (Lodgepole Rd., 559/565-4436, 7am-7pm daily May-Oct., hours vary in spring and fall) is one of the major information centers run by the National Park Service. Visitors can get books, maps, and souvenirs and join a ranger talk or walk. Wilderness permits (summer $15, off-season free) are available inside the visitors center when it's open. Self-register outside when it's closed. Crystal Cave tour tickets are sold here (daily mid-May-late Oct.) until the visitors center closes for the winter. It's about an hour's drive to Lodgepole from either park entrance.

Wolverton

Wolverton is a picnic area two miles north of the General Sherman Tree. It's a wide-open space with plenty of room for sledding in winter and barbecue and dinner theater events in summer (tickets sold at Lodgepole or Wuksachi Lodge).

★ General Sherman Tree

The **General Sherman Tree** (Wolverton Rd., off Generals Hwy., 4 miles north of the Giant Forest Museum) is not the tallest tree, at just under 275 feet, nor is it the widest, at about 103 feet in circumference, nor the oldest, at 2,200 years old, but by sheer volume of wood it is the largest tree known on earth. These superlatives are part of the fun. It can be difficult to imagine just how tall, and big, and old these trees are; scientists and park officials have devised ways to help us get our minds around it all. For example, General Sherman is about the same height as the Statue of Liberty.

Pick up some of the literature available at the visitors centers and discover the locations of the world's 30 largest giant sequoias, among other fun facts. There are some things that facts and figures cannot communicate—such as being in the presence of the General Sherman Tree. It's an easy 0.5-mile walk down from the parking lot or from the shuttle stop at Wolverton Road. When you get to the viewing area, you'll find masses of people paying their respects. This enormous attraction can get crowded on summer weekends, so if you're able to visit on a weekday, or early in the morning, you may enjoy the experience even more.

General Sherman Tree

★ Giant Forest Museum

The **Giant Forest Museum** (Generals Hwy., 16 miles from the Ash Mountain Entrance, 559/565-4480, 9am-4:30pm daily) is a lively place full of giant sequoias that grow only here in the Sierra Nevada range. Children and adults alike love the touchable exhibits that provide context to all the facts and figures about the trees. This museum goes into great detail about the importance of fire in the life of a giant sequoia (and other plants and trees that grow in the same areas). You'll also learn how the park used to look, and why many of the buildings have been removed to make way for more trees. This is a great stop for families, especially if the kids need a rest from hiking or from long intervals in the car. Numerous hikes branch out into the Giant Forest Sequoia Grove. Crystal Cave tour tickets are sold here (daily 9am-90 minutes before day's last tour) in November after the Lodgepole Visitors Center closes for the winter.

★ Crystal Cave

Magical **Crystal Cave** (Generals Hwy., 3 miles south of the General Sherman Tree) is one of the most beautiful of the 200 or so caves that occur naturally in the park. Its immense underground rooms are filled with sparkling stalagmites and stalactites made of limestone that has metamorphosed into marble over time. The Sequoia Natural History Association (559/565-3759, www.sequoiahistory.org) offers 45-minute guided tours of the cave (daily mid-May-late Oct., adults $16, ages 5-12 $8). A more challenging two-hour tour takes you deeper into the caverns and gives you a much more detailed lesson on the cave's history and geology. Best of all, serious spelunkers can sign up for the Adventure Tour (559/565-4222, $135), a four- to six-hour crawl off the well-lit trails and into the depths of Crystal Cave. You must be at least 16 years old and in good physical condition to join this expedition. Caving gear is provided.

You can't buy a ticket for a tour at the entrance to Crystal Cave. Stop at either the Foothills Visitor Center (one mile north of the Ash Mountain Entrance, 559/565-4212, ticket sales 8am daily May-Nov.), the Lodgepole Visitor Center (Lodgepole Rd., 559/565-4436, Lodgepole Rd., 559/565-4436, ticket sales 8am daily May-late Oct.), or the Giant Forest Museum (ticket sales 9am daily Nov.) in advance to purchase tickets. Then drive the long, winding, dirt road to the cave parking lot; the trip can take more than an hour from either visitors center. No trailers or RVs over 22 feet are allowed on the road to Crystal Cave. Be aware that even in the fall, tours fill up quickly, so if possible get your tickets early in the morning or even a day in advance. Ticket sales close daily at the visitors centers about 90 minutes before each day's final tour.

★ Moro Rock

Moro Rock stands starkly alone in the middle of the landscape, providing an amazing vantage point for much of the park. This granite dome was formed by exfoliation, a repetitive process in which outer layers drop off, the remaining rock is no longer as compressed, so it expands farther, and further peeling occurs. The end result is the rock's smooth, rounded dome. If you can, try to be here for one of the ranger talks that occasionally happen on top, or visit at sunset to see it in full color.

For maximum impact, park in the lot at the

Crystal Cave

Moro Rock

base of the rock and climb the 400 steps to the top, a distance of about 0.25 mile. (The climb to Moro Rock is not for those with an extreme fear of heights, but most people should be able to manage it.) The stairs are solid, and there are handrails all along the way. You'll want to take it slow, in any case; the entire route is filled with photo ops as you look down on the canyons of the Great Western Divide and across the canyons to some of the most beautiful peaks of the Sierra Nevada—Triple Divide Peak, Mount Silliman, Alta Peak, and Castle Rocks.

To reach the parking area from Generals Highway, take Moro Rock/Crescent Meadow Road south. There are restrooms and interpretive signage in the large parking lot. A free shuttle is available in summer (9am-6pm). The road is closed to vehicles weekends and holidays.

Crescent Meadow

A sort of oasis beside the Giant Forest, **Crescent Meadow** is a bright green and yellow plain, thick with grasses and teeming with wildlife. You can walk around the whole meadow in about an hour, watching for all manner of birds, squirrels, chipmunks, marmots, and even black bears. To reach the parking area from Generals Highway, take Moro Rock/Crescent Meadow Road south, past Moro Rock to the road's terminus. A free shuttle is available in summer (9am-6pm). The road is closed to vehicles weekends and holidays.

RECREATION

Hiking

Numerous trails characterize this region, offering options for hikers of all levels and abilities. Hard-core hikers willing to brave steep climbs at high altitudes can either take day hikes or obtain overnight backcountry passes for the region's major trails. The following are just a sample; pick up trail maps ($1.50-3.50) at the visitors centers for even more hikes.

LITTLE BALDY

How can you resist a hike to a granite formation called **Little Baldy** (nine miles north of the General Sherman Tree, 3.4 miles round-trip)? This moderate climb takes you up about 700 feet to the top of the granite dome. Look down from the peak, which tops out at over 8,000 feet, into the Giant Forest and snap a few photos.

TOKOPAH FALLS

To cool off, head for **Tokopah Falls** (trailhead near Marble Fork Bridge in Lodgepole Campground, 3.4 miles round-trip, easy). Early summer, when the flow is at its peak, is the best time to trek out the almost two miles along the Marble Fork of the Kaweah River to this fantastic 1,200-foot waterfall.

LAKES TRAILS

The **Lakes Trails** (trailhead at Wolverton Picnic Area, 8-12.5 miles, strenuous) vary in length, but you're definitely going to have to climb a ways up to the glacial lakes. From the trail, you can visit Heather Lake, Emerald Lake, and Pear Lake. The minimum distance round-trip for a day hike to **Heather Lake** is eight miles. To go all the way to **Pear Lake** and back is at least 12.5 miles. The daily quota is 25 people. Request a first-come, first-served wilderness permit from Lodgepole Visitor Center before beginning this hike.

ALTA TRAIL

Peak-baggers choose the **Alta Trail** (trailhead at Wolverton Picnic Area, 14-15 miles, very strenuous), which ascends all the way up to the 11,204-foot summit of Alta Peak. Pick a clear day for this challenging hike and you'll get a view of Mount Whitney across the Great Western Divide. As you climb, you'll also see Pear Lake, Moose Lake, and the granite Tablelands below. If you make it all the way, you'll gain more than 4,300 feet in altitude—but turn around if conditions feel treacherous. (Some rock-scrambling near the top is not for the faint of heart, and at this altitude it is likely you'll run into snow and ice year-round.) Exercise caution, especially if you encounter large ice fields; they can be slippery and dangerous to traverse. Tharp's Rock, at 10,400 feet, is an impressive destination in itself, and a good place to stop and turn around if you've had enough.

CONGRESS TRAIL

One of the best short trails in the whole area is the **Congress Trail** (trailhead at General Sherman Tree, 2 miles, easy), which begins from the parking lot for the General Sherman Tree off Wolverton Road. Pick up a pamphlet and map to get the best experience on this

Crescent Meadow

trail, which includes many of the park's most famous giant sequoias—Chief Sequoyah, General Lee, and President McKinley—as well as the House and Senate Groups. This round-trip trail is paved, making it wheelchair accessible and an easy walk even for people who usually aren't big hikers.

BIG TREES TRAIL

A level loop hike, **Big Trees Trail** (trailhead at Giant Forest Museum, 1.2 miles, easy) travels around Round Meadow near the Giant Forest Museum. Interpretive panels make this a fun walk for kids, and the paved boardwalk is wheelchair accessible. Accessible parking is available at the Big Trees trailhead. Otherwise, park at the Giant Forest Museum and follow the hike from the Trail Center trailhead.

HAZELWOOD NATURE TRAIL

For a charming interpretive walk, head down the **Hazelwood Nature Trail** (trailhead at Giant Forest Museum, 1 mile, easy). Signs along this flat stroll detail the history of humans' relationship with the giant sequoia trees—both beneficial and destructive. This walk works well for families with children. From the Giant Forest Museum, take the Alta Trail to the Hazelwood Loop.

In the same vicinity, you can putter along the 0.25-mile **Trail for All People.** This interpretive nature walk is best in spring, when the wildflowers bloom.

MORO ROCK

If you do only one hike, it should be the 300-foot ascent to the summit of **Moro Rock** at 6,725 feet. From the parking lot off Morro Rock/Crescent Meadow Road, climb the 400 steps to the top (0.25 mile, moderate) where you'll be greeted by the canyons of the Great Western Divide and the Sierra Nevada peaks. To extend this hike another three miles, start instead from the Giant Forest Museum and hike the Moro Rock Trail 1.5 miles south along a mostly wooded trail to the base of Moro Rock, enjoying a couple of spectacular overlooks along the way.

You can also begin this hike at the General Sherman Tree for a 10-mile loop with Moro Rock in the middle. Begin by taking the Congress Trail past The Cloister; then follow the Alta Trail south past the Bedrock Mortars. At the second junction, follow the Soldiers Trail south, walking along Circle Meadow and continuing all the way to the base of Moro Rock. After your climb, follow the Moro Rock Trail to turn east onto Sugar Pine Trail. You'll walk alongside Crescent Meadow, Log Meadow, past Tharp's Log (the oldest pioneer cabin still in the park) and the Chimney Tree. At the junction of the Huckleberry Trail with the Crescent Meadow Loop, hike north to return to the Congress Trail and your starting point near the General Sherman Tree.

CRESCENT MEADOW-LOG MEADOW LOOP TRAIL

The **Crescent Meadow-Log Meadow Loop Trail** (1.6 miles, easy) starts at the Crescent Meadow parking lot and picnic area. This short loop lets you experience more wildflowers and forest. It also takes you past Tharp's Log, the park's oldest cabin. Start by following the High Sierra Trail a short distance to its intersection with the Crescent Meadow Loop (you'll see signs for Tharp's Log). Take the Tharp's Log Trail north to the namesake cabin along Log Meadow. Explore the "cabin," then turn west to visit the Chimney Tree at the northern edge of Crescent Meadow. Follow the Crescent Meadow Loop south to return to the parking area.

ACCOMMODATIONS

Built in 1999, the ★ **Wuksachi Lodge** (64740 Wuksachi Way, off Generals Hwy. west of Lodgepole, 866/807-3598, www.visitsequoia.com, $215-276) offers the most luxurious accommodations available inside the parks. With 102 rooms in various sizes, the Wuksachi Lodge offers ample luxury housing for tree-lovers who just can't give up their creature comforts. Rooms have a woodsy-motel decor, with colorful Native American print bedspreads and mission-style wooden furniture. Each room has a private bath, a TV, a phone, a coffeemaker, a fridge, ski racks, and daily maid service, and Internet access is available at no extra charge both in the rooms and in the common areas. The Wuksachi's superior rooms offer space and comfort, particularly for families who like digital entertainment on their vacations. An on-site restaurant (the best in the parks), a Native American-themed gift shop, and close access to the Lodgepole visitors complex round out the attractions of this popular lodge. Although it's a bit pricey in summer, the Wuksachi can be quite affordable in winter, with nonholiday rates as low as $109. Ask for the bed-and-breakfast special year-round, which adds an excellent buffet breakfast ($25-30) for two to your room rate.

CAMPING

Lodgepole Campground (214 sites, year-round, reservations summer only 877/444-6777, www.recreation.gov, May-Sept., $22) is located along the Kaweah River, 21 miles from the Ash Mountain park entrance. The campground has flush toilets, picnic tables, and bear-proof containers, and it's less than 0.25 mile from Lodgepole Village, where you'll find showers, laundry, and groceries. Off-season, only 16 first-come, first-served walk-in tent sites are available.

Dorst Creek Campground (222 sites, reservations 877/444-6777, www.recreation.gov, late June-Labor Day, $22-60) is located along Generals Highway, six miles north of Wuksachi Village. This is one of only two campgrounds (the other is Lodgepole) in the parks that accept reservations, and they are definitely recommended; Dorst fills up fast in summer. The campground has flush toilets, drinking water, picnic tables, fire rings, bear-proof containers, and a dump station.

Adventurous campers should check out the **Bearpaw High Sierra Camp** (888/252-5757, www.visitsequoia.com, June-mid-Sept., 2 people $350). This camp takes a leaf from Yosemite's book with its accommodations and amenities, featuring six tent cabins that sleep two people apiece with bedding, towels, and sleeping pads. (You can even fit a third person on the floor of your cabin.) A bathhouse offers flush toilets and hot showers, and each stay comes with a full dinner and breakfast, served family-style. You can even buy a box lunch to take with you on your next day's journey. To reach this backcountry camp from the Crescent Meadow parking area, hike the wide, well-marked High Sierra Trail for 11.5 miles to Bearpaw Meadow at 7,800 feet.

If you have overnight reservations at High Sierra Camp, you do not have to pay the $15 wilderness camping fee, but you do still need a wilderness permit from the Lodgepole Visitor Center.

FOOD

The closest thing to an upscale restaurant in Sequoia and Kings Canyon is the ★ **Peaks Restaurant** (64740 Wuksachi Way, off Generals Hwy., 2 miles north of Lodgepole, 559/565-4070 or 866/807-3598, www.visitsequoia.com, 7am-10am, 11:30am-3pm, 5pm-9:30pm daily summer, 7:30am-9:30am, 11:30am-2:30pm, 5pm-8:30pm daily winter, $13-34) in Wuksachi Lodge. The elegant dining room features white tablecloths and sweeping forest views outside the picture windows. The Wuksachi Restaurant offers three meals daily and nonguests are welcome. Dinner is especially good, with creative menus and fine California-style ingredients, and includes vegan options. Make a reservation if you plan to dine at the Wuksachi on a summer weekend.

You'll find basic groceries and other necessary camping supplies at the **Lodgepole Market** (Generals Hwy., Lodgepole, 559/565-3301, 8am-9pm daily early May-late Oct., 9am-6pm daily late Mar.-early May).

The **Watchtower Deli** (559/565-3301, 9am-6pm daily early Mar.-early May, 8am-8pm daily early May-late Oct.) at Lodgepole Village serves pizza, pre-made sandwiches, and other light snacks.

GETTING THERE

Lodgepole is located on Generals Highway 22 miles north of the Ash Mountain (south) Entrance and 27 miles south of the Big Stump (northwest) Entrance. It takes about an hour to drive to Lodgepole from either entrance. Wuksachi Village is just two miles northwest of Lodgepole, and the General Sherman Tree parking lot is 2.5 miles south of Lodgepole off Wolverton Road.

Foothills

The Foothills area of Sequoia National Park is in the southern part of the park, with lower elevations and drier snow-free weather. It is accessed from the Ash Mountain Entrance on Highway 123, east of Three Rivers.

SIGHTS

Foothills Visitor Center

The **Foothills Visitor Center** (559/565-4212, 8am-4:30pm daily) is one mile north of the Ash Mountain Entrance and also serves as the park headquarters. It includes a bookstore and exhibits about the nearby area, and ranger talks and walks begin here. You can also buy Crystal Cave tickets (ticket sales 8am daily May-late Oct.) or get a wilderness permit (late May-late Sept., $15 for up to 15 people). Check the office behind the visitors center in summer, or self-register for a permit outside the rest of the year for free.

Hospital Rock

Hospital Rock is the former home of the Western Mono people. Exhibits help identify the markings they left behind when they vacated the area in the 1870s. One of the major indicators of their way of life is the grinding holes on the rocks, where they ground flour out of acorns. The short **Hospital Rock River Trail** is nearby and there is a picnic area. Hospital Rock is on Generals Highway six miles northeast of the Foothills Visitor Center.

RECREATION

Hiking

MARBLE FORK TRAIL

For a vigorous adventure with a big payoff, take the **Marble Fork Trail** (upper end of Potwisha Campground, 7.4 miles, moderate-strenuous) to Marble Falls. This hike starts in the Potwisha Campground near site 14. (You aren't allowed to park in Potwisha unless you're camping here, but there's some room across the street for parking.) The trail is named after the Marble Fork of the Kaweah River, and you'll hear its pleasant sounds as you hike. Start out on a forest road, and you'll soon see a sign directing you to keep left; the way becomes more trail-like, winding upward through the woods. After 2.5 miles, you'll emerge from the trees for sweeping views of the canyons around you and the water below. In four miles or less you'll come to Marble Falls. The falls are beautiful, noisy, and dramatic, and you'll see why they got their name—the viewpoint actually looks like a very large slab of white marble. Sit and enjoy the falls for a while as you rest up from your climb, and then return the way you came.

PARADISE CREEK

A nice short nature walk in the Foothills area starts in Buckeye Flat Campground and leads alongside **Paradise Creek** (Buckeye Flat Campground, three miles, easy). Start by crossing the footbridge near campsite 28 and then bear right to follow the trail beside the creek. The Middle Fork of the Kaweah River heads off to the left. In about 1.5 miles the trail will start to peter out. At that point, turn around and return the same way. No day parking is allowed at Buckeye Flat; park at Hospital Rock Picnic Area and walk about a mile on a paved road to Buckeye Flat.

CAMPING

Potwisha (42 sites, year-round, $22) is on the Kaweah River, about four miles north of the Ash Mountain Entrance. Amenities at this first-come, first-served campground include flush toilets, drinking water, a dump station, and bear-proof containers.

Just a few miles farther north along Generals Highway, and on a little spur to the east, you'll find **Buckeye Flat** (28 sites, May-Sept., $22) in a lovely spot along the Kaweah River. This tent-only campground is first-come, first-served and has flush toilets; it does not accommodate RVs or trailers.

The **South Fork** (10 sites, year-round, May-Oct., $12, Oct.-May. free) is a tent-only campground 13 miles off Highway 198 on South Fork Drive near Three Rivers. The campground is first-come, first-served with pit toilets and bear-proof containers, but no drinking water.

GETTING THERE

The Foothills area is easily accessed from the south via Highway 198; it's the first part of the park you encounter after the Ash Mountain Entrance.

Mineral King

All of the national park and national forest lands here have extensive unspoiled natural beauty and are remote from civilization, but the Mineral King section (Mineral King Rd., 25 miles east of Hwy. 198) of Sequoia National park is really out there. This glacial valley was annexed into the park in 1978 and is now its southernmost section. The region includes just a few examples of human intervention: the Mineral King Ranger Station, the Silver City Mountain Resort, a few private cabins, and two campgrounds (Atwell and Cold Springs). Otherwise, you're fully communing with nature, so plan accordingly. The nearest food and gas are in the town of Three Rivers, and the 22-mile road to get there is so rough that it takes at least 1.5 hours to drive—and that's in good weather. It's a one-lane road open to two-way traffic, so expect to pull over and wait now and then.

Interestingly, the once booming town of Mineral King never had a successful mining industry nearby. Silver was discovered here in the 19th century, and mining began in 1873, but not many minerals moved out of the mountain. Instead, the road built in 1879 attracted loggers and the hydroelectric industry, and the town managed to flourish for a while. Today visitors drive up the long winding road to enjoy the resurgence of nature at the expense of human construction. Mineral King Valley draws both geology and botany buffs with its glacier-carved array of rocks and minerals, some overgrown with a variety of native plants. The Atwell Mill that once cut first-growth sequoia timber has been reduced to a few relics—a steam engine, a wheel, miscellaneous junk—while all around, young giant sequoias reclaim their territory. High above the former town, Sawtooth Peak, at more than 12,000 feet, looms large and reminiscent of similar mountains in the Rockies. The peak is perfect for intrepid day hikers and backpackers.

Marmots frequent the Mineral King area, and these furry critters won't seem quite so cute after you discover they've chewed through your radiator hoses. Check with the ranger station about their current activity, and notify the rangers if your car has been disabled.

SIGHTS

Mineral King Ranger Station

The **Mineral King Ranger Station** (Mineral King Rd., 559/565-3768, 8am-4pm daily May-Sept.) is located near the end of Mineral King Road, beyond the Silver City Resort and close to Cold Springs Campground. You can get information and wilderness permits here, and there is a self-service wilderness permit box ($15 summer, free winter) on the porch so you can get a permit even when the ranger station is closed.

RECREATION

Hiking

Many hikes begin in Mineral King Valley, and you can visit a number of charming alpine lakes if you're up for a hike of 7-12 miles. However, at 7,500 feet elevation hikes in the Mineral King area are demanding and strenuous. Bring lots of water and honestly gauge the fitness level of yourself and others before hitting the trail.

COLD SPRINGS NATURE TRAIL

A good place to start walking in Mineral King is the **Cold Springs Nature Trail** (1 mile). This easy interpretive walk describes and displays the natural wonders and the formation of the valley.

TIMBER GAP

The **Timber Gap Trail** (4 miles round-trip) follows an old mining road through a forest of red fir trees. You'll enjoy pretty views out to Alta Peak and the Middle Fork of the Kaweah River. Remember that you're at over 7,500 feet elevation, so you may feel you're getting a workout even on this short hike.

MONARCH LAKES

Upper and Lower Monarch Lakes (8.5 miles round-trip) sit nestled beneath majestic Sawtooth Peak. The trek is mostly flat and easy walking through forest and meadows with views of the Great Divide. Bring a picnic to enjoy beside the lakes.

Those in great shape and looking for tremendous views can keep hiking 1.3 miles past the lakes to the top of **Sawtooth Peak** (11,700 feet). This trail isn't for the faint of breath or shaky of leg—it climbs 1,200 vertical feet in just over a mile of loose difficult ground. But once you're at the top, you'll get a fine chance to rest as you soak in the majestic peaks all around.

Another option is to explore the trail to **Crystal Lake** (roughly 10 miles round-trip) where it splits from the Monarch Lakes hike at Chihuahua Bowl. The trail passes the relics of an old mine before climbing steeply to end at the lake.

EAGLE AND MOSQUITO LAKES

Plan to spend all day on the hike out to **Eagle and Mosquito Lakes** (7 miles round-trip), which lies in the backcountry beyond the Mineral Creek Ranger Station. The Eagle and Mosquito Lakes Trailhead is at the end of Mineral King Road. From the trailhead, climb two miles up Mineral King Valley to Eagle Basin. Where the trail splits, head left to Eagle Lake (3.4 miles from trailhead) or right to Mosquito Lake (3.6 miles from trailhead).

WHITE CHIEF TRAIL

The **White Chief Trail** (5.8 miles round-trip) begins at the Eagle and Mosquito Lakes Trailhead at the end of Mineral King Road. The trail leads to the abandoned mine site at White Chief Bowl. It's a fairly steep climb at times, but the rewards include scenic views of the Mineral King Valley and a look at some remnants from the area's mining history, including the Crabtree Cabin, which dates to the 1870s.

ACCOMMODATIONS AND FOOD

Silver City Mountain Resort (559/561-3223, www.silvercityresort.com, May-mid-Oct.) is the sort of place that isn't supposed to exist: a privately owned resort on national park land. That's because it was already there when the Mineral King area was annexed to the southern part of Sequoia National Park in the 1970s, and so it was grandfathered in. The resort has 13 different cabins. The most economical are the three small "historical cabins" built in the 1930s ($100-150). A step up in comfort are the three "family cabins" that sleep up to five people ($195). Finally, five luxurious modern "chalets" ($250-395) are outfitted with decks, fireplaces, showers, phones, and outstanding mountain views. Wi-Fi is included in the rates, and it sometimes works outdoors near the cabins and chalets.

The **Silver City Resort Restaurant** (8am-8pm Thurs.-Mon., 9am-5pm Tues.-Wed., $10-17.50) is the only place to get food, so it's important to know that the only thing they serve on Tuesday and Wednesday is pie and beverages. The homemade pies are very good, but if you want a real meal, make sure you bring food of your own. No food is left on the premises by the time Tuesday rolls around, and the kitchen staff is off making the long drive into town to restock. The food is good while it lasts, though, and they serve beer and wine. The souvenir shop (8am-8pm Thurs.-Mon., 9am-5pm Tues.-Wed.) in the restaurant building usually only has energy bars and sodas.

CAMPING

There are two campgrounds in the Mineral King area: **Atwell Mill** (21 sites, May-Oct., $12) and **Cold Springs** (40 sites, May-Oct., $12). Both are first-come, first-served and have vault toilets. If you want showers or food, you can drive to Silver City, 0.5 mile east of Atwell Mill and 2.5 miles west of Cold Spring. Both campgrounds have drinking water available May through mid-October. The water is turned off the rest of the year. The Mineral King Ranger Station is located beside the Cold Spring campground.

GETTING THERE

To get to Mineral King, approach Sequoia National Park from the south on Highway 198, and instead of entering the park, make a right turn onto Mineral King Road, two miles before the Ash Mountain Entrance, and drive 25 miles east. It will take about 30 minutes to come to the end of this narrow winding road; trailers and RVs are not allowed. Along the way, you will enter the boundaries of Sequoia National Park through the small Lookout Point entrance (May-Oct., $20) and pay the entrance fee at a self-serve station. November-April, the gate is locked for the season.

Eagle and Mosquito Lakes

Sequoia National Forest

As you explore Kings Canyon and Sequoia National Parks, you'll find yourself crossing in and out of park boundaries almost without noticing. Signs announce the entrance of Sequoia National Forest, then a national park, and then back again. Both the national forest and the parks are full of scenery, hiking trails, and interesting things to do, but the rules in each are a little different.

Inside national park boundaries, you can camp only in designated campgrounds; in Sequoia National Forest, you can camp almost anywhere as long as you have a wilderness permit. Services also vary.

Companies doing business on national park land must either work for the National Park Service or be an official concessionaire hired by the National Park Service and subject to its restrictions. In Sequoia National Forest, the government can lease areas to private operators who are free to run their businesses their own way. The Hume Lake Christian Camp and the Kings Canyon Lodge are two such properties; they're located in the Sequoia National Forest, but they are privately owned and operated. In addition, Sequoia-Kings Canyon Park Services Company operates the Montecito Sequoia Lodge and Stony Creek Village in the Sequoia National Forest.

Free dispersed camping (camping outside developed campgrounds) is allowed throughout most of the Sequoia National Forest. The only areas where it is not allowed are the Hume Lake and Stony Creek recreation areas. Be careful to check where you're camping. Forest lands run seamlessly into the national parks here, and dispersed camping in Sequoia and Kings Canyon National Parks is not allowed unless you have a backcountry permit. You do not need a backcountry permit to camp in the national forest, but you do need a campfire permit if you want to have a fire or use a stove. You can pick one up at the **Kings Canyon Visitor Center** (Grant Grove, 83918 Hwy. 180 E., Miramonte, 559/565-4307, 9am-4:30pm daily) or the **Hume Lake Ranger District** (Hwy. 180, 19 miles west of the Big Stump Entrance, 559/338-2251, 8am-4:30pm Mon.-Fri.).

HUME LAKE

The **Hume Lake Ranger District office** (35860 E. Kings Canyon Rd., Dunlap, 559/338-2251, 8am-4:30pm Mon.-Fri.) for the Sequoia National Forest and Giant Sequoia National Monument is 19 miles west of Kings Canyon National Park on Highway 180. At the district office, you can get forest information and free campfire permits. You may want to stop by even if they're closed. Not only is there a self-serve station for permits, there are outdoor exhibits about the area and information about the 13 giant sequoia (*Sequoiadendron giganteum*) groves that lie within the Hume Lake Ranger District. The 1882 Dolbeer Donkey displayed outside dates from Hume Lake's past as a logging site. Plenty of literature is available outside to take with you as well.

Hume Lake Christian Camp

Hume Lake is a lovely 87-acre body of water located along the Generals Highway about eight miles northeast of Grant Grove Village. The lake itself is part of the national forest, and anyone may use it. Most of the facilities on the lake are owned and operated by the private **Hume Lake Christian Camp** (559/305-7770, www.humelake.org), which has been here since 1946. The Christian Camp is a lively bustling place with a lodge, a dining room, a conference center, four swimming pools, a snack shop, a general store, a small laundry, and fleets of bicycles, kayaks, and golf carts. Most of the facilities are primarily for the use of the organization and its constituents. However, when the camp isn't full, it becomes available to visitors.

The **Lodge at Hume Lake Christian**

Camp (800/965-4863, www.humelake.org, $140-160, including breakfast) rents rooms to the public whenever space is available beyond the needs of their own programs. Rooms are spacious and modern, with phones, ceiling fans, coffeemakers, and other niceties. They're tastefully decorated in woodsy style, so you won't feel you're in a generic motel. Guests at the lodge can use the camp's swimming pools at no extra charge. Rates can run as low as $105 during the off-season.

The **Pine Tree Dining Room** (6:30am-8:30am, 11:30am-1:30pm, 4:30pm-6:30pm daily summer, 6:45am-7:30am, 11:45am-12:30pm, 4:45pm-5:30pm daily fall-spring, $5.50-9.50) is open to the public when space is available. Meals are served buffet-style in a large modern building with wonderful views of the lake and forest from its picture windows. If you're staying in the Grant Grove area, this can be a nice alternative to the village offerings; in good weather the drive takes less than 30 minutes. A snack shop (11am-11pm daily summer, limited hours Sat.-Sun. fall-spring) on the premises serves ice cream, pizza, and a few other things at a walk-up counter.

Groceries and other basic supplies, as well as fishing licenses, are available at the **Hume Lake General Store** (559/305-7770, www.humelake.org, 8am-11pm Mon.-Thurs., 8am-9pm Fri., 7am-7pm Sat., 8am-10:30am, 12:30pm-11pm Sun. summer, 8am-5pm Sun.-Thurs., 8am-11pm Fri., 8am-5:30pm, 8:30pm-10pm Sat. winter; hours subject to change). A **post office** (64144 Hume Lake Rd., 559/336-2542, 8am-3pm Mon.-Fri.) is located in the middle of the Hume Lake development and is open to the public.

Camping

Campgrounds are managed by the Hume Lake Ranger District of the Sequoia National Forest/Giant Sequoia National Monument (559/338-2251, www.fs.fed.us/r5/sequoia). To check weather and to verify campground availability, call 559/565-3341. Campgrounds in the area include **Princess Campground** (Hwy. 180, 877/444-6777, www.recreation.gov, June-Sept., $18), six miles north of Grant Grove Village, with 88 sites and vault toilets; **Hume Lake** (Generals Hwy., 877/444-6777, www.recreation.gov, May-Sept., $20), 10

Hume Lake

miles northeast of Grant Grove, with 74 sites and flush toilets; **Tenmile** (Generals Hwy., May-Sept., $16), five miles northeast of Grant Grove, with 13 first-come, first-served sites. It allows RVs up to 22 feet long but has no drinking water and has vault toilets; **Landslide** (Generals Hwy., summer only, $16), 13 miles northeast of Grant Grove, with nine first-come, first-served sites and vault toilets; and **Convict Flat** (Hwy. 180, summer only, free) 19 miles northeast of Grant Grove, with five first-come, first-served sites.

KINGS CANYON LODGE

As you drive the scenic road from Grant Grove to Cedar Grove, you'll eventually come upon a large roadside sign that says "Caution Ice." It's not an unusual warning in these parts, but below, a sort of addendum to the sign continues: "Cream Ahead." Sure enough, you're just 0.25 mile from quirky **Kings Canyon Lodge** (67751 E. Kings Canyon Rd., 13 miles east of Grant Grove Village, 559/335-2405, www.kingscanyonlodge.com, Apr.-Nov., $109-199), which offers ice cream, beer, food, accommodations, and gas. If ever there was a mountain resort that time forgot, this is it. The main building is a ramshackle wooden cabin with a counter and about a dozen barstools inside. Upstairs are three rooms and two baths, and out on the grounds are seven cabins, each of which sleeps 2-8 people. The main attraction is a pair of antique gas pumps, which date to 1928 and claim to be the country's oldest double gravity pumps. (The owners are a little touchy about people stopping by just to take pictures with the gas pumps, so enjoy a look but be respectful.) This family-owned and oddly charming complex has no Wi-Fi, no cell service, no laundry, and no guaranteed hours of operation.

Kings Canyon Lodge Restaurant (67751 E. Kings Canyon Rd., 13 miles east of Grant Grove Village, 559/335-2405, hours vary, usually 8am-8pm daily summer, 9am-6pm spring and fall, $6-9) is the only place to buy food between Grant Grove and Cedar Grove. It's far from fancy, but if you've ever fantasized about dining in an Old West saloon, you'll enjoy the experience. The food is mostly sandwiches, burgers, milk shakes, and ice cream, but the cold beer and soda will be especially welcome to summer travelers taking a break.

BOYDEN CAVE

Tucked back in the wilds of the Sequoia National Forest, between Grant Grove and Cedar Grove, **Boyden Cave** (74101 E. Kings Canyon Rd., 888/965-8243, www.caverntours.com, tours 10am-5pm daily May-Sept., some tours offered in Oct., adults $14.50, under age 12 $8.75) gives visitors an up-close cave experience. Inside Boyden, "please try not to touch the formations" takes on a new meaning—you have to turn sideways to avoid the walls and duck to keep from hitting your head on stalactites that are many thousands of years old. The cavern network contains plenty of draperies, pancakes, stalactites, and other calcite structures; you can stare right at them, up into them, and in some cases walk all the way around them.

Boyden Cave is operated on national forest land by Boyden Cavern Adventures and Tours, a private company. Due to its location along Highway 180 (Kings Canyon Scenic Byway/E. Kings Canyon Rd.), visitors must first enter Kings Canyon National Park and pay the park entry fee ($20) before driving to the cavern. However, the cavern is not in the park or operated by the government, so you must also pay a fee for the tour.

BIG MEADOWS

In the Big Meadows area, you'll find one of those funky one-of-a-kind lodging options that the U.S. Forest Service sometimes surprises you with. The 900-square-foot **Big Meadows Guard Station** (35860 Kings Canyon Rd., Dunlap, 877/444-6777, www.recreation.gov, June-Oct., $125) was built by the Civilian Conservation Corps between 1933 and 1935 as a residence for firefighting personnel. The one-story cabin has a refrigerator, a stove, a hot-water heater, pots, pans, and dishes, a table and chairs, and beds for six people (one queen, two bunks, and a double-size fold-out sofa). Bring your own sleeping bags or blankets and all your own food. The station is located in one of the higher areas of the forest, at 7,600 feet elevation, so expect cool nights even in midsummer.

The U.S. Forest Service maintains the **Horse Camp** (Big Meadow Rd., June-Oct., first-come, first-served, free), 13 miles southeast of Grant Grove via Generals Highway, with five equestrian sites, no drinking water, and vault toilets; and the **Big Meadows Campground** (Big Meadow Rd., June-Oct., first-come, first-served, free), 13 miles southeast of Grant Grove via Generals Highway, with 45 sites, vault toilets, and no drinking water.

MONTECITO SEQUOIA LODGE

Montecito Sequoia Lodge (63410 Generals Hwy., 559/565-3388 or 800/227-9900, www.mslodge.com, year-round), also known as the Montecito Lake Resort, is a rustic full-service resort located on Generals Highway nine miles southeast of Grant Grove Village. The main lodge has 22 rooms, four smaller lodges that sleep up to five people each, and eight heated cabins that sleep up to eight people each. The cabins do not have private baths, but bathhouses with free showers are nearby. Four deluxe two-story cabins each accommodate up to five people; all four cabins have full baths.

In summer, Montecito operates primarily as a family camp (800/227-9900, Sun.-Fri. mid-June-mid-Aug., six-day minimum). The weekly rates range from $1,495 for one person to $5,995 for a family of 3-6 people in one of the better suites. Lodging, meals, and all sorts of activities are included, from guided hikes to canoeing on the lake to swimming in the large outdoor pool. Supervised activities for children ages 2-17 are also included. In summer, the lodge is available to noncampers ($100-400) on Saturday only.

Outside the summer season, Montecito Lake Resort is a regular resort with nightly accommodations (mid-Aug.-mid-June, $99-318, meals included). The pool is closed, but the outdoor hot tub is open and can be ideal after a day of cross-country skiing, backcountry snowboarding, tubing on Montecito's 40 miles of groomed trails, or ice-skating on Montecito Lake. The resort rent skis and snowshoes ($15-25 per day), and lessons are available ($15). The staff also offers group activities for children, such as snow sculpture and igloo-building.

Free wireless Internet access is available in the lodge, and a business center for guests has a hard-wired computer, printer, and satellite TV. A gift shop is located inside the main lodge (hours vary), but there are no groceries available. The nearest gas in summer is at Stony Creek, 3.5 miles south.

The restaurant at **Montecito Sequoia Lodge** (7:30am-9am, noon-1:30pm, 5:30pm-7pm daily mid-June-mid-Aug., 8am-9am, noon-1pm, 6pm-7pm daily mid-Aug.-mid-June, $9-30) is open to nonguests year-round. Buffet-style meals are served at massive wooden tables that seat 10 people each, which encourages mingling among the campers. For those who plan to spend the day hiking or skiing, the staff will prepare trail lunches ($9-10) on request. The **Pine Box Bar** (5:30pm-8:30pm daily and available by request) is in the back room of the main lodge.

Montecito Lake Resort is run by Asilomar Management Company (800/227-9900), which also operates the Stony Creek Village. If you're staying at the lodge in Stony Creek, you can receive a 25 percent discount on meals here.

STONY CREEK

Stony Creek Village (May-Sept. or Oct.) is located in the Sequoia National Forest on Generals Highway, just north of the boundary of Sequoia National Park. Facilities here are operated by the Sequoia-Kings Canyon Park Services Company (877/828-1440) and include a lodge, a restaurant, a market and gift shop (7am-8pm daily), a coin laundry (9am-6pm daily), showers (9am-6pm daily, $4), an

ATM, and a gas station (with credit card 24 hours daily).

The **Stony Creek Lodge** (559/565-3909, www.sequoia-kingscanyon.com, $159-179) has 12 rooms, each with either one queen bed and a patio or a combination of queen and twin beds. Rooms include satellite TV, phones, private baths, maid service, and continental breakfast. The on-site **restaurant** (11am-6pm daily, $10-25) specializes in pizza.

In addition, the U.S. Forest Service maintains two campgrounds near Stony Creek Village. **Stony Creek Campground** (Generals Hwy., 14 miles southeast of Grant Grove, 49 sites, 877/444-6777, www.recreation.gov, May-Oct., $20) has tent and RV sites with fire rings, flush toilets, water, and food storage. **Upper Stony Creek Campground** (Generals Hwy., 14 miles southeast of Grant Grove, 18 sites, first-come, first-served, $16) has fire rings, picnic tables, water, and pit toilets.

Practicalities

There are three entrances to Sequoia and Kings Canyon National Parks. The **entrance fee** is $20, good for up to seven days, and it is valid for both Sequoia and Kings Canyon National Parks. (No additional fees are necessary for access to Sequoia National Forest or Giant Sequoia National Monument.) Upon entering the park, you'll receive a glossy pamphlet with a basic map of the parks and an up-to-date park guide for Sequoia and Kings Canyon. These will provide you with all the in-park information you need to have a great time and keep up on any activities and events.

INFORMATION AND SERVICES

Banks and Post Offices

There are no banks inside the park, but you can find ATMs at the major visitors complexes at Grant Grove (inside the restaurant and in the grocery market), Lodgepole, Wuksachi, and Cedar Grove (summer only).

Although you can no longer mail a letter from the old log cabin post office, you can make use of the **Park Post Office at Lodgepole** (Lodgepole Visitor Center, 63228 Generals Hwy., 559/565-3678, 8am-1pm, 2pm-4pm Mon.-Fri.). Another post office is beside the market in **Grant Grove Village** (86724 Hwy. 180, 559/335-2499, 9am-4pm Mon.-Fri., lobby 24 hours daily), and one other is within the **Hume Lake Christian Camp** (64144 Hume Lake Rd., 559/336-2542, 8am-3pm Mon.-Fri.).

Fishing Licenses

Fishing is not a major sport in Kings Canyon and Sequoia, but the many lakes and streams in the park do allow fishing provided you have a valid California fishing license and follow state regulations. You can purchase tackle at the Lodgepole, Grant Grove, and Cedar Grove markets. Licenses are available at the Hume Lake General Store. Get up-to-date information on fishing regulations in the parks at the various visitors centers, and ask for recommendations about good spots to try. In most of the parks, trout season is late April to mid-November. Check online with the Department of Fish and Game (www.dfg.ca.gov) for information on seasons and rules.

Gas and Automotive Services

Technically, there is no gas available within Sequoia or Kings Canyon National Parks. However, there are several gas-station locations outside and very close to the park boundaries.

The **Kings Canyon Lodge Gas Station** (67751 E. Kings Canyon Rd., 13 miles east of Grant Grove Village, 559/335-2405, Apr.-Nov.) can be found on Kings Canyon Road between Grant Grove and Cedar Grove; however, it is in Sequoia National Forest rather than Kings

Canyon National Park. Many visitors are dubious when they see the genuine antique gas pumps sitting outside the funky old lodge. The pumps actually work, though they're not self-service, so ask the owners for assistance. There's also a gas station at **Stony Creek Village** (Generals Hwy., 559/565-3909, 24 hours daily with credit card, summer only), between Wuksachi and Grant Grove.

West of the Big Stump Entrance, gas is available at the **Valero Station** (Hwy. 180, Squaw Valley, 20 miles west of Grant Grove). The station also has a grocery store, **Clingan's** (559/338-2404, 7am-9pm Sun.-Thurs., 7am-10pm Fri.-Sat. summer, 7am-8pm Sun.-Thurs., 7am-9pm Fri.-Sat. winter), and it has free Wi-Fi access. A **Chevron Station** (41907 Sierra Dr., Three Rivers, 559/561-3835) is approximately six miles west of the Foothills Entrance off Highway 198.

Laundry and Showers

Laundry facilities are available at **Cedar Grove Village** (8am-9pm daily), **Stony Creek Resort** (9am-6pm daily summer), and **Lodgepole Village** (8am-7pm daily summer, shorter hours spring-fall). There's also a very small coin laundry at Hume Lake in the Christian Camp facilities. Nonguests are welcome to use it, but it's quite busy. At **Montecito Sequoia Lodge** (63410 Generals Hwy., 559/565-3388 or 800/227-9900, www.mslodge.com, year-round), the housekeeping staff will launder items for a fee. If you drive out to Stony Creek Resort to do laundry, bring your own soap—only large boxes of laundry soap are available.

Cedar Grove Village (8am-1pm, 3pm-9pm daily May-Oct., $3.50) has seasonal showers. Showers are also available at **Grant Grove Village** (11am-4pm daily May-Oct., $1 for 3 minutes) in the Meadow Camp cabins area. Ask for a map at the visitors center. **Stony Creek Village** has showers (9am-6pm daily May-Sept., $4) available seasonally. Campers can clean up at **Lodgepole Village** (9am-1pm, 3pm-5pm daily Apr.-May, 8am-1pm, 3pm-8pm daily June-Oct., $1 for 3 minutes). Bring quarters for all laundry services and showers.

Media and Communications

You're a long way from civilization when you visit Sequoia and Kings Canyon National Parks—don't expect cell-phone or 4G service. Instead, you'll rely on landlines at the visitors centers and the lodgings for the duration of your stay. **Pay telephones** are available outside most visitors centers, at Cold Springs Campground and Silver City Mountain Resort in the Mineral King Area, at Stony Creek Village and the Dorst Campground on Generals Highway, and at Hume Lake and Kings Canyon Lodge (summer only).

Internet access is becoming reasonably common in heavily trafficked areas. Several park lodges (John Muir, Montecito-Sequoia, and Wuksachi) offer free unsecured wireless access; you can also connect in the Grant Grove Restaurant, in the lodging desk lobby area beside the restaurant, and at the Valero Station, 20 miles outside the park on Highway 180. Of course, it's also nice to forget about the laptop and unplug for a few days.

Medical Services

There are no medical services available in Sequoia and Kings Canyon beyond the first aid provided by rangers. In a medical emergency, dial 911. The nearest hospitals are in Fresno at **St. Agnes Medical Center** (1303 E. Herndon Ave., 559/450-3000, www.samc.com) or **Community Regional Medical Center** (2823 Fresno St., 559/459-6000, www.communitymedical.org).

GETTING THERE

Car

There are three entrances to Sequoia and Kings Canyon National Parks. Visitors can enter Sequoia National Park at the Ash Mountain Entrance on Highway 198. The Big Stump Entrance is north in Kings Canyon National Park on Highway 180. The main road running through the two parks is Generals Highway; it connects Highway 180

(Kings Canyon Hwy.) in the north to Highway 198 in the south. The little-used Lookout Point Entrance provides seasonal access to the Mineral King area of Sequoia National Park. There are no road entrances on the east side of the parks.

The closest major highway is Highway 99. From Highway 99, turn east onto Highway 180 at Fresno to reach the Big Stump Entrance of Kings Canyon National Park. From San Francisco, the drive to the Big Stump Entrance takes about 4.5 hours. If entering from the south, take Highway 99 to Visalia, and then turn east onto Highway 198 to reach the Ash Mountain Entrance of Sequoia National Park.

BIG STUMP ENTRANCE

The main portal on the west side of Kings Canyon National Park is the Big Stump Entrance, located on Highway 180. Big Stump is the most direct route to either park from the west or north. At the entrance station, pay the park entry fee ($20) and receive your park map and official *Guide*. When leaving the pay station, turn left to return to Highway 180 heading north into the park. If your goal is Kings Canyon National Park, continue straight; you'll be at Grant Grove Village in about 3.5 miles. To reach Sequoia National Park, turn right onto Generals Highway at the next junction and head south toward Lodgepole Visitor Center and Village.

ASH MOUNTAIN ENTRANCE

The Ash Mountain Entrance is located on Highway 198, which enters Sequoia National Park from the south. Once inside the park, Highway 198 becomes Generals Highway. As you continue north, you'll pass the Foothills Visitor Center, Giant Forest Museum, the General Sherman Tree, and, after many curves and switchbacks, the Lodgepole Visitor Center and Village. This road can be slow going thanks to a combination of heavy traffic (especially in summer) and ongoing road construction.

In winter, the Ash Mountain Entrance is probably the better choice. This southern section of Generals Highway is plowed sooner and more thoroughly than the stretch from Grant Grove to Lodgepole. To check road conditions in advance, call 559/565-3341 or Caltrans Highway (800/427-7623).

LOOKOUT POINT ENTRANCE

Located on Mineral King Road, east of the Ash Mountain Entrance, the Lookout Point Entrance is only used by travelers headed for the Mineral King area of Sequoia National Park. It is much less trafficked than the other two entrances. The entrance fee ($20) can be paid at a self-serve kiosk. Mineral King Road is narrow, winding, and closed in winter (Nov.-May) and cannot be used by RVs or trailers.

Air

The nearest airport is the **Visalia Municipal Airport** (VIS, 9501 Airport Dr., Visalia, 559/713-4201, www.flyvisalia.com), with daily flights from Los Angeles and Las Vegas on Great Lakes Airlines. Driving distance from the airport to the park's Ash Mountain Entrance is about 36 miles.

The **Fresno-Yosemite International Airport** (FAT, 5175 E. Clinton Way, Fresno, 800/244-2359, www.flyfresno.gov) is served by a number of airlines; it is about 50 miles west of the Big Stump Entrance to Kings Canyon National Park. Larger airports include **Sacramento International Airport** (SMF, 6900 Airport Blvd., Sacramento, 916/929-5411, www.sacramento.aero) or **San Francisco International Airport** (SFO, Hwy. 101, San Francisco, 650/821-8211 or 800/435-9736, www.flysfo.com).

GETTING AROUND

Car

Generals Highway is the main road running north-south through the two parks; it connects Highway 180 (Kings Canyon National Park) in the north to Highway 198 (Sequoia National Park) in the south. It might be called a "highway," but the Generals Highway is a steep, narrow, twisting mountain road that can be treacherous in bad weather or when driven too fast. Road construction may also create delays. The maximum allowed RV length on Generals Highway is 22 feet, and trailers are not permitted. Neither RVs nor trailers are permitted on Mineral King Road or Moro Rock-Crescent Meadow Road.

Parking lots are available at most major attractions, but these can fill up quickly in summer; some parking is permitted along the roadside. In summer, various shuttles provide convenient access to some of the park's biggest sights.

Shuttles

Sequoia National Park provides free shuttle service (559/565-3341, www.nps.gov/seki, 9am-6pm daily late May-Sept.) within the park. The **Giant Forest Route** (30 min. round-trip) connects the Giant Forest Museum to the Lodgepole Visitor Center, stopping at the General Sherman Tree. The **Moro Rock-Crescent Meadow Route** (15 min. each way) connects the Giant Forest Museum to Moro Rock (outbound only) and Crescent Meadow. The **Lodgepole-Wuksachi-Dorst Route** (20 minutes one way) takes visitors from Lodgepole to the Dorst Creek Campground, stopping at Wuksachi Lodge. The **Wolverton-General Sherman Route** (30 min. each way) runs service between Wolverton and the General Sherman Tree.

The **Giant Forest-Visalia Route** is operated by Sequoia Shuttle (877/287-4453, www.sequoiashuttle.com, $15 round-trip, Memorial-Labor Day). Buses leave Visalia hourly (6am-10am, 2 hours one-way) for the Giant Forest Museum, returning in the afternoon (2:30pm-6:30pm). And since you don't have to pay the $20 entry fee when you come in by bus, this is a real bargain. Call for reservations in advance.

Winter Access

Several of the park's roads close in winter. **Mineral King Road, Crystal Cave Road,** and **Panoramic Point** close from the beginning of November to the end of May each year. Generals Highway remains open, at least officially; however, heavy snows make it difficult to predict how quickly even the major roads will be plowed. The top priorities for plowing are Highway 198 from the Ash Mountain Entrance to Lodgepole and Highway 180 from the Big Stump Entrance through Grant Grove Village, as far north as the Princess Campground junction. After that, the remainder of Generals Highway, through the middle of the parks, will be cleared if possible. If you have reservations in winter at Montecito Sequoia Lodge (63410 Generals Hwy., 559/565-3388 or 800/227-9900, www.mslodge.com, year-round), don't worry. If the road conditions are difficult, call the resort when you get to Grant Grove and they will send an escort to help you get there safely. Check www.nps.gov/seki or call 559/565-3341 for current road conditions.

Central Coast

Here begins the California coast that movies and literature have made legendary. Soaring cliffs drop straight down into the sea in some areas, making the white sand beaches that occasionally appear all the more inviting.

From north to south, the Pacific Ocean changes from slate gray to a gentler blue. Scents of salt and kelp waft up the beaches, and the endless crash of the breakers against the shore is a constant lullaby in the coastal towns.

The coastal city of Santa Cruz, with its ultraliberal culture, redwood-clad university, and general sense of funky fun, prides itself on keeping things weird. The beach and Boardwalk are prime attractions for surfing and enjoying the sun.

Gorgeous Monterey Bay is famous for its sealife. Sea otters dive and play at the world-renowned aquarium while sea lions sun themselves on offshore rocks. The historic Cannery Row was immortalized by Steinbeck in his novel of the same name, but the tourist district now bears only a superficial resemblance to its fishing past.

On the other side of the Monterey Peninsula, Carmel basks in the beauty of the Central Coast with white sand beaches, storybook cottages, and a history of art, literature, and theater. Its allure has drawn not only bohemians, but also millionaires, as it, and particularly the ultraexclusive Pebble Beach to the north, boasts some of the most expensive real estate in the country.

South of Carmel, Highway 1 begins its scenic tour down Big Sur. The Big Sur coast might be the single most beautiful part of California. The rugged cliffs and protected forests have little development to mar their natural charms. Travelers called to the wilderness will feel right at home in Big Sur. Waterfalls and redwoods beckon hikers and campers, while cliffside resorts pamper guests.

Nearing San Simeon and Cambria, the coast becomes less rugged, though no less beautiful. Seaside Cambria makes a good base from which to visit the grand Hearst Castle, an homage to excess.

Previous: Bixby Bridge in Big Sur; inquisitive sea otter at Monterey Bay Aquarium. **Above:** a ride at Santa Cruz Beach Boardwalk.

Look for ★ to find recommended sights, activities, dining, and lodging.

Highlights

★ **Santa Cruz Beach Boardwalk:** This is the best beach boardwalk in the state (page 555).

★ **Big Basin Redwoods State Park:** California's first state park still awes with some of the tallest redwoods in the world, gushing waterfalls, and over 80 miles of hiking, including the backcountry Skyline to the Sea Trail (page 572).

★ **Monterey Bay Aquarium:** This mammoth aquarium was the first of its kind in the United States and still astonishes with a vast array of sea life and exhibits (page 573).

★ **San Juan Bautista State Historic Park:** Step back in time to the heyday of mission-era California at this jewel of a historic park surrounded by the bucolic rolling hills of San Bonito County (page 590).

★ **Pinnacles National Park:** Climbers, hikers, and campers can't get enough of the huge rock formations, deep caves, and amazing topography found in this tucked-away treasure (page 592).

★ **Carmel Mission:** Father Junípero Serra's favorite California mission is still a working parish, with an informative museum and stunning gilded altar (page 594).

★ **Point Lobos State Natural Reserve:** This tiny peninsula captures the essence of the Central Coast with its deep underwater canyons, ancient cypress, and secluded cove (page 604).

★ **Big Sur Coast Highway:** This twisty coastal drive is iconic Big Sur, with jutting cliffs, crashing surf, and epic views (page 606).

★ **McWay Falls:** The ribbon-like stream crashing into the pristine beach below is *the* photo-op of Big Sur (page 608).

★ **Hearst Castle:** No visit to the Central Coast is complete without a tour of this grand mansion on a hill conceived and built by publishing magnate William Randolph Hearst (page 620).

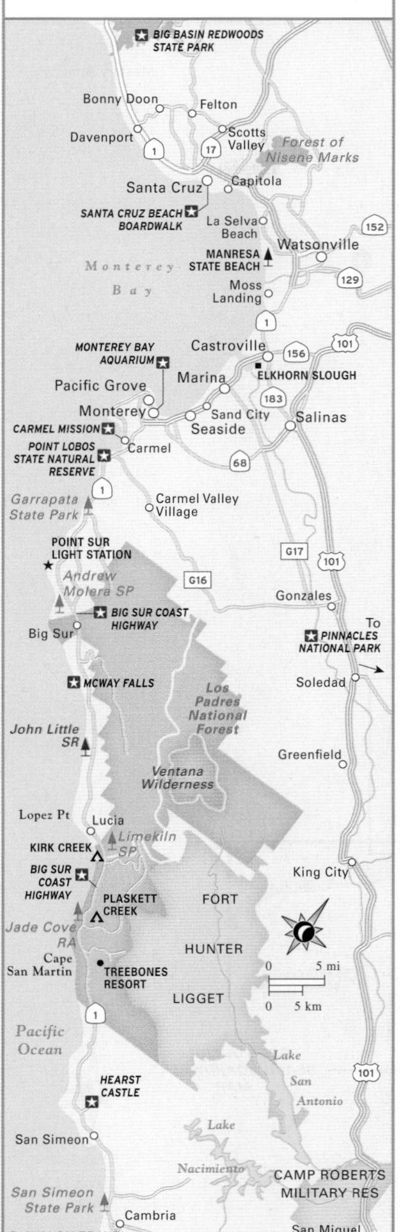

PLANNING YOUR TIME

The Central Coast is a favorite of many California residents for romantic weekend getaways. If you're coming for a weekend, pick an area and explore it in depth. Don't try to get everywhere in only two days—this is a big region and driving from one spot to another can take hours. Plan ahead: Reservations at hotels, campgrounds, and some must-eat restaurants fill up fast.

For a relaxed weekend, focus your trip on Santa Cruz, Monterey, or Big Sur. If you're up for more adventure, add a day of wine-tasting in Carmel Valley, or continue to San Simeon and Cambria to complete a fantastic drive down the coast.

Santa Cruz

There's no place like Santa Cruz. Not even in the Bay Area can you find another town that has embraced the radical fringe of the nation and made it into a municipal-cultural statement. In Santa Cruz, you'll find surfers on the waves, nudists on the beaches, tree huggers in the redwood forests, tattooed and pierced punks on the main drag, and families walking the dog along West Cliff Drive.

Most visitors come to Santa Cruz to hit the Boardwalk and the beaches, while locals and UCSC students tend to hang out on Pacific Avenue and stroll on West Cliff. The sizeable town is broken up into neighborhoods such as Seabright and the West Side, which themselves resemble small towns. Beyond the city limits there is a ton to explore, from the rocky northern coast and the redwood backcountry inland, to the beach town of Capitola, east of the city.

SIGHTS

★ Santa Cruz Beach Boardwalk

Since 1907, the **Santa Cruz Beach Boardwalk** (400 Beach St., 831/423-5590,

Santa Cruz and Vicinity

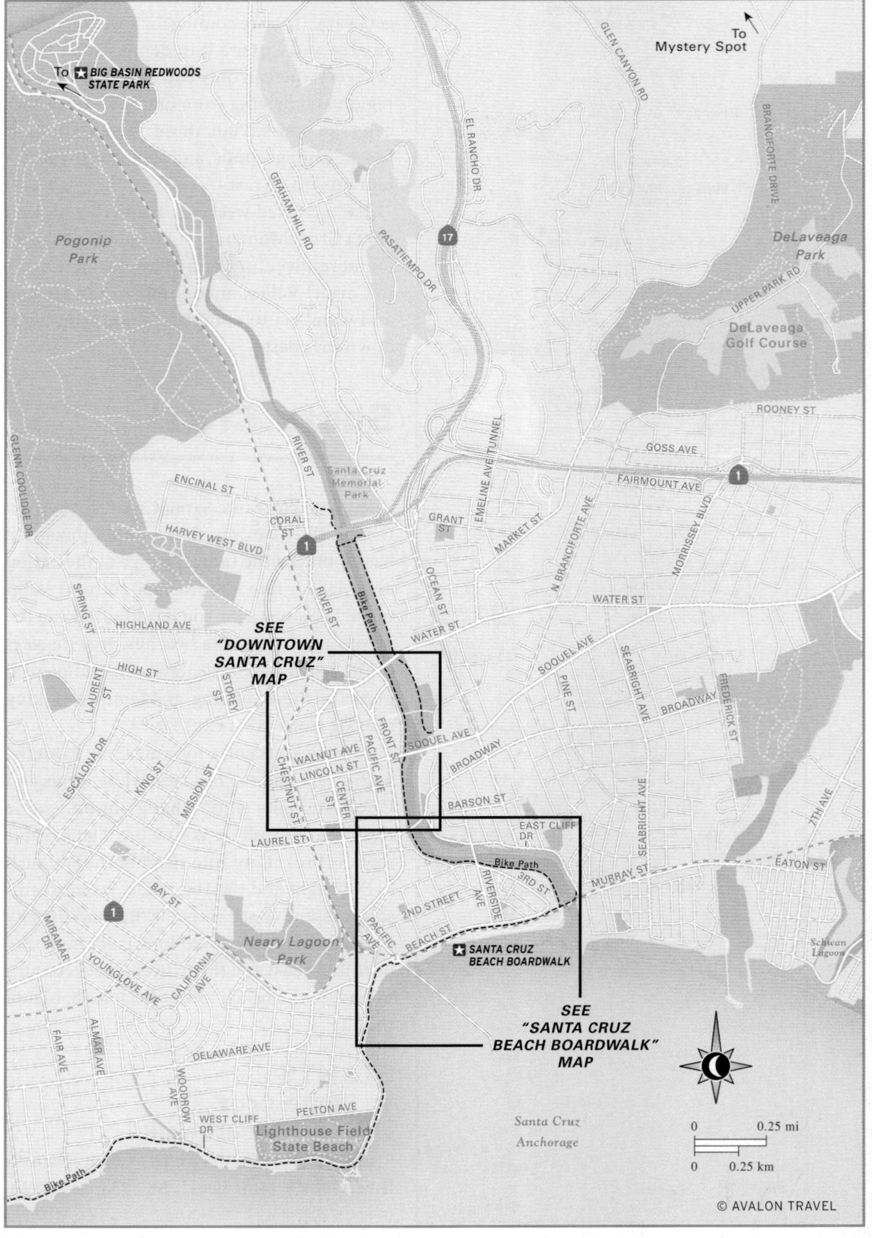

www.beachboardwalk.com, 11am-close daily June-Aug., hours vary Sept.-May, parking $6-15) has beckoned to young children, too-cool teenagers, and adults of all ages.

The amusement park rambles along the Boardwalk. Entry is free, but you must buy either ride tickets ($3-6 per ride) or an unlimited ride wristband ($24-34). The 34 rides keep the whole family entertained. The Great Dipper boasts a history as the oldest wooden roller coaster in the state, still giving riders a thrill. The Undertow and the Fireball tend to be more fun for kids (or at least folks with hardy stomachs and inner ears). In summer, a log ride cools down guests hot from hours of tromping around. Ten rides are geared toward toddlers and young kids, while avid gamesters choose between the lure of prizes from the traditional midway games and the large arcade. Throw baseballs at things, try your arm at Skee-Ball, or take a pass at classic or newer video games. At the 1911 carousel, reach for the brass ring.

After you've worn yourself out, you can take the stairs down to the broad, sandy beach below the Boardwalk or grab a cool drink and a corn dog at one of the many food-on-a-stick stands. A trip to the Boardwalk wouldn't be complete without a bag of saltwater taffy or a piece of chocolate-covered bacon from the family-owned **Marnini's Candies** (9am-10pm daily).

Across the beach, more food, shopping, and parking can be found along the **Santa Cruz Municipal Wharf** (831/420-6025, www.cityofsantacruz.com, parking $1-3/hour or $12-24/day). The wharf was built in 1914 to accommodate steamships and eventually became a home for warehouses and a cannery. Today, it has given way to tourism, offering caramel apples, seashell tchotchkes, Santa Cruz apparel, and views of the Monterey Bay.

For a little fun-filled education to go with your hot dog and kettle corn, stop by the **Monterey Bay Aquarium's Sanctuary Exploration Center** (35 Pacific Ave., 831/421-9993, http://montereybay.noaa.gov, 10am-5pm Wed.-Sun., free). Designed for kids and adults, this free museum is filled with interactive exhibits that illuminate not only the wonders of the undersea canyon just off the coast, but also humans' impact, positive and negative, on the ocean.

Santa Cruz Surfing Museum

It's fitting that the original "Surf City" has its own museum dedicated to the sport. Perched above the famous Steamers Lane break, the

the Santa Cruz Beach Boardwalk

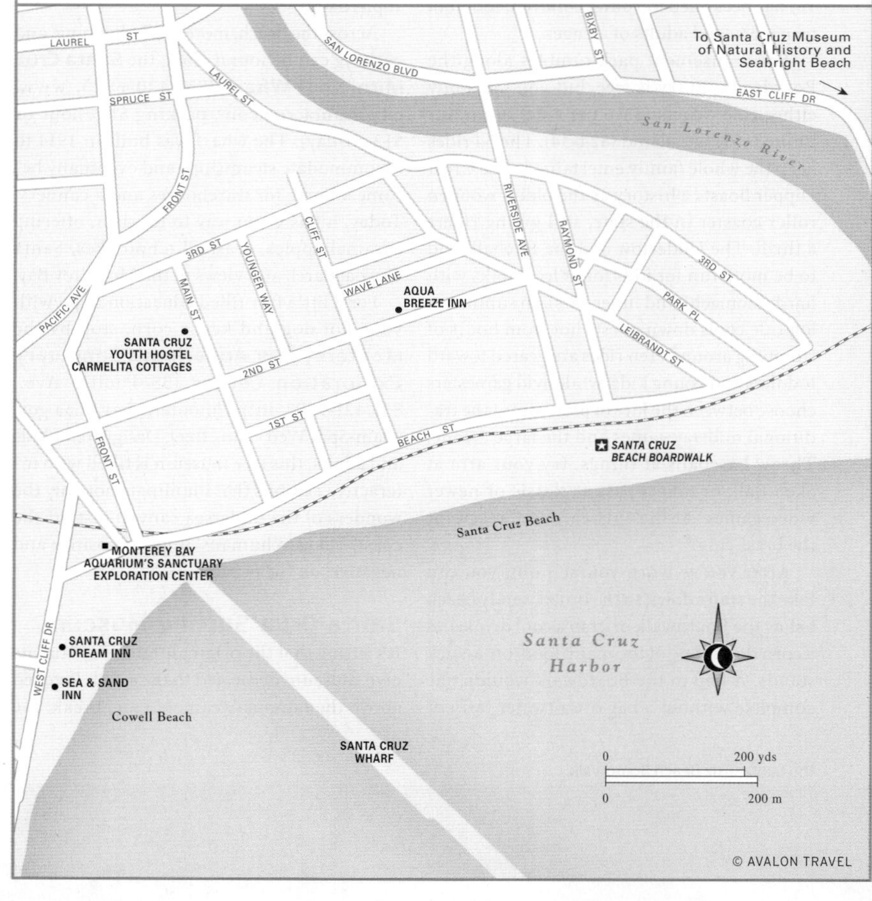

Santa Cruz Surfing Museum (701 W. Cliff Dr., 831/420-6289, www.santacruzsurfingmuseum.org, 10am-5pm Wed.-Mon. July-Aug., noon-4pm Thurs.-Mon. Sept.-June, free), housed inside the small but handsome Mark Abbott Memorial Lighthouse, showcases vintage surfboards, nostalgia-inducing photos, and a motley collection of memorabilia from the 1930s through the 1990s. Learn about the early origins of surfing in Hawaii and how three Hawaiian princes surfed the mouth of the San Lorenzo River on plank boards in 1885, forever embedding surfing into Santa Cruz culture.

Santa Cruz Museum of Natural History

Santa Cruz's very first museum was the **Santa Cruz Museum of Natural History** (1305 E. Cliff Dr., 831/420-6115, 10am-5pm Tues.-Sat., adults $4, seniors $2, youth under 18 free), opening its doors in 1904. Inside, find plenty of exhibits highlighting the Ohlone (the original Santa Cruz residents), plus the geology,

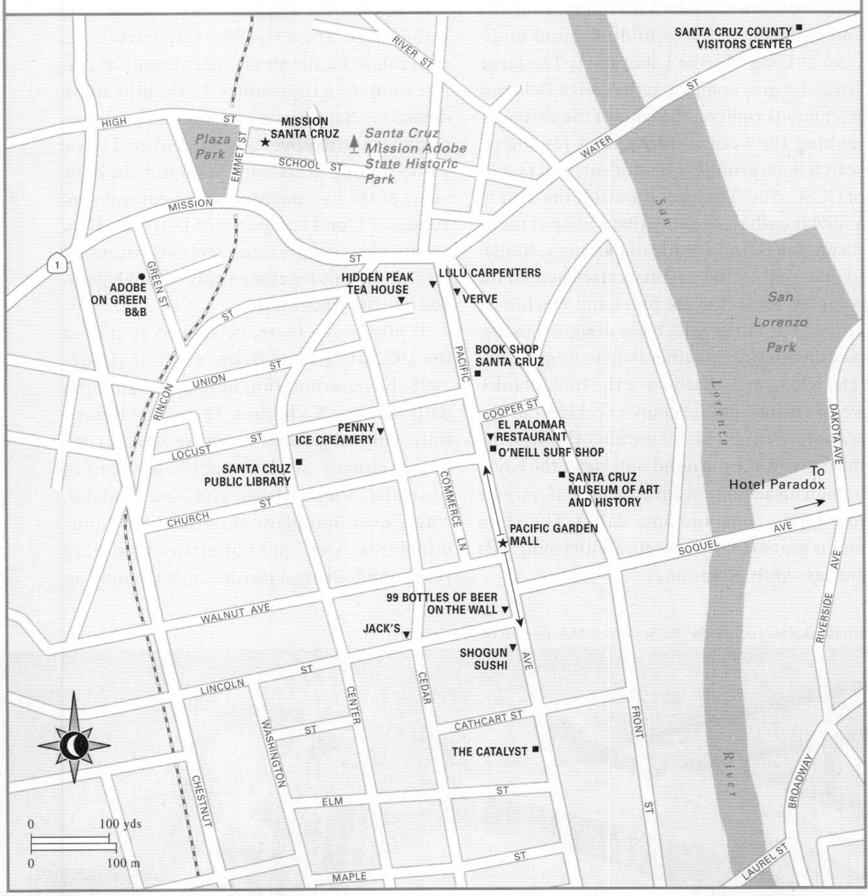

ecology, and marine ecosystems of Santa Cruz and its surrounding environs.

Santa Cruz Mission State Historic Park

Believe it or not, weird and funky Santa Cruz started out as a mission town. **Santa Cruz Mission State Historic Park** (144 School St., 831/425-5849, www.parks.ca.gov, 10am-4pm Mon. and Thurs.-Sat., noon-4pm Sun., free) tells was dedicated in 1791 and destroyed by an earthquake in 1857. Stroll the peaceful grounds on top of Mission Hill, peek into the last building of the original complex, and browse the exhibits at the visitors center. Nearby, the 1889 Holy Cross Church (126 High St.) sits on the original site of the mission. Behind the attractive church is a half-scale replica of the original mission.

Seymour Marine Discovery Center

Take a tour of the **Seymour Marine Discovery Center** (100 Shaffer Rd.,

831/459-3800, http://seymourcenter.ucsc.edu, 10am-5pm daily July-Aug., 10am-5pm Tues.-Sun. Sept.-June, adults $8, seniors, students, and children 3-16 $6, children 2 and under free) at Long Marine Laboratory. The large, attractive gray complex at the end of Delaware Avenue sits right on the edge of the cliff overlooking the ocean—convenient for the research done primarily by students and faculty of UCSC. You'll be greeted outside the door by a full blue whale skeleton that's lit up at night. Inside you'll find a marine laboratory, similar to that used by the scientists elsewhere in the complex. Expect to see pipes and machinery around the tanks, which are designed to display their residents rather than to mimic habitats. Kids particularly love the touch tanks, while curious adults enjoy checking out the seasonal tank, which contains the wildlife that's swimming around outside in the bay.

Sign up an hour in advance for a 45-minute tour (1pm, 2pm, and 3pm daily). The 11am tour is geared toward families with young kids and lasts only 30 minutes.

University of California, Santa Cruz

The **University of California, Santa Cruz** (1156 High St., 831/459-0111, www.ucsc.edu) might be the single most beautiful college campus in the country. In the hills above downtown Santa Cruz, classrooms and dorms sit underneath groves of coast redwood trees, while sloping grasslands yield unbelievable views of the bay and Monterey Peninsula beyond. Call for a campus tour (831/459-4118, groups of six or more, reservations required). Or simply wander along trails through campus like the students do.

While you're there, be sure to stop in at the **UC Santa Cruz Arboretum** (831/502-2998, http://arboretum.ucsc.edu, 9am-5pm daily, adults $5, children $2), where beautifully sculpted gardens showcase Santa Cruz's unique climate. Stroll through ecosystems of Australia, South Africa, and New Zealand, where over 300 plant varieties keep hummingbirds, bees, and butterflies humming year-round. Bring a picnic lunch to enjoy on

whale skeleton outside the Seymour Marine Discovery Center

one of the many quiet benches or join the free tour the first Saturday of every month and pick up tips for your own garden.

Mystery Spot

This old-fashioned roadside attraction has drawn visitors young and old since the 1940s. At the **Mystery Spot** (465 Mystery Spot Rd., 831/423-8897, www.mysteryspot.com, 10am-4pm Mon.-Fri., 10am-5pm Sat.-Sun., $6, children under 4 free, parking $5), gravity doesn't work as it does everywhere else. Inside this wooded hill, experience balls rolling uphill and brooms standing on end and walk up walls while your friends seem to shrink. Tours last 45 minutes, and you'll get a chance to hear the many theories of this anomaly, including that of extraterrestrial intervention.

Wilder Ranch State Park

To the north, **Wilder Ranch State Park** (1401 Old Coast Rd., 831/423-9703, www.parks.ca.gov, 8am-sunset daily, $8) is where you'll find many Santa Cruz residents on weekend mornings. Its 34 miles of trails draws hikers, mountain bikers, and equestrians, while its sheltered beaches and tide pools provide hours of sandy fun. The park encompasses the historical ranch of the Wilder family. Their 19th-century farmhouse and creamery still dot the landscape, coming alive in tours and living-history demonstrations scheduled throughout the year (call for details; 831/426-0505). However, what attracts locals is the ranch's wide-open space from the beach and coastal prairie, through the fir and redwood canyons, and up to oak-studded grassland and chaparral. The **Ohlone Bluff Trail** (4 miles, easy) follows the bluffs at the southern end of the park to its northern tip above **Four Mile Beach.** To get your heart pounding, cross Highway 1 at the Cultural Preserve parking lot (the trail goes under the road) and head inland and up. On the **Engleman Loop** (4 miles, moderate), you'll get it all: You'll pass historical structures, walk through buckeye and bay laurel, and eventually pass through deep canyons of redwoods

Surfing is a big part of Santa Cruz life.

and expansive grasslands with views of the bay and the Monterey Peninsula. And best of all, it is short enough that you'll have plenty of time to catch lunch at a West Side eatery.

ENTERTAINMENT AND EVENTS

Nightlife

Down on Pacific Avenue, stroll upstairs to **Rosie McCann's** (1220 Pacific Ave., 831/426-9930, www.rosiemccanns.com) for a pint and a bite. This dark-paneled, Irish-style saloon serves Guinness, black and tans, snakebites, and several tasty draft beers. You can also get a hefty meal of pub food. A largely local crowd hangs out here, and you'll find the bar crowded and noisy, but the vibe friendly and entertaining.

The hippest place in town is **515 Kitchen & Cocktails** (515 Cedar St., 831/425-5051, http://515santacruz.com, 4pm-2am daily). Reminiscent of a college student's apartment, there are two levels strewn with beat-up Victorian couches, cut-glass chandeliers, and the odd crooked print. The cocktails are top tier, with originals such as the Violent Femme and Cinder and Smoke (made with mescal and barbecue and habanero bitters). Snack on the truffle *pommes frites*, dine on Bavette steak, or come for a brunch of crab cake Benedict and mimosas.

The deliciously divey **Red Room** (1003 Cedar St., 831/426-2994, 3pm-1:30am daily) is illuminated mainly by the red lights above the bar. This spot is all black and red vinyl, a great juke box, whiskey, and cigarette smoke. On weekend nights, the crowd can make getting a table or booth near impossible.

Beer lovers will be in heaven at **99 Bottles of Beer on the Wall** (110 Walnut Ave., 831/459-9999, 11:30am-1:30am Mon.-Thurs., 11:30am-2am Fri.-Sat., 11:30am-midnight Sun.). Yes, the bar does have 99 different varieties of beer, many of which are local microbrews. Hearty pub food is served until midnight on Friday and Saturday nights. Another beer lover's paradise is **Santa Cruz Mountain Brewing** (402 Ingalls St., 831/425-4900, www.scmbrew.com, 11:30am-10pm daily). Located in the laid-back West Side in a hip commercial hub, the organic brewery is a dog-friendly, kid-friendly spot with an eclectic tasting room and a friendly beer garden. Nibble on food made at the scrumptious Kelly's Bakery around the corner and order a flight of the seven flagship ales. You can also opt for a pint of one of their seasonal brews.

The best Irish bar is tucked off a downtown alley and is named **The Poet & The Patriot** (320 Cedar St., 831/426-8620, 11am-2am daily). With dartboards, low ceilings, and memorabilia cluttering the place, The Poet & The Patriot feels like a private club hidden away from the world. Grab a pint of Guinness or a snakebite and hang out with the largely local crowd.

The **Blue Lagoon** (923 Pacific Ave., 831/423-7117, www.thebluelagoon.com, 4pm-2am daily) has thumping beats, glittery cocktails, and a sweaty collegiate crowd every day of the week. Drop in for DJs spinning Top 40 on Saturdays, standup comedy followed by '80s tunes on Thursdays, and hip-hop on Tuesdays.

The Catalyst (1011 Pacific Ave., 831/423-1338, advance tickets 866/384-3060, www.catalystclub.com, $12-35), right downtown on Pacific Avenue, is *the* Santa Cruz nightclub. This live rock venue hosts all sorts of big-name national acts and DJ dance nights. Be sure to check the calendar when you buy tickets—some shows are 21 and over. The main concert hall is standing room only, while the balconies offer seating. A bar sits downstairs, adjacent to the concert space. The vibe at the Catalyst tends to be low-key. Some of the more retro acts draw an older crowd, while the techno-DJ dance parties cater to the UCSC set.

South of downtown, the small, clubby **Moe's Alley** (1535 Commercial Way, 831/479-1854, www.moesalley.com, $5-45) hosts live acts six nights a week. You'll get your pick of ska, hip-hop, salsa, and legends like Los Lobos and the English Beat. The full bar and small stage give it the vibe of a cozy dive joint, while the patio outside provides a great respite, where you can grab a taco or a smoke.

Performing Arts

Big acts play the relatively small **Santa Cruz Civic Auditorium** (307 Church St., 831/420-5240, https://santacruztickets.com). Opened in 1940, the art deco Civic is run by the city and acts as both a community center and an event venue. It seats 2,000 and has surprisingly good acoustics. Acts at the Civic could be anything from Bill Maher, roller derby, Cake, and mixed martial arts fights to Emmylou Harris.

In such an expressive town, it's no surprise that Santa Cruz is home to several community theaters. The most well known, drawing theatergoers from around the Bay Area, is the annual summer Shakespeare festival, **Shakespeare Santa Cruz** (831/460-6396, www.santacruzshakespeare.org, adults $36-48, seniors $30-42, students and children $16), put on by UCSC. This six-week festival usually runs July through mid-August. Each year the festival puts up at least two Shakespeare plays—2015 selections included *Much Ado About Nothing* and *Macbeth*—plus at least one other production (often a more contemporary play). At performances at the outdoor Sinsheimer-Stanley Festival Glen on campus, audience members are encouraged to bring their own picnics. This can make for the perfect romantic date or a fun outing for the whole family.

SHOPPING

Pacific Avenue, which comprises Santa Cruz's downtown, runs from the clock tower down to Laurel Street. At the north end, shoppers peruse antiques, boutique clothing, fantastic footwear, and kitchen supplies. Down at the south end of the mall, visitors can get shiny new body jewelry or a great tattoo. Two independent movie theaters provide a break from afternoon shopping, and throughout the mall you can find a bite to eat, a cappuccino, or a cocktail in one of the many independent eateries. The middle of the mall is anchored by the flagship **O'Neill Surf Shop** (110 Cooper St., 831/469-4377, www.oneill.com, 10am-8pm Sun.-Thurs., 10am-9pm Fri.-Sat.). It is a good place to start if your trip to California has gotten you hooked on riding the waves. You'll find only a select few chain stores on the mall. Even through the closure of larger bookstores, the scrappy, independent **Book Shop Santa Cruz** (1520 Pacific Ave., 831/423-0900, www.bookshopsantacruz.com, 9am-10pm Sun.-Thurs., 9am-11pm Fri.-Sat.) stays strong.

Tucked away in the West Side, the **Swift and Ingalls Streets Courtyards** (402 Ingalls St.) are the place to go for hip home furnishings, wine-tasting, foodie delights, and hand-crafted beer. Once a Brussels sprouts packing plant, this collection of corrugated metal buildings is home to nearly 20 retailers. Join a yoga class, get a facial, sift through French antiques, pack your picnic basket with locally cured meat, or simply relax with a glass of local wine and watch the afternoon go by.

SPORTS AND RECREATION

Beaches

Natural Bridges State Park (2531 W. Cliff Dr., 831/423-4609, www.parks.ca.gov, 8am-sunset daily) may not be the best beach for catching some rays with a paperback, but this wonderful state park offers fantastic wildlife viewing from butterflies to whales. The unique rock formations create an inconsistent break, making surfing at Natural Bridges fun on occasion, and it's a diverse habitat where seals, sea otters, and porpoises frolic. From atop the cliffs, it's possible to see migrating whales farther out. The deep-set beach is cut by Moore Creek, which creates wetlands perfect for shorebirds. Tide pools are found west side of the beach, which are accessed by a somewhat scrambling short hike (0.25-0.5 mile) on the rocky cliffs. These odd little holes filled with sea life aren't like most tide pools—many are nearly perfect round depressions in the sandstone cliffs worn away by harder stones as the tides move tirelessly back and forth.

Monarch butterflies migrate here year after year. The best time to see them is October-February, when nearly 100,000 monarchs come to winter in the park's Eucalyptus Grove. Rangers offer guided tours of the monarch reserve (11am, 2pm Sat.-Sun. Oct.-Feb.) and the tide pools (year-round) at low tide.

At **Main Beach** (108 Beach St., 831/420-5270, www.cityofsantacruz.com), everyone comes to stroll, surf, and sunbathe. Just below the Boardwalk, the beach stretches from the mouth of the San Lorenzo River to the wharf. There are year-round volleyball courts, and the waves are perfect for body-boarding. Beyond the wharf is **Cowell Beach** (101 Beach St.), a good surf spot for beginners. There are free outdoor showers to rinse off the sand and salt. Lifeguards stand watch to keep everyone safe.

Residents flock to **Seabright Beach** (E. Cliff Dr. at Seabright Ave., 831/685-6500, www.thatsmypark.org, 6am-10pm daily, free) all summer long. This miles-long stretch of sand, protected by the cliffs from the worst of the winds, is a favorite retreat for sunbathers and loungers. While there's little in the way of facilities, you can still have a great time at Seabright. There's no surfing here—Seabright has a shore break that delights skim-boarders, but makes wave-riding impossible. Seabright is the site of an annual Fourth of July extravaganza. If you love fireworks and don't mind crowds, get here early.

Six miles east of Santa Cruz, Capitola is the quintessential beach town. Capitola life centers around the beautiful **New Brighton State Beach** (1500 Park Ave., Capitola, 831/464-6330, www.parks.ca.gov, 8am-sunset daily). This forest-backed beach has everything: a strip of sand that's perfect for lounging, calm water for cold-water swimming, two miles of hiking trails, and ranger-led nature programs. The forest-shaded campground ($35) has 111 sites for both tent and RV campers, plus hot showers. If you plan to camp, call in advance to make reservations at this popular state park. New Brighton can get crowded on sunny summer days. Capitola's combination of beauty along with quaint and narrow streets is a perfect recipe for traffic. Bear this in mind when venturing that way on beautiful weekend days.

Surfing

The coastline of Santa Cruz has more than its share of great surf breaks. The water is cold, demanding full wetsuits year-round, and the shoreline is rough and rocky. But that doesn't

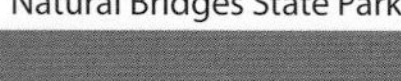

Natural Bridges State Park

deter the hordes of locals who ply the waves every day they can. The surfing culture pervades the town—if you stroll along West Cliff Drive, you'll pass the *To Honor Surfing* sculpture. Santa Cruz loves this statue, and it's often dressed up and always gets a costume for Halloween.

At **Cowell Beach** (stairs at W. Cliff Dr. and Cowell Beach), it is all about surfing. If you're a beginner, this is the best place to start surfing in Santa Cruz. The waves are low and long, making for fun longboard rides perfect for surfers just getting their balance. Because the Cowell's break is acknowledged as the newbie spot, the often sizeable crowd tends to be polite to newcomers and tourists. Not far away, the most famous break in all of Santa Cruz can also be the most hostile to newcomers. **Steamer Lane** (W. Cliff Dr. btwn. Cowell's and the Lighthouse) has both a fiercely protective crew of locals and a dangerous break that actually kills someone about every other year. But if you're into adrenaline and there's a swell coming in, you'll be hard pressed to find a more exciting ride on the Central Coast, or indeed in most of California.

Visitors who know their surfing lore will want to surf the more famous spots along the Santa Cruz shore. **Pleasure Point** (btwn. 32nd Ave. and 41st Ave., Soquel) encompasses a number of different breaks. You may have heard of **The Hook** (steps at 41st Ave.), a well-known experienced longboarder's paradise. But don't mistake The Hook for a beginner's break; the locals feel protective of the waves here and aren't always friendly toward inexperienced tourists. The break at **36th and East Cliff** (steps at 36th Ave.) can be a better place to go on weekdays—on the weekends, the crowd makes catching your own wave a challenge. Up at **30th and East Cliff** (steps at 36th Ave.), you'll find challenging sets and hot-dogging shortboarders.

Farther south, advanced surfers looking for smaller crowds in the water will find that **Manresa State Beach** (San Andreas Rd., Aptos, 831/761-1795, www.parks.ca.gov) offers fun rides under the right conditions. Manresa is several minutes' drive south toward Aptos. You'll usually find a good beach break, and the waves can get big when there's a north swell.

The **Santa Cruz Surf School** (131 Center St., 831/426-7072, www.santacruzsurfschool.com, $45-120 per hour) and the **Richard Schmidt School of Surfing** (849 Almar Ave., 831/423-0928, www.richardschmidt.com, $45-150 per hour) offer private and semi-private lessons, as does **Club Ed** (2350 Paul Minnie Ave., 831/464-0177, http://club-ed.com, $38-120 per hour). You can also get stand-up paddleboard lessons as well as surfing rentals, from boards to booties, at Ed's.

Windsurfing and Kiteboarding

If you prefer to let the wind help you catch the waves, you probably already know that Santa Cruz has some prize windsurfing and kiteboarding locales. Beginning windsurfers vie with longboarders for space at **Cowell's,** which sits right next to the City Wharf (stairs at W. Cliff Dr. and Cowell Beach). For a bigger breeze, head up West Cliff to **Natural Bridges State Park** (W. Cliff Dr., www.parks.ca.gov, $8 parking). Natural Bridges offers the best spot to set up, plus restroom facilities and ample parking.

Kayaking

The semi-protected coves around Santa Cruz offer some great kayaking. At the tip of Monterey Bay, you'll enjoy rich marine life, fun swells, and plenty of company. The best places to launch are **Main Beach** (108 Beach St., 831/420-5270, www.cityofsantacruz.com) and the **Santa Cruz Harbor** (135 5th Ave., 831/475-6161, www.santacruzharbor.org). At Main Beach, you can enter the water near the Boardwalk and by Cowell's break. Paddling out from the Boardwalk will be a more relaxing ride, but if you want a thrill, chase the waves over at Cowell's. Rentals are available at **Venture Quest Kayaking** (2 Santa Cruz Wharf, 831/425-8445, http://kayaksantacruz.com, 10am-7pm Mon.-Fri., 9am-7pm Sat.-Sun. May-Oct., by appointment Oct.-Apr.) on the wharf. You can pick open or closed kayaks, single ($35-60) or double ($55-100) for three hours or all day. If you're new to paddling in Santa Cruz, join a tour. Explore sea caves, the wildlife below the wharf and beyond, or paddle alongside gray whales in the spring ($58-100). This is a largely seasonal operation, so if you plan on paddling between October and April, call ahead.

On the east side of the harbor, the launch ramp is close to parking, making getting in and out of the water easy. The harbor itself is fun to explore, as it is a haven for barking sea lions, and extends all the way to Woods Lagoon. You can also opt for a more adventurous paddle by cruising past the breakwaters onto the open sea. For rentals at the harbor, **Kayak Connection** (413 Lake Ave. no. 3, 831/479-1121, 10am-5pm Mon.-Fri., 9am-5pm Sat.-Sun., 4 hours $35 single, $55 double) is the place to go. They also have the gear you'll need to keep warm, in addition to stand-up paddleboards. The company also offers whale-watching tours, one to Natural Bridges, and a full moon tour. All last about three hours and cost $60.

Fishing and Whale-Watching Tours

With the Monterey Bay Sanctuary just off shore and teeming with life, it is no surprise that Santa Cruz has some excellent fishing and whale-watching trips. Many companies wear both hats: Taking folks fishing in the morning, and taking others to look for porpoises, sea otters, and migrating whales later in the day. One such operation is **Stagnaro Fishing** (1718 Brommer St., 831/427-0230, www.stagnaros.com). Throughout the year, they lead fishing trips for salmon, albacore, cod, and sand dab. Trips cost $50-85 and do not include your license or rod and reel, which can be purchased or rented from Stagnaro. If just observing the ocean's bounty is more your thing, you can pick from a number of sea life tours ($48 for 3-4 hours) or the one-hour scenic Bay Cruise ($20).

Another option is **Monterey Bay Charters** (Santa Cruz Harbor Dock S, 831/818-8808, www.montereybaycharters.com), run by Tom Dolan, a veteran of Monterey fishing since 1974. Aboard his six-person boat you'll fish for albacore, snapper, crab, lingcod, and salmon, depending on the time of year. Trips cost $135-350, which includes the price of the bait and tackle, but not the license. If it seems expensive compared to other outfits, remember that you are paying for expertise.

Sailing

If all you're looking for is a chance to get out on the water, book an hour-long tour with **O'Neill Yacht Charters** (275 Lake Ave., 831/818-3645, $20/hour). The catamaran sails past the wharf, Boardwalk, and the Walton Lighthouse. You'll get a chance to check out surfers as they ride Steamers Lane and otters while they lounge on the bed of a kelp forest. For little ones, this is especially fun, because the center of the catamaran is made of trampoline netting, perfect for lounging and watching what passes beneath the boat.

A wide variety of sailing options await you at ***Chardonnay II* Sailing Charters** (790 Mariner Park Way, Dock FF, 831/423-1213, https://chardonnay.cernesystems.com, adults $56, children $30). Pick from Sushi Sunday Charter, the taste of Santa Cruz Charter, the weekend Sunset Charter, and the Brewmaster Charter. On the two-hour cruises, you'll be fed by many of Santa Cruz's top restaurants aboard the 70-foot sailing yacht. The best deal is the brown bag (bring your own food and drink) Thursday Night Special (adults $40, children $24), which sails 5pm-7pm, just in time to watch the sun go down.

ACCOMMODATIONS

Under $100

The **Santa Cruz Youth Hostel Carmelita Cottages** (321 Main St., 831/423-8304, www.hi-santacruz.org, $23-26 dorm, $55-90 private room) offers a great local atmosphere, and it's clean, cheap, friendly, and close to the beach. You'll even find a spot to store your surfboard or bike. The big, homey kitchen is open for guest use, and might even be housing some free food in its cupboards. Expect all the usual hostel amenities, a nice garden out back, free linens, laundry facilities, and a free Internet kiosk.

Cheap digs can also be found across the street from the Boardwalk at the **Aqua Breeze Inn** (204 2nd St., 831/426-7878, http://aquabreezeinn.com, $55-80). The rooms are small but clean and decorated in questionably bright colors. While this classic beach motel may not be the most charming accommodation in town, you will get a mini-fridge, microwave, use of the heated pool, and a place for Fido to lay his head at night.

$100-150

Conveniently located on Highway 1, the Spanish-style **Mission Inn** (2250 Mission St., 831/425-5455 or 800/895-5455, http://missioninn.com, $150) is an easy jog to downtown, the beach, and points north. It has 53 clean, standard motel rooms with cable TV, coffee makers, and free Wi-Fi, and some rooms have whirlpool tubs. All guests can enjoy the outdoor hot tub and sauna, and are treated to a complimentary continental breakfast.

$150-250

Hidden in a hillside residential neighborhood perched above downtown, the four-room bed-and-breakfast ★ **Adobe on Green Street** (103 Green St., 831/469-9866, www.adobeongreen.com, $129-219) lets you soak in the local atmosphere. Each room has a queen bed, a private bathroom (most with tubs and colorful tile work), a small TV with DVD player, and lots of other comforting amenities. Visit the dining room for an expanded continental spread each morning 8am-10:30am. Expect local pastries, organic and soy yogurts, and eggs laid by a neighbor's flock of chickens. Adobe runs on solar power.

For a room overlooking the ocean, stay at the **Sea & Sand Inn** (201 W. Cliff Dr., 831/427-3400, www.santacruzmotels.com, $129-319). Thanks to its unbeatable location on the ocean side of West Cliff in a quiet neighborhood, you'll be close enough to downtown and the Boardwalk to enjoy the action of Santa Cruz. Rooms are smartly but simply decorated. Suites have hot tubs and private patios. Other than the complimentary breakfast and wine and cheese hour in the afternoon, you won't find fancy amenities.

Sophisticated urban chic can be found at the 162-room **Hotel Paradox** (611 Ocean St., 831/425-7100, www.thehotelparadox.com, $219-349). At the higher end of the price range, expect plenty of designer touches that incorporate Santa Cruz's woodland environs, as well as plush beds, flat screen TVs, and mini-fridges. Completing the posh accommodations are an outdoor pool and hot tub with rentable cabanas and poolside service from the hotel's bar and restaurant.

Over $250

High above Santa Cruz, **Chaminade** (1 Chaminade Ln., 831/475-5600, www.chaminade.com, $225-375) is *the* resort in Santa Cruz. There are 156 rooms scattered around this 300-acre compound, each with feather beds and down duvets, flat screen TVs, and views of natural open space, and some have private patios. All have access to three miles of hiking trails, the heated outdoor pool, yoga and pilates classes, and the full spa. With two restaurants, Chaminade offers little reason to leave.

You won't get closer to the beach than the **Santa Cruz Dream Inn** (175 W. Cliff Dr., 831/426-4330, http://jdvhotels.com, $240-480), which channels a classic throwback kitsch. Take your morning coffee out on your private deck or lounge poolside beneath bright umbrellas. Since it's across from the Boardwalk and close to downtown, you'll never have to change out of your flip-flops.

FOOD

The combination of beach and college town vibes makes Santa Cruz a casual and eclectic dining scene. You'll find excellent cafés, burger joints, and ethnic eateries that tend to have an old-school vibe. The fancier meals tend to be at the established seafood restaurants, and most bars also serve excellent food.

Downtown

One of the favorites on Pacific Avenue is ★ **El Palomar** (1336 Pacific Ave., 831/425-7575, 11am-3pm, 5pm-10pm Mon.-Fri., 10am-3pm, 5pm-10pm Sat.-Sun., $8-15). This family-owned Mexican joint has been serving family recipes since 1983. The salsa and tortillas are handmade, and the flavors are fresh and comforting, with the appropriate amount of spice. Don't pass up a margarita—their bar has scores of tequilas and their drinks have scored critical attention.

A couple blocks away, **Shogun Sushi** (1123 Pacific Ave., 831/469-4477, noon-2:30pm, 5pm-9pm Mon.-Wed., noon-2:30pm, 5pm-10pm Thurs.-Fri.., Sat. 3pm-10pm, $12-30) is the place locals go when they need their sushi fix. The *nigiri* arrives at your table in big, fresh slabs, and you'll have an interesting collection of rolls to choose from. The restaurant is relatively small, so expect a wait for a table in the evenings and on weekends.

For an all-American meal, head over to **Jack's** (202 Lincoln St., 831/423-4421, 10am-7pm Mon.-Thurs., 10am-8pm Fri.-Sat., $5-10). While hipster burger joints have started to infiltrate the Santa Cruz scene, Jack's still has the best cheeseburger in town. The walk-up window, outside seating, and simple selection of burgers, fries, dogs, and shakes can't help but charm.

Since 1937, **Stagnaro Bros. Restaurant** (59 Municipal Wharf, 831/423-2180, http://stagnarobros.com, 11am-9pm daily, $11-27) has been selling fish to the people of Santa Cruz. Come and check out the outdoor fish market or go upstairs to the nautically themed restaurant. Pick from over 50 seafood dishes, ranging from crab melt sandwiches to blackened ahi. Many items have an Italian bent, and the must-try is the cioppino.

The denizens of Santa Cruz love the ice cream from **Penny Ice Creamery** (913 Cedar St., 831/204-2523, http://thepennyicecreamery.com, noon-11pm daily). Everything is made from scratch, including the marshmallows in the Rocky Lane flavor and the cones. Using only local and organic ingredients, Penny offers strawberry in spring, peach in summer, and pumpkin in the fall. Vanilla, salted caramel, chocolate, and coffee are available year-round.

The perpetual influx of students, thinkers, and foodies means Santa Cruz has plenty of excellent places to pick up a cup of coffee. **Verve** (1540 Pacific Ave., 831/600-7784, www.vervecoffeeroasters.com, 6:30am-9pm daily), with its reclaimed wood, subway tile, and soot-colored walls, receives the most buzz. If the loud music and hipster vibe are too much for you, venture across the street to **Lulu Carpenter's** (1545 Pacific Ave., 831/439-9200, www.lulucarpenters.com, 6am-midnight daily). The exposed brick and beam interior speaks to the 1990s wave of cafés, while the small tables and lush outdoor patio create the perfect atmosphere to read or study. Unplug at **Hidden Peak Tea House** (1541 Pacific Ave., 831/423-4200, www.hiddenpeakteahouse.com, 11am-10pm Thurs.-Sat., 11am-9pm Sun.-Wed.). The range of teas here rivals traditional tea houses in San Francisco's Chinatown. You'll find white, black, green, and oolong teas, as well as the fermented *pu-erhs*. Poke around the storefront and learn about tea from the owner himself or duck back into the tea room for a serene tea service surrounded by Asian antiques and ambient lighting. No electronics are allowed.

West Side

The West Side neighborhood draws locals with a love of good food. Opened in 1991, **Cafe Brasil** (1410 Mission St., 831/429-1855, www.cafebrasil.us, 8am-3pm daily, $7-10) has been serving up Brazilian fare since well before there was a foodie craze, and it is still packed every weekend morning. At the brightly painted café, the breakfast fare runs to omelets, while lunch includes pressed sandwiches, meat and tofu dishes, and Brazilian house specials. A juice bar provides rich but healthy meal accompaniments that can act as light meals on their own.

Anchoring Ingalls Street Courtyard is the Santa Cruz favorite **Kelly's French Bakery** (402 Ingalls St., 831/423-9059, www.kellysfrenchbakery.com, 7am-8pm Fri., 7am-7pm Sat.-Thurs., $10). Located in an old packing shed, Kelly's sells bread, pastries, hot and cold sandwiches, and breakfast dishes. It's got both indoor and outdoor seating, or you can take your food to go. Don't pass up the opportunity to try the divine coffee cake.

The best gastropub in town is along Ingalls Street at **West End Tap & Kitchen** (334D Ingalls St., 831/471-8115, http://westendtap.com, 11:30am-9:30pm Sun.-Thurs., 11:30am-10pm Fri.-Sat., $11-22). Angus tenders, smoked mac and cheese, tomatillo-braised pork flatbread, and duck fat popcorn complement West End's small-batch beer. With the exception of a couple surfboards on the walls, the pub has an urban feel rare in Santa Cruz. It's a great place to catch a game, as multiple flat screen TVs hang above the bar.

Seabright

Seabright expresses a laid-back beach vibe. For coffee, pastries, and sandwiches to go, stop by ★ **The Buttery** (702 Soquel Ave., 831/458-3020, www.butterybakery.com, 7am-7pm daily, $3-10). At the corner of Soquel and Branciforte in a large Victorian building, The Buttery bustles with locals. Grab a number before you peruse the rich assortment in the deli cases. For a hot meal, the counter on the left side is the place to go, and the outside patio, beneath the blooming wild roses, is perfect for coffee and a pastry.

One of the best casual eateries in Seabright is the **Harbor Café** (535 7th Ave., 831/475-4948, www.harborcafesantacruz.com, 8am-2pm daily, $7-13). This diner has tropical ocean flair with bright colors, corrugated metal, leafy greenery, and marlins propped on the walls. Outside, the patio is sheltered by palms and warmed by heat lamps. The food is a hearty mash-up of tri-tip and carnitas omelets, eggs Benedicts (served on croissants), burgers, and rice bowls. The full bar and excellent service make the tasty grub go down even easier.

Perched above the harbor in a handsome building, ★ **Johnny's Harborside** (493 Lake Ave., 831/479-3430, www.johnnysharborside.com, 11:30am-8:30pm Mon.-Thurs., 11:30am-9:30pm Fri.-Sat., 10am-8:30pm

Kelly's French Bakery, West Side Santa Cruz

Sun., $12-32) delivers plates of fish-and-chips, blackened New York steak, and tempura ahi. The dining room is spare, and the menu is eclectic, revolving mainly around seafood. Johnny's offers an extensive gluten-free menu as well as happy hour drink specials.

To eat right on the water, take an outside table at **Aldo's** (616 Atlantic Ave., 831/426-3736, www.aldos-cruz.com, 8am-4pm Mon.-Thurs., 8am-8:30pm Fri., 7am-8:30pm Sat., 7am-5pm Sun., $11-23), on the west side of the harbor. While the food may not be quite the caliber found at Johnny's Harborside, you'll soak in the sunshine, hear seals bark in the harbor, and smell the ocean breeze over a bloody Mary or a glass of wine and a plate of fried calamari or house-made pasta with fresh seafood.

Capitola

Undoubtedly the most romantic restaurant in the region is Capitola's ★ **Shadowbrook** (1750 Wharf Rd., 831/475-1511, www.shadowbrook-capitola.com, 5pm-8:45pm Mon.-Fri., 4pm-9:45pm Sat., 4pm-8:45pm Sun., $23-45). The restaurant is down a steep and lush ravine along Soquel Creek. To get there, diners take a trip aboard the antique cable car, or by foot along the winding illuminated path through thick flora. The restaurant is inviting, with roses, candlelight, and robust plates of lobster and black truffle gnocchi, followed by fine chocolate desserts. The adjacent **Rock Room Lounge** (4pm-10pm Mon.-Fri., 3:30pm-10pm Sat., 2:30pm-10pm Sun., $13-27) offers a more casual atmosphere and menu. The Rock Room does not take reservations, unlike Shadowbrook, where they are a must.

INFORMATION AND SERVICES

Tourist Information

While it can be fun to explore Santa Cruz on your own, those who want a bit more structure can hit the **Santa Cruz Visitors Center** (303 Water St., 831/425-1234, www.santacruzca.org, 9am-4pm Mon.-Fri., 11am-3pm Sat.-Sun.) for maps, advice, and information. If you're on Pacific Avenue, the Downtown Association has a **Visitors Kiosk** (1130 Pacific Ave., 831/332-7422, www.downtownsantacruz.com, 11am-5pm Sun.-Thurs., 11am-7pm Fri.-Sat.) at the corner of Pacific and Soquel Avenues.

Despite its reputation as a funky bohemian beach town, Santa Cruz's dense population dictates that it have at least one full-fledged hospital of its own. You can get medical treatment and emergency care at **Dominican Hospital** (1555 Soquel Ave., 831/426-7700, www.dominicanhospital.org). For less life-threatening issues, the Palo Alto Medical Foundation (www.pamf.org) has two urgent care clinics in Santa Cruz: the **Main Clinic** (2025 Soquel Ave., 831/458-5537, 8am-9pm daily) and the **Westside Clinic** (1301 Mission St., 831/458-6310, 9am-9pm Mon.-Thurs., 9am-6pm Fri.-Sun.).

TRANSPORTATION

From San Francisco, Santa Cruz is 75 miles south, about 1.5 hours away. Take either U.S. 101 or I-280 south (101 can be slightly faster, but less scenic and more prone to traffic) to Highway 17 toward Santa Cruz. Most locals take this 50-mile-per hour corridor fast—probably faster than they should. Each year, several people die in accidents on Highway 17, so keep to the right and take it slow, no matter what the traffic to the left of you is doing. Check traffic reports before you head out; Highway 17 is known as one of the worst commuting roads in the Bay Area, and weekend beach traffic in the summer jams up fast in both directions.

For a more leisurely drive, opt for two-lane Highway 1. Utterly scenic, with plenty of beach stops along the way, it's not a bad way to travel down to Santa Cruz. Once in town, Highway 1 becomes Mission Street on the West Side and acts as the main artery through Santa Cruz and down to Capitola, Soquel, Aptos, and coastal points farther south. Visitors planning to drive or bike around Santa Cruz should get themselves a good map, either before they arrive or at the visitors center in town. Navigating the winding, occasionally broken-up streets of this oddly shaped town isn't for the faint of heart. Neither is the traffic, which is endemic (at commute times and off) throughout town and along the highways.

Parking in Santa Cruz can be challenging. Downtown, head straight for the parking structures one block away from Pacific Avenue on either side. They're much easier to deal with than trying to find street parking. The same goes for the beach and Boardwalk areas. At the Boardwalk, just pay the fee to park in the big parking lot adjacent to the attractions. You'll save an hour and a possible car break-in or theft trying to find street parking in the sketchy neighborhoods that surround the Boardwalk.

Santa Cruz METRO (831/425-8600, www.scmtd.com, $2/single ride, passes available) runs 42 bus routes in Santa Cruz County, helping you get nearly anywhere you'd want to go. In the summer, take advantage of the **Santa Cruz Trolley** (831/420-5150, http://santacruztrolley.com, 11am-9pm daily May-Sept., $0.25). The vintage trolley car connects the Boardwalk and downtown via a three-stop route run every 15-20 minutes. And it only costs a quarter.

SANTA CRUZ MOUNTAINS

If you haven't been sufficiently wowed by the splendor and diversity of the Santa Cruz landscape, head east into the mountains. Highway 9, the main road snaking through the redwood-dense mountains, is lined with the towns of **Felton, Ben Lomond,** and **Boulder Creek,** in addition to the stellar state parks of **Henry Cowell Redwoods** and **Big Basin.** Less than 20 minutes from downtown Santa Cruz, residents commute for work and school, but tucked into the forest, these mountain towns still feel worlds away.

Henry Cowell Redwoods State Park

Before entering the town of Felton, Highway 9 slows to wind through the bottom of a steep river gorge. This is the beginning of the 4,600-acre **Henry Cowell Redwoods State Park** (101 N. Big Trees Park Rd., Felton, 831/335-4598, www.parks.ca.gov, $10). Encompassing old-growth redwoods, waterfalls, and, high in the hills, views of Monterey Bay, the park offers 20 miles of trails as well as campsites. There is also swimming at the sandy **Frisbee** and **Cable Car Beaches** along the San Lorenzo River.

The park is broken up into two large swaths. The main section is in the heart of Felton and has a ranger kiosk, a **Nature Center** with nature displays and interactive exhibits, and the accessible **Redwood Grove Loop,** an interpretive trail winding through giant trees. Trails crisscross this entire section of park, making any number of moderate loops possible. Longer, backcountry trails can be found in the northern **Fall Creek** section of the park. Trailheads line the Felton-Empire Grade Road, including for the **Fall Creek Trail**, a 3.2-mile loop via the **Ridge Trail.** To make this into a full day adventure, take **Fall Creek Trail,** then turn left onto **Big Ben Trail,** followed by another left onto **Lost Empire Trail,** and back to **Fall Creek** via the **Cape Horn** and **South Fork Trails.** On this strenuous nine-mile loop, you'll pass the famous giant Big Ben redwood tree and the old lime kilns along South Fall Creek.

Camping ($35) is available at Henry Cowell April through October. Sites are near the creek, nestled in the redwoods, and come with fire rings, lockers, and picnic tables, with flush toilets and hot showers close by.

Roaring Camp Railroads

If the river and the redwoods aren't enough, walk over to **Roaring Camp Railroads** (5401 Graham Hill Rd., Felton, 831/335-4484, www.roaringcamp.com, 9am-5pm daily, 13 and over $27-29, children 2-12 $20-23, parking $8). Running out of a re-created 1880s logging town, antique steam engines wind through the Santa Cruz Mountains, over trestles and beneath towering redwoods, on hour-long tours. You can jump aboard a three-hour round-trip down to the Boardwalk for a whole day of fun. Picnicking is encouraged at the camp, as is exploring the myriad of activities, from gold panning and blacksmithing to volleyball.

★ Big Basin Redwoods State Park

Redwoods are common throughout the Santa Cruz Mountains, but **Big Basin Redwoods State Park** (21600 Big Basin Way, Boulder Creek, 831/338-8860, www.parks.ca.gov, $10) is special. Big Basin is home to the largest continuous stand of old-growth coast redwoods south of San Francisco and owes this distinction to becoming California's first state park in 1902, at the height of the logging frenzy. Today this means an area rich in biodiversity. You'll find oak, madrone, and Douglas fir, in addition to redwoods. At higher elevations, sun-loving chaparral communities dominate the landscape.

Big Basin Redwoods State Park

Big Basin has 80 miles of trails to explore, stretching from the crown of the Santa Cruz Mountains down to the mouth of Waddell Creek just south of Año Nuevo. One of the most popular hikes is to **Berry Creek Falls** (12 miles, strenuous), a series of four waterfalls cascading through old-growth redwoods. Usually done as a one-way trek, **Skyline to the Sea** to **Waddell Creek Beach** (12.5 miles, strenuous) is a rite of passage for many local outdoor enthusiasts. There are plenty of shorter and more moderate hikes, like the **Shadowbrook Trail** (4.7 miles, moderate) and **Sequoia Trail** (4 miles, easy), which both lead to Sempervirens Falls.

At the main entrance, 146 traditional campsites ($35) are divided into four areas. These all have access to bathroom facilities, showers, and a group amphitheater where campers are often entertained by music or ghost stories. Tent cabins are also available ($75), as are backpacking sites ($15). Reservations can be made by phone or online (800/444-7275, www.reserveamerica.com). Backpacking sites must be reserved in advance by phone (831/338-8861). The park is big, but all the visitor services are clustered together. You'll find a general store, a gift store, and a museum near the visitors center, where you can pay fees, buy a trail map, and query a happy-to-oblige ranger. Docent-led hikes leave from here and generally occur every Saturday morning.

Big Basin is located 25 miles northeast of Santa Cruz, smack in the middle of the mountains, near the intersections of Highways 35 and 9. The park's main entrance is seven miles down Highway 236 (also known as Big Basin Highway). Boulder Creek is the closest town, nine miles south on Highway 9.

Food

Dining options along Highway 9 are a motley collection of roadhouses, breweries, and family-owned restaurants. Nothing is terribly cheap or ultrasophisticated. For breakfast, lunch, or dinner stop in at the sunlit **Oak Tree Ristorante** (5447 Hwy. 9, Felton, 831/335-5551, www.oaktreeristorante.com,

4pm-10pm Mon.-Tues. and Thurs., 8:30am-10pm Fri.-Sun., $17-32), a nice Italian restaurant beneath a giant oak tree. Expect delicious frittatas for breakfast, panini for lunch, and plenty of house-made pastas for dinner. The wine selection is extensive and mostly hails from the Santa Cruz Mountains and Italy.

In Boulder Creek, the place to go is the **Boulder Creek Brewery & Café** (13040 Hwy. 9, Boulder Creek, 831/338-7882, 11:30am-10pm Sun.-Thurs., 11:30am-10:30pm Fri.-Sat., $10-22). Since 1989, the modest-looking brewery has been a mainstay here, pouring its handcrafted beers to locals and fans driving from Santa Cruz. Big juicy burgers, fat onion rings, and their famous avocado fries make great accompaniments after a long day out on the trail.

To fill your backpack for a day out in the redwoods, swing by **New Leaf Community Market** (13159 Central Ave., Boulder Creek, 831/338-7211, 9am-9pm daily), Santa Cruz's answer to Whole Foods. This excellent, locally owned health food store chain began at this Boulder Creek location. In its well-stocked selection of natural foods, including prepared salads and sandwiches, a full deli counter, and bakery, you'll find everything you need and more.

Monterey

Surrounded by fields of lettuce, artichokes, and Brussels sprouts and a forest of pine, the Monterey Peninsula juts out from the California coast to create the wide and magnificent Monterey Bay. It has been a draw to the native Ohlone people, Spanish settlers, farmers, commercial fishers, writers, poets, and painters. Over the years, the charm of the peninsula and its waters has also attracted luxury hotels and high-wattage restaurants. Recognizing that Monterey's bounty was not unlimited, the creation of the Monterey Bay National Marine Sanctuary in 1992 protected the bay's astounding biological diversity, including its kelp forests and the Monterey Submarine Canyon, one of the deepest in the world.

Monterey is many things. It is the commercial hub of the Monterey Peninsula, filled with law and doctors' offices, malls, and parks, and it's he launch point to the protected waters just off the coast. Founded in 1770, Monterey was "California's first city." It was the capital of Alta California and had a thriving port and bustling military Presidio. Whaling and fishing soon followed, as did the canneries and their workers, a collection of immigrants from Oklahoma to the Philippines; a tough and hard-working world captured by John Steinbeck. Pacific Grove (PG to locals) is sandwiched between Monterey and Pebble Beach. David Avenue is the border between Monterey and PG.

SIGHTS

★ Monterey Bay Aquarium

At the **Monterey Bay Aquarium** (886 Cannery Row, 831/648-4800, www.montereybayaquarium.org, 9:30am-6pm daily Sept.-June, 9:30am-6pm Mon.-Fri., 9:30am-8pm Sat.-Sun. July-Aug., adults $40, seniors and students 13-17 $35, children 3-12 $25, under 3 free), you'll get to explore the ocean beyond the beach, where sharks roam the deep, sardines circle forests of kelp, and sea otters relax over a lunch of abalone. All the exhibits you'll see in this mammoth complex contain only local sea life and convey a message of sustainability. The exhibits and shows put on by the residents of Monterey Bay delight children and adults alike, especially the playful sea otters, the intelligent and stealthy giant octopus, and the bat rays, who love a good petting.

The aquarium is one of the best places to eat on Cannery Row. Try for a table at the full-service restaurant and bar, complete with

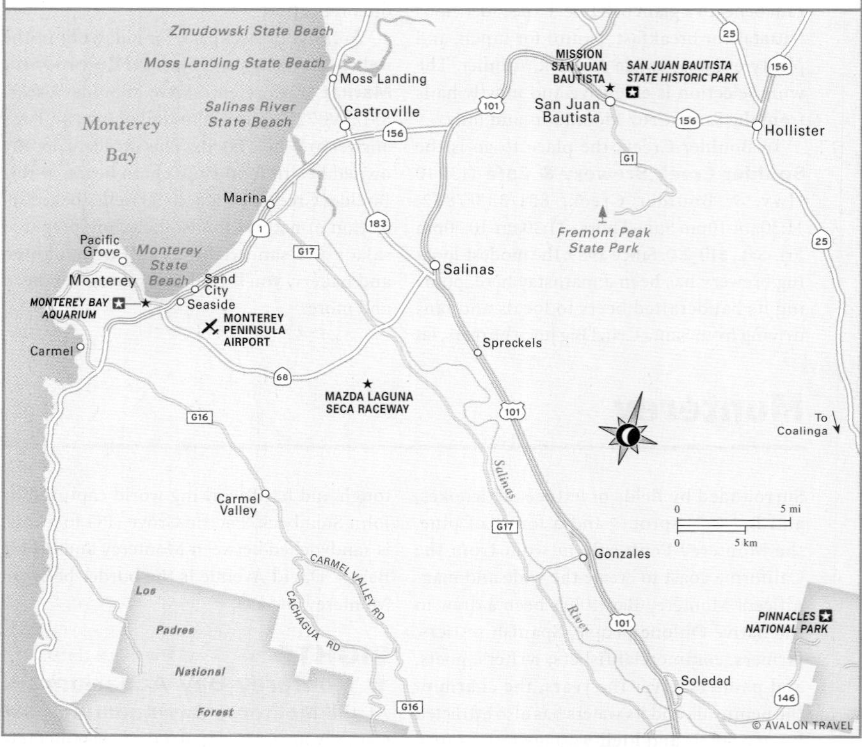

white tablecloths and a view of the bay. A self-service café offers sandwiches, salads, and international dishes for decent prices and with equally excellent views. Everything served is sustainable.

Cannery Row and Fisherman's Wharf

Cannery Row (www.canneryrow.com) and **Fisherman's Wharf** (www.montereywharf.com) are Monterey's manufactured tourist meccas. There are the places that most locals avoid. Filled with boutique hotels, big seafood restaurants, and cheesy souvenir stores, it's hard to imagine that this stretch of coastline, extending past the lower tip of the Presidio to Fisherman's Wharf, was the center of Monterey's booming fishing industry in the early 20th century. Here, thousands of tons of sardines were hauled in, processed, and canned by low-wage workers at the 16 canning plants and 14 reduction plants lining Cannery Row. In the 1950s the industry collapsed.

If you look close enough, you can still traces of John Steinbeck's Cannery Row. Ed Rickett's lab still looks as it did, complete with the concrete specimen tanks out back, and the city has maintained several of the one-room cottages that housed Filipino and Japanese workers. Inside the aquarium, itself housed in an old cannery, you can check out old steam boilers.

Monterey State Historic Park

For history that is beautifully preserved, uncrowded, and still an active part of the city,

The Monterey Bay Aquarium is known for integrating inside and outside spaces.

visit **Monterey State Historic Park** (20 Custom House Plaza, 831/649-7118, www.parks.ca.gov, 10am-5pm daily, free). Usually called Old Monterey by locals, "the park" is a collection of 55 historical sites along a 2.5-mile trail that weaves through downtown Monterey. It provides a peek into Monterey as it was in the middle of the 19th century—a busy place filled with dock workers, fishermen, bureaucrats, and soldiers. And yet it blends into the modern town of Monterey as well, and modern stores, galleries, and restaurants sit next to historic adobe structures.

To find all the historic sites, follow the yellow medallions embedded in the sidewalks. Organized walking tours (10:30am, 12:30pm Fri.-Sun., $5) meet at the Pacific House Museum and last 45 minutes. Tours of several of the brick and adobe buildings are also available. Although many of the structures are not (or at least are rarely) open to the public, you are encouraged to spend time in their splendid gardens, which are open daily.

The best place to start is the **Custom House Plaza** at the base of Fisherman's Wharf. Here, the **Custom House** (10am-4pm Fri.-Sun., adults $3, children 12 and under free) is California State Historic Landmark Number 1, and the oldest bureaucratic building to still stand in the state. You can spend some time wandering through the adobe building, checking out the artifacts on display, or even just looking out the upstairs window toward the sea. Also included in the entrance fee is admittance to the neighboring **Pacific House Museum** (10am-4pm Fri.-Sun.). Built in 1847, it was at varying points a courthouse, hotel, and tavern and now houses exhibits of Native American artifacts. Other nearby historic sites are **California's First Theater** (Pacific St. and Scott St.); the **Old Whaling Station** (391 Decatur St.), with its whalebone sidewalk out front; and the **Casa del Oro** (210 Oliver St., 11am-3pm Thurs.-Sun.), a two-story adobe building home to the quaint Boston Store and Picket Fence Garden Shop.

Downtown, another great starting point is **Colton Hall** (351 Pacific St., 831/646-5640, www.monterey.org, 10am-4pm daily). Though technically not part of the Monterey State Historic Park, Colton Hall is a city museum honoring the drafting of California's

Downtown Monterey

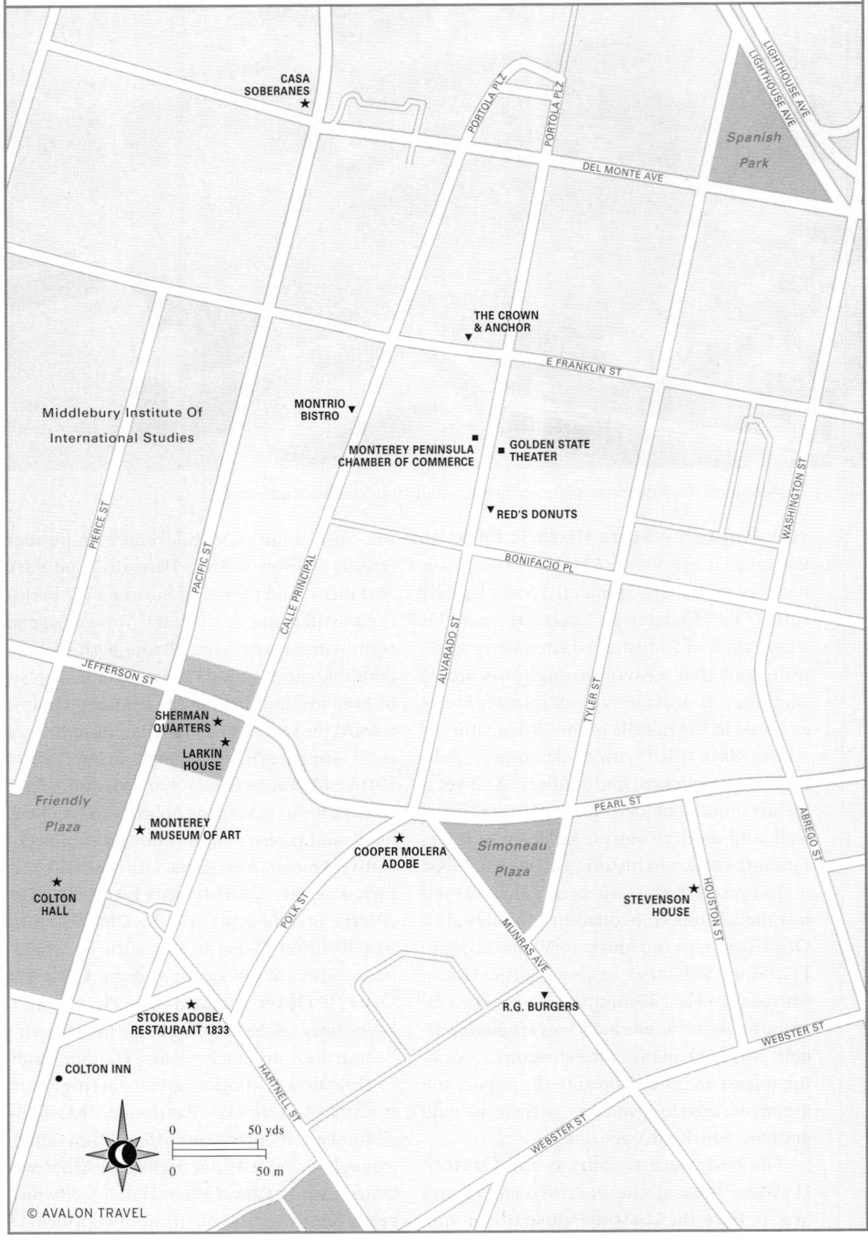

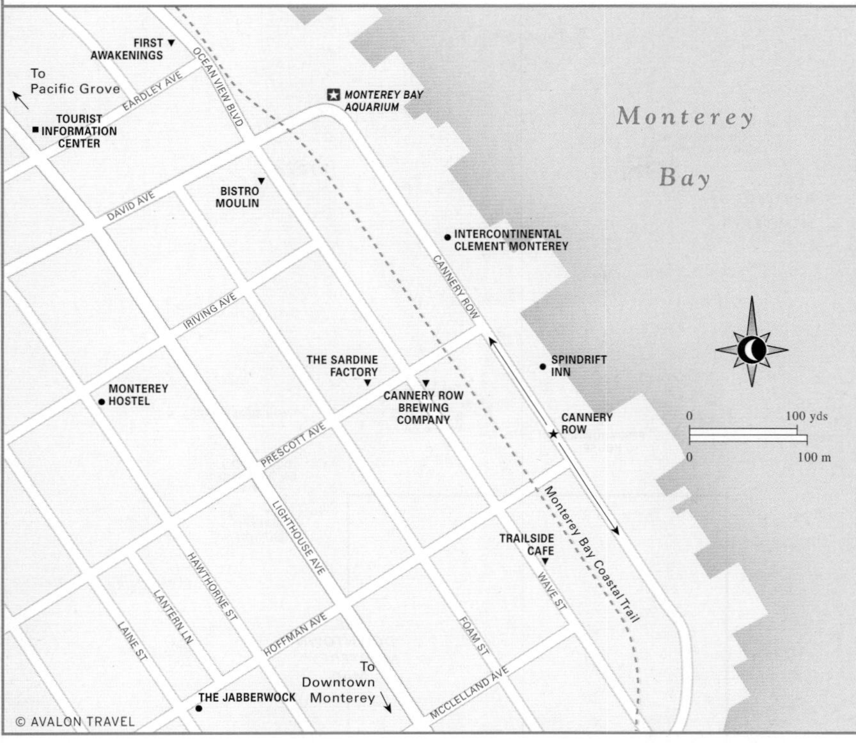

first constitution in 1849. Directly behind the stately building is the **Old Monterey Jail** (831/646-5640, www.monterey.org, 10am-4pm daily), which served as the city's jail from 1854 to1956.

Sites along the Monterey State Historic Park walk include **Casa Soberanes** (Pacific St. and Del Monte Ave.), where the garden path is lined with old bottles, whalebones, antique china, and abalone shells; the **Larkin House** (464 Calle Principal, tours noon and 1pm Fri.-Sun., $5); **Sherman Quarters** (Calle Principal), once the home of Lieutenant William T. Sherman of Civil War fame; **Stevenson House** (530 Houston St., 10am-4pm Sat.-Sun.), the hotel where author Robert Louis Stevenson stayed; and the **Cooper-Molera Adobe** (525 Polk St., store and garden 10am-4pm daily, tours 10:30am, 2pm Fri.-Sun., $5), a two-acre, 1840s compound of gardens, a barn, a tallow room, and a great gift store, selling thoughtful trinkets that celebrate the era.

Museum of Monterey

More history can be found at the **Museum of Monterey** (5 Custom House Plaza, 831/372-2608, http://museumofmonterey.org, 11am-5pm Wed.-Sat., noon-5pm Sun., free). The large modern facility in the middle of Custom House Plaza provides plenty of space for art and historic artifacts collected over the decades. You can explore the history of the native Rumisen and Ohlone people, going

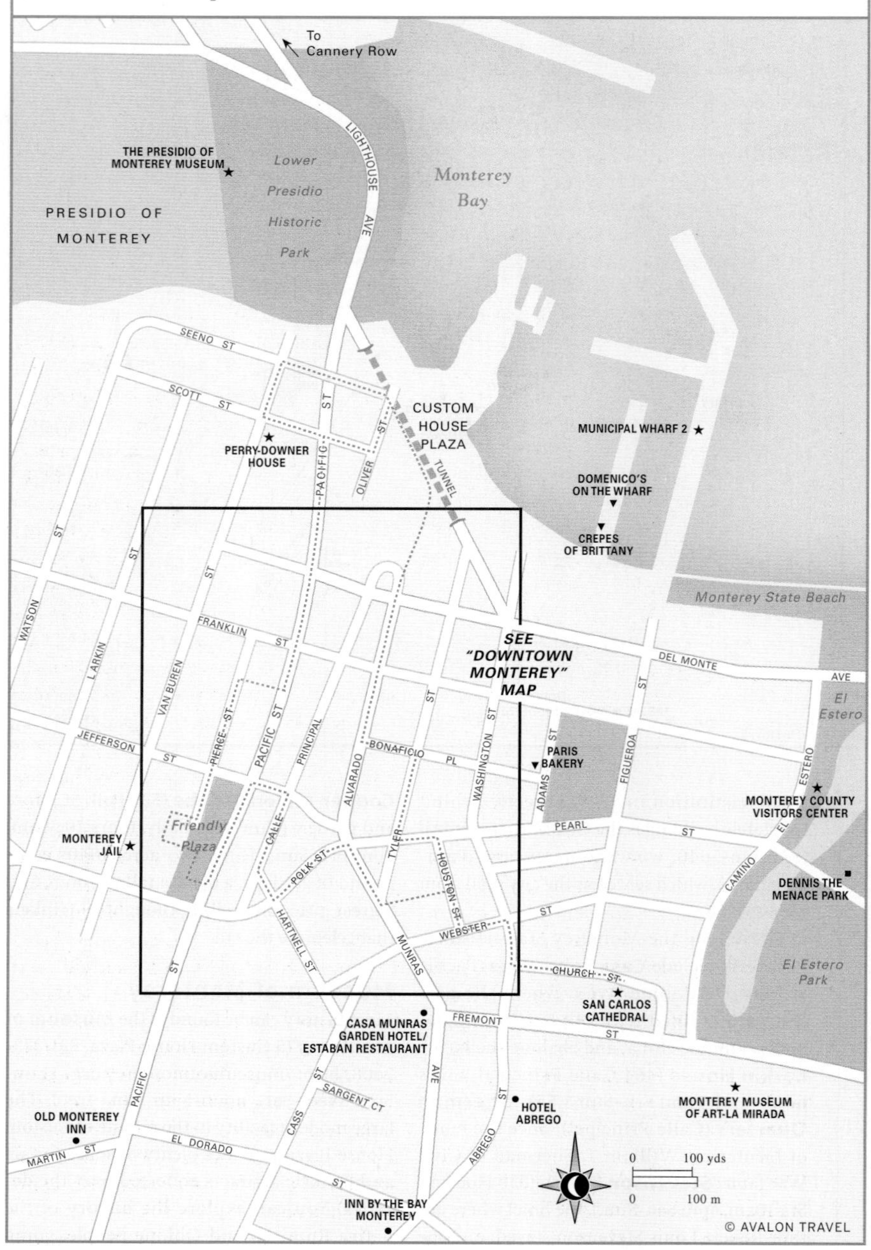
Monterey State Historic Park
To Cannery Row
THE PRESIDIO OF MONTEREY MUSEUM
Lower Presidio Historic Park
Monterey Bay
PRESIDIO OF MONTEREY
LIGHTHOUSE AVE
SEENO ST
SCOTT ST
CUSTOM HOUSE PLAZA
MUNICIPAL WHARF 2
PERRY-DOWNER HOUSE
PACIFIC ST
OLIVER ST
TUNNEL
DOMENICO'S ON THE WHARF
CREPES OF BRITTANY
Monterey State Beach
WATSON
LARKIN
VAN BUREN
FRANKLIN ST
SEE "DOWNTOWN MONTEREY" MAP
DEL MONTE AVE
El Estero
JEFFERSON ST
PIERCE ST
PRINCIPAL
ALVARADO
BONAFICIO PL
WASHINGTON ST
ADAMS ST
PARIS BAKERY
FIGUEROA
ESTERO
MONTEREY COUNTY VISITORS CENTER
Friendly Plaza
CALLE
TYLER
PEARL ST
MONTEREY JAIL
POLK ST
HOUSTON ST
CAMINO EL ESTERO
DENNIS THE MENACE PARK
HARTNELL ST
WEBSTER ST
MUNRAS
CHURCH ST
El Estero Park
SAN CARLOS CATHEDRAL
CASA MUNRAS GARDEN HOTEL/ ESTABAN RESTAURANT
FREMONT ST
AVE
SARGENT CT
HOTEL ABREGO
MONTEREY MUSEUM OF ART-LA MIRADA
OLD MONTEREY INN
CASS ST
EL DORADO ST
MARTIN ST
ABREGO ST
0 100 yds
0 100 m
INN BY THE BAY MONTEREY
© AVALON TRAVEL

through the Spanish exploration and conquistador era, and on into the American military and fishing presence on the Central Coast. The original Fresnel lens from the Point Sur light station sits in here, as does an array of sardine fishing equipment.

Monterey Museum of Art

Surrounded by historical adobe, the **Monterey Museum of Art** (559 Pacific St., 831/372-5477, www.montereyart.org, 11am-5pm Thurs.-Mon., adults $10, students and children 18 and under free) adds a splash of contemporary color to Old Monterey. The three-story museum showcases art, from early California landscapes to modern sculpture and abstract painting. You'll also find fresh, rotating exhibits exploring a number of California-related themes.

Presidio of Monterey

Since its establishment in 1770, Monterey has had a strong military presence. All that remains of the original Spanish Presidio is the **San Carlos Cathedral** (500 Church St.), then known as the Royal Presidio Chapel and California's first cathedral. Where the Spanish installed 11 cannons to protect the bay is the current site of the **Presidio of Monterey** (between Hwy. 68 and Lighthouse Ave., 831/242-5000, www.monterey.army.mil).

As it is still an active army base, visitors are restricted from entering most of the Presidio. The 26-acre **Lower Presidio Historic Park** (Lighthouse Ave. and Artillery St.) has ruins of Fort Mervine (the first American installation on the site), remains of a Native American Rumsen village, a few monuments, and trails with beautiful views of the bay. You'll also find the **Presidio of Monterey Museum** (Bldg. 113, Corporal Ewing Rd., 831/646-3456, http://monterey.org, 10am-1pm Mon., 10am-4pm Thurs.-Sat., 1pm-4pm Sun., free), a must-see for any military buff.

Pacific Grove Monarch Sanctuary

From November to February, the best place to see the nearly 10,000 monarch butterflies that travel thousands of miles to winter in the eucalyptus and pine forests of Pacific Grove is in the **Monarch Sanctuary** (250 Ridge Rd., off Lighthouse Ave.). Here they hang in great clusters, resembling clumps of dead leaves, until the fluttering of their wings seem to make the trees take flight. During this time, museum docents armed with viewing scopes come to answer questions every day (noon-3pm).

ENTERTAINMENT AND EVENTS

Live music and a wild time can be had at **Carbone's Bar** (214 Lighthouse Ave., 831/643-9169, 4pm-2am Mon., 3pm-2am Tues.-Fri., noon-2am Sat.-Sun.). The slender bar hosts live music most nights, while a lively jukebox, pool tables, and dart boards keep the atmosphere perpetually loud and festive. The fire pit in the crowded back patio will keep you warm. Smoking is allowed on the patio.

Channeling a British vibe is **Crown & Anchor** (150 W. Franklin St., 831/649-6496, http://crownandanchor.net, 11am-1:30am daily). With considerably more polish, it pours aged bourbons and vintage port, in addition to 20 beers on tap. Decorated in rich leather, gleaming nautical devices, and high-backed booths, the imperial atmosphere will impress. The outside patio is also a great place to relax, and the kitchen serves food until midnight.

You won't miss the **Cannery Row Brewing Company** (95 Prescott Ave., 831/643-2722, www.canneryrowbrewingcompany.com, 11:30am-midnight Sun.-Thurs., 11:30am-2am Fri.-Sat.), with its installation of giant kegs fixed to the side of its brick building. Boasting the second-largest selection of beer on tap in Northern California, this is a microbrew pub Cannery Row-style. The large, industrial-chic space is loud, often crowded, and serves a large and tasty selection of pub food. Live music, multiple TVs broadcasting sports, and outdoor seating with roaring fire pits add to mix.

One of the coolest small-rock venues in

California is the **Golden State Theatre** (417 Alvarado St., 831/649-1070, www.goldenstatetheatre.com). This beautiful theater has retained its 1920s-era Middle Eastern chic. It features relatively large acts like Ozomatli, Robert Cray, and Kenny Wayne Shepard. On other nights, the theater hosts touring musicals and National Geographic talks.

The **Monterey County Fairgrounds** has hosted some of the most significant music events in American music history. In 1967, the Monterey Pop Festival introduced Janis Joplin and Jimi Hendrix to the world. Today it remains home to one of the biggest music festivals in California, the **Monterey Jazz Festival** (2004 Fairground Rd., 831/373-3366, www.montereyjazzfestival.org). As the site of the longest-running jazz festival on earth, Monterey attracts top performers from around the world. Held each September—the best month for beautiful weather on Monterey Bay—this long weekend of amazing music can leave you happy for the whole year. Eight stages put up acts day and night, making it easy to either find your favorite stage and settle in for a long stay and multiple musicians or wander the length and breadth of the fairgrounds to sample the acts at each unique venue.

SPORTS AND RECREATION

Beaches

Much of the coastline between Cannery Row and Fisherman's Wharf is rocky, but a couple postage-stamp-size beaches are perfect places to get your toes wet or build a sand castle. **San Carlos Beach** (Cannery Row at Reese Ave.) is a protected little cove, with both sand and a grassy area upon which to throw down your picnic blanket. Even smaller is **McAbee Beach** (Cannery Row and Hoffman Ave.). Here you'll find tide pools as well as offshore kelp forests, where you may spy sea otters if you keep your eyes peeled.

The widest, flattest beach in Monterey can be found on the other side of the municipal pier at **Monterey State Beach** (Del Monte Ave. and Park Ave., 831/649-2836, www.parks.ca.gov), a 21-mile long network of beaches stretching from Monterey to north of Moss Landing. The two-mile stretch between Monterey and Seaside is a favorite with families and beachcombers.

The beach, particularly the section known as **Del Monte Beach** (just east of the pier), is also a draw for surfers who favor the long rollers, ideal for beginners. More seasoned surfers may want to continue north to

Explore the tide pools at Monterey Bay.

Marina State Beach (off Reservation Rd.), also within the Monterey State Beach system. Here, the crowds are thinner and the steady winds, strong riptides, and heavy currents create a moderate-to-challenging ride. Gear, rentals, and advice can be found at **On the Beach** (693 Lighthouse Ave., 831/646-9283, 10am-6pm Sun.-Thurs., 10am-7pm Fri.-Sat., surfboards $20 half day or $30 full day, bodyboards $5 half day or $10 full day, wetsuits $10 half day or $15 full day), a local surf shop since 1986.

In Pacific Grove, **Asilomar State Beach** (Sunset Dr. near Asilomar Ave., www.parks.ca.gov, 831/646-6440, sunrise-sunset daily) is a beautiful stretch of sand. Rocky, with tons of tide pools and plenty of wind, Asilomar is the place to go to look for tiny sea creatures or fly a kite. Continuous breakers also draw lots of surfers. Aside from the maintained trail down to the beach, don't expect anything in the way of comforts like bathrooms or picnic tables.

Scuba

The allure of Monterey is not just the beach, but what lies beyond. The Monterey Bay Marine Sanctuary, with its underwater canyons, kelp forests, and rich biological diversity, is a world-class place to dive. Accordingly, dozens of dive schools cluster in and around Monterey, and several companies lead trips from shore or by boat.

One of these is **Aquarius Dive Shop** (2040 Del Monte Ave., 831/375-1933, www.aquariusdivers.com, 9am-6pm Mon.-Fri., 7am-6pm Sat.-Sun.), which sits across from Monterey State Beach and offers everything you need to go diving out in Monterey Bay, including air and nitrox fills, equipment rental, certification courses, guided shore tours, and help booking a trip on a local dive boat. Aquarius works with four boats to create great trips for divers of all interests and ability levels. Call or check the website for current local dive conditions.

Near Cannery Row, **Bamboo Reef Enterprises** (614 Lighthouse Ave., 831/372-1685, http://bambooreef.com, 9am-6pm Mon.-Fri., 7am-6pm Sat.-Sun.) is a full dive shop and has equipment rentals, certification classes, and tours that leave from different points around the bay.

If you are an experienced diver, eager to explore the depths beyond the shore, the ***Monterey Express*** (831/915-0752, www.montereyexpress.com) will take you there. This popular dive boat knows all the great spots and has scheduled 3.5-hour trips (8am, 1:30pm Sat.-Sun., $90).

Kayaking

With all the focus on sustainable tourism in Monterey, coupled with the lovely recreation area formed by Monterey Bay, it's no wonder that sea kayaking is popular here. Whether you want to try paddling your first kayak, or you're an expert who needs to rent gear, you'll find a local outfit ready and willing to hook you up. Fisherman's Wharf is a great launch point with an easy paddle through the harbor. Once you're on the bay, passing over the kelp can slow the kayak, as paddles can become tangled. Dolphins in the distance and sea otters are the rewards: In spring, you are likely to spy otter mothers holding baby pups on their bellies.

To get outfitted, **Adventures by the Sea** (299 Cannery Row, 831/372-1807, www.adventuresbythesea.com, 9am-6pm daily winter, 9am-8pm daily summer, tours $60/person, rentals $30/day) rents kayaks for full days to let you choose your own route around the magnificent Monterey Bay kelp forest. If you're not confident enough to go off on your own, Adventures offers tours from Cannery Row. Your guide can tell you all about the wildlife you're seeing: harbor seals, sea otters, pelicans, seagulls, and maybe even a whale in the winter. The tour lasts about 2.5 hours, and the available tandem sit-on-top kayaks make it a great experience for school-age children. Adventures by the Sea also runs a tour of Stillwater Cove at Pebble Beach ($85). Reservations are recommended for all tours, but during the summer, the Cannery Row tour leaves regularly at 10am and 2pm, so you can stop by on a whim and see if there's a spot available.

Monterey Bay Kayaks (693 Del Monte Ave., 831/373-5357, www.montereybaykayaks.com, 8:30am-5pm daily winter, 8:30am-6:30pm daily summer, tours $55-85) specializes in tours of central Monterey and Elkhorn Slough. You can choose between open-deck and closed-deck tours, beginning tours (perfect for kids), romantic sunset or full moon paddles, or even long paddles designed for more experienced sea kayakers. If you prefer to rent a kayak and explore the bay or slough on your own, Monterey Bay Kayaks can help you out there, too. If you really get into it, you can also sign up for closed-deck sea kayaking classes to learn about safety, rescue techniques, tides, currents, and paddling techniques.

Fishing and Whale-Watching

Whales pass quite near the shores of Monterey year-round. Although you can sometimes even see them from the beach, boats can take you out for a closer look at the great beasts as they travel north and south. The area hosts many humpbacks, blue whales, and gray whales, plus the occasional killer whale, minke whale, and pod of dolphins. Bring your own binoculars for a better view, but the experienced boat captains will do all they can to get you as close as possible. Most tours last 2-3 hours and leave from Fisherman's Wharf, which is easy to get to and has ample parking. If you prefer not to rise with the sun, pick a tour that leaves in the afternoon.

Monterey Bay Whale Watch (84 Fisherman's Wharf, 831/375-4658, www.montereybaywhalewatch.com, half-day trips adults $41-49, children 4-12 $29-39, children 3 and under $15, full-day trips adults only $145) leaves right from an easy-to-find red building on Fisherman's Wharf and runs tours in every season. You must make a reservation in advance, even for regularly scheduled tours. Morning, afternoon, and all-day tours are available.

Another popular choice is ***Princess Monterey* Whale-Watching** (96 Fisherman's Wharf, 831/372-2203, www.montereywhalewatching.com). It prides itself on its knowledgeable guides and its comfortable, spacious vessels. The *Princess Monterey* offers morning and afternoon tours, and you can buy tickets online or by phone. Tours last 2.5 hours and cost $45.

If you'd rather catch fish than watch mammals, **Randy's Fishing and Whale-Watching Trips** (66 Fisherman's Wharf, 800/251-7440 or 831/372-7440, www.randysfishingtrips.com, fishing trips $75-300, whale-watching adults $40, children 12 and under $20) can take you out for salmon, halibut, albacore, mackerel, rock cod, flatfish, and even squid and Dungeness crab in season. They can also take you out for a whale-watching trip if that's your preference. Trips begin early in the morning and can last for several hours. You can bring your own food—catering is not provided—including a small cooler for your drinks. If you don't have a California fishing license, you can purchase a one-day license through Randy. Although you can try to walk up to the bright teal-painted shop at Fisherman's Wharf, it's best to get tickets for your trip in advance. Like his fishing trips, whale-watching excursions change with the seasons. Call or check the website for the current schedule.

Chris's Fishing Trips and Whale-Watching (48 Fisherman's Wharf, 831/372-5951, www.chrissfishing.com, fishing adults $75-80, children $50, whale-watching adults $37, children $22) offers both scheduled deep sea trips for cod and salmon in addition to boats for charter. You can get your license, bait, and tackle here, but it will cost extra. Chris also offers whale-watching trips. Tours depart daily at 10am and 1:30pm and last three hours.

Biking

The **Monterey Bay Coastal Recreation Trail** (http://monterey.org) is a two-lane bike trail that stretches 18 miles from Castroville to Pacific Grove. Relatively flat and hugging the coast much of the way, it is an easy and safe way to see the sights around Monterey. If you have left your bike at home, there are many bike outfits happy to rent you one. Located on Cannery Row, **Bay Bike** (585 Cannery Row, 831/655-2453, www.baybikes.com, 9am-5pm Sun.-Thurs., 9am-5:30pm Fri., 9am-6pm Sat.) has a wide selection of bike rentals from cruisers ($8/hour, $32/day), road bikes ($12/hour, $48/day), and tandem bikes ($16/hour, $48/day), plus kids' bikes, and all sorts of gear. Another choice with several locations is **Adventures by the Sea** (299 Cannery Row, 831/372-1807, http://adventuresbythesea.com, 9am-5pm Mon.-Fri., 9am-6pm Sat.-Sun.). They have cruisers ($8/hour, $30/day) and tandem bikes ($16/hour, $60/day), plus large family surreys ($20-30/hour, $120-180/day).

ACCOMMODATIONS

Under $100

The **Monterey Hostel** (778 Hawthorne St., 831/649-0375, http://montereyhostel.com, dorm $26-37, room $79-199) offers inexpensive accommodations within walking distance of the major attractions of Monterey. The kitchen serves a free pancake breakfast every morning, linens are included with your bed, and there are comfy, casual common spaces with couches and musical instruments. There's no laundry facility on-site, and the dorm rooms can be pretty crowded. But you can't beat the location for the prices.

$100-150

A cute, small, budget motel, the **Monterey Bay Lodge** (55 Camino Aguajito, 831/372-8057 or 800/558-1900, www.montereybaylodge.com, $119-199) brings a bit of the Côte d'Azur to Monterey. With small rooms decorated in classic yellows and blues and a sparkling pool with a fountain in the shallow end, the lodge makes a perfect base for budget-minded families.

If you're on a budget and all you're really looking for is a room with an ocean view, **Borg's Ocean Front Motel** (635 Ocean View Blvd., Pacific Grove, 831/375-2406, www.borgsoceanfrontmotel.com, $114-179) in Pacific Grove may be the place for you. This classic, independently owned economy hotel sits directly across the street from Lovers Point and the Monterey Bay Coastal Recreation Trail. There is little in the way of amenities aside from a clean bed to lay your head, but with this location and the money you'll save, who needs them?

$150-250

The **Colton Inn** (707 Pacific St., 831/649-6500, www.coltoninn.com, $149-199) offers a touch of class above that of a standard beach-town motel. Located in the midst of downtown Monterey, the inn has queen and king bedrooms that boast attractive fabrics, designer bathrooms, and pretty appointments. Although you'll find restaurants and historic adobe buildings adjacent to the Colton, expect to drive or take public transit to Cannery Row and the aquarium.

Down along bustling Alvarado Street, the **Monterey Hotel** (406 Alvarado St., 831/375-3184 or 800/966-6490, www.montereyhotel.com, $175-206) has welcomed guests since 1904. The 45 rooms reflect its Victorian heyday with carved details, antique furnishings, and floral prints. Continental breakfast is included in the room rates, and the convenient location makes it easy to explore Old Monterey on foot.

One of the better bargains can be found at the **Casa Munras Hotel and Spa** (700 Munras Ave., 831/375-2411, www.hotelcasamunras.com, $150-240), a large, updated downtown hotel with historical roots. Part of the hotel's original structure was built in 1824. Although the original adobe walls can been seen in one part of the hotel, the rest of it is decorated with a contemporary chic that feels right at home in Monterey. Book a spa treatment or dine at the Estéban Restaurant, which serves daily breakfast, lunch, and dinner, leaning heavily on Spanish cuisine.

Call well in advance to get a room at ★ **The Jabberwock** (598 Laine St., 831/372-4777, www.jabberwockinn.com, $199-309), a favorite with frequent visitors to Monterey. This Alice in Wonderland-themed B&B is both whimsical and elegant. Expect to find a copy of the namesake novel in your tastefully appointed room. Join the owners at their daily wine and cheese reception in the afternoon. Though located up a steep hill, the Jabberwock is within walking distance of Cannery Row and all its adjacent attractions (it's worth the extra exercise to avoid the cost and hassle of parking in the tourist lots).

In Pacific Grove, the ★ **Asilomar Conference Grounds** (800 Asilomar Ave., 888/635-5310, www.visitasilomar.com, $120-284), originally built in 1913 as a YWCA Leadership Camp, is a part of Asilomar State Beach and makes it a mission to be accessible to non-profit groups and individuals. Designed by Julia Morgan, Asilomar is feet away from one of the most beautiful beaches on the peninsula. With amenities like a heated pool, in-room massage, and an outdoor fire pit, where you can roast gourmet s'mores, Asilomar is spread out like a compound. To make the most of the location, book one of the Surf rooms, nestled in the dunes with a private deck. Be sure to enjoy Morgan's work by wandering around the grounds and poking your head in the chapel, Social Hall, and Merrill Hall.

Over $250

Monterey visitors looking for elegant accommodations love the ★ **Old Monterey Inn** (500 Martin St., 831/375-8284, www.oldmontereyinn.com, $199-379). The lovely old edifice stands in the midst of mature gardens that blossom all spring and summer. Inside the inn, the 10 rooms carry the garden motif, and all have private bathrooms and some have fireplaces. Additional amenities include a full breakfast (often served in the garden, or brought to your room) and a menu of spa treatments that can be enjoyed downstairs in the serene treatment room.

You'll pay handsomely to stay on the water, but it's worth it at the **Monterey Plaza Hotel & Spa** (400 Cannery Row, 831/646-1700 or 800/334-3999, www.montereyplazahotel.com, $219-369). This waterside luxury hotel has it all: a restaurant, café, and lounge, plus a spa, a private beach, room service, and upscale goodies. Rooms range from "budget" garden and Cannery Row-facing accommodations to ocean-view rooms with private balconies and huge suites that mimic a posh private apartment.

With the arrival of the **InterContinental Clement Monterey** (750 Cannery Row, 831/375-4500 or 877/834-3613, www.intercontinental.com, $299-419), Cannery Row went from being a loud tourist attraction to the center of Monterey's new wave of luxury. The minimal, sleek interior provides a serene respite from the outside noise. There are 110 rooms that hover over the water, while 98 sit across the street, adjoined by a covered walkway bridge. The rooms have chic appointments, but what you are really paying for is the location. There is also convenient access to the stellar restaurant and lounge, spa services, in-room yoga, and child care.

FOOD

Monterey is blessed with the bountiful sea and surrounding fertile fields, plus thousands of tourists visiting each year, which makes for a varied and high-quality dining scene. Prices climb the closer you get to Cannery Row and Fisherman's Wharf.

Cannery Row and Fisherman's Wharf

In Cannery Row, fill up for a day of sight-seeing, kayaking, and whale-watching at **First Awakenings** (125 Ocean View Blvd., Pacific Grove, 831/372-1125, www.firstawakenings.net, 7am-2pm Mon.-Fri., 7am-2:30pm Sat.-Sun., $8-12). Technically in Pacific Grove, First Awakenings is on the other side of the aquarium, with great views, but away from the hubbub. While you are relaxing on the patio with your first cup of coffee, your server will bring out enormous plates full of eggs, waffles, bacon, and sausage. If you're in the mood for lunch, this laid-back joint also has an extensive menu of burgers, sandwiches, and salads, and the portions are just as huge.

On a beautiful sunny morning, it's hard to pass up an espresso and a basket of home-baked beignets at the leafy outdoor patio of **Trailside Café** (550 Wave St., 831/649-8600, www.trailsidecafe.com, 8am-3pm Mon.-Fri., 8am-4pm Sat.-Sun., $10-14, cash only). Breakfast, filled with plenty of eggs Benedicts and blueberry pancakes, is served all day, as is lunch, with its assortment of gourmet salads, grilled sandwiches, and tasty entrées like mac and cheese, fish tacos, and linguini primavera. Extensive beer and wine lists accompany both menus, including pitchers of mimosas, which are also served all day.

The Sardine Factory (701 Wave St., 831/373-3775, www.sardinefactory.com, 5pm-9:30pm Sun.-Thurs., 5pm-10pm Fri.-Sat., $27-44) is *the* Monterey restaurant. Opened in 1968 on what was the then-rundown Cannery Row, The Sardine Factory saw the potential in this abandoned stretch of real estate. The restaurant has made an appearance in a Clint Eastwood movie and its signature abalone dish was served at President Reagan's inaugural dinner. Still an old-school joint, the Factory serves steak and Italian-inspired seafood dishes. The wine list has won awards, and for those who don't want to splurge on a whole dinner here, the lounge offers a scaled-down menu with plenty of stiff drinks, live music, and a chance to soak in the ambience.

The **C Restaurant & Bar** (750 Cannery Row, 831/375-4800, www.thecrestaurant-monterey.com, 6:30am-10pm daily, $32-58) represents Monterey's next generation of dining chic. On the ground floor of the InterContinental Clement Monterey, the restaurant has a minimalist décor, while the dishes explode with a variety of seafood, heritage vegetables, and high-quality meat and artisan cheese. The price for dinner may be out of reach for many, but locals know that the best place to grab a late lunch is on the patio overlooking the water. The bar menu, served on the patio from the beginning of lunch through late night, has a number of à la carte plates such as oysters, flatbreads, and burgers. Don't forget to order a glass of white wine or a high-wattage cocktail while you're at it.

Steinbeck would be shocked if he saw all the high-dollar joints filling his poetically soiled Cannery Row, but the one locals swear by is ★ **Bistro Moulin** (867 Wave St., 831/333-1200, www.bistromoulin.com, 5pm-9:30pm daily, $19-29). Owned and operated by a veteran of Carmel's Casanova, Bistro Moulin serves authentic French and Belgian cuisine in a small, intimate setting. Expect bountiful local seafood, continental-style vegetables, and a wine list that is both Californian and European.

Downtown

In general, downtown is where you will find more causal spots that are less expensive and less anxious to show what they've got. **Restaurant 1833** (500 Hartnell St., 831/643-1833, www.restaurant1833.com, 5:30pm-10pm Sun.-Thurs., 5:30pm-1am Fri.-Sat., $24-39) is the exception. Housed in the historical Stokes Adobe building built in 1833, it has had the foodie community buzzing since it opened in 2011. The food is amazing. The chef has a pedigree that includes time at Thomas Keller's Per Se, among others. His pairings of cactus pear and shrimp, charred octopus and romesco, and grilled sourdough, bone marrow, and horseradish hint at the next wave of California cuisine. However, Restaurant 1833 is really about the house. Maintaining the original rooms as dining rooms, the restaurant digs into history to create a romantic mood of Old Monterey. Cocktails are aged in barrels behind the bar, but some dining rooms verge on being *too* dark, and the music can be incongruously loud.

In Old Monterey is the mellow **Montrio Bistro** (414 Calle Principal, 831/648-8880, www.montrio.com, $16-31). Since 1995, this bistro has been serving sustainably sourced food prepared in a California-French style. Look for fun small bites like the duck popcorn, truffle tater tots, and legendary crab cakes, while the bigger dishes—seafood, steak, and pasta—won't disappoint. Montrio is located in the historic 1910 firehouse, but makes little of the ambience, letting you enjoy the decor quietly on your own.

When locals crave seafood, they head to the **Monterey Fish House** (2114 Del Monte Ave., 831/373-4647, 11:30am-2:30pm, 5pm-9:30pm Mon.-Fri., 5pm-9:30pm Sat.-Sun., $15-30). The tiny dining room serves cioppino, fish and chips, grilled oysters, and seafood pastas and entrées at almost-reasonable prices.

"Real Good" is what the "R.G." stands for in **R.G. Burgers** (570 Munras Ave., 831/372-4930, www.rgburgers.com, 11am-9pm Sun.-Thurs., 11am-10pm Fri.-Sat., $8-11). And they're not kidding. The menu offers dozens of burgers, dogs, sandwiches, sides, and salads that are cooked to big, juicy, American standards. Then there are the shakes: With over 20 selections, it is almost enough to make your brain freeze.

Since 1950, **Red's Donuts** (433 Alvarado St., 831/372-9761, www.redsdonuts.com) has anchored the end of Alvarado Street, pouring black cups of coffee and serving dangerously good donuts to locals. Once you've picked from the nearly 40 varieties available, head off to your adventure for the day or pull up a stool at the counter and take a load off.

Pacific Grove

The food in PG is unpretentious, reasonably affordable, and high quality. Undoubtedly, the best location is ★ **Beach House** (620 Ocean View Blvd., 831/375-2345, www.beachhousepg.com, 4pm-close daily, $13-34). At the only restaurant on Lovers Point, every seat is treated to fantastic views of the bay and the French-inspired food is equally rave-worthy. Prices are extremely reasonable, especially if you come in time for the Sunset Supper Menu. If seated by 5:30pm, you'll pay only $10 for your entrée (including the beloved bacon-wrapped meatloaf) and only $3 for wine or beer. This is one of the best deals on the bay.

For a special evening out, make a reservation at the excellent **Fandango** (223 17th St., 831/372-3456, http://fandangorestaurant.com, 11:30am-2:30pm, 5pm-close daily, $20-34). Housed in an old, rambling wood house, the European restaurant is known for the quality of its food (steaks, paella, duck à l'orange), the breadth of its wine selection, and its charming continental interior. Five dining rooms allow for maximum intimacy, giving diners the feeling of eating in a cozy European inn.

After visiting the aquarium, you will likely be picking your seafood selections carefully. At ★ **Passionfish** (701 Lighthouse Ave., 831/655-3311, www.passionfish.net, 5pm-close daily, $16-36) there is no need to worry. Since opening in 1997, Passionfish has been serving sustainable seafood. The menu changes constantly in accordance to what's available, but expect beautiful dishes such as basil-stuffed rainbow trout and shrimp mousseline ravioli. For those wanting something of the turf instead of the surf, grass-fed tenderloin and "spoonable" 12-hour lamb are equally rave-worthy.

INFORMATION AND SERVICES

Across from Monterey State Beach at Lake El Estero, the **El Estero Visitors Center** (401 Camino El Estero, www.seemonterey.com, 9am-6pm Mon.-Sat., 9am-5pm Sun. summer, 9am-5pm Mon.-Sat., 10am-4pm Sun. winter) is the local outlet of the Monterey Country Convention & Visitors Bureau. They have a wall dedicated to information and pamphlets about the area, as well as a helpful staff.

For medical needs, the **Community Hospital of the Monterey Peninsula** (23625 Holman Hwy., 831/624-5311, www.chomp.org) provides emergency services to the area.

TRANSPORTATION

Most visitors drive into Monterey via the scenic Highway 1. From San Francisco, the drive down the coast is 120 miles and takes a little less than 2.5 hours. Others opt for taking U.S. 101 south to Prunedale, jumping over to the coast on Highway 156. Highway 68 connects directly to U.S. 101 at Salinas for travelers coming from the south.

For a more leisurely ride, the *Coast Starlight* route of **Amtrak** (11 Station Pl., Salinas, 800/872-7245, www.amtrak.com) travels through Salinas daily. Amtrak provides a bus into downtown Monterey. Along Highway 68, you'll also find the **Monterey Peninsula Airport** (MRY, 200 Fred Kane Dr., 831/648-7000, www.montereyairport.com). The small but efficient airport has daily service by Alaska Airlines, American Airlines, Allegiant, United, and US Airways. The airport has several national car rental agencies.

Once you're in Monterey, the **Monterey-Salinas Transit** (888/678-2871, http://mst.org, $1.50-2.50) runs routes all over the Monterey Peninsula and into Salinas, Carmel, and Big Sur. Many of the lines connect at the **Monterey Transit Plaza,** conveniently located in downtown Monterey at the intersection of Munras Avenue and Alvarado Street. The agency also operates the free **Monterey Trolley** (10am-7pm daily), which makes stops all around historic Monterey and Cannery Row every 10-15 minutes.

PEBBLE BEACH

Polo grounds, manned gates, large estates shrouded in cypress and Spanish moss, and the odd Bentley in grocery store parking lots are all part of the scenery in Pebble Beach. Even the annual community events, like the **Concours d'Elegance** (www.pebblebeachconcours.net) and the celebrity-filled **AT&T Pebble Beach National Pro-Am** (www.pebblebeach.com), are rarified gatherings. But it is not just the air of exclusivity that is attractive. The land inside the gates of Pebble Beach is some of the area's most beautiful, making the price of admission worth it, at least once.

17-Mile Drive

If you're a first-time visitor to the Monterey area, **17-Mile Drive** ($10/vehicle) can introduce you to some of the most beautiful and representative land- and seascapes on the Central Coast. But don't get too excited yet—long ago, the powerful Pebble Beach Corporation realized what a precious commodity they held in this road, and began charging a toll. The good news is that when you pay your fee at the gatehouse, you'll get a map of the drive that describes the parks and sights that you will pass as you make your way along the winding coastal road. These include the much-photographed Lone Cypress (now held up by cables), the beaches of Spanish Bay, and Pebble Beach's golf courses, and some of the outsized mansions.

There are plenty of turnouts where you can stop to take photos of the stunning ocean and the iconic cypress trees. You can picnic at many of the beaches, most of which have basic restroom facilities and ample parking lots. The only food and gas to be had are at the Inn at Spanish Bay and the Lodge at Pebble Beach. If you're in a great hurry, you can get from one end of the 17-Mile Drive to the other in 20 minutes—but that would defeat the main purpose of taking the drive, which is to go slowly and stop often to enjoy the beauty of the area.

Golf Courses

There's no place for golfing in all of California like Pebble Beach. You can play courses trodden by the likes of Tiger Woods and actor Jack Nicholson, pause a moment before you putt to take in the sight of the stunning Pacific Ocean, and pay $300 or more for a single round of golf. Golf has been a major pastime on the peninsula since the late 19th century, and today avid golfers come from around the world to tee off in Pebble Beach. There are two highly exclusive private golf clubs, and six public courses, five of which are owned and operated by the Pebble Beach Company.

The crème de la crème is the **Pebble Beach Golf Links** (1700 17-Mile Dr., 800/877-0597, www.pebblebeach.com, 18-hole par 72, $495), which is both the priciest in the region and the most acclaimed. Visible from Carmel Beach, the manicured greens blanket Pebble Beach's southern coastline for stellar views and wide open spaces. In operation since 1919, it is home to the annual AT&T Pebble Beach National Pro-Am, and has hosted five U.S. Open Championships.

Spyglass Hill (1700 17-Mile Dr., Pebble Beach, 800/654-9300, www.pebblebeach.com, 18-hole par 72, $385) gets its moniker from the Robert Louis Stevenson novel *Treasure Island*. But don't be fooled—the holes on this beautiful course may be named for fictional characters, but that doesn't mean they're easy. Spyglass Hill boasts some of the most challenging play even in this golf course-laden region. Expect a few bogeys if you choose to play here, and tee off from the Championship level at your own (ego's) risk.

Links in Scotland may refer to sandy, windswept wasteland, but make no mistake about it—the wasteland here at the **Links at Spanish Bay** (2700 17-Mile Dr., 800/877-0597, www.pebblebeach.com, 18-hole par 72, $270) is extremely posh and scenic. Designed to evoke golf's early days in Scotland, the course is set amid native grasses, waterways, and the never-ending prevailing wind. There is even a bagpiper who closes the course each evening.

For those who don't want to fork over a chunk of their rent for a round of golf, the **Peter Hay Golf Course** (1700 17-Mile Dr., 831/622-8723, www.pebblebeach.com, adults $30, students 13-17 $10, children 12 and under free) is an excellent deal. You still get the views and the prestige of teeing off in Pebble Beach but at a fraction of the cost. Plus, it is a 9-hole par-3 course, making it ideal for kids and beginners.

Accommodations and Food

The digs in Pebble Beach are almost entirely run by the Pebble Beach Company and so are just as exclusive as its fairways. The only restaurants you will find are attached to the high-priced hotels. If you're willing to pay for it, the food, service, and accommodations stand nothing short of excellent.

Sitting at the edge of a secluded bay, the **Inn at Spanish Bay** (2700 17-Mile Dr., 831/647-7500 or 800/877-0597, www.pebblebeach.com, $650-975) has 269 rooms and suites, each with its own fireplace and modern decor. The large hotel has large outdoor fire pits to enjoy the evening, a health club, retail area, and an award-winning golf course. On-site, you'll also find three restaurants and two lounges that serve cocktails and bar food: **Peppoli at Pebble Beach** (831/647-7433, 6pm-10pm daily, $25-65) serves northern Italian food in a fine-dining setting overlooking the bay.

Spyglass Hill golf course

Hawaiian fusion is not what you might expect in Pebble Beach, but **Roy's at Pebble Beach** (831/647-7423, 5:30pm-10pm daily, $18-45) serves a variety of fresh sushi and elaborate meat dishes in a relaxed casual atmosphere. Catch the game and grab a beer and burger at **Sticks** (831/647-7470, 6:30am-4pm, 5pm-8pm daily, $10-25), the resort's version of a sports bar. Late-night bites can be found at **Traps** (831/647-7210, 5:30pm-midnight daily, $15-25).

Since 1919, the **Lodge at Pebble Beach** (1700 17-Mile Dr., www.pebblebeach.com, 831/647-7500 or 800/877-0597, $765-980) has accommodated the well-heeled. The 161 modern rooms have fireplaces and lovely views of the ocean and the golf course. The lodge is Pebble Beach's only pet-friendly hotel (extra $70 per night). It is also the hub of Pebble Beach, and here you'll find the greatest variety of shopping, activities, and food. Inside the lodge are four restaurants and one bar. For breakfast and lunch, the place to go is the sunny **Gallery Café** (831/625-8577, 6am-2pm daily, $13-21) where you'll find standard breakfast dishes and a slew of American lunch standards. If you're looking for hipster fare (think pork belly, mac and cheese, duck-fat potatoes, and retro-fresh cocktails), ★ **The Bench** (800/877-0597, 11am-10pm daily, $11-31) overlooks the 18th Hole, one of the most iconic spots in Pebble Beach. The **Stillwater Bar & Grill** (831/625-8524, $39-68) serves seafood in a white tablecloth setting, in addition to a slightly more casual (but still expensive) breakfast and lunch.

Transportation

There are five entry gates to Pebble Beach. The main ones are the **Highway 1 Gate** at the intersection of Highways 1 and 68 west; the **Carmel Gate** (N. San Antonio Ave. and 2nd Ave.); and the **Sunset Gate** (Sunset Dr./Hwy. 68 and 17-Mile Dr.) in Pacific Grove. Once you're inside, stick to 17-Mile Drive, as the roads in the forest wind randomly and are perfect for getting lost. It costs $10 to drive in, which is reimbursed if you are a guest at one of the lodges or spend at least $25 at one of the restaurants, not a difficult feat. Pebble Beach is very easy to navigate on bike; bicyclists don't have to pay the toll.

Inland Monterey County

Twenty miles east of the sparkling waters of Monterey Bay, eastern Monterey County is hard at work, growing the lettuce for our salads, the strawberries for our ice cream, and tomatoes for our pasta sauce. Nicknamed the "Salad Bowl of the World," the region, with its wide open spaces, fertile soil, and mild climate, was also the site of thriving Californio (Spanish-Californians) communities during the Mexican period. Today the towns are small, mostly agricultural, and are home to large Latino populations.

SAN JUAN BAUTISTA

To touch a piece of early California's past, visit romantic San Juan Bautista. With less than 2,000 residents, the small town has one of the best historic parks in the state and a charming independent main street, and it's surrounded by the fertile fields and bucolic rolling hills that were once a part of San Justo Rancho, a 34,000-acre 1839 Mexican land grant.

Mission San Juan Bautista

Founded in 1797, the **Mission San Juan Bautista** (406 2nd St., 831/623-4528, http://oldmissionsjb.org, 9:30am-4:30pm daily) was the 15th in the chain, and one of California's richest missions. It also has the dubious distinction of having one of the largest Native American populations, which at one point reached 1,200 people. Taken and held largely by force, this mix of Mutsun and Yokut people suffered under the yoke of hard labor and succumbed to many waves of disease. A mass graveyard beside the mission is where an estimated 4,000-5,000 souls are buried.

The mission holds mass at 8am Monday-Friday, 5pm Saturday, and 8:30am and 10am on Sunday. Visitors are welcome to stroll the grounds and explore many of the buildings. There is a small museum and gift shop, as well as daily tours (adults $4, seniors $3, children 5 and over $2, under 5 free).

★ San Juan Bautista State Historic Park

Adjoining the mission is the wonderful **San Juan Bautista State Historic Park** (2nd St. at Washington and Mariposa Sts., 831/623-4881, www.parks.ca.gov, 10am-4:30pm daily). Centered around the large plaza, the park is home to many of the original 19th-century wood and adobe buildings that made up the once-largest town in Central California. Poke your head into a fashionable period parlor at the **Plaza Hall-Zanetta House.** Explore the grounds around the 1841 **Castro-Breen Adobe.** Learn more about San Juan Bautista's history in the museum located in the adobe **Plaza Hotel.** The best exhibit is found at the **Plaza Stables and Blacksmith Shop,** a perfectly preserved blacksmith shop complete with a full set of tools. Stagecoaches, a fire wagon, and carriages are also on display.

Try to time your visit during one of the **Living History Days** (11am-4pm first Sat. of every month), when docents dress in period costumes, giving a taste what life was like in this Californio (Spanish-Californian) town. A more unusual look at the park can be had at ***Vertigo* Day at the Park** (tour $15, dinner $35, check website for dates). You'll get a tour of the film's shooting locations, dinner catered by a local Mexican restaurant, and an outdoor showing of *Vertigo,* Hitchcock's classic 1957 film about a woman who could not escape her Californio past.

Fremont Peak State Park

History was also made at the top of **Fremont Peak State Park** (end of San Juan Canyon Rd., 831/623-4526, www.parks.ca.gov, 8am-sunset daily), as the U.S. Army captain John C. Fremont first hoisted the American flag over the bustling town of San Juan Bautista in 1846. Fremont picked the perfect place to escalate tensions between the United States and Mexico, as Fremont Peak, at 3,169 feet, is one of the tallest mountains around. From it, on a clear day, you can see Monterey Bay, Salinas Valley, the three nearby mountain

San Juan Bautista State Historic Park

ranges, and, if you're lucky, the snow-capped Sierra Nevada. From the parking lot, the peak is accessible by the relatively easy one-mile **Fremont Peak Trail.**

The views at night are not bad, either. The height and isolation of Fremont Peak gives viewers a perfect view of the solar system without the light pollution of urban centers. To make the most of it, the **Fremont Peak Observatory** (831/623-2465, www.fpoa.net, 8pm-midnight Sat. Apr.-Oct.) hosts viewings of the night sky through its 30-inch diameter telescope. The program starts with a 30-minute talk, followed by viewings, plus plenty of discussion. It's a casual affair and reservations are not required. Visit their website for a schedule, which includes rare solar viewings.

Food

The ideal lunch spot in San Juan Bautista is **Jardines de San Juan** (115 3rd St., 831/623-4466, www.jardinesrestaurant.com, 11:30am-9pm Sun.-Thurs., 11:30am-10pm Fri.-Sat., $7-16). The northern Mexican restaurant serves classic comfort dishes in a flower-filled courtyard and charming historic dining room. With an excellent beer, wine, and cocktail menu, which includes margaritas, mojitos, and sangria, it's easy to spend the whole afternoon here, lounging in the San Juan Bautista sun.

Although San Juan Bautista is not known for its Basque community, the food and atmosphere at **Basque Matxian Etxea Restaurant** (206 4th St., 831/623-4472, 4pm-9pm Wed.-Thurs., noon-9pm Fri.-Sat., 1pm-9pm Sun., $14-22) fits right in. Traditional tapas and entrées like oxtail stew, *bacalao,* and paella fill the menu, while the ambience is homey and casual.

Getting There

San Juan Bautista is located off Highway 156, three miles east of the intersection with U.S. 101. From San Francisco, the 93-mile trip takes 1.5 hours. From Monterey, 33 miles away, it takes 40 minutes. Once you reach San Juan Bautista, turn left at the light onto the Alameda. It will take you directly to the historic downtown.

SALINAS

East of Eden, Steinbeck's 1952 novel, made a star out of hard-scrabble Salinas. The working-class hub of the region, Salinas is surrounded by fertile fields, while in town, big-rig truck yards, packing plants, and the business center of industrial agriculture keep everything humming. Over the years, there has been an effort to revitalize the city's historic downtown (christened Oldtown) and celebrate the rich heritage of generations of hardworking farmers. But make no mistake about it: Salinas is still a tough town, just as it was in Steinbeck's day.

National Steinbeck Center

Standing at the entrance of Salinas's historic Main Street is the **National Steinbeck Center** (1 Main St., 831/775-4721, www.steinbeck.org, 10am-5pm daily, adults $15, seniors and students $9, students 13-17 $8, children 6-12 $6, children under 6 free). You'll learn through engaging, artistic, and interactive displays about the life of John Steinbeck, his body of work, which includes *Cannery Row, Of Mice and Men, East of Eden, Tortilla Flat,* and *The Grapes of Wrath*, and the impact his work had on American culture. The museum showcases Salinas Valley, as well as the lives of its workers, a cause which Steinbeck was passionate about.

Mazda Raceway Laguna Seca

If you're feeling the need for speed, you can get lots of it at the **Mazda Raceway Laguna Seca** (1021 Monterey-Salinas Hwy., 831/242-8201, www.mazdaraceway.com), one of the country's premier road-racing venues. Here you can see historic auto races, superbikes, speed festivals, and an array of Grand Prix events. The major racing season runs May-October. In addition to big events, Laguna Seca hosts innumerable auto clubs and small sports car and stock car races.

Food

Near the Steinbeck Center in Oldtown Salinas, there are a number of good places to grab a casual bite to eat. Across the street from the Steinbeck Center, **XL Taproom** (127 Main St., 831/754-2337, 4pm-10pm Mon.-Wed., 4pm-midnight Thurs.-Fri., 2pm-midnight Sat., 2pm-10pm Sun.) is the hipster take on Salinas. The exposed beam and brick interior lacks a designer's polish, giving an old-time Salinas vibe. Bartenders, serving a wide variety of handcrafted beer, are friendly and will happily chat about their selections, even offering a taste or two. They don't serve food, but the Mexican joint next door will deliver.

For a quick bite to take with you on the road, the place to go is **Farm Fresh Deli Café** (145 Main St., 831/422-2777, 11am-7pm Mon.-Thurs., 11am-9pm Fri.-Sat., $8). Locals rave about the oversized sandwiches, wraps, and salads. You can also grab a fresh smoothie or frozen yogurt to cool down on hot summer day.

Salinas has a number of good taquerias. Across from the train station, **El Charrito** (122 W. Market St., 831/424-9446, www.elcharritoburrito.com, 6am-7pm Mon.-Sat., 7am-6pm Sun., $8) serves big burritos wrapped in homemade tortillas, tamales, chiles rellenos, fish tacos, and, for dessert, dangerously good churros. The taqueria is in the back of the busy El Charrito Market, where the family-owned business sells its handmade tortillas, masa, salsas, fresh meats, and other groceries. Expect a line at lunch.

Salinas is lucky to have several highly regarded Japanese restaurants. One of the favorites is the downtown **KoKoRo Sushi** (36 W. Galiban St., 831/424-7553, 11am-2pm, 5pm-9pm Mon.-Thurs., 11am-2pm, 5pm-9:30pm Fri.-Sat., $10-30). This tiny restaurant is known for its wide selection of fresh rolls, grilled meats, noodles, and bento box specials. The sushi entrées, with various *nigiri,* sashimi, and roll combos, are a great deal, while the Steinbeck roll (asparagus, cream cheese, and *unagi*) is a tasty nod to the area. Service can be slow, so only go if you have time to spare.

Information and Services

To better explore Salinas, stop by the **California Welcome Center** (1213 N. Davis Rd., 831/757-8687, www.visitcalifornia.com, 9am-5pm daily). The state visitors center not only has information about the Central Coast, but the staff, largely Salinas locals, will tell you the best places to visit in their city.

Transportation

Salinas sits on U.S. 101, nearly two hours and a little over 100 miles south of San Francisco. It is 20 miles and nearly 30 minutes from Monterey via Highway 68, which runs through Salinas, just south of Oldtown. If you are coming south on Highway 1, but not going to the Monterey Peninsula, Highway 183 starts in Castroville, 11 miles north of Monterey, and cuts east through the valley's agricultural fields to Salinas.

Train lovers will delight at the old west **Amtrak station** (11 Station Pl., 800/872-7245, www.amtrak.com). The *Coast Starlight* train travels through Salinas daily, and Amtrak provides a bus into downtown Monterey.

Once you're in Salinas, stick to Oldtown. It's easy to get lost in the sprawling town, and some neighborhoods are a bit dodgy. Oldtown is located between Monterey and Salinas Streets and John and Main Streets. There are U.S. 101 exits at John and Main Streets.

★ Pinnacles National Park

East of the Salinas Valley, in the parched hills of the Galiban Mountains, **Pinnacles National Park** (5000 Hwy. 146, Paicines, 831/389-4486, www.nps.gov/pinn, $10) attracts hikers, rock climbers, cave explorers, and birders. True to its name, the 26,000-acre park is studded with huge rock formations jutting up into the sky. The unusual geography is thanks to an ancient volcano that erupted 26 million years ago. It was then split in two and moved 200 miles north by the San Andreas

Pinnacles National Park

Fault. Today the park teems with life. Coyotes, bobcats, and mountain lions call the park home, as do California condors, hawks, and prairie and peregrine falcons. Thirteen species of bats live in talus caves, and the park has roughly 400 different species of bees, more than anywhere else on earth.

The park has two entrances and no road that connects them. Plenty of hiking trails can be found at both entrances. The park is generally warm and dry throughout the year and blazing hot in the summer. It is essential to bring plenty of water. In western Pinnacles, the **Balconies Cliffs-Cave Loop** (2.4-miles round-trip, easy to moderate) passes through the famous caves and is a great introduction to the area. To see more of the park, make this trail into a loop by taking **High Peaks Trail to Balconies Cave Loop** (8.4 miles, strenuous). You'll get into the heart of the park, but be sure to start with the High Peaks Trail, as the elevation gain is significantly easier. Not only will you need to take a flashlight to navigate through the caves, it is important to check and see if they are open. The caves can close because of high water from rain or when bat colonies are raising their young, generally from mid-May through mid-July.

More trails can be found at the east end of the park. You'll get a bit of everything, including a reservoir, on the **Moses Spring to Rim Trail Loop** (2.2 miles, moderate). After climbing up the peaks, you'll enjoy the meadows and shade of sycamore, buckeye, and oak trees on the **High Peaks to Bear Gulch Loop** (6.7 miles, strenuous). Most of the park's best **rock climbing** can be found at the east end of the park, where there are beginning to advanced routes. For more information, visit **Friends of Pinnacles** (www.pinnacles.org), an organization dedicated to climbing at Pinnacles.

Accommodations

The **Pinnacles Campground** (831/389-4538, reservations 877/444-6777 or www.recreation.gov, tents $23, RVs $36) is located at the east entrance and has 99 tent sites, 36 RV sites, and 14 group sites. Most are shaded by oaks and all come with a picnic table, fire ring, and bathrooms, with showers nearby. To accommodate RVs, there is a dump station, and all sites have electrical hook ups. A general store helps with any forgotten food or necessities.

If you plan on hiking in the west side of the park and want a soft bed to sleep in afterward, **Inn at the Pinnacles** (32025 Stonewall Canyon Rd., 831/678-2400, www.innatthepinnacles.com, $235-260) is roughly between Soledad and Pinnacles off Highway 146. Surrounded by vineyards deep in the Galiban Mountains, you'll enjoy the surroundings of Pinnacles with creature comforts. There are six suites at the inn, each equipped with a refrigerator, microwave, and gas grill. The inn also has a whirlpool tub and gas fireplace.

Getting There

Pinnacles has two entrances, but no road that connects them, making the drive from one to the other a two-hour endeavor. To reach the **east entrance** from the north, take

U.S. 101 to Highway 25 through the town of Hollister. After another 30 miles, turn right on Highway 146 to the park entrance, which is not much farther. From San Francisco, the trip is 130 miles and takes nearly 2.5 hours. From Monterey, it is 75 miles and 1.5 hours.

For the **west entrance,** continue south on U.S. 101, past Salinas to Highway 146 in Soledad. Take Highway 146 east for a very slow 14 miles. There are no services at this entrance. The trip from San Francisco is a 2.5-hour, 145-mile drive. From Monterey, via Highway 68, it is 60 miles, taking a little over an hour.

Carmel

Carmel's landscape is divided into three distinct parts: Carmel-by-the-Sea, Carmel Valley, and the Carmel Highlands. The village of Carmel-by-the-Sea sits above white sand beaches, nestled in a forest of pine and cypress. The streets are filled with storybook cottages, art galleries, and stately old hotels. The yin to its yang is Carmel Valley, the long east-west valley carved by the Carmel River. Here, forest gives way to sunbaked land, and tasting rooms replace galleries. There are plenty of outdoor activities to take advantage of the perfect weather, and the wineries and restaurants clustered in tiny Carmel Valley Village offer the ideal repose. Both Carmel-by-the-Sea and Carmel Valley residents love dogs. Your pooch is welcome at many establishments, and a number of stores and restaurants offer doggie treats and keep fresh water outside for the canine set.

About five miles south of town on the way to Big Sur, the Carmel Highlands stand perched above the rich Carmel Bay. The jewel of this area is the splendid Point Lobos State Natural Reserve. Farther south, several upscale resorts take full advantage of the views.

CARMEL-BY-THE-SEA

When most Californians talk about Carmel, they mean Carmel-by-the-Sea. Beginning as an artist colony in the early 20th century, the picturesque cove drew artists, painters, writers, and dancers, who built cheap cottages and pursued their art. Outdoor theater, literary salons, and scores of paintings characterized Carmel in its heyday. But now the secret is out, and the hamlet is not so cheap anymore. Crowds have replaced artists, and many galleries hawk standard seascapes in place of truly inspired work. However, Carmel remains a magical place. Sparkling beaches, winding streets with neither sidewalks nor streetlights, friendly shops, and quaint restaurants still make the mood and are capable of moving even the most hardened cynic.

If you are wondering where the business gets done in Carmel, banks, office buildings, and large supermarkets sit at what locals call the "mouth of the valley." At the intersection of Carmel Valley Road, Rio Road, and Highway 1 are two major developments, the Barnyard and the Crossroads. These have additional shops, restaurants, and cafés, should the abundance in town not be enough.

SIGHTS

★ Carmel Mission

The **Carmel Mission** (3080 Rio Rd., 831/624-1271, www.carmelmission.org, 9:30am-7pm daily, adults $6.50, seniors $4, children 7-18 $2, children under 7 free), formally called the San Carlos Borromeo de Carmelo Mission, was Father Junípero Serra's personal favorite among his California mission churches. He lived, worked, and eventually died here, and visitors today can see a replica of his cell. A working Catholic parish remains part of the complex, so be respectful when taking the self-guided tour. The Carmel Mission has a small memorial museum in a building off the second courtyard, but exhibits run through many of the buildings, showing a small slice of the lives of the

Carmel

17-MILE DRIVE
Pebble Beach Golf Course
CARMEL WAY
1ST AVE
2ND AVE
3RD AVE
4TH AVE
5TH AVE
6TH AVE
OCEAN AVE
7TH AVE
8TH AVE
9TH AVE
10TH AVE
11TH AVE
12TH AVE
13TH AVE
SANTA LUCIA AVE
14TH AVE
15TH AVE
WALKER AVE
16TH AVE
17TH AVE
N SAN ANTONIO AVE
N CARMELO ST
N CAMINO REAL
LOPEZ AVE
PALOU AVE
N CASANOVA ST
MONTE VERDE ST
LINCOLN ST
DOLORES ST
SAN CARLOS ST
MISSION ST
JUNIPERO ST
TORRES ST
SANTA FE ST
SANTA RITA ST
MOUNTAIN VIEW AVE
VIZCAINO AVE
SCENIC RD
SAN ANTONIO AVE
CARMELO ST
CAMINO REAL
CASANOVA ST
RIO RD
FRANCISCAN WAY
LASUEN DR
BAY VIEW AVE
ISABELLA AVE
VALLEY VIEW AVE
STEWART WAY
OCEAN VIEW AVE
RIO AVE
CASANOVA
CARMEL VISITOR CENTER
KATY'S PLACE
STARLIGHT 65 ROOFTOP TERRACE AT VESUVIO
CARMEL ART ASSOCIATION
EM LE'S
AKAONI
BRUNO'S MARKET
LOBOS LODGE
To CA-1
CARMEL BEACH
CARMEL VALLEY ROASTING COMPANY
DAMETRA CAFÉ
CARMEL BAY COMPANY
SALUMERIA LUCA
TUCK BOX
BICYCLETTE
Carmel Plaza
CYPRESS INN
THE FOREST THEATER
LA PLAYA HOTEL
GOLDEN BOUGH PLAHOUSE
SUNSET CENTER
Carmel Bay
Mission Trail Park
CARMEL MISSION
MISSION RANCH
RESTAURANT AT MISSION RANCH
Carmel River State Beach
0
500 yds
0
500 m
© AVALON TRAVEL

18th- and 19th-century friars. The highlight of the complex is the church, with its gilded altar front, its shrine to the Virgin Mary, the grave of Father Serra, and ancillary chapel dedicated to the memory of Father Serra. Round out your visit by walking out to the gardens to admire the flowers and fountains and to read the grave markers in the small cemetery.

Tor House

When poet Robinson Jeffers began hauling great granite boulders up from the beach to this spot in 1919, Carmel was young and Carmel Point was a barren and treeless outcropping. Jeffers named the family home he built **Tor House** (26304 Ocean View Ave., 831/624-1813, www.torhouse.org, tours hourly 10am-3pm Fri.-Sat., adults $10, students 12 and over $5, children under 12 not permitted) for its rocky location. A year later he began construction on Hawk Tower, named for a hawk that he saw daily as he built the Irish-style stone structure. It was here where Jeffers wrote his most enduring work. Filled with celebrations of nature's truths and denunciation of man's many follies, Jeffers in his time was known as "the dark prince of poetry," and later hailed as one of America's earliest environmental poets.

Since then, Carmel has grown up, as have the towering cypress trees on Carmel Point, but Tor House remains, as if preserved in amber. Two days a week, visitors can tour the stone cottage and tower, stroll the lush English garden, and imagine what it was like to live here surrounded only by the forest and the pounding surf, before electricity (installed in 1949), during the innocent and dark romance of this poetic era.

Carmel Beach

The mile-long **Carmel Beach** (Ocean Ave. and Scenic Rd., 831/620-2000, 6am-10pm daily) lies at the foot of Ocean Avenue and is known for its sparkly white sand that squeaks beneath your feet. Its aqua-blue waters teem with life, including sea otters, dolphins, surfers, and body boarders. There is a price for the beauty, though, as the beach is often windy and rarely offers a goose-pimple-free day of sunbathing. Dogs and small bonfires are allowed on the beach south of 10th Avenue. You can park at a relatively large lot at the base of Ocean Avenue or along the one-way Scenic Road, which also has a pleasant footpath above the beach to catch the views without getting your shoes sandy.

Carmel Mission

Carmel River State Beach

Around the point from Carmel Beach is **Carmel River State Beach** (Scenic Rd. and Carmelo St., 831/649-2836, www.parks.ca.gov, sunrise-sunset daily, free). Sheltered from the wind and with stellar views of Point Lobos, this is a favorite with families. Cutting though the beach is the Carmel River, which makes a tidy lagoon, home to a diverse community of shore birds and perfect for kids to wade and swim in its warm water. The beach is less well known than the popular Carmel Beach, making it the less crowded option on the rare hot and sunny day.

ENTERTAINMENT AND EVENTS

Carmel's nightlife has long consisted of a good dinner out and an evening of classical music or theater. Recently, some bars have entered the scene (live music in bars was illegal until 2006), but expect last call to be around 10pm or 11pm. To watch the game or groove to some live music, **Jack London's Bar & Grill** (Dolores St. and 5th Ave., 831/624-2336, 11:30am-midnight daily) is the place. Big-screen TVs tuned to the games of the day, live blues each Friday, and music on the weekends keep this place hopping, but, being Carmel, the interior is all dark wood, fancy ceiling, and quiet elegance. It's also no surprise that Jack London's has a full menu of fancier-than-average bar food and a wine list that would make a high-end restaurant proud. If you've brought your favorite canine companion, you'll find a welcoming seat outside on the patio, where the full menu is served.

According to many, the best happy hour can be found at the **Starlight 65 Rooftop Terrace at Vesuvio** (Junipero St. and 6th Ave., 831/626-7373, 4pm-11pm daily). From 4pm to 6pm you'll find $5 cocktails and half off the bar menu. The terrace, with small wood fires, throw blankets, and cozy seats beneath tiny white lights, makes for a lovely pre-dinner drink or a hip evening out.

Some of the biggest foodies in town will recommend a drink at **Terry's Lounge** (Lincoln St. and 7th St., 831/624-3871, noon-11pm Sun.-Thurs., noon-midnight Fri.-Sat.) at the Cypress Inn as the quintessential Carmel cocktail. Originally opening its doors in 1929, the hotel retains the cool elegance of the era, with a drink menu filled with historical cocktails that pack a punch. The Cypress Inn is co-owned by actress Doris Day, a Carmel local and avid animal rights advocate. Not

Carmel River State Beach

only will you see touches of Hollywood history throughout the bar, you can also bet that your pooch will be as welcome are you are.

To get back to Carmel's roots, see a play at the historical **Forest Theater** (Mountain View St. and Santa Rita St., 831/626-1681, www.foresttheaterguild.org). Built in 1910, this outdoor theater is surrounded by towering pine trees and is home to the annual **Carmel Shakespeare Festival.** Performed by the **Pacific Repertory Theater** (831/622-0100, www.pacrep.org, adults $20-42, students $10-16, children 12 and under $8), this short showing of Shakespeare is good enough to draw the notice of Bay Area theater buffs. Pac, as the locals know it, is the only professional theater company on the Monterey Peninsula and performs primarily at **Golden Bough Playhouse** (Monte Verde St. and 8th Ave.) and the tiny **Circle Theater** (Casanova St. between 8th and 9th Aves.), within the Golden Bough complex. The company also performs fun productions like *The Full Monty* and heavy hitters like Patrick Shanley's *Doubt.*

One of the most prestigious festivals in Northern California is the **Carmel Bach Festival** (831/624-1521, www.bachfestival.org). For two weeks each July, Carmel-by-the-Sea and its surrounding towns host dozens of classical concerts. Naturally the works of J. S. Bach are featured, but you can also hear renditions of Mozart, Vivaldi, Handel, and other heavyweights of Bach's era. Choose between big concerts in major venues or intimate performances in smaller spaces, with only a small audience between you and the beautiful music. Concerts and recitals take place every day of the week, so budget-conscious music lovers can enjoy cheaper shows in the middle of the week.

SHOPPING

The quaint streets of Carmel-by-the-Sea cry out to shoppers. The heart of downtown Carmel lies along Ocean Avenue between Junipero and Monte Verde Streets. Here, you'll find a noteworthy selection of high-end apparel, jewelers, sweet shops, specialty soap and beauty care boutiques, and a couple excellent toy stores. To find upmarket chains, be sure to stop at the **Carmel Plaza** (Mission St. and Ocean Ave., 831/624-1385, http://carmelplaza.com, 10am-6pm Mon.-Sat., 11am-5pm Sun.,) where stores like Tiffany &Co., Anthropologie, and Kate Spade fill the three-story open air mall. Farther down Ocean Avenue, the **Carmel Bay Company** (Ocean Ave. and Lincoln St., 831/624-3868, 10am-5pm daily) is a two-story emporium that has everything from cookware and delicate decorative candles to side-splitting coffee table books, plus a fine selection of hats, clothes, and scarves upstairs. It is the ideal place to get lost while looking for a gift or a special souvenir.

For many, Carmel means art galleries. Collections of landscapes, modern art, photography, sculpture, and jewelry can be found throughout downtown Carmel. You'll find many galleries along Ocean Avenue, but the greatest concentration is on Dolores Street between 5th and 7th Avenues and on Mission Street between Ocean Avenue and 5th Avenue. If you only want to make one stop, be sure it's at the **Carmel Art Association** (Dolores St. between 5th and 6th Aves., 831/624-6176, www.carmelart.org, 10am-5pm daily). The oldest gallery in Carmel is operated by a non-profit that only shows artists local to the Monterey Peninsula. Housed in a historical building, the gallery is broken up into multiple galleries, which helps showcase the diverse, rotating collection and gives it a museum-like quality.

ACCOMMODATIONS

It's virtually impossible to walk 10 feet without passing a unique Carmel inn or hotel. You'll find a collection of cottages tucked in a stand of oaks down an unlit neighborhood street, stately old hotels dating from the 1920s, and sprawling modern hotels that feature suites, private decks, and kitchenettes. None of the options are chains, but none are cheap, either.

The best deals are at the rambling and pink **Hofsas House** (San Carlos St. and 3rd Ave., 831/624-2745, www.hofsashouse.com, $125-160). Evoking a quaint inn set in the

Netherlands countryside, the Hofsas House sits in a quiet neighborhood within easy walking distance of downtown Carmel. Rooms in the multi-story structure are spacious, and amenities include a year-round heated swimming pool, two dry saunas, and off-street parking, a rarity in Carmel. Get an ocean-view room with a patio or balcony, buy a bottle of wine, and spend some time sitting outside.

Pink **La Playa Hotel** (Camino Real and 8th Ave., 831/293-6100 or 800/582-8900, www.laplayahotel.com, $249-399) is considered by many to be "Grande Dame of Carmel." Built in 1905 for a member of the Ghirardelli family, the hotel has a Mediterranean elegance and an intimate feel, despite its 75 rooms. It's only blocks from the beach and boasts manicured gardens, a giant outdoor chess set, and a secluded pool. Splurge for an ocean-view room to experience the best of the hotel. Indulge in the complimentary champagne breakfast, with a bounty of pastries, hot egg dishes, fruit, and an expansive waffle bar, out on the patio.

The **Cypress Inn** (Lincoln St. and 7th St., 831/624-3871 or 800/443-7443, www.cypress-inn.com, $249-549) competes with La Playa for the most charm and luxury. Built in the Mediterranean style of the day, it features wrought iron, box-beam ceilings, and coved windows. You'll also find a touch of old Hollywood: Doris Day is a co-owner. Day is a well-known animal rights advocate, and her hotel is one of the most pet-friendly around.

Owned since 1986 by Clint Eastwood, ★ **Mission Ranch** (26270 Dolores St., 831/624-6436 or 800/538-8221, www.missionranchcarmel.com, $125-300) sits on 22 acres (some with grazing sheep) and has 31 rooms spread over 10 buildings, a well-respected restaurant, and spectacular views of Point Lobos and River Beach. There are plenty of rooms where you can spend a chunk of your rent payment, but the ranch also offers a number of "economy rooms" in the Main Barn and Farmhouse. Either way, your stay will be graced with historical charm, great views, and a quiet setting.

FOOD

There is a surplus of great food in Carmel. The king of Carmel dining is **Casanova** (5th Ave. and Mission St., 831/625-0501, 11:30am-3pm, 5pm-10pm Sun.-Thurs., 11:30am-3pm, 5pm-10:30pm Fri.-Sat., $22-49). The rebuilt old house is designed after a Belgian farmhouse with low ceilings and intimate dining rooms. There is also a covered terrace and a heated patio. The cuisine is rustic French-Italian and is made in-house, including all the pasta and bread. Reservations, even for lunch, are strongly encouraged.

★ **La Bicyclette** (Dolores St. and 7th Ave., 831/622-9899, www.labicycletterestaurant.com, 8am-11am, 11:30am-3:30pm, 5pm-10pm daily, $14-26) is owned by the same folks as Casanova. The dining room houses a long bar that pours beer and a selection of French and Monterey County wines (wine-tasting is available all day). The food is rustic Italian-French, with an emphasis on thin-crust, wood-fired pizza. The simple margherita and the butternut squash, speck, and Gruyère pizzas are standouts. La Bicyclette's simple and superb Velo burger is another top option.

Winning raves is **Dametra Café** (Ocean Ave. and Lincoln St., 831/622-7766, http://dametracafe.com, 11am-11pm daily, $13-28). Serving Greek and Mediterranean food, Dametra is perfect for a casual meal that won't break the bank. Pizza, pasta, gyros, and kebabs, plus a burger and New York steak fill the large menu. The restaurant is family run, and great care has been taken to make the interior cozy and charming. If you want to eat here on a Saturday night, you may want to call ahead.

Some of the best sushi on the Central Coast is at the tiny **Akaoni** (Mission St. and 6th Ave., 831/620-1516, 5:30pm-8:45pm Tues.-Wed., 11:30am-1:15pm, 5:30pm-8:45pm Thurs.-Sun., $20-40). Surrounded by galleries, the small, multisided restaurant serves a dizzying selection of sashimi, *nigiri*, rolls, noodles, and homemade tofu dishes. The breaded Monterey sardine fillets are nods to the bounty of the local waters, as are the abalone and sea urchin sashimi, both elegantly served in their stunning shells, making presentation half the experience at this exceptional, no-nonsense eatery.

Carmel has held onto its breakfast joints, all unchanged over the years. The oldest is **Em Le's** (Dolores St. and 5th Ave., 831/625-6780, http://emlescarmel.com, 7am-3pm Mon.-Tues., 7am-3pm, 4:30pm-8pm Wed.-Sun., $12-25). Established in 1955, Em Le's sits in one of Carmel's storybook cottages. The large menu is boldly American: big plates of homemade meatloaf, hearty pasta dishes, steak, and seafood. Breakfast, served all day, is the biggest draw, with bottomless coffee and plates piled high with eggs, pancakes, and French toast.

Serving breakfast in a cuter-than-cute Carmel cottage is the **Tuck Box** (Dolores St. and 7th Ave., 831/624-3396, www.tuckbox.com, 7:30am-2:30pm daily, $6-12). A Carmel institution, the Tuck Box has been around in some form since 1931. Today it serves straightforward and extremely affordable breakfast and lunch. You can also swing by for afternoon tea.

The local joint is **Katy's Place** (Mission St. and 6th Ave., 831/624-0199, www.katysplace-carmel.com, 7am-2pm daily, $10-23). In the plain dining room and on the charming deck overlooking Mission Street, Katy's serves only breakfast and lunch, but the menu is huge. Burgers, salads, quesadillas, crab cakes, omelets, and pancakes all come in a wide variety, but the true king is the eggs Benedict. Offered 16 different ways, this is what locals come for. Portions are hearty, as are the prices, but the food is excellent.

You won't find Starbucks or Peet's in Carmel, but you will find the **Carmel Valley Roasting Company** (Ocean Ave. and Lincoln St., 831/626-2913, www.carmel-coffeeroasters.com, 6am-6pm Sun.-Thurs., 6am-7pm Fri.-Sat., $5). Coffee, espresso, and pastries are served, and a few tables fill the delightful shop.

If the weather is right, a picnic on the beach may win out over a bistro lunch. **Bruno's Market** (Junipero Ave. and 6th Ave., 831/624-3821, www.brunosmarket.com, 7am-8pm daily, $8) is the local pick for provisions, which include huge deli sandwiches, premade salads, and daily barbecue. With a foodie polish is the Italian **Salumeria Luca** (Dolores St. and 7th Ave., 831/625-0264, http://salumerialuca.

The Tuck Box is housed in one of Carmel's classic storybook cottages.

com, 11am-6pm Sun.-Thurs., 11am-7pm Fri.-Sat., $8). In addition to a deli case stocked with Italian cheese and house-made *salumi*, it has cold sandwiches, grilled panini, and pizza by the slice.

INFORMATION AND SERVICES

You'll find the **Carmel Visitors Center** (San Carlos St. and 5th Ave., 831/624-2522, www.carmelcalifornia.org, 10am-5pm daily) right in the midst of downtown Carmel-by-the-Sea. The nearest major medical center to Carmel-by-the-Sea is in nearby Monterey. For major or minor issues, head for the **Community Hospital of Monterey** (23625 Holman Hwy., Monterey, 831/622-2746, www.chomp.org).

TRANSPORTATION

If you've made it to the Monterey Peninsula by car, getting to Carmel is a piece of cake. Simply take Highway 1 south and then turn right on Ocean Avenue into the middle of downtown Carmel. **Monterey-Salinas Transit** (MST, 888/678-2871, http://mst.org, $2.50) runs a bus daily from Monterey to downtown Carmel.

CARMEL VALLEY

In many ways, Carmel Valley is everything that Carmel-by-the-Sea isn't—expansive, laid back, hot in the summer, and more about outdoor recreation than indoor poetry. But what it does have in common with its more famous neighbor is natural beauty. The narrow valley,

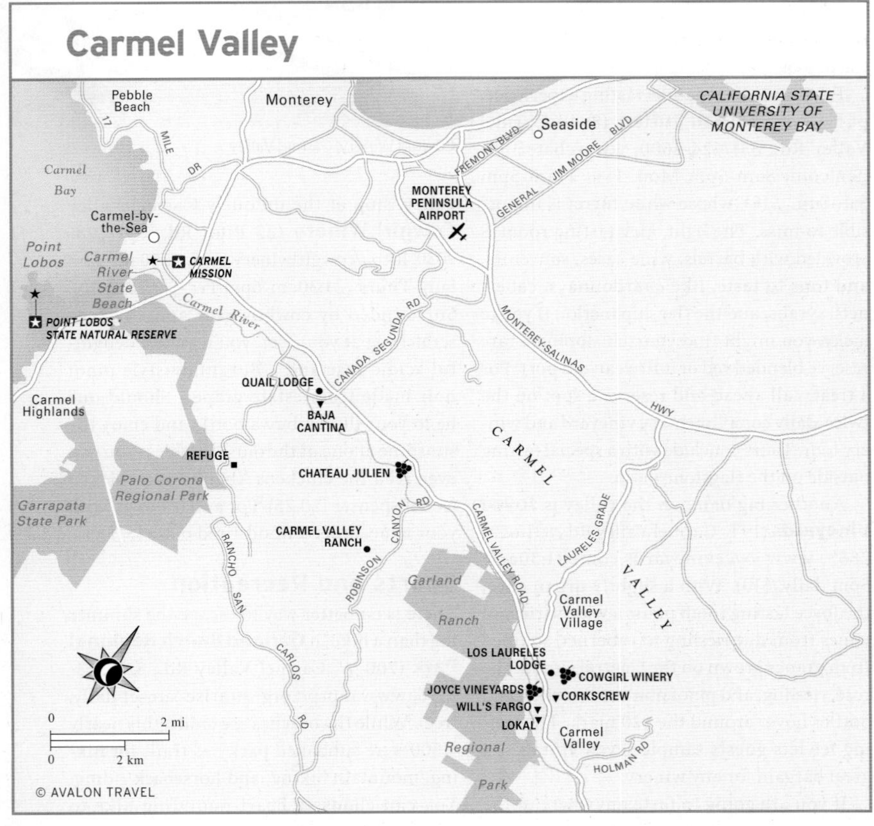

carved by the lazy Carmel River, stands on its own as a sublime destination. Over the years, the valley, once home to ranchers and retirees, has been discovered by golfers, and, more recently, vintners. Now several world-class golf courses blanket the valley floor, while vines of syrah, merlot, and pinot noir climb the hills. Even with these upscale pursuits, the valley retains its casual, unpretentious vibe.

Wineries

Carmel Valley is a relative newcomer to the California wine world, and as such, it has an undiscovered quality. The crowds are light, families own most of the wineries, and there is more charm and personal attention than in other California wine regions. There are few wineries that offer tastings in view of vineyards. Most often, the wine is made from grapes grown farther up the valley in Cachagua.

For the most Napa-like tasting experience, pull into **Chateau Julien** (8940 Carmel Valley Rd., 831/624-2600, www.chateaujulien.com, 8am-5pm Mon.-Fri., 11am-5pm Sat.-Sun., $15), whose white turret is impossible to miss. The light, airy tasting room is crowded with barrels, wine cases, souvenirs, and tons to taste, like chardonnays, cabernets, syrahs, and the flagship merlot. If you're lucky, you might find yourself sipping a rare reserve blended red or a 10-year-old port. For a treat, call ahead and reserve a spot on the twice-daily complimentary vineyard and winery tour. Tours conclude with a special tasting outside on the flagstone patio.

Another big name in the valley is **Joyce Vineyards** (19 E. Carmel Valley Rd., 831/659-2885, www.joycevineyards.com, 11:30am-5pm daily, $10). With a slightly urban edge, the Joyce tasting room pours a wide variety of wines from dry riesling to cabernet, sourced from grapes grown on the Central Coast. The rosé, riesling, and pinot noir are favorites, and bottles hover around the $20 mark. The tasting fee lets guests sample seven vintages, a great bargain for any winery.

If you are going to taste anywhere in the

Cowgirl Winery, Carmel Valley

valley, stop at the uniquely Carmel Valley **Cowgirl Winery** (25 Pilot Rd., 831/298-7030, http://cowgirlwinery.com, 11:30am-5pm Sun.-Thurs., 11:30am-6pm Fri.-Sat., $13-20). Surrounded by cowboy gear and chickens scratching at your feet, you'll taste a delightful acidic rosé and a Burgundy-style pinot noir made from estate grapes. Should one be to your liking, buy a bottle and enjoy the sunshine at one of the outside tables. You can even feed the chickens, thanks to a chicken feed dispenser ($0.25). For a snack to go with your wine, order a wood-fired pizza ($15).

Sports and Recreation

There is no better way to escape the summer fog than a hike in **Garland Ranch Regional Park** (700 W. Carmel Valley Rd., 831/372-3196, www.mprpd.org, sunrise-sunset daily, free). While the beaches are chilly, this nearly 4,500-acre sunbaked park has trails for hiking, mountain biking, and horseback riding. You can choose a heart-pounding hike to

Vasquez Saddle (9 miles round-trip, strenuous), a leisurely stroll along the **Lupine Loop** (1.4 miles, easy), or a visit to the seasonal waterfall up in **Redwood Canyon** (4.8 miles round-trip, moderate). Along the way, you'll pass historical buildings, as this was a working ranch until 1975, plus a variety of ecosystems. Well-controlled dogs are welcome in Garland Ranch. Should you need any advice, a ranger at the visitors center will gladly assist.

More manicured outdoor recreation can be had at one of the valley's three stellar golf courses, each of which is designed to dip in and out of the natural landscape. Near the mouth of the valley is the public **Rancho Canada Golf Course** (4860 Carmel Valley Rd., 800/536-9459, www.ranchocanada.com, $25-70). The two 18-hole courses, the East Course and the West Course, vary in difficulty and length and cross back and forth over the river. The West Course is considered to be the more advanced.

Farther up the valley, you'll find **Quail Lodge** (8205 Valley Greens Dr., 831/624-2888, www.quaillodge.com, $50-185), a par-71 championship course. Ten lakes and the Carmel River provide some challenges, but the course is comfortably walkable, for those who want to take in the scenery. For visitors, club rental ($60) and shoe rental ($20) are available.

At **Carmel Valley Ranch** (1 Old Ranch Rd., 831/620-6406, $95-175), a championship 18-hole course, you'll get the challenge of elevation gain when you climb the hills from the valley floor. The only Northern California course designed by Pete Dye, the course takes full advantage of the stunning scenery, including the 11th and 13th holes, where steep drop-offs frame the valley in all its glory and might induce vertigo. Carmel Valley Ranch boasts T1 Bentgrass on the fairways and flat screen TVs and outdoor patio fire pits at the upscale clubhouse.

Whether it's hiking through sycamores and dusty chaparral or teeing off on a verdant driving range, the end of the day will probably call for a respite at **Refuge** (27300 Rancho San Carlos Rd., 831/620-7360, www.refuge.com, 10am-10pm daily, $44). At this outdoor, coed spa, the focus is on the hot/cold plunge, silence, and maximum relaxation. Guests can heat up in the cedar saunas, eucalyptus steam room, or the thermal pools, complete with rocky waterfalls, and then cool down in tubs the temperature of the ocean. Adirondack chairs circling fire pits and overlooking the hills complete the experience. If that isn't enough, you can book a massage ($109, includes price of soak), which is best made in advance.

Accommodations

Carmel Valley boasts some funky and rather inexpensive digs. If you're traveling with kids, the place to go is **Los Laureles Lodge** (65 W. Carmel Valley Rd., 831/659-2233, http://loslaureles.com, $115-250). Sitting at the foot of the Los Laureles Grade, the lodge has a pool, restaurant, bar, and affordable family-friendly (and dog-friendly) accommodations that include suites and cottages. Established in the 1830s, the lodge was the first in the valley, giving it a historical charm. The lodge has a casual, fun atmosphere and opens its pool to the public for $7 a person.

Called a "summer camp for all ages," the luxurious **Carmel Valley Ranch** (1 Old Ranch Rd., 831/625-9500, www.carmelvalleyranch.com, $450) offers yoga, gardens, hiking trails, activities for kids, an excellent restaurant, spa, pool, and golf. With dining and recreation for all, and suites as large as some city apartments, with fireplaces, soaking tubs, and private patios with expansive views, there is no reason to ever leave. Most activities fall under the resort fee ($30), but some are extra and require reservations.

Food

Locals love **Lokal** (13762 Center St., 831/659-5886, 8am-3pm Wed., 8am-3pm, 6pm-9pm Thurs.-Sun., $20). Tucked in a quaint shopping center on Carmel Valley Road, Lokal adds a youthful edge to the valley. At the reclaimed wood bar, you can order a West Coast microbrew, a hard cider, or a glass of fine local wine. The restaurant's down-home fare includes a juicy burger with duck fat fries, lamb chops, and steamed mussels. Save room for dessert, like the homemade olive oil doughnuts or the burnt Jack Daniels bread pudding.

At the entrance of the village sits **Corkscrew Cafe** (55 W. Carmel Valley Rd., 831/659-8888, http://corkscrewcafe.com, 11:30am-9pm daily, $15-32), a Carmel Valley bistro with rustic flair. Take a table inside or outside on the sun-dappled patio and marvel at the collection of antique corkscrews; then select from pizza, wood-fired trout, cod tacos, and rib-eye steak. The staff is knowledgeable, friendly, and can help you pick the best wine to round out a perfect meal.

Will's Fargo (16 W. Carmel Valley Rd., 831/659-2774, http://wfrestaurant.com, 4:30pm-9pm Mon.-Sat., 4:30pm-8:30pm Sun., $20-40) opened in 1959 as a "dressed-up saloon," serving hearty meat, fish, and pasta dishes and sides of creamed spinach and twice-baked potatoes. There is a reason it has stuck around so long: The food is solid and the atmosphere can't be beat.

Cluttered with nostalgia is the cheerful mid-valley **Baja Cantina** (7166 Carmel Valley Rd., 831/625-2252, www.carmelcantina.com, 11:30am-9pm Mon.-Fri., 10am-9pm Sat.-Sun., $12-28). Bright dishes of huevos rancheros, organic vegetarian tamales, and a slew of tacos make their way to diners sunning themselves on the outdoor patio. The cantina also serves a tempting selection of mouth-watering margaritas that can be the perfect reward after a long hike or quickly derail any ambitious afternoon plans.

Information and Services

Carmel Valley is rural, so don't expect much in the way of services. Cell reception can be spotty. Gas and ATMs can be found at the Mid-Valley Shopping Center (7 miles east of Carmel), and in the village (13 miles east of Carmel).

Transportation

From Carmel, the valley is due east along Carmel Valley Road, which intersects with Highway 1 at the south end of town, known locally as the mouth of the valley. Parks, golf courses, and wineries cluster along the edge of the road, while, 13 miles in, Carmel Valley Village is the place to park, browse, and sip wine. You may also reach Carmel Valley from Highway 68, which connects Salinas and U.S. 101 to Monterey. Simply take the Los Laureles Grade south and over the hill. Be sure you have good brakes, as it is a steep descent.

CARMEL HIGHLANDS

Carmel Highlands is a small, unincorporated, wealthy community five miles south of Carmel. It is notable for its stunning scenery, luxurious accommodations, proximity to Point Lobos, and as a gateway to Big Sur.

★ Point Lobos State Natural Reserve

Early-20th-century painter Francis McComas called Point Lobos "the greatest meeting of land and water in the world," and he may be right. Jutting out into the sea three miles south of Carmel, **Point Lobos State Natural Reserve** (Hwy. 1 and Point Lobos St., 831/624-4909, www.parks.ca.gov, 8am-sunset daily, $10) is filled with ragged cliffs, hidden coves, rich marine ecosystems, lovely meadows, and dense pine and cypress forests. Hiking trails crisscross the reserve, the most spectacular of which hug the coastline, including the **North Shore Trail** (0.75 mile), which rises dramatically above the crashing sea, and the **Cypress Grove Trail** (2.4 miles), a loop that passes through one of only two wild groves of Monterey cypress. **South Shore Trail** (1 mile) runs along the southern edge of the point. Take it to **Bird Island Trail** (0.8 mile) where you will get a view of not only a loud and messy bird colony, but also China Cove, one of the most splendid sites at Point Lobos. A popular stroll, particularly if you walk into the park, is the **Granite Point Trail** (0.5 mile, easy) along Whalers Cove. Not only will you get a taste of the diverse landscape and wildlife, but you can also visit the

Whalers Cabin Museum (9am-5pm daily), which shows off the history of Point Lobos with artifacts from Native Americans and Chinese, Japanese, and Portuguese whalers and fishers, along with whale bones.

Point Lobos might be even more famous for what lies beneath the water than above it, which is nearly half the preserve's total acreage. The protected areas lie just south of the deep Carmel Submarine Canyon, making them home to a diverse marine ecosystem that includes 70-foot high kelp forests, wolf eels, rockfish, crabs, abalone, and giant sunflower stars, along with seals, sea otters, and the occasional shark. Add in the incredible underwater topography and the amazingly clear waters, and it's easy to see why Point Lobos is a divers' paradise. Diving is permitted at **Whalers Cove** and **Blue Fish Cove,** but permits (831/624-8413, http://pointlobos.org) are required. These can be obtained at the front gate, but reservations are strongly recommended, as only a limited number of divers are allowed per day. It's best to call or make a reservation online. Kayaking and boating are also allowed, and there is a boat launch at Whalers Cove, an easy entrance.

Accommodations

Despite its name, the cliff-top **Tickle Pink Inn** (155 Highlands Dr., 831/624-1244, www.ticklepinkinn.com, $314) offers tasteful luxury. Each room has a view of the ocean, an array of high-end furniture and linens, and all the top-end amenities you'd expect from a distinctive Carmel hostelry. For a special treat, shell out for the spa bath suite and watch the ocean while you soak in the tub with your sweetie.

The **Hyatt Carmel Highlands** (120 Highlands Dr., 831/620-1234, http://highlandsinn.hyatt.com, from $499) is an all-inclusive resort. Take a yoga class, swim in the heated pool, book a massage and spa treatment, or stay tucked away in your stylish, modern room with breathtaking views from a private porch. For food, choose from the upscale **Pacific's Edge** (831/622-5445, 5:30pm-9pm daily, $24-65) and the more casual **California Market** (831/622-5450, 7am-3pm daily, $15-30), where breakfast and lunch are served on an expansive patio, or sip cocktails in the glassed-in **Sunset Lounge** (831/622-5445, 3:30pm-close daily). Reservations are recommended for Pacific's Edge, but all are open to non-guests.

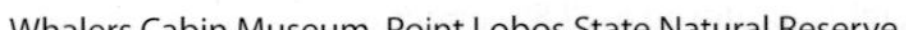

Whalers Cabin Museum, Point Lobos State Natural Reserve

Big Sur

Beguiling artists, writers, spiritual seekers, and dreamers, Big Sur is the spectacular collision of land and sea between Carmel and Cambria. It is home to coastal redwoods, high desert-like chaparral, thermal hot springs, jade deposits, grassy fields of wildflowers, the California condor, and, some would say, a spiritual energy vortex. In years with too little rain it is prone to fires; with too much rain there are mudslides, which keeps residents living on the edge in paradise.

This 90-mile stretch of road was completed in the 1930s and many of the inns and restaurants along it retain a midcentury hideaway atmosphere. There are plenty of places to jump off the road and explore the beaches and backcountry.

SIGHTS

★ Big Sur Coast Highway

Even if you're not up to tackling the endless hiking trails and deep wilderness backcountry of Big Sur, you can take in the glory of this region just by driving through it. The **Big Sur Coast Highway,** a 90-mile stretch of Highway 1, runs along jagged cliffs and rocky beaches, through dense redwood forest, over historical bridges, and past innumerable parks. Construction on this stretch of road was completed in the 1930s, connecting Cambria to Carmel. You can start at either of these towns and spend a whole day making your way to the other end of the road. The road has plenty of wide turnouts set into picturesque cliffs, making easy to stop and admire the glittering ocean and stunning wooded cliffs running right out to the water. Be sure to bring a camera—you'll find yourself wanting to take photos every mile for hours on end.

Bixby Bridge

You'll probably recognize the **Bixby Bridge** when you come upon it on Highway 1 in Big Sur. The picturesque cement open-spandrel arched bridge is one of the most photographed bridges in the nation, and it's been used in countless car commercials over the years. The bridge was built in the early 1930s as part of the massive project that completed Highway 1 through the Big Sur area to connect the road from the north end of California to the south. Today you can pull out either to the north or south of the bridge to take photos or just look out at the attractive span and Bixby Creek flowing into the Pacific far below.

The Rocky Creek Bridge (north of Bixby Bridge on Hwy. 1) is similar in design, if not quite as grand and picturesque.

Point Sur Lighthouse

Sitting lonely and isolated out on its 360-foot rock, the **Point Sur Lighthouse** (Hwy. 1 at milepost 54.1, 831/625-4419, www.pointsur.org, tours 10am Sat.-Sun., 1pm Wed. Nov.-Mar., 10am, 2pm Sat. and Wed., 10am Sun. Apr.-June and Oct., 10am, 2pm Sat. and Wed., 10am Thurs. and Sun. July-Aug., adults $12, children 6-17 $5, under 6 free) has been keeping watch over ships near the rocky waters of Big Sur since 1889. It's the only complete 19th-century light station in California that you can visit, and even here, access is severely limited.

You can't make a reservation for a Point Sur tour (but calling ahead is encouraged), so you must park your car off Highway 1 on the west side by the farm gate and wait for the tour guide. Tours are filled on a first-come, first-served basis, so be on time and ready to go. You will be led to the base of the paved road and walk for 0.5 mile, then climb a number of stairs to the light station (wear comfortable shoes). The tour lasts three hours, and you'll get to explore the restored keepers' homes and service buildings and walk out to the cliff edge. Expect to see a great variety of wildlife, from brilliant wildflowers in the spring and

Big Sur

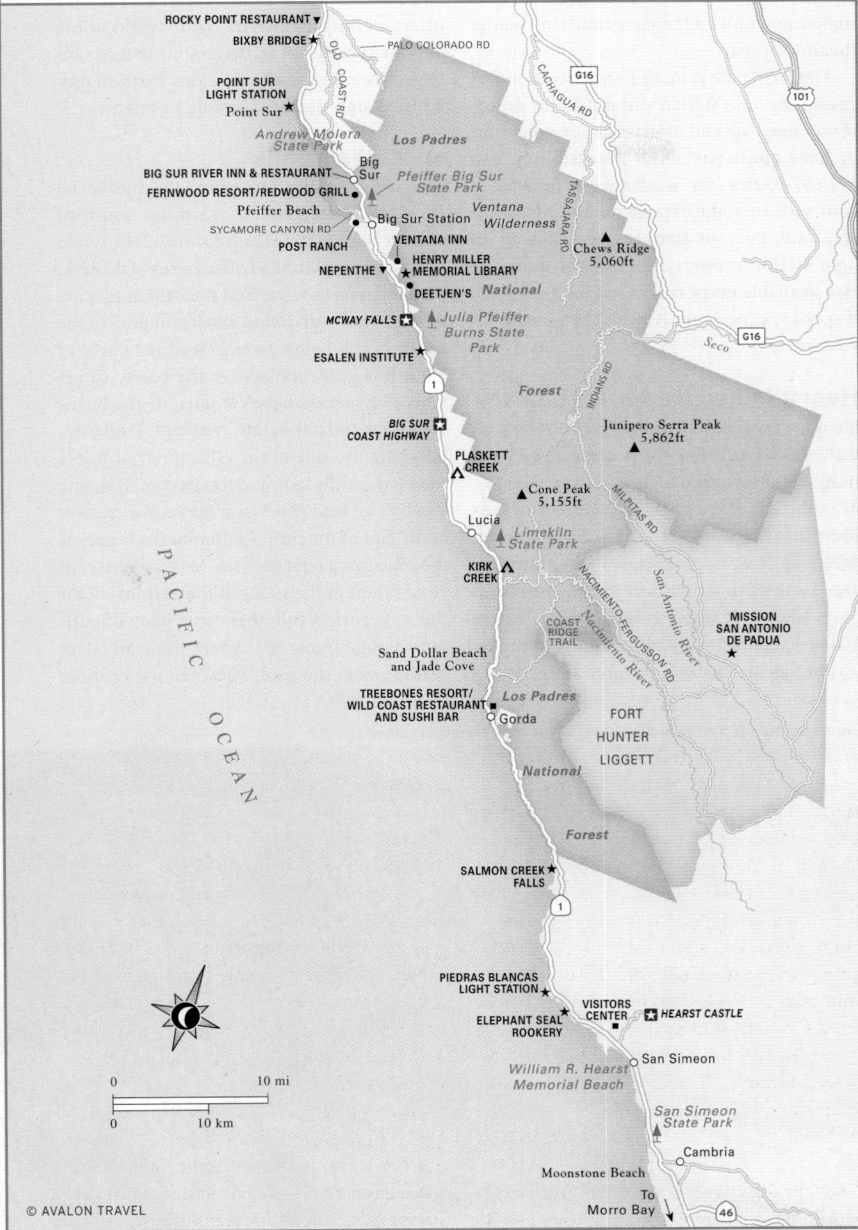

ROCKY POINT RESTAURANT
BIXBY BRIDGE
OLD COAST RD
PALO COLORADO RD
CACHAGUA RD
G16
101
POINT SUR LIGHT STATION
Point Sur
Andrew Molera State Park
Los Padres
BIG SUR RIVER INN & RESTAURANT
Big Sur
Pfeiffer Big Sur State Park
FERNWOOD RESORT/REDWOOD GRILL
Pfeiffer Beach
SYCAMORE CANYON RD
Big Sur Station
Ventana Wilderness
TASSAJARA RD
POST RANCH
VENTANA INN
Chews Ridge 5,060ft
HENRY MILLER MEMORIAL LIBRARY
NEPENTHE
DEETJEN'S
National
MCWAY FALLS
Julia Pfeiffer Burns State Park
G16
Seco
ESALEN INSTITUTE
1
Forest
INDIANS RD
BIG SUR COAST HIGHWAY
Junipero Serra Peak 5,862ft
PLASKETT CREEK
Cone Peak 5,155ft
MILPITAS RD
Lucia
Limekiln State Park
PACIFIC OCEAN
KIRK CREEK
NACIMIENTO-FERGUSSON RD
San Antonio River
COAST RIDGE TRAIL
Nacimiento River
MISSION SAN ANTONIO DE PADUA
Sand Dollar Beach and Jade Cove
TREEBONES RESORT/ WILD COAST RESTAURANT AND SUSHI BAR
Los Padres
Gorda
FORT HUNTER LIGGETT
National
Forest
SALMON CREEK FALLS
1
PIEDRAS BLANCAS LIGHT STATION
ELEPHANT SEAL ROOKERY
VISITORS CENTER
HEARST CASTLE
San Simeon
William R. Hearst Memorial Beach
0
10 mi
0
10 km
San Simeon State Park
Cambria
Moonstone Beach
To Morro Bay
46
© AVALON TRAVEL

gray whales in the winter to flocks of pelicans at any time of year. Be sure to dress in layers; it can be sunny and hot or foggy and cold (and sometimes both on the same tour!), no matter the time of year.

The farm gate is locked and there's no access to the light station without a tour group. If you need special assistance for your tour or have questions about accessibility, call 831/667-0528 as far in advance as possible of your visit to make arrangements. No strollers, food, pets, or smoking are allowed on light station property. Moonlight tours are also available every full moon for a magical, if spooky, experience. Check the website for schedules.

Henry Miller Memorial Library

It is quite possible that the coolest bookstore on the Central Coast (for avant-garde literary fiction, at least) is found tucked in the redwoods, near the edge of a cliff. The **Henry Miller Memorial Library** (Hwy. 1, 0.25 mile south of Nepenthe, 831/667-2574, www.henrymiller.org, 11am-6pm daily) is neither a memorial nor a library. It is not even the home where Miller lived and worked for the 18 years he was in Big Sur. Instead, the bookstore, sitting in a sun-dappled meadow, encourages visitors to browse, pour themselves a cup of coffee, and meditate on art and beauty. The library offers a glimpse into the "real" world of Big Sur as a spread-out artists' colony that has inspired countless works. Just look for the hand-painted sign on the east side of Highway 1.

★ McWay Falls

The ultimate Big Sur photo op has to be **McWay Falls** (Hwy. 1, 12 miles south of Pfeiffer Big Sur State Park, 831/667-2315, www.parks.ca.gov) at Julia Pfeiffer Burns State Park. The aquamarine cove and the ribbon-like arc of this small year-round creek plunging to the sandy beach below have graced the cover of countless guidebooks over the years. To get your own snapshot, park at Julia Pfeiffer Burns State Park and follow the **Overlook Trail** west. Hugging the side of the cliff, the trail is less than half a mile long and has its own dramatic views. The best place to snap your picture is at the end of the trail. Adding to the beauty is the remaining terrace of the McWay Waterfall House built in the 1920s. If the parking lot for the state park is full, there are plenty of pullouts along Highway 1 where the trail is accessible from the road. However, use caution.

Every turnout on the Big Sur Coast Highway offers beautiful views.

McWay Falls

Esalen Institute

To sink into the spiritual vortex of Big Sur, book a massage at the **Esalen Institute** (55000 Hwy. 1, 888/837-2536, www.esalen.org). Founded in 1962, Esalen's mission is to delve into the human condition. Seekers and neophytes come from around the world to attend retreats and workshops at this spiritual and ecological think tank, also known as "The New Age Harvard." Such enlightenment may cost $400-1,750 for a weekend workshop.

For those who just want to dip their toes into Esalen's healing ways, the place to go is the institute's mineral-fed hot tubs perched over the Pacific. To do so, you'll need to make an appointment for a massage (831/837-2536 or 831/667-3002, 11am or 4pm Mon.-Thurs and Sat., 11am Fri. and Sun., $165). You are granted access to the hot tubs for an hour before and an hour after your 75-minute treatment session. If you just want to sit in the mineral water, you'll need to stay up very late. Inexpensive access ($25) to the Esalen tubs begins on a first-come, first-served basis at 1am and ends at 3am daily (reservations 831/667-3047). Many locals consider the sleep deprivation well worth it to enjoy the mineral waters and the stunning astronomical shows. The tubs are clothing-optional.

HIKING

The main reason people come to Big Sur is to hike its beaches and forests.

Garrapata State Park

Covering a long, thin line of coast and steep terrain to the east of Highway 1, **Garrapata State Park** (Hwy. 1, 6.7 miles south of Carmel, 831/624-4909, www.parks.ca.gov) is the first state park you'll reach as you travel south after Point Lobos. It's a great place to get out and stretch your legs. With few facilities, numbered gates are what you must rely on for orientation. The **Soberanes Point Trails** wind through the windswept area and offer wonderful views of the coastline, including seals, sea otters, and sea lions, and migrating whales in the winter. This area is accessible at gates 8, 9, and 10. For something more strenuous, head east. Just north of Soberanes Point, **Soberanes Canyon Trail** and the **Rocky Ridge Trail** together form a strenuous 4.5-mile loop through a trickling creek, lush forest, fields of poppies, and unrelenting chaparral. If you're feeling up to it, take the 1.5-mile spur **Peak Trail** to Doud Peak. At 1,977 feet, it is a truly breathtaking hike.

Andrew Molera State Park

The first "Big Sur" park you'll encounter coming south from Carmel is **Andrew Molera State Park** (Hwy. 1, 22 miles south of Carmel, 831/667-2315, www.parks.ca.gov, $8). Once home to small camps of Esselen Native Americans, this chunk of Big Sur eventually became the Molera Ranch. The land was used to grow crops and ranch animals and as a hunting and fishing retreat for family and friends. It was turned over to the California state park system in 1965. Today the **Molera Ranch House Museum** (11am-3pm Sat.-Sun. June-Aug.) displays stories of the life and times of Big Sur's pioneers and artists as well as the wildlife and plants of the region. Take the road toward the horse tours to get to the ranch house. To learn more about the natural history of the region, visit the **Big Sur Discovery Center** (831/624-1202, www.ventanaws.org, 10am-4pm Sat.-Sun. June-Aug.) nearby. Interactive exhibits and enthusiastic volunteers tell the story of the flora and fauna that call Big Sur home, including information on the heroic effort to bring back the California condor from the edge of extinction.

The park has numerous hiking trails that run down to the beach and up into the forest along the river—many are open to biking and horseback riding as well. Most of the park trails lie to the west of the highway. The beach is a one-mile walk down the easy, multi-use **Trail Camp.** From there, climb on out on the **Headlands Trail,** a 0.25-mile loop, for a beautiful view from the headlands. If you prefer to get a better look at the Big Sur River, take the flat, moderate **Bobcat Trail** (5.5 miles round-trip) and perhaps a few of its ancillary loops. You'll walk right along the riverbanks, enjoying the local microhabitats. Just be sure to look out for bicycles and the occasional horse and rider. For an even longer and more difficult trek up the mountains and down to the beach, take the eight-mile **Ridge Bluff Loop.** You'll start at the parking lot on the **Creamery Meadow Beach Trail** (0.7 mile, easy) then make a left onto the long and fairly steep **Ridge Trail** (2 miles, moderate to strenuous) to get a sense of the local ecosystem. Then turn left again onto the **Panorama Trail** (3.4 miles, easy to moderate), which runs down to the coastal scrublands and finally out to the Bluffs Trail, which takes you back to Creamery Meadow.

At the park entrance, you'll find bathrooms but no drinkable water and no food concessions. If you're camping here, be sure to bring plenty of your own water for washing dishes as well as drinking. If you're hiking for the day, pack in bottled water and snacks.

Pfeiffer Big Sur State Park

The biggest, most developed park in Big Sur is **Pfeiffer Big Sur State Park** (47225 Hwy. 1, 831/667-2315, www.parks.ca.gov, $8). It's got the Big Sur Lodge, a restaurant and café, a shop, an amphitheater, a softball field, plenty of hiking trails, and lovely redwood-shaded campsites. The park is up in the coastal redwood forest, with a network of roads that can be driven or biked up into the trees and along the Big Sur River.

Andrew Molera State Park

Pfeiffer Big Sur has the tiny **Ernest Ewoldsen Memorial Nature Center,** which features taxidermy examples of local wildlife. It's open seasonally; call the park for days and hours. Another historical exhibit is the **Homestead Cabin,** once the home to part of the Pfeiffer family—the first European immigrants to settle in Big Sur. Day-trippers and overnight visitors can take a stroll through the cabins of the Big Sur Lodge, built by the Civilian Conservation Corps during the Great Depression.

No bikes or horses are allowed on the trails in this park, which makes it quite peaceful for hikers. For a starter walk, take the easy, 0.7-mile **Nature Trail** in a loop from Day Use Parking Lot 2. Grab a brochure at the lodge to learn about the park's plant life as you walk the trail. For a longer stroll, head out on the popular **Pfeiffer Falls Trail** (1.5 miles round-trip, moderate). You'll find stairs on the steep sections and footbridges across the creek, then a lovely platform at the base of the 60-foot waterfall, where you can rest and relax midway through your hike. Ocean views can be found at the end of **Buzzards Roost Trail** (3 miles, moderate). It leaves from the Parking Lot 2, crosses the Big Sur River, travels through redwoods, and crests a ridge west of the highway. While moderate, the trail may have you huffing and puffing at times.

Julia Pfeiffer Burns State Park

One of the best-known and easiest hikes in all of the Big Sur region sits in **Julia Pfeiffer Burns State Park** (Hwy. 1, 12 miles south of Pfeiffer Big Sur State Park, 831/667-2315, www.parks.ca.gov). The **Overlook Trail** runs only two-thirds of a mile round-trip, along a level, wheelchair-accessible boardwalk. Stroll under Highway 1, past the Pelton wheel house, and out to the observation deck and the stunning view of McWay Falls. The medium-sized waterfall cascades year-round off a cliff and onto the beach of a remote cove, where the water wets the sand and trickles out into the bright blue sea. Anyone with an ounce of love for the ocean will want to build a hut right there beside the waterfall. But you can't—in fact, the reason you'll look down on a pristine and empty stretch of sand is that there's no way down to the cove.

If you're up for a longer hike after taking in the falls, go back the other way to pick up the **Ewoldsen Trail** (5 miles round-trip, moderate-difficult). This trek takes you through McWay Canyon, and you'll see the creek and surrounding lush greenery as you walk. Then you'll loop away from the water and climb up into the hills. Be sure to bring water, as this hike can take several hours.

If you want to spend all day at Julia Pfeiffer Burns State Park, drive north from the park entrance to the Partington Cove pullout and park along the side of the highway. On the east side of the highway, start out along the **Tan Bark Trail** (6.4 miles round-trip, difficult). You'll head through redwood groves and up steep switchbacks to the top of the coastal ridge where the trail ends at the historical Tin House. Here, the **Tinhouse Fire Road** (2.3 miles, difficult) eventually makes its way back down to Highway 1, though too far away from Partington Cove to make this into a loop.

Ventana Wilderness

What makes the state parks in Big Sur seem endless is the spectacular backdrop of the vast **Ventana Wilderness** (831/385-5434 or 831/667-2315, www.fs.usda.gov). Its nearly 250,000 acres stretches from Palo Colorado Road, east of the Bixby Bridge, to the rangeland below Hearst Castle. There are 273 miles of trails that cross up, over, and across its steep hillsides, sharp ridges, and dramatic V-shaped valleys with waterfalls and thermal springs. You'll find abundant wildlife, including condors, black bears, and rattlesnakes and 55 designated primitive campsites where you can recharge after a long day of hiking.

Trails are geared toward backpackers and offer few scenic loops. Still, there are plenty of opportunities for day hikers. From **Bottchers Gap** (end of Palo Colorado Rd., 831/667-2315, $5), the **Skinner Ridge Trail** is a popular option, traveling through redwood forests and rocky canyons and up to hilly, challenging terrain. A spur takes you up to **Mount Carmel** (9.8-miles round-trip, strenuous). This is a tough hike, but the rewards are views of Monterey Bay.

The highest coastal peak in the continental United States is an extremely doable day hike just south of the one-stop town of Lucia. **Cone Peak** is 5,158 feet. You can hike that arduous climb through a set of grueling switchbacks via the **Kirk Creek/Vicente Flat, Stone Ridge,** and **Gamboa Trails** (22 miles, difficult) or you could cut out much of the huffing and puffing and enjoy a scenic drive to the trailhead. From Highway 1, take the Nacimiento-Ferguson Road to Cone Peak Road (during heavy rainy seasons, the road is often closed). Turn left and the trailhead will be near the end of the road. From there, the **Cone Peak Trail** (6 miles round-trip, moderate to strenuous) ambles through oaks and chaparral, quickly turning into rocky switchbacks. The pain doesn't last long, as it is only two miles to the top, where a fire lookout station provides an additional boost to enjoy the views.

Farther south, just remote enough not to attract a whole lot of hikers, is the **Buckeye Trail** (7 miles round-trip, strenuous), which climbs the side of the coast range. If climbing nearly 600 feet in the first mile sounds like a deal breaker, you can start on the **Soda Springs Trail,** which departs Highway 1 at a higher elevation. Soda Springs and Buckeye Trails meet, eventually reaching Buckeye Camp, a small dip from the trail's spectacular coastal panorama, where a shady oak, a spring, and a few picnic tables greet hikers.

As you may have noticed, most of the trails in Ventana Wilderness, thanks to the dramatic terrain, are strenuous and exposed. Plan with care. Bring plenty of water, sunscreen, layers, and even a map. Getting lost out here is no joke. For help planning your adventure call or visit the rangers at the multi-agency **Big Sur Station** (just south of Pfeiffer Big Sur State Park, 831/667-2315, 9am-4pm daily).

Limekiln State Park

At the southern end of Big Sur, **Limekiln State Park** (63025 Hwy. 1, 805/434-1996, www.parks.ca.gov, $8), named for the limekilns that cured the mountain's limestone (used in San Francisco's earliest brick buildings), offers a couple easy strolls through this redwood rich gulch. From the parking lot, the **Limekiln Trail** (1 mile round-trip, easy) ventures back into the canyon where the enormous furnaces still stand. Halfway there, **Falls Trail** is a short spur to a 100-foot waterfall. Also leaving from the parking lot, the **Hare Trail** follows the creek for a gentle 0.5-mile stroll.

BEACHES

Big Sur may be all about the intersection of the land and the sea, but beaches are not as common as you would think. Perhaps scarcity breeds selection, but the sandy stretches you do find are sublime. The first major beach past the Carmel Headlands is the two-mile **Garrapata State Beach** (Hwy. 1, 6.7 miles south of Carmel, 831/624-4909, www.parks.ca.gov). Dip your toes in the cerulean blue Pacific while keeping your eyes open for seals, dolphins, and whales. There is plenty of room for walking, and the view of the rocky coastline is expansive. To access the beach, use gates 18 and 19.

Certainly not the biggest beach, **Pfeiffer Beach** (Sycamore Canyon Rd., 805/434-1995, www.fs.usda.gov, 9am-8pm daily, $10) is undoubtedly the best-known beach in Big Sur and certainly its most photographed. Located directly across Highway 1 from Big Sur Station, it sits at the end of a pretty, slightly residential coastal road, nestled in a cove. From the parking lot, you'll walk through a canopy of cypress, then out to the beach. Here, huge rock formations, with arches and caves, keep the brilliant blue waves foamy and alive while the white sand, flecked with red and black, changes color from every angle.

To surf Big Sur, the place to go is **Sand Dollar Beach** (Hwy. 1, 60 miles south of Carmel and across from Plaskett Creek

Campground, 805/434-1996, 9am-8pm daily, $10). For surfers, the waves break far enough from shore for a pleasant ride, and low tide exposes a cave to the north, for adventurous explorers. The longest stretch of sand in Big Sur, this beach is perfect for long walks, beachcombing, and sunbathing (weather permitting, of course).

To add to the splendors of the Big Sur coast is the presence of jade along the shore. **Jade Cove** (Hwy. 1, 2 miles south of Sand Dollar Beach), has, over the years, attracted beachcombers and divers to its rocky shore in search of the semiprecious stone. You won't find any impressive pieces like in the art galleries of Big Sur (unless you take to the water, and this is for skilled divers only), but searching may yield a few small treasures, and you can still reach out and touch a multi-ton boulder shot through with jade. A road sign marks the area, but there's not much in the way of a formal parking lot or anything else to denote the treasures of this jagged stretch of Big Sur. Park in the dirt/gravel strip off the road and head past the fence and into the park. Once you get to the edge of the cliff, the short trail gets rough. It's only 0.25 mile, but it's almost straight down a rocky, slippery cliff. Good shoes are a must, and keep your hands free for support. Don't try to climb down if you're not in reasonably good condition. For mineral hunting that is a little less hair-raising, the rocky beach at **Willow Creek** (Hwy. 1, 62 miles south of Carmel) has jade scattered about. Better yet, the descent from the parking lot is an easy walk, doable in flip-flops.

SPORTS AND RECREATION

Horseback Riding

You can take a guided horseback ride through Andrew Molera State Park with **Molera Horseback Tours** (831/625-5486, http://molerahorsebacktours.com, Apr.-Oct., $60-84,). Tours of 1-2.5 hours depart each day starting at 9am—call ahead to guarantee your spot, or take a chance and just show up at the stables 15 minutes ahead of the ride you want to take. It's also possible to book a private guided ride for yourself and your party. Each ride takes you from the modest corral area along multi-use trails through forests or meadows or along the Big Sur River and down to Molera Beach. You'll guide your horse along the solid sands as you admire the beauty of the wild Pacific Ocean.

Garrapata State Beach

Backpacking

If you are going backpacking in the **Ventana Wilderness** (831/385-5434 or 831/667-2315, http://www.fs.usda.gov), everyone will tell you to go to **Sykes Hot Springs** (20 miles round-trip, strenuous). Departing from Big Sur Station, via the **Pine Ridge Trail,** you'll get a workout traversing switchbacks as the trail climbs to the Big Sur River Gorge and the thermal springs. Terraced in deep pools on either side of the river, the spring average 100°F. If you long for the lonely peace of backcountry camping, this may not be the trip for you. April through October, the trail and tubs are crowded, but thankfully, Sykes is nestled in a forested section of the river, which can add some quietude and privacy amidst the crowds.

To feel like you're alone on top of the world, hike from Bottchers Gap to the **Skinner Ridge** and the **Ventana Double Cone Trails,** which ride the ridgeline to the lookout of the 4,856-foot mountain (12 miles one way, strenuous). While providing plenty of scenery and sunshine perfect for a winter trek, the trails dip in and out of steep gorges, challenging the most seasoned of hikers. Thankfully, you'll find plenty of primitive camps along the way to rest for the night.

Bottchers Gap is also an excellent jumping-off point for shorter backpacking excursions, with multiple camps clustered within 10 miles of the trailhead. These include **Jackson Camp** (5 miles, easy to moderate), **Pico Blanco Camp** (7 miles, easy to moderate), **Apple Tree Camp** (3 miles, strenuous), and **Turner Creek Camp** (5 miles, strenuous). If you really don't want to walk far, there is even a camp at the trailhead at Bottchers Gap, but locals love **Litter Sur Camp** (5 miles, easy to moderate), found off the private Boy Scouts of America road, nestled in a grove of redwoods.

Contact the ranger station (Forest Service, 831/385-5434) or the Big Sur Station (831/667-2315) to get the most up-to-date information on trail conditions. A fire permit is required, which can be obtained at Big Sur Station or online (www.fs.usda.gov).

Scuba Diving

There's not much for beginner divers in Big Sur, but if you've got some underwater experience, you'll want to bring your gear when you visit. Expect cold water. Temperatures range in the mid-50s in the shallows, dipping into the 40s as you dive deeper down. Visibility is 20-30 feet, though rough conditions can diminish this significantly. The best season for clear water is September through November.

The biggest and most interesting dive locale here is the **Julia Pfeiffer Burns State Park** (Hwy. 1, 12 miles south of Pfeiffer Big Sur, 831/667-2315, www.parks.ca.gov, sunrise-sunset daily). You'll need to acquire a special permit at Big Sur Station and prove your experience to dive at this protected underwater park. The park, along with the rest of the Big Sur coast, is part of the Monterey Bay National Marine Sanctuary. Enter the water at Partington Point, and check out the ecosystems as you go, beginning with the busy life of the beach sands and heading out to the rocky reefs, then into the lush green kelp forests.

Divers at access-hostile **Jade Cove** (Hwy. 1, 2 miles south of Sand Dollar Beach) aren't usually interested in cute, colorful nudibranchs or even majestic gray whales. Jade Cove divers come to stalk the wily jade pebbles and rocks that cluster in this special spot. The semiprecious stone striates the coastline right here, and storms tear clumps of jade out of the cliffs. Much of it settles just off the shore of the tiny cove, and divers hope to find jewelry-quality stones to sell for a huge profit.

If you're looking for a guided scuba dive of the Big Sur region, contact **Adventure Sports Unlimited** (303 Potrero St., no. 15, Santa Cruz, 831/458-3648, www.asudoit.com).

Spas

Physical exertion is one side of the Big Sur experience; relaxation is the other. At **The Spa at Ventana** (48123 Hwy. 1, 831/667-4222, www.ventanainn.com, 10am-7pm daily, $140/50-minute massage), you'll love the serene atmosphere of the treatment and waiting areas. Greenery and weathered wood create a unique space that helps to put you in a tranquil state of mind. Indulge in a soothing massage, purifying body treatment, or rejuvenating or beautifying facial. Take your spa experience a step farther in true Big Sur fashion with a reiki or craniosacral treatment. If you're a guest of Ventana, you can choose to have your spa treatment in the comfort of your own room or out on your private deck.

CAMPING

Many visitors to Big Sur want to experience the unspoiled beauty of the landscape daily. To accommodate true outdoors lovers, many of the parks and lodges in the area have campgrounds. You'll find all types of camping here, from full-service, RV-accessible areas to environmental tent campsites and wilderness backpacking. You can camp in a state park or out behind one of the small resort motels near the Big Sur River.

Andrew Molera State Park

Andrew Molera State Park (Hwy. 1, 22 miles south of Carmel, 831/667-2315, www.parks.ca.gov, $35/night) offers 24 walk-in, tent-only campsites located 0.25-0.5 mile from the parking lot via a level, well-maintained trail. You'll pitch your tent in a pretty meadow near the Big Sur River, in a site that includes a picnic table and a fire ring. No reservations are taken, so come early in summer to get one of the prime spots under a tree. Look out for bobcats, foxes, deer, raccoons (stow your food securely!), and any number of birds. Camping here requires you bring your own water; there is no potable water available. Pit toilets sit a short walk from the camping area.

Fernwood Resort

The **Fernwood Resort** (47520 Hwy. 1, 831/667-2422, www.fernwoodbigsur.com) maintains a large campground on both sides of the Big Sur River. You can choose between pitching your own tent, pulling in your RV, and renting a tent cabin. The resort has easy access to the river, where you can swim, inner tube, and hike. You'll also have access to the restaurant, store, and tavern.

Tent cabins ($90-120 for 2 people) offer small canvas spaces that sleep up to four, with a double and two twins. You can pull your car right up to the back of your cabin, and pick the more affordable, bring-your-own linens-tent or the "glamping" option, in which a larger tent is made up for you. Hot showers and bathrooms are a short walk away. Tent campsites ($55-65) are scattered in great places—tucked down by the river under vast, shady redwood trees. You can even park your RV under a tree and then hook it up to water and electricity.

Pfeiffer Big Sur State Park

The biggest and most developed campground in Big Sur sits at **Pfeiffer Big Sur State Park** (47225 Hwy. 1, 831/667-2315, www.parks.ca.gov, reservations 800/444-7275 or www.reserveamerica.com, $35). With 150 individual sites that sit along the Big Sur River, each of which can take two vehicles and eight people or an RV (32 feet or shorter, trailers 27 feet max, dump station on-site). During the summer, a grocery store and laundry facilities operate within the campground for those who don't want to hike down to the lodge, and plenty of flush toilets and hot showers are scattered throughout the campground. In the evenings, walk down to the Campfire Center for entertaining and educational programs. If you prefer a quieter and less asphalt-oriented camping experience, check out the hike-in and bike-in campgrounds that make up part of the Pfeiffer Big Sur complex. Advanced reservations, particularly in the summer and on weekends, are strongly encouraged.

Limekiln State Park

The small but pretty campground at **Limekiln State Park** (63025 Hwy. 1, 805/434-1996 or 831/649-2836, www.parks.ca.gov, reservations 800/444-7275, summer only, $35) offers 29 campsites with hot showers and flush toilets along an attractive creek and abutting the beach. RVs (up to 24 feet) and trailers (up to 15 feet) can stay anywhere but the Redwood

Sites, and hookups and dump stations aren't available. In summer, the park recommends making reservations early. In winter, no reservations are available and many sites are closed. Call for more information if you want to camp here in the off-season.

Treebones Resort

For the ultimate high-end California camping experience, book a yurt at the ★ **Treebones Resort** (71895 Hwy. 1, 877/424-4787, www.treebonesresort.com, $95-215). The resort got its name from the locals' description of this scrap of land, which was once a wood recycling plant with sun-bleached logs lying about—"tree bones." Yurts ($215) at Treebones are spacious and charming, with polished wood floors, queen beds, seating areas, and outdoor decks for lounging. There are also walk-in campsites ($95 for two people), which include "Ocean View" sites—a round canvas tent on a wood platform ($130). In the central lodge, you'll find hot showers and clean restroom facilities, plus a heated pool and hot tub. Treebones offers a somewhat pricey casual dinner each night and basic linens. Check the website for a list of items to bring. Treebones does not recommend bringing kids under 6 years old.

ACCOMMODATIONS

Under $100-150

It doesn't look like a spot where famous writers, artists, and Hollywood stars have laid their heads, but ★ **Deetjens Big Sur Inn** (48865 Hwy. 1, 831/667-2378, www.deetjens.com, $115-270) can indeed boast a guest register that many hostelries in Beverly Hills would kill for. The inn prides itself on its artfully decorated rooms and rustic historical construction. Expect thin, weathered walls, funky cabin construction, and no outdoor locks on the doors. Many rooms have shared baths, but you can request a private bath when you make reservations. Deetjens asks that families with children under eight rent both rooms of a two-room building. Deetjens has no TVs or stereos, no phones in rooms, and no cell phone service. Two pay phones are available for emergencies.

In the town of Big Sur, you'll find a couple small motels. A popular one is the **Fernwood Resort** (47520 Hwy. 1, 831/667-2422, www.fernwoodbigsur.com, $135-165), which includes a 12-room motel, convenience store, restaurant, and tavern that passes for the local nighttime hot spot. Farther down the road are the resort's campgrounds, which include tent cabins as well as tent and RV sites. Not much sunlight gets into the motel rooms, but the decor is light and reasonably attractive. Rooms have queen beds and private bathrooms, but no TVs. Cabins accommodating six along with full kitchens are also available ($215). In the summer, book in advance, especially on weekends.

First opened in the 1930s by a member of the Pfeiffer family, the **Big Sur River Inn** (46840 Hwy. 1, 831/667-2700 or 800/548-3610, www.bigsurriverinn.com, $130-350) has been in continuous operation ever since. It boasts 20 rooms, a restaurant, and a gift shop. Rooms are small but comfortable. Families and small groups can choose between standard rooms with two queen beds and two-room suites with multiple beds and attractive decks that look out over the Big Sur River. Enjoy the attractive pool with its surrounding lawn that leads down to the river.

$150-250

If you want to stay in one of the parks but tents aren't your style, book a cabin at the **Big Sur Lodge** (47225 Hwy. 1, 831/667-3100 or 800/424-4787, www.bigsurlodge.com, $159-399) in Pfeiffer Big Sur State Park. The lodge was built in the 1930s. Set in the redwood forest along an array of paths and small roads, the cabins feature rustic furniture and simple but clean bathrooms. Many cabins have lots of beds, and the largest cabins have fireplaces and kitchens. Stock your kitchen at the on-site grocery store, or just get a meal at the restaurant or café. The lodge has a swimming pool, but the real attraction is its access to the Pfeiffer Big Sur trails.

Ragged Point Inn (19019 Hwy. 1, 805/927-4502, http://raggedpointinn.net, $149-339) perches on one of Big Sur's famous cliffs, offering stellar views from the glass walls and private balconies or patios of almost every room. Budget rooms still have plenty of space, a comfy king or two double beds, and ocean views. Enjoy a meal in the restaurant, get picnic supplies from the snack bar or the mini-mart, fill up for a day trip at the on-site gas station, or peruse the works of local artists in the gift shop or in the jewelry gallery. The hotel has its own hiking trail, which travels past a waterfall to Ragged Point's private beach.

Over $250

At ★ **Ventana** (48123 Hwy. 1, 800/628-6500, www.ventanainn.com, $670), the panoramic ocean views begin in the parking lot. Home-baked pastries, fresh yogurt, in-season fruit, and organic coffee are delivered to your room in the morning. Enjoy that sumptuous breakfast outdoors on a private patio overlooking a wildflower-strewn meadow. Next, don a plush spa robe and rubber slippers and head for the Japanese bathhouse. Two swimming pools offer a cool respite: The lower pool is clothing-optional, and the upper pool perches on a high spot for enthralling views. Many other amenities are available, including daily complimentary yoga classes. Rooms range from the standard rooms, with king beds and exposed cedar walls, up to full-sized multi-bedroom houses.

Sleek, modern, and built into the landscape as is only possible in Big Sur, **Post Ranch** (47900 Hwy. 1, 831/667-2200 or 800/527-2200, www.postranchinn.com, $675-995) sits directly across Highway 1 from Ventana, rivaling its New Age luxury. Spa, yoga, hot and cold pools, and a unique yet rustic atmosphere are just a few of its perks.

FOOD

Casual Dining

The first restaurant you'll find south of the Carmel Highlands is the isolated **Rocky Point Restaurant** (36700 Hwy. 1, 831/624-2933, www.rocky-point.com, 11:30am-8pm daily, $15-36). Built in 1947, it offers your standard American lunch and dinner. Find hearty steaks, a few pasta dishes, calorie-laden salads, and plenty of seafood. The full bar and plate glass windows complete the midcentury vibe and provide a lovely (if not the most epicurean) break from the road.

In the heart of Big Sur, you'll find a selection of ultracasual restaurants attached to hotels that offer good, reasonably priced food, frothy pints of beer, and shady creekside tables. The **Redwood Grill** (Hwy. 1, 831/667-2129, www.fernwoodbigsur.com, 11am-9pm daily, $15-205) at Fernwood Resort looks and feels like a grill in the woods ought to: rustic, in need of some repair, and like a living room for locals. Burgers, fish and chips, pizza, and barbecue ribs go perfectly with a cold beer from the bar.

A locals' choice is the **Restaurant at the River Inn** (46840 Hwy. 1, 831/667-2700 or 800/548-3610, www.bigsurriverinn.com, 8am-9pm daily, $15-33). With a welcoming stone fireplace and full bar inside, the restaurant serves big plates of standard American breakfast, lunch, and dinner fare. If you can, order the Roadhouse Ribs at the backyard barbecue and enjoy the sunshine on the creekside porch. If you need something on the go, the inn's General Store has a **burrito bar** (11am-7pm daily) where you can build your own hearty lunch.

Serving three meals each day to lodge guests and passersby, the **Big Sur Lodge Café and Restaurant** (47225 Hwy. 1, 800/242-4787, www.bigsurlodge.com, 8am-9pm daily, $14-32) has a dining room as well as a cute espresso bar and deli out front. The dining room dishes up a full menu of American classics for every meal, or you can grab a quick sandwich and cappuccino to go.

The ★ **Big Sur Bakery** (47540 Hwy. 1, 831/667-0520, www.bigsurbakery.com, 9am-3:30pm Mon., 9am-3:30pm 5:30pm-close Tues.-Fri., 10:30am-2:30pm, 5:30pm-close Sat.-Sun., $17-32) might sound like a casual, walk-up spot, and, sure enough, you can get a homemade jelly donut or a flaky croissant sandwich along with a latte. But in the dining room, an elegant surprise awaits diners. Be sure to make reservations so you can experience the wood-fired pizza, pan-roasted halibut, and grilled octopus.

If you're going to eat anywhere in Big Sur, save your appetite for ★ **Nepenthe** (48510 Hwy. 1, 831/667-2345, www.nepenthebigsur.com, 11:30am-10pm daily, $15-45). Since 1949, Nepenthe has been entertaining guests in its cool midcentury modern building and out on the terraced patio warmed by the open fire pit, overlooking perhaps the most brilliant vista in Big Sur. The menu is short, but carefully selected, and the full bar pours a healthy variety of beer, wine, and cocktails. For something warm on a foggy afternoon, order the Hot Apple Pie (cider and *tuaca*, topped with whipped cream), a Big Sur original. The downside of Nepenthe is the crowds. If you stop in on a sunny weekend or during the summer, expect a wait. Luckily, you can lounge on the patio with a drink from the bar. Should the wait be too excruciating, the seasonal **Cafe Kevah** (Mar.-Jan., $10-16) serves soup, salads, and sandwiches, along with coffee and pastries, from a walk-up window.

According to Big Sur locals, the best breakfast in the area can be had at ★ **Deetjens** (48865 Hwy. 1, 831/667-2378, www.deetjens.com, 8am-noon, 6pm-9pm Mon.-Fri., 8am-12:30pm, 6pm-9pm Sat.-Sun., $24-42). The funky dining room, with its mismatched tables, dark wooden chairs, and cluttered wall decor, accentuates the high quality of the cuisine served. Dinner veers toward the epicurean, with plates of seared duck and filet mignon, but breakfast is more down to earth, filled with fresh eggs, bright berries, and maple syrup.

Past Deetjens, dining options get slimmer. With a perpetual wait for a table at Treebone's **Wild Coast Restaurant and Sushi Bar** (71895 Hwy. 1, 805/927-2390, www.treebonesresort.com, noon-2pm, 6pm-8:30pm daily, sushi bar 5:30pm-8:30pm Wed.-Mon. Mar.-Dec., $25-33), this eco-lodge is doing something right. Utilizing the large garden, the restaurant serves a select menu of locally inspired dishes. The 12-seat sushi bar delivers a dizzying array of sashimi and sushi rolls. Can't get enough of the view? Take a table outside on the wraparound deck.

Two options on this remote part of the coast are **Lucia Lodge Restaurant** (62400 Hwy. 1, 831/667-2718 or 866/424-4787, www.

dining at Nepenthe

lucialodge.com, 11am-4pm, 5pm-8pm daily, $15-32) and **Ragged Point Inn** (19019 Hwy. 1, 805/927-4502, http://raggedpointinn.com, 8am-11am, noon-4pm, 5pm-9pm daily, $22-40). Both boast spectacular views and French-inspired California cuisine. The fish and chips at the Lucia Lodge is rave-worthy, and the cozy dining room, built in the 1930s, is charming. At the Ragged Point Inn, lunch is the best deal, as the eclectic menu is the most affordable and appeals to more palates. In summer, the restaurant opens a sandwich stand, serving classic American fast food along with locally made ice cream, while live music keeps the mood festive.

Fine Dining

You don't need to be a guest at the Ventana to enjoy a refined dinner at the **Restaurant at Ventana** (Hwy. 1, 831/667-4242, www.ventanainn.com, 7:30am-4:30pm, 6pm-9pm daily, $28-38). The spacious dining room boasts a wood fire, open kitchen, and comfortable banquettes with throw pillows to lounge against. Request a table outside to enjoy the stunning views. The dining room also has great views, along with a forest of wood lining the walls, floors, and bars. The chef offers a daily spread of haute California dishes, many of which feature organic or homegrown produce and local meats. Ventana's menu is heavy on sustainable seafood offerings.

The **Sierra Mar** (47900 Hwy. 1, 831/667-2800, www.postranchinn.com, 12:15pm-3pm, 5:30pm-9pm daily, $125) restaurant at the Post Ranch Inn offers decadent prix fixe lunch and dinner in a stunning ocean-view setting. The highbrow menus seek to celebrate the Big Sur experience with such inventive delicacies as bay laurel brioche, venison tartare, and red abalone.

INFORMATION AND SERVICES

It is not surprising that the place to go for visitor information is the multi-agency, ranger-led **Big Sur Station** (just south of Pfeiffer Big Sur State Park, 831/667-2315, 9am-4pm daily). The fairly large complex is run by Caltrans, the Los Padres National Forest, and the California State Parks. Its staff can help you with everything from getting a backcountry permit to deciding where to eat for dinner.

Information for the whole region can also be found at the visitor kiosk at **Pfeiffer Big Sur State Park** (47225 Hwy. 1, 831/667-2315, www.parks.ca.gov). The ranger will even point you in the direction of a launderette, in case you need to wash a quick load of grubby backpacking gear. This large park also offers some basic staples at the store, as does **Fernwood Resort** (47200 Hwy. 1, 831/667-2422, www.fernwoodbigsur.com). There are no supermarkets anywhere on the 90-mile stretch of road.

Gas stations are rare, too. A couple of the resorts have their own filling stations, but you pay for that convenience. Best to fuel up before you leave Carmel or San Simeon. This is especially important to remember, as cell phones do not work on much of the coast. Call boxes are set at regular intervals along the highway in case of an emergency.

Should a medical emergency arise, the **Big Sur Health Center** (46896 Hwy. 1, Big Sur, 831/667-2580, http://bigsurhealthcenter.org, 10am-5pm Mon.-Fri.) can take care of minor medical needs and limited emergency care. The **Big Sur Fire Volunteer Fire Brigade** (831/667-2113, http://bigsurfire.org) is the emergency responder for the area and has an ambulance and a 24-hour paramedic team.

TRANSPORTATION

The heart of Big Sur lies about 22 miles south of Carmel, but for many locals, Big Sur starts once you exit the Carmel Highlands. The ride is slow, as Highway 1 hugs the plunging cliffs and crosses steep river gorges. The scenery competes with the road for your attention, but there are plenty of wide turnouts if you need to take a moment and catch the view.

Cambria and San Simeon

Where the towering cliffs of Big Sur flatten out to rolling coastal grassland, San Simeon and Cambria offer travelers a remarkable final stop at the end of a remarkable road. Many artists have made this stop permanent, including one of the greatest art appreciators, mining scions, and newspaper magnates, in U.S. history, William Randolph Hearst. The castle he built on the hill became key to the economies of both San Simeon and Cambria, which originally began as whaling and mining towns, respectively. Today Hearst Castle draws thousands of visitors each year, and the region is now fully reliant on the tourist trade.

Tiny San Simeon remains largely as it did in Hearst's time, with the exception of the large chain hotels catering to summer tourists. Less than five miles south on Highway 1, Cambria is a picturesque small town with an artist colony pedigree. Along Main Street, art galleries, tasting rooms, and gift shops fill the antique buildings nestled in the pine forest. San Simeon is where the main attraction is, but Cambria has the restaurants, accommodations, and shopping to round out a weekend away.

SIGHTS

★ Hearst Castle

There's nothing in California quite like **Hearst Castle** (Hwy. 1 and Hearst Castle Rd., 800/444-4445, www.hearstcastle.com, tours 9am-3:40pm daily, adults $25, children 5-12 $12, under 5 free). Newspaper magnate William Randolph Hearst conceived the idea of a grand mansion on the land where he and his parents camped above the Pacific. He hired Julia Morgan, the first female civil engineering graduate from UC Berkeley, to design and build the house for him. She did a brilliant job with every detail, despite the ever-changing wishes of her employer. The house was to be a museum, of sorts, for Hearst's vast holding of European medieval and Renaissance antiquities, from tiny tchotchkes to whole gilded ceilings. As most of these pieces were from the Mediterranean region, the castle was modeled after a Mediterranean village, complete with a plaza and grand church facade. Because Hearst adored exotic animals, he created one of the largest private zoos in the nation on his land. Though most of the zoo is gone now, you can still see the occasional zebra grazing peacefully along Highway 1, south of the castle.

Like the estate itself, visiting is no small affair. The castle sits five miles up the hill from the visitors center, along a steep and winding road. The only way there is aboard the shuttle bus run by the park, and the only way to board the bus is by purchasing a ticket to one of the four tours offered, each focusing on a different space and aspect of the castle. The **Grand**

Hearst Castle

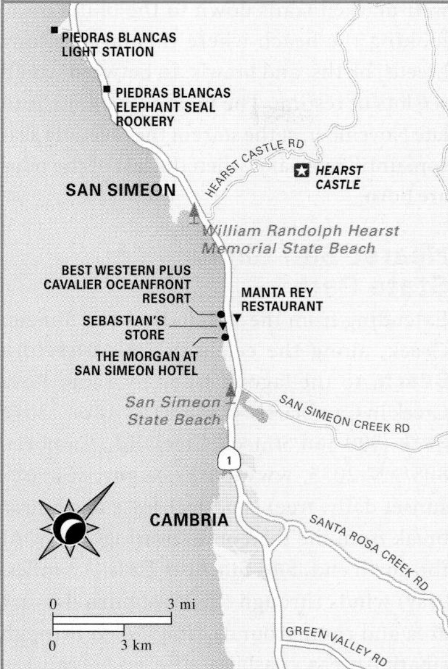

Rooms Tour is recommended for first-time visitors, and you can tack on other tours (the **Upstairs Suites Tour** and the **Cottages and Kitchen Tour**), if you have the time, interest, and money. For those who wish to get a glimpse of the glamour of Hearst Castle, the **Evening Tour** (adults $65, children 5-12 $18) offered in spring and fall, takes you through a wider swath of rooms populated by docents in 1930s attire.

Tours last 45 minutes, with the exception of the Evening Tour, which lasts 100 minutes. Expect to walk for at least an hour on whichever tour you choose and to climb up and down many stairs. Even the most jaded traveler can't help but be amazed by the beauty and opulence that drips from every room in the house. Afterward, you are free to explore the grounds until the last shuttle departs, around 5pm.

The park recommends that visitors buy tour tickets at least a few days in advance, and even farther ahead for the Evening Tour and on summer weekends. For visitors with limited mobility, a special wheelchair-accessible tour is available. Strollers, food, drink, and gum are not permitted. The visitors center is quite impressive, built to accommodate the large volume of guests that visit each day. A line of ticket windows have screens that illuminate up-to-the minute tour departure times. A theater plays the much-touted film *Hearst Castle—Building the Dream* (ticket included in the tour price). There are also a gift shop, a café selling wares from Hearst Ranch, and a bank of portable toilets lining the massive parking lot.

Historic San Simeon

The hamlet of San Simeon was established to support the construction of Hearst Castle. Its motley collection of warehouses housed Hearst's art, the dock brought in materials for construction, the general store and post office acted as a central gathering place for the community, and the tiny schoolhouse educated their children. Like the castle visible above, San Simeon remains mostly unchanged. You can still walk up the weathered wooden steps of **Sebastian's Store** (442 Slo San Simeon, 805/927-3307, 11am-4pm Tues.-Sun.) and buy a bite to eat. Or taste wine from **Hearst Ranch Winery** (805/927-4100, www.hearstranchwinery.com, 11am-5pm daily, $10), which produces a number of tasty Central Coast varietals.

William Randolph Hearst Memorial State Beach

The cove where ships unloaded tons of marble and piles of antiques for Hearst Castle is now a part of the **William Randolph Hearst Memorial State Beach** (750 Hearst Castle Rd., San Simeon, 805/927-2020, www.parks.ca.gov, dawn-dusk daily). The sheltered beach is popular with beachcombers, sunbathers, kayakers, and surfers. Near the parking lot and overlooking the remaining structure of the old pier are 24 picnic sites with barbecue grills. To get the most of the scenery, take the **San Simeon Bay Trail** to San Simeon Point for an easy, six-mile out-and-back hike. You can also learn more about the unique ecology here at the **Coastal Discovery Center** (805/927-6575, http://montereybay.noaa.gov, 11am-5pm Fri.-Sun., free), a joint project between the Monterey Bay Aquarium and the California state park system.

Piedras Blancas Lighthouse

Visible from Hearst Castle is the **Piedras Blancas Lighthouse** (15950 Cabrillo Hwy., 805/927-7361, www.piedrasblancas.org, tours 9:45am Tues., Thurs., and Sat., adult $12, children 6-17 $5, under 6 free). Six miles north of San Simeon, the handsomely restored lighthouse was established in 1875 and sits surrounded by protected coastal prairie. The immense white rock outcroppings just offshore not only give the lighthouse its name, but also are home to a rich array of shorebirds and marine wildlife. To visit the lighthouse, you must be a part of a tour. These occur three mornings a week, do not require reservations, and leave promptly from the old Piedras Blancas Motel, 1.5 miles north of the lighthouse.

Just south of the lighthouse is the popular **Northern Elephant Seal Rookery** (Hwy. 1, 805/924-1628, www.elephantseal.org), home to nearly 16,000 giant elephant seals. From the large parking lot off the highway, take the well-marked trails down to the bluffs overlooking the beach where this large colony breeds, births, and brawls. In between, you'll see lots of resting. The most active time is in late November, at the start of the breeding season, until February, when the last of the pups are born.

Hearst San Simeon State Park

Extending from the wetlands of San Simeon Creek, along the celebrated **Moonstone Beach,** to the lagoon filled by Santa Rosa Creek in Cambia, **Hearst San Simeon State Park** (500 San Simeon Creek Rd., Cambria, 805/927-2035, www.parks.ca.gov, sunrise-sunset daily, free) is perfect for a few hours' break from the road or an overnight stay. At the north end, **San Simeon Trail** (3.3 miles, easy) winds through the Washburn day-use area and campgrounds. You'll pass through riparian areas, coastal prairie, and ocean-top bluffs. There are two large campgrounds at this end of the park. Closest to the ocean, **San Simeon Creek Campground** ($20-25) has

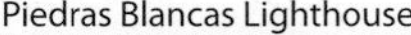

Piedras Blancas Lighthouse

Cambria

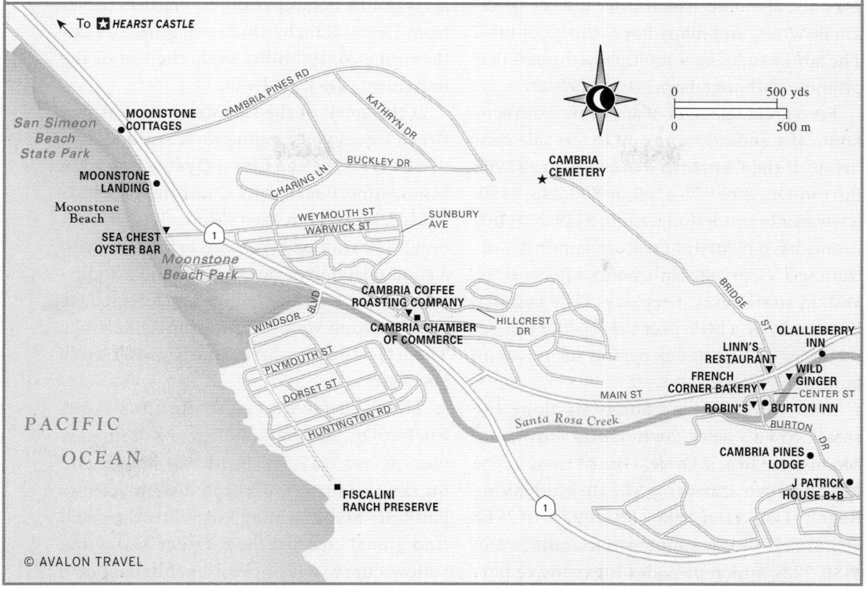

134 sites for tents and RVs, plus flush toilets, coin operated showers, a sanitation dump, and water fill stations. An additional 56 primitive sites are located roughly a mile inland at the **Washburn Campground**.

To get the most out of the coast, the mile-long **Moonstone Boardwalk** hugs the beach. It starts at the parking lot of **Leffingwell Landing,** where you will also find a boat launch and excellent opportunities for tide pooling. The boardwalk and the beach are both open to dogs.

ACCOMMODATIONS

A number of large chains and chain-like hotels line Highway 1 in San Simeon near Hearst Castle. For little-to-no difference in price, opt to stay a few miles away in picturesque Cambria. The accommodations here do their best to charm guests without charging an arm and a leg.

A favorite among the many inns of Cambria, the **Olallieberry Inn** (2476 Main St., Cambria, 805/927-3222, www.olallieberry.com, $140-225) sits in a charming 19th-century Greek Revival home and adjacent cottage, walking distance from downtown. Each of the nine rooms features its own quaint Victorian-inspired decor, with comfortable beds and attractive appointments. Six rooms have private baths. A full daily breakfast (complete with olallieberry jam) rounds out the comfortable and personal experience.

Perched on the wooded hill above downtown, a charming log cabin shelters the seven rooms of the **J. Patrick House Bed and Breakfast** (2990 Burton Dr., Cambria, 805/927-3812 or 800/341-5258, www.jpatrickhouse.com, $175-185). Each room is decorated with classic dark wood antiques, with a simple modern aesthetic, a private bath, and plenty of amenities. They're dedicated to feeding you at J. Patrick, with a big breakfast in the morning, hors d'oeuvres in the afternoon, and chocolate chip cookies at bedtime.

The Burton Inn (4022 Burton Dr.,

805/927-5125, www.burtoninn.com, $135-225) offers modernity in an attractive setting. Even the standard rooms offer tons of space, kitchenettes, and many have whirlpool tubs. The family suites have multiple bedrooms that promote both togetherness and privacy.

For a great selection of anything from economical standard rooms up to sizeable cabins, pick the **Cambria Pines Lodge** (2905 Burton Dr., 805/927-4200 or 800/445-6490, www.cambriapineslodge.com, $129-259). All rooms have plenty of creature comforts, including TVs, private bathrooms, kitchenettes, and, in some cases, fireplaces. The country kitsch may be a little over the top, but this resort does its best and is perfect for traveling families.

Many of Cambria's hotels sit along the small town's very own Hotel Row, aka Moonstone Beach Drive. One of these is the **Moonstone Landing** (6240 Moonstone Beach Dr., Cambria, 805/927-0012 or 800/830-4540, www.moonstonelanding.com, $180-272), which provides inexpensive partial-view rooms with the decor and amenities of a mid-tier chain motel, as well as oceanfront luxury rooms featuring travertine marble bathrooms.

One of the cuter and more interesting lodgings on Moonstone Beach Drive, **Moonstone Cottages** (6580 Moonstone Beach Dr., Cambria, 805/927-1366 or 800/222-9157, http://moonstonecottages.com, $250-369) offers peace and luxury along with proximity to the sea. Expect your cottage to include a fireplace, a marble bathroom with a whirlpool tub, a flat screen TV with a DVD player, Internet access, and a view of the ocean.

FOOD

As with accommodations, the best food options in the area are found in Cambria. The one shining exception is the historical ★ **Sebastian's Store** (442 Slo San Simeon Rd., San Simeon, 805/927-3307, 11am-4pm daily, $8-12). Built in 1852 and established as the town's general store in 1914, Sebastian's Store serves burgers, hot sandwiches, and sides from a walk-up counter. The beef comes from Hearst Ranch, which still grazes its cattle on the coastal hills, while the rest of the ingredients are farm fresh.

If the smell of the salt air on Moonstone Beach leaves you longing for a seafood dinner, head for the **Sea Chest Oyster Bar** (6216 Moonstone Beach Dr., Cambria, 805/927-4514, 5:30pm-9pm Wed.-Mon., $20-30, cash only). The seafood here tends to be fresh, with a good selection of raw oysters, and it's tourist-friendly. No reservations are accepted, so expect a long wait for a window-side table. There is a fire pit where wine is served while you wait.

The local favorite is ★ **Robin's** (4095 Burton Dr., 805/927-5007, www.robinsrestaurant.com, $17-34). Inside the homey and quirky restaurant, decorated with eclectic paintings and charming knick-knacks, you'll find global comfort food. Order Malaysian yellow curry, wild prawn enchiladas, or a Kansas City-style New York steak. The kids menu is reasonably priced. Take a table outside on the patio, draped in flowering vines and adorned with wooden birdhouses.

If you can't get a table at Robin's, walk over to **Linn's Restaurant** (2277 Main St., Cambria, 805/927-0371, www.linnsfruitbin.com, 8am-9pm daily, $17-29). Part of an expansive, but still local, family business, Linn's serves tasty, unpretentious American favorites in a casual, family-friendly atmosphere. Order the famous olallieberry pie.

One of the best bargains in town is ★ **Wild Ginger** (2380 Main St., Cambria, 805/927-1001, www.wildgingercambria.com, 11am-2:30pm, 5pm-9pm Mon.-Wed. and Fri.-Sat., 5pm-9pm Sun., $14-19). This tiny pan-Asian café serves delicious, fresh food at its few tables and carries an array of take-out fare displayed in a glass case crammed into the back of the dining room. Come early for the best selection of dishes.

For something on the go, the **French Corner Bakery** (2214 Main St., 805/927-8227, www.frenchcornerbakery.com, 6:30am-6pm daily, $6-8) serves a selection of pastries and hot and cold sandwiches in a cute, homey atmosphere.

As suggested by the long line and crowded tables below its yellow awning, *the* place to go for coffee in Cambria is the **Cambria Coffee Roasting Company** (761 Main St., 805/927-0670, http://cambriacoffeeroasting.com, 7am-5:30pm daily). Expect a perfect cup of joe, whether it's a fancy macchiato or a filtered drip.

INFORMATION AND SERVICES

The **Hearst Castle Visitors Center and Exhibition Hall** (750 Hearst Castle Rd., 800/444-4445, www.parks.ca.gov, 8am-5pm daily) has all the information you need on visiting Hearst Castle.

There is an ATM at **Bank of America** (734 Main St.) in downtown Cambria. For medical assistance, contact the **Cambria Community Health Center** (2515 Main St., Cambia, 805/927-5292, http://communityhealthcenters.org, 8:30am-5:30pm Mon.-Fri.). The nearest emergency room to Cambria is the **Twin Cities Hospital** (1100 Las Tablas Rd., Templeton, 805/434-3500, www.twincitieshospital.com), 25 miles east, near at the junction of U.S. 101and Highway 46.

TRANSPORTATION

San Simeon sits roughly 140 miles south of Carmel on the slow and scenic Highway 1. Cambria is less than five miles south of that. From San Francisco, take U.S. 101 to the Paso Robles area and then turn west onto Highway 46, which brings you right to the town of Cambria. This route is 230 miles, which is a four-hour drive.

There's not much to navigating San Simeon. To get to downtown Cambria, exit Highway 1 at Windsor Boulevard, turning right on to Main Street. Shops, restaurants, and galleries cluster on Main between Windsor and Cambria Road, and then again around the intersection of Main and Burton Drive to the east. There are a number of large churches and newish housing developments in between.

Background

The Landscape

GEOGRAPHY

Northern California's geographic profile is as diverse as its population. At nearly 159,000 square miles, California is the third-largest state in the United States, stretching 770 miles from the Oregon state line to its southern border with Mexico. Northern California includes the Sierra Nevada mountain range, numerous national parks and monuments, coastal and giant redwoods, volcanoes, the agricultural Central Valley, and the tallest mountain in the continental United States, Mount Whitney, at 14,505 feet. In addition, two major tectonic plates—the north-moving Pacific and south-moving North American Plate—give Northern California a reputation for shaking things up a bit.

Mountain Ranges

The Northern California coast is characterized by craggy cliffs, rocky beaches, and enormous coast redwoods (*Sequoia sempervirens*) that reach heights up to 380 feet. The coast is bounded by the aptly named Coast Range, ruggedly steep mountains formed 30 million years ago when part of the Pacific Plate jammed, folded, and compressed to form the Coast Range and Transverse Range. In addition to the Coast Range, there are two other significant high-elevation regions in the state. In the north, the Cascade Mountains evolved through volcanic activity 10 million years ago when the Juan de Fuca Plate, the earth's smallest tectonic plate (between the North American and Pacific Plates), collided with the North American Plate and was forced under the larger plate. Magma from the melting plate raised a series of mountains, including California's two active volcanoes—Mount Lassen and Mount Shasta. Mount Lassen (10,462 feet) last blew its top in 1915; today the surrounding park offers a glimpse into the earth's formation. Majestic Mount Shasta, along I-5 north of Redding, has not erupted in quite some time. At 14,179 feet, Mount Shasta's extreme height creates its own weather system.

To the east is the Sierra Nevada, stretching 400 miles north-south and forming the eastern spine of the state. Its peaks and valleys include Mount Whitney, Lake Tahoe, Yosemite, and the giant sequoias (*Sequoiadendron giganteum*) in Sequoia and Kings Canyon National Parks. The Sierra Nevada formed 60 million years ago when magma seeped up between the Pacific and North American Plates. It created a massive pool of granite that slowly cooled to form a batholith, a massive dome-shaped formation of intrusive igneous rock. For the past 12 million years the formation has been pushing upward.

Earthquakes and Faults

Earthquakes occur when the tectonic plates that compose the earth's crust shift along faults, the boundaries between the plates—and Northern California's seat on the Pacific Ring of Fire is well established. The North American Plate and Pacific Plate came together about 150 million years ago, causing compression and folding of the earth's crust that created the Sierra Nevada; it eventually eroded to fill with sediments what would become the Central Valley. About 30 million years ago a ridge of the Pacific Plate became jammed and caused the folding and compression that formed the Coast and Transverse Ranges. More importantly, the contact caused the Pacific Plate to change direction and move northward, forming the San Andreas Fault.

Previous: Yosemite in autumn; colorful Victorians in San Francisco.

Earthquake Tips

Visitors from outside California may have the impression that big earthquakes happen here all the time. Well, that's only partly correct. Earthquakes do happen all the time, but most shakers are measurable only by sophisticated equipment and remain unfelt by most residents. According to the California Office of Emergency Services, there are some things you can do to protect yourself during an earthquake:

- Drop! Cover! Hold on! California schoolchildren learn this early on through education programs. It means that if an earthquake begins, drop to the ground. Find cover under a sturdy desk or table, or stand in a corner or doorway. Hold on to something sturdy if the ground begins to pitch.
- If you're in a high-rise building, avoid elevators, windows, and outside areas.
- If you're outside, move to a clear area away from trees, buildings, overpasses, walls, and power lines—anything that could fall on you.
- If you're in a car, pull over to the side of the road. Make sure you're not parked underneath a structure that could collapse.
- If you're inside a crowded place, do not rush to the exit. Instead, squat down and protect your head and neck with your hands and arms.

It's important to stay as calm as possible after an earthquake; the ground may start shaking again. Aftershocks, usually smaller, often follow a sizeable earthquake and originate near the same location. A mild earthquake might cause anxiety, but it should not affect your travel plans aside from slight delays in public transportation and other inconveniences. A major earthquake—magnitude 4.5 and larger—is a different story, but these earthquakes are pretty uncommon (it's more likely that you'll win the state lottery than experience a major earthquake).

For more information on what to do before, during, and after an earthquake, visit the California Office of Emergency Services (www.calema.ca.gov) and the U.S. Geological Survey (www.usgs.gov).

This infamous strike-slip fault, where two tectonic plates move horizontally, the North American Plate moving mostly southward and the Pacific Plate moving mostly northward, runs along the North Coast, near San Francisco, and east of Los Angeles before branching off into Mexico and the Pacific Ocean.

The plates frequently catch as they move past each other, storing energy and causing tension to build. When the plates jolt past one another, they release this energy in the form of an earthquake. The San Andreas Fault is not the only fault in Northern California; earthquakes along numerous faults happen daily, 10,000-37,000 times each year. Most register less than magnitude 3 and go unnoticed by Californians used to the shake, rattle, and roll. However, there have been several significant earthquakes in Northern California history. The 1906 San Francisco earthquake had a magnitude of 7.7-8.3 and involved the "rupturing" of the northern 300 miles of the San Andreas Fault from San Juan Bautista to Cape Mendocino. The 1989 Loma Prieta earthquake, with an epicenter near Loma Prieta Peak in the Santa Cruz Mountains, was small by comparison at magnitude 6.9

and with only 25 miles of ruptured fault. California's stringent building codes, developed in the wake of deadly and destructive earthquakes, include an extensive seismic retrofit program that has brought older buildings, overpasses, bridges, and other structures up to strict standards.

CLIMATE

Vast in size and varied in geography, Northern California also has a vastly varied climate, from boiling heat in the Central Valley to subarctic temperatures at mountain summits.

Along the North Coast, the weather stays fairly constant: chilly, windy, and foggy. Summer days rarely reach 80°F, and winter rainstorms can pound the area. San Francisco shares its cool and foggy climate, with temperatures in the 50s and 60s well into summer. South on the peninsula or across the bay in Marin County and the East Bay, the temperature may rise 20-30 degrees and the fog often makes way for sun.

North of San Francisco, the Wine Country is graced with milder weather and warm summers, perfect for growing grapes. Inland, Sacramento and the Central Valley can be very hot. Daily temperatures in summer can peak well over 100°F and often worsen air quality, causing Spare the Air alerts. Winters in the Central Valley are cool and usually clear, though the nearby Sierra Nevada foothills often receive snow in the winter, and roads can become impassable.

Expect harsh weather if you head to Yosemite, Lake Tahoe, Mount Shasta, Mount Lassen, or the Eastern Sierra in the winter. Snowfall in a 24-hour period can be measured in feet, forcing road closures and power outages that wreak havoc with travel plans. But activities such as skiing, snowboarding, sledding, snowshoeing, and snow camping abound. The short hot summers draw campers, hikers, and mountain bikers.

The Central Coast is a bit warmer than the San Francisco Bay Area, but still, expect cool temperatures and fog in summer. A chilly wind accompanies the rain in the winter, often closing mountain roads and highways, including Highway 1.

ENVIRONMENTAL ISSUES

Californians face several major environmental issues. The state battles drought, so water for crops, farms, and human consumption is in short supply. Conservation measures include limiting development and urban sprawl, restricting water usage, and designating set periods for personal and recreational use, such as watering lawns.

Water pollution is also an issue. Most tap water is safe to drink, but swimming in California's plentiful bays, lakes, and rivers as well as the Pacific Ocean requires more caution. Pollution may cause *E. coli* outbreaks at beaches, affecting wildlife and beachgoers alike. Fishing is no longer permitted in San Francisco Bay because of high mercury levels in the bay's fish.

Northern California's lakes have also been affected by infestations of invasive zebra mussels, which grow so quickly and profusely that they can clog water intakes and outcompete native mussels and clams. Many boat restrictions are in effect at coastal waterways and mountain lakes to control the spread of the infestation; check with the Department of Fish and Game (916/445-0411, www.dfg.ca.gov) for more information.

Many of the state's grand oak trees have succumbed to sudden oak death, a disease that spreads through spores to eventually kill live oaks, black oaks, and tan oaks. To control its spread, travelers are advised to clean all camping equipment thoroughly and to buy and burn local firewood rather than importing it from elsewhere.

Plants and Animals

PLANTS

Redwoods

A visit to Northern California's famous redwoods should be on every traveler's list. The coast redwood (*Sequoia sempervirens*) grows along the North Coast as far south as Big Sur. Coast redwoods are characterized by their towering height, flaky red bark, and moist understory. Among the tallest trees on earth, they are also some of the oldest, with some individuals almost 2,000 years old. Coast redwoods occupy a narrow strip of coastal California, growing less than 50 miles inland to collect moisture from the ocean and fog. Their tannin-rich bark is crucial to their ability to survive wildfires and regenerate afterward. The best places to marvel at the giants are within the Redwood National and State Parks, Muir Woods, and Big Basin State Park.

The giant sequoia (*Sequoiadendron giganteum*) grows farther inland in a 260-mile belt at 2,700-8,900 feet elevation in the Sierra Nevada mountain range. Giant sequoias are the largest trees by volume on earth; they can grow to heights of 280 feet with a diameter up to 26 feet and can live for thousands of years. Giant sequoias share the ruddy bark of the coast sequoia as well as its fire-resistant qualities. The best places to see giant sequoias up close are at Sequoia and Kings Canyon National Parks, Calaveras Big Trees, and the Mariposa Grove at Yosemite National Park.

Sequoia Gate in Mariposa Grove at Yosemite National Park

Oaks

Northern California is home to many native oaks. The most common are the valley oak, black oak, live oak, and coastal live oak. The deciduous valley oak (*Quercus lobata*) commonly grows on slopes, valleys, and wooded foothills in the Central Valley. The black oak, also deciduous, grows throughout the foothills of the Coast Range and Sierra Nevada; it is unfortunately one of the victims of sudden oak death. The live oak habitat is in the Central Valley, and the coastal live oak occupies the Coast Range. The acorns of all these oaks were an important food supply for California's Native American population and continue to be an important food source for wildlife.

Wildflowers

California's state flower is the California poppy (*Eschscholzia californica*). The pretty little perennial grows just about everywhere, even on the sides of the busiest highways. The flowers of most California poppies are bright orange, but they also appear occasionally in white, cream, and an even deeper red-orange.

ANIMALS

Mountain Lions

Mountain lions (*Felis concolor*) are an example of powerful and potentially deadly

a California poppy, the state's official flower

beauty. Their solitary territorial hunting habits make them elusive, but human contact has increased as more homes are built in mountain lion habitat throughout California. Many parks in or near mountain lion territory post signs with warnings and advice: Do not run if you come across a mountain lion; instead make noise and raise and wave your arms so that you look bigger. The California Fish and Game Department (www.dfg.ca.gov) offers a downloadable brochure on encounters and other tips.

Black Bears

Don't take the name black bear (*Ursus americanus*) too literally. The black bear can actually have brown and even cinnamon-colored fur, sometimes with a white patch on the chest. The black bear is pretty common throughout North America, including in the forests of Northern California south to Sonoma County, the Sierra Nevada, and the Transverse Range. Although the black bear can appear cuddly from a distance, distance is exactly what should separate bears and humans—at least 25 feet or more. These are wild animals; do not attempt to feed or approach them, and never come between a mama bear and her cubs. Bears can run up to 30 mph, and they can definitely outrun you. Campers should use bear-proof food lockers at campgrounds or a bear canister in the backcountry; never keep food or any scented products (toothpaste, energy bars, hair products) in a tent or in view inside a car. Bears can be crafty and destructive—some, especially in Yosemite National Park, have broken into cars and shredded the interiors looking for food. Bears are mostly nocturnal but can be seen out during the day, and they do not always hibernate in winter.

Coyote

Coyotes (*Canis latrans*), a wild canine related to wolves, are everywhere in California—even suburbs and city parks, and especially on the trail. Coyotes have a storied place in the tall tales and native legends of the West, often portrayed as a wily and shrewd beast with a shrill "yip-yip-yip" howl that's downright spooky. Like black bears, coyotes usually won't hurt humans; these resourceful critters mostly hunt small mammals and reptiles or even medium-sized livestock like pigs and sheep. Coyotes don't have the fearsome reputation of wolves, but nonetheless, be careful and don't feed them; though incidents are uncommon, coyotes have been known to attack humans.

Tule Elk

Tule elk (*Cervus elaphus nannodes*, also known as wapiti, California elk, or dwarf elk) are the smallest elk in North America and once thrived in the Central Valley, but were nearly hunted to extinction to feed Gold Rush settlers. There are now almost 3,000 tule elk in approximately 20 free-range and protected herds in several grassland habitats in the Central Valley and Point Reyes National Seashore. Usually pale gray, brown, or tan with thick chestnut brown necks, the male bull can grow antlers that stretch five feet or more. In the fall, the bull gives a low bellow followed by a distinctive far-carrying whistle or bugle, and the female whistles in spring.

Whales

The massive, majestic gray whale (*Eschrichtius robustus*) was once endangered, but its numbers have rebounded with international protection. The gray whale measures about 40 feet long and has mottled shades of gray with black fins; its habitat is inshore ocean waters, so there is a chance to get a glimpse of them from headlands up and down the coast. Gray whales generally migrate south along the coast November-January, and closer to shore February-June when they migrate northward. Mendocino County is a perfect place to watch the water for a glimpse of whales breaching.

Perhaps a more recognizable behemoth is the humpback whale (*Megaptera novaeangliae*). At 45-55 feet long, the humpback is the only large whale to breach regularly, then roll and crash back into the water, providing one of the best shows in nature; the whale also rolls from side to side on the surface, slapping its long flippers. Humpbacks generally stay a little farther from shore, so it may be necessary to take a whale-watching cruise to catch a glimpse of them, but their 20-foot spouts can help landlubbers spot them from shore. Look for humpbacks April-early December off the coast near Big Sur, particularly at Julia Pfeiffer Burns State Park.

The blue whale (*Balaenoptera musculus*) is the largest animal on earth. At 70-90 feet long, the blue whale even exceeds dinosaurs in size. With a blue-gray top and a yellowish bottom,

a black bear in Sequoia National Park

sea lions at Pier 39 in San Francisco

the blue whale has a heart the size of a small car, along with two blowholes, but alas does not breach. They can be seen June-November off the Northern California coast, but especially at Monterey and north of Point Reyes.

California Sea Lions

Watching a beach full of California sea lions (*Zalophus californianus*) sunning themselves and noisily honking away can be a pleasure. Sea lions are migratory, so they come and go at will, especially in the fall when they head to the Channel Islands for breeding. If you have a serious hankering to see California sea lions, try Pier 39 near Fisherman's Wharf or on the coast at Seal Rocks, both in San Francisco.

Sea Otters

Much higher on the cuteness scale is the sea otter (*Enhydra lutris*), which can be spotted just off shore in shallow kelp beds. Once near extinction, the endearing playful sea otter has survived; now there are more than 2,000 in California waters. It can be a bit mesmerizing to witness a sea otter roll on its back in the water and use a rock to break open mollusks for lunch. Sea otter habitat runs mainly from Monterey Bay to Big Sur, but they have also been spotted in the waters near Mendocino.

Birds

California has a wide range of habitat with accessible food and water that makes it perfect for hundreds of bird species to nest, raise their young, or just stop over and rest during long migrations. Nearly 600 species have been spotted in California, so it may be just the place for a bird-watcher's vacation.

Among the most regal of California's bird species are raptors. The red-tailed hawk (*Buteo jamaicensis*) is found throughout California and is frequently sighted perched in trees along the North Coast highway, in the Central Valley, and even in urban areas such as San Francisco. The red-tailed hawk features a light underbelly with a dark band and a distinctive red tail that gives the bird its name.

Although not as common as it once was, Swainson's hawk (*Buteo swainsoni*) has been an indicator species in California's environment. The Swainson's hawk population has declined from loss of habitat and excessive pesticide use in agricultural lands in the Central Valley; its main diet consists of the locusts and grasshoppers that feed on these crops, passing the contaminants on to the birds. These hawks are smaller than the red-tailed hawk, with dark brown coloring and some white underparts either on the chest or under the tail.

Reptiles

Several varieties of rattlesnakes are indigenous to the state. The Pacific Northwest rattler makes its home in Northern California, while more than half a dozen different rattlesnake varieties live in Southern California, including the western diamondback and the Mojave rattlesnake.

If you spot California's most infamous native reptile, keep your distance. All rattlesnakes are venomous, though death by snakebite is extremely rare in California. Most parks with known rattlesnake populations post signs alerting hikers to their presence; hikers should stay on marked trails and avoid tromping off into meadows or brush. Pay attention when hiking, especially when negotiating rocks and woodpiles, and never put a foot or a hand down in a spot you can't see first. Wear long pants and heavy hiking boots for protection from snakes as well as insects, other critters, and unfriendly plants you might encounter.

Butterflies

California's vast population of wildflowers attracts an array of gorgeous butterflies. The monarch butterfly (*Danaus plexippus*) is emblematic of the state. These large orange-and-black butterflies have a migratory pattern that's reminiscent of birds. Starting in August, they begin migrating south to cluster in groves of eucalyptus trees. As they crowd together and close up their wings to hibernate, their dull outer wing color camouflages them as clumps of dried leaves, thus protecting them from predators. In spring, the butterflies begin to wake up, fluttering lazily in the groves for a while before flying north to seek out milkweed on which to lay their eggs. Pacific Grove, Santa Cruz, and Cambria are great places to visit these California "butterfly trees."

History

THE FIRST RESIDENTS

The diverse ecology of California allowed Native Americans to adapt to the land in various ways. Communities settled from the border of present-day Oregon south through the mountain ranges and valleys, along the coast, into the Sierra Nevada, and in the arid lands that stretch into Mexico. These groups include the Maidu, Miwok, Yurok, and Pomo. More than 100 Native American languages were spoken in California, and each language had several dialects, all of which were identified with geographic areas. There are about two dozen distinct Native American groups in the Del Norte-Humboldt-Mendocino area alone. Here is an overview of the groups most commonly encountered when traveling around the state.

Yurok

The Yurok people are the largest Native American population in California, and they continue to live along the Klamath River and the Humboldt County coast near Redwood National Park, north of Eureka and south of Crescent City. Spanish explorers arriving in 1775 were the Yurok's first contact with Europeans. Fur traders and trappers from the Hudson's Bay Company arrived in about 1827, but it wasn't until gold miners arrived in 1850 that the Yurok faced disease and destruction that diminished their population by 75 percent. Researchers put the 1770 population at 2,500-3,100, which dropped to 669-700 by 1910. Today more than 5,000 Yurok live in California, and about 6,000 live in the United States overall.

Pomo

The name for the Pomo people and their language first meant "those who live at the red earth hole," possibly referring to the magnesite used for red beads or the reddish earth and clay mined in the area. It was also once the name of a village near the present-day community of Pomo in Potter Valley. The Pomo territory was large, bounded by the Pacific Ocean to the west and extending inland to Clear Lake in Lake County. Today the territory includes present-day Santa Rosa and much of the Sonoma County wine country.

In 1800 there were 10,000-18,000 Pomo living in approximately 70 communities that spoke seven Pomo languages. But as the Pomo interacted and traded with the Russians at Fort Ross, added pressure came from the

a Pomo woman gathering seeds (1924 photo by Edward S. Curtis)

Spanish missionaries and American settlers pressing in from the south and east. European encroachment may have been the reason Pomo villages became more centralized and why many Pomo retreated to remote areas to band together in defense.

The Pomo suffered not only from lifestyle changes and loss of territory but from diseases for which they had no immunity. Missionaries, traders, and settlers brought with them measles, smallpox, and other diseases that devastated indigenous populations. In 1850 miners began settling in the Russian River Valley, and the Lake Sonoma Valley was homesteaded. As a result, the U.S. government forced the Pomo off their land and onto reservations. Historians believe there were 3,500-5,000 Pomo in 1851, but only 777-1,200 by 1910. There were nearly 5,000 Pomo by the early 1990s.

Miwok

Before contact with white settlers in 1769, the Miwok people lived in small bands in separate parts of California. The Plains and Sierra Miwok lived on the Sacramento-San Joaquin Delta, parts of the San Joaquin and Sacramento Valleys, and the foothills and western slopes of the Sierra Nevada. The Coast Miwok—including the Bodega Bay Miwok and the Marin Miwok—lived in what is now Marin County and southern Sonoma County. Lake Miwok people were found in the Clear Lake Basin of Lake County. The Bay Miwok were in present-day Contra Costa County. Miwok domesticated dogs and grew tobacco but otherwise depended on hunting, fishing, and gathering for food. Miwok in the Sierra exploited the California black oak for acorns, and it is believed that they cultivated the tree in parts of what is now Yosemite National Park.

Like so many indigenous people in California, the Miwok suffered after explorers, missionaries, miners, and settlers arrived. Historians estimate there were at least 11,000 Miwok in 1770, but in all four regions there were only about 671 Miwok in 1910 and 491 in 1930. Today there are about 3,500 Miwok.

Ohlone

The Ohlone people once occupied what is now San Francisco, Berkeley, Oakland, Silicon Valley, Santa Cruz, Monterey, and the lower Salinas Valley. The Ohlone (a Miwok word meaning "western people") lived in permanent villages, only moving temporarily to gather seasonal foods such as acorns and berries. The Ohlone formed an association of about 50 different communities with an average of 200 members each. The villages interacted through trade, marriages, and ceremonies. Basket weaving, ceremonial dancing, piercings and tattoos, and general ornamentation indicated status within the community and were all part of Ohlone life. Like other Native Americans in the region, the Ohlone depended on hunting, fishing, gathering, and agrarian skills such as burning off old growth each year to get a better yield from seeds.

The Ohlone culture remained fairly stable until the first Spanish missionaries arrived to spread Christianity and to expand Spanish territorial claims. Spanish explorer Sebastián Vizcaíno reached present-day Monterey in December 1602, and the Rumsen group of Ohlone were the first they encountered. Father Junípero Serra's missionaries built seven missions on Ohlone land, and most of the Ohlone people were brought to the missions to live and work. For the next 60 years, the Ohlone suffered, as did most indigenous people at the missions. Along with the culture shock of subjugation came the diseases for which they had no immunity—measles, smallpox, syphilis, and others. It wasn't until 1834 that the California missions were abolished and the Mexican government redistributed the mission land holdings.

The Ohlone lost the vast majority of their population between 1780 and 1850 because of disease, social upheaval from European incursion, and low birth rates. Estimates are that there were 7,000-26,000 Ohlone when Spanish soldiers and missionaries arrived, and about 3,000 in 1800 and 864-1,000 by 1852. There are 1,500-2,000 Ohlone people today.

Yokut

The Yokut people have inhabited the Central Valley for at least 8,000 years; they may even have been the first people to settle here. The Yokuts live in the San Joaquin Valley from the Sacramento-San Joaquin River Delta south to Bakersfield and east to the Sierra foothills. Sequoia and Kings Canyon National Parks are included in this area, as are the cities of Fresno and Modesto. Like other Native Americans, the Yokuts developed water transportation, harvesting abundant tule reeds to work them into canoes.

Spanish explorers entered the valley in 1772 and found 63 different Yokut groups scattered up and down the Central Valley. Many of the Yokuts were taken to the various missions, where they suffered from European subjugation and diseases. Later, as miners entered the region, the Yokut people were forced from their lands. There may have been as many as 4,500 Yokuts when the Spaniards arrived, but the last full-blooded member of the Southern Yokuts is said to have died in 1960. Yokut descendants today live on the Tule River Reservation near Porterville and at the Santa Rosa Rancheria near Lemoore.

Paiute basket weaver in Yosemite (1900 photo by C. C. Pierce)

Paiute

The Paiute people are grouped by their language—despite location, political connection, or even genetic similarity. For the Northern Paiutes and the Southern Paiutes, that language is the Numic branch of the Uto-Aztecan family of Native American languages. The Northern Paiutes live in the Great Basin; the Southern Paiutes lived in the Mojave Desert on the edge of present-day Death Valley National Park. Between the Northern Paiutes and the Southern Paiutes are the Mono Lake Northern Paiutes and the Owens Valley Paiutes.

The Northern Paiute lifestyle was well adapted to the harsh environment of the Great Basin. Each band occupied a territory usually centered around a lake or other water source that also provided fish and waterfowl. Food drives to capture rabbits and pronghorn were communal and often involved nearby bands. Piñon nuts were gathered and stored for winter, and grass seeds and roots were part of the diet. Because of their remoteness, the Northern Paiutes may have completely avoided the hardships of the mission period. Their first contact with European Americans may have occurred in 1820, but sustained contact did not happen until the 1840s; several violent confrontations over land and other conflicts occurred in this period. In the end, smallpox did more to decimate the Northern Paiutes than warfare. The Northern Paiutes established colonies that were joined by Shoshone and Washoe people and eventually received recognition by the federal government.

The Southern Paiutes were not as fortunate as the Northern Paiutes. The first contact with Europeans came in 1776, when the priests Silvestre Vélez de Escalante and Francisco Atanasio Domínguez met them while seeking an overland route to the California missions. The Southern Paiutes suffered slave raids by the Navajo and Ute before Europeans arrived, and the raids increased afterward. In 1851, Mormon settlers arrived and occupied local water sources, and the slave raids ended. Settlers and their agrarian practices, such as cattle herding, drove away game and limited the Southern Paiutes' ability to gather food, disrupting their traditional lifestyle.

EXPLORATION

Juan Rodríguez Cabrillo, a Portuguese explorer and adventurer, was commissioned in 1542 by the Viceroy of New Spain (Mexico) to sail into what is now San Diego Bay. He continued north as far as Point Reyes before heading to Santa Catalina Island in late November 1542 to winter and make repairs to his ship. On Christmas Eve, Cabrillo tripped, splintering his shin, and the injury developed gangrene. He died on January 3, 1543, and is buried on Catalina. The rest of his party arrived in Barra de Navidad on April 14, 1543. Having found no wealth, advanced Native American civilization or agriculture, nor northwest passage, Portuguese interest in exploring California lapsed for more than 200 years.

Francis Drake, an English explorer, claimed a chunk of the Northern California coast in 1579. It is thought that Drake landed somewhere along Point Reyes to make extensive repairs to his only surviving ship, *The Golden Hind.* Drakes Bay, just east of Point Reyes, is marked as the spot of his landing, but the actual location is disputed. Drake eventually left California and completed the second recorded circumnavigation of the world (Ferdinand Magellan's was the first).

THE MISSION PERIOD

In the mid-1700s, Spain pushed for colonization of Alta California, rushing to occupy North America before the British beat them to it. The effort was overly ambitious and underfunded, but missionaries started to sweep into present-day California.

The priest Junípero Serra is credited with influencing the early development of California—and not necessarily for the better. A Franciscan monk, Serra played a prominent role in bringing Christianity and European diseases to Native American people from San Diego north to Sonoma County. The Franciscan order built a string of missions; each was intended to act as a self-sufficient parish that grew its own food, maintained its own buildings, and took care of its own people. However, mission structures were limited by a lack of suitable building materials and skilled labor. Later, the forced labor of Native Americans was used to cut and haul timbers and to make adobe bricks. By the time the missions were operating, they claimed about 15 percent of the land in California, or about one million acres per mission.

Spanish soldiers used subjugation to control indigenous people, pulling them from their villages and lands to the missions. Presidios (royal forts) were built near some of the missions to establish land claims, intimidate indigenous people, and carry out the overall

Carmel Mission

goal of finding wealth in the New World. The presidios housed the Spanish soldiers that accompanied the missionaries. The cities of San Francisco, Santa Barbara, San Jose, and later Santa Cruz grew from the establishment of these missions and the presidios.

In 1821, Mexico gained independence from Spain along with control of Alta California and the missions. The Franciscans resisted giving up the land and free labor, and Native Americans continued to be treated as slaves. From 1824 to 1834 the Mexican government handed out 51 land grants to colonists for land that had belonged to Native Americans and was held by nearby missions. From 1834 to 1836 the Mexican government revoked the power of the Franciscans to use Native American labor and to redistribute the vast mission land holdings.

In the 20th century, interest in the history of the missions was rekindled, and funds were invested to restore many of the churches and complexes. Today many of the missions have been restored as Catholic parishes, with visitors centers and museum displays of various levels of quality and polish. Some have been restored as state parks.

THE BEAR FLAG REVOLT

Mexico gained independence in 1821, claiming the Spanish lands that would become California and the U.S. Southwest. Hostilities between U.S. and Mexican troops began in April 1846 when a number of U.S. Army troops in the future state of Texas were attacked and killed. The first major battle of the Mexican-American War was fought the following month, and Congress responded with a declaration of war.

Rumors of possible Mexican military action against newly arrived settlers in California led a group of 30 settlers to seize the small Sonoma garrison in 1846. The uprising became known as the Bear Flag Revolt after a hastily designed flag depicting a grizzly bear and a five-point star was raised over Sonoma as the revolutionaries declared independence from Mexico.

Captain John C. Frémont, who was leading a U.S. Army Corps of Topographical Engineers Exploratory Force, returned to Northern California when he received word that war with Mexico was imminent and that a revolt had occurred. The Bear Flag Revolt was short-lived; Frémont took over the rebellion and replaced the Bear Flag with the U.S. flag. Without orders and without knowing about the declaration of war, Frémont went on to the San Francisco Presidio to spike, or disable, the cannons there. More U.S. ships, marines, and sailors arrived and took control of California ports up and down the coast. Frémont's forces grew into the California Battalion, whose members were used mainly to garrison and keep order in the rapidly surrendering towns.

THE GOLD RUSH

James Marshall was a carpenter employed by John Sutter to build a sawmill in Coloma near Placerville. Marshall made a glittery discovery on January 24, 1848, in a nearby stream—gold. Soon news spread to Sacramento and San Francisco that chunks of gold were on the riverbeds for the taking, and the Gold Rush was on. Thousands of people streamed into Northern California seeking gold. After panning streams and water-blasting hillsides for gold, the famous hard-rock mines of California began construction. Although panning continued, by the 1860s most of the rough men had taken jobs working in the dangerous mines. The most productive region was a swath of land nearly 200 miles long, roughly from El Dorado south to Mariposa, known as the Mother Lode or Gold Country. Mining towns such as Sonora, Volcano, Placerville, Sutter's Creek, and Nevada City swelled to huge proportions, only to shrink back into obscurity as the mines eventually closed one by one. Today Highway 49 winds from one historical Gold Rush town to the next, and gold mining has mostly given way to tourism.

As American and European men came to Northern California to seek their fortunes in gold, a few wives and children joined them, but the number of families in the average mining town was small. A few lone women joined in the rush to the gold fields in the oldest profession, serving the population of single male miners and laborers with female companionship.

Another major group of immigrants came to Northern California from China—not to mine but to labor and serve the white miners. Most were forced to pass through the wretched immigration facilities on Angel Island in the middle of San Francisco Bay before being allowed onto the mainland; others were summarily shipped back to China. San Francisco's Chinatown became a hub for the immigrants, a place where their language was spoken and their culture understood. Thousands headed east, becoming low-level laborers in the industry surrounding the mines or workers on the railroads continuously being built to connect Gold Country to the rest of the country.

The dramatic population boom caused by the Gold Rush ensured that California would be on the fast track to admission into the United States, bypassing the territorial phase. California became a state in 1850—it had gone from a Mexican province to the 31st U.S. state in little more than four years.

THE RAILROADS

California's population swelled to more than 250,000 within three years of the Gold Rush. To avoid the grueling cross-country trip, eastern industrialists pushed for a railroad to open the West. While politicians argued, Theodore D. Judah got to work. Judah came to California from New York at the bidding of the promoters of the Sacramento Valley Railroad. The route linked the Embarcadero along the Sacramento River to Folsom, the jumping-off point to the gold fields. When the Sacramento Valley Railroad project ended in 1856, Judah became a passionate advocate for a transcontinental railroad. He lobbied in Washington DC and in 1861 convinced a group of merchants—men who would become known as the Big Four—to incorporate the Central Pacific Railroad in Sacramento.

The Big Four were Leland Stanford, Charles Crocker, Collis Huntington, and Mark Hopkins, and they were instrumental in developing the state railroad system from 1861 to 1900. Stanford operated a general store for miners before becoming an American tycoon, industrialist, politician, and the founder of Stanford University. Crocker founded a small independent iron forge, invested in the railroad venture, and eventually gained a controlling interest in Wells Fargo Bank before buying the rest of the bank for his son. Huntington was a Sacramento merchant who later went on to build other railroads. Hopkins was another Sacramento merchant who formed a partnership with Huntington before joining him in investing in the transcontinental railroad.

In mid-1862 President Abraham Lincoln signed the Pacific Railroad Act, giving the Central Pacific Railroad the go-ahead to build the railroad east from Sacramento and the Union Pacific Railroad to build west from Omaha. The government used land grants and government loans to fund the project. Workers for the two companies met May 10, 1869, at Promontory Summit, Utah, to complete the nation's first transcontinental railroad with a ceremonial golden spike.

THE GREAT DEPRESSION

The stock market crash of 1929 led to the Great Depression. Many property owners lost their farms and homes, and unemployment in California hit 28 percent in 1932; by 1935, about 20 percent of all Californians were on public relief.

The Great Depression transformed the nation. Beyond the economic agony was an optimism that moved people to migrate to California. Settling primarily in the Central Valley, these Midwest transplants preserved their ways and retained identities separate from other Californians. The Midwest migrant plight was captured in John Steinbeck's 1939 novel *The Grapes of Wrath*. Steinbeck, a Salinas native, gathered information by viewing firsthand the deplorable living and labor conditions under which Okie families existed. The novel was widely read and was turned into a movie in 1940. Government agencies banned the book from public schools, and libraries and large landowners campaigned to have it banned elsewhere. That effort lost steam, however, when Steinbeck won the 1940 Pulitzer Prize.

Even during the worst economic depression in U.S. history, Californians continued to build and move forward. The San Francisco-Oakland Bay Bridge was completed in 1936 and the Golden Gate Bridge in 1937, connecting the land around San Francisco Bay and putting people to work. The 1939 Golden Gate International Exposition on Treasure Island in San Francisco Bay helped show the Great Depression the door.

WORLD WAR II

During World War II, San Francisco become home to the liberty ships, a fleet of like-design ships built quickly to help supply the war effort. Some liberty ships, known as the Mothball Fleet, are now tied together farther up Carquinez Strait and can be seen while driving south on I-680 near one of the state's first capitals, Benicia.

Unfortunately, Northern California was also home to a deplorable chapter in the war—the internment camps for Japanese people and Japanese Americans. In reaction to the attack on Pearl Harbor, President Franklin Roosevelt signed Executive Order 9066 in 1942, creating "military exclusion zones" for people of Japanese ancestry. Approximately 110,000 Japanese Americans were uprooted and sent to war relocation camps in desolate areas such as Manzanar, in the dry basin of the eastern Sierra, Tulelake; in the remote northeast corner of the state; and as far away as North Dakota and Oklahoma.

In San Francisco, the immigration station on Angel Island became a deportation center in addition to holding Japanese prisoners of war. Today examples of their carved inscriptions on the prison walls remain as part of the museum in the old barracks building.

THE 1960S

Few places in the country felt the impact of the radical changes of the 1960s more than

California. It's arguable that the peace and free-love movements began here, probably on the campus of the indomitable University of California, Berkeley. Certainly Berkeley helped to shape and foster the culture of hippies, peaceniks, and radical politics. The college campus was the home of the Black Panthers, anti-Vietnam War sit-ins, and numerous protests for many progressive causes.

If Berkeley was the de facto home of 1960s political movements, then San Francisco was the base of its social and cultural phenomena. Free concerts in Golden Gate Park and the growing fame of the hippie community taking over a neighborhood called Haight-Ashbury drew young people from across the country. Many found themselves living on Haight Street for months and experimenting with the mind-altering chemicals emblematic of the era. The music scene became the stuff of legend. The Grateful Dead—one of the most famous and longest-lasting of the 1960s rock bands—hailed from the Bay Area.

THE DOT-COM ERA

The spectacular growth of the electronics industry started in Silicon Valley, south of San Francisco. Many firms settled in the area of Palo Alto, Santa Clara, Sunnyvale, and San Jose, producing innovations such as personal computers, video games, and networking systems at an incredible pace. All these firms were based in the Santa Clara Valley, dubbed Silicon Valley after the material used to produce integrated circuits. Hewlett-Packard and Varian Associates were among the early companies that grew here. Even today the tenant list is impressive: Facebook, Google, LinkedIn, Adobe, Apple, Cisco Systems, Intel, eBay, Oracle Corporation, SanDisk, and Symantec.

The demand for skilled technical professionals was so great in the high-tech industry that firms had difficulty filling openings and began lobbying to have visa restrictions eased, so they could recruit professionals from abroad. Later, however, the dot-com financial bubble that formed in the mid-1990s burst, and tech-industry stock values plummeted in April 2000; many tech companies went into bankruptcy or were sold for a fraction of their worth, and jobs evaporated overnight. Within a few years, it seemed that many of the coveted high-tech jobs were "off-shored" (sent to India for 10 percent of the U.S. labor cost) or "on-shored" by recruiting among newcomers from China and India.

Those lean days appear long gone, and Silicon Valley continues to be the technological hub of the state. Among metropolitan areas, Silicon Valley has the highest concentration of tech workers, with more than 33 percent of the local workforce employed in science and technological fields. And the money is good too—Silicon Valley's start-up companies receive about half of all venture capital investment in the United States.

Government and Economy

GOVERNMENT

Northern California is often viewed as a place where liberalism has run amok. It's true that Northern California is home to what many consider liberal views: political protests and free speech, legalized medical marijuana use, environmental activism, and gay and lesbian rights. These beliefs are not incorporated as a whole throughout the state, however. Major metropolitan areas, such as San Francisco, and areas along the coast have become havens for artists, musicians, and those seeking alternatives to mainstream America. Populations in the Central Valley and the Sierra Nevada foothills often show more conservative leanings at the polls.

California is overwhelmingly Democratic, but when it comes to politics, not everything

Saving California's State Parks

California's state finances suffered during the nation's recent economic crisis, and the budget for state parks continues to be under threat as a result. A few state parks closed in 2011, while others have had services or hours reduced or campgrounds shut. Despite an uptick in the state's economy, there is a fair amount of uncertainty about the future of many of California's parks.

Before planning your trip, check the status of state parks first to avoid disappointment. For updates on park closings and service changes, check online (www.parks.ca.gov), call the park directly, or contact the main office in Sacramento (800/777-0369, 8am-5pm Mon.-Fri.).

To become involved in keeping California's parks open to the public, join the Save Our State Parks Campaign, run by the **California State Parks Foundation** (916/442-2119, www.savestateparks.org). Of course, nothing speaks louder about the value of our parks than visiting them. If you love the parks, use them: go camping, take a hike, learn about the state's cultural and natural history, or even volunteer. Using the parks is one of the best ways to signal your support and to help ensure that they'll thrive in the future.

is predictable. In 2012 California voters rejected Proposition 37, which called for labels on GMO foods, by 51.4 percent to 48.6 percent. Voters also rejected a measure to ban the death penalty the same year. The California Democratic Party supported both proposals. Yet Californians did support two other liberal measures in 2012: one to to raise taxes on wealthy individuals and the other to reform the state's tough crime laws. The Golden State might seem blue, but with 38 million people spread across a vast expanse of varying terrain and economic zones, sometimes California can still surprise.

ECONOMY

California boasts the eighth-largest economy in the world, though the ongoing global economic downturn may put a dent in that ranking in the years to come. Still, California's contribution to the United States outpaces even its immense size and population; it continues to be the country's number-one economy.

Northern California's number-one economic sector is farming. The Central Valley's agricultural juggernaut supplies the world with crops that include grapefruit, grass-fed beef, rice, corn, and tomatoes. Sweet strawberries and spiky artichokes grow in abundance in the cooler Central Coast region. As the fog gets colder and drippier in Marin, ranchers take advantage of the naturally growing grasses for herds of cattle. Agriculture, including fruit, vegetables, nuts, dairy, and wine production, helps make California the world's fifth-largest supplier of food and agricultural commodities.

Today organic farms and ranches are proliferating across the state. In addition to the giant factory farms prevalent in the Central Valley, you'll also see an increasing number of small farms and ranches growing crops using organic, sustainable, and even biodynamic practices. Most of these farmers sell directly to consumers by way of farmers markets and farm stands—almost every town or county in the Northern California has a weekly farmer's market in the summer, and many last year-round.

And then there's the wine. It seems like every square inch of free agricultural land has a grapevine growing on it. The vineyards that were once seen primarily in Napa and Sonoma can now be found on the slopes of the Sierra foothills, on the northern Mendocino coast, and in Carmel. It's actually the wine industry that's leading the charge beyond mere organic and into biodynamic growing practices—like using sheep to graze weeds in vineyards, purchasing natural fertilizer, harvesting grapes, and pruning vines.

Essentials

Transportation

GETTING THERE

Air

Northern California is easy to fly to, particularly if you're heading for one of the major metropolitan areas. Reaching the more rural outlying regions is a bit trickier, and you'll probably find yourself driving—possibly for hours—from one of the major airports.

San Francisco's major airport is **San Francisco International Airport** (SFO, U.S. 101, Millbrae, 800/435-9736, www.flysfo.com), located approximately 13 miles south of the city. Plan to arrive at the airport up to three hours before your flight leaves. Airport lines, especially on weekends and holidays, are notoriously long, and planes can be grounded due to fog.

To avoid the SFO crowds, consider booking a flight into one of the Bay Area's less crowded airports. **Oakland International Airport** (OAK, 1 Airport Dr., Oakland, 510/563-3300, www.flyoakland.com) serves the East Bay with access to San Francisco via the Bay Bridge and BART, the regional commuter train. **Mineta San Jose International Airport** (SJC, Airport Blvd., San Jose, 408/392-3600, www.flysanjose.com) is south of San Francisco in the heart of Silicon Valley. These airports are quite a bit smaller than SFO, but service is brisk from many U.S. destinations.

Sacramento International Airport (SMF, Airport Blvd., Sacramento, 916/929-5411, www.sacramento.aero) is a good launching point for trips in the Central Valley, Gold Country, or the Sierra Nevada and Lake Tahoe areas.

Southwest Airlines (www.southwest.com, 800/435-9792) offers many affordable connecting flights among these Northern California airports. To reach the small but user-friendly airports in Monterey, Eureka, Crescent City, and Redding from the Bay Area, check with **United Airlines** (www.united.com, 800/864-8331).

AIRPORT TRANSPORTATION

Several public and private transportation options can get you into San Francisco. **Bay Area Rapid Transit** (BART, www.bart.gov) connects directly with SFO's international terminal, providing a simple and relatively fast (under 1 hour) and inexpensive ($8.65) trip to downtown San Francisco. The BART station is an easy walk or a free shuttle ride from any point in the airport. **Caltrain** (www.caltrain.com, $3-13) is a good option if you are staying farther south on the peninsula. To access Caltrain from the airport, you must first take BART to the Millbrae stop, where the two lines meet. This station is designed for folks jumping from one line to the other. SJC is also serviced by Caltrain via the free **Valley Transit Authority Airport Flyer** (VTA, www.vta.org), and BART runs a connector shuttle from OAK, making both airports accessible by public transit.

Shuttle vans are another cost-effective option for door-to-door service, though these make several stops along the way. Rates typically range $17-35 per person, and the vans congregate outside the baggage claim areas of both the domestic and international terminals. Advance reservations guarantee a seat, but these aren't required and don't necessarily speed the process. Quake City Shuttle (415/255-4899, www.quakecityshuttle.com) services SFO, SJC, and OAK, while SuperShuttle (800/258-3826, www.

Previous: San Francisco cable car; scenic Highway 1.

Winter Driving

It can snow in the Northern California mountains anytime between November and April; if you plan on crossing any high passes, make sure you have tire chains in your vehicle. In winter, the mountain passes on I-5 near Mount Shasta and on I-80 to Tahoe and over the Sierra Nevada can be very hazardous and may require chains, snow tires, or both. Close to Tahoe, many roadside chain installers set up in pullouts along the side of I-80 and will install tire chains for a hefty fee. Chains can also be rented at certain automotive stores and service stations.

Road closures elsewhere in the state can be common in winter. Highway 1 along the coast can shut down because of flooding or landslides. I-5 through the Central Valley can either close or be subject to hazardous driving conditions resulting from tule fog, which can reduce visibility to only a few feet. Some highways avoid these problems altogether by closing for part of the year. Highway 120, which runs over Tioga Pass and connects Yosemite Valley with the Eastern Sierra, is generally closed October-April.

The **California Department of Transportation** (Caltrans, 800/427-7623, http://dot.ca.gov) has a very user-friendly website to check current road conditions before your trip.

supershuttle.com) can be found at all Bay Area airports and Sacramento.

For **taxis,** the average fare to downtown San Francisco is around $40.

Train

Several long-distance **Amtrak** (www.amtrak.com) trains rumble through Northern California daily. There are eight train routes that serve the region: The *California Zephyr* runs from Chicago and Denver to Emeryville; the *Capitol Corridor* serves Auburn, Sacramento, Emeryville, Oakland, and San Jose, and is a popular route with local commuters; the *Coast Starlight* travels down the West Coast from Seattle and Portland as far as Los Angeles; the *Pacific Surfliner* will get you to the Central Coast from Southern California; and the *San Joaquin* connects the southern Central Valley to the Bay Area. There is no train depot in San Francisco; the closest station is in Emeryville in the East Bay. Fortunately, comfortable coach buses ferry travelers to and from the Emeryville Amtrak station with many stops in downtown San Francisco.

Car

The main transportation artery in Northern California is **I-5,** which runs north-south from Oregon through Sacramento and ending at the Mexican border.

Highway 1, also known as the Pacific Coast Highway, follows the North Coast from Leggett to San Luis Obispo on the Central Coast and points south. Running parallel and intertwining with Highway 1 for much of its length, **U.S. 101** stretches north-south from Oregon to Mexico. These alternate routes are longer but prettier than I-5.

The main east-west conduit is **I-80,** which begins as part of the Bay Bridge in San Francisco and runs east through Sacramento to Tahoe and over the Sierras into Nevada. I-80 can close because of heavy winter snows.

Highway speeds in Northern California are generally 55 mph, unless otherwise posted. Larger freeways, such as I-80 and I-5, may have posted speed limits of 65-70 mph.

California law requires that all drivers carry liability insurance for their vehicles.

GETTING AROUND

Air

Domestic flights can be an economical and faster option when traversing between major cities within the state. San Francisco International Airport (SFO, www.flysfo.com), Oakland International Airport (OAK, www.flyoakland.com), San Jose International

Airport (SJC, www.flysanjose.com), and Sacramento International Airport (SMF, www.sacramento.aero) connect with several smaller regional airports in Northern California. These include the **Monterey Regional Airport** (MRY, www.montereyairport.com), the **Redding Municipal Airport** (RDD, www.ci.redding.ca.us), and the **Arcata-Eureka Airport** (ACV, http://co.humboldt.ca.us/aviation). Southwest Airlines (www.southwest.com) provides affordable flights among the larger airports, while United Airlines (www.united.com) has regular flights to regional airports. Geared toward commuters, flights are generally frequent but a bit pricy.

Train

Amtrak (www.amtrak.com) runs several trains through the state. The *California Zephyr, Capitol Corridor, Coast Starlight,* and *San Joaquin* routes offer services to Auburn, Sacramento, Emeryville, Oakland, San Jose, the Central Coast, and the Central Valley. Trains are roomy, comfortable, and offer a dining car for affordable snacks and meals. While there is no train station in San Francisco, Amtrak provides bus service between downtown San Francisco and Emeryville in the East Bay, the main Amtrak hub for this part of the state. In the San Francisco Bay Area, **Bay Area Rapid Transit** (BART) is a high-speed train that runs from San Francisco south to the airport and across to the East Bay. **Caltrain** (www.caltrain.com) is largely a commuter train that runs from San Francisco down the peninsula as far as Gilroy, south of San Jose.

Bus

A very affordable way to get around Northern California is on **Greyhound** (800/231-2222, www.greyhound.com). The San Francisco Station (200 Folsom St., 415/495-1569) is a hub for Greyhound bus lines serving Northern California. Other major stations include Oakland (2103 San Pablo Ave., 510/823-4730), San Jose (70 S. Almaden Ave., 408/295-4151), and Sacramento (420 Richards Blvd., 916/444-6858). Greyhound routes generally follow the major highways, traveling up U.S. 101 through Santa Rosa to Arcata, along I-5 through Redding and Mount Shasta, near I-80 to Reno, and south through San Jose to Santa Cruz. Greyhound does not go to destinations like Wine Country, Gold Country, and the Monterey Peninsula.

Most counties and municipalities have bus service with routes to outlying areas.

Car and RV

California is great for road trips. Scenic coastal routes such as Highway 1 and U.S. 101 are often destinations in themselves, while inland I-5 is the most direct route north-south through the state. However, traffic congestion, accidents, mudslides, fires, and snow can affect highways at any time. To explore Northern California safely, have a good map and check road conditions online with the **California Department of Transportation** (Caltrans, 800/427-7623, http://dot.ca.gov) before departure. The *Thomas Guide Road Atlas* (www.mapbooks4u.com, $15) is a reliable and detailed map and road guide and a great insurance policy against getting lost.

Larger highways like I-5 and I-80 are relatively easy to navigate, but many smaller two-lane highways that connect Northern California's rural destinations offer scenic and leisurely alternatives. Mountain passes such as I-80 to Tahoe and I-5 in the Shasta and Lassen regions may require snow tires or chains at any time. In rural areas, gas stations may be few and far between.

The left lanes of most major Bay Area freeways become **carpool lanes** during the heaviest commute times (generally 7am-10am and 3pm-7pm). Posted signs list the hours of operation, the number of people you have to have in your car to use the lanes, and the often hefty fine for violating.

In addition, bridge tolls are charges to cross the bridges throughout the Bay Area. The toll is $5 one way for all bridges except for the **Bay Bridge,** for which the toll changes according to commute times (midnight-5am, 10am-3pm, and 7pm-midnight Mon.-Fri. $4, 5am-10am and 3pm-7pm Mon.-Fri. $6, midnight Fri.-midnight Sun., $5). The **Golden Gate Bridge** is the other exception. There is a $7 toll for southbound traffic, which is collected electronically and presented as a bill in the mail. Should you have a rental car, ask about their toll program if you are planning a trip across the Golden Gate. You can also visit http://goldengate.org for more information. To avoid all these ins and outs, many savvy Bay Area commuters pay electronically via **FasTrak** (www.bayareafastrak.org), a transponder in their cars that deducts the toll from the user's account as they pass through the toll plaza.

CAR AND RV RENTAL

Most car-rental companies are located at each of the major Northern California airports. To reserve a car in advance, contact **Budget Rent A Car** (800/527-0700, www.budget.com), **Dollar Rent A Car** (800/800-4000, www.dollar.com), **Enterprise** (800/261-7331, www.enterprise.com), or **Hertz** (800/654-3131, www.hertz.com).

To rent a car, drivers in California must be at least 21 years of age and have a valid driver's license. California law also requires that all vehicles carry liability insurance. You can purchase insurance with your rental car, but it generally costs an additional $10 per day, which can add up quickly. Most private auto insurance will also cover rental cars. Before buying rental insurance, check your car insurance policy to see if rental-car coverage is included.

The average cost of a rental car is $50 per day or $250 per week; however, rates vary greatly based on the time of year and distance traveled. Weekend and summer rentals cost significantly more. Generally, it is more expensive to rent from car rental agencies at an airport. To avoid excessive rates, first plan travel to areas where a car is not required, then rent a car from an agency branch in town to explore more rural areas. Rental agencies occasionally allow vehicle drop-off at a different location from where it was picked up for an additional fee.

If you rent an RV, you won't have to worry about camping or lodging options, and many facilities, particularly farther north, accommodate RVs. However, RVs are difficult to maneuver and park, limiting your access to metropolitan areas. They are also expensive, in terms of both gas and the rental rates. Rates during the summer average $650 per week and $400 for three days, the standard minimum rental. **Cruise America** (800/671-8042, www.cruiseamerica.com) has branches in San Jose, Sacramento, Santa Rosa, and San Mateo.

Travel Tips

VISAS AND OFFICIALDOM

Passports and Visas

If visiting from another country, you must have a valid passport and a visa to enter the United States. In most other countries, the local U.S. embassy should be able to provide a tourist visa. The average fee for a visa is US$160. While a visa may be processed as quickly as 24 hours on request, plan at least a couple of weeks, as there can be unexpected delays, particularly during the busy summer season (June-Aug.). However, before doing so, check with the U.S. Department of Homeland Security (www.cbp.gov) to see if you qualify for the Visa Waiver Program. Passport holders of certain countries can apply online with the Electronic System for Travel Authorization at least 72 hours before traveling. Have a return plane or cruise ticket to your country of origin dated less than 90 days from your date of entry. Holders of Canadian passports don't need visas or visa waivers.

Embassies

San Francisco has embassies and consulates from many countries around the globe. If you should lose your passport or find yourself in some other trouble while visiting California, contact your country's offices for assistance. To find an embassy, check online at www.state.gov/s/cpr/rls/dpl/32122.htm, which lists the websites for all foreign embassies in the United States. A representative will be able to direct you to the nearest embassy or consulate.

Customs

Before you enter the United States from another country by sea or by air, you'll be required to fill out a customs form. Check with the U.S. embassy in your country or the Customs and Border Protection website (www.cbp.gov) for an updated list of items you must declare.

If you require medication administered by injection, you must pack your syringes in a checked bag; syringes are not permitted in carry-ons coming into the United States.

Also, pack documentation describing your need for any narcotic medications you've brought with you. Failure to produce documentation for narcotics on request can result in severe penalties in the United States.

If you're driving into California along I-5 or another major highway, prepare to stop at Agricultural Inspection Stations a few miles inside the state line. You don't need to present a passport, a visa, or even a driver's license; instead, you must be prepared to present all your fruits and vegetables. California's largest economic sector is agriculture, and a number of the major crops grown here are sensitive to pests and diseases. If you've got produce, especially homegrown or from a farm stand, it could be infected by a known problem pest or disease. Expect it to be confiscated on the spot.

TOURIST INFORMATION

When visiting California, you might be tempted to stop in at one of several **Golden State Welcome Centers** (www.visitcwc.com) scattered throughout the state. If you're in an area that doesn't have its own visitors center, the State Welcome Center might be a useful place to pick up maps and brochures. Otherwise, stick with local, regional, and national park visitors centers, which tend to be staffed by volunteers or rangers who feel a real passion for their locale.

If you are looking for maps, almost all gas stations and drugstores sell maps both of the place you're in and of the whole state. **AAA of Northern California** (www.csaa.com) is the auto club for Northern California, and it offers free maps to auto club members.

Many local and regional visitors centers also offer maps, but you'll need to pay a few dollars for the bigger and better ones. But if all you need is a wine-tasting map in a known wine region, you can probably get one for free along with a few tasting coupons at the nearest regional visitors center. Basic national park maps come with your admission payment. State park maps can be free or cost a few dollars at the visitors centers.

The state's **California Travel and Tourism Commission** (916/444-4429, http://gocalif.ca.gov) also provides helpful and free tips, information, and downloadable maps and guides.

California is in the Pacific time zone (PST and PDT) and observes daylight saving time March-November.

Money

California businesses use the U.S. dollar ($). Most businesses also accept the major credit cards Visa, MasterCard, Discover, and American Express. ATM and debit cards work at many stores and restaurants, and ATMs are available throughout the region. In more remote areas, such as Gold Country and the North Coast, some business may only accept cash, so don't depend entirely on your plastic.

You can change currency at any international airport in the state. Currency exchange points also crop up in downtown San Francisco and at some of the major business hotels in urban areas.

California is not a particularly expensive place to travel, but keeping an eye on your budget is still important. San Francisco and the Wine Country are the priciest regions for visitors, especially with the amount of high-quality food and luxury accommodations. Advance reservations for hotels and marquee restaurants in these areas are recommended.

Banks

As with anywhere, traveling with a huge amount of cash is not recommended, which may make frequent trips to the bank necessary. Fortunately, most destinations have at least one major bank. Usually Bank of America or Wells Fargo can be found on the main drags through towns. Banking hours tend to be 8am-5pm Monday-Friday, 9am-noon Saturday. Never count on a bank being open on Sunday or federal holidays. If you need cash when the banks are closed, there is generally a 24-hour ATM available. Furthermore, many cash-only businesses have an ATM on-site for those who don't have enough cash ready in their wallets. The unfortunate downside to this convenience is a fee of $2-4 per transaction. This also applies to ATMs at banks at which you don't have an account.

Tax

Sales tax in California varies by city and county, but the average rate is around 8.5 percent. All goods are taxable with the exception of food not eaten on the premises. For example, your bill at a restaurant will include tax, but your bill at a grocery store will not. The hotel tax is another unexpected added expense to traveling in California. Most cities have enacted a tax on hotel rooms largely to make up for budget shortfalls. As you would expect, these taxes are higher in areas more popular with visitors. In Wine County you can expect to add an additional 12-14 percent onto your hotel bill, while in San Francisco the tax tops 15 percent. Some areas, like Eureka, have a lower hotel tax of 10 percent.

Tipping

Tipping is expected and appreciated, and a 15 percent tip for restaurants is about the norm. When ordering in bars, tip the bartender or waitstaff $1 per drink. For taxis, plan to tip 15-20 percent of the fare, or simply round the cost up to the nearest dollar. Cafés and coffee shops often have tip jars out. There is no consensus on what is appropriate when purchasing a $3 beverage. Often $0.50 is enough, depending on the quality and service.

Tipping is also expected in hotels and B&Bs. Often you'll find an envelope on the desk for the housekeeping staff. Depending on the type of accommodations, $1-5 per night is the standard rate.

Communications and Media

With the exception of rural and wilderness areas, Northern California is fairly well connected. Cell phone reception is good except in places far from any large town. Likewise, you can find Internet access just about anywhere. The bigger cities are well wired, but even in small towns you can log on either at a library or in a café with a computer in the back. Be prepared to pay a per-minute usage fee.

The main newspaper in Northern California is the *San Francisco Chronicle*. You can usually find it on sale from Monterey to Crescent City and east to Lake Tahoe. Of course, there are other regional papers that may offer some international news in addition to the local color. As for radio, there are some news stations on the FM dial, and in most regions you can count on finding a National Public Radio (NPR) affiliate. While they will all offer some NPR news coverage, some will be more geared toward music and local concerns. KQED (88.5 FM) is the hometown San Francisco station that can also be heard in Sacramento (89.3 FM). Nearly all California radio stations report traffic conditions during commuting hours.

Because of California's size both geographically and in terms of population, you will have to contend with multiple area codes—the numbers that prefix the seven-digit phone number—throughout the state. In Northern California, 415 is San Francisco north to Novato; 650 is San Mateo County, including Palo Alto; 831 is Monterey County; 408 is San Jose; 510 is the East Bay; 925 is the far-east East Bay; 707 is Wine Country and the North Coast; 916 is Sacramento and part of Gold Country; and 530 is the Sacramento Valley north to Oregon and east to Lake Tahoe. The 800 or 866 area codes are toll-free numbers. Any time you are dialing out of the area, you must dial 1, plus the area code, followed by the seven-digit number.

To mail a letter, find a blue post office box, which are found on the main streets of any town. Postage rates vary by destination. You can purchase stamps at the local post office, where you can also mail packages. Stamps can also be bought at some ATMs and online at www.usps.com, which can also give you the location and hours of the nearest post office. Post offices are generally open Monday-Friday, with limited hours on Saturday. They are always closed on Sunday and federal holidays.

CONDUCT AND CUSTOMS

The legal drinking age in California is 21. Expect to have your ID checked if you look under age 30, especially in bars and clubs, but also in restaurants and wineries. Most California bars and clubs close at 2am; you'll find the occasional after-hours nightspot in San Francisco.

Smoking has been banned in many places throughout California. Don't expect to find a smoking section in any restaurant or an ashtray in any bar. Smoking is illegal in all bars and clubs, but your new favorite watering hole might have an outdoor patio where smokers can huddle. Taking the ban one step further, many hotels, motels, and inns throughout Northern California are strictly nonsmoking, and you'll be subject to fees of hundreds of dollars if your room smells of smoke when you leave.

There's no smoking in any public building, and even some of the state parks don't allow cigarettes. There's often good reason for this; the fire danger in California is extreme in the summer, and one carelessly thrown butt can cause a genuine catastrophe.

ACCESS FOR TRAVELERS WITH DISABILITIES

Most Northern California attractions, hotels, and restaurants are accessible for travelers with disabilities. State law requires that public transportation must accommodate the special needs of travelers with disabilities and that public spaces and businesses have adequate restroom facilities and equal access. This includes national parks and historical structures, many of which have been refitted with ramps and wider doors. Most parks have one or two trails that are accessible to wheelchairs, and most campgrounds designate specific campsites that meet the Americans with Disabilities Act standards. The state of California also provides a free telephone TDD-to-voice relay service; just dial 711.

If you are traveling with a disability, there are many resources to help you plan your trip. **Access Northern California** (http://accessnca.org) is a nonprofit organization that offers general travel tips, including recommendations on accommodations, parks and trails, transportation, and travel equipment. For a comprehensive guide to wheelchair-accessible beaches, rivers, and shorelines from Santa Cruz to Marin County, including the East Bay and Wine Country, contact the **California Coastal Conservancy** (510/286-1015, www.scc.ca.gov), which publishes a free and downloadable guide. San Francisco's **Wheelchair Getaways** (800/642-2042, www.wheelchairgetaways.com, $95-110 per day) rents wheelchair-accessible vans and offers pickup and drop-off service from San Francisco, Oakland, San Jose, and Sacramento airports ($100-300). Likewise, **Avis Access** (888/879-4273, www.avis.com) rents cars, scooters, and other products to make traveling with a disability easier; click on the "Services" link on the website.

TRAVELING WITH CHILDREN

Many spots in California are ideal destinations for families with children of all ages. Amusement parks, interactive museums, zoos, parks, beaches, and playgrounds all make for family-friendly fun. On the other hand, there are a few spots in the Golden State that beckon more to adults than to children. Frankly, there aren't many family activities in Wine Country. This adult playground is all about alcoholic beverages and high-end dining. Similarly, the North Coast's focus on original art and romantic B&Bs brings out couples looking for weekend getaways rather than families. In fact, before you book a room at a B&B that you expect to share with your kids, check to be sure that the inn can accommodate extra people in the guest rooms and whether they allow guests under age 16.

WOMEN TRAVELING ALONE

California is a pretty friendly place for women traveling alone. Most of the major outdoor attractions are incredibly safe, and even many of the urban areas boast pleasant neighborhoods that welcome lone female travelers. But you'll need to take some basic precautions and pay attention to your surroundings, just as you would in any unfamiliar place. When you're walking down a city street, be alert and keep an eye on your surroundings and on anyone who might be following you. In rural areas, don't go tromping into unlit wooded areas or out into grassy fields alone at night without a flashlight; many of California's critters are nocturnal. Of course, this caution applies to men as well; mountain lions and rattlesnakes don't tend to discriminate.

SENIOR TRAVELERS

Throughout the state you'll find senior discounts nearly every place you go, including restaurants, golf courses, major attractions, and even some hotels, though the minimum age can range 50-65. Just ask, and be prepared to produce ID if you look young or are requesting a senior discount. You can often get additional discounts on rental cars, hotels, and tour packages as a member of **AARP** (888/687-2277, www.aarp.org). If you're not a member, its website can also offer helpful travel tips and advice. **Elderhostel** (800/454-5768, www.roadscholar.org) is another great resource for senior travelers. Dedicated to providing educational opportunities for older travelers, Elderhostel provides package trips to beautiful and interesting destinations. Called "Educational Adventures," these trips are generally 3-9 days long and emphasize history, natural history, art, music, or a combination thereof.

GAY AND LESBIAN TRAVELERS

The Golden State is a golden place for gay travel—especially in the bigger cities and even in some of the smaller towns around the state. As with much of the country, the farther you venture into rural and agricultural regions, the less likely you are to experience the liberal acceptance the state is known for.

the Gay Pride flag hanging outside San Francisco City Hall

San Francisco has the biggest and arguably best **Gay Pride Festival** (www.sfpride.org) in the nation, usually held on Market Street on the last weekend in June. Year-round, the Castro District offers fun of all kinds, from theater to clubs to shopping, mostly targeted at gay men but with a few places sprinkled in for lesbians. If the Castro is your primary destination, you can even find a place to stay in the middle of the action.

Santa Cruz on the Central Coast is a quirky town specially known for its lesbian-friendly culture. A relaxed vibe informs everything from underground clubs to unofficial nude beaches to live-action role-playing games in the middle of downtown. Even the lingerie and adult toy shops tend to be woman-owned and -operated.

Many gay and lesbian San Francisco residents go to Guerneville for a weekend escape. This outdoorsy town on the Russian River has rustic lodges, vacation rentals, and cabins down by the river; rafting and kayaking companies offer summertime adventures, and nearby wineries offer relaxation. The short but colorful Main Street is home to queer-friendly bars and festivals.

The oh-so-fabulous California vibe has even made it to the interior of the state—Sacramento's newly revitalized Midtown neighborhood offers a more low-key but visible gay evening scene.

Health and Safety

MEDICAL SERVICES

For an emergency anywhere in California, dial 911. Inside hotels and resorts, check your emergency number as soon as you get to your guest room. In urban and suburban areas, full-service hospitals and medical centers abound, but in more remote regions, help can be more than an hour away.

WILDERNESS SAFETY

If you're planning a backcountry expedition, follow all rules and guidelines for obtaining wilderness permits and for self-registration at trailheads. These are for your safety, letting the rangers know roughly where you plan to be and when to expect you back. National and state park visitors centers can advise in more detail on any health or wilderness alerts in the area. It is also advisable to let someone outside your party know your route and expected date of return.

Extreme Temperatures

Being out in the elements can present its own set of challenges. Despite Northern California's relatively mild climate, heat exhaustion and heat stroke can affect anyone during the hot summer months, particularly during a long strenuous hike in the sun. Common symptoms include nausea, lightheadedness, headache, or muscle cramps. Dehydration and loss of electrolytes are the common causes of heat exhaustion. If you or anyone in your group develops any of these symptoms, get out of the sun immediately, stop all physical activity, and drink plenty of water. Heat exhaustion can be severe, and if untreated can lead to heat stroke, in which the body's core temperature reaches 105°F. Fainting, seizures, confusion, and rapid heartbeat and breathing can indicate the situation has moved beyond heat exhaustion. If you suspect this, call 911 immediately.

Similar precautions hold true for hypothermia, which is caused by prolonged exposure to cold water or weather. For many in California, this can happen on a hike or backpacking trip without sufficient rain gear, or by staying too long in the ocean or another cold body of water without a wetsuit. Symptoms include shivering, weak pulse, drowsiness, confusion, slurred speech, or stumbling. To treat hypothermia, immediately remove the wet clothing, cover the person with blankets, and feed him or her hot liquids. If symptoms don't improve, call 911.

Altitude

You don't have to be outdoors to suffer from altitude sickness. A flu-like illness, it can affect anyone who has made a quick transition from low to high elevation. It occurs most commonly above 8,000 feet, but some individuals suffer at lower elevations. Headaches are the most common symptom, followed by nausea, dizziness, fatigue, and even the swelling of hands, feet, and face. Symptoms either go away once the individual has acclimated to the thinner air and lower oxygen levels or they don't, requiring either medical attention or a return to lower elevation. To prevent altitude sickness, avoid any strenuous exercise, including hiking, for the first 24 hours of your stay. Drinking alcohol also exacerbates altitude sickness because it can cause dehydration.

Wildlife

Many places are still wild in California, making it important to use precautions with regard to wildlife. While California no longer has any grizzly bears, black bears thrive and are often seen in the mountains foraging for food in the spring, summer, and fall. Black bears certainly don't have the size or reputation of grizzlies, but there is good reason to exercise caution. Never get between a bear and her cub, and if a bear sees you, identify yourself as human by waving your hands above your head, speaking in calm voice, and backing away slowly. If a bear charges, do not run. One of the best precautions against an unwanted bear encounter is to keep a clean camp, store all food in airtight bear-proof containers, and strictly follow any guidelines given by the park or rangers.

Even more common than bears are mountain lions, which can be found in the Sierra foothills, the Coast Range, grasslands, and forests. Because of their solitary nature, it is unlikely you will see one, even on long trips in the backcountry. Still, there are a couple things to remember. If you come across a kill, probably a large partly eaten deer, leave immediately. And if you see a mountain lion and it sees you, identify yourself as human, making your body appear as big as possible, just as with a bear. And remember: Never run. As with any cat, large or small, running triggers its hunting instincts. If a mountain lion should attack, fight back; cats don't like to get hurt.

The other treacherous critter in the backcountry is the rattlesnake. They can be found in summer in generally hot and dry areas from the coast to the Sierra Nevada. When hiking in this type of terrain—many parks will indicate if rattlesnakes are a problem in the area—keep your eyes on the ground and an ear out for the telltale rattle. Snakes like to warn you to keep away. The only time this is not the case is with baby rattlesnakes that have not yet developed their rattles. Unfortunately, they have developed their fangs and venom, which is particularly potent. Should you get bitten, seek immediate medical help.

Mosquitoes can be found throughout the state, particularly in the Central Valley and the Sierra Nevada. At higher elevations they can be worse, prompting many hikers and backpackers to don head nets and apply potent repellents, usually DEET. The high season for mosquitoes in this area is late spring-early summer, at the end of snowmelt when there is lots of still freshwater in which to multiply. In the Central Valley, there has been concern over West Nile virus, which can cause nausea, diarrhea, and fever for 3-6 days. In very rare cases, the illness becomes more serious, and medical attention becomes necessary.

Ticks live in many of the forests and grasslands throughout the state, except at higher elevations. Tick season generally runs late fall-early summer. If you are hiking through brushy areas, wear pants and long-sleeve shirts. Ticks like to crawl to warm moist places (armpits are a favorite) on their host. If a tick is engorged, it can be difficult to remove. There are two main types of ticks found in Northern California: dog ticks and deer ticks. Dog ticks are larger, brown, and have a gold spot on their backs, while deer ticks are small, tear-shaped, and black. Deer ticks are known to carry Lyme disease. While Lyme disease is relatively rare in California—there are more cases in the northernmost part of the state—it is very serious. If you get bitten by a deer tick and the bite leaves a red ring, seek medical attention. Lyme disease can be successfully treated with early rounds of antibiotics.

There is only one major variety of plant in California that can cause an adverse reaction in humans if you touch the leaves or stems: poison oak, a common shrub that inhabits forests throughout the state. Poison oak has a characteristic three-leaf configuration, with scalloped leaves that are shiny green in the spring and then turn yellow, orange, and red in late summer-fall. In fall the leaves drop, leaving a cluster of innocuous-looking branches. The oil in poison oak is present year-round in both the leaves and branches. Your best protection is to wear long sleeves and long pants when hiking, no matter how hot it is. A product called Tecnu is available at most California drugstores—slather it on before you go hiking to protect yourself from poison oak. If your skin comes into contact with poison oak, expect an itchy, irritating rash. Poison oak is also extremely transferable, so avoid touching your eyes, face, or other parts of your body. Calamine lotion can help, and in extreme cases a doctor can administer cortisone to help decrease the inflammation.

Poison oak is common throughout Northern California.

CRIME AND SAFETY PRECAUTIONS

The outdoors is not the only place that harbors danger. In both rural and urban areas, theft can be a problem. When parking at a trailhead or in park or at a beach, don't leave any valuables in the car. If you must, place them out of sight either in a locked glove box or in the trunk. The same holds true for urban areas. Furthermore, avoid keeping your wallet, camera, and other expensive items, including lots of cash, easily accessible in backpacks; keep them within your sight at all times. Certain neighborhoods in San Francisco and Oakland are best avoided at night. However, many of them, like the Mission and Tenderloin districts in San Francisco or downtown Oakland, are also home to great restaurants, clubs, and music venues. If you find yourself in these areas after dark, consider taking a cab to avoid walking blocks and blocks to get to your car or to wait for public transportation. In case of a theft or any other emergency, call 911.

Resources

Suggested Reading

FICTION

Kerouac, Jack. *Big Sur.* New York: Penguin, 2011.

London, Jack. *The Valley of the Moon.* Los Angeles: Aegypan, 2007.

Muir, John, *The Mountains of California.* San Francisco: Sierra Club Books, 1988.

Muir, John. *My First Summer in the Sierra.* New York: Penguin Books, 1997.

Steinbeck, John. *The Grapes of Wrath.* New York: Penguin, 2006.

Stegner, Wallace. *Angle of Repose.* New York: Penguin, 2000.

Stevenson, Robert Louis. *The Complete Short Stories of Robert Louis Stevenson: With a Selection of the Best Short Novels.* New York: Modern Library, 2002.

Tan, Amy. *The Joy Luck Club.* New York: Putnam's, 1989.

Twain, Mark. *Great Short Works of Mark Twain.* New York: HarperCollins, 2004.

FIELD GUIDES

Alden, Peter, and Fred Heath. *National Audubon Field Guide to California.* New York: Knopf, 1998.

Arno, Stephen F. *Discovering Sierra Trees.* Yosemite National Park: Yosemite Association and Sequoia Natural History Association, 1986.

Blackwell, Laird R. *Wildflowers of the Tahoe Sierra: From Forest Deep to Mountain Peak.* Redmond, WA: Lone Pine Publishing, 1997.

Hill, Mary. *Geology of the Sierra Nevada.* Berkeley, CA: University of California Press, 2006.

Horn, Elizabeth L. *Sierra Nevada Wildflowers.* Missoula, MT: Mountain Press Publishing Company, 1998.

Tekiela, Stan. *Birds of California Field Guide.* Cambridge, MN: Adventure Publications, 2003.

HISTORY

Brand, H.W. *The Age of Gold: The California Gold Rush and the New American Dream.* New York, NY: Doubleday, 2003.

Belden, L. Burr, and Mary DeDecker. *Death Valley to Yosemite: Frontier Mining Camps and Ghost Towns.* Bishop, CA: Spotted Dog Press, 2000.

Gutiérrez, Ramon A., and Richard J. Orsi, eds. *Contested Eden: California Before the Gold Rush.* Berkeley, CA: University of California Press, 1998.

Heizer, Robert F., and Albert B. Elsasser. *The Natural World of the California Indians.* Berkeley, CA: University of California Press, 1981.

Holiday, James. *The World Rushed In: The California Gold Rush Experience: An Eyewitness Account of a Nation Heading West.* Norman, OK: University of Oklahoma Press, 2002.

Kamiya, Gary. *Cool Gray City of Love.* New York: Bloomsbury, 2013.

Rayner, Richard. *The Associates: Four Capitalists Who Created California.* New York: W. W. Norton and Company, 2008.

Reisner, Marc. *Cadillac Desert: The American West and Its Disappearing Water.* New York: Penguin, 1993.

Rice, Richard, William Bullough, and Richard Orsi. *The Elusive Eden: A New History of California.* Columbus, OH: McGraw Hill, 2001.

Stone, Irving. Men to Match My Mountains. New York: Berkley Trade, 1987.

Sullivan, Charles. *A Companion to California Wine: An Encyclopedia of Wine and Winemaking from the Mission Period to the Present.* Berkeley, CA: University of California Press, 1998.

Varney, Philip. *Ghost Towns of Northern California.* Stillwater, MN: Voyageur Press, 2001.

NATURAL HISTORY

Bakker, Elna, and Gordy Slack. *An Island Called California.* Berkeley, CA: University of California Press, 1985.

Barbour, Michael, Bruce Pavlik, Susan Lindstrom, and Frank Drysdale. *California's Changing Landscapes: Diversity and Conservation of California Vegetation.* Sacramento, CA: California Native Plant Society Press, 1991.

Gudde, Erwin G., and William O. Bright. *California Place Names: The Origin and Etymology of Current Geographical Names.* Berkeley, CA: University of California Press, 2010.

Guyton, Bill. *Glaciers of California: Modern Glaciers, Ice Age Glaciers, the Origin of Yosemite Valley, and a Glacier Tour in the Sierra Nevada.* Berkeley, CA: University of California Press, 2001.

McPhee, John. *Assembling California.* New York: Farrar, Straus and Giroux, 1994.

Schoenherr, Allan A. *A Natural History of California.* Berkeley, CA: University of California Press, 1995.

TRAVEL

Arns, Christopher. *Moon Sacramento and the Gold Country.* Berkeley, CA: Avalon Travel, 2013.

Brown, Ann Marie. *Moon 101 Great Hikes of the San Francisco Bay Area.* Berkeley, CA: Avalon Travel, 2014.

Brown, Ann Marie. *Moon Tahoe.* Berkeley, CA: Avalon Travel, 2015.

California Coastal Commission, State of California. *The California Coastal Access Guide.* Berkeley, CA: University of California Press, 2003.

Linhart Veneman, Elizabeth. *Moon Napa & Sonoma.* Berkeley, CA: Avalon Travel, 2013.

Soares, Marc J. *Best Coast Hikes of Northern California: A Guide to the Top Trails from Big Sur to the Oregon Border.* San Francisco: Sierra Club Books, 1998.

Stienstra, Tom, and Ann Marie Brown. *Moon California Hiking*. Berkeley, CA: Avalon Travel, 2013.

Stienstra, Tom. *Moon California Camping*. Berkeley, CA: Avalon Travel, 2015.

Thornton, Stuart. *Moon California Road Trip*. Berkeley, CA: Avalon Travel, 2015.

Thornton, Stuart. *Moon Coastal California*. Berkeley, CA: Avalon Travel, 2013.

Thornton, Stuart. *Moon Monterey & Carmel*. Berkeley, CA: Avalon Travel, 2015.

Internet Resources

CALIFORNIA

California Department of Transportation

www.dot.ca.gov

Contains state map and highway information.

Visit California

www.visitcalifornia.com

The official tourism site of the state of California.

REGIONAL SITES

Central Coast Regional Tourism

www.centralcoast-tourism.com

A guide to the Central Coast region, including Santa Cruz and Monterey.

NapaValley.com

www.napavalley.com

A Napa Valley tourism website from WineCountry.com.

Sacramento Convention and Visitors Bureau

www.vistsacramento.org

The official website of the Sacramento Convention and Visitors Bureau.

Shasta and Lassen Regional Tourism

www.shastacascade.org

The California Travel and Tourism Information Network includes information and a downloadable visitors guide to Mount Shasta, Shasta Lake, Redding, and Lassen.

Visit California Gold Country

www.calgold.org

The website from the Gold Country Visitors Association, with information about Grass Valley, Nevada City, Placer Country, Sacramento, and Amador Country.

PARKS AND OUTDOORS

California Outdoor and Recreational Information

www.caoutdoors.com

This recreation-focused website includes links to maps, local newspapers, festivals, and events as well as a wide variety of recreational activities throughout the state.

California State Parks

www.parks.ca.gov

The official website lists hours, accessibility, activities, camping areas, fees, and more information for all parks in the state system.

Lassen Volcanic National Park

www.nps.gov/lavo

The official website for Lassen Volcanic National Park.

Recreation.gov

www.recreation.gov

Recreation.gov is the reservation website for numerous California campgrounds.

Redwood National Park
www.nps.gov/redw
The official website for all Redwood National and State Parks.

Sequoia and Kings Canyon National Parks
www.nps.gov/seki
The official website for Sequoia and Kings Canyon.

State of California
www.ca.gov/visitplay/greatoutdoors
Outdoor resources for California state and government organizations. Check for information about fishing and hunting licenses, backcountry permits, boating regulations, and more.

Yosemite National Park
www.nps.gov/yose
The National Park Service website for Yosemite National Park.

Yosemite National Park Vacation and Lodging Information
www.yosemitepark.com
The concessionaire website for Yosemite National Park lodging, dining, and reservations.

Index

A

B

D

E

F

G

H

M

QR

INDEX

S

T

UV

WXYZ

List of Maps

Front map

Discover Northern California

San Francisco

San Francisco Bay Area

Wine Country

North Coast

Shasta and Lassen

Lake Tahoe

Sacramento and Gold Country

Yosemite and the Eastern Sierra

Sequoia and Kings Canyon

Central Coast

Photo Credits

Photo Credits

Title page photo: © kavram/123rf.com; page 4 © Masterlu | Dreamstime.com; page 5 (top) © Yoleven | Dreamstime.com, (bottom) © Jeffrey Banke/123rf.com; page 6 (top left) © Biolifepics | Dreamstime.com, (top right) © Tryder | Dreamstime.com, (bottom) © Masterlu | Dreamstime.com; page 7 (top) © Nalukai | Dreamstime.com, (bottom left) © Mike7777777 | Dreamstime.com, (bottom right) © Mjwalters | Dreamstime.com; page 8 (top) © Hotshotsworldwide | Dreamstime.com, (bottom left) © Elizabeth Linhart Veneman, (bottom right) © Elizabeth Linhart Veneman; page 9 © Egomezta | Dreamstime.com; page 10 © Mblach | Dreamstime.com; page 11 © Minyun9260 | Dreamstime.com; page 12 © Andrew Zarivny/123rf.com; page 13 © Lunamarina | Dreamstime.com; page 14 © Raferrier | Dreamstime.com; page 15 © Valis2 | Dreamstime.com; page 16 (top) © Christopher Arns, (bottom) © Radkol | Dreamstime.com; page 17 © Luckyphotographer | Dreamstime.com; page 19 © Thicoz | Dreamstime.com; page 20 © Snyfer | Dreamstime.com; page 21 © Haydn5 | Dreamstime.com; page 23 (left) © Chrisboswell | Dreamstime.com, (right) © Christopher Arns; page 24 © Christopher Arns; page 25 (top) © Heyengel | Dreamstime.com, (bottom) © Zepherwind | Dreamstime.com; page 27 © Zhukovsky | Dreamstime.com; page 30 © Elizabeth Linhart Veneman; page 31 © Andreykr | Dreamstime.com; page 36 © Chee-Onn Leong/123rf.com; page 37 © Elizabeth Linhart Veneman; page 40 © Elizabeth Linhart Veneman; page 41 © Chee-Onn Leong/123rf.com; page 42 © Afagundes | Dreamstime.com; page 43 © Elizabeth Linhart Veneman; page 44 © Lunamarina | Dreamstime.com; page 45 © Rafael Ramirez Lee/123rf.com; page 46 © imagezebra/123rf.com; page 47 © Elizabeth Linhart Veneman; page 58 © Masterlu | Dreamstime.com; page 62 © F8grapher | Dreamstime.com; page 79 © Elizabeth Linhart Veneman; page 89 (top) © Jropelato2 | Dreamstime.com, (bottom) © Chao Kusollerschariya/123rf.com; page 91 © Aspenrock | Dreamstime.com; page 99 © Brunoseara | Dreamstime.com; page 104 © Layfphoto | Dreamstime.com; page 106 © Elizabeth Linhart Veneman; page 112 © Luckyphotographer | Dreamstime.com; page 120 © Dexchao | Dreamstime.com; page 125 © Rue Flaherty; page 132 © Digital94086 | Dreamstime.com; page 136 © Elizabeth Linhart Veneman; page 137 photo by Jurvetson on flickr; page 139 © Jim Allen; page 141 © Graham Prentice/123rf.com; page 146 © Elizabeth Linhart Veneman; page 150 (top) © Elizabeth Linhart Veneman, (bottom) © Kitleong | Dreamstime.com; page 151 © Spvvkr | Dreamstime.com; page 157 © Elizabeth Linhart Veneman; page 163 © Elizabeth Linhart Veneman; page 170 © Elizabeth Linhart Veneman; page 171 © Elizabeth Linhart Veneman; page 179 © Elizabeth Linhart Veneman; page 183 © Elizabeth Linhart Veneman; page 186 (top) © Elizabeth Linhart Veneman, (bottom) © Elizabeth Linhart Veneman; page 198 © Elizabeth Linhart Veneman; page 202 © Elizabeth Linhart Veneman; page 204 © Fernley | Dreamstime.com; page 212 © Elizabeth Linhart Veneman; page 215 (top) © Photoquest | Dreamstime.com, (bottom) © Sekarb | Dreamstime.com; page 217 © Jbatt | Dreamstime.com; page 223 © Meinzahn | Dreamstime.com; page 226 © Elizabeth Linhart Veneman; page 227 © Willyb007 | Dreamstime.com; page 232 © Elizabeth Linhart Veneman; page 236 © Elizabeth Linhart Veneman; page 241 © Elizabeth Linhart Veneman; page 250 © Elizabeth Linhart Veneman; page 256 © Elizabeth Linhart Veneman; page 261 © Elizabeth Linhart Veneman; page 265 © Elizabeth Linhart Veneman; page 268 © Johnandersonphoto | Dreamstime.com; page 278 (top) © Christopher Arns, (bottom) © Kojihirano | Dreamstime.com; page 279 © Harasahani | Dreamstime.com; page 286 © Akstp | Dreamstime.com; page 292 © Maislam | Dreamstime.com; page 293 © Mariusz Jurgielewicz/123rf.com; page 294 © Photoquest | Dreamstime.com; page 302 © Mirekdeml | Dreamstime.com; page 303 © Miker37 | Dreamstime.com; page 305 © Maislam | Dreamstime.com; page 307 © Miker37 | Dreamstime.com; page 314 © Christopher Arns; page 316 © Christopher Arns; page 324 © Christopher Arns; page 326 © Christopher Arns; page 328 © Christopher Arns; page 330 (top) © Myleapyear | Dreamstime.com, (bottom) © Celsodiniz | Dreamstime.com; page 331 © Christopher Arns; page 336 © Christopher Arns; page 337 © Christopher Arns; page 342 © Goldenangel | Dreamstime.com; page 343 © Christopher Arns; page 355 © Christopher Arns; page 366 © Christopher Arns; page 368 © Christopher Arns; page 374 © Christopher Arns; page 380 © Christopher Arns; page 384 (top) © Christopher Arns, (bottom) © Christopher Arns; page 385 © Christopher Arns; page 389 © Christopher Arns; page 391 © Christopher Arns; page 397 © Christopher Arns; page 399 © Christopher Arns; page 404 © Nora Jang; page 406 © Christopher Arns; page 411 © Christopher Arns; page 412 © Christopher Arns;

page 417 © Christopher Arns; page 427 © Christopher Arns; page 428 © Christopher Arns; page 429 © Christopher Arns; page 439 © Tono Balaguer/123rf.com; page 443 © Christopher Arns; page 445 (top) © Christopher Arns, (bottom) © Christopher Arns; page 447 © Lorcel | Dreamstime.com; page 451 (top) © Svecchiotti | Dreamstime.com, (bottom) © Christopher Arns; page 454 © Srongkrod | Dreamstime.com; page 455 © Mblach | Dreamstime.com; page 459 © Christopher Arns; page 464 © Pepperboxdesign | Dreamstime.com; page 466 © Christopher Arns; page 467 © Jarnogz | Dreamstime.com; page 469 © Christopher Arns; page 470 © Snyfer | Dreamstime.com; page 471 © Bertl123 | Dreamstime.com; page 476 © Christopher Arns; page 478 © Djschreiber | Dreamstime.com; page 480 © Christopher Arns; page 481 © Lightphoto | Dreamstime.com; page 488 © Christopher Arns; page 495 © Christopher Arns; page 500 © Christopher Arns; page 501 © Christopher Arns; page 506 © Disorderly | Dreamstime.com; page 514 © Juliengrondin | Dreamstime.com; page 518 (top) © Martinmolcan | Dreamstime.com, (bottom) © Kathicof | Dreamstime.com; page 519 © Hotshotsworldwide | Dreamstime.com; page 522 © Demerzel21 | Dreamstime.com; page 527 © Kreulen | Dreamstime.com; page 530 © Sashabuzko | Dreamstime.com; page 531 © Galyna Andrushko/123rf.com; page 534 © Nstanev | Dreamstime.com; page 535 © Meinzahn | Dreamstime.com; page 536 © Nstanev | Dreamstime.com; page 537 © Urosr | Dreamstime.com; page 543 © Sburel | Dreamstime.com; page 545 © Sashabuzko | Dreamstime.com; page 552 (top) © Lunamarina | Dreamstime.com, (bottom) © Courtesy of Monterey Bay Aquarium; page 553 © Violafattore | Dreamstime.com; page 557 © Wolterk | Dreamstime.com; page 560 © Mariusz Jurgielewicz/123rf.com; page 561 © Elizabeth Linhart Veneman; page 564 © A4ndreas | Dreamstime.com; page 569 © Elizabeth Linhart Veneman; page 572 © Elizabeth Linhart Veneman; page 575 © Elizabeth Linhart Veneman; page 580 © Elizabeth Linhart Veneman; page 588 © Elizabeth Linhart Veneman; page 590 © Elizabeth Linhart Veneman; page 593 © Elizabeth Linhart Veneman; page 596 © Elizabeth Linhart Veneman; page 597 © Snovitsky | Dreamstime.com; page 600 © Elizabeth Linhart Veneman; page 602 © Elizabeth Linhart Veneman; page 605 © Elizabeth Linhart Veneman; page 608 © Maislam | Dreamstime.com; page 609 © Luckyphotographer | Dreamstime.com; page 610 © Azahirar | Dreamstime.com; page 613 © Ffennema | Dreamstime.com; page 618 © Elizabeth Linhart Veneman; page 620 © Elizabeth Linhart Veneman; page 622 © Randyandy101 | Dreamstime.com; page 626 (top) © Diomedes66 | Dreamstime.com, (bottom) © Lunamarina | Dreamstime.com; page 630 © Lunamarina | Dreamstime.com; page 631 © Christopher Arns; page 632 © Nstanev | Dreamstime.com; page 633 © Pikappa | Dreamstime.com; page 635 photo by Edward S. Curtis/Public Domain/Wikimedia Commons/Library of Congress; page 636 photo by Charles C. Pierce/Public Domain/Wikimedia Commons/Library of Congress; page 638 © Danielschreurs | Dreamstime.com; page 643 (top) © Kropic | Dreamstime.com, (bottom) © Miaomiaoyaya | Dreamstime.com; page 651 © Lindsay Douglas/123rf.com; page 654 © Elizabeth Linhart Veneman

Also Available

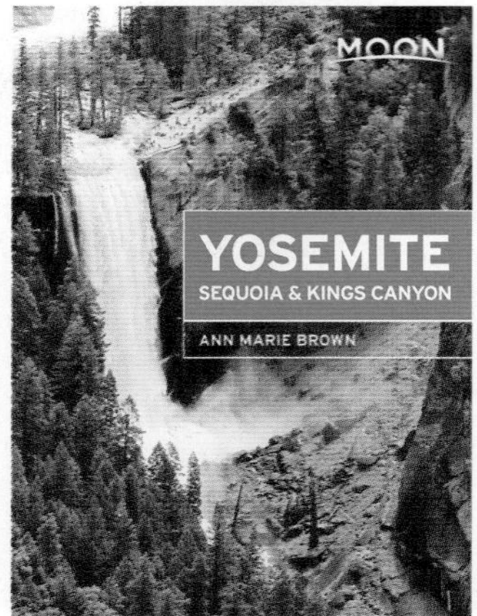

MAP SYMBOLS

- Expressway
- Primary Road
- Secondary Road
- Unpaved Road
- Feature Trail
- Other Trail
- Ferry
- Pedestrian Walkway
- Stairs
- City/Town
- State Capital
- National Capital
- Point of Interest
- Accommodation
- Restaurant/Bar
- Other Location
- Campground
- Airport
- Airfield
- Mountain
- Unique Natural Feature
- Waterfall
- Park
- Trailhead
- Skiing Area
- Golf Course
- Parking Area
- Archaeological Site
- Church
- Gas Station
- Glacier
- Mangrove
- Reef
- Swamp

CONVERSION TABLES

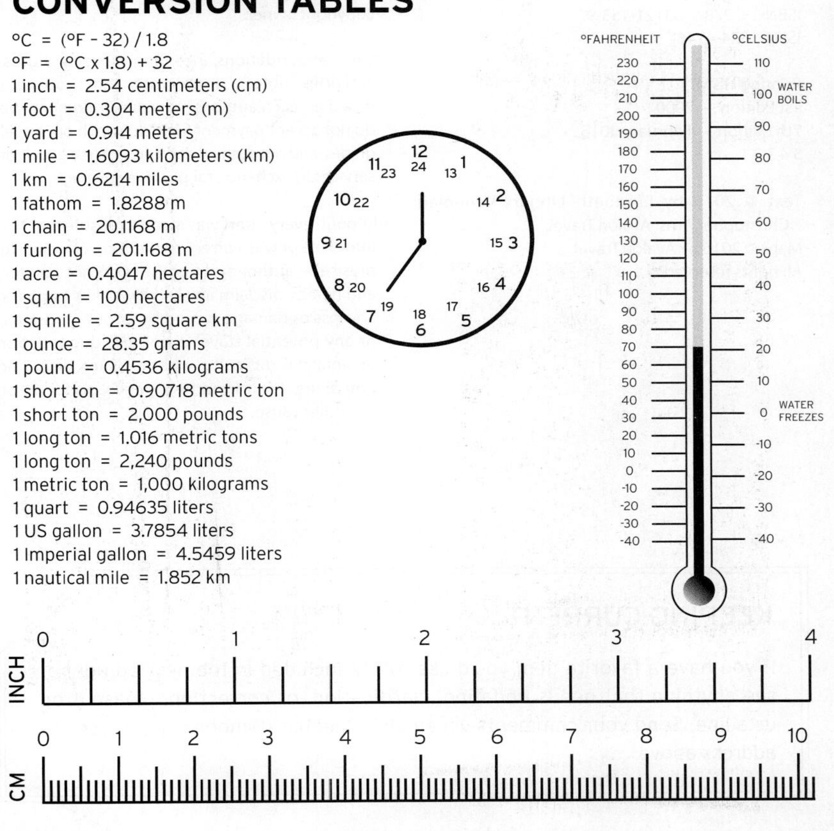

°C = (°F - 32) / 1.8
°F = (°C x 1.8) + 32
1 inch = 2.54 centimeters (cm)
1 foot = 0.304 meters (m)
1 yard = 0.914 meters
1 mile = 1.6093 kilometers (km)
1 km = 0.6214 miles
1 fathom = 1.8288 m
1 chain = 20.1168 m
1 furlong = 201.168 m
1 acre = 0.4047 hectares
1 sq km = 100 hectares
1 sq mile = 2.59 square km
1 ounce = 28.35 grams
1 pound = 0.4536 kilograms
1 short ton = 0.90718 metric ton
1 short ton = 2,000 pounds
1 long ton = 1.016 metric tons
1 long ton = 2,240 pounds
1 metric ton = 1,000 kilograms
1 quart = 0.94635 liters
1 US gallon = 3.7854 liters
1 Imperial gallon = 4.5459 liters
1 nautical mile = 1.852 km

MOON NORTHERN CALIFORNIA
Avalon Travel
a member of the Perseus Books Group
1700 Fourth Street
Berkeley, CA 94710, USA
www.moon.com

Editor: Leah Gordon
Series Manager: Kathryn Ettinger
Copy Editor: Carolyn Cotney
Graphics Coordinator: Elizabeth Jang
Production Coordinator: Elizabeth Jang
Cover Design: Faceout Studios, Charles Brock
Moon Logo: Tim McGrath
Map Editor: Albert Angulo
Cartographer: Brian Shotwell
Proofreaders: Megan Mulholland, Deana Shields
Indexer: Rachel Kuhn

ISBN-13: 978-1-63121-153-9
ISSN: 1524-4148

Printing History
1st Edition — 2000
7th Edition — February 2016
5 4 3 2 1

Front cover photo: bicyclist on a country road in Napa Valley © Jerry Alexander/Getty Images

Back cover photo: San Francisco's Golden Gate Bridge © Nickolay Stanev | Dreamstime.com

Printed in China by RRD Shenzhen

All recommendations, including those for sights, activities, hotels, restaurants, and shops, are based on each author's individual judgment. We do not accept payment for inclusion in our travel guides, and our authors don't accept free goods or services in exchange for positive coverage.

KEEPING CURRENT

If you have a favorite gem you'd like to see included in the next edition, or see anything that needs updating, clarification, or correction, please drop us a line. Send your comments via email to feedback@moon.com, or use the address above.